Bioethics in a Changing World

Bioethics in a Changing World

Jennifer A. Parks
Loyola University, Chicago

Victoria S. Wike
Loyola University, Chicago

Prentice Hall

Upper Saddle River   London   Singapore
Toronto   Tokyo   Sydney   Hong Kong   Mexico City

Editor in Chief: Dickson Musslewhite
Publisher: Nancy Roberts
Editorial Assistant: Nart Varoqua
Editorial Project Manager: Sarah Holle
Director of Marketing: Brandy Dawson
Senior Marketing Manager: Laura Lee Manley
Marketing Assistant: Pat Walsh
Assistant Managing Editor: Melissa Feimer
Production Project Manager: Jean Lapidus
Composition/Full-Service Management: Laserwords Maine
Project Manager: Sunitha Arun Bhaskar
Arts & Sciences: Nick Sklitsis
Operations Specialist: Cathy Petersen

Visual Research Manager: Beth Brenzel
Image Permission Coordinator: Nancy Seise
Manager, Visual Research & Permissions: Karen Sanatar
Cover Design: Bruce Kenselaar
Cover Photos:
Top Left: © Getty Images, Inc.
Middle Left: © Getty Images, Inc.
Bottom Left: © Getty Images, Inc.
Bottom Middle: © Getty Images, Inc.
Bottom Right: HIV/AIDS patient in hospital, Garoua, Cameroon, Africa. © Heiner Heine/Imagebroker/Alamy.

Credits and acknowledgments borrowed from other sources and reproduced, with permission, in this textbook appear on appropriate page within text.

Library of Congress Cataloging-in-Publication Data

Parks, Jennifer A.
 Bioethics in a changing world / Jennifer A. Parks, Victoria S. Wike. —
1st ed.
    p. ; cm.
 Includes bibliographical references.
 ISBN-13: 978-0-13-615164-7 (alk. paper)
 ISBN-10: 0-13-615164-7 (alk. paper)
 1. Medical ethics—Textbooks. 2. Bioethics—Textbooks. I. Wike, Victoria
S. II. Title.
 [DNLM: 1. Bioethical Issues. 2. Delivery of Health Care—ethics. 3.
Ethics, Medical. WB 60 P252b 2009]
 R724.P245 2009
 174.2—dc22

                    2009021127

Prentice Hall
is an imprint of

www.pearsonhighered.com

ISBN-10:   0-13-615164-7
ISBN-13: 978-0-13-615164-7

Contents

Chapter 8   **ORGAN DONATION AND TRANSPLANTATION**   517

Chapter 11   FUTURE DIRECTIONS IN BIOETHICS   756

Preface

Bioethics in a Changing World is an introductory textbook for individuals who are new to the study of bioethics. This interdisciplinary field, which encompasses philosophy, religion, sociology, gerontology, psychiatry, biomedical science, law, and nursing (to name a few), has been rapidly growing and developing over the last half-century. In order to get a handle on what "doing" bioethics entails, it is helpful to start with the basic philosophical foundations of bioethical theory and then consider a variety of trenchant issues that arise from the practice of medicine and the provision of health care services within an age of technology.

In constructing this textbook, our central aim has been to guide readers in developing a clear sense of how theory and practice are linked in the dynamic field of bioethics. Though new problems and issues in bioethics are constantly arising, we see the persistence of foundational questions that apply in new contexts. For example, fundamental questions that arise within the abortion debate (Does the fetus have moral status? Should fetuses be counted as persons? When does "life" begin?) also apply to newer problems surrounding stem cell research and assisted reproductive technologies. Likewise, some of the newest life-saving and life-extending technologies raise long-standing questions that have been addressed by the euthanasia debate, such as: What kind of life is worth living? Under what conditions does an individual have the right to refuse treatment? What does it mean to have a "good death"? It is our hope that this text will help readers to think through bioethical issues from a variety of perspectives, with a number of philosophical approaches as "tools" at hand to do the job.

ORGANIZATION AND CONCEPTUAL FRAMEWORK

Bioethics in a Changing World is divided into 11 chapters, each dealing with an important area of bioethical study. Each chapter includes an opening creative piece, a case study presentation, and a chapter introduction that briefly outlines for readers what has happened and what is currently happening with regard to the topic at hand. We have also included in Chapters 2–10 a "Looking Ahead" section that anticipates related ethical issues that we are likely to encounter in the near future.

The chapters are laid out as follows:

- Chapter 1 concerns the theories and principles of biomedical ethics.
- Chapter 2 treats a variety of roles and responsibilities attached to bioethics (including the role of doctors, nurses, and genetic counselors).
- Chapter 3 addresses issues of justice and health care.
- Chapter 4 considers experimentation and research on human subjects.
- Chapter 5 concerns health, normalcy, and the "abnormal" patient.
- Chapter 6 addresses issues at the beginning of life.
- Chapter 7 treats genetic technologies.
- Chapter 8 covers organ donation and transplantation.
- Chapter 9 considers topics in aging and ethics.
- Chapter 10 highlights issues at the end of life.
- Chapter 11 is a consideration of "future directions" in bioethics.

Each of the readings included in the volume has been selected by virtue of its impact on the field of bioethics, its raising of important perspectives or questions, and/or its current relevance. For example, we have included foundational articles by Judith Jarvis Thomson (abortion) and James Rachels (euthanasia), as well as new essays that address problems in the pharmaceutical industry, gene "doping" in athletics, and emergency preparedness for pandemics and bioterrorism.

While we recognize that there is much more to learning bioethics than simply applying theories and principles to case studies, we nevertheless believe that the use of case studies for ethical investigation of concepts and viewpoints can be very instructive and stimulating. To this end, we have organized all of Chapter 1 around a case study to which we repeatedly return as an example. The idea behind this is to give a common reference point for all the theories and principles presented in Chapter 1 so that our readers can clearly see how they address and resolve a case differently. Again, while this in no way implies that doing bioethics boils down to solving cases, it *is* the case that much of the thinking and talking about bioethics is done by way of narratives. Likewise, in this text we repeatedly return to case study narratives to provide context and flavor for the ethical dilemmas at hand and to highlight those occasions when theory and practice come together.

DISTINGUISHING FEATURES

There are five unique features that make *Bioethics in a Changing World* distinctive:

- The chapter on theories and principles in bioethics treats one case study from a variety of theoretical perspectives so that readers can clearly grasp how different theories and principles approach the same moral problem from different points of view and so may derive different answers.
- *Bioethics in a Changing World* includes novel and timely chapters on (a) aging and long-term care; (2) health, normalcy, and "abnormalcy"; and (3) future directions, none of which appears in other leading textbooks.
- Every chapter includes articles that address issues of race, class, gender, and sexual orientation, so that these issues permeate the text and are not treated as "add-on" concerns.
- Each chapter contains a creative work (including poetry, newspaper clippings, and Internet websites) to help situate the chapter's overall theme and to offer a new context for thinking about the issue at hand.
- Chapters 2–10 include a "Looking Ahead" section to offer some ideas of where the bioethical issues are pointing.

PEDAGOGICAL AIDS

This textbook includes an online instructor's manual that offers additional teaching materials. In it, we provide web sites and films relevant to each chapter as well as suggested additional readings, supplementary cases, discussion questions, and some model test questions.

ACKNOWLEDGMENTS

A number of colleagues, friends, and graduate students have helped us in the preparation and successful completion of this textbook. First, we would like to thank Mical Moser for bringing this project to us for consideration, and for having a clear vision and enthusiasm for the material. We sincerely thank our graduate assistants Merritt Foy, Kristina Grob, and Hillary Bussell for their willingness to complete much of the tedious labor associated with the production of this text. Our colleague Mark Waymack was very helpful in providing suggestions for readings and sections in the textbook, and he kindly allowed us to adapt in Chapter 10 a case study he wrote on Alzheimer's disease and long-term care.

We greatly appreciate the input and guidance offered by the staff at Prentice Hall: our managing editor, Sarah Holle; Lisa Black, who so patiently worked through the permissions for this textbook; and the following reviewers who provided essential and extremely helpful feedback while the text was under construction.

Anthon Preus
Binghamton University
Binghamton, NY

David Paul
Western Michigan University
Sturgis, MI

Laura Newhart
Eastern Kentucky University
Richmond, KY

Lorraine Landry
Oklahoma State University
Stillwater, OK

James Nelson
Michigan State University
East Lansing, MI

Christopher Williams
University of Nevada — Reno
Reno, NV

Benjamin Hale
University of Colorado — Boulder
Boulder, CO

John M. Doris
Washington University
St. Louis, MO

Deborah Heikes
University of Alabama — Huntsville
Huntsville, AL

Finally, we are grateful to our spouses, Ed Wike and David Ingram, who offered their advice and support as we pursued this enormous undertaking.

PHOTO CREDITS

Page 7: Getty Images, Inc./Hulton Archive Photos; Page 15: Harvard Graduate School of Education; Page 21 George Dodson/Pearson Education/PH College; Page 32: Mark Richards/PhotoEdit Inc.; Page 39: Robin Nelson/PhotoEdit Inc.; Page 124: Robert Trippet/SIPA Press; Page 126: Steven Rubin/The Image Works; Page 127: Bryan Sikora/istockphoto; Page 204: Anat Givon/AP WideWorld Photos; Page 205: Greg Gibson/AP WideWorld Photos; Page 206: The Museum of Disability History; Page 279: Michael Newman/PhotoEdit, Inc.; Page 281: AP WideWorld Photos; Page 283: Fotandy/Dreamstime; Page 345: Photolibrary.com; Page 353: Knut Mueller/Das Fotoarchive/Peter Arnold, Inc,: Page 354: © CORBIS/All Rights Reserved.; Page 440: Steve Uzzell, 111; Page 518: K.M. Chaudary/AP WideWorld Photos; Page 520: Pat Sullivan/AP WideWorld Photos; Page 521: Ed Andrieski/AP WideWorld Photos; Page 591: Angela Hampton/Picture Library/ALAMY; Page 593: Cornor Caffrey/Photo Researcher, Inc.; Page 594: Getty Images, Inc./Hulton Archive Photos: Page 672: UPI/CORBIS-NY; Page 674: John C. Hillery/Reuters/CORBIS-NY; Page 675: Getty Images, Inc.; Page 758: AP WideWorld Photos.

Chapter 1

Theories and Values in Bioethics

Welcome to the study of bioethics. We are confident that you will find the issues and problems of bioethics challenging and engaging. In keeping with the methods of bioethics, let us start with a case study that relates a common, but ethically difficult, issue in medicine. Case studies enable us to use moral, philosophical, and theoretical reasoning to illuminate real-world scenarios. While case studies are not all that bioethics is about, they are a good beginning point. We return to the case throughout this chapter as we discuss theories, values, and issues in bioethics.

> At age 89, Sam Levine is admitted to the hospital with bronchial pneumonia, advanced pulmonary edema (fluid in the lungs), and urinary tract infection. When he checks in he is presented with information about advance directives, as are all hospital admits. When the question of cardiopulmonary resuscitation (CPR) is raised, Sam responds by saying, "If my heart stops beating, just get it going again." Gladys, Sam's wife, agrees with her husband's request. In order to ensure valid consent, they are given general information about the nature of the treatment (that it may require chest compressions, artificial respiration, intubation, defibrillation, and/or ventilation) and the effectiveness of the treatment. Though it is uncertain whether either of them fully understands, their physician, Dr. Anuradha Gupta, agrees to respect their wishes.
>
> After 10 days in the hospital Sam is responding poorly to treatment. His prognosis is dismal and in the words of Dr. Gupta, "Sam's vital processes just seem to be shutting down." The nurses want to know what to do if he goes into cardiac arrest. Dr. Gupta decides to speak to Gladys.
>
> After raising the question of CPR with her, Gladys insists she still wants "everything done for Sam, including CPR." When the physician proposes talking again to Sam, Gladys becomes quite agitated and says, "Don't harass my husband with such a sensitive question at a time like this. It would give him the wrong message. How can you ask, 'Do you want to be resuscitated?' without making it sound like a rhetorical question that invites 'no' for an answer? I won't let you do that to him. He already expressed his wish about CPR ten days ago. He was more lucid then than now. So I think we should go with his earlier decision."
>
> The Levines' daughter, Anne, who has been regularly visiting her father at the hospital, strongly disagrees. "Mom," she says, "Dad is 89 years old and has lived a good life. The doctor doesn't think resuscitation makes any sense for him. Neither do I. When dad said he wanted CPR, I don't think he had any idea what kind of condition he would be in. It's cruel to think of putting him through that. We need to think about what he would want now, not what he said 10 days ago!"
>
> "Well, Anne," Gladys replies, "I was always taught that where there's life there's hope. And your dad made his wishes very clear."
>
> Given what has already happened, Sam's condition, and the disagreement between Gladys and her daughter, Anne, what should Dr. Gupta do?

WHAT IS BIOETHICS?

Any initial introduction to biomedical ethics should begin with the most basic of questions: What exactly is biomedical ethics? In some ways, the question is easily answered by almost anyone who reads the newspaper, watches popular television, or listens to the radio. Issues of ethical importance are raised by programs like *ER, Grey's Anatomy, House,* and *Law & Order*; and the newspaper and radio often present ethical, legal, and economic issues that arise in medicine. So, in some sense, bioethics is familiar to all of us, whether through personal experiences in medicine or the media.

But presentations by the popular media and press do not give us the clearest picture of bioethics. Sensationalist television programs emphasize "ripped from the headlines" issues, making biomedical ethics appear to be all about cutting-edge technologies and acute medical emergencies. To gain a deeper understanding of what bioethics is, then, we must bypass these popular presentations to consider a broader definition of it. While popular programs present issues of bioethical importance, they wrongly give the idea that this is all bioethics is about. Such depictions overlook some of the important but commonplace ethical issues that arise in medicine, such as the ethical problem that arises in the case involving Dr. Gupta and the Levine family.

Certain terminology is used in this text to denote different applications of ethics. The term "medical ethics" is used in application to ethical issues in the medical clinic, and the kinds of issues that may arise for physicians in providing care for patients. "Health care ethics" is used when referring to ethical issues relating to the provision of health care (including the allocation of health care dollars or concerns for the provision of health care). We treat the terms "biomedical ethics" and "bioethics" as meaning the same thing: the attempt to address ethical issues within biomedical research and biotechnologies broadly construed. The terms "bioethics" or "biomedical ethics" are most often used in the literature, and are the terms we use throughout this textbook, since they are most inclusive. Biomedical ethics, then, concerns a broad range of practices and questions, covering everything from the more cutting-edge issues presented by the media (stem cell research, cloning, abortion, physician-assisted suicide, reproductive technologies) to the more mundane, housekeeping issues that arise (providing care at home for older adults, paying for health care, dealing with chronic care needs).

While the field of biomedical ethics may appear to have only sprung up within the past few decades, codes of ethics that set out moral behavior for medical practitioners have a very long history. The often-cited *Hippocratic Oath* (4th century B.C.), though specific to its time, sets out the enduring values of confidentiality, respect for the medical profession, and the obligation to benefit patients. Jewish philosopher and physician Maimonides (1138–1204) wrote various tracts on a number of diseases and their cures. Much of the current concern regarding the ethics of medical research and experimentation came out of the post–World War II Nuremberg Trials which took place from 1945 to 1949, resulting in the Nuremberg Code, which helps to provide current ethical guidelines surrounding human research and experimentation. And long before bioethics became a discrete area of study, theologians were discussing and debating issues of medical importance, such as abortion, euthanasia, and the use of children in medical research. Thus, while modern bioethics can be said to have started within the past three decades, when medical technologies bourgeoned, the ability to significantly extend life grew, and health care costs skyrocketed, we can see that it has a much longer history extending back thousands of years.

Currently, biomedical ethics makes up its own large area of study in ethics: ethical issues in health care are now treated as an entirely separate area of ethics. Bioethicists—those who are formally trained through Master's and PhD programs of various types—may teach bioethics at colleges, universities, or medical schools, may serve on hospital ethics committees or research ethics boards, and may work as clinical ethicists (ethics consultants in hospitals). There have now been so many books and articles written on ethical issues in medicine that they could not possibly be listed in their entirety.

Like experts in other fields, bioethicists have a common way of "doing" bioethics. Ethical problems in medicine are explored by the use of case studies, like the one that opens this chapter. In order to achieve the deepest possible understanding of the ethical particulars of a medical issue, a case study narrative is used to relate the case. In it, the different roles and relationships can be conveyed and the complex ethical issues can be laid out; bioethicists take such cases as instructive examples of common problems in medicine, and use them as thought experiments to work through what should be done in similar kinds of situations. However, where case studies are presented to hospital ethics committees, they are just as often real cases that are occurring in hospitals, cases that raise ethical dilemmas for those involved in the patients' care. The discussion and resolution to these situations is instructive for health care teams, who often invite the patients' families to attend the ethics consults.

It is critical to remember that biomedical ethics is a kind of applied ethics—it is ethics applied to problems in medicine and medical research. As such, it is important that one have the necessary tools to apply to moral problems and to find a reasonable solution to them. There are different ways of approaching biomedical ethics, each coming with its own strengths and weaknesses. Some moral philosophers such as Immanuel Kant and John Stuart Mill have ethical theories that can be applied to bioethical problems. Other ways of addressing ethics in medicine are to apply perspectives that derive from a justice ethic, from virtue ethics, or from a feminist ethic of care. Another approach is to focus on the values or principles inherent in bioethical situations. This approach, known as the **"four principles approach"** is described by Tom Beauchamp and James Childress. And one must also think multiculturally about religious, racial, ethnic, and cultural differences in medicine.

As we will see, each theory or perspective has something valuable to contribute to bioethics, a unique approach to ethical issues that reflects important values in medical care, such as an openness to whichever principle is most suitable to a particular case; the importance of duty; achieving the best possible outcomes; being a virtuous health care professional who is committed to personal excellence; a commitment to caring, nurturing, and maintaining relationships, especially those involving the weak, ill, frail, and young; or concern for difference between caregivers and patients.

Equally important in the medical setting is that one has the tools to achieve a *fast* solution, since one often lacks the luxury of time to debate the problem at hand. The need to make effective but swift decisions in medicine is what in part motivated Beauchamp and Childress to forego a theoretical approach to medical ethics, opting instead for a much simpler "principles" approach, which avoids the need for a cumbersome theoretical framework. More will be said about this in what follows.

Imagine that you are Dr. Gupta—the doctor dealing with Mr. and Mrs. Levine in the case that opened this chapter. A decision must be made about Sam Levine's treatment, and it is clear that there is not agreement about what should be done. Mrs. Levine is strongly in favor of continuing treatment for her husband, despite the likelihood that cardiopulmonary resuscitation (CPR) will be of no benefit to him, and even though it might lead to further harm. Anne, their daughter, is equally convinced that her father should not be resuscitated when the need arises. Dr. Gupta's professional opinion is that Sam is slipping away, and that CPR will be of no further benefit to him. Given that her patient could code at any time, it is necessary to come to a mutually agreeable solution so that the doctor has a plan of action if and when Sam needs CPR. Here is an example of an ethical dilemma that requires a quick resolution, since much hangs on whether to offer CPR or to write a "do not resuscitate" (DNR) order.

Before looking at any particular moral theories, we must add a general word of caution. When you are using a moral approach or theory to shed light on a case, remember that you are offering *an* interpretation, not *the* interpretation. Even those who share a moral theory, say, deontology, do not always agree about cases. Thus, there may not be just one deontological "answer" to the problem that a moral situation raises. In some situations, it may be clear how a certain moral approach or theory illuminates a case but in others it may not. On top of that, remember that what distinguishes moral approaches and theories from one another is not the actions or decisions they prescribe but the reasoning they employ to arrive at decisions. It is quite possible that a single decision could be supported by multiple moral approaches or theories. Moral theories can and often do recommend the same action or decision, say, to tell the truth to one's patient. In fact, when this happens, it comes as something of a relief because it means that even when adopting different moral frameworks and different principles and rules, there is agreement on what is the right decision. The harder, more morally difficult, cases are the ones where the various moral approaches or theories seem to lead in different directions. When that happens, the theories as tools of moral thinking are insufficient by themselves to solve a problem. The moral agent—that is, you the moral thinker—must then decide that the perspective of one moral theory or approach is better than the others or that there is a way of combining several approaches or theories. You are required to do more interpreting and more judging when the moral theories do not all lead to the same decision. In other words, you must find a reason to prefer the perspective of one moral approach or theory over the others or else you must find a creative solution that allows you to utilize the insights and values of several moral approaches or theories. In these cases, you will work harder as a moral thinker than in those situations where moral frameworks come together to recommend a decision.

MORAL THEORIES AND BIOMEDICAL ETHICS

A moral theory is a systematic perspective to moral problems that ranks or prioritizes the principles and rules valued by the approach. Put simply, it is a way of approaching ethical situations and of ordering principles (values) and rules. It is a view on what is important in ethical life and a view that people can carry with them from situation to situation. So, for example, some moral theories include the view that persons are essentially social beings and take their identity and meaning from their participation in a social community whereas other moral theories focus on persons as individuals and on their unique characteristics or their individual rights or capacities. Depending on your worldview, your beliefs about the nature and meaning of human lives, your thoughts on relationships and responsibilities, you may find certain moral theories more convincing and more helpful than others. However, our concern is not to advocate any particular moral theory, but rather to recommend them all. Moral theories are themselves tools—they may help us to see aspects of moral situations that we might otherwise have overlooked. And they may point us toward solutions to moral questions and thus help us to resolve problems and to defend our solutions.

In what follows we characterize the five major types of moral theories and consider the "four principles" approach to biomedical ethics. Then we show how they work and describe some problems they face.

Deontology

The theory called **"deontology"** views moral life in the context of duties, obligations, and what is right. Simply, it says that we have acted morally when we perform actions that are right, that is, that are required by moral law or duty. A deontologist believes that the rightness or wrongness of an action does not depend on what sort of consequences follow from the action but on whether or not the action is the right sort of action, namely, an action that has a good intention and is done for the sake of duty.

W.D. Ross formulated one version of a deontological ethical theory. For him, actions are right or wrong depending on the kind of actions that they are. Actions are right not because they bring about good consequences but because they are acts that fulfill duties. According to Ross, there are three kinds of duties: reparation, gratitude, and keeping faith. Actions that are of a certain kind (say, paying off a debt; that is, reparation) are right. Ross calls these actions that are right "prima facie duties." This means that all of them are on the face of things, initially, our duties. But since prima facie duties can conflict (perhaps one can't both pay off a debt and keep faith by paying one's taxes), there can be only one "actual duty." The moral person must figure out which of these prima facie duties is "more of a duty" and thereby carry out his or her actual duty.

Certainly the most famous version of deontology is the ethical theory of Immanuel Kant, a German philosopher from the 18th century (Figure 1.1).

Kant focuses on the fact that reason can identify what is right and what is wrong. He puts forward a rule called the "Categorical Imperative" that is a law of reason that commands (hence, "imperative") unconditionally, necessarily, and universally (hence, "categorically"). It commands that we act in ways consistent with reason and logic, regardless of our wishes, desires, feelings, emotions, and circumstances. To act in this rational way is, according to **Kantian deontology**, to act with autonomy. So we are autonomous when we act rationally, logically, and for the sake of the categorical imperative and, contrary to popular opinion, we are not autonomous when following our whims and desires.

The categorical imperative can be formulated in two primary ways. Kant claims that the two formulations are equivalent so that either one of them can be used. The first version of the categorical imperative is called the "Formula of Universal Law." It says:

Act in such a way that the maxim of your action could be willed to be a universal law.

In other words, we should only act in ways that we are willing to allow others to act. Similarly, we should only act for reasons (maxims) we are willing to allow others to use. If you think it is morally

FIGURE 1.1   Immanuel Kant 1724–1804.

acceptable for you to tell a lie but you are not willing to consider it morally acceptable for everyone to lie, then you are not truly acting morally. The Universal Law version is based on a principle or value of universalizability, that is, that something is right only if it is right for everyone. No one can make an exception of herself or act for reasons that can be used only by her.

The second version of the categorical imperative is called the "Formula of Humanity." It demands:

> Act in such a way that you treat persons as ends in themselves and not merely as means.

That is, an action is moral only if it recognizes the dignity, the intrinsic value, and the autonomy of persons. Persons are not things. We do inevitably use people as means (patients use nurses to improve their health and comfort and nurses use patients as a means to wage-earning). This kind of usefulness to each other is fine, according to Kant, as long as we also consider each other as intrinsically valuable and as worthy of respect. Because persons have autonomy, there are certain ways of acting toward them that will be unacceptable, such as belittling, enslaving, and manipulating them. Respect for persons is a central value for deontology.

Now, we return to the case of Sam. The case concludes with the question: What should the physician do? As we know, a deontologist expects the physician to perform the right action for the right reason, in other words, to act according to reason and to do her duty. A deontologist ignores possible consequences, family dynamics, and circumstances that may be unique to this situation. The concern is not for the future but for the present and the past. How do we uphold universality, autonomy, and respect for persons and how do we honor commitments, promises, and act in ways that can be universalized? The short answer for the deontologist is: We use reason to determine what our duty is. Now suppose the physician does this. What will her reasoning look like?

As a deontologist, Dr. Gupta brings to this situation certain beliefs and values. Her moral thinking is governed by her belief that some actions and policies are inherently right while others are necessarily wrong. She is convinced that there are rational moral rules that govern this situation. Hence, her job is to figure out what those rules are and apply them to Sam's case. For her, Sam's case is not unique; it is rather a type of case. Others may have been in similar situations in the past and so there may be actions or policies for cases like Sam's that are well established and defended. Or at least there will be other cases like Sam's in the future and it is important to determine the right action or policy in Sam's case in order to have a guide for the cases to come.

More specifically as a Kantian deontologist, Dr. Gupta would think about whether her proposed maxim or reason for action is logically consistent when universalized. That is, she would want to ensure that the rule she follows is one that could be logically followed by others as well. She would also be careful that whatever action she decided on must treat the people involved as valuable, as ends in themselves, not merely as means to others' ends. Deontologists of all kinds figure out what is morally right through an understanding of reason and our rational nature.

One problem is that it is not always obvious when maxims or rules or policies are contradictory or contrary to reason. Deontology seems to require a certain logical precision in moral decision making that is not evident in most people's experience. Finding logical inconsistency among moral maxims may be difficult and in fact may be wrong-headed. Why should we assume that the realm of morality follows the same rules as logic? Moral life may not be subject to the kind of precision that deontology asserts.

A related problem is that deontology takes rules very seriously. Rules and actions are universalizable, that is, they are the same for all rational beings. However, many people find this requirement unrealistic and false. Do we all reason in the same way? Are there some duties that arise only in relationships (say, physician–patient) or apply more strongly to some people and not to others (say, duties to benefit our families and friends more than strangers)? It may be that deontology overlooks important distinctions and differences among people and types of circumstances.

Finally, deontology is criticized because it ignores human emotions and relationships, special circumstances, and future consequences. In Sam's case, the deontologist may not explore Gladys' agitation, Anne's concern about the cruelty of the CPR treatment, or the relationships among the various parties. The deontologist is applying a rule, looking at types of reasons and actions, and not attending to special circumstances or estimating future consequences. The harm or benefit that might come to people as a result of adopting a rule or performing an action is not a concern to the deontologist. But this seems to ignore the obvious fact that it is important to people and it is morally relevant whether good or bad consequences follow from an action.

These are some of the objections made to deontology and especially to Kantian deontology. They are serious criticisms but they are not enough to make us reject deontology entirely. As we will see, no theory is free from problems and there is value to the particular perspective each theory provides. In fact, because deontology sets uncompromising standards, it has played an important role in discussions of bioethical issues such as truth-telling, confidentiality, patient rights, reproductive issues, stem cell research, cloning, and death and dying. Bioethicists have used deontology to argue against the practice of surrogate mothers on the grounds that it is wrong to create a child intending to give it away (this treats the child as simply a thing and fails to acknowledge the dignity of human lives). Stem cell research has been opposed by some deontologists because it destroys a human life in the attempt to better the lives of others (it appeals to good consequences to try to justify a morally wrong action). Finally, deontology's emphasis on rationality and moral laws inherent to our nature highlights the worth and dignity of individuals and the moral obligation to respect persons and value autonomy. This emphasis can be seen concretely in bioethics in the ways that patients' wishes and decisions are solicited on informed consent documents and advance directives.

Consequentialism

Consequentialism refers to moral theories that focus entirely on the consequences or results of actions and rules. For consequentialists, an action or rule is right if it produces or is likely to produce more good consequences (or fewer bad consequences) than any alternative action or rule. The most influential version of consequentialism is **utilitarianism**. Utilitarianism is the product of two English philosophers from the nineteenth century, Jeremy Bentham and John Stuart Mill (Figure 1.2).

They began from the view that what is important to human beings is pleasure and the avoidance of pain. These are the goods at which a moral life aims and together they are called "happiness." There

FIGURE 1.2   John Stuart Mill 1806–1873.

may be other goods that people desire such as health, knowledge, self-realization, virtue, and so on, but Bentham and Mill believed that none of these were desired in themselves. All of these ends are desired because they bring us pleasure and help us to avoid pain and so happiness remains the one true goal of human life. Furthermore, because we live in communities and have social feelings, namely, sympathy for others, it is not just our own happiness at which we aim but rather the happiness of all. So the basis of utilitarianism is "Utility" or the "Greatest Happiness." The "Greatest Happiness for All" is thus the principle or value of utilitarianism and its rule is: "Act in such a way that you maximize the greatest happiness for the greatest number of people."

For a utilitarian, an action or rule is right if it tends to maximize more happiness than unhappiness for all and wrong if it tends to maximize more unhappiness than happiness for all. Utilitarianism maintains that the right action or rule is one whose consequences are best; in other words, an act or rule is right if its consequences are good, namely, it brings about happiness. Utilitarianism focuses on the future—what will bring about the happiness we all desire? In addition, utilitarianism is a theory that takes a broad social view. Unlike deontology, which focuses on individuals and duty, utilitarianism is concerned with the social good and with bringing about the best consequences.

In order to determine what action or policy is right, utilitarians must compare the amount of happiness produced by several possible actions or policies. It is impossible to look at one action and tell whether or not it maximizes the "most happiness." Instead, all possible alternatives must be compared in order to see how much happiness and unhappiness each produces and hence which one results in the most overall happiness. Also, utilitarians must measure the various happinesses and unhappinesses that follow from each alternative. It is not enough to observe that three people receive happiness from action A while eight people receive happiness from action B. A utilitarian wants to know how much (and even for Mill, what kind of) happiness each of those persons gets. It is possible that the amount of happiness that the three people get from action A is greater than the amount of happiness the eight people get from action B. To deal with this issue, Bentham called utilitarianism a "hedonistic calculus," meaning that it is a mathematical calculation focused on pleasure and the avoidance of pain. He listed several ways of measuring the value of a pleasure or pain: (1) intensity (a more intense pleasure is worth more than a dimly felt pleasure), (2) duration (a long-lasting pleasure is worth more than a short-term pleasure), (3) purity (a pleasure free from pain is worth more than a pleasure laced with pain), (4) fecundity (a pleasure likely to produce more pleasure is worth more than a dead-end pleasure), and so on. Pains are measured in the same way. A pain is greater and hence the unhappiness is greater when it is more intense, or long lasting, or free from any pleasure, or likely to produce more pain. So, a utilitarian perspective on a moral situation aims, via a mathematical-type equation, to determine which of several alternatives is likely to bring about the best overall consequences.

There are also two different types of utilitarians, known as "act utilitarians" and "rule utilitarians." What distinguishes them is the way that they employ the greatest happiness principle. Act utilitarians maintain that the principle of greatest happiness must be applied in every action, every situation one encounters. There are no shortcuts. Act utilitarians approach moral situations and ask: What *act* maximizes the greatest amount of happiness for all? Rule utilitarians, however, insist that the principle of greatest happiness is applied to rules. Thus, to save time and to be more efficient and more consistent, rule utilitarians approach moral situations and ask: What *rule* maximizes the greatest amount of happiness for all? Each of these types of utilitarianism is critical of the other. Act utilitarians accuse rule utilitarians of not being truly faithful to the greatest happiness. Sometimes rules that in general maximize the greatest utility fail to realize the greatest utility in particular cases. For example, as a rule, telling the truth brings the greatest happiness to all but we can imagine a case in which withholding the truth is more productive of utility. Rule utilitarians are not sensitive to important differences between cases. On the other hand, rule utilitarians insist that act utilitarians make impossible demands on our time and our abilities to assess and evaluate. That is, act utilitarians apparently believe that we have the time and the capabilities in each and every situation to morally assess the features of the case without relying on rules that provide direction on how to deal with types of cases. Without this direction, act utilitarians are bogged down by having to take the time to describe, analyze, and judge every moral situation. In spite of these critiques and without choosing sides, we note that utilitarianism can be practiced either at the level of acts or at the level of rules.

Consider the case of Sam and his physician and how the utilitarian perspective can help the physician with her predicament. First, we know that Dr. Gupta is concerned with maximizing the greatest happiness for all in whatever decision she makes. So she pays attention to Sam, Gladys, Anne, the nurses, herself, and any others whose happiness is at stake in this situation. She is searching for the best possible outcome for everyone. Dr. Gupta, as a utilitarian physician, is single-minded—she is thinking only of the future well-being of those affected by her decision, and not about intentions, duties, virtues, good character, moral rights, and other components of moral situations. Second, contrary to what you might think, given that she is Sam's physician, she is not automatically awarding more value to Sam's happiness than to the happiness of others. She cannot privilege Sam's good over the good of other people affected by her decision just because Sam is her patient. She must objectively assess the amount of happiness and unhappiness coming to each and not accord special value to someone in the calculation of the consequences just because of who he or she is. It may be that Gladys' happiness is affected to a greater degree than Sam's by what Dr. Gupta decides and hence Gladys' happiness will count more in her deliberation than Sam's. It is the amount of total happiness that utilitarians focus on and not whose happiness it happens to be. This is what utilitarians mean when they say that each counts equally in the hedonistic calculation—it is happiness that is being measured and valued and not specific persons.

Now, as a utilitarian, Sam's physician will follow a procedure like this one:

1. Consider all options (the possible actions or rules that could be adopted).
2. Consider all those whose happiness will be affected by the action or rule that is chosen.
3. Assign a value, a measure, to how much happiness or unhappiness each of the persons listed above would obtain if each of the possible options was acted on.
4. Add up the amount of total happiness each option produces and then subtract from that the amount of unhappiness each option produces.
5. Choose the option that realizes the greatest amount of overall happiness.

This utilitarian procedure enables Dr. Gupta to be concerned with all those who will be affected positively or negatively by the choice she makes and it requires her to act in such a way as to maximize benefits and minimize harms.

Now let us turn a critical eye on utilitarianism and draw attention to some of the difficulties with utilitarian reasoning. One problem for utilitarians is that they must *predict* the consequences of the various possible actions or rules they might adopt. In other words, they have to look into the future and imagine what will happen if they act in a certain way. Now sometimes it is fairly simple to make this sort of prediction. If the physician bypasses Gladys's wishes, Gladys will be angry. But the larger issue is that realistically it is sometimes very hard to predict exactly what the consequences will be. In this case, if the physician ignores Gladys's wishes, will Anne unexpectedly join Gladys's side and defend her mother against the physician? Will they complain to hospital administrators? Will they hire a lawyer? Often it is just not humanly possible to predict what consequences are likely to follow from a decision. And if you cannot predict consequences, then you cannot make decisions as a utilitarian.

A second concern is that utilitarians have to make calculative judgments regarding how much happiness or unhappiness each action or rule will bring. This is hard to do and there is no guarantee that any two utilitarians will weigh the consequences in the same way and hence reach the same conclusion as to what is right. Some call this the "subjectivism" that is built into utilitarianism—we are forced to depend on our subjective measurements of the amount of pleasure or pain that would result from particular choices.

A final objection to utilitarianism is that it seems to some people to be an inappropriate way to make moral decisions. This criticism can take two forms. On the one hand, some critics argue that the best moral decisions could not possibly follow from the kind of adding up and subtracting that utilitarians must do to determine whether more good comes from this or that action or rule. They ask, is the question of what is moral just a mathematical problem? Is morality subject to the kind of exactness and precision that mathematics is? The way to appreciate this criticism in terms of Sam's case is to ask whether there are any important moral considerations that cannot be quantified. On the other hand, some complain that the decisions that are reached by means of a utilitarian calculation may very well be the most *efficient* or *cost-effective* decisions but they are not necessarily the most moral or just decisions. The decision made by Sam's physician may be designed to satisfy the greatest number of people and achieve the most good. But sometimes the interest of one person is morally decisive—that is, justice and morality sometimes demand that we take the side of the one person even if the majority are ignored or overruled. Look at slavery or child labor, where utility is perhaps furthered by the enslavement or oppression of individuals but we do not believe that morality justifies slavery or child labor. Critics argue that what produces the greatest happiness is not necessarily synonymous with what is *moral*. So even if Dr. Gupta figures out what action or rule is most efficient or useful, she may have dodged the issue of morality altogether.

Nevertheless, utilitarianism in particular and consequentialism in general recognize several basic facts about human beings that are relevant to moral reasoning. We value happiness, we sympathize with others, and we assess the likely consequences of possible actions and rules we might adopt. Utilitarianism offers an important perspective on bioethical issues and it has played a pivotal role in discussions of issues such as health care systems and access to health care, euthanasia and physician-assisted suicide, reproductive technologies, organ donation, and research ethics. When discussions are held about how to allocate money for medical research, it is reasonable to consider what decisions would best maximize the overall good. In the case of a woman who is pregnant with multiple embryos, utilitarians ask, how can we bring about the greatest amount of good for all? It may be that the selective reduction of some embryos would be likely to generate more overall good than attempting to bring all of the embryos to term. However, the harm to the embryos who are selected against as well as possible physical or psychological harm to the parents and remaining embryos may lead a utilitarian to conclude that not selectively reducing the embryos avoids the greatest harm and so is the right action or rule. Utilitarian thinking is evident whenever individuals or policymakers reach decisions by means of cost–benefit calculations that gauge, for example, the social effects of policies that legalize physician-assisted suicide or of rules that prioritize candidates for organ transplants.

Justice theory

Now let's turn our attention to a third type of ethical theory called **"justice theory"** or "rights theory." This theory is not identified with a single moral thinker, although Aristotle (4th century B.C.) and John Rawls (*A Theory of Justice*, 1971) are often considered its architects and proponents. Like deontology and utilitarianism, justice theory aims at providing a standard for right and wrong action. As the name indicates, justice theory privileges the principle or value of justice. The justice theorist views moral situations as arenas where justice is in question and where the claims of justice can often be addressed by identifying rights. Before we can go further with justice theory we need some definitions and explanations.

Justice means getting what one deserves or is owed. It includes having one's rights respected and being treated fairly. To be treated fairly is to be treated in a way that is appropriate or that one deserves. What a person deserves or is owed may vary from situation to situation. For example, if Mary is a U.S. military veteran, she deserves to receive medical treatment from a Veterans Administration hospital, whereas if she is not a U.S. military veteran, she does not deserve to be treated there. In this case, the criterion for what a person deserves or is owed happens to be participation in the U.S. military. But obviously this is not always the standard. There are many cases in which being a veteran has nothing to do with what one deserves, for example, in the distribution of organs for transplant. Hence, there are multiple criteria for determining what a person deserves and we will have to figure out which criterion applies in which cases.

But first, let us return to our previous question concerning the definition of justice theory. Justice theory is rooted in a broad, social perspective that views people as members of a community. Given that our lives are lived in the context of this community, we must coexist and share the benefits and the burdens of communal living. Some justice theories have explanations for how and why these communities come to be. For instance, philosophers as diverse as Plato, Hobbes, and Rawls have developed "social contract" theories that propose a real or hypothetical "contract" to which members of a community commit themselves. In return for certain benefits (say, protection from attack, a legal system, a system of private property and commerce), citizens agree to accept certain burdens (such as taxation and the obligation to defend the community). According to this social contract, citizens have both rights—these are the benefits of living in a community—and duties—these are the burdens of such living. Hence, justice theory employs the language of rights and duties.

We need not debate the plausibility of this social contract. For our purposes, it is enough to know that justice theory and rights theory arise in the context of social and political accounts of community.

There are two practical lessons to draw from the social contract background of justice theory. The first is that justice is often applied and understood *comparatively*. This means that in order to determine what is just for one person we must compare him or her to others and decide what is just for them as well. What one person deserves is figured out in light of what others deserve. We'll return to this shortly. The second practical point is that although there are several types of justice—compensatory (reimbursing for past wrongs), retributive (assigning punishment for crimes), and distributive (allocating benefits and burdens)—distributive justice is most relevant to bioethics and it applies to *situations of scarcity*. Distributive justice asks: How can we fairly pass out the benefits and the burdens of living in a community when resources are scarce? If resources (time, money, expertise, medicine, and so on) were not scarce, then there would be no distributive justice problems. Everyone could get as much of everything as they need or want. Sometimes people act as if resources are not scarce. But realistically, given the global world in which we live, rapid population growth, and limited resources, we must acknowledge that finding a way to fairly pass out scarce resources such as medicine, health care, and research funding depends on distributive justice theory.

Notice that we have not identified justice with equality. Often justice requires treating people equally, but not always. For example, it would be equality if we were to divide up the amount of pain medication (say, morphine) presently available in the United States and distribute an equal amount to every U.S. resident. But that would hardly be just. A more just system would be to distribute to those who need pain medication an amount appropriate to their level of need while providing no pain medication to those with no need for it.

Often justice theory employs the concept of "rights." Here we mean moral rights, not legal rights. For example, bioethicists have spoken of a right to health care, a right to die, reproductive rights, the right to privacy, and so on. A **"right"** is a morally justified claim or demand that someone else do something (positive right) or not do something (negative right). Rights imply duties. If someone has a right to something, then someone else has a duty to either do something or not do something to facilitate that right. Supposing there is a right to health care, it follows that society or someone else has a duty to provide health care. Or if there is a right to privacy—a right not to have one's personal life made public—then others have duties not to spy on people, read their mail, or publicize their health records, to name a few. Thus, justice theory can address bioethical situations in terms of rights (which imply duties) or duties (which do not imply rights). "Duty" is a broader category than "rights" since there can be duties even in the absence of rights (for instance, one may have a duty to be generous even though no specific person has a right to demand one's generosity).

With this background we are ready to consider the specific rules and procedures employed by justice theory. Reflect again on the situation facing Sam's physician. This time imagine that Dr. Gupta thinks from the point of view of justice theory. She will then approach the problem of what to do by focusing on distributive justice and related rights and duties. She might think about whether Sam has a right to updated information on his condition, whether Gladys has the right to speak on Sam's behalf, and what is fair for everyone.

Justice theory aims to achieve fairness by upholding rights and treating persons as they deserve to be treated. Persons deserve to be treated like those to whom they are similar and unlike those to whom they are dissimilar, that is, who differ from them in morally significant ways (such as need, merit, or social contribution). Thus, Dr. Gupta may need to think comparatively about Sam and assess whether he is like or unlike other patients. The just choice will take account of rights and fairness.

Justice theory identifies some of the morally relevant ways in which people are different in terms of their levels of need, merit, and social contribution and it prescribes that people deserve to be treated differently because of these differences. That is, there are times when it is just to treat people differently because of their level of need (distributing pain medication), merit (promotion to head nurse), and social contribution (Nobel prize). These differences stand in contrast to differences that are not generally morally relevant, such as race, nationality, sex, and religion. These latter differences, though morally irrelevant, have often been used wrongly to justify the unequal treatment of people.

Of course, justice theory, like all ethical theories, is subject to criticism. One problem is the identification of rights; that is, there is uncertainty at the basic level concerning what rights people possess. It can be hard to say what rights people have. A related concern is where rights come from. Ethicists debate what justifies or backs up claims about rights and whether we must adopt a complicated theory about the nature of political communities in order to explain what gives rise to rights. Perhaps rights are God-given or natural, but then again it seems we would need to formulate some kind of foundational account to explain how and why rights come about.

Another problem is what to do when rights come into conflict. The debate about the morality of abortion is often cast as a conflict between the rights of the mother (say, her right to control her body) and the rights of the fetus (say, its right to life). This leads to the question of whether some rights are more important, more basic, more "inalienable" than others. What rule would we use to decide which rights are more important or whose rights take priority when rights seem to conflict? Justice theory may be incomplete if it cannot answer this question. Possibly, we need another moral theory, like utilitarianism, in order to decide how to order or rank rights.

Finally, taking a critical point of view, it can be said that justice theory is too general to be of much help. While it is a morally valuable insight to observe that similar persons deserve similar treatment, this does not direct us to a specific action. Justice theory provides a kind of procedural rule but no details on how to act toward similar people. If seriously injured people have been turned away from hospital emergency rooms because they cannot pay for their care, does it follow, is it just or moral, that this particular patient, who is similarly injured and unable to pay for care, should be similarly turned away? There must certainly be a broader picture of what is moral, even of what is just, than this "precedent-following" rule of justice theory. Yes, justice theory tells us that it is fair to treat people dissimilarly when they differ in terms of merit, need, or social contribution, but how do we know which differences to focus on and which are relevant to a specific situation? It seems that we need more direction on the nature and content of right and wrong actions than a justice theory alone can offer.

In spite of these concerns, justice theory brings an important perspective to bioethics. It requires bioethicists to acknowledge the social context, the community, within which bioethical issues arise. It takes account not only of the social effects of bioethical decisions (as consequentialism does) but also the social milieu or context that gives rise to bioethical issues and influences bioethical decision making. For example, justice theory focuses attention on the rights of patients, families, and health care professionals and the duties and responsibilities that correspond to those rights. But these rights and responsibilities may take different forms in different societies in part because those societies understand differently the role and authority of the health care provider, the dynamics of family life, and the relationship between individuals and communities. Acting justly or fairly requires paying attention to the resources of a community and determining how to distribute the benefits and burdens of living in a community equitably.

Justice theory often emphasizes the big picture—whether there is a right to health care, which diseases should receive the greatest medical attention and research support, and whether laws and institutional policies are just in setting up criteria for who is offered specialized care, who may speak on behalf of a patient, and who may utilize physician-assisted suicide. Justice theory also moves bioethics beyond national boundaries as it considers and aims to set standards for medical research in developing countries and the responsibilities wealthy countries and pharmaceutical companies have to provide medical care and low-cost medicines to the poor.

Virtue ethics

Virtue ethics is another moral perspective to consider. When ancient philosophers such as Plato and Aristotle discussed questions of morality, they did so from a virtue perspective. Some contemporary thinkers, such as Philippa Foot, Alastair MacIntyre, and Martha Nussbaum, have recently argued for the superiority of the virtue approach. The distinguishing feature of this perspective is that it focuses on persons and not actions. It is concerned more with the people who act and less with the actions they perform. Virtue ethics is all about becoming and being a good person, that is, a person who is virtuous, whose character reflects virtues.

The virtue approach notes that there is a difference between being good and doing right actions. A person can do the right action, namely, act in a morally correct way, without being good in the sense of being the sort of person who consistently acts in right ways. For example, performing an honest action accidentally or unthinkingly or while coerced is not the same as choosing to become a person who values and exemplifies honesty. Being good requires more than doing the right thing. Morality, from the virtue perspective, concerns people and their characters and dispositions, and not rules and requirements for actions.

Aristotle formulated one of the most complete virtue approaches so we will describe his view, although the strengths and weaknesses that we consider apply more broadly to all virtue approaches. Aristotle defined virtue as a kind of excellence of the human soul, a way of living in accordance with rationality. Examples of virtues are courage, temperance, generosity, and friendliness. Virtues are states of character, ways of being, and not specific directions on how to act. Aristotle believed that a virtuous person tends to act in virtuous ways, although there is a difference between a right action performed by a virtuous person and a right action done by a nonvirtuous person. The latter's action fails to be performed for the right reason or in the right way. It lacks the authority of the virtuous character expressed by the action of the virtuous person.

Since virtue ethics describes a person's character, it must have something to say about how we become virtuous people. Aristotle's claim is that people become virtuous by practicing right actions, namely, by habitually acting in morally correct ways. And how does the nonvirtuous person know what the right actions are? He or she looks to virtuous people as the standard and follows what they do. Thus, people like Socrates, Jesus, Muhammad, or in more contemporary terms, Martin Luther King, Jr. or Albert Schweitzer or Mother Theresa become the models, the "exemplars," of how we ought to act. We, the not yet virtuous, imitate them until we become virtuous and then serve as models for others.

There is one other guideline that Aristotle offers to help us act in virtuous ways. He explains that virtue is a "mean," that is, it is an intermediate state between two vices that are "extremes." One vice is excess, doing too much, while the other is deficiency, doing too little. Virtue is the mean; it recommends the moderate action. Courage is a virtue; it requires actions that fall midway between recklessness (excess) and cowardliness (deficiency). Similarly, generosity is a mean between extravagance (excess) and stinginess (deficiency). The key to virtue then is to practice actions that are moderate.

There is also an ethical theory known as **natural law** that developed out of Aristotle's virtue theory. Natural law theorists believe that a moral life is a life based on reason. For them, moral standards and laws are "natural," that is, built in to the fabric of the universe and ourselves. Moral laws and rules are in some ways like other natural laws such as the law of gravity; they apply to everyone, they hold necessarily, and we can know them by using our faculty of reason. But in another way they are different from other natural laws. We can't help but follow the law of gravity while we must choose to follow the moral laws that are natural to us. Many natural law theorists are Christian, especially Catholic, ethicists. Saint Thomas Aquinas, for one, advocates for natural law theory. These natural law theorists maintain that God, a perfectly rational being, has endowed human beings with rationality. Since we are created in God's image, our moral lives are to be lived in accordance with our nature, our reason.

Now, in the case involving Sam and his physician, Dr. Gupta, suppose that Dr. Gupta is committed to the virtue ethics perspective. Her task then is to determine how a virtuous person would act in her situation. She is likely to consider what it means to be a virtuous physician and how best to realize virtues such as courage, generosity, friendliness, and benevolence. Finally, she will probably assess what is the moderate course of action for her to take. In sum, she will use reason and what she knows of human nature to help her decide how to be virtuous in this situation.

Next, let us take a look at some of the problems of virtue ethics. One concern is that virtue ethics does not seem to provide clear direction. It does not tell us exactly what to do. Of course, as we have said, its focus is not on action but on character, so it is not surprising that it does not recommend or prohibit specific actions. But the criticism can apply as well to character traits and to virtues. It is not clear how many virtues there are and what the virtues are. We can ask whether virtues are universal and timeless or whether there are different virtues for different sorts of people or people living in different historical circumstances. Some may identify as a virtuous trait something that others would fail to consider virtuous (say, humility). Thus, a virtue approach may not offer sufficient direction in identifying virtues.

Another issue is that it is not obvious how to best exemplify and express virtue. One person may decide that a certain choice is the moderate choice, although others would have trouble seeing it as such. Aristotle recognized this aspect of virtue ethics and commented that virtue is a "relative" mean. It is not a mathematical mean, absolutely halfway between each extreme. Instead, it is a mean that is relative to us and to the situation. Sometimes the courageous way of being, while still moderate, is closer to recklessness and other times it is closer to cowardice. The "mean" is a broad expanse. Different people will locate virtue at different points in this expanse. Therefore, critics object to the inevitable subjectivity that seems to occur in applying the virtues.

Finally, it may be that what seemed to be an advantage of virtue ethics, namely, its focus on the character and nature of the person acting, turns out to be a disadvantage. While it successfully draws ethics away from a narrow concern with actions and rules and emphasizes the desired characteristics of moral people, it assumes that human beings have purposes or excellences, namely, certain goals at which they are naturally aimed. The goal of the virtue ethicist is to live a good life, according to Aristotle, a flourishing life. This belief may have seemed obvious to Aristotle and Aquinas, but it does not seem obvious to everyone today. Science, for example, does not speak of the natural purposes and ends of things. If we are not comfortable with the notion of natural purposes and laws then virtue ethics loses some of its attractiveness.

In spite of these concerns, virtue ethics plays a significant role in the field of bioethics. The professional codes of ethics can be seen as efforts to describe the commitments and virtues of the various health care professionals. Catholic bioethicists have used the notion of natural law to explain why abortion, in vitro fertilization technologies, and suicide are wrong. They violate our purposes, our excellences, and what God intends for us. Evidence of virtue ethics can be found in discussions of the physician's role in certain cosmetic surgeries and in physician-assisted suicides. There is debate over whether it is consistent with the nature and goals of medicine for physicians to participate in procedures that are not medically required or that hasten a patient's death.

Virtue ethics enables us to move beyond what we think physicians, family members, and patients should *do* to what they should *exemplify*. Medical professionals should not only obtain patient consent prior to surgery but they should do so in ways that show integrity, are caring, sensitive, conscientious, and more. These virtuous character traits are a part of what it means in the full sense to act morally. Virtue ethics gives us a way of explaining why even people who follow moral rules and do good things may not yet be the kind of people we choose for our friends and caregivers. We look for those who not only embody moral rules but also enact those rules in thoughtful, compassionate, conscientious, and thus, in virtuous ways.

Next, we consider another approach to bioethics that shares some points in common with virtue ethics. A feminist ethic of care offers us yet another tool for analyzing ethical problems in medicine, this time from a perspective of care, maintaining relationships, and recognizing the essential interdependence of human beings. Like virtue ethics, an ethic of care emphasizes the person acting, and not so much the action itself.

Care ethics

Some feminist approaches to ethics start with a unique moral perspective that is thought to be reflective of many women's experience: an **"ethic of care."** This ethic is characterized by an understanding of the individual as an interdependent, socially embedded being. Such a view of the individual goes against the more traditional accounts according to which we are independent subjects who relate to others in a detached manner. It also goes against traditional views about the nature of moral decision making. Traditional ethical theories like those of Kantian deontology and utilitarianism demand that we make our moral decisions objectively and impartially. According to these theories, we must use our reasoning capacity and, as independent rational agents, make our moral decisions based on objective considerations.

But feminist ethicists question the value placed on objectivity, impartiality, reason, and independence. Instead, they argue that we are born into a web of relationships beginning with our immediate families and extending later in life to include friends, significant others, and colleagues. Our social embeddedness means that we are not the independent, objective, and impartial beings that traditional accounts have emphasized. On the contrary, we are *inter*dependent beings who need one another for emotional and physical support. Furthermore, who we are—and what duties and rights we have with respect to others—is at least partly a function of the social roles we have taken on. For example, being a mother means having certain obligations with respect to your child that are not shared by others. Being socially embedded also means that our moral understanding of ourselves and others is always contextually situated (e.g., a poor black woman will perceive certain aspects of social reality differently than a wealthy white man). Thus, feminist ethicists emphasize the contextual features of our lives over the abstract universal humanity that traditional ethicists claim is the ground of morality, and they stress the importance of caring for others as the basis for our moral decision making.

Indeed, some care ethicists go even further in arguing that traditional approaches to ethics are actually immoral because they tend to ignore important contextual features of our lives. Moral theorist Nel Noddings argues that human relationships are based not on respect for individuals' abstract rights but rather on meeting the concrete needs of particular individuals. By demanding that we be detached, impartial agents, these traditional approaches deny our lived experiences and chasten us to ignore the particular features of our situations. Noddings goes so far as to reject Kantian and utilitarian-style approaches to moral reasoning because they are too ambiguous and tend to separate us from others. She and other feminist ethicists claim that a care approach is a superior one because it takes seriously our caring relationships and the impact those relationships have on our moral decision making. Instead of focusing on contractual human relationships, say some care ethicists, we ought rather to take the mother–child relationship as the paradigm for all human relationships, since this relationship is at least as representative of human interactions as the more contractual view of human relationships promoted by Kantian deontology and utilitarianism.

Carol Gilligan was first to identify an ethic of care that tends to represent women's lives and provides them with a moral identity different from men's (Figure 1.3).

Gilligan identified this "ethic of care" in response to the work of Lawrence Kohlberg, a moral development theorist who argued that women are largely incapable of reaching the highest stages of moral development. Kohlberg conducted studies that showed boys' ability to reach the highest stages of moral development (that is, the capacity to reason impartially based on abstract rules and principles such as justice) and that showed girls' widespread incapacity to think independently outside of particular relationships. Gilligan indicates that the girls in Kohlberg's study were merely using a "different voice" to identify the moral features of a situation: the "care" voice. (It is important to note that Gilligan does not claim a biologically based notion of women as "care" ethicists and men as "justice" ethicists. On the contrary, she suggests that gender role socialization may be the cause of these gendered ways of moral reasoning; furthermore, she suggests that some men may think from the perspective of an ethic of care whereas some women may think from a justice perspective.)

Gilligan's work allowed women to embrace the ethic of care, since it was found to be no less justified than (and thus not inferior to) the "justice" perspective—or focus on principles, objectivity,

FIGURE 1.3 Carol Gilligan b. 1936.

and impartiality that mark the traditional moral approach into which men are socialized. The ethic of care liberated women in that it embraced women's particular ways of "doing" moral reasoning and allowed for the inclusion of more personal considerations in moral theory. Rather than working from the level of abstract moral theories to determine what should be done in specific circumstances, the ethic of care begins with the particular features of one's own personal relationships with others.

While an ethic of care identifies a legitimate moral perspective that derives from our human relationships, it lacks a social and political component that raises questions such as: Who does the caring? At what cost? What presuppositions and theoretical assumptions are behind it? Some feminist ethicists have argued for a more socially and politically engaged version of care ethics.

In her work, Susan Sherwin critiques systems of health care from a politicized care perspective. She identifies the care ethic as a "feminine" ethic and distinguishes it from a more explicitly political feminist perspective, where women's oppression is treated as being politically and morally unacceptable. On her view, while we must respect the unique moral perspective of women, we must also ensure justice by examining the oppressive practices by which women are subordinated. In short, this requires setting up moral criteria for determining when to offer and when to withhold care, an element of caring that is not addressed by care ethicists like Noddings.

Helga Kuhse is equally critical of an ethic of care that lacks a social and political basis. In her work on nursing ethics, Kuhse argues that without being balanced by concerns for justice, a nursing ethic of care is ultimately conservative and oppressive for women. This nursing ethic has been identified as a way of distinguishing the nurse's focus on caring from medicine's concern with curing. By embracing an ethic of care, some nursing theorists have argued, nurses can identify an ethic that is unique to the practice of nursing, that is, caring and patient advocacy. Yet the nursing profession is still dominated by women, so appealing to a nursing ethic of care can be politically dangerous. It robs nurses of the moral grounds to petition for fair wages, to strike, to speak out when they are treated unjustly by patients, and to resist being overburdened by huge patient loads. Kuhse argues that along with care, nursing ethics requires justice and impartiality to ensure that nurses are not exploited.

Other feminist ethicists have also cautioned against being too enthusiastic about an ethic of care. While these feminists do not reject the value of caregiving, nurturing, and investing in others, they do question the wholehearted embracing of "womanly" virtues. For example, the uncritical embracing of what Sherwin calls a "feminine" care ethic glosses over the history of women's nurturance and care work, in which women give freely while expecting nothing in return. There are dangers in reclaiming the "womanly" virtues, primarily the danger of gender essentialism and glorifying women's oppression.

Most contemporary care ethicists now argue that we need a blend of the relational concerns raised by care ethics along with an emphasis on principled moral theorizing that stresses objectivity, universalizability, and justice.

With this background in mind, what might care ethics have to say about the case involving Sam Levine and Dr. Gupta? Let us now consider the kinds of ethical issues that a care ethic would address in this case, issues that some of the other moral theories and principles do not consider.

A care ethicist would begin from the concern with maintaining and sustaining human relationships by considering what relationships are at stake in this dilemma. Clearly the problem does not involve a lone patient, Sam Levine, but also his wife and daughter, who are closely bound to him by their loving, familial bond. Both Gladys and Anne are concerned that Sam not suffer, that he receive the best care possible, and that he be treated as he would *wish* to be treated. Clearly there are other relationships at stake, too. Dr. Gupta and the nurses who are taking care of Sam are bound in a relationship of care, so their interests and views cannot simply be sidelined. It is important that the relationships among the patient, family, and health care staff be harmonious so that everyone involved can feel respected and cared about, and so that the patient and his or her family can receive the best care possible. A breakdown in the therapeutic relationship can be very detrimental to both the good care of the patient and to the flourishing of all the individuals who are part of the relationship.

Also, if we place Sam's medical situation within the social and political context of care that has been emphasized by some feminist ethicists, we need to consider more than just what will support the care and nurturance of Sam. We would also need to consider the implications for Gladys and Anne of whatever course of action is followed. While the original version of the care ethic only emphasizes the importance of caring, of maintaining relationships *no matter the consequences* for the caretaker and others, a more politicized version would ask: What are the implications for Gladys and for Anne should CPR be done for Sam? If Sam is resuscitated but left in an extremely frail and dependent state, then the care burden on Gladys and Anne could be extreme. Furthermore, since Anne is apparently their only adult daughter, she is likely to have the responsibility of care for Gladys. The stress and physical demands of caring for Sam could place Gladys in such ill health that Anne would be left with the intensive care demands of a very sick mother; this could affect her work and other relationships, which could strain her relationship with her mother.

When considering what care requires, it is not simply an issue of choosing an option, but of acting so as not to violate relationships or hurt the others with whom one is in relationships. It is too easy to confuse a failure to care with a failure to provide further medical interventions. But an ethic of care may involve rejecting medical interventions, which can actually impede relationships by rendering patients unconscious, or by applying medical technologies to the point where family members can no longer even touch, lie down with, or interact with their ill loved ones. A loving relationship between family members can be permanently fractured if a loved one is hooked up to tubes and machines, in only a semi-conscious state so that a true relationship is no longer possible. The failure to provide such invasive care is not equivalent to the failure to *care about* the patient. Care ethicists recognize that sometimes the most caring thing to do is refuse the endless number of medical interventions and instead opt for a more natural death within the circle of a loving, close family.

Like all other moral theories and approaches, there are particular problems raised by the ethic of care. First, though one might initially be able to narrow down whose concerns should be highlighted based on maintaining and sustaining relationships of care, it is much more difficult to determine what "care" requires. How can one determine if Gladys or Anne has the most caring approach to dealing with Sam's situation? It doesn't seem that care ethics offers a good answer to this question, since both are speaking as family members who know Sam well, who are deeply concerned for his welfare, and who will be directly impacted by the decision.

Second, critics charge that care ethics suffers from a lack of rules by which to effectively make moral decisions. In a reversal of the concerns raised against Kantian and utilitarian theories—that they may be too formulaic to address the complexities of human emotions and relationships—feminist care ethics suffers from the lack of a clear framework for making judgments and decisions. Individuals who try to apply a care ethic approach to moral dilemmas may find themselves without clear guidance in terms of how to proceed because the approach is so context-specific. In the field of bioethics, if there is no clear decision procedure in place then the theory or approach may be of little help.

Third, the ethic of care in its original form does not require that we radically change our caregiving practices or values. Feminists who are concerned about the degree to which women carry the care burden in society reject the care approach because it tends to result in much of the same old thing: women doing most of the care work with little to no remuneration. An ethic of care doesn't necessarily require that nurses be paid well, that new mothers have help learning how to care for their infants, or that families caring for their elderly family members are not "burned out" by the burden of care. So, some critics argue, a justice-based approach may better serve female caregivers because it petitions for the rights of care workers in a way that the care ethic simply cannot.

Clearly, an ethic of care draws on different strengths from those of traditional moral theories. It rejects the abstract, absolute, universal rules set by Kantian and utilitarian approaches and instead emphasizes the particulars of each case, the relationships involved, and the demands of care. Care ethics does not allow us to determine objectively what should be done; on the contrary, it violates the spirit of care ethics to try and consider a case "objectively." For this reason, the ethic of care has been applied most often in health care contexts where questions of relationships and caregiving arise. Bioethicists have applied the ethic of care in the context of abortion, where a woman's individual life conditions inform her decision making, and where her relationship to her fetus impacts her emotional and psychological state. In cases of long-term care for older adults, decisions about whether and when to move an elderly person from home to a care facility involves the elderly person and his or her adult children, and can have a long-lasting impact on those family relations. For this reason, the ethic of care is particularly well suited to dealing with these situations. Finally, despite some of its problems, the ethic of care really is best suited to the nursing profession, since like nursing it takes care to be the fundamental good of human relationships.

THE "FOUR PRINCIPLES" APPROACH TO BIOMEDICAL ETHICS

It is in part because ethical solutions to medical problems require urgent responses that Tom Beauchamp and James Childress came up with the "four principles" approach to biomedical ethics. Their 1977 text, *Principles of Biomedical Ethics*, was groundbreaking in its approach to ethics in medicine, and it was the beginning of biomedical ethics as we currently practice it.

These authors claim that the answers to bioethical problems can be quickly and efficiently discovered by appealing to four principles that are core to the practice of good medicine: autonomy (self-rule or self-government); justice (fairness, often defined as treating like cases alike); beneficence (to do good); and nonmaleficence (to do no harm). Quite simply, Beauchamp and Childress argue that these four principles are the most important because they address different aspects of medical ethics: that as much as possible one should respect the patient and his or her wishes; that when practicing medicine one should ensure the fair and equal treatment of all patients; that the purpose of medicine is to benefit patients by making them better off than they were before the medical intervention; and finally, that at the very least in medical practice one should always avoid doing harm. While other principles or values may be important in medicine, these authors claim that we can capture the important aspects of medical ethics in these four basic principles.

Furthermore, the four principles are of particular value because people from widely different faith and philosophical commitments can accept and agree upon them, even if their reasons for accepting them and how they interpret them may differ. Individuals may not agree on their conceptions of what is good or what is right, but they may agree that the principles of autonomy, beneficence, nonmaleficence, and justice are significant.

Over the past few decades *Principles of Biomedical Ethics* has become a foundational text in biomedical ethics. There is a simplicity to the approach that is appealing, and the four principles do allow one to address the most important concerns in medicine and medical research. For example, the principle of autonomy is essential to medical research because it ensures that the research subjects' rights are respected and that they are not used simply to advance the interests of society. And in allocating medical resources, one must consider the principle of justice to ensure that patients are being treated fairly and equally. The "four principles" approach is thus appealing to practitioners because it is easily learned and allows for a quick decision-making process that is so essential in medicine. While theory-based approaches to doing bioethics require a deeper grounding for principles (one begins with a theory—then derives a principle—from the principle derives a rule—and then from the rule determines the appropriate action), principled approaches like that of Beauchamp and Childress cut out the necessity for the theory. Instead, one determines the most relevant or important principle in a case—then derives a rule from the principle—and finally, determines the appropriate action. By eliminating the level of theory, one saves a great deal of work to justify the principle, and removes a layer of unnecessary philosophizing that can get in the way of effective (and swift) action in medicine, at the same time allowing for a broad interpretation of what the four principles entail.

The principle of respect for autonomy

The principle of respect for autonomy demands that each rational, competent person be given the right to make medical decisions that affect his or her life. Since each individual knows his or her own values, beliefs, and preferences best, we must let each person decide for him- or herself. For several reasons, this principle is now considered essential to the good practice of medicine. First, there is a long history of **paternalism** in medicine. Paternalism literally means "rule by the father" (where the father makes decisions for the child in the child's best interests) and in medicine it resulted in physicians making decisions for their patients without consulting them. Doctors used to withhold information from patients, lie to them, dictate treatment, and sometimes force treatment against the patient's will, all under the rubric of paternalistic medicine.

Second, respecting autonomy ensures that patients have given their free, informed consent for treatment. The process of informed consent is taken very seriously in medicine, given the importance of protecting individual rights and dignity. Informed consent is not only an important legal procedure, but is symbolic of the respect that is owed to patients. Thus, the signing of the consent form indicates a patient's understanding of the procedure and a willingness to submit to the consequences of the intervention.

Finally, the possibility of lawsuits now weighs heavily on the minds of health care providers. Especially in the United States, where health care is often run on a for-profit model, caregivers do not want to do anything to patients (or deny patients any treatment) that could result in litigation. By focusing on patient autonomy, it is better ensured that patients' wishes will be respected and staff members are far less likely to be sued for medical malpractice.

The principle of justice

The principle of justice speaks to other ethical worries in medicine: that people should be treated justly, fairly, and equally, and that when patients are in similar medical situations we should treat their cases the same. Beauchamp and Childress were right that justice is important to the practice of medicine: We need to always be sure that medicine is practiced fairly, with equal concern for all patients.

Issues of justice in health care become especially important when one addresses questions about allocating and rationing health care. Because health care is a scarce resource—it is very expensive, and eats up a huge portion of the federal budget—decisions about how to allocate it must be made very carefully. When society is deciding how to distribute health care dollars or, on a more personal level, which patients should get medical resources and which ones not, we need a principle of justice to determine how to ration in a way that is fair and respectful, but that also makes good sense. The principle of justice leads to questions such as: Should 90-year-olds have access to organ transplants? Should we spend more research money on AIDS or cancer? If we have time to operate on only one patient, but two require emergency care, which one should we choose?

While some Americans receive the best health care in the world, others have no access to health care at all. If we all have equal need of care, and it is a basic need without which one cannot lead a flourishing life, then it is arguably unjust that some Americans go without it. Some ethicists appeal to the principle of justice to argue for a universal system of health care.

The principle of beneficence

The principle of beneficence—to "do good" for patients—addresses a concern that is basic to medical care: that the whole purpose of medical practice is to make lives better, to improve patients' situations, and to make people well again. The principle of beneficence is what motivated the kind of medical paternalism that reigned supreme until very recently. Physicians wanted to do good for their patients, and believed that doing good sometimes requires lying to them, or withholding medical information, or dictating the one correct treatment option.

Still, the practice of medicine without beneficence would be unthinkable, given that when it is practiced correctly (and when it is at its best) medical care can return people to levels of function they experienced prior to their illnesses. It is important to consider what it would mean to "do good" for a patient, since presumably that is why patients seek medical care: to be benefited by the skill and expertise of health care professionals.

The principle of nonmaleficence

The principle of nonmaleficence may be considered a minimalist principle in medical practice. This principle tells health care providers that, if they can no longer benefit or do good for patients because their condition has drastically worsened, then they should at least not harm them. This does not mean, however, that physicians are prohibited from cutting patients open for surgical interventions, from inserting needles into patients, or from giving painful treatments. While these procedures do inflict harm, in the long run they benefit the patients in question and so can be morally justified based on the health benefits that will result. The principle of nonmaleficence is rather a caution against taking serious risks with patients, or doing things that have no immediate or long-term benefit for them.

There are sometimes problems, however, in interpreting what it means to "harm" someone. As a doctor one may refuse to do abortions because one does not want to harm a woman or her fetus; but the pregnant woman herself might not see the abortion as a "harm" at all. Or a patient might demand a treatment that a doctor believes to be of no benefit; one must then wonder whether it is harming the patient to let her have the desired treatment.

Having reviewed the principles, it is now important to ask how the four principles approach works. It is one thing to identify some important principles in medicine and another thing to know how one will reason when he or she puts those principles into action. Beauchamp and Childress claim that one can determine which principle is most relevant to a medical situation by briefly considering the situation at hand. In some cases, autonomy will be central; in other cases, justice will surface as the most important and relevant principle; and in still others, the principles of beneficence or nonmaleficence will prevail. But there is no simple or clear-cut way to determine which of the four principles is most relevant in any given case; one must use his or her powers of reflection to determine which principle is overriding, and then consider what action the principle requires. At various points we might need to rank and rerank our principles as the particulars of a case unfold.

The easiest way to understand how the four principles approach might work is to apply it to a situation. By returning to the scenario of Dr. Gupta and the Levine family, we can consider the four principles and how one might reflect upon them in an actual case. Let us now consider how Dr. Gupta might think about this difficult situation.

When considering Sam's current position, Dr. Gupta will reflect upon the principles of *Beneficence* and *Nonmaleficence*. As a physician, her goal is certainly to not harm Sam or his family and, in the best case scenario, to actually do good in some way. This patient has a bronchial infection, pulmonary edema, and a urinary tract infection. At 89 years of age, his health is declining rapidly, and it is very uncertain whether CPR will be of any benefit whatsoever to him. It is especially important, given his many and complex health issues, that Mr. Levine not be made any worse off than he already is.

The principles of *Justice* and *Autonomy* would also be part of Dr. Gupta's thinking about this case. She might ask herself whether it is fair for an 89-year-old man to use limited health resources with little likelihood of benefit, when the cost for Sam's care could be put toward a child or young adult with a much stronger chance of benefiting from the care. If the principle of Justice demands that we "treat like cases alike" then Dr. Gupta must determine what this means. And with respect to the principle of Respect for Autonomy, Dr. Gupta would be reflecting on the importance of Sam's stated wishes and the disagreement between Anne and Gladys about whether Sam should be approached again for a follow-up conversation. The principle of Respect for Autonomy would lead Dr. Gupta to reflect on the different autonomous claims (including her own!) that are at stake in this situation.

The four principles approach is meant to be useful and expeditious because it does not require a complicated theoretical framework that one must work through prior to considering what principles are at stake. It is also intended to have broad appeal to individuals, no matter what their particular theoretical or religious commitments may be. Yet as we can see in attempting to apply the four principles in this case, it is very difficult to know how to interpret the principles if there is no theoretical framework within which to *ground* those principles. And this is one of the most serious flaws with the four principles approach, a critique that has been leveled against the principles by those who favor a theory-based approach to resolving ethical dilemmas in health care: One needs a theoretical framework to understand and interpret the relevant principles. Theories may provide more complex ways of resolving moral problems and justifying moral decisions. They add a layer of complexity to moral reasoning—this may be a negative—but in turn they provide unified and integrated approaches to moral situations—this is a positive.

Nevertheless, the principles approach has proven effective in treating complex situations that have a number of variables to take into consideration. It allows for persons with different theoretical and/or religious frameworks to deliberate together over principles that, all things being equal, people can agree upon. Furthermore, the principles approach does not require the deliberators to have a background in philosophical theory such that they can reason through from a Kantian or utilitarian perspective; the principles are intuitive to clinicians, and so may prove most useful to them in the end.

To sum up these sections, recall that we have described five kinds of moral theories or approaches (deontology, consequentialism, justice theory, virtue ethics, and care ethics) and one principle-based framework. We have also explained how to use them in a case. None of these theories or perspectives is perfect, but all of them have something important to contribute to moral thinking about bioethics. Bioethicists use them as tools; together they help us to better understand moral situations and therefore to reach better resolutions to moral conflicts.

ADDRESSING MULTICULTURALISM IN MEDICINE

Finally, we turn to a whole other set of issues that are not addressed by the theories, principles, and approaches we have covered thus far: cultural differences among the health care staff, their patients, and their patients' families. While these cultural considerations do not at all constitute a theoretical framework for addressing bioethics, they are important to any theory or approach one uses, since religious, cultural, ethnic, racial, and other differences may enter into the picture no matter which framework one is using.

In the past couple of decades, bioethicists have begun considering cultural differences in health care, and how those differences affect the choices and relationships of the people involved. As more and more people from all different parts of the world immigrate to the United States, we see within the practice of medicine an increasingly complex set of relationships that must be negotiated. An awareness of **multiculturalism** highlights the ethical importance of racial, ethnic, religious, and cultural differences that arise among patients, their families, and the hospital staff (Figure 1.4).

The United States now has one of the most ethnically, racially, and religiously diverse populations in the world. As a result of this diverse population, we enjoy a wide variety of cuisine, music, clothing, and language. And along with these enriching aspects of multiculturalism come new challenges to our

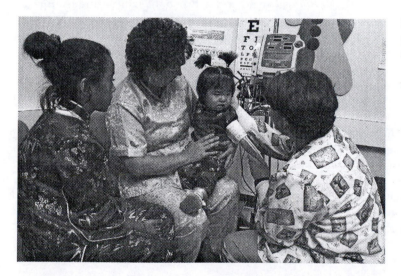

FIGURE 1.4   Nurse taking blood pressure of a Chinese child accompanied by her family.

beliefs and practices. Nowhere are these challenges more obvious than in the health care setting, where differences of religion, culture, language, race, and ethnicity can affect the physician–patient relationship, sometimes creating extreme differences of opinion.

In contrast to the old "melting pot" theory of immigration, where newcomers to the United States were expected to strictly adopt American ways and set their "old ways" aside, the new multiculturalism emphasizes the value of cultural diversity and difference. Over the past several decades we have seen the building of mosques and Buddhist temples to reflect the needs of immigrants of non-Christian faiths; and we have seen an explosion in communities of Hispanic, Southeast Asian, West Indian, and Middle Eastern people who may not speak English, and who may continue in their traditional religious, spiritual, and cultural practices.

As a result, a white, American-born physician who has been trained to practice Western medicine will increasingly meet patients who do not share his or her religious or spiritual beliefs, language, or customs—and who may also have very different beliefs about the appropriate practice of medicine. Conversely, a white, American-born patient will increasingly meet health care staff who differ vastly from his or her background. When crises or difficult medical decisions arise, and the parties involved become stressed, one sometimes sees a breakdown in the physician–patient–family relationship as these cultural, religious, and medical belief systems come into conflict with one another.

For example, some cultures within the United States are rooted in spiritual beliefs that include a concern for bad or evil spirits that may opportunistically invade human bodies. So for a Vietnamese culture like the Hmong, when a person is suffering convulsions it is a sign that spirits (Dabs) have invaded the body and the way to deal with them is to practice ritualistic burning to drive them out. To a physician trained in Western medicine the very idea that spirits invade human bodies and repeatedly throw them to the ground is nonsensical; such behavior is medically diagnosed as epilepsy, and proper medical treatment is provided to prevent it from happening again. When these two different sets of beliefs come into contact, tensions arise because the patient's family may wish to follow their customary rituals while the health care staff may see such rituals as medically useless and even abusive to the patient. When such differences arise, it is not always clear how to best negotiate them.

In other circumstances, there may be cultural clashes over the value of medicating a patient to prevent pain and suffering, since some people believe (on spiritual grounds) that it is better to face pain than to face death in a foggy and drugged state. Or one may see cases where a patient's extended Mexican family keeps vigil with their very ill family member, causing the health care staff to complain because there are many people in the hospital room, and they cannot get near the patient to do routine medical care. In yet another example, some Native American patients and/or their families may refuse to be given a medical diagnosis because it is "bad luck" or disrespectful to discuss negative conditions like cancer, despite the strong American cultural (and medical) emphasis on autonomy and informed consent. As one can see through such examples, the tensions often arise not just between the patient and health care team, but also between the patient's family and staff.

There are no easy answers to these complex medical situations. But bioethicists are certainly addressing these cultural differences, and offering some ethical and practical guidelines for negotiating them. For example, some have suggested that when dealing with non-Western cancer patients and their families, a conversation should be held well in advance of diagnosis to find out how they wish to be informed of their condition. If an elderly female Chinese patient indicates that the physician should talk to her adult son, and that she does not want to know her diagnosis, then the physician should follow her wishes. In almost all cases, many of the differences and clashes can be prevented by a clear and honest conversation early on in the medical relationship. By taking time to work out a mode of relating to one another, physicians, patients, and their families can at least aim at respectful, effective, and cooperative relationships.

Let us briefly consider these multicultural concerns as they relate to the case of Sam Levine and Dr. Gupta. There is a point of contention between Dr. Gupta and the Levines that centers around the appropriateness of providing CPR if Sam's heart should stop beating. In this case, no real religious, cultural, or spiritually-based reasons are given for why Sam would want CPR at all costs. But the situation between the Levines and Dr. Gupta may be intensified by the fact that there are racial and ethnic differences between them. As an elderly couple who were raised in an era of medicine where physicians were mostly white men, being faced with a young, female Indian physician may increase their degree of discomfort, and may lead to a distrust of the doctor's opinions. Depending on their religious or spiritual backgrounds, they may not all share the same views about the end of life or the value of aggressive medical interventions.

If we alter the case a little and suppose the Levines are an African American couple, then we raise other culturally sensitive issues that may relate to Sam's and Gladys's demand for CPR. As a later chapter in this textbook outlines, African Americans have historically faced discrimination and abuse within the U.S. medical system, most strongly exemplified by the United States Public Health Service syphilis study, where a group of African American men from the rural South were studied by the public health service and denied available treatments—without their knowledge or consent—to understand the effects of untreated syphilis. This study, which was done in Tuskegee, Alabama, is a major cause of what has been labeled the "Tuskegee effect," a widespread and deep distrust among African Americans of the American medical system. So, if Sam and Gladys were African American, one might better understand their strong reaction against Dr. Gupta's suggestion that nothing further should be done for Sam; they might see it as a failure to respect Sam by valuing his life less because he is black.

The case could be altered in a number of ways to highlight the way that differences among health professionals, patients, and their families affect health care. The point is simply that we need to be mindful of how ethnic, religious, and cultural differences can affect the practice of medicine and the attitudes of the people involved. How far a medical team needs to go to accommodate the views and wishes of patients and their families is not easily settled; but these differences must be addressed and negotiated, preferably before the disagreement arises.

These concerns for negotiating cultural and religious differences in health care point to one obvious response; that we should have respect for others' beliefs, values, and practices and not impose our own upon them. So, one might argue, a Western white physician should simply respect the wishes of an elderly Asian woman who rejects informed consent and sends him to speak to her eldest son. In her culture one addresses the eldest son directly, and does not trouble the ill elderly patient with the particulars of her disease. Whatever the case at hand, some critics argue that respect for cultural differences should be the overriding value that guides the practice of health care.

Here we enter into an interesting debate concerning the question of **cultural relativism**. Cultural relativists are those who are opposed to giving absolute authority to moral claims, that is, they believe that rightness and wrongness are not absolute but are different from culture to culture. Their concern arises because throughout history, human beings have used moral authority to interfere with other cultures and to force their beliefs on them. This has especially been the case where more powerful European and North American cultures have colonized and dominated those less industrialized cultures that are rooted in mystical or spiritual beliefs—in the African continent, the West Indies, and India, for example.

Cultural relativists are motivated by the concern that if we insist on imposing our moral ideas because we believe that they are the only true (universally valid) ones, we will run roughshod over other, more vulnerable cultures. But there are even more arguments that have been summoned in favor of cultural relativism, namely:

- Different societies have different moral beliefs and practices, and we have no way of judging one culture's beliefs or practices to be better than another's. Where ethics is concerned, right and wrong are matters of opinion, and opinion differs from culture to culture.
- There are vast cultural differences in views of right and wrong, so there is vast disagreement between cultures about moral values.
- Individuals should conform to the moral code of their society, and people visiting other cultures should conform to those moral codes as well.

Cultural relativists hold the view that there is no objective right and wrong in ethics; it boils down to what a particular culture thinks is right and wrong. If something is practiced in a culture, then it is right and cannot be criticized by outsiders. As the famous sociologist William Sumner claimed,

"In the folkways, whatever is, is right." By this Sumner meant that whatever customs, beliefs, or traditions are at work in a culture are right simply because they belong to that culture.

Consider some of these different cultural practices that have raised strong disagreements within Western medicine:

1. Some non-Western cultures practice female genital cutting (FGC), which involves either cutting off a young girl's clitoris or sewing her vulva shut, leaving only a small opening to urinate and maybe another for menstrual flow, so that she cannot experience sexual pleasure when she grows into adulthood. In some instances, practitioners within the United States have been asked by parents to aid and assist in these rituals for their daughters.

2. The Christian Science faith requires its practitioners to reject medical assistance and instead pray over the ill individual. There have been instances in the United States where parents have refused treatment for their children because they wanted to opt instead for prayer, so that God's will would determine the final outcome for their child.

3. The medical practice of implanting cochlear implants into children born deaf has come under strong criticism by some individuals from within the deaf community. These critics argue that it constitutes genocide to "kill off" deaf children by permanently removing them from deaf culture, and robbing them of the opportunity to learn American Sign Language.

When faced with such examples, cultural relativists would say these beliefs and practices are no better or worse than others' beliefs and practices. They are simply different, but should not and cannot be judged to be morally deficient.

But is that true? In cultures where FGC is accepted and still practiced, do we really want to take such a sanguine view that it is simply "different" from our North American ways? In North America, most people think that women should have the same protections and rights as men— but do we mean that only North American women have these same rights, or do we mean that *all* women should have these rights? As we saw from the discussion of Kant's ethics, he did not claim that one's actions are based on mere personal or cultural opinion. When one is forbidden to do an action because it cannot be universalized, that act is forbidden for everyone in all cultures; in short, no one should ever do it.

This raises a related problem with cultural relativism: it leaves one powerless to speak about ethics in any meaningful way. The claim "X is wrong" reduces to "in this culture, X is wrong," which is an extremely weak moral claim. Usually when people make moral statements (like "abortion is wrong" or "operating on patients without proper training is wrong") they are not only applying their claims to their own cultures; they mean it is *universally* wrong to abort fetuses, and that all individuals performing surgery should be properly trained. But cultural relativists would deny the universal application of such statements, thus gutting them of any real moral substance.

Furthermore, cultural relativists assume that everybody in a culture agrees on the moral code of that society. But one cannot assume this, since many people who come to the United States reject their traditions and cultural practices, and may have left their home countries for that reason. Indeed, even *within* communities that practice FGC we find strong opposition to the practice on the part of clerics, teachers, doctors, and other educated professionals, not to mention women. So it is a mistake to claim that there is agreement within a culture on what is morally right or wrong, since even within a culture individuals and groups may sharply disagree about certain practices.

Finally, cultural relativists point to the fact that cultures often come into sharp disagreement, a fact they claim proves there is no universal truth. Yet just because two cultures disagree about something does not mean that there is no truth of the matter. It could be that we simply have not yet discovered the truth; or it could be that one culture is right and the other is wrong. Sometimes the problem may be different interpretations of the facts, and not a huge difference in values. All cultures might agree that older adults should be treated with respect. For some cultures, however, this means not burdening them with bad news about their medical situation, but instead speaking to the eldest son; while in other cultures, respect for older adults means speaking directly to the elderly patient so that she is free to make decisions for herself.

There is an important lesson to be learned here: One must not automatically assume that different cultural practices indicate a totally different system of values. We might have the same values and just have different ways of expressing them. Cultures may not have such different values. There may be more commonalities among cultures than one might initially think.

Thus, while cultural relativism tries to address conflicts caused by difference (whether cultural, religious, or ethnic), it cannot resolve them. If one takes a relativist position seriously, then one loses the ability to look critically at other people's (and other culture's) practices. Returning to a previous example, a physician would have no grounds for refusing to participate in cutting a girl's genitals if her father was requesting it and he claimed it was an important and common practice in his culture. A relativist position would leave a health care provider virtually powerless to criticize the values, beliefs, or practices of her patients, even if she believed them to be harmful to her patients' health. Thus, this is another reason to reject the cultural relativist's claim. Certainly, the ethical theories and approaches we discussed earlier in this chapter all reject cultural relativism, although some leave room for or are more sensitive to cultural diversity than others.

ACCOUNTING FOR RELIGION IN BIOETHICS

As we pointed out in the previous section, one difference that can drive a wedge between patients, their caregivers, and patients' families is religious difference. Like other kinds of differences (racial, ethnic, linguistic, and cultural), religious differences can serve to interfere both with good communication between patients and staff and with good patient care.

However, religion is much more than a "problem" to be dealt with in the realm of bioethics. It is fundamental to many of the beliefs and values that are held by individuals, and can be the world-view that gives individuals comfort in times of illness, dying, and death. So despite sometimes posing problems in terms of patient-staff interactions, religion also serves as the rock that grounds people in very difficult times.

The role of religion in bioethics discourse has been hotly debated by religious and secular bioethicists. Philosophical approaches to bioethics are almost entirely governed by a secular approach that sets aside religious arguments in favor of rational argumentation, the best reasons for and against a practice, and the philosophical foundations for grounding decisions and actions. Religious approaches to bioethics start with the assumption that there is a higher power, and a set of religious texts, that determine for us the parameters for human action. If we want to know whether certain practices (such as aborting the embryo or fetus) are morally acceptable, we simply need to turn to religious texts and authority for answers. Generally speaking, students of bioethics will find a secular approach is taken in their philosophical bioethics courses and a religious approach is taken in their theological bioethics courses. The articles collected in this textbook tend to reflect a philosophical approach to bioethics, with many of them presenting different reasons and arguments— stemming from different philosophical frameworks—for thinking practices in medicine are right or wrong.

As an example of the difference between philosopher-bioethicists and religious bioethicists, consider human dignity—a concept that derives from the Bible and other religious texts. Secular bioethicists like Ruth Macklin advocate eliminating the term "human dignity" from bioethical discourse because it comes from religious sources, and because it has no meaning, she says "over and above respect for persons or for their autonomy."[1] Other secular bioethicists have argued that the term is just a cover for a religious tradition that views "the order of nature as divinely sanctioned."[2] Religious bioethicists respond, however, by questioning the basis for the secularist's view that we should have respect for persons and their autonomy. If this respect for persons and their autonomy is not grounded in a belief in their Creator, that endows them with inalienable rights, then what *does* ground it?

Since many health care interactions will involve religious worldviews, in this section we briefly highlight some of the major religious traditions and the distinctive approaches these religious groups take to modern problems in medicine. The information contained here is by no means exhaustive, but is meant to paint in broad brushstrokes the similarities and differences between Catholic, Jewish, and Islamic traditions.

Catholic approaches to bioethics

As one commentator smartly claims, "Strictly speaking, there is no such science as 'Catholic Bioethics' just as there is no such thing as 'Catholic Baseball,' 'Catholic Dentistry,' 'Catholic Garbage Collection,' or 'Catholic Plumbing.'"[3] Yet one can identify in the bioethics literature a distinct approach that is reflective of Catholic systematic thought. Catholic teaching in medicine "uses reason to understand what kinds of activity done by doctors are in accord with human dignity and flourishing, and what kinds are only apparently so and actually undermine, mutilate or destroy the goods of human beings."[4]

The foundation for Catholic bioethics is Natural Law Theory, which has been briefly outlined in this chapter. Catholic bioethicists are not against the development of medical technology or medical science per se, but they *are* concerned with the lure of science to reduce human beings to just another material substance to be experimented upon, analyzed, and manipulated according to empirical methods. According to natural law, each human life is unique, has inherent value, and must not be used in the service of ends that pervert our nature or our innate dignity. The unique status of human beings derives from our creation in the image and likeness of God, and from being the only living thing created by God "for its own sake."[5]

Furthermore, according to Catholic bioethicists, God is the sole creator of life, and imbues every human being with a fundamental right to life from the moment of conception. From this assertion one can appreciate why these bioethicists so strongly defend the right to life in all contexts: abortion, euthanasia, stem cell research, assisted reproductive technologies, cloning, genetic technologies, and care of older adults. To take a human life—whatever its form, level of development, or cognitive state may be—is immoral, even if doing so may serve important ends (such as leading to cures for Parkinson's disease or preventing the suffering caused by genetic disease).

Beyond this, Catholic bioethics also takes as foundational treating the "whole person," meaning that we cannot divide the body and soul so that treatment of the body does not impact the person overall. Whatever we do to our bodies (in terms of cosmetic alteration, reproduction, and so on) we do to the whole person, and we cannot divorce the two. Thus, we do not have dominion over our bodies to do anything we want with them; rather, we are stewards called to respect ourselves and others through a respect for bodily integrity.

Jewish approaches to bioethics

As is the case for the Catholic faith, Judaism adheres to certain principles relating to life and death that directly impact medical practice. While the principles are similar to those found in the Catholic tradition (the general prohibition against taking a life, for example), the religious grounding for these principles comes out of a distinctively Jewish religious and social history. As Philip Cohen claims,

> Louis Newman, in his essay "Jewish Theology and Bioethics," identifies five principles of Jewish ethics particularly important for bioethics: (1) human life possesses intrinsic value; (2) the preservation of life is the highest moral imperative; (3) all human lives are equal; (4) our lives are not really our own—they belong to God; and (5) the sacredness of human life inheres in the human being as a whole. I would add a sixth: the imitation of God is manifested through my actions toward the other.[6]

These principles are uniquely defined within the Jewish tradition by appeal to the Hebrew Bible and to the Talmud, a body of literature that forms the center of Jewish law. But what *is* Jewish bioethics, and is there a body of literature (as is the case in Catholic teaching) that sets out an absolute set of Jewish laws? The answer is no, given the ancient and diverse tradition of Judaism. Much of Jewish ethics derives from interpretations of Talmudic and extra-Talmudic sources, and these interpretations can come into conflict so that no single conclusion may be reached in some situations. The problem is not in finding principles that ground Jewish bioethical thought (see the list above), but in coming up with rules that derive from those principles so that some kind of ethical action is possible.[7]

Generally speaking, traditional Jewish thought rejects practices of abortion (unless the pregnant woman's life is at risk), suicide, euthanasia, and the withholding or withdrawing of treatment. As is the case in Catholicism, an observant Jew would not consider it morally licit to take her life to prevent her suffering from terminal disease, since human beings do not "own" their bodies, our lives are not our own to take as we see fit. And with regard to the body, traditional or religious Jews may feel strongly about protecting their modesty by, for example, having a hospital gown that fully covers them or having a physician of the same sex examine them. As within the Muslim faith (see below), more religious practitioners of Judaism may require brief periods for prayer and to complete important rituals.

Islamic approaches to bioethics

Islamic bioethics results from a combination of principles, duties, and rights in connection with an emphasis on virtues. As within the Catholic and Jewish traditions, Islamic bioethical decision making is carried out within a framework of values derived from revelation and tradition. It is closely tied to the ethical instruction provided by the Qur'an and the tradition of the Prophet Muhammad, which together make up the basis for Islamic law. Islamic bioethics encourages preventive measures and instructs practitioners that Muslim patients must be treated with respect and compassion: physical, mental, and spiritual dimensions of illness must be taken into account. Because Islam shares some of the core principles that ground Judaism and Christianity, practitioners from these other religious traditions will already be acquainted with much of what is contained within Islamic bioethics.[8]

The Islamic faith holds positions on major issues (such as beginning and end of life) that are similar to those of the Jewish and Catholic religions. Where abortion is concerned, Muslims believe that full human rights begin at the moment of ensoulment, which is interpreted by some scholars to be 120 days after conception, and by others as 40 days. (Shiites and Sunnis may sometimes differ on the interpretation of Islamic laws.) In any case, in practice most Muslims allow abortion after implantation and before ensoulment for serious reasons, such as in the case of rape. After ensoulment, abortion is prohibited unless it is necessary to save the pregnant woman's life. And the Islamic faith determines an individual to be dead at the point when the soul leaves the body, though there is no way of determining this beyond the physical signs displayed by the body.

As with traditional Jewish patients, there are certain practical measures that health care professionals need to follow when caring for Muslim patients. For example, the privacy and modesty of women is held in high regard within the Islamic faith. Medical exams should be performed with a chaperone present, and it is preferable to have a female physician, especially for gynecological visits. Where possible, physicians should ask Muslim women to reveal only one part of their body at a time in order to do an examination. There are also religious-based dietary restrictions, and hygiene requirements that should be respected. Finally, more devout Muslims and those who are physically able may wish to carry out religious observances that require running water for washing and a quiet area with room for a prayer mat that faces Mecca.[9]

All three of these religious traditions, though widely differing in cultural and religious practices, share some common beliefs and concepts. Respect and concern for human dignity is something shared by all three faiths; the requirement that we should respect life from its earliest stages, and that we should never take a life through euthanasia or physician-assisted suicide is also something they hold in common. The Islamic faith stands alone from the Catholic and Jewish traditions in possibly allowing stem cell research. According to this faith, if a given technology is for serious benefit and the good that results is proportional to the harm done, then it may be permitted.

From this brief overview of these three major religious traditions, one can newly appreciate the connection between religion and bioethics. Though some bioethicists would prefer to entirely avoid religious approaches to issues in bioethics, and insist on the separation of church and state, in practice it may prove difficult to do so. In our pluralistic and multicultural society, health care staff will be faced with medical demands that stem from patients' religious beliefs and practices; to ignore these demands and reject religious approaches to medical practices is to cut a very large portion of the population out of the conversation concerning the ethical practice of medicine.

CONCLUSION

Finally, not all of the work performed by bioethicists involves solving a case study. Sometimes bioethicists address professional groups of bioethicists or physicians or philosophers (and others) and sometimes they meet with families, committees, or individual patients. In such contexts, the bioethicist may not be asked to resolve a case. Instead, he or she may be involved in critiquing or formulating policy, providing information, facilitating communication, or debating current topics or issues. A good bioethicist must do more than resolve cases, but on the other hand resolving cases is a good place to begin. A good bioethicist cannot refuse to solve cases. As we said at the beginning of this chapter, the field of bioethics has been led by cases, that is, by particular situations in which particular people find themselves. Coming to understand these situations and their specific circumstances helps us to recognize and deal with future situations. Therefore, the practice of the best bioethicists is always intensely specific because it is informed by particular people in particular cases. But it is also broadly theoretical since it reflects on particular people and cases in the context of rules, values, principles, theories, and perspectives and draws from this reflection conclusions that will apply to other people and cases. Case-based reasoning is central to bioethics but it is not the whole of bioethics.

Now let's take all of these tools that we have discussed—values, principles, rules, approaches, theories, and multiculturalism—and move on to the issues and problems of bioethics.

Endnotes

1. Ruth Macklin, "Dignity is a Useless Concept," *British Medical Journal* 327 (2003), 1419–1420, available online at www.bmj .com/cgi/content/full/327/7429/1419?etoc.
2. Dieter Birnbacher, "Human Cloning and Human Dignity," *Reproductive Biomedicine Online*, 10 (Suppl. 1) (2005), 50–55.
3. See http://bioethics.catholicexchange.com/2008/07/13/what-is-catholic-bioethics/ [Accessed on September 8, 2008].
4. Ibid.
5. Catechism for the Catholic Church, no. 2258 (2nd ed., English Translation, September 8, 1997), available online at http://www .scborromeo.org/ccc.htm.
6. See http://www.parkridgecenter.org/Page20.html [Accessed on September 10, 2008].
7. This is not to say there is no agreement surrounding the principles that guide medical practice, just that the Judaic tradition involves a rich history of textual interpretation that has involved some degree of dispute amongst Jewish scholars. As one source indicates:

   > In Judaism, life is valued above almost all else. The Talmud notes that all people are descended from a single person, thus taking a single life is like destroying an entire world, and saving a single life is like saving an entire world.
   >   Of the 613 commandments, only the prohibitions against murder, idolatry, incest and adultery are so important that they cannot be violated to save a life. Judaism not only permits, but often *requires* a person to violate the commandments if necessary to save a life. A person who is extremely ill, for example, or a woman in labor, is not permitted to fast on Yom Kippur, because fasting at such a time would endanger the person's life. Doctors are permitted to answer emergency calls on Shabbat, even though this may violate many Shabbat prohibitions. Abortions where necessary to save the life of a mother are mandatory (the unborn are not considered human life in Jewish law, thus the mother's human life overrides).
   >   Because life is so valuable, we are not permitted to do anything that may hasten death, not even to prevent suffering. Euthanasia, suicide and assisted suicide are strictly forbidden by Jewish law. The Talmud states that you may not even move a dying person's arms if that would shorten his life.
   >   However, where death is imminent and certain, and the patient is suffering, Jewish law does permit one to cease artificially prolonging life. Thus, in certain circumstances, Jewish law permits "pulling the plug" or refusing extraordinary means of prolonging life. (http://www.jewfaq.org/death.htm) [Accessed on September 11, 2008].

8. Abdallah S. Daar and A. Binsumeit Al Khitamy, "Bioethics for clinicians: 21. Islamic bioethics," *Canadian Medical Association Journal*, 164:1 (2001), 60–63.
9. Ibid.

Chapter 2

Roles, Responsibilities, and Relationships

What the Nurse Likes

*I like looking into patients' ears
and seeing what they can never see.*

It's like owning them.

*I like patients' honesty—
they trust me with simple things:*

> *They wake at night and count heartbeats.
> They search for lumps.*

I am also afraid.

*I like the way women look at me
and feel safe.
Then I lean across them
and they smell my perfume.*

*I like the way men become shy.
Even angry men bow their heads
when they are naked.*

*I like lifting a woman's hair
to place stethoscope to skin,
the way everyone breathes differently—*

*the way men make suggestive groans
when I listen to their hearts.*

*I like eccentric patients:
Old women who wear people knit hats
and black eyeliner. Men
who put makeup over their age spots.*

*I like talking about patients
as if they aren't real, calling them
"the fracture" or "the hysterectomy."*

It makes illness seem trivial.

I like saying

> **You shouldn't smoke!
> You must have this test!**

*I like that patients don't always
do what I say.*

*I like the way we stop the blood,
pump the lungs,
turn hearts off and on with electricity.*

*I don't like when it's over
and then I realize*

I know nothing.

*I like being the one to give bad news;
I am not embarrassed by grief.*

*I like the way patients gather their hearts,
their bones, their arms and legs,
that have spun away momentarily.*

*At the end of the gathering they sigh
and look up.*

I like how dying patients become beautiful.

Their eyes concentrate light. Their skin
becomes thin and delicate as fog.
Nothing matters anymore
but sheets, pain, a radio, the time of day.

■

I like watching patients die.

First they are living,
then something comes up from within
and moves from them.

They become vacant and yet
their bodies are heavy
and sink into the sheets.

I like how emptiness is seen first
in the eyes, then in the hands.

■

I like taking care of patients
and I like forgetting them,

going home and sitting on my porch
while they stand away from me
talking among themselves.

I like how they look back
when I turn their way.

"What the Nurse Likes" from DETAILS OF FLESH by Cortney Davis.
Copyright © 1987 by Cortney Davis. Reprinted by permission of Calyx Books.

Irene

After the third stroke,
her words fell off
to a few soft syllables.
When I enter the room
and enter those red-rimmed eyes
that can't help
looking toward the left,
she cocks her jaw
and her cheekbones swell.
With what looks like weakness,
she wobbles
her left hand to my wrist,
but that grip
is the grip of a woman
who clings by a root
to the face of a cliff.

When she speaks, her words
are small stones
and loosened particles
of meaning
that tumble to their deaths
before my ear
is quick or close enough
to save them. Irene,
tell me again, *I say,*
after the words
in her bits of chopped breath
are gone. But George
takes his cap from my desk
and puts it on his head, and says
Her gulps don't make no sense.

Coulehan, Jack. "Irene" Copyright © 1991 from THE KNITTED GLOVE (Troy, ME: Nightshade Press, 1991).
Copyright © 1991 by Jack Coulehan. Reprinted by permission of the author.

In these two poems, we experience some of what it means to be a nurse and a doctor. We feel the intimacy of their contact with a patient's hair and eyes and grip and words. We appreciate the way that patients feel safe with them and count on them to listen even when family members no longer try to listen. The nurse loves both the immediacy and the uniqueness of the people for whom she cares and her separation and distance from them. The physician enters both the patient's room and the patient's eyes. In these poems, it is obvious that the relationships between providers and patients are intense and personal. The provider encounters not only the patient but the patient's fear, vanity, contrariness, quiet dignity, and despair. And in all this, the nurse likes taking care of patients and the doctor hopes to be able to catch the words of his patient.

This gives us a first glimpse of what health care professionals do. In this chapter, we look at the roles, responsibilities, and relationships that characterize some of those who work in health care and bioethics. We focus on physicians, nurses, and genetic counselors and by understanding their professional roles and rules we can better reflect on the questions and topics of health care practice and bioethics. Consider this case:

CASE STUDY: CARMEN DIAZ'S SURGERY

Carmen Diaz, a 30-year-old Mexican citizen who legally resides and works in the United States, has been suffering from serious pelvic pain for 3 months. She finds it hard to work because of the pain and even harder to perform the chores required by daily living. Her physician finally refers her to a surgeon, Dr. Henrietta Wilson. Dr. Wilson recommends that Carmen undergo diagnostic laparoscopy, a minimally invasive surgery that involves viewing the abdominal cavity by means of a thin, lighted telescope. Carmen agrees to the surgery and comes to the hospital at the scheduled time. Before the surgery, a colleague of Dr. Wilson's comes to Carmen's room with a consent form. The colleague offers to explain the surgical procedure to Carmen but she indicates that she already understands the nature of the surgery. The consent form includes a statement that grants to the surgeon the right to do what is medically necessary and advisable if unexpected circumstances arise during the surgery. Carmen signs the form.

Dr. Kai Wang, the anesthesiologist, puts Carmen under anesthesia and Dr. Wilson begins the surgery. Dr. Wilson discovers that Carmen has several large fibroid tumors of the uterus. These tumors are benign (i.e., noncancerous), but they can be quite large and painful. Dr. Wilson declares that she will go ahead and perform a laparoscopic hysterectomy (removal of the uterus via laparoscopy) because the tumors are very large and surgery is the best way to eliminate fibroid tumors that are large and painful. Dr. Wang informs Dr. Wilson that he is unwilling to continue the anesthesia for that surgery since his understanding was that the present surgery was merely for diagnostic purposes. He is unsure whether Carmen has given consent for the hysterectomy and wonders whether the hysterectomy is medically indicated. He states that he will bring Carmen back to a wakeful and conscious state and that the hysterectomy surgery may then be performed at a future date. Dr. Wilson grits her teeth but says nothing.

This case, like many, is loaded with uncertainty and incomplete information. The people involved in the case have not communicated well and so they have different ideas about what actions are appropriate and how to proceed. On top of that, the case ends with an angry surgeon and a patient who may have to undergo a second surgical procedure.

As this case reveals, medical care is often provided by teams of health care professionals. Surgeons work alongside anesthesiologists, internal medicine physicians, pediatricians, and more, not to mention nurses, X-ray technicians, and so on. As the pool of those caring for the patient expands, so do the opportunities for misunderstandings. In this case, Carmen's team of Dr. Wilson and Dr. Wang are not working well together, to put it mildly! They have different conceptions of the purpose and goal of the surgery and they disagree about what Carmen has consented to. This makes for a very unstable working relationship and risks either acting too precipitously and possibly going against Carmen's wishes or acting too cautiously and forcing Carmen to undergo the risks of a second surgery. It would be wise therefore for us to consider the nature and roles of those involved in the delivery of medical and health care services and to reflect on the relationships among all those involved in providing the services and among those providers and the ones receiving the services.

Carmen's case also reminds us that while health care professionals can recommend treatments and procedures, it is patients or clients who must decide whether or not to make use of these techniques. Here Carmen had to agree to the surgery and had to indicate her agreement by signing a consent document (Figure 2.1).

She had to express an "informed consent." Thus, in some cases, there will be legal documents by means of which patients or subjects in an experiment can indicate their wishes and the extent of their willingness to participate. These documents give priority to the patient's choices and goals and reflect the fact that in medical contexts in the United States in the 21st century, there is a clear recognition of the patient's or client's autonomy and hence of his or her "right" to be informed, to

FIGURE 2.1   Woman reviewing and signing documents before receiving a flu vaccine.

Source: Photo by photoedit Inc

deliberate, and to choose. In Carmen's case, her medical doctors, Dr. Wilson and Dr. Wang, may have conflicting views on the nature of Carmen's wishes and choices.

In addition, Carmen's case leads us to consider questions pertaining to information-sharing, disclosure of information, and ultimately, truth-telling. We wonder what information Carmen received about her surgery before consenting to it and we wonder how much consultation there was between her doctors. In order for Carmen to make a well-thought-out decision, it would be necessary for her to understand her situation and the proposed treatment. Similarly, for the medical team to work together to promote Carmen's best interests they must understand her situation, her wishes, and the nature of the surgery. All of this understanding is possible only if the relevant information has been disclosed and shared and there has been no withholding of information or deception. The relationships at stake—Carmen and her doctors, doctor to doctor—and the care of the patient here depend on honesty and truthfulness. If the medical personnel involved in Carmen's care do not share a similar view of her condition, her wishes, and the plan for her treatment, then Carmen's care may be compromised. And if Carmen and her physicians are not truthful and open with one another, then again Carmen is at risk of inappropriate or inadequate care. Hence, the signing of a consent form leads inevitably to questions about whether sufficient information has been shared, whether it has been shared with the appropriate people, and whether adequate understanding of that information has occurred. These topics are often discussed under such headings as disclosure, truth-telling, competency, and confidentiality.

You may see other bioethical issues in Carmen's case, beyond those we have discussed. For example, one such issue might be who should have access to medical resources or who will pay for medical procedures (remember that Carmen is not a U.S. citizen). Another might be whether or not Carmen has signed an advance directive, indicating her end-of-life wishes, prior to her surgery. If something were to go drastically wrong during or after the surgery and Carmen's life could be saved only through the use of advanced life support systems, would Carmen want her life extended? If you do recognize other issues, this is a good sign. It means that you have begun to think as a bioethicist, that is, as a person who identifies, cares about, and works to clarify the moral questions and values inherent in health care, medicine, and public health. For now, let us return to the questions surrounding the relationships at stake in Carmen's case and her consent form. It is to these topics that this chapter is directed.

As seen in the case of Carmen's surgery, there is nothing more fundamental to health care than the relationship between the patient and the health care provider. No health care can be initiated, no diagnosis can be made, in the absence of some contact between a patient and a health care provider. This point seems obvious but because it sets the stage for everything that follows we must pay special attention to it. How do physicians, nurses, genetic counselors, physical therapists, and so on meet and care for patients? Where does care take place—in community hospitals, private offices, free clinics, teaching hospitals, and so on? How do the various parties involved in these relationships understand their roles? Is the nurse's expectation of what his or her role is the same as the patient's? What responsibilities do the various parties have to one another? As basic as these questions are, as simple as the relationship between patient and provider seems, the issues raised are complex. For instance, a patient and a doctor may disagree about the desirability of a medical treatment. This disagreement may be due to the fact that one party is working toward the goal of life extension (i.e., longevity), whereas the other is working toward the goal of quality of life (i.e., comfortable living). These different goals or ends can complicate the working relationships of patient to provider and of provider to provider. In short, we need to reflect on the nature and complexity of these roles and relationships before we move on to specific topics in bioethics, such as, reproductive technologies and end-of-life care.

ROLES AND RELATIONSHIPS

In the readings that follow in this chapter, we focus our attention on three professional roles: physician, nurse, and genetic counselor. A particular case may involve one of these professionals or all of them. Physicians and nurses provide patients with health care services and comfort care. Genetic counselors evaluate patients for genetic risks, may recommend testing, and interpret test results. Let's start by considering what these three roles have in common.

The practices of medicine, nursing, and genetic counseling are governed by codes of ethics. One of the earliest codes is the **Hippocratic Oath**, a code of ethics for physicians from the 4th century B.C. This code, like other, more modern codes, aims to set standards, role expectations, and responsibilities for the members of a profession. It defines the purpose of the work, the central values upheld by the profession, and rules for professional practice. For example, the American Medical Association Principles of Medical Ethics says: "As a member of this profession, a physician must recognize responsibility to patients first and foremost, as well as to society, to other health professionals, and to self." The Code of Ethics for Nurses says: "The nurse's primary commitment is to the patient, whether an individual, family, group, or community." The Code of Ethics for the National Society of Genetic Counselors asserts: "The primary concern of genetic counselors is the interests of their clients." These codes agree in making the patient's interests the focus of the professional's action.

You might be surprised not to find the well-known tenet of medicine in the above statements. "*Primum non nocere*" or "Above all, do no harm" is widely understood to be the first principle of medical practice. This translates into the claim that physicians must above all not harm the patient and that the physician's treatments must not leave the patient worse off than he was before treatment. People also tend to identify the goal of medical care as saving lives, curing illnesses, and treating diseases. But as we all know, medicine cannot always save lives, death is inevitable, and sometimes medicine has no effective treatments to offer. In these cases, we need to think more broadly about what medicine—and for that matter, nursing and genetic counseling—can accomplish. Perhaps these professions work in the service of patients in other ways. These professions can provide information to a patient that may be helpful in planning the rest of the patient's life. They can also provide support, compassionate care, and services that contribute to the quality of life experienced by the patient. As evidence for this expanding idea of what it means to "put the patient first," observe that the ancient Hippocratic Oath says that the physician "will come for the benefit of the sick." The American Medical Association Principles of Medical Ethics states that the physician works for "the benefit of the patient" and then explains that this means in part "providing competent medical care, with compassion and respect for human dignity and rights." Today, medicine treats not just the sick but those patients who have dignity and rights and are in need of compassion and good medical care. The Code of Ethics for Nurses also states that the nurse "practices with compassion and respect for the inherent dignity, worth and uniqueness of every individual."

This is not to say that "Above all, do no harm" is not important or that saving lives is not a part of medicine. Rather, it is a reminder that the older, more simplistic ways of describing the nature of the health care professions must be supplemented with newer understandings of the professions that reflect their current state (their capabilities and their technologies) and the current social views (what society allows and expects of them). It is noteworthy that the newer codes require not just certain *acts* of benefiting but certain *ways* of benefiting, namely, those that are compassionate and respectful.

Still there are several problems in depending on these codes of ethics to inform us about the roles and responsibilities of the professionals who work in health care. First, as we have seen, codes of ethics change over time. As social views on issues change and as technology offers new opportunities, our sense of what is morally acceptable in medicine, nursing, or genetic counseling may change. The "Code for Professional Nurses" from 1952 states: "The nurse is obligated to carry out the physician's orders intelligently, to avoid misunderstanding and inaccuracies by verifying orders and to refuse to participate in unethical procedures." The 2001 edition of the Code says instead: "The nurse is responsible and accountable for individual nursing practice and determines the appropriate delegation of tasks consistent with the nurse's obligation to provide optimum patient care." This change reveals how nurses are now recognized as health care practitioners with their own set of standards and expertise. Similarly, the 1957 version of the American Medical Association Principles of Medical Ethics states that: "He [the physician] should not solicit patients." But today physicians advertise their services in newspapers and on billboards. These changes to the codes reflect deeper social changes in the nature of these professions and in our understanding of what medicine and nursing mean. Medicine has taken on some of the characteristics of a business and the service nature of the profession has been redefined. Nursing has incorporated the values of independence and autonomy and so the profession no longer views itself as subservient to medicine or as practicing as the "right hand" of the doctor (Figure 2.2).

Second, codes of ethics are written by members of professional associations, such as the American Medical Association, American Nurses Association, and National Society of Genetic Counselors. Not all providers may be members of these organizations. The American Nurses Association reports that it has approximately 150,000 nurses as individual members, although it represents the almost 2.7 million registered nurses. There are about 800,000 active physicians in the United States and approximately 240,000 physicians are members of the American Medical Association.[1] Do the codes apply to those who are not members?

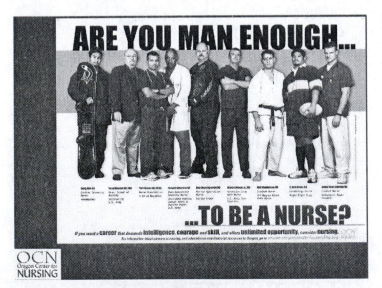

FIGURE 2.2   Nursing advertisement.

Source: Photo by the Oregon Center for Nursing. the Oregon Center for Nursing www.oregoncenterfornursing.org

Finally, note that the codes speak broadly about standards and responsibilities. They don't give specific and exact directions on how to uphold the values and enact the responsibilities. What exactly does it mean to put the patient first? To Paul Farmer, MD, who treats the poor in Haiti, it means hiking long distances to check on a patient who did not return to the clinic for his TB medicine. Farmer acknowledges, "Some people would argue this wasn't worth a five-hour walk.... But you can never invest too much in making sure this stuff works."[2] Individual doctors, nurses, and genetic counselors must interpret and apply the rules of the codes and thus decision making and judgment are crucial. There are, no doubt, many ways to provide competent medical and nursing care and many ways of serving patients' interests.

RESPONSIBILITIES AND RELATIONSHIPS

Aside from these general goals for the health care professions, the practice of medicine and health care as well as the codes of ethics also speak of more specific responsibilities. These responsibilities focus on three aspects of the provider and patient relationship: confidentiality, truth-telling, and informed consent. To better understand these components of health care relationships, we can look once again at the codes of ethics as well as to precedent-setting legal cases and to standard practice.

"Confidentiality" refers to the practice of keeping to oneself personal and intimate details that one may know about another's life. It is often associated with the value of privacy. Many professional relationships between a professional and a client are governed by confidentiality, for instance, investigative reporters and their sources, therapists and their clients, and priests and those confessing to them. And many personal relationships assume or take for granted there will be confidentiality. Spouses assume that their quirks and idiosyncratic habits will not be relayed by their spouses to their employers. Friends may keep silent about the infidelities of their friends. In most of these cases, there is no explicit promise of confidentiality; rather, there is presumed confidentiality. The reason for upholding confidentiality is that "keeping silent" or maintaining privacy is thought to protect the other from harm and to be for the good of the other.

Confidentiality has long been a part of health care relationships. The Hippocratic Oath asserts that the physician will keep to himself whatever he sees or hears in the course of treatment. The AMA Principles of Medical Ethics confirm that physicians "shall safeguard patient confidences and privacy within the constraints of the law." In a statement issued by the House of Delegates of the AMA in 2001, physicians pledge to: "Protect the privacy and confidentiality of those for whom we care and breach that confidence only when keeping it would seriously threaten their health and safety or that of others." The Code of Ethics for genetic counselors states that they will: "Maintain information received from clients as confidential, unless released by the client or disclosure is required by law."

The importance of confidentiality in health care relationships is confirmed by **HIPAA (the Health Insurance Portability and Accountability Act),** which Congress enacted in 1996. Specifically, its Privacy Rule (put into effect in 2003) states that a patient's medical record and payment history are considered "protected health information." This protected information can be shared with others when the law requires, when patients authorize its release, or when it is necessary to facilitate treatment or payment. Thus, HIPAA aims to enhance the confidentiality of medical records and medical communications in light of electronic record-keeping and information-sharing.

Several points become evident in these rules from the codes and laws. First, for health professionals, there is no absolute duty to uphold confidentiality. Instead, confidentiality is important but it is a value that can be overridden by other, more important values or concerns. Second, there is no agreement concerning when it is acceptable to violate confidentiality for the sake of some other good. The codes disagree. Two of the codes recognize that the law can mandate a breach of confidentiality. Many state laws in the United States require health professionals or hospitals to report cases of suspected child abuse and gunshot wounds. State laws also typically require that patients who suffer from seizure disorders must be reported to the Division of Motor Vehicles. Many infectious diseases such as tuberculosis must by law be reported to public health authorities. But one of the codes also mentions other reasons to violate confidentiality, namely, when the patient's health or safety is at risk and when the health and safety of others are at risk. To break a confidence on grounds that the patient's health or safety requires it is to act in a paternalistic way. As we said in Chapter 1, paternalism is acting on behalf of someone else in that other person's best interest. If the patient is in fact a competent adult, then violating his or her confidence in order to protect him from his own decisions is difficult to justify. Adults have the right to make decisions even if those decisions put them at risk. On the other hand, violating a confidence in order to protect someone else, someone who may be unaware of the fact that they are at risk, seems more morally acceptable. Here you are breaching the trust implicit in the confidential relationship (committing a wrong) but you are doing it to prevent a greater harm (acting to avoid a greater wrong). According to an ethics survey conducted by the magazine *Medical Economics* in 2002, 28% of physicians answered "Yes" when they were asked: "Have you ever revealed confidential information about a patient if his or her condition could affect others?"[3]

The Tarasoff case has been influential in understanding the limits of confidentiality.

> In August 1969, Prosenjit Poddar was a voluntary outpatient receiving therapy from a psychologist employed by the hospital at the University of California at Berkeley. Poddar told his psychologist that he intended to kill Tatiana Tarasoff when she returned from a summer in Brazil. The psychologist notified campus police that he would request commitment of Poddar to a mental hospital for observation. Three campus policemen briefly questioned and held Poddar but released him because he appeared to be rational. The psychologist's superior at the hospital determined that no further action should be taken to commit Poddar. On October 27, 1969, Poddar killed Tatiana Tarasoff.[4]

The majority opinion, in the lawsuit that was brought against the University of California, asserted that when a therapist determines that his or her patient presents a serious risk of danger to another, the therapist has an obligation to use reasonable care to protect the intended victim. It argued that the confidentiality of the therapist–patient relationship must be broken when disclosure is necessary to save others from danger.

"Truth-telling" is a rule that is associated with the value of honesty. Acting honestly means to refrain from lying and deceiving and withholding the truth. Some of these ways of acting dishonestly, namely, lying, deceiving, and withholding truth, may be morally worse than others. To lie to a person is to pass off as true something that is false or the reverse, to pass off as false something that is actually true. If the truth is eventually discovered by the person, then the relationship that presupposed honesty and trust is broken. But if a person is not told the whole entire truth, it is still possible to disclose the whole truth later on and hence to sustain the relationship. In other words, a partial truth may not be as damaging to a relationship as a lie. There are therefore degrees of truth-telling, as well as different manners of truth-telling, and so we can expect that questions about the truth-telling responsibilities of health care professionals will be complicated.

Observe that truth-telling responsibilities really exist for both members of a relationship. The health care professional may have a moral duty to be truthful and honest with a patient, but the patient would have a similar duty to be truthful and forthcoming with his or her health care provider. It would seem that good health care cannot be provided in relationships where the patient isn't accurately reporting her symptoms and the physician, for example, is not offering the patient true and adequate information about treatments and options. So while we tend to focus on the truth-telling responsibilities of the health care provider, we should remember that patients, clients, and subjects in medical experiments and clinical trials also have duties to tell the truth.

Also, be aware that truth-telling and honesty are issues not just in doctor–patient relationships but in all kinds of relationships in bioethics. We can ask whether a surgeon has been honest with his office staff, whether a nurse has told the truth to his shift replacement, whether a family physician has been honest in submitting insurance claims for a patient, and on and on. In a survey conducted by the Association of American Physicians and Surgeons, 78% of the physicians who responded indicated that they had withheld information from a patient's record due to privacy and confidentiality concerns.[5] As you can see, there are many occasions in health care situations where information is asked for or provided and in all of these occasions the value of honesty is at stake.

Again, we start by looking at what the professional codes of ethics have to say about truth-telling, veracity, and honesty. The AMA code states that physicians must "be honest in all professional interactions." The code of ethics for genetic counselors says that: "Genetic counselors value...veracity" and hence that they will "[a]ccurately represent their experience, competence and credentials" and will "[e]nable their clients to make informed decisions, free of coercion, by providing or illuminating the necessary facts." Both physicians and genetic counselors value honesty and truth-telling, although the code of ethics for genetic counselors is much more specific about what those values mean. Now, why is it that only these two codes refer to honesty? Primarily the codes aim to set standards for provider–patient relationships and it is mainly doctors who communicate with patients about their health and disease. A nurse or physical therapist is not the appropriate person for a patient to ask for information about his or her diagnosis and prognosis. On the other hand, they may be exactly the right people to ask for information about pain medication or pain in a joint while exercising. The point is that not all those who know the facts about a patient's case are in a position to give the patient or family that information. Physicians are primarily responsible for communicating the truth about diagnosis and prognosis to patients. Hence, only the physician and the genetic counselor codes speak about truth-telling responsibilities to the patient, although in a larger sense, not focusing on diagnosis and prognosis, all health care professionals have a responsibility to be honest in their dealings with patients.

One reason why physicians have been cautious about adopting strict rules of truth-telling is the traditional concept of "**therapeutic privilege**." According to this idea, physicians have the right to do what is necessary to further the patient's best interests or health. If telling the patient the "whole truth and nothing but the truth" would overwhelm the patient, compromise healing, or make the patient suicidal, then out of concern for the patient's health, truth-telling is not morally required. This is another example of paternalistic thinking (paternalism). Nevertheless, given the physician's professed commitment to the patient's best interests, the concept of therapeutic privilege provides a reason to rank truth-telling second to the patient's well-being (nonmaleficence and beneficence).

There are several other reasons that have been given for why health care professionals may not always have a responsibility to tell the truth. First, some have claimed that patients in fact do not want to know the truth about their situations. If so, the argument goes, then health care professionals have no responsibility to tell the truth. But this is not a very good argument. Studies have shown that patients do want to know the truth. Even if they did not want to know the truth, it still would not necessarily follow that physicians have no responsibility to provide the truth. For a Kantian, our duties and responsibilities arise independently of what we or others happen to want or desire. Second, it has been argued that doctors often do not know the truth and hence that they could not have any responsibility to convey what they do not know. Sometimes prognosis is uncertain or no diagnosis can be made. But the response to this is to agree that there is no duty to say what one does not know. Usually, however, there is still plenty that the doctor does know—statistics may be available on how others have fared, and certain diseases may have been eliminated by testing even if none has been confirmed. The responsibility to tell the truth and be honest means only that physicians must share what they do know and even perhaps what they think is likely or probable.

The strongest reasons against truth-telling and honesty are beneficence and nonmaleficence. That is, there may be cases or even types of cases in which to avoid harm or to benefit someone the truth should be omitted. Like all the complex questions in bioethics, these cases must be judged by individuals using their abilities to morally deliberate and decide.

On the other side of the question, why do we think it is important in health care situations to tell the truth and be honest? Simply, it is better for the patient or client to know. The patient or experimental subject must make choices—take the test or don't take the test, have the surgery or don't have the surgery, try this treatment or that treatment, agree to be in the clinical study or refuse to participate, and so on. To make good choices, the patient must understand what he or she is choosing.

Furthermore, even if there are no treatment decisions for the patient to make, say the cancer is inoperable and terminal, the patient still has life choices to make, say whether or not to reconcile with an estranged relative. The autonomy and dignity of patients are respected by providing them with the information that they need to be fully self-determining.

One other reason in favor of truth-telling and honesty in health care relationships is utility. It is not only patients who benefit from honest relationships—so do health care providers. By informing patients of the truth, doctors are able to allow patients to make decisions about their care and thus to eliminate some of the risks and liabilities of treating them. Physicians benefit because patients who are treated honestly feel respected and so they are more likely to trust and less likely to sue these physicians.

One final comment on truth-telling responsibilities in health care is that standards and expectations can change over time and can vary from culture to culture. A study performed in the 1960s showed that 88% of physicians said they would not tell a patient he or she had cancer.[6] A similar study in the 1970s revealed that 98% of physicians would disclose a cancer diagnosis.[7] In some cultures, patients expect to hear the truth from their physicians; in other cultures, it is the patient's family that is to be told and not the patient. For example, in 1995, one study showed that 63% of African Americans believed a patient should be told of a terminal condition while only 48% of Mexican Americans and 35% of Korean Americans believed this (Figure 2.3).[8]

Finally, the health care professions have a responsibility to provide "**informed consent**." This means that health care providers must receive a patient's or experimental subject's "consent" prior to treatment or study and this consent must be "informed," that is, based on a correct understanding of the medical situation. Though the codes of ethics do not speak directly of this responsibility, it has been legally recognized in the United States since the late 1960s. The concept of informed consent is based on the acknowledgment (in the codes) that the rights and dignity of patients are important values. In order to act autonomously and in their own best interests, patients and subjects need to be able to act knowledgeably, in informed ways. Informed consent also furthers utility. If patients and subjects make their own decisions about treatments and procedures, then health care providers may bear less blame for unsuccessful treatments. The Sadie Nemser case was an early influential case.

Sadie Nemser, 80 years old and a widow, had lived in the Jewish Home and Hospital for the Aged in New York City from May 1964 until August 1966. She had arteriosclerotic heart disease and had suffered at least three strokes. In a medical emergency she was admitted to Beth Israel Hospital with extensive gangrene of her right foot and heel. The attending physician recommended an amputation above the ankle and said that if the gangrene was allowed to progress, death would follow. Mrs. Nemser said she did not want her foot amputated, although she wanted to live. An attending psychiatrist reported that she was not

FIGURE 2.3   Chart on disclosing terminal illness diagnoses to patients.

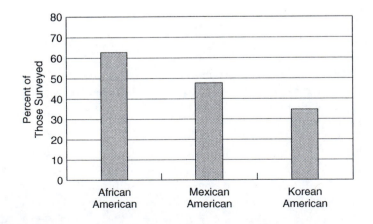

Favor Disclosing Terminal Illness to Patients

capable of understanding any permission for surgery she might be asked for. The hospital and surgeon would not proceed without consent from Mrs. Nemser's next-of-kin. She had three sons. Two of them, one a lawyer, agreed to the amputation. But the third, a physician, refused to consent on grounds that she may not be able to survive the surgery and anesthesia and that the gangrenous parts would slough off themselves through auto-amputation.[9]

In this case, surgery was recommended but the problem was whether or not to go ahead with it. Mrs. Nemser offers contradictory opinions—she does not want the amputation surgery, but she wants to live. Is she able to give an informed consent or to refuse consent in an informed way? Is she competent to decide for herself? If not, who should decide for her? And are there any guidelines for how her sons (or someone else) should make this choice for her? All of these are questions that pertain to issues surrounding informed consent.

An informed consent must meet four criteria: competency, disclosure, understanding, and voluntariness. **Competency** is satisfied when the person consenting is capable of rational deliberation and decision making. This is decided not by looking at what a person decides but by observing how he or she came to that decision. Often there will be difficult cases where a patient may be competent in making certain decisions for themselves but not competent in making others. The bias is to presume that adults are competent unless there is evidence to the contrary. **Disclosure** is met when health care providers inform the person consenting, namely, give the person sufficient information that is relevant to making a decision. There has been adequate disclosure when the one consenting is told what a reasonable person would want to know to make this decision. Minimally, this would include the benefits and risks of the procedure, the nature of the procedure, alternatives, the cost of the treatment, and even the qualifications of those performing the treatment (Figure 2.4).

Understanding is accomplished when the person consenting adequately comprehends the situation. Voluntariness is satisfied when the one consenting is free from undue influence or constraint in making a decision. Often there is pressure—financial, familial, and so on—to choose or forego a treatment but as long as the pressure is not controlling, then we say the person has acted voluntarily.

FIGURE 2.4   A genetics counselor talking with an expectant couple in her office in Georgia.

Source: Photo by photoedit Inc

Because people are not always able to make decisions for themselves—think, for example, of children, those with dementia, those who are in comas or unconscious—it is necessary for someone else to act on their behalf. These stand-in decision-makers are called "**surrogates**" in bioethics. A surrogate ideally is someone who knows the patient well, usually a close relative, or perhaps someone who has been appointed by the patient. Sometimes, as in Sadie Nemser's case, a patient's family members may disagree about what to do in a case and it can be difficult to determine whose decision counts. As a general rule, surrogates are expected to follow a **substituted judgment** standard in cases where the patient in question was formerly competent. The surrogate acts on the basis of what the patient would have wanted if he or she could still speak for themselves. Here the patient's autonomy, wishes, and values are directing the surrogate. But where the patient's wishes are not known or where the patient has never been competent, a surrogate is expected to follow a **best interest** standard. This means that the surrogate must weigh the benefits and burdens of the proposed treatment to the patient and decide what best serves the patient's interests.

Thus, health care providers and researchers will be in relationships with patients, subjects, and surrogates and will have responsibilities to ensure that their decision-making satisfies the conditions for an informed decision. They also have responsibilities to confidentiality and to truth-telling. Now, as we look to the future, consider the following developments that will challenge our understanding of the roles, relationships, and responsibilities of health care professionals.

Looking Ahead

- People enter the United States health care system from a wide variety of backgrounds with different ethnicities and diverse cultural and religious beliefs. There is increased pressure on health care providers to understand and accommodate these diverse beliefs. Physicians, as well as other health care providers, will have to develop "cultural competencies" in order to be sensitive to and respectful of cultural beliefs about health and disease that are different from their own. For example, Harvard Medical School's Center of Excellence in Women's Health (in conjunction with four other universities) developed a curriculum called "Cultural Competency in Women's Health" for training health care providers in the "unique needs of minority and other underserved women."[10] Health care providers will face difficult decisions when patients come to them asking for treatments that coincide with their home cultural or religious beliefs but are contrary to the best practices of medicine in the United States.

- Increasingly, patients come to health care providers with requests for certain medications and treatments. They have seen a drug advertised on television and would like to try it. Or they would like a cosmetic surgery or enhancement. These requests imply that medicine should serve to satisfy patients' desires, in addition to patients' needs. This suggests a kind of consumer mentality. Medical techniques and drugs would become available to those who desire to use them (and can pay for them). Is the profession of medicine willing to be used in this way? Are physicians prepared to practice in this way? In New York City, some podiatrists are doing "toe shortening" surgeries so that their female clients can wear stylish shoes comfortably.[11] What are the ends and goals of medicine?

- The United States is projected to have a serious shortage of registered nurses by 2020.[12] Already many nurses are recruited from countries such as the Philippines, various countries in Africa, and India. These countries have their own serious medical needs and these needs become worse as they lose trained nurses. How will we address these problems globally and locally? Already there are "signing bonuses" paid to some nurses.[13] Will we increase the bonuses and the salaries in order to attract more nurses? Will we offer bonuses to students to entice them to go to nursing school? Will licensed nurses or nurses' aides take over some of the work previously done by registered nurses? Will families be forced to provide some of the nursing care for their hospitalized relatives?

Endnotes

1. See information from the AMA's 2006 Annual Report and from a 2005 article in *USA Today* on the doctor shortage (http://www.usatoday.com/news/health/2005-03-02-doctor-shortage_x.htm) [Accessed on April 21, 2008].

2. Tracy Kidder, *Mountains Beyond Mountains: The Quest of Dr. Paul Farmer, A Man Who Would Cure the World* (New York: Random House, 2003), 42.

3. See http://www.memag.com/memag/article/articleDetail.jsp?id=116463 [Accessed on April 21, 2008].

4. This is summarized in Tom L. Beauchamp and James F. Childress, *Principles of Biomedical Ethics*, 5th ed. (New York: Oxford University Press, 2001), 415–418.

5. See http://hr.blr.com/news.aspx?id=3515 [Accessed on April 21, 2008].

6. Donald Oken, "What to Tell Cancer Patients: A Study of Medical Attitudes," *Journal of the American Medical Association* 175 (1961), 1120–1128.

7. Dennis H. Novack, et al., "Changes in Physicians' Attitudes Toward Telling the Cancer Patient," *Journal of the American Medical Association* 241 (1979), 897–900.

8. Leslie J. Blackhall, Sheila T. Murphy, Gelya Frank, et al., "Ethnicity and Attitudes toward Patient Autonomy," *Journal of the American Medical Association* 274 (1995), 820–825. For more examples, see Joseph A. Carrese and Lorna A. Rhodes, "Western Bioethics on the Navajo Reservation: Benefit or Harm?" *Journal of the American Medical Association* 274 (1995), 826–829; Yali Cong, "Doctor–Family–Patient Relationship: The Chinese Paradigm of Informed Consent," *Journal of Medicine and Philosophy* 29:2 (2004), 149–178.

9. Robert M. Veatch, *Case Studies in Medical Ethics* (Cambridge, MA: Harvard University Press, 1977), 43–44 (from *In re Nemser*, 273 NYS 2 d [Sup. Ct. 1966]).

10. See the website http://www.hms.harvard.edu/coewh/cultural/index.html [Accessed on April 21, 2008].

11. Dr. Suzanne Levine spoke to the *New York Post* and was quoted saying this by Fox News on September 8, 2003 (http://www.foxnews.com/story/0,2933,96659,00.html) [Accessed on April 21, 2008].

12. According to a study by Dr. Peter Buerhaus and colleagues published in the *Journal of the American Medical Association* on June 14, 2000, the United States will experience a 20% shortage in the number of nurses needed in our nation's health care system by the year 2020. This translates into a shortage of more than 400,000 RNs nationwide. See http://jama.ama-assn.org/cgi/content/full/283/22/2948 [Accessed on April 21, 2008].

13. See Robert Steinbrook's article, "Nursing in the Crossfire," *New England Journal of Medicine* 346:22 (May 30, 2002), 1757–1766, where he refers to signing bonuses to nurses of $1,000 to $5,000 and more.

PHYSICIAN

Decision-Making in the Physician–Patient Encounter: Revisiting the Shared Treatment Decision-Making Model

Cathy Charles, Amiram Gafni, and Tim Whelan

INTRODUCTION

Although shared treatment decision-making is a concept that has gained widespread appeal to both physicians and patients in recent years, there is still confusion about what the concept means. To help clarify this issue, we published a paper which tried to define shared treatment decision-making and its key characteristics and to show how this interactional model differs from other commonly cited approaches to treatment decision-making such as the paternalistic and the informed models[1]. The paternalistic model is by now well known and articulated. Hence, we concentrated on exploring the differences between the informed and the shared models because these two labels have often been used interchangeably to describe quite different types of interaction between physician and patient in treatment decision-making.

The context for our discussion was a life threatening disease where several treatment options were available with different possible outcomes (benefits and risks or side effects), outcomes could vary in their impact on the patient's physical and psychological well-being and outcomes in the individual case were uncertain. In this context, we argued that a shared treatment decision-making model could be identified as such by reference to four necessary characteristics as follows:

1. At a minimum, both the physician and patient are involved in the treatment decision-making process.

2. Both the physician and patient share information with each other.

3. Both the physician and the patient take steps to participate in the decision-making process by expressing treatment preferences.

4. A treatment decision is made and both the physician and patient agree on the treatment to implement.

In this paper we revisit and add elements to our conceptual framework based on further analytic thinking and our current research on the meaning of shared decision-making to women with early stage breast cancer and to physicians who specialize in this area. Our revised framework (1) identifies different analytic stages in the treatment decision-making process; (2) provides a dynamic view of treatment decision-making by recognizing that the approach adopted at the outset of any given physician-patient encounter may change during the course of that encounter; (3) identifies different approaches that lie in between the three predominant treatment decision-making models and (4) has practical applications for clinical practice, research and medical education. Before exploring these issues, we briefly review factors that have led to the development of new treatment decision-making models as alternatives to the traditional paternalistic approach.

THE RISE AND FALL OF PATERNALISM

Prior to the 1980s, the most prevalent approach to treatment decision-making in North America was paternalistic with physicians assuming the dominant role.

Abridged from Charles, Cathy, Amiram Gafni, and Tim Whelan, "Decision-making in the Physician-Patient Encounter: Revisiting the Shared Treatment Decision-making Model," *Social Science & Medicine* 49 (1999), 651–666. Copyright © 1999. Reprinted by permission of Elsevier.

[1]There is a fourth model of treatment decision-making derived from health economics called the physician-as-agent for the patient. This model stresses the informational asymmetry between physician and patient. Physicians, in the usual case, are seen as possessing more technical expertise about various treatments and their benefits and risks than patients, while patients are seen as possessing superior knowledge about how these different treatments resonate with their lifestyle, health beliefs and desired health states. This model assumes that both knowledge and preferences are needed to make the best decision, yet a dilemma arises because each of these components resides in a different person. To resolve this dilemma, the model specifies that the patient communicate her preferences to the physician. The latter, who then becomes the sole decision-maker, "assumes responsibility for directing the health care utilization of the patient, as an agent trying to choose what the patient would have chosen, had she been as well-informed as the professional." (Evans, 1984, p. 75). An alternative way to bring values and preferences together in one person is for the physician to communicate the technical knowledge about treatment benefits to the patient. She will then possess the relevant knowledge, preferences and values to enable her to make the decision. This is called the informed model of decision-making. In another paper (Gafni et al., 1998) we have compared these two models and argued that the informed model appears to be superior to the physician-as-agent model in terms of feasibility of implementation.

Underlying this deference to professional authority were a number of assumptions. First, that for most illnesses, a single best treatment existed and that physicians generally would be well versed in the most current and valid clinical thinking. Second, physicians would not only know the best treatments available, they would consistently apply this information when selecting treatments for their own patients. Third, because of their expertise and experience, physicians were in the best position to evaluate tradeoffs between different treatments and to make the treatment decision. Fourth, because of their professional concern for the welfare of their patients, physicians had a legitimate investment in each treatment decision. This legitimation of physician control was further buttressed by professional codes of ethics which bound physicians to act in the best interests of their patients. All of these assumptions led both physicians and patients to expect a dominant role for physicians in treatment decision-making. Status differences between physicians and patients in terms of education, income and gender also contributed to power differentials in the medical encounter.

During the 1980s and beyond, the credibility of the above assumptions began to be questioned. For an increasing number of illnesses, for example, there was no one best treatment and a more murky and complex decisional context evolved where different treatments had different types of tradeoffs between benefits and risks. Since the patient rather than the physician would have to live with the consequences of these tradeoffs, the assumption that physicians were in the best position to evaluate and weigh these was increasingly challenged. At the same time, research into the quality of medical care began to focus on the effectiveness and appropriateness of a wide range of services delivered by physicians. The research on small area variations, for example, found consistent evidence that physician procedures for the same disease often varied considerably across small geographic areas and that these variations did not seem to be related to differences in the health status of the respective populations. Variations in treatment patterns were also found for diseases for which clinical guidelines had been developed on best practices. Patient preferences may have accounted for some of this variation, but the data also suggested that either some physicians were unaware of recommended best practices for the treatment of particular diseases or that they were aware, but were not implementing the recommended guidelines.

Concern with rising health care costs in both Canada and the United States was another health policy issue focusing attention on the medical profession. The joining together of cost and quality concerns resulted in

recommendations to make physicians more explicitly accountable to patients, the public, and in the case of the United States, to third party payers. In addition, the twin principles of caveat emptor (let the buyer beware) and consumer sovereignty gained popularity, as manifested in new legislation precluding treatment implementation without informed consent and in legislation safeguarding the rights of patients to be informed about all available treatment options. These two principles were also evident in the emergent interest among both patients and physicians in developing and advocating new approaches to treatment decision-making which would incorporate a larger role for patients in the decision-making process.

MODELS OF TREATMENT DECISION-MAKING

Both the informed and the shared models of treatment decision-making were developed largely in reaction to the paternalistic model and to compensate for alleged flaws in the latter approach. These three models are the most prominent and widely discussed in the treatment decision-making literature. Key characteristics of each model and how they differ from one another are summarized in Table 1. In Table 1 treatment decision-making is subdivided into three analytically distinct stages, even though, in reality, these may occur together or in an iterative process. The steps are: information exchange, deliberation about treatment options and deciding on the treatment to implement. The latter is the outcome of the deliberation process.

Information exchange

Information exchange refers to the type and amount of information exchanged between physician and patient and whether information flow is one or two way. Types of information that the physician might communicate to the patient include: the natural history of the disease, the benefits and risks (side effects) of various treatment alternatives, a description of the treatment procedure(s) to be used and community resources and information that the patient could access about her disease. These are primarily technical types of knowledge which most patients will not have. Information that the patient might reveal to the physician include: aspects of the patient's health history, her lifestyle, her social

TABLE 1   Models of Treatment Decision-Making[a]

Analytical stages	Models	Paternalistic (in between approaches)	Shared (in between approaches)	Informed
Information exchange	Flow	One way (largely)	Two way	One way (largely)
	Direction	Physician → patient	Physician ⇄ patient	Physician → patient
	Type	Medical	Medical and personal	Medical
	Amount[b]	Minimum legally required	All relevant for decision-making	All relevant for decision-making
Deliberation		Physician alone or with other physicians	Physician and patient (plus potential others)	Patient (plus potential others)
Deciding on treatment to implement		Physicians	Physician and patient	Patient

[a]Illustration for an encounter focusing on the case of a (treating) physician–patient dyad. For more complex cases see text.
[b]Minimum required.

context (e.g. work and family responsibilities and relationships), her beliefs and fears about her disease and her knowledge of various treatment options obtained from lay networks and/or other information sources. Except for the latter, these are primarily types of self-knowledge that the patient brings to the encounter and that the physician typically has no way of knowing except through direct communication with the patient in this or in prior consultations. In addition, at the outset of the encounter, either the physician, the patient, or both may exchange preferences regarding their own and each other's role in the decision-making process. The goal of this exchange is to make explicit how each expects the decision-making process to proceed.

The flow of information exchange may be one way or two way. In the paternalistic model, the exchange is largely one way and the direction is from physician to patient. At a minimum, the physician must provide the patient with legally required information on treatment options and obtain informed consent to the treatment recommended. Beyond this, the patient as depicted in this model is a passive recipient of whatever amount and type of information the physician chooses to reveal. In some cases, the physician may ask the patient about specific issues such as pain tolerance or allergies that could affect the latter's reaction to the treatment selected by the physician. In general, this model assumes that the physician knows best and will make the best treatment decision for the patient. In addition, information exchange from patient to physician is not seen as a major prerequisite to completing this task.

In a shared decision-making model, the information exchange is two way. At a minimum, the physician must inform the patient of all information that is relevant to making the decision, i.e. information about available treatment options, the benefits and risks of each and potential effects on the patient's psychological and social well being. The patient needs to provide information to the physician on issues raised above, e.g. her values, preferences, lifestyle, beliefs and knowledge about her illness and its treatment. The first type of information exchange ensures that all relevant treatment options are on the table; the second ensures that both the physician and patient evaluate these within the context of the patient's specific situation and needs rather than as a standard menu of options whose impact and outcomes are assumed to be similar for clinically similar patients.

In the informed model, information exchange is one way, from physician to patient. This exchange is the very crux of the model, defining the boundaries of the physician's clinical role in decision-making. The physician in this model is assumed to be the primary source of information to the patient on medical/scientific issues about the patient's disease and treatment options. To fulfill this role, the physician, at a minimum, needs to give the patient all relevant information from the highest quality research evidence on the benefits and risks of various treatments so that she will be enabled to make an informed decision. Beyond information transfer, the physician has no further role in the decision-making process. The remaining tasks of deliberation and decision-making are the patient's alone. Eddy (1990, p. 442) describes the rationale for restricting physician involvement in these latter two steps as follows:

> …the people whose preferences count are the patients, because they are the ones who will have to live (or die) with the outcomes.…Ideally, you and I are not even in the picture. What matters is what Mrs. Smith thinks…It is also quite possible that Mrs. Smith's preferences will differ from Mrs. Brown's preferences. If so, both are correct, because 'correct' is defined separately for each woman. Assuming that both women are accurately informed regarding the outcomes, neither should be persuaded to change her mind.

Not only the direction of information exchange but also the amount of information exchanged can vary across decision-making models. So far, we have focused on minimum amounts for each model but have not specified outer boundaries. The amount of information that the physician could convey to the patient, for example, is, theoretically, infinite. The physician could provide detailed information on issues like the biology of the disease or detailed aspects of the molecular basis for the disease. However, in practice, the amount of information exchanged will be influenced by time and money constraints, both of which raise issues of equity and costs. Time spent by physicians with a given patient, for example, depletes the time available to them for other needy patients in their practice. This issue seems particularly salient to a shared decision-making approach. Because the information exchange is two way rather than one way, as are processes of deliberation and decision-making, this approach is likely to take more time than either the paternalistic or informed approaches, each of which requires less interaction and consensus building.

Given the importance of information transfer from physician to patient in both the shared and informed models, it is not surprising that various sorts of decision aids have been and are being developed to help physicians communicate treatment information to patients and to present the information in a standardized way. These aids range from high technology interactive videos to low technology flip charts with audio tapes. Decision boards are another form of communication aid that lie between the high and low technology options. Each of these types of decision aids has been developed, for the most part, in isolation from one another and by different research teams. Although each type has its own supporters and advocates, to our knowledge, few, if any, empirical studies have been undertaken that compare the different decision aids in terms of criteria such as effectiveness, efficiency and patient satisfaction.

In addition, one important role for decision aids has received little attention. This is their potential for relationship building between the physician and patient. Exchanging information is a process which enables the physician and patient to get to know each other and to determine how well they can work together. This issue is particularly important for the patient. Through the process of information exchange, the patient has the opportunity to assess the extent to which the physician's practice style, attitudes and behaviour will match her own expectations of and preferences for how she wants the physician to interact with her. Building trust is one part of this process but does not capture all the important ingredients of the relationship.

In our current study of women with early stage breast cancer, for example, we found that women stressed the importance not only of finding a physician they could trust, but also one who would treat them as individuals. Patients' assessments of these physician attributes rested, in large part, on their perceptions of the physician's ability and willingness to contextualize the decision-making process by framing the discussion in terms of each patient's unique background, characteristics and life experience.

Decision aids used within the context of the physician-patient relationship provide another piece of information for patients to use in assessing their level of compatibility and comfort with a given physician's practice style. Some decision aids, however, can be self-administered and used outside the context of the physician/patient interaction. What effect, if any, information tools that are self-administered might have on a patient's relationship with her physician is an issue requiring further study.

Decision aids which present scientific information to patients about treatment benefits and risks are developed to create more informed patients and to encourage 'evidence-based decision-making'. This approach assumes that if only physicians knew how to transfer scientific information to patients in an accurate and unbiased way, the latter could be filled up (like an empty glass) with new knowledge and thereby transformed into informed and willing decision-makers. However, patients are not empty vessels. They come to the medical encounter with their own beliefs, values, fears, illness experiences and, increasingly, information about various treatment options. Moreover, patients are not so much interested in average outcomes for aggregate groups of patients as they are in knowing what this information means for themselves specifically. Patients interpret information on average treatment outcomes in order to make them personally meaningful within the decision-making context they face. In so doing, their own values and beliefs act as filters in processing what information is allowed in and how it is understood. In this interpretive process, the intended message to the patient may be lost, altered or transformed. Research into decision aids and other communication mechanisms that focus only on defining the specific message to be conveyed and the most appropriate means of doing so, fail to consider patient factors that might also affect how information is processed and understood. This latter type of data would be useful to clinicians who want to be part of the deliberation process, to better understand their patients and to recognize potential differences between lay and medical world views.

Deliberation

The deliberation stage of decision-making refers to the process of expressing and discussing treatment preferences. The minimum requirement for who is involved in this process varies across decision-making models. In the paternalistic approach, the treating physician weighs the benefits and risks of each option alone or in consultation with other physicians. The treating physician dominates the deliberation process while the patient passively listens. Physician dominance is justified by clinical judgement and experience. The label paternalistic is an apt term for this model because it evokes the image of a parent-child relationship where the authority figure (physician) has the right to decide what is best for the child (patient), even if the child disagrees.

The treating physician may verbally communicate to the patient only the ultimate treatment decision, failing to reveal knowledge and values considered in the selection process and how these were weighted. Decision-making in this context can be completed fairly quickly if the physician feels well informed to make the decision and unrestrained by the need to have patient input into this process. Of course, the lack of patient input is precisely the reason why this model is viewed by many as undesirable.

The defining characteristic of deliberation in the shared decision-making model is its interactional nature. This is both its major strength and weakness. The emphasis on interaction ensures patient input into the process; but it also makes the process more cumbersome and time consuming. Both physician and patient are assumed to have a legitimate investment in the treatment decision, the patient because her health is at stake and the physician out of concern for the patient's welfare.

For a shared model to work, both physicians and patients have to perceive that there are treatment choices. Otherwise, there is nothing to decide. Patients typically face one of two alternative treatment decisional contexts. The first is a choice between two different treatments; the second is a choice between doing nothing (e.g. watchful waiting) and doing something (e.g. implementing a specific intervention such as radiation). In an earlier study, we found that women with early stage breast cancer attending a regional cancer centre for consultation re: adjuvant therapy did not perceive the latter situation as one of choice. Many women felt they had no choice but to accept the treatment offered so that they could reassure themselves that they had done everything possible to fight the disease and to alleviate the possibility of post-decision regret should the disease return. As one woman said: "Doing nothing is no choice".

In a shared approach, each person needs to be willing to engage in the decision-making process by expressing treatment preferences, in addition to whatever information they exchange. Some have argued that if information is exchanged, this is sufficient to view the interaction as shared. We view information as only the first step in the overall treatment decision-making process. It is the basic building block to enable a shared process to occur but it does not, in and of itself, constitute that process.

In a shared model, the interaction process to be used to reach an agreement may be explicitly discussed at the outset of the encounter or may evolve implicitly as the interaction unfolds. The process is likely to be consensual if both parties start out fairly close together in their thinking about the preferred treatment. If they are wider apart in their views, a process of negotiation is likely to occur. Negotiating as equal partners, however, is not easy for the patient because of the inherent information and power imbalance in the relationship. Physicians, in the usual case, will have superior knowledge of the technical issues involved in treatment decision-making and perhaps years of clinical experience with similar types of patients. The physician bears the officially legitimized title of 'expert' while the patient may feel particularly vulnerable and frightened during the medical encounter. When education, income, culture and/or gender differences also exist between the physician and patient, the patient may feel too intimidated to freely and openly express her preferences, let alone negotiate for them with the physician. Creating a safe environment for the patient so that she feels comfortable in exploring information and expressing opinions is probably the highest challenge for physicians who want to practise a shared approach. At the other end of the patient spectrum are those who are well informed about their illness and various treatment options and who have no difficulty expressing preferences. Some of these patients may have already made the treatment decision before entering the physician's office. If the patient's preference is different from the physician's and the physician is not able to change the patient's view, then the process will become conflictual.

In a shared model, both physicians and patients are assumed to have an investment in the treatment decision. The physician can legitimately give a treatment recommendation to patients and try to persuade them to accept the recommendation. However, physicians would also have to concentrate on listening to and understanding why patients might favour a different treatment option. Perhaps the decision will be resolved through further discussion and clarification of values, preferences and information, but perhaps not. In the latter case, physicians would have to decide whether they could endorse patients' preferences as part of a negotiated agreement in which patients' views count, or whether the strength of their own views of the best possible treatment for each patient would preclude endorsement of any other option. If a physician cannot, in good conscience, endorse the patient's preference, then there is no agreement on the decision to implement even though the deliberation process was shared. In this case, the patient would have to go elsewhere and begin the process over again with another physician if she hopes to have her preferred treatment implemented (unless, of course, her preferred option was to do nothing). This example illustrates that patients face constraints in that their preferences for specific treatments can only be implemented if a physician agrees to do so. On the other hand, physicians also face constraints. A patient turned down by one physician, can make the same treatment request to another physician. A refusal from the first physician does not preclude her from receiving the desired service from the second.

Each of the above examples assumes that only two parties are involved in the decision-making process. This is the most simple case but probably not the usual case. The patient may decide to share any or all of the decision-making steps with persons other than or in addition to the physician. For example, some women with early stage breast cancer in our study of shared treatment decision-making shared the information exchange component of the process with their oncologist but consulted with family, friends or their family physician in selecting the most appropriate treatment for themselves. These latter individuals knew the patient personally and, were sought out during the deliberation and decision-making stages precisely for this reason. Including others in the decision-making process introduces additional complexity since it expands both the nature and the number of decisions to be made as well as increasing the need for co-ordination so that consultations with all persons involved can occur. In addition, some decisions require third party agreement as a necessary pre-condition for implementation. For example, a physician and patient may decide that the latter would do better being cared for at home, even though a high level of constant and close supervision is required. If there is no care-giver willing to step in and either organize or undertake this task, the decision cannot be implemented.

These examples illustrate that, in many instances, a given physician-patient interaction is only one slice of a larger decision-making process that involves others in key roles and that takes place outside the context of the medical encounter. To the extent that our conceptualizations of treatment decision-making fail to incorporate these others or to recognize their influence, they fail to capture important slices of the reality of this process. Concepts, particularly sensitizing concepts, serve as analytic guides, defining, at least initially, the boundaries of what to look for empirically to better understand a phenomenon or process of interest. If conceptualizations of treatment decision-making fail to incorporate a potential role for significant others outside the physician-patient dyad, empirical research will focus solely on this micro-system, excluding important external influences. Focusing on the physician-patient dyad may yield a lot of information about this particular slice of reality, but relatively little about the importance of this slice in the overall treatment decision-making process.

In the informed model, as noted earlier, the patient proceeds through the deliberation and decision-making process on her own. The physician's role is limited to providing medical/scientific information that will enable her to make an informed decision. Underlying this model are two assumptions. The first is that as long as patients possess current scientific information on treatment benefits and risks, they will be able to make the best decision for themselves. The second is that physicians should not have an investment in the decision-making process or in the decision made. To do so, would go beyond the boundaries of an appropriate clinical role because the physician might harm the patient by inadvertently steering her in a certain direction which reflects the physician's own bias. Underlying this concern is the assumption that the interests and motivations of the physician and patient may not be the same. This consumer oriented model emphasizes patient sovereignty and patients' rights to make independent, autonomous choices.

The view that physicians have no legitimate role to play in the discussion or recommendation of treatments may be difficult for many physicians to accept since it runs counter to decades of professional medical training and practice in which clinical experience expertise and knowledge, have been assumed to be the quintessential skills that physicians have to offer. The informed model may meet patients' needs for autonomy in decision-making (for those who value this goal) but it may not meet the needs of physicians who want to participate in treatment decision-making and who consider this a key part of their clinical role. The identification of needs raises the issue of whose needs and goals should be served in the medical encounter: the physician's, the patient's or both? Few (hopefully) would argue for the physician's needs alone. However, there may well be disagreement over the latter two options.

The use of evidence-based clinical guidelines in treatment decision-making provides a useful context within which to consider this issue. Increasingly, clinical guidelines are being developed, based on the highest quality research evidence available, to inform treatment decision-making. Underlying the evidence-based approach is an assumption that whatever treatment is shown by the evidence to be the most effective is the best treatment and the 'rational' choice to implement. Some physicians go further to argue that if an informed patient with an expressed desire to 'get well' chooses a different treatment, this choice must be the result of 'irrational' thinking and it is the physician's duty to try to change the patient's mind. In such situations, evidence may be used by the physician to prescribe the 'right' treatment. Consumer sovereignty takes second place to the physician's own belief system about what ought to determine the treatment decision. This role for evidence is not compatible with either a shared or an informed model of treatment decision-making. A role that is compatible lies in using scientific information to help create more informed patients and to enhance patient choice.

When physicians and patients have different ideas about which decision-making model should be used to structure the decision-making interaction, they are headed for conflict. Decision-making using any of the above models will be prone to setbacks if the physician and patient are not in step with each other. In our earlier paper, we made the analogy that shared decision-making takes 'two to tango'. For the two parties to dance together, the physician needs to know what kind of dance the patient prefers and the steps that this involves. Otherwise, the dance will be punctuated with false starts and missteps, creating tension between the partners and impeding their ability to work together. This analogy can be extended. For a certain type of dance, it seems appropriate that the physician take the lead (for example, in transferring technical information to patients). However, when the music changes to another type of dance, the patient may well take the lead, being more of an expert in the new steps required to fit with this particular beat (for example, patient preferences for different health states). In a shared treatment decision-making model both the physician and patient can take turns 'leading' specific discussions depending on which person has more expertise and experience to contribute on a given issue.

Decision on the treatment to implement

The final task in the decision-making process is choosing a treatment to implement. In the paternalistic and informed models, the decision-maker is one person; in the first case, the physician and in the second, the patient. However, in both cases the decision-maker is not totally autonomous because each faces constraints in actually implementing the decision. The physician must have the patient's informed consent before proceeding and the patient needs the physician's agreement to implement her preferred treatment (unless no treatment or an alternative therapy is preferred). In the shared model, both parties, through the deliberation process, work towards reaching an agreement and both parties have an investment in the ultimate decision made. The extent to which patient involvement in decision-making is associated with a greater commitment to the agreed upon treatment is an important area for study.

PRACTICAL APPLICATIONS
OF THE FRAMEWORK

Our revised and updated framework depicted in Table 1 is more flexible and incorporates a more dynamic perspective on treatment decision-making than our earlier model. We think it is also clearer in terms of practical applications for physicians and others. First, the framework provides a description of the various analytical stages in the decision-making process. The framework can be used to educate physicians about these stages and about the defining characteristics of each model. The framework also describes the general path each model follows and more specifically, behavioural expectations of both physicians and patients for implementing each model.

Second, physicians can use the framework to help explain to patients the different approaches that can be used to make treatment decisions. They can also use the framework as a tool in assessing patient preferences (as well as their own) in this regard.

Third, the framework makes explicit the possibility that not only can the decision-making approach used in one physician–patient interaction change in the next interaction, it can also change within a single interaction. For example, a physician who starts the consultation with an informed approach may need to switch mid-stream to a more shared approach if it becomes evident that the patient does not want to make the decision on her own. In this case, what started as an informed approach changes to one in which the physician plays a more active role in making the decision. Alternatively, even though a physician may be more comfortable with a paternalistic approach, a given patient may want more of a role in decision-making than the former expects or is used to. To respond to this patient's preferences, the physician will need to move towards a shared model. The framework can help physicians identify the changes required of them to move from a particular decision-making approach adopted at the outset of a medical encounter to a different one that better meets the needs of a specific patient in the later stages of decision-making. Said another way, a single treatment decision-making process can combine elements from different models at different stages in the overall process.

Fourth, the framework makes explicit that switching models during the encounter is easier in some circumstances than in others. In fact, some movements across models are not possible within a single interaction unless the whole process is started anew. For example,

a shared model, where both the physician and patient decide on the treatment to implement requires as a precondition that two way information exchange and deliberation have already taken place. If the physician starts the decision-making process with a paternalistic approach, the information gap would need to be filled before a switch to a more shared approach could be made.

Fifth, the framework recognizes that, in reality, there are multiple approaches that lie between the three ideal types. Starting with the paternalistic model, for example, the more that each step moves from a physician dominated encounter to one where the patient's input is recognized, nourished and valued, the more the model evolves into a shared approach. Similarly, as the physician's role fades into the background in steps 2 and 3 of the decision-making process, the approach moves towards the informed model.

It would be difficult to pinpoint the exact point where one model ends and another begins. We think of the three prominent approaches discussed above as markers or anchor points that reflect the most well known and best described models, recognizing that there are many combinations in between. While each could be labeled, this would be a time consuming and difficult task. In addition, we doubt that this would be a useful exercise since labels seem to generate normative judgements about what are 'good' and 'bad' ways of decision-making rather than focusing on the specific situational context in which one approach would be more appropriate than another. The identification in the framework, not only of general approaches to treatment decision-making but also of combinations in between increases options for physicians. It also reinforces the importance of flexibility so that physicians are able to recognize and respond to changes in patient preferences for the nature of the interaction as the decision-making process unfolds.

Sixth, identifying the interactional dynamics required of each model highlights the added 'costs' of engaging in shared decision-making relative to the other models. While advocates of shared decision-making have stressed the benefits of this approach in promoting patient participation and patient-centred care, few have focused on its financial costs. If shared decision-making turns out to require more time on average than other approaches in order to facilitate interaction and to build consensus, then physicians may respond by either advocating for increased fees or seeing fewer patients. However, there may also be costs for not involving patients, in the form of repeat visits, second opinions and doctor shopping.

The potential system-wide policy impacts of a shared decision-making approach have not yet received much systematic research or public policy attention.

Seventh, the framework can assist in the evaluation of different components of the overall treatment decision-making process. For example, if the goal of treatment decision aids is limited to improving information transfer then the framework can be used to identify the specific decision-making stage which forms the relevant context for the evaluation. However, if the goal of decision aids goes beyond this to also incorporate relationship building within a shared decision-making approach, then the relevant evaluation context will have to be broadened. As another example, the identification of explicit and analytically distinct phases of the decision-making process makes it possible to target specific questions regarding patient satisfaction to each of these stages and to determine which contributes most to a patient's overall satisfaction level.

Eighth, the framework can be used as an educational tool in medical training to stimulate discussion about professional orientations to and roles in treatment decision-making. For example,

1. Whose views of the meaning of shared decision-making should count: those of academics and researchers who advocate specific normative models in professional journals, or those of physicians and patients in non-academic settings whose views might be quite different?

2. Should physicians try to influence the treatment decision-making process and outcome or should the clinical role be limited to transferring relevant treatment information to the patient?

3. If a patient and her physician both prefer a paternalistic approach, is there anything 'wrong' with making the decision in this manner?

4. If a physician prefers that a patient make the treatment decision (the informed model), should the patient be 'forced' to do so, even if she does not want to?

5. Given the power, status and informational asymmetry between physician and patient, is it realistic to expect patients, even informed patients, to be able to hold their own in negotiations with physicians about treatment preferences? What steps can physicians take to create a safe environment where this can occur?

6. What is the most effective strategy available to physicians to elicit patient preferences for involvement in treatment decision-making?

CONCLUSION

In this paper we have revisited and expanded our earlier conceptual framework of different treatment decision-making models. We think this framework is more flexible than its predecessor and recognizes more clearly the dynamic nature of treatment decision-making. Practical applications of the framework have also been discussed. Over the course of our research we have learned that treatment decision-making is a complex process that takes place over time and can involve many individuals rather than an event that takes place at a fixed point in time and is restricted to the physician-patient dyad. Our thinking on treatment decision-making will continue to evolve as we move in an iterative process, empirically studying different aspects of this process and using the information to clarify our conceptual thinking.

The Calling

Abraham Verghese

I grew up in Africa, the younger of two sons of Indian parents who taught college physics. Around the time that my brother's precocious ability with numbers was revealing itself, I discovered that I had no head for math—or for any other subject in the school curriculum.

Middle-class Indian parents worshipped the professions, and only three existed for them: medicine, engineering, and law. When my brother announced, while still in short pants, that he was going to be an engineer, my parents' joy was astonishing to behold.

Nothing I had ever said had produced such a reaction. I promptly proclaimed that I intended to be a doctor. What made this remotely plausible, even to me, was that I had more than a passing familiarity with blood, mostly my own, because I was always getting into scrapes. Moreover, my unseemly interest in witnessing chicken and sheep being slaughtered for the kitchen and my fascination with watching animals give birth could now be viewed as a form of scholarship.

Having announced this bogus call to medicine so early in life, I did not give it another thought. Which is why when the true call to medicine arrived when I was 12 years old, I was flabbergasted. The moment did not have the high drama of Saint Paul's revelation on the road to Damascus. My call came quietly, but there was no mistaking it. It came in the form of a book.

I loved to read and did so with little discrimination and with a prejudice toward works that I thought might be titillating. I picked up *Of Human Bondage* by Somerset Maugham because the title was promising, and I had already read *Lolita* and *Lady Chatterley's Lover.* Of course, the book was nothing like what the title had suggested to me; it was better. The opening scene—in which Philip, a club-footed child, is ushered to his mother's deathbed to say goodbye—still haunts me. Orphaned and raised by stern relatives, and taunted in school because of his clubfoot, Philip finds solace in painting. After high school, he sets off to Paris to become an artist. Money is tight, and he lives on the brink of starvation. One day, he persuades his art teacher, Monsieur Foinet, to assess his paintings and tell him whether he should continue. The teacher studies Philip's work and makes a brilliant speech about money and its connection to the arts: "Money is like a sixth sense without which you cannot make a complete use of the other five … I pity with all my heart the artist, whether he writes or paints, who is entirely dependent for subsistence upon his art." As to his opinion on Philip's art, he offers this: "take your courage in both hands and try your luck at something else."[1]

Philip, crushed and disappointed but also relieved to have discovered what is not to be his calling, returns to London and enters medical school. The learning is grueling, and the life hard. But when he enters the outpatient clinic, he realizes he has made the right choice:

He found the work of absorbing interest. There was humanity there in the rough, the materials the artist worked on; and Philip felt a curious thrill when it occurred to him that he was in the position of the artist and the patients were like clay in his hands … Philip found that he was less shy with these people than he had ever been with others; he felt not exactly sympathy, for sympathy suggests condescension; but he felt at home with them. He found that he was able to put them at their ease, and, when he had been given a case to find out what he could about it, it seemed to him that the patient delivered himself into his hands with a peculiar confidence. "Perhaps," he thought to himself, with a smile, "perhaps I'm cut out to be a doctor. It would be rather a lark if I'd hit upon the one thing I'm fit for."[1]

The phrase "humanity there in the rough" spoke directly to my 12-year-old mind. I took it to mean that even if one did not have the talent to be an artist (or mathematician), one could aspire to be a doctor, perhaps even a good one; medicine was proletarian, and the prime prerequisite was to have an interest in humanity in the rough.

I could not tell my family how much *Of Human Bondage* had affected me or that I had now found my calling, because they believed I already had. And I was also learning, from books, that grand outward pronouncements of passion were not as significant as quiet inner convictions.

Of Human Bondage reinforced another lesson, that good literature, particularly fiction, has the power to transform. A good book can give the reader insight into his or her own life and may reveal its purpose.

Soon after this experience, another book affirmed my choice of career. A.J. Cronin, the author of *The Citadel* (1938), was, like Somerset Maugham, a physician, although he eventually gave up medicine to write novels. *The Citadel* traces the career of the doctor Andrew Manson from his idealistic youth, through his succumbing to temptation in a high-society practice, to his reclaiming of his true values—a triumph that, tragically, coincides with the sudden death of his dear wife. An immensely popular writer, Cronin was ostracized by his medical peers for his liberal views, but it is said that his books documenting the terrible state of medical care in England were instrumental in the later creation of the National Health Service.

When I arrived in the United States as an intern in 1980, I diffidently mentioned to one of my attending physicians the two books that had brought me to medicine. He was unfamiliar with the particular books but not surprised by the phenomenon. He noted that Sinclair Lewis's Pulitzer Prize-winning 1926 novel, *Arrowsmith*, about a man torn between pure scientific inquiry and the exigencies of medical practice, and Paul de Kruif's *Microbe Hunters* had had a similar influence on young prospective physicians in this country.

How and why do such books inspire young people at the threshold of their careers? The most obvious answer is that the protagonist in these novels is often wrestling with and finding his or her calling, and the reader (or perhaps a certain kind of reader) identifies with and is drawn to the character facing such a crisis. Such novels often celebrate the quietly heroic aspect of medicine, fashioning physicians in the mold of Joseph Campbell's archetypal hero—those who have dedicated their lives to something bigger than themselves.

But a good novel can offer a formative experience to prospective doctors that is both broader and deeper than identification with an admirable or sympathetic hero, and I worry that today's students may be missing out. On the one hand, students seem to me to be coming to medical school with a greater number and diversity of talents than the students of a generation ago, not only playing myriad musical instruments but also pursuing athletic hobbies ranging from spelunking to pole vaulting. On the other hand, our entering classes don't seem to include as many avid readers as they once did. This may simply reflect a societal trend, but it is one that I, as an educator, cannot be complacent about. John Fowles talks about a "prevalent form of blindness, directly caused by the terrible and crippling atrophy of the imaginative faculty (being unable to slip down the magical passage from the little signals we call words into far richer worlds than any film or TV 'version' will ever be able to present)."[2] Indeed, watching films and television are passive activities; reading, by contrast, is dynamic and collaborative: the reader uses the writer's words to construct a rich fictional dream of his or her own. As readers, we enjoy this creative process best when the writer provides just enough, but not so much that our imagination has no work to do.

Reading fiction is an easy skill, but it is also easy to avoid. The couch and the remote control beckon and compete. But the diagnosis Fowles outlines comes with an obvious prescription—a few hours spent with Gabriel Garcia Márquez's *Love in the Time of Cholera* will inoculate against cortical atrophy and preserve and expand the clinical imagination. The activity is just as salutary as a 20-minute run and easier on the knees. But there's more to it than that. As Joanne Trautmann says, "A fully imagined world is far richer than our own."[3] A well-developed fiction-reading capacity allows us to imagine our patients' worlds fully and put ourselves in their shoes. I have marveled at the way in which selected fiction discussed in a medical school class effectively conveys the tenets of professionalism and multiculturalism without ever invoking those soporific words. "Fiction," says the writer Dorothy Allison, "is the great lie that tells the truth as to how the rest of the world lives."[4]

In this visual and cyber age, when the death of the novel has been predicted for decades, one must wonder where medical students of future generations will find their *Arrowsmiths*, their *Citadels*, their *Of Human Bondages*. Where will their sense of calling come from? From television shows like *ER* and *Scrubs*? The thought is chilling.

Perhaps the whole idea of a calling is old-fashioned anyway. The sheer volume of information that today's medical students must assimilate, the debt most have to take on, and the increasingly technological nature of medicine surely dampen the sense of calling. By the end of their studies, students are often less idealistic and more pragmatic than when they began. The pressures of managed care, the malpractice crisis, and rising health care costs loom in their future.

And yet students continue to enroll in medical school, coming to the profession for timeless reasons—because of a physician they admire, or because they want to serve, or because they have suffered or witnessed suffering. Perhaps some lucky ones even today have been called to medicine through the medium of a book. If they have a love of literature, reading may well help them to discover a way to understand and identify with the ambitions, sorrows, and joy of the people whose lives are put in their hands. In medicine, we often separate life events from their meaning for those who live them. In literature, the two are united. That is reason enough to keep reading. And writing.

NOTES

1. Maugham WS. Of human bondage. New York: Bantam Books, 1991.

2. Fraser A, ed. The pleasure of reading. London: Bloomsbury, 1992:74–8.

3. Trautmann J. The wonders of literature in medical education. Mobius 1982;2(3):23–31.

4. Allison D. Skin: talking about sex, class & literature. Ithaca, N.Y.: Firebrand Books, 1994.

NURSE

The Nurse as Patient Advocate

Ellen W. Bernal

Since the 1970s an extensive discussion in nursing literature has been devoted to the suggestion that nurses be "patient advocates" whose primary responsibility is to protect patient rights and interests in the health care setting.[1] The obligation to patients represents an ideal: in actual practice, institutional and hierarchical constraints often prevent nurses from acting as advocates. Consequently, those espousing patient advocacy argue that unless nurses achieve greater professional autonomy, patients' rights will not be fully protected in hospital settings.[2]

The intertwining of professional and ethical concerns, whereby principles such as patient rights and autonomy are considered in the same context as the professional issue of freedom to practice, is worthy of note. Indeed, such intertwining is a distinguishing feature of nursing ethics in general. While medical ethics rarely needs to address the physician's freedom to establish a professional relationship with patients, nursing ethics has had to deal with ongoing challenges to the freedom to practice, especially in hospital settings.

But even within the context of nursing ethics and its characteristic focus on professional issues, the advocacy literature is distinguished by the frequently explicit claim that patients' rights and interests can only be fully protected in hospital settings if nurses achieve greater professional autonomy. The claim may be misguided. Potential confusions may arise when a call for protection of patient rights is combined with a call for increased political power for nurses.[3]

While the specific features of patient advocacy continue to be debated, it is clear that the central idea—that the primary obligation of nurses is to patients, rather than to physicians or hierarchies within hospitals—has gained wide acceptance within the profession.

Revisions in the American Nurses' Association's *Code for Nurses* reflect this shift in professional viewpoint. The 1976 code not only omits statements, present in earlier versions, that obliged nurses to maintain confidence in physicians and obey their orders, but also explicitly uses the language of advocacy in its interpretive statements: "In the role of client advocate, the nurse must be alert to and take appropriate action regarding any instances of incompetent, unethical, or illegal practice(s) by any member of the health care team or the health care system itself, or any action on the part of others that is prejudicial to the client's best interests."[4]

The debate over nurses' role as patient advocate affords an opportunity to consider several key issues. First, over the past two decades, nurses' perception of their primary allegiance has shifted from physicians and hospitals to patients. Second, some of the advocacy literature explicitly combines professional aspirations with the expression of obligations to patients. To what extent is this combination of moral and political claims legitimate? Third, patient advocacy assumes that nurses bring a special moral perspective to hospital settings. What is the nature of this moral contribution, and do nurses in fact wish to accept this as a feature of their professional role?

The advocacy literature asserts the moral primacy of autonomy, currently accepted in Western culture, and as a result may risk an impoverished view of illness, suffering, and the obligations of the professional to the patient. Alternative models of the nurse-patient relationship, such as the covenantal models already described in nursing literature, may offer a better construction of the relationship between nursing and the public.

THE ADVOCACY MODEL

Before the advocacy model gained wide acceptance, nurses believed that their primary obligation was to obey physicians and maintain order within hospitals. This military sense of nursing identity originated in the context of the Crimean war, when Florence Nightingale brought order and greatly improved conditions to military hospitals. Upon her return to England in 1856, Nightingale worked to establish a training school for nurses that would eventually impart the same military discipline to civilian hospitals, through an emphasis on improved education and obedience to institutional hierarchies. Elements of the military ideal included unquestioning loyalty and obedience to the nurse's training school, hospital, and physician's orders; protection of the patient's faith in the physician, even in cases of physician error or incompetence; self-sacrifice under difficult working conditions; and routine indications of discipline such as uniforms and deference to physicians. Despite evidence that some nursing leaders called attention to the conflicts in loyalty that could come about under this model, the military ideal provided an early sense of professional nursing identity.

The military language prevalent during the Nightingale era was gradually replaced by the language of advocacy. The primary role of advocacy is defined as the protection of patients' rights and interests. In one of the earliest pieces on the topic, Mary F. Kohnke suggests that advocacy means informing patients about their rights, providing facts about their health care situation, and supporting them in the decisions they make.[5] A more extensive development of this idea is found in a series of articles by George J. Annas, who claims that patients' rights need protection in hospital settings, and that nurses may be able to fill the role of "patient rights advocate."[6]

From the outset, the advocacy literature has frequently associated protection of patient rights with professional development. For example, Annas notes that advocacy will require a level of assertiveness that many nurses may not currently possess. If nurses provided organized support for the idea of patient rights, and taught students the art of advocacy in nursing schools, the position of the patient in the hospital and the public image of the nurse would both be enhanced. "Nurses so trained can act not only as independent practitioners, but can also move into the direct care of patients as partners of doctors rather than servants to them." Similarly, Nancy Quinn and Anne Somers Walsh predict that if nurses support the consumers' movement in health care and become patient advocates, health care and nurses' professional status will improve, while Elsie and Bertram Bandman claim that "patient advocacy is integral with the expanding relationships nurses have in the care of their patients. Models of nurse-patient-physician relationships show that patient advocacy by nurses is essential to patients' health care rights."[7]

The next move in the debate was the claim that hospital power structures prevent nurses from identifying unsafe or unethical practices by instilling a fear of reprisal. That is to say, hospital nurses are limited in their ability to serve as patient advocates because they are *unable* to protect patients' rights. Unless hospital power structures are changed to permit greater autonomy for nurses, patient rights within hospitals will be compromised. In this view, set forth in an influential article by Roland R. Yarling and Beverly J. McElmurry, optimal protection of patient rights can only be achieved through the development of nurses' professional power:

> unless nursing, through the reform of the institution in which the majority of its members practice, acquires a balance of controlling power in that institution or creates new structures for the organization of practice, it cannot effectively implement standards of care for its own practice. If it cannot realize reform it will compromise the integrity of the nurse-patient relationship, which is the moral foundation of nursing, and it will have lost its status as a profession. Furthermore, the public will have lost its most valuable ally within the health care system. The one action that would most improve the quality of health care in this society is simple and direct: set the nurses free, set the nurses free.[8]

AN ETHICAL ANALYSIS OF THE ADVOCACY ARGUMENT

The advocacy literature expresses professional identity and aspirations in the context of present nursing practice, displaying a concern for public and interprofessional recognition of nursing's professional status along with the concern to promote patients' rights and best interests. The literature often describes nurses as symbols of moral order within hospitals, and may have captured the imagination of nurses because it seems to offer a constructive way out of current difficult practice conditions, while simultaneously enhancing patients' rights.

The use of autonomy in the arguments for patient advocacy is also worth noting. The image of the autonomous person is invoked for both the patient whose rights are threatened in the hospital and for the nurse whose moral agency is compromised by institutional power structures. In the most extreme formulation of patient advocacy, the autonomy of the patient is held to be contingent upon the autonomy of the nurse.

The combination of references to actual circumstances, professional frustration and aspiration, and powerful moral ideals tends to promote uncritical assent to the claims for patient advocacy.[9] Criticism of any one of these elements may lead to a defense of advocacy through an appeal to another component. For example, any empirical question raised about nurses' working conditions within hospital settings might be answered by an appeal to nurses' professional aspirations. In a similar fashion, criticism of the search for professional power can be turned aside through a reference to the ideal of autonomy. The complex relationships among the components of the argument may have contributed to the persistence of the advocacy model.

But it is important to distinguish between the interest generated by a model and its adequacy in describing professional realities, values, and ideals. Professional nursing needs to determine whether the current description of patient advocacy actually enhances, or is in fact a detriment to professional development. Toward this end, the elements of the model should be considered separately. For example, the empirical claims and assumptions present in the advocacy literature should be examined. Is the typical nurse more likely to identify ethical issues than members of other professions, or than the general public? Do nurses currently have adequate freedom to practice? What courses of action are available to nurses when they observe less than optimal care in hospitals or other settings? Do nurses exercise these options, if they are in fact currently available? When nurses hesitate to act because of fear of reprisal, how realistic is this fear? What is the relevance of the advocacy role to situations involving deficiencies in the practice of other nurses? Research in nursing ethics is currently examining related issues that could be extended and brought to bear on the concept of advocacy if the empirical claims used to argue for it could be separated from the accompanying moral principles and professional aspirations.

Professional identity also requires clear conceptual distinctions between intrinsic professional values, the instrumental need for adequate freedom to practice, and the more self-serving goal of increased professional status. Without this differentiation, a key feature of professional identity may be lost: the promise to provide services to the public as an intrinsic value, rather than as a means to achieve professional power. Professional autonomy is not an intrinsic value of nursing and does not constitute part of the services offered to the public.[10] Instead, the ability to take action is a condition for the exercise of other values that are intrinsic to the profession. While freedom to practice is certainly necessary, the advocacy literature repeatedly confuses the distinction between freedom to practice and the less disinterested goal of professional nursing development.

ON THE MORAL CONTRIBUTION OF NURSES TO HOSPITALS

The patient advocacy literature presents symbolic images of the nurse as an individual who identifies ethical concerns, yet because of institutional constraints must either set these concerns aside or take unusually forceful action. If she sets the concerns aside, the nurse compromises personal integrity and the adequacy of patient care; if she takes action, she risks personal and professional harm.

Christine Mitchell's argument for nursing integrity signals the end of the notion that the military model of obedience can provide effective patient care in hospitals, and the beginning of the advocacy literature's claim that the nurse's freedom to act with integrity is essential to the support of patient rights and best interests. In a fictional account, Mitchell describes the moral discord faced by Nurse Andrews, who is caring for two neurologically injured patients, one an alert quadriplegic and the other a comatose individual with a poor prognosis. The two patients are attended by different physicians whose perspectives on cardiopulmonary resuscitation are different. The military model of obedience at the heart of Nurse Andrews's practice leads to inconsistency: she resuscitates the comatose patient several times, but allows the alert quadriplegic to die, despite his interest in recovering. Mitchell comments that "the individual nurse is severely handicapped in acting with integrity. Nurses' interprofessional relationships with physicians come into direct conflict with their relationships with patients. Consequently, the integrity of the whole health care system is threatened."[11] In this story, the nurse is portrayed as central to the protection of moral standards and consistent care within the hospital. When her integrity is compromised, the integrity of the institution is compromised as well.

In other advocacy stories the nurse attempts to champion patient rights and in the process either experiences or narrowly avoids personal harm. Leah Curtin provides a description of an actual situation. Jean S. is a staff nurse who is assigned to care for William R., a recently widowed man in his late sixties who was admitted to the hospital through the emergency room, where he presented with probable bowel obstruction. When the house surgeon operated, he found that Mr. R. had cancer; however, the physician believed that this diagnosis should not be shared with the patient. Jean S. attempted to convince the physician that this lack of disclosure was contrary to the rights of the patient and counterproductive to his well-being, but without success. When the patient continued to ask pointed questions regarding his health, the nurse did inform the patient about his condition. The grateful patient was then able to obtain assistance with home care through a local hospice association and later died peacefully at home. The attending physician was angry with the nurse and lodged a complaint of insubordination against her, but the director of nursing, social work services, and the chaplain's office supported her decision to share information. In Curtin's commentary upon this case, she observes that "although nurses have a moral duty to be honest in answering patients' questions, ... it is unlikely that nurses will do so (at least in any great numbers) as long as physicians have the professional and institutional power to coerce and punish them."[12]

Whether the nurse in the advocacy stories chooses to act or to remain passive, she brings a moral point of view to patient care. The expectation that nurses are to display a special moral sensitivity, while a key feature of the notion of advocacy, is by no means new. In the culture of ancient Greece and Rome, the perception that women have a natural altruism and an ability to care for others gave a sense of moral obligation to their traditional domestic occupations, such as caring for the sick. But because these occupations were regarded as chores somehow natural to women, and because of women's comparative social invisibility, their work did not appear to merit special notice. Although some of the services performed by women were highly respected, such as preparing the dead for burial and assisting at childbirth, the surrounding culture did not confer professional status on women who performed these activities.[13]

Modern culture persists in the belief that women are naturally altruistic, and altruism is a foundational assumption in the professional development of nursing. The establishment of modern hospitals "played upon the contemporary assumption that there was a necessary and laudable conjunction between nursing and femininity; the trained sensibility of a middle-class woman could alone bring order and morality to the hospital's grim wards."[14] But the view that women are naturally altruistic has restricted the ability of nurses to achieve professional status. Demands for professional autonomy when made by women are taken to be self-interested rather than oriented toward the needs of others, and so are seen as unfeminine.[15]

Patient advocacy appears to offer a way out of this difficulty, as it draws upon the traditional belief that nurses bring a civilizing, altruistic influence to hospitals, but is based on a changed notion of civic virtue.

Instead of military obedience, the surrounding culture now values individual rights. Proponents of patient advocacy imply that nurses are the professionals who—given adequate professional freedom—can best ensure the protecting of patient rights within hospitals. Through this maneuver nurses can make a claim for professional power without jeopardizing their traditional image of altruism, self-sacrifice, and high moral ideals.

The advocacy stories, however, contain questionable implications that should be considered carefully by anyone tempted to define nurses as patient advocates. First of all, they suggest that the core values of nursing are ephemeral, and that the profession will take up whatever values are current in the surrounding culture. The stories also contribute to the likelihood that the public will continue to perceive the nursing profession sentimentally, perpetuating longstanding stereotypes of nurses as martyrs or heroes. The martyr, a victim of circumstance, is sacrificed to save others who will not at first honor the sacrifice or recognize its importance. This is the nurse under the military model, who works long hours and sacrifices her own interests to care for the suffering and to save lives. In contrast, the hero, possessing unusual strength and courage, is engaged in a socially visible struggle. This is the nurse under the advocacy model, who both defends patients' rights and seeks to elevate nurses' professional status, in an adversarial struggle against the forces of institutional oppression. Both images are highly unrealistic. Professional authority has legitimate origins in nursing expertise and history, not in romantic images of nurses as guardians of morality. When nurses are portrayed in this fashion, nursing practice is burdened with unrealistic demands and barriers are erected between nurses and the other professionals with whom they cooperate.

THE IDEAL OF AUTONOMY

Those who promote patient advocacy often confuse the need for an adequate level of professional freedom to practice with an idealized image of autonomy that has attained a privileged moral status in Western culture. In this idealized image, persons select actions from a wide array of choices and are unlimited by situational constraints. Such a vision of autonomy impoverishes our view of social relationships, illness, suffering, and the obligations of the professional to the patient.

On the patient advocate model, social relationships within the hospital are essentially adversarial and manipulative. The rights of the patient are threatened by caregivers and by the institution itself. Nurses' rights too are abridged by physicians, other professionals, and bureaucratic structures. The model assumes that most relationships within hospitals are based on self-preservation and self-interest, rather than on mutual cooperation toward a common end. Within this context, nurses become professionals who assert their own rights and the rights of patients when they are threatened by others. There is a tendency to protest and unmask others' motivations rather than to explore the purposes and ends of social relationships and one's own responsibilities in promoting them.

A misplaced emphasis on autonomy obscures the frequently positive aspects of social relationships within hospitals: the mutually affirmed goals of promoting the patient's best interest in accordance with patient choices and the responsible use of resources in the service of those ends. Although hospitals may sometimes fail in their efforts to achieve their goals, it is not clear that failures are due to a deficit in nursing autonomy. The call for an abstract and unadulterated ideal of autonomy disregards the freedom of action that nurses already have.[16]

It is also not clear that the vision of autonomy invoked by proponents of patient advocacy sufficiently honors the experience of illness for the patient in the hospital. When the patient is suffering and vulnerable, an emphasis on individual rights cannot fully characterize the nurse-client relationship, as Sally Gadow observes when she urges nurses to assist the patient to find meaning in the experience of illness.[17] The interests of third parties and communities are also not encompassed by notions of patient autonomy.

The ascendancy of autonomy in modern culture contributes to the likelihood that the role of nurse as patient advocate will be accepted uncritically, especially by those nurses who actually experience repressive working conditions in hospital settings. Nurses should consider whether a more effective contribution to the growth of professional identity might not be achieved by defining patient advocacy more precisely.

As it now stands, advocacy refers to situations in which the nurse protects the patient from the incompetent or unethical practice of another professional. But other professionals, such as patient representatives, also describe themselves as patient advocates. Are nurses to practice a distinctive, nurse-specific form of advocacy, or is their advocacy to overlap that of other professionals?

Professional nursing might also wish to examine the public's perception of nursing's contributions to health care, and in particular whether the public wishes

nurses to assume the role of patient advocate. While public expectations should not define professional identity, extreme disparities between them are an indication that professionals need to examine their assumptions regarding their role.

Nurses should also consider setting aside the idea that they are powerless within hospitals. It would seem to be far more productive to identify and extend currently available resources for action, rather than seeking an idealized version of autonomy that no one working in hospitals actually possesses. If nurses do have restricted autonomy, they are not alone. Increasingly, physicians have their autonomy limited by third-party payers, utilization review, and hospital administration. In any case, what is needed is not greater individuation for nurses but greater cooperation among all professionals who provide health care in a hospital setting.

PROFESSIONAL VIRTUE AND THE MODEL OF A COVENANT

With its perplexing claim that patient autonomy is contingent upon nursing autonomy, proponents of patient advocacy tend to disregard crucial empirical questions relating to nursing practice, and to offer an overly romanticized image of the nurse as a moral guardian within the hospital. It would seem important to investigate other descriptions of nursing authority to assess their contribution to the further development of professional identity.

A covenantal model of the professional-public relationship is one alternative that has been suggested. On William May's account, covenantal agreements described in the Bible are based on three elements that provide clues to authentic professional-public relationships: (1) an exchange of gifts, symbolizing mutual indebtedness; (2) an exchange of promises, establishing a set of mutually affirmed intrinsic values; and (3) an ontological change in the persons who create the covenantal agreement. The individual becomes a professional when he or she is given freedom to practice by the public, on the basis of the professional's promise to remain faithful to the ideal of service.[18] These elements, which have their origins in ancient Hebrew thought, afford a different interpretation of issues raised by the proponents of patient advocacy: the relationship between professions and the public, the meaning of personal autonomy and illness, and intrinsic professional values.

A covenantal model calls attention to the reciprocal indebtedness of the public and the profession, suggesting that professional power is a gift from the public to the profession given in exchange for its expertise and orientation toward the service of others. Those who have adopted the notion that nurses should be patient advocates should consider whether the current model of advocacy can fully encompass the extent of services nursing traditionally offers. While protecting patient self-determination is certainly essential, nursing is also, in the language of the American Nurses' Association,

> the protection, promotion and restoration of health; the prevention of illness, and the alleviation of suffering in the care of clients, including individuals, family groups, and communities. In the context of these functions, nursing is defined as the diagnosis and treatment of human responses to actual or potential health problems.[19]

Patient advocacy represents only one feature of the range of professional services nursing provides.

Under a covenantal model, gifts are to some degree responsive to the needs and expectations of the recipients. Although the full extent of nursing's gift to the public may not be completely defined by the needs that the public perceives, if patients do not in fact expect or want nurses to be their advocates, the nurse's gift of advocacy may well go unappreciated. Patients presumably regard themselves and their families or other surrogates, rather than nurses, as the primary sources of self-determination, and expect nurses to respond to the wider variety of needs occasioned by illness and health care.

A related concern involves the connection between patient advocacy and professional autonomy. A gift given by the profession to the public should strengthen the covenantal relationship between the nurse and the patient rather than strengthen the profession's independent claim to professional status. A gift with this secondary motivation risks becoming illegitimately self-interested. The risk seems greater when the nurse is presented as the key to moral practice within hospital settings. Surely other professionals within hospitals also provide support for patient self-determination, rights, and interests. Nurses must carefully consider whether they wish to retain this image of moral centrality or whether it is in fact counter-productive to professional development.

A covenantal model describes persons as free to enter into agreements, establish moral principles, and keep promises. This account of practical autonomy, or autonomy within a situation, is an alternative to the more sweeping description of professional autonomy underlying the argument for patient advocacy, which tends to view persons as though they were abstracted from the social obligations, relationships, and contingencies that characterize actual social settings. A covenantal model more clearly engages actual experience, including the need to change institutions that are repressive and inimical to the covenantal relationship.

At present, patient advocacy does not provide a comprehensive description of the role and contributions of nursing. But the question of whether nurses currently possess adequate professional freedom to establish covenantal relationships with patients still remains. It seems clear that professional nursing has an extensive and historically based covenant with the general public. However, especially for nurses who practice in hospitals, the possibility of professional covenants with clients faces several challenges, not only because of the bureaucratic structures of hospitals and the history of the nurse-physician relationship, but also because of the way that nursing services within hospitals are allocated. When patients are admitted to hospitals by physicians, they have little choice regarding which nurses will take care of them. Changes in nursing personnel due to staffing patterns and the frequent lack of primary care nursing also contribute to discontinuity in nurse-patient relationships. These structures place real limitations on hospital nurses' ability to enter into caregiving agreements with individual patients. At the same time, institutions do provide opportunities for cooperative change, which is especially likely to occur if nurses continue to demonstrate the essential contribution that the profession makes to overall patient well-being. The adversarial stance of the advocacy model may not be the best way to achieve needed change.

Professions modify their intrinsic values over time, in response to historical and social conditions. The conditions that prompted the call for patient advocacy should also prompt a consideration of alternative models, given advocacy's theoretical and practical shortcomings. Such consideration will contribute to an expression of professional identity that reflects both the history and traditions of nursing and the challenges of modern practice.

REFERENCES

1. Barbara K. Miller, Thomas J. Mansen, and Helen Lee, "Patient Advocacy: Do Nurses Have the Power and Authority to Act as Patient Advocate?" *Nursing Leadership* 6 (June 1983): 56–60; Gerald R. Winslow, "From Loyalty to Advocacy: A New Metaphor for Nursing," *Hastings Center Report* 14, no. 3 (1984): 32–40; and Terry Pence and Janice Cantrall, eds., *Ethics in Nursing: An Anthology* (New York: National League for Nursing, 1990).

2. George J. Annas, "The Patient Rights Advocate: Can Nurses Fill the Role?" *Supervisor Nurse* 5 (July 1974): 20–23, 25; Mary F. Kohnke, "The Nurse as Advocate," *American Journal of Nursing* 80 (November 1980): 2038–40; Christine Mitchell, "Integrity in Interprofessional Relationships," in *Responsibility in Health Care*, ed. George J. Agich (Dordrecht: D. Reidel, 1982); Darlene Trandel-Korenchuk and Keith Trandel-Korenchuk, "Nursing Advocacy of Patients' Rights: Myth or Reality?" *Nurse Practitioner* 8 (April 1983): 40–42.

3. See George J. Agich, "Professionalism and Ethics in Health Care," *Journal of Medicine and Philosophy* 5, no. 3 (1980): 186–99.

4. American Nurses' Association, *Code for Nurses with Interpretive Statements* (Kansas City: American Nurses' Association, 1976; 1985).

5. Kohnke, "The Nurse as Advocate."

6. George J. Annas, "Patient Rights: An Agenda for the '80s," *Nursing Law and Ethics* 3 (April 1981), reprinted in *Ethics in Nursing*, ed. Pence and Cantrall, pp. 75–82.

7. Annas, "The Patient Rights Advocate," p. 25; Nancy Quinn and Anne Somers, "The Patient's Bill of Rights: A Significant Aspect of the Consumer Revolution," *Nursing Outlook* 22 (April 1974): 240–44; Elsie L. Bandman and Bertram Bandman, *Nursing Ethics Across the Life Span*, 2d ed. (Norwalk: Appleton and Lange, 1990), p. 21.

8. Roland R. Yarling and Beverly J. McElmurry, "The Moral Foundation of Nursing," *Advances in Nursing Science* 8, no. 2 (1986): 63–73.

9. Michael Polanyi, *Personal Knowledge: Towards a Post-Critical Philosophy* (New York: Harper Torchbooks, 1964).

10. John S. Packard and Mary Ferrara, "In Search of the Moral Foundation of Nursing," *Advances in Nursing Science* 10, no. 4 (1988): 60–71.

11. Mitchell, "Integrity in Interprofessional Relationships," pp. 163–84.

12. Leah Curtin and Josephine Flaherty, *Nursing Ethics: Theories and Pragmatics* (Bowie, Md.: Robert J. Brady Co., 1982), p. 333.

13. Natalie B. Kampen, "Before Florence Nightingale: A Prehistory of Nursing in Painting and Sculpture," in *Images of Nurses: Perspectives from History, Art, and Literature*, ed. Anne Hudson Jones (Philadelphia: University of Pennsylvania Press, 1988), pp. 6–39.

14. Charles E. Rosenberg, *The Care of Strangers: The Rise of America's Hospital System* (New York: Basic Books, 1987), p. 212.

15. Susan Reverby, "A Caring Dilemma: Womanhood and Nursing in Historical Perspective," *Nursing Research* 36, no. 1 (1987): 5–11.

16. Anne H. Bishop and John R. Scudder, Jr., *The Practical, Moral and Personal Sense of Nursing: A Phenomenological Philosophy of Practice* (Albany: State University of New York Press, 1990).

17. Sally Gadow, "Existential Advocacy: Philosophical Foundation of Nursing," in *Nursing Images and Ideals: Opening Dialogue with the Humanities*, ed. Stuart F. Spicker and Sally Gadow (New York: Springer, 1980), pp. 79–101.

18. William F. May, "Code and Covenant or Philanthropy and Contract?" in *Ethics in Medicine: Historical Perspectives and Contemporary Concerns*, ed. Stanley Joel Reiser, Arthur J. Dyck, and William J. Curran (Cambridge, Mass.: M.I.T. Press, 1977), pp. 65–76; see also Mary Carolyn Cooper, "Convenantal Relationships: Grounding for the Nursing Ethic," *Advances in Nursing Science* 10, no. 4 (1988): 48–59.

19. American Nurses' Association, *Code for Nurses*, Preamble.

Nurse Autonomy as Relational

Chris MacDonald

INTRODUCTION: AUTONOMY

This article seeks an improved understanding of nurse autonomy by looking at nursing through the lens of what recent feminist scholars have called 'relational' autonomy. The main claim made here is that nurse autonomy is, indeed, relational. Attention to the social and contextual factors that facilitate meaningfully autonomous action is crucial to advancing our understanding of the relationships between professionals and patients, as well as between different groups of professionals.

AUTONOMY: DESCRIPTIVE AND PRESCRIPTIVE

Autonomy has both a descriptive and a prescriptive aspect, and the two are interrelated. Descriptively, autonomy is the capacity for self-governance. Prescriptively, respect for autonomy means (at least) not interfering with persons' control over their own lives and (perhaps) taking active steps to facilitate such control. Our understanding of the factual aspect of autonomy is, however, bound to influence the steps we need to take (or to avoid) in our attempts to respect people's autonomy. If our factual understanding of the preconditions for autonomous action are flawed, so will be our ethical reaction to that autonomy. For example, as Sherwin notes, if our basic understanding of human autonomy is built on 'a model of articulate, intelligent patients who are accustomed to making decisions about the course of their lives and who possess the resources necessary to allow them a range of options to choose among', then respect for autonomy in the clinical setting will require only that we adhere to the standard for informed consent. That standard requires (roughly) that patients be suitably informed about their prognosis and options, and be allowed to choose

Abridged from MacDonald, Chris. "Nurse Autonomy as Relational," *Nursing Ethics* 9:2 (2002), 194–197, 198–201. Copyright © 2002. Reprinted by permission of Sage Publications Ltd.

among them. Such an approach ignores (albeit perhaps as a pragmatic necessity) numerous contextual factors that may prevent patients from experiencing the possibility of real choice, even though they are informed, capable, uncoerced and so on. Similarly, giving health professionals the formal authority to make a decision about patient care does not constitute professional autonomy in any meaningful sense if the institutional culture in which they are situated is not supportive of their capacity for independent judgement.

Recent feminist work on the concept of autonomy has brought attention to the networks of social relationships and interdependencies that facilitate autonomous action. Feminist scholars such as Susan Sherwin and Anne Donchin have argued that older, liberal understanding of autonomous agents as free and independent individuals is inadequate, and that we will understand autonomy better if we examine the complex webs of personal and institutional relationships that make possible, or sometimes hinder, the making of real choices. This new understanding of autonomy—known as 'relational' autonomy—claims to be a more accurate description of the actual basis for autonomous action, as well as a better grounding for our obligation to respect each other's autonomy. It is interesting that, as Sherwin herself notes, this new understanding of autonomy continues to focus on the autonomy of individuals (rather than of groups or institutions), albeit individuals who are socially situated.

Autonomy has been, and continues to be, a central notion in modern health care ethics. It is understood as the ability to direct one's own life and to make one's own decisions. It is generally seen as having two components: control of one's own actions (that is, the absence of constraint) and the capacity for rational deliberation. The focus of discussions of autonomy within bioethics has typically been patient autonomy. The point generally made here is that competent patients have the right—both ethically and legally—to exercise a significant degree of control over their own health care. The relational perspective on autonomy, as it gains prominence within the health care ethics literature, will have important implications for a wide range of issues, including among others our understandings of informed consent, advocacy and confidentiality. The focus of this article, however, is the implications of the relational perspective for our understanding of the professional autonomy of nurses.

PROFESSIONAL AUTONOMY

Autonomy is a notion that applies to more than just patients; it also applies to health professionals. Although respect for patient autonomy means that patients should have (other things being equal) as much control as possible over their own care, respect for professional autonomy means allowing professionals to have substantial control over professional practice, including significant room for exercise of their judgement.

A 'professional' is (roughly) a member of a self-regulating occupational group granted (usually by legislation) the exclusive right to practice in a particular field. Standard examples of professionals in this sense include physicians, nurses, lawyers and engineers. (Which occupational groups will count as professions, in this model, will vary according to jurisdiction. In some provinces in Canada, for example, social work is a regulated profession, while in others it is not. Although the argument here applies most strongly to the legislated professions, it will apply also, with varying degrees of strength, to other protected and service-orientated occupational groups.)

Nurses have not always been members of a 'profession' in the sense intended here; hence they have not always been accorded professional autonomy. During the American Civil War, for example, the very word 'nurse' could be used to describe a wide range of trained and untrained caregivers. During the early years of professionalization, nurses were often told to think of the physician-nurse-patient triad as a family, with the physician as the head of the family and the nurse playing a watchful supportive role. As nursing roles and educational experiences have become standardized, their recognition as a profession has grown. In most modern health care systems, nursing is a licensed, self-regulating profession. Today, nurses have their own professional standards, which imply a right and a wrong way of doing things; no physician order has sufficient moral weight to override those.

The concept of 'professional autonomy' applies to nurses both as a profession and as individuals. As it applies to the profession of nursing, we use the term 'professional autonomy' to indicate the privilege of self-governance. Nurses—like other professionals in professions such as medicine, law, and engineering—are given the freedom to set, within broad limits, their own standards and to enforce those standards among their members. Today, in modern health care systems, the members of the nursing profession, as a group, are given by society the privilege of setting their own standards of both technical and ethical excellence. Thus, professional bodies typically have the authority to determine educational and licensing standards, to set and enforce standards of technical excellence and ethical propriety, and to grant and revoke licenses to practice. This relative freedom that the nursing profession has from outside scrutiny and control constitutes an important kind of autonomy.

As it applies to individual nurses, the notion of professional autonomy has to do with the ability of particular nurses to make at least some decisions that are not subject to authoritative review by those outside of the profession. When we speak of the professional autonomy of an individual nurse, what we are really considering is the right—indeed, the responsibility—of a member of the nursing profession to act according to the shared standards of that profession. Professional autonomy implies the right to exercise professional judgement—in adherence to professional standards—in the face of countervailing pressures from institutional authorities, disagreement with members of other professions, or inappropriate demands on the part of patients or clients or the general public.

For example, professional autonomy provides justification for nurses acting according to their own professional judgement, rather than simply being told by physicians what to do. The professional autonomy that nurses so rightly claim means that nursing expertise carries with it its own authority. It means that nursing expertise is independent of, rather than subordinate to, medical expertise. Even when nurses are carrying out physicians' orders, they typically retain a sphere of autonomous judgement regarding how those orders are fulfilled. Nurses receive formal training and gain experience in activities about which physicians typically know less. Nurses may (depending upon specialization) know more, for example, than physicians do about performing phlebotomy or the appropriate procedures for sterile dressings. When a physician's orders conflict with nursing standards or with a nurse's expert judgement, the nurse's professional autonomy implies a right to object.

EXTENDING THE RELATIONAL VIEW

In particular, I argue that professional autonomy—the autonomy of both the profession as a collective and individual nurses in their work—is relational in nature. That is, I contend that professional autonomy finds its sources in supportive social relations and is threatened when those relations are either weak or absent.

Autonomy of the profession

In what sense, then, should professional autonomy be understood as relational, as it applies to the profession of nursing? The most obvious way in which the autonomy of the profession depends on social structures is in the fact that nursing, as a self-governing profession, depends on legislation—an external enabling factor—for its very existence. The privilege of self-regulation is granted by society, usually by means of provincial or state legislation. Thus, the profession's ability to grant licenses, for example, and to take legal action against those who attempt to practice without a license, is a direct result of empowering legislation. It is the consent of society—represented by the executive and legislative branches of government—that gives the profession this range of freedom and authority.

Furthermore, the relative autonomy of the profession as a group results, in part, from the reluctance of courts to question the wisdom of standards of proficiency and ethical conduct set by professional bodies. The relative freedom from judicial review enjoyed by most professions finds its source in the common-law understanding that, for the most part, only members of a given profession possess the expertise required to judge the standards set by that profession. Professions may have either more or less autonomy, depending on the extent to which the courts are willing to defer to the profession on questions such as this. As it happens, most professions enjoy a great deal of autonomy in this regard.

The freedom that the nursing profession has to regulate the activities of its own members is therefore deeply influenced by the profession's relationship with other segments of society, including the executive, legislative and judicial branches of government.

Autonomy of the professional

Next, in what sense should professional autonomy be understood as relational as it applies to individual nurses? The ability to do the things that nurses do depends crucially on a whole range of social relations and social institutions. Nurses' freedom to care for patients according to their best judgement, for example, is a direct result of their membership of a supporting institution, namely a self-regulating professional body. When they act according to the shared standards of their profession, their colleagues will (normally) lend them their support.

Individual nurses' capacity for autonomous action depends on a number of features of the health care institution within which they practice. In an article on accepting and refusing assignments, Judith Powers notes the importance of an 'enabling practice environment', which 'supports autonomous nursing giving nurses the opportunity, the authority, and the accountability to identify and solve practice related problems'. Among the factors Powers points to as enabling autonomous nursing is adequate staffing. Without this nurses may find their ability—their freedom—to meet the demands of professional standards jeopardized. Other examples of ways in which health institutions can support autonomous nursing include providing ancillary personnel to assist nurses with such non-nursing tasks as laundry and food tray pick-up, and supporting 'collaborative practice through monthly meetings between unit nurses and the physicians who work on those units'.

Regulations also play an important role in facilitating—and limiting—individual nurses' autonomy. They do not generally have the autonomy, for example, to engage in the range of practices granted by legislation to physicians. As a particular example, Cullen notes that nurses' '[d]ecision-making autonomy is inhibited in the UK by the restrictions on nurse prescribing'.

Some nursing roles provide for a greater degree of autonomy, by design. Nurse practitioners, for example, are granted autonomy within a broader range of practices than are registered nurses. Even when legislation permits autonomous practice (e.g. for nurse practitioners), the ability actually to practice autonomously depends upon a range of factors, including public perceptions, institutional arrangements and the support and respect of other health professions. Cullen notes that 'the development of clearly defined, accessible, cost effective nursing care will open up further opportunities' for nurse practitioners to practice autonomously. The greater ability of nurse practitioners to practice autonomously springs from a combination of additional education and enabling legislation, both of which find their source in social relations of the sort that make this additional autonomy count as relational.

If we are to see clearly the distinction between personal and professional autonomy, it may help to look at an example of (relational) personal autonomy as it applies to nurses' work within a professional context. An example of the degree to which nurses' personal autonomy, within their work environment, is relational can be seen in cases of conscientious objection. To the extent to which nurses have the freedom to decline assignments that they oppose ethically, they have this freedom because their rights of conscience are supported by their professional code of conduct, by institutional policies, and by the courts. It is important to see, however, that this is an instance of personal, not professional autonomy. The right not to participate in activities that one finds

objectionable springs not from one's membership of a profession, but from one's dignity as a human being. Indeed, membership of the nursing profession puts distinct limits on one's personal autonomy. For example, as Davino notes, 'once you begin treating a patient, you're legally responsible for him until he has been placed in the care of someone else'. This requirement applies regardless of whether one has reason to object, for personal reasons, to the assignment.

IMPLICATIONS OF A RELATIONAL MODEL

What implications spring from understanding nurses' professional autonomy as relational? Two spring readily to mind.

First, understanding autonomy as relational may help nurses (or nursing students) to understand better the differences between their own capacities for autonomous action and the capacities of the patients for whom they care. As Michael Yeo notes: 'Power, knowledge, and vulnerability are not evenly balanced in the client-professional relationship'. It is all too easy for people in positions of relative power to underestimate their own advantages. A focus on the relational nature of autonomy reminds professionals that their own capacities for autonomous action—including their skills, their education, their self-confidence—have their source in certain enabling experiences and relationships that may not be similarly available to particular patients. As Donchin points out, 'Some women are inevitably better prepared to be assertive than others because social, educational, and economic class obviously influence one's self-assurance in the face of authority'. This realization may facilitate appropriate empathy, on the part of nurses, for disempowered patients.

Secondly, a relational understanding of nurse autonomy may help us to understand better those situations in which nurses themselves are seen as having inadequate autonomy. The study of the relational nature of autonomy, as exemplified by Sherwin and Donchin, is rooted in a desire to understand better the relative lack of autonomy of oppressed groups. Applying the lens of relationality to professional autonomy may seem odd to some because professionals have traditionally been understood as enjoying a relative abundance of autonomy. Indeed, the scope of autonomous judgement is one of the identifying marks of a professional, but it is clear that not all professions enjoy an equal scope of autonomous action. Health care, in particular, is notoriously hierarchical in this regard. Physicians have traditionally had the lion's share of authority, with nursing and pharmacy, for example, only more recently asserting themselves as autonomous professions with their own bodies of knowledge and their own responsibilities to patients. As nurses and other health care professionals move towards greater autonomy, and also towards collaboration with (rather than subordination to) physicians, it will be crucial to understand the social and institutional factors that enable autonomous action. Clearly, a relational understanding of autonomy is essential here. Autonomy does not and cannot mean independence. For nurses, increasing professional autonomy must mean finding ways to facilitate meaningful self-direction within the context of an interdependent health care team.

GENETIC COUNSELOR

Neutrality Is Not Morality: The Ethics of Genetic Counseling

Arthur L. Caplan

THE ETHOS OF NEUTRALITY IN GENETIC COUNSELING

Those who do genetic counseling agree that it should always be done in a morally neutral manner. This is reflected in professional discussions of the goals of genetic counseling, in the norms that should govern the behavior of clinical geneticists and counselors, and in discussions of the techniques and methods that counselors should use to attain their goals. The long dominant view of the goals, norms, and methods thought appropriate in genetic counseling can be accurately described as an ethos of value neutrality.

GOALS

The Code of Ethics recently promulgated by the National Society of Genetic Counselors provides a useful summary of the goals that professionals agree ought to guide the process of counseling.

The goal of counseling is simple: The counselor is to empower the patient/client to make autonomous decisions. Autonomous decisions must be informed and free from coercion, but short of these ethical side-constraints, the values of the counselor should not play a role in setting the goals of clients.

The goal of simply providing information that the client can use to make a decision guided by his or her own values has been omnipresent throughout the evolution of the specialty of clinical genetics in the United States over the past 20 years or so. W. S. Sly in a classic article, "What Is Genetic Counseling?" maintained that the goal of counseling

is the delivery of professional advice concerning the magnitude of, the implication of and the alternatives for dealing with the risk of occurrence of a hereditary disorder within a family. (Sly 1973)

The counselor is to provide accurate and understandable information. The responsibility for doing something with that information is not the counselor's, it is the client's.

NORMS

The norms of genetic counseling, as articulated in numerous books, articles, and codes of ethics, have—despite changes in the professional identity of those doing the counseling—remained relatively constant for the past 20 years. They exemplify the norm of value neutrality made famous by the fictional Sergeant Joe Friday on television's long-running detective series, "Dragnet." Sergeant Friday, when called to the scene of a crime, would ask the victim to provide, "just the facts." Fridayism, the provision of the facts and only the facts, is entirely consistent with the textbook picture of the goals of genetic counseling, which sees the provision of purely factual information in the service of enhancing autonomous decision making by the client as the sole legitimate norm in the counseling process.

The presumption behind the norms guiding the actual conduct and methods of clinical genetics work is that autonomy, especially with respect to reproductive choices, can flourish only in a purely factual environment.

Clients are informed of all genetic risks, the methods available to refine the risks, the options available to deal with these risks, and the consequences likely to follow from each of the options. (Yarborough, Scott, and Dixon 1989)

A very influential article that appeared in the *American Journal of Human Genetics* discouraged the provision of anything other than the facts:

> This process [genetic counseling] involves...helping the individual or the family to (1) comprehend the medical facts, ... (2) appreciate the way in which heredity contributes to the disorder, (3) understand the options for dealing with risk of recurrence, (4) choose the course of action that seems appropriate to them in view of their risk and their family goals, ... (5) make the best possible adjustment to the disorder. (Fraser 1974)

METHODS

If the goal of counseling for the past 20 years has been to provide information to maximize client choices, and the norm for doing so has been "Fridayism," the methods and techniques prescribed for achieving this goal while respecting this norm have, throughout this same period of time, been inhospitable to the overt appearance of professional values. Counseling has, for decades, been taught and depicted as an activity requiring moral neutrality concerning the actions, statements, and conduct of the counselor.

The commitment to moral neutrality concerning the counselor's behavior is best illustrated by the methodological recommendation that counseling be nondirective. It is the client's values and only the client's values that have any place in guiding decisions. Yarborough, Scott, and Dixon observe that the dominant view of genetic counseling insists that it be done

> in a nondirective manner wherein the counselor maintains a morally neutral attitude about the particular choices clients may eventually make. (Yarborough et al. 1989)

Another clinical geneticist echoes this view when he writes,

> There is ... general agreement that the doctor should respect the conscience and moral beliefs of the patient and not impose his personal moral values. (West 1988) ...

The ethos of value neutrality that dominates genetic counseling in America consists of three elements: the goal of maximizing patient or client choice, the norm of supplying only the facts, and the technique of nondirectiveness in the provision of information. Each of these elements has very little room for the expression of the values of the counselor.

THE DISTINCTIVE NATURE OF THE ETHOS OF COUNSELING

It is remarkable how the goals of enhancing patient autonomy, the technique of nondirectiveness, and the normative stance of absolute value neutrality differ from the goals, norms, and methods associated with other sorts of health care professional–patient encounters. Most areas of clinical medicine make no pretense of value neutrality.

If a test of a patient's blood lipid levels were to reveal a cholesterol count of 350, most doctors and public health experts would be astounded if this fact were merely reported to the patient with no prescriptive or normative recommendation. If a pediatrician were to examine a child and see a spine that displayed severe scoliosis, and then give the parent of that child only a diagnosis with no recommendation for or against treatment, that physician certainly would not be praised by his or her peers for respecting the autonomous decision-making authority of the parent. The failure to offer a prescriptive recommendation concerning treatment would probably be seen as grounds for a malpractice charge due to culpable negligence...

But this [prescriptive attitude] is not the ethos that prevails in the domain of clinical human genetics. Those doing counseling have been taught for more than 20 years that their goals, their norms, and their methods must be morally neutral. Counseling ought to aim at nothing more than the provision of facts about hereditary conditions and the options for choices available to the client in light of those facts. Counselors are taught to provide facts about heredity without giving any hint as to their own values concerning the decision that a client ought to reach. It would be considered a gross violation of the ethos of counseling by most counselors for a counselor to criticize or disagree with the ultimate reproductive decision of a client.

THE CHALLENGE OF THE GENOME PROJECT TO THE ETHIC OF NEUTRALITY

The question of whether moral neutrality is an adequate morality for clinical genetics and genetic counseling does not arise because those who do the counseling are ridden with self-doubt about the adequacy of the ethos that has dominated their work for more than two decades. It is not a result of ontological or epistemological challenges to the very possibility of value neutrality. Nor is it provoked by complaints or disquiet on the part of clients, other health care providers, or the general public. Quite the opposite is true. Many experts in clinical genetics and counseling believe that it is the strict adherence to an ethos of value neutrality that has allowed the field to flourish.

My concern regarding the adequacy of the ethos of neutrality for counseling is rooted in the likelihood that those doing counseling will soon have a wealth of new information about the genetic makeup of eggs, sperm, embryos, fetuses, parents, and would-be parents as a result of ongoing efforts to map and sequence the human genome. If the genome project succeeds and a flood of new knowledge concerning the genetic contributions to human disease and disability becomes available, the ethos of moral neutrality will come under severe pressure for at least three reasons: the absence of enough adequately trained genetic counselors, uncertainty about what constitutes disease and health in the realm of genetics, and pressures to apply newly acquired genetic information in the service of containing the ever-escalating cost of health care....

UNCERTAINTY ABOUT THE MEANING OF NEW GENETIC KNOWLEDGE

The field of clinical genetics has been confined until relatively recently to the detection of and counseling about highly unusual, uncommon, and often devastating genetic anomalies. The detection of extra or missing chromosomes, structural chromosomal abnormalities, or inborn errors of metabolism, although not simple, has, nevertheless, as its goal, the detection of clear-cut biological anomalies. The majority of these anomalies result, given certain developmental and environmental circumstances, in readily detectable phenotypic conditions, states, or symptoms. The consequences of most of the genetic conditions now at the center of genetic counseling are incapacitating, life-threatening, or both....

While most agree that anencephaly, spina bifida, Tay-Sachs disease, or trisomy 18 are to be disvalued because they are associated with impairment, dysfunction, or premature death, the prospect for obtaining agreement about the meaning, significance, and disease status of soon-to-be-discovered genetic differences among human beings is far from clear. Simply finding polymorphisms at the genome level (e.g., within genes coding for blood types or skin colors) can be viewed as having little or great import depending on how such discoveries are presented and understood. For some prospective parents, telling them that their fetus is "different" or that they are carriers of "unusual" genotypes may be enough to affect their reproductive behavior.

The genetic contribution to many common diseases and disorders whose disvalued status is not in dispute (i.e., cancer, Alzheimer's disease, severe depression) will be made clearer as scientific understanding of the structure and composition of the genome increases. But more will also be learned about the genetic basis of other conditions (i.e., allergies, phobias, anxiety, short stature, poor dexterity, poor complexion) where there are fewer obvious points of agreement as to whether or not they should be disvalued, much less classified, as diseases or impairments.

The genome project is also likely to reveal a good deal of structural and anatomic information about variation among genomes for which there will be no clear understanding of the function of variation. Greater knowledge of structure without a corresponding knowledge of function provides ample opportunities for confusion, dispute, and disagreement about the significance of this information for determinations of the health or diseased state of those persons or groups who possess different or rare genomes. An ethics of neutrality is not likely to be as serviceable when the "facts" about heredity are much more controversial than they have been for most of the history of genetic counseling.

COST CONTAINMENT AND COUNSELING

The ethos of neutrality with respect to counseling will also be challenged by the impact that new knowledge resulting from the genome project will have in the arena of health policy. There is every reason to presume that the costs of health care will continue to increase well into the first few decades of the next century. Many experts are convinced that the explicit rationing of access to health care as a matter of public policy is the only solution to controlling the high costs associated with modern health care.

If it is possible to reduce the cost of care by preventing the birth or compelling the early treatment of those likely to have costly diseases and disorders, then the ethos of neutrality dominant today with respect to both goals and conduct in genetic counseling will be fiercely challenged. Many will see the application of new knowledge concerning the genome as a legitimate and ethical way for society to decrease the burden of paying the costs associated with disease, disorder, and dysfunction. Historically, new information about the genetic basis of behavior has led to powerful movements in American public policy for the utilization of that information for the good of society (Reilly 1991).

Political pressure for genetic counselors to take a normative stance, which accommodates society's need to decrease the cost of diseases and disorders with strong hereditary origins, will escalate as more becomes known about the role played by heredity in human health. Public health will incorporate more and more information about the hereditary basis of disease into its increasingly proactive and prophylactic stance toward the goal of disease prevention. It will become increasingly difficult to remain value neutral if the information supplied by the genome project permits cost savings through "prudent" or "responsible" reproductive choices.

IF GENETIC COUNSELING IS NONDIRECTIVE IS IT MORALLY NEUTRAL?

How inhospitable to the impending assault on value neutrality will genetic counseling be? Is the ethos of neutrality likely to yield as the work of the genome project proceeds in the United States and other nations, and the knowledge base for testing, screening, and counseling grows? If, despite the oft-professed allegiance to an ethos of neutrality, genetic counseling is not, and has not ever really been, conducted in accordance with that ethos, then the absorption of new genetic knowledge into counseling may meet with less resistance than might be expected.

While those who teach and write about counseling depict the goals, norms, and methods used in morally neutral terms, there are many reasons to think they are simply kidding themselves as to the moral content of their actual work. The few studies that have been done of the content of genetic counseling and of the attitudes of genetic counselors reveal wide variations in their beliefs and practices (Wertz and Fletcher 1989). In practice, an ethos of neutrality exists alongside a wide spectrum of beliefs, attitudes, and conduct. These differences suggest that value neutrality is hardly the order of the day in genetic counseling . . . .

Could genetic counseling be morally neutral? What would it look like if it was? The only way to answer this question is to clarify what might be meant by prescriptions requiring that counseling be morally neutral.

One of the reasons why it is possible to argue that genetic counseling is not morally neutral is that it is not exactly obvious, despite the frequency with which such claims are made, what an ethos of neutrality entails. The most frequent injunctions as to how to achieve an ethos of neutrality are exemplified in warnings that

counseling must be nondirective. Moral neutrality is often equated with nondirectiveness.

Of all of the possible ways in which counseling might be seen as value neutral, nondirectiveness seems to have been of the greatest historical importance to professionals who have written about the ethics of this activity. Yet, oddly, the issue of directiveness does not seem to have anything to do with avoiding or eliminating a specific set of norms, values, or principles. Rather, nondirectiveness is used to describe the stance that the counselor should adopt toward the counselee, one of openness along with a willingness to listen. Nondirectiveness has its roots in a theoretical position within psychiatry, social work, and psycho-analysis that prescribes nondirectiveness as the best stance for eliciting information from a patient, so that the patient may come to have insight about his or her psychological problems.

Directive counseling would permit or require the counselor to be active, willing to engage in challenge, argument, and confrontation with clients. Those who favor nondirective counseling among genetic counseling professionals are usually referring not to a neutral or indifferent moral outlook but, rather, to a passive role in which counselors try to be responsive to client needs and questions and avoid challenges or confrontations in seeking to accomplish their educational goals.

Seen in this light, it quickly becomes obvious that the discussions of the appropriateness of "directiveness" with respect to genetic counseling have little to do with ethics or values. Those who insist on nondirective counseling do so because they believe that counselors will be most effective at communicating and conveying information if they listen carefully to those who seek their help and avoid directly challenging or confronting their clients. But, the effectiveness of nondirectiveness as a technique, or the best technique, for ascertaining client needs and conveying information is amenable to empirical assessment. It is simply a mistake to equate nondirectiveness in counseling with value neutrality. Nondirective counseling need not presuppose any particular moral outlook but it is quite compatible with many prescriptive stances.

Admittedly, there are moral constraints over the kinds of techniques that are permissible to use in the context of a counseling session, be it directive or not (i.e., no coercion, no hectoring, no threats, no rudeness, etc.). But imposing such constraints over the process of counseling is surely not to advocate adhering to an ethic of moral neutrality.

Passivity and responsiveness may be preferable to aggression and proactivity in trying to talk about genetic information (or anything else for that matter!). But those who insist on the desirability of nondirective counseling are doing so on grounds that have little to do with morality, but rather a lot to do with their beliefs concerning what is and is not effective in facilitating communication. The limits on what counselors can do and how they ought to behave are set by beliefs about what allows successful communication—they do not redefine the adoption of a value-neutral ethic for genetic counseling....

The other important reason evident in the literature of clinical genetics from the past two decades for an ethic of value neutrality for genetic counseling is to prohibit counselors from making particular recommendations or from prescribing specific courses of action to their clients. The insistence on nonprescriptiveness in counseling has its roots in the history of the goals that have fueled clinical genetics.

When genetic counseling first appeared, it was clearly, explicitly, and unabashedly linked to achieving eugenic goals. At the turn of the century, and for roughly the next three decades, health care professionals sought to make genetic counseling available to persons in the hope that they would discourage those likely to have impaired, diseased, or mentally defective children from having them. Some also hoped to encourage those whom they saw as having positive genetic endowments to have lots of children. As the scientific underpinnings for both negative and positive eugenics came under challenge in the 1940s and 1950s, and as the horrors of social policies built on race hygiene in Nazi Germany were revealed (Reilly 1991), the emphasis shifted from eugenic goals to the goals of prevention....

However, [today's] shift away from an ethical stance favoring the prescription of eugenic or preventative goals toward one favoring respect for the autonomy of client decision making is [not] morally neutral. On the contrary, the shift toward an ethic that elevates client or patient autonomy above all other values is highly value-laden and prescriptive.

Touting a nonprescriptive ethic is not the same thing as touting a morally neutral ethic. In reality, those who believe genetic counseling should be both nonprescriptive and nondirective maintain these views because they believe that clients should have the final word over decisions and actions, and that they will be in a better position to make decisions if these norms are followed by counselors. This means that respect for autonomy and the desirability of informed, "rational" decision making are norms of

critical importance. And this means that the ethic being taught, recommended, and defended is anything but morally neutral or value free (Yarborough, Scott, and Dixon 1989).

The advocacy of a morally neutral ethic by those in genetic counseling may be intended to avoid certain other problems. Sometimes those who advocate an ethic of moral neutrality warn against the counselor being judgmental toward clients. Moral neutrality is a way of indicating that counselors must be nonjudgmental about those they serve.

Similarly, an ethic of value neutrality is sometimes advanced as a way to warn against the covert smuggling of professional or personal counselor values into the counseling situation. It is intended to prohibit the utilization of tacit or covert values in the selection of information that is passed along to counselees.

Avoiding the use of covert values and advocating that counselors remain nonjudgmental may be sound strategies for effective genetic counseling. But they are also norms that are clearly motivated by the belief that the client's autonomy can be allowed to flourish only in certain environments. Respect for patient or client autonomy is clearly the ethic that underpins these sorts of recommendations.

Finally, the notion that genetic counseling must be morally neutral may be motivated by the concern that values not be allowed to influence or color the facts with respect to the presentation of information about the risks and consequences of particular genetic conditions or states. The facts must be given objectively (West 1988).

One commonly hears counselors say that they feel obligated to present all the facts and all the options to their clients. Strictly adhering to the admonition to be morally neutral in the selection and transmission of information may lead counselors to simply dump information onto their clients. At its worst, informed consent in any area of health care can be treated as an exercise in truth-dumping, in which every fact, every option, every risk, and every benefit is unleashed on an unwitting and sometimes unwilling patient, because the person giving the information feels that he or she must do so in a way that is completely value free. Such an exercise often leads to frustration rather than the enhancement of autonomy.

Since the ethic of genetic counseling is surely committed to autonomy enhancement, the idea that information is value free or can be presented in a value free manner makes little sense. Surely the counselor must exercise some judgment over what information to present and how to best present it. Trying to preserve the objectivity of information about heredity by insisting on the value free nature of counseling leads to information overload—not informed decision making.

WHY HAS AN ETHIC OF MORAL NEUTRALITY DOMINATED GENETIC COUNSELING FOR THE PAST TWENTY YEARS?

Why has a distinctive ethos of moral neutrality dominated genetic counseling in the United States and other Western nations for the past two decades? Abuse carried out under the banner of eugenics and the controversy over elective abortion are key reasons.

Those who established the field of clinical genetics in the years after World War II were keenly aware of the tie that existed between genetics and the Holocaust. They also knew that there were powerful strains of racism and bigotry in evidence in the field of genetics in the United States, Canada, the United Kingdom, and other countries in the prewar years. The emphasis on moral neutrality as the guiding ethic of clinical genetics was a reaction against the utilization of genetics and clinical genetics in the service of an ideology that led to mass genocide in Germany (Proctor 1988) and coercive sterilization in the United States and other nations (Reilly 1991).

Few areas of science have had to live with the historical legacy of abuse that haunts clinical genetics. The history of the twentieth century ends all arguments about whether or not it is possible to abuse genetic information. As a result, few areas of science or medicine have been so keen to restrict or confine the role played by professionals to matters of fact, not value as genetic counseling.

The other major reason for the emergence of an ethic of value neutrality in genetic counseling is the link between counseling and reproduction. In the United States, genetic counseling came of age at the same time as a political movement to carve out a fundamental right to privacy with respect to reproduction regarding contraception, abortion, and sexual conduct was emerging. The right of a woman to choose whether or not to bear a child emerged in the late 1960s and early 1970s. At the time this right was being articulated, a shift was taking place in the composition of those doing genetic counseling from M.D.s to M.A.s and from men to women. The women who began to dominate the counseling field

were hardly unaware of the importance of reproductive rights for women and the controversy over the right to abortion on demand. The right to privacy meant that women had to remain free to choose whether or not they would have a child regardless of what genetic testing revealed. The fragility of that right could not have been lost on the women who were beginning to dominate the field of genetic counseling.

Not only did genetic counseling emerge in tandem with the right to reproductive privacy, but it was also inextricably intertwined with the issue of abortion. The only option available to women or parents in almost all situations where congenital anomalies were discovered prenatally was abortion. Abortion was, and remains, a subject that generates enormous moral conflict. An ethic of value neutrality provided some space for clinical genetics from the abortion controversy. Genetic counselors could not be accused of favoring or promoting abortion if they adhered to a strict ethic of value neutrality.

THE TIME HAS COME TO ABANDON THE ETHIC OF NEUTRALITY

Are there sufficient reasons to abandon the ideal of moral neutrality in genetic counseling and attempt to initiate a debate about what ethos should be put in its place? This question is especially acute when the focus of moral discussion shifts from the clinical to that of public health policy. The danger of misunderstanding and misapplication of the information likely to be created by the Human Genome Project suggests that the time has come to abandon the pretense of moral neutrality, both in the clinical setting and in the public policy arena.

CLINICAL PRACTICE

The avowal of an ethic of neutrality probably did provide room for clinical genetics to grow despite the long shadow cast by Nazi eugenics. The ethic of neutrality was indisputably helpful in providing a buffer for the field from the heated controversy over the right of women to elect abortions.

But promoting value neutrality as the moral ideal for counselors no longer makes sense. The abuses of the Nazi era no longer threaten the existence of the field. And an ethic of neutrality is unlikely to provide much cover from the current divisive debates about abortion in which you are seen as either for or against it. Moreover, the flood of new information soon to sweep into clinical genetics from the findings of the Human Genome Project raises many other questions about the aims and goals of clinical genetics that go beyond the question of the morality of elective abortion.

Value neutrality is no longer healthy for the practice of clinical genetics. It deflects attention away from the question of whether neutrality actually prevails in counseling sessions and, if it does, what counselors and clients think it actually means. The relative paucity of studies of the actual practices of genetic counselors is partly a result of the dominance of the value neutral ethos among those in the field.

Value neutrality discourages those in the field from coming to grips with the central ethical question that now confronts the field—how to define genetic disease and disorder in order to lay out appropriate targets for testing and counseling. When the genetic abnormalities, which were the object of testing and counseling, were relatively noncontroversial in terms of their dysfunctional and disvalued status, the definition of genetic disease could be put aside. As more and more information becomes available on more and more genetic conditions, this question can no longer be avoided. Ducking the question of what it is that clinical genetics seeks to detect and possibly treat has led many persons with disabilities to distrust the motives and goals of those in clinical genetics.

With a mountain of new information about the human genome looming in the not-so-distant future, genetic counseling can no longer afford to ignore the question of what sorts of disorders and diseases it wishes to discover, why, and what exactly it wants to say about them. Definitions of genetic disease and disorder must be spelled out so that they are available for criticism and challenge by clients as well as by those inside and outside the field.

An ethos of value neutrality also makes it very difficult for patients to hold counselors accountable for their conduct. If neutrality is the avowed ethos but no clear consensus exists as to what the ethos involves in terms of actual behavior and conduct, then it will be difficult for clients to know when and if a counselor is deviating from neutrality in the provision of information. If any and all behavior is compatible with an avowed stance of value neutrality, then the ability to ensure quality in genetic counseling is severely impaired.

Value neutrality also leaves counselors powerless in the face of what may be immoral requests on the part of clients. If families come seeking testing and counseling so that they can indulge their taste for a child of a particular sex, or if, for some personal reasons, they want a child with a particular disease or handicap, or they hope to create a tissue donor, the counselor bound by strict value neutrality can say nothing. As the range of traits and conditions correlated with genetic states begins to grow, the requests of parents are likely to grow as well. At some point parents are likely to begin making requests for testing and counseling that clearly fall in the realm of genetic improvement and enhancement rather than in the domain of dysfunction and disease. An ethic of value neutrality provides no foundation for counselors to try and dissuade parents from making choices that are frivolous, silly, or malicious. ...

PUBLIC HEALTH AND PUBLIC POLICY

... Lastly, a stance of value neutrality may foster a sense of irresponsibility about reproduction and genetics. If reproductive choice is simply a matter of individual choice and nothing more, if no moral argument or persuasion is considered licit, then the message the profession is sending to its clients and the public is that you can do with your gametes as you please. It may be true that we ought not to allow government to take a strong hand in legislating who can and cannot reproduce (although this is hardly a value neutral position!). But there is a big difference between not wanting to become involved in legislative and judicial matters pertaining to the use of genetic information in making reproductive choices, and not having anything to say about the rights, duties, and responsibilities of those who choose to reproduce.

Ethics is not the same as the law. It is possible to believe that something is morally wrong and yet not believe it should be outlawed. Similarly, it is possible to believe that an act or policy is morally right or good without believing that there is a role for the state, the courts, or the legislature.

If those in genetic counseling still believe that the lessons of history indicate that a gap must be allowed to exist between the practice of clinical genetics and public policy, this does not mean that the only way to ensure that that gap exists is to cling to an ethos of value neutrality. Ironically, to do so is to leave the field to others who will not necessarily be so like-minded.

There are many who will see the influx of new information from the Human Genome Project as providing an opportunity to advance their social, ideological, racial, or economic goals. Value neutrality, whether possible or not in the clinical setting, is simply not an adequate ethic in the public policy arena. It is precisely the information sought by those involved in the genome project that points toward the inadequacies of the current ethic in genetic counseling.

REFERENCES

Fraser, F. C. 1974. "Genetic Counseling." *American Journal of Human Genetics* 26:636–659.

Proctor, R. 1988. *Racial Hygiene: Medicine Under the Nazis.* Cambridge: Harvard University Press.

Reilly, P. R. 1991. *The Surgical Solution: A History of Involuntary Sterilization in the United States.* Baltimore: Johns Hopkins University Press.

Sly, W. S. 1973. "What Is Genetic Counseling?" In *Contemporary Genetic Counseling,* edited by D. Bergsma. White Plains, NY: The National Foundation–March of Dimes.

Wertz, D. C. and J. C. Fletcher. 1989. *Ethics and Human Genetics: A Cross-Cultural Perspective.* New York: Springer-Verlag.

West, R. 1988. "Ethical Aspects of Genetic Disease and Genetic Counseling." *Journal of Medical Ethics* 14:194–197.

Yarborough, M., J. Scott, and L. Dixon. 1989. "The Role of Beneficence in Clinical Genetics: Nondirective Counseling Reconsidered." *Theoretical Medicine* 10:139–148.

Psychosocial Genetic Counseling in the Post-Nondirective Era: A Point of View

Jon Weil

For thirty years nondirectiveness has been the guiding principle or central ethos of genetic counseling. For the individual genetic counselor it has provided practical and ethical guidance to the complex tasks of presenting technical information, giving emotional support, and assisting in the process of decision making. At the professional level it has served as a basis for developing ethical standards, counseling techniques, and professional identity. From the public perspective it has sent a strong message of support for the beliefs and values of individual counselees as they make difficult decisions, often while confronting the compelling pressures of medical technology, medical paternalism, and public health approaches to disease reduction.

Despite its deep historical roots, I believe the role of nondirectiveness as the central ethos of genetic counseling has become an impediment to the continued development of the profession and to its ability to meet the multiple challenges it now faces. In what follows I will discuss the basis for this position as well as the ways in which removing nondirectiveness from its central role (while retaining it as a component of practice) would contribute to the future development of genetic counseling. One consequence of such a step would be to open discussion and debate concerning other potential guiding principles, to which I make an initial contribution.

A BRIEF HISTORY

Nondirective approaches to genetic counseling arose in the 1950s and 1960s for multiple reasons (Weil, 2000). What is now called genetic counseling was initially provided by PhD research geneticists and MD clinical geneticists who, because of their academic affiliations and research orientation, were not fully imbued with the paternalistic approach to patients that characterized most medical practice of the time (Sorenson, 1993). In addition, the earliest genetic counseling could only provide recurrence risks based on Mendelian genetics and, when amniocentesis was developed, could only provide a fetal diagnosis. The response was up to the clients and involved reproductive decisions—Have children and run the risk, or don't. Continue the pregnancy or abort. While some practitioners almost certainly gave advice and exerted pressure to avoid having seriously affected children, it was also recognized that these profoundly personal decisions were ultimately the responsibility of the individuals who would be most affected (Fine, 1993; Resta, 1997; Sorenson, 1993).

There was, in addition, a need to dissociate genetic counseling from eugenics. The eugenics movement was strong in the early part of the twentieth century, but support then declined due to social and political changes, a more sophisticated understanding of population

Weil, Jon. "Psychosocial Genetic Counseling in the Post-Nondirective Era: A Point of View," *Journal of Genetic Counseling* 12:3 (2003), 199–211.

genetics and the genetics of complex characteristics, and the use of eugenics as a rationale for Nazi genocide in World War II (Caplan, 1993; Sorenson, 1993). Sheldon Reed, who originated the term genetic counseling, defined it as "a kind of genetic social work without eugenic connotations" which, in his opinion, "contributed to [its] rapid growth" (Reed, 1974, p. 335).

The founding of the first masters degree training programs, beginning with Sarah Lawrence College in 1969, initiated a period of more organized theory and education in genetic counseling. Several factors again contributed to the consolidation of nondirectiveness in the period that followed. In the search for psychological and counseling theories that could serve the developing profession, the Sarah Lawrence Program adopted Carl Roger's theory of nondirective counseling as the basis for an interview skills course that, among the counseling courses offered, "had the greatest overall impact on" the Sarah Lawrence students (Marks, 1993, p. 20). Roger's concepts and terminology subsequently became a central component of genetic counseling theory and practice (Fine, 1993). During this period, a growing understanding of the psychosocial dimensions of genetic counseling also led to concern for supporting the beliefs, values, and decision making process of the counselee (Kessler, 1980). Changing social and political attitudes also played a role, with the abortion rights, patient rights, disability rights, and feminist movements all providing support for reproductive decision making based on the beliefs and values of the individuals involved (Caplan, 1993; Rapp, 1999).

Nondirective genetic counseling was supported by the influential and frequently cited definition of genetic counseling formulated by a committee of the American Society of Human Genetics in 1975. It states in part that the process of genetic counseling involves "help[ing] the individual or family ... choose the course of action which seems appropriate to them" (Ad Hoc Committee on Genetic Counseling, 1975, p. 241). The Code of Ethics of the National Society of Genetic Counselors (NSGC) also states in part that genetic counselors "Respect their clients' beliefs, cultural traditions, inclinations, circumstances, and feelings," and "Enable their clients to make informed independent decisions, free of coercion" (National Society of Genetic Counselors, 1992, p. 42). More recently, a "Code of Ethical Principles for Genetics Professionals" states that genetic professionals "Provide counseling that is *nondirective*...and [that] respect[s] the choices of

patients and families" (italics added; Baumiller *et al.*, 1996, p. 180).

In 1988 a survey of MDs and PhDs providing genetic counseling found strong endorsement of nondirectiveness in the United States and, with some exceptions, in other countries (Wertz and Fletcher, 1988). A later survey of NSGC members reported that 96% of respondents considered nondirectiveness to be important or extremely important in their clinical practice. When asked to define nondirectiveness in their own words, "The majority of responses fell into three major categories ... Present both (all) sides ... Allow client values to determine the outcome ... and Be objective" (Bartels *et al.*, 1997, p. 175).

In reviewing this brief history, the most relevant aspect for the present discussion is the diversity of factors—scientific, medical, technological, professional, and social-political—that led to the current status of nondirectiveness. Each of these continues to evolve, thus necessitating an on-going evaluation of the role of nondirectiveness in the practice of genetic counseling.

PROBLEMS AND CRITIQUES

Despite broad support for nondirective genetic counseling, there are a number of problematic issues. The term has frequently been used without precise definition. When defined, the definitions have varied. On the one hand are narrow definitions. These are based on the ethical principle of value neutrality and primarily specify what the genetic counselor should not do: She should refrain from expressing or revealing her own emotions or beliefs, giving advice, telling counselees what to do, or making therapeutic recommendations (Kessler, 1997b; White, 1997). If the counselee asks "What would you do?" the basic approach is to say, with an appropriate explanation, "I am not in a position to tell you what you should do."

In addition to issues of definition, it has been argued that nondirectiveness is ethically insufficient as a central ethos, given that decisions involving abortion and selective termination for birth defects raise moral and ethical questions for individual counselees and in society at large. A nondirective stance can be construed as avoiding these difficult ethical issues—under the banner of the counselee's freedom of choice, genetic counseling attempts to isolate itself from the moral, ethical, and political issues that its practices raise (Caplan, 1993; Wolff and Jung, 1995).

Finally, it is clear that narrowly defined nondirectiveness is not an achievable absolute. It is, at best, a goal toward which to strive. There are four broad reasons why this is the case:

Inadvertent Directiveness.   The genetic counselor's attitudes or values "show" despite efforts to remain and/or appear neutral.

Inevitable Directiveness.   This results from the inevitable choices the genetic counselor must make concerning the information provided and counseling approaches used.

Institutional Directiveness.   The institutional message and/or setting implies one course of action is preferable or advisable. For example, state support for expanded alphafetoprotein (XAFP) screening implies that prenatal diagnosis and abortion are the appropriate courses of action for test-positive XAFP and medically positive prenatal diagnosis results, respectively (Clarke, 1991).

Meta-Directiveness.   Nondirectiveness is a specific approach to counseling and is thus directive with respect to the counseling process and the approach to decision making. As Kessler (1992, p. 11) states "In the case of directiveness, the counselor wishes to influence the counselee's behavior, whereas in the case of nondirectiveness, the counselor attempts to influence the way the counselee thinks about a specific problem."

MOVING BEYOND NARROW DEFINITIONS

The practical and conceptual limitations imposed by narrow definitions of nondirectiveness inhibit clinical practice and the ability to develop active, effective counseling techniques. Burke and Kolker (1994), Brunger and Lippman (1995), and Bower *et al.* (2002) report the experiences of genetic counselors who feel torn between the realities of providing counseling to actual counselees and the narrow definition of nondirectiveness in which they were trained. In the course of providing clinical supervision to students in the University of California, Berkeley, Program in Genetic Counseling, I observed the vigilance and inhibition that narrow definitions impose, even in a training program that specifically promotes active counseling techniques and a psychosocial orientation. I believe that for many genetic counselors and genetic counseling students there remains an underlying anxiety about what it is and is not appropriate to do in genetic counseling, because of a fear that active counseling approaches will be perceived as "directive."

Broad definitions of nondirectiveness have evolved in an attempt to circumvent these limitations. They define nondirectiveness in the larger ethical context of supporting client autonomy and promoting active, self-confident decision making (Kessler, 1997b; White, 1997). They are predicated upon and promote active, skill-based counseling techniques that fully utilize the genetic counselor's knowledge of medical—genetic, psychosocial, and ethical issues. Illustrative of this perspective is the approach to the question "What would you do?" Rather than treating this as a situation to be avoided or circumvented, genetic counseling based on broad definitions treats the question as an opportunity to identify and address the underlying issues, such as confusion, anxiety, or couple disagreement, that led to the question being asked (Djurdjinovic, 1998; Kessler, 1997b; Weil, 2000).

Seymour Kessler's keynote address to the 1996 NSGC Annual Education Convention (Kessler, 1997b) made a major contribution to the process of developing a broad definition of nondirectiveness. Kessler proposed that counselees are more emotionally and cognitively robust than they are given credit for, such that they can absorb and utilize attitudes and opinions expressed by the genetic counselor without being inappropriately influenced. He argued that narrow definitions of nondirectiveness are inhibiting and limit the genetic counselor's ability to effectively serve the counselee. He then proposed a more expansive definition as the appropriate guiding ethos for genetic counseling.

> [S]ince the beginning, there has been a second aspect of nondirective methods that practitioners recognized, namely their ability to promote the autonomous functioning of the client. This aspect of ND is clearly applicable to genetic counseling and I offer it as a definition: ND describes procedures aimed at promoting the autonomy and self-directedness of the client. (p. 166)

Drawing on this, he then argued that what genetic counseling needs is not more discussion of nondirectiveness, but rather the development of more active, effective counseling skills, a position that he has consistently and effectively promoted for many years (Abrams and Kessler, 2002; Resta, 2000).

Since Kessler's presentation, a substantial body of literature has developed in which a broad definition of nondirectiveness is used, implicitly or explicitly, to promote active, knowledgeable counseling that supports counselee autonomy, facilitates informed decision making, and allows the counselee(s) to benefit from the full range of the genetic counselor's knowledge and skills (e.g., Djurdjinovic, 1998; Eunpu, 1997; Kessler, 1997a, 1998, 1999; McCarthy Veach *et al.*, 2003; Weil, 2000; White, 1997).

GENETIC COUNSELING SHOULD NOW MOVE BEYOND BROAD DEFINITIONS AS A CENTRAL ETHOS—A PROPOSAL

Broad definitions of nondirectiveness represent a substantial step forward. Nevertheless, as long as nondirectiveness continues to serve as the central ethos of genetic counseling, the profession faces a fundamental limitation or stasis. This results from the need to tie discussions of theory and practice to the concept of nondirectiveness and to filter perceptions and ideas through the lens, or more aptly the bottleneck, of nondirectiveness.

This can be illustrated by returning to Kessler's (1997b) definition, quoted above,

> [Nondirectiveness] describes procedures aimed at promoting the autonomy and self-directedness of the client.[1]

Consider an alternative statement:

> A guiding principle for genetic counseling should be to promote the autonomy and self-directedness of the client.

This alternative loses nothing in terms of its contribution to a discussion of genetic counseling. However, it provides a freer, fresher perspective from which to consider how it might be implemented.

This example illustrates a more general situation: As the definition of nondirectiveness evolves in the direction of promoting counseling skills and patient autonomy, the term "nondirective" becomes less and less relevant and appears increasingly to be a historic relic, albeit an honorable one. Retaining the term adds nothing substantive to the discussion, but its connotations, including the continuing legacy of narrow definitions, are inhibiting.

For these reasons, I make the following proposal:

Nondirectiveness should be replaced as the guiding principle for the clinical practice and professional conceptualization of genetic counseling.

In so doing, I am not suggesting that the concept of nondirective genetic counseling should be eliminated from professional consideration. There is value to the underlying principles such as providing balanced information, not imposing the genetic counselor's values

on the counselee, and supporting counselee autonomy. These should be retained as important components of the practice and ethics of genetic counseling. However, the term and concept of nondirectiveness should no longer serve as the central ethos.

Recent work by Bower and coworkers (Bower *et al.*, 2002) supports this proposal. A questionnaire concerning ethical and professional dilemmas faced by genetic counselors found that one fifth of the respondents reported issues related to nondirectiveness occur "frequently." Relevant situations included counselee decisions that the genetic counselor felt were based on incomplete informed consent or information. The predominant strategies suggested by the respondents for addressing these situations were active: seek consultation, make a referral, or discuss the issue with the counselee. In discussing these findings in an accompanying paper, the authors strongly support a broad definition of nondirectiveness. However, they go further:

> Nondirectiveness... has failed to provide a framework for determining when and how to take a more proactive stance with clients....Genetic counselors need guidance and support from the profession regarding how to have a conversation with clients in which the counselors' values can be appropriately shared and incorporated into a session. (McCarthy Veach *et al.*, 2002, pp. 188–189)

And they place this in a yet larger context:

> Genetic counseling is a unique activity that warrants its own model and methods. It is time for the profession to *find itself* by articulating the *genetic counseling model* of genetic counseling (p. 190, italics in original).

I believe the continuing development and articulation of such a model will be facilitated by removing the historical constraint of nondirectiveness as the central ethos.

While the arguments presented thus far draw on general counseling principles and clinical experience within genetic counseling, the proposal is also relevant to the evolving medical, professional and social context within which genetic counseling functions. With the impetus of the Human Genome Project, genetics will play an increasingly important role in many aspects of medicine, including the testing, diagnosis, and treatment of common adult onset disorders (Collins and McKusick, 2001). The expansion of genetic counseling into cancer risk genetics and recent developments in cardiovascular and neurogenetics represent early

---

[1]The use of this example is not a criticism of it. It is chosen because it is a clear example of a "broad" definition, and it was presented in the context of promoting more active, skill-based, effective counseling.

steps in this process. These developments, which have been referred to as "genomic medicine," raise critical questions concerning the type of genetic counseling appropriate to different medical situations as well as which professionals should provide them (Greendale and Pyeritz, 2001; Guttmacher *et al.*, 2001).

In contrast to prenatal or pediatric genetic counseling, in which decisions commonly involve reproductive choices, decision making in cancer risk counseling and many other medical areas often involves complex issues related to the value of genetic testing and to medical interventions and health care practices with varying degrees of, sometimes uncertain, efficacy. In these circumstances, the knowledge, recommendations and clinical experience of the health care provider(s) may have an essential role in helping the patient reach an appropriate decision. It has been argued that nondirective counseling is inadequate under these circumstances, and that the needs of patients are better served by an interactive process in which the health care provider(s) make specific recommendations while the counselee retains a crucial role in making the final decision. This has been referred to as shared decision making (Burke *et al.*, 2001; Elwyn *et al.*, 2000), a deliberative relationship (Jansen, 2001) and a medical recommendation from an appropriate specialist (Peters and Stopfer, 1996).

This is a complex issue, with multiple viewpoints, whose resolution will vary depending upon the circumstances. Genetic counseling can more effectively contribute to these deliberations if nondirectiveness is presented as one option—with an extensive body of experience and theory behind it—rather than as the central professional ethos which must be circumvented if other approaches are to be considered.

This issue also impacts the question of who should provide genetic counseling as genetics expands into many areas of medicine. Jansen (2001) argues that nurses, especially advanced practice nurses, are more suited than are genetic counselors. She states that nurses have an established role as patient advocates and utilize a deliberative counseling approach that enhances patient autonomy and "assist[s] client[s] in thinking critically about values that bear on [a] decision" (p. 138). In contrast, she asserts that genetic counselors have a nondirective approach which presents "information in a clear and neutral manner…leaving [clients] free to interpret this information according to their own values" (p. 135). A comparable position is presented by Anderson (1999).

These authors imply that genetic counselors work from a narrow definition of nondirectiveness. Their arguments can be countered with an explanation of broad definitions and the adoption of such definitions by the genetic counseling profession. However, the authors' position illustrates a persistent, if somewhat outmoded, perception of genetic counseling that has important potential ramifications. Critical decisions concerning professional roles and scope of practice in the evolving practice of genomic medicine will be made by health care providers, health care managers, and government personnel in policy, regulatory and legislative capacities. Perceptions and stereotypes of genetic counseling, as well as the reality of contemporary practice, may play a role in these decisions. Genetic counseling can address arguments such as Jansen's more effectively if the principles and practice of the profession can be stated directly, rather than through the limiting and historically laden principle of nondirectiveness.

DOES GENETIC COUNSELING NEED A DEFINING ETHOS?—A SECOND PROPOSAL

Eliminating nondirectiveness as the central ethos for genetic counseling would also raise a set of fundamental questions that can be fruitfully explored:

Does genetic counseling need a guiding principle or central ethos? If so, should it be a single concept or a suite of concepts? And if so, what should it or they be? To promote the discussion to which these questions lead I make the following second proposal:

The central ethos of genetic counseling should be to bring the psychosocial component into every aspect of the work.

A number of arguments support this proposal. First, it embodies the fundamental role of genetic counseling: To help individuals use the information and technology of medical genetics to meet the difficult situations that arise due to the occurrence or risk of occurrence of genetic diseases and birth defects. In spite of the large body of relevant information and technology, this is a fundamentally humanistic undertaking. The situations that counselees confront are often painful, frightening, and ethically complex. They affect the hopes and fears, and the emotional, cognitive, moral, family and social lives of those who are involved, i.e., the psychosocial domain.

Second, the ever-increasing flow of information and technology creates great pressure on genetic counselors to attend to the medical-genetic side of genetic counseling, in their training and continuing education as well as in their work with counselees. No "central ethos" is required to promote this imperative. The proposed central ethos would provide a counterbalance. In practical and ethical terms it would support the difficult and continuing effort to make time and place for the psychosocial aspects of genetic counseling, and it would provide a basis for requesting sufficient time, personnel and budgetary resources to do so. It would also serve as an important message in presenting the services and profession of genetic counseling to the public and other professionals.

Third, if the counselee's psychosocial needs are to be adequately addressed, this must be done in a manner appropriate to his or her ethnocultural experience and background (Greb, 1998; Weil, 2000). Stated differently, the approach to psychosocial issues must be multicultural, not monocultural (Weil and Mittman, 1993). Given the complexity of psychosocial issues and of ethnocultural issues, ethnocultural issues are frequently treated as a separate topic rather than being integrated into a discussion of psychosocial issues (e.g., Baker *et al.*, 1998; Weil, 2000). There is no easy solution to this problem. However, if the central ethos of genetic counseling were to bring the psychosocial component into every aspect of the work, it would help achieve the desired integration by providing additional impetus to understand the psychosocial needs of the individual counselee in the multitude of ethnocultural contexts in which genetic counseling takes place.

As with nondirectiveness, adopting a psychosocial orientation as the guiding principle represents a goal to work towards, not an absolute. Indeed, the same four types of limitations discussed above with respect to nondirectiveness would also apply to the new ethos. They can be stated as follows:

Inadvertent Limitations. Sometimes the genetic counselor doesn't have the understanding, insight or resources to fully invoke the psychosocial dimension.

Inevitable Limitations. Sometimes circumstances require that the genetic counselor focus primarily or exclusively on the informational or technical issues.

Institutional Limitations. Sometimes the institutional message and/or setting focuses the discussion almost exclusively on informational or technical issues.

Meta-Limitation. The proposition that all aspects of genetic counseling should be considered from a psychosocial perspective is a specific approach to genetic counseling, not an absolute.

Adopting a psychosocial orientation as the central ethos would require that the genetic counselor strive to recognize these limitations and, insofar as possible, reduce them or adapt counseling to them. This would support an aware, knowledgeable application of the psychosocial approach in the face of the multiple scientific,

financial and workday pressures that tend to inhibit it, and it would lessen the tendency to simply reduce, bypass or avoid the psychosocial when there are impediments.

The adoption of a central ethos implies that, consciously or unconsciously, the genetic counselor exercises vigilance while counseling to meet the indicated standard of practice. It is useful to consider how this vigilance might be characterized for three different central principles:

Narrow nondirectiveness. Am I being nondirective?

Broad nondirectiveness. Am I supporting and facilitating the counselee's autonomy?

Psychosocial orientation. Am I using the best counseling techniques I can to meet the psychosocial needs of the counselee(s)?

I believe the last of these would serve as an important and valuable orientation for genetic counseling as it draws on its many professional accomplishments to meet the challenges of the future.

CONCLUSIONS

Recent discussions and presentations in which I have participated convince me that a significant proportion of genetic counselors are concerned about the continuing legacy of nondirectiveness as the central ethos, due to the inhibitory influence it has on theory and practice. However, in every such discussion important questions and concerns have been raised about the consequences of replacing nondirectiveness as the central ethos. These are complex issues, and the process of considering them may be at least as valuable as is any specific decision or outcome.

My first proposal is to replace nondirectiveness as the central ethos. This would provide a more creative, unencumbered environment for the intrinsic development of the profession and for meeting the opportunities and challenges of providing services in an expanding medical arena. The proposal raises a number of fundamental questions that are useful to examine in their own right: Should genetic counseling have a central ethos? If so, what should it be? What should be the role of nondirectiveness in genetic counseling? How should nondirectiveness be defined? How should it be implemented?

The second proposal is one response to the first two questions: The central ethos of genetic counseling should be to bring the psychosocial component into every aspect of the work. This promotes the continuing development of the psychosocial domain through a counterbalancing imperative to the multiple forces that motivate teaching, research, and clinical services in the medical-genetic domain. There are a wide variety of published resources upon which genetic counselors with all levels of training and experience can draw to develop their own skills and advance the profession (e.g., Djurdjinovic, 1998; Eunpu, 1997; Kessler, 1979; McCarthy Veach *et al.*, 2003; McConkie-Rosell and Sullivan, 1999; O'Daniel and Wells, 2002; Resta, 2000; Weil, 2000). They represent different theoretical approaches presented by authors with diverse backgrounds. Other resources include workshops and presentations at the NSGC Annual Education Convention, educational opportunities presented by the continuing education requirement for recertification by the American Board of Genetic Counseling and in proposed legislation and regulations for state licensure, and various forms of clinical supervision (Kennedy, 2000). Most important, however, is the continued commitment to teaching, research, and clinical services that address the psychosocial needs of counselees.

It is my hope that the opinions and proposals presented in this Point of View will promote additional discussion and debate.

REFERENCES

Abrams, L. J., & Kessler, S. (2002). The Inner World of the Genetic Counselor. *J Genet Counsel, 11*, 5–17.

Ad Hoc Committee on Genetic Counseling (1975). Genetic Counseling. *Am J Hum Genet, 27*, 240–242.

Anderson, G. (1999). Nondirectiveness in Prenatal Genetics: Patients Read Between the Lines. *Nurs Ethics, 6*, 126–136.

Baker, D. L., Schuette, J. L., & Uhlmann, W. R. (1998). *A Guide to Genetic Counseling*. New York: Wiley.

Bartels, D. M., LeRoy, B. S., McCarthy, P., & Caplan, A. L. (1997). Nondirectiveness in Genetic Counseling: A Survey of Practitioners. *Am J Med Genet, 72*, 172–179.

Basmiller, R. C., Cunningham, G., Fisher, N., Fox, L., Henderson, M., Lebel, R., *et al.* (1996). Code of Ethical Principles for Genetics Professionals: An Explication. *Am J Med Genet, 65*, 179–183.

Bower, M. A., McCarthy Veach, P., Bartels, D. M., & LeRoy, B. S. (2002). A Survey of Genetic Counselors' Strategies for Addressing Ethical and Professional Challenges in Practice. *J Genet Counsel, 11*, 163–186.

Brunger, F., & Lippman, A. (1995). Resistance and Adherence to the Norms of Genetic Counseling. *J Genet Counsel, 4*, 151–168.

Burke, B. M., & Kolker, A. (1994). Directiveness in Prenatal Genetic Counseling. *Women Health, 22*, 31–53.

Burke, W., Pinsky, L. E., & Press, N. A. (2001). Categorizing Genetic Tests to Identify Their Ethical, Legal, and Social Implications. *Am J Med Genet, 106*, 233–240.

Caplan, A. L. (1993). Neutrality is not morality: the ethics of genetic counseling. In D. M. Bartels, B. S. LeRoy, & A. L. Caplan (Eds.), *Prescribing our future: ethical challenges in genetic counseling* (pp. 149–165). New York: Aldine de Gruyter.

Clarke, A. (1991). Is Non-Directive Genetic Counseling Possible? *Lancet, 338*, 998–1001.

Collins, F. S., & McKusick, V. A. (2001). Implications of the Human Genome Project for Medical Science. *JAMA, 285*, 540–544.

Djurdjinovic, L. (1998). Psychosocial counseling. In D. I. Baker, J. L. Schuette, & W. R. Uhlmann (Eds.), *A guide to genetic counseling* (pp. 127–166). New York: Wiley.

Elwyn, G., Gray, J., & Clarke, A. (2000). Shared Decision Making and Non-Directiveness in Genetic Counselling. *J Med Genet, 37*, 135–138.

Eunpu, D. L. (1997). Systemically-Based Psychotherapeutic Techniques in Genetic Counseling. *J Genet Counsel, 6*, 1–20.

Fine, B. A. (1993). The evolution of nondirectiveness in genetic counseling and implications of the human genome project. In D. M. Bartels, B. S. LeRoy, & A. L. Caplan (Eds.), *Prescribing our future: ethical challenges in genetic counseling* (pp. 101–117). New York: Aldine de Gruyter.

Greb, A. (1998). Multiculturalism and the practice of genetic counseling. In D. L. Baker, J. L. Schuette, & W. R. Uhlmann (Eds.), *A guide to genetic counseling* (pp. 171–198). New York: Wiley.

Greendale, K., & Pyeritz, R. E. (2001). Empowering Primary Care Health Professionals in Medical Genetics: How Soon? How Fast? How Far? *Am J Med Genet, 106*, 223–232.

Guttmacher, A. E., Jenkins, J., & Uhlmann, W. R. (2001). Genomic Medicine: Who Will Practice It? A Call to Open Arms. *Am J Med Genet, 106*, 216–222.

Jansen, L. A. (2001). Role of the nurse in clinical genetics. In M. B. Mahowald, A. S. Scheuerle, & T. J. Aspinwall (Eds.), *Genetics in the clinic: clinical, ethical, and social implications for primary care* (pp. 133–141). St. Louis: Mosby.

Kennedy, A. L. (2000). Supervision for Practicing Genetic Counselors: An Overview of Models. *J Genet Counsel, 9*, 379–390.

Kessler, S. (1979). *Genetic Counseling: Psychological Dimensions*. New York: Academic Press.

Kessler, S. (1980). The Psychological Paradigm Shift in Genetic Counseling. *Soc Biol, 27*, 167–185.

Kessler, S. (1992). Psychological Aspects of Genetic Counseling. VII. Thoughts on Directiveness. *J Genet Counsel, 1*, 9–18.

Kessler, S. (1997a). Psychological Aspects of Genetic Counseling. IX. Teaching and Counseling. *J Genet Counsel, 6*, 287–295.

Kessler, S. (1997b). Psychological Aspects of Genetic Counseling. XI. Nondirectiveness Revisited. *Am J Med Genet, 72*, 164–171.

Kessler, S. (1998). Psychological Aspects of Genetic Counseling: XII. More on Counseling Skills. *J Genet Counsel, 7*, 263–278.

Kessler, S. (1999). Psychological Aspects of Genetic Counseling: XIII. Empathy and Decency. *J Genet Counsel, 8*, 333–343.

Marks, J. H. (1993). The training of genetic counselors: origins of a psychosocial model. In D. M. Bartels, B. S. LeRoy, & A. L. Caplan (Eds.), *Prescribing our future: ethical challenges in genetic counseling* (pp. 15–24). New York: Aldine de Gruyter.

McCarthy Veach, P., Bartels, D. M., & LeRoy, B. S. (2002). Commentary on Genetic Counseling—A Profession in Search of Itself. *J Genet Counsel, 11*, 187–191.

McCarthy Veach, P., LeRoy, B. S., & Bartels, D. M. (2003). *Facilitating the Genetic Counseling Process: A Manual for Practice*. New York: Springer-Verlag.

McConkie-Rosell, A., & Sullivan, J. A. (1999). Genetic Counseling—Stress, Coping, and the Empowerment Perspective. *J Genet Counsel, 8*, 345–357.

National Society of Genetic Counselors (1992). Code of Ethics. *J Genet Counsel, 1*, 41–43.

O'Daniel, J. M., & Wells, D. (2002). Approaching Complex Cases With a Crisis Intervention Model and Teamwork. *J Genet Counsel, 11*, 369–376.

Peters, J. A., & Stopfer, J. E. (1996). Role of the Genetic Counselor in Familial Cancer. *Oncology, 10*, 159–166.

Rapp, R. (1999). *Testing Women, Testing the Fetus: The Social Impact of Amniocentesis in America.* New York: Routledge.

Reed, S. (1974). A Short History of Genetic Counseling. *Soc Biol, 21,* 332–339.

Resta, R. G. (1997). Eugenics and Non-Directiveness in Genetic Counseling. *J Genet Counsel, 6,* 255–258.

Resta, R. G. (2000). *Psyche and Helix: Psychological Aspects of Genetic Counseling—Essays by Seymour Kessler: Ph.D.* New York: Wiley.

Sorenson, J. R. (1993). Genetic counseling: values that have mattered. In D. M. Bartels, B. S. LeRoy, & A. L. Caplan (Eds.), *Prescribing our future: ethical challenges in genetic counseling* (pp. 3–14). New York: Aldine de Gruyter.

Weil, J. (2000). *Psychosocial Genetic Counseling.* New York: Oxford University Press.

Weil, J., & Mittman, I. (1993). A Teaching Framework for Cross-Cultural Genetic Counseling. *J Genet Counsel, 2,* 159–170.

Wertz, D. C., & Fletcher, J. C. (1988). Attitudes of Genetic Counselors: A Multinational Survey. *Am J Hum Genet, 42,* 592–600.

White, M. T. (1997). "Respect for Autonomy" in Genetic Counseling: An Analysis and a Proposal. *J Genet Counsel, 6,* 297–313.

Wolff, G., & Jung, C. (1995). Nondirectiveness and Genetic Counseling. *J Genet Counsel, 4,* 3–26.

CONFIDENTIALITY

Confidentiality in Medicine—A Decrepit Concept

Mark Siegler

MEDICAL confidentiality, as it has traditionally been understood by patients and doctors, no longer exists. This ancient medical principle, which has been included in every physician's oath and code of ethics since Hippocratic times, has become old, worn-out, and useless; it is a decrepit concept. Efforts to preserve it appear doomed to failure and often give rise to more problems than solutions. Psychiatrists have tacitly acknowledged the impossibility of ensuring the confidentiality of medical records by choosing to establish a separate, more secret record. The following case illustrates how the confidentiality principle is compromised systematically in the course of routine medical care.

A patient of mine with mild chronic obstructive pulmonary disease was transferred from the surgical intensive-care unit to a surgical nursing floor two days after an elective cholecystectomy. On the day of transfer, the patient saw a respiratory therapist writing in his medical chart (the therapist was recording the results of an arterial blood gas analysis) and became concerned about the confidentiality of his hospital records. The patient threatened to leave the hospital prematurely unless I could guarantee that the confidentiality of his hospital record would be respected.

This patient's complaint prompted me to enumerate the number of persons who had both access to his hospital record and a reason to examine it. I was amazed to learn that at least 25 and possibly as many as 100 health professionals and administrative personnel at our university hospital had access to the patient's record and that all of them had a legitimate need, indeed a professional responsibility, to open and use that chart. These persons included 6 attending physicians (the primary physician, the surgeon, the pulmonary consultant, and others); 12 house officers (medical, surgical, intensive-care unit, and "covering" house staff); 20 nursing personnel (on three shifts); 6 respiratory therapists; 3 nutritionists; 2 clinical pharmacists; 15 students (from medicine, nursing, respiratory therapy, and clinical pharmacy); 4 unit secretaries; 4 hospital financial officers; and 4 chart reviewers (utilization review, quality assurance review, tissue review, and insurance auditor). It is of interest that this patient's problem was straightforward, and he therefore did not require many other technical and support services that the modern hospital provides. For example, he did not need multiple consultants and fellows, such specialized procedures as dialysis, or social workers, chaplains, physical therapists, occupational therapists, and the like.

Upon completing my survey I reported to the patient that I estimated that at least 75 health professionals and hospital personnel had access to his medical record. I suggested to the patient that these people were all involved in providing or supporting his health-care services. They were, I assured him, working for him. Despite my reassurances the patient was obviously distressed and retorted, "I always believed that medical confidentiality was part of a doctor's code of ethics. Perhaps you should tell me just what you people mean by 'confidentiality'!"

TWO ASPECTS OF MEDICAL CONFIDENTIALITY

Confidentiality and Third-Party Interests

Previous discussions of medical confidentiality usually have focused on the tension between a physician's responsibility to keep information divulged by patients secret and a physician's legal and moral duty, on occasion, to reveal such confidences to third parties, such as families, employers, public-health authorities, or police authorities. In all these instances, the central question relates to the stringency of the physician's obligation to maintain patient confidentiality when the health, well-being, and safety of identifiable others or of society in general would be threatened by a failure to reveal information about the patient. The tension in such cases is between the good of the patient and the good of others.

Confidentiality and the Patient's Interest

As the example above illustrates, further challenges to confidentiality arise because the patient's personal interest in maintaining confidentiality comes into conflict with his personal interest in receiving the best possible health care. Modern high-technology health care is available principally in hospitals (often, teaching hospitals), requires many trained and specialized workers (a "health-care team"), and is very costly. The existence of such teams means that information that previously had been held in confidence by an individual physician will now necessarily be disseminated to many members of the team. Furthermore, since health-care teams are expensive and few patients can afford to pay such costs directly, it becomes essential to grant access to the patient's medical record to persons who are responsible for obtaining third-party payment. These persons include chart reviewers, financial officers, insurance auditors, and quality-of-care assessors. Finally, as medicine expands from a narrow, disease-based model to a model that encompasses psychological, social, and economic problems, not only will the size of the health-care team and medical costs increase, but more sensitive information (such as one's personal habits and financial condition) will now be included in the medical record and will no longer be confidential.

The point I wish to establish is that hospital medicine, the rise of health-care teams, the existence of third-party insurance programs, and the expanding limits of medicine all appear to be responses to the wishes of people for better and more comprehensive medical care. But each of these developments necessarily modifies our traditional understanding of medical confidentiality.

THE ROLE OF CONFIDENTIALITY IN MEDICINE

Confidentiality serves a dual purpose in medicine. In the first place, it acknowledges respect for the patient's sense of individuality and privacy. The patient's most personal physical and psychological secrets are kept confidential in order to decrease a sense of shame and vulnerability. Secondly, confidentiality is important in improving the patient's health care—a basic goal of medicine. The promise of confidentiality permits people to trust (i.e., have confidence) that information revealed to a physician in the course of a medical encounter will not be disseminated further. In this way patients are encouraged to communicate honestly and forthrightly with their doctors. This bond of trust between patient and doctor is vitally important both in the diagnostic process (which relies on an accurate history) and subsequently in the treatment phase, which often depends as much on the patient's trust in the physician as it does on medications and surgery. These two important functions of confidentiality are as important now as they were in the past. They will not be supplanted entirely either by improvements in medical technology or by recent changes in relations between some patients and doctors toward a rights-based, consumerist model.

POSSIBLE SOLUTIONS TO THE CONFIDENTIALITY PROBLEM

First of all, in all nonbureaucratic, noninstitutional medical encounters—that is, in the millions of doctor-patient encounters that take place in physicians' offices, where more privacy can be preserved—meticulous care should be taken to guarantee that patients' medical and personal information will be kept confidential.

Secondly, in such settings as hospitals or large-scale group practices, where many persons have opportunities to examine the medical record, we should aim to provide access only to those who have "a need to know." This could be accomplished through such administrative changes as dividing the entire record into several sections—for example, a medical and financial section—and permitting only health professionals access to the medical information.

The approach favored by many psychiatrists—that of keeping a psychiatric record separate from the general medical record—is an understandable strategy but one that is not entirely satisfactory and that should not be generalized. The keeping of separate psychiatric records implies that psychiatry and medicine are different undertakings and thus drives deeper the wedge between them and between physical and psychological illness. Furthermore, it is often vitally important for internists or surgeons to know that a patient is being seen by a psychiatrist or is taking a particular medication. When separate records are kept, this information may not be available. Finally, if generalized, the practice of keeping a separate psychiatric record could lead to the unacceptable consequence of having a separate record for each type of medical problem.

Patients should be informed about what is meant by "medical confidentiality." We should establish the distinction between information about the patient that generally will be kept confidential regardless of the interest of third parties and information that will be exchanged among members of the health-care team in order to provide care for the patient. Patients should be made aware of the large number of persons in the modern hospital who require access to the medical record in order to serve the patient's medical and financial interests.

Finally, at some point most patients should have an opportunity to review their medical record and to make informed choices about whether their entire record is to be available to everyone or whether certain portions of the record are privileged and should be accessible only to their principal physician or to others designated explicitly by the patient. This approach would rely on traditional informed-consent procedural standards and might permit the patient to balance the personal value of medical confidentiality against the personal value of high-technology, team health care. There is no reason that the same procedure should not be used with psychiatric records instead of the arbitrary system now employed, in which everything related to psychiatry is kept secret.

AFTERTHOUGHT: CONFIDENTIALITY AND INDISCRETION

There is one additional aspect of confidentiality that is rarely included in discussions of the subject. I am referring here to the wanton, often inadvertent, but avoidable exchanges of confidential information that occur frequently in hospital rooms, elevators, cafeterias, doctors' offices, and at cocktail parties. Of course, as more people have access to medical information about the patient the potential for this irresponsible abuse of confidentiality increases geometrically.

Such mundane breaches of confidentiality are probably of greater concern to most patients than the broader issue of whether their medical records may be entered into a computerized data bank or whether a respiratory therapist is reviewing the results of an arterial blood gas determination. Somehow, privacy is violated and a sense of shame is heightened when intimate secrets are revealed to people one knows or is close to—friends, neighbors, acquaintances, or hospital roommates—rather than when they are disclosed to an anonymous bureaucrat sitting at a computer terminal in a distant city or to a health professional who is acting in an official capacity.

I suspect that the principles of medical confidentiality, particularly those reflected in most medical codes of ethics, were designed principally to prevent just this sort of embarrassing personal indiscretion rather than to maintain (for social, political, or economic reasons) the absolute secrecy of doctor-patient communications. In this regard, it is worth noting that Percival's Code of Medical Ethics (1803) includes the following admonition: "Patients should be interrogated concerning their complaint in a tone of voice which cannot be overheard." We in the medical profession frequently neglect these simple courtesies.

CONCLUSION

The principle of medical confidentiality described in medical codes of ethics and still believed in by patients no longer exists. In this respect, it is a decrepit concept. Rather than perpetuate the myth of confidentiality and invest energy vainly to preserve it, the public and the profession would be better served if they devoted their attention to determining which aspects of the original principle of confidentiality are worth retaining. Efforts could then be directed to salvaging those.

Caring for Patients while Respecting Their Privacy: Renewing Our Commitment

Jeanette Ives Erickson and Sally Millar

Privacy and confidentiality are basic rights in our society. Safeguarding those rights, with respect to an individual's personal health information, is our ethical and legal obligation as health care providers. Doing so in today's health care environment is increasingly challenging.

Every nurse understands and respects the need for patient confidentiality. As professionals, our connection to our patients and our colleagues depends on it. But, the truth is, advanced technology, new demands in health care, and developments in the world-at-large, make it more and more difficult to keep this promise. But keep it we must!

As nurses, through the Nightingale Pledge and all subsequent nursing codes, we have identified the need for confidentiality; we made this point long before national legislation was ever contemplated. The Code for Nurses, published by the American Nurses Association (ANA) Ethics Committees, "is the standard by which ethical conduct is guided and evaluated by the profession" (ANA, 1994, p.1). Provision 3 of the current Code of Ethics for Nurses states: "The nurse promotes, advocates for, and strives to protect the health, safety, and rights of the patient" (ANA, 2001). The interpretive statements, 3.1 and 3.2, are explicit in their language regarding privacy and confidentiality (ANA, 2001), and should be used by nurses to guide clinical practice and to set organizational policy.

As health care workers, we see and hear confidential information every day. Our practice is full of this kind of information. Occasionally, we become so comfortable with patient information that it can be easy to forget how important it is to keep information private. Thus, it is important to review the Privacy Section of the Health Insurance Portability and Accountability Act (HIPAA) and use it to identify opportunities to better protect patient confidentiality. This article will remind nurses about the importance of keeping patient information private. This reminder will come first as HIPAA is reviewed and the implications of this Act for nurses are discussed. The reminder will also come as challenges to maintaining privacy and strategies for promoting privacy are presented.

HEALTH INSURANCE PORTABILITY AND ACCOUNTABILITY ACT

HIPAA, or the Health Insurance Portability and Accountability Act (Public Law 104–191), was the first national legislation to assure every patient across the nation protection of their health insurance information. The privacy portion of the new law limits those who may have access to a patient's health information and how it may be used. Hospitals and providers may use this information only for treatment, obtaining payment for care, and for specified operational purposes like improving quality of care. They must inform patients in writing of how their health data will be used; establish systems to track disclosure; and allow patients to review, obtain copies, and amend their own health information.

HIPAA established standards and requirements for the electronic transmission of certain health information (eligibility requirements, referrals to other physicians, and health claims) (American Hospital Association, 2002). HIPAA protects a patient's rights to the confidentiality of his/her medical information and, for the first time, creates federal civil and criminal penalties for improper use or disclosure of protected health information.

Understanding the full meaning of the word confidentiality is key to ensuring a successful rollout of HIPAA and any policy or training that results from the introduction of this law. Confidentiality applies to protected patient information, including basic identifiers of the patient's past, present, or future physical or mental health conditions, including the provision of health services and payment for those services. Under this law, patients are given significant new rights to understand and control how their health information and insurance is used or shared (American Hospital Association, 2002).

Before reviewing the implications of HIPAA for nurses, it is important to understand a patient's health information (record) from a conceptual framework. The patient's health record is the collection of all health information in all media generated on a patient under a unique personal identifier and

Erickson, Jeanette Ives and Sally Millar. "Caring for Patients while Respecting their Privacy: Renewing our Commitment," *Online Journal of Issues in Nursing* 10:2 (May 31, 2005) available at www.nursingworld.org/ojin/topic27/tpc27_1.htm. Reprinted by permission of the publisher.

across the continuum of care. The record is created for every patient who receives treatment, care, or services at each institution or health network, and is maintained for the primary purpose of providing patient care. In addition, it is used for financial and other administrative processes, outcome measurement, research, education, patient self-management, disease prevention, and public health activities. The record contains sufficient information to identify the patient, support the diagnosis(es), justify the treatment, document the course and results of treatments, and facilitate the continuity of each patient's care. The health information or data contained in the record belongs to the patient even though the physical record (either electronic or paper) belongs to the institution.

HIPAA'S IMPLICATIONS FOR NURSES

Establishing and maintaining patients' trust in their caregivers is critical to obtaining a complete history, an accurate health record, and carrying out an effective treatment plan. If a nurse fails to protect the patient's privacy, the erosion in the relationship can have dire consequences to the nurse/patient relationship.

At the same time, the reality of the world in which we practice raises troubling confidentiality questions:

- Nurses are frequently put in the tenuous position of being asked for patient information by patients' families and well-wishers. An example is another employee checking to see how a friend is doing. On the surface this seems harmless. But, is it really?
- A key patient safety initiative is better improved labeling of drugs and devices. IV bags and medicines are now routinely labeled with the patient's name, a step we take to assure we are delivering the right care to the right patient. When they are discarded in open trash receptacles in patient rooms, have we compromised the patient's confidentiality?
- Busy, frequently overcrowded, hospitals are less than perfect environments. Conversations with patients can easily be overheard. What can we do to lessen the chances of inadvertent disclosure?
- Are we confident that we have correctly determined who "needs-to-know" for every patient? How are we teaching the next generation of caregivers to think about confidentiality? Are there new tools we can give them?
- The consumer can access almost anything on the Internet today. Sophisticated search engines enable us to find everything ever written about any person or topic. Equally sophisticated efforts must be made by health care providers to prevent unauthorized access to patient information. How much information should we provide and what can we provide under HIPAA? What would our patients prefer?

Our commitment to protecting patients' privacy must advance from the abstract realm of tacit understanding to a more conscious, active, and visible place. We need to let our colleagues know that we will not engage in, nor will we tolerate in others, anything less than full compliance (personal communication, Massachusetts General Hospital Privacy and Confidentiality Committee, 2004).

There are two criteria to always come back to in discussions about confidentiality. One is to ask yourself, "What you would want if it were your medical information in question?" The other is to ask yourself, "Do I really need-to-know this information in order to do my job?" Most of the time, if you have to ask, you probably don't need-to-know.

CHALLENGES OF MAINTAINING PRIVACY AND CONFIDENTIALITY

Knowing the difference between privacy and confidentiality can be confusing. Privacy is the right of individuals to keep information about themselves from being disclosed; that is, people (our patients) are in control of others' access to themselves or information about themselves. Patients decide who, when, and where to share their health information. On the other hand, confidentiality is how we, as nurses, treat private information once it has been disclosed to others or ourselves. This disclosure of information usually results from a relationship of trust; it assumes that health information is given with the expectation that it will not be divulged except in ways that have been previously agreed upon, e.g., for treatment, for payment of services, or for use in monitoring the quality of care that is being delivered. With the increasing use of technology for the provision of care in our fast-paced clinical environments, maintaining privacy and confidentiality can be a daunting task.

The impact of technology

Electronic messaging and new computer technology, though quick and efficient, might not be as secure as we would want it to be. This is an unfortunate reality, but one we must consider. If it is not absolutely necessary to include patients' names in electronic correspondences, then we should refrain from doing so. We must be smart and sensitive when communicating patient information, be it by fax, telephone, email, or other technologies yet to be developed (Ives Erickson, 1999). When communicating with another clinician, remember this:

- Others besides the addressee may process messages during addressee's usual business hours or during addressee's vacation or illness
- Electronic messages can occasionally go to the wrong party
- Electronic communication can be accessed from various locations
- Information written by one clinician may be sent electronically to other care providers
- The Internet does not typically provide a secure media for transporting confidential information unless both parties are using encryption technologies.

Fax machines are perhaps the least secure technology when it comes to transmitting patient information. Certain types of information are prohibited by law from being faxed outside of an institution without appropriate written authorization, e.g., genetic test results, HIV information, and sexual assault counseling. All fax cover sheets should contain the standard warning that reads: "The information contained in this electronic message and any attachments to this message are intended for the exclusive use of the addressee(s) and may contain confidential or privileged information. If you are not the intended recipient, please notify me immediately and destroy all copies of this message and any attachments."

Palm pilots, PDAs, and Blackberries are an exploding technology. Many clinicians have health information stored or available on these hand-held devices. Yet, how many users have their PDA's password protected in order to prevent access if the device is inadvertently left somewhere?

Busy people cutting corners

It is not enough anymore to assume we're maintaining confidentiality as we go about our daily work. There are too many opportunities for private information to be inadvertently read, faxed, overheard, transmitted, or otherwise unintentionally disclosed. As nurses and as leaders of the health care industry, we need to sharpen our awareness and redouble our efforts to protect our patients' rights to privacy (American Hospital Association, 2002).

Each of us has witnessed situations that demonstrate this point. For example, as you've walked through a hospital, health center, or ambulatory practice, have you ever seen a trash bag that has been accidentally ripped open, and there on the floor in front

of you is patient information? The person who discarded this information did so with the best of intentions, never foreseeing that it would re-surface in a torn-up trash bag. Confidential papers should be appropriately disposed of, e.g., torn or shredded, when they are no longer needed. Yet, how many times is this not done?

Now, think back on rides you've taken in an elevator along with other health care employees and a few visitors. How often have you overheard clinicians discussing a patient in a code situation, not mentioning the patient's name, but talking in great detail about the specifics of the case? Though they never identify the patient by name, the discussion still breaches a very important aspect of our code of conduct. It creates the perception that we don't care about confidentiality.

It is clear in confidentiality guidelines that, "Patient information should not be discussed where others can overhear the conversation (in hallways, on elevators, in the cafeteria, in restaurants, etc.). It is not okay to discuss clinical information in public areas even if a patient's name is not used. This can raise doubts among patients and visitors about our respect for their privacy" (personal communication, Massachusetts General Hospital, Privacy and Confidentiality Committee, 2004). If you put yourself in the patient's place, you'll agree that this raises serious doubts about the employee's commitment to confidentiality.

STRATEGIES FOR PROMOTING PRIVACY

Many view the extra steps that may need to be taken by nurses in the commitment to assuring privacy to be a burden. But, in reality, who is better positioned than nurses to advocate for patient privacy and safety? Thinking with a patient-first philosophy, our work puts us in a position of strength. For example, on the patient care units, nurses routinely field calls from patients' families and friends, and occasionally the media, who are inquiring about a patient's status and prognosis. Nurses are strategically placed in managing this personal patient information. If it is a member of your organization's public relations department, but a person you don't know, you can say, "I'll call you back in your office." This ensures that the person calling you is who he says he is. Remember: it is the patient's right to decide what information is shared about them and when.

In clinical care a patient's condition can change at a moment's notice. Imagine this situation—a patient assigned to a semi-private room takes a sudden turn for the worse and it becomes apparent that death is near. Nurses are empowered to make the necessary changes in bed and room assignments to afford patients and families the privacy that is warranted in a particular patient care situation. Again, this puts nursing in a position of strength.

However, what if a private room can't be found and the patient's roommate objects to having the roommate's family spend the night because they feel unsafe? As nurses, we need to balance patient safety and treatment with a respect for privacy. If you must choose, always choose patient safety first. Use your professional judgment that moves this added demand from a perception of extra work to a position of strength in patient advocacy.

The following are other strategies to address confidentiality challenges facing nurses.

- Communication with family members—always keep the patient's best interest in mind. This may translate into adequately informing long-distance family members so they are able to properly respond and support elderly or demented parent's needs. Verify identity as legal guardian or executor, if necessary.
- Never assume you have the right to look at any type of health information unless you need it in order to do your job. HIPAA assumes there is a need-to-know. For example, co-workers' phone numbers for personal reasons may be looked up by the interested party on the Internet or the phone book. Phone numbers needed for work-related reasons may be obtained from the supervisor or the employee database if you have been authorized for access. Always ask yourself, "Do I need-to-know this information?" Need-to-Know is defined as that which is necessary for one to adequately perform one's specific job responsibilities.
- Hold your colleagues as accountable as you hold yourself when it comes to respecting patient privacy. When you see a nurse or physician carrying progress notes on their tray in the cafeteria for others to see, gently and politely remind them to turn them over in the name of confidentiality. When you are hearing a conversation between two care providers in the elevator or the hospital shuttle, politely ask them to please continue their discussion in a private area.
- Be a privacy mentor to nursing students just starting out in the profession. For example, keep medical records closed on desktops, close out results on computer screens, send out text paging with minimum necessary information (last name first initial), restrict excessive printing of health information from computers, restrict the removal of all copies of health information from the hospital, even if reports have been de-identified.
- Stand up to peer pressure when friends or neighbors ask you to do a favor by obtaining for them copies of their records or copies of a family member's records. Always get written authorization and follow proper procedure. In many organizations, failure to follow proper procedures regarding release of information may result in disciplinary action, up to and including termination of employment or suspension of privileges.

If in doubt when releasing health information to patients, confer with your health information services department or privacy office for advice and assistance. Use opportunities to share Confidentiality Quizzes (Exhibit A) in order to educate staff. There are guidelines in place to help reduce risk for you and the hospital while meeting patients' needs—know and use these guidelines.

SUMMARY

Patient confidentiality is a sacred trust. Nurses are important in ensuring that organizations create an environment to safeguard patients' rights to confidentiality. As stated in the ANA Code of Ethics, "The nurse advocates for an environment that provides for sufficient physical privacy, including auditory privacy for discussions of a personal nature and policies and practices that protect the confidentiality of information" (ANA, 2001).

Our patient's health record serves as the instrument of care. Increased regulatory scrutiny has emerged to protect the rights of the patient which, in turn, has allowed the patient to be the recognized owner of his or her care. Nurses, physicians, and all who provide care, are entrusted with the patient's health information solely to be of service to that patient.

It is our duty to protect the well being of those who are entrusted to our care. Protecting the integrity of the nurse-patient relationship and patient rights is a sacred trust. It is also our duty to periodically remind other nurses of the importance of keeping patient information private. This reminder has come in this article as HIPAA has been reviewed and the implications of this Act for nurses have been discussed. The reminder has also come as challenges to maintaining privacy and strategies for promoting privacy have been presented...and presented again.

Exhibit A. Confidentiality Awareness Quiz

1. A patient named John has just completed his procedure and is wheeled into the recovery area. The nurse comes to talk with John about the procedure and to discuss discharge plans. There are other patients around them and a closed privacy curtain only separates them.

   Should the nurse have this discussion with the patient in the recovery room?

   Answer: Yes, this is considered an "incidental disclosure." It is unrealistic for care to always be provided in a private room. Incidental disclosure is when patients hear health information during the normal course of providing health care. This is not considered a HIPAA violation.

2. Robert is the pastor of your church. He comes to you as you are leaving the Sunday service and tells you about a parishioner who is now an inpatient at your hospital. You are very good friends with the pastor and he asks you to find out what her diagnosis and prognosis is. Because of your position you have access to this information.

   Can you look this up because your pastor asked you to?

   Answer: No, this is considered a breach of that patient's confidentiality. If asked about anyone who is a patient, simply reply, "I'm sorry, out of respect to that patient, that information is confidential. Of course, if Mr. X tells me it is OK to share his health information, then I'm happy to do that."

3. An environmental worker is scrubbing the floor in a semi-private room when the nurse comes in to talk to a patient about discharge plans. The environmental worker overhears the nurse even though the curtain was pulled around for privacy. The worker recognizes the patient as a teacher at her son's school. She hears the nurse tell him he has cancer and only weeks to live. The worker feels very badly and wants to tell her son and husband.

   What should the environmental worker do?

   What are the risks here?

   Answer: The environmental worker has to pretend that she never heard anything about this patient or that she even knows he is in the hospital. The worker should have signed an annually-signed confidentiality agreement that acknowledges she will keep any information she sees or hears in the course of doing her job confidential.

4. You are an Orthopedic nurse at your hospital. Your spouse is here as an inpatient following exploratory surgery. You finish your work and go up to your spouse's room to visit. Your spouse has not awakened from the procedure at this point. You go out to the nurses' station and pull the chart.

   Is this allowed because you are her spouse and practice at this hospital?

   Answer: No, being the spouse does not give you special access, nor does having access to your hospital's health system give you authorization. You must have a signed "Authorization to Release Information" form signed by your spouse giving you authorization to review the protected health information.

5. One of your nurse colleagues is expecting and it's been decided that you will organize the baby shower. Not having access to co-workers' addresses, you only look in the demographics portion of the electronic medical record to obtain this information. You do not look at any clinical information. Would this be OK?

   Answer: No, even demographic (address, phone number, etc) information is considered protected health information under the privacy regulations and should not be accessed without approval of the patient.

6. You are a nurse manager and one of your staff needs to be out on a medical leave for a minor procedure. She is expected to return in a week but calls and states she will need an additional week. You see her surgeon in the hallway the next day and ask him about the procedure and the additional time out of work. As her employer, do you have the right to ask this information?

   Answer: No. This is personal and protected health information that should not be requested without patient consent, even for employment reasons. There are no special privileges afforded to managers regarding the specific details of an employee's health status.

7. You have a very good friend who is a nurse practitioner and is away from the hospital on vacation. While she is out, her breast biopsy results come back. Because she had told you she was having this procedure, you felt it would be the right thing to do out of concern to look up her results and call her with this information. Is this appropriate?

   Answer: No, just because a colleague chooses to disclose certain portions of her health information with you, it does not mean you have the right to continue and follow up on any related results or findings.

8. A patient came into the ED to be treated for depression. When asked by the triage nurse for his reason for the visit the patient refused to tell her until she would agree to take him to a confidential room to discuss one-on-one,

rather than be interviewed at her own desk which was partitioned from the waiting area and the public. The nurse refused to take the patient to an individual room to speak to him so he reported that she had breached his confidentiality. Would this be a violation that the Office of Civil Rights (OCR) would penalize the hospital for? Under HIPAA, violations to the regulations may be investigated by the Department of Health and Human Services Office of Civil Rights (U.S. Department of Health and Human Services, n.d.). If an individual or organization is found to be non-compliant, penalties may occur, such as fines and imprisonment.

Answer: No. They would review the hospital policy on triaging patients in the ED, they may even come by to see the area in which patients are interviewed. However, the OCR knows the urgent issues that arise in the ED and allows for flexibility in carrying out hospital operations that are both safe and appropriate for the patient and the staff. One of the roles of the triage nurse is to assess the patient's safety before bringing them to a room alone, this is optimal patient care in an ED situation. Because the triage desk was also constructed in a way to offer some separation and privacy to the patients being interviewed, this would also be in the hospital's favor. Had she stood openly in the waiting room among other patients discussing details of his health information they would find fault with the lack of privacy measures.

Source/Used with permission: Adapted from Massachusetts General Hospital Privacy and Confidentiality Committee, Eileen Bryan, Privacy Manager

REFERENCES

American Hospital Association (2002). *HIPAA Privacy Standards.* Retrieved January 21, 2005 www.hospitalconnect.com/hospitalconnect/jsp/keyissues.jsp?topic=HIPAA.

American Nurses Association (2001, February). *Code of Ethics for Nurses.* Retrieved March 24, 2005 from http://nursingworld.org/ethics/ecode.htm.

American Nurses Association (1994). Position Statements. *The Non-negotiable Nature of this ANA Code for Nurses with Interpretive Statements.* New York: American Nurses Association.

Federal Register 82462. (Volume 65). (2001, December 28). *Standards of Privacy of Individually Identifiable Health Information; Final Rule.*

Federal Register No. 157. (Volume 67). (August 14, 2002). *Standards of Privacy of Individually Identifiable Health Information; Final Rule.*

Ives Erickson, J. (1999, December 2). Revisiting patient confidentiality. *Caring Headlines.* MA: Massachusetts General Hospital.

U.S. Department of Health and Human Services Office for Civil Rights. (n.d.). *Privacy and your health information.* Retrieved March 24, 2005 from www.hhs.gov/ocr/hipaa/consumer_summary.pdf

TRUTH-TELLING

Lying to Insurance Companies: The Desire to Deceive among Physicians and the Public

Rachel M. Werner, G. Caleb Alexander, Angela Fagerlin, and Peter A. Ubel

INTRODUCTION

In an effort to contain rising health care costs, many third-party payers have developed mechanisms to limit physicians' ability to order expensive tests, treatments, or referrals for their patients. One common mechanism is to limit insurance coverage of services unless a patient meets certain clinical criteria. These restrictions are designed to guide physicians away from expensive tests in favor of less expensive tests. In some cases, these restrictions force physicians to use less expensive tests that also have less benefit, and thus make cost-quality tradeoffs. In these cases, lack of coverage for expensive health care services that bring only a small marginal benefit may force physicians to use less expensive services.

Third-party payer restrictions often impede physicians' abilities to provide what they deem to be medically necessary health care for their patients, instead asking them to rely on insurers to define medical

Werner, Rachel M., G. Caleb Alexander, Angela Fagerlin, and Peter A. Ubel. "Lying to Insurance Companies: The Desire to Deceive among Physicians and the Public," *The American Journal of Bioethics* 4:4 (2004), 53–59. Copyright © 2004. Reprinted by permission of Copyright Clearance Center on behalf of the publisher.

necessity. These restrictions have forced physicians to balance their roles as patient advocates with their obligations to third-party payers. Because of the conflict this balance causes, some physicians have responded by misrepresenting the truth to insurers in order to obtain desired health care services (Morreim 1991). Previous research has shown that in many circumstances physicians are willing to deceive insurers to obtain specific health care benefits (Freeman et al. 1999; Werner et al. 2002; Wynia et al. 2000). Over one-third of physicians reported manipulating the reimbursement rules on behalf of their patients (Wynia et al. 2000).

Physicians' support for deception of insurers varies based on a number of factors, such as how sick the patient is and the health service in question. In addition, physicians' willingness to use deception varies with the hassle of the appeals process. As the appeals process becomes more burdensome, lengthier, and with a lower likelihood of having a successful outcome, physicians are more likely to misrepresent the truth to insurers in order to obtain approval for medical services (Werner et al. 2002).

Recently, we found that the public supports deception. Twenty-six percent of the surveyed public sanctioned the use of deception to obtain health care services. While the support for deception was substantial among the public, as a whole respondents were largely unaware that many physicians feel they do not have enough time to appeal insurance company decisions. Among the subset of the public who thought physicians had *inadequate* time to appeal coverage decisions, the proportion of people who support physicians' use of deception was substantially higher (Alexander et al. 2003). If the public had increased awareness of the time pressures that physicians face, their support for deception might increase substantially. No research has directly compared the public's and physicians' support for deception or if perceptions about the hassle of the appeals process differentially impacts the public's and physicians' support for deception of insurance companies.

We undertook this study to directly compare differences between the public's and physicians' support for insurance deception. Additionally, we sought to quantify the difference between the public's and physicians' perceptions of physicians' time pressures, and how this difference affects the likelihood of support for insurance company deception.

METHODS

Participants

During the fall of 1999, we surveyed a convenience sample of 700 prospective jurors at the Philadelphia County Courthouse. All jurors in the juror reading room were invited to participate and were given a candy bar for completing a written survey. In previous studies, over 75% of prospective jurors completed surveys (Armstrong et al. 2002), but we did not track participation in this study.

We also conducted an anonymous mail survey of 1617 physicians (general internists, family practitioners, general practitioners, and internal medicine subspecialists) in the United States. Subjects were selected randomly from the American Medical Association (AMA) master file, which is the most comprehensive available mailing list of physicians, as it includes AMA members and nonmembers. Each physician received a five-dollar bill in the first mailing to encourage participation (Asch et al. 1998). Nonresponders were sent a second mailing without financial incentive.

Materials

Each survey included one of two clinical vignettes (see the appendix), several attitudinal questions, and demographic information. Each vignette featured a patient who had been denied insurance coverage for a medical procedure by his or her insurance company and asked the respondent if the physician in the scenario should (1) accept the insurance company's decision, (2) appeal the insurance company's decision, or (3) misrepresent the facts to the insurance company in order to obtain coverage. Vignettes differed by severity of the medical condition (severe angina versus moderate low-back pain), time required for the physician to appeal the insurance company's decision (60 minutes versus 5–10 minutes), and likelihood of having a successful appeal (50% versus 95%). Beliefs about time pressures faced by physicians were assessed using a five-point Likert scale.

Statistical analysis

Chi-square tests and independent sample t-tests were used to (1) compare juror and physician responses across questionnaire versions, (2) compare juror and physician demographics across questionnaire versions, and (3) compare demographic character-istics of physician responders and non-responders. No data was gathered on non-responders among jurors.

Our primary interest was in differences in support for deception between jurors and physicians. Data was initially analyzed separately for each of the three variables that changed across vignettes (severity of disease, length of the appeals process, and likelihood of success). Because differences in support for deception between jurors and physicians were independent of vignette version, we collapsed data across the versions. We first calculated the proportion of respondents recommending that the physician in the vignette appeal the restriction, accept the restriction, or misrepresent the facts to the insurance company. Next, we used chi-square tests for differences in these proportions among jurors versus physicians. We then calculated the proportion of jurors and physicians agreeing with the attitudinal item about time pressures. To focus on the relationship between respondent agreement with the attitudinal item and the choice to sanction deception, the responses to the Likert scale were grouped into "agree" and "disagree," excluding those who responded "not sure." Finally, we used multinomial logistic regression to study the relationship between the physician's hypothetical management decision (accept, appeal, or misrepresent) and respondent (juror vs. physician). This model was re-estimated, controlling for perception of physician time pressures. Data were analyzed using STATA 7.0 (Stata Corporation, College Station, TX).

RESULTS

Of the 700 members of the public we surveyed, the mean age was 43 years (range 19–80 years), 56% were white, and 66% were female. Of the 1617 surveys mailed to physicians, 50 were undeliverable and 890 were returned completed, for an overall response rate of 57%. Physicians were predominately male (77%) and white (75%), with a mean age of 48 years (range 28–89 years). The majority were family practitioners (48%) or general internists (43%). Most respondents worked in solo or small group practices (58%), while 5% worked in managed care organizations. Across survey versions, there were no differences in physician response rate or in physician or juror demographics (all p-values >0.05). Physician responders did not differ

from nonresponders in regard to age, gender, or medical specialty (all p-values >0.05).

Differences in sanctioning of deception between jurors and physicians

There were significant differences in the likelihood of endorsing deception rather than appealing the insurance company's decision between jurors and physicians. Overall, jurors were more than twice as likely as physicians to choose to misrepresent facts to the insurance company by reporting that a patient is having fictitious symptoms (26% vs. 11%; see Table 1), while fewer jurors than physicians recommended to appeal (70% vs. 77%) or accept (4% vs. 12%) the insurance company's restriction ($\chi^2 = 76.14$, $p < 0.0001$).

The impact of perception of physician time pressures on decision to misrepresent

Jurors and physicians had significantly different responses to the statement "My physician has [I have] enough time to appeal coverage decisions that are denied by the insurance company." Almost three times as many jurors agreed with the statement as physicians (59% vs. 22%, $\chi^2 = 209$, $p < 0.0001$).

To further assess whether these differences in attitude played a role in sanctioning of deception, willingness to appeal insurance company restrictions or misrepresent the facts to the insurance company was stratified by each group's perception of the amount of time physicians have to appeal coverage decisions (Figure 1). Jurors who thought that physicians had insufficient time to appeal coverage decisions were much more likely to support misrepresentation than physicians were. Specifically, among respondents who thought that physicians have inadequate time to appeal insurance company restriction, 50% of jurors endorsed misrepresentation compared to 13% of physicians.

To further explore the hypothesis that perceptions about time impact a respondent's willingness to endorse misrepresentation, we calculated the odds of endorsing misrepresentation with and without controlling for perceptions of time pressures (Table 1). Without adjustment, the odds of jurors endorsing misrepresentation were more than double that of physicians (OR 2.48, CI 1.89–3.25). After adjusting for the disparity in perceptions of physicians' time pressures, the odds that jurors would endorse misrepresentation

TABLE 1   Jurors' and Physicians' Support for Misrepresentation as Percent Supporting Misrepresentation and Odds Ratios of Jurors' Willingness to Endorse Misrepresentation of Patient Symptoms Compared to Physicians*

	Support for misrepresentation
Jurors	26%
Physicians	11%
Unadjusted OR (95% CI)	2.48 (1.89–3.25)
Adjusted OR[†] (95% CI)	4.64 (3.38–6.37)

OR = Odds ratio; CI = 95% confidence interval.
*For example, an odds ratio of 2.48 means that the odds of endorsing misrepresentation of patient symptoms are 2.48 times higher among jurors than among physicians.
[†]Odds ratios are adjusted for perceptions of physician time pressures.

compared to physicians became even larger, rising from 2.48 to 4.64 (CI 3.38–6.37).

DISCUSSION

We found that the public was significantly more likely to endorse misrepresentation of a patient's medical condition than physicians were. In addition, the public's greater support for physician deception increased substantially after accounting for different perceptions of physicians' time pressures.

To practicing clinicians, the fact that physicians misrepresent the truth to insurance companies may not be surprising. Clinicians often face busy schedules of patients with challenging problems. As the prevalence of managed care has increased in the United States, Physicians report feeling more strapped for time (Hadley et al. 1999), experiencing higher administrative burden for each patient they see (Lasker and Marquis 1999), and having decreasing autonomy to take care of patients as they see fit (Burdi and Baker 1999). Part of physicians' response to these pressures may be to choose to deceive insurance companies rather than play by their rules.

The decision to deceive might be easy to see from the perspective of a busy physician who is an hour behind schedule, whose pager has been going off steadily, and who is seeing a woman with chest pain. In this physician's eyes, this woman clearly needs surgery. Is it in the physician's best interest to spend the extra time it would take to appeal to the insurance company to cover the needed surgery, putting him even further behind in caring for his patients that day,

when in his view, the surgery should have been covered to begin with? Or is it better to simply exaggerate the woman's symptoms during his routine documentation of the visit knowing that this will guarantee coverage of a medically necessary procedure? The right answer is unclear. However, it is clear that at times some physicians will choose the option that is less hassle: deceiving the insurer.

Would physicians' support for misrepresentation be negligible if it were not for the time pressures they face? It is unlikely. Our study suggests that even after controlling for time pressures, some physicians still choose to misrepresent facts to third-party payers. Previous studies have suggested that patient expectations may play a role in physicians' sanctioning of deception (Wilson et al. 2001; Zemencuk et al. 1999). Other studies have suggested that in the era of cost containment in health care, physicians' ethics may be compromised, and cost containment arrangements have increased the likelihood that physicians will resort to deception (Connelly and DalleMura 1988; Novack et al. 1989; Sulmasy et al. 2000). Our findings of high rates of public support for deception may add to the numerous pressures that physicians face in their day-to-day practice.

It is noteworthy that not all physicians are willing to deceive insurers to benefit their patients. Some view the issue of misrepresentation in the context of the declining professionalism of medicine and thus are reluctant to endorse deception. One recent study documenting physicians' willingness to deceive insurance companies noted that "physicians consistently assumed that society would provide greater justification ratings (for deception) than they (the physicians) would" (Freeman et al. 1999). Indeed, many professional organizations specifically denounce gaming the system (American College of Physicians 1998; American Medical Association 1997), and the majority of doctors surveyed find the practice unethical (Wynia et al. 2000). While physicians face enormous pressures to obtain health care for their patients, when these goals are in direct conflict with insurance companies' goals of cutting costs, physicians continue to struggle to maintain professionalism.

There are good reasons, beyond ethics and legalities, for physicians to be wary of misrepresentation, including the medical consequences to misrepresenting the truth to the insurers. When physicians fabricate medical information for insurers, the information becomes part of their patients' medical records. Not only can this mistakenly impact the decisions future

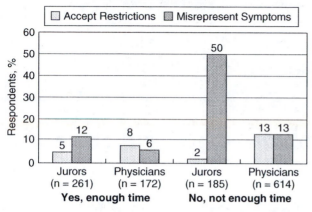

Do physicians have enough time to appeal insurance company restrictions?

FIGURE 1 Comparison of jurors' and physicians' Willingness to accept an insurance company restriction or to misrepresent patient symptoms to the insurance company stratified by perceptions of physicians' time pressures.

physicians make about patients; it can directly impact patients if they are unaware of the misrepresentation and believe the chart lore is the truth about their medical condition.

There are ways for physicians to avoid deceiving insurers while still obtaining necessary services. For some services, such as vaccinations, some patients may be able to pay for the needed but uncovered health care out of pocket. For other, more expensive services, physicians can devote resources to navigating the reimbursement system—if not with their own time, then with the efforts of support staff.

Our study demonstrates that not only do physicians support deception of insurance companies, but the public seems to agree with this practice more often than physicians do. Unlike physicians, patients may be less likely to be motivated by the level of professionalism in medicine. Instead, the primary concern of many patients may be the health care they receive. Patients may see tests and procedures as necessary, not optional. Thus, the benefits of any health care service are high, and making cost-quality trade-offs may in and of itself seem unethical. Additionally, patients are concerned about the quality of care they receive and may view obtaining tests and procedures as being an important part of high-quality care. Thus, a general desire to have access to tests and procedures may partially explain the public's greater support for insurance company deception. Finally, the public may be less concerned with the potential legal ramifications that physicians face

when they deceive insurance companies on behalf of their patients. All of these reasons may motivate patients to support deception at higher rates than physicians do.

Not only is the public's support for physician deception high, but among those who know how busy physicians are, the odds of support for deception is almost five times higher among the public than it is among physicians. It seems that if more patients knew how busy their physicians were, they would wonder why doctors don't routinely deceive insurance companies. Physicians may feel that the managed care system has increased their burden. Patients, on the other hand, may have simply lost faith in the whole system.

Our study has several limitations. The primary limitation is that we ask how people *would* behave under certain conditions rather than how they *actually* behave. However, our results are consistent with prior studies demonstrating that a substantial minority of physicians admit they have deceived insurance companies in the past (Freeman et al. 1999; Wynia et al. 2000). Another limitation is that some of our respondents are drawn from a jury pool in one large northeastern city and do not reflect a representative national sample. Although we found no significant association between jurors' sociodemographic characteristics or self-reported health and the sanctioning of deception, support for physicians' use of deception may vary substantially by geographic region. Finally, it is possible that we overestimated the public's support for deception due to the nature of the question we asked. Physicians and jurors were asked what the doctor in the scenario should do. This may have allowed jurors to make a recommendation for unethical physician behavior without feeling like they were shouldering any of the burdens of lying themselves.

In some circumstances, many physicians and patients support deceiving insurers in order to obtain health care services. Our findings of substantially higher support for deception among the public than among physicians highlight the ethical challenge facing physicians and patients in balancing patient advocacy with honesty in the setting of limited societal resources.

REFERENCES

Alexander, G. C., R. M. Werner, A. Fagerlin, and P. A. Ubel. 2003. Support for physician deception of insurance companies among a sample of Philadelphia residents. *Annals of Internal Medicine* 138(6):472–475.

American College of Physicians. 1998. Ethics manual, fourth edition. *Annals of Internal Medicine* 128:576–594.

American Medical Association. 1997. *Health care fraud and abuse: Report of the Council on Ethical and Judicial Affairs and the Council on Medical Service of the American Medical Association.* Chicago: AMA Press.

Armstrong, K., J. S. Schwartz, G. Fitzgerald, and P. A. Ubel. 2002. Effect of framing as gain vs. loss on understanding and hypothetical treatment choices: Survival and mortality curves. *Medical Decision Making* 22:76–83.

Asch, D. A., N. A. Christakis, and P. A. Ubel. 1998. Conducting physician mail surveys on a limited budget: A randomized trial comparing $2 bill versus $5 bill incentives. *Medical Care* 36:95–99.

Burdi, M. D., and L. C. Baker. 1999. Physicians' perceptions of autonomy and satisfaction in California. *Health Affairs (Millwood)* 18(4):134–145.

Campion, E. W. 2001. A symptom of discontent. *New England Journal of Medicine* 344:223–225.

Connelly, J. E., and S. DalleMura. 1988. Ethical problems in the medical office. *Journal of the American Medical Association* 260:812–815.

Freeman, V. G., S. S. Rathore, K. P. Weinfurt, K. A. Schulman, and D. P. Sulmasy. 1999. Lying for patients: Physician deception of third-party payers. *Archives of Internal Medicine* 159:2263–2270.

Grumbach, K., D. Osmond, K. Vranizan, D. Jaffe, and A. B. Bindman. 1998. Primary care physicians' experience of financial incentives in managed-care systems. *New England Journal of Medicine* 339:1516–1521.

Hadley, J., J. M. Mitchell, D. P. Sulmasy, and M. G. Bloche. 1999. Perceived financial incentives, HMO market penetration, and physicians' practice styles and satisfaction. *Health Services Research* 34(1, pt. 2):307–321.

Lasker, R. D., and M. S. Marquis. 1999. The intensity of physicians' work in patient visits—implications for the coding of patient evaluation and management services. *New England Journal of Medicine* 341:337–341.

Mechanic, D., D. D. McAlpine, and M. Rosenthal. 2001. Are patients' office visits with physicians getting shorter? *New England Journal of Medicine* 344:198–204.

Morreim, E. H. 1991. Gaming the system: Dodging the rules, ruling the dodgers, *Archives of Internal Medicine* 151(3):443–447.

Novack, D. H., B. J. Detering, R. Arnold, L. Forrow, M. Ladinsky, and J. C. Pezzullo. 1989. Physicians' attitudes toward using deception to resolve difficult ethical problems. *Journal of the American Medical Association* 261:2980–2985.

St. Peter, R. F., M. C. Reed, P. Kemper, and D. Blumenthal. 1999. Changes in the scope of care provided by primary care physicians. *New England Journal of Medicine* 341:1980–1985.

Sulmasy, D. P., M. G. Bioche, J. M. Mitchell, and J. Hadley. 2000. Physicians' ethical beliefs about cost-control arrangements. *Archives of Internal Medicine* 160:649–657.

Werner, R. M., G. C. Alexander, A. Fagerlin, and P. A. Ubel. 2002. The "hassle factor": What motivates physicians to manipulate reimbursement rules? *Archives of Internal Medicine* 162:1134–1139.

Wilson, I. B., K. Dukes, S. Greenfield, S. Kaplan, and B. Hillman. 2001. Patients' role in the use of radiology testing for common office practice complaints. *Archives of Internal Medicine* 161:256–263.

Wynia, M. K., D. S. Cummins, J. B. VanGeest, and I. B. Wilson. 2000. Physician manipulation of reimbursement rules for patients: Between a rock and a hard place. *Journal of the American Medical Association* 283:1858–1865.

Zemencuk, J. K., R. A. Hayward, K. A. Skarupski, and S. J. Katz. 1999. Patients' desires and expectations for medical care: A challenge to improving patient satisfaction. *American Journal of Medical Quality* 14:21–27.

APPENDIX

The following is the text that was used in the surveys sent to physicians. The same survey, except without medical jargon, was given to jurors.

One of the following vignettes was included in each survey:

Severe angina

A 55-year-old woman who just moved to a new city comes to her new doctor. She asks to be referred to a surgeon of heart bypass surgery. She is homebound because of chest pains. Before moving, she had an angiogram and it showed that she had triple vessel disease. She is on maximal medical therapy, but continues to have severe chest pain when she walks up a flight of stairs or tries to carry groceries in from the car.

Based on the medical literature and the degree of stenosis in her coronary arteries, her new doctor believes that bypass surgery is needed. However, the patient's insurance company will not pay for bypass surgery for this pre-existing condition because her chest pain has been stable for several months. The insurance company will pay for bypass surgery in this woman only if her chest pain gets worse.

Moderate low back pain

A 55-year-old man who has just moved to a new city comes to his new doctor. He asks whether he can receive an MRI to evaluate his low back pain. He says that four months ago he injured his back while doing some heavy lifting. Since then, he has continued to have low back pain that limits him from doing many of his normal daily activities. He has undergone conservative therapy for four months, but has had no significant relief from his pain.

Based on the medical literature, the doctor believes that after four months of continuous low back pain, the patient needs to be evaluated for surgery by receiving an MRI. However, the patient's new insurance company will not pay for an MRI until he has had six months of conservative medical therapy, unless the patient develops leg weakness.

For both vignettes, the respondent was told the doctor had one of the following three options:

- *Accept* the insurance company's decision. In this case, the patient must either delay surgery until her symptoms worsen or pay for the surgery with her own money.
- *Appeal* the insurance company's decision. To do this, the doctor has to make a *ten-minute* phone call. (*Or:* To do this, the doctor has to make several phone calls and fill out some forms. This process takes about *an hour.*) In the past, the doctor has been *successful 95% of the time* in obtaining coverage for bypass surgery in patients like this. (*Or:* In the past, the doctor has been *successful 50% of the time* in obtaining coverage for bypass surgery in patients like this.) Appeals, however, take time away from the doctor's ability to see other patients and, if unsuccessful, the patient will not receive the bypass unless her symptoms worsen.
- *Misrepresent* the facts to the insurance company and report that the woman's chest pains are getting worse. This would guarantee that the insurance company will pay for the surgery.

Respondents were then asked what the doctor in the vignette should do:

- *Accept* the insurance company's decision not to pay for surgery.
- *Appeal* the insurance company's decision not to pay for surgery.
- *Misrepresent* the facts to the insurance company and report that the patient is having increasing frequency of chest pain.

Hope for the Best, and Prepare for the Worst

Anthony L. Back, Robert M. Arnold, and Timothy E. Quill

Mr. J., a 40-year-old father of two young children, has metastatic non–small-cell lung cancer that has not responded to two different chemotherapy regimens. His physician, Dr. B., explains that the cancer is progressing. Mr. J. says. "Isn't there something you can do? Please don't give up on me." Dr. B. pauses and says, "Well, there is an experimental protocol we could try."

When faced with life-threatening illness, patients and physicians often feel that they must choose between hoping for disease remission and preparing for death. Mr. J. wants to fight the cancer in hope of living longer, and his physician is reluctant to discuss palliative care issues because she does not want to "destroy his hope" (1). Dr. B. knows that a patient in Mr. J.'s situation rarely benefits from third-line chemotherapy, and she also knows that by offering aggressive treatment she may be colluding with Mr. J. to avoid discussing the most likely prospect—that he is dying (2). Dr. B. is unsure how to proceed.

When patients and physicians discuss life-threatening illness by focusing exclusively on hope, they may miss important opportunities to improve pain and symptom management (3, 4), respond to underlying fears and concerns, explore life closure (5), and deepen the patient-physician relationship. The difficulty for physicians is acknowledging and supporting the patient's hopes while recognizing the severity of the patient's disease, thus offering an opportunity to discuss end-of-life concerns.

Hoping for a cure and preparing for potential death need not be mutually exclusive. Both patients and physicians want to hope for the best. At the same time, some patients also want to discuss their concerns about dying, and others probably should prepare because they are likely to die sooner rather than later. Although it may seem contradictory, hoping for the best while *at the same time* preparing for the worst is a useful strategy for approaching patients with potentially life-limiting illness. By acknowledging all the possible outcomes, patients and their physicians can expand their medical focus to include disease-modifying and symptomatic treatments and attend to underlying psychological, spiritual, and existential issues.

FRAMING THE DISCUSSION

This strategy of simultaneously hoping for the best and preparing for the worst may initially seem inconsistent and contradictory: How can you talk about chemotherapy *and* palliative care? Our strategy embraces the divided thinking many patients, families, and even health care providers have, which is often not logically consistent because of the profound ambivalence and vacillation they experience.

This strategy is derived, in part, from classic studies of human behavior during illness. Sociologists Glaser and Strauss (6) described patients who experienced an "open awareness" of their impending deaths and discussed it explicitly with family and caregivers. Kubler-Ross (7) built on this work by describing stages of dying, culminating in a stage she called "acceptance." However, most patients do not progress linearly through Kubler-Ross's stages. Living with a terminal illness is often marked by ambivalence about being a dying person. Weisman (8) described a period of "middle knowledge," in which patients vacillate between the state of continuing to live and plan and the state of preparing for death. Similarly, McCormick and Conley (9) interviewed patients who spoke of a "living-dying" period late in their illness. These studies and others (10, 11) indicate that vacillation between living and dying is common to many patients like Mr. J.

Using this strategy frames the discussion to include both living and dying. It may seem paradoxical to simultaneously explore living and dying, since these states are mutually exclusive in common parlance. However, this framing may enable Dr. B., Mr. J., and Mr. J.'s family to have a deeper conversation than if they focused just on dying or living. The following guidelines are useful.

1. Give Equal Air Time to Hoping and Preparing

Dr. B. wants to be empathic and realistic: I want to work with you, and I will do everything I can to optimize your chances. I am hoping for the best. I think that, at the same time, we need to prepare for the worst in case the treatment is not effective.

Mr. J.: Hope is really important to me.

Back, A. L., Arnold, R. M., Quill, T. E. "Hope for the Best, and Prepare for the Worst," *Annals of Internal Medicine* 138 (2003), 439–443. Copyright © 2003 by American College of Physicians. Reprinted by permission of the publisher.

By articulating hope and preparation at the outset, Dr. B. gives Mr. J. permission to discuss a wide range of topics. An introductory statement such as "I have found it helpful to hope for the best and, at the same time, prepare for the worst" allows the patient to discuss the topic he feels is most important or is most comfortable with. For patients like Mr. J., who want to discuss hopes first, we recommend following the patient's lead to fully explore hopes and place those hopes in the context of the patient's disease process. Other patients may need to prepare for their potential death before they can commit wholeheartedly to active treatment.

2. Align Patient and Physician Hopes
Dr. B: Could you tell me more about what you are hoping for? That will help me do a better job for you.

There are legitimate reasons why physicians should encourage patients to hope, such as disease remission or improvement in health status. Hope is a critical element for coping with illness (12). Most patients expect and want physicians to be advocates for health and longevity. Even if the media frequently exaggerate the power of medicine, many patients have beaten the odds. Patients frequently cite hope as the most important element of their coping and seek clinicians who will search every avenue of hope (13).

Physicians also want to hope for the best. Many physicians pursued medicine because they wanted to cure diseases, make patients feel better, and help relieve suffering (14). Articulating hopes for extending a patient's life can affirm this aspect of medicine. Some medical therapies, such as chemotherapy, make patients feel worse in the short run. To give these therapies day after day requires that oncologists believe in their ability to provide long-term benefit. Providing hope to patients is psychologically gratifying because patients and families are often grateful to doctors who hope. Shared hopes offer physicians an opportunity to align with their patient.

3. Encourage but Do Not Impose the Dual Agenda of Hoping and Preparing
Dr. B.: It's good for me to know about your hopes. It helps me get to know you better. Do you also want to talk about your concerns if things do not go as we hope?

Mr. J.: I'm really committed to trying this new treatment, and I feel like you are kind of giving up on me with this "preparing for the worst" stuff.

Dr. B.: I share your hope that the new treatment will benefit you. I want you to have the best medicine available. I talk about hoping for the best and preparing for the worst with all my patients who are seriously ill. Preparing for the worst doesn't mean I'm giving up on you; it helps me arrange the best medical care for you, no matter what happens.

When physicians initiate a conversation about preparing for the worst, patients and family members may react with fear, sadness, anxiety, or anger. Blocking or ignoring such emotions sends a nonverbal message that the physician is uncomfortable in discussing the worst and discourages patients from honestly discussing their concerns (15).

There can be positive consequences for patients who prepare for the worst, which physicians can underscore, and these can be powerful motivators. By preparing for the worst—by making a living will, naming a health care proxy, preparing financial matters, or settling family affairs—patients can address fears, clarify priorities, and strengthen relationships with loved ones, all components of a good death identified in empirical studies of patients with life-threatening illnesses (16, 17). Furthermore, some patients may be thinking about the worst but are afraid to discuss it for fear of frightening their family or disappointing their physician. One study indicates that unarticulated concerns correlate with increased anxiety and depression (18). Naming and discussing these concerns, which often deal with spiritual and existential issues, is an important first step for patients.

Physicians can also benefit from discussing the worst. These discussions allow physicians to feel that they are being honest with patients and, if done in the context of a supportive relationship, can increase patient trust. Patients and families who prepare for a range of outcomes may be less likely to blame their physicians for the consequences of disease progression.

4. Support the Evolution of Hope and Preparation over Time
Mr. J.: I don't want to think about preparing for the worst.

Dr. B.: It sounds like this is hard to think about.

Mr. J.: You bet it is.

Dr. B.: I wonder if you could say what makes it hard to think about?

Mr. J.: [pause] I'm worried that my wife won't be able to deal with this.

Knowing why a patient is reluctant to discuss these matters is important data for the physician. It may be enough to note the patient's hesitance about the discussion and plan to return to the issue at a future visit. Often the seed is planted even if it is not specifically discussed. Mr. J.'s willingness to talk about preparing for the worst may slowly increase over successive discussions as he begins to trust that his physician will hope and prepare at the same time.

Time the initial discussion early in the illness, and revisit the issues regularly. Talking about hope and preparation allows "big picture" discussions to begin. By regularly visiting the issues, physicians can normalize the idea that talking about death is one aspect of discussions between a patient and physician. The issues can then be revisited at times when a change in strategy is contemplated and the relative emphasis on relief of suffering and treatment of disease is brought into question. Time and disease progression may enable a patient to acknowledge his illness and the potential consequences. A physician may need to be more direct late in the patient's illness, while acknowledging that these topics are difficult. By revisiting hope and preparation regularly during the illness, Dr. B. can enable Mr. J.'s thinking to evolve and foster constructive ways of coping. Physicians should judge success in communication by the quality and depth of discussion and the adequacy of the plans jointly developed to guide medical care. However, if a patient has made reasonable plans but does not wish to talk in depth about dying, that patient's desires should be respected.

5. Respect Hopes and Fears, and Respond to Emotions

Mr. J.: You know, I'm really worried about my wife. I'm worried about leaving her alone.

Dr. B.: It sounds like you care a great deal about her.

Physicians can use communication strategies of responding to emotions, including acknowledgment, exploration, legitimation, and empathy (19) (Table 1). These strategies enable physicians to frame their concerns for the patient relative to the patient's concerns (*Mr J., I can see that taking care of your family is a major priority, and I have some ideas about how to do that in case the treatment doesn't go the way we hope.*). This framing can help patient and physician reach common ground. Most patients want to hear their physician's true opinions and recommendations as long as the physician is not too blunt (20, 21). Compassion can take the form of giving recommendations in light of what the physician knows about the patient's values, medical situation, goals, and fears. A physician need not fully share a patient's hopes or fears to respect, learn about, and respond to them.

Physicians often have emotional responses to their patients, and these emotions shape their relationship with the patient and family. These emotions, if unmonitored, can influence the physician-patient communication and relationship in unintended ways. For example, physicians may feel like the patient "does not get it" and feel angry that they are

TABLE 1 Responding to Hopes and Fears[*]

Patient Says:	Physician Responds:
"I hope that I can live a little longer."	"I hope you can live longer, too. What would be most important for you in that time?"
"I hope that the treatment will help me."	"I'm also hoping that the treatment will help you. If it works, what will be most important for you to do? I wonder, also, if you would be willing to talk about what we should do in case the treatment doesn't work?"
"I'm concerned that talking about the worst will be overwhelming."	"Hmmm . . . . Talking about the worst can be frightening at first, but most of the patients I have worked with have found it helpful in the long run."
"I'm worried that talking about the worst would be giving up."	"I understand your concern, but we are not talking about giving up on treatment. We are asking you to consider what would be most important if treatment does not work as we both hope."
"I don't want to talk about what I'm worried about."	"Okay. I realize that talking about worries can be a hard thing to do. If you do want to talk about these issues in the future, I would be open to it."

[*]These examples show how physicians can respond to both hopes and fears as they discuss hoping for the best and preparing for the worst with their patients. To use this strategy effectively, physicians should explore patients' hopes and fears and respect patients' boundaries. Note that the suggested physician responses do not move immediately toward solving problems or reassuring. Premature reassurance can make patients feel their concerns are not heard. These responses suggest ways to deepen the conversation and better understand patient concerns.

being asked to provide care that is unlikely to work (22). Sometimes a physician's emotions can be a clue to how the patient is feeling; other times, physicians may come to understand that they are reacting to personal feelings of their own about death and dying (23). When trying to sort out one's own strong reactions, conversation with a trusted colleague can be clarifying.

OTHER CLINICAL SCENARIOS

Not every patient approaches a life-threatening illness like Mr. J. A patient who primarily prepares for the worst might benefit from a physician invitation to hope for the best. For example, a 65-year-old woman with breast cancer that is estrogen receptor positive and metastatic to bone but not visceral organs says that she is terrified of dying in pain and, consequently, is stockpiling pain medication. Her physician might explore this fear and learn that the patient had a difficult experience with a close friend who died of cancer and that her other fears include missing her first grandchild's birth expected in 3 months. The physician could reassure her and also invite her to hope (*I can assure you that sophisticated pain control will be available if you need it. I think we can also hope that the tamoxifen will control the cancer for many months with minimal toxicity. It is entirely possible to hope that you will be present when your grandchild is born.*).

This approach is also applicable to patients with noncancer illnesses. For example, a 55-year-old man with endstage congestive heart failure who is waiting for a heart transplant might also benefit from a discussion about hoping and preparing (*I am hoping that a heart will become available for you, and we want to do everything we can to keep you ready. I also want to be prepared if a heart does not come up and your own heart gets worse.*). The question "If time turns out to be short, what would be most important for you to accomplish?" may facilitate an important conversation.

PITFALLS OF FOCUSING EXCLUSIVELY ON HOPING OR PREPARING

Hoping and preparing minimizes the weakness of each strategy on its own. Focusing only on hope may leave patients unaware of their limited life expectancy (24). Such patients are more likely to choose life-prolonging therapies such as cardiopulmonary resuscitation in

situations where these therapies are rarely effective (25, 26). Thus, when physicians focus only on hope, patients may unrealistically focus their time and energy on treatments that are unlikely to work. Physicians who focus exclusively on hope also may feel that they have not been honest with patients, which can make it more difficult for them to confront the limitations of medicine (22). These physicians withdraw when it becomes clear that a patient is dying; patients sense withdrawal, feel abandoned, and may respond by demanding even more medical attention (27).

LIMITATIONS

This dual-track approach may not work for everyone. Patients may not wish to live with the cognitive and emotional dissonance of hoping for the best and preparing for the worst. Some cultures place negative values on talking explicitly about death or potential bad outcomes, feeling it is dangerous, harmful, and even cruel. Once the meaning of such conversation is fully understood, physicians should attempt to find alternative, culturally appropriate processes that may not involve open discussion to make critical end-of-life decisions (30, 31).

This approach requires that the physician maintain dual roles, providing two kinds of coaching: optimism (*Let's hope*) and realism (*Let's prepare*). Physicians using this approach will need to be careful about checking in with the patient's emotional state to ensure that the patient understands the physician's intention. Physicians may need to explain this strategy to other clinicians and family members, who may be concerned that the approach presents a confusing, mixed message.

Other physicians may feel that the terminology "preparing for the worst" is too harsh, casting death as the enemy or suggesting that death always is accompanied by severe suffering. A more tempered phrase, such as "preparing for the possibility that the treatment fails" may allow patient and physician to gradually work toward a common understanding of the difficult issues presented by dying.

Finally, there are few data linking hope and preparation to other outcomes. Although descriptive data indicate the importance of both of these approaches, no studies have examined how supporting hope and preparing for death might affect medical outcomes such as survival, quality of life, symptom management, and quality of death.

CONCLUSION

Physicians often deal with hope as something they must embrace or negate completely. But this exclusive focus on hope constricts options for discussing how a patient, family, and physician can work together with a life-threatening illness. Embracing a dual approach of hoping for the best and preparing for the worst helps physicians join with patients and families, yet plan medical care that is responsive to a range of potential outcomes for the patient. These conversations can enrich the patient-physician relationship and provide a fresh source of meaning for the work of medicine (32, 33).

REFERENCES

1. Delvecchio Good MJ, Good BJ, Schaffer C, Lind SE. American oncology and the discourse on hope. Cult Med Psychiatry. 1990;14:59–79. [PMID: 2340733]

2. The AM, Hak T, Koëter G, van Der Wal G. Collusion in doctor-patient communication about imminent death: an ethnographic study. BMJ. 2000;231:1376–81. [PMID: 11099281]

3. Ersek M, Kraybill BM, Pen AD. Factors hindering patients' use of medications for cancer pain. Cancer Pract. 1999;7:226–32. [PMID: 10687591]

4. Cleeland CS, Gonin R, Hatfield AK, Edmonson JH, Blum RH, Stewart JA, et al. Pain and its treatment in outpatients with metastatic cancer. N Engl J Med. 1994;330:592–6. [PMID: 7508092]

5. Byock IR. The nature of suffering and the nature of opportunity at the end of life. Clin Geriatr Med. 1996;12:237–52. [PMID: 8799345]

6. Glaser BG, Strauss AL. Awareness of Dying. Chicago: Aldine Publishing; 1965.

7. Kubler-Ross E. On Death and Dying. New York: Macmillan; 1969.

8. Weisman A. On Dying and Denying: A Psychiatric Study of Terminality. New York: Behavioral Publications; 1972.

9. McCornick TR, Conley BJ. Patients' perspectives on dying and on the care of dying patients. West J Med. 1995;163:236–43. [PMID: 7571586]

10. Barnard D, Boston P, Towers AM, Lambrinidou Y. Crossing Over. Narratives of Palliative Care. New York: Oxford Univ Pr; 2000.

11. Kuhl D. What Dying People Want: Practical Wisdom for the End of Life. New York: PublicAffairs; 2002.

12. Herth K. Fostering hope in terminally-ill people. J Adv Nurs. 1990;15: 1250–9. [PMID: 2269747]

13. Quill TE, Cassel CK. Nonabandonment: a central obligation for physicians. Ann Intern Med. 1995;122:368–74. [PMID: 7847649]

14. Crawshaw R, Rogers DE, Pellegrino ED, Bulger RJ, Lundberg GD, Bristow LR, et al. Patient-physician covenant. JAMA. 1995;273:1553. [PMID: 7739086]

15. Maguire P. Improving communication with cancer patients. Eur J Cancer. 1999;35:1415–22. [PMID: 10673972]

16. Steinhauser KE, Christakis NA, Clipp EC, McNeilly M, McIntyre L, Tulsky JA. Factors considered important at the end of life by patients, family, physicians, and other care providers. JAMA. 2000;284:2476–82. [PMID: 11074777]

17. Singer PA, Martin DK, Kelner M. Quality end-of-life care: patients' perspectives. JAMA. 1999;281:163–8. [PMID: 9917120]

18. Heaven CM, Maguire P. Disclosure of concerns by hospice patients and their identification by nurses. Palliat Med. 1997;11:283–90. [PMID: 9373579]

19. Quill TE. Recognizing and adjusting to barriers in doctor-patient communication. Ann Intern Med. 1989;111:51–7. [PMID: 2660647]

20. Quill TE, Brody H. Physician recommendations and patient autonomy: finding a balance between physician power and patient choice. Ann Intern Med. 1996;125:763–9. [PMID: 8929011]

21. Curtis JR, Wenrich MD, Carline JD, Shannon SE, Ambrozy DM, Ramsey PG. Understanding physicians' skills at providing end-of-life care perspectives of patients, families, and health care workers. J Gen Intern Med. 2001;16:41–9. [PMID: 11251749]

22. Quill TE, Suchman AL. Uncertainty and control: learning to live with medicine's limitations. Humane Med. 1993;9:109–20. [PMID: 11656250]

23. Meier DE, Back AL, Morrison RS. The inner life of physicians and care of the seriously ill. JAMA. 2001;286:3007–14. [PMID: 11743845]

24. Lamont EB, Christakis NA. Prognostic disclosure to patients with cancer near the end of life. Ann Intern Med. 2001;134:1096–105. [PMID: 11412049]

25. Weeks JC, Cook EF, O'Day SJ, Peterson LM, Wenger N, Reding D, et al. Relationship between cancer patients' predictions of prognosis and their treatment preferences. JAMA. 1998;279:1709–14. [PMID: 9624023]

26. Emanuel EJ, Young-Xu Y, Ash A, Gazelle G, Levinsky N, Moskowitz M. How much chemotherapy are cancer patients receiving at the end of life? [Abstract] Proceedings of the 37th Annual Meeting of the American Society of Clinical Oncology, San Francisco, CA; 12–15 May 2001. Abstract no. 953.

27. Shapiro A. The Vigil. Chicago: Univ of Chicago Pr; 1997.

28. Waisel DB. The hazards of "hanging crepe" or stating overly pessimistic prognoses. J Clin Ethics. 2000;11:171–4. [PMID: 11056876]

29. Siegler M. Remarks on 'crepe hanging'—or ethics in everyday practice. Am Med News. 1977;20:22. [PMID: 11664719]

30. Kagawa-Singer M, Blackhall LJ. Negotiating cross-cultural issues at the end of life: "You got to go where he lives." JAMA. 2001;286:2993–3001. [PMID: 11743841]

31. Crawley L, Payne R, Bolden J, Payne T, Washington P, Williams S, et al. Palliative and end-of-life care in the African American community. JAMA. 2000; 284:2518–21. [PMID: 11074786]

32. Quill TE, Williamson PR. Healthy approaches to physician stress. Arch Intern Med. 1990;150:1857–61. [PMID: 2393317]

33. Remen RN. Recapturing the soul of medicine: physicians need to reclaim meaning in their working lives. West J Med. 2001;174:4–5. [PMID: 11154646]

INFORMED CONSENT

Transparency: Informed Consent in Primary Care

Howard Brody

While the patient's right to give informed consent to medical treatment is now well-established both in U.S. law and in biomedical ethics, evidence continues to suggest that the concept has been poorly integrated into American medical practice, and that in many instances the needs and desires of patients are not being well met by current policies.[1] It appears that the theory and the practice of informed consent are out of joint in some crucial ways. This is particularly true for primary care settings, a context typically ignored by medical ethics literature, but where the majority of doctor-patient encounters occur. Indeed, some have suggested that the concept of informed consent is virtually foreign to primary care medicine where benign paternalism appropriately reigns and where respect for patient autonomy is almost completely absent.[2]

It is worth asking whether current legal standards for informed consent tend to resolve the problem or to exacerbate it. I will maintain that accepted legal standards, at least in the form commonly employed by courts, send physicians the wrong message about what is expected of them. An alternative standard that would send physicians the correct message, a conversation standard, is probably unworkable legally. As an alternative, I will propose a transparency standard as a compromise that gives physicians a doable task and allows courts to review appropriately. I must begin, however, by briefly identifying some assumptions crucial to the development of this position even though space precludes complete argumentation and documentation.

CRUCIAL ASSUMPTIONS

Informed consent is a meaningful ethical concept only to the extent that it can be realized and promoted within the ongoing practice of good medicine. This need not imply diminished respect for patient autonomy, for there are excellent reasons to regard respect for patient autonomy as a central feature of good medical care. Informed consent, properly understood, must be considered an essential ingredient of good patient care, and a physician who lacks the skills to inform patients appropriately and obtain proper consent should be viewed as lacking essential medical skills necessary for practice. It is not enough to see informed consent as a nonmedical, legalistic exercise designed to promote patient autonomy, one that interrupts the process of medical care.

However, available empirical evidence strongly suggests that this is precisely how physicians currently view informed consent practices. Informed consent is still seen as bureaucratic legalism rather than as part of patient care. Physicians often deny the existence of realistic treatment alternatives, thereby attenuating the perceived need to inform the patient of meaningful options. While patients may be informed, efforts are seldom made to assess accurately the patient's actual need or desire for information, or what the patient then proceeds to do with the information provided. Physicians typically underestimate patients' desire to be informed and overestimate their desire to be involved in decisionmaking. Physicians may also view informed consent as an empty charade, since they are confident in their abilities to manipulate consent by how they discuss or divulge information.[3]

A third assumption is that there are important differences between the practice of primary care medicine and the tertiary care settings that have been most frequently discussed in the literature on informed consent. The models of informed consent discussed below typically take as the paradigm case something like surgery for breast cancer or the performance of an invasive and risky radiologic procedure. It is assumed that the risks to the patient are significant, and the values placed on alternative forms of treatment are quite weighty. Moreover, it is assumed that the specialist physician performing the procedure probably does a fairly limited number of procedures and thus could be expected to know exhaustively the precise risks, benefits, and alternatives for each.

Primary care medicine, however, fails to fit this model. The primary care physician, instead of performing five or six complicated and risky procedures frequently, may engage in several hundred treatment modalities during an average week of practice. In many cases, risks to the patient are negligible and conflicts over patient values and the goals of treatment or nontreatment are of little consequence. Moreover, in contrast to the tertiary care patient, the typical ambulatory patient is much better able to exercise freedom of choice and somewhat less likely to be intimidated by either the severity of the disease or the expertise of the physician; the opportunities for changing one's mind once treatment has begun are also much greater. Indeed, in primary care, it is much more likely for the full process of informed consent to treatment (such as the beginning and the dose adjustment of an antihypertensive medication) to occur over several office visits rather than at one single point in time.

It might be argued that for all these reasons, the stakes are so low in primary care that it is fully appropriate for informed consent to be interpreted only with regard to the specialized or tertiary care setting. I believe that this is quite incorrect for three reasons. First, good primary care medicine ought to embrace respect for patient autonomy, and if patient autonomy is operationalized in informed consent, properly understood, then it ought to be part and parcel of good primary care. Second, the claim that the primary care physician cannot be expected to obtain the patient's informed consent seems to undermine the idea that informed consent could or ought to be part of the daily practice of medicine. Third, primary care encounters are statistically more common than the highly specialized encounters previously used as models for the concept of informed consent.[4]

ACCEPTED LEGAL STANDARDS

Most of the literature on legal approaches to informed consent addresses the tension between the community practice standard and the reasonable patient standard, with the latter seen as the more satisfactory, emerging legal standard.[5] However, neither standard sends the proper message to the physician about what is expected of her to promote patient autonomy effectively and to serve the informational needs of patients in daily practice.

The community practice standard sends the wrong message because it leaves the door open too wide for physician paternalism. The physician is instructed to behave as other physicians in that specialty behave, regardless of how well or how poorly that behavior serves patients' needs. Certainly, behaving the way other physicians behave is a task we might expect physicians to readily accomplish; unfortunately, the standard fails to inform them of the end toward which the task is aimed.

The reasonable patient standard does a much better job of indicating the centrality of respect for patient autonomy and the desired outcome of the informed consent process, which is revealing the information that a reasonable person would need to make an informed and rational decision. This standard is particularly valuable when modified to include the specific informational and decisional needs of a particular patient.

If certain things were true about the relationship between medicine and law in today's society, the reasonable patient standard would provide acceptable guidance to physicians. One feature would be that physicians esteem the law as a positive force in guiding their practice, rather than as a threat to their well-being that must be handled defensively. Another element would be a prospective consideration by the law of what the physician could reasonably have been expected to do in practice, rather than a retrospective review armed with the foreknowledge that some significant patient harm has already occurred.

Unfortunately, given the present legal climate, the physician is much more likely to get a mixed or an undesirable message from the reasonable patient standard. The message the physician hears from the reasonable patient standard is that one must exhaustively lay out all possible risks as well as benefits and alternatives of the proposed procedure. If one remembers to discuss fifty possible risks, and the patient in a particular case suffers the fifty-first, the physician might subsequently be found liable for incomplete disclosure. Since lawsuits are triggered when patients suffer harm, disclosure of risk becomes relatively more important than disclosure of benefits. Moreover, disclosure of information becomes much more critical than effective patient participation in decisionmaking. Physicians consider it more important to document what they said to the patient than to document how the patient used or thought about that information subsequently.

In specialty practice, many of these concerns can be nicely met by detailed written or videotaped consent documents, which can provide the depth of information required while still putting the benefits and alternatives in proper context. This is workable when one engages in a limited number of procedures and can have a complete document or videotape for each.[6]

However, this approach is not feasible for primary care, when the number of procedures may be much more numerous and the time available with each patient may be considerably less. Moreover, it is simply not realistic to expect even the best educated of primary care physicians to rattle off at a moment's notice a detailed list of significant risks attached to any of the many drugs and therapeutic modalities they recommend.

This sets informed consent apart from all other aspects of medical practice in a way that I believe is widely perceived by nonpaternalistic primary care physicians, but which is almost never commented upon in the medical ethics literature. To the physician obtaining informed consent, *you never know when you are finished*. When a primary care physician is told to treat a patient for strep throat or to counsel a person suffering a normal grief reaction from the recent death of a relative, the physician has a good sense of what it means to complete the task at hand. When a physician is told to obtain the patient's informed consent for a medical intervention, the impression is quite different. A list of as many possible risks as can be thought of may still omit some significant ones. A list of all the risks that actually have occurred may still not have dealt with the patient's need to know risks in relation to benefits and alternatives. A description of all benefits, risks, and alternatives may not establish whether the patient has understood the information. If the patient says he understands, the physician has to wonder whether he really understands or whether he is simply saying this to be accommodating. As the law currently *appears* to operate (in the perception of the defensively minded physician), there never comes a point at which you can be certain that you have adequately completed your legal as well as your ethical task.

The point is not simply that physicians are paranoid about the law; more fundamentally, physicians are getting a message that informed consent is very different from any other task they are asked to perform in medicine. If physicians conclude that informed consent is therefore not properly part of medicine at all, but is rather a legalistic and bureaucratic hurdle they must overcome at their own peril, blame cannot be attributed to paternalistic attitudes or lack of respect for patient autonomy.

THE CONVERSATION MODEL

A metaphor employed by Jay Katz, informed consent as conversation, provides an approach to respect for patient autonomy that can be readily integrated within primary care practice.[7] Just as the specific needs of an individual patient for information, or the meaning that patient will attach to the information as it is presented, cannot be known in advance, one cannot always tell in advance how a conversation is going to turn out. One must follow the process along and take one's cues from the unfolding conversation itself. Despite the absence of any formal rules for carrying out or completing a conversation on a specific subject, most people have a good intuitive grasp of what it means for a conversation to be finished, what it means to change the subject in the middle of a conversation, and what it means to later reopen a conversation one had thought was completed when something new has just arisen. Thus, the metaphor suggests that informed consent consists not in a formal process carried out strictly by protocol but in a conversation designed to encourage patient participation in all medical decisions to the extent that the patient wishes to be included. The idea of informed consent as physician-patient conversation could, when properly developed, be a useful analytic tool for ethical issues in informed consent, and could also be a powerful educational tool for highlighting the skills and attitudes that a physician needs to successfully integrate this process within patient care.

If primary care physicians understand informed consent as this sort of conversation process, the idea that exact rules cannot be given for its successful management could cease to be a mystery. Physicians would instead be guided to rely on their own intuitions and communication skills, with careful attention to information received from the patient, to determine when an adequate job had been done in the informed consent process. Moreover, physicians would be encouraged to see informed consent as a genuinely mutual and participatory process, instead of being reduced to the one-way disclosure of information. In effect, informed consent could be demystified, and located within the context of the everyday relationships between physician and patient, albeit with a renewed emphasis on patient participation.[8]

Unfortunately, the conversation metaphor does not lend itself to ready translation into a legal standard for determining whether or not the physician has satisfied her basic responsibilities to the patient. There seems to be an inherently subjective element to conversation that makes it ill-suited as a legal standard for review of controversial cases. A conversation in which one participates is by its nature a very different thing from the same conversation described to an outsider. It is hard to imagine how a jury could be instructed to determine in retrospect whether or not a particular conversation was adequate for its purposes. However, without the possibility for legal review, the message that patient autonomy is an important value and that patients have important rights within primary care would seem to be severely undermined. The question then is whether some of the important strengths of the conversation model can be retained in another model that does allow better guidance.

THE TRANSPARENCY STANDARD

I propose the transparency standard as a means to operationalize the best features of the conversation model in medical practice. According to this standard, adequate informed consent is obtained when a reasonably informed patient is allowed to participate in the medical decision to the extent that patient wishes. In turn, "reasonably informed" consists of two features: (1) the physician discloses the basis on which the proposed treatment, or alternative possible treatments, have been chosen; and (2) the patient is allowed to ask questions suggested by the disclosure of the physician's reasoning, and those questions are answered to the patient's satisfaction.

According to the transparency model, the key to reasonable disclosure is not adherence to existing standards of other practitioners, nor is it adherence to a list of risks that a hypothetical reasonable patient would want to know. Instead, disclosure is adequate when the physician's basic thinking has been rendered transparent to the patient. If the physician arrives at a recommended therapeutic or diagnostic intervention only after carefully examining a list of risks and benefits, then rendering the physician's thinking transparent requires that those risks and benefits be detailed for the patient. If the physician's thinking has not followed that route but has reached its conclusion by other considerations, then what needs to be disclosed to the patient is accordingly different. Essentially, the transparency standard requires the physician to engage in the typical patient-management thought process, only to *do it out loud in language understandable to the patient.*[9]

To see how this might work in practice, consider the following as possible general decision-making strategies that might be used by a primary physician:

1. The intervention, in addition to being presumably low-risk, is also routine and automatic. The physician, faced with a case like that presented by the patient, almost always chooses this treatment.

2. The decision is not routine but seems to offer clear benefit with minimal risk.

3. The proposed procedure offers substantial chances for benefit, but also very substantial risks.

4. The proposed intervention offers substantial risks and extremely questionable benefits. Unfortunately, possible alternative courses of action also have high risk and uncertain benefit.

The exact risks entailed by treatment loom much larger in the physician's own thinking in cases 3 and 4 than in cases 1 and 2. The transparency standard would require that physicians at least mention the various risks to patients in scenarios 3 and 4, but would not necessarily require physicians exhaustively to describe risks, unless the patient asked, in scenarios 1 and 2.

The transparency standard seems to offer some considerable advantages for informing physicians what can legitimately be expected of them in the promotion of patient autonomy while carrying out the activities of primary care medicine. We would hope that the well-trained primary care physician generally thinks before acting. On that assumption, the physician can be told exactly when she is finished obtaining informed consent—first, she has to share her thinking with the patient; secondly, she has to encourage and answer questions; and third, she has to discover how participatory he wishes to be and facilitate that level of participation. This seems a much more reasonable task within primary care than an exhaustive listing of often irrelevant risk factors.

There are also considerable advantages for the patient in this approach. The patient retains the right to ask for an exhaustive recital of risks and alternatives. However, the vast majority of patients, in a primary care setting particularly, would wish to supplement a standardized recital of risks and benefits of treatment with some questions like, "Yes, doctor, but what does this really mean for me? What meaning am I supposed to attach to the information that you've just given?" For example, in scenarios 1 and 2, the precise and specific risk probabilities and possibilities are very small considerations in the thinking of the physician, and reciting an exhaustive list of risks would seriously misstate just what the physician was thinking. If the physician did detail a laundry list of risk factors, the patient might very well ask, "Well, doctor, just what should I think about what you have just told me?" and the thoughtful and concerned physician might well reply, "There's certainly a small possibility that one of these bad things will happen to you; but I think the chance is extremely remote and in my own practice I have never seen anything like that occur." The patient is very likely to give much more weight to that statement, putting the risks in perspective, than he is to the listing of risks. And that emphasis corresponds with an understanding of how the physician herself has reached the decision.

The transparency standard should further facilitate and encourage useful questions from patients. If a patient is given a routine list of risks and benefits and then is asked "Do you have any questions?" the response may well be perfunctory and automatic. If the patient is told precisely the grounds on which the physician has made her recommendation, and then asked the same question, the response is much more likely to be individualized and meaningful.

There certainly would be problems in applying the transparency standard in the courtroom, but these do not appear to be materially more difficult than those encountered in applying other standards; moreover, this standard could call attention to more important features in the ethical relationship between physician and patient. Consider the fairly typical case, in which a patient suffers harm from the occurrence of a rare but predictable complication of a procedure, and then claims that he would not have consented had he known about that risk. Under the present "enlightened" court standards, the jury would examine whether a reasonable patient would have needed to know about that risk factor prior to making a decision on the proposed intervention. Under the transparency standard, the question would instead be whether the physician thought about that risk factor as a relevant consideration prior to recommending the course of action to the patient. If the physician did seriously consider that risk factor, but failed to reveal that to the patient, he was in effect making up the patient's mind in advance about what risks were worth accepting. In that situation, the physician could easily be held liable. If, on the other hand, that risk was considered too insignificant to play a role in determining which intervention ought to be performed, the physician may still have rendered his thinking completely transparent to the patient even though that specific risk factor was not mentioned. In this circumstance, the physician would be held to have done an adequate job of disclosing information.[10] A question would still exist as to whether a competent physician ought to have known about that risk factor and ought to have considered it more carefully prior to doing the procedure. But that question raises the issue of negligence, which is where such considerations properly belong, and removes the problem from the context of informed consent. Obviously, the standard of informed consent is misapplied if it is intended by itself to prevent the practice of negligent medicine.

TRANSPARENCY IN MEDICAL PRACTICE

Will adopting a legal standard like transparency change medical practice for the better? Ultimately only empirical research will answer this question. We know almost nothing about the sorts of conversations primary care physicians now have with their patients, or what would happen if these physicians routinely tried harder to share their basic thinking about therapeutic choices. In this setting it is possible to argue that the transparency standard will have deleterious effects. Perhaps the physician's basic thinking will fail to include risk issues that patients, from their perspective, would regard as substantial. Perhaps how physicians think about therapeutic choice will prove to be too idiosyncratic and variable to serve as any sort of standard. Perhaps disclosing basic thinking processes will impede rather than promote optimal patient participation in decisions.

But the transparency standard must be judged, not only against ideal medical practice, but also against the present-day standard and the message it sends to practitioners. I have argued that that message is, "You can protect yourself legally only by guessing all bad outcomes that might occur and warning each patient explicitly that he might suffer any of them." The transparency standard is an attempt to send the message, "You can protect yourself legally by conversing with your patients in a way that promotes their participation in medical decisions, and more specifically by making sure that they see the basic reasoning you used to arrive at the recommended treatment." It seems at least plausible to me that the attempt is worth making.

The reasonable person standard may still be the best way to view informed consent in highly specialized settings where a relatively small number of discrete and potentially risky procedures are the daily order of business. In primary care settings, the best ethical advice we can give physicians is to view informed consent as an ongoing process of conversation designed to maximize patient participation after adequately revealing the key facts. Because the conversation metaphor does not by itself suggest measures for later judicial review, a transparency standard, or something like it, may be a reasonable way to operationalize that concept in primary care practice. Some positive side-effects of this might be more focus on good diagnostic and therapeutic decisionmaking on the physician's part, since it will be understood that the patient will be made aware of what the physician's reasoning process has been like, and better documentation of management decisions in the patient record. If these occur, then it will be clearer that the standard of informed consent has promoted rather than impeded high quality patient care.

REFERENCES

1. Charles W. Lidz *et al.*, "Barriers to Informed Consent," *Annals of Internal Medicine* 99:4 (1983), 539–43.

2. Tom L. Beauchamp and Laurence McCullough, *Medical Ethics: The Moral Responsibilities of Physicians* (Englewood Cliffs, NJ: Prentice-Hall, 1984).

3. For a concise overview of empirical data about contemporary informed consent practices see Ruth R. Faden and Tom L. Beauchamp, *A History and Theory of Informed Consent* (New York: Oxford University Press, 1986), 98–99 and associated footnotes.

4. For efforts to address ethical aspects of primary care practice, see Ronald J. Christie and Barry Hoffmaster, *Ethical Issues in Family Medicine* (New York: Oxford University Press, 1986); and Harmon L. Smith and Larry R. Churchill, *Professional Ethics and Primary Care Medicine* (Durham, NC: Duke University Press, 1986).

5. Faden and Beauchamp, *A History and Theory of Informed Consent*, 23–49 and 114–50. I have also greatly benefited from an unpublished paper by Margaret Wallace.

6. For a specialty opinion to the contrary, see W. H. Coles *et al.*, "Teaching Informed Consent," in *Further Developments in Assessing Clinical Competence*, Ian R. Hart and Ronald M. Harden, eds. (Montreal: Can-Heal Publications, 1987), 241–70. This paper is interesting in applying to specialty care a model very much like the one I propose for primary care.

7. Jay Katz, *The Silent World of Doctor and Patient* (New York: Free Press, 1984).

8. Howard Brody, *Stories of Sickness* (New Haven: Yale University Press, 1987), 171–81.

9. For an interesting study of physicians' practices on this point, see William C. Wu and Robert A. Pearlman, "Consent in Medical Decisionmaking: The Role of Communication," *Journal of General Internal Medicine* 3:1 (1988), 9–14.

10. A court case that might point the way toward this line of reasoning is *Precourt v. Frederick*, 395 Mass. 689 (1985). See William J. Curran, "Informed Consent in Malpractice Cases: A Turn Toward Reality," *New England Journal of Medicine* 314:7 (1986), 429–31.

Reconceiving the Family
The Process of Consent in Medical Decisionmaking

Mark G. Kuczewski

Medical ethics has rediscovered the family. At least two factors have contributed to widening the focus from the individual. There has been a general revival of communitarian rhetoric in the United States that, of course, brings the role of social relations to the fore. Similarly, we should not underestimate the natural progression and development of medical ethics. Having focused on the rights of the patient for so long, it follows that ethicists now wish to map the relationships surrounding the individual that may affect medical decisionmaking. Because this interest in the family is a concern with the significant relationships that surround the patient, the family is described in terms of "closeness," not biology. This way of describing the family is commonplace in medical ethics and is a meritorious convention.[1] Thus, when John Hardwig asks, "What about the Family?"[2] he asks whether there is any role in medical decision making for those close to the patient. This is *the* question because our thinking about medical decisionmaking is entirely patient-centered.

This patient-centered ethic is systematized as the doctrine of informed consent.

Without much exaggeration it can be said that all of medical ethics is but a footnote to informed consent. It is the concept that first called medicine out of its paternalistic slumber and into the open light of public scrutiny. Informed consent serves as the foundation upon which answers to new questions and problems are constructed. Informed consent is a kind of doctrine, that is, an amalgam of legal and philosophical reasoning with a conceptual framework and a number of specific prescriptions. This framework entails a few basic actions and presupposes certain conditions. At the heart of the doctrine is the legal principle that "the right of a competent person to refuse medical treatment is virtually absolute."[3] The exercise of this right presupposes that the patient must receive all information relevant to the decision to undergo or forgo a proposed treatment and that he or she must comprehend the information. The legal principle indicates that the

Kuczewski, Mark G. "Reconceiving the Family: The Process of Consent in Medical Decisionmaking," *Hastings Center Report* 26:2 (1996), 30–37. Copyright © 1996. Reprinted by permission of The Hastings Center.

patient needs to be competent and it is also implicit that the choice is relatively freely made. Although influence is acceptable, all forms of coercion are beyond the pale.[4]

The individualistic nature of this line of thought is clear. The person is conceptualized as possessing a sphere of protected activity or privacy free from unwanted interference. Within this zone of privacy, one is able to exercise his or her liberty and discretion. Within this protected sphere take place disclosure, comprehension, and choice, which express the patient's right of self-determination over her body.[5] Of course, these are legal formulations. The philosophical justification for them draws on egalitarian or democratic intuitions regarding personhood.

The person is opaque to others and therefore the best judge and guardian of his or her own interests. Although the physician may be the expert on the medical "facts," the patient is the only individual with genuine insight into his private sphere of "values." Because treatment plans should reflect personal values as well as medical realities, the patient must be the ultimate decisionmaker.[6] Once we sketch the person in this way, the problem for ethicists is obvious. The doctrine of informed consent is based on an individual profile rather than a family portrait. The individual is outlined first, and only then do we ask where close others may be added to the picture. Because the philosophical and legal premises of the doctrine leave few other reasonable options, the family is usually conceived as comprising competing interests. Such a result is not adequate to our ordinary intuitions regarding the relationship of the patient to the family. Furthermore, these premises limit ethicists to arguing about the relative merits of these rival bundles of interests.

Once we understand the relationship between the doctrine of informed consent and the inability of medical ethicists to adequately describe the role of the family in medical decisionmaking, the tasks become clear. To follow the communitarian impulse and characterize the family in a way that transcends an atomistic view of human relations will require a several-part investigation. First, I must critique the traditional doctrine of informed consent and show how it has "hijacked" what questions can be asked about the role of the family. By examining the doctrine's major assumptions and fixing the limits of its application, we can find room for the family in situations where such legalistic thought is inappropriate. Second, I shall explain how several promising "process" models of informed consent better describe the role of the family in medical decisionmaking. Finally, I shall apply these process models to a case and show how they also demand a different role for the physician in the decisionmaking process. Only by exploring the traditional doctrine of informed consent and escaping its individualistic and legalistic assumptions, can we hope to enrich the theoretical picture of the family in the decisionmaking process.

SUBVERTING INDIVIDUALISM IN MEDICAL ETHICS

The communitarian impulse that has revived inquiry into the family represents a dissatisfaction with the "rugged individualism"[7] that a patient-centered ethic implies. Medical ethicists sometimes investigate the family in the hope of finding a way to place the interests of the patient in proper perspective. Of course, the only way to describe the role of the family is in terms of the doctrine of informed consent, since it is the foundation of medical decisionmaking. In addition to the patient, each member of the family also has his or her sphere of privacy, values, and interests. The obvious question follows: what are the family's rights? Another way of formulating the same question is to ask how we should balance the rights of the individual patient and those of the family when they conflict. This is the framework that virtually every medical ethicist investigating the family has accepted. As a result, the answers vary little in substance even though, at first glance, there seems to be wide disagreement. In this kind of rights-based investigation, the family usually loses to the patient.

John Hardwig advances the most radical view by advocating that we abandon our current patient-centered ethic in favor of a presumption of the equality of interests, both medical and nonmedical, of each family member. This presumption can and usually will be overridden by the patient's interests in optimal health and a longer life.[8] On some occasions, however, the family's interests may outweigh those of the patient and should receive preference. Hardwig's essay is paradigmatic in a number of ways for those which have followed. All agree that the patient is usually vulnerable and in need of advocacy and protection. Therefore, they begin with a strong presumption in favor of the patient's right to be the primary decisionmaker. However, the advance these authors make is that they do not characterize the patient's rights as a trump card. Instead, they model their arguments on a scale of justice. The patient's claims are usually weighty compared to the side of the balance on which family rights rest. On occasion, however, the interests of the patient are not very compelling while the family may have a great stake, financially or emotionally, in what course is followed. All argue that family interests should hold sway to some extent under such circumstances.

Jeffrey Blustein sums up this position when he says, "because treatment decisions often do have a dramatic impact on family members, procedures need to be devised, short of giving family members a share of decisional authority, that acknowledge the moral weight of their legitimate interests."[9] Blustein argues that patients be encouraged to include the interests of family members in thinking about choices but that the choice per se belongs to the patient. James Nelson tilts the scales slightly more in favor of the family. He argues that we should begin with a presumption that the competent patient is the decisionmaker, but acknowledge that this presumption is rebuttable by showing that family interests are sufficiently compelling to override the patient's wishes. Hardwig's position can be interpreted as virtually identical with Nelson's. These arguments are framed in terms of a conflict between the interests of the patient and those of the family. With some exceptions, most such conflicts must be settled in favor of the patient.[10] This is hardly a satisfactory outcome for these inquiries.

Hardwig's essay is, at first glance, provocative and radical because he argues that morality requires heeding family interests. Unfortunately, he asks questions of individual and group rights that must be answered in either/or terms. But it is the dissatisfaction with this kind of rights-oriented individualism that revived discussion of the family in the first place. Furthermore, it is not obvious that the role of the family in decisionmaking is exhausted by discussions of such conflicts. The profundity of the links and bonds between family members is hidden from view in these legalistic discussions of interests and rights. This failure to escape the limitations of rights-based thinking clearly emanates from the acceptance of the doctrine of informed consent. While trying to subvert individualism in medical ethics, these ethicists remain trapped by the individualism implicit in the doctrine. To overcome such individualism, informed consent will have to be rethought. We must also be clear regarding the question to which the doctrine is the answer.

THE FAMILY: WHAT'S THE QUESTION?

We can see that there is an ambiguity regarding the question medical ethicists ask about the family. Is the question, Whose interests and wishes should take precedence when those of the patient and family conflict? or What are the respective roles of the patient, family, and physician in medical decisionmaking? In other words, are we asking what to do in a particular event, such as when wishes irresolubly conflict, or are we sketching the process of decisionmaking? The question of unresolvable conflict has an initial attraction because of its clarity and practicality. Its answer is also clear. The patient's wishes and interests must take priority, but there can be exceptions. This conclusion follows from the legalistic aspect of the doctrine of informed consent. Persons are defined in terms of rights and interests and so conflicts must be resolved in such terms. Answering this question, however, does not explain the more general phenomenon of the family's place in medical decisionmaking, such as in the vast majority of cases that lack an unresolvable conflict.

We noted at the outset that informed consent is not only a legal doctrine, but also includes certain philosophical justifications. The legal doctrine is supported by philosophical notions of self-determination and the opacity of an individual's values. These notions, however, are usually considered tenets of political philosophy. That political philosophy should supply the justifications is natural because the legal notion of informed consent is, in large part, an outgrowth of the right to be free from unwanted government interference in one's affairs.[11] Political philosophy is thereby called upon to justify an essentially political doctrine. The political notions of liberty and the right to base decisions on one's private values also do important philosophical work in cases of unresolvable conflict because these are instances in which the state must adjudicate claims. However, when recourse to the conflict resolution mechanisms of the state is not necessary, these conceptions of liberty and privacy seem out of place.

Most major writers on the family in medical decisionmaking implicitly accept the political view of the person contained in the legalistic aspect of the doctrine of informed consent. The competent adult person has developed values and preferences. Informed consent involves a conference in which the physician discloses treatment options along with risks, costs, and benefits to the patient or to the patient and family. A calculation is made regarding what is in the patient's best interest or in the interest of the family unit and the treatment is thereby chosen. When illness transforms a person into a patient, his autonomy is compromised and needs to be restored. Jeffrey Blustein suggests that this is a temporary situation caused by the emotionally traumatic nature of illness and the need to cognize the situation, the treatment options, and the interests of all those affected. Thus, the family can primarily assist with the patient's "thinking" and thereby help to "restore" the patient's autonomy.[12] According to this view, the family's role when there is no unresolvable conflict is trivial and uninteresting.

In sum, certain presuppositions of the traditional legalistic vision of informed consent have caused the dialogue to focus on familial conflict and prevented the question of the family's role in medical decision-making from being addressed. These assumptions are that the person is mainly a cognitive animal in need of information and, perhaps, assistance due to impairment in mental functioning, and has a developed set of private and opaque values from which the patient's treatment preferences readily flow. These assumptions not only emphasize the legalistic aspects of the doctrine of informed consent, but lead to conceiving consent as an event. Consent takes place during a conference when information is exchanged and comprehended, and the patient makes a choice evidenced in the signing of the consent form. We see that the legalistic, event model of informed consent and its implicit notion of the person is preventing us from seeing the family in all its richness. Fortunately, as we move away from the literature on the family and examine recent scholarship on informed consent, we find resources on which to draw. Rugged individualism is not the only conception of consent in contemporary bioethics.[13]

RECONCEIVING INFORMED CONSENT

Bioethicists such as Charles Lidz,[14] Howard Brody,[15] and Ezekiel and Linda Emanuel[16] have developed models of informed consent and the physician-patient relationship that do not assume patients have a developed set of private values. Instead, they see informed consent as a process of shared decision-making in which the thinking and values of the patient and physician gradually take shape. The legalistic, event model of informed consent conceived the patient and physician as experts over their distinctly private realms with the patient reigning over his or her private values. Process models view the physician and patient as each having access to interrelated and evolving facts and values. They mutually monitor each other in order that their thinking and evaluations become transparent. Once informed consent is conceived in this manner, more integral roles for the physician and for others close to the patient are apparent. Let us illustrate this with a case.

Mrs. L was a fifty-year-old female who was transferred to this tertiary care facility from a primary care hospital. Her husband visited daily. She also had several brothers and sisters but no children. Mrs. L's recent problem concerned multiple external lacerations on her hands, chest, and groin area as well as kidney failure. These health problems are related to her long-term insulin-dependent diabetes. She had suffered from diabetes since childhood, but the complications and consequences of this illness have increased recently with a leg amputation being necessary about a year ago. Shortly thereafter, dialysis was begun.

The patient was transferred to the tertiary care facility to have her lesions biopsied for diagnostic purposes. These were open, draining, and very painful to the patient. Initial work-up ruled out vasculitis as the causal agent. Finding the source of the lesions proved difficult and the hospitalization became prolonged as other complications developed. Ms. L was in great pain and was placed on a sand bed and given a patient-controlled analgesia machine to help provide relief. Despite these measures, pain continued to be a factor in the slow process of diagnostic testing.

Mrs. L began to ask the nurses to stop dialysis. These requests began about one month into this hospitalization and continued at intervals. Each time the requests became frequent, a discussion would be held with Mrs. L, her husband, and the attending physician. In these meetings, Mr. L would often ask Mrs. L to change her mind regarding the dialysis or other tests she was resisting "for him." Each time, this request was granted by the patient after some resistance. On a couple of occasions, the patient agreed to further diagnostic work if her husband would be able to be with her through the test. The nursing staff became increasingly unnerved by the situation as Mrs. L would often continue to tell the nurses that she "really" wished to stop and "just wanted to die in peace." This particular wish was always superseded by the results of the patient-husband-physician conferences. Eventually, it seemed that the patient's husband also grew tired of the long hospital stay.

About eight weeks into her hospitalization, Mrs. L remained adamant in her treatment refusals during a conference with her husband and physician. Mr. L then agreed to accept her wishes and agreed to stay by her during her death. The physician wrote a DNR order on the chart along with orders to discontinue dialysis.

Palliative care continued to be provided. The patient died within forty-eight hours accompanied by her grieving husband.[17]

This case is likely to be reported to an ethics consultation service as involving a familial conflict. Such conflicts are supposedly what the literature on the family analyzes. Nevertheless, these analyses cannot help because a legalistic, event model of informed consent does not explain the difficulties between Mr. and Mrs. L. Any view of informed consent or the family premised upon a patient with a sturdy set of interests and values must necessarily be beside the point. Mrs. L's wishes and values are not clear or are somewhat inaccessible to her.

The legalistic view of the doctrine of informed consent tells us that a competent patient has a right to refuse treatment and therefore counsels that we call for a determination of the patient's decisionmaking capacity or competence to give consent. If the patient is competent, then we should stand by her wishes (of course, with some occasional exceptions). Competence typically requires that the patient understand the situation, base her choices on relatively stable values, and be able to communicate her wishes. Unfortunately, this means we must determine which utterances represent fleeting whims and which disclose underlying values. To verify when Mrs. L is "being herself" requires input from someone who knows her well and can place the current episode in a larger context. This role, as the verifier of the patient's competence, has been the most widely accepted role accorded the family. Nevertheless, this approach makes us nervous. Even if we discount selfish motives on the part of family members, it is difficult to know if Mrs. L really has a single set of preferences or values to be verified. Thus, we must take a different, process-oriented approach.

We can view the process of informed consent in cases like the one at hand in one of two related ways. Each emphasizes a different element of the patient's decisional capacity and undermines slightly different assumptions of the event model of informed consent. We can take a clue from event models of informed consent that emphasize the patient's cognitive nature. We then advance the suggestion that the role of the family is to assist the patient's "thinking." This approach is sometimes called the *interpretive model*[18] because the physician and family assist the patient in interpreting her values and translating them into treatment preferences. This process model allows that the patient has

relatively well-developed and stable values but stresses that they may not only be opaque to others, but can also be unclear to the patient. Thus, translating values into treatment choices is not merely logical "thinking" but is a process of self-discovery.

A more radical process model of informed consent is required in those cases, perhaps including that of Mrs. L, where the fundamental layer of necessary values is lacking and needs to be developed. This process of value development is the *deliberative model*. Which of these two process models is more applicable in a given case can be difficult to know. It is seldom clear whether we are helping a patient to uncover her values and translate them into preferences or to develop new values. Thus, these two ways of viewing the process of informed consent, two types of process models, are complementary aspects of one and the same theory of consent.

AN INTERPRETIVE PROCESS OF CONSENT: RESTORING "THINKING"

The interpretive model of consent starts from the assumption that there is a gap between the fundamental core of a human being that we call her values and her "preferences" that are relatively transient, circumstantial expressions of her personality. In many common situations, our preferences reflect no more than taste or whimsy. In choices of gravity, we wish our preferences to reflect who we are, that is, to follow from the values at our core. Sometimes people come to situations with their values and preferences already developed and in harmony. Nevertheless, to assume that this is generally the case in clinical situations is not plausible. Why think a patient has preferences applicable to situations that are rather new? Her prognosis changes, new treatment choices are presented, and the relative merits of ongoing treatments may change. Additionally, the patient gains new appreciation for various treatments as she accumulates experiential information from undergoing them. This continuous refinement of knowledge and development of preferences are important aspects of process approaches to consent.

The interpretive approach focuses on the articulation of preferences from the patient's underlying values. The patient may possess stable values, for example, love of her husband, desire to be relatively pain free, etc., but not yet know how to apply these values to particular treatment choices. Hence, as she gains experience with the treatment and refines her understanding of her illness, the choices follow. This *interpretive process* model differs from an *event* model of informed consent in two ways. First, the process model sees the family's role in restoring the patient's thinking as primarily one of providing the appropriate surrounding and context through presence and interaction. "Restoring the patient's thinking" is an experiential and interactive process of which the cognitive deduction from values to preferences is a small moment. Second, the idea that the patient's values and preferences are opaque to others while the patient has privileged access is rejected.

Interpreting our values usually involves the feedback of those close to us and often the advice of persons with professional expertise. Just as we are uncomfortable with the idea that a family member can gain access to the patient's real values and definitively say when she is being herself, so too there is something unrealistic in thinking that the patient has private and privileged access to her values. The feedback of others is necessary to one's reality testing and the construction of an interpersonal narrative that forms the framework for choices. Thus, the process of decisionmaking is interpretive in nature.

Although Blustein recognized the need for family to help patients with their thinking, we see that a process model of consent goes beyond this in making "thinking" a metaphor. Though the patient may be quite capable of a syllogistic deduction of treatment choices from her values, illness somehow distances her from her identity and causes a loss of touch with her everyday values. Family members do not merely help the patient to clarify his or her thinking. They take part in the patient's narrative self-discovery that helps her to reconnect with her values and give them meaning as expressed in choices. This self-discovery is not prior to the event of giving consent, but, in a sense, is the process of informed consent.

Our initial hope in cases like Mrs. L's is that matters unfold as the interpretive model suggests: a changing prognosis and new treatment options will interact over time with a relatively stable set of values to produce rational treatment preferences. Values, however, do not always prove to be the kind of unchanging thing that can serve as such an Archimedean point. Mrs. L's values or vision of the good may not be sufficiently developed to make the choices confronting her. In other words, her values are also in process. The patient is not only uncovering values; she is also creating them. For instance, one may never have developed values or

virtues relating to extreme pain or never needed to develop more than the sketchiest concept of personal dignity. Perhaps, such dispositions and character traits exist but are undergoing radical shifts. If so, the justification for family involvement becomes all the clearer. When values must be constructed, this construction process is unlikely to be an individual affair.

A DELIBERATIVE PROCESS OF CONSENT: DEVELOPING VALUES

Ezekiel and Linda Emanuel explore the process of choosing oneself and one's values, that is, the deliberative model of physician-patient encounters.[19] In this model, the physician assists the patient by elucidating the values embodied in the different treatment options. Because the patient's values are not fixed, the physician is free, even obligated, to advocate certain values. He is helping to shape the patient's values through his recommendations. The Emanuels do not mention the family in this process, but the justification for familial involvement flows from the same sources. Because we discover our values in dialogue with those closest to us, the family is naturally an integral part of this process. In Mrs. L's encounter with her physician and husband, she is coming to choose her values over time.

If we assume that values do not simply emanate from some ineffable core within us but take shape through interaction with our environment, the family is a natural part of this process. Much of our youth is spent internalizing the values of close others. In adult life our values usually are not acquired through mere passive internalization, but this process has a dialectical character. Furthermore, we seldom decide our values in a single, irrevocable act of will. Instead, values must become sturdy and defined if they are to form the foundation for our preferences. They must take shape and concretize. By "trying out" expressions of these developing values with close others, they begin to take shape and become firm. There is still a further reason for including the family. As in Mrs. L's case, these values are often about them. In part, the values Mrs. L is developing or re-ranking are about her love for and relationship to her husband. To truly know whether she has arrived at the proper ordering may require testing them together with him. Similarly, his values may also be developing and changing, and these values are about her.

In an ongoing dialogue between intimates, there will be a mutual discovery and shaping of values. In the particular case at hand, Mr. L may simply have the more stable values, or his are challenged less by the present situation. For whatever reason, he does not seem to experience the vacillation that his wife undergoes. This is merely the fact of this case. Nevertheless, a family member, especially one who is often the patient's primary caregiver, may undergo a process of self-discovery and adoption of a new value structure in the same way that patients often do. In this particular case, Mr. L eventually tires from the prolonged course and then supports his wife's treatment refusal. We do not know whether this is adapting his same long-held values to a changing situation (the interpretive model) or a fundamental reordering of priorities (the deliberative model). Either way, informed consent is a process of mutual self-discovery. Family does not simply provide the context for the patient's thinking in the way a familiar object would. In the process of decisionmaking, the context is also dynamic.

In sum, we see that process models of informed consent are comfortable with active roles for physicians and families in the medical decisionmaking process. This comfort with collaborative decisionmaking grows from the assumption that values are not the hidden and privileged property of the individual. They take shape publicly, and when they are opaque or absent their discovery or construction is also a communal process. Nevertheless, several questions may trouble us. On what basis might the physician legitimately advocate certain values? Should the physician advocate these values only to the patient or also to the family since the family's values are also in process? Is the physician simply one more person in the process of informed consent or does he occupy a particular role in the relationship between the patient and family? In other words, the process models of informed consent suggest active roles for the physician and family and we must more clearly define and circumscribe these roles. In cases like the one at hand, these are not abstract questions. There is something about Mr. L's behavior that makes us uneasy and raises the question of the physician's obligation to the patient and to him.

RECONCEIVING THE ROLES OF THE PHYSICIAN AND FAMILY

The physician's role requires justification for two reasons. First, the physician is being characterized as an advocate of certain values, and we must provide appropriate content and reasons for this advocacy. Second, we have allowed a much greater role for the family,

and we need a counter-weight to prevent the family's role from becoming a coercive one. We must be careful to avoid justifying unbridled paternalism in the name of family values. Ezekiel and Linda Emanuel propose that the physician's advocacy is legitimate because she only advocates health-related values. Certain of these are deemed more worthy than others. It is easy to imagine that health is more worthwhile than sickness, and therefore good eating, hygiene, and exercise habits can uncontroversially be advocated. But what should the physician advocate in Mrs. L's case? How can the doctor avoid his professional bias to treat this patient as long as there is a medical treatment at hand? Perhaps we can take a cue from the literature on patient competency and suggest a sliding scale or risk-related standard of advocacy.[20]

In assessing patient capacity to give informed consent, the standard of competence is based upon the risks and benefits of a proposed course of treatment. When patients wish to consent to a treatment that poses few risks and whose benefits are considerable and clear, they do not need great comprehension of the situation. Mere awareness will justify allowing the patient to make this decision. However, to refuse this same treatment, especially if the refusal will place the patient in great jeopardy, we need to be sure the patient truly appreciates the ramifications of her choice. As the risks of a treatment increase and the benefits become more dubious, one again relaxes the standard of competence needed to refuse. The physician need only require that the patient understands what she is being told. This same schema may be transposed upon the present case. Instead of focusing on the patient's cognitive capacity, we can apply this scale to the relative stability of her values. For instance, to refuse a clearly beneficial treatment that poses few burdens, the decision must represent rather stable values of the patient. If the refusal does not, the physician is justified in more strenuously advocating for the treatment. Thus, by advocating "health-related values only," we are talking about common notions of clear benefits to health. When such benefits are not so clear, advocacy recedes. This same schema can guide the physician in deciding how intense to allow the family's persuasive efforts to become.

Mrs. L's case reflects this sliding-scale model of decisionmaking. Early in the patient's treatment course, it was thought that diagnostic work would reveal the cause of her lesions. The caregivers hoped that once the etiology was revealed, the lesions could be treated and the patient restored to a more comfortable state. Refusals of treatment and diagnostic work at that point would have run counter to a commonsense notion of a risk/benefit calculation. Thus, the physician was justified in further investigating the strength of the patient's views and whether this refusal was "in character," that is, reflective of relatively stable values. In this kind of investigation, the family can be helpful. If the refusal was firm enough to stand up to the influence of the physician and husband, of course, the refusal should have been honored. But it was not.

As the course of diagnostic work and treatment grew longer, the expected benefits of the medical interventions declined in value. At the same time, the persistence of Mrs. L's requests to stop dialysis indicated that this desire reflected a new value that was becoming stable or that she was interpreting this treatment refusal as indicative of her long-held values. Thus, the exertion of influence to persuade the patient differently became less and less justified. Fortunately, the influencing family member also came to discover and hold the same values or same reinterpretation of old values as the patient. He engaged in the process of mutual self-discovery with her. Had Mr. L failed to evolve in the way Mrs. L did, the sliding-scale approach would have justified the physician's influencing Mr. L to acquiesce to his wife's wishes and persuading Mr. L to be supportive of her desires in the conferences. If this effort had failed, the physician should have sought formal institutional mechanisms to protect the patient from her husband's influence. In other words, although Mr. L's behavior might have remained the same, the changing clinical situation and the development of stable wishes or values in the patient meant that his persistence would no longer be seen as influence, but as coercion.

The physician remains the patient advocate. He tries to relieve the patient's pain and suffering and restore her to health. To actually determine the means of doing this, and to be sure that such means do not violate the patient's autonomy, the physician must engage in the process of informed consent with the patient. In some cases, the family will provide assistance merely by verifying the patient's competence by vouching for the stability of the patient's values and wishes. In other cases, these values may be below the surface and need to emerge to meet the weighty challenges posed by the illness and choices that must be made. The family provides a kind of personal and social context for the exploration of the meaning of values for the present situation. Sometimes, however, the situation requires that new values be chosen or developed because there are none available that adequately address the changing situation. In these situations, the physician is truly "treating the family" because they are the soil out of which the patient's values and preferences grow.

As we have noted, the physician must be careful to monitor the emergence of such values in both the patient and family and to assess their relative stability. In doing this, he is doing no more than has traditionally been seen as assessing competence to give informed consent. In these assessments, he must muddle through with his professional and commonsense evaluations of the merit of proposed treatments and the rationality of choices that are made. Ultimately, he must be willing to engage in a process that strains the limits of his clinical judgment.

RECONCEIVING THE FAMILY

Clinicians may be running well ahead of medical ethicists in dealing with families. This is a surprising situation for bioethics because of clinicians' initial resistance to the development of informed consent procedures. However, when it comes to the role of the family in medical decisionmaking, ethicists have fallen prey to "either/or" thinking; for example, the patient's wishes versus the family's.

Bioethicists argue that either the patient must make the decision or the family must make it. This disjunction is resolved in the patient's favor, relegating the family to an after-thought in the process. This argument is sound but limited in its range of application. Arguments that affirm patient rights are important mainly in cases in which the patient has developed and stable views. In such cases of unresolvable conflict between patient and family, a legalistic, event model of consent is appropriate. In the cases that demand more profound self-discovery, the family should be described in a more nuanced manner.

When the values, wishes, preferences, and thoughts of the persons involved are in transformation, only the family truly can be said to exist. The previously existing individuals have metaphorically dissolved into this group due to crisis—but also are in the process of emerging from the unit with developed and stable values. In other words, they will again become individuals. Then, communitarian formulations should recede as interests and rights can be identified and become weightier considerations. This process of vacillation between identity and difference makes the family a metaphysically mysterious entity that has eluded capture by legalistic models. In sum, I am advocating that we view the development of patient autonomy as the goal of the process of informed consent rather than as something given or in need of restoration. The family, as those who have been reciprocal participants in the attainment of the patient's personhood,[21] have a natural place in the ongoing process.

REFERENCES

1. See The President's Commission for the Study of Ethical Problems in Biomedical and Behavioral Research, *Deciding to Forego Life-Sustaining Treatment* (Washington, D.C.: U.S. Government Printing Office, 1983), p. 127; Allen E. Buchanan and Dan W. Brock, *Deciding for Others: The Ethics of Surrogate Decision Making* (New York: Cambridge University Press, 1989), p. 136.

2. John Hardwig, "What about the Family?" *Hastings Center Report* 20, no. 2 (1990): 5–10.

3. Alan Meisel, "The Legal Consensus about Forgoing Life-Sustaining Treatment: Its Status and Prospects," *Kennedy Institute of Ethics Journal* 2, no. 4 (1992): 309–45, at 319.

4. Ruth R. Faden and Tom L Beauchamp, *A History and Theory of Informed Consent* (New York: Oxford University Press, 1986), p. 274.

5. Faden and Beauchamp, *A History and Theory of Informed Consent*, p. 123.

6. Edmund G. Pellegrino and David Thomasma, *The Virtues in Medical Practice* (New York: Oxford University Press, 1993), p. 74.

7. James Lindemann Nelson, "Taking Families Seriously," *Hastings Center Report* 22, no. 4 (1992): 6–12, at 7.

8. Hardwig, "What about the Family?" p. 7.

9. Jeffrey Blustein, "The Family in Medical Decisionmaking," *Hastings Center Report* 23, no. 3 (1993): 6–13, at 11.

10. See also, Carson Strong, "Patients Should Not Always Come First in Treatment Decisions, *Journal of Clinical Ethics* 4, no. 1 (1993): 63–65, 75.

11. Faden and Beauchamp, *A History and Theory of Informed Consent*, p. 40.

12. Blustein, "The Family in Medical Decisionmaking," p. 12.

13. Thomas A. Mappes and Jane S. Zembaty, "Patient Choices, Family Interests, and Physician Obligations," *Kennedy Institute of Ethics Journal* 4, no. 1(1994): 27–46, at 31.

14. Charles W. Lidz, Paul S. Appelbaum, and Alan Meisel, "Two Models of Implementing Informed Consent," *Archives of Internal Medicine* 148 (1988): 1385–89.

15. Howard Brody, "Transparency: Informed Consent in Primary Care," *Hastings Center Report* 19, no. 5 (1989): 5–9.

16. Ezekiel J. Emanuel and Linda L. Emanuel, "Four Models of the Physician-Patient Relationship," *JAMA* 267 (1992): 2221–26.

17. Adapted from Mark G. Kuczewski and Rosa Lynn Pinkus, eds., *An Ethics Casebook for Community Hospitals* (unpublished manuscript).

18. Emanuel and Emanuel, "Four Models," p. 2221.

19. Emanuel and Emanuel, "Four Models," p. 2222.

20. For detailed discussion of the sliding-scale model or risk-related standards of competence see two articles by James F. Drane, "Competency to Give Informed Consent," *JAMA* 252, (1984): 925–27, and "The Many Faces of Competency," *Hastings Center Report* 15, no. 2 (1985): 17–21, as well as Buchanan and Brock, *Deciding for Others*, pp. 47–59.

21. For a detailed account of this process and how it can be extended to decisionmaking for the incompetent patient, see Mark G. Kuczewski, "Whose Will Is It, Anyway? A Discussion of Advance Directives, Personal Identity, and Consensus in Medical Ethics," *Bioethics* 8, no. 1 (1994): 27–48.

Families, Patients, and Physicians in Medical Decisionmaking: A Pakistani Perspective

Farhat Moazam

After training and practicing as a physician in the United States for many years, I accepted an academic position at a medical university in Pakistan. One of my first experiences there was to tell two brothers sitting across the desk from me that all investigations indicated their elderly father had widespread metastatic cancer, and therefore not long to live. The patient, who lived with the oldest son and his family, was not present during this conversation, although an unmarried daughter, a daughter-in-law, and an adult grandson were. After listening attentively to what I had to say, and obviously upset at this news, one of the sons said, "We do not want him to know that he has cancer. How long he lives is in the hands of God in any case, and it is not right to make my father lose hope while

he is so ill." He then added, "Doctor *Sahib*, tell us what we should do next. You know best. You are not just our doctor, you are like our mother."

In these words lies the essence of decisionmaking when illness strikes a member of the family in Pakistan. It is the family rather than the patient who takes center stage in this process. In the case of a conscious patient, the family and physician will generally protect the patient from the anxiety and distress associated with the knowledge of impending death. This is done by not disclosing the diagnosis or disclosing it in ambiguous terms. The "doctor sahib," (*sahib* has an Arabic root meaning "lord") remains the authority in matters relating to disease and medical interventions. She or he is often symbolically inducted into the family and is expected to direct rather than just facilitate medical management. In the final analysis, however, God, not man, controls life and death.

This model, in which religion and the extended family play a primary role in matters dealing with illnesses, particularly terminal illnesses, is shared by many Eastern cultures, but contrasts significantly with the situation prevalent in many western countries. In secular Western societies, patient autonomy is generally accepted as the cornerstone of medical ethics when it comes to choices involving medical care and end of life decisions. The competent patient is considered an autonomous and rational agent who is sovereign over her fate and the locus for all choices regarding therapeutic interventions[1]—witness the fact that by 1991 more than forty states in the U.S. had enacted "living will" statutes that allow competent people to refuse therapeutic measures in the event of terminal illness even if they are no longer competent, and that trump opinions of family members and physicians. In that year also the federal Patient Self-determination Act went into effect, requiring that all adult patients admitted to a hospital be told of their right to formulate an advance directive.[2]

The principle of autonomy has also been extended to incompetent patients who do not have advance directives through court rulings and the legislature.[3] The substituted judgment standard works on the premise that the personal autonomy of the once competent patient must be extended to her current state of incompetency, with the surrogate functioning as an instrument to determine what the patient would have wished done under the circumstances, if he or she were still competent.

The autonomy model is not without critics, however, especially in a pluralistic society. Joseph Carrese and Lorna Rhodes, for example, have noted that many Navajo consider advance care planning to violate their traditional values.[4] Nor is the exclusion of families from decisionmaking universally valued. Empirical research by Leslie Blackhall and colleagues has shown that Korean and Mexican Americans, among others in the United States, feel that families—not patients—should hear a terminal diagnosis and be the primary decisionmakers.[5]

Undoubtedly the realities of American society, an amalgam of people from many different ethnic groups, have helped bring such issues to the forefront. In recent years, medical, bioethical, and legal literature has begun to address the need for families to have a greater role in medical decisionmaking.[6] A number of court decisions and legislative actions in the last decade have moved toward giving families greater decisional authority in the area of disputes about terminal care as well.[7] More importantly, almost 80 percent of the world's population resides outside North America and Western Europe. For many, families play a major if not primary role in therapeutic decisions, including end of life situations.

Medical decisionmaking in Pakistan offers interesting contrasts to secular societies. Although the country came into being as an independent nation in 1947, its people have longstanding cultural traditions and religious beliefs that place the family at the center of one's existence. Lives are spent within extended families in which power structures are clearly defined. Familial relationships are not merely horizontal but also vertical across three or more generations. In such societies, Arthur Kleinman notes, the individual is viewed as "sociocentrically enmeshed in inextricable social bonds, ties that make interpersonal processes the source of vital decisions."[8] In Pakistan, family-centered decisionmaking works in tandem with an active, directive role assumed by the physician that stresses the principles of beneficence and nonmaleficence rather than patient autonomy. In this deeply religious society, morality is rooted primarily in what is perceived as the religious obligations of the family and the physician toward the patient rather than stemming from a secular, reason-based philosophy that emphasizes the legal rights of individuals.

The following reflections on the interconnectedness of the patient and the family, the dominant role of the physician, and the impact of religious beliefs and socioeconomic realities on medical decisionmaking flow from my experience of having practiced both in the United States and, for more than a decade, in Pakistan.

FAMILIES: TIES THAT BIND

The family is the fundamental unit of society in Pakistan, a country with over 130 million people. Almost 65 percent of the population is rural, and 95 percent of the citizens are Muslims. In contrast to the pluralistic society of the United States, Pakistan offers a fairly homogenous milieu insofar as values and sociocultural norms are concerned. Religious belief plays a central role in the life of men and women from all social strata and is a major influence on all public and private activities. Historically, Islamic teachings have regarded all fields of human activity as coming under the umbrella of religion. There is no separation of state and religion, and no activity is considered purely secular in the life of a Muslim.[9] Moral authority and a sense of right and wrong are derived from religious tenets.

Although the functioning of the judiciary is based on the British legal system, Article 198 of the Constitution of the Islamic Republic of Pakistan states that no law shall be enacted that is considered "repugnant" to the injunctions of Islam.[10] Islam does not recognize a central church or religious priesthood and ministries. Direction is sought through the *Quran*, the Muslim holy book considered to be the Word of God, and the Traditions, *Sunna*, of the Prophet Muhammad. These sources form the basis of Islamic law, the *Shari'a*, that guides all private and public conduct, and is similar in many ways to the Jewish *Halakhah*. If no direct answer to a moral or ethical dilemma in personal life can be gleaned through the *Shari'a*, "subordinate sources," in the form of opinions from Muslim scholars or jurists, are sought.

For Muslims, religion defines the role of the individual, the family, and the physician in life passages including birth, illness, and death. It frames familial and filial responsibilities, obligations of physicians, decisions that involve end of life situations, and how death itself is to be viewed. This remains a seminal difference from many Western societies, in which moral direction for these events is usually sought through human reason, a concept rooted in the secular philosophy of Kant and Mill. Whereas rationalism fuels the ethical and legal discourse of human relationships in secular societies, in Pakistan religion and an interpretation of divine injunctions are the driving forces.

People generally live together in extended families, and it is not uncommon to have three generations living under one roof or in close proximity to each other. It is not unusual for children, particularly sons, to continue to live with their parents following marriage, leading to strong vertical, intergenerational relationships. Personal identity takes second place to the collective family identity and consciousness. Family obligations and harmonious living are considered moral imperatives, second in importance only to submission to the will of God. Discourses that revolve around the rights of individual members in a family, including what one owes to another or the issue of rights between parents and their children, are alien.[11] Mark Kuczewski's observation, while discussing the family's role in decisionmaking in the United States, that medical ethics has rediscovered the family, would be incomprehensible to most Pakistanis.[12] In Pakistan, for the vast majority of the population, you *are* your family, and your family is you.

Family obligations are considered a moral injunction from God. Aging parents in particular are to be treated with patience and humility.[13] The Prophet said, the best beloved of God is one who loves his family the most.[14] Increasing wisdom is attributed to advancement in years and the gray-haired elders of a family are to be respected and obeyed. Relationships and connectedness are defined through mutual trust, care, and obligations rather than competing rights of individual members. This forms the paradigm for the way humans must relate to one another within a family, not only in life but also when death is at hand. Concerns regarding erosion of the patient's autonomy and subordination of the patient's interest to competing interests of other members in the family would not resonate well in the social context of Pakistan.[15] A legal concept of advance directives and living wills by an individual regarding her end of life care is alien to Pakistani cultural norms.

Family members generally avoid disclosure of terminal diseases like cancer to patients to avoid burdening them further and to allow dying in peace. This is perceived as a form of caring, particularly toward elderly family members. Death with dignity, oft repeated in English literature, is seldom raised as an issue in Pakistan. Members of the extended family with whom the patient resides generally undertake decisions regarding terminal care for both competent and incompetent patients. Nursing homes for those who are aged, terminally ill, or incompetent are unknown in Pakistan; such individuals are cared for at home by the family. Although affluent families may hire nurses for home care of a family member who is ill, caregiving in most cases is a shared responsibility of the female members of the extended family. These may include a wife, unmarried daughters, or daughters-in-law. As families are both hierarchical and patrilineal, the oldest male member plays a pivotal role in major decisions, with a varying degree of input from the patient and other family members.

The physician is often adopted into the family unit by being referred to as mother, father, or older sibling. After being addressed by pediatric patients in the United States as Doctor for many years, it was a novel experience for me when children in my clinic in Pakistan were instructed to call me Aunty or Doctor Aunty. Male physicians are referred to as uncles. Parents and even grandparents accompanying the child, while conversing with me, often expressed their respect by referring to me as being like a mother or an older sister to them. It is interesting that in this strongly patriarchal society, the mother is awarded a position of respect that is superior to all other relationships. This is based on the Prophet having said that *janat* (paradise) lies under the feet of a mother. Therefore, equating a female physician with a mother is indicative of reverence and can confer an incredible degree of authority.

The phenomenon of placing a health care professional in the role of a family member has received some attention in psychosocial literature emanating from Pakistan. Riffat Zaman, an American-trained psychologist, notes that the cultural pattern is generally one in which one confides in and trusts family members rather than strangers.[16] Thus even when the therapist is a stranger to begin with, the patient eventually begins to see the therapist in the role of a family member. In her opinion, Pakistani patients will often feel more comfortable seeking therapy from someone known to them or their family rather than a stranger. Similarly, I believe that awarding physicians an adoptive kinship reflects a collectivistic culture (as opposed to one that is individualistic) that experiences life primarily as a mosaic of interdependent family relationships that extend from the cradle to the grave.

Within the extended family, relationships are generally well defined based on gender and age. From childhood, members are taught to respect authority, a characteristic that has also been observed in other non-Western cultures.[17] In Pakistan, according to Zaman, help is usually sought from an authority figure within the family, usually a parent or older sibling, who is expected to be not only supportive and facilitative, but also directive in the advice given.[18] This is construed as a sign of caring rather than as an intrusive act. Zaman, when comparing her experience as a psychotherapist in the United States to that in Pakistan, states that the "idealized neutrality" of the therapist in the West does not hold up well in such a culture. According to her, in Pakistan, at the end of a session patients wait expectantly for the therapist to provide a "solution on which they should or would act."

In my own practice I often sensed a prototype of a parent-child interaction, with many families expecting me to play the role of an "elder." In the United States I was sometimes asked by a patient, "What would you do if you were in my place?" In Pakistan this is more likely to be phrased "What do you think I should do?" Interaction with a physician thus takes the form of recourse to an authority figure and not merely a consultation with a medical expert.

THE PHYSICIAN: AN INSTRUMENT OF GOD

In Pakistan, the physician is held in high esteem by a society that respects authority and condones hierarchical systems. This is also true of other oriental societies, such as Japan.[19] In Pakistan, however, reverence and respect toward physicians is due not only to their knowledge and scientific expertise but also to the historical position accorded the art and science of medicine in Islam. The privileged position of physicians is derived through a historical understanding of the healer as an instrument of divine mercy. This became clear to me through several personal experiences caring for patients in Pakistan.

One was a conversation I had with the father of a frail newborn in the neonatal intensive care unit. The baby was critically ill and close to death. He had a perforated intestine, but there was a small chance that surgical intervention might save his life. The father interrupted my explanation—a product of my own "Western" education in the necessity for seeking the decisionmaker's informed consent—of the patient's disease and the nature and risks of the surgery we were contemplating. He told me that I did not need his permission because while he believed in God up there (he pointed to the sky), here on earth he held the same trust in me. In effect, he was signifying to me that just as he could not question God's wisdom and His divine plans, when it came to decisions regarding corporal matters of his ill child he put the same faith in me, the physician. Another instance was my conversation with a grateful mother taking her child home after a long hospitalization and several surgical procedures. After thanking me for my surgical, scientific expertise, she added a caveat. It was clear, she said, that I was a good doctor because God had put *shifa* (the power of healing) in my hands. Again, I was perceived as having a kind of connection with God in my role as a physician.

According to al-Ruhavi, a famous Muslim physician of the ninth century, a physician "imitates the acts of God as much as he can." One of the Arabic words for a physician is *Hakim*. It means one who has knowledge and wisdom and is also a name for God.[20] According to a Muslim scholar of the fourteenth century, "after performing God's worship and the basic duties of Islam, there is no greater service to God than to treat patients."[21] In Islam, many scholars have historically assigned a high religious priority to medicine, second only to ritual worship. Al-Ghazali, an eleventh century Muslim theologian and philosopher, considered the profession of medicine to be a *fard-ki-faya*, collective duty, of Muslims, in which some members must assume this religious responsibility for the good of the community.[22]

Under the auspices of the Islamic Organization of Medical Sciences, a conference on Islamic medicine was held in Kuwait in 1981 to mark the beginning of the fifteenth Islamic century.[23] Participants, consisting of physicians and theologians of Muslim countries, met with a view that there was a need to integrate Islamic medical ethics with modern medicine. The *Quran* and *Sunna* were used as the basis for arriving at a consensus. The conference ended with the formulation of a detailed Islamic Code of Medical Ethics that described the practice of medicine as "an act of worship" and the physician as an "instrument of God."[24] This reinforces the belief that respect and reverence for the physician are due not only for her scientific knowledge and expertise but also for her religious responsibility, a striking contrast to a secular understanding of the physician as a well-trained expert who provides a service to consumers and clients in a contractual relationship.

There are strong religious prohibitions in Islam against physician-assisted suicide or direct actions that hasten death. This is related to a Quranic verse that for one who takes a life it is "as if he killed all humankind."[25] The language of the Islamic Code of Medical Ethics is one of obligations and duties of the physician with a lesser focus on the rights of the patient. The code states that "it is the process of life that the doctor aims to maintain and not the process of dying," and prohibits the physician from taking any "positive measure to terminate the patient's life." It forbids ending the life of a patient "even when motivated by mercy." The issue of a patient's right to request assistance or take steps to end his or her life is therefore not an option in Islam.

The code mentions that physicians must obtain consent from patients. However, when urgent intervention is required "to save life" the physician is stated to be morally obligated to proceed with what he or she believes is essential. This is based on a rule by Muslim jurists that "necessities override prohibitions."[26] Among many Muslim physicians this is applied in instances when saving a life may require medical intervention without consent from the patient. Pakistani physicians will also usually turn to family members for consent when a patient is reluctant to accept an intervention that is considered essential to save his or her life. For example, an anxious, elderly woman with congestive heart failure needed an urgent coronary bypass, but developed dangerous arrhythmias each time the issue of this major surgery was broached with her. Following a discussion with her son, with whom she lived, the consent for the surgery was obtained from him. The patient was merely informed that the surgeon needed to do "a test," and the surgery was undertaken uneventfully. Such collusion between the family and the physician would have been ethically and legally problematic in many Western societies. In this case, at the time of discharge, the patient, having been informed of the subterfuge following her recovery from surgery, warmly thanked the surgeon for proceeding with the necessary intervention and saw her son's decision to assume responsibility for consenting on her behalf as an act of filial love.

Although family members are taken into confidence, physicians in Pakistan generally use substantial discretion when it comes to disclosing a grave prognosis or terminal illness to the patient. In the absence of a legal requirement or a tradition of living wills, physicians rarely disclose terminal disease to the patient or often do so in ambiguous terms. Portions of the Islamic Code of Medical Ethics dealing with the issue of disclosure state that the patient has "a right" to know about his illness, but that the physician's "way of answering should be tailored to the particular patient in question." The physician is advised to find "suitable vocabulary" depending on the situation and delete "frightening nomenclature." If necessary, "coinage of new names, expressions or descriptions" is suggested. This is very much the case in Pakistan, where physicians tend to interpret informed consent contextually, tailoring the extent, time, and nature of disclosure based on their and the family's belief as to what and how much the patient should be told.

Avoiding full disclosure of terminal disease and using ambiguous terminology has also been reported from other societies, particularly in regard to cancer. In an international survey of the attitude of physicians in revealing the diagnosis of cancer to patients, fewer than 40 percent of oncologists from Africa, Hungary, Japan, Portugal, Italy, and Spain were reported as using the word *cancer* when talking to patients.[27] Commonly substituted words included "growth," "tumor," "mass," etc. Although recent studies, particularly in Japan, indicate a trend toward greater acceptance of revealing the true diagnosis to the patient, a reluctance for full disclosure is still not uncommon in many cultures. The 1995 survey by Carrese and Rhodes reported a strong Navajo cultural belief that presenting such information to patients is detrimental to their health and welfare— "negative words" could hurt the patient.[28]

In Pakistan, reluctance to reveal the diagnosis of terminal disease appears to be largely based on the family's concern to protect the patient from additional distress. In my experience, at times this mirrored a cultural reluctance on the part of some patients to learn all the facts even when they suspected a grim prognosis. Since Muslims believe in a divinely predestined time of death, which no human has the power to alter, discussions regarding the duration of remaining life are seen as meaningless.

RELIGIOUS BELIEFS AND CONCEPTS OF DEATH

A few governmental and many private health care institutions in the country now offer tertiary level medical and surgical interventions, including open-heart surgery, major joint replacements, in vitro fertilization, and neonatal surgical interventions. Although poverty and lack of third-party payers limit access to private institutions, government-run health services are heavily subsidized and available to the general population. Life-prolonging measures in the event of terminal illnesses are beginning to gain ground, particularly in urbanized parts of the country, through progressive importation of scientific technology and increasing numbers of Western-trained physicians. Despite the secular and scientific nature of medical science, religious beliefs continue to shape how patients and educated families perceive terminal disease and impending death. Death, when it occurs, is generally considered to be through divine ordinance and not necessarily a failure of science. Malpractice suits against physicians and hospitals do occur, but the cases are few and far between due to a legal system that is not conducive to this form of litigation.

There is a strong belief that life is merely one stage of human existence and that death can occur only at a divinely appointed hour. Following physical death, humans are believed to return to God and a spiritual life.[29] The focus for a patient and her family when critical illness strikes is often not so much on a fear of death but rather on preparation for the "next" life through worship and prayer. A conversation with the grieving father of a dying five-year-old boy demonstrated to me the role of religious faith in making sense of even the tragic deaths of children. Despite radical surgery and chemotherapy for a renal tumor, the child's cancer had spread rapidly. The parents had maintained a vigil at their son's bedside for days as the battle to save his life was slowly lost. With tears in his eyes, the father (a lawyer) told me it seemed that God had ordained just so many days on earth for his son, and expressed his belief that medical science could never defeat death. Human intellect could not comprehend God's plans or question His will. Thus medical science and technology are accepted as having limits, and death is seen as the will of God.

The conversation among patients, families, and often the most "scientifically" trained physicians is usually peppered with references to the will of *Allah* and His control of events on earth. While transmitting news of a successfully performed surgical procedure that is expected to have a good outcome, a surgeon will invariably add *inshallah*, "if God wills." A family reporting that the patient is recovering well from an extensive medical intervention will always remember to end this news with *mashallah*, "with the grace of God" or *subhanallah*, "praise be to God."

Hospitals with technology that can extend the life of those who are terminally ill are not yet as widely available in Pakistan as in the industrialized world, and most patients die at home amidst their families. The final hours are spent in prayers and recitation of the Quran, activities in which all members of the extended family and close friends participate. Whether the relentless march of science in prolonging life and postponing death in intensive care units and a greater accessibility of this technology in Pakistan over time will change the prevalent attitude toward life and death remains to be seen.

ECONOMICS AND FAMILY DECISIONMAKING

Despite a small affluent sector, in Pakistan the average per capita income is approximately $430. (The 1997 Encarta lists this figure as $19,000 for the United States.) Health care—often not the best—is provided free in overcrowded government-run clinics and hospitals, but patients usually pay cash for medications as well as a fee for specialized investigations. There are no third-party payers and few health insurance schemes in the private and public sectors. Private hospitals, with a better standard of care, sometimes maintain a budget for the treatment of the indigent, but primarily run on a system of fee for service.

Poor and middle class family units often consist of three-generation households with one or more breadwinners who pool their resources for the extended family. Familial obligations, particularly to aging parents and the care of several children in the household, can have serious financial implications for the family in case of protracted illness of any one member. In his analysis of the decisionmaking process in Japan, Michael Fetters uses the term "family autonomy" to refer to the societal norm for dealing with medical issues.[30] In his opinion, although physician paternalism characterizes patient-physician relationships in Japan, the family, particularly the male head of the household, forms the locus for decisionmaking. By necessity, decisions must take into consideration the financial survival of the family rather than preferentially emphasize any one member's rights in isolation. The same is often painfully evident in Pakistan, a much less affluent society than Japan, where there are no public financial aid programs to cover health costs in the case of protracted or life-threatening illnesses. Such situations can be morally troubling and a source of considerable anguish for physicians, who believe that professional and moral obligations to provide medical care should be based on need rather than an ability to pay.

I was faced with such a situation when a three-year-old girl was brought to the emergency room severely dehydrated from prolonged diarrhea that had been refractory to treatment by a general practitioner. Her only chance for survival, I believed, was through admission and parenteral hydration. The grandmother and father accompanying her refused admission, requesting instead a prescription for medications that could be given to her at home. The father was a tailor, the sole breadwinner in a family with six children and two elderly grandparents. Due to a festival later that week he had a large number of requests to stitch clothes and thus an opportunity to earn much needed money. The entire family, including the children, were needed at home to cope with the additional work. Admitting the child to the hospital at this point would not only be an added expense, but would also reduce the manpower for work as one family member would have to stay with the child in the hospital. When I insisted on the admission, the grandmother pointed out to me that while my concern as a physician was for this one child, the family had another five at home who needed food and clothing.

This case presents a stark example of the socioeconomic realities in Pakistan that force families with limited resources to make distressing choices and leave physicians in a moral quandary. The survival of the entire family unit superceding the interest of an individual member is an extreme example of family autonomy and a form of distributive justice at the micro level. In countries with effective social services and government financial aid programs this degree of family autonomy would perhaps not arise. In Pakistan,

it remains a daily reality for families and health care professionals.

On another occasion I was asked to consult on a sixteen-year-old boy with Down syndrome who was left a quadriplegic due to cervical spine subluxation. All surgical attempts to stabilize his spine had failed and the progressive and complete paralysis of his respiratory muscles now made him ventilator dependent. He was unable to breathe without mechanical support, but remained awake and fully conscious. Prior to this event he had lived in a remote village with his extended, middle class family composed of twelve people. The family, very fond of their youngest member, had pooled resources to bring the patient to the private, tertiary care, university hospital in the city hoping for a cure. During the subsequent two months of hospitalization, the family sold their only car and part of their land to help defray the cost. They were now not in a position to pay any more. A brother, one of the family breadwinners, had lost his job because he would not leave the patient alone in the unfamiliar surroundings of the hospital. After two months in the hospital, the life of the patient was evidently pitted against the survival of his entire family. Distressed at what he saw as prolonged suffering on the part of the patient, the brother told me that if they had known of this outcome, they would never have brought him to this hospital with its "machines and specialists" and his brother "would have died at home in peace."

In Pakistan and other developing countries, skilled physicians and surgeons are no longer difficult to find. State of the art technology is beginning to take root in the public and private sectors. The opportunities for prolonging life are on the rise, but there are few support services outside hospitals and the associated increase in health care costs can bring with it devastating financial and emotional burdens for many families. The issue of arriving at a fair distribution of health care services in the face of limited resources is becoming a vexing one for even affluent countries. Recently, it has been suggested by some that in "futile" cases at least (with the admitted difficulty in agreeing on the definition of futility), it may be morally justifiable to give family interests and the issue of distributive justice decisive weight over the interests of the individual.[31] But the circumstances in impoverished countries like Pakistan can lead to even more intensely troubling dilemmas for physicians. Patients like the two I have described, who do not fit even the broadest definition of "medical" futility, can raise wrenching issues about which is the morally correct choice—or indeed, whether a morally correct choice exists at all.

FINDING A MIDDLE GROUND

In recent years, a narrow focus on patient autonomy has been criticized as being noncontextual and based on an abstract concept that the individual is isolated and disconnected from the many relationships within which he or she actually exists. The Pakistani family-centered model of decisionmaking, in contrast, works on the premise that the family exists in mutually trusting and interdependent relationships that stress caring and love rather than individual rights. When illness strikes, the physician is expected to act as an authority figure who is seldom questioned in the therapeutic arena.

Decisionmaking by the family, if strictly authoritarian, may hold inherent risks for some members of the family unit. In patrilineal families, the norm in many Eastern societies, there can be inadequate representation of the interests and wishes of certain family members, often women, who are economically dependent on the male head of the family or are powerless for other reasons. An unquestioned acceptance by the physician of implicit agreement on the part of such members to every decision that is made on their behalf can carry risks for the most vulnerable family members. This was illustrated in a case that was brought to my attention by a Pakistani surgeon. An elderly woman came with her son, with whom she had lived for many years, to be scheduled for an elective biopsy of a breast mass. During the meeting with the surgeon, the son mentioned that his mother also had gallstones and requested that a cholecystectomy be done along with the breast biopsy. The patient, who was present during this exchange with the surgeon, did not disagree and accepted without questioning the son's signature for both procedures on her behalf. As a son consenting for the mother is not an unusual occurrence in Pakistan, the surgeon—interestingly, also a woman—made no attempt to question the patient directly regarding her wish.

Just prior to being administered general anesthesia in the operating room, the patient told the surgeon that she did not wish the cholecystectomy to be done, something she had not verbalized in the presence of her son. Much to the anger of the son when he was informed later, the surgeon complied with the woman's request. The son expressed his concern that it was in the best interest of his mother to have had her gallbladder removed to avoid another anesthetic and surgical procedure in the future. When she shared this episode with me, the surgeon confessed that instead of accepting the common tradition of a male in a family signing the informed consent for female members, she should have probed the patient's own wishes and been sensitive to what might have been fear and anxiety on the patient's part regarding the cholecystectomy.

Although in this case the patient did eventually voice her preference in the absence of her son (perhaps due to the gender of the surgeon), undoubtedly many cases occur in which the concerns and wishes of a competent patient are ignored or overridden in a nonparticipatory process of decisionmaking. An unquestioned, face-value acceptance by the physician of cultural norms can jeopardize respect for the individual as a person, a prerequisite for the covenant between a physician and her patient. It is often easier and certainly less time-consuming to take refuge behind a veil of uncritical respect for cultural norms. In societies like Pakistan, physicians can utilize the tremendous respect they command to assess each encounter with a patient and family carefully to strive for a participatory process of decisionmaking, particularly when some members of the unit have been dealt a stronger hand culturally.

With rising literacy rates (albeit slower in women) and greater awareness, in time Pakistani physicians may well face an increase in the number of patients who wish to know more about their illness and prognosis. An automatic assumption that family members must be given the details of the disease while this information is withheld from the patient may become difficult to defend. However, my own experience suggests that in the social context of Pakistan there can be considerable variation in patients' responses to offers of full disclosure of illness. A measure of sensitivity and discrimination is needed in the context of the prevalent, widely accepted societal belief that caring involves shielding one's family members from distressing news.

This was illustrated for me by the case of an intelligent, educated, sixty-year-old woman hospitalized with abdominal pain and diagnosed to have a large, unresectable malignant liver tumor. As is accepted, I gave this news first to her only son, with whom she had lived since the death of her husband a few years previously. He felt strongly that telling his mother she had cancer would depress her and make her "lose hope." He felt she should be told that she had a liver "infection." He added that since her husband's death, she had always relied on him for all major decisions. Conceding that he knew his mother better than I did, I told him that as his older sister—a kinship he had bestowed on me—I felt it was important to judge first whether his mother would indeed not wish to know a diagnosis that carried major implications for her. After a while we reached a compromise: I would not use the word cancer but would tell her she had a large "tumor," but I would not lie to her if she asked me a direct question regarding the nature of the tumor, including whether it was malignant. The son assured me that she would not and he was right. During several conversations with the patient in which we talked about her "tumor," despite several openings I offered her, she never once questioned me about what kind of tumor it was or whether this would affect the duration of time she had left to live—information I had been certain she would wish to obtain. On the other hand, I have come across other patients over the years who have not only asked questions of varying depth, but have also indicated their preferences in decisions regarding their medical care.

A shift away from an authoritarian family decisionmaking process is possible, but the physician must use discrimination, judging encounters with each patient and family on their own merit. With appropriate rapport with the family and sensitivity to the wishes of a particular patient, cultural norms can be challenged. In Pakistan, the physician as a matriarch can also work toward neutralizing some of the unfair leverage that one family member may have over another in the decisionmaking process. A young couple brought their infant to me with a nonfunctioning kidney that needed to be excised. When the time came to discuss the surgery, the husband asked the wife to take the child out to another room to feed her. He then requested that I give him the details of the nephrectomy but tell his wife only that a "biopsy" was needed. He was concerned that she was too tender hearted to stand the shock of being told that the kidney would have to be removed and he did not wish to upset her. As I had already been inducted into the position of mother by the young man, I informed him that mothers had the right to decide themselves how much they wished to know about the medical plans for their children. The anxious woman was called back into the room and, on my questioning, expressed a wish to be told exactly what surgery was needed for the child. As I proceeded to do so in my role as the "wise" matriarch, the husband's apprehension gradually subsided.

Deeply entrenched religious beliefs and cultural norms that emphasize the primacy of the family and well-defined roles within it are realities in Pakistan. I believe that replacing a system of supportive interdependent relationships within families with another that focuses on disconnected individual rights exclusive of family interests is neither feasible nor desirable. However, a shift

to some kind of middle ground is necessary. This can be facilitated if physicians play a role befitting a *Hakim*, bestowed on them through long-held cultural and religious traditions. As my own experience illustrates, there is room for flexibility between a rights-based, patient-centered model of decisionmaking and another in which the identity of the patient and individual members may be lost in the collective consciousness of the family unit. A dynamic balance can be found that preserves important cultural values of duty and caring within families and introduces a possibility for individual members to participate in their own medical decisions. In Pakistan the physician, with her unique standing in society, is ideally suited to serve as the catalyst to begin a move toward such a middle ground.

This being said, the other risk to patients in Pakistan ironically comes from the physician herself. It lies in the potential for abuse of this unchallenged power that physicians command in a country where the population is largely illiterate and economically disadvantaged. Unquestioned authority of the medical profession and a fatalistic belief among the population regarding illness and death can leave patients open to exploitation by unscrupulous physicians. I am aware of instances in which improper care or medical negligence was camouflaged by references to divine predestination leading to the death of a patient. Institutional and organizational checks and balances of physicians and the medical profession as a whole are variable in effectiveness even in many institutions where they exist. Furthermore, there is a general lack of awareness of individual rights and redress through the judicial system, which is not accessible to most. All these factors combine to leave patients and their families exposed to exploitation by health care professionals.

In religious societies like Pakistan, physicians have been expected traditionally to draw their professional morality from duties and obligations. But times are changing. The medical education of physicians for some years now has been occurring in a secular, scientific milieu, and Pakistani physicians are no exception. According to Fazlur Rahman, a professor of Islamic thought at the University of Chicago, the medical tradition in Muslim societies is losing "the warmth of the cultural home in spiritual terms."[14] With the progressive shift to medical specialization and increased use of impersonal technology, all with undoubted benefits, physicians in Pakistan are moving away from close relationships with patients and their families to an approach that is distant and akin to the contractual model prevalent in the West. Such relationships require an informed, literate population and a society with well-established, effective checks and balances through institutional, professional, and governmental bodies. If these are absent or do not function well, patients and their families have little recourse against exploitation. In the Pakistani context at least, within the family-physician-patient triad it is the physician who can be the most influential in working toward a model that respects a cultural tradition of family caring yet draws the patient into the decisionmaking process.

REFERENCES

1. T.L. Beauchamp and J.L. Childress, *Principles of Biomedical Ethics*, 4th ed. (New York: Oxford University Press, 1994).

2. G.J. Annas, "The Health Care Proxy and the Living Will," *NEJM* 324 (1991), 1210–13.

3. R.S. Dresser and J.A. Robertson, "Quality of Life and Nontreatment Decisions for Incompetent Patients," *Law, Medicine and Health Care* 17 (1989): 234–44; N.K. Rhoden, "Litigating Life and Death," *Harvard Law Review* 102 (1988), 375–446.

4. J.A. Carrese and L.A. Rhodes, "Western Bioethics on the Navajo Reservation," *JAMA* 274 (1995), 826–29.

5. L. Blackhall et al., "Ethnicity and Attitudes towards Patient Autonomy," *JAMA* 274, no. 10 (1995), 820–25.

6. H.L. Nelson and J.L. Nelson, "Family," in *Encyclopedia of Bioethics*, ed. W.T. Reich, rev. ed. (New York: Simon and Schuster MacMillan, 1995), 801–808; M.G. Kuczewski, "Reconceiving the Family: The Process of Consent in Medical Decisionmaking," *Hastings Center Report* 26, no. 2 (1996): 30–37; J. Hardwig, "What about the Family?" *Hastings Center Report* 20, no. 2 (1990): 5–10; J.L. Nelson, "Critical Interests and Sources of Familial Decision-Making Authority for Incapacitated Patients," *Journal of Law, Medicine and Ethics* 23 (1995), 143–48.

7. J. Areen, "Advance Directives under State Law and Judicial Decisions," *Law, Medicine and Health Care* 19 (1991), 91–100.

8. A. Kleinman, "Anthropology of Medicine," in *Encyclopedia of Bioethics*, ed. W.T. Reich, rev. ed. (New York: Simon and Schuster MacMillan,), 1667–73.

9. F. Rahman, *Health and Medicine in the Islamic Tradition* (Chicago: ABC International Group, 1998), 1–3.

10. R. Patel, *Islamization of Laws in Pakistan* (Karichi: Saad Publications, 1986), p. 9.

11. J. English, "What Do Grown Children Owe Their Parents?" in *Having Children: Philosophical and Legal Reflections on Parenthood*, ed. O. O'Neill and W. Ruddick (New York: Oxford University Press, 1979), 351–56.

12. See ref. 6, Kuczewski, "Reconceiving the Family."

13. *Quran*, Chapter 17, Verse 23: "Your Lord has commanded that you worship none but Him, and do good to your parents. If either or both of them attain old age in your company, show them no impatience, but speak to them kind words. Lower to them the wing of humility"; Chapter 4, Verse 36: "To everyone

14. See ref. 9, Rahman, "Health and Medicine in the Islamic Tradition". 30–31.

15. J. Blustein, "The Family in Medical Decisionmaking," *Hastings Center Report* 23, no. 3 (1993), 6–13.

16. R.M. Zaman, "Psychotherapy in the Third World: Some Impressions from Pakistan," in *Psychology in Internal Perspective*, ed. U.P Gielen, L.L. Adler, N.A. Milgram (Amsterdam: Swets and Zeitlinger, 1992), 314–20.

17. M. Fetters, "The Family in Medical Decision Making: Japanese Perspectives," *Journal of Clinical Ethics* 9 (1998): 132–46; P.J.L. Donnely, "The Impact of Culture on Psychotherapy: Korean Clients' Expectations in Psychotherapy," *Journal of the New York State Nurses Association* 23 (1993): 12–15; T.M. McLntyre, "Family Therapy in Portugal and the U.S.: A Culturally Sensitive Approach," in *International Approaches to Family and Family Therapy*, ed. U.P. Gielen and A.L. Comunian (Padua: CDEM, 1997), 1–51; R.M. Zaman, "The Adaptation of Western Psychotherapeutic Methods to Muslim Societies," *World Psychology* 3 (1997), 65–87.

18. See ref. 17, Zaman, "The Adaptation of Western Psychotherapeutic Methods."

19. See ref. 17, Fetters, "The Family in Medical Decision Making."

20. See ref. 11, English, "What Do Grown Children Owe Their Parents?"

21. F. Rahman, "Islam and Medicine," *Perspectives in Biology and Medicine* 27 (1984), 585–97.

22. H. Hathout, *Topics in Islamic Medicine* (Kuwait: Publications of Islamic Medicine Organization, 1983).

23. First International Conference on Islamic Medicine, *Islamic Code of Medical Ethics*, Kuwait Documentary, Kuwait Rabi 1, January 1981.

24. See ref. 22, Hathout, "Topics in Islamic Medicine"; ref. 23, First International Conference, *Islamic Code of Medical Ethics.*

25. *Quran*, Chapter 5, Verse 32: "Whosoever takes a life, except to combat murder and villainy on earth, it is as if he killed all mankind."

26. M.A.S. Abdel Haleem, "Medical Ethics in Islam," In *Choices and Decisions in Health Care*, ed. A. Grubb (London: John Wiley and Sons Ltd., 1993), 1–20.

27. J.C. Holland, N. Geary, A. Marchum, S. Tross, "An International Survey of Physicians' Attitudes and Practice in Regard to Revealing the Diagnosis of Cancer," *Cancer Investigation* 5 (1987), 151–54.

28. See ref. 4, Carrese and Rhodes, "Western Bioethics on the Navajo Reservation."

29. *Quran*, Chapter 16, Verse 6:1 "When their term is come, they would not put it back by a single hour, nor put it forward"; Chapter 2, Verse 28: "He gave you life, then He shall make you dead, then He shall give you life, then unto Him you shall be returned."

30. See ref. 17, Fetters, "The Family in Medical Decision Making."

31. D.W. Brock, "What is the Moral Authority of Family Members to Act as Surrogates for Incapacitated Patients?" *Millbank Quarterly* 74 (1996): 599–618, J. Hardwig, "The Problem of Proxies with Interests of Their Own," *Journal of Clinical Ethics* 4 (1993), 20–27.

Chapter *3*

Justice and Health Care

US Seniors Group Attacks Pharmaceutical Industry "Fronts"

The giant US seniors group AARP, which has 35 million members aged over 50, has accused the pharmaceutical industry of funding "front" groups that purport to represent older Americans but instead push industry friendly political messages.

An investigation by the AARP Bulletin *has discovered that three key organisations, the United Seniors Association, the Seniors Coalition, and the 60 Plus Association, have all received substantial contributions in recent years from the drug industry.*

"When the pharmaceutical industry speaks these days, many Americans may not be able to recognize its voice. That's because the industry often uses 'front groups' that work to advance its agenda under the veil of other interests," says the article.

AARP is one of the strongest citizens groups in the United States, and it is currently lobbying hard for a national pharmaceutical scheme to help older people to meet their drug costs. Proposals for a new scheme have split the US congress, with Democrats favouring a government-run approach, and the Republicans supporting a more privatised market based plan, also being promoted by the pharmaceutical industry.

The AARP article gave detailed figures of drug company funding for the three seniors groups, and cited examples of pro-industry campaigning, including multimillion dollar television advertisements in the closing weeks of the congressional elections in November 2002. The 60 Plus Association is accused of being involved with "astro-turfing," allegedly helping to create a false grass roots campaign to defeat proposed state laws on prescription drugs.

The AARP's policy director, John Rother, said his organisation was now considering calling for new laws mandating disclosure of sponsors' names in any political advertising. He told the BMJ *that apart from Pfizer, which mounted a campaign in its own name before the 2002 elections, "the rest of the industry hid behind this device of using phoney seniors' organisations."*

A spokesperson for Pfizer said that its campaign was designed to improve understanding of the industry's involvement in research and generate support for a prescription drug scheme.

Jeff Trewhitt, spokesman for the Washington based lobby group, the Pharmaceutical Research and Manufacturers of America, refused to respond to the specific allegations that industry was hiding behind front groups, saying that industry did not discuss its tactics: "I don't see a problem here."

The 60 Plus Association's president, Jim Martin, rejected the accusations about front groups, telling the BMJ *that his 10 year old group started taking money from drug companies only two years ago. He said his association had 225,000 donors but that to protect privacy it had a policy of not revealing names.*

Ray Moynihan, Washington

Moynahan, Ray "US Seniors Group Attacks Pharmaceutical Industry 'Fronts'" *British Medical Journal*, 326:351, 15 February, 2005. Copyright © 2005. Reprinted by permission of The BMJ Publishing Group Ltd.

This article raises an ethical question that is hotly debated within the bioethics literature: whether consumers can truly enact informed consent in making decisions about prescription drug use in our current American context. The American Association of Retired Persons (AARP) contends that pharmaceutical companies are funding "front" groups that use the seniors' groups to advance pro-pharmaceutical industry messages. If this is true, then the industry is behaving unethically and seniors are being duped into thinking that what amounts to ad campaigns for drug companies is actually education and information.

Yet some critics point out that the pharmaceutical industry is not unique in this regard. Many industries, companies, and church organizations have and do use friendly front organizations to help advance their cause. As far back as forty years ago, the pharmaceutical industry has paid honoraria for services rendered by Grand Round speakers—chosen by the hospitals presenting the rounds—to enable hospital health personnel to learn about the latest health situations and treatments. As a result of this pharmaceutical industry support for non-partisan speakers, health care professionals have kept abreast of available treatments and services, and the public has arguably benefited from the information presented to them.

Still, this issue reflects an important ethical question with regard to the presentation of information to the public. Is it honest—truth in advertising—to present pro-industry political messages as mere information or public education? What should be the rules regarding disclosure, and how can we ensure that citizens can tell the difference between propaganda and educational messages?

CASE STUDY: THE PROBLEM THAT WON'T GO AWAY

Paul Oberlin is a substitute janitor at a junior high school in Gary, Indiana. Because he is only employed part time, he is not eligible for insurance benefits. He does not qualify for Medicaid or, at 53 years old, for Medicare. He comes into a student-run free health clinic on Chicago's West side after a long commute from Gary. A year earlier, he had been referred to the clinic by a county public hospital. He had been diagnosed and treated for chronic recurrent prostatitis on multiple previous visits to the free health clinic, and on the current visit he reports having pain in his pelvic region and upon urination. He is sexually active but refrains from sex with his girlfriend when his symptoms flare up for fear of transmitting an infection.

During a recent visit to the clinic, Mr. Oberlin tested negative for sexually transmitted infections, had a negative urine dip, no glucose in his urine, normal prostate specific antigen (PSA) levels, and an enlarged prostate but no nodules. He has traveled to the clinic almost monthly during the past year and has kept all scheduled appointments but one. His health literacy appears high according to a triage volunteer who read his medical history, and he is conscientious about choosing healthy behaviors.

Usually, the physician or fourth-year medical student at the clinic recommends a course of antibiotics for Mr. Oberlin, which helps relieve his symptoms during the treatment course. Some antibiotics have seemed to work while others have not. A few days or a few weeks after each antibiotic regimen his symptoms return. He has been experiencing this pattern for almost 2 years and takes Flomax regularly to help relieve his enlarged prostate. During his last visit, the physician recommended Levaquin, which the patient said worked best for him in the past. For some undocumented reason, the physician noted offering it to Mr. Oberlin on this visit only if he could pay for a prescription. If not, the physician recommended doxycycline.

A fourth-year medical student, Peter Mills, having just reviewed Mr. Oberlin's chart and test results before walking into his room, felt the status quo needed to change starting with this visit. He was frustrated with the lack of continuity of care for Mr. Oberlin and the often incomplete or inadequate documentation in his chart. Mr. Mills noted that no referral had been suggested for Mr. Oberlin. He thought he knew why since the average wait period for an urologist at Cook County Hospital for the uninsured was at least 5 months. Mr. Oberlin was becoming increasingly frustrated, as he all too quickly let Mr. Mills know.

Mr. Mills researched chronic prostatitis quickly and determined that there were additional imaging services and procedural tests that might help diagnose Mr. Oberlin's disease and treat it more effectively than the perpetual and often ineffective antibiotic treatments. None of these had been discussed with Mr. Oberlin. Mr. Mills explained that the clinic did not provide these services and recommended that Mr. Oberlin approach Cook County Hospital or a federally qualified health care center for more affordable, out-of-pocket testing if he did not feel he could wait the year or so it may take to eventually get the tests through Cook County.

The tests would be expensive, and Mr. Oberlin expresses his concerns over his ability to pay for them. Mr. Mills thinks Mr.Oberlin should get tested sooner rather than later due to the recurring symptoms, and he ponders how he might be able to "hurry the system" along. It is apparent to Mr. Mills that Mr. Oberlin is not receiving the standard of care, given his symptoms. He does not know what other alternatives he can recommend to this patient. Should he refer him to a private physician where he would accrue debt but at least receive more timely and comprehensive care? Should he just continue the status quo and provide yet another antibiotic? Should Mr. Mills just accept the unfortunate aspects of the system for his patient?

This scenario has become all too familiar within the context of the United States, where an increasing number of people lack comprehensive health care coverage. Many average citizens, who, like Paul Oberlin, are employed in some capacity, fall between the cracks. They may not receive health insurance benefits through their full- or part-time employment, but their incomes are also too high to receive **Medicaid,** and they are not old enough to qualify for **Medicare** benefits. Indeed, in the year 2006, 58.7% of the uninsured were working either full or part time; and adults between the ages of 18 and 34 comprised the largest group of uninsured persons, at 40.4% of those without coverage.[1] Clearly, then, one does not have to be devastatingly poor or unemployed to suffer the lack of decent health care (Figure 3.1).

The fourth-year medical student in this case is just another provider who is passing through Mr. Oberlin's life. But this student, Mr. Mills, recognizes that this patient has suffered a serious lack of continuity of care, which results in a negative impact on Mr. Oberlin's health. His medical records are incomplete and inadequate, and no referrals have been made for him, perhaps because the previous providers recognize the futility of making such referrals. Mr. Oberlin would either have several months to more than a year's wait for testing at the county hospital, or he would have to pay out of pocket to see a specialist. Either option is problematic, and does not solve his most urgent health needs—to treat the pain caused by his recurring prostatitis.

The problem that any physician faces in such a case involves both the individual and the societal levels. On the societal level, a physician must question why patients are left without adequate health insurance coverage, and how such a problem can be addressed through changes in health insurance and the provision of health care. Yet on the individual level, a physician must still deal with the patient that is sitting before her, and do her best to address that patient's condition. Mr. Mills is in such a situation, where he must now decide whether to make a referral—perhaps even a costly one—for Mr. Oberlin, or whether he should do as his predecessors and send him away with yet another prescription in the hopes that it might relieve Mr. Oberlin's pain for another short period of time.

The situation in which we find Mr. Oberlin is a sharp reminder of the deteriorating state of the U.S. medical system. Many citizens are similarly under- or unemployed such that they lack sufficient health insurance coverage. One may wonder why health insurance in the United States is linked to employment at all, whereas in most other developed countries one's employment status is not relevant to one's level of health insurance coverage. The reasons for this connection come from a particular moment in U.S. history that set the stage for our current system of **employment-based health insurance** coverage.

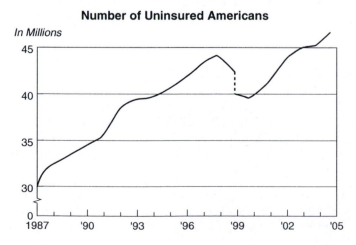

Number of Uninsured Americans

In Millions

FIGURE 3.1   U.S. census bureau graph indicating number of uninsured Americans.

U.S. census bureau, current population survey, 1988 to 2006 annual social and economic supplements.

THE RISE OF EMPLOYMENT–BASED HEALTH INSURANCE IN THE UNITED STATES

Many supporters of the current system of health insurance assume a certain natural connection between employment and the provision of health insurance. Yet the connection forged between them arises from very specific needs that arose during World War II. At that time, employers were competing for employees to work in their factories. Munitions factories and other war-related industries were desperate for workers, and there were only a limited number of workers available given the large number of individuals off at war. Employers were prohibited from luring workers to their factories through wage competition because of the freeze on salaries; they had to find other ways of attracting employees. One way of doing so was by offering benefits packages that included health insurance coverage. Since this point during the 1940s, health insurance in the United States has been increasingly employment-based, with coverage now being a standard part of employment benefits packages.

By inheriting this system of employment-based health insurance we have also inherited the problems that go with it. One such problem is the sharply rising costs of health care. Employers now struggle to offer their employees comprehensive, affordable health care plans. As the costs to employers continue to rise, they find it necessary to cut their level of contribution to the plans, resulting in foisting the costs upon employees. Many employees find they cannot afford the increased costs given that their salaries are not keeping up with the rise in health insurance premiums, so they are forced to drop their coverage. The problem of skyrocketing insurance costs is persisting, and employers are now looking for other ways to address the rising cost of insuring their employees.

In the 1980s, in one attempt to address the rising costs of health insurance, the Reagan administration brought in a system of Managed Care. This system was intended to keep in check the rate of health care inflation: By organizing and managing health care such that there were caps on fees and patient referrals, and incentives for physicians to see fewer patients in clinic, it was hoped that health care could be provided in a way that would be more economical, less duplicative, and that would be better for both patients and the employers who pay a large portion of the health plans. The idea of managed care is not problematic in itself; however, the fact that it was introduced within a system of for-profit medicine, in which **managed care organizations (MCOs)** stood to make a great deal of money by keeping patient costs as low as possible, was a recipe for disaster. Instead of focusing on what is best for patients, MCOs have focused on making profits for their shareholders; rather than recognizing health care as a basic need, something that should especially be provided to the sick and needy, MCOs have avoided insuring the sickest and most vulnerable persons because they are the most costly to insure.

Indeed, since the rise of managed care in the United States, the number of un- and under-insured citizens has sharply increased; if anything, the practice of managed care has served to drive up health care costs and cause even more citizens to lose coverage. Over the past number of years, some experts have looked to our neighbor to the north, Canada, as a model for universal access to health care.

CANADA'S SYSTEM OF UNIVERSAL HEALTH CARE

Under the directives of the Canada Health Act, each and every Canadian citizen has the right to receive decent, basic health care. The Act's five principles ensure that all Canadians are covered, that there are no periods during which a citizen is without coverage, and that, no matter where one is living in Canada, one has reasonable access to necessary care, including emergency care. The five principles of the Canada Health Act are as follows:

- *Portability:* if one switches jobs or relocates from one province or territory to another, the home province in which the person previously resided is responsible for providing care until coverage commences in the new province or territory. At no point is a Canadian citizen left without health care insurance.

- *Accessibility:* the health insurance plans of each province or territory must provide reasonable access to insured health services without regard to age, health status, or financial circumstances; and each citizen must physically have access to necessary medical services where and as they are available.
- *Universality:* One hundred percent of a province's or territory's insured residents must have access to insured health services provided by the plans; the services must be offered on uniform terms and conditions.
- *Comprehensiveness:* the health insurance plans of the provinces and territories must cover all insured health services (including hospital, physician, surgical, etc.). No province or territory is permitted to refuse coverage for any health service that is insured by the province.
- *Public Administration:* the health insurance plans of all provinces and territories are to be administered and operated on a nonprofit basis by a public authority. They are responsible to the provincial/territorial governments and are subject to audits of their financial accounts and transactions.

While each province and territory in Canada oversees its own health care plan, each is responsible for adhering to and upholding the five principles. Thus, while the government attempts to ensure uniformity of treatment and access across Canada (whether one lives in British Columbia or Newfoundland), the Act also allows for each province or territory to uniquely address its citizens' health care needs.

The Canadian system of health care has been referred to variously as **universal health care, socialized medicine,** and as a **single-payer system.** Supporters of the Canadian model point out the significantly lower cost of providing care because administrative oversight of the system is simplified, with each provincial government responsible for reimbursing physicians and other providers for their services. Unlike the United States, where multiple agencies and organizations reimburse for services, and where one faces administrative bureaucracy of nightmarish proportions, the Canadian system of reimbursement is simple and efficient, with few delays in reimbursing and little paperwork to fill out. For example, the province of Ontario provides the Ontario Health Insurance Plan (OHIP); to receive reimbursement for services rendered, health care providers in Ontario simply submit their billing to OHIP and they are directly reimbursed by the government.

As with any system, the Canadian system of health care is experiencing problems. Since the 1990s, the federal government has reduced transfer payments to the provinces such that there is less federal money being offered to support each province's health care plan. Services that were previously insured have been cut in an attempt to control provincial health care costs; so citizens are now complaining that services have either been deinsured or significantly reduced, meaning that they are responsible for paying for them out-of-pocket. The process of **deinsurance** has generated disparities in provincial health care coverage. For example, the removal of warts is no longer covered in Nova Scotia, New Brunswick, Ontario, Manitoba, Alberta, Saskatchewan, and British Columbia, but it remains publicly insured in Newfoundland, Quebec, and Prince Edward Island. Although stomach stapling is covered in most provinces, it is not insured in New Brunswick, Nova Scotia, and the Yukon, and patients in these provinces/territories must pay for this procedure. In addition, coverage varies widely across the country in the areas of reproductive services.[2]

More recently, across Canada private facilities have been cropping up that deliver both insured and uninsured services, leading many to worry about the genesis of a two-tiered system that allows some to pay for more or better care while others are left relying on whatever insured services remain. Finally, there is a shift toward noninstitutional care, where many Canadians are receiving care in their homes and in their communities. As a result, many services that are deemed medically necessary today are not publicly insured because they are not provided in hospitals or by physicians. Given the Canada Health Act's focus on hospitals and physician services, the provision of care and treatments in noninstitutional settings is simply not covered. This problem has led some Canadian health policymakers to argue that the Act should "fund the care, not the institution."

Despite these problems, and some Canadians' complaints about long waits for medical services, Canadians tend to do better overall in terms of health and longevity when compared to Americans.

Though in 2004 the U.S. spent 15.2% of the gross domestic product on health in comparison to Canada's 9.7%, Americans fare no better in terms of overall health outcomes.[3]

Those who admire universal forms of health care have attempted to find ways to import it to the United States. One such admirer was President Bill Clinton, who in 1993 presented a comprehensive health plan for ensuring that all Americans would have health insurance coverage. Clinton attempted to adopt a system that reflected American values (in that the health care system would still be run on a market-based model), but that ensured that no citizen would be left without access to decent health care.

THE CLINTON PLAN: A FAILED ATTEMPT AT UNIVERSAL HEALTH CARE

On September 22, 1993, President Bill Clinton made the following health care speech to a joint session of Congress:

> Millions of Americans are just a pink slip away from losing their health insurance, and one serious illness away from losing all their savings. Millions more are locked into the jobs they have now just because they or someone in their family has once been sick and they have what is called the preexisting condition. And on any given day, over 37 million Americans—most of them working people and their little children—have no health insurance at all. And in spite of all this, our medical bills are growing at over twice the rate of inflation, and the United States spends over a third more of its income on health care than any other nation on Earth.[4]

The Clinton health plan, if passed, would have effectively brought universal health care to the United States, though it would not have ended the system of for-profit medical care. In the plan, Clinton required that each U.S. citizen and permanent resident become enrolled in a qualified health plan. His program did not allow disenrollment until individuals had coverage through another plan (addressing the need for continuous coverage so that individuals would not have been left without health insurance for periods of time while switching jobs or moving from state-to-state). The Clinton plan listed minimum coverage and maximum annual out-of-pocket expenses for each plan. To address citizens living in poverty, people below a certain set income level were to pay nothing. The act listed funding to be sent to the states for the administration of this plan, beginning at $4.5 billion in 1993 and reaching $38.3 billion in 2003.

Clinton's Task Force on National Health Care Reform was headed by First Lady Hillary Rodham Clinton (Figure 3.2). Starting on September 28, 1993, she appeared for several days of testimony in front of five congressional committees on health care. Those who opposed the bill organized against it before it was presented to the Democratic-controlled Congress on November 20, 1993. The bill (called the "Health Security Act") was a complex proposal running more than 1,000 pages, which had as its

FIGURE 3.2 Hillary Rodham Clinton speaking out about health care reform in 1993.

core mandate that employers must provide health insurance coverage to all of their employees through competitive but closely regulated **health maintenance organizations (HMOs)**.[5]

The Clinton plan ultimately failed, in large part because of the insurance industry campaign against it. These lobbyists criticized the plan for being too bureaucratic and too restrictive of patient choice. For a country built on the foundation of individual liberties, a health care plan that is heavily regulated by the government may appear to be seriously problematic, and for this reason, the plan never did make it to a vote by Congress.

HEALTH CARE FOR ILLEGAL IMMIGRANTS?

Ana Puente was an infant with a liver disorder when her aunt brought her illegally to the United States to seek medical care. She underwent two liver transplants at UCLA Medical Center as a child in 1989 and a third in 1998, each paid for by the state. But when Puente turned 21, she aged out of her state-funded health insurance and was unable to continue treatment at UCLA.

Puente's liver began failing again and she was hospitalized at County-USC Medical Center. In her Medi-Cal application, a USC doctor wrote, "Her current clinical course is irreversible, progressive and will lead to death without another liver transplant." The application was denied. The county gave her medication but does not have the resources to perform transplants.

Puente then learned of another, little-known option for patients with certain health care needs. If she notified U.S. Citizenship and Immigration Services that she was in the country illegally, state health officials might grant her full Medi-Cal coverage. Puente did so, her benefits were restored, and she then awaited a fourth transplant at UCLA.

Puente's case highlights two controversial issues: Should illegal immigrants receive liver transplants in the United States and should taxpayers pick up the cost?[6]

The United States is one of the most diverse and multicultural countries in the world; because of its degree of wealth and perceived opportunity, it is a desirable place to live for many immigrants, both legal and illegal. Indeed, the large number of illegal immigrants coming to the United States has led to many questions about the moral, social, and legal responsibility to provide them with a decent minimum of health care. While some ethicists argue in favor of providing health care for undocumented workers, others argue that by offering such care we validate illegal border crossings and siphon off health care resources that should be placed with U.S. citizens.

Undocumented workers can get emergency care in the United States through the provisions of the Emergency Medical Treatment and Active Labor Act of 1985 (EMTALA). The Act obliges hospitals that have emergency departments and that receive federal funding to treat uninsured individuals without reimbursement. Undocumented workers cannot, however, receive nonemergency care unless they pay; and they are not eligible for most other public benefits.

The arguments against providing nonemergency and preventive health care for undocumented workers focuses on the concern that illegal immigrants do not pay taxes, and so do not pay into the system from which they are taking health care resources. Critics also point out that, with millions of uninsured U.S. citizens, we can hardly afford to "take all comers" by offering free care to noncitizens or those who are not permanent residents. Furthermore, when we look at states like Texas, which is situated along the Mexican border (the gateway through which many illegal immigrants from South and Central America and Mexico are entering the United States), we see that the emergency rooms are crowded with patients seeking medical care (Figure 3.3).

Yet ethicists that support the provision of nonemergency and preventive health care for illegal immigrants point out the ethical, financial, and legal arguments in favor of this practice. First, they argue that undocumented workers are, indeed, paying taxes, and so are not taking "free rides" on taxpayers' money. These workers pay sales tax on purchases they make; they pay tax on their rentals or home ownership; and some pay into Social Security, Medicare, and workers' compensation through their payroll deductions. Second, advocates point out that we cannot afford *not* to offer nonemergency and preventive health care to illegal immigrants, since offering services prevents public health issues (such as the spreading of preventable, communicable diseases) and avoids greater costs down the road. For

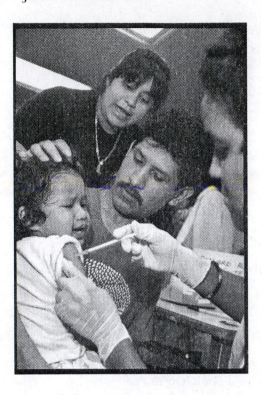

FIGURE 3.3   Doctors immunize a Mexican child at a health clinic in New York City.

example, offering good prenatal care to women who are undocumented workers (but whose children will, after all, be born as American citizens) helps to minimize the need for expensive, invasive care, ensuring that the children will be born with the potential to be healthy and productive citizens. Finally, it is argued that border states such as Texas suffer from an overflow of patients, not because illegal immigrants are filling the emergency rooms, but because American citizens who lack health insurance are looking for facilities where care is available.

Nevertheless, when some citizens hear of cases such as that of Ana Puente, they are angered by the very idea that she—an illegal immigrant—has had four opportunities to receive expensive, rare transplants while some citizens have not yet had the chance at one. The debate concerning non-emergency and preventive health care for undocumented workers will likely continue for a long time to come.

THE PHARMACEUTICAL INDUSTRY

In 1892 William Osler, known as the "Father of Modern Medicine," claimed, "One of the first duties of the physician is to educate the masses, not to take medicine." Yet we are now a culture so obsessed with disease (and pharmaceutical responses to disease) that we take more medications than any other culture at any other time in history. Indeed, despite the fact that many Americans cannot afford necessary medications, the United States has a particularly booming pharmaceutical industry. Though showing steady growth for several years, it was during the last decade that the growth could be considered phenomenal, escalating from $22 billion in 1980 to $149 billion in the year 2000.[7]

The most interesting statistics concern the amount of money that the industry spends on marketing and lobbying. According to the *New England Journal of Medicine,* the major pharmaceutical companies now spend more than $5.5 billion to promote drugs to doctors—more than what all U.S. medical schools spend to educate medical students.[8] Major drug companies employ about 90,000 sales representatives—one for every 4.7 doctors in the United States; the total pharmaceutical marketing budget is $25 billion. And in terms of lobbying power, drug firms have spent $800 million since 1998 on what one might call "buying influence," including $675 million on direct lobbying of Congress.[9] No other interest group has spent more money to sway public policy (Figure 3.4).

As some bioethicists have pointed out, these costs for aggressive marketing have serious implications for all of us, since the marketing and lobbying costs get passed on to the public through the high cost of medications. While defenders of the industry claim that there are very high costs associated with research and development of new pharmaceuticals, and that those costs are reflected in the market price of new medications brought to market, critics claim that not enough emphasis in the United States is placed on research and development, and that most of the industry's money goes toward marketing copycat drugs (those that replicate other available drugs) to the public.

The pharmaceutical industry's practice of **direct-to-consumer advertising** has also spawned debate over its appropriateness and the ethical implications of pitching medications to the general public. This practice of magazine, television, radio, and Internet advertising is defended by arguing that it is a form of public education; the ads help to educate citizens concerning new disease findings and possible treatments for those diseases. However, critics of this practice point out that education is neither the intention nor the end result of these ad campaigns. Rather, the intention is to persuade individuals that they have a certain condition (restless leg syndrome, for example) and that they need a (usually expensive) medication to help them deal with the problem. Absent a background in medicine or pharmacology, the average citizen is in no position to affirm or deny the claims made in the pharmaceutical ads, so their value as a form of public education is seriously questioned.

Clearly, there is not widespread agreement on these justice issues such as health care for immigrants, the need for a universal system of health care, or whether advertising by the pharmaceutical industry is desirable or not. What is clear, however, is that we are going to have to decide how to address these important issues, as the demand to provide health care for noncitizens is only going to increase, the number of un- and underinsured Americans will continue to grow, and as the pharmaceutical industry plays a bigger and bigger role in people's lives via advertising on television, the Internet, and billboards.

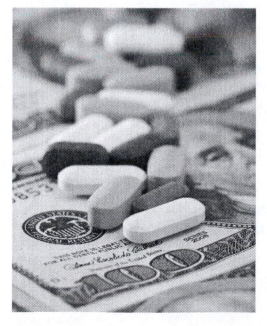

FIGURE 3.4   Many Americans struggle to pay for their medications given the high cost of prescription drugs in the United States.

Looking Ahead

- In an attempt by some physicians to minimize their involvement in health care bureaucracy, an increasing number of them may turn toward offering "concierge care" or "boutique services." In such circumstances, doctors require extra fees of patients (starting at over $1,000 per year and running much higher) to keep them "on retainer"; in return, patients receive top-notch care, with special personal attention from their physicians. By offering such boutique services, physicians can significantly reduce their patient loads, cutting their numbers of patients by as much as 75 percent. In doing this, they are able to offer a small patient group better, more personalized care, and they can minimize their involvement with Medicare, Medicaid, and managed care. The likely increase in this practice may lead to concerns over a greater divide between the "haves" and the "have-nots."

- Given the high cost of pharmaceuticals in the United States, and the competition from countries (such as Mexico and Canada) where prescription drugs are less expensive, we will likely see attempts by the U.S. pharmaceutical industry to lobby U.S. lawmakers either to strictly enforce laws already on the books or write new legislation banning the cross-border pharmaceutical trade. The inability for patients to purchase necessary drugs will likely worsen with the financial crisis, and we may see many citizens (especially older adults) becoming more vocal about their difficult situations in accessing medications.

- An increasing number of employers and employees will turn to health savings accounts (HSAs) as a way of coping with the high cost of health insurance. Instead of providing group health insurance, more employers will favor placing a set, finite amount into each employee's HSA, which employees can then use to defray health care costs. These accounts require holders to have a high-deductible health plan, meaning that individuals pay much more of the initial costs of their health care, so there is more risk involved than traditional insurance, which carries much lower deductibles. These plans are already being touted as ways to ensure individuals take responsibility for their health care costs, and as ways to get individuals to be as thrifty as possible when seeking health care.

Endnotes

1. Information taken from http://www.kaisernetwork.org/daily_reports/rep_index.cfm?DR_ID=47178. [Accessed on May 2, 2008].
2. Information taken from http://www.parl.gc.ca/information/library/prbpubs/944-e.htm [Accessed on May 2, 2008].
3. Information taken from the World Health Organization at http://www.who.int/whosis/database/core/core_select_process.cfm?countries=all&indicators=nha [Accessed on June 18, 2008].
4. President Clinton's entire speech can be found at http://www.clintonpresidentialcenter.org/legacy/092293-speech-by-president-address-to-joint-session-of-congress-as-delivered.htm [Accessed on May 5, 2008].
5. The full text of the November 20 bill (the "Health Security Act") is available online at http://thomas.loc.gov/cgi-bin/query/z?c103:H.R.3600.IH [Accessed on May 5, 2008].
6. Case taken from the *Los Angeles Times*, April 13, 2008. Available online at http://www.latimes.com/news/local/la-me-liver13apr13,0,6444372.story [Accessed on May 5, 2008].
7. See Conchetta White Fulton, "Despite the National Economic Downturn, the Pharmaceutical Industry Remains Strong," at http://www.black-collegian.com/career/industry-reports/pharmacy2002-2nd.shtml [Accessed on May 6, 2008].
8. "The Lessons of Vioxx," *New England Journal of Medicine,* June 23, 2005.
9. See the Center for Public Integrity online at http://www.publicintegrity.org/Content.aspx?src=search&context=article&id=723 [Accessed on May 6, 2008].

ISSUES IN ACCESS TO HEALTH CARE

A Lifespan Approach to Health Care[1]

Norman Daniels

CONFLICTING MESSAGES ABOUT OUR HEALTH CARE SYSTEM

The next few years will bring many proposals intended to reform the financing and the design of our health care system. Major reforms are necessary because we simultaneously face several critical issues: a growing insurance gap now involving nearly 40 million people; rapidly rising health care costs whose long-term rate of increase is unaffected by current cost-containment measures; and a pattern of resource allocation that leaves many fundamental health care needs unmet. In thinking about what we want reforms to accomplish, I think we should try to answer such questions as these: Do we get from the spectrum of care we receive over the lifespan what we need and most want? Does our health care system allocate resources over the whole lifespan in a way that is fair to all age groups? How should we as citizens and as health professionals think about what we want our health care system to do for us? What are our social obligations to design a system that delivers care to both rich and poor, black and white, male and female, young and old? What does justice require in the way of health care over the lifespan?

These are hard questions, and it is no surprise that our society has not faced them as squarely and directly as it should have. Part of what makes answering them so difficult is the very different messages we, the public, get about our health care system. One message we get is that *medical technology can do just about anything, at all points in the lifespan, given the resources.* The media dramatize the latest ventures in in vitro fertilization, the microsurgery on minute neonates, and the saving of children with biliary atresia by liver transplants. A young worker who loses a hand in an industrial accident can have it reattached; genetic engineering gives us new drugs to treat heart attacks; whole hip sockets can be replaced for the elderly. We are experimenting with transplanting neural tissue to repair spinal damage and even to treat Alzheimer's and Parkinson's diseases. Cosmetic surgeons are vying with Henry Moore as sculptors of fatty tissue. We use technology in confusion and desperation: we can keep alive through heroic measures those who have lost central features of their personhood,

sometimes in disregard of their wishes. The message here is that from the marriage bed to the deathbed we can hold death, disability, and ugliness at bay if we are willing.

There are darker messages, too. We read that 40 million Americans have no health care insurance at all and that we are the only industrial democracy that fails to provide universal access to basic health care, let alone these technological miracles. We read that, when prenatal maternal care programs were eliminated from federal funding as a result of budget-cutting in the early Reagan years, infant mortality rates rose—at the same time we invested heavily in neonatal intensive care units. We read that millions of partially disabled elderly are unable to get adequate home care or social support services. We read that millions of mentally ill people are unable to get treatment at all—and they live in our streets among the homeless.

Yet, despite all these things that we fail to do—thereby "saving" health care dollars, we also read that health care costs are rising at rates above inflation. This rise takes place despite federal DRG capping of Medicare hospital payments, increased cost-sharing by Medicare patients, decreased tax deductions for medical care, state capping of hospital budgets, and measures taken by employers and third-party payers intended to promote price competition in health care or prospective payment wherever possible. Because these measures have not greatly slowed rising costs, and because some economists do not think we can succeed just by measures that try to trim the waste or fat out of the system—indeed, this is the central dispute among the experts—we hear more and more calls for the *rationing* of medical care.

In fact, of course, we already ration beneficial care by ability to pay, for that is what leaving 40 million people without insurance coverage amounts to. Similarly, some beneficial care (and not just unnecessary care) is denied patients as a result of DRGs and other cost-containment measures, and some studies have shown a slight increase in death rates for the elderly as a result of shortened hospital stays following surgery. However, the new call for rationing is a request for more explicit measures. It is a call for us to make decisions about the priorities that should govern the dissemination of medical technologies.

Daniels, Norman. "A Lifespan Approach to Health Care," *Aging and Ethics: Philosophical Problems in Gerontology,* Nancy Jecker, ed., Clifton, NJ: Humana Press (1991), 227–246. Copyright © 1991. Reprinted by permission of Springer Science and Business Media.

This call for rationing in the United States is striking. We are not in wartime. We do not require national sacrifice to keep our soldiers in battle. Can we not have both guns and bandages? Can we not give up some guns for some bandages? This is not a depression. Productivity is not so low that we cannot keep Reeboks on our feet and a chicken in every microwave. Yet, what many are saying is that spending 11 or 12% of GNP on health care may be approaching the limit of what it is reasonable to invest in health care, and that our current cost-containment measures can at best squeeze a small amount of fat out of the system. Also, they say, quite plausibly, that if we do not figure out what kinds of medical technologies are most important to disseminate, then our costs will continue to rise rapidly, even though we will only achieve marginal gains in health status. What is worse, there is great reluctance to introduce entitlement schemes that eliminate the shameful gaps in health care insurance without some demonstration that we know how to control health care costs, through rationing or otherwise. In effect, we are being told that the price for making health care more accessible to all is that we may have to make some forms of it less accessible to all—and this means we will have to face hard policy choices.

There is much truth in all of these messages about health care: we do amazing things; we fail to do equally important things; we will have to refrain from doing other important things. It will be difficult to expand entitlement to health care without controlling health care costs, but controlling costs involves our making hard choices about what technologies to use. When not everyone can get what he or she wants or needs, we must find principles of justice or fair procedures for determining who should get what, but this kind of talk about competition for scarce resources has its political costs, and I would like to say a few things about them.

THE ELDERLY IN THE HOT SEAT

When public talk turns to claims about scarcity and the need for rationing, there is a tendency to blame one group for the problems of another. In recent years, there has been considerable finger-pointing at the elderly—not by the public as a whole, which continues to support programs aimed at the needs of the elderly, but at least by some scholars, planners, and even legislators. What has emerged is a growing perception that the old and the young are locked in fierce competition for critical but scarce resources, namely, public funds for human services. It is in this regard that we hear complaints that the old are benefiting at the direct expense of children, of the poor, and of younger workers. It is

in this context that some call for "intergenerational equity"—indeed, there is a Washington lobby called AGE (Americans for Generational Equality).

The most plaintive cries are about competition between the elderly and children—between grandparent or great-grandparents and grandchildren.

Since 1970, expanded Social Security benefits have reduced poverty among the elderly from double the national incidence to a level slightly below the average rate of poverty. There are now proportionally more poor children than poor elderly, a switch from 15 years ago.

- Children now receive a smaller proportion of Medicaid dollars than in earlier years, despite an increase in the number of poor children.
- In 1971, we spent less on the elderly than on national defense, but in the 1980s we spent more.
- Federal per capita expenditures on children are only nine percent of per capita expenditures on the elderly.

More generally, we spend four-and-a-half times as much on federal retirement programs, including Medicare, which benefit rich and poor alike, than we do on all welfare programs aimed specifically at the poor.

The elderly are thus seen as competitors with children and the poor. However, they are also portrayed as competitors with other birth cohorts: each retiree is now supported by 3.4 workers, but when the Baby Boom retires, only two workers will contribute for every retiree.

The conflict between the elderly and other groups over public money sometimes penetrates right to the level of the family. Currently, families provide about 80% of all home health care to the partially disabled elderly. This care is costly to adult children and other family members, in terms of money, expended time, and the stress of sustaining care over extended periods. As one daughter put it:

> We put her in the shower and brush her teeth. . . . We put lipstick on her and put her hair in a french twist with floral combs. . . . When we go away overnight, we take her with us. . . . I put paper on the floor 'cause she doesn't always make it to the bathroom. . . . I'll paint her apartment, change the light bulbs, and wash the windows.[2]

Despite these high levels of care provided by some families, rising public expenditure on long-term care have led some legislators in the early 1980s to propose "family responsibility initiatives" in about half the states. If passed, such laws would hold family members legally responsible for costs currently paid by Medicaid. Shifting costs out of public budgets, however, will not eliminate competition between the elderly and the young for resources. It will only shift the locus and burden of that competition from public budgets to family budgets.

Though we spend heavily—and some say too heavily—to meet the needs of the elderly, their needs are far from met by existing institutions. Perhaps the clearest example of the failure to meet important needs is our long-term care system. This system forces the premature institutionalization of many partially disabled elderly and leaves millions of others without adequate home care services to enable them to function without extreme hardship. Families that provide care get little relief from their burdens. Yet it is this already inadequate system that will be most strained by the rapid growth of age groups over 75. At the same time, we continue to provide intensive acute care treatments to the dying elderly. We point to this glamorous challenge to death as if it proved we value highly every last minute of their lives—and indeed it is the last minute we appear to value the most, though we do not always know which that minute will be. Yet it is far from obvious that prolonging the process of dying in these ways meets an important health care need. We often trap the elderly in treatments they and their families do not want, even ignoring explicit preferences to discontinue treatment. Children often insist on treating their parents more aggressively than they would want to be treated themselves.

I already noted that the proportion of the elderly who are poor is comparable to that of the population as a whole, which represents great progress. However, this still means that millions of elderly live in poverty and millions more live near the poverty line. Moreover, this poverty is concentrated by race and sex. We can reduce expenditures to meet the needs of the elderly only by pushing many more into poverty or by excluding them from medical care.

The problems we face are especially difficult because it is the basic needs of different groups that lead to conflict and competition. The old and the young both need health care. What do we do if competition means a choice between health care for the elderly and education for their grandchildren, or between the immediate need of elderly parents and the future needs of their adult children?

Underlying the common perception of competition between the old and the young, underlying the call for "generational equity" in our aging society, there lurks a challenging new problem: what is a just or fair distribution of social resources among the different age groups competing for them? I shall argue that we can solve this problem only if we think about the competition among age groups in a radically different way. Indeed, we will have to stop thinking about competition between groups altogether.

JUSTICE AND HEALTH CARE OVER THE LIFESPAN

I have given an overview of the problems we face in our health care system because I want to emphasize one central fact: the time for piecemeal thought about individual problems and merely incremental modifications of the system is past. Of course, we can continue to improve it with legislation aimed at meeting specific needs, for example, by providing for long-term care needs of the elderly or by closing the insurance gap. However, we really face a much bigger challenge: we must rethink what we want out of our health care investment, and, in a principled way, we must consider what our social obligations are in the allocation of resources and the provision of access to care. We have never squarely faced these big tasks, at least not in the way other societies, such as Canada, have when they designed systems that guarantee universal access to adequate health care and provide for regional planning about the dissemination of technology and the allocation of health care resources.

Concerns about these larger issues are already surfacing at the state level. Massachusetts has passed legislation intended to guarantee access to care to all in the state, but there are serious questions whether it has developed an adequate plan to control costs.[3] Oregon has attracted national attention with its decision to provide no state funding for organ transplants for the poor. It argues that prenatal maternal outreach programs will save twice as many lives per dollar spent as such transplant programs, and its senate president, a physician, has argued that, as long as many citizens are without access to any insurance, it is wrong to spend enormous sums to provide benefits to but a few. Of course, by denying access to expensive high-technology treatments that may be available to other citizens or to those who move to another state, or that may be available if pleas for charity funds are successful, Oregon risks creating other inequities that are highly problematic and very visible.[4] Nevertheless, my point is that these problems of access and resource allocation must be faced everywhere and must be based on an attempt to figure out what justice requires. Massachusetts and Oregon are at least trying to face the right issues.

To address these issues of access and resource allocation, we must raise some basic questions about what justice requires in the design of our health care system.[5] Let us begin with a very general question: Is health care *special?* Is it social good that we should distinguish from other goods, say video recorders, because of its special importance? Does it have special moral importance? Also, does that moral importance mean that there are social obligations to distribute it in ways that might not coincide with the results of market distribution? I believe the answer to all these questions is "yes."

Health care—I mean the term quite broadly—does many important things for people. Some extends lives, some reduces pain and suffering, some merely gives important information about one's condition, and much health care affects the quality of life in other ways. Yet, we do not think all things that improve quality of life are comparable in importance: the *way* quality is improved seems critical. I have argued elsewhere that a central unifying function of health care is to maintain and restore functioning that is typical or normal for our species. Health care derives its moral importance from the following fact: normal functioning has a central effect on the opportunity open to an individual. It helps guarantee individuals a fair chance to enjoy the normal opportunity range for their society. The *normal opportunity range* for a given society is the array of life plans reasonable persons in it are likely to construct for themselves. An individual's fair share of the normal opportunity range is the array of life plans he or she may reasonably choose, given his or her talents and skills. Disease and disability shrinks that share from what is fair; health care protects it. Health care lets a person enjoy that portion of the normal range to which his or her full range of skill and talents would give him or her access assuming these too are not impaired by special social disadvantages. The suggestion that emerges from this account is that we should use impairment of the normal opportunity range as a fairly crude measure of the relative moral importance of health care needs at the macro level.

Some general theories of justice, most notably Rawls',[6] provide foundations for a principle protecting fair equality of opportunity. If such a principle is indeed a requirement of an acceptable general theory of justice, then I believe we have a natural way to extend such general theories to govern the distribution of health care. We should include health care institutions among those basic institutions of a society that are governed by the fair equality of opportunity principle.[7] If this approach to a theory of just health care is correct, it means that there are social obligations to provide health care services that protect and restore normal functioning. In short, the principle of justice that should govern the design of health care institutions is a principle that calls for guaranteeing fair equality of opportunity.

This principle of justice has implications for both access and resource allocation. It implies that there should be no financial, geographical, or discriminatory barriers to a level of care that promotes normal functioning. It also implies that resources be allocated in ways that are effective in promoting normal functioning. That is, since we can use the effect on normal opportunity range as a crude way of ranking the moral importance of health care services we can guide hard public policy choices about which services are more important to provide. Thus, the principle does not imply that every technology that might have a positive impact on normal functioning for some individuals should be introduced: we must weigh new technologies against alternatives to judge the overall impact of introducing them on fair equality of opportunity—this gives a slightly new sense to the term "opportunity cost." The point is that social obligations to provide just health care must be met within the conditions of moderate scarcity that we face. This is not an approach that gives individuals a basic right to have all their health care needs met. There are social obligations to provide individuals only with those services that are part of the design of a system that, on the whole, protects equal opportunity.

We must refine this account so that it applies more directly to the problem of allocating health care over the lifespan—among different age groups. I draw on three basic observations. First, there is the banal fact we have all noticed: we age. By contrast, we do not change sex or race. This contrast has important implications for the problem of equality. If I treat blacks and whites or men and women differently, then I produce an inequality, and such inequalities raise questions about justice. If I treat the old and the young differently, I may or may not produce an inequality. If I treat them differently just occasionally and arbitrarily, then I will treat different persons unequally, but if I treat as a matter of policy the old one way and the young another, and I do so over their whole lives, then I treat all persons the same way. No inequality is produced. Thus, the fact that we all notice, that we age, means age is different from race or sex when we think about distributive justice.

Second, as we age, we pass through institutions that redistribute wealth and income in a way that performs a "savings" function. The observation is trivial with regard to income support institutions, such as the Social Security system. It is not often noticed that our health care system does the same thing. When we reach age 65, we consume health care resources at about 3.5 times the rate (in dollars) that we do prior to age 65. However, we pay, as working people, a combined health care insurance premium—through private premiums, through employee contributions, and through Social Security taxes—that covers not just our actuarially fair costs, but the costs of the elderly and of children as well. If this system continues as we age, others will pay "inflated premiums" that will cover our higher costs when we are elderly. In effect, the system allows us to defer the use of resources from one stage of our lives to a later one. It "saves" health care for our old age—when we need more of it.

Third, our health care system is not prudently designed, given that it plays this role as a savings institution. It lavishes life-extending resources on us as we are dying, but it withholds other kinds of services, such as personal care and social support services, which may be crucial to our well-being when our lives are not under immediate threat. The system could be far more prudently designed. It could pay better attention to matching services to needs at different stages of our lives and, thus, be more effective in its savings function.

Earlier, I claimed that the just design of our health care institutions should rest on a principle protecting fair equality of opportunity. Imagine that each of us has a lifetime allocation of health care services, which we can claim only if the appropriate needs arise, as a result of appealing to such a principle. Our task now is to allocate that fair share over the lifespan—and to do so prudently. In this exercise, we will find out what is just or fair between age groups by discovering what it is prudent to do between stages of life, over the whole lifespan. One way to make sure we do not bias this allocation, favoring one stage of life and, thus, one age group over another is to pretend that we do not know how old we are. We must allocate these resources imagining that we must live our whole lives with the result of our choices. One way we would refine our earlier principle of justice is to conclude that we should protect our fair shares of the normal opportunity range at each stage of life. Since we must live through each stage, we will not treat any one stage as less important than another.[8]

Notice what this rather abstract perspective—I call it the Prudential Lifespan Account—accomplishes: it tells us that we should not think of age groups as competing with each other, but as sharing a whole life. We want to make that life go as well as possible, and we must therefore make the appropriate decisions about what needs it is most important to meet at each stage of life. If we do this prudently, we will learn how it is fair to treat each age group. Instead of focusing on competition, we have

a unifying perspective or vision. I am suggesting that, as individuals and as a society, we must think through the decisions we must make about our health care system from this perspective.

IMPLICATIONS FOR RESOURCE ALLOCATION

There are important implications of this perspective. How would prudent deliberators view the importance of various personal care and social support services for the partially disabled as compared to personal medical services? From the perspective of these deliberators, both types of care would have the same rationale and the same general importance. Personal medical services restore normal functioning and, thus, have a great impact on an individual's share of the normal opportunity range at each stage of life. However, so too do personal care and support services for the partially disabled. They compensate for losses of normal functioning in ways that enhance individual opportunity. It is not prudent to design a system such as ours, which ignores these health care needs, since they affect such a substantial portion of the later stages of life. If we pay attention only to acute care needs, then we are "saving" the wrong kinds of resources, or not enough resources.

A major criticism of the US health care system—that it encourages premature and inappropriate institutionalization of the elderly—should be assessed in this light. The issue becomes not just one of costs and the relative cost-effectiveness of institutionalization vs home care. Rather, opportunity range for many disabled persons will be enhanced if they are helped to function normally outside institutions. They will have more opportunity to complete projects and pursue relationships of great importance to them, or even to modify the remaining stages of their plans of life. Often, this issue is discussed in terms of the loss of dignity and self-respect that accompanies premature institutionalization or inappropriate levels of care. The underlying issue, however, is loss of opportunity range, which obviously has an effect on autonomy, dignity, and self-respect. Viewed in this light, the British and Canadian systems (which are quite different from each other), in which extensive home care services exist (at least in some Canadian provinces), far more respect the importance of normal opportunity range for the elderly than does our system. They put more of their resources into improving opportunity range for the substantial number of elderly who are disabled over significant periods of the late stages of life. We put our resources into marginally extending life when it is threatened in old age by acute episodes. I am suggesting their approach may be more prudent, because it better protects age-relative opportunity range than ours.

There is another implication of this approach that is quite controversial. Under certain resource constraints, prudent deliberators would prefer a distributive scheme that improves their chances of reaching a normal lifespan (normal life expectancy) to one that gives them a reduced chance of reaching normal lifespan, but a greater chance to live an extended span once normal life expectancy is reached. It would be prudent, in other words, to put more resources into reducing early death than into adding years very late in life. Under some conditions of resource scarcity, this might imply rationing some life-extending technologies by age, but this implication very much depends on how the scarcity works in the society.[9] In contrast to Callahan,[10] I am not advocating such rationing as general policy, either because it would help contain costs or because it would add meaning to our old age, as Callahan would ironically have it. In contrast to Callahan, I do not think there is only one way to add meaning to old age. My argument leads only to a very modest conclusion: under certain conditions of scarcity, rationing by age would not be impermissible and could be the fair way to allocate scarce resources. Of course, such rationing would have to meet other stringent conditions, including that the policy and its rationale be public and democratically selected. Nevertheless, there are far more important things we can do to make our current system both more effective and more just in its use of resources than introducing rationing by age, even for those cases where scarcity may have the effects required by the argument I have sketched.

There are important practical implications of the Prudential Lifespan Account for the young as well as the old. The most basic implication of this view is that the insurance gap that excludes about 1 in 5 children from any form of medical insurance is simply intolerable. Important groups are addressing this problem in the traditional American way—patch as patch can. The Academy of Pediatrics is supporting legislation calling for universal health coverage for children and mothers—mirroring Medicare's protection at the end of life. Similarly, the Children's Defense Fund calls for expansion of Medicaid eligibility requirements (covering all children in families living below 200% of

poverty). These proposals are consistent with the approach to justice I have been describing—provided they really solve the problems of access. There are good reasons now to consider solving this problem in an unAmerican way—through a truly universal insurance scheme. Incremental proposals will always leave some groups unprotected; means-based coverage will always leave the poor vulnerable when the political will to meet social obligations flags.

One thing that is striking about the literature on children's health is the broad consensus that certain preventive and monitoring services—beginning prenatally and going through adolescence—are essential to protecting the health status of children. Many of the inequalities in health status between poor children, especially minorities, and richer children are traceable to lack of access to such services. At the same time, however, society is willing to lavish very expensive technologies on the "identified victims" that result from the absence of such preventive services. The point was brought home to me when I was taken on a tour of Houston a couple of years ago. I was shown the Jefferson Davis Memorial Hospital, which is located in a Chicano ghetto. It boasts, I was told, one of the most expensive neonatal intensive care units in the country—state of the art. Yet there was absolutely no prenatal maternal care outreach program in the area of the hospital. Moreover, after an infant surviving such treatment is released, it could end up uninsured again, since Texas has one of the most restrictive Medicaid eligibility standards of all states.

Is ours a prudently designed system? I will say something shortly about "big-ticket" items, like neonatal intensive care, and I am not saying that we should abandon such services. However, if I were designing a system I would have to live through at all stages of life, and if I wanted it to meet my needs early in life, I would prefer one that guaranteed access to prenatal maternal care to one that had no such services but offered neonatal intensive care instead. Prudence requires me to attend to the fact that the preventive program more cost-effectively protects and maintains normal functioning—and thus, my opportunity range—than neonatal intensive care. If resources were scarce, I would also prefer the prenatal maternal care program to various technologies that deliver less protection of opportunity range at higher cost at later stages of my life, e.g., aggressive chemotherapy for metastatic solid tumors. I am here not arguing rigorously, but only using the device of prudent lifespan allocation heuristically to help us see that certain allocations in our health system more effectively protect opportunity over the lifespan than others. On the theory that I am sketching, prudent allocations are the ones that are fair to different age groups, the ones that justice requires.

Similar points could be made about the recommendations of the Academy of Pediatrics and the Children's Defense Fund: the key difference in the health status of children will be made by relatively inexpensive, but labor-intensive services. Fetuses need their mothers to be adequately nourished, free of sexually transmitted diseases, and free of drugs. Children need immunizations, they need to be monitored for their physical and mental development, they need access to psychological and dental services, they need lead removed from their homes, and they need education and counseling as adolescents about sex and drugs. If we knew that we had to budget a lifetime fair share of health care so that it made our lives as a whole go as well as possible and so that it protected opportunity at each stage of life, we would not be stingy about these services. Indeed, we would trade access to them for access to many acute care services that are now provided as a matter of course and without any real concern about their costs. A very similar set of points could be made about access to long-term care for chronic diseases and disabilities: these services may be more important to protecting opportunity over the lifespan than lavishing certain technologies on the dying—elderly or young.

My point here is not that we should now ration big-ticket items, such as organ transplantation or neonatal intensive care, even if they would be less prudent to include in our system than services we now omit. I doubt that, in our wealthy system, the rationing of these big-ticket items is really necessary. In any case, we have hardly eliminated all services that are less cost-effective than these big-ticket ones—indeed, we are not even sure which ones they are. Nevertheless, under some conditions of scarcity—including the natural scarcity of organs—justice requires that we ration fairly, and so we must be clear about what principle should govern such rationing, including the dissemination of technologies whose opportunity costs are too high.

INSTITUTIONAL OBSTACLES TO JUST RATIONING

I want to conclude by noting that it is not enough simply to have a good idea what an ideally just allocation of health care resource would be.[11] Suppose we conclude that protecting equality of opportunity over the lifespan implies that we should not disseminate as widely as we do certain big-ticket technologies, such as organ substitution technologies. Suppose, that is, that Oregon is right and that opportunity is better protected for the system as a whole by using our resources on other technologies.[12] The point is sometimes put by saying that the "opportunity costs" of some big-ticket technologies is too high. Knowing that a more just allocation would not include the widespread dissemination of these technologies will not stop their dissemination, for there are institutional obstacles to acting on these concerns about what justice requires.

Much of our health care decision making is not regionally or nationally coordinated. Different providers often directly compete with each other, which gives them some different, merely agent-relative rather than common, goals. Even where there is no direct competition, there is still no coordination or cooperation. When these providers pursue their goals—when they successfully pursue them—they may still produce outcomes that are collectively worse for them and us. It is important to see how this problem arises.

Suppose that we agree that, in an ideally just arrangement, the health care system would invest resources in services other than certain organ substitution technologies. On the other hand, if we forgo introducing this technology (supposing we are on a hospital board making such a decision), some other providers we compete with may do so anyway. Then those providers will be seen as the technologically most advanced hospitals and medical centers. They will attract physicians who seek the glamor and profit involved in offering such services; they will attract patients. They will be in a superior competitive situation to us. So if other providers introduce the new technology, we are better off if we do, too. On the other hand, if other providers refrain from introducing the technology although we add it, then we will enhance our competitive situation relative to them. Of course, each provider will reason this way. In the absence of political constraints that compel us to do otherwise, each will add the technology, and we will move farther from what we agreed would be a more just allocation of resources. Thus, when we all introduce the big-ticket items, the system works less well than it should, and our competitive situation is, in any case, no better than it would have been had we all refrained from disseminating the inappropriate technology.

It may seem that only bad motives could drive us to reason in this way, but this is not the case. Good motives can produce the same bad results. For example, we may be motivated to do the best we can for our patients; we may think that we have a special obligation to deliver all medically feasible benefits to our own patients. These motives will lead each provider to reason that it should introduce the new technology or risk, losing the opportunity to benefit its patients as much as it can.

Two important features of the US health care system create this problem. We allow health care institutions to operate competitively instead of requiring them to act cooperatively and collectively. Also, we do not force each institution to pay the price for introducing technologies with highly problematic opportunity costs. Together, these features create a context in which claims that justice requires spending resources in ways that do not involve certain technologies fail to obtain a grip on allocation decisions. This argument suggests that macro allocation decisions at the federal and state levels will have to establish specific priorities for technology dissemination and will have to provide the regulative and legislative muscle needed to produce cooperative and not merely competitive decision making.

Eliminating these features of our institutions will have to be an explicit priority for those who wish to make our system conform to acceptable ideals of justice for health care. Medical and other health care technologies have made it possible for us to make improvements in our well-being at all points in the lifespan. However, under real world conditions of scarcity, we cannot meet everyone's needs, and so we must figure out how it is fair to allocate limited resources. I have suggested a perspective from which to think about some of those questions. I have emphasized the importance of fair equality of opportunity in thinking about health care in general, and I have suggested that we use the device of thinking about prudent allocation over the lifespan as a way of answering questions about justice between age groups.

In pointing out that there are institutional obstacles that stand in the way of making our system more just, however, I do not intend to build skepticism about the relevance of thinking about justice to practical decisions. It is important to know that, even if people understand what would be just, institutional arrangements may make it impossible for them to make appropriate decisions. Even when we know we cannot fully achieve the ideal, it is still important to know just what stands in our way. What stands in our way in this case is not sacred or immutable, but only institutions that we have constructed and can alter.

The central thesis of this chapter has been that prudential allocation over the lifespan can guide us toward a policy that is fair to all age groups. My own account of justice for health care requires that the Prudential Lifespan Account be applied within a general framework that protects fair equality of opportunity. In the United States, two crucial features of the system stand in the way of it even approximating the requirements of justice. First, the financing of the system means that almost 40 million citizens are uninsured and many millions more are underinsured. Second, there is no mechanism for allocating resources in accordance with principles of fairness; indeed, the institutional obstacles we have just examined stand in the way. Together, these point to a policy conclusion. The most effective way to move the system into compliance with what justice requires would be to implement a national health insurance scheme that guarantees universal coverage and provides the means to carry out appropriate resource allocation measures, including rationing of beneficial services. I have not argued for this policy conclusion here, but do not see any way justice can be done without measures along these lines.

NOTES AND REFERENCES

1. This chapter is based on a talk delivered at the Conference on Justice Between Generations, University of Maryland at Baltimore, October 1988. I draw on material in N. Daniels (1988a) *Am I My Parents' Keeper? An Essay on Justice Between the Young and the Old.* Oxford University Press, New York, NY, with permission.

2. D.L. Frankfather, M.J. Smith, and F.G. Caro (1981) *Family Care of the Elderly.* Lexington Books, Lexington, MA, p. 1.

3. I believe there are also problems with its retention of an employer-based system of private insurance.

4. Oregon's position can be understood as follows: given that politically imposed resource limitations mean that some rationing by ability will take place, it is better to ration extrarenal organ transplants by ability to pay than prenatal maternal care services. *See* N. Daniels (1989) Comment: Ability to pay and access to transplantation. *Transplantation Proceedings* **21:3**, 3424–3425.

5. *See* N. Daniels (1985) *Just Health Care.* Cambridge University Press, New York, NY, and (1988a) for a developed discussion of the approach to justice and health care sketched above.

6. *See* J. Rawls (1971) *A Theory of Justice.* Harvard University Press, Cambridge, MA, pp. 75–90, 150–161, 175–183.

7. This requires modifications of Rawls' equal opportunity principle, however. Cf Daniels, *Just Health Care,* pp. 39–55.

8. The justification for this approach and many of its details are necessarily omitted here. *See* Daniels 1988a.

9. For the details of the argument for this conclusion, *see* Daniels (1988a, Ch. 5). It would be very easy to misunderstand this argument if its more developed version is not examined carefully.

10. D. Callahan (1987) *Setting Limits: Medical Goals in an Aging Society.* Simon and Schuster, New York, NY.

11. The next several paragraphs draw on material in Daniels (1988b) Justice and the dissemination of big-ticket technologies, in *Organ Substitution Technology: Ethical, Legal, and Public Policy Issues.* Westview Press, Boulder, CO, pp. 211–220.

12. *See* N. Daniels (1989) Comment: Ability to pay and access to transplantation. *Transplantation Proceedings* **21:3**, 3424–3425, for further discussion of Oregon and "ability to pay" as a criterion for organ transplantation.

Health Care Reform: Still Possible

Ezekiel Emanuel

Now might be the time, if the proposal is crafted right.

Without much public notice, health care is entering a crisis. The events of 11 September and the Enron collapse have made that crisis more imminent, serious, and even more likely to come on the American public and politicians unnoticed. September 11 gave the economy another major hit, led to a military build up that will consume whatever budget surplus there might have been, and drew whatever political and public attention exists away from domestic issues. Nevertheless, we should attend to health care reform. There will soon be a major crisis, and we need to be ready with a reasonable policy for politicians who will suddenly find themselves in need of answers.

Consider four descriptive and five prescriptive propositions that lead to the outlines of a politically palatable and ethically justifiable strategy.

1. No one is happy with the current health care system. Doctors and patients hate the encroachment on their choice, feel they have no control over their health plan, and trust no one. Managed care organizations and employers feel that doctors and patients have unrealistic demands, are unwilling to confront the need to cut costs, and are unwilling to be held accountable; managed care is asked to do the impossible to simultaneously improve quality and keep costs down.

2. Health care costs are going up and will continue to go up in the foreseeable future. Whatever savings there were in the 1990s from managed care, they are gone, and they will not return. With pharmaceuticals rising at 20 to 30 percent per year, and hospitals and doctors demanding more money, premiums are heading up at double digit rates with no end in sight.

3. The number of uninsured Americans is going up and the range of health benefits for those who are insured is going down. Increases in unemployment and increases in health care premiums mean more people will lose their health insurance. Decreases in corporate profits mean that those still insured will have skimpier benefit packages and bear more of the premium price with higher copayments.

4. Pressure on state budgets will also mean close looks at Medicaid budgets. As the economy declines, state coffers shrink. Coincidentally, rises in unemployment and health care costs will increase Medicaid expenditures, further squeezing state budgets and crowding out other vital state programs, including education and infrastructure improvements.

This is the crisis. But we have been here before. This was almost exactly the situation in the early 1990s, except that then managed care had the potential to constrain costs. And yet, as we all know, health care reform failed. In part, it failed because Clinton spectacularly misplayed the politics of health care reform, and in part because employers embraced managed care—and abandoned Clinton's plan—on the premise that managed care was a more certain path to controlling costs.

What better proof is there that everyone makes big—multibillion dollar—mistakes? But we can learn five key lessons from that stunning and tragic failure that might help develop universal health care coverage.

5. The big hurdle for health care reform is not ethics or economics but politics. Ethics supports universal coverage. Both ethics and economics urge the need for cost constraint. But even when everyone agrees that there is a problem, that is no guarantee they all—or even a majority of them—will support the same solution. The key is to provide a solution that both liberals and conservatives can endorse, making it harder for any single interest group to kill it.

6. Retain a private health care delivery system. "Harry and Louise" ads proved that the health care insurance industry is strong and can torpedo almost any reform package that tries to eliminate it. After all, its survival is at stake, and the industry has nothing to lose in such a life-and-death struggle. More importantly, no delivery system that is dominantly public will have any chance of widespread public support in the United States. It is important to emphasize ad nauseum that there is a difference between finance and delivery and that predominantly public finance can happily coexist with private delivery. This occurs in lots of spheres—defense procurement, biomedical research, highway construction. But recall Lyndon Johnson's problem with selling Medicare to the American medical establishment and don't underestimate the difficulty of communicating this basic distinction between finance and delivery.

7. Break the employer-health insurance link. This is purely a quirk of history and it persists because of inertia. No reasonable person defends it. With the end of life-time employment, with American residential and employment mobility, with small businesses as the driving force behind job creation, it makes no sense to have health coverage provided by employers. More importantly, employers no longer want this responsibility. Health care costs are unpredictable and rising; employers need predictability. They would rather compete for employees on salary than on health benefits. For employees, having the employer control which insurance company they get and which doctor they see is odious and constraining.

8. Some kind of managed delivery system is here to stay. While everyone has the managed care blues and many people are writing its obituary, some form of managed health care seems here to stay. Leaving health care decisions to each doctor's discretion has been undermined by quality and cost data. When everyone is talking about the importance of systems for delivering safe, high quality, and cost effective care it is hard to imagine that we will dismantle the very delivery system capable of doing this. It is much more likely that a new form of management will arise.

9. Permit a multitiered delivery system as long as the bottom rung is reasonable. Ethicists often worry about tiered systems in which the the rich have access to better medical care. This worry is mistaken. Justice does not require that every person receive the same health care services. The only key ethical questions are whether the range of medical services guaranteed to all as the minimum is just, and whether allowing the rich to buy more undermines what the less well-off get. We should expect the rich to spend their money to get more of everything, but this should not disturb us if the poor are guaranteed a sufficient package.

So the question is: Is there a health care system that retains private, managed care delivery, breaks the employer link, will not break the bank, and can be politically palatable to both liberals and conservatives? After a century of repeated failures to enact a national health care system, the most hopeful answer that can be given is *maybe.*

The only thing I can imagine that fulfills these requirements is a universal health care voucher system. Vouchers would be provided to individuals and families by the government or by private employers who prefer—or are forced by union contracts—to retain this responsibility. Individuals and families would use vouchers to purchase health insurance from a private managed care or insurance system. A quasi-public body would certify managed care or health insurance companies based on their ability to provide the minimum services, fiscal health, and adequate delivery capacity. This body would also have responsibility for monitoring quality of these delivery systems.

Could this work? This is the barest of outlines and there are a huge number of details to be worked out. I can only sketch some answers to the most critical questions. Politically it has certain attractive qualities. "Universal health care voucher" is a simple sound-bite slogan. The public will like the control it provides over choice of insurance company, as well as the prospect of secure coverage that does not change with every change in employer. For liberals it provides for universality in health insurance—a long-sought goal. Liberals have opposed vouchers in education and for Medicare. But these are existing universal, public provision programs in which a voucher system seems to take something away. There is no universal entitlement in health care; a voucher may well be the only way to achieve that cherished goal. For conservatives it is a voucher that gives individuals choice over their own health coverage. Conservatives have never met a voucher system they did not like. This would be especially popular with conservatives if Medicare and Medicaid were included either immediately or phased in with new beneficiaries, thereby getting the government completely out of health care.

To ensure fiscal responsibility the value of the voucher would have to be established. The infusion of money required to establish its value would be a net redistribution from the rich to the poor, politically the most problematic of its characteristics. But then the value of the voucher would increase with overall inflation, plus a bit for the aging of the population. This would provide a perfect fiscal rheostat. People who want more services would pay higher premiums and copayments. As prices increase, people would opt for fewer added services and use their services more prudently and cost consciously. When the gap between the value of the voucher and the premiums increased too much, requiring more out-of-pocket payments, there would be political pressure by the public to significantly increase the value of voucher. But that would require raising taxes to pay for a higher voucher value. Thus the system would provide perfect individual and social incentive to control costs.

To minimize cherry picking by the managed care and insurance companies, the value of the voucher payment to the companies would be "risk adjusted" or based on partial capitation. This would mean that incentives to exclude the sickest members of society would be minimized or eliminated. Simultaneously, to the public the voucher would appear the same, ensuring universality and popular support.

If we are to have any chance of reforming the health care system to ensure universal health care coverage while controlling costs in a politically palatable form, I think the universal health care voucher is the only way forward. Will it solve all problems? Clearly not. Is a universal health care voucher better than what we have? Definitely.

Health Care and Equality of Opportunity

Gopal Sreenivasan

In many civilized societies, universal access to health care—or, at least, to a decent minimum of health care—is regarded as a requirement of justice. Indeed, for many, its status as a requirement of justice may be fairly described as axiomatic. Still, even those who already subscribe to this consensus (as I do) may hope that a more articulate rationale can also be provided. One prominent rationale appeals to a principle of "equality of opportunity."[1] Its rough idea is that good *health* is required to secure individuals in the share of opportunity, whatever it is exactly, that they are due under the principle of equality of opportunity. Furthermore, since access to a decent minimum of health care is manifestly required to secure an individual's good health, access to health care will likewise be required for everyone under the same principle.

My aim here is to argue that, despite appearances, an equality of opportunity framework actually fails to supply us with the desired rationale. I shall argue that when due account is taken of important data on the so-called "social determinants" of health, the conclusion to which the equal opportunity framework leads is that universal access to health care is not required by justice. I do not mean to endorse this conclusion; instead I think we should seek an alternative rationale for the requirement of universal access. Neither do I mean to impugn the equal opportunity principle. As a matter of justice, I believe in both universal access to health care and equality of opportunity. I simply contend that the one does not follow from the other. Not all good things grow on the same tree.

THE EQUALITY OF OPPORTUNITY RATIONALE

To set the stage, let me bring the idea of an equal opportunity account into better focus. Any principle of equality of opportunity will assign each individual a protected share of opportunity. The equality of opportunity rationale for universal access to health care begins from that protected share. We can refer to it as the individual's *fair share* of opportunity. Different principles will define this share differently. But the aim of the argument is to extend the moral protection accorded an individual's fair share of opportunity to a share of health care.

The central insight on which the argument rests is that there is a strong instrumental connection between good health and an individual's (effective) opportunities: without good health, an individual would have markedly fewer opportunities.[2] In that sense, protecting an individual's health is required in order to maintain her existing share of opportunities. Not only is this point difficult to deny, but it also holds for a very wide range of interpretations of what an "opportunity" is. This makes it possible for the argument to proceed despite the fact that few advocates for equality of opportunity are very specific about the nature of the relevant opportunities.[3]

What the equal opportunity account infers from its central insight is that individuals require good health in order to maintain their fair share of opportunity. Let's call the "magnitude" of health required to maintain an individual's fair share of opportunity a "fair share of health." The first step in the argument is thus from a fair share of opportunity to a fair share of health. To end up with a rationale for universal access to health care, we still need a further step, from health to health *care*. Continuing the instrumental strategy, we must be able to affirm that individuals require access to health care in order to secure their fair share of health. But this is perfectly intuitive. The cumulative upshot of the argument, therefore, is that each individual requires a fair share of health care to retain her fair share of opportunity.

So conceived, the equal opportunity rationale is simple and appealing. Unfortunately, it is also invalid.

Despite the connection between health and opportunity, we are not entitled to infer "violation of equal opportunity" merely from "loss of health." To be sure, someone in ill health will have fewer opportunities than when she was in good health, but this shows only that health was required to maintain her *existing* share of opportunity. Since that share may well have exceeded her *fair* share, it does not follow that she now has less than her fair share of opportunity. It may simply be that illness has reduced the opportunities she had in excess of her fair share.

To license the inference from loss of health to violation of equal opportunity, the argument has to establish that the opportunities an individual stands to lose with a loss of health will leave her with *less* than her fair share of opportunity. I know of only one demonstrably successful way to establish this crucial point. It requires that "equality" of opportunity be interpreted in relative terms, so that a "fair share of opportunity" is defined in comparison to the shares held by others in society: each person's share of opportunity ought to be (more or less) the same as everyone else's share.[4] Let me explain how this interpretation enables us to restore the validity of the equal opportunity rationale.

On the relative interpretation, an individual's fair share of opportunity refers, by definition, to other people's opportunities. Her share has to be more or less the same *as theirs*. This comparison to others makes it possible to locate the lower limit on a fair share of opportunity by combining two known quantities. The first quantity is supplied by the relevant others—for example, by the average level of opportunity in society. The second quantity is the permissible variance in a fair share—the "more or less" in "more or less equal," which can be estimated. Combining these two quantities tells us that no one's level of opportunity is permitted to fall below the average by more than half of the permissible variance in a fair share.

To generate a valid rationale for access to health care, it only remains to establish that the "magnitude" of opportunity that a given individual stands to lose with a loss of health will drop her below this permissible lower limit. In that case, a loss of health will indeed leave her with less than her fair share of opportunity. A rough and ready argument along the required lines is not difficult to supply. The following premises would suffice: The magnitude of opportunity that individuals stand to lose with a loss of health will leave them far below the average, whereas the permissible lower limit on their fair share of opportunity is not far below the average. Despite their vagueness, these premises are fairly plausible, and they license the rationale's crucial

inference from loss of health to violation of equal opportunity.

Now, although it is the most familiar interpretation of equality of opportunity, the relative interpretation is not strictly compulsory. For present purposes, however, the fact that it demonstrably restores the validity—and therefore, the appeal—of the equal opportunity rationale for universal access is sufficient reason to adopt it.[5] From here on, then, I shall understand fair shares of opportunity as *relative* shares.

At this point we should also note a further consequence of adopting this interpretation, which is that fair shares of health also have to be understood as relative shares. This follows because the moral significance of health derives, on the equal opportunity account, simply from its connection to a fair share of opportunity. Variations in health matter, in other words, only insofar as they have an effect on opportunity. Yet by the definition above, only relative variations in opportunity affect anyone's fair share of opportunity. Accordingly, the only variations in health that matter are relative variations, since only relative variations in health produce relative variations in opportunity.[6]

In summary, the equal opportunity argument for universal access to health care has two main steps. The first step takes us from a fair share of opportunity to a fair share of health; and the second step takes us from this fair share of health to a fair share of health care. While it can easily seem that the challenge for the argument centers on the first step, we may now actually ignore that step. My criticism will focus entirely on the *second* step, the most intuitive one. All one will need to bear in mind is that my target requires both steps and that the fair shares to which it refers are relative shares.

SOCIAL DETERMINENTS OF HEALTH

Let us therefore turn to examine the equal opportunity rationale's step from a fair share of health to a fair share of health care. Intuitively, this step seems eminently reasonable. But it is instructive to ask why access to health care should be necessary for conserving one's fair share of health. The simplest position is that health care is the only *socially controllable* factor that makes a significant causal contribution to health. Since the other obvious determinants of health—biology and luck—are not socially controllable, this position is certainly plausible. Still, I shall argue that it is false.

The empirical data to which I shall appeal in this connection concern what have been called the "social determinants" of health.[7] These data have been well known to public health researchers for at least two decades, but have only caught the attention of a wider audience relatively recently.[8] The *social determinants* of health, roughly speaking, are those social factors outside the traditional health care system that have an effect—either positive or negative—on the health status of individuals in a given population.

An example will help. Consider the distribution of class or socioeconomic status (SES).[9] I chose this example because there is a lot of data on SES. However, it also has the independent merit of falling clearly *outside* the health care system, no matter how broadly the system is plausibly defined.

Perhaps the best evidence on the relation between class and health comes from the Whitehall studies, conducted in England by Michael Marmot.[10] Between 1967 and 1969, Marmot examined some eighteen thousand male civil servants ranging in age from forty to sixty-nine. By placing a flag on their records at the National Health Service (NHS) Central Registry, Marmot was able to track the cause and date of death for each subject who later died. His data are unusually good. To begin with, they are generated from data points on specific individuals. Each datum reports the relation between the class position of a particular person and the lifespan (and cause of death) of the very same person. By contrast, almost every other study begins from aggregate data. In addition, a number of important background factors are held constant for this study population. Notably, all of the subjects are stably employed, live in the same region (greater London), and have free access to health care provided by the NHS.

Figure 1 presents the Whitehall data after twenty-five years of follow-up. It reports age-adjusted, all-cause mortality rate ratios by employment grade for three periods of follow-up.[11] There are four grades in the British Civil Service employment hierarchy: administrative at the top, followed by professional/executive, clerical, and "other." The professional/executive grade was used as the reference group, so its mortality rate ratio is 1.0 by definition.

The striking and important feature of these data is that the relationship between employment grade and mortality exhibits a marked gradient. It is natural to think that, below some threshold of deprivation, there will be disproportionate ill-health. Yet in this study population, there is no deprivation, not even in the lowest grade. They are all government employees, and they all have free access to health care. More to the point, however, there is no threshold, either. Rather, there is a *step-wise* improvement in health outcomes as one climbs the class ladder. During the first

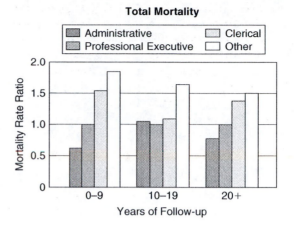

FIGURE 1 Social gradient in total mortality, Whitehall 25-year follow-up.

C. Van Rossum et al., "Employment grade differences in cause specific mortality," *Journal of Epidemiology and Community Health* 54 (2000): 181. Figure reproduced with permission from the BMJ publishing group.

nine years of follow-up, clerical civil servants have a significantly lower mortality rate than the "others," and the mortality rate for professionals is more than a third lower than that for clericals. Most surprising perhaps, the mortality rate for administrators is, in turn, a third lower again than that for professionals. The gradient does flatten in the middle follow-up period, but a clear step-wise pattern reemerges after twenty to twenty-seven years of follow-up.

Moreover, these marked gradients persist even after the mortality rates have been adjusted for standard risk factors. For example, standard risk factors for coronary heart disease include smoking, blood pressure, cholesterol and blood sugar levels, and height.[12] Figure 2 presents the Whitehall data on mortality from coronary heart disease, again after twenty-five years of follow-up. It reports relative rates of death from coronary heart disease by employment grade, with administrators having a rate of 1.0 by definition. The left bar in each pair displays the relative rate adjusted for age alone, while the right bar adjusts it for all the standard risk factors. Correcting for standard risk factors explains some of the gradient in coronary heart disease mortality, but no more than a third. The remaining gradient is still marked.

It seems clear, then, that SES either makes a fairly strong contribution to the distribution of health across the population or stands proxy for something else that does. That is a straightforward consequence of the marked social gradient in health.[13] Moreover, this gradient is manifest even when access to health care is

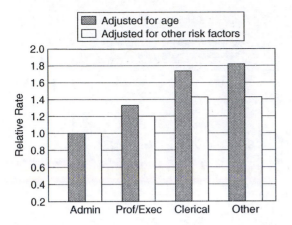

FIGURE 2 Risk factor adjusted social gradient in coronary heart disease mortality, Whitehall 25-year follow-up.

M.G. Marmot, "Multilevel approaches to understanding social determinants," in *Social Epidemology*, ed. L. Berkman and I. Kawachi (Oxford, U.K.: Oxford University Press, 2000), 363. Figure reproduced with the permission of Oxford University Press.

held constant. We should therefore conclude that health care is not the only socially controllable factor that makes a significant contribution to health.

HOW MUCH DOES HEALTH CARE CONTRIBUTE TO HEALTH?

Of course, access to health care may still be necessary to conserve one's fair share of health, even if other socially controllable factors also make significant contributions to health. Hence, by itself, the argument so far is not sufficient to undermine the equal opportunity rationale for universal access. All the equal opportunity rationale requires is that, relative to the other socially controllable factors, the contribution health care makes to health is strong enough to make access to health care indispensable to a fair share of health. But is health care's relative contribution as critical as that?

I shall develop my answer in stages. I begin by describing a generic scenario in which health care makes a *weak* contribution to the distribution of health, and the strong contribution that SES makes or stands proxy for is also socially *controllable*. I start with a generic description because that makes it easier to specify where the equal opportunity rationale goes wrong. However, I want to emphasize at the outset that my scenario is far from an idle conjecture. On the contrary, its defining assumptions are empirically quite realistic, as I shall go on to show.

Let's say our society does not have universal access to health care: we have no national health insurance scheme, and many of our citizens do not have private health insurance. Let's say, furthermore, that our society has a social gradient in health status similar to the one exhibited in Figures 1 and 2. Now imagine the following scenario: First, suppose our society introduces a national health insurance scheme and this makes *no* difference to the social gradient in health—the distribution of health outcomes across society remains essentially unchanged. Second, suppose that if, instead of introducing a national health insurance scheme, we had spent the same amount of money on equalizing the distribution of social status—on equalizing the distribution of income, say, or of education—then our society's social gradient in health would have been significantly reduced.

In this scenario, our society actually moves its citizens *closer* to their "fair share of health" by devoting the entire cost of the national health insurance scheme to ameliorating the social determinants of health—closer, that is, than it does by maintaining a national health insurance scheme. It follows that the equal opportunity account does not require universal access to health care.

To defend these two claims, let us first ask how, for these purposes, a "fair share of health" should be understood. On the equal opportunity account, as we have seen, a fair share of health is the share of health required to preserve an individual's fair share of opportunity. To illustrate what this means, let us make do initially with two crude simplifications. (We shall refine them presently.) Let us say that "fair" means equal and that the "health" required to preserve an equal share of opportunity is a matter of lifespan. Let us say, in other words, that having a *fair share of health* means living the average lifespan.

In that case, a society's citizens are closer to their fair share of health to the extent that each of their lifespans approaches the average—when there is less variance in the distribution of life expectancy around the mean. On this interpretation, flattening our society's social gradient in mortality is the same thing as moving its citizens closer to their fair share of health. By hypothesis, spending the entire national health care budget on ameliorating the distribution of social status flattens the social gradient in mortality, whereas spending it on the health insurance scheme does not. Hence, the first course moves the citizens of our society closer to their fair share of health, and the second does not.

Notice that relaxing the first simplification does not affect this conclusion. If a fair share need not be an equal share, but only a "more or less equal" share, then a fair share of health will correspond to a *range* of lifespans centered on the mean. In that case, it will be possible to achieve a completely fair distribution of health without altogether eliminating the variance in a society's distribution of life expectancy. This certainly seems plausible. However, as long as the actual variance exceeds the variance permitted by fairness, flattening the social gradient—and so reducing the variance in life expectancy—will still move citizens *closer* to their fair share of health.

A similar point can be made about the second simplification. As long as more sophisticated measures of health themselves exhibit a marked social gradient, the conclusion will stand. Presumably, the most sophisticated measures of health will combine mortality and morbidity in some fashion. But we need not inquire into the details of the combination here, since it turns out that both of these dimensions manifest a steep social gradient. In a subsequent study, "Whitehall II," Marmot and his colleagues went on to demonstrate that many measures of *morbidity* also exhibit a steep social gradient.[14] Moreover, these gradients in morbidity persist in the face of adjustment for standard risk factors as well.[15] Replacing "life expectancy" with a more sophisticated measure of health would not, therefore, disturb the basic conclusion that devoting our society's entire health care budget to improving the social determinants of health does better than running a national health insurance scheme at moving the citizens closer to their fair share of health.

Now let me vindicate the two key assumptions that license this conclusion. The first assumption was that our society introduces a national health insurance scheme, and it makes no difference to the social gradient in health. This assumption describes what actually happened in Britain in the twentieth century, as documented in 1980 by the "Report of the Working Group on Inequalities in Health" (generally known as the Black Report). Figure 3 presents mortality data by social class for men fifteen to sixty-four years old in England and Wales. Social class is measured here in the terms of the U.K. Registrar General's classification scheme, which ranges from professional (class I) through to unskilled (class V).

The mortality data in Figure 3 are reported as standardized mortality ratios (SMRs). The SMR for a given social class is a ratio of two mortality levels: the actual number who died in that class, and the number

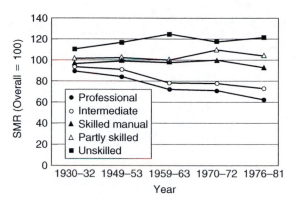

FIGURE 3   Social gradient in relative mortality, English men aged 15–64.

Black report, in *Inequalities in Health*, ed. P. Townsend, N. Davidson, and M. Whitehead (London, U.K.:Penguin books, 1992), 59. The last data point is taken from M. Whitehead, "The health divide," also in *Inequalities in Health*, 231.

who would have died in it had the class had the same mortality rate as the population as a whole. By definition, the SMR for the population as a whole is one hundred. Thus, an SMR greater (or lesser) than one hundred indicates that the mortality rate in the relevant social class is greater (or lesser) than it is in the population as a whole (and by how much).

The series begins in 1930–32 and runs through 1976–81. The National Health Service (NHS) was introduced in July 1948, just before the second data point (1949–53). Any way you look at it, the introduction of the NHS is at least consistent with a *widening* of the social gradient in mortality.[16]

Of course, this is *not* to say that health care makes no difference to life expectancy at all. We need to distinguish between *absolute* levels of life expectancy (or mortality) and *relative* levels. The data in Figure 3, as indeed in Figures 1 and 2, are relative mortality data. They represent the mortality rates of a given social class relative to those of the population as a whole. These data clearly suggest—or at least are surprisingly consistent with the hypothesis—that universal access to health care in Britain did very little to equalize relative levels of life expectancy across its various social classes.[17] Nevertheless, it remains possible that universal access to health care made an important contribution to *absolute* levels of life expectancy in this period, even for social classes whose relative mortality level did not improve. To assess this possibility, we need to examine absolute mortality data.

Figure 4 presents mortality data by social class, in a slightly longer time frame, for men and married women

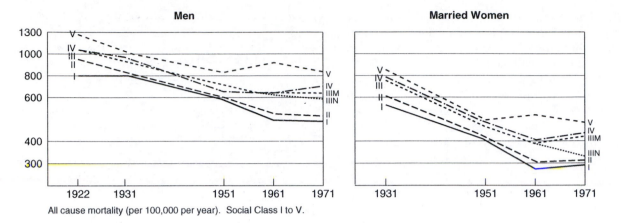

FIGURE 4   Social gradient in absolute mortality, England and Wales.

M.G. Marmot et al., "Social/Economic status and disease," *Annual Review of Public Health* (1987): 117. Figure reproduced with permission from *Annual Reviews*.

in England and Wales. Again, social class is measured by the Registrar General's classifications. But here the mortality rates are reported in absolute terms, as deaths per one hundred thousand per year. There is a clear decline in absolute mortality for all social classes, at least over the first half of the century, even though there is also a gradient across classes. This is certainly consistent with the hypothesis that health care makes an important contribution to absolute life expectancy.

For our purposes, however, the relevant data are those presented in Figure 3.7. As I emphasized at the very beginning, the fair shares of opportunity—and so of health—on which the equal opportunity account focuses are defined in relative terms. As far as relative levels of health are concerned, we really should conclude that the contribution made by universal access to health care is weak. I shall return to this point.

The second assumption was that if, instead of introducing a national health insurance scheme, we had spent the same amount of money on equalizing the distribution of social status, then our society's social gradient in health would have been significantly reduced. I shall have to leave this assumption closer to the status of a conjecture. But let me at least bolster it with a few remarks. To begin with, given that Britain actually spends almost 7 percent of its gross domestic product on the NHS, what this assumption supposes is that spending almost 7 percent of Britain's GDP on equalizing the distribution of some core component of social status there would do *significantly more than nothing* to reduce the social gradient in health status.

Now in order to consider the evidence for this proposition, we need to specify a core component of social status. In principle, we are free to specify whichever

component promises to be the most efficacious lever for policy purposes. But here we are seriously hampered by the primitive state of our understanding of the pathways through which SES affects health.[18] So we have to fall back on income, the component of SES that has received the most attention, despite the fact that it is presumably a fairly crude health policy lever.

No one denies that equalizing the distribution of income in a society will improve average life expectancy *provided* that the relationship between individual income and individual life expectancy is causal and "concave"—meaning that there are diminishing marginal returns of health to income.[19] Thus, the second assumption will be confirmed—at least in principle— if the relationship between individual income and individual life expectancy is causal and concave.[20] Most people agree that the relationship between individual income and life expectancy is indeed concave, and there is also clear empirical evidence that it is.[21]

Both of the assumptions that define my generic scenario turn out, therefore, to be plausible and realistic. What I concluded on their basis was that a society does more to move its citizens toward their fair share of health when it devotes the equivalent of the health care budget to improving the social determinants of health than when it runs a national health care system.

It follows, I also said, that an equal opportunity account does not require universal access to health care. In fact, a stronger contention can be defended. In the Britain we have described, an equal opportunity account requires that society spend *none* of its health budget on health care and all of it on ameliorating the social determinants instead. That is because the goal of health policy, on the equal opportunity account, is to provide each citizen with a fair share of opportunity. The goal, in other words, is a *distribution of opportunity* in which each citizen's share is as close as possible to the fair share. As far as health is concerned, this means a distribution in which each citizen's share of health is as close as possible to the fair share. In the Britain described, that distribution is achieved by devoting the equivalent of the entire NHS budget to ameliorating the social determinants. Accordingly, that is what the equal opportunity account requires.

What complaint of justice can be raised against the failure to provide health care? On the equal opportunity account, variations in access to care matter only insofar as they have an impact on the distribution of opportunity; and they can do *that* only insofar as they have an impact on the distribution of health. Yet by hypothesis, failure to provide health care has no adverse impact on the distribution of health. Hence, on the equal opportunity account, no complaint of justice can be raised against the failure to provide health care. A fortiori, none can be raised against the failure to provide universal access to health care.

OBJECTIONS AND REPLIES

Simply implausible. One immediate objection may be that it is simply implausible to suppose that the optimum allocation of a fixed health budget would allocate nothing to traditional health care. Even if the data show that the contribution health care makes to the distribution of health is weak relative to other socially controllable factors, that hardly establishes that a society should spend *nothing* on health care.

This objection makes two important mistakes. First, it wrongly supposes that my argument offers its own policy prescription (on the basis of the data reviewed). But I am not arguing for or against any policy; I am simply scrutinizing the policy commitments of the equal opportunity account. My aim is to identify the policy that follows from the data, *given that account's goal* of achieving the best distribution of health outcomes (and ignoring all other goals).

Second, the objection trains its attention on the wrong policy question. The dramatic scenario from the previous section, in which nothing is allocated to health care, illustrates the equal opportunity account's answers to *two* policy questions at once. One question is how best to allocate a fixed health budget between health care and the social determinants of health. The other question is whether access to health care should be provided *to everyone*. In addition to being dramatic,

the previous scenario had the advantage of making the answer to the second question (no) especially clear: distribution of a zero budget evidently provides no health care to anyone. However, while the objection focuses on the first question, only the second matters for our purposes. My central conclusion is simply that the equal opportunity account does not require that access to health care be provided to everyone.

What bears particular emphasis here is that my conclusion in no way depends upon the point contested by the objection. To make this clear, let us stipulate that the optimum subdivision of the health budget allocates *something* (rather than nothing) to health care. We still have to face the critical question of how these resources should be distributed across the citizenry, thereby determining their access to health care.[22] Is the best distribution of health outcomes secured by making health care available to everyone? In other words, does the equal opportunity account require *universal* access to health care?

Why should we believe that it does? Even when our attention is restricted to socially controllable factors, the final distribution of health outcomes in society must now be seen as the result of a package of distributions: as the *joint* upshot of a distribution of health care and a distribution of the social determinants of health. The effects of a given distribution of health care, so far as the final upshot in health is concerned, are therefore mediated by the distribution of social determinants with which it is packaged (and vice versa). This introduces the possibility of trade-offs within a given package: one person's relative disadvantage with respect to a distribution of health care, say, may be offset by a relative advantage with respect to a complementary distribution of the social determinants. Moreover, since it is *relative* advantage that is at issue, this offsetting can be achieved either by changing the person's own absolute position or by changing the absolute position of others. It seems, then, that various packages of distributions (of health care and of the social determinants) can result in the same final distribution of health outcomes. There is no reason to suppose that the best final distribution results from a distribution of health care that makes at least some health care available to every citizen.

In fact, since universal access to health care has as little effect on the social gradient in mortality as we have seen, there is good reason to suppose that certain groups could be excluded from health care altogether—either random groups (blondes, people with odd social security numbers) or more plausibly, nonrandom groups (the rich, the suburban, the impregnable)—and this *without adverse effects* on the final distribution of health outcomes. Indeed, if the resources saved by excluding some people from health care are put to use in effectively promoting health by other means, this new package may well result in a *better* final distribution of health outcomes.[23]

In any case, a distribution of health care that has no adverse effects on the final distribution of health outcomes, and hence none on the distribution of opportunity, is unimpeachable from the standpoint of justice according to an equal opportunity account. Since the evidence suggests that a distribution of health care *excluding some citizens* from health care altogether cannot be impeached on these terms, it still follows that an equal opportunity account does not require universal access to health care.

Britain is a special case

Various empirical objections can also be lodged against this claim. Some may wonder, for example, whether Britain is a special case, perhaps because of its entrenched class divisions. But this is not plausible. I concentrated on Britain for two main reasons: the unique character of the Whitehall studies, which allows us to sidestep the many problems associated with aggregate data, and the exceptional time span for which reliable public health statistics are available there. But for the record, a marked social gradient in mortality has been documented in many countries,[24] including Sweden, Canada, the Netherlands, and Australia.[25] In Canada, where we also have data that address the issue, the introduction of universal access to health care did not reduce the mortality gradient either.[26]

NHS access is not really universal

Another empirical objection one might raise is that Britain's National Health Service does not really provide universal access to health care in the relevant sense. If the NHS does not actually provide everyone with comparable access to health care, then perhaps the persistence of the social gradient in mortality in Britain can be explained away by reference to the remaining inequalities in access to health care. This objection is not taken very seriously in the public health literature.[27] The consensus in that literature is that most of the improvements in mortality over the past century and a half are not the result of advances in medical care.[28] It is also doubted that the inequalities in access to health care remaining under the NHS suffice to explain much of the gradient in mortality.

This skepticism is fully consistent with the available evidence. For example, employing utilization of general practitioner and outpatient services as a proxy for access to health care, one study found "little inequality in access to care" in Britain for the period from 1984 to 1994,[29] confirming earlier findings to the same effect.[30] More specific evidence comes from studies of mortality in England and Wales caused by conditions *newly* amenable to medical intervention.[31] Between 1961 and 1981, the decline in relative mortality from conditions newly amenable to intervention does not appreciably favor the higher occupational classes.[32] By contrast, in the same period, the decline in relative mortality from conditions *not* amenable to medical intervention significantly favors the higher occupational classes; and these conditions also account for a much greater proportion of total mortality.[33] This makes it difficult to attribute very much of the widening social gradient in mortality under the NHS to residual inequalities in access to health care.

SES is no better

Finally, one may object that insufficient *causality* has been demonstrated in the relationship between life expectancy and any component of social status to make equalizing the distribution of some such component (for example, income) a reliable means of reducing the social gradient in health. The second assumption defining my generic scenario therefore lacks adequate empirical support. Hence, the most that follows from the argument above is that the equal opportunity rationale fails to license spending the health budget on either policy—neither on universal access to health care nor on improving the social determinants of health.

Having myself described the second assumption as a conjecture, I can accept most of this objection. (There is room to dispute where the balance of empirical plausibility lies, but no need to settle the matter here.) For present purposes, the important thing is to appreciate that the assumption contested by the objection is, strictly speaking, dispensable in my critique. What the objection rightly concedes is itself enough to undermine the equal opportunity rationale.

Recall that, according to the equal opportunity account, the following condition is both necessary and sufficient to support a given health policy: implementing the policy improves the relative distribution of health—and so, of opportunity—in society. Since universal access to health care makes no difference to the social gradient in health, and hence none to the relative distribution of opportunity, this policy does not satisfy the account's necessary condition. As a result, it remains true that the equal opportunity argument fails to license universal access to health care—and this given only the first "assumption" (really, an uncontested fact) defining the generic scenario above. Now if the objector is right, the argument also fails to license spending on the social determinants. However, this is cold comfort, as it leaves in place the conclusion that the equal opportunity account provides *no rationale for universal access* to health care, which is the bottom line of my critique.

Naturally, since my claim is fundamentally empirical, it remains open to being overturned, either by new facts or by a more comprehensive accounting of the old facts. One way or another, then, it may yet be established that the best final distribution of health outcomes is secured by universal access to health care after all. Still, a rather detailed empirical case will be required to establish this. In the meantime, we should believe what the mass of available evidence plainly indicates—namely, that the best final distribution of health does *not* require universal access to health care.

WHAT ABOUT THE ABSOLUTE INTERPRETATION?

As should now be clear, the decisive philosophical feature making the equal opportunity account vulnerable to my empirical critique is that its notion of a fair share of opportunity, and therefore of health, has been interpreted as a relative share. That is why the relevant data are to be found in Figure 3 rather than Figure 4. An obvious reaction is to wonder whether the account can be rescued by interpreting equality of opportunity in *absolute* terms instead.

The answer depends on whether a valid argument can be preserved under the absolute interpretation. As we saw at the beginning, a valid equal opportunity argument for universal access to health care has to establish that the opportunities an individual stands to lose with a loss of health will leave her with less than her fair share of opportunity. Thus, to preserve the argument's validity, we must at least be able to *locate* the permissible lower limit of an individual's fair share of opportunity.[34] The signal advantage of the relative interpretation was its demonstrable ability to set this lower limit by means of tractable *comparisons with others* in the society.

On the absolute interpretation, by contrast, an individual's fair share of opportunity must be defined without recourse to comparisons with others. Hence, to specify the permissible lower limit of "opportunity" in absolute terms, one must first define a noncomparative scale of opportunity and then locate a given individual's permissible lower limit somewhere on that scale. I am not sure how to do this.[35] The challenge is exacerbated by the fact that one must discharge these tasks while eschewing not only explicit comparisons (reference to other individuals), but also *implicit* ones (as happens when one refers to a given society, for example).[36] As yet, no one has even attempted to make this interpretation work. For the time being, then, the absolute interpretation is more of an aspiration than a completed argument.

NEW FRAMEWORKS

Let us take stock. The equal opportunity argument for universal access to health care has two basic steps. Each step is beset by a significant difficulty. The first step is the inference that anyone who suffers a loss of health also suffers a violation of her fair share of opportunity. Unfortunately, this inference is invalid unless the permissible lower limit on the individual's fair share of opportunity has been suitably located. We can locate a serviceable lower limit by relying on our sense of the permissible variance in a person's relative share of opportunity, but this means we must interpret "fair share" in relative terms.

The second step is the inference that anyone entitled to a fair share of health is also entitled to a fair share of health care. This inference is licensed by the intuitively plausible premise that access to health care is necessary to conserve an individual's fair share of health. However, when a fair share is a relative share, and we take account of some little-appreciated but well-established facts about the social determinants of health, this premise turns out to be false. The best final distribution of health turns out to be consistent with some citizens having no access to health care at all.

Either way one interprets it, then, the equal opportunity argument fails to yield a rationale for universal access. Under the absolute interpretation, the first step is invalid, and under the relative interpretation, the second step requires a false premise.

But let me be clear. This critique is by no means an indictment of the policy of universal access. I continue to believe firmly that universal access to health care is a requirement of justice. The present analysis simply demonstrates that appeals to equality of opportunity—attractive though they may be—are of no use in justifying this widespread conviction. We need an alternative rationale, which we shall do better to seek in a different framework altogether.

REFERENCES

1. This rationale is invoked, for example, by the official commentary on Article 12 of the "International Covenant on Economic, Cultural, and Social Rights," which enshrines a "right to health." See General Comment 14, "The right to the highest attainable standard of health," Part I, sec. 8, U.N. Committee on Economic, Cultural, and Social Rights. E/C.12/2000/4. See also N. Daniels, *Just Health Care* (Cambridge, U.K.: Cambridge University Press, 1985).

2. Compare Daniels, *Just Health Care*, 27: "[My] account turns on this basic fact: impairments of normal species functioning reduce the range of opportunity open to the individual in which he may construct his 'plan of life.'"

3. Consider John Rawls's principle of fair equality of opportunity, which requires positions and offices in society to be open to all. Even though Rawls does not say a lot about how to interpret "opportunities to achieve positions and offices," it is intuitively clear that, without good health, an individual would have markedly fewer of them. J. Rawls, *A Theory of Justice*, rev. ed. (Cambridge, Mass.: Harvard University Press, 1999), sections 11–17.

4. The alternative is to interpret it in absolute terms. In that case, each individual's fair share of opportunity is defined non-comparatively—that is, without reference to anyone else. I return to consider this alternative at the end. On the distinction between relative and absolute interpretations of equality, see D. Parfit, *Equality or Priority?* (Lindley Lecture, University of Kansas, 1991).

5. A good case can also be made that textual indications in Daniels's seminal version of the argument favor the relative interpretation. See Daniels, *Just Health Care*, 45: "Because meeting healthcare needs has an important effect on the distribution of opportunity, the health care institutions are regulated by a fair equality of opportunity principle." Compare also pages 33–34.

6. Imagine a world with only two inhabitants, Billy and Bob. Suppose they both experience the same loss of health and consequently the same loss of opportunity. Their relative shares of opportunity remain unchanged, so neither has a claim under the equal opportunity principle. In that case, their absolute loss of health is morally irrelevant, at least as far as this principle is concerned.

7. For an introduction, see P. Townsend, N. Davidson, and M. Whitehead, eds., *Inequalities in Health* (London, U.K.: Penguin Books, 1992); M. Marmot and R.G. Wilkinson, eds., *Social Determinants of Health* (Oxford, U.K.: Oxford University Press, 1999); and R.G. Evans, M.L. Barer, and T.R. Marmor, eds., *Why Are Some People Healthy and Others Not?* (New York: de Gruyter, 1994).

8. They would not come as news to Daniels himself. See N. Daniels, B. Kennedy, and I. Kawachi, "Why Justice Is Good for Our Health: The Social Determinants of Health Inequalities," *Daedalus* 128, no. 4 (1999): 215–51. More recently, other philosophers have begun to attend to these data, but their attention does not extend to the implications to be established here. See S. Anand, F. Peter, and A. Sen, eds., *Public Health, Ethics, and Equity* (Oxford, U.K.: Oxford University Press, 2004).

9. I leave open the question of whether SES itself makes a causal contribution to health, or whether it is merely a proxy for other factors that do. It seems likely that SES—a composite measure if ever there was one—is largely a proxy, though in fact this is not altogether uncontroversial. In any case, the identification of the "pathways" through which SES affects health is something of a fledgling enterprise. See N.E. Adler and J.M. Ostrove, "Socioeconomic Status and Health: What We Know and What We Don't," in N.E. Adler et al., eds., *Socioeconomic Status and Health in Industrial Nations: Social, Psychological, and Biological Pathways* (New York: New York Academy of Sciences, 1999), 3–15.

10. For the original study, see M.G. Marmot et al., "Employment Grade and Coronary Heart Disease in British Civil Servants," *Journal of Epidemiology and Community Health* 32 (1978): 244–49. Twenty-five-year follow-up data are presented in C. van Rossum et al., "Employment Grade Differences in Cause Specific Mortality," *Journal of Epidemiology and Community Health* 54 (2000): 178–84.

11. A mortality rate ratio reports the proportion of deaths in a given group divided by the proportion of deaths in the reference group.

12. This is not a random example. Coronary heart disease accounted for 43 percent of the deaths in the Whitehall study at ten years of follow-up. M.G. Marmot, M.J. Shipley, and G. Rose, "Inequalities in Death—Specific Explanations of a General Pattern?" *Lancet* 323 (1984): 1003.

13. Unless, of course, the gradient can be explained away. But that strategy has not fared very well, as the discussion of risk factors partly illustrates. See also my replies to objections below.

14. See M.G. Marmot et al., "Health Inequalities among British Civil Servants: The Whitehall II Study," *Lancet* 337 (1991): 1387–93; and M.G. Marmot, "Social Differentials in Health within and between Populations," *Daedalus* 123, no. 4 (1994): 203.

15. Marmot, "Social Differentials in Health within and between Populations," 212.

16. More recent evidence suggests the gradient has continued to widen. M. Shaw et al., "Increasing Mortality Differentials by Residential Area Level of Poverty: Britain 1981–1997," *Social Science and Medicine* 51 (2000): 151–53.

17. The qualification is required because it is always at least possible that relative levels of life expectancy in Britain would have become even more unequal had the NHS *not* been introduced. There is no evidence to support this. But strictly, the possibility can only be excluded by a controlled study, which plainly cannot be run. However, in this case, note that other data suggest a similar conclusion for a different country (Canada) at a later date.

18. A similar point is made by A. Deaton, "Policy Implications of the Health and Wealth Gradient," *Health Affairs* 21, no. 2 (2002): 21.

19. For a nice illustration, see H. Gravelle, "How Much of the Relation between Population Mortality and Unequal Distribution of Income Is a Statistical Artefact?" *British Medical Journal* 316 (1998): 382–85. As Deaton observes, the expression "statistical artefact" is unfortunate because it suggests "that there is no real link between income inequality and health, and that redistributive policy cannot improve average population health. This is far from the case." A. Deaton, "Health, Inequality, and Economic Development," *Journal of Economic Literature* 41 (2003): 118.

20. Of course, redistributing income may not improve average life expectancy in practice, even if this relationship is causal and concave. One reason is that not everything taken from the rich may wind up in the pockets of the poor: the proverbial redistributive bucket may be leaky. Deaton refers to this as "dead-weight loss"; "Policy Implications," 23.

21. See M. Wolfson et al., "Relationship between Income Inequality and Mortality: Empirical Demonstration," *British Medical Journal* 319 (1999): 953–55; and also Deaton, "Health, Inequality, and Economic Development," 115–18, and Figure 2. Notice that most of this literature focuses on whether equalizing income promotes *average* life expectancy. My assumption requires only that greater income equality improve the relative mortality levels of the worse off. There is no specific evidence demonstrating that the relationship is causal. That is why I describe the second assumption as closer to a conjecture.

22. In this context, a policy that merely permits citizens to spend private resources on health care still counts as "distributing" resources to them for the provision of health care.

23. Compare J.P Mackenbach, K.E. Stronks, and A.E. Kunst, "The Contribution of Medical Care to Inequalities in Health," *Social Science and Medicine* 29, no. 3 (1989): 376: "A truly egalitarian health care policy, aiming at the equalization of health status in the population, would therefore require a radical redistribution of medical care in favor of those most in need."

24. See J. Fox, ed., *Health Inequalities in European Countries* (Aldershot, U.K.: Gower, 1989); and N.E. Adler et al., "Socioeconomic Status and Health: The Challenge of the Gradient," *American Psychologist* 49 (1994): 15–24.

25. D. Vågerö and O. Lundberg, "Health Inequalities in Britain and Sweden," *Lancet* 334 (1989): 35–36; J.P. Mackenbach, "Socio-Economic Health Differences in the Netherlands: A Review of Recent Empirical Findings," *Social Science and Medicine* 34 (1992): 213–26; G. Turrell and C. Mathers, "Socioeconomic Inequalities in All-Cause and Specific-Cause Mortality in Australia: 1985–1987 and 1995–1997," *International Journal of Epidemiology* 30 (2001): 231–39.

26. R. Wilkins, O. Adams, and A. Brancker, "Changes in Mortality by Income in Urban Canada from 1971 to 1986," *Health Reports* 1, no. 2 (1989): 137–74.

27. See Marmot, "Introduction," to Marmot and Wilkinson, *Social Determinants of Health,* 2–3; and Marmot, "Social Differentials in Health within and between Populations," 200–201.

28. See T. McKeown, *The Role of Medicine* (Princeton, N.J.: Princeton University Press, 1979).

29. M. Whitehead et al., "As the Health Divide Widens in Sweden and Britain, What's Happening to Access to Care?" *British Medical Journal* 315 (1997): 1006–1009.

30. See M. Blaxter, "Equity and Consultation Rates in General Practice," *British Medical Journal* 288 (1984): 1963–67.

31. Mackenbach et al., "The Contribution of Medical Care to Inequalities in Health," 369–76.

32. Ibid. Mackenbach et al. found that the corresponding decline does favor the higher occupational classes between 1931 and 1961. However, this period is largely prior to the creation of the NHS. Moreover, the differential decline in question is overwhelmed by the differential decline in relative mortality from conditions not amenable to medical intervention.

33. For a graphic presentation of these data, see M. Marmot, M. Bobak, and G. Davey Smith, "Explanations for Social Inequalities in Health," in *Society and Health,* ed. B. Amick et al. (Oxford, U.K.: Oxford University Press, 1995), Figure 6–13, p. 197.

34. This is not sufficient to preserve the argument's validity. The location of the permissible lower limit also has to make it plausible that a loss of health threatens to leave an individual with *less than* her fair share of opportunity. Not any old location will do.

35. It is far from clear, for example, how an absolute scale of opportunity would be constructed from Daniels's account. For a useful critical discussion of the indeterminacy in Daniels's notion of opportunity, albeit in a different context, see E.J. Emanuel, *The Ends of Human Life* (Cambridge, Mass.: Harvard University Press, 1991), 129–35.

36. Daniels is explicit that his fair shares of opportunity are defined relative to a given society. This implicit comparison in his definition is not motivated under the absolute interpretation, which is one of my reasons for not attributing that interpretation to him; *Just Health Care,* 33–34.

THE ETHICS OF MANAGED CARE

Managed Care and Public Health: Conflict and Collaboration

Sara Rosenbaum and Brian Kamoie

This article reviews the relationship between managed care and public health. Managed care, with its seemingly infinite structural and organizational variation, dominates the modern American health-care system for the non-elderly U.S. population. Through its emphasis on standardized practice norms and performance measurement, coupled with industrial purchasing techniques, prepayment, risk downstreaming, and incentives-based compensation, managed care has the potential to exert considerable influence over the manner in which the health-care system is organized and functions. Given the degree to which the attainment of the basic public health goal of protecting the public against population health threats for which there are known and effective medical interventions depends on the successful interaction between public health policy and the medical care system, the importance of a viable working relationship between public health and managed care is difficult to overstate.

The potential for conflict between public health and medical care is nothing new; indeed, delineating the boundaries of public health to shape and influence medical practice has occupied the energies of policy-makers and the medical industry for well over a century.[1] But the transformation to managed care raises this ongoing dialogue to new levels of significance because of the enormous implications that flow from the modern approach to organizing, buying, and furnishing

Rosenbaum, Sara, and Brian Kamoie. "Managed Care and Public Health: Conflict and Collaboration," *Journal of Law, Medicine, and Ethics,* 30:2 (2002), 191–200. Copyright © 2002. Reprinted by permission of Blackwell Publishing Ltd.

health care. Through its merger of the functions of medical care and resource allocation, and its overlay of the conventions of the commercial insurance industry directly onto the medical care enterprise itself,[2] managed care (whether tightly or loosely organized) has grafted risk avoidance[3] directly into medical practice. There is no greater conceptual gulf than that which exists between this core concept of insurance and the fundamental principles that underlie public health. Thus, while the essence of the struggle between medical care and public health previously lay in the tensions between *professional* autonomy and state control, the modern challenge arises from the tensions between broad public health considerations on the one hand and contractual and *risk avoidance* autonomy on the other.

Whether one side of this struggle is more powerful is unclear. What is clear is that the central public policy question in the coming years is whether and under what circumstances the basic characteristics of the modern approach to medical care delivery and financing will give way to certain basic imperatives in public health.

This article begins with an overview of the core structural and design elements of managed care. The article then places the core functions of public health in a managed care context. The article then turns to one of the most important aspects of the managed care/public health relationship: the power to set and finance the clinical standard of care for the assessment, diagnosis, and treatment of conditions and diseases that carry with them basic public health implications. The article concludes with a discussion of the current national debate over managed care and public accountability and the degree to which it addresses basic public health concerns.

BACKGROUND AND OVERVIEW

As recently as 1980, virtually all insured Americans, whether publicly or privately insured, had coverage that existed independent of the practice of medicine itself.[4] A very small minority of all insured individuals were enrolled in prepaid health-care plans, the structural (even if not philosophical) precursors of the modern managed care enterprise. Public and private health insurers already had begun to make limited use of cost management techniques, such as prospective assessment of the medical necessity of covered benefits and services. But these limited steps met with controversy among the public and in the courts; indeed, even as late as 1977, an Illinois court was willing to reject an

insurer's claims that it had the contractual authority to prospectively limit care, and in doing so stated:

> It is a reasonable conclusion that a layman would not think that "medical necessity" would be construed as a limitation so that his insurer, not his doctor, would pass final judgment on the necessity for his hospitalization . . . .[5]

Twenty years later, the landscape has been completely altered. In a single generation, the American health system was transformed into a "stunning array of new health care financing and delivery entities" that "took responsibility for managing resources," and for channeling "enrollees to providers with whom preferential contracts had been renegotiated."[6] As of 2000, more than 90 percent of all persons with employer-based health insurance coverage were enrolled in some form of managed care,[7] and 79 percent of covered workers had only managed care options to choose from.[8] Half of all Medicaid beneficiaries were enrolled in managed care, and for most, enrollment in managed care was compulsory. Managed care had gained a foothold in Medicare, although the relationship has been relatively rocky. Managed care contracts and practice techniques have become staples of the Defense Department, the Department of Veterans Affairs (which runs the nation's single largest health-care system), and the Indian health system. Even in the case of the State Children's Health Insurance Program (SCHIP), studies suggest that more than two-thirds of states with separately administered SCHIP plans (i.e., programs that are separate from Medicaid) use their SCHIP allotments to purchase managed care arrangements.[9] As a result of this pervasiveness, managed care operates in spheres once dominated by public health-care delivery systems and principles.

The roots of the modern managed care era can be found in the efforts of employers in the early 1980s to bring industrial techniques to health-care purchasing through the use of preset cost and quality expectations. This development arose in the face of rampant medical care cost escalation and a recessionary economy, coupled with the rejection of the "learned profession" exemption from federal and state anti-trust law.[10] These two advances—the first on the demand side and the second on the supply side—revolutionized the power of group sponsors to buy medical care from health professionals and other medical suppliers in accordance with preset cost and quality expectations. As employers brought industrial techniques to health-care purchasing, public sponsors also began to enthusiastically follow suit. In leading the way, employers pursued these purchasing strategies in their employer-sponsored health plans. As a result, this foray into large-scale purchasing of medical care from organized groups operating in accordance with specifications set by the purchaser was grounded in the principles and conventions of employer-sponsored health insurance.

The basic elements of managed care

Experts in managed care note that "there is no universally accepted managed care terminology."[11] Despite its various forms, managed care can be defined as any arrangement in which, for a preset fee (i.e., a premium or a capitation payment), an entity sells a defined set of medical care and administrative services to a sponsor or purchaser and offers services to enrollees through a network of participating providers that operate under written contractual or employment agreements and whose selection and authority to furnish covered treatments is controlled by the entity. This definition captures the essence of managed care, regardless of whether the plan is labeled as a health maintenance organization (HMO), an individual practice association (IPA), a preferred provider organization (PPO), an integrated service network, a disease management company, a provider services organization (PSO), or some other name.

Regardless of the label they use, managed care organizations (MCOs) combine the elements of insurance and prepayment with medical care itself, selling care from members of their provider networks to purchasers for a pre-negotiated fee.[12] Thus, the essence of managed care is the merger of coverage and care.[13] More specifically, MCOs merge medical care and the conventions and norms of commercial health insurance financing, with its extensive limitations on coverage, its delineation of contractual responsibilities, and its techniques for minimizing sponsors' and insurers' exposure to financial risk.

Most managed care plans (other than traditional staff model companies that employ their medical and administrative staff) tend to operate as virtual health systems. That is, the companies build their products through a cascade of contractual agreements between the MCO and group sponsor on the one hand, and the company and its medical, financial, and administrative subcontractors and suppliers on the other. The contracts and subcontracts that spell out the structural and financial framework of the relationship typically are not visible to the naked eye. Indeed, with the exception of the prime contracts between certain public purchasers and managed care companies, these agreements are considered proprietary. A typical managed care contract between a sponsor and an MCO will contain specifications in the areas of coverage, provider network composition and capabilities, service access, quality improvement and oversight, provision of information, and business terms and conditions.[14]

Regardless of the terminology under which they conduct business, managed care entities possess certain features, each of which plays a significant role in making the managed care enterprise function. Understanding how the enterprise functions is critical to understanding the constraints inherent in the relationship between managed care and public health.

The first basic element of the managed care enterprise is the contract between the managed care entity and a prime sponsor (an employer, the Medicaid program, or some other group purchaser).[15] This contract describes covered treatments and procedures and the terms of payment. It also sets forth the basic duty on the part of the entity to undertake care itself through the organization and oversight of a participating provider network that meets certain specifications of adequacy.[16] This dual obligation on the part of managed care entities to both finance care and furnish it has been recognized by the courts, which have viewed MCOs as wearing the two hats of insurer and health-care provider.[17]

With the exception of Medicaid managed care contracts, which, like Medicaid itself, frequently cover treatments and services for chronic illness and disability,[18] the standard managed care prime contract reflects the rules of conventional insurance. These rules seek to constrain the outer limits of insurance to interventions that are described as precisely as possible in order to avoid financial risk. This means that coverage is limited to services and treatments that diagnose and treat illnesses and injuries and other specified conditions. Most forms of preventive coverage are excluded as outside the scope of risk financing.[19] Because the conventions of insurance are designed to respond to the health needs of a working, healthy population,[20] medical necessity may be either overtly or implicitly measured in accordance with a definition that turns on the concepts of significant improvement and a return to normal functioning. While social norms have shifted considerably and the public has come to expect the integration of persons with disabilities into the work world, these changes in social expectations have had only the most limited impact on the design of health insurance. Although there have been federal and state public policy efforts to make conventional insurance more responsive to persons with greater health needs, public reforms have yielded little other than the most limited steps to curb the use of preexisting condition exclusions and the most overt disparities in physical and mental health coverage.[21]

A second key element of managed care is the formation and oversight of a provider network through which contracted services are delivered. Members can be restricted to this network or alternatively can be incentivized to use the network through cost-sharing differentials. Regardless, the network is the realization of the managed care entity's medical care contractual undertaking through a series of cascading contracts with individual and group medical practices, institutions, and other health-care providers and suppliers. This provider network, selected by the prime contractor, operates under the direction of the prime sponsor, which assumes quality oversight responsibilities. A prime contractor also may contract with "sub-prime" entities such as behavioral health organizations, pharmacy benefit management companies, and disease management firms, to manage portions of the prime contract. By 1995, over 80 percent of the more than 600,000 practicing physicians in the United States reported that they were either employed by or had entered into at least one contractual arrangement with a managed care plan. This represents a one-third increase in 5 years in the proportion of practicing physicians who report participating in managed care.[22] Managed care participation thus has become fundamental to the ability to practice medicine in the United States.

As health-care purchasers, MCOs have exceedingly broad power to compose their networks and negotiate the terms of participation, and network selection is among the most closely guarded types of information maintained by managed care plans. Recent developments at the state level have broadened the body of law applicable to network selection and de-selection, and industry accreditation standards also address this issue. However, other than broadly drafted "any willing provider" statutes confined to very narrow classes of providers such as physicians, dentists, or pharmacists, neither the law nor accreditation standards dictate the structure or composition of networks.[23]

A third essential element of managed care is the use of preset pricing to control the cost and flow of medical care. To be sure, recent evidence of a growing escalation in health-care costs shows the limits of this strategy (no single purchaser, however powerful, can control the larger events that affect the price of goods and services).[24] At the same time, there is a general consensus that managed care did in fact reduce the rate of health-care cost growth for many years and remains a powerful tool for controlling the rate of cost increase.[25] Because managed care is at its core a health-care undertaking for

a fixed price, risk downstreaming becomes essential,[26] as does the use of financial incentives and penalties aimed at encouraging reductions in resource utilization.[27] In sum, risk sharing between MCOs and their providers is a basic feature of managed care;[28] this is true regardless of whether the prime contract includes financial risk for the prime contractor or, in the case of a self-insuring plan, is for third-party administration only.[29]

The final structural element of the managed care enterprise for purposes of this article is control over the treatment practices of physicians. Harold Luft and Robert Miller have observed that physician conduct is the element that is managed in managed care.[30] In the early stages of the modern managed care movement, MCOs exercised this control through the close utilization management of individual patient treatment decisions made by physicians. As this approach increasingly came under scrutiny, companies moved to more structural strategies, emphasizing practice guidelines, disease management, case management, and pharmaceutical restrictions.[31] Despite the movement away from close management, managed care focuses on the basic issue of physician practice style and essentially seeks to minimize the frequency of individual physician judgment in favor of greater levels of standardization. Proponents of this effort to move toward more standardized approaches to medicine can justifiably point to studies by Wennberg and others documenting the astonishing breadth of medical judgment in the absence of physical or other characteristics to explain these differences.[32]

PUBLIC HEALTH IN A MANAGED CARE CONTEXT

The core functions of public health[33] (assessment, assurance, and policy development[34]) not only remain valid in a managed care era, but may in fact grow in importance in the modern health-care environment. This is because the ability to measure the health of a population over time and adjust resources to meet evidence-based needs—a basic goal of public health—also is essential to the success of the managed care enterprise. Viewed in this context, the successful execution of the core functions of public health can be said to be consistent with the managed care enterprise. Managed care may best succeed when evidence on the health of a population is available and timely, thereby allowing, to the maximum extent possible, the calibration of health resources (in both amount and availability) to meet population needs.

At the same time, however, fundamental differences exist between the duties of public health agencies and those of managed care companies. These structural issues are shaped by legal/jurisdictional, financial, and traditional worldview considerations.

Legal/jurisdictional differences

A public health agency's jurisdiction extends to the entire community that the agency is authorized to serve. Public health agencies have a social compact with their communities as well as a legal duty to serve the community at large; however, no individual within the community has a legally enforceable entitlement to population-based public health services. For example, communicable disease control and surveillance must be accomplished without regard to a particular individual's eligibility for Medicaid or any other form of insurance. Every member of the community, insured or not, "belongs" to public health, and public health agencies must attempt to maximize their resources on the community's behalf.

In contrast, MCOs possess very different duties. As fiduciaries, managed care entities owe a duty to their sponsors to restrict expenditures on members and to hold expenditures to preset premiums or, in the case of self-insured plans, capitation payments. Investments whose payments extend beyond the period of the contract may place the enterprise at major risk for losses. This problem is further magnified by the fact that unlike residents of a public health agency's service area, MCO enrollees have a legally enforceable right to coverage for the defined benefits in their contracts. This entitlement further complicates the power of MCOs to divert resources away from expressly covered medical benefits and into broad public health clinical and administrative investments, regardless of their contractual status.

At some point, the obligation to serve members properly may require that MCOs engage in services and activities that may also have the effect of benefiting nonmembers. MCOs also may elect to engage in certain community-wide service activities, and anecdotal evidence suggests that like other health-care providers, MCOs frequently are actively involved in numerous community-wide programs. Nonetheless, the duty of an MCO is defined by those members who have a legal entitlement to coverage and care, while the duty of public health agencies is defined by their community jurisdiction.

Financial considerations

As noted earlier, MCOs operate on a financial risk basis—they sign contracts that require them to provide defined contractual services to enrollees for a fixed fee (typically paid monthly). Thus, for example, an MCO that contracts to furnish certain services cannot arbitrarily discontinue coverage for certain services (e.g., childhood immunizations or drugs) during the term of its contract. This, of course, does not mean that an MCO cannot institute rationing procedures to slow consumption or seek to interpret its contract to reduce the scope and extent of its legal obligations. But regardless of their ability to control resource consumption, MCOs are bound to live up to their coverage contracts.

Public health agencies, on the other hand, typically manage costs within global budgets, as supported by state, federal, and local categorical grants, as well as third-party payments generated by participation in state and private insurance programs, especially Medicaid. Because no individual is legally entitled to certain defined benefits offered by public health agencies, an agency typically has the legal power to reduce or eliminate services and activities if funds run out during a budget year.

Because public health agencies do not have legally enforceable duties to individuals, they also have greater latitude to commingle funds and engage in cross-subsidization practices in order to keep their basic activities afloat. Thus, for example, a public health agency may pool revenues derived from grants, contracts, patient fees, and third-party payments (most typically Medicaid) to support the provision of subsidized personal health-care activities for the uninsured. In this way, shortages in one area can be compensated for via budgetary reallocations where not prohibited by law. Because grant and contract funding for public health activities tends to be modest, and because a large proportion of the patient population is poor, third-party revenues, especially Medicaid, take on crucial importance.

Differences in worldviews and perspectives

Differences in the traditional worldview perspectives of public health and managed care present complex challenges for understanding and collaboration. Managed care combines health-care delivery with the financial and structural principles of insurance, and managed care companies focus on their members rather than the entire community population. Meeting the needs of members over the time period of the contract and within the constraints of premium or capitation payments, while still achieving an adequate profit margin or return on investment, causes MCOs to focus intensively on short-range timeframes. Public health, by contrast, takes a longer view of improving community health, which may take many months, or even years, to achieve. Public health agencies must also be equipped to respond rapidly to disease outbreaks with short-term dedication of labor- and resource-intensive efforts to contain the spread of a particular disease. MCOs are an outgrowth of the world of employment-based health insurance. They gear their operations and activities to relatively healthy, relatively easy-to-manage patients. Public health agencies frequently specialize in the care, management, and oversight of complex patients with public insurance or other sources of public financing who present management challenges that include the provision of social supports to ensure completion of treatment (e.g., transportation, translation, "cultural competency" capacity). A key question that is fundamental to any discussion of the possibility of public health and managed care collaboration, therefore, is the extent to which each domain is aware of the other's perspectives and traditions.

The realities of managed care can put MCOs into conflict with public health agencies in a number of respects. First, managed care companies may alter existing health-care delivery systems through their contractual network arrangements in ways that interrupt previously established relationships between public health agencies and providers of health care. MCOs may shift members away from clinical care arrangements that either are part of or that work in collaboration with public health agencies and into other systems that do not share public health traditions. The shift away from "health-care safety net" providers, such as publicly managed maternity clinics, in favor of private health providers represents an example of this trend. Not only is the provider eliminated from the network, but the insurance funds that might have helped subsidize care for uninsured maternity patients are lost.[35]

Second, in altering health-care delivery arrangements and in establishing ownership over certain purchased services, MCOs may disrupt access to certain health-care data on which public health agencies historically have depended. As health care is purchased, the information generated by the care falls within the scope of the purchasing agreement. Such information may become inaccessible in the absence of special laws regulating disclosure. An example of this phenomenon is the tendency of MCOs to use out-of-state clinical laboratories in lieu of in-state public health laboratories.[36] Not only are the in-state labs cut out of the health-care (and health-care financing) loop, but their access to specimens for the purpose of secondary public health and epidemiological analysis may be lost.

Third, managed care entities may establish standards of treatment that differ from those recommended by

public health agencies. The remainder of this article focuses on this important effect of managed care on public health.

PUBLIC HEALTH AND THE STANDARD OF CARE: TREATMENT GUIDELINES

From a legal point of view, treatment guidelines are the most significant effect of managed care on the management of medical care. Without knowing anything more about them, one would imagine them to be legally non-binding guides to treatment, accompanied by financial and other incentives to persuade practitioners to adopt them. However, recent evidence from a judicial decision related to employer plan coverage and medical liability indicates that treatment guidelines may have moved to a new legal level of absolute contractual limitations on treatment itself.[37] As such, the guidelines may leave no room for variation in the choice of what is considered contractually permissible, even within the broad classes of benefits that may be enumerated within a coverage contract.

The power of practice guidelines to actually set the contractual standard of care has been recognized by leading experts in managed care such as Dr. David Eddy, who has written:

> Coverage criteria [in insurance plans] constitute a contract between health plans and their members on how the members' money will be spent .... [They function] to ensure that plans do not waste the members' money on non-medical, ineffective, or harmful practices .... A second purpose that evolved over the last two decades is to improve quality .... [G]aps in knowledge [about the effectiveness of medical practices] exist because practices that provide some hope of benefit are disseminated before the ... actual benefit can be confirmed through clinical research .... The best way to correct this problem is to insist on good evidence of effectiveness before allowing a practice to be disseminated. Because coverage criteria sit astride the flow of money, they are in an excellent position to do this .... [C]overage criteria help plans achieve the seemingly contradictory objectives of controlling costs while simultaneously increasing quality.[38]

Other experts have written on the advisability of elevating practice guidelines to a level at which they no longer function as guides to treatment but as an actual articulation of the limits of a contractual health-care undertaking itself.[39]

Such a vast elevation in the status of clinical treatment guidelines from advisory to binding legal limits on treatment, of course, raises major issues regarding the quality of the guidelines themselves and the manner in which they are developed and applied. The potential for guidelines to actually lower the standard of care beneath what is considered clinically acceptable and to leave patients without recourse to challenge can be seen in a recent decision from the U.S. Court of Appeals for the Tenth Circuit.

In *Jones v. Kodak Medical Assistance Plan,*[40] the court treated certain alcoholism treatment guidelines as a matter of basic contract design, and thus completely non-reviewable under an individual appeal by a plan member. The member had been denied a particular form of alcoholism treatment in favor of a treatment procedure that was incorporated directly into the plan documents as part of the plan's contract of coverage. Like many other persons with employer-sponsored coverage, the insured sought to appeal the plan's medical necessity denial and to argue for another form of treatment. The court did not merely reject her arguments. It characterized her case as non-justifiable (even though there was evidence that the plan administrator had determined that the treatment was inappropriate to the member's particular condition) because as part of the contract itself, the guidelines became part of the plan design and thus non-challengeable.[41]

Because health plan contracting practices are considered proprietary, they are extremely difficult to meassure, and litigation becomes the means by which contracting trends come to light. To the extent that the employer-sponsored health plan practices in *Jones* in fact signal a trend toward contractual treatment and a contractual standard of care, the health system may indeed be evolving into one in which insurance coverage is used not merely to establish coverage design, but to actually establish the clinical standard of care. In this event, the use of practice guidelines takes on heightened importance (to put it mildly), since in combination with network selection and compensation techniques the guidelines become the industry standard of care.[42]

The nascent emergence of fixed treatment guidelines as a determinant of the clinical treatment of a population holds major implications for public health practice and policy. Public health policy is aimed at containing, controlling, and minimizing broad public health threats. Some of these threats are addressed through population-wide initiatives, such as efforts to promote water and air quality safety; these types of interventions transcend personal medical care to any individual. Other interventions turn on the ability to assure that personal medical care services are both available and performed in a manner that comports with public health

standards of quality and appropriateness.[43] Examples of public health goals reached through medical care are the earliest possible diagnosis and complete treatment of communicable disease, the prevention of disease through immunization, and the prevention of premature death and disability through early intervention and management. To this end, the Centers for Disease Control and Prevention (CDC), through numerous scientific advisory groups, has developed scientific guidelines for the prevention, treatment, and control of communicable diseases as well as chronic diseases with broad public health implications, such as asthma and diabetes.[44]

The modern managed care movement, with its use of treatment guidelines, offers public health authorities unparalleled opportunities to disseminate scientific standards to the medical community with unusual speed and power. Indeed, one of the most troubling problems with medical quality prior to the advent of managed care was the absence of any means for decisively moving toward evidence-based standards of care that would lessen the risk of unjustifiable variations in practice style. In this respect, managed care represents a potentially great advance in the techniques for adopting health-care standards.

At the same time, the dangers are also equally apparent. To the extent that managed care entities turn to science to calibrate treatment and use treatment guidelines with due regard for the need to make individual variations when the facts of particular patients' cases warrant alternative approaches, the evolution is positive. But to the extent that the guidelines incorporated into a contract are scientifically unsound in either structure or application and operate to withdraw all treatment other than that which is contractually specified, the results can be a lowering of the standard of care rather than its improvement. Courts have begun to recognize this result in managed care corporate liability cases.[45] Indeed, eliminating all forms of covered treatment other than that enumerated in a specific guideline would reduce an MCO's contractual obligation to zero in any instance in which a particular guideline's treatment was inappropriate for a member due to underlying complications such as a co-occurring condition. Depending on how the contract was written, rather than defaulting in coverage to the medical judgment of the physician and the plan, the contract would effectively default to a complete absence of treatment.

Although malpractice liability actions against a provider or an MCO may be available for patients harmed by substandard care (whether or not delivered pursuant to practice guidelines), these actions provide recourse only after the fact of injury.[46] Moreover, malpractice actions do not address the fundamental coverage design issues raised by the use of treatment guidelines as a contractual limitation of coverage.[47] It remains to be seen whether future litigation will confirm or reject the approach outlined in *Jones*.

The potential for inappropriate guidelines or for guidelines to be used in ways that create medical treatment vacuums is considerable, however. Despite the plethora of treatment guidelines, there are relatively few in relation to the entire body of medical care. There are even fewer that can be said to have been scientifically developed (i.e., those grounded in the results of valid research rather than actuarial estimates). The number of usable guidelines shrinks to almost zero if even the best guidelines are used irrebuttably and without consideration of underlying patient factors that can render even the strongest guideline utterly irrelevant. For example, the use of the routine childhood immunization guidelines established by the CDC Advisory Committee on Immunization Practices (ACIP) is inappropriate where a child has certain immune system-related health conditions.

There are few studies of the scientific soundness or application of managed care industry treatment guidelines. What is apparent is that despite their availability, CDC scientific guidelines appear to be seldom used. One recent review of all Medicaid managed care contracts conducted for the CDC revealed that fewer than 10 percent specify adult immunization in accordance with ACIP standards as a basic duty of care for contractors, and fewer than half incorporate the ACIP standard of care in the area of pediatric immunizations.[48]

In another study, which focused on managed care plan adherence to public health standards, researchers surveyed Medicaid-participating managed care entities for their compliance with CDC assessment and treatment guidelines in the area of sexually transmitted disease prevention, treatment, and management.[49] The researchers found that MCOs overwhelmingly failed to follow the CDC practices or even recommend them for their primary care physicians.[50] The reasons given by the MCOs for not using or recommending the CDC standards included cost, legal liability, conflicts with networks, and a desire to give network physicians autonomy (a striking finding in light of the growing emphasis on guidelines in managed care as a means of contractually limiting coverage itself).[51] Most importantly perhaps, and consistent with their primary adherence to the time periods of contracts, MCOs noted the low priority they placed on upgrading preventive health services given the high rate of turnover in Medicaid enrollees.[52]

The fact that so little is known about treatment guidelines and managed care (other than a few isolated studies and court decisions) is extraordinary given their importance in health quality. The Institute of Medicine (IOM), which has studied guidelines, defines treatment guidelines as "systematically developed statements to assist practitioner and patient decisions about appropriate health care for specific clinical circumstances."[53] The IOM also has identified certain prerequisites to their use, including the credibility of the development process, their scientific grounding, their development through a multidisciplinary approach, and their ability to be "specific, comprehensive and yet flexible enough to be useful in the varied settings and circumstances of everyday medical practice."[54] Most importantly perhaps, in the IOM's view, guidelines should "specify what information about the clinical problem, the patient's circumstances and preferences, and the delivery setting should be recorded to permit later evaluation of the appropriateness of care."[55]

Despite the criteria for the development and use of treatment guidelines established by the IOM, the practice of structuring managed care through guidelines remains basically unstudied and unregulated. No state appears to have established minimum criteria for either the adoption of guidelines or their application to individual treatment decisions; there are no laws setting up minimum conditions before a guideline can be incorporated into a contract of insurance as a fixed standard of care. State laws enacted in recent years to permit independent review of MCO treatment decisions do not address the evidentiary weight to be given treatment guidelines, nor do they address the power of an independent review organization (IRO) to set aside a decision of a plan when otherwise covered treatment is limited via a practice guideline to one particular type of medical intervention.

Similarly, federal managed care quality legislation basically does not address this issue. Both the House and Senate bills passed in the summer of 2001[56] prescribe a federal independent review system and provide broad evidentiary standards for the conduct of external reviews. In addition, both measures establish certain basic patient "rights" that generally focus on emergency care, access to certain covered treatments and network providers, and coverage for treatment furnished as part of a clinical trial. Neither bill sets standards for measuring when a treatment guideline can be directly incorporated into an employer-sponsored health plan, as in the *Jones* case, nor does either bill limit how the guideline can be applied. Both bills potentially allow members greater latitude to externally challenge the application of a treatment guideline in a case in which the care would be medically inappropriate, but because the measures do not reach the content of coverage itself, neither would permit a hearing officer to override a guideline and authorize other treatment unless it was covered under the contract. Thus, even where a treatment guideline is subject to challenge in an external review, the effects of such a challenge may be to eliminate treatment entirely in the case of a health plan that limits covered treatments for certain conditions to those specified in guidelines.

DISCUSSION

In the American health-care system, the complexities of the relationship between medical care and public health are historic and deeply ingrained. In the early period of the modern era of American medicine, tensions arose from the clash between professionalism on the one hand and the imperative for public accountability on the other. In today's world, tensions flow from the demand for contractual autonomy on the one hand and the need for public accountability on the other. It is not possible to say which set of tensions presents the greater public policy challenge; indeed, Americans prize their independence over all else, whether as professionals or as contractors.

It is difficult to say how the managed care/public health relationship will resolve itself. There are many issues that bear scrutiny in the quest for a public accountability framework, including access to data and information for public health measurement and surveillance purposes,[57] and the use of performance measures that incorporate public health goals and objectives, such as the reduction of vaccine-preventable or communicable disease. But one of the most abiding of public health concerns is the extent to which managed care, in moving to a world in which treatment is determined through fixed guidelines, designs its contracts to reflect the standards of prevention, assessment, diagnosis, and treatment that are essential to achieve not only individual health, but the success of broader public health objectives. In the absence of this melding of contractual treatment and public health concerns, the goals of public health will remain extra-contractual at best and dependent on supplemental sources of health-care financing, which are increasingly difficult to secure.

From a public health perspective, policymakers have two concerns regarding treatment guidelines. The first is the soundness of a guideline itself; the second is the soundness of its application. Guidelines that do not meet minimum standards for science have no place in the medical care system, whether used to guide or determine treatment. In this regard, the IOM's recommendations should be considered carefully. Furthermore, where scientific guidelines have been developed and promulgated by government agencies, managed care plans, like courts,[58] should be required to give them great weight, setting them aside only if the plans can prove the guidelines' lack of soundness.

Equally important, however, is guarding against the misapplication of even sound treatment guidelines to cases that do not meet the guidelines' own underlying scientific and practice assumptions. This type of health-care quality danger can be avoided only through individualized determinations based on an evidentiary standard that is designed to consider all relevant and reliable evidence regarding an individual patient.[59] Furthermore, in those situations in which an otherwise applicable treatment guideline is considered inappropriate based on the evidence, the "default" standard of treatment must be covered treatment that reflects individualized medical judgment, not *no* treatment.

Managed care may represent a basic advance in how emerging consensus regarding standards of care is disseminated and applied to the patient population. But the degree to which the advance is valid and not in fact a retrenchment in quality and public health depends on the degree to which public health authorities and policymakers are willing to temper the autonomy of contractual design, a tall order in a market-driven society in which the goal of quality too often takes second chair to the cost of achieving quality. In the end, policymakers must ask the hard question: What good is the nation's unprecedented level of medical expenditures if these expenditures advance only substandard care?

REFERENCES

1. See, e.g., L. Gostin, *Public Health Law: Power, Duty, Restraint* (California: University of California Press, 2000): at 11; Paul Starr, *The Social Transformation of American Medicine* (New York: Basic Books, 1982): at 180–97.

2. Perhaps the single finest exploration of the conventions of commercial insurance and their implications for public policy in health care is Deborah Stone's seminal article, "The Struggle for the Soul of Health Insurance," *Journal of Health Politics, Policy and Law,* 18 (1993): 287–317.

3. By "risk avoidance," we mean managed care's delineation of covered treatment and the extensive limitations placed on coverage

to minimize exposure to unanticipated financial risk. Managed care products, like conventional insurance, typically limit coverage for services not designed to return an individual to prior normal functioning (e.g., treatment for chronic illnesses). As a result of these coverage limitations and the contractual shifting of financial risk to providers, managed care injects conventional insurance principles directly into medical practice.

4. This background and overview is adapted from R. Rosenblatt, S. Law, and S. Rosenbaum, *Law and the American Health Care System* (New York: Foundation Press, 1997): at 543–73.

5. *Van Vector v. Blue Cross Ass'n*, 365 N.E.2d 638, 645 (Ill. App. Ct. 1977).

6. J. Weiner and G. de Lissovoy, "Razing a Tower of Babel: A Taxonomy for Managed Care and Health Insurance Plans," *Journal of Health Politics, Policy and Law,* 18 (1993): 75–103, at 73–77.

7. R.A. Dudley and H. Luft, "Managed Care in Transition," *N. Engl. J. Med.,* 344 (2001): 1087–92, at 1087.

8. L. Levitt et al., Kaiser Family Foundation and Health Research and Educational Trust, *Employer Health Benefits: 2000 Annual Survey* (Chicago: Kaiser Family Foundation and Health Research and Educational Trust, 2000): at 55.

9. S. Rosenbaum et al., *Policy Brief #2: State Benefit Design Choices under SCHIP—Implications for Pediatric Health Care* (Washington, D.C.: George Washington University School of Public Health and Health Services, Center for Health Services Research and Policy, 2001), *available at* <http://www.gwhealthpolicy.org/downloads/issue_brief_2.pdf>; C. Pernice et al., *Charting SCHIP: Report of the Second National Survey of the State Children's Health Insurance Program* (Washington, D.C.: National Academy for State Health Policy, 2001).

10. Rosenblatt, Law, and Rosenbaum, *supra* note 4, at 550, 656.

11. R.H. Miller and H. Luft, "Managed Care Plan Performance Since 1980: A Literature Analysis," *JAMA,* 271, no. 19 (1994): 1512–19, at 1512. See also J. Hacker and T. Marmor, "How Not to Think About 'Managed Care,' " *University of Michigan Journal of Law Reform,* 32 (Summer, 1999): 661–84, at 661 (arguing that the application of "managed care" to many diverse trends in the organization and financing of health care is a barrier to meaningful analysis).

12. For a more detailed description of the structure and organization of various types of managed care organizations, see Rosenblatt, Law, and Rosenbaum, *supra* note 4, at 551–73.

13. Weiner and de Lissovoy, *supra* note 6, at 85–86.

14. See Rosenblatt, Law, and Rosenbaum, *supra* note 4, at 551–73.

15. A very small amount of managed care enrollment can be attributed to direct purchase memberships held by persons who have individual coverage.

16. S. Rosenbaum et al., *Negotiating the New Health System: A Nationwide Study of Medicaid Managed Care Contracts,* 3rd ed. (Washington, D.C.: George Washington University School of Public Health and Health Services, Center for Health Services Research and Policy, 1999), *available at* <http://www.gwu.edu/~chsrp/contracts.html>; *Boyd v. Albert Einstein Medical Ctr.,* 547 A.2d 1229 (Pa. Super. Ct. 1988).

17. See *Pegram v. Herdrich*, 530 U.S. 211 (2000); *Pappas v. Asbel,* 768 A.2d 1089 (Pa. 2001); *Boyd v. Albert Einstein Medical Ctr.,* 547 A.2d 1229 (Pa. Super. Ct. 1988).

18. Rosenbaum et al., *supra* note 16, vol. 2, at 1–2.

19. A typical private insurance contract will cover specified forms of preventive services, such as certain immunizations, well baby and well child care, and periodic mammograms. But generalized assessments of health and well-being and preventive screening interventions to detect the presence of a wide range of conditions frequently are excluded or else not identified as included.

20. The growth in public acceptance of and pressure to encourage persons with disabilities to work as a result of the Americans with Disabilities Act and changing social norms has created new challenges for conventional employment-based insurance design. However, federal and state public policy efforts to make conventional insurance more responsive to persons with greater health needs has yielded little. See text accompanying note 21 and note 21, *infra.*

21. The Health Insurance Portability and Accountability Act (HIPAA) and the Mental Health Parity Act are two examples of such legislation. See HIPAA, Pub. L. No. 104–191 (codified in scattered sections of 42 U.S.C.); Mental Health Parity Act, 42 U.S.C. § 300gg-5 (2001). HIPAA sets minimal restrictions on the use of preexisting condition exclusions and waiting periods. Under HIPAA, the maximum length of such an exclusion is 12 months after the date the individual first enrolls in a new group plan. Second, the preexisting condition exclusion cannot apply to a condition for which the person received no services within the 6-month period prior to enrollment. Third, HIPAA can allow an individual to completely bypass any preexisting condition exclusion by providing evidence of 12 months of prior group or individual health coverage, including federal health coverage such as Medicaid or Medicare. See 42 U.S.C. § 300gg (2001). Despite these protections, however, enforcement of these limitations is difficult. The Mental Health Parity Act prohibits only the grossest of all limits, annual and lifetime dollar caps, and leaves untouched diagnostically based variations in treatment. See 42 U.S.C. §§ 300gg-5(a) and (b) (2001).

22. D. Segal, "Doctors Who Dodge a Managed Care Stampede," *Washington Post,* May 20, 1996, Health Section, at S.

23. One notable exception is the state of Washington, which requires MCOs to include alternative medicine providers (e.g., acupuncturists, massage therapists, naturopaths, and chiropractors) in their network. See *Washington Physicians Ass'n v. Gregoire,* 147 F.3d 1039 (9th Cir. 1998).

24. See S. Heffler et al., "Health Spending Growth Up in 1999; Faster Growth Expected in the Future," *Health Affairs,* 20, no. 2 (2001): 193–203, at 193.

25. See Miller and Luft, *supra* note 11, at 1516, 1994; E. Wagner and T. Bledsoe, "The Rand Health Insurance Experiment and HMOs," *Medical Care,* 28, no. 3, (1990): 191–200. At least one scholar, however, has questioned the general consensus. See K. Sullivan, "On the 'Efficiency' of Managed Care Plans," *Health Affairs,* 19, no. 4 (2001): 139–48 (arguing that the evidence supporting the claim that managed care controls costs is inconclusive).

26. See J. Robinson, "Physician Organization in California: Crisis and Opportunity," *Health Affairs,* 20, no. 4 (2001): 81–96; J. Robinson, "The Future of Managed Care Organization," *Health Affairs,* 18, no. 2 (1999): 7–24; *Pegram v. Herdrich,* 530 U.S. 211 (2000).

27. To encourage a reduction in hospital days for Medicare patients, Humana Health Plans' contracts with hospitals include a bonus level for every 100 patient days under a specified utilization target (contracts on file with authors).

28. *Pegram v. Herdrich,* 530 U.S. 211 (2000).

29. Rosenblatt, Law, and Rosenbaum, *supra* note 4, at 565.

30. Miller and Luft, *supra* note 11, at 1512.

31. Dudley and Luft, *supra* note 7, at 1087–88.

32. J. Wennberg, "Dealing with Medical Practice Variations: A Proposal for Action," *Health Affairs,* 3, no. 2 (1984): 6–32, at 6, 9–10.

33. Our use of "public health" in this article encompasses both traditional definitions of public health (collective actions to assure the conditions that allow people to be healthy) and other aspects of public health that include the delivery of health care by public health departments as safety net providers.

34. Institute of Medicine, *The Future of Public Health* (Washington, D.C.: National Academy Press, 1988): at 1–18.

35. For a detailed discussion of the role of managed care and Medicaid in the larger context of "welfare medicine" (poor people and the health-care professionals and institutions that serve them), see S. Watson, "Commercialization of Medicaid," *St. Louis Law Journal,* 45 (Winter 2001): 53–78.

36. See Gostin, *supra* note 1, at 119.

37. *Jones v. Kodak Medical Assistance Plan,* 169 F.3d 1287 (10th Cir. 1999).

38. D. Eddy, "Benefit Language: Criteria That Will Improve Quality While Reducing Costs," *JAMA,* 275 (1996): 650–57, at 650–651.

39. See R. Epstein, "Medical Malpractice: The Case for Contract," *American Bar Foundation Research Journal* (1976): 87–149; C. Havighurst, "Altering the Applicable Standard of Care," *Law & Contemporary Problems,* 49 (Spring 1986): 265–75; C. Havighurst, "Prospective Self-Denial: Can Consumers Contract Today to Accept Health Care Rationing Tomorrow?," *University of Pennsylvania Law Review,* 140 (1992): 1755–808; E.H. Morreim, "The Futility of Medical Necessity Regulation," *Regulation* (Summer 2001): 22–26.

40. *Jones v. Kodak Medical Assistance Plan,* 169 F.3d 1287 (10th Cir: 1999).

41. See *id.* at 1292. The record in the case showed that the plan's own administrator questioned the quality of the treatment that the plan was prepared to permit in light of the facts in the plaintiff's case.

42. For additional discussion of the role of practice guidelines and other standards of care in procedural protections for health-care consumers, see E.D. Kinney, *Protecting American Health Care Consumers* (Durham, North Carolina: Duke University Press, 2002).

43. Institute of Medicine, *supra* note 34, at 1–18.

44. See, e.g., Centers for Disease Control and Prevention, 1998 Guidelines for the Treatment of Sexually Transmitted Diseases (January 23, 1998); Prevention and Control of Influenza: Recommendations of the Advisory Committee on Immunization Practices (May 1, 1998); Treatment of Tuberculosis and Tuberculosis Infection in Adults and Children (January 1, 1994); The Prevention and Treatment of Complications of Diabetes Mellitus: A Guide for Primary Care Practitioners (January 1, 1991). The guidelines are available at <http://aepo-xdv-www.epo.cdc.gov/wonder/PrevGuid/titles_a.shtml> (last visited May 1, 2002).

45. See *Lazorko v. Pennsylvania Hosp.,* 237 F.3d 242 (3d Cir. 2000); *Bauman v. U.S. Healthcare (In re U.S. Healthcare),* 193 F.3d 151 (3d Cir. 1999), *cert. denied,* 530 U.S. 1242 (2000); *Moscovitch v. Danbury Hosp.,* 25 F. Supp. 2d 74 (D. Conn. 1998); *Shannon v. McNulty,* 718 A.2d 828, 831 (Pa. Super. Ct. 1998).

46. See *Lazorko v. Pennsylvania Hosp.,* 237 F.3d 242 (3d Cir. 2000). After his wife committed suicide, Lazorko brought suit in state court against his wife's physician and HMO. After being discharged from a 6-month hospitalization following a prior

47. suicide attempt, the wife requested re-hospitalization. 237 F.3d at 236. Her physician denied the request, and Lazorko alleged that the HMO was directly and vicariously liable for his wife's death because the HMO imposed financial disincentives on the physician that discouraged him from recommitting her for additional treatment. *Id.* Despite the HMO's argument that the refusal to hospitalize the wife was a denial of benefits (and, therefore, preempted by ERISA), the court allowed the suit to proceed as a liability action for substandard care, See *id.* at 249–50.

47. A detailed discussion of malpractice liability for MCOs and providers rendering substandard care under MCO treatment guidelines is beyond the scope of this article, which focuses on the implication of the use of such guidelines for the interaction between managed care and public health.

48. Rosenbaum et al., *supra* note 16, vol. 1, at 14, vol. 2, at 2–808.

49. E.R. Brown et al., *Delivery of Sexually Transmitted Disease Services in Medicaid Managed Care* (Los Angeles: UCLA Center for Health Policy Research, 2000).

50. *Id.* at *v-vi.*

51. *Id.* at *vi-vii.*

52. *Id.* at *vi.*

53. Institute of Medicine, *Clinical Practice Guidelines: Directions for a New Program* (Washington, D.C., 1990): at 8.

54. *Id.* at 12.

55. *Id.*

56. Bipartisan Patient Protection Act, S. 1052 and H.R. 2563, 107th Cong. (1st Sess. 2001).

57. See Gostin, *supra* note 1, at 113. In addition, the HIPAA privacy regulation permits the disclosure of individually identifiable health information without patient consent for public health activities mandated by law, such as the collection of information to prevent or control disease or to conduct public health surveillance. See 45 C.F.R. § 164.512(b), 65 Fed. Reg. 82,813–14 (December 28, 2000). Therefore, the privacy regulation does not impede public health agencies' access to data for these purposes. On the other hand, when providing direct patient care, public health providers must comply with the rule's consent and security standards for activities that fall outside public health activities mandated by law. See generally 45 C.F.R. § 160.103, 65 Fed. Reg. 82,799 (December 28, 2000).

58. See *Bragdon v. Abbott,* 524 U.S. 624, 649 (1998) (Kennedy, J., writing for the majority, noted, "the views of public health authorities, such as the U.S. Public Health Service, CDC, and the National Institutes of Health, are of special weight and authority.... A health care professional who disagrees with the prevailing medical consensus may refute it by citing a credible scientific basis for deviating from the accepted norm.").

59. S. Rosenbaum et al., "Who Should Determine When Health Care Is Medically Necessary?," *N. Engl. J. Med.,* 340 (1999): 229–33.

Managed Care and the Goals of Medicine

Daniel Callahan

The recent dramatic increase in managed care plans, the increase in the number of people affected by these plans, and the post-1994 enthusiasm generated by them in some quarters raise a basic question. Are some means of financing and delivering health care more (or less) compatible with the goals of medicine? Or, to add a slightly different twist, are some means more open, in practice, to corrupting the goals of medicine even if, in principle, they are compatible with those goals?

Callahan, Daniel. "Managed Care and the Goals of Medicine," *Journal of the American Geriatrics Society,* 46:3 (1998), 385–388. Copyright © 1998. Reprinted by permission of Blackwell Publishing Ltd.

I ask these questions because, as I will argue, there is no reason, *in principle,* that managed care cannot be harmonious with the goals of medicine, but there is every reason to worry that, *in practice,* there will be significant conflict. In the end, much will depend on (1) the place managed care attains in the American healthcare system, (2) the way its programs are organized and administered, and (3) the extent to which market and profit motives come to dominate the programs.

In addition to making that particular argument, however, I want also to press the claim that when debating the meaning and possibilities of managed care, we should also engage in a parallel debate about the goals of medicine. Just as we would do well to assume that much is still ambiguous and uncertain about the nature and future of managed care, we should also recognize that the goals of medicine are not—in our contemporary context—clear or self-evident. A general problem with most recent healthcare debates, both in the United States and abroad, has been a dissociation of ends and means: the debates are almost entirely about means— organizational, financial, political—and too little about what medicine should now be seeking. Procedural questions have come to dominate substantive ones. I will first discuss the goals of medicine and then move on to the relationship between these goals and managed care.

THE GOALS OF MEDICINE

Modern scientific medicine has been ambitious in its aims and expansionary in its scope. It has believed in the value and necessity of constant medical progress, in the superiority of scientific medicine and a reductionistic organically oriented methodology, and in serving human needs that transcend the narrow confines of health as it has been traditionally conceived. In recent years, this set of medical values has been combined with a number of important cultural values. These include the right of autonomy and self-determination and the need for an equitable distribution of healthcare resources.

All of these values, medical and social, have had their critics, and I do not want to paint a monochromatic picture. Scepticism has been expressed about the possibilities of medical progress, and there have been calls for a medical paradigm that is biopsy chosocial rather than reductionistic and some worries about the medicalization of all of life's problems. Autonomy has by no means been embraced by all physicians, or by all patients, and the struggles over equitable resource distribution have seen market proponents arrayed against those who believe in a more centrally organized and government-oriented system.

Despite these arguments, however, there has been much common agreement about the central importance of the doctor-patient relationship, the necessity of high quality medical care, and the need for medicine to maintain its internal integrity. Given the earlier cited assorted disagreements, however—some of them profound—one might well ask if some goals of medicine could now command general assent and, if so, whether it will be possible for managed care to serve them well.

Let me address the first question by listing the goals that were specified by a recent international project on the goals of medicine of which I was a part:

- The prevention of disease and injury and the promotion and maintenance of health
- The relief of pain and suffering caused by maladies
- The care and cure of those with a malady, and the care of those who cannot be cured
- The avoidance of premature death and the pursuit of a peaceful death

I do not believe there would be much dispute about these four goals as listed. The problem arises when one wants to know whether some are more important than, or should take priority over, others; what the meaning of those goals might be in different cultural and social contexts; and whether age, gender, and other social characteristics should make a difference in the interpretation of those goals. I will not pursue those questions here because they are explored at length in *The Goals of Medicine: Setting New Priorities.*[1] Instead, I will examine the goals stated above and ask, generally, about their compatibility with managed care.

First the aims of managed care must be specified. I believe it fair to say that managed care is meant to be the provision of health care in a way that integrates the various elements of health care while controlling the costs of that care. In short, managed care has both a medical goal, the integration of care, and a financial goal, controlling the costs of that care. That is the theory and the ideal. At the same time, proponents of managed care have also espoused a commitment to the welfare of patients, to a grounding in the best scientific information, and to high quality of care. For-profit organizations have added the further specification that they seek a decent financial return to their shareholders.

Now if one is interested only in comparing the ideal goals of medicine with the ideal goals of managed care, no apparent conflicts exist. Do not managed care organizations espouse the value of health promotion and disease prevention? Do they not espouse the relief of pain and suffering? Do they not pursue the cure of those who can be cured and the care of those who cannot? Do they not espouse the avoidance of a premature death and the pursuit of a peaceful death?

THE REAL AND THE IDEAL WORLD

What about the ways things are, that real world that so commonly impinges on our ideals? Everything is not so clear there. Whereas health promotion and disease prevention are ideals, the time pressures on physician gatekeepers are frequently such that they have little time to do the kind of counseling necessary for good health promotion. There is no evidence that the relief of pain and suffering is handled better by managed care organizations than by earlier financial and organizational arrangements; medicine as a whole has not done well with this kind of care. Managed care, by common agreement, has not done well with chronic illness and disability; in fact, it seems to be doing quite poorly. In regard to the care of the dying, managed care has yet to make any special mark although there is some, but not much, evidence to suggest it is going to do a better job in the near future than the rest of medicine has in the past, which has not been exemplary.

Nevertheless, the managed care world is now complex, diverse, and changing rapidly. One can find grist for any mill, with good examples and bad, horror stories and uplifting stories. Just how managed care will shake out in the long run is anything but clear, and, thus, it is probably premature to take either the good reports or the unsettling ones as symbols of models of the future. Much will depend on the responsiveness of managed care organizations to public and professional criticism, the effects of market competition, the extent to which the organizations are able (and not just willing) to change their ways, and the degree and kind of government regulations that develop concerning the quality of the care they provide.

It is all too easy to forget the kinds of abuses that fee-for-service medicine spawned, not only in generating excessive costs and flagrant waste but also in exposing patients to the hazards of unnecessary and even harmful treatments, treatments generated by that most noxious of combinations: an infatuation with technology and action wedded to a belief that it is just fine if doctors, particularly specialists, do well even as they do good. What managed care has going for it at the moment is that even those members of the public who are critical still, on the whole, accept the trade-off between the kind of quality they would like and the amount of money that are willing to pay for it. A lower quality, if the price is right, seems not unacceptable to the public.

FORMS OF CARE, FORMS OF ORGANIZATION

However, I am still skimming what I take to be the surface of the problem. I asked at the outset whether some forms of delivering health care are more or less compatible with the goals of medicine and whether some are more open than others to corrupting the goals of medicine. On the surface, there seems no inherent conflict between the ideal goals of medicine and the ideals of managed care. Even if numerous complaints abound about some of the actual practices of managed care, they may turn out to be correctable when the dust of the present rapid change settles a bit.

There are three serious soft spots—real points of hazard—that need closer examination: (1) the profit motive in managed care; (2) the effect on physician integrity of managerial oversight and practice guidelines; and (3) the effect of the present emphasis on managed care on the American health system as a whole. It is not easy to show the kind of compatibility between the goals of medicine and those of managed care to which I have so far pointed.

Profits, the market, and managed care

Managed care comes in two economic forms, nonprofit and for-profit. Because I have spent my entire career in the nonprofit world, I am under no illusion that altruism and economic self-denial are always the norm there. Many people make a very good living from nonprofit medicine—think of the salaries of those who manage large systems or hospitals—and few of those who do will tell those with money to give them less of it. Even so, the purpose of nonprofit organizations is not making money or pleasing outside stockholders. There is in that sense no fundamental conflict between the altruistic goals of medicine as an institution and the altruistic goals of (most) nonprofit organizations, including those in health care. That some or many individuals in those organizations are not swept away personally by fits of altruism does not conflict with the general organizational point.

It is a different matter with for-profit organizations. Conflict of interest is built in at the heart of their enterprise: the good of the organization and those who own it against the good that medicine would do. Even worse, actually, the principal aim of for-profit medicine (or so I believe) is to make money. The ethics, goals, and ethos of medicine may be operative in that context, but more as a secondary aim than as an equally competitive primary value.

Now I do not doubt that some, perhaps many, people in for-profit medicine may have chosen that field for their entrepreneurial ventures because they could combine doing good and doing (very) well. Many of us want to find means of succeeding both ways in this world, of doing something valuable for others while, at the same time, doing something for ourselves. In this case, however, the controlling principle of for-profit organizations has to be their capacity to turn a profit. Why? The answer is not simply to keep everyone in the organization happy and well-fed, which nonprofits can do, but also to turn a profit for those who have invested their money in the organization and who expect not just to feel good but to get a good financial return on their investment.

Whereas a good excuse in the nonprofit world might be that no money was made, that the organization just broke even for the year (which is in fact what it should do), this is intolerable in the for-profit world. Few investors would be happy to know that their money was doing many wonderful things but not making them any money. That's fine with their personal eleemosynary contributions but not their financial investments.

In short, an inherent and fundamental conflict exists between the goals of medicine and the goals of for-profit managed care organizations. Because the latter might occasionally accomplish some or even much good while turning a profit does not eliminate the conflict. In hard times, or in highly competitive situations, those organizations will have to make a choice about their moral and financial priorities. It is hard to see how a responsible for-profit manager could justify harming the stake of his or her investors in the name of the higher goals of medicine. That is not what he is supposed to do. It would be a form of managerial irresponsibility in the context of the purpose for which he was hired. We might salute that person for personal courage and integrity, but there would be no management prizes.

It seems no less obvious that when financial or other incentives exist for physicians to hold down costs, the same fundamental conflict arises. The situation is not different from the one that applied earlier in fee-for-service medicine, in which there was at least a tacit financial incentive to treat patients (by calling for more tests, more visits, more shifting of therapies, etc.). In that situation, however, the conflict of interest was self-imposed: the physicians did not have to do what, absent compelling medical reasons, they did not see a need to do. In the case of managed care incentives, however, they are built into the system, allowing no choice of escape.

Managerial oversight and physician integrity

The problem of financial incentives for physicians touches directly on a broader issue, the effect of managerial oversight on physician integrity. This oversight can take the form of pressures to stay within certain parameters in treatment patterns, to withhold referrals to specialists, and to gain permission for certain forms of diagnostic or therapeutic interventions. There are two separate issues here. The first is whether, speaking objectively, there is any necessary harm to patients as a result of such pressures. The second is whether the subjective harm to her integrity that a physician might feel constitutes a moral real harm.

On the first issue, the answer, I believe, is that patients will not necessarily be harmed by managerial oversight of their physicians. Those pressures may force a physician to practice better medicine than he otherwise might on his own, might protect patients from unnecessary diagnostic and therapeutic procedures, and might ensure that the most scientifically based medicine is practiced. I say "not necessarily" because there is nothing in managerial oversight per se that threatens harm to patients. Everything will depend on how that oversight is managed as well as its general quality, which can be good or bad.

On the second issue, a different kind of judgment is necessary. If by "physician integrity" one means the notion that a physician should be free to practice medicine in a way that is in accord with her considered medical and moral judgment, then managerial oversight can pose a threat to that integrity. This threat would be possible even in those cases where, in fact, the patient might be better off because of the oversight. However, that is irrelevant where integrity is concerned for medical integrity concerns how a physician evaluates the competence and correctness of her actions. The importance of the ancient Socratic maxim that one should "know oneself" is matched by the more modern notion that one should be "true to oneself," but that may be impossible if managerial decisions force conduct that one would not choose oneself.

Managed care and the American health system

In 1993 and 1994, there was a strong push for some form of universal health care. That push failed, abysmally so, opening the way for a powerful private sector turn toward managed care. However, the purpose of managed care is to organize the operation and procedures of a healthcare system, not to extend health care to those who do not have it. The way it has worked out is that managed care is being applied to those who already have or can afford coverage, not to those who have none at all. Whereas managed care organizations have financial incentives to increase their membership, those incentives do not apply to those who cannot pay (or are poorly subsidized by government) or to those who might increase costs significantly.

I have not heard of any managed care organization whose ambition is to capture the entire population and, thus, to achieve universal care, nor do I expect to in this or any other world. If this comment is true of nonprofit managed care organizations, it will be true in spades for for-profit managed care organizations. Indeed, so strong are the financial incentives *not* to enroll an unlimited number of people indiscriminately that one can say an inherent conflict exists between the goal of universal care and the actual operation of managed care organizations.

However, could it happen that, with sufficient competition and a truly free market, universal care might—by a kind of ink-blot creep—eventually cover everyone? That is not likely, at least without government subvention, because a large group of people would remain who could not pay out of their own pockets or have employers who could pay for them. Managed care, in any event, is designed not to be a form of equitable national health care allocation but to be a way of organizing the inner life of a particular system.

MEDICAL GOALS, ECONOMIC MEANS

I have pointed to three places where an achievement of the goals of medicine could be compromised by managed care, particularly in its for-profit manifestation. Unlike other problems with managed care, those I have pointed to appear to be intrinsic to that form of care and would not be overcome easily. The attempt to mix the altruistic aims of medicine as an institution with the self-seeking that is native to a profit motive poses the most fundamental conflict. The only possible guard against this kind of conflict—impossible to imagine—would be some kind of corporate dedication to risk financial ruin rather than compromise medical goals. If ever a manager were tempted to go in that direction, one could well imagine a quick objection from his colleagues, but will our patients be better off if we go under altogether? The tyranny of survival would no doubt take over at that point.

The only way to overcome the threat to the subjective sense of physician integrity is to give physicians an active and cooperative role in fashioning the incentives and pressures under which they would live. Even if this role were of some help, however, there would still be some individual physicians whose judgment would deviate from that of their peers and the common consensus. There would be no obvious relief for them, except for an organization that would tolerate some deviance. But how much deviance could an organization tolerate if it began posing a threat to the bottom line or, more benignly, allowed some physicians to flaunt the standards by which their peers agreed to live?

Finally, what more might be said about managed care and universal health coverage? It would be a fool's mission to look to the managed care fraternity and industry to take the lead in a new drive for universal healthcare coverage. That kind of coverage also faces a general legislative and taxpayer unwillingness to see taxes raised in any significant way to provide universal care. In a universal health care system, the techniques of managed care might well insure the most efficient kind of care, but only government support, over and beyond those techniques, would bring about the needed universality.

We seem, then, to be stuck where we began in 1994. Managed care is sweeping the land, mainly because it has seemed the best way to control costs, whether those of government entitlement programs or those of private employers providing benefits for their employees. Nevertheless, it has left unaddressed, and will continue to leave unaddressed, the needs of those who cannot pay. At this point, only some kind of moral or entitlement revolution seems sufficient to bring universal health care. There is, unhappily, little evidence that any such revolution is brewing. In the meantime, as we wait, great creativity will be needed to find ways for managed care to overcome its practical problems, reassure its legitimate critics, and ameliorate the intrinsic conflict it poses for a proper pursuit of the goals of medicine.

REFERENCE

1. The goals of medicine: Setting new priorities. Hastings Cent Rep 1992 (special supplement); 26:1–27.

Lifestyles of the Risky and Infamous

E. Haavi Morreim

FROM MANAGED CARE TO MANAGED LIVES

As managed care organizations provide an increasing proportion of citizen's health care, the move toward asking individuals to help control costs by taking more responsibility for their health is likely to intensify. Economic, medical and legal responses to lifestyle-induced health care costs raise concerns as well as possibilities for using resources responsibly.

The house officer groans inwardly as the alcoholic reappears in the emergency room with his eighteenth—or is that nineteenth?—bout of acute pancreatitis. The internist sighs as she examines the obese, diabetic, hypertensive man who doesn't take his medication but still manages to take in plenty of greasy, salty foods. The surgeon is shocked as his patient, now on the mend after Medicare paid $275,000 for Intensive care of his ruptured abdominal aortic aneurism, refuses to spend $75 of his own money for the new dentures that will enable him to eat solid food and regain his strength.[1] Why can't people take a little responsibility for their health, these physicians wonder.

The nation is beginning to wonder, as well. Many commentators have proposed that citizens should help tame costs by trying to stay healthy and helping to pay for their care. That move is likely to intensify and accelerate in the next few years, as managed care organizations provide an increasing proportion of citizens' health care.

According to senior analysts, managed care evolves through three stages.[2] In stage one, intensive utilization review controls expenditures via rules that limit physicians' decisions. Stage two replaces this costly, intrusive monitoring with economic incentives. Physicians regain clinical autonomy by assuming financial risk. The third stage is dubbed "true managed care": health plans "actually reduce the health risks of their enrollees. 'Plans' competitive advantages will not come from premiums, which are already nearly the same, but from proving that ... they actually did something about health care risks."[3] Health plans' main vehicle for reducing health care risks is, of course, to reduce health risks. And that, inevitably, means addressing patients' lifestyles. When managed care organizations are integrated delivery systems,[4] they provide all the health care that patients need. Reducing need is thus crucial to containing costs.

The move has already begun. Like the man who finally realized what actually causes cancer in laboratory animals—scientists cause the cancer!!—managed care organizations recognize that the real cause of health care costs is patients' illnesses and injuries. They are undertaking or considering a variety of lifestyle initiatives via economic, medical, and even legal means.

Economic responses to lifestyle-induced costs are becoming more common. Some employers and insurers charge higher premiums for people with unhealthy habits,[5] or deny benefits if injuries were caused by reckless behavior like drunk driving.[6] One analyst predicts that managed care organizations "will eventually require enrollees to pay a portion of their medical bills if they neglect their health. A motorcycle-accident victim, for example, will have to pony up part of his medical bill if he wasn't wearing a helmet."[7]

Medical approaches begin with preventive care, which consists of three kinds of interventions: preventing illness and injury, early detection of illness, and preventing or reducing recurrences and exacerbations of a chronic illness. Each can involve lifestyle issues. Preventing illness and injury, for instance, almost always concerns patients' conduct outside the physician's office, since smoking, overeating, and hazardous sports all have predictable morbidities. Early detection of illness requires that patients undergo screening tests that in turn require them to spend their time, undergo some measure of discomfort if not risk, and perhaps pay for extra childcare or experience other inconveniences. Preventing recurrence or exacerbation of chronic illnesses usually requires rigorous adherence to therapy.

Such adherence can be tracked. Because the care provided by managed care organizations usually includes medications, they can (and some now do) use their computer databases to determine which patients receive immunizations and mammograms, and who fills and refills their prescriptions.[8] Noncompliance may result in a note from the physician's orifice, and some organizations already use "telephone naggers" who phone often to ensure that patients are taking their medications.[9] In other cases, managed care organizations might bypass the problem by administering treatments that do not require compliance at all—as with a one-time (but painful) injection of bicillin, instead of oral antibiotics, for a sexually transmitted disease.

In the ultimate response to non-compliance, some managed care organizations may use their data documenting patients' noncompliance to disenroll them from membership. Although fee-for-service insurers and managed care organizations more commonly disenroll patients for reason of nonpayment or fraud (for example, by using their policies to obtain benefits for another person), documented, systematic noncompliance with medical recommendations can also be cause for removing the patient.

Legal controls can be expected as well. One managed care organization successfully lobbied a state legislature to defeat a smokers' rights bill and simultaneously secured the agreement of a local newspaper not to carry cigarette ads. Given that many managed care organizations are currently earning billions of dollars in profit,[10] well-funded lobbying on all sorts of lifestyle issues can be anticipated, ostensibly to improve public health but which also, not coincidentally, save the organizations money.

Managed care plans may look beyond the legislature in their efforts to restrict health risks. Many are already working closely with employers to institute wellness programs and health risk monitoring. While these programs in themselves may be excellent, more coercive measures could also be tried, as by charging higher premiums unless employers institute such measures as smoking bans, mandated safety measures, and the like. Here members are directly coerced, not by health care providers, but by their employers. But the impetus could come from the plan.

Managed care organizations may also raise lifestyle issues in civil litigation. In one recent case a deceased patient's family sued a health maintenance organization physician, alleging inadequate treatment of his heart condition. The physician argued that this patient had effectively committed suicide, based on his years of refusal to take his medications; eat properly, exercise, and quit smoking. The court judged these factors too remote to be the "proximate cause" of the patient's death, though it did find relevant his conduct during the hours immediately before his death—particularly his refusal to return for additional medical attention, as instructed, when his chest pain returned.[11]

This listing is not to suggest that attention to lifestyles is inevitably bad. Preventive care has been too long overlooked. And many managed care organizations are instituting voluntary programs such as exercise and nutrition classes, telephone consultation to help subscribers make intelligent use of the system, and other measures that can be a great boon to patients and plans alike. And not all attempts at lifestyle control come through managed care. Other providers and payers, including employers, can be expected to try similar approaches.

Because most of us may thus find ourselves subject to lifestyle monitoring, and because virtually all of us are concerned about the costs that others' carelessness may generate for the rest of us, it is time to take a closer look. Although there are good reasons to expect people to live prudent lifestyles and accept some consequences when they do not, this essay argues that virtually any mechanism to enforce such responsibility—legal, medical, or economic is seriously flawed. The more important question concerns the responsible use of resources overall, because needless expense from irresponsible living is just one of many ways to misuse health resources. A more comprehensive approach is needed.

Instead of placing financial incentives on physicians and restrictive rules on patients, patients should be brought into the financial incentives in ways that reward prudence without creating barriers to care. A variety of approaches is available, usable under traditional insurance as well as in managed care. Each lets patients experience moderate economic consequences of their health and health care decisions while, at the same time, enhancing patients' control over their care and reducing some of the economic pressures that now drive wedges between patients and physicians.

TAKING RESPONSIBILITY SERIOUSLY

There are good reasons to expect responsibility in matters of health. People can harm others directly, as careless sexual practices transmit lethal disease, or indirectly, as unhealthy living consumes limited financial and medical resources. More fundamentally, the concept of personal responsibility lies at the heart of morality. The very idea of a moral order presupposes that some actions are right, some wrong. Moral agents are not merely "encouraged" or "enabled" to be responsible.[12] They are required to and must be held to answer, perhaps to atone, if they do not.[13]

There is a catch, however. These robust responsibility requirements apply only to autonomous-agents who can choose their own actions for their own reasons. We do not blame people for what is beyond their control. Disease often strikes more out of bad luck than bad behavior, and ill people may lack their usual capacity to make responsible decisions.

But there is an opposing catch. Much of our health is in our own hands, through factors such as tobacco, diet and activity patterns, alcohol and drugs, firearms, sexual behavior, and motor vehicles.[14] In non-medical contexts people are routinely held responsible: the bully who commits assault is not less guilty because he was drunk; the robber is no less culpable because he was high on cocaine; the lover who knowingly transmits a lethal virus can be liable. Surely we are not exempt in matters of health.

Further, although serious illness can impair decision-making, the majority of people visiting a physician are not seriously ill. Many medical visits are for preventive care, symptomatic relief of self-limited illnesses like colds and flu, and routine management of chronic illnesses such as diabetes and hypertension. Most of these people are just as capable of being responsible in health care as they are elsewhere in life.

Unfortunately, although enforcing lifestyle responsibility through law, medicine, or economics can perhaps have some limited legitimate role, there are also major problems.

LEGAL ENFORCEMENT

Enforcement of healthy lifestyle choices through the courts or legislation might prohibit or require specified conduct, as with motorcycle helmet laws or smoking bans. These restrictions have long been controversial because, when government says "we forbid you to live as you see fit because you might burden the rest of us," it invites major intrusions on human liberty.[15] Such intrusions can penetrate beyond conduct, into private beliefs and values. Optimal health is just one value, alongside others ranging from risky sports for entertainment to unhealthy ethnic diets. And not everyone agrees what health is. Medical concepts of health and illness are based on scientific notions of cause and effect that, from some or folk perspectives, appear shallow.[16] Enforcement itself could also be highly intrusive—spying and prying to see who's smoking on the sly.

Still, law does have some legitimate voice regarding personal responsibility in health care. In contract negotiations, the law regards medical patients as vulnerable and gives them a strong benefit of the doubt in their interactions with health insurers, hospitals, and physicians.[17] Nevertheless, patients are expected to be responsible adults. They must not deliberately or intentionally harm others, and their contributory negligence, such as noncompliance with medical instructions, can reduce or preclude damage awards for malpractice injuries[18] Sometimes a patient who knowingly consents to risks, such as an unconventional medical treatment, may simply have to live with the bad outcome, with no right of recovery for injuries. And if a patient consistently refuses to cooperate with therapy, eventually the physician is no longer obligated to care for her.

In sum, though these limited legal measures seem appropriate, the problems caused by irresponsible living do not generally warrant the coercive power of the state. Unfortunately, once we agree that people should mostly be permitted to live as they wish, we face the burdens their freedom can impose on the rest of us. Since the idea of responsibility requires people to live with the consequences of their decisions, perhaps we should expect them to bear the natural consequences of their unhealthy lifestyles by denying medical rescue.

MEDICAL ENFORCEMENT

Lifestyle-based restrictions on medical care are not limited to managed care organizations. In the early days of renal dialysis, committees determined who would live, not just on the basis of medical eligibility, but candidates' value to the community.[19] Today, some physicians refuse to offer coronary bypass surgery to patients who refuse to stop smoking,[20] while others might deny multiple valve replacements to a patient whose continued intravenous drug use keeps reinfecting his heart.[21]

It is generally wrong to deny medical care because of patients' lifestyles for four reasons. First, denying treatment can be unreasonably harsh. Many ostensibly voluntary behaviors are mediated by genetic predispositions, while other bad habits have an addictive dimension, and chronic illnesses can render some patients psychologically less able to act rationally according to their values.[22] The harshness goes further. Requiring someone to live with the consequences of his actions can, in medicine, be deadly. Failing to use a seatbelt is foolish—especially if one is driving to a store to buy cigarettes and greasy junk food. But the person does not deserve to die for it, which is just what may happen if the offender is denied medical care after his auto accident. If we are unwilling to criminalize such activity, we should not seek to make its consequences even worse than incarceration.

Second, medical punishment for lifestyle vices raises important problems of science and evidence. Just as there is insufficient evidence to determine when bad habits have been caused by factors other than voluntary choice, those habits in turn may play an uncertain role in the actual development of illness. Triggers for lung cancer, for instance, can include genetic and environmental factors, and it may be impossible to determine which factors play what role.

The problem runs deeper. Epidemiological evidence is too frequently overthrown. A claim that coffee causes pancreatic cancer is followed by a retraction.[23] Moderate caffeine during pregnancy might—or then again might not—be harmful.[24] Women in their forties should get a mammogram every year or two—until new evidence suggests that it does not save lives in this age group, and one (but not another) cancer agency changes its screening recommendations.[25] Alcohol can be good for your health, while exercise can kill you.[26]

Sometimes our beliefs about patients are even flimsier. It would be easy to assume that liver transplant for an alcoholic is pointless—surely the person will ruin a second liver the same way he did the first. Yet studies suggest these patients' one year survival after the procedure appears comparable to other patients', and return to alcohol is uncommon.[27]

Using science as the basis for behavior control is also a hazard to science itself. The more forcefully science is used to curtail people's behavior, the more it is resented when the mandate later turns out to be wrong. Reciprocally, science that shapes medical, political, and economic policy is itself in danger of being shaped more by economic mandates and political correctness than by intellectual rigor.

Problem number three arises if, at the policy level, we construct broad rules forbidding certain resources for certain kinds of patients, as by refusing liver transplant for alcoholics. Aside from possibly offending anti-discrimination laws, such policies would ignore potentially important differences between patients. One person may be only a minimal smoker whose cancer was primarily caused by hereditary factors, while another may truly have smoked his way into a heart attack. Under a policy denying surgeries to smokers; both would be denied care. Institutions do, of course, need to create resource priorities, such as hospital policies governing the use of intensive care beds and extra-corporeal membrane oxygenation (ECMO).[28] But these should be based on medical indications, not personal lifestyle.

The alternative, namely expecting physicians to determine case-by-case which patients truly caused their own problems, raises the fourth even more serious concern. Denying medical care for lifestyle vices conflicts with a deep moral conviction of medicine: compassion for the patient as a human being in need. Let judges condemn the guilty, but let physicians help the suffering. The physician who denies medical care as a penalty for irresponsible conduct is no longer a healer with a fiduciary commitment to each patient, but an enforcer of social policy.

Moreover, the enforcer role can be medically counterproductive. Good care requires a complete and honest history from the patient, a requirement so important that stout principles of confidentiality assure patients that disclosures to physicians will not find their way to third parties who could do them harm. Where the physician stands as judge and jury of the patient's failure to live responsibly, as by denying bypass surgery to smokers; the enemy threatening harm is the physician himself. Here, the patient who tells his physician the truth is a fool.

This is not to say that physicians cannot expect patients to be responsible partners within their relationship. Patients are obligated to provide an accurate history, to participate in decisions about treatment, and to carry out or else renegotiate their agreements. The patient who routinely deceives, or refuses to comply with treatment and yet demands un-flagging devotion,

unfairly manipulates the physician and demeans his integrity.

Determining just how physicians should respond, however, poses a challenge. The physician's personal or professional integrity may require him to refuse some patient demands. And sometimes it may be acceptable to deny specified medical services if a patient is unwilling to provide cooperation that is essential to the treatment's success. A patient who refuses to take antirejection medications has exempted himself from organ transplant. On the whole, however, such denials are hazardous. They can tempt the physician to exercise his superior knowledge and power of prescription as a weapon to manipulate patients into submission, bypassing the necessary discussion, negotiation, and free consent. The patient should not fear abandonment every time he disagrees with the physician.

At the same time, the physician should not be expected indefinitely to pick up the pieces left by abusively irresponsible patients. In such cases it is probably best for the physician simply to withdraw from the relationship, with appropriate notice and perhaps an explanation that circumstances have shown he is unable to meet this particular patient's needs.

In the final analysis, patients should not generally have to pay for lifestyle indiscretions by forfeiting medical care, either by social policy or by physician discretion. Medical vigilantism is repugnant.

ECONOMIC ENFORCEMENT

Economic responsibility can be imposed prior to unhealthy conduct or concurrently with its consequences. Taxes on cigarettes and alcohol, for example, aim to deter the unwanted conduct and to collect in advance the money to treat the anticipated health problems, as do higher insurance premiums for people with high-risk habits.

These levies seem partly fair, partly not. The more one smokes, the higher the risks and taxes. Stop smoking, and pay no more taxes. On the other hand, it is difficult to tax other vices, such as overeating. And cigarette taxes are also paid by smokers who never become ill. Still, even if we can't get at all unhealthy behaviors, it is not necessarily unfair to collect from offenders when we can.[29] And even if someone is never hurt, he is still generating extra risk.

There are other problems. A heavy tax on cigarettes can spawn a ferocious black market, consuming more money to catch crooks than it raises for health care.[30]

Higher insurance premiums either require risk takers to be honest in ways that will raise their premiums or necessitate unsavory intrusions into privacy to overcome the expected dishonesty. Furthermore, economic facts don't always support the taxes. Smokers do generate health care costs. Yet they often die of relatively inexpensive causes, right around the time of retirement—saving considerably on pension plans.[31]

The pay-as-you-go approach is already in place to some extent. When insurers require substantial cost sharing, those who are ill more, pay more. Similarly, coverage for behavior-caused illnesses and injuries might be reduced. Several large corporations pay reduced death benefits if the deceased was not wearing a seatbelt during a fatal auto accident; another company will pay 60 percent rather than the usual 100 percent of prenatal care if the pregnant employee or family member delayed seeking that care.[32] Here, however, familiar problems arise, such as determining whether the illness was caused by truly voluntary conduct. In other cases high costs levied on patients could bar them from health care altogether, an unduly punitive outcome. Incentives, such as paying regular bonuses to a pregnant cocaine user for remaining drug free until delivery, can perversely backfire. Paying only those who originally test positive for drugs would be a powerful incentive to take up drugs as soon as one knows one is pregnant; but paying everyone to "be good" would be prohibitively costly.

BROADER CONCEPTS OF RESPONSIBLE RESOURCE USE

For better or worse, then, it seems there is little we should do to enforce clean living. Annoying though it is to see common resources depleted by people who will not behave as responsible adults, the price of coercing goodness may be even worse for us all. Limiting patients' recovery in civil suits for the consequences of their own foolishness is only right. But legally prohibiting risky conduct, while justifiable in a few circumstances, invades important liberties. And if an activity is not pernicious enough to be declared illegal, punishing it by withholding medical care would be harsh, ill-founded, and contrary to medicine's most cherished values. And economic remedies, such as heavy taxes and post hoc fees for health vices, can often be unfair, impractical, and empirically unjustified. Thus, these various measures offer a few legitimate ways to enforce limited accountability, but hardly a satisfactory comprehensive solution.

Perhaps we must resign ourselves to rescue and resent. Common decency will not let us turn someone away, bleeding or dying, just because he was foolish. In this way we partly generate our own problem. It is difficult to take seriously an admonition to behave if one knows he will be rescued. A washed-out homeowner may be told that if he rebuilds his home on a flood plain, we will not bail him out of the next flood. But if we take pity on his suffering after that next flood and cover his losses again, we have taught him that irresponsibility pays, exacerbating the free-rider problem for future disasters. We may believe that individuals should experience the consequences of their choices, yet we must find a way that is not so punitive that it either harms suffering individuals or triggers our own urge to rescue regardless of irresponsibility.

A better answer requires us to reformulate the question. Lifestyle issues are just one part of a larger challenge: more responsible use of health care resources, generally. There are many ways to use health care resources irresponsibly—doing too much, too little, or the wrong thing—and virtually anyone in the health care system can behave irresponsibly. Patients can fail to wear bike helmets or demand antibiotics for vital infections. Physicians can order tests and treatments more justified by habit than by science or to ward off purely hypothetical malpractice liability. Hospitals may open more beds than they can fill or acquire technology they cannot fully use. Administrative inefficiency can waste time and money without enhancing care or profits.

Currently, health plans are largely in charge of resource use. Businesses and governments insist on moderate premium prices and good quality of care, but the health plans usually determine the specifics. Health plans have two basic ways to contain costs: direct controls, in which they directly determine which interventions will be authorized for which patients under what conditions, and incentives inspiring physicians and other providers toward conservative resource use.

Recently plans have begun to realize that these utilization controls can be expensive, intrusive, economically ineffective, and medically harmful. Hence we see the shift described above, from stage one to stage two in the evolution of managed care, in which clinicians are left to deliver care as they see fit, but under the pressures of economic incentives. Increasingly, those incentives are not cash rewards for specific cost-saving decisions, but broad constraints such as capitation, in which all patients' care is covered by a flat fee, and profiling of physicians' overall performance with the threat of being "deselected," or fired, by the managed care organizations. These arrangements attempt to bring physicians into the plans' overall goals for containing costs without dictating the specifics of care.

The langue du jour speaks of "aligning" incentives among physicians, employers, managed care organizations and other payers.[33] Significantly in these discussions, patients are not listed among the financial players. Daniel Sulmasy, for example, notes that "[w]hat is envisioned under managed competition is thus a three-layered system. The government manages HMOs, HMOs manage physicians, and physicians manage patients. All three would have strong incentives to spend less on health care."[34] Note that although the passage identifies four parties—government, HMOs, physicians, and patients—only three are contemplated as players in managing care.

Of course, managed care organizations do not ignore patients in containing costs. Just as with physicians, such plans and other payers have two basic options regarding patients' role: they can control, or they can offer incentives. Currently, controls on patients' choices of plans, providers, and treatments are the main instrument. Most patients have little or no choice among health plans. Of businesses that provide health care insurance, almost 84 percent provide only one option.[35] Many of the others provide only two or three choices, and now "more and more people are shifted into managed care" with or without their agreement.[36]

Within plans, patients' choices of providers and treatments are likewise limited, except where they can afford to pay substantial out-of-pocket costs for out-of-plan options. Limiting patients' choices is essential to managed care.[37] Patients may even find controls exerted by their own physicians. As health economist Mark Crane notes, "Some doctors discourage their capitated patients by forcing them to wait weeks for office visits, giving only 'non-prime time' appointments, using the telephone as a roadblock, and erecting other obstacles to prevent the patient from seeing the physician."[38]

But patients' role in containing costs will not be limited to controlling choices among plans, physicians, and treatments. Lifestyle management will inevitably enter. Such measures can, of course, be medically beneficial. However, the very idea of patient autonomy suggests that patients are entitled to have a different opinion about their best interests, medical and otherwise. The hypertensive patient may find that the medications permitted by his managed care organization's stringently limited formulary have unacceptable side-effects; or the inner-city dweller may find that walking for exercise in his neighborhood is far more dangerous than being overweight. Equally ominous, many managed care organizations are beginning to require physicians to police these

lifestyle rules. For example, many plans now have incentives rewarding physicians for quality of care. The concept is laudable, but in many cases quality is measured in part by how successfully the physician gets his patients to come in for designated services and to comply with their medications.[39] The physician must demand ever more insistently that patients follow all sorts of medical orders that may or may not suit their preferences.

Perhaps most disturbing of all, under current economic arrangements, successful regulation of patients' health habits translates directly into cash in the pockets of employers, payers, health plans, and physicians. The patient gives up his favorite vices so that others can pocket the savings.

Currently most patients have little or no incentive toward cost-consciousness, particularly in managed care, where copays are almost negligible. But it is also true elsewhere in the health care system, where cost sharing is generally modest, and many patients purchase "gap" insurance, or urge physicians to waive the copays, or simply refuse to pay them. So long as this is true, patients will inevitably be subject to others' control—because there are only the two options: controls and incentives.

If patients are to avoid being subjected to extensive, offensive, and often rather insidious forms of health care limits and lifestyle coercion, it would seem that the only alternative is to bring them into the same "alignment" of incentives that now is beginning to unify all the other players in the health care scene. At the same time, such economic involvement should not pose barriers to care. Fortunately, several approaches are available, and some are already being successfully used.

ECONOMIC ACCOUNTABILITY

The objective of these approaches is to place patients systematically in closer contact with the economic consequences of all their health care decisions, not just those associated with unhealthy habits. They do so not by installing financial barriers to care, but by rewarding prudent resource use. Thus the incentives are positive, not negative.

For example, a Medical Savings Account is a tax-free fund, perhaps $3,000, to cover the routine costs of care, while catastrophic insurance covers health care exceeding that amount. The fund might be filled by the individual, the employer, or even the government so that everyone—including the poor—could afford it. On one version, money left at the end of each year would roll over into the next year's account for future medical expenses and also, after retirement, for general living expenses.[40] In another version, patients keep the remainder at the end of each year. Medical savings accounts have been endorsed by the American Medical Association and a number of political leaders.

Managed care organizations could do something similar. One approach would place a specified number of points (say, 3,000) into an account for each subscriber at the beginning of the year. The patient would "spend" those points, for example for ordinary physician visits or medications that are costlier than those on the formulary. Reciprocally, extra points might be awarded to encourage important preventive care such as immunizations and prenatal care, or needed follow-up for chronic illness or serious injury. Points remaining at the end of the year might be returned as cash or reduced premiums, banked for the next year, or perhaps spent in a catalogue of goods such as health club memberships or household items.[41]

Such approaches have important advantages. Financial barriers to care are eliminated as patients enjoy either first-dollar coverage through a dedicated account or all needed care directly from the managed care organizations. At the same time, patients have a real reward for prudent resource use, unlike the current situation. Managed care patients with minimal copayments sometimes make needless visits for minor or self-limited problems ("it's free, so I might as well go"), or insist on exotic treatments that are not medically indicated ("I paid my premium, so I'm entitled").[42] Patients with indemnity insurance sometimes urge their physicians to extract extra resources by "gaming the system."

In contrast, deducting such care directly from patients' medical savings accounts or managed care points could prompt more careful use of resources. Similarly, the indigent person with a government-funded account would be rewarded for seeking care from a primary care physician rather than an emergency room. Additionally, these incentives would expose patients to some of the costs of unhealthy habits. As those with a medical savings account pay directly for the first $3,000 of their care, fellow subscribers don't have to. The account would cover most if not all of the physician visits necessitated by smokers' extra respiratory infections, for example. Similarly, managed care points diminish as extra illnesses from unhealthy habits require more physician visits. And on both approaches, patients may be less likely to demand unnecessary care, such as antibiotics for vital ailments. In the process, people with serious or chronic illnesses would enjoy what, for them, is the best prize of all: more and better health care. A system less clogged with demands for marginal care can be more fully dedicated to those who really need it.

Reciprocally, such a system need not foster another kind of irresponsibility: forgoing necessary care in order to save money. There are several reasons.

First, the money or points in these accounts cannot be directly traded for beer or other commodities. More importantly, the principle of autonomy permits competent patients to forgo care for whatever reason they see fit, and people are entitled to define for themselves what care is "necessary" and what is not. If they are entitled to refuse care on religious, personal, or even frivolous grounds, surely they are entitled to do so on economic grounds if they have determined that some other use of their money is more important. No rule requires that health needs must be met before all other needs, any more than all people must buy the safest possible automobile regardless of the cost. A society in which Prudent Purchase Police barred the door to fast-food stands would be oppressive indeed.

Further, greater patient cost-consciousness should diminish the need for outside micromanagement, with commensurate reductions in administrative costs of care, annoying hassle-factor, and even premium costs. More important, if patients help curb over-utilization, then insurers and managed care organizations may find less need for the financial incentives that place physicians in conflicts of interest by encouraging them to cut back on care. Indeed, when the money at stake is the patient's rather than the physician's, the physician who discusses costs is not an adversary guarding his and third parties' money, but an ally looking at the patient's broader interests, helping him both to ensure that the value of care is worth its cost and to avoid medically short-sighted cost-cutting.

Just as compelling, perhaps, is evidence indicating that people who are actually in such systems use them well. Several corporations use variations of medical savings accounts with significant success. Golden Rule Insurance Company, for example, instituted a savings account option for its own employees, in addition to their usual indemnity option. The 80 percent who chose the medical savings account during the first year received a total of $468,000 in rebates at the end of the year. The following year, with even more employees enrolled, the plan returned $743,000, or over $1,000 per worker. The savings came several ways. Some individuals needing outpatient diagnostic testing, for instance, did price-shopping that revealed wide variations in the costs of the same test from one provider to the next, with no identifiable difference in quality. Higher-priced providers began cutting their rates to compete. Claim costs on catastrophic insurance decreased, with subsequent lowering of premiums. And equally important, some health care utilization actually increased. For many low-wage families, the typical indemnity deductible of several hundred dollars effectively prohibited many forms of preventive care. For them, medical savings accounts represented first-dollar coverage permitting easy access to these important services.[43] Other companies have tried similar approaches, also with striking success.

DOING THE BEST WE CAN

There would be little reason to care about bad habits that harm only the individual if it weren't for the fact that the rest of us pay for the repairs. Admittedly, the mild incentives in this approach do not solve the problem of irresponsible lifestyles. Deducting a few dollars or points from an account is unlikely to transform smokers and drinkers into paragons of health virtue. But there is no fully satisfactory solution. Any serious legal, medical, or economic enforcements against unpalatable lifestyles will usually be worse than the vices they attack. Fortunately, this recognition does not constitute a defeat, for it helps us to redirect our focus.

The real question is much broader: how do we ensure that all those with an important stake in the health care system—payers, providers, and patients alike—use its resources more wisely? The value of greater economic accountability for patients is found not in its power to change their lifestyles, but in its capacity to foster more responsible use of health care resources generally, to return to patients a greater measure of control over their health care, and to avert the potentially major and illegitimate intrusions into personal lives that are surely around the corner if patients are not brought into resource management in more constructive ways. It is no panacea, but it is probably the best we can do.

REFERENCES

1. J.P. Weaver, "The Best Care Other People's Money Can Buy," Wall Street Journal, 19 November 1992.
2. Anita J. Slomski, "Maybe Bigger Isn't Better After All," Medical Economics 72, no. 4 (1995): 55–58.
3. Slomski, "Maybe Bigger Isn't Better," p. 58.
4. The term managed care can refer to a variety of arrangements, some consisting of no more than a utilization review system. A managed care organization, however, is normally an entity that provides complete care for a single, fixed monthly or annual premium. These include health maintenance organizations and hospital-based integrated delivery systems.
5. New York Life Ins. Co. v. Johnson, 923 F.2d 279 (3rd. Cir. 1991); Robert L. Schwartz, "Life Style, Health Status, and Distributive Justice," Health Matrix 3 (1993): 195–217.
6. Hoag Memorial Hosp. v. Managed Care Administrators, 820 F.Supp. 1232 (C.D.Cal. 1993).
7. Slomski, "Maybe Bigger Isn't Better," p. 58.
8. Robert S. Thompson, Stephen H. Taplin, Timothy A. McAfee et al, "Primary and Secondary Prevention Services in Clinical Practice: Twenty Years' Experience in Development, Implementation, and Evaluation," JAMA 273 (1995): 113035; Wayne Katon, Michael Von Korff, Elizabeth Lin et al., "Collaborative Management to Achieve Treatment Guidelines: Impact on Depression in Primary Care," JAMA 273 (1995): 1026–31.
9. George Anders, "Drug Makers Help Manage Patient Care," Wall Street Journal, 17 May 1995; Ron Winslow, "An HMO Tries Talking Members into Healthy Habits," Wall Street Journal, 6 April 1994; S. Stevens; "Capitation Seen No Bar to Profits and Control," Physicians Financial News: Managed Care Report, 30 April 1995, S-I, S-19; H. Meyer, "HMOs May Improve Preventive Care, But Reform Must Create Proper Incentives," American Medical News, 23–30 May 1994.

An increasingly popular approach, called "disease management," involves intensive monitoring of patients' compliance with treatment, among other measures. See Carl Peterson, "Disease Management: A Team Approach to Chronic Care," HMO Magazine 36, no. 3 (1995): 39–47.
10. George Anders, "HMOs Pile Up Billions in Cash, Try to Decide What to Do with It," Wall Street Journal, 21 December 1994.
11. Van Vacter v. Hierholzer, 865 S.W. 2d 355 (Mo. App. W.D. 1993).
12. Reinhold Priester, "A Values Framework for Health System Reform," Health Affairs 11 (1992): 84–107, at 99.
13. E. Haavi Morreim, "Impairments and Impediments in Patients' Decision Making: Reframing the Competence Question," Journal of Clinical Ethics 4 (1993): 294–307.
14. J. Michael McGinnis and William H. Foege, "Actual Causes of Death in the United States," JAMA 270 (1993): 2207–12.
15. Daniel I. Wikler, "Persuasion and Coercion for Health: Ethical Issues in Government Efforts to Change LifeStyles," Milbank Memorial Fund Quarterly 56 (19.78): 303–37.
16. Faith Fitzgerald, "The Tyranny of Health," NEJM 331 (1994): 196–98; L. M. Pachter, "Culture and Clinical Care: Folk Illness Beliefs and Behaviors and Their Implications for Health Care Delivery," JAMA 271 (1994): 690–94.
17. E. Haavi Morreim, "Redefining Quality by Reassigning Responsibility," American Journal of Law and Medicine 20 (1994): 79–104.
18. Barry R. Furrow, Sandra H. Johnson, Timothy S. Jost, and Robert L. Schwartz, Liability and Quality Issues in Health Care (St. Paul: West Publishing Co., 1991) at 188–98.
19. D. Sanders and J. Dukeminier, Jr., "Medical Advance and Legal Lag: Hemodialysis and Kidney Transplantation," University of California Law Review 15 (1968): 357–413.
20. M.J. Underwood and J. S. Balley, "Coronary Bypass Surgery Should Not Be Offered to Smokers," British Medical Journal 306 (1993): 1047–48.
21. Lance K. Stell, "The Noncompliant Substance Abuser," Hastings Center Report 21, no. 2 (1991): 31–32.
22. Roger Higgs, "Human Frailty Should Not Be Penalised," British Medical Journal 306 (1993): 1049–50; David Orentlicher, "Denying Treatment to the Non-compliant Patient," JAMA 265 (1991): 1579–82.
23. A.R. Feinstein, "Scientific Standards in Epidemiologic Studies of the Menace of Daily Life," JAMA 242 (1988): 125763.
24. Brenda Eskenazi, "Caffeine During Pregnancy: Grounds for Concern?" JAMA 270 (1993): 2973–74.

25. Marilyn Chase, "Mammogram Starting Age Rises to 50 Under New Federal Recommendations," Wall Street Journal, 6 December 1993.

26. Gary D. Friedman and Arthur L. Klatsky, "Is Alcohol Good for Your Health?" NEJM 329 (1993): 1882–83; Gregory D. Curfman, "Is Exercise Beneficial—or Hazardous—to Your Health?" NEJM 329 (1993): 1730–31.

27. Kenneth R. McCurry, Prabhaker Baliga, Robert M. Merion et al., "Resource Utilization and Outcome for Liver Transplantation for Alcoholic Cirrhosis," Archives of Surgery 127 (1992): 772–77; Carl Cohen et al., "Alcoholics and Liver Transplantation," JAMA 256 (1991): 1299–1301.

28. John J. Paris, Michael D. Schreiber, Mindy Statter et al., "Beyond Autonomy—Physicians' Refusal to Use Life-Prolonging Extra-corporeal Membrane Oxygenation," NEJM 329 (1993): 354–57.

29. Robert M. Veatch, "Voluntary Risks to Health: The Ethical Issues," JAMA 243 (1980): 50–55.

30. "Canada Mulls Tobacco Tax Cuts to Hit Smugglers," American Medical News 7 March 1994.

31. W.G. Manning, B. K Emmett, J. P. Newhouse et al., "The Taxes of Sin: Do Smokers and Drinkers Pay Their Way?" JAMA 261 (1989): 1604–9.

32. Schwartz, "Life Style, Health Status, and Distributive Justice," at 197.

33. E. Haavi Morreim, "The Ethics of Incentives in Managed Care," Trends in Health Care, Law & Ethics I O (1995): 56–62.

34. Daniel P. Sulmasy, "Managed Care and Managed Death," Archives of Internal Medicine 155 (1995): 33–36.

35. Robert J. Blendon, Mollyann Brodie, and John Benson, "What Should Be Done Now that National Health System Reform Is Dead?" JAMA 273 (1995): 24344, at 243.

36. D. Murray, "The Four Market Stages, and Where You Fit In," Medical Economics 72, no. 5 (1995): 44–57, at 52.

37. B. Weise, "Managed Care: There's No Stopping It Now," Medical Economics 72; no. 5 (1995): 26–43.

38. Mark Crane, "It Doesn't Pay to Shortchange Managed-Care Patients," Medical Economics 72, no. 5 (1995): 95–104, at 96.

39. C. Appleby, "HEDIS: Managed Care's Emerging Gold Standard," Managed Care 4 (1995): 19–24; Slomski, "Maybe Bigger Isn't Better."

40. John C. Goodman and Gerald L. Musgrave, Patient Power (Washington D.C.: Cato Institute, 1992).

41. E. Haavi Morreim, "Diverse and Perverse Incentives in Managed Care"; forthcoming in Widener Law Symposium Journal 1995.

42. A 1993 study commissioned by the American Hospital Association found that health maintenance organization patients see their physicians more frequently than fee-for-service patients: 3.63 outpatient visits per year compared with 3.35. See R. L. Lowes, "Exactly How Busy Are Physicians?" Medical Economics 72, no. 6 (1995): 59.

43. Personal communication: J. Patrick Rooney, Chairman of the Board, Golden Rule Insurance Company, 7 March 1995.

Canadians Confront Health Care Reform

Julia Abelson, Matthew Mendelsohn, John N. Lavis, Steven G. Morgan, Pierre-Gerlier Forest, and Marilyn Swinton

A 2002 survey shows that Canadians' attitudes toward health system changes are in a state of flux.

Canadians have recently been through a series of soul-searching exercises to consider the problems facing their health care system and options for its reform. The provincial and national commissions that have led these exercises have reacted to growing perceptions that the system needs major reform. The most recent national inquiry, the Commission on the Future of Health Care in Canada (also known as the Romanow Commission), provided advice about the sustainability of the health care system and about how best to bring about change. The results of our survey of public opinion, which was conducted at the time of the commission's final report, may be particularly instructive for the United States, given that both Americans and Canadians are grappling with what should constitute "core" services within their respective Medicare programs and the role for the for-profit sector in delivering these services.

Beginning in the 1990s Canadians expressed growing concern that their health care system was failing to deliver timely access to high-quality care when needed; that Canadian Medicare—built around universal public insurance for hospitals and doctors—inadequately addresses increasing expenditures on prescription drugs and home care; and that an increased role for private financing and for-profit delivery may be necessary to sustain the health care system. Our survey updates measures of Canadians' concerns about timely access to high-quality care and solicits views about perceived problems with the health care system, attitudes toward widely debated options for transforming the health care system, and the values underpinning these attitudes. The use of a series of tracking questions in our 2002 survey allowed us to reflect on the evolution of Canadians' opinions about their health care system in comparison with other countries, namely the United States and the United Kingdom.

Two private financing options were examined: user fees for medically necessary hospital and physician care,

Abridged from Abelson, Julia, Matthew Mendelsohn, John N. Lavis, Steven G. Morgan, Pierre-Gerlier Forest, and Marilyn Swinton. "Canadians Confront Health Care Reform" *Health Affairs*, 23:3 (May/June 2004), 186–193. Copyright © 2004. Reprinted by permission of Copyright Clearance Center on behalf of the publisher.

and "two-tier" physician and hospital care that would allow people to pay for faster or higher-quality care or both. These financing options were selected because they are now prohibited in the Canadian Medicare system yet are routinely presented as options for alleviating perceived access problems. For-profit delivery was also examined because it, too, is prohibited and has been much debated. We compared attitudes toward financing and delivery options for physician and hospital care versus attitudes toward the same options applied to high-tech care (for example, diagnostic equipment) and home care to determine whether Canadians viewed core Canadian Medicare services (financed publicly and delivered on a not-for-profit basis for more than thirty years) differently from rapidly expanding forms of care (financed and delivered through varied arrangements across the country).

SURVEY FINDINGS

Perceived problems with the Canadian health care system

Previous international surveys published in *Health Affairs* documented a decline in public confidence in the Canadian health care system during the 1990s. Using a question from these surveys, we compared Canadians' views in 2002 with the views in Canada, the United States, and the United Kingdom in 1988 and 1998. Among the three countries, Canadians were uniquely satisfied with their system in 1988. But by 1998 Canadians had radically reevaluated the performance of their system. Their responses more closely matched U.S. views and were notably less positive than those in the United Kingdom. By 2002 views about the extent of system change required had changed considerably: More Canadians believed that major changes are needed, but fewer believed that complete rebuilding is needed.

Concerns about the quality of the health care system and concerns about access to services follow the same pattern of peaking over a similar time period. That said, in 2002 Canadians no longer believed that their system is excellent, as they did in the early 1990s, and they were clearly experiencing more difficulty obtaining needed health care than in the late 1980s, even if the worst of the perceived accessibility crisis appeared to be over in 2002.

Perceived sources of problems

In 2002 a substantial majority of Canadians held the view that patients and, to a lesser and decreasing extent, doctors abuse the health care system. However, Canadians did not believe that the public financing model that underpins Medicare is fundamentally unaffordable: only about one-third of respondents agreed with this statement, and these views have not changed since the late 1990s. Despite the widespread use of cost sharing for patients and utilization controls for physicians in the United States, which would at first glance appear to be possible solutions to health system abuse, Canadians have not embraced the U.S. model of health care delivery. The Canadian health system remains an important component of Canadians' sense of differentiation from the United States; however, the intensity of this feeling has subsided In our 2002 survey, 12 percent of respondents stated a preference for being treated in the United States, compared with 7 percent stating this preference in 1995.

Attitudes toward reform options

In 2002 Canadians were firm in their beliefs that health care is a right of citizenship (93 percent agreed, and only 6 percent disagreed), but they were divided on the issue of the role that the market versus the state should play in the financing and delivery of health care. More than half (51 percent) of respondents believed that profit making in the health care system can be justified (42 percent disagreed), and 62 percent believed that there is nothing wrong with having private, for-profit companies and competition play a role in the health care system (34 percent disagreed). But at the same time, 57 percent also believed that more money should be put into the system even if it means paying more in taxes (40 percent disagreed).

To obtain more specific views about these complex issues, we presented respondents with several scenarios, each of which tapped views about a different aspect of the public/private financing and not-for-profit/for-profit delivery debates. Through these scenarios we sought to discern public attitudes toward three options for transforming the health care system: (1) user fees, defined as "a patient paying part of the cost for the health care they receive"; (2) two-tier delivery, defined as "people being allowed to pay for faster and/or higher quality care"; and (3) for-profit care, defined as "private firms setting up alongside the not for profit health care system and competing with it."

Canadians make a distinction between doctors and hospitals on the one hand and home care and high-tech care on the other, and they more strongly oppose changes to the traditional domains of doctors and hospitals. Governments' roles in maintaining free and equitably delivered doctor and hospital care are highly visible in Canada and have been since the introduction of Medicare more than thirty years ago. Notwithstanding Canadians' views about patients' abusing the health care system, the majority of them remained opposed to user fees in 2002. The same solidaristic principles, however, have not informed how governments treat home care and high-tech care, and views did not appear to be held as strongly for these forms of care. Moreover, Canadians were more receptive to two-tier options for expanding some forms of care (such as high-tech care and home care) than for hospital care. They also appeared to be more supportive of for-profit over two-tier options when they considered these within the context of high-tech care and home care.

We conducted exploratory regression analysis to identify drivers of support for transformative changes to the health care system, as defined by our user fee, two-tier, and for-profit scenarios. We provide a brief summary of reactions to these options here. First, contact with the health care system, such as whether one had been hospitalized in the previous year or is now providing home care, is not an important predictor of attitudes toward these options. Second, those who know more about the health care system, as measured by their knowledge of the Commission on the Future of Health Care in Canada, are somewhat more opposed to these changes. Third, most sociodemographic factors were not very important in explaining opinions about these options. However, a consistent pattern of age effects was found. Younger Canadians were consistently more supportive of the scenarios presented to them, while older Canadians were particularly opposed to two-tier options. Fourth, what appears to emerge most strongly as an explanation for support or opposition to these options is competing values. Support for private and for-profit scenarios comes from those who are generally more supportive of science, technology, and individualism; more socially conservative; and more opposed to equity and solidarity as overarching principles. Although these relationships warrant further examination, a combination of these deeper core values—an embrace of technology, individualism, social conservatism, and a rejection of equity—characterize attitudinal support for user fee, two-tier, and for-profit scenarios.

DISCUSSION

Papering over problems with money (for now)

Our survey data reveal that in 2002 Canadians were less anxious about their health care system than they were a few years earlier, when perceptions peaked that the system needed major reform and was failing to deliver timely access to high-quality care when needed. Canadians' anxiety seems to have peaked when reductions in federal government health care contributions were most severe. Since then, the federal government increased its contributions as part of its 2000 pre-election "health care budget." Although long-term concerns still remain, our survey results demonstrate that the Canadian public has acknowledged that governments have been responding to their concerns about the health system. But there may be a limit to how much can be accomplished simply by putting more money into the system. There may also be a backlash if the new money does not translate, or is not shown to translate, into shorter waiting times and other improvements in system performance.

Holding on strongly to free, single-tier doctor and hospital care

Despite dramatic shifts in the delivery of health care over the past two decades, with more and more services being provided outside the hospital and by health care professionals other than doctors, in 2002 Canadians still viewed doctors and hospitals as the pillars of their health care system and were staunchly opposed to changes in their financing arrangements. The principle of universal access to health care based on need and not ability to pay was less vigorously supported when it came to home care and high-tech care, which were still perceived to be "outside" the public system, despite the increasing proportion of each provincial government's health care budget taken up by these services. These findings suggest the powerful influence of past policies (that is, first-dollar coverage for medically necessary physician and hospital care) on current and future policy-making processes and the policies that they produce. A vast majority of the Canadian public appeared to have internalized the policy legacy of "private practice, public payment" for physician and hospital care that has created and reinforced institutional barriers to change.

As Canadians move further away from the familiarity of these "core" services and the longstanding policy debates associated with reform in these areas (that is, user charges for doctor and hospital care), their views about transformative options that have been the subject of more recent debate are less assured. In the absence of tracking data for these options, in large part because of the conflating of private and for-profit delivery in previous public opinion surveys, we cannot say whether Canadians have reached a settled judgment about these options. When the defining features of two-tier care and for-profit delivery were explained to them, Canadians appeared to be slightly more open to for-profit delivery than two-tier care for "non-care" high-tech and home care services. Of the two options, two-tier care may be perceived to pose a greater challenge to universality, a defining feature of their health care system.

Predictors of support for change

The generally weak and inconsistent results for experiential and sociodemographic variables suggest the need to consider other predictors of support for change. Our exploratory analysis revealed core values to be the strongest, most consistent set of predictors, which suggests consistent set of predictors, which suggests the relevance of exploring more fully the relationships between values and attitudes toward health care reform, particularly in domains with differing policy legacies, such as "core" and "non-core" services.

Prospects for the future

As new and reoriented health care investments are realized within Canadian Medicare, through the processes set into action by the Commission on the Future of Health Care in Canada and the federal and provincial first ministers' health care accord, Canadians' attitudes toward these changes will continue to evolve and, in turn, be shaped by future policies. The same may hold true for parts of U.S. Medicare. Elderly Americans have grown accustomed to seeing hospitals and physicians as "core" services, and they may soon grow accustomed to seeing prescription drugs in the same light.

IMMIGRANTS

Illegal Immigrants, Health Care, and Social Responsibility

James Dwyer

Illegal immigrants form a large and disputed group in many countries. Indeed, even the name is in dispute. People in this group are referred to as illegal immigrants, illegal aliens, irregular migrants, undocumented workers, or, in French, as *sans papiers*. Whatever they are called, their existence raises an important ethical question: Do societies have an ethical responsibility to provide health care for them and to promote their health?

This question often elicits two different answers. Some people—call them nationalists—say that the answer is obviously no. They argue that people who have no right to be in a country should not have rights to benefits in that country. Other people—call them humanists—say that the answer is obviously yes. They argue that all people should have access to health care. It's a basic human right.

I think both these answers are off the mark. The first focuses too narrowly on what we owe people based on legal rules and formal citizenship. The other answer focuses too broadly, on what we owe people qua human beings. We need a perspective that is in between, that adequately responds to the phenomenon of illegal immigration and adequately reflects the complexity of moral thought. There may be important ethical distinctions, for example, among the following groups: U.S. citizens who lack health insurance, undocumented workers who lack health insurance in spite of working full time, medical visitors who fly to the United States as tourists in order to obtain care at public hospitals, foreign citizens who work abroad for subcontractors of American firms, and foreign citizens who live in impoverished countries. I believe that we—U.S. citizens—have ethical duties in all of these situations, but I see important differences in what these duties demand and how they are to be explained.

In this paper, I want to focus on the situation of illegal immigrants. I will discuss several different answers to the question about what ethical responsibility we have to provide health care to illegal immigrants. (I shall simply assume that societies have an ethical obligation to provide their own citizens with a reasonably comprehensive package of health benefits.) The answers that I shall discuss tend to conceptualize the ethical issues in terms of individual desert, professional ethics, or human rights. I want to discuss the limitations of each of these approaches and to offer an alternative. I shall approach the issues in

Dwyer, James. "Illegal immigrants, Health Care, and Social Responsibility," *Hastings Center Report*, 34:1 (2004), 34–41. Copyright © 2004. Reprinted by permission of The Hastings Center.

terms of social responsibility and discuss the moral relevance of work. In doing so, I tend to pull bioethics in the direction of social ethics and political philosophy. That's the direction I think it should be heading. But before I begin the ethical discussion, I need to say more about the phenomenon of illegal immigration.

HUMAN MIGRATION

People have always moved around. They have moved for political, environmental, economic, and familial reasons. They have tried to escape war, persecution, discrimination, famine, environmental degradation, poverty, and a variety of other problems. They have tried to find places to build better lives, earn more money, and provide better support for their families. A strong sense of family responsibility has always been an important factor behind migration.[1]

But while human migration is not new, *illegal* immigration is, since only recently have nation-states tried to control and regulate the flow of immigration. Societies have always tried to exclude people they viewed as undesirable: criminals, people unable to support themselves, people with contagious diseases, and certain ethnic or racial groups. But only in the last hundred years or so have states tried in a systematic way to control the number and kinds of immigrants.

In contrast, what the Athenian polis tried to control was not immigration, but citizenship. Workers, merchants, and scholars came to Athens from all over the Mediterranean world. They were free to work, trade, and study in Athens, although they were excluded from the rich political life that citizens enjoyed. Today, political states try to control both citizenship and residency.

Modern attempts to control residency are not remarkably effective. There are illegal immigrants residing and working all over the globe. When people think about illegal immigrants, they tend to focus on Mexicans in the United States or North-Africans in France. But the phenomenon is really much more diverse and complex. Illegal immigrants come from hundreds of countries and go wherever they can get work. There are undocumented workers from Indonesia in Malaysia, undocumented workers from Haiti in the Dominican Republic, and undocumented workers from Myanmar in Thailand. Thailand is an interesting example because it is both a source of and a destination for undocumented workers: while many people from poorer countries have gone to work in Thailand, many Thais have gone to work in richer countries.

Since illegal activities are difficult to measure, and people are difficult to count, we do not know exactly how many people are illegal immigrants. The following estimates provide a rough idea. The total number of illegal immigrants in the U.S. is probably between five and eight million. About 30–40 percent of these people entered the country legally, but overstayed their visas. Of all the immigrants in Europe, about one third are probably illegal immigrants. A small country like Israel has about 125,000 foreign workers (not counting Palestinians). About 50,000 of these are in the country illegally.[2]

I believe that a sound ethical response to the question of illegal immigration requires some understanding of the work that illegal immigrants do. Most undocumented workers do the jobs that citizens often eschew. They do difficult and disagreeable work at low wages for small firms in the informal sector of the economy. In general, they have the worst jobs and work in the worst conditions in such sectors of the economy as agriculture, construction, manufacturing, and the food industry. They pick fruit, wash dishes, move dirt, sew clothes, clean toilets.

Japan is a good example of this. In the 1980s many foreign workers came to Japan from the Philippines, Thailand, China, and other countries. Yoshio Sugimoto summarizes the situation:

> The unprecedented flow of foreign workers into Japan stemmed from the situations in both the domestic and foreign labor markets. "Pull" factors within Japan included the ageing of the Japanese workforce and the accompanying shortage of labor in unskilled, manual, and physically demanding areas. In addition, the changing work ethic of Japanese youth has made it difficult for employers to recruit them for this type of work, which is described in terms of the three undesirable Ks (or Ds in English): kitanai (dirty), kitsui (difficult), and kiken (dangerous). Under these circumstances, a number of employers found illegal migrants, in particular from Asia, a remedy for their labor shortage.[3] The pattern is much the same in other countries.

In the global economy, in which a company can shift its manufacturing base with relative ease to a country with cheaper labor, illegal immigrants often perform work that cannot be shifted overseas. Toilets have to be cleaned, dishes have to be washed, and children have to be watched *locally*. This local demand may help to explain a relatively new trend: the feminization of migration. Migrants used to be predominantly young men, seeking work in areas such as agriculture and construction. But that pattern is changing. More and more women migrants are employed in the service sector as, for example, maids, nannies, and health care aides.

Women migrants are also employed as sex workers. The connection between commercial sex and illegal immigration is quite striking. As women in some societies have more money, choices, schooling, and power, they are unwilling to work as prostitutes. These societies seem to be supplying their demands for commercial sex by using undocumented workers from poorer countries. Before brothels were legalized in the Netherlands, about 40 to 75 percent of the prostitutes who worked in Amsterdam were undocumented workers. About 3,000 of the 7,000 prostitutes in Berlin are from Thailand. Japan has over 150,000 foreign prostitutes, most of them from Thailand, China, and the Philippines. Thailand has about 25,000 prostitutes from Myanmar.[4]

Even when prostitution is voluntary, it is difficult and dangerous. Leah Platt notes that prostitution is

a job without overtime pay, health insurance, or sick leave—and usually without recourse against the abuses of one's employer, which can include being required to have sex without a condom and being forced to turn tricks in order to work off crushing debts.[5]

And for some illegal immigrants, prostitution is not a voluntary choice. Some are deceived and delivered into prostitution. Others are coerced, their lives controlled by pimps, criminal gangs, and human traffickers.

Some of the worst moral offenses occur in the trafficking of human beings, but even here it is important to see a continuum of activities. Sometimes traffickers simply provide transportation in exchange for payment. Sometimes, they recruit people with deceptive promises and false accounts of jobs, then transport them under horrible and dangerous conditions. If and when the immigrants arrive in the destination country, they are controlled by debt, threat, and force. Some become indentured servants, working without pay for a period of time. Others are controlled by physical threats or threats to expose their illegal status. A few are enslaved and held as property.

Not all illegal immigrants are victims, however, and an accurate account of illegal immigration, even if only sketched, must capture some of its complexity. My task is to consider how well different ethical frameworks deal with that complexity.

A MATTER OF DESERT

The abstract ethical question of whether societies have a responsibility to provide health care for illegal immigrants sometimes becomes a concrete political issue. Rising health care costs, budget reduction programs, and feelings of resentment sometimes transform the ethical question into a political debate. This has happened several times in the United States. In 1996, the Congress debated and passed the "Illegal Immigration Reform and Immigrant Responsibility Act." This law made all immigrants ineligible for Medicaid, although it did allow the federal government to reimburse states for emergency treatment of illegal immigrants.

In 1994, the citizens of California debated Proposition 187, an even more restrictive measure. This ballot initiative proposed to deny publicly funded health care, social services, and education to illegal immigrants. This law would have required publicly funded health care facilities to deny care, except in medical emergencies, to people who could not prove that they were U.S. citizens or legal residents.

This proposition was approved by 59 percent of the voters. It was never implemented because courts found that parts of it conflicted with other laws, but the deepest arguments for and against it remain very much alive. Because they will probably surface again, at a different time or in different place, it is worthwhile evaluating the ethical frameworks that they assume.

The first argument put forward is that illegal aliens should be denied public benefits because they are in the country illegally. Although it is true that illegal aliens have violated a law by entering or remaining in the country, it is not clear what the moral implication of this point is. Nothing about access to health care follows from the mere fact that illegal aliens have violated a law. Many people break many different laws. Whether a violation of a law should disqualify people from public services probably depends on the nature and purpose of the services, the nature and the gravity of the violation, and many other matters.

Consider one example of a violation of the law. People sometimes break tax laws by working off the books. They do certain jobs for cash in order to avoid paying taxes or losing benefits. Moreover, this practice is probably quite common. I recently asked students in two of my classes if they or anyone in their extended family had earned money that was not reported as taxable income. In one class, all but two students raised their hands. In the other class, every hand went up.

No one has suggested that health care facilities deny care to people suspected of working off the books. But undocumented work is also a violation of the law. Furthermore, it involves an issue of fairness because it shifts burdens onto others and diminishes funding for important purposes. Of course, working off the books and working without a visa are not alike in all respects. But without further argument, nothing much follows about whether it is right to deny benefits to people who have violated a law.

Proponents of restrictive measures also appeal to an argument that combines a particular conception of desert with the need to make trade-offs. Proponents of California's Proposition 187 stated that, "while our own citizens and legal residents go wanting, those who chose to enter our country ILLEGALLY get royal treatment at the expense of the California taxpayer."[6] Proponents noted that the legislature maintained programs that included free prenatal care for illegal aliens but increased the amount that senior citizens must pay for prescription drugs. They then asked, "Why should we give more comfort and consideration to illegal aliens than to *our* own needy American citizens?"

The rhetorical question is part of the argument. I would restate the argument in the following way: Given the limited public budget for health care, U.S. citizens and legal residents are more deserving of benefits than are illegal aliens. This argument frames the issue as a choice between competing goods in a situation of limited resources.

There is something right and something wrong about this way of framing the issue. What is right is the idea that in all of life, individual and political, we have to choose between competing goods. A society cannot have everything: comprehensive and universal health care, good public schools, extensive public parks and beaches, public services, and very low taxes. What is false is the idea that we have to choose between basic health care for illegal aliens and basic health care for citizens. Many other tradeoffs are possible, including an increase in public funding.

The narrow framework of the debate pits poor citizens against illegal aliens in a battle for health care resources. Within this framework, the issue is posed as one of desert. Avoiding the idea of desert is impossible. After all, justice is a matter of giving people their due—giving them what they deserve. But a narrow conception of desert seems most at home in allocating particular goods that go beyond basic needs, in situations where the criteria of achievement and effort are very clear. For example, if we are asked to give an award for the best student in chemistry, a narrow notion of desert is appropriate and useful. But publicly funded health care is different and requires a broader view of desert.

The discussion of restrictive measures often focuses on desert, taxation, and benefits. Proponents tend to picture illegal immigrants as free riders who are taking advantage of public services without contributing to public funding. Opponents are quick to note that illegal immigrants do pay taxes. They pay sales tax, gas tax, and value-added tax. They often pay income tax and property tax. But do they pay enough tax to cover the cost of the services they use? Or more generally, are illegal immigrants a net economic gain or a net economic loss for society?

Instead of trying to answer the economic question, I want to point out a problem with the question itself. The question about taxation and benefits tends to portray society as a private business venture. On the business model, investors should benefit in proportion to the funds they put into the venture. This may be an appropriate model for some business ventures, but it is not an adequate model for all social institutions and benefits. The business model is not an adequate model for thinking about voting, legal defense, library services, minimum wages, occupational safety, and many other social benefits.

Consider my favorite social institution: the public library. The important question here is not whether some people use more library services than they pay for through taxation, which is obviously true. Some people pay relatively high taxes but never use the library, while others pay relatively low taxes but use the library quite often. In thinking about the public library, we should consider questions such as the following. What purposes does the library serve? Does it promote education, provide opportunity, and foster public life? Does it tend to ameliorate or exacerbate social injustice? Given the library's purposes, who should count as its constituents or members? And what are the rights and responsibilities of the library users? In the following sections, I shall consider analogous questions about illegal immigrants and the social institutions that promote health.

A MATTER OF PROFESSIONAL ETHICS

Some of the most vigorous responses to restrictive measures have come from those who consider the issue within the framework of professional ethics. Tal Ann Ziv and Bernard Lo, for example, argue that "cooperating with Proposition 187 would undermine professional ethics."[7] In particular, they argue that cooperating with this kind of restrictive measure is inconsistent with physicians' "ethical responsibilities to protect the public health, care for persons in medical need, and respect patient confidentiality."[8]

Restrictive measures may indeed have adverse effects on the public health. For example, measures that deny care to illegal aliens, or make them afraid to seek care, could lead to an increase in tuberculosis.

And physicians do have a professional obligation to oppose measures that would significantly harm the public health. But the public health argument has a serious failing, if taken by itself. It avoids the big issue of whether illegal immigrants should be considered part of the public and whether public institutions should serve their health needs. Instead of appealing to an inclusive notion of social justice, the argument suggests how the health of illegal immigrants may influence citizens' health, and then appeals to citizens' sense of prudence. The appeal to prudence is not wrong, but it avoids the larger ethical issues.

The second argument against Proposition 187 is that it restricts confidentiality in ways that are not justified. It requires health care facilities to report people suspected of being in the country illegally and to disclose additional information to authorities. Ziv and Lo argue that "Proposition 187 fails to provide the usual ethical justifications for overriding patient confidentiality."[9] Reporting a patient's "immigration status serves no medical or public health purpose, involves no medical expertise, and is not a routine part of medical care."[10] Thus this restriction on confidentiality is a serious violation of professional ethics.

But if restrictive measures work as designed, issues of confidentiality may not even arise. Illegal aliens will be deterred from seeking medical care or will be screened out before they see a doctor. Thus the issue of screening may be more important than the issue of confidentiality. First, if the screening is carried out, it should not be by physicians, because it is not their role to act as agents for the police or the immigration service. Professional ethics requires some separation of social roles, and terrible things have happened when physicians have become agents of political regimes. The bigger issue, though, is not who should do the screening, but whether it should be done at all.

Ziv and Lo note that "clerks will probably screen patients for their immigration status, just as they currently screen them for their insurance status."[11] They object to this arrangement, and they argue that physicians bear some responsibility for arrangements that conflict with professional ethics. In their view, screening out illegal aliens conflicts with physicians' ethical responsibility to "care for persons in medical need."[12]

This claim is important, but ambiguous. It could mean simply that physicians have an obligation to attend to anyone who presents to them in need of emergency care. That seems right. It would be wrong not to stabilize and save someone in a medical emergency. It would be inhumane, even morally absurd, to let someone die because her visa had expired. But a claim that physicians have an enduring obligation to provide emergency care is consistent with measures like Proposition 187 and the 1996 federal law.

The claim might also mean that the selection of patients should be based only on medical need, never on such factors as nationality, residency, immigration status, or ability to pay. This is a very strong claim. It means that all private practice is morally wrong. It means that most national health care systems are too restrictive. It means that transplant lists for organs donated in a particular country should be open to everyone in the world. It might even mean that physicians have an ethical responsibility to relocate to places where the medical need is the greatest. I shall say more about the strong claim in the next section. Here I just want to note one point. This claim goes well beyond professional ethics. It is an ethical claim that seems to be based on a belief about the nature of human needs and human rights.

Finally, Ziv and Lo's claim about physicians' responsibility to care for people in medical need might be stronger than the claim about emergency care but weaker than the universal claim. Perhaps we should interpret it to mean that it is wrong to turn patients away when society has no other provisions and institutions to provide them with basic care. The idea then is that society should provide all members with basic health care and that physicians have some responsibility to work to realize this idea.

There is something appealing and plausible about this interpretation, but it too goes beyond professional ethics. It has more to do with the nature of social justice and social institutions than with the nature of medical practice. It makes an ethical claim based on a belief about social responsibility and an assumption that illegal aliens are to be counted as members of society. I shall try to elaborate this belief and assumption later.

Let me sum up my main points so far. Political measures that restrict medical care for illegal immigrants often involve violations of professional ethics, and health care professionals should oppose such measures. But the framework of professional ethics is not adequate for thinking about the larger ethical issues. It fails to illuminate the obligation to provide medical care. Furthermore, it fails to consider factors such as work and housing that may have a profound impact on health. In the next two sections I shall consider broader frameworks and discourses.

A MATTER OF HUMAN RIGHTS

To deal with the issue of health care and illegal immigrants, some adopt a humanistic framework and employ a discourse of human rights. They tend to emphasize the right of all human beings to medical treatment, as well as the common humanity of aliens and citizens, pointing to the arbitrary nature of national borders.

National borders can seem arbitrary. Distinctions based on national borders seem even more arbitrary when one studies how borders were established and the disparities in wealth and health that exist between countries. Since it doesn't seem just that some people should be disadvantaged by arbitrary boundaries, it may also seem that people should have the right to emigrate from wherever they are and to immigrate to wherever they wish. But does this follow from the fact that national borders can be seen as arbitrary?

John Rawls thinks not. He writes:

> It does not follow from the fact that boundaries are historically arbitrary that their role in the Law of Peoples cannot be justified. On the contrary, to fix on their arbitrariness is to fix on the wrong thing. In the absence of a world state, there *must* be boundaries of some kind, which when viewed in isolation will seem arbitrary, and depend to some degree on historical circumstances.[13]

Even if boundaries depend on historical circumstances, a defined territory may allow a people to form a government that acts as their agent in a fair and effective way. A defined territory may allow a people to form a government that enables them to take responsibility for the natural environment, promote the well-being of the human population, deal with social problems, and cultivate just political institutions.[14]

From functions like these, governments derive a qualified right to regulate immigration. This right is not an unlimited right of communal self-determination. Societies do not have a right to protect institutions and ways of life that are deeply unjust. Furthermore, even when a society has a right to regulate immigration, there are ethical questions about whether and how the society should exercise that right. And there are ethical questions about how immigrants should be treated in that society.

The committed humanist, who begins with reflections on the arbitrary nature of national boundaries, sometimes reaches the same conclusion as the global capitalist: that all restrictions on labor mobility are unjustified. In their different ways, both the humanist and the capitalist devalue distinctions based on political community. To be sure, there is much to criticize about existing political communities, but we need to be cautious about some of the alternatives. Michael Walzer warns us about two possibilities. He says that to "tear down the walls of the state is not . . . to create a world without walls, but rather to create a thousand petty fortresses."[15] Without state

regulation of immigration, local communities may become more exclusionary, parochial, and xenophobic. Walzer also notes another possibility: "The fortresses, too, could be torn down: all that is necessary is a global state sufficiently powerful to overwhelm the local communities. Then the result would be . . . a world of radically deracinated men and women."[16]

Of course, the humanist need not be committed to an abstract position about open borders. The humanist might accept that states have a qualified right to regulate immigration, but insist that all states must respect the human rights of all immigrants—legal and illegal. That idea makes a lot of sense, although much depends on how we specify the content of human rights.

The idea that all human beings should have equal access to all beneficial health care is often used to critique both national and international arrangements. In an editorial in the *New England Journal of Medicine*, Paul Farmer reflects on the number of people who go untreated for diseases such as tuberculosis and HIV. He writes:

> Prevention is, of course, always preferable to treatment. But epidemics of treatable infectious diseases should remind us that although science has revolutionized medicine, we still need a plan for ensuring equal access to care. As study after study shows the power of effective therapies to alter the course of infectious disease, we should be increasingly reluctant to reserve these therapies for the affluent, low-incidence regions of the world where most medical resources are concentrated. Excellence without equity looms as the chief human-rights dilemma of health care in the 21st century.[17]

I too am critical of the gross inequalities in health within countries and between countries, but here I only want to make explicit the framework and discourse of Farmer's critique. His critique appeals to two ideas: that there is a lack of proportion between the medical resources and the burden of disease and that there is a human right to equal access.

What is wrong with the claim that equal access to health care is a human right? First, to claim something as a right is more of a conclusion than an argument. Such claims function more to summarize a position than to further moral discussion. A quick and simple appeal to a comprehensive right avoids all the hard questions about duties and priorities. When faced with grave injustices and huge inequalities, claiming that all human beings have a right to health care is easy. Specifying the kind of care to which people are entitled is harder. Specifying duties is harder yet. And getting those duties institutionalized is hardest of all.

In addition to the general problems with claims about rights, a problem more specific to the issue of illegal immigration exists. Since a claim based on a human right is a claim based on people's common humanity, it tends to collapse distinctions between people. Yet for certain purposes, it may be important to make distinctions and emphasize different responsibilities. We may owe different things to, for example, the poor undocumented worker in our country, the middle-class visitor who needs dialysis, the prince who wants a transplant, people enmeshed in the global economy, and the most marginalized people in poor countries.

Rather than claiming an essentially limitless right, it makes more sense to recognize a modest core of human rights and to supplement those rights with a robust account of social responsibility, social justice, and international justice. I do not know if there is a principled way to delineate exactly what should be included in the core of human rights.[18] But even a short list of circumscribed rights would have important consequences if societies took responsibility for trying to protect everyone from violations of these rights. Illegal immigrants are sometimes killed in transport, physically or sexually abused, held as slaves, kept in indentured servitude, forced to work in occupations, and denied personal property. These are clear violations of what should be recognized as human rights. But this core of recognized rights should be supplemented with an account of social justice and responsibility.

A MATTER OF SOCIAL RESPONSIBILITY

Framing the issue in terms of social responsibility helps to highlight one of the most striking features of illegal immigration: the employment pattern within society. As I noted before, illegal immigrants often perform the worst work for the lowest wages. Illegal immigrants are part of a pattern that is older and deeper than the recent globalization of the economy. Societies have often used the most powerless and marginalized people to do the most disagreeable and difficult work. Societies have used slaves, indentured servants, castes, minorities, orphans, poor children, internal migrants, and foreign migrants. Of course, the pattern is not exactly the same in every society, not even in every industry within a society, but the similarities are striking.

I see the use of illegal immigrants as the contemporary form of the old pattern. But it is not a natural phenomenon beyond human control. It is the result of laws, norms, institutions, habits, and conditions in society, and of the conditions in the world at large. It is a social construction that we could try to reconstruct.

Some might object that no one forces illegal immigrants to take unsavory jobs and that they can return home if they wish. This objection is too simple. Although most undocumented workers made a voluntary choice to go to another country, they often had inadequate information and dismal alternatives, and voluntary return is not an attractive option when they have substantial debts and poor earning potential at home. More importantly, even a fully informed and voluntary choice does not settle the question of social justice and responsibility. We have gone through this debate before. As the industrial revolution developed, many people agreed to work under horrible conditions in shops, factories, and mines. Yet most societies eventually saw that freedom of contract was a limited part of a larger social ethic. They accepted a responsibility to address conditions of work and to empower workers, at least in basic ways. Decent societies now try to regulate child labor, workplace safety, minimum rates of pay, workers' rights to unionize, background conditions, and much more. But because of their illegal status, undocumented workers are often unable to challenge or report employers who violate even the basic standards of a decent society.

We need to take responsibility for preventing the old pattern from continuing, and the key idea is that of "taking responsibility." It is not the same as legal accountability, which leads one to think about determining causation, proving intention or negligence, examining excuses, apportioning blame, and assigning costs. Taking responsibility is more about seeing patterns and problems, examining background conditions, not passing the buck, and responding in appropriate ways. A society need not bear full causal responsibility in order to assume social responsibility.

Why should society take responsibility for people it tried to keep out of its territory, for people who are not social members? Because in many respects illegal immigrants are social members. Although they are not citizens or legal residents, they may be diligent workers, good neighbors, concerned parents, and active participants in community life. They are workers, involved in complex schemes of social co-operation. Many of the most exploited workers in the industrial revolution—children, women, men without property—were also not full citizens, but they were vulnerable people, doing often undesirable work, for whom society needed to take some responsibility. Undocumented workers' similar role in society is one reason that the social responsibility to care for them is different from the responsibility to care for medical visitors.

If a given society had the ethical conviction and political will, it could develop practical measures to transform the worst aspects of some work, empower the most disadvantaged workers, and shape the background conditions in which the labor market operates. The interests of the worst-off citizens and the interests of illegal immigrants need not be opposed. Practical measures may raise labor costs and increase the price of goods and services, as they should. We should not rely on undocumented workers to keep down prices on everything from strawberries to sex.

I can already hear the objection. "What you propose is a perfect recipe for increasing illegal immigration. All the practical measures that you suggest would encourage more illegal immigration." Whether improving the situation of the worst-off workers will increase illegal immigration is a complex empirical question. The answer probably depends on many factors. But even if transforming the worst work and empowering the worst-off workers leads to an increase in illegal immigration, countries should take those steps. Although we have a right to regulate immigration, considerations of justice constrain the ways we can pursue that aim. A society might also decrease illegal immigration by decriminalizing the killing of illegal immigrants, but no one thinks that would be a reasonable and ethical social policy. Nor do I think that the old pattern of using marginalized people is a reasonable and ethical way to regulate immigration.

I have left out of my account the very point with which I began, namely, health and health care, and I ended up talking about work and social responsibility. Surely work and social responsibility are at the heart of the matter. Where then does health care fit in?

Good health care can, among other things, prevent death and suffering, promote health and well-being, respond to basic needs and vulnerabilities, express care and solidarity, contribute to equality of opportunity, monitor social problems (such as child abuse or pesticide exposure), and accomplish other important aims. But health care is just one means, and not always the most effective means, to these ends. To focus on access to and payment of health care is to focus our ethical concern too narrowly.

I believe that societies that attract illegal immigrants should pursue policies and practices that (1) improve the pay for and conditions of the worst forms of work; (2) structure and organize work so as to give workers more voice, power, and opportunity to develop their capacities; and (3) connect labor to unions, associations, and communities in ways that increase social respect for all workers. I cannot justify these claims in this paper, but I want to note how they are connected to health care. Providing health care for all workers

and their families is a very good way to improve the benefit that workers receive for the worst forms of work, to render workers less vulnerable, and to express social and communal respect for them. These are good reasons for providing health care for all workers, documented and undocumented alike. And they express ethical concerns that are not captured by talking about human rights, public health, or the rights of citizens.

THE RIGHT DISCUSSION

I have examined the frameworks that are employed in discussions about illegal immigrants and health care. I argued against conceptualizing the issues in terms of desert, professional ethics, or even human rights. Although all of these concepts highlight something important, they tend to be too narrow or too broad. And because they provide the wrong perspective, they fail to focus attention on the crux of the matter.

I have suggested that the issues should be framed in terms of social justice and social responsibility. I realize that I did not fully justify my view, and that other people may give a different account of what social justice requires. But I had a different aim. I did not want to convince everyone of the rectitude of my account, but to shift the discussion into the realm of social justice and responsibility.

REFERENCES

1. See P. Warshall, "Human Flow," *Whole Earth* 108 (2002): 39–43.

2. These statistics are taken from the following sources: U.S. Immigration and Naturalization Service, "Illegal Alien Resident Population," available at http://www.ins.gov/graphics/aboutins/statistics/illegalalien/illegal.pdf, accessed October 1, 2002; B. Ghosh, *Huddled Masses and Uncertain Shores* (The Hague: Matinus Nijhoff Publishers, 1998); L. Platt, "The Working Caste," *The American Prospect* 13, Part 8 (2001): 32–36.

3. Y. Sumimoto, *An Introduction to Japanese Society* (Cambridge: Cambridge University Press, 1997), 187.

4. These statistics are taken from the following sources: L. Platt, "Regulating the Global Brothel," *The American Prospect,* Special Supplement, Summer 2001: 10–14; Ghosh, *Huddled Masses and Uncertain Shores,* 27; P. Phongpaichit, "Trafficking in People in Thailand," in *Illegal Immigration and Commercial Sex,* ed. P. Williams (London: Frank Cass, 1999), 89–90.

5. Platt, *Regulating the Global Brothel,* 11.

6. This and the following quorations are from the California Ballot Pamphlet, 1994, available at http://www.holmes.uchastings.edu/cgibin/starfinder/5640/calprop/txt, accessed September 30, 2002.

7. T.A. Ziv and B. Lo, "Denial of Care to Illegal Immigrants," *NEJM* 332 (1995): 1095–1098.

8. Ibid., 1096.

9. Ibid., 1097.

10. Ibid.

11. Ibid., 1096.

12. Ibid.

13. J. Rawls, *The Law of Peoples* (Cambridge, Mass.: Harvard University Press, 1999), 39.

14. Compare Rawls, *The Law of Peoples*, 8.

15. M. Walzer, *Spheres of Justice* (New York: Basic Books, 1983), 39.

16. Ibid.

17. P. Farmer, "The Major Infectious Disease in the World-To Treat or Not to Treat?" *NEJM* 345 (2001): 208–210.

18. Compare Rawls, *The Law of Peoples*, 79–80.

Restrictions on Undocumented Immigrants' Access to Health Services: The Public Health Implications of Welfare Reform

Jeffrey T. Kullgren

The Federal Personal Responsibility and Work Opportunity Reconciliation Act (PRWORA) of 1996 greatly restricts the provision of many federal, state, and local publicly funded services to undocumented immigrants. Many public health and health care institutions have wrestled with the legal, administrative, and ethical conflicts generated by these limitations. The debate has been most visible in the state of Texas, where the legality of several public hospitals' provision of free primary and preventive health care to undocumented immigrants has been challenged.

Instead of serving their intended purpose of reducing illegal immigration and conserving public resources, PRWORA'S restrictions on undocumented immigrants' access to publicly financed health services unduly burden health care providers and threaten the health of the community at large. These deleterious effects warrant the public health community's support of strategies to both repeal these restrictions and sustain the provision of health services irrespective of immigration status.

INTENT AND SUBSTANCE OF PRWORA'S RESTRICTIONS

The enactment of PRWORA in 1996 went further than simply ending welfare as we knew it. The law also broke significant new ground in immigration policy by declaring that "current eligibility rules for public assistance and unenforceable financial support agreements have proved wholly incapable of assuring that individual aliens not burden the public benefits system" and that "it is a compelling government interest to remove the incentive for illegal immigration provided by the availability of public benefits."[1] To these ends, the law outlines standards in regard to legal and undocumented immigrants' eligibility for—and the provision of—services supported by the federal government and by state and local governments.

With respect to state and local public benefits, PRWORA declares that undocumented immigrants are ineligible for "any retirement, welfare, health, disability ... or any other similar benefit for which payments or assistance are provided to an individual, household, or family eligibility unit by an agency of a State or local government or by appropriated funds of a State or local government."[1] Exceptions include "assistance for health care items and services that are necessary for the treatment of an emergency medical condition" and "public health assistance for immunizations with respect to immunizable diseases and for testing and treatment of symptoms of communicable diseases whether or not such symptoms are caused by a communicable disease."[1] PRWORA also allows provision of public benefits to undocumented immigrants if states enacted legislation after August 22, 1996, that "affirmatively provides for such eligibility" or if the US attorney general declares additional services exempt from the law's restrictions.[1]

UNDOCUMENTED IMMIGRANTS' HEALTH AND ACCESS TO SERVICES

The 300,000 to 500,000 undocumented immigrants that enter the United States each year arrive bearing a disproportionate burden of undiagnosed illness—including communicable diseases such as tuberculosis and HIV—and frequently lack basic preventive care and immunizations.[2-5] The adverse circumstances under which some undocumented immigrants enter the country, and the substandard conditions in which many live following their arrival, only exacerbate poor health.[6]

These health burdens are sustained and magnified by language barriers, lack of knowledge about the US health care system, and fear of detection by immigration authorities, all of which limit undocumented immigrants' ability to effectively access health services.[4,5,7] Undocumented immigrants are also frequently limited in their ability to access care by a lack of both health insurance and sufficient financial resources to pay for services.[5]

The consequences of undocumented immigrants' health burdens and barriers to accessing services extend beyond the individual to the entire community. The agricultural and food service settings in which many undocumented immigrants work, for example, can facilitate the spread of communicable diseases to other segments of the population.[5] Johns and Varkoutas also suggest that fear of detection has driven undocumented immigrants to pursue treatments through underground channels, which may have helped fuel the emergence of drug-resistant microbes.[8]

RESPONSES TO PRWORA'S RESTRICTIONS

For the most part, PRWORA'S limitations on the provision of health services to undocumented immigrants have not been embraced by state and local officials. In light of the threats that undocumented immigrants' health conditions pose to communities, relatively few local jurisdictions have established policies explicitly limiting provision of health services based on immigration status.[9] Many publicly supported health care institutions in Texas, for example, have long provided free and discounted nonemergency care to all residents, even after the enactment of welfare reform legislation.[10] There are, however, a few notable exceptions to this trend, including institutions in San Diego, Albuquerque, and Fort Worth.[9,11]

In response to the ambiguity generated by this seemingly pervasive disconnection between policy and practice, administrators of the Harris County Hospital District, which includes the city of Houston and constitutes the third-busiest public health care system in the United States, sought guidance from Texas Attorney General John Cornyn in late 2000 to ascertain whether its proposed payment policy revisions (which would have permitted the district to provide free or discounted care to anyone who could show county residency and financial need) violated PRWORA and to

determine the possible penalties for any such violations.[12] Attorney General Cornyn's subsequent opinion concluded that the welfare reform law prohibits the district from providing free or discounted nonemergency health care to undocumented immigrants, even if they reside within the district's boundaries, and that no state laws enacted since 1996 "expressly state the legislature's intent that undocumented aliens are to be eligible for certain public benefits."[13] With respect to potential penalties, the attorney general decided that, while PRWORA does not explicitly describe a penalty for providing public benefits to undocumented immigrants, "there may be sanctions to the district pursuant to conditions attached to federal funding" and that "there may also be legal consequences pursuant to state law for spending public funds for an unauthorized purpose."[13]

Cornyn's opinion has stirred an intense debate both in Texas and around the nation. Some of the state's local advocates and district attorneys have pressed for public inquiries into the activities of jurisdictions that choose to continue to provide free and discounted services; in Harris County, the local district attorney initiated a criminal investigation of the hospital district and its leadership.[14] Fearful of similar investigations in their own jurisdictions, some health care institutions in Nueces County, which includes Corpus Christi, and Montgomery County, just outside of Houston, have chosen to limit the services provided to undocumented individuals rather than leave their organizations and administrators exposed to prosecution.[9,10] Other parties that support hospitals' long-standing policies have obtained alternative legal interpretations of applicable state and federal laws that they claim justify the continued provision of discounted services to all residents irrespective of immigration status.[15]

While Harris County's district attorney has withdrawn his criminal investigation in an effort to achieve a workable compromise with health administrators, and calls for the initiation of similar inquiries around the state appear to have subsided, Attorney General Cornyn's opinion still stands to shape public health policy regarding undocumented immigrants not only in Texas but across the country.[16] Attorneys general and local prosecutors in other jurisdictions may draw on the opinion to initiate legal action against institutions that provide discounted services irrespective of immigration status. Should a court uphold Cornyn's opinion and related legal challenges, institutions that have not amended their policies to accommodate PRWORA's restrictions may face increased scrutiny.

Institutions in states such as California and New York, which have relatively large undocumented populations but so far appear to have been spared from legal inquiries, could conceivably be the next targets. Even if other jurisdictions' policies are not contested in court, the Cornyn opinion itself may have a chilling effect by discouraging undocumented immigrants from accessing health care as well as discouraging individual institutions from providing discounted services to undocumented populations.

HOW THE RESTRICTIONS JEOPARDIZE PUBLIC HEALTH

The divergent reactions to Cornyn's opinion, the differing responses of health care providers, and the absence of definitive guidance from any level of government leave many publicly supported institutions in a state of legal and administrative uncertainty. The public health community should recognize, call attention to, and press for resolution of the threats posed to community health and welfare by this uncertainty and PRWORA's limitations on provision of health services.

First, these restrictions fail to consider the power and responsibility of state and local governments, and the institutions they fund, to protect the health, safety, and welfare of all who reside within the state's borders. While regulation of immigration has traditionally been a federal responsibility, Gostin notes that "part of the constitutional compact of our Union was that states would remain free to govern within the traditional sphere of health, safety, and morals."[17] Indeed, PRWORA's restrictions on the provision of health care infringe on states' "police power" and limit their ability to protect the health of their residents.[17,18]

Second, prohibiting the provision of discounted health care endangers access to services among undocumented immigrants' children, many of whom are born in the United States and are therefore eligible for publicly funded health care programs.[19]

Findings of the Kaiser Commission on Medicaid and the Uninsured suggest that immigrants are often confused by state and federal eligibility restrictions and are intimidated by the threat of being discovered and deported.[20] As a result, even though PRWORA allows for provision of discounted immunizations and emergency services—and children born in the United States are eligible for government-funded health coverage—fear of immigration authorities or beliefs that their children do not qualify for services may prevent undocumented parents from seeking health care for their native-born children. A similar argument—that improving adults' access to services will improve children's access to care—has been offered as a rationale for expanding public health insurance coverage to parents of children enrolled in state Children's Health Insurance programs.[21]

Third, PRWORA's restrictions on the provision of health care services contradict the long-standing ethical obligations of clinicians by requiring providers to assume responsibilities traditionally reserved for federal immigration officials.[5,18] Ziv and Lo note that physicians who comply with mandates to deny services to undocumented immigrants "forgo the ethical ideal that patients' medical needs should be attended to without regard to their social, political, or citizenship status."[22] In addition, while PRWORA does not place as great a burden on health professionals as Proposition 187, the ballot initiative that sought to deny many public services to undocumented immigrants and require clinicians to report undocumented individuals to the Immigration and Naturalization Service, a legislative order to deny services leaves the door open for further, more invasive intrusions on the confidentiality that facilitates trust between patients and providers.

Fourth, the administrative complexities generated by limits on the provision of services by publicly supported health care providers endanger access to care among legal residents. Guidelines issued by the US Department of Justice require that all patients be treated equally; therefore, all patients should be required to provide evidence of their immigration status.[9] Sorting through immigration documents for each patient, and turning away those who lack sufficient documentation but are unable to pay for the full cost of services, would increase administrative costs and waiting times, reducing the efficiency of already overburdened safety-net institutions.[2]

Fifth, restricting access to preventive services while requiring institutions to continue to provide care for emergency conditions prevents administrators from putting public resources to their most cost-effective use. Laws such as the Emergency Medical Treatment and Labor Act require institutions to provide expensive acute health care to undocumented individuals when they present with emergency medical conditions.[6,23] In many cases, such as management of diabetes, asthma, or hypertension, preventive care can thwart the need for costly services to treat conditions that have progressed to emergency status.[24] Providing prenatal care to undocumented mothers has also been shown to be cost-effective.[25,26] Prohibiting the provision of these services prevents administrators from managing taxpayers' resources in the most cost-effective manner and may ultimately limit the health care safety net's ability to finance both public health and individual medical services.

Finally, limiting undocumented immigrants' access to health services weakens efforts to fight the spread of communicable diseases among the general population. While PRWORA's exemptions include the treatment of infectious diseases and their symptoms, conditions such as tuberculosis are not always easily detected as communicable diseases.[8] In addition, many cases of infectious disease are identified not when symptoms manifest themselves but when patients seek medical care for other unrelated conditions.[24] Consequently, identifying and treating communicable diseases in their earliest stages requires that undocumented immigrants be able to access services for all health conditions—not just those that have progressed to an emergency level or include symptoms of infectious disease—before others in the community are exposed.

STRATEGIES FOR PROTECTING ACCESS TO HEALTH SERVICES

Given the significant threats posed by limits on undocumented immigrants' access to health services, the public health community should pursue a range of strategies to circumvent the barriers erected by PRWORA and avert the spread of legal challenges to other jurisdictions. The most obvious way in which institutions could unambiguously provide free or discounted primary and preventive health services to undocumented immigrants would be for states to "enact legislation which affirmatively provides for such eligibility."[1] The pursuit of state legislation, however, may fail to provide a sweeping and immediate solution to the problem, in that legislative action is subject to individual states' political climates, competing demands on lawmakers' attention, and the limited schedules of many legislatures.

PRWORA also allows publicly supported health care services to be exempted from eligibility restrictions under a determination by the US attorney general. Since the terrorist attacks on New York and Washington, however, there have been demands from the public to increase border security and heighten scrutiny of individuals illegally residing in the United States, and this situation almost certainly precludes

the current US attorney general from advocating for the protection of additional public benefits for undocumented immigrants.

Federal legislation provides another opportunity for a solution. Representatives Sheila Jackson-Lee and Gene Green of Texas both introduced bills in the 107th Congress to amend PRWORA to include primary and preventive care among the list of services exempted from restriction. Should Congress fail to pass these or similar pieces of legislation, reauthorization of PRWORA could offer a sweeping resolution to the debate, and public health advocates should work to ensure that this issue is not overshadowed by other policy debates as lawmakers revisit welfare reform. In advocating for legislative solutions, public health advocates should, when feasible, seek untraditional alliances. Many business leaders, for example, have supported more generous immigration policies and could be effective allies.

If Congress chooses not to lift the restrictions on undocumented immigrants' access to services, health administrators should continue to work with law enforcement officials, particularly district attorneys in their respective communities, to reach agreements that permit institutions to sustain the provision of services critical to protecting the public's health, allocate resources to their most cost-effective uses, and avoid both criminal prosecutions of administrators and reductions in public funding. Hospital districts and public health institutions should also continue to provide free and discounted primary and preventive care services regardless of immigration status and allow the judicial system to determine what a reasonable outcome for this situation might be. Finally, public health leaders should be prepared to offer expert knowledge and file amicus curiae briefs on behalf of organizations and individuals who might face criminal prosecution or civil suits as a result of providing services to undocumented immigrants.

CONCLUSIONS

The public health community has an important role to play in advocating for a resolution of this debate that is based on sound public health and public management principles. Little to no evidence exists to suggest that public benefits, particularly health care services, lure undocumented immigrants to the United States. To the contrary, significant evidence does suggest that undocumented immigrants' use of public benefits is relatively low and that job opportunities and family issues are the primary factors motivating illegal immigration.[2,18,27,28] Furthermore, restricting undocumented immigrants' access to services unduly burdens health care institutions and threatens the health of entire communities. Consequently, public health advocates should work to ensure that policymakers seeking to reduce the number of undocumented immigrants in the United States focus their attention on strengthening border control and weakening the "pull factors" that actually drive illegal immigration, instead of endangering the public's health through misguided restrictions on provision of health services.

REFERENCES

1. Pub L No. 104–193, 110 Stat 2260.

2. *Hearings Before the U.S. House of Representatives Subcommittee on Immigration and Claims,* 104th Congress, 1st Sess (1995) (testimony of Michael Fix and Jeffrey S. Passel).

3. Illegal alien resident population. Available at: http://www.ins.usdoj.gov/graphics/aboutins/statistics/illegalalien/index. Accessed January 15, 2002.

4. Committee on Community Health Services. American Academy of Pediatrics. *Health Care for Children of Immigrant Families.* Chicago, Ill: American Academy of Pediatrics: 1997.

5. Loue S. Access to health care and the undocumented alien. *J Legal Med.* 1992:13:271–332.

6. Fallek S. Health care for illegal aliens: why it is a necessity. *Houston J Int Law.* 1997;19:951.

7. Berk M. Schur C. The effect of fear on access to care among undocumented immigrants. *J Immigrant Health.* 2001;3:151–156.

8. Johns K. Varkoutas C. The tuberculosis crisis: the deadly consequence of immigration policies and welfare reform. *J Contemp Health Law Policy.* 1998;15:101.

9. Center for Public Policy Priorities. The straight story: health care for uninsured undocumented immigrants in Texas. *Policy Page.* August 14, 2001:138.

10. Yardley J. Immigrants' medical care is focus of Texas dispute. *New York Times.* August 11, 2001:A18.

11. Jaklevic M. This side of the ethical border. *Modern Healthcare.* 2001;36:52–54.

12. Jaklevic M. Texas prosecutor probes free care. *Modern Healthcare.* 2002;37:20.

13. Office of the Attorney General of the State of Texas. Opinion No. JC-0394 (2001 Tex AG LEXIS 84).

14. Landa A. Illegal care? *Am Med News.* 2001;37:5.

15. Suval J. Paying the price. *Houston Press.* October 11, 2001;News and features.

16. Brewer S. DA drops investigation of immigrant health care. *Houston Chronicle* [online]. Available at http://www.HoustonChronicle.com. Accessed December 11, 2001.

17. Gostin LO. *Public Health Law: Power, Duty, Restraint.* Los Angeles, Calif: University of California Press; 2000:48.

18. Fee A. Forbidding states from providing essential social services to illegal immigrants: the constitutionality of recent federal action. *Boston Public Interest Law J.* 1998;93.

19. Brenner E. The invisible children of illegal aliens. *New York Times.* March 28, 2001:A1.

20. Feld P, Power B. *Immigrants' Access to Health Care After Welfare Reform: Findings From Focus Groups in Four Cities.* Washington, DC: Kaiser Commission on Medicaid and the Uninsured; 2000.

21. Dubay L. Kenney G. *Covering Parents Through Medicaid and SCHIP: Potential Benefits to Low-Income Parents and Children.* Washington, DC: Kaiser Commission on Medicaid and the Uninsured; 2001.

22. Ziv TA, Lo B. Denial of care to illegal immigrants—Proposition 187 in California. *N Engl J Med.* 1995;332:1095–1098.

23. Bilchik G. No easy answers. *Hospitals Health Networks.* 2001;5:58–60.

24. Brown E. Proposed immigrant care cuts threaten everyone. *Am Med News.* 1996;24:38.

25. Kuiper H, Richwald GA, Rotblatt H, Asch S. The communicable disease impact of eliminating publicly funded prenatal care for undocumented immigrants. *Maternal Child Health J.* 1999;3:39–52.

26. Lu Mc, Lin YG, Prietto NM. Garite TJ. Elimination of public funding of prenatal care for undocumented immigrants in California: a cost/benefit analysis. *Am J Obstet Gynecol.* 2000;182: 233–239.

27. Berk ML, Schur CL, Chavez LR, Frankel M. Health care use among undocumented Latino immigrants. *Health Aff.* 2000;4:51–63.

28. Rivera-Batiz F. Underground on American soil: undocumented workers and immigration policy. *J Int Aff.* 2000; 2:485–501.

Left Out: Immigrants' Access to Health Care and Insurance

Leighton Ku and Sheetal Matani

Even when insured, noncitizens and their children have less access to care than insured American citizens have.

Public attention has recently focused on racial and ethnic disparities in access to health care, and research indicates that Latinos have the highest uninsurance rates among racial/ethnic groups living in the United States. But there has been surprisingly little discussion of the importance of immigration status, although one-third of U.S. Hispanics and two-thirds of U.S. Asians are foreign-born. Immigrants are a large and growing segment of American society and are disproportionately low-income and uninsured. Thus, the status of immigrants has broader implications for national and state efforts to improve access to health care.

The 1996 federal welfare reform law (Personal Responsibility and Work Opportunity Reconciliation Act, or PRWORA) restricted Medicaid eligibility of immigrants, so that those admitted to the United States after August 1996 cannot receive coverage, except for emergencies, in their first five years in the country. Historically, legally admitted immigrants were eligible for Medicaid and other benefits on the same terms as citizens were, but PRWORA signaled an important change in the social contract. These policies exacerbated immigrants' fears that began after the enactment of California's Proposition 187 and after publicity about the Immigration and Naturalization Service (INS) efforts to apply "public charge" enforcement to Medicaid, asking immigrants to repay the value of Medicaid benefits received or else jeopardize their U.S. residency status. Collectively, these policies signaled that legal immigrants should avoid Medicaid, even if they were uninsured and eligible.

The Medicaid participation of low-income noncitizens fell and uninsurance rates climbed from 1995 to 1998. Since PRWORA changed eligibility for only the fraction of immigrants admitted after 1996, many analysts ascribe these changes to a "chilling effect" that affected immigrants who still were eligible. These fears affected U.S.-born children of immigrants (who are legal citizens), impeding efforts to enroll children in Medicaid and the State Children's Health Insurance Program (SCHIP). About one-fifth of all children in the United States are immigrants (3 percent) or U.S.-born children of immigrants (16 percent).

This paper presents data from the National Survey of America's Families (NSAF) on how immigrant status affects insurance coverage and the use of medical, dental, and mental health services by adults and children. A key advantage of NSAF is that it includes data about citizenship, insurance status, and health care use. By contrast, the Current Population Survey (CPS) lacks information about health care use, while the National Health Interview and Medical Expenditure Panel Surveys do not report citizenship status.

INSURANCE COVERAGE AND USUAL SOURCE OF CARE

More than half of the low-income noncitizen adults and children in the sample were uninsured. Noncitizen adults and their children were much less likely than native-born citizens were to have Medicaid and/or job-based or other insurance and were more likely to be uninsured. Some have claimed that immigrants are more likely than native-born citizens are to use Medicaid but fail to account for their disproportionate poverty.

Noncitizens and their children also were less likely to have a usual source of health care. Given the low level of insurance coverage, it is not surprising that noncitizen families were relatively less likely to use private doctors or health maintenance organizations (HMOs). Community clinics and hospital outpatient departments are the most common sources of ambulatory care for immigrants. Very few said that the emergency room was their usual source.

Effect of immigrant status

To what extent are the differences in insurance status and usual source of care related to being immigrant, as opposed to other social and economic differences?

For adults, being a noncitizen was associated with a 2.5 percent reduction in Medicaid coverage, an 8.9 percent decrease in job-based insurance coverage, and an 8.5 percent increase in the probability of being uninsured, compared with native citizens. Noncitizen adults were less likely to have a usual source of care than native citizens were. Naturalized citizens' insurance status did not significantly differ from that of native citizens after multivariate controls, but they were more likely to lack a usual source of care.

Noncitizen children had 14 percent less Medicaid, 15 percent less job-based insurance, and 16 percent greater risk of being uninsured, compared with children whose parents were citizens. They also were less likely to have a usual source of care. After controlling for the other factors, citizen children whose parents were noncitizens had about 5 percent less Medicaid and 8 percent less job-based insurance and were about 8 percent more likely to be uninsured. They also were more likely than children of citizens were to lack a usual source of care. While citizen children with noncitizen parents were eligible for Medicaid, they were still less likely to participate, perhaps because of their parents' fears or other perceived barriers.

After we controlled for immigrant status and the other factors, the insurance coverage of Hispanics was not significantly different from that of non-Hispanic whites, except for employer-sponsored insurance for children. A major reason for the low insurance coverage of Latinos is that so many are in noncitizen families.

IMMIGRANTS AND THEIR CHILDREN'S ACCESS TO CARE

How is immigrant status related to access to and use of services? First, we examined what factors determined whether a person had any visits to a doctor/nurse or an emergency room in the past year, as a measure of health care access. Next we examined how these factors affected the number of visits, among those who had at least one visit, as a measure of the quantity of health care received.

Ambulatory care

After many other social and economic factors are controlled for, being a noncitizen adult or child was associated with a substantial and significant reduction in access to regular ambulatory health care (visits to a doctor or nurse) and to the emergency room, compared with native citizens or their children. Further, citizen children with noncitizen parents had significantly fewer doctor/nurse and emergency room visits than did children of citizens. Noncitizen adults and children also had fewer emergency room visits, among those with any.

Noncitizen families had less initial access to ambulatory medical and emergency medical care and, even when they had access, often received less care. These data show that immigrants faced serious barriers in getting both regular ambulatory care and emergency room care. This is in contrast to the common assumption that people with less access to primary care use emergency rooms more often for routine problems. To help put this in perspective, the extent to which noncitizens and their children had no doctor/nurse or emergency room visits in a year (41 percent for noncitizen adults, 38 percent for noncitizen children, and 21 percent for citizen children with noncitizen parents) was roughly double the rate of native adults (21 percent) and children of citizens (13 percent).

Hispanics' access to care

Even after immigration status was controlled for, being Hispanic was associated with getting less medical care.

Both citizen and noncitizen Latinos had poorer access to care than white citizens had (in contrast to the findings for insurance coverage).

Being Hispanic also modified the relationship of health status to medical care use. In the NSAF, as in most other surveys, Latinos reported poorer health status than non-Latinos did. It has been speculated that this might be caused by cultural differences in how Hispanics describe their health status, as compared to differences in more clinical or objective measures of health. People who reported fair or poor health status used much more health care, but this relationship was smaller for Hispanics. This is consistent with the view that Latinos report health status differently than non-Latinos do, although an alternative interpretation is that a similar level of impairment leads to less additional medical care for Latinos.

In the models, having health insurance was associated with much better access to regular ambulatory care for immigrants and non-immigrants alike but had relatively little effect (except for Medicaid) on emergency room access. Although insured noncitizens had less access to care than insured citizens did, they have much better access to care than uninsured noncitizens.

General patterns

Looking across the analyses, general patterns can be inferred. Being a noncitizen adult or the child of noncitizen parents reduces access to ambulatory medical care and emergency room care, after factors such as health status, income, and race/ethnicity are controlled for. For children of noncitizen parents, the access gaps are larger for noncitizen children than for citizen children, but both types of children have less access to medical care than do children of citizens. The health care access of naturalized citizens is generally similar to that of native-born citizens, suggesting that immigrants' health care use increases as they acculturate.

CONCLUSIONS AND POLICY IMPLICATIONS

Noncitizen immigrants and their children have large gaps in their health insurance coverage and access to health care, even when the children are citizens. The disparity in access has two components. First, noncitizens and their children are much more likely to be uninsured. Since insurance strongly increases access to care, uninsurance reduces immigrants' ability to get care. Second, even insured noncitizens and their children have less access to medical care than insured native-born citizens have. Immigrants encounter non-financial health care barriers.

From a policy perspective, the insurance gaps for citizen children in immigrant families are distressing, since they are eligible for Medicaid and SCHIP and are a major target of outreach campaigns. The insurance coverage of U.S.-born children of immigrants has fallen in recent years.

Noncitizen families have poor access to both ambulatory medical and emergency room care. The gap in emergency care is particularly relevant because federal policy lets noncitizen immigrants, including undocumented aliens, receive emergency Medicaid services, even if they are ineligible for full coverage. In principle, this policy should permit more Medicaid emergency room care as a "safety valve" for both patients and providers. Our finding suggests that the current policies are not effective and that states could do more to facilitate emergency Medicaid access for immigrants. An earlier study found that use of emergency Medicaid benefits appeared to be higher in California, which provides a Medicaid card that gives immigrants limited emergency coverage, than in other states that mostly determine Medicaid eligibility only after an emergency occurs.

Even before the welfare reform changes of the mid-1990s, immigrant families had problems with insurance coverage and access to care. Their situation appears to have worsened during the late 1990s. It is hard to disentangle the comparative effects of immigrant eligibility changes under welfare reform, public charge, and other factors, since the policies occurred in roughly the same time period and all sought to discourage immigrants from using public services. Nevertheless, it seems reasonable to conclude that the combined effect was negative.

Some remedial actions have begun or have been proposed. In 1999 the INS clarified that getting Medicaid should not endanger immigrants' legal status under public charge provisions, and the governor of California cancelled efforts to implement Proposition 187. Many states, such as California, Washington, and Massachusetts, have chosen to use state funds to provide Medicaid or SCHIP coverage to postenactment immigrants, supplementing federally funded benefits. Recent congressional proposals would give states the option to restore immigrants' eligibility for Medicaid and SCHIP for children and pregnant women. It also is important to consider strategies to foster private job-based health insurance for immigrant workers and their families. A recent study found that noncitizen workers in California were offered health insurance less often than citizens were, but that their take-up of insurance offers was similar.

Finally, health care systems need to reduce access barriers. Language problems were the leading barrier to child health services cited by Latino parents; they may also increase medical errors because of misdiagnosis and misunderstanding of physicians' orders. Federal policy already states that providers must ensure that people with limited English proficiency can get interpreter services, but problems remain commonplace. Clinics, hospitals, managed care plans, and Medicaid eligibility offices need to provide adequate interpreter and translation services.

THE PHARMACEUTICAL INDUSTRY

Big Pharma, Bad Science

Nathan Newman

In June, the *New England Journal of Medicine*, one of the most respected medical journals, made a startling announcement. The editors declared that they were dropping their policy stipulating that authors of review articles of medical studies could not have financial ties to drug companies whose medicines were being analyzed.

The reason? The journal could no longer find enough independent experts. Drug company gifts and "consulting fees" are so pervasive that in any given field, you cannot find an expert who has not been paid off in some way by the industry. So the journal settled for a new standard: Their reviewers can have received no more than $10,000 from companies whose work they judge. Isn't that comforting?

This announcement by the *New England Journal of Medicine* is just the tip of the iceberg of a scientific

Newman, Nathan. "Big Pharma, Bad Science," *The Nation*, July 25, 2002. Online article at http://www.thenation.com/doc/20020805/newman200220725. Reprinted with permission from the July 25, 2002 issue of The Nation. For subscription information, call 1-800-333-8536. Portions of each week's Nation Magazine can be accessed at http://www.thenation.com.

establishment that has been pervasively corrupted by conflicts of interest and bias, throwing doubt on almost all scientific claims made in the biomedical field.

The standard announced in June was only for the reviewers. The actual authors of scientific studies in medical journals are often bought and paid for by private drug companies with a stake in the scientific results. While the NEJM and some other journals disclose these conflicts, others do not. Unknown to many readers is the fact that the data being discussed was often collected and analyzed by the maker of the drug involved in the test. An independent 1996 study found that 98 percent of scientific papers based on research sponsored by corporations promoted the effectiveness of a company's drug. By comparison, 79 percent of independent studies found that a new drug was effective. This corruption reaches from the doctors prescribing a drug to government review boards to university research centers.

There have long been worries about the advertising and promotional gifts given to doctors to influence which drugs they prescribe. But it turns out that even deeper financial ties extend to the medical experts setting nationwide professional guidelines for treating conditions ranging from heart disease to diabetes. Surveys have found that nine out of ten experts writing such guidelines have financial ties to the pharmaceutical industry, yet those ties are almost never disclosed in the treatment guidelines, which are often published in medical journals and endorsed by medical societies.

The Food and Drug Administration, for reasons similar to those of the medical journals, routinely allows researchers with ties to the industry to sit on drug approval advisory committees. In many cases, half the panelists on such committees have a financial stake in the outcome, through links to the drug manufacturer or to a competitor.

Increasingly, the industry has converted academic research centers into subsidiaries of the companies. The billions of dollars of academic government funding essentially pays to flush out negative results, while private industry gets to profit from any successful result. Industry now provides 7 percent of university research funding, but they are manipulating the system to gain a far more substantial benefit. At the University of California at Berkeley, Novartis agreed to pay $25 million to the campus in exchange for the first right to patent a range of basic plant research produced by the university.

Where once university research was oriented to producing independent knowledge that any other researcher could access and improve upon, university research is increasingly being locked up in patents. What's more, scientists at universities are often allowed to have stock options in companies benefiting from the research they are conducting. As Dr. Marcia Angell, a former editor of *The New England Journal of Medicine,* noted in the *Baltimore Sun,* "What would be considered a grotesque conflict of interest if a politician or judge did it is somehow not in a physician."

And the results are expensive and sometimes tragic for the public. Experimental clinical drug trials are hazardous to participants and, more broadly, critical to those with life threatening conditions who need to know which treatments are fruitless to pursue. Yet researchers on industry payrolls end up pressured to suppress negative results.

At the most basic level, researchers who defy their corporate sponsors know they may lose their funding. When one Toronto scientist revealed in 1998 a serious side effect of deferiprone, a drug for a blood disorder, her contract was terminated. More dramatically, when a number of researchers concluded that Remune, an anti-AIDS therapy, was of little benefit to patients, the company funding their research, the Immune Response Corporation, sued the scientists in 2001 for $10 million for damaging its business.

And these are the examples of scientists who spoke out. Many others just go along with the demands of their corporate sponsors and suppress negative evidence. In the early 1990s, a pharmacologist at the University of California at San Francisco, Betty Dong, found that a generic thyroid hormone worked as well as Synthroid, the brand-name drug made by the funder of the research. According to the *Washington Post,* the company, Knoll Pharmaceuticals, successfully blocked publication of the findings for seven years. Only in 1997 was this fraud discovered, and in 1999 Knoll had to pay 37 states $42 million to settle a suit for consumer fraud in promoting the superiority of its drug.

This pattern of suppression means that medical knowledge is being stunted and delayed, as other researchers aren't informed of dead ends that might have helped steer their own research. And by locking up knowledge produced at academic centers in patents, what should be free knowledge for the public (free in both the intellectual and economic sense) instead feeds the profit margins of the pharmaceutical industry.

Universities once opposed patents for any academic research. Yale University's 1948 policy on patents stated, "It is, in general, undesirable and contrary to the best interests of medicine and the public to patent any discovery or invention applicable in the fields of public health or medicine." That policy was later abandoned and Yale now holds a key anti-AIDS drug patent jointly with Bristol Myers. Facing massive global protest, Yale last year agreed to relax its patent rules, but the fact that universities routinely now balance who will live and die against their own profit motive is a degradation of their public purpose.

This corruption of academic science is pervasive and the costs are extremely clear, but what is remarkable is how easy it would be to end. Federal and state governments still supply the overwhelming percentage of university research funding. If all such funding was conditioned on ending non-disclosure agreements and on barring the licensing of government-funded results to private industry, the public would benefit both scientifically and financially. We've paid for the knowledge once. We shouldn't have to do so again in increased costs of medicine and increased deaths due to suppressed knowledge.

The Educational Potential Of Direct-To-Consumer Prescription Drug Advertising

Kimberly A. Kaphingst and William DeJong

Many consumers would have difficulty learning risk information from DTC television ads and supplemental materials.

The volume of prescription drug advertising directed to consumers grew remarkably during the 1990s. In 1990 pharmaceutical manufacturers spent an estimated $47 million on direct-to-consumer (DTC) advertising; by 2001 this figure had climbed to $2.7 billion.[1] Television has claimed an increasing share of the DTC advertising pie. In 2001 about 64 percent of spending for DTC advertising was for television ads, up from 13 percent in 1994.[2]

FDA policies

According to U.S. Food and Drug Administration (FDA) regulations, prescription drug ads cannot be false or misleading, cannot omit facts that are material to representations made in the advertisement, and must have "fair balance" in the presentation of risks and benefits.[3] DTC ads in print formats must include information in "brief summary" about side effects, contraindications, and effectiveness.[4] This requirement is often met by including the complete risk-related sections of the FDA-approved professional product labeling, which is generally intended for physicians, pharmacists, nurses, and other health care professionals.[5]

Broadcast DTC ads have somewhat different requirements. Those ads that mention the name and use of a specific drug and have efficacy and safety claims—called product-specific ads—must include a "major statement" of chief adverse effects and contraindications.[6] These ads must also include either the brief summary or "adequate provision" for dissemination of the drug's approved product labeling.[7]

In a guidance finalized in 1999, the FDA suggested that broadcast DTC ads could meet the "adequate provision" requirement by referring consumers to physicians and pharmacists and to more detailed product information available through a Web site, a toll-free telephone number, and a concurrently running DTC print ad.[8] The guidance also stated that "consumer-friendly language" should be used to present information on indications and the major statement of chief adverse effects and contraindications.

In 2002 an estimated 6,000 pieces of promotional material aimed at consumers were submitted to the FDA, including 486 broadcast ads.[9] FDA approval of materials prior to dissemination is generally not required; ads are submitted for approval as they go out to the public.[10] In practice, a majority of companies voluntarily submit draft broadcast ads to reduce the likelihood of later enforcement action.[11] Although advertisers are not obligated to follow FDA advice regarding draft submissions, this gives the FDA influence over content prior to dissemination.

Given the volume of submitted material, the FDA concentrates on pieces such as television ads and widely circulated print ads.[12] Upon finding that an ad

Kamphingist, Kimberly, and William DeJong. "The Educational Potential of Direct-to-Consumer Prescription Drug Advertising," *Health Affairs*, 23:4 (2004), 143–150.

violates regulations, the FDA sends a regulatory letter to the company. Only a small percentage of advertisements have been so cited. The FDA has yet to employ more severe remedies, such as initiating court action to seize products for which there is false or misleading advertising.[13]

DTC advertising controversy

DTC advertising is the subject of intense debate. Proponents argue that it can educate consumers about new treatments, increase treatment for underdiagnosed conditions, and help patients make better-informed health care decisions.[14] Opponents contend that it could interfere with the physician-patient relationship; raise health care costs; and increase consumption of new, more costly products over older, cheaper, and safer alternatives.[15] Opponents also argue that DTC ads oversimplify complex issues and may confuse consumers who lack specialized medical knowledge.[16]

THREE STUDIES OF DTC ADVERTISING

FDA regulations allow broadcast DTC advertisements with incomplete risk information if the ads meet the adequate provision requirement. This raises a number of important questions, including whether consumers can understand the brief risk presentations included in broadcast DTC ads and the more complete information found in supplemental text materials. These questions are of particular importance for adults with limited literacy.

With colleagues Lawren Daltroy and Rima Rudd, we addressed these questions with a series of three studies. We summarize these studies below, followed by a discussion of policy implications.

Content analysis of television ads

We conducted a descriptive content analysis of twenty-three product-specific DTC television ads, focusing on how information was presented.[17] The ads were broadcast on one of the three major network affiliates in Boston, in February or March 2001. The twenty-three ads were for twenty-two different indications.

We observed that the ads gave an average of 30 percent fewer benefit facts per second than risk facts per second. Eighty-three percent of the ads presented risk information in one continuous segment, rather than interspersing the information throughout the ad. During the presentation of risk information, only positive or neutral visual images were shown; images were never negative. Most ads (91 percent) did not use techniques such as changes in speed, tone, or volume to distinguish the risk information from the rest of the ad.

Seventy percent of the ads used both medical and lay terms to convey medical ideas, and 70 percent did not provide any information about risk factors or symptoms that might raise awareness among undiagnosed people. Only 34 percent informed consumers that the drug might not work for everyone.

More than four-fifths of the ads told consumers to talk to their doctors about the advertised drug, but only one ad directed consumers to seek information about the portrayed indication. References to additional sources of product information (such as Web sites, print ads, and toll-free numbers) were presented exclusively in text, usually without explaining what would be found there.

Consumers' comprehension of television ads

We also directly assessed comprehension of DTC television ads among a sample of adults with limited literacy.[18] We selected three DTC television ads from the content analysis sample: Nasacort AQ (for allergies), Singulair (for asthma), and Zocor (for high cholesterol). We conducted individual interviews with fifty adults recruited from adult education centers in Massachusetts. After viewing each ad, participants answered a series of orally administered true/false questions focused on key content. At the end of the interview, participants answered sociodemographic and health-related questions. The measure of health literacy was the Rapid Estimate of Adult Literacy in Medicine (REALM), which assesses ability to read and pronounce sixty-six common medical and health-related terms.[19]

Participants correctly answered an average of 59 percent of the true/false questions. A multivariate analysis showed that the odds of a correct answer were lower for risk information than other types of information (odds ratio = 0.28, 95 percent confidence interval: 0.20, 0.40) and lower if the information had been given in text, with or without accompanying audio, rather than in audio only (OR = 0.64, 95 percent CI: 0.44, 0.93), controlling for place of birth, literacy level, health status, family history, the ad to which the question referred, and the order in which the ad was shown.

Reading difficulty of text materials

In our third study we examined the supplemental sources of information cited in the twenty-three television ads from the content analysis—in each case, a DTC magazine ad, a Web site, and a brochure obtained through a toll-free number.[20] We used the SMOG readability formula to estimate the reading difficulty of the materials.[21] We also applied the Suitability Assessment of Materials (SAM) instrument to examine specific features that might contribute to reading difficulty.[22] The SAM includes twenty-two variables organized into six categories: content, literacy demand, graphics, layout and typography, learning stimulation and motivation, and cultural appropriateness. We assessed the required brief summary section separately from the main body of the material.

All of the materials except one had SMOG scores for both the main body and brief summary sections that exceeded the maximum eighth-grade reading level recommended for materials used with the general public.[23] College-level reading ability would be needed to read the average brief summary section.

The SAM results indicated specific features of the materials that increased reading difficulty, including (1) presentation of extensive information not essential for consumers (for example, pharmacokinetic data); (2) lack of key idea summaries; (3) use of passive voice, complex sentence structure, and technical vocabularly; (4) lack of illustrations for key ideas; (5) lack of visual and typographic cues to highlight key content; (6) use of small type, long line lengths, and crowded layout; and (7) presentation of text without subdivisions.

POLICY IMPLICATIONS

Television ads

Fair balance. Our content analysis suggested several reasons to question whether DTC television ads provide balance in the presentation of risks and benefits. First, the ads gave consumers about 30 percent less time to absorb facts about risks than about benefits. Clearly, fair balance cannot be achieved if statements about benefits are more fully explicated than those about risks.

Second, we observed that some risk statements lacked important contextual information. For example, with a statement such as "Tell your doctor what other medications you are taking," a consumer might not know the unspoken contextual message that other medications could interact with the advertised drug and cause adverse effects. Such assumed background knowledge might be particularly problematic with consumers who have limited literacy.[24] The FDA has

reported that it monitors DTC advertising to ensure that adequate contextual and risk information is presented in understandable language, but consumers' limited background knowledge must be considered in this assessment.[25]

Third, most of the ads presented risk information in one continuous segment. FDA studies show that consumers perceive ads in which risk information is given in one continuous segment by a different announcer as emphasizing risks to a lesser extent than ads in which that information is interspersed.[26] The impact of having the same announcer present risk information in one continuous segment has not been studied. Benefit information is typically interspersed throughout DTC ads.

Fourth, closer examination of the visual images shown during the risk segment is also warranted. An ad with contradictory visual and audio messages that minimizes risk information compared with benefit information fails to provide fair balance.[27]

Our study assessing comprehension of DTC television ads among adults with limited literacy showed that the ads were less successful in communicating risk information than other information, which is consistent with previous research.[28] Our content analysis suggests reasons why comprehension of risk information might be lower, but additional research is needed to evaluate the effects of specific ad features.

Consumer-friendly language. An additional concern arises from our finding that a majority of the DTC television ads used some medical vocabulary. Consumers' understanding of medical terms should not be assumed, particularly among people with limited literacy.[29] Use of medical terminology should be carefully scrutinized to ensure that it does not obscure key information.

Adequate provision. Our research also has implications for the adequate-provision requirement. We found that in the television ads, complete references to supplemental information sources were presented exclusively in text. This may be problematic for many consumers, including those with low literacy. Importantly, a previous study found limited recall of sources of additional information cited in DTC television ads.[30]

Research indicates that relatively few consumers are using supplemental text information sources.[31] In one study, consumers who had looked for more information as a result of a DTC ad seldom consulted toll-free numbers (15 percent), the Internet (38 percent), or magazines (18 percent), but 89 percent consulted a physician. These consumers most often reported looking for side-effect information.[32] More research is needed to investigate whether low consumer recall of the availability of these sources explains their limited use or if other factors are involved.

Text materials

The adequate-provision requirement is meant to ensure that consumers have access to detailed product information, particularly the risk information that is incompletely presented in television DTC ads. However, our assessment of these written materials suggested that they are too difficult to be used by the general public. The average reading difficulty scores of the materials were well above the reading ability of the average adult American.[33]

The brief summary sections containing detailed risk information were often particularly difficult. Some of these sections included many unexplained medical terms and extensive clinical research data drawn directly from the approved professional labeling. The FDA has recognized that such information might be difficult for consumers to understand and recently suggested alternatives, such as FDA-approved patient labeling that addresses a drug's most serious and common risks.[34] The FDA recognizes that information intended for consumers should optimally be communicated in language understandable to lay readers and presented in easily readable formats, but the agency only encourages such approaches and does not require them.[35]

RECOMMENDATIONS

Based on our analysis, we have developed recommendations for DTC television ads and supplemental sources of information. Improving ads' educational quality will increase their usefulness to consumers and better meet the spirit of the FDA regulations. These recommendations can be implemented through either voluntary agreements or additional FDA regulations.

Balance risk and benefit information more effectively in television ads. Many different aspects of information presentation should be considered: (1) how fully explicated benefit statements are, compared with risk statements; (2) whether presentation of risk information in a single continuous segment gives the information less prominence than the more interspersed benefit information; (3) whether visual images shown during the risk presentation reinforce benefit rather than risk messages; and (4) whether more difficult vocabulary is used for risk statements than for benefit statements.

Always use consumer-friendly language. As stated by the FDA, it is particularly important that indications and risk information be provided in simple language.[36] Ads directed at consumers should use lay terminology wherever possible. If medical terms must be used, they should be defined or examples provided. The background knowledge and vocabulary of consumers with limited literacy should be taken into account.

Sources of additional information should be given in both audio and visual channels. This step is necessary to ensure that consumers, especially those with limited literacy, can find additional information. The ads should also state what information consumers could find in these sources.

Text materials should be prepared according to "plain language" guidelines. These materials should have a reading difficulty score no higher than the reading level of the average adult American—about eighth grade.[37] Other plain language guidelines include the following: (1) present only essential information; (2) summarize key ideas; (3) use the active voice, simple sentence structure, and common words and definitions; (4) illustrate key ideas; (5) highlight key content with visual and typographic cues; (6) use at least twelve-point type, short line lengths, and adequate white space; and (7) subdivide the text with headings and subheadings.[38] The FDA could outline such guidelines as strategies to make DTC print materials more useful to consumers. Consumers' understanding of materials with and without such changes should be compared in future research. In addition, our findings indicate that the FDA should require, not simply recommend, the use of consumer-friendly language in DTC print ads, mailed brochures, and Web sites.

DTC advertising should provide more information about the portrayed indication. If the purpose of DTC advertising is to educate consumers and increase treatment for underdiagnosed conditions, as claimed by the pharmaceutical industry, then DTC ads should provide information about symptoms and risk factors. Our findings are consistent with a prior content analysis of DTC magazine advertisements, which showed that few advertisements provided information about causes, risk factors, and prevalence of conditions or clarified common misconceptions.[39] DTC advertisements should also provide information on the efficacy of the drug, alternative treatments, and nonpharmacological approaches.[40]

Continued research is needed to evaluate consumers' comprehension of DTC advertising. Several studies have assessed topics that consumers remember being included in DTC ads, but few have directly tested what consumers actually recall and comprehend.[41] Studies testing comprehension of both print and broadcast ads are needed. Such studies should include participants with a range of literacy skills. Further research should explore how confusion about risk information affects consumers' attitudes and perceptions of risk. Future studies should also evaluate specific ad features that affect consumers' comprehension of risk information.

Require prior approval of ads. The current post hoc review of advertisements allows for widespread communication of potentially misleading information. A 2002 report by the U.S. General Accounting Office (GAO) indicated a number of problems with the current system.[42] First, the FDA cannot verify that it receives all newly disseminated ads from drug companies. Second, a policy change requiring legal review of regulatory letters has increased the time it takes to issue the letters, which can extend consumers' exposure to misleading ads before the FDA takes regulatory action. This is particularly problematic because the number of FDA enforcement actions against false or misleading ads continued to decline in 2003, while enforcement delays increased.[43] Furthermore, while drug companies have complied with FDA requests to stop dissemination of misleading DTC ads, some companies have made misleading claims in subsequent ads. Requiring approval prior to dissemination can help to ensure that misleading information does not reach consumers.

CONCLUSIONS

The results of our research suggest that consumers would have a difficult time learning risk information from DTC television ads and the supplemental text materials linked to those ads. Our recommendations for improving the educational quality of DTC advertising are intended for policymakers, reviewers, and advertisers, as well as for researchers, health care providers, and consumer advocacy groups interested in monitoring DTC advertising.

A central question remains, however: Can DTC advertising truly educate consumers? Some have argued that drug makers are well poised to provide educational information about prescription drugs because of their greater resources and incentive to advertise.[44] Critics have countered that such education is too important to be relegated to promotions intended to sell pharmaceutical products.[45]

As a first step, we recommend that drug companies implement our proposed policy changes, either voluntarily or through revised FDA regulations. If consumers continue to be exposed to misleading or confusing ads, then we propose the development of alternative, neutral sources of information that could compare different pharmacological and nonpharmacological treatments. In the end, governments and third-party payers might need to work with the medical and public health communities to provide consumers with the information they need to make truly educated decisions.

NOTES

1. J.C. Schommer, W.R. Doucette, and B.H. Mehta, "Rote Learning after Exposure to a Direct-to-Consumer Television Advertisement for a Prescription Drug," *Clinical Therapeutics* 20, no. 3 (1998): 617–632; and U.S. General Accounting Office, *Prescription Drugs: FDA Oversight of Direct-to-Consumer Advertising Has Limitations,* Pub. no. GAO-03-177 (Washington: GAO, 2002).

2. R.G. Frank et al., *Trends in Direct-to-Consumer Advertising of Prescription Drugs* (Menlo Park, Calif.: Henry J. Kaiser Family Foundation, 2002); and GAO, *Prescription Drugs.*

3. M. Baylor-Henry and N.A. Drezin, "Regulation of Prescription Drug Promotion: Direct-to-Consumer Advertising," *Clinical Therapeutics* 20, Supp. C (1998): C86–C95; T. Nordenberg, "Direct to You: TV Drug Ads That Make Sense," *FDA Consumer* 32, no. 1 (1998): 7–10; and GAO, *Prescription Drugs.*

4. D.A. Kessler and W.L. Pines, "The Federal Regulation of Prescription Drug Advertising and Promotion," *Journal of the American Medical Association* 264, no. 18 (1990): 2409–2415; and U.S. Food and Drug Administration, "Frequently Asked Questions (FAQs)," 28 May 2003, www.fda.gov/cder/ddmac/FAQS.htm (26 March 2004).

5. L.R. Bradley and J.M. Zito, "Direct-to-Consumer Prescription Drug Advertising," *Medical Care* 35, no. 1 (1997): 86–92; Nordenberg, "Direct to You"; and FDA, "Draft Guidance for Industry—Brief Summary: Disclosing Risk Information in Consumer-Directed Print Advertisements," January 2004, www.fda.gov/cder/guidance/5669dft.pdf (19 April 2004).

6. C.R. Talley, "Direct-to-Consumer Prescription Drug Advertising," *American Journal of Health-System Pharmacy* 54, no. 19 (1997): 2181; and Baylor-Henry and Drezin, "Regulation of Prescription Drug Promotion."

7. Bradley and Zito, "Direct-to-Consumer Prescription Drug Advertising"; and Nordenberg, "Direct to You."

8. Talley, "Direct-to-Consumer Prescription Drug Advertising"; and FDA, "Guidance for Industry: Consumer-Directed Broadcast Advertisements," August 1999, www.fda.gov/cder/guidance/1804fnl.pdf (19 April 2004).

9. Janet Woodcock, director, FDA Center for Drug Evaluation and Research, statement before the Senate Special Committee on Aging, 22 July 2003, www.fda.gov/ola/2003/AdvertisingofPrescriptionDrugs0722.html (19 April 2004).

10. Ibid.; and M.T. Gahart et al., "Examining the FDA's Oversight of Direct-to-Consumer Advertising," *Health Affairs,* 12 February 2003, content healthaffairs.org/cgi/content/abstract/hlthaff.w3.120 (19 April 2004).

11. Statement by Janet Woodcock.

12. GAO, *Prescription Drugs;* and Gahart et al., "Examining the FDA's Oversight."

13. GAO, *Prescription Drugs.*

14. A. Masson and P.H. Rubin, "Matching Prescription Drugs and Consumers," *New England Journal of Medicine* 313, no. 8 (1985): 513–515: J. Whyte, "Direct Consumer Advertising of Prescription Drugs," *Journal of the American Medical Association* 268, no. 25 (1993): 146, 150; Bradley and Zito, "Direct-to-Consumer Prescription Drug Advertising"; A.F. Holmer, "Direct-to-Consumer Prescription Drug Advertising Builds Bridges between Patients and Physicians," *Journal of the American Medical Association* 281, no. 4 (1999): 380–382; and T.V. Terzian, "Direct-to-Consumer Prescription Drug Advertising," *American Journal of Law and Medicine* 25, no. 1 (1999): 149–167.

15. E. 't Hoen, "Direct-to-Consumer Advertising: For Better Profits or for Better Health," *American Journal of Health-System Pharmacy* 55, no. 6 (1998): 594–597; J.R. Hoffman and M. Wilkes, "Direct to Consumer Advertising of Prescription Drugs: An Idea Whose Time Should Not Come," *British Medical Journal* 318, no. 7194 (1999): 1301–1302; and M.S. Wilkes, R.A. Bell, and R.L. Kravitz, "Direct-to-Consumer Prescription Drug Advertising: Trends, Impact, and Implications," *Health Affairs* 19, no. 2 (2000): 110–128.

16. Committee on Drugs, "Prescription Drug Advertising Direct to the Consumer," *Pediatrics* 88, no. 1 (1991): 174–175; Bradley and Zito, "Direct-to-Consumer Prescription Drug Advertising"; and Terzian, "Direct-to-Consumer Prescription Drug Advertising."

17. K.A. Kaphingst et al., "A Content Analysis of Direct-to-Consumer Television Prescription Drug Advertisements," *Journal of Health Communication* (forthcoming); and K.A. Kaphingst, *Examining the Educational Potential of Direct-to-Consumer Prescription Drug Advertising* (Boston: Harvard School of Public Health, 2002).

18. K.A. Kaphingst et al., "Comprehension of Information in Direct-to-Consumer Television Prescription Drug Advertisements among Adults with Limited Literacy" (Unpublished paper, Harvard School of Public Health, 2004); and Kaphingst, *Examining the Educational Potential.*

19. T.C. Davis et al., "Rapid Estimate of Adult Literacy in Medicine: A Shortened Screening Instrument," *Family Medicine* 25, no. 6 (1993): 391–395.

20. K.A. Kaphingst et al., "Literacy Demands of Product Information Intended to Supplement Television Direct-to-Consumer Prescription Drug Advertisements," *Patient Education and Counseling* (forthcoming); and Kaphingst, *Examining the Educational Potential.*

21. G. McLaughlin, "SMOG Grading—A New Readability Formula," *Journal of Reading* 12, no. 8 (1969): 639–646.

22. C.C. Doak, L.G. Doak, and J.H. Root, *Teaching Patients with Low Literacy Skills* (Philadelphia: J.B. Lippincott Company, 1996).

23. J. Root and S. Stableford, "Easy-to-Read Consumer Communications: A Missing Link in Medicaid Managed Care," *Journal of Health Politics, Policy and Law* 24, no. 1 (1999): 1–26.

24. D.W. Baker et al., "Inadequate Functional Health Literacy" (letter), *Journal of the American Medical Association* 275, no. 11 (1996): 840.

25. Nancy M. Ostrove, deputy director, Division of Drug Marketing, Advertising, and Communications. FDA Center for Drug Evaluation and Research, statement before the Senate Subcommittee on Consumer Affairs, Foreign Commerce, and Tourism, 24 July 2001, www.fda.gov/ola/2001/drugpromo0724.html (26 March 2004).

26. L.A. Morris et al., "Consumer Attitudes about Advertisements for Medicinal Drugs," *Social Science and Medicine* 22, no. 6 (1986): 629–638.

27. K.N. Reeves, "Direct-to-Consumer Broadcast Advertising: Empowering the Consumer or Manipulating a Vulnerable Population?" *Food and Drug Law Journal* 53, no. 4 (1998): 661–679.

28. Henry J. Kaiser Family Foundation, *Understanding the Effects of Direct-to-Consumer Prescription Drug Advertising* (Menlo Park, Calif: Kaiser Family Foundation, 2001).

29. Baker et al., "Inadequate Functional Health Literacy"; E.J. Mayeaux et al., "Improving Patient Education for Patients with Low Literacy Skills," *American Family Physician* 53, no. 1 (1996): 205–211; and A.E. Cunningham and K.E. Stanovich, "What Reading Does for the Mind," *American Educator* 22, nos. 1–2 (1998): 8–15.

30. Kaiser Family Foundation, *Understanding the Effects.*

31. *Prevention Magazine,* "Fifth Annual Survey: Consumer Reaction to DTC Advertising of Prescription Medicines" (Emmaus, Pa.: Rodale Inc., 2002).

32. K.J. Aikin, "Direct-to-Consumer Advertising of Prescription Drugs: Patient Survey Results," 19 September 2002, www.fda.gov/cder/ddmac/presentations/kitHMCC2002out/index.htm (20 April 2004).

33. Doak et al., *Teaching Patients with Low Literacy Skills.*

34. FDA, "Draft Guidance for Industry: Brief Summary."

35. Ibid.

36. FDA, "Guidance for Industry: Consumer-Directed Broadcast Advertisements."

37. Root and Stableford, "Easy-to-Read Consumer Communications."

38. Doak et al., *Teaching Patients with Low Literacy Skills.*

39. R.A. Bell, M.S. Wilkes, and R.L. Kravitz, "The Educational Value of Consumer-Targeted Prescription Drug Print Advertising," *Journal of Family Practice* 49, no. 12 (2000): 1092–1098.

40. Wilkes et al., "Direct-to-Consumer Prescription Drug Advertising."

41. Aikin, "Direct-to-Consumer Advertising of Prescription Drugs"; and Kaiser Family Foundation, *Understanding the Effects.*

42. GAO, *Prescription Drugs.*

43. U.S. House of Representatives, Committee on Government Reform—Minority Staff, "FDA Enforcement Actions against False and Misleading Prescription Drug Advertisements Declined in 2003," January 2004, www.house.gov/reform/min/inves_prescrip/index_drug_ads_2003.htm (13 February 2004).

44. R.W. Dubois, "Pharmaceutical Promotion: Don't Throw the Baby Out with the Bathwater," *Health Affairs,* 26 February 2003, content.healthaffairs.org/cgi/content/abstract/hlthaff.w3.96 (20 April 2004).

45. B. Mintzes, *Blurring the Boundaries: New Trends in Drug Promotion,* 1998, www.haiweb.org/pubs/blurring/blurring.intro.html (26 March 2004); S.M. Wolfe, "Direct-to-Consumer Advertising—Education or Emotion Promotion?" *New England Journal of Medicine* 346, no. 7 (2002): 524–526; and J. Avorn, "Advertising and Prescription Drugs: Promotion, Education, and the Public's Health," *Health Affairs,* 21 April 2003, content.health affairs.org/cgi/content/abstract/hlthaff.w3.104 (20 April 2004).

Pushing the Borders:
The Moral Dilemma of International Internet Pharmacies

Jillian Clare Cohen

When we think about drug access issues, typically we turn to the appalling lack of access in developing countries where, as the World Health Organization reports, one-third of the population does not have regular access to needed medicines. But the issue of drug access has also recently become a politically charged topic in the United States, the world's most lucrative pharmaceutical market. There have been several populist initiatives to buy pharmaceuticals over the border. Unfortunately, although these initiatives are well intentioned, once the rhetoric is cast aside and the purchases are analyzed impartially, it becomes evident that they are an unfair solution for the long term. Some people would benefit from them, but many more would pay.

In the United States, pharmaceutical firms price their products at whatever the market will bear, atypical for an OECD country, resulting in inadequate coverage for many people. Moreover, an estimated 35 percent of Medicare beneficiaries lack drug benefits.[1] The Congressional Budget Office (CBO) has projected that rising drug prices will continue to assume a large share of seniors' incomes. It also reported that for the lowest income quintile, the projected increase in drug expenditures, measured as a share of after-tax income, is about 25 percent from 2000 to 2013.

American consumers are increasingly unable or unwilling to pay these prices and are seeking better government coverage of pharmaceutical products as well as relief from unaffordable medicines. Cross-border pharmaceutical purchases, particularly from Canada, have acquired political currency as a possible solution, and they became even more popular during 2003. Whether or not the recent Medicare reform will offer enough relief from high prescription drug prices for those in need and the middle class is uncertain at best.

For American consumers, purchasing medicines from Internet pharmacies in Canada makes economic sense because Canadian prices are significantly lower, and Canada's pharmaceutical system has secure and excellent quality assurance.

The Canadian Patented Medicines Prices Review Board (PMPRB) and provincial and territorial governments regulate drug prices for drugs that are available on their formulary (such as the Ontario Drug Benefit Program). Price regulation and a weaker Canadian dollar have contributed to comparatively much lower pharmaceutical prices in Canada. Although Canadian drug prices are not low by international standards, they are on a par with drug prices in other jurisdictions, such as France, Italy, and Sweden. The PMPRB, for example, noted that in 2002, Canadian prices in the Canadian pharmaceutical market were only about 1 percent higher than median foreign prices.

The right to purchase medicines from Canada through the Internet or through other means is increasingly perceived as making moral sense, despite being potentially illegal. A senior citizen action group recently launched a campaign calling Americans to support their grandparents and parents by boycotting GlaxoSmithKline, the first pharmaceutical company to take action against the sale of Canadian pharmaceutical products in the United States. A Wall Street Journal Online/Harris Interactive poll released in October 2003, found that 77 percent of Americans surveyed said they think it is "unreasonable" for pharmaceutical companies to stop Canadian pharmacies from selling drugs over the Internet to Americans.[2]

In recognition of the widespread popularity of cross-border pharmaceutical purchases, the Pharmaceutical Market Access Act, a bill with broad-based support, was passed in July 2003 in Congress and is currently referred to the Senate Committee on Health, Education, Labor, and Pensions. The bill would permit Americans to purchase medicines from Canada and other countries. Internet pharmacy entrepreneurs in Canada, when questioned about the ethics of their business, state that they are doing their duty and providing a service to those in need. The international, research-based pharmaceutical industry, on the other hand, argues that Internet pharmacies are concerned with profit and not the patient.

For many Americans, particularly seniors who tend to consume more drugs more often for chronic conditions, purchasing pharmaceuticals from Canadian Internet pharmacies, while a potential breach of law, appears to be as good a way to deal with a public policy failure and a health necessity. When 22 percent of seniors cannot fill prescriptions or skip doses to make

Cohen, Jillian Clare. "Pushing the Borders: The Moral Dilemma of International Internet Pharmacies," *Hastings Center Report*, 34:2 (2004), 15–17. Copyright © 2004. Reprinted by permission of The Hastings Center.

prescriptions last longer, even breaching the law can appear justifiable.[3] Further, while pharmaceutical imports into the United States are illegal if they are not FDA approved, the law is subject to interpretation. For example, it states that Food and Drug Administration personnel "may use their discretion to allow entry of shipments of violative FDA-regulated products when the quantity and purpose are clearly for personal use, and the product does not present an unreasonable risk to the user."[4] Until recently, the FDA has tended to show benign disregard toward cross-border pharmaceutical purchases. Even if the FDA tries to scale up its governance of cross-border pharmaceutical purchases, it has limited resources to do so. Custom workers apparently inspect less than 1 percent of an estimated two million packages of medicine that enter into the United States each year.[5]

Many U.S. public figures have supported the re-importation of pharmaceuticals. William Novelli, head of the American Associations of Retired Persons, recently stated that while reimportation is not a policy solution, it may put increased pressure on the pharmaceutical market and ease double-digit growth in prescription drug costs. Rod Blagojevich, the democratic governor of Illinois, commissioned a study in September 2003 to determine how much the state could save by purchasing medicines from Canada. The governor emphasized, "We're not going to violate what the FDA's rules are, but we are going to try to get the FDA to change its position and one way to do it is through the U.S. Congress. The FDA cannot ignore the people forever."[6]

The study found that the state, its employees, and retirees could save about $90 million annually if all eligible prescriptions were filled through a Canadian Mail Order Plan. The study also found that employees and retirees enrolled in the plan using three prescriptions a month would save up to $1,008 per year on their prescription co-payments.[7] And the mayor of Springfield, Massachusetts, Mike Albano, made national headlines in July 2003 with his program to encourage the importation of drugs from Canada for city employees and retirees. He claims that by purchasing pharmaceuticals from Canada, the public would save anywhere from four to nine million dollars a year.[8]

International pharmaceutical companies, such as GlaxoSmithKline, Pfizer, AstraZeneca, and Wyeth, have also taken measures to respond to a perceived failure of governments to regulate Internet pharmacy purchases. Since January 2003, all of them have taken individual measures, including limiting the supply of pharmaceuticals or stopping the sale of pharmaceutical products to Internet pharmacies, to stop the flow of their products across the Canadian-American border. GlaxoSmithKline made public its intent to stop selling to Canadian pharmacies that sell to Americans over the Internet. Pfizer notified fifty Canadian pharmacies that they would have to order their drugs directly through Pfizer, again as a strategy to limit the sale of their products from Canada into the United States. The pharmaceutical firms argue that products arriving from Canada are not safe. While this may be overstated, there is some truth to the claim, since some Americans may purchase their medicines from questionable suppliers. But it is not clear that pharmaceutical firms are motivated by anything other than the potential threat to loss of profits in the U.S. market.

Echoing the safety concern, the Canadian Pharmacists Association (CphA) has stated that it does not support the international purchase of pharmaceuticals through the Internet because it compromises the relationship between the patient and the health care professional; it violates local (and international) laws; and it presents a credible threat to drug supply and to Canadian drug prices. In its "Statement on International Prescription Services and Distance Provision of Pharmaceuticals," CphA notes that "the public protection safety net can be bypassed with the purchase of pharmaceuticals through the Internet."[9]

The cross-border pharmaceutical purchasing phenomenon raises some knotty policy and ethical issues. On the one hand, it is a convenient solution to the issue of limited pharmaceutical access in the United States. If American consumers are struggling to pay their pharmaceutical bills, why not purchase much cheaper medicines from Canada? It also sends a signal to pharmaceutical firms that drugs need to be priced at affordable levels and that price regulation is a necessity. In part, the American demand for lower-priced drugs may also be attributed to the lowering of pharmaceutical prices for antiretrovirals predominantly in Sub-Saharan Africa. The international research-based pharmaceutical firms have demonstrated that they are willing to lower prices significantly if the pressure and the need are great enough. If pharmaceutical firms are willing to lower prices in developing countries, the reasoning goes, should they not do the same at home?

However, when looked at impartially, it becomes clear that populist initiatives that foster cross-border shopping are unrealistic and unfair. For starters, Canada represents a little less than 3 percent of the global pharmaceutical market, and even if all Canadian drugs were shipped to the United States, the United States would still have shortages. And the consequences for Canada would be severe. Canada is facing pharmaceutical shortages in locations, such as Manitoba, where Internet pharmacies that cater to American consumers are thriving. Second, much-needed pharmacists are diverted from personal customer care in Canada and deployed for cross-border commerce. The prescriptions used in the Internet purchases are often co-signed by a Canadian physician who has never seen the patient receiving the prescription. Thus the patient-pharmacist and patient-physician relationships are compromised. While current claims of safety hazards may indeed be overstated, the use of cross-border pharmaceutical purchases through cyberspace undeniably creates greater openings for the sale of counterfeit medicines. Consumers may have a hard time determining a legitimate Internet pharmacy from a rogue pharmacy. Finally, it presents a threat to a Canadian social policy norm—regulated pharmaceutical prices.

While many Americans regard the Internet pharmacy trade as an expeditious policy solution to drug access, it is replete with complications and potentially unsavory consequences. It might benefit some Americans who are hard hit by high pharmaceutical prices (although the poorest Americans do have pharmaceutical coverage through Medicaid). It presents a

number of various health security threats to Canada and also to the American patient who relies on cross-border pharmaceutical purchases. Rather than looking outside itself to Canada for a solution to its drug access problem, the United States should focus on improving access to pharmaceuticals locally through a more comprehensive drug benefit program or by rethinking pharmaceutical pricing regulations.

NOTES

1. Families USA, "Medicaid and Prescription Drugs," October 2002, www.familiesusa.org.

2. G. Lamb, "Cheap Drug Imports: Who Wins?" *Christian Science Monitor,* October 16, 2003.

3. See comm-org.utoledo.edu/pipermail/announce/2003-February/000352.html; accessed December 17, 2003.

4. www.fda.gov/ora/compliance_ref/rpm_new2/ch9pers.html.

5. See www.affordabledrugs.il.gov; accessed December 26, 2003.

6. M. Dorning, "Law Makers Target Rogue E-Pharmacies," *Chicago Tribune,* October 14, 2003.

7. See www.illinois.gov/PressReleases; accessed December 26, 2003.

8. Dorning, "Law Makers Target Rogue E- Pharmacies."

9. CPhA's Statement on Internet Pharmacy in Canada notes that "online prescription services from Canadian pharmacies are not legal."

Chapter 4

Experimentation and Research on Human Subjects

From a May 30, 2007, Article, "Pfizer Faces Criminal Charges in Nigeria"

Officials in Nigeria have brought criminal charges against pharmaceutical giant Pfizer for the company's alleged role in the deaths of children who received an unapproved drug during a meningitis epidemic. . . . They also filed a civil lawsuit seeking more than $2 billion in damages and restitution from Pfizer. . . .

The government alleges that Pfizer researchers selected 200 children and infants from crowds at a makeshift epidemic camp in Kano and gave about half of the group an untested antibiotic called Trovan. Researchers gave the other children what the lawsuit describes as a dangerously low dose of a comparison drug. . . . Nigerian officials say Pfizer's actions resulted in the deaths of an unspecified number of children and left others deaf, paralyzed, blind or brain-damaged.

The lawsuit says that the researchers did not obtain consent from the children's families and that the researchers knew Trovan to be an experimental drug with life-threatening side effects that was "unfit for human use." Parents were banned from the ward where the drug trial occurred, the suit says, and the company left no medical records in Nigeria. . . .

Internal Pfizer records obtained by The Washington Post show that five children died after being treated with the experimental antibiotic, though there is no indication in the documents that the drug was responsible for the deaths. Six children died while taking the comparison drug. . . .

In a statement, Pfizer said it thinks it did nothing wrong and emphasized that children with meningitis have a high fatality rate. "It is indeed regrettable that, more than a decade after the meningitis epidemic in Kano, the Nigerian government has taken legal action against Pfizer and others for an effort that provided significant benefit to some of Nigeria's youngest citizens," the statement said.

"Pfizer continues to emphasize—in the strongest terms—that the 1996 Trovan clinical study was conducted with the full knowledge of the Nigerian government and in a responsible and ethical way consistent with the company's abiding commitment to patient safety. Any allegations in these lawsuits to the contrary are simply untrue—they weren't valid when they were first raised years ago and they're not valid today." . . .

Last year, The Post obtained a copy [of a final report submitted by a panel of experts to the Nigerian health minister] . . . . The panel said Pfizer administered an oral form of Trovan that apparently had never been given to children with meningitis. It said there were no records documenting that Pfizer told the children or their parents that they were part of a drug trial. And it said an approval letter from a Nigerian ethics committee, which Pfizer used to justify its actions, was a sham concocted long after the trial ended.[1]

The 1996 clinical study described above continues to have far-reaching effects. In December 2007, a Nigerian court ordered the arrests of three local Pfizer executives who were not present for a hearing.[2] Pfizer argued that the executives were not properly served with criminal summons and that therefore they had no obligation to appear in court. There are legal issues at stake here in addition to the many moral issues, but let us begin with several points that both parties to the dispute agree on. First, Pfizer performed a clinical study on 200 Nigerian children suffering from meningitis. Half of the children were given an experimental antibiotic while the other half received a comparison drug. Second, 11 children died while in the study and others suffered significant impairments. Third, there do not seem to be any records of written consent forms.

Beyond these three points of agreement, there are many disputed points. How were children chosen to be subjects in the study and was that selection fair? Did the experimental antibiotic cause the children's deaths or impairments? Did it treat or fail to treat meningitis? Did the parents of the children understand that the study was experimental? Were they informed of the risks and benefits of the experimental drug? Did they know that there were other alternative medicines available? The Doctors Without Borders group was apparently offering traditional antibiotics in a different part of the medical camp. Who, if anyone, is responsible for the children's deaths and impairments? Is it morally acceptable to test new drugs on people in developing countries? Should the study have been halted at some point and medicines known to be effective against meningitis have been provided? The answers to some of these questions as they pertain to the Pfizer study of 1996 may come out in the course of the legal proceedings or subsequent scientific studies. But many of them are questions that arise perennially when clinical studies and experimental research studies are performed on human beings. These are the moral questions and we will highlight them and the important values raised by them. But first let us consider another case of medical experimentation.

CASE STUDY: TOBIAS, THE RESEARCH SUBJECT?

Tobias Reznick is a 24-year-old lab technician who works in the medical center of a top-notch university. He works in a lab where several scientists are doing malaria research. Part of his job is to manage the mosquito colonies and laboratory mice that are used in the experiments.

Tobias is a bright and committed scientist. He believes strongly in the value of the lab's work. He thinks it is possible that significant results in the way of methods to block malaria transmission and even vaccines against malaria may follow from the work of the lab. He is proud to be a part of the scientific community working to save the lives of people around the world. In fact, he believes that scientists are the ones who contribute the most to the improvement of human lives.

One day on his way into work, he notices a posting at a lab down the hall. This lab is working on better understanding, treating, and preventing asthma. The posting is for a study that is just beginning and is recruiting healthy volunteers. The study requires several hours of a volunteer's time. The volunteers will be given a drug that constricts their air passages and hence mimics asthma. Then, they will inhale another chemical in order to determine whether it blocks signals from the brain to the lungs to reopen the air passages. He notes that the study has been approved by the university's Institutional Review Board.

Tobias thinks that since he has no breathing difficulties he could easily participate in this study and make a contribution to the advancement of science. He wonders if he could take Friday off and volunteer in the study.

The case of Tobias, the research subject, is in many ways different from the case of the 200 Nigerian children who were research subjects. Tobias is healthy; they were ill. Tobias does not stand to benefit personally from his research participation (except perhaps from the feeling of satisfaction he would receive by helping to further scientific knowledge); the 200 children were in need of medical treatment. Tobias appears to be able to make an informed decision about whether or not to participate in the study. Or, to put it differently, there is nothing to suggest that Tobias's participation is coerced or manipulated (unless you think he might be pressured by the proximity of the neighboring lab, his familiarity with the workers in that lab, or the likelihood that his lab director and the institution will look favorably on his participation in this study). On the other hand, in the case of the Nigerian children, there are many reasons to question whether the decision to have them participate was informed and free from coercion. They were ill, in great need, children, and citizens in a developing country where most medical care is difficult to obtain. But in other ways, both Tobias's case and the case of the Nigerian children are typical cases of medical experimentation. Consider what these cases have in common.

COMMON CHARACTERISTICS OF CASES OF CLINICAL RESEARCH ON HUMANS

All cases of medical research on human beings share the following three characteristics:

1. The experiment or clinical trial takes place because there is something that we do not know and are trying to find out. Experiments are performed in order to advance knowledge and to better understand, treat, prevent, and cure diseases or other unfavorable conditions. While researchers may hypothesize or believe that a certain disease can be treated in a specific way, until we conduct experiments we cannot know this about a disease. We may have tested a specific medication in the lab and on animals, but until it is tested on human beings we do not know that it is safe or effective. Thus, the reason for human experiments is that we believe they will ultimately benefit human beings, in other words, they promote beneficence or utility.

2. Given that research happens in the context of what is unknown, it is not surprising that there is always a component of risk. The reason the experiment is being conducted is to determine the safety and efficacy of a treatment or medication. And we do not already know the safety and efficacy of the treatment on human beings. Thus, there is risk. The medication may or may not be safe or effective. It may or may not have side effects in human beings that are similar to or comparable to its side effects in animals. There may be unexpected harms or risks and of course unforeseen benefits. Thus, the principles of nonmaleficence and beneficence are especially relevant to medical experimentation on human beings.

3. The relationship between the scientist who is the medical researcher and the person who is the experimental subject is by definition an unequal partnership. The researcher is the one testing a hypothesis, working to advance knowledge and the treatment of disease. The research subject is being used to advance knowledge and treatment. There is no way to get around this. The subject must be asked for his consent to participate, he must be a willing and informed volunteer, but he is still being manipulated and used in ways that may benefit him or others. It is logical to ask under what conditions would it be morally acceptable to consent to being used in this way? Autonomy is relevant here, as is informed consent, the dignity of human persons, and the responsibility to respect human persons.

   But in addition to the role inequality between the researcher (the user) and the experimental subject (the used), there is often also a kind of political or social inequality. Since the researcher is the one who has proposed the research study, he or she understands it, believes in its value, and has a stake in its success. The researcher is committed to making sure that the experiment takes place and the researcher has the resources to carry out the study. In recruiting subjects for the experiment, it is not necessary that they understand or believe in the study to the same extent. Hence, researchers may be—and in the past, have been—tempted to recruit subjects who can be manipulated and controlled. These have included prisoners, children, those with mental illness, members of the armed services, the poor, and citizens of developing countries. Thus, some people who lack mental, physical, financial, and other resources may find it very difficult to choose not to participate in an experimental study. They may not clearly understand that an experimental study is not a treatment regimen. And, in other cases, people may have a great need for an effective treatment for their disease and hence they may be overly eager to participate in an experimental drug trial. In both of these types of cases, the research subject is vulnerable, easily convinced to participate, and because of limited resources or great need, does not have the political or social clout of the researcher. Therefore, as research subjects are chosen for a medical experiment, justice—meaning the fair and appropriate treatment of people—is an important moral consideration.

HISTORY AND GUIDELINES

We have seen in the two cases we considered above how beneficence, nonmaleficence, autonomy, and justice are at stake. Let us look more concretely at the ethical guidelines that apply to cases of medical research on human beings.

The issue of experimenting on human beings first came to public attention during and after World War II. As information about the Nazis' medical or medically supervised experiments became known, there was outrage over the nature of the experiments and the horrors inflicted on the human subjects. During the Nuremberg Trials in 1946–1947, 20 Nazi doctors were prosecuted for war crimes and crimes against humanity, specifically for engaging in medical experiments without the subjects' consent where the subjects were prisoners of war and civilians (Figure 4.1).

Some received the death penalty, others were imprisoned or acquitted. But as information about their medical experiments became known, two bioethical issues came to the forefront.

First, measures needed to be taken to protect human subjects. To address this, the **Nuremberg Code** (1947) was formulated. Its 10 statements formalized the conditions necessary for morally acceptable experimentation on human subjects. Briefly, it requires that the human subjects have voluntarily consented to participate; some good for society will result from the experiment; and the risks are reasonable and proportional to the benefits (it is unreasonable for any experiment to lead knowingly to death or disabling injury). Second, scientists had to decide whether or not to use information generated from the Nazi experiments. There has been a great deal of debate, especially concerning the Nazi hypothermia experiments, concerning whether use of the information they gathered should be prohibited (since using it seems to validate and condone the experiment) or allowed (it is wasteful and may cost other lives not to use the information gathered and perhaps using it honors the sacrifices of the victims).[3]

But it is not only Nazi experiments that have raised questions about the protection of human subjects. Two famous examples of research studies in the United States that treated research subjects in questionable and immoral ways were the **United States Public Health Service Syphilis Study** (sometimes called the **Tuskegee Syphilis Study**) and the **Willowbrook State Hospital Study**. The former was a clinical study that took place between 1932 and 1972 in Tuskegee, Alabama. It was designed to document the natural course of syphilis. The study subjects were 399 poor, mostly illiterate African American men who had syphilis and 201 African American men without syphilis. The 399 men were not told that they had syphilis; they were told that they were being "treated" for "bad blood." In fact, they were offered no treatment; their disease was left to run its course, even though there were some treatments for syphilis in 1932 and as of 1947 penicillin was known to be an effective treatment for syphilis.

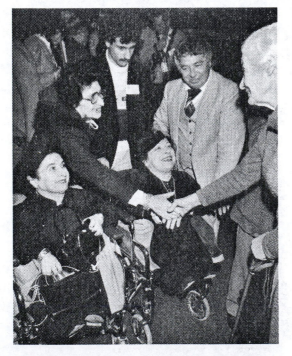

FIGURE 4.1   Ella Lingens (R), a Viennese doctor incarcerateed in Auschwitz for aiding jews, shakes hands with Sarah Qoici and her sister Perla who were victims of Nazi doctor Josef Mengele's experiments on dwarfs.

They were not told they were participating in a research study. Hence, as human subjects, they were not protected but exposed to great risks (many of their wives were infected and some of their children were born with congenital syphilis) and their consent to participate in this study does not constitute an informed voluntary consent because they were unaware that they were in fact research subjects. In addition, charges of racism were leveled against the study due to its selection of research subjects. In 1997, President Bill Clinton issued a formal apology to the survivors of the experiment and their families and admitted that what the United States government did was wrong (Figure 4.2).[4]

The Willowbrook State Hospital was a New York State institution that housed children with severe mental illness (Figure 4.3).

There were not many alternatives for parents of children with mental illness, so there was a waiting list for admission even though the sanitary conditions were poor and hepatitis was rampant in the hospital. A research study took place in the 1950s and 1960s with the purpose of working toward a vaccine or other preventive treatment for hepatitis. Researchers admitted some children directly into the research study at the hospital. These children were infected with hepatitis and then monitored. Researchers argued that the children would likely have gotten hepatitis anyway and that the infected children in the study would be better off than other children in the hospital because they would be better cared for and isolated from other illnesses and strains of hepatitis. Moreover, the waiting list was shorter for those willing to enter the research study. The ethical objections to this study focused on three main points. First, research subjects were not protected but in fact given a disease. Second, there appears to have been very little respect for persons, their dignity, and their autonomy. Parents were pressured to enroll their children in this experiment in hopes of finding appropriate care for their children. The children obviously could not consent for themselves to be research subjects. Finally, there is the question of justice, of the fairness of selecting subjects from such a vulnerable, already disadvantaged group.[5]

Since the Nuremberg Code, international and national organizations have formulated other codes designed to set standards for research on human subjects. The two most important codes are the **Declaration of Helsinki** (1964) and the **Belmont Report** (1997). The Declaration of Helsinki is the product of the World Medical Association. It reiterates that human subjects must be informed and willing participants and that any risks or burdens to subjects must be minimized and balanced by the benefits to be achieved. But it adds several additional requirements. One such requirement is that proposals for medical research must be reviewed and evaluated by an independent "ethical

FIGURE 4.2   Herman Shaw, 94, a Tuskegee syphilis study victim, receives an official apology from President Clinton Friday, May 16, 1997 in Washington.

FIGURE 4.3 Willowbrook State Hospital (formerly known as Halloran General Hospital).

review committee." This requirement provides an independent and unbiased check or policing mechanism on the process for undertaking experimental research on humans. In the United States, we have **institutional review boards** that serve as clearinghouses for proposals that require research on humans. Another contribution of the Declaration of Helsinki is the recognition of what constitutes an "informed consent" by a human subject. The Declaration states:

> Each potential subject must be adequately informed of the aims, methods, sources of funding, any possible conflicts of interest, institutional affiliations of the researcher, the anticipated benefits and potential risks of the study and the discomfort it may entail. The subject should be informed of the right to abstain from participation in the study or to withdraw consent to participate at any time without reprisal. (Principle 22, Declaration of Helsinki)

Finally, the Declaration also allowed that for research subjects who are incompetent—that is, those who are minors or who are physically or mentally unable to consent—consent may be obtained from their legal representatives. This expands the potential pool of research subjects by including those who are not able to consent for themselves.

In 1979, the United States Department of Health, Education, and Welfare (now renamed Health and Human Services) issued a set of ethical guidelines for the protection of human research subjects. Called the "Belmont Report," it begins by identifying the ethical values and principles to be upheld in medical research. These include respect for persons, beneficence, and justice. Respect for persons requires that researchers treat subjects with courtesy and respect and allow for their autonomy. Informed consent is one specific way in which human subjects are respected. Beneficence demands that researchers maximize good outcomes but minimize harms and risks to subjects. Justice requires that the procedures of the research experiment be fair, that risks and benefits be dispersed fairly, and that research subjects be selected and assigned to treatment groups in ways that are fair. The novel contribution of the Belmont Report to the codes governing medical research is this last point. It is because of this justice requirement that questions are raised about the fairness of excluding women from research on heart disease until the 1990s[6] or including only Nigerian children in the research on an experimental antibiotic for meningitis.

Finally, the United States Department of Health and Human Services has a document relating to the protection of human subjects that governs all research supported by any federal department or agency.[7] This policy provides directions on the makeup and work of an institutional review board (IRB) committee, the informed consent procedures, plus details about special protections as well. These additional protections apply to pregnant women, human fetuses and neonates, prisoners, and children. This document provides another example of how medical research on humans in addition to promoting beneficence must be mindful of autonomy, respect for and dignity of persons, nonmaleficence, and justice.

Let us note, however, that these policies regarding the treatment of human subjects in research do not by themselves prevent unacceptable and immoral research. Some of the guidelines were in existence at the time of the U.S. Public Health Service Syphilis Study and the Willowbrook State Hospital

Study. As shown in the Pfizer study of an antibiotic in Nigeria and current debate over the standards of the United States Environmental Protection Agency (EPA) for testing pesticides on humans,[8] we need to be vigilant in upholding, enforcing, and improving the guidelines.

CONTEMPORARY TERMS

Clinical research can be done in different ways and we can distinguish between cases of medical research and **clinical trials**. The U.S. National Institutes of Health (NIH) explains that clinical research includes trials that test new treatments and therapies in addition to long-term natural history studies that chart information on how disease and health progress.[9] Clinical trials thus are a type of clinical research; they are drug or treatment trials.

Clinical research is carried out in accordance with a protocol. The protocol explains who is eligible to participate in the research, what tests, procedures, and medications will be administered, how long the study will take, and what information will be collected. Clinical research protocols must be reviewed and approved by an IRB. All institutions that conduct or support clinical medical research on human beings must have an IRB to facilitate these reviews.

Clinical trials can be funded by individuals, institutions, or organizations. For example, some governmental agencies (the NIH, the Department of Defense, etc.) support clinical trials, as do universities, medical institutions, foundations, and pharmaceutical companies. The NIH keeps a registry of federally and privately funded clinical trials. In December 2007, the list included 48,392 clinical trials that were taking place in 153 countries (Figure 4.4).[10]

Clinical trials take place in "phases" and each phase of a clinical trial has a different purpose and aims to answer a different question. Phase I trials involve a small group of subjects (20–80) and aim to test the safety of the drug or treatment and identify side effects. Phase II trials include 100–300 subjects and try to determine the effectiveness of the treatment and further test its safety. In Phase III trials,

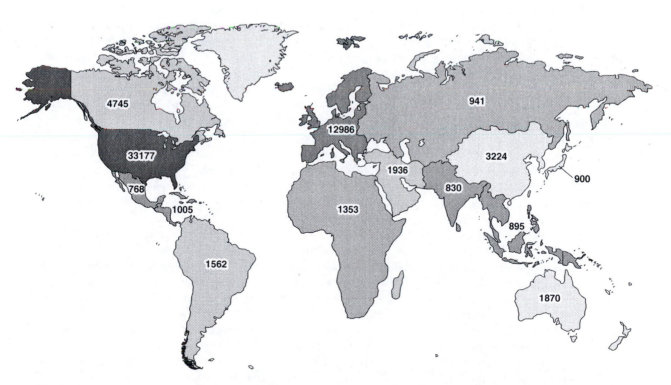

FIGURE 4.4 Map of countries with clinical trials.

1,000–3,000 subjects are enrolled and the treatment's effectiveness and side effects are monitored and compared with standard or other available treatments. Phases II and III usually involve control groups (i.e., groups that are compared to the experimental group and that may have received no treatment), a **placebo** (i.e., a product that has no treatment value [e.g., a "sugar" pill]), or some alternative treatment. If those in the experimental group benefit from their treatment more than those who are receiving no treatment, a placebo, or an alternative treatment, then there is pressure to discontinue the study in order to provide the best treatment to all. The worry then is that without the completion of the study we may not have the long-term data on the side effects or safety of the treatment that we need. Placebos are not used if it is known that they would put subjects at risk. Phase IV trials take place after a drug or treatment has been approved by the Food and Drug Administration (FDA). These are long term studies including large numbers of subjects and designed to monitor the safety, benefits, and side effects of the drug or treatment.

Two other terms are important in distinguishing various kinds of research studies. Clinical studies that are randomized and single- or double-blind are preferred because of the objectivity that they provide. **Randomization** occurs when two or more drug or treatment alternatives are randomly assigned to subjects. In this way there can be no bias, no unfair treatment, on the part of researchers in terms of which subjects receive which treatments. **Single-blind** refers to a research study in which the volunteer subject is unaware of which treatment group he is assigned to. **Double-blind** means that both the researcher and the subject do not know which drug or treatment the subject is receiving. This enables the researcher and the subject to describe and observe symptoms and side effects objectively, without being influenced by knowledge of what drug or treatment is being administered.

In the United States, it is the FDA that decides when a drug is approved as a treatment for a specific condition or disease in human beings.[11] They monitor the safety and effectiveness of drugs, both prescription and over-the-counter drugs. Thus, experimentation and research on human beings is a necessary part of the process by which medications are officially tested, monitored, and approved.

At the beginning of this chapter we introduced the case of Tobias who is making a decision about whether or not to participate in a clinical trial. Tobias's case is modeled on the actual case of Ellen Roche, who in 2001 participated in a clinical study and ultimately died.[12]

Roche was a healthy 24-year-old volunteer, a lab technician at Johns Hopkins University, and she agreed to be a subject in an asthma study that had been approved by the university's IRB. After her death, many ethical problems surfaced. The drug she inhaled was not approved by the FDA and that fact was not mentioned in the consent form she was asked to sign. It appears that the principal investigator in the study failed to discover or cite some earlier studies that suggested the drug might damage the lungs. Therefore, neither Roche nor the IRB had adequate disclosure of the risks of the experiment. The Johns Hopkins investigating committee concluded that the IRB should have required more evidence of the safety of the drug. One lesson to be learned from Roche's unfortunate death is that an IRB committee's approval does not guarantee that a research study is safe. It is also clear that the standards for the ethical treatment of human subjects must be constantly reevaluated and updated. While the ethical codes that we have developed since 1947 highlight important ethical values and demand informed consent, and so on, the specific ways of enacting these values and demands must evolve as our knowledge grows, as we learn how drugs work and how consent forms and institutional review boards function.

The articles to follow in this chapter take up many issues concerning human experimentation, including international research studies, HIV studies, the meaning of the principles of autonomy, beneficence, nonmaleficence, and justice in human research studies, and research on children. There is much more that needs to be discussed and decided about the ethics of human experimentation; however, we have made progress in our understanding of what is ethically troublesome in this field and what broad principles ought to guide such experimentation. As bioethicists, if we return to the decision that Tobias is making, there is important advice that we can offer. First, we can thank Tobias for his commitment to improving the health and well-being of others and commend him for recognizing the vital role that research on human subjects plays in advancing human well-being. We can refer Tobias to the national and international documents aimed at protecting research subjects. We can encourage him to learn more about the purpose and aims of the clinical study, the good outcome it is designed to further, the risks and harms to subjects, the qualifications of the researchers, the nature of the drug being tested, and the process by which subjects are selected. We can recommend that he ask the researchers any questions he may have about the study and that he should not make his decision whether or not to participate based solely on institutional loyalty, feelings of friendship, or financial inducements. After that, it will be Tobias's decision to make.

Looking Ahead

- Researchers will be required to undergo specialized training modules prior to conducting research studies. Web courses on topics such as these will proliferate: protecting human subjects, constructing a consent form, fair selection of human subjects, and so on. Similarly, there will be increased pressure on IRBs and government agencies to set requirements, raise standards, and monitor researchers and research studies. This will lead to increased training for IRB members. With the extra training required and the increased responsibility of the board, there will be fewer people willing to serve on these boards.
- Consent forms will get more detailed, more complex, and longer. This will not help the typical human subject to better understand what he is agreeing to or what his rights are.
- There will continue to be research protocols involving human subjects that exaggerate the benefits of the research, obtain consent in misleading ways, inflict significant risk on human subjects, and take advantage of persons who are vulnerable, poorly informed, or powerless. The need for ethical oversight will remain.

Endnotes

1. See the complete article by Joe Stephens at *washingtonpost.com,* May 30, 2007, http://www.washingtonpost.com/wp-dyn/content/article/2007/05/29/AR2007052902107.html [Accessed on April 26, 2008]. Also see Joe Stephens's article "Where Profits and Lives Hang in Balance," December 17, 2000, at *washingtonpost.com* and Wikipedia's report on Pfizer and Nigeria at http://en.wikipedia.org/wiki/Pfizer [Accessed on April 26, 2008].

2. See http://www.reuters.com/article/latestCrisis/idUSL24679549 [Accessed on April 26, 2008].

3. See, for example, Kristine Moe, "Should the Nazi Research Data be Cited?" *Hastings Center Report* 14:6 (1984), 5–7; A. Schafer, "On Using Nazi Data: The Case Against," *Dialogue (Canadian Philosophical Association)* 25:3 (1986), 413–419; and R.M. Martin, "Using Nazi Scientific Data," *Dialogue (Canadian Philosophical Association)* 25:3 (1986), 403–411.

4. See reports of the study at http://www.tuskegee.edu/Global/Story.asp?s=1207598 [Accessed on April 26, 2008] and http://www.cdc.gov/tuskegee/ [Accessed on April 26, 2008].

5. See the discussions of the Willowbrook State Hospital study at http://www.emhr.net/search.php?heading=7 [Accessed on April 26, 2008], http://hss.energy.gov/healthsafety/ohre/roadmap/achre/chap3_2.html [Accessed on May 7, 2008], and Lainie Friedman Ross, "Children in Medical Research: Balancing Protection and Access: Has the Pendulum Swung Too Far?" *Perspectives in Biology and Medicine* 47:4 (2004), 519–536.

6. See, for example, Rebecca Dresser, "Wanted: Single, White Male for Medical Research," *Hastings Center Report* 22:1 (1992), 24–30; Marcia Angell, "Caring for Women's Health: What is the Problem?" *New England Journal of Medicine* 329:4 (1993), 271–272.

7. See U.S. Department of Health & Human Services, Code of Federal Regulations, Title 45: Public Welfare, Part 46: Protection of Human Subjects at http://www.hhs.gov/ohrp/humansubjects/guidance/45cfr46.htm [Accessed on April 26, 2008].

8. On the debate over EPA standards, see Sheldon Krimsky and Tania Simoncelli, "Testing Pesticides in Humans: Of Mice and Men Divided by Ten," *Journal of the American Medical Association* 297:21 (2007), 2405–2407; and "Human Experiment Ethics Remain Unsettled at EPA—Controversy Surrounding EPA Pesticide Experiments on Infants Lingers," at http://www.healthy.net/scr/news.asp?Id=9514&action=print [Accessed on April 26, 2008].

9. See the Frequently Asked Questions at NIH and Clinical Research (http://clinicalresearch.nih.gov/how.html) [Accessed on April 26, 2008].

10. See ClinicalTrials.gov at http://www.clinicaltrials.gov/ct2/home [Accessed on April 26, 2008].

11. See information on the work of the FDA at http://www.fda.gov/cder/index.html [Accessed on April 26, 2008].

12. See these accounts of the case of Ellen Roche: http://www.pbs.org/newshour/bb/health/july-dec01/hopkins_7–20.html [Accessed on April 26, 2008], http://query.nytimes.com/gst/fullpage.html?res=9501E2DE1E3BF934A25754C0A9679C8B63 [Accessed on April 26, 2008], and http://www.hopkinsmedicine.org/mediaII/press_kits/patient_safety/roche.html [Accessed on April 26, 2008].

CLINICAL RESEARCH AND MEDICINE

The Principles of the Belmont Report Revisited: How Have Respect for Persons, Beneficence, and Justice Been Applied to Clinical Medicine?

Eric J. Cassell

In 1954 a man in his fifties was admitted to a teaching hospital with a heart attack of a few hours' duration. He was to be the first subject of an innovative treatment (intravenous streptokinase and streptodornase) to dissolve the thrombosis in his coronary artery.

The patient was chosen because he was a derelict with no living relatives. In the fashion of the day, he was not told what was to be done and no consent was requested or obtained. An attending physician, resident, and medical student were in constant attendance. After a number of hours of receiving the new medication, an irregularity of his heart rhythm developed. The treatment was stopped out of fear for his safety.

In 1997 a thirty-eight-year-old woman with stage IV (metastatic) cancer of the breast received high-dose chemotherapy followed by a bone marrow stem-cell transplant at a major western medical center, after almost three years of continuous disease and multiple treatments. Months later a routine CT scan revealed what appeared to the transplant oncologist to be recurrent cancer in the spine. The implication was that the chemotherapy and bone marrow transplant had failed.

The transplant oncologist sent the following letter to the patient, her radiation oncologist, and the chief of the breast service at a major cancer center in the patient's home city:

> Dear Olga [the patient], Cheryl, and Jimmy:
>
> Enclosed is the relevant bone window from Olga's 11–12–97 CT Scan (as well as the formal reading) demonstrating the new sclerotic focus in the left pedicle of L2. I have circled it in red. It looks real to me and I would have Cheryl buzz [radiate] that area.
>
> Olga, this is our only copy so will you send that one sheet back to us for our files? Hope all is well with the three of you. Talk to you soon.
>
> **Sincerely**
>
> **[Signed]**
>
> **Associate Director,**
>
> **Bone Marrow Transplant Program**

In the forty-three years between these cases both medicine and the society around it have changed significantly under the influence of complex and intertwining forces. Scientific and technological advance have come to drive medical practice; the organization and financing of medical services have been remodeled in response both to new therapeutic capabilities and to the increasing costs of those therapies; chronic disease has displaced infectious and other acute diseases as the leading reason for seeking medical care and the leading cause of death; and the relationship between the patient and the physician has shifted not only toward "patient-centered" care but equally toward consumerism.

American society, of course, has undergone equally deep changes as government and authority were challenged in the social unrest of the '60s and '70s, rights movements of all kinds (civil rights, women's rights, patients' rights, gay rights, disability rights, and others) have gained prominence, individualism and pride in ethnicity have superceded the metaphor of the American "melting pot," and information technologies and financial and economic forces have captured the social imagination, allowing an ever-widening gap to open between rich and poor.

Like the wider society, neither the profession of medicine nor medical education is what it was a scant four decades ago.

Just about midway through these forty years of transformation, in 1978, the National Commission for the Protection of Human Subjects in Biomedical and Behavioral Research published the *Belmont Report*, introducing the principles of respect for persons, beneficence, and justice into research with human subjects—and foreclosing scenarios like the opening case. The Belmont principles have permeated clinical medicine as well. For example, recognition of the importance of freedom of choice as an aspect of respect for persons is now instantiated in informed consent documents, laws, and court rulings. Similarly, the principles of respect for persons and beneficence are institutionalized in hospital functions that monitor quality of care, such as the tissue committees that insure that surgical procedures are appropriate. Patterns of practice, professional ideals, and the everyday behavior of both doctors and patients also demonstrate the definitions and application of the principles. They show what patients expect or demand and what physicians feel obligated to do. But what the principles mean is closely bound up with the changes in medicine and the social context in which medicine is practiced.

BENEFICENCE

I begin with the principle of beneficence because the place of respect for persons and justice in clinical practice is easier to understand when one becomes aware of the changes since the 1950s in what counts as beneficence in medicine. Beneficent (or benevolent) actions or behaviors are those that actively do good or that actively protect from harm. Initially, the idea of doing good and avoiding harm was seen as resulting from both physicians' personal characteristics and medical effectiveness. The former, if ideal, would be devoid of overweening pride, venality, impure motives, untrustworthiness, and carelessness. The latter was a function of technical knowledge and proficiency. The physicians of the derelict with the heart attack suffered both moral and technical inadequacies of which they were largely unaware. They were, however, unquestionably aware of the dangers and fearful of harming him.

The intervening period in medicine has seen an explosion of technical capacity and a great increase in moral awareness, but the concept of benevolence has shrunk pari passu. The personal characteristics of physicians that served beneficence and were believed to be of great importance in previous generations now serve nostalgia more than clinical medicine.

In the early 1950s, being made better was often defined as having the burdens of disease lifted. Benevolence had to do with making patients better. During my training and early years of medical practice, disease manifestations were treated because they were there. Hernias, hemorrhoids that made any trouble, and most varicose veins of the legs were surgically removed, as were many superficial tumors and abnormalities. By the late 1950s, psychological determinants of illness began to be better known, leading to the attribution of many common complaints to psychological causes. With that awareness, the psychotherapies began to displace the sympathetic ear that had been part of medical benevolence since antiquity.

Increasingly, the focus of medicine has come to be understanding functional abnormalities and pathophysiology—the chain of bodily events that lead to and define the abnormal state as well as explaining its manifestations. This important conceptual evolution has been supported by a number of trends. In medical science primacy is given to research on mechanisms of disease, including molecular biology. Newer diagnostic technologies facilitate study of the body and its parts in motion, replacing the static view of disease afforded by, for example, plain X-rays, electrocardiograms, and biopsies. Pharmacological innovation has produced legions of drugs that give excellent symptom control for complaints as diverse as migraine headaches, angina pectoris, asthma, and panic attacks. The old belief that one should treat the disease not the symptoms gave way to the understanding that in many conditions the symptoms *are* the disease.

The good of patients that was identified with making them better has changed as a structural understanding of disease has been superseded to a large extent by a pathophysiological perspective that focuses on the function of parts. This encourages measuring benefit by the good done to only a part of the patient. With the rise of scientific medicine, what doctors had long done out of kindness, sympathy, patience, and personal interest—attentions directed solely at the person rather than the disease—were derogated as handholding or bedside manner, were not scientific medicine. As therapeutic effectiveness and scientific medicine came into bloom, the sick person lost standing to the body or disease as the place of clinical interventions and was no longer the primary locus of benevolence. The code of what was called medical ethics in times past was devoted to protecting patients (among other goals). Now termed medical etiquette, it has largely disappeared.

Patients were also gaining power as a result of the rights movements, their increasing knowledge of medicine and science, and of the erosion of respect for authority in general and the authority of physicians specifically. The profession's view of benevolence as the cure of disease or the relief of its manifestations came under public scrutiny, as did the view of physicians as benevolent helpmates in general. For example, the 1973 self-help book *Our*

Bodies, Our Selves was published to promote what the authors saw as the need for women to take back their bodies from physicians, whose motives and actions were viewed with increasing suspicion. Doing "what the doctor ordered" without question and out of respect for his or her benevolence and authority had long been the mode when I went into practice in 1961. It was largely gone by the end of the decade and has not returned.

With increasing knowledge about science and medicine, the public bought into medical definitions of treatment, improvement, and cure—largely devoted to parts of the patient rather than to the person of the patient—as evidence of the benevolence of the medical profession. It is, however—if one can imagine such an attribute—a disembodied benevolence. It is not doctors, one might guess from the attitude of the public, but their scientific knowledge and technology that diagnose, treat, and cure diseases. Knowledge of medical science and information about medicine began to pervade the media. With the advent of the Internet, patients have an ever-increasing array of options from which to choose, leading to a kind of evidence-based and guideline-driven "cafeteria medicine." Patients, now at center stage in medicine, define benevolence, while physicians retreat or are forced by managed care to retreat from taking responsibility for the whole patient.

Over the same forty-some years there have been countervailing trends within and outside medicine as well. Response to wounds suffered during WWII started the rehabilitation medicine movement, which brought new understandings of function, thereafter defined not solely by the action of a body part but by the ability of a person to participate in a social role. Rehabilitation may not correct the underlying pathogenic mechanism, but it can restore function by retraining abnormal parts, utilizing other body mechanisms to compensate for lost function, and teaching persons to accommodate to their impairments.

When the goal is removing diseased tissues or restoring a diseased organ to normal—defined structurally—professional standards can define benevolence. But when the idea is to restore function to a part, or actively relieve symptoms, or return the patient to social function, then the sick person is the final arbiter of success. Only the patient knows when he or she is better.

In the care of the dying, the paradoxes of beneficence are easily seen. The goal of keeping people alive first entered medicine in the nineteenth century, well before the necessary technical capability existed. As time went on doctors became better able to support one physiological function after another apart from the state of the whole patient. Kidney dialysis replaced lost renal function, better ventilators replaced failed lungs and supported oxygenation, pacemakers and defibrillators maintained heart rhythm, total intravenous nutrition took over when oral nutrition failed, various methods of blood pressure support and volume replacement maintained circulation. Transfusions of various blood components as well as means for stimulating production of blood elements allowed for continued function of the blood as an organ. By the 1980s intensive care units contained patients on life support even though they had no chance of returning to meaningful life, whatever the outcome of their therapies. These patients lay alongside others with diseases for which resuscitation and life support were appropriate because, if they could be maintained long enough, their return to full function was probable. These excesses led to a reaction among the public and physicians. The importance of a good death, first brought to public awareness by Elisabeth Kübler-Ross in her 1972 book *On Death and Dying*, received increasing support and was the subject of widespread discussion. Advance directives and "do not resuscitate" orders became more common, and the assignment of surrogates for medical purposes became easier and more frequent. The hospice movement provided an alternative for the care of the terminally ill and focused attention on the relief of pain. Nonetheless, as in other aspects of medical care, technical proficiency and scientific knowledge continued to define medical benevolence, again most often as the good done to a part. Patients were constantly told what was wrong and what was happening in considerable technical detail, and then given technical options to choose from, as was the case with Olga, the patient with breast cancer mentioned earlier. She, like others with similar end-stage diseases, chose to accept the physicians' recommendations, because choices were described to her only in terms of technical procedures.

The patient has become increasingly central, but codes, guidelines, laws, and legal actions have pushed the notion of wronging the patient to the fore, while the calculus of benefit and harm has receded as physicians have withdrawn even more from the ideals of the past.

RESPECT FOR PERSONS

The physicians of the derelict with the heart attack probably did not entertain the notion that he had a right to decide whether to participate in the experiment or that he was wronged by not having been asked for his consent. They chose a derelict with no family because more sophisticated patients were always wary of being "experimented on." By the standards of the time they did the right thing: they protected the patient from harm. He was after all a patient, not a person. When persons became patients, their social status changed. In the late 1960s I admitted a mentally fit corporate president with pneumonia to the hospital. After I explained to him what I thought was wrong and what would take place, his wife and I went out into the corridor for a full discussion of his case—a discussion that would not now take place without his participation. Patienthood had in minutes deprived him of his status as a self-determined person. This was the fashion of the times.

The letter to Olga, the young woman with stage IV breast cancer, suggests that to the physicians Olga is clearly a person; it is the sick patient part of her identity that seems to have diminished. She has gained rights as a person, but no longer commands obligations due a patient.

The idea of respect for persons as described in the *Belmont Report*—or even the concept of persons qua persons—was not present in medicine in 1954. Benevolence and the avoidance of harm were the expressions of respect for the humanity of patients. Patients were to be treated as fully human. Persons, in contrast, are not merely human; they are social, moral, legal, and political entities with rights, to whom obligations are due. Because of this persons can not only be harmed, they can be wronged. It seems probable that the idea of person as we use it today—derivative as it is from the evolving concept of atomistic individuality—was just beginning to take full form after WWII. In the time period covered in this essay, the nature of persons changed, society changed, and medicine changed, resulting in a change in the meaning of respect for persons and autonomy. In the 1950s and early 1960s, women in public were not persons in their present sense, nor were people with disabilities, nor gay people. The civil rights movement achieved legal rights for blacks and other ethnic minorities but also changed their social status by making them persons in the wider American community

in a legal and political sense. These changes were not the end of the matter; they were the official beginning of a process that had started well before the civil rights movement and that continues to this day.

In *The Patient as Person: Explorations in Medical Ethics* (published in 1970), Paul Ramsey discusses the bond between physician and patient and how that bond defines both. Before the patient became fully a person, physicians were patients' decision-makers: doctors made decisions about the best thing to do and about what and how to tell patients about their circumstances. It was part of physicians' obligations and part of their patients' expectations. Good physicians knew that patients had to be informed about what was happening because too much uncertainty was considered bad.

But full disclosure of fatal or dangerous diagnoses or situations was thought to be harmful because it would be followed by hopelessness. When one patient I cared for was back in his room after his surgery for inoperable cancer of the stomach, he asked his surgeon what he had found. The surgeon said, "We did a lot of cuttin' and schnitten and removed a lotta junk and you're gonna be fine." I took care of the patient until he died months later. A few days before he died he said, "Sometimes lately I think maybe I'm not getting better."

Medicine was only a few decades into the beginning of the therapeutic revolution that now is taken for granted. Then, despite great expectations of the bounty to be expected from medical science, there was little optimism about the outcome of diseases such as cancer, strokes, heart attacks, heart failure, advanced diabetes, and emphysema. Only for children had everything improved, as their death rates from now curable infectious diseases dropped precipitously in the Western World.

It is important to understand the relation among the fall in death rates, the improvement in health and well-being, the optimism fed by scientific advances, and the notions of respect for persons and freedom of choice. Previously, if you believed that your cancer inevitably meant a hopeless outcome and a painful death, and if your physicians believed that there was nothing beyond surgery that could be done for you, you might not have been so eager for knowledge or the freedom to choose. Beyond refusing or agreeing to (say) surgery, there was not much choice. One did the mastectomy and waited for the patient to get a recurrence and die, or be lucky. So doctors lied, not because they were morally defective but because, in their eyes, all they had to offer was an attitude of optimism and denial of a bad truth. Especially since at that time personal matters that might arise from these illnesses and the doctors' lies—lost hopes, unhappiness, anxieties, sadness, suffering, death, and grief—were personal matters kept from the view of others, even physicians (unless they looked).

On the other hand, if death rates are falling and the expectation of becoming hopelessly ill is disappearing in the face of new treatments, if persons with disabilities are entering active life in increasing numbers, if optimism pervades medicine, and if the world around is encouraging a further blossoming of individualism, then telling the truth and freedom of choice have new meaning.

The effects of the change in disease burden, the advance of medical science, change in social status, and personal freedom are easily seen in the rise of the women's movement. Would the continuing emergence of women to their present social and political state have been possible without a low birthrate, effective contraception, the virtual disappearance of the complications of childbirth, and the increased survival of children? As recently as 1928 Virginia Woolf, in *A Room of One's Own*, could decry the paucity of women in letters or any other profession. At that time, none of the four benefits mentioned above were available to women. Is widespread freedom of choice possible in their absence? Virginia Woolf did not think so.

Like WWI, WWII had put women in the work force, but I believe it took these medical changes to continue their advance. By the end of the social turmoil of the 1960s, as the women's movement grew, abortion had become legal, common venereal diseases were easily treatable (although new ones were appearing), and the physical constraints on the emergence of women were disappearing. Further, the opinion held by physicians about women gradually changed with the changing social milieu so that their climate of choice was also altered—even in advance of the entrance of large numbers of women into medicine. Women seized the locus of choice from physicians prior, I believe, to a similar change in the general population.

The bioethics movement was also a major force in spreading the importance of patient autonomy in clinical medicine. Publications, public discussions, the education of interested physicians and individuals who were making bioethics their academic field, and increased public interest brought power to the idea of patient autonomy.

By 1997 when Olga came to be making decisions about how her breast cancer would be treated, respect for persons in clinical medicine had become identical in many minds with autonomy defined solely as freedom of choice.

As time went on, the emphasis in the meaning of freedom of choice in medical practice shifted from choice from among the reasonable alternatives offered by physicians to whatever the patient (or surrogate) wanted. This was most evident in intensive care units where unconscious patients with no possibility of survival in the absence of support equipment were kept alive because (the physicians said) the family wanted a "full court press." It was not unusual at this time for the family and the medical staff to become adversaries. Influential guidelines in the bioethics literature (such as the Hastings Center Guidelines) supported the right of the family or patient to insist on resuscitation no matter what the clinical situation or the patient's prognosis.

In earlier years, learning to base clinical decisions on prognostication—carefully considered alternative possible outcomes (not merely what a physician wanted to do)—had been an important part of clinical training. With freedom of choice, this element began to disappear from clinical medicine. (Surgeons remained constant in this regard. They remained firmly in control of the decision to operate—if the patient agreed.) Absent concern about the impact of the past and the future on a clinical decision (what prognostication is all about), the exercise of autonomy in medicine came to be marked by immediacy.

Issues such as the nature of the person, the impact of illness on decisionmaking capacity, the problems of autonomy that were specific to medicine and care of the sick, and the meaning of autonomy in the context of the special relationship between patient and physician were buried under the tide of legal interpretations of these concepts and rise of the language of rights. As required by law, in every hospital in New York State a "Patients' Bill of Rights" was posted prominently next to elevators or other visible sites. The tone of the document was adversarial, as though everything that could be undertaken by physicians was determined by patient rights and medical obligations rather than patient needs and medical responsibilities. The balance of power had clearly shifted to the patient. For many physicians it became easier to acquiesce when patients wanted medications or diagnostic technologies than to assert medical authority or negotiate a middle ground. Patients and the public at large had become so knowledgeable that their choices were often well informed and cogent.

There can be no freedom of choice in the absence of knowledge on which to base choices. As previously noted, until the 1970s physicians commonly withheld the truth from patients who had life-threatening diseases. Earlier, doctors did not tell patients about the facts of their illnesses even when they were not serious. For example, doctors frequently did not reveal blood pressure to patients. Why would they want to know? After all, it was thought, they did not know what a specific blood pressure meant. The reasons for a specific medication might be revealed because it had been shown that explanations increased compliance (otherwise only about half of prescriptions were ever filled), not because it was believed that patients wanted to participate in the decision. Why would they? That was the doctor's job. It was commonly believed that doctors did not tell the truth—that they hid bad news. By the late 1970s patients were increasingly told the truth. By the late 1980s, any reticence on the part of the physician about revealing the truth was gone. The criterion for telling something to a patient became its truth.

From the destructiveness of complete lies to the destructiveness of unmediated truth took less than three decades. Attempts to teach the harm that could be done by "truth bombs" and "truth fragments" fell on deaf ears. But the truth of information is only one of its aspects. Of importance also are accuracy, reliability, and completeness, the meaning to the patient of the information, its relevance to the patient's problem, whether it increases or decreases uncertainty, what it indicates about appropriate or possible action, and what impact it has on the relationship between patient and physician. The understanding that information is a tool that can be used for healing or hurting disappeared under the new avalanche of truth revealed to patients in the service of autonomy. Deciding what should be said when, where, and how requires knowledge of not just the medical facts, but the nature of the sick person and his or her needs beyond the simply "medical." Physicians who have distanced themselves from their patients cannot obtain this kind of personal knowledge.

Decisions made in the name of respect for persons and their autonomy can result in different conclusions about the right thing to do. Consider, for example, the following two cases: A terminally ill patient with terminal respiratory disease decided against further treatment and entered a home hospice program. He soon became very sick and was brought to an emergency room in respiratory failure. Severely short of breath, he chose to go on a respirator despite having previously decided against resuscitation. His request was granted, although he could have been made comfortable without a respirator, and ultimately he will again be in the terminal state he was in before entering the emergency room. The second instance is that of a patient who had been on dialysis for a long time and decided to stop treatment. When he was close to death he requested that he be restarted on dialysis. His physicians chose not to do so and he soon died.

In the first instance the decision was justified by saying that the patient wanted to be resuscitated despite his previous refusal of further treatment. In the second instance the decision was justified by saying that the patient's previous decision against dialysis carried more weight than his current request for dialysis. The first case probably represents the more common contemporary occurrence. Here the patient's choice is atemporal—as though the person of the past does not count in the present and as if there is no future. Choice is exercised as if it were independent of circumstances, as if the panic of respiratory distress had no impact on the choice and the patient in his profoundly sick circumstances is as representative of the person as the less sick voice of the recent past. It is the immediate, individual choice that counts.

In the second case the physicians take responsibility for deciding that the previous decision to stop dialysis is more representative of the person than the current choice to restart dialysis. How do they know that they are correct, that they are not condemning the patient to death based solely on their judgment? They cannot know; it is merely a judgment. Their decision is based on their knowledge of endstage renal disease, the life of a dialysand, and this patient's previous experience with both. The patient will die of renal disease—no action or decision will change that fact. His previous decision was made over time and was justified over time. No patient is removed from dialysis without a lot of discussion with his or her physicians—it is in the nature of dialysis units. To honor his immediate choice would return him to the situation that he opted to end with death rather than face its continuance. Here the decision acknowledges the effect of illness and, perhaps most important, entwines the acts of the physicians with those of the patient.

In the years since the early 1950s, clinical medicine has moved away from respect for persons expressed primarily by benevolence and the avoidance of harm toward respect for persons defined by autonomous freedom of choice with little regard for other aspects of autonomy. Before the current era, patients were not accorded full status as persons by society—sickness removed them from the community of equals, impaired their autonomy, and required that physicians accept full responsibility for their benevolent treatment. At present, in the absence of obviously diminished mental capacity, the easily demonstrable impairment in the very sick of the ability to make reasoned decisions is essentially denied and they are accorded the full autonomy of normal persons who make decisions in which their physicians no longer share much responsibility.

JUSTICE

In 1981 I was asked to discuss justice as it applied at the patient's bedside. I argued that "love of humanity, compassion, and mercy, not justice, are the appropriate concepts to guide actions at the bedside."[1] But in the years that have followed, society and medicine itself have come to realize that no nation is rich enough to make available all that medicine has to offer. Accordingly, there have been many discussions of the need for some kinds of rationing or the awareness that covert rationing already exists. With that awakening has come concern for fairness in distribution, whether the problem is seen as one of large-scale social institutions such as governments, or of more local institutions such as transplant teams, hospitals, or other medical care organizations.

Inevitably, this involves the belief that individual physicians should play a part in preserving society's medical resources. Simply put, this means that the physician should be thinking not solely about a particular patient, but also about how the resources used in that patient's care affect conservation of the general resource supply. Only a few decades ago, such an idea would have met with strong opposition. The ethos held that physicians' primary obligation is to their patients and all else comes second—including physicians themselves, their institutions, and society.

The rise of managed care in the last decade has highlighted the distributive issues that arise when cost becomes the primary value by which services are measured. Eliminating services from a plan's benefit package, reducing the level of reimbursement for specific services, and reducing the time allotted for services can directly reduce costs. Each of these cost-saving strategies raises the question whether these medical services are not merely commodities that can be allocated fairly or unfairly.

It is not surprising that in this changing climate attention has turned to issues of justice arising from the individual physician's attention to an individual patient. The idea of concepts of justice applying to the physician's acts at the bedside, to which I denied legitimacy in 1981, has now become a focus of attention. In *Local Justice*, published in 1992, Jon Elster explores allocation of resources in situations not usually considered matters of justice, including military draft, admission to colleges, and certain larger medical allocation problems such as organ transplantation, which he discusses at some length.[2] Elster cites previous work by others, including Michael Walzer, that has focused on similar local issues. *Local Justice*, however, allows me to demonstrate the application of these ideas to clinical medicine.

The values underlying Elster's arguments are simple. To meet the standard of justice, the distribution of scarce resources should be both equitable and efficient. The existing norms of clinical medicine appear to conflict with justice as a principle of clinical medicine. The following excerpt from Elster makes the point:

In many cases, professional norms are self-explanatory. There is no need to ask why colleges want good students, why firms want to retain the most qualified workers, or why generals want their soldiers to be fit for combat. The norms of medical ethics, however, are somewhat more puzzling. I shall offer some conjectures concerning the origins of two central medical norms with important allocative consequences. Neither norm is outcome oriented, in the sense of aiming at the most efficient use of scarce medical resources. Instead, one might say that the norms are *patient oriented*, in a sense that will become clear in a moment. [Italics in the original.]

The first is what I have called "the norm of compassion," that is, the principle of channeling medical resources toward the critically ill patients, even when they would do more good in others. In addition to spontaneous empathy, I believe some cognitive factors could be involved in this norm . . . Instead of comparing the fates of different individuals if treated, doctors compare their fates if left untreated . . . .

Next, there is what I shall call "the norm of thoroughness." Rational-choice theory tells us that when allocating scarce resources, whether as input for production or as goods for consumption, one should equalize the marginal productivity or the marginal utility of all units .... A rational consumer would, therefore, spread his income more thinly over a large number of goods, rather than concentrate it on just a few.

We can apply similar reasoning to the behavior of doctors. With respect to any given patient, the doctor's time has decreasing marginal productivity, at least beyond a certain point .... This implies that if a doctor makes a very thorough examination of his patient, his behavior is not instrumentally rational with respect to the objective of saving lives or improving overall health. Other patients might benefit much more from the time he spends on the last and most esoteric tests. Nevertheless, doctors seem to follow a norm of thoroughness, which tells them that once a patient has been admitted, he or she should get "the full treatment.". . .

In Norway, a recent parliamentary commission found that eye specialists tend to admit too few patients and treat each of them excessively thoroughly. When I confronted my own eye doctor with this claim, she refuted it by telling me about a case in which she had been able to diagnose a rare eye disease only after exhaustive examination, thereby saving her patient's sight. I did not remind her of the cases that go undetected because the patient never gets to see a doctor at all. (pp. 146–48)

In the 1950s such an application of economic theory to medicine was unlikely. Even today, many clinicians would be upset at the conclusions Elster has drawn, but he is not alone. As F. H. Bradley once said, "When you are perplexed, you have made an assumption and it is up to you to find out what it is." Elster's assumption, which led to his puzzlement about the norms of medical ethics and on which his argument stands, is that medicine is devoted to saving lives and promoting overall health.

Historically, *clinical* medicine has been devoted to caring for individual patients, one at a time. Elster can be excused his error. He has probably been reading medicine's public relations slogans, in common with the rest of the population. The medical industry—clinical, teaching, and research—supports itself by spreading the belief that it is about saving lives and promoting health. The error is really an error in systems theory. The level of the medical system devoted to these goals is not medicine as a profession of individual doctors treating individual patients—what most people think of when they speak of medicine. It is medicine as a social system, concerned with keeping the population alive and healthy. The United States does not have an institution responsible for the social system of medicine—certainly it is not the Surgeon General's Office or the Department of Health and Human Services. The nation depends instead on the outmoded and demonstrably false assumptions that the health of the population is the sum of the health of individuals and that lives are best saved by the actions of individual physicians.

In the last few decades, however, as the economics of medical care have come under increasing scrutiny, addressing questions of equity and efficiency in the care of patients has come to be seen as necessary and reasonable. But the goal has not necessarily been the best medicine for the overall health of the population and the lowest death rate, but the most medical care for the money. Perhaps the closest thing to an arbiter of medicine as a social system has been the Healthcare Financing Administration, in conjunction with various organizations concerned with technology assessment, epidemiology (The Centers for Disease Control), and health policy.

It is probably true that at the present time more than one set of norms are applied to clinical medicine and the care of patients—patients who persist in clinging to historical values in the belief that when they are actively the patient they are their doctor's primary concern. Their health insurance organization is probably dedicated primarily to efficiency and, hopefully, equity—whatever its public advertising may say. But the matter does not end here. A recent paper by Lynn Jansen, a nurse who has a doctorate in political theory, allows us to move a step further.[3] Drawing on Elster's work, she applies the concept of local justice to the treatment of pain. As have many others, she finds that pain is under treated. She states that "an important factor affecting the distribution of [pain management] resources was the decisions made by individual clinicians at the bedside. Since these decisions affect the distribution of important health care resources, they should be understood as raising an issue of justice." After citing as an objection to her conclusions the belief of others that individual treatment decisions should be discussed in terms of beneficence, she states, "It is the actual distribution of resources, however, that should be assessed in terms of justice. *Ultimately, what matters from the standpoint of justice is who actually gets what resources.* If, therefore, this distribution is influenced in part by the decisions of individual physicians, then it is entirely appropriate that these decisions be assessed in terms of justice" (italics in the original). (In a footnote she states that not every decision by a physician raises an issue of justice.)

Why does it matter whether these local decisions are viewed in terms of justice? "As the case of pain management resources aptly demonstrates, many of these resources cannot be distributed properly according to a uniform policy or guideline. Yet they are sufficiently important to require a stronger distributive justification than simply relying on market forces or professional discretion." And finally, "When decisions . . . come to be viewed in terms of justice, there is greater pressure, both social and legal, for those who make these decisions to defend and justify them in public."

Whether one agrees with Jansen's argument is not the issue; what is important is the concept on which her discussion is based. For Jansen, and for many others in these last decades, the actions of the doctor have become *resources* for which physicians are socially and legally accountable. Take away the concept of resources and the argument that the idea of justice applies at the bedside disappears. The overriding belief that physicians' acts represent the exemplification of the *personal* duties of individual physicians toward individual patients—that this is the moral framework of clinical medicine—has lost considerable currency.

A number of things follow from the shift to a framework of justice. It presupposes people or groups pressing claims for scarce goods as their *right* and justifying those claims by rules or standards. It suggests the utility of rules and guidelines, and evidence-based medicine that can provide the basis for the social and legal evaluation of the distribution of the physicians' resources. It provides a basis for diminishing the importance of the personal judgment of physicians.

In quoting both Jon Elster and Lynn Jansen perhaps I have presented an overdrawn account of the place of justice in contemporary clinical medicine. This idea is not usually so baldly stated because, in a period of changing values, people often talk the old values but act on the new. Whether the word justice is used or not, the idea of physicians' services as scarce commodities discussed in marketplace terms is, by now, widely accepted. Similarly, the utility of guidelines, evidence-based medicine, and rules of practice are increasingly accepted. When physician commentators point out that such a medicine dismisses the importance of the physician's personal judgment based on the evaluation of the individual patient in context, they are correct but they miss the point. To a medicine guided by marketplace principles and the socially based ethics of justice, the loss of the personal is irrelevant. The classical norms of clinical medicine—dedication to the patient, constancy, thoroughness, self-discipline, compassion—are not about saving lives and improving overall health; they are about *this patient's* life and health.

These are the values of a professional ethos that at the moment of action knows no other patient. It is the physician's difficult task, accepted since antiquity, to keep these values in the forefront despite the fact that at any time there are many other patients. They are values that arise in relationships; they presume a relationship between doctor and patient. In this relationship, fairness—justice—is only one duty among others and probably not preeminent, judging from its absence in classical discussions of the obligations of physicians. Although Eric Cassell could rise in outrage at the idea of the concept of justice at the bedside in 1981, less than twenty years later it has a secure place at the head of the patient's bed to insure that the patient gets a fair share (but not more) of the medical resources and that the social system gets its money's worth.

FROM TREATING PATIENTS TO MAKING TREATMENT DECISIONS

We no longer understand the Belmont principles as we did in 1978, or 1954. The meaning of benevolence has shifted from acting for the good of the sick person to acting for the good of a body part or physiological system. Respect for persons has been redefined from overriding concern for the sick person (almost solely) to the right of the patient to choose independently from among all options. Justice was originally not seen to apply to clinical medicine; now it is apposite because we no longer understand the medical act as that of an individual clinician caring for an individual patient within a relationship, but as a commodity or a resource within a marketplace.

Their relationship devalued, the actors in the medical drama have become atomistic individuals, and treatment the increasingly successful therapy of body parts or systems. Scientific, legal, and marketplace world views have increasingly defined the participants and their actions, with medicine reflecting changes that have occurred in the surrounding society. There are, of course, countervailing forces in which the patient rather than the disease is the object of medicine, but they offer no more than an alternative viewpoint at this time.

A final case.

A forty-nine-year-old woman developed recurrent breast cancer three years after a lumpectomy, radiation, and chemotherapy. It progressed very rapidly so that within a few weeks she had extensive spread of her cancer to the lungs, bones, and liver. The severity of her liver disease made adequate chemotherapy impossible, but her oncologist continued to talk of cure "once the liver is better." When she became sicker and deeply jaundiced, she was admitted to a major teaching hospital. Because of gross edema and abnormalities of electrolytes, a nephrologist was called who took over the problem of kidney function. Her liver function worsened, but the oncologist's stated optimism did not wane. The house staff were kind and attentive, but busied themselves with her abnormal liver function. She and her partner, supported by the physicians, continued to make plans for her future and would not hear of the possibility that she might die. Reluctantly, she accepted the advice that her parents be told of her illness. She was discharged from the hospital but was readmitted in three days with a pathologic fracture of the hip. The hip was pinned, but postoperatively her liver function worsened and her blood pressure fell. She was transferred to an intensive care unit. The oncologist said that as soon as the problems with her liver and kidneys were straightened out, he could start treating her cancer. In a few days the nephrologist announced that her kidneys were now doing well. Her sickness deepened and she became confused. The orthopedist came and pronounced the wound healing well. He asked the nurses whether they could get her up and walking. She died the next morning.

REFERENCES

1. E.J. Cassell, "Do Justice, Love Mercy: The Inappropriateness of the Concept of Justice Applied to Bedside Decisions," in *Justice and Health Care*, ed. E.E. Sharp (Boston, Mass.: D. Raidel Publishing Company, 1981).
2. J. Elster, *Local Justice: How Institutions Allocate Scarce Goods and Necessary Burdens* (New York: Russell Sage Foundation, 1992).
3. L.A. Jansen, "Local Justice and Health Care: The Case of Pain Management," delivered at a medical ethics meeting at Johns Hopkins University, Baltimore, Maryland, 1999.

A Critique of Clinical Equipoise: Therapeutic Misconception in the Ethics of Clinical Trials

Franklin G. Miller and Howard Brody

The Hypericum Depression Trial Study Group published in 2002 the results of a randomized trial comparing hypericum (St. John's Wort), sertraline (Zoloft), and placebo in the treatment of major depression.[1] In the study, funded by the National Institutes of Health, 340 subjects from twelve participating centers were randomized to three trial arms for an eight-week period, with careful monitoring to assure that patients who worsened significantly or who became suicidal were removed from the study and received adequate treatment. Neither hypericum nor sertraline was found to be superior to placebo on the primary outcome measures. The authors noted, "From a methodological point of view, this study can be considered an example of the importance of including inactive and active comparators in trials testing the possible antidepressant effects of medications. In fact, without a placebo, hypericum could easily have been considered as effective as sertraline."[2]

What can we conclude about the ethics of this trial? One dominant viewpoint in research ethics would have prohibited the study. On this viewpoint, a randomized trial is ethical only in circumstances of "clinical equipoise"—a genuine uncertainty within the medical community as to whether (in this case) any of the three treatment arms are superior to the other two. No such uncertainty exists. Approximately twenty-five clinically available antidepressants, including sertraline, have been shown to be superior to placebo.[3] Moreover, the majority opinion within psychiatry probably holds that sertraline is definitely superior to hypericum for major depression, even if hypericum has potential for the treatment of mild to moderate depression. But another widespread viewpoint would hold that the trial was ethically sound. Depressed individuals widely use hypericum, a "natural" agent, despite the lack of proven efficacy. Accordingly, a rigorous evaluation offered scientific, clinical, and social value. According to the report of trial results, the study was approved by institutional review boards (IRBs) at twelve sites and subjects provided written informed consent.

But if clinical equipoise is a basic requirement for ethical research, how could all these review boards be blind to the unethical nature of this trial? And how could two such radically divergent viewpoints exist, without research ethics being widely regarded as in a state of crisis?

THERAPEUTIC MISCONCEPTIONS

The prevailing ethical perspective on clinical trials holds that physician-investigators can discharge their "therapeutic obligation" to patients in the context of randomized clinical trials (RCTs) as long as treatments being tested scientifically satisfy clinical equipoise. We contend that this ethical perspective is fundamentally flawed. An ethical framework that provides normative guidance about a practice should accurately characterize the practice. The prevailing ethical perspective fails this test: All sound ethical thinking about clinical research, and the regulatory framework for review of protocols for clinical investigation, depends on a basic distinction between research and therapy. But the claims in the prevailing ethical perspective on clinical trials conflate research and therapy. These claims are that the ethics of the physician-patient relationship must govern RCTs, that physicians who conduct these trials have a "therapeutic obligation" to patients enrolled in them, and that RCTs must be compatible with some form of equipoise.

Certainly, investigators and ethicists recognize that clinical trials are scientific experiments, which differ from standard medical care. They also recognize that they are subject to regulatory requirements which do not apply to routine medical practice. However, the prevailing ethical framework views clinical trials through a therapeutic lens. The mainstream ethical approach to clinical trials attempts to have it both ways: to view the clinical trial as a scientific experiment, aimed at producing knowledge that can help improve the care of future patients, and as treatment conducted by physicians who retain fidelity to the principles of therapeutic beneficence and therapeutic non-maleficence that govern the ethics of clinical medicine. The doctrine of clinical equipoise has emerged as the bridge between medical care and scientific experimentation, allegedly making it possible to conduct RCTs without sacrificing the therapeutic obligation of physicians to provide treatment according to a scientifically validated standard of care. This constitutes a "therapeutic misconception" concerning the ethics of clinical trials, analogous to the tendency of patient volunteers to confuse treatment in the context of RCTs with routine medical care.[4] As Paul Appelbaum has recently observed, "In fact, this confusion between the ethics of research and of ordinary clinical care appears rampant in the world of clinical trials."[5]

The therapeutic misconception in the ethics of clinical trials is reflected in the language commonly used within the clinical research enterprise. Clinical trials are often described as "therapeutic research," and investigators are regarded as having a "therapeutic intent." Research participants who are being studied because they have a medical condition under investigation are referred to as "patients," and investigators as "physicians" or "doctors," without qualification.

To demonstrate our contention about the mainstream approach to the ethics of clinical trials, we will offer an intellectual reconstruction of some of the history of research ethics since the 1970s. This history is characterized by incoherence resulting from commitment to two incompatible positions, each approaching research ethics in a fundamentally different way. The therapeutic misconception about the ethics of clinical trials has emerged from the "similarity position," which argues that ultimately, the ethics of clinical trials rest on the same moral considerations that underlie the ethics of therapeutic medicine. The "difference position" argues that the ethics of clinical trials must start with the realization that medical research and medical treatment are two distinct forms of activity, governed by different ethical principles.

The reigning ethical paradigm for clinical trials has coexisted with clinical trials practice that departs from its guidance. Clinical equipoise, the cornerstone of the similarity position, rules out placebo-controlled trials whenever there is a proven effective treatment for the disorder under investigation.[6] However, IRBs have routinely approved such placebo-controlled trials. These two anomalies—unappreciated theoretical incoherence and conflict between the theoretical paradigm and the practice of ethical review of clinical trials—call for critical examination of the similarity position and the doctrine of clinical equipoise.

THE DISTINCTION BETWEEN RESEARCH AND THERAPY

In 1979, Robert Levine summarized "the most important achievements of the National Commission" for the Protection of Human Subjects of Biomedical and Behavioral Research in "correcting the conceptual and semantic errors that had undermined virtually all previous attempts to develop rational public policy on research involving human subjects."[7] Two portions of Levine's summary capture the essential ingredients of the difference position: recognizing the distinction between research and therapy and, accordingly, abandoning the distinction between therapeutic and nontherapeutic research.

Clinical research shares with medical care the fact that both are performed by physicians in clinical settings, and both often use similar diagnostic and treatment interventions. When the commission began its work, physicians commonly regarded clinical research and medical therapy as inextricably connected. One authority quoted by Levine claimed that "Every time a physician administers a drug to a patient, he is in a sense performing an experiment." But the commission recognized the importance of determining the boundaries between routine medical practice and research. For Levine, the commission's conceptual breakthrough came with the realization that the physicians of the day were thinking about clinical research in the wrong way, and that the boundary between research and therapy was clear rather than fuzzy. The commission came to hold that clinical research is fundamentally different from medical practice.[8]

Clinical medicine aims at providing optimal medical care for individual patients. Ethically, it is governed by the principles of therapeutic beneficence and therapeutic nonmaleficence. Therapeutic beneficence directs physicians to practice medicine with primary fidelity to promoting the health of particular patients. According to therapeutic nonmaleficence, the risks of medical care to which a patient is exposed are to be justified by the prospect of compensating medical benefits for that patient. The physician uses scientific knowledge to care for the patient and engages in therapeutic experimentation with the aim only of finding optimal treatment. It is not part of the role of the physician in providing medical care to develop scientific knowledge that can help future patients.

Clinical research, in contrast, is not a therapeutic activity devoted to the personal care of patients. It is designed for answering a scientific question, with the aim of producing "generalizable knowledge." The investigator seeks to learn about disease and its treatment in *groups* of patients, with the ultimate aim of improving medical care. Scientific interest in any particular patient concerns what can be learned that is applicable to other patients. In view of the nature and purpose of clinical research, the principles of beneficence and nonmaleficence applicable to clinical research lack the therapeutic meaning that guides their application to medical care. Clinical research is dedicated primarily to promoting the medical good of future patients by means of scientific knowledge derived from experimentation with current research participants—a frankly utilitarian purpose.

A major reason for distinguishing research from therapy is to underscore that clinical research has an inherent potential for exploiting research participants.[9] Exploitation also may occur in clinical medicine—venal physicians sometimes perform medically unnecessary procedures for the sake of profit, for example. Yet when physicians of integrity practice medicine, physicians' and patients' interests converge. The patient desires to regain or maintain health or to relieve suffering; the physician is dedicated to providing the medical help that the patient needs.

In clinical research, by contrast, the interests of investigators and patient volunteers are likely to diverge, even when the investigator acts with complete integrity. Patient volunteers, especially in clinical trials, typically seek therapeutic benefit, though they also may be motivated by altruism.[10] Investigators are interested primarily in developing scientific knowledge about groups of patients. Regardless of investigators' motivations, patient volunteers are at risk of having their well-being compromised in the course of scientific investigation. Clinical research involves an inherent tension between pursuing rigorous science and protecting research participants from harm.[11]

Historically, the ethical distinction between research and therapy emerged out of concern about exploitive abuses of patients in clinical research. Reflection on this dark history gave rise to a major development in the ethics of clinical research: the requirement for independent, prospective review and approval of research protocols.[12] Prior independent review was considered necessary for clinical research because of the divergence between the interests of the investigator and the research participant. Self-regulation by physician-investigators could not be trusted in the research context to the same extent that self-regulation by physician was appropriate in the therapeutic context. The basic rationale for prospective, independent research review depends on the distinction between research and therapy.

The point of distinguishing research and therapy is not to make an invidious comparison, implying that clinical trials are more risky or ethically problematic than routine clinical practice. Indeed, there is some evidence that patients receive more favorable medical outcomes in many clinical trials,[13] and clinical medicine is certainly rife with ethical problems. Further, since research is more carefully regulated than medical practice, it is quite likely that fewer ethical violations occur in research. To say that two activities are ethically different is not to say that either is inherently better than the other.

ABANDONING THE DISTINCTION

The distinction between research and therapy is most likely to be obfuscated in the context of clinical trials, which test the safety or efficacy of investigational and standard treatments. Since patients may derive medical benefit from trial participation, especially in phase III RCTs (the final stage of testing, which many investigational drugs never even reach), clinical trials are often characterized as "therapeutic research."

Nonetheless, the process of treatment in RCTs differs radically from routine clinical practice.[14] Consider the contrast between the hypericumsertraline trial and routine medical care for depression. If a physician treated 340 patients for major depression, she would not decide which drug to administer by flipping a coin. If the physician elected to use sertraline, she would judge each case individually to determine dose, when to change the dose, and whether to prescribe a second antidepressant or recommend other treatment. We would expect to find considerable variation in the treatment administered to those 340 patients after eight weeks or so. From the vantage point of therapy, this is what it means to provide care to patients.

From the vantage point of research, such variation would wreak havoc on experimental design and the validity and generalizability of findings. So when patients are randomized to one or another experimental drug, and are treated according to relatively inflexible protocols, the activity is very different from therapeutic medicine.

In many other ways, too, routine aspects of research deviate from what would be required by the duties of therapeutic beneficence and nonmaleficence. Volunteer patients and physician investigators are often ignorant of assignment to the experimental or control treatment, which may be a placebo. Trials often include interventions such as blood draws, lumbar punctures, radiation imaging, or biopsies that measure trial outcomes but in no way benefit participants. RCTs often contain a drug "washout" phase before randomization to avoid confounding the evaluation of the investigational treatment with the effects of medication that patients were receiving prior to the trial. These various features of research design promote scientific validity; they carry risks to participants without the prospect of compensating therapeutic benefit.

For these reasons, Levine argued that the second major contribution of the commission was to abandon the "illogical" distinction between therapeutic and nontherapeutic research, which previous policymakers thought was essential to the proper regulation of research and the protection of human subjects.[15] Because research and therapy are distinct activities, and the ethics of therapeutic medicine therefore cannot be automatically extended to guide research, it is mistaken to label research as "therapeutic" or "nontherapeutic," as if that made any fundamental ethical difference. Many research trials consist of a complex mix of therapeutic and nontherapeutic elements—the placebo-controlled trial being only one obvious example—such that labeling the trial as a whole as "therapeutic" or "nontherapeutic" is

misleading. In addition, the therapeutic-nontherapeutic distinction diverts attention from key ethical issues. Consider a nontherapeutic trial in which one interviews subjects and takes saliva samples, and a therapeutic trial in which one is testing a new cancer drug that has some promise for creating remission, but also has potentially life-threatening toxicity. Is the latter trial less in need of stringent regulatory oversight because it is "therapeutic"? Or does the therapeutic-nontherapeutic distinction distract the observer from those aspects of the trials that assume far greater moral weight, such as the level of risks and the potential vulnerability of subjects?

Once one understands the distinction between research and therapy, one realizes that "therapeutic" research is still research, and that the ethical rules appropriate to it are those appropriate for clinical research generally. Even though the patient may derive benefit from treatment being evaluated, the basic goal of the activity is not personal therapy, but rather the acquisition of generally applicable scientific knowledge. The basic goal and nature of the activity determines the ethical standards that ought to apply.

Writing in 1993, Jay Katz affirmed the vital importance of the distinction between research and therapy and deplored its blurring in practice: "The astronomical increase in clinical research has, in practice, not led to a clear demarcation between therapy and research, bioethical theories notwithstanding. This vital distinction remains blurred when physician-investigators view subjects as patients, and then believe that patients' interests and not science's are being served by participation in randomized clinical trials that are so commonly conducted in today's world."[16] One of the reasons investigators (and bioethicists) have failed to appreciate the distinction between research and therapy is that the similarity position has conceived the ethics of clinical trials within the context of the physician-patient relationship.

CHARLES FRIED AND THE SIMILARITY POSITION

In 1974, Fried published *Medical Experimentation: Personal Integrity and Social Policy*, which launched the similarity position within bioethics.[17] Fried assumed that answers to ethical dilemmas in research would have to be found within the ethics of therapeutic medicine. He defended fidelity to the interests of the individual patient against a model in which "medicine is to be viewed as caring for populations."[18] What made the RCT ethically suspect was that it seemed to him a prime example of population-focused—rather than individualized—and utilitarian medicine.

Fried devoted most of his book to defending patients' "rights in personal care."[19] Returning to medical research, he took issue with trials in which patients were randomized to receive either the experimental intervention or standard care. Fried coined the term "equipoise" to describe the ethically necessary condition for conducting an RCT: physician-investigators must be indifferent to the therapeutic value of the experimental and control treatments evaluated in the trial. The basic idea of equipoise had previously been articulated by Bradford Hill, a pioneer in the development of RCTs.[20] But what Fried objected to primarily in RCTs was not randomization per se, but the fact that no informed consent had been obtained. Fried saw the threat of "care for groups" (instead of "care for individuals") as residing primarily in the idea that it was legitimate to enroll subjects in an RCT without explicit, informed consent because the results of the trial would provide new medical knowledge that would improve the lot of future patients.[21] Because Fried was concerned chiefly about informed consent, an essential ingredient of both medical research and therapeutic medicine, he saw no problem in applying the ethics of medical therapy to medical research.

In the 1970s, the "respect for patient autonomy" movement was gaining steam as a replacement for the old Hippocratic ethic of paternalistic beneficence. Since both Fried and the National Commission seemed on the surface to be championing patient autonomy, it was easy to miss the point that they were proposing two fundamentally different strategies for approaching the ethics of clinical trials. Put another way, so long as the bioethics debate of the moment has to do with whether research ethics requires all competent subjects to give fully informed consent, any fundamental divergence between the similarity and the difference positions is likely to be obscured.

THE EMERGENCE OF CLINICAL EQUIPOISE

During the 1980s, philosophers interested in research ethics recognized a tension between the obligation of physicians to offer optimal care to their patients ("the therapeutic obligation") and the provision of medical treatment in the context of clinical trials. Don Marquis addressed this problem in a 1983 essay, "Leaving Therapy to Chance."[22] The title is significant, suggesting that the RCT is a form of therapy rather than an ethically distinct activity. Marquis began his essay, "Consider this

dilemma: according to an argument that is hard to refute, the procedure for conducting randomized clinical trials of anticancer drugs is incompatible with the ethics of the physician-patient relationship. If this problem is to be resolved, then either a key procedure for achieving scientific knowledge in medicine must be given up or unethical behavior by physicians must be tolerated."[23] In framing this "RCT dilemma," Marquis assumed that the appropriate ethic for clinical trials was that of the (therapeutic) physician-patient relationship.

Fred Gifford, following the lead of Marquis, examined the RCT dilemma in greater depth: "The central dilemma concerning randomized clinical trials (RCTs) arises out of some simple facts about causal methodology (RCTs are the best way to generate the reliable causal knowledge necessary for optimally-informed action) and a *prima facie* plausible principle concerning how physicians should treat their patients (always do what it is most reasonable to believe will be best for the patient)."[24] Neither Marquis nor Gifford found what they regarded as a satisfactory solution, and neither considered the possibility that the difference position could dismiss the "RCT dilemma" as misguided to begin with.

In a landmark 1987 article, Benjamin Freedman offered a solution to the RCT dilemma that gained widespread acceptance within bioethics. He argued that the tension between ethically legitimate scientific experimentation and the therapeutic obligation of physicians could be overcome by the principle of "clinical equipoise."[25] Freedman agreed with Fried and Marquis that ethical clinical trials had to be compatible with therapeutic beneficence and nonmaleficence. But he argued that Fried's formulation of equipoise was too constraining. Freedman called Fried's original concept "theoretical equipoise" (sometimes called "individual equipoise") and contrasted it with his favored concept of "clinical equipoise" (sometimes called "collective equipoise"). In the latter sense of equipoise, any individual investigator or physician might have reasons to believe that one arm of the RCT offers a therapeutic benefit over the other arm, but the medical profession as a whole remains divided. According to Freedman, an RCT is ethical so long as the professional community has not yet reached a consensus, which recognizes that "medicine is social rather than individual in nature."[26] When, and only when, clinical equipoise is satisfied will patients enrolled in a clinical trial be assured that they will not be randomized to treatment known to be inferior. Freedman thus asserted in a later article that clinical equipoise is "grounded in the normative nature of clinical practice, the view that a patient is ethically entitled to expect treatment from his or her physician—an entitlement that cannot be sacrificed to scientific curiosity."[27]

The bioethics community perceived Freedman's concept of clinical equipoise as both a theoretical and a practical advance. Theoretically, it appeared to offer a more intellectually compelling argument than Fried's initial formulation. Practically, it would permit useful RCTs that would otherwise be ethically proscribed to go forward. Since it appeared to solve the RCT dilemma by accommodating the conduct of clinical trials with the therapeutic obligation of physicians to offer optimal medical care, clinical equipoise gained wide currency as a fundamental concept of the ethics of clinical trials.[28] The persuasive way in which Freedman fortified the similarity position diverted attention from the fact that clinical equipoise collapsed the distinction between research and therapy.

The similarity position and clinical equipoise have been popular not only among bioethicists, but also among investigators. We speculate that this ethical perspective helps to address investigators' psychological needs. Physician-investigators, after all, went to medical school, not investigator school. To think of research with patients outside the ethical framework of the physician-patient relationship, as the difference position requires, may be difficult and threatening to them. Clinical equipoise offers a formula that seems to allow them to mix both physician and investigator roles—even if the psychological comfort is purchased at the price of ethical obfuscation.

The anomaly therefore exists that much of today's bioethical thinking accepts clinical equipoise as an outgrowth of the similarity position, while the Federal regulations grew out of the work of the National Commission, which largely endorsed the difference position. One would imagine that sooner or later proponents of clinical equipoise would realize the need to defend this doctrine from the charge that it conflates the ethics of clinical trials with the ethics of medical care. But this is precisely what has not yet happened.

THE CASE OF PLACEBO-CONTROLLED TRIALS

Although the similarity position, bolstered by clinical equipoise, became the reigning paradigm in the ethics of clinical trials, its dominion over practice was limited. This divorce between theory and practice has been particularly pronounced in the case of placebo-controlled trials. Freedman and his colleagues argued that the use of placebo controls is unethical whenever proven effective treatment exists for the medical condition under investigation in a clinical trial because those randomized to placebo would receive treatment known to be inferior.[29]

Despite the clear implications of clinical equipoise for the ethics of placebo-controlled trials, numerous trials, such as the hypericum-sertraline trial, continued to use placebo controls despite proven effective treatment. Placebo controls have typically been used in trials of new treatments for a wide range of chronic conditions—including mood and anxiety disorders, asthma, stable angina, hypertension, and migraine headaches—all of which can be treated with medication of proven efficacy.

There are two explanations for this incoherence between theory and practice. First, the FDA has encouraged the use of placebo controls in trials concerning these and other chronic conditions.[30] Active-controlled trials designed to test the equivalence of the experimental treatment with a standard treatment suffer from serious methodological limitations. Whenever active-controlled trials show no statistically significant difference between the investigational treatment and an active comparator, two conclusions are possible. Either both were effective in the trial sample of patients, or neither was effective. Without the use of a placebo control, such trials lack internal validity. Accordingly, the FDA has insisted that pharmaceutical companies use placebo controls in trials of new treatments for conditions characterized by fluctuating symptoms and high rates of placebo response.[31] Second, the U.S. federal regulations governing human subjects research do not provide any explicit guidance on the use of placebo controls.[32] IRBs have been free to approve such placebo-controlled trials, provided that they meet regulatory requirements for a favorable risk-benefit ratio, including the potential value of knowledge to be gained and informed consent.

For the most part, this lack of fit between theory and practice received little critical attention until the publication in 1994 of an article in the *New England Journal of Medicine* entitled "The Continuing Unethical Use of Placebo Controls."[33] Kenneth Rothman and Karin Michels castigated the practice of placebo-controlled trials in the face of proven effective treatment and the role of the FDA in encouraging these trials. They cited the Declaration of Helsinki, which relies heavily on the similarity position, as prohibiting this widespread "unethical" practice.

Their article stimulated a lively debate over the ethics of placebo-controlled trials. Freedman and his colleagues attacked "the placebo orthodoxy" in a two-part article that challenged the scientific value of placebo-controlled trials and reiterated that they are unethical when proven effective treatments exist because they contravene clinical equipoise.[34] Other commentators, writing in leading medical journals, defended more or less extensive use of placebo-controlled trials on methodological and ethical grounds.[35] Without directly challenging the doctrine of clinical equipoise, they implied that clinical equipoise provides erroneous ethical guidance for placebo-controlled trials. Accordingly, the debate over placebo-controlled trials jeopardizes the reigning ethical paradigm of the similarity position and clinical equipoise.

CRITIQUE OF THE SIMILARITY POSITION AND CLINICAL EQUIPOISE

Our reconstruction of the recent history of the ethics of clinical trials has traced the emergence and dominance of the similarity position. This history also reveals cracks in the foundation of this ethical paradigm. Simultaneous endorsement of the difference position, reflected in the federal regulatory system and the Belmont Report, and the similarity position, which invokes the doctrine of clinical equipoise, has left the ethics of clinical trials in a state of incoherence. Although this incoherence has not received critical attention, it becomes apparent once the assumptions underlying the similarity position and clinical equipoise are challenged. In addition, the divorce between research ethics theory and clinical trials practice in the case of placebo-controlled trials suggests that a critique of the similarity position and clinical equipoise is overdue.

We contend that clinical equipoise is fundamentally mistaken because "the RCT dilemma," for which it was proposed as a solution, is false. Clinical equipoise and all other forms of equipoise make sense as a normative requirement for clinical trials only on the assumption that investigators have a therapeutic obligation to the research participants. The "therapeutic obligation" of investigators, forming one horn of the RCT dilemma, constitutes a therapeutic misconception about the ethics of clinical trials. The presumption that RCTs must be compatible with the ethics of the physician-patient relationship assumes erroneously that the RCT is a form of therapy, thus inappropriately applying the principles of therapeutic beneficence and nonmaleficence that govern clinical medicine to the fundamentally different practice of clinical research. It is impossible to maintain fidelity to doing what is best medically for patients in the context of RCTs because these are not designed for, and may conflict with, personalized care. Although ethically appealing, the project of bridging the gap between therapy and research via the doctrine of clinical equipoise is doomed to fail.

The insight that the RCT contravenes the ethics of the physician-patient relationship led Samuel Hellman and Debra Hellman to argue that the RCT is unethical and that other methods of evaluating treatments should be employed.[36] This stance, however, would deprive patients and society of the benefits that flow from rigorous scientific evaluation of experimental and standard treatments. The more reasonable conclusion is that RCTs should be governed by ethical norms appropriate to clinical research, which are distinct from therapeutic beneficence and therapeutic nonmaleficence.

Clinical equipoise is neither necessary nor sufficient for ethically justifiable RCTs. The use of placebo controls when proven effective treatment exists violates clinical equipoise; however, when methodologically indicated, their use is no different in principle from any research intervention that poses risks to subjects without the prospect of benefiting them.[37] In many cases, the risks of withholding effective treatment are excessive, and the use of placebo controls would thus be unethical. Nevertheless, it is the unacceptable level of risk, not the violation of investigators' alleged "therapeutic obligation," that makes these trials unethical. In other cases, including the hypericum-sertraline trial, use of placebo controls when proven effective treatment exists is ethically justifiable.

By conflating the ethics of clinical trials with the ethics of therapeutic medicine, proponents of the similarity position may also contribute to the lack of adequate informed consent. If investigators view the ethics of clinical trials through a therapeutic lens, they may explicitly or implicitly foster the therapeutic misconception among research participants—that is, the tendency of participants in trials to confuse clinical trials with medical care. Research participants need to know that the overall activity is aimed not at their own ultimate benefit, but at discovering new knowledge to help future patients. If they think that clinical trial participation is a form of therapy, then they cannot give informed consent. Moreover, unlike the therapeutic context, the patient-subject cannot delegate the decision to the physician-researcher. In the therapeutic setting, a patient can decide to trust the physician to choose the best treatment because the physician has the patient's best interests at heart. The investigator has the interests of future patients at heart, and so cannot decide for the subject whether or not to participate in the research. To be trustworthy, investigators must themselves understand clearly the ways in which clinical research differs from clinical practice and convey this forthrightly to potential research subjects.

It is worth pondering, however, the practical consequences that might ensue if physicians, investigators, patients, and ethicists understood clinical trials without distortion by therapeutic misconceptions. Would recruitment of participants for valuable clinical trials become substantially more difficult, slowing progress in medical care? The fact that clinical trials are no longer seen as a mode of therapy leaves unchanged the real prospect of therapeutic benefits offered to patients from trial participation, including the opportunity to receive promising investigational agents, ancillary medical care, expert diagnostic evaluations, and education about their disorder. Nonetheless, some patients might be less inclined to participate in clinical trials when they appreciate the differences between these scientific experiments and medical care.

To attract enough subjects, researchers might have to pay people for their participation, as researchers in industry-sponsored clinical trials already do with increasing frequency. Payments would add to the cost of conducting clinical trials, but it might help prevent the therapeutic misconception among trial participants.[38] To be paid signifies that the trial participant is not merely a patient seeking therapy. If additional expenditure is necessary to motivate clinical trial participation, then this is a price worth paying for enhanced professional integrity and informed consent.

AN ALTERNATIVE ETHICAL FRAMEWORK

In view of the theoretical and practical problems associated with the similarity position and its logical offspring, clinical equipoise, an alternative framework for the ethics of clinical trials is needed. The most promising recent treatment of research ethics has been developed by Ezekiel Emanuel, David Wendler, and Christine Grady.[39] They propose seven ethical requirements for all clinical research: (1) scientific or social value; (2) scientific validity; (3) fair subject selection; (4) favorable risk-benefit ratio; (5) independent review; (6) informed consent; and (7) respect for enrolled research participants. This framework is built on the difference between research and therapy and on the core value of *protecting research participants from exploitation*.

Yet even this formulation of an ethical framework appropriate to clinical research testifies to the hold of the similarity position. The authors endorse clinical equipoise, claiming it is implied by the requirements of value, validity, and risk-benefit ratio. We contend, by contrast, that the endorsement of clinical equipoise renders incoherent any account that arises from the difference position. The most important next step for research ethics is to develop this "non-exploitation" framework systematically in a way that avoids any conflation of clinical research with medical care.

Those who agree that physician-investigators who conduct clinical trials are not governed by therapeutic beneficence still might argue that clinical equipoise provides important methodological guidance for justifying clinical trials. Freedman and his colleagues have argued that clinical equipoise is both an ethical and a scientific principle: "That principle can be put into normative or scientific language. As a normative matter, it defines ethical trial design as prohibiting any compromise of a patient's right to medical treatment by enrolling in a study. The same concern is often stated scientifically when we assert that a study must start with an honest null hypothesis, genuine medical uncertainty concerning the relative merits of the various treatment arms included in the trial's design."[40] Nevertheless, whatever is valid methodologically in clinical equipoise—the honest null hypothesis—can be stated more clearly and without confusion with the therapeutic obligation, by appeal to the requirement of scientific value: no research participants should be exposed to the risks of valueless research. Clinical trials must be designed to answer valuable scientific questions. If the answer is already known or the question is trivial, then there is no honest null hypothesis, and a clinical trial should not be conducted. But this is logically independent of whether all the patients enrolled in the trial would receive medical treatment that is believed by the expert medical community to be at least as good as the standard of care.

This alternative framework provides accurate ethical guidance concerning clinical research without presuming that the ethics of therapeutic medicine should govern clinical trials. We illustrate this by applying the seven ethical requirements to the example of the hypericum-sertraline trial.

Scientific or social value and scientific validity

The study has social value owing to the widespread use of herbal remedies. Since the efficacy of hypericum in treating depression (especially major depression) was uncertain, there was an honest null hypothesis that hypericum would be no better than placebo. It would have been unreasonable to design the trial as an active-controlled superiority trial, since it is highly unlikely that hypericum could be shown to be more effective than sertraline. An active-controlled equivalence trial would lack "assay sensitivity" because the finding that the reduction in symptoms of depression experienced by those trial participants receiving hypericum was not significantly different for those receiving sertaline would not validly support the inference that hypericum was effective.[41] It would remain possible that neither treatment was effective in the study sample—as was in fact shown. The study, therefore, was properly designed as a three-arm placebo-controlled trial.

Fair subject selection

There is no evidence to suggest that particularly vulnerable patients were recruited inappropriately for this study, which included a sample representative of depressed patients.

Favorable risk-benefit ratio

Risk-benefit assessment of research protocols ultimately comes down to a matter of judgment. With respect to the use of the placebo control—the aspect of the trial that violated clinical equipoise—the risks to participants from an eight-week trial, with careful exclusionary criteria and monitoring, were not excessive and were justifiable by the anticipated value of the knowledge to be gained from the research. Hence, the placebo component of the study had a favorable risk-benefit ratio. Eliminating the placebo would have made the risk-benefit ratio unfavorable by virtue of undermining the scientific validity of the research.

Independent review, informed consent, and respect for enrolled research participants

The report of the study asserted that IRB approval was obtained at all sites and that all subjects gave informed consent. In addition, the described procedures for monitoring subjects for possible risk of harm indicated an acceptable level of respect.

In sum, this study was ethically justifiable despite violating clinical equipoise; moreover, had it been designed in accordance with clinical equipoise, it would have been methodologically deficient and therefore ethically questionable.

Charles Weijer, a leading advocate of clinical equipoise and the similarity position, has recently claimed that "Placebo-controlled trials in the context of serious illnesses such as depression or schizophrenia are ethically egregious precisely because no competent physician would fail to offer therapy to a patient with the condition."[42] Although we agree that depression is a serious illness, the hypericum-sertraline trial demonstrates that there is nothing "ethically egregious" about the use of placebo controls in trials of treatment for depression, as

long as the ethical requirements for clinical research are satisfied. Whether or not one agrees that, all things considered, the placebo control was ethical in this trial, the ethical justification of placebo controls has nothing to do with the therapeutic practice of competent physicians. In any case, the alternative ethical framework with its seven requirements provides adequate guidance for clinical trials without appeal to the incoherent doctrine of clinical equipoise and without conflating the ethics of research with the ethics of therapy.

REFERENCES

1. Hypericum Depression Trial Study Group, "Effect of *Hypericum Perforatum* (St John's Wort) in Major Depressive Disorder: a Randomized Controlled Trial," *JAMA 287* (2002):1807–1814.
2. Ibid., 1813.
3. S.M. Stahl, *Essential Psychopharmacology of Depression and Bipolar Disorder* (New York: Cambridge University Press, 2000).
4. P.S. Appelbaum, L.H. Roth, C.W. Lidz, P. Benson, and W. Winslade, "False Hopes and Best Data: Consent to Research and the Therapeutic Misconception." *Hastings Center Report 17*, no. 2 (1987):20–24.
5. P.S. Appelbaum, "Clarifying the Ethics of Clinical Research: a Path Toward Avoiding the Therapeutic Misconception," *American Journal of Bioethics* 2, no. 2 (2002):22.
6. B. Freedman, "Placebo-Controlled Trials and the Logic of Clinical Purpose," *IRB* 12, no. 6 (1990):1–6.
7. R.J. Levine, "Clarifying the Concepts of Research Ethics," *Hastings Center Report* 9, no. 3 (1979):21–26.
8. National Commission for the Protection of Human Subjects of Biomedical and Behavioral Research, *The Belmont Report* (Washington, D.C.: U.S. Government Printing Office, 1979) p. 3.
9. E.J. Emanuel, D. Wendler, and C. Grady, "What Makes Clinical Research Ethical?" *JAMA* 283 (2000):2701–2711.
10. J. Sugarman, N.E. Kass, S.N. Goodman, P. Perentesis, P. Fernandes, and R.R.Faden, "What Patients Say About Medical Research," *IRB* 20, no. 4 (1998):1–7.
11. F.G. Miller, D.L. Rosenstein, and E.G. DeRenzo, "Professional Integrity in Clinical Research," *JAMA* 280 (1998):1449–54.
12. R.R. Faden and T.L. Beauchamp, A *History and Theory of Informed Consent* (New York: Oxford University Press, 1986):200–232.
13. D.A. Braunholtz, S.J.L. Edwards and R.J. Lilford, "Are Randomized Clinical Trials Good For Us (in the Short term)? Evidence for a 'Trial Effect,'" *Journal of Clinical Epidemiology* 54 (2001):217–224.
14. J.W. Berg, P.S. Appelbaum, C.W.Lidz, and L.S. Parker, *Informed Consent: Legal Theory and Clinical Practice*, 2nd edition (New York: Oxford University Press, 2001):280–283.
15. R.J. Levine, *Ethics and Regulation of Clinical Research*, 2nd ed. (New Haven: Yale University Press, 1986):8–10.
16. J. Katz, "'Ethics and clinical research' revisited: a tribute to Henry K. Beecher," *Hastings Center Report* 23, no. 5 (1993):36.
17. C. Fried, *Medical Experimentation: Personal Integrity and Social Policy* (New York: American Elsevier, 1974).
18. Ibid., 5.
19. Ibid., 94.
20. A.B. Hill, "Medical ethics and controlled trials," *British Medical Journal* 1 (1963):1043–1049.
21. C. Fried, *Medical Experimentation: Personal Integrity and Social Policy* (New York: American Elsevier, 1974):8.

22. D. Marquis, "Leaving therapy to chance," *Hastings Center Report* 13, no. 4 (1983):40–47.

23. Ibid., 40.

24. F. Gifford, "The Conflict Between Randomized Clinical Trials and the Therapeutic Obligation," *Journal of Medicine and Philosophy* 11 (1986):347–366.

25. B. Freedman, "Equipoise and the Ethics of Clinical Research," *NEJM* 317 (1987):141–145.

26. Ibid., 144.

27. B. Freedman, "Placebo-Controlled Trials and the Logic of Scientific Purpose," *IRB* 12, no. 6 (1990):5.

28. T.L. Beauchamp, and J.F. Childress, *Principles of Biomedical Ethic*, 5th edition (New York: Oxford University Press, 2001):323–327.

29. B. Freedman, K.C. Glass, and C. Weijer, "Placebo Orthodoxy in Clinical Research. II: Ethical, Legal and Regulatory Myths," *Journal of Law, Medicine & Ethics* 24 (1996):252–259.

30. R. Temple and S. E. Ellenberg, "Placebo-Controlled Trials and Active-Control Trials in the Evaluation of New Treatments: Part 1: Ethical and Scientific Issues," *Annals of Internal Medicine* 133 (2000):455–63.

31. T.P. Laughren, "The Scientific and Ethical Basis for Placebo-Controlled Trials in Depression and Schizophrenia: an FDA Perspective," *European Psychiatry* 16 (2001):418–423.

32. Department of Health and Human Services. Protection of Human Subjects. Code of Federal Regulations. 45CFR46, 1991.

33. K.J. Rothman and K.B. Michels, "The Continuing Unethical Use of Placebo Controls," *NEJM* 331 (1994):394–8.

34. See B. Freedman, K.C. Glass, and C. Weijer, "Placebo Orthodoxy in Clinical Research. I: Empirical and Methodological Myths," *Journal of Law, Medicine & Ethics* 24 (1996):243–51; and B. Freedman, K.C. Glass, and C. Weijer, "Placebo Orthodoxy in Clinical Research. II: Ethical, Legal and Regulatory Myths," *Journal of Law, Medicine & Ethics* 24 (1996):252–259.

35. R. Temple and S.E. Ellenberg, "Placebo-Controlled Trials and Active-Control Trials in the Evaluation of New Treatments: Part 1: Ethical and Scientific Issues," Annals of Internal Medicine 133 (2000):455–63; E.J. Emanuel and F.G. Miller, "The Ethics of Placebo-Controlled Trials—a Middle Ground," *NEJM* 345 (2001):915–919.

36. S. Hellman and D.S. Hellman, "Of Mice But Not Men: Problems of the Randomized Controlled Trial," *NEJM* 324 (1991):1585–1589.

37. F.G. Miller and H. Brody, "What Makes Placebo-Controlled Trials Unethical?" *American Journal of Bioethics* 2, no. 2 (2002):3–9.

38. N. Dickert and C. Grady, "What's the Price of a Research Subject? Approaches to Payment for Research Participation," *New England Journal of Medicine* 341 (1999):198–203.

39. See E.J. Emanuel, D. Wendler, and C. Grady, "What Makes Clinical Research Ethical?" *JAMA* 283 (2000):2701–2711.

40. B. Freedman, K.C. Glass, and C. Weijer, "Placebo Orthodoxy in Clinical Research. II: Ethical, Legal and Regulatory Myths." *Journal of Law, Medicine & Ethics* 24 (1996):253.

41. R. Temple and S.E., "Placebo-Controlled Trials and Active-Control trials in the Evaluation of New Treatments: Part 1: Ethical and Scientific Issues," *Annals of Internal Medicine* 133 (2000):455–63.

42. C. Weijer, "When Argument Fails," *American Journal of Bioethics* 2, no. 2 (2002):10.

Rethinking Research Ethics

Rosamond Rhodes

A NOVEL PROPOSAL

To allow you to vividly appreciate the role that I see for informed consent and the concept of autonomy in research regulation, I put forward a hypothetical policy suggestion on human subject research participation, a novel proposal. Imagine that after sharing information (e.g., about actual harms that have been suffered by research subjects since the institution of research regulations, advantages achieved through previous studies, options for improved research oversight, etc.), opportunity for discussion, and a period of lively free and open debate, a social consensus emerges, and with bi-partisan support our legislature passes a bill that requires every U.S. resident to perform some research service every ten years. According to the carefully crafted measure, while each of us would be required to serve as a subject in some research study, we would be left the freedom to choose the particular project for our service from among all of the projects listed on a national web-site for which we meet the selection criteria.

In such a context, the research participation policy would embody our autonomous choice of a principle for ruling our own action in the first-person sense of autonomy [the ideal of autonomy]. The policy's allowance for individual decision-making would express the commitment to respect for autonomy in the second-person sense [the respect for autonomy]. In this context, informed consent would have to do new kinds of work.

First, informed consent would help to assure the trust and trustworthiness of biomedical research. In an informed consent environment, people would not volunteer to serve as research subjects or endorse and comply with a policy of required research participation unless they could trust biomedical research as an institution and the individual researchers who conducted studies under its auspices. Without subjects' trust that studies would actually produce valuable information and trust

Abridged from Rhodes, Rosamond. "Rethinking Research Ethics," *The American Journal of Bioethics* 5:1 (2005), 15–17, 21–22, 23–25. Copyright © 2005. Reprinted by permission of Copyright Clearance Center on behalf of the publisher.

that subjects were unlikely to be significantly harmed or to experience more burdens than they had been given to expect, the research enterprise could not go forward. Developing subject trust and assuring the trustworthiness of biomedical research practices is, therefore, essential for the practice of human subject research.

Medical science's need for trust and medical researchers' need for trust provides them with reasons for taking steps to assure the trustworthiness of their practice and to secure the trust of subjects (Rhodes and Strain 2000). For research to be trustworthy, medical science would have to take its fiduciary responsibility seriously and pay significant attention to research oversight (e.g., by IRBs). The commitment would allow subjects to be reasonably confident that studies would impose no unreasonable risks or burdens, that each research project was well designed, properly conducted, and could conceivably produce its promised results (Freedman, Fuks, and Weijer 1993; Fuchs and Westervelt 1996).

Second, we know that the same thing can look very different from different perspectives. From the point of view of a researcher, whose judgment may be colored by self-interest or theoretical commitment (Medawar 1983), or even a relatively objective review body, some risks and burdens could appear quite reasonable. But they might not appear quite so reasonable from the point of view of some potential subjects. Allowing subjects the option of choosing their participation with full disclosure, of at least the usual kinds of information required by current legislative guidelines, would allow their judgment to serve as a check on researcher bias.

Third, informed and voluntary selection of projects by subject-participants would keep research design to an ethically reasonable standard because researchers would be reluctant to publicly describe procedures that they should not undertake. When subjects are kept in the dark and researchers can conceal the nature of what they are doing behind masks of deception and duplicity, some researchers, as if rendered invisible by the magical powers of the ring of Gyges, could be tempted to do things they otherwise would not. In the light of full disclosure, a well-nurtured sense of shame is likely to inhibit at least non-sociopaths who might be tempted to stretch moral limits. In other words, a publicity condition that makes research proposals transparent to the biomedical research community and to the larger public will inhibit researchers from proposing unreasonable study designs.

Fourth, informed consent in subjects' selection of projects would be the principal mechanism for assuring respect for subject autonomy, in the second-person sense. It would allow individuals to fulfill their research

obligations within a framework of recognition and respect for their other values, goals, and commitments. Family responsibilities, career agendas, personal projects, tastes, attitudes toward risk and pain, and an individual's comprehensive moral view make some particular project choices reasonable and acceptable to some and different ones reasonable and acceptable to others. For a person who has suffered from schizophrenia and found the burdens associated with current drug regimes very onerous, the risks associated with a drug-free wash out period for a trial of a new drug could be worth taking. For another with a family history of Alzheimer's disease, the discomfort and inconvenience of a study that could advance the scientific understanding of that particular degenerative process could be worth taking. For someone else, it could be important to find a project that could be done from home or completed in a single day. For another, a study that involved new technology would be most interesting. And, for another, the more human interaction the better. Leaving the judgment to the involved individuals is likely to actually expand the parameters of acceptable research beyond those set by disinterested "protectors" of research subjects because individuals' personal values and personal attitudes toward risk vary significantly. That's precisely the point of respect for autonomy.

To some, a universal policy of required participation in some research project may appear to violate autonomy. But we must take care to avoid a superficial understanding of this complex concept. Protective thinking of the currently prevailing sort misses the point of autonomy as the rule-giving, self-legislating capacity to undertake responsibility and to create influences to control one's own behavior. Every principle and every policy that a person endorses constrains her own future behavior. That's what all laws do. Unless every principle, policy, and law violates autonomy, there is no special reason to believe that a personal commitment or a legislative requirement for research participation is, or should be, different. To respect another as an autonomous being is to allow the other to make choices about research participation by assessing the personal and societal advantages and disadvantages. This allows individuals to factor their personal values and experience into their choice.

When those engaged in research oversight in the name of autonomy take the stance of "protector," they express a willingness to deny genuine respect for autonomy out of fear of possibly allowing someone to make a less than ideally autonomous choice. However, as Mill has taught us, respect for autonomy requires the opposite approach by recognizing the illegitimacy of limitations on personal choice out of concern for the personal safety of others. Yet, research subject protectors seek ever more demanding mechanisms of protection and search out more and more groups that may be less than ideally rational and, so, in need of their protection. I am arguing that these well-meaning efforts are misdirected and counterproductive in that many may do more harm than good in terms of safe-guarding personal autonomy and supporting autonomous choices.

Although my "novel proposal" of periodic required research service is contrived, it was only put forward as an example of how commitments to equality and the importance of research could be implemented. For the most part, people want biomedical science to pursue therapeutic advances, and they are prepared to do their fair share when others do so as well. And, just as other laws apply to those who cannot consent to them, there is no obvious reason why a research participation policy should be different. No groups should be exempt from research participation. People with all sorts of special needs have to be investigated so that researchers can learn about them and so that they, and others who are similarly situated, can benefit from advances in biomedical science. For these reasons, even those incapable of giving consent (e.g., children, the demented) should be considered legitimate research subjects. Modern medical technology carries potentially huge benefits, serious dangers, and immense costs. Wasting opportunities to gather evidence while subjecting people to avoidable hazards associated with unstudied "therapy" benefits no one and is, therefore, an immoral approach to research policy. Because those who cannot consent, as well as others who are classified in vulnerable groups, have been systematically excluded from full research participation, we have an underdeveloped understanding of their medical treatment.

RETHINKING RESEARCH ETHICS

Protective thinking of the currently prevailing sort misses the point of autonomy as the rule-giving, self-legislating capacity to undertake responsibility and to create influences that control one's own behavior. In research, respect for another as an autonomous being requires allowing the other to make choices about research participation by assessing the personal and societal advantages and disadvantages according to her own priorities.

Lack of autonomy is an excellent reason for refusing to leave decisions about research participation with those who lack decisional capacity. It does not, however, justify a limitation on their research participation. The

reason for limiting anyone's participation in research should relate to the vulnerability that we all share. On the one hand, we are all vulnerable to the emotional effects of a serious illness. Frequently, our judgment and decisions are impacted by the pressures inherent in the situations that we confront. Nevertheless, to the extent that emotional impact allows subjects or surrogates to meet a threshold level of autonomy, they should be allowed to decide for themselves (Oshana 2003). Any sweeping move to limit or usurp self-determination in research decisions based on emotional vulnerability should be recognized as the unjustified paternalism that it is, and expunged from research ethics policies. On the other hand, we are all vulnerable to death, pain, and disability, to the loss of pleasure and freedom. If the likelihood of any of these is a credible consequence of a research study, and if the circumstances make it unreasonable to take the chance, the research community should prevent the study from going forward.

In other words, IRBs should change the focus of their study review from an attitude of protecting the vulnerable from Nazi-like researchers to assuring that the risks and burdens of research are reasonable, that the design is sound, and that the research is conducted with caring and respect: When that is done, a study conforms with the highest ethical standards. In that light, IRBs should examine protocols with an eye toward prohibiting those studies that would impose an unreasonable risk of significant harm and devote attention to oversight of ongoing studies. If IRBs actually embraced these responsibilities, they would permit only research with reasonable risks and burdens to go forward and assure the ethical conduct of human subject research. This new approach should leave neither the decisionally competent nor the decisionally incompetent without protection: Everyone should be protected from unreasonable risks and burdens. The worry about accepting the consent of someone who was less than ideally autonomous should also be negligible because there should be no exposure to unreasonable risk.

IMPLICATIONS OF RETHINKING THE ETHICAL CONDUCT OF RESEARCH

Policies and their associated sanctions and rewards should be designed to promote important goals. Current research policies are counter-productive because they tend to discourage studies that we need for guiding medical practice. In that respect, policies are ethically flawed. Whereas research policy preambles pay lip service to equality, respect, and the importance of studying children, the policy focus on protection and beneficence frequently impedes studies that could provide immediate benefit or evidence that could improve the medical treatment of patients later on.

Although individuals today may want to avoid serving as guinea pigs (just as they prefer to avoid jury duty and paying taxes), expanding the use of research would make study service part of the fabric of life. Because we need to learn about the long-term consequences of treatments, their side-effects and complications, we should strive to make research a common component of treatment instead of an unusual exception. This approach has led to amazing advances in pediatric oncology and it should become the reigning standard.

Society may not yet be ready to embrace my novel proposal for compulsory research participation. Yet, the perspective on research that I am urging has several obvious and not so obvious implications that should be given immediate attention. No doubt, most studies that would be prohibited under current policy would also be disallowed under the revised framework I propose. Yet, a model that discards the reigning dogmas and conducts human subject research with assurance of no more than reasonable risk and attention to oversight differs significantly from the current approach. This change in perspective should also promote a more just distribution of researcher attention.

CONCLUSIONS

Each of us has a stake in the outcomes of biomedical research. This suggests that we should each contribute our fair share and endorse rules and procedures that allow the research agenda to move forward with safety, efficacy, and trust in the scientific community. We now need to face up to the flaws in research policy, use what we have learned about the ethical conduct of human subject research, and start over again to formulate reasonable research policies:

- We need to change our view of researchers and subjects. When we regard them as exploiters and exploited, dedicated scientists are demonized and courageous subjects are devalued. Instead, we should see both as cooperative partners engaged in and committed to socially important collaborative projects constrained within bounds of reasonable risk (Katz 1992).
- We need to change the focus of IRB review from an attitude of protecting the vulnerable against the exploitation of Nazi-like researchers to assuring that research is conducted according to the highest ethical standards. IRBs need to redefine their role and to appreciate their charge as protectors of the trust and trustworthiness of the biomedical research enterprise. This will require

increased attention to the evaluation of the scientific merits and conduct of studies, the assessment of potential risks and burdens, and investment into oversight of ongoing projects.
- No groups should be exempt from research participation. People with all sorts of special needs have to be investigated so that they can benefit from advances in biomedical science. Even those incapable of giving consent should be considered legitimate research subjects because participation is the rule we should presume them to endorse if they had the requisite capacities.
- The judgment of individuals who lack decisional capacity cannot serve the oversight role. New procedures will have to be developed for monitoring the conduct of research involving individuals who cannot consent for themselves in order to assess and assure the reasonableness of burdens and risks.
- A health care system that accepts the social contribution of all research subjects without making the benefits available to all is grossly unjust. The U.S. has tolerated a health care allocation system that leaves approximately 45,000,000 people without any form of medical insurance. Society has turned a blind eye and accepted a situation in which some poor people with chronic disease can only receive drugs by serving as research subjects in the development of treatments for the benefit of the insured (Kolata and Eichenwald 1999). Adopting a system of universal participation in biomedical research would make universal access to health care a conspicuous moral imperative and require research benefits to be distributed along with the burdens.
- A variety of different reasons justify numerous limitations on research practices. Research policy should reflect the range of broadly shared reasonable concerns. For example, health, life, and disability insurance for research participants should be a requisite feature of studies that involve hazards. Most subjects would want to minimize their risks and burdens by having insurance. Yet, unless regulations required it for everyone, it would be very difficult for any individual subject to negotiate that coverage. Providing a benefit that reasonable people would want is a good reason for making it a condition of hazardous research. Notice, however, that this is a "hard paternalism" justification of insurance for subjects, and not the "soft paternalism" justification that follows from declaring them "vulnerable" and denying them the presumption of autonomy. Another example is a limitation on inducements for prisoners. Because the criminal justice system involves meting out punishment (i.e., a morally precarious activity of deliberately inflicting harm, a violation of ordinary rules of morality that requires serious justification) it is important to protect the system from contamination by any outside influences and to safeguard it against avoidable conflicts of interest. Again, the justification does not rely upon any aspersion of prisoner decisional capacity.

Informed consent has been seen as the primary standard for the ethical conduct of research, and protecting groups branded "vulnerable" (e.g., children, the mentally ill, the elderly, prisoners) has been taken as the single easy answer to every vexing question about the proper conduct of human subject research. But different questions require different answers. There is no obvious reason to presume that informed consent is the primary consideration for the ethical conduct of research or that protecting groups classified as "vulnerable" provides the answer to every moral question concerning research.

Ethics is not simple. At this point in our evolving understanding of the moral requirements for the ethical conduct of research, it is crucial that we rethink the role and requirements for the ethical conduct of research with sensitivity to complexity and awareness of the range of contexts in which clinical studies are and should be conducted. At this point in the development of biomedical science, failure to reexamine and reassess the reigning research dogmas of the primacy of informed consent, protection for the vulnerable, and beneficence constitutes self-righteous, but culpable, moral blindness.

DEVELOPING COUNTRIES

It Takes a Village: Medical Research and Ethics in Mali

Ogobara K. Doumbo

The world is populated by rich and poor nations filled with a diversity of peoples and customs. For those scientists and physicians trying to have an impact on global health, conducting clinical trials and other types of medical research in these varied places, and among these different cultures, is central to the cause. It also is imperative that these efforts are undertaken in ethical ways that respect and honor those many individuals and communities that agree to participate in the investigations. To do that, researchers need to develop an understanding of the unique ways in which different cultural groups make decisions. Only then can the investigators feel assured that the human beings who consent to partake in their studies are fully informed about the possible risks and benefits of such participation.

Without knowing it at the time, I began to develop a sensibility to these issues as an 8-year-old child when I used to follow my grandfather while he practiced traditional medicine in the Dogon country in northeast Mali. I was impressed by his attitude toward his patients. He was very close to them, talked to them with respect and consideration, and showed compassion for their suffering. The patient and the caregiver in this care-providing system are so intimately connected that my grandfather considered the patients as part of his family, sharing the same food and shelter. Because of my grandfather's fame, and because he specialized in two diseases—pharyngitis and breast tumor/infection—some patients came to him from very remote areas.

The respect my grandfather showed while interacting with his patients marked my life. At the age of 10, I decided to become a medical doctor, and 7 years later I began my medical studies at the National School of Medicine and Pharmacy in Bamako, Mali. There, in my second year of medical studies, during rounds with the late Bernard Duflo of the Internal Medicine ward of the National hospital "Point G," I witnessed a similar intensely ethical attitude in the patient-physician relationship. My grandfather and Dr. Duflo, a French physician, were from two completely different cultures, but they shared the same attitude in healing patients.

My "indoctrination" in the importance of ethics continued when I started my own medical research career in 1984. I was fortunate at that time to have been at the University of Marseille where I worked with parasitologist Philippe Ranque in the first Phase II trials in Mali of ivermectin, then a new drug for the treatment of onchocerciasis, or river blindness. Like my grandfather, Dr. Ranque's priority was to show his patients attention, care, and compassion. Dr. Ranque believed that protection of volunteers in medical trials was more important than achieving scientific goals.

Over time, my exposure to this sort of ethics-in-the-field, as well as to more academic discussions of ethics, convinced me that scientists must consider ethical issues throughout the entire research process, from identifying a research question to analyzing and interpreting data.

In Mali, where most of the population cannot read and where the social structures demand that decision-making be done more communally than in the West, we have had to develop new procedures for obtaining informed consent from participants in our malaria research. The process doesn't always work, takes a long time, and requires more discussion and leg work than in the West, but it generates mutual understanding, medical care for the participants and often their entire communities, and valuable scientific results.*

ETHICS IN THE FIELD: INFORMED CONSENT

At the Malaria Research and Training Center (MRTC) of the University of Bamako, Mali, we conduct different types of research, including laboratory-based studies, field research, and clinical trials. For us, ethical considerations constitute a dynamic process and are an integral part of the research enterprise. Here, I will focus on some study designs used at the MRTC and how we incorporate ethical considerations in our procedures for obtaining informed consent. I will also compare the strategies for getting documented and signed informed consent in developing countries, on the one hand, and in North America or Europe, on the other.

In recent years, we conducted an observational study of the natural history of malaria in the field as part of the Mali-Tulane Tropical Medicine Research Center (TMRC) project, funded by the National Institute of Allergy and Infectious Diseases (NIAID). The grant included three projects all located at Bancoumana, a large rural village in Mali with 12,000 inhabitants.

In Project I we studied a cohort of about 3500 children under 9 years of age, all of whom had been exposed to malaria. We recorded data on the natural history of malaria with the aim of identifying risk factors for infection or disease.

Because our studies were being done in the field and in a variety of social structures that respond differently to medical researchers coming into their lives, we needed to develop a dynamic approach to obtaining informed consent and to maintaining it over time. Usually, this was a stepwise process. First, we needed to get permission from the community to proceed. This began as a discussion with the group of village elders. Next, we convened focused group discussions with the heads of extended families. Then we held similar discussions with mothers whose children might become part of the malaria study. Finally, we obtained consent of the individual families involved in our cohort. The consent process was open and better suited to the needs of the population than were more conventional approaches. It generated more confidence by the villagers in the research project and a better understanding for us of the village culture and behavior. In developing this approach, I always had my grandfather and other ethics mentors in mind.

The villagers in the study received a tangible benefit too. Because we needed to examine the children many times during the course of the study, it meant that the villagers benefited from repeated contacts with the study physicians who lived in the village. Previous malaria studies in Africa commonly used a design typical of developing countries in which the interaction between study subjects and investigators is more limited and usually confined to clinical settings.

The second TMRC project was also unique in the strategy of getting informed consent. We wanted to test gametocyte infectivity in the community by directly exposing members already carrying the gametocytes to *Anopheles gambiae* mosquitoes—the most effective vector of the malaria parasite, *Plasmodium falciparum*, in Mali—collected in that village. Our aim was to determine the factors that influence how efficiently the mosquitoes would pick up the gametocytes from the infected villagers to initiate the sporogonic cycle during which the infective form of the malaria parasite proliferates inside the insects. Such direct exposure to these mosquitoes—even ones that were themselves not yet carrying the parasite and grown under controlled conditions—generates many ethical concerns. How could we prove to ourselves and to the community that the lab-reared *Anopheles* really were safe? How should we select the volunteers? How should we approach the community and document the process of community permission and individual consent (versus assent)? How should we explain the malaria life cycle to a population where 70 to 80% of its members are illiterate?

The first time we presented our protocol to the Institutional Review Board (IRB) of the Faculty of Medicine, Pharmacy and Odonto-stomatology, which oversees informed consent procedures, and to the village community, the design was rejected. The IRB deemed that it was not acceptable to expose humans to *Anopheles* even if the insects were reared in a well-qualified laboratory. We had to spend days and nights explaining the protocol to the villagers and to the Malian IRB members. Part of the process involved bringing representatives from two villages to visit our center at Bamako so that they could see how the exposure procedure would unfold.

They spent 2 days with us and questioned us about all aspects of the experiment. In the end, the protocol was accepted, providing testimony to the ways in which responsible, open, and patient explanation of well-designed studies sometimes can alleviate participants' fears and misgivings.[†]

The third NIAID-funded project—in collaboration with colleagues at the U.S. Centers for Disease Control in Atlanta, GA, and the National Malaria Control Program of Mali—was designed as a supplement to the original TMRC project. It was particularly ethically charged because it involved a vulnerable population of pregnant women. We wanted to conduct this study to generate data important for developing public health policies to help protect pregnant women from contracting malaria in ways that minimize risks to the fetus.[‡]

We designed a community-based open label trial to compare three prophylactic drug regimens in pregnant women. Given the special importance of pregnant women in African culture, we knew that we needed to be extremely careful about ethical considerations. Although these drugs were recommended by the National Malaria Control Program and the World Health Organization, their use in pregnant women needed rigorous ethical scrutiny.

Central to the project, of course, was to obtain the community's permission to conduct the study. A key early step was to discuss the benefit of learning more about these drugs with the women's local council. Then we met with the mothers-in-law of each pregnant woman. After all of these discussions, we met with the individual pregnant woman. Toward the end of the process, the women requested that we meet with their husbands and fathers-in-law as well. (It is a widespread custom in African cultures that a pregnant woman belongs to the family-in-law, which is responsible for her care.) The overall goal of this project was to determine risk factors for contracting malaria, and we were able to offer the community the benefit of yearly feedback of all the results about the likely infectivity of their local mosquito population, before the next transmission season.

CONSENTING PARTNERS

These three experiences show how different the informed consent process needs to be in different places in the world. For one thing, the issue of who "signs off" on consent must be carefully considered. Informed consent in Europe and in North America usually involves written documents, which the prospective volunteer must read and sign in order to participate in a study. The emphasis is on the autonomy of individuals.

In some developing countries, however, individual and community consent are part of the same process. We cannot separate them in our countries, and this reality should be understood by sponsors and funding agencies and northern research institutions. We need to think about the protection, safety, risks, and benefits of individuals and of the community at large. We have learned in particular that the initial focus and discussion should be with the leaders of the community, rather than individuals. By approaching individuals first, one is likely to introduce social conflict in the village, and this could be unethical.

Another challenge is the need to document the consent process using a signed document. At the beginning of our TMRC projects, the villagers we approached were opposed to signing any document, because they strongly believed that "they gave their words" and that that should be sufficient. It took very careful explanation and patience to overcome this resistance. Informed consent must be based on a thorough understanding of the society in which the study is to take place. For outsiders, the role of local guides, local investigators, and socio-anthropologists is critical.

Documents and legal language also pose difficulties. One of them is that in developed countries, the heavy use of legal language and documents makes it increasingly difficult and murky for participants to discern the risks and benefits of participating in studies. The goal of these legal documents seems to have more to do with protecting the investigators and sponsors than the volunteers. What's more, legal language is hard enough for a highly educated person to understand. In Mali, less than 20% of adults are literate, so written documents can easily discourage rural populations from participating in studies. Also, for rural communities, paper often means trouble with the government.

From both ethical and biological standpoints, the particular case of pregnant women needs special attention. In Malian traditional communities there is a very good but discreet representation of women in decisions concerning the village's affairs. Foreign researchers may overlook this important involvement of women and thereby lose the confidence of the community. Similar decision-making subtleties go with enrolling children in medical trials.

In the developed countries, children normally are excluded from medical trials of new medicines, but in Africa we have to test products on children because the target populations for malaria and many infectious diseases are children and pregnant women. It can be especially challenging to convince the community that it ultimately is in its best interest to allow children to participate in trials that could have widespread medical benefits in the future.

One way to earn the confidence of the community is to provide medical care for the community while the study is being conducted. In rural regions of developing countries where medical care is limited or nonexistent, the research team often has to set up its own clinic. Providing standard care for both study participants and others in the community during a research project where the team is the sole source of medical care can be a form of community compensation. Almost all studies in developing countries should guarantee care for volunteers who experience serious adverse events during the study and after it has been completed. Care must be taken to ensure that the provision of these services, and the establishment of a clinic, do not induce the community to participate in the study when in fact it might not be in the community's interest to do so. This ethical dilemma is not yet solved and remains a big concern.

The challenge of obtaining informed consent for medical research from communities in developing countries can be daunting, especially from rural and mostly illiterate populations in rural regions. Even so, our 15 years of international research experience in dealing with these complex issues of informed consent in Mali shows that these difficulties can be overcome in a way that benefits medical science and public health.

NOTES

*O. Doumbo, Multilateral Initiative on Malaria (MIM), Durban, South Africa, March 1999.

†Y.T. Touré et al., Am. J. Trop. Med. Hyg. **59**, 481 (1998).

‡K. Kayentao et al., J. Infect. Dis. **191**, 109 (2005).

HIV/AIDS Clinical Research, and the Claims of Beneficence, Justice, and Integrity

Deborah Zion

INTRODUCTION

In a recent edition of the *Medical Journal of Australia*, Greg Dore and David Cooper called on persons in developed nations like Australia to bridge the divide between resource-rich countries to nations in the developing world, where therapies to ease or halt the ravages of the virus are nonexistent or in short supply.[1]

Indeed, Rob Moodie has suggested that HIV is an issue that pertains above all to development. He states:

> In sub-Saharan Africa, the single most important risk factor for women is simply being married. For young women in rural Thailand and Laos or Myanmar, the main risk factor is being poor. (p. 6)[2]

HIV is a disease that reveals much to us about both the best and worst of human behavior. About manly courage among gay men, many of whom were themselves unwell, but who cared compassionately for their friends, while establishing sophisticated mechanisms to supply treatment and halt the spread of the disease. But it also reveals the worst, as the virus spreads most rapidly among disempowered persons.

When we consider the world of HIV medical research, we also see the best of ethical practice and, conversely, studies that must be described as ethically questionable. The purpose of this paper is to ask two questions:

1. On what basis can we ground duties that some or all persons here might have toward persons who are participants in HIV clinical trials in the developing world?
2. If we can, how can we go about fulfilling our obligations toward them?

Before I attempt to answer these questions, I want to establish why I think that a great deal of the research in question is, at best, ethically questionable. To do so, I will briefly look at two recent trials that epitomize what is wrong with HIV clinical research in the developing world.

RAKAI

The first of the trials in question took place in the Rakai district of Uganda. There were two objectives:

1. to see how other kinds of sexually transmitted diseases affected HIV transmission in heterosexual couples
2. to see how HIV transmission was affected by viral load.[3]

To test these hypotheses, a cluster of 10 villages in the Rakai district of Uganda were selected, and within them 415 couples, in which one partner was negative and the other positive. Investigators gave residents of five of the 10 villages antibiotic treatment every 10 months, whereas the persons in the control group were given an anthelmintic drug, an iron-folate tablet, and from the second survey round, a single low-dose vitamin pill.[4] At the same time, viral load was monitored and correlated with the rate of new infection. Participants in the trial were provided with condoms and safe sex counseling.

WHAT THEN IS UNETHICAL ABOUT THESE TRIALS?

Subjects who were HIV positive were observed for up to 30 months but not treated. Seropositive partners were interviewed but not informed of their partners' serostatus. Finally, those in the control arm who had treatable sexually transmitted diseases were left to seek their own treatment.[5] But most importantly, the results of the second part of the trial—that the level of viral load has a direct bearing on the rate of new infections—is of absolutely no use to the subjects of the study or their communities, as they cannot afford treatments that will halt the virus or reduce its levels. This trial, on the other hand, is of great use to people in developed countries, where effective antiretroviral treatment is available.

A trial of this kind could not be carried out in a developed country, where a fatal but treatable illness— be it HIV or syphilis—would have had to be treated as part of the trial. But when investigators can rely on the best local standards of treatment, the way is left open for trials that exploit populations in developing countries for the good of the developed world.

THE MOMBASSA NON-OXYNOL 9 PHASE 3 PREVENTATIVE TRIAL

In early 1997, the World Health Organization began a phase 3 trial of vaginal gels to determine their effect in lowering the transmission of HIV among women in Kenya.[6] Consent was obtained from the largely illiterate population. The trial was a double-blind placebo controlled trial, and organizers relied on providing treatment to participants at the best local standard rather than the best international standard. One investigator wrote:

> Anti-retroviral therapy is not routinely available in Kenya. We provide a basic level of primary care to all women in the trial. As the women who acquire HIV-1 are recent seroconverters, they are not yet having HIV related illnesses.[7]

Given that a placebo was used, it is clear that, even if the gels had proved to be 100 percent efficacious, some people would have contracted HIV, for which no treatment was then offered to them. Clinical researchers, however, relied on the idea that the participants were personally responsible for their exposure to the virus, as they received counseling about the importance of condoms, and the condoms most liked by the women were provided free of charge. Women kept a coitel log, on which the use of gel and condoms was recorded. Women who were inconsistent in gel and condom use were counseled to use gels and condoms at each sexual encounter.[8]

Despite these interventions, it is clear that cultural practices and economic desperation undermined the provision of condoms. In a recent study, Jackson et al. implied that African women do not receive much cooperation concerning the use of condoms.[9] Their study also points out that "seropositive male partners may be less likely to use condoms if they knew that the woman was participating in a vaccine trial."[10] This last point is particularly pertinent to the argument that being on a trial could actually increase the risk of infection. As well, recent research suggests that the product in question actually increased the women's chances of contracting the virus, as the gel seems to contribute to the development of lesions.[11]

SUMMARY OF ETHICAL PROBLEMS

- The trials exploited the desperation of subjects.
- The trials, although applying a formal definition of informed consent, did not take into account a different understanding of the fallibility of Western medicine.
- They did not take into account the power structures inherent within the communities in question, particularly as related to gender.
- The trials produced results that were more applicable for the Western world than the trial population (Rakai).
- The trials actually increased the risk of HIV transmission for some participants, without backup care being offered to them (non-oxynol 9).

THE DUTY OF BENEFICENCE

Let me return to my original questions. How can we establish that we owe anything to persons taking part in such trials? If we can establish such a claim, what is it that we should do? On whom should they fall? To answer these questions I will begin with a discussion of the duty of beneficence.

In his formulation of the duty of beneficence, Peter Singer suggests that:

> if it is in our power to prevent something bad from happening, without thereby sacrificing anything of comparable moral importance, we ought, morally, to do it. (p. 28)[12]

If, for example, we see a child drowning in a shallow pond and have only to sacrifice a few minutes and the slight inconvenience of wet clothes, then we have a duty to give assistance. Singer uses this example as a kind of paradigm, suggesting that in many other situations, such as helping the severely impoverished, rendering aid would cost as little effort, and do as much good, as rescuing the drowning child.

Singer is responding to the assertion that "charity begins at home"—that is, the argument that people close to us either physically or emotionally have some special claim. He argues, on the contrary, that particular attachments of this kind are irrelevant when considering our obligations to others. The only important issue, according to Singer, is that our rendering assistance does not exacerbate a bad situation or in itself bring about comparable harm.

Singer's "obligation to assist"[13] has been criticized by many on the basis that it is unrealistically overdemanding.[14] John Arthur, for example, suggests that Singer's formulation produces a duty for healthy people to donate one eye or one kidney, on the grounds that the inconvenience caused to the donating agent is seriously outweighed by the good such organs might do to the blind or dying. What is problematic about this kind of argument is best summed up by Michael Slote, in his discussion of Singer's "duty to assist" when he suggests that persons should not have their major life plans disrupted by the duty to help others.[15] Slote's limitation of the duty makes more sense if we consider the lives of the moderately well off than if we apply it to exploitative millionaires. However, his point—that limits must be set to beneficence—is significant.

THE DUTY OF BENEFICENCE AND COLLECTIVITY

How then do we set such limits when considering what we might owe others? The bioethicists Beauchamp and Childress respond to the excessive burden objection in their formulation of the duty of beneficence by discussing the way in which *collectivity* is an important factor in fulfilling the obligation to help others, pointing out that group action both lessens the burden on each

individual and also increases the chance that the action undertaken will actually make some difference.

The importance of collective action is also central to Robert Goodin's work *Protecting the Vulnerable*, especially in his discussion of foreign aid and world hunger.[16] He suggests that personal donations to schemes that target individuals like "sponsor a child" do not take into account the massive restructuring that is needed in impoverished communities. Thus, Goodin contends that, when considering aid to the severely impoverished, giving money is not enough—individuals must also engage in political action to organize efficacious schemes.[17] The main advantages of collective action are, therefore, efficacy and an easing of the burden on individual donors, thus once again answering to some degree the "overdemandingness" objection.

The relationship between collectivity and the duty of beneficence is particularly significant because the problems raised by HIV/AIDS trials in developing countries are not limited to research alone and do indeed have the potential to impose a significant burden. I suggest that chronic poverty, and in many cases the lack of political freedoms, meant that a considerable number of subjects were deprived of basic rights and were thus easily exploitable. If we consider Singer's account, then it is easy to establish a duty to donate aid that is logically prior to any obligation that might be engendered by the trials themselves, in the same way that we might have a duty to help any chronically impoverished and deprived population. In the creation of a just world, where basic rights were intact, many of the problems that vex clinical trials would cease to exist. The question of the need to create a more equitable world, however, distracts us from specific problems that beset clinical trials and the important ways in which specific groups of people might respond to them. Without such a focus, the ongoing issues of exploitation of research subjects might be lost among claims that relate to other kinds of deprivation.

JUSTICE

Singer's work alerts us to the possibility of a different way of functioning in the world, whereas writers like Goodin show us that collective action might resolve some of the "overdemandingness" objection. However, if we focus on issues related to justice, we might see more clearly why some of us might have specific duties to those engaged in the trials in question and what they might look like.

The political philosopher Kok-Chor Tan suggests that "[t]he intricate economic, social, and political interdependencies of the global community draw virtually everyone, some more deeply than others, into social arrangements with each other" (p. 62).[18]

In the case of HIV/AIDS clinical trials, I have already argued that decisions made in the developed world have an important part to play in the ongoing development of unethical research, particularly patents and generic antiretroviral therapy. It follows, then, that those who have benefited from such research have a duty to redress the imbalance that such involvement has caused. Tan, for example, suggests that, if I witness a bank robbery and the thief hands me a wad of $100 bills, I have gained from an unjust act, even though I was neither involved in the robbery nor its intended beneficiary.

This argument is significant in the case of HIV/AIDS trials under discussion, not only because those using the results in question benefit but also because their use of the results—in some cases—is an incentive for such research to continue. Before we can draw such a conclusion, however, we must examine carefully the issue of justice as it is related to HIV/AIDS research and consider some competing formulations of justice that challenge the assumption that there are indeed grounds for the existence of such claims.

JUSTICE: THE PROBLEM OF DISTRIBUTION

Many formulations of justice are pertinent to HIV/AIDS research. One of the most significant is that which Allen Buchanan refers to as "justice as fair reciprocity."[19] According to this version of justice, we are entitled to social resources only if we can contribute to the cooperative surplus.[20] Thus, by this account, severely disabled persons, for example, would not be entitled to be allocated resources, as they would never be in a position to enter into schemes that might generate goods.

Other formulations of justice pertinent to clinical trials in developing countries rely on the idea that justice can be equated with compensating people for ill fortune.[21] As Richard Arneson suggests:

The concern of distributive justice is to compensate individuals for misfortune. Some people are blessed with good luck, some are cursed with bad luck, and it is the responsibility of society—all of us regarded collectively—to alter the distribution of goods and evils that arises from the jumble of lotteries that constitute human life as we know it.[22]

This view of justice as fair distribution is based on the work of John Rawls and has at its heart the idea that persons have intrinsic moral worth and entitlements, regardless of their actual or potential contributions. Central to Rawls's formulation of justice as fairness is the creation of a level playing field, on which equitable relationships can be built. He states:

All social primary goods—liberty and opportunity, income and wealth, and the bases of self-respect—are to be distributed equally unless an unequal distribution of any or all of these goods is to the advantage of the least favoured.[23]

In many situations, justice as fair reciprocity and the allocation of goods based on a system of equitable distribution can coexist. Buchanan points out that the generation of special rights might come about "through voluntary participation in cooperative schemes."[24] That is, everyone would be entitled to basic rights simply by virtue of personhood, and reciprocal rights when they entered into certain schemes.

When we consider the guidelines that govern clinical trials, we see both of these versions of justice. For example, the Committee for International Organization of Medical Sciences (CIOMS) guideline 10 states that:

Individuals or communities to be invited to be subjects of research will be selected in such a way that the burdens and benefits of the research will be equally distributed. Special justification is required for inviting vulnerable individuals, and if they are selected, the means of protecting their rights and welfare must be particularly strictly applied. (p. 600)[25]

This particular guideline sought to redress the exploitative practice of using vulnerable populations, such as prisoners, to test therapies that were to be used by others. It also states that, should such persons become research subjects, they must share in the goods created through their participation. However, what is not clearly explained in the CIOMS guidelines is that justice as fair reciprocity—a share in the profits of an enterprise—is not a substitute for the kinds of basic rights that help to ensure that such trials do not exploit the subjects taking part in them in the first place. Nor does it ensure that research is carried out so that clinical investigators know exactly which rights and goods participants consider to be important. Significantly, there are almost no follow-up studies that are routinely done after clinical trials.

If the claims of justice cannot be met by simply repaying subjects for their participation with drugs that have been developed by the trials in which they have been involved, then my original questions need further attention; that is, what obligations and duties might persons in a first world country like Australia have toward those involved in HIV/AIDS research in the developing world? To whom might these duties apply?

NEGATIVE AND POSITIVE DUTIES

In the first instance, those who have profited from unfair bargains in the production of HIV/AIDS drugs can be seen to have a particular duty. Kok-Chor Tan suggests that Kantian duties based on justice can be extended to "preventing pending violations."[26] He states:

> Because everyone is inadvertently a participant in an economic bargaining scheme and some of these participants are particularly vulnerable to coercion and deception, there is a duty of justice on the part of other participants to render them less vulnerable to coercion and deception.[27]

This view of justice is somewhat different from the idea of redressing past wrongs. Instead, it bears some resemblance to the idea of "subject centred justice,"[28] as expressed by writers like John Rawls. In particular, Tan seems to be suggesting that it is incumbent on everyone to create a just foundation on which other enterprises can be negotiated. The kinds of positive duties that we might have then would be to ensure that all enterprises in which we were involved *began* on a just basis.

In a similar vein, the political theorist Henry Shue describes the way in which collectivity might also give claims based on justice more force. Although negative duties—that is, duties not to harm others—are relatively easy to maintain, positive duties, according to Shue, require some "division of labour."[29] One reason for this is to do with the "overdemandingness" objection that I discussed in relation to the Utilitarian formulation of the duty of beneficence. Another is the degree of efficacy that institutions can achieve in fulfilling basic needs. However, Shue goes further. He also describes an important relationship between institutions and the fulfilment of positive duties through the story of two men, Benny and Al. Benny is relatively wealthy, whereas Al is deprived of the most basic of rights and goods. In his commentary on their situation, Shue asks the important question: why should Benny, who shares neither culture nor any institutions with Al, have a duty to protect and fulfill his rights?[30]

Shue's answer to this question is that these two men do indeed share crude and primitive institutions connected to the global economy. However, these institutions do not assign rights and duties. According to Shue, individuals therefore have duties "for the design and creation of positive-duty-performing institutions" in order for rights to be fulfilled.[31]

The idea that there might be some duty to create "mediating institutions" is an important one when we consider HIV/AIDS research.[32] It might create a duty for those involved in the research at every level and those who use the drugs created by it. In particular, those involved in conducting pretrial research into the communities from which subjects could be drawn, as well as the medical researchers, might be seen to have particular duties to *create* mechanisms through which some problems relating to vulnerability might be addressed. Moreover, the rights of subjects should be protected, and issues related to justice addressed before and after the commencement of clinical trials. Tessa Tan-Torres Edejer puts it as follows:

> Increasingly, there is an awareness that the success of North-South research collaboration should not be judged solely on the results of scientific research activities. This awareness must be coupled with a learning approach to create a sustainable, mutually beneficial working relationship, that aside from advancing science must address inequity and put local priorities first, develop capacity with a long term perspective and preserve the dignity of local people by ensuring that the benefits of research will truly uplift their status.[33]

A discussion of the kinds of claims justice might generate help us to not only define more specifically the nature of claims but go some way to fulfilling them. I want briefly to add a final argument and illustrate it with a case study. This argument relates to integrity and shows us why some persons might feel particular duties to the research subjects under discussion.

AFAO AND BANGKOK HIV PREVENTATIVE VACCINE PREPARATION

In 2003 the Australian federation of AIDS organizations received a commission from NIH to run the social research arm of the HIV preventative phase 2 trial that will start shortly in Bangkok. It seems that this kind of organization has particularly strong duties to make sure that the trial in question is ethical—duties that are, in fact, reflected in the care that they are taking to involve genuine community representatives and ensure distribution of any drugs produced.

Why, then, is the issue of integrity particularly important in relation to AFAO? Those working for this organization are accountable to many activist groups who have been involved in negotiating new ways to conduct HIV/AIDS clinical trials in which research subjects were able to enter into a just partnership with clinical investigators. Therefore, it would seem inconsistent for persons engaged in creating such a research tradition to fail to apply its principles elsewhere.[34] The kind of integrity I am talking about is reliant on the work of Cheshire Calhoun. Calhoun talks about integrity as both an interactive and a social virtue, rather than merely a personal one.

According to Calhoun, integrity is a social virtue because when a subject sticks by her best judgment about "what is worth doing" she stands for something. Thus, "[h]er standing for something is not just something she does for herself. She takes a stand for, and before, all deliberators who share her goal of determining what is worth doing" (p. 257).[35] Central to Calhoun's argument is also the idea that a person who acts with integrity must treat others' best judgments in the same way. She suggests that "[i]ntegrity calls us simultaneously to stand behind our convictions and to take seriously others' doubts about them."[36]

This view seems important because it is also directive about *how* to act. That is, to act with integrity on this definition and in this context is to enter into a true negotiation with research subjects, so that they can reveal exactly which rights and goods they consider to be important. In this way, we move toward a view of justice that is reliant not on goods but on empowering all persons engaged in the research process. As the philosopher Elizabeth Anderson puts it:

> The proper negative aim of equalitarian justice is not to eliminate the impact of brute bad luck from human affairs, but to end oppression, which by definition is socially imposed. Its proper positive aim is not to ensure that everyone gets what they morally deserve, but to create a community in which people stand in relations of equality to others.[37]

NOTES

1. Dore G, Cooper D. Bridging the divide: global inequalities in access to HIV/AIDS therapy. *Medical Journal of Australia* 2001;175:570–2.

2. Moodie R. Should HIV be on the development agenda? *Development Bulletin* 2000;52:6–8.

3. Quinn TC, Wawer MJ, Sewankambo N, Serwadda D, Li C, Wabwire-Mangen F et al. Viral load and heterosexual transmission of human immunodeficiency virus type 1. *New England Journal of Medicine* 2000;342:921–9. See also: Wawer MJ, Sewankambo NK, Serwadda D. Quinn TC, Paxton LA, Kiwanuka N et al. Control of sexually transmitted diseases for AIDS prevention in Uganda: a randomised community trial. *Lancet* 1999;353(9512):525–35. For commentaries on this trial, see: Angell M. Investigator's responsibilities for human subjects in developing countries. *New England Journal of Medicine* 2000;342(13)967–9; and Groopman J. In an AIDS study, the devil is in the details. *New York Times* 2 Apr 2000.

4. See note 3, Wawer, Sewankambo, Serwadda, Quinn, Paxton, Kiwannka et al. 1999; see note 3, Quinn, Wawer, Sewankambo, Serwadda, Li, Wabwire-Mangen et al 2000:921; see note 3, Angell 2000:967.

5. See note 3, Angell 2000:967.

6. See: Zion D. "Moral taint" or ethical responsibility? unethical information and the problem of HIV clinical trials in developing countries. *Journal of Applied Philosophy* 1998;15(3):231–41.

7. Personal correspondence from Hal Martin, clinical investigator, non-oxynol 9 trial, Kenya, University of Washington. 11 Feb 1997.

8. See note 7, Martin 1997.

9. Jackson DJ, Martin H Jr, Bwayo J, Nyange P, Rakwar J, Kashonga F et al. Acceptability of HIV vaccine trials in high-risk heterosexual cohorts in Mombassa, Kenya. *AIDS* 1995;9(11):1279–83, at 1282.

10. See note 9, Jackson, Martin, Bwayo, Nyange, Rakwar, Kashonga et al. 1995:1282.

11. Microbicide may increase risk of HIV. *Business Day* 13 Jul 2000.

12. Singer P. Famine, affluence, and morality. In: Aiken W, LaFollette H, eds. *World Hunger and Morality*, 2nd ed. Englewood Cliffs, NJ: Prentice Hall; 1996:26–38.

13. Singer P. *Practical Ethics.* New York: Cambridge University Press; 1979:128ff. See also: Beauchamp TL, Childress J. *Principles of Biomedical Ethics*, 3rd. ed. New York: Oxford University Press, 1989.

14. Arthur J. Rights and the duty to bring aid. In: Aiken W, LaFollette H, eds. *World Hunger and Morality*, 2nd ed. Englewood Cliffs, NJ: Prentice Hall; 1996:39–50, at 43–4.

15. Slote M. The morality of wealth. In: Aiken W, LaFollette H, eds. *World Hunger and Moral Obligation.* Englewood Cliffs, NJ: Prentice Hall; 1977:124–47, at 125–7.

16. Goodin R. *Protecting the Vulnerable: A Reanalysis of Our Social Responsibilities.* Chicago: University of Chicago Press; 1985:163.

17. See note 16, Goodin 1985:164.

18. Tan KC. Kantian ethics and global justice. *Social Theory and Practice* 1997;23(1):53–73. See also: Shue H. Mediating duties. *Ethics* 1988;98:687–704, at 693.

19. Buchanan A. Justice as reciprocity versus subject centred justice. *Philosophy and Public Affairs* 1990;19(3):227–52, at 229–31.

20. See note 19, Buchanan 1990:230.

21. Buchanan refers to this as "subject centred justice." See note 19, Buchanan 1990:230.

22. Arneson R. Rawls, responsibility, and distributive justice. In: Salles M, Weymark JA, eds. *Justice, Political Liberalism, and Utilitarianism; Themes front Harsanyi and Rawls.* New York: Cambridge University Press; forthcoming. Quoted in: Anderson ES. What is the point of equality? *Ethics* 1999;109(2):287–337. See also; Rawls J. *A Theory of Justice.* Cambridge, MA: Harvard University Press; 1971:100–4, see also: Anderson 1999.

23. See note 22, Rawls 1971:303.

24. See note 19, Buchanan 1990:231.

25. CIOMS, WHO. International ethical guidelines for biomedical research involving human subjects. In: Arras J, Steinbock B, eds. *Ethical Issues in Modern Medicine*, 5th ed. Mountain View, CA: Mayfield Publishing; 1999:597–601.

26. See note 18, Tan 1997:66.

27. See note 18, Tan 1997.

28. This term is Allen Buchanan's. See note 19, Buchanan 1990.

29. See note 18, Shue 1988:690.

30. See note 18, Shue 1988:700–4.

31. See note 18, Shue 1988:703.

32. In fact, I am suggesting that the trials themselves, if properly designed, become mediating institutions. For an example of how this could be achieved, see: Edejer TTT. North-South research partnerships: the ethics of carrying out research in developing countries. *BMJ* 1999;319:438–41.

33. See note 32, Edejer 1999:440.

34. A similar example relates to the action of the AIDS Healthcare Foundation, one of the largest providers of specialized AIDS care in the United States. It says that it will bar GlaxoSmithKline from marketing drugs at its outpatient sites, in protest against the company's pricing policy. The foundation claims that the drug manufacturer still charges twice as much as its competitors for drugs in the developing world. See: Avery S. AIDS group bars Glaxo marketing. *Los Angeles Times* 2002 May 28; home ed. C3.

35. Calhoun C. Standing for something. *Journal of Philosophy* 1995;92(5):235–61.

36. See note 35, Calhoun 1995:260.

37. See note 22, Anderson 1999:288–9.

Moral Standards for Research in Developing Countries From "Reasonable Availability" to "Fair Benefits"

The Participants in the 2001 Conference on Ethical Aspects of Research in Developing Countries

Over the last decade, clinical research conducted by sponsors and researchers from developed countries in developing countries has grown very controversial.[1] The perinatal HIV transmission studies that were sponsored by the National Institutes of Health and the Centers for Disease Control and conducted in Southeast Asia and Africa inflamed this controversy and focused it on the standard of care—that is, on whether treatments tested in developing countries should be compared to the treatments provided locally or to the best interventions available anywhere.[2] Since then, this debate has expanded to include concerns about informed consent.

A subject that has received less discussion but is potentially even more important is the requirement that any drugs proven effective in the trial be made available to the host population after the trial.[3] There seems to be general agreement that "reasonable availability" is necessary in order to ensure that the subject population is not exploited.

This consensus is mistaken, however. A "fair benefits" framework offers a more reliable and justifiable way to avoid exploitation. In this paper we develop the argument for the fair benefits framework in detail and compare the two approaches in a specific case—the trial of hepatitis A vaccine in Thailand.

CURRENT VIEWS ON THE REASONABLE AVAILABILITY REQUIREMENT

The idea of making interventions reasonably available was emphasized in the *International Ethical Guidelines* issued in 1993 by the Council for International Organizations of Medical Sciences (CIOMS), and it was reiterated in the 2002 revision in Guideline 10 and its commentary.

As a general rule, the sponsoring agency should agree in advance of the research that any product developed through such research will be made reasonably available to the inhabitants of the host community or country at the completion of successful testing. Exceptions to this general requirement should be justified and agreed to by all concerned parties before the research begins.[4]

Four issues have generated disagreement. First, how strong or explicit should the commitment to provide the drug or vaccine be at the initiation of the research trial? CIOMS required an explicit, contract-like mechanism, agreed to before the trial, and it assigns this responsibility to the sponsors of research. The Declaration of Helsinki's 2000 revision endorses a less stringent guarantee that does not require availability of interventions to be "ensured" "in advance."[5] Several other ethical guidelines suggest "discussion in advance" but do not require formal, prior agreements.[6] Conversely, some commentators insist that the CIOMS guarantee is "not strong or specific enough."[7] For instance, the chair and executive director of the U.S. National Bioethics Advisory Commission (NBAC) contended:

> If the intervention being tested is not likely to be affordable in the host country or if the health care infrastructure cannot support its proper distribution and use, it is unethical to ask persons in that country to participate in the research, since they will not enjoy any of its potential benefits.[8]

To address these concerns, others advocate that research in developing countries ethically requires a formal and explicit prior agreement that "includes identified funding" and specifies improvements necessary in the "country's health care delivery capabilities."[9]

The second area of disagreement has concerned who is responsible for ensuring reasonable availability. Are sponsors responsible, as the original CIOMS

The Participants in the 2001 Conference on Ethical Aspects of Research in Developing Countries, "Moral Standards for Research in Developing Countries: From 'Reasonable Availability' to 'Fair Benefits,'" *Hastings Center Report* 34:3 (2004), 17–27. Copyright © 2004. Reprinted by permission of The Hastings Center.

guideline called for? Does responsibility rest with host country governments? Or international aid organizations? The third area of disagreement focuses on what it means for drugs to be made reasonably available. Does it require that the drug or vaccine be free, subsidized, or at market prices?

Finally, to whom should interventions be made reasonably available? Should they be restricted to participants in the research study? Should they include the village or tribe from which individual participants were enrolled? Or the whole country in which the research was conducted?

THE JUSTIFICATION OF REASONABLE AVAILABILITY

Why is reasonable availability thought to be a requirement for ethical research in developing countries? Research uses participants to develop generalizable knowledge that can improve health and health care for others.[10] The potential for exploitation of individual participants enrolled in research as well as communities that support and bear the burdens of research is inherent in every research trial. Historically, favorable risk-benefit ratios, informed consent, and respect for enrolled participants have been the primary mechanisms for minimizing the potential exploitation of individual research participants.[11] In developed countries, exploitation of populations has been a less significant concern because there is a process, albeit an imperfect one, for ensuring that interventions proven effective through clinical research are introduced into the health care system and benefit the general population.[12] In contrast, the potential for exploitation is acute in research trials in developing countries. Target populations may lack access to regular health care, political power, and an understanding of research. Hence, they may be exposed to the risks of research with few tangible benefits. The benefits of research—access to new effective drugs and vaccines—may be predominantly for people in developed countries with profits to the pharmaceutical industry. Many consider this scenario the quintessential case of exploitation.[13]

Supporters deem that reasonable availability is necessary to prevent such exploitation of communities. As one group of commentators put it:

> [I]n order for research to be ethically conducted [in a developing country] it must offer the potential of actual benefit to the inhabitants of that developing country....[F]or underdeveloped communities to derive potential benefit from research, they must have access to the *fruits* of such research.[14] (emphasis added)

Or as the commentary to the 2002 CIOMS Guideline 10 put it:

> [I]f the knowledge gained from the research in such a country [with limited resources] is used primarily for the benefit of populations that can afford the tested product, the research may rightly be characterized as exploitative and, therefore, unethical.[15]

WHAT IS EXPLOITATION?

Even though it seems initially plausible, there are a number of problems with making reasonable availability a necessary ethical requirement for multinational research in developing countries. The most important problem is that the reasonable availability requirement embodies a mistaken conception of exploitation and therefore offers wrong solution to the problem of exploitation.

There are numerous ways of harming other individuals, only one of which is exploitation. Oppression, coercion, assault, deception, betrayal, and discrimination are all distinct ways of harming people. They are frequently all conflated and confused with exploitation.[16] One reason for distinguishing these different wrongs is that they require very different remedies. Addressing coercion requires removing threats, and addressing deception requires full disclosure, yet removing threats and requiring full disclosure will not necessarily prevent exploitation.

What is exploitation? In the useful analysis developed by Alan Wertheimer, Party A exploits party B when B receives an unfair level of benefits as a result of B's interactions with A.[17] Whether B's benefits are fair depends upon the burdens that B bears as part of the interaction and the benefits that A and others receive as a result of B's participation in the interaction. If B runs his car into a snow bank and A offers to tow him out but only at the cost of $200—when the normal and fair price for the tow is $75—then A exploits B.

Wertheimer's conception of exploitation is distinct from the conventional idea that exploitation entails the "use" of someone else for one's own benefit. There are many problems with this familiar conception. Most importantly, if exploitation is made to depend only on instrumental use of another person, then almost all human interactions are exploitative. We constantly and necessarily use other people.[18] In the example above, not only does A exploit B, but B also exploits A, because B uses A to get his car out of the snow bank. Sometimes the word "exploit" refers to a *neutral* use—as when we say that a person exploited the minerals or his own strength. However, in discussions of research, especially but not exclusively when the research occurs in developing countries, exploitation is never neutral; it is always a moral wrong. Consequently, we do not need to mark out all cases of use. We need only to identify those that are morally problematic.[19]

The Wertheimerian conception of exploitation also departs from the commonly cited Kantian conception. As Allan Buchanan characterizes the Kantian conception, "To exploit a person involves the *harmful, merely instrumental utilization* of him or his capacities, for one's own advantage or for the sake of one's own ends."[20] The Kantian conception of exploitation seems to expand beyond use to include a separate harm. But in the case of exploitation, what is this "other harm"? For a Kantian, *to exploit* must mean to use in a way that the other person could not consent to, a way that undermines their autonomy.[21] However in many cases, people consent—with full knowledge and without threats—and yet we think they are exploited. People in developing countries could consent to being on a research study after full informed consent and still be exploited. Similarly, snow bank-bound B seems exploited even if he consents to being towed out for $200. Thus the Kantian conception seems mistaken in fusing exploitation with inadequate consent.

In any event, the reasonable availability requirement is not grounded in Kantian claims about use and violation of autonomy. Rather, it is aimed at ensuring that people have access to the interventions that they helped to demonstrate were effective. It is related to the benefits people receive from participating in a research study, not to their autonomy in consent. Consequently, whatever the merits of the Kantian conception of exploitation, it seems irrelevant to deciding whether making the trial intervention reasonably available can prevent exploitation. In contrast, the Wertheimerian view, which locates the core moral issue inherent in exploitation in the fair level of benefits each party of an interaction receives, captures the ethical concern underlying the reasonable availability requirement.

In determining whether exploitation has occurred in any case, the Wertheimerian conception gives us at least six important considerations to bear in mind. First, exploitation is a micro-level concern. Exploitation is about harms from discrete interactions, rather than about the larger social justice of the distribution of background rights and resources. Certainly macro-level distributions of resources can influence exploitation, but the actual exploitation is distinct. Furthermore, while past events may lead people to feel and claim that they have been exploited, whether exploitation occurred does not depend either on their feelings or on historical injustices. Exploitation is about the fairness of an individual exchange. Indeed, as we shall note below, exploitation can happen even in a just society, and it can fail to occur even when there is gross inequality between the parties. As Wertheimer argues:

> [W]hile the background conditions shape our existence, the primary experiences occur at the micro-level. Exploitation matters to people. People who can accept an unjust set of aggregate resources with considerable equanimity will recoil when they feel exploited in an individual or local transaction.... Furthermore, micro-level exploitation is not as closely linked to macro-level injustice as might be thought. Even in a reasonably just society, people will find themselves in situations [that] will give rise to allegations of exploitation.[22]

The reasonable availability requirement recognizes the possibility of exploitation associated with a particular study, and it does not require ensuring the just distribution of all rights and resources or a just international social order. This is more than just a pragmatic point; it reflects the deep experience that exploitation is transactional.

Second, because exploitation is about interactions at a micro-level, between researcher and community, it can occur only once an interaction is initiated. In this sense, the obligations to avoid exploitation are obligations that coexist with initiating an interaction.

Third, exploitation is about "how much," not "what," each party receives. The key issue is fairness in the level of benefits. Moreover, exploitation depends upon fairness, not "equalness." An unequal distribution of benefits may be fair if there are differences in the burdens and contributions of each party. Fairness in the distribution of benefits is common to both Wertheimer's theory of exploitation and Rawls's theory of justice, but the notion of fairness important for exploitation is not Rawlsian. They differ in that Rawls addresses macro- and Wertheimer micro-level distributions of benefits. The Rawlsian conception of fairness addresses the distribution of rights, liberties, and resources for the basic structure of society within which individual transactions occur.[23] In other words, Rawlsian fairness is about constitutional arrangements, taxes, and opportunities. Rawls's conception has often but wrongly been applied to micro-level decisions, where it usually issues in implausible and indefensible recommendations. Fairness in individual interactions, which is the concern of exploitation, is based on ideal market transactions.[24] Thus a fair distribution of benefits at the micro-level is based on the level of benefits that would occur in a market transaction devoid of fraud, deception, or force, in which the parties have full information. While this is always idealized—in just the way that economic theory is idealized—it is the powerful ideal informing the notion of fairness of micro-level transactions. This notion of fairness is also relative: just as fair price in a market is based on comparability, so too is the determination of fair benefits based on comparisons to the level of benefits received by other parties interacting in similar circumstances.

Fourth, that one party is vulnerable may make exploitation more likely, but does not inherently entail exploitation. Since exploitation involves the distribution of benefits and burdens, vulnerability is neither necessary nor sufficient for its occurrence. The status of the parties is irrelevant in determining whether exploitation has occurred. If the exchange is fair to both parties, then no one is exploited, regardless of whether one party is poor, uneducated, or otherwise vulnerable and disadvantaged. In the case of snowbound B, if A charges B $75 for towing the car out, then B is not exploited even though B is vulnerable.

Fifth, since exploitation is about the fairness of micro-level interactions, the key question is the level of benefits provided to the parties *who interact*. Determining whether exploitation has occurred does not involve weighing the benefits received by people who do not participate in the interaction.

Finally, because fairness depends on idealized market transactions, determining when exploitation occurs—when the level of benefits is unfair—will require interpretation. As with the application of legal principles and constitutional provisions, the inevitability of interpretation means that reasonable people can and will disagree. But such interpretation and controversy does not invalidate either judicial or moral judgments.

PROBLEMS WITH THE REASONABLE AVAILABILITY REQUIREMENT

The fundamental problem with the reasonable availability standard is that it guarantees a benefit—the proven intervention—but not a *fair level* of benefits, and therefore it does not necessarily prevent exploitation. Reasonable availability focuses on *what*—the products of research—but exploitation requires addressing *how much*—the level of benefit. For some research in which either the subjects would be exposed to great risks or the sponsor stands to gain enormously, reasonable availability might be inadequate and unfair. Conversely, for very low- or no-risk research in which the population would obtain other benefits, or in which the benefits to the sponsor are minimal, requiring the sponsor to make a product reasonably available could be excessive and unfair.

There are also other problems with the reasonable availability standard. First, it embodies a very narrow notion of benefits. It suggests that only one type of benefit—a proven intervention—can justify participation in clinical research. But a population in a developing country could consider a diverse range of other benefits from research, including the training of health care or research personnel, the construction of health care facilities and other physical infrastructure, and the provision of public health measures and health services beyond those required as part of the research trial. The reasonable availability standard ignores such benefits, and hence cannot reliably determine when exploitation has occurred.

Second, at least as originally formulated by CIOMS, the reasonable availability standard applies to only a narrow range of clinical research—successful Phase III testing of interventions.[25] It does not apply to Phase I and II drug and vaccine testing, or to genetic, epidemiology, and natural history research, which are all necessary and common types of research in developing countries but may be conducted years or decades before any intervention is proven safe and effective. Consequently, either the reasonable availability requirement suggests that Phase I and II studies cannot be ethically conducted in developing countries—a position articulated in the original CIOMS guidelines but widely repudiated—or there is no ethical requirement to provide benefits to the population when conducting such early phase research, or reasonable availability is not the only way to provide benefits from a clinical research study.

To address this gap, CIOMS altered the reasonable availability requirement in 2002:

> Before undertaking research in a population or community with limited resources, the sponsor and the investigator must make every effort to ensure that ... any intervention or product developed, or *knowledge generated*, will be made reasonably available for the benefit of that population or community.[26] (emphasis added)

According to CIOMS some knowledge alone may constitute a fair level of benefits for some non-Phase III studies. But in many non-Phase III studies, it may not match either the risks to subjects or the benefits to others. Indeed, the requirement could permit pharmaceutically sponsored Phase I and II testing of drugs in developing countries while shifting Phase III testing and sales to developed countries as long as data from the early studies are provided to the developing countries. This modification to encompass non-Phase III studies might actually invite *more* exploitation of developing countries.

Third, even in Phase III studies, the reasonable availability requirement provides an *uncertain* benefit to the population, since it makes benefit depend on whether the trial is a "successful testing" of a new product. If there is true clinical equipoise at the beginning of Phase III trials conducted in developing countries, then the new intervention should be proven more effective in only about half of the trials.[27] Consequently, reliance on reasonable availability alone to provide benefits implies that the host country will receive sufficient benefits from half or fewer of all Phase III studies.

Fourth, assuring reasonable availability does not avert the potential for undue inducement of a deprived population. One worry about research in developing countries is that collateral benefits will be escalated to induce the population to enroll in excessively risky research. If the population lacks access to public health measures, routine vaccines, medications for common ailments, and even trained health care personnel, then providing these services as part of a research study might induce them to consent to the project despite its risks, and despite the fact that it disproportionately benefits people in developed countries.[28] Similarly, guaranteeing reasonable availability to a safe and effective drug or vaccine after a study could also function as an undue inducement if the population lacks basic health care.

Fifth, it is beyond the authority of researchers and even of many sponsors of research to guarantee reasonable availability. Clinical researchers and even some sponsors in developed countries, such as the NIH and Medical Research Council, do not control drug approval processes in their own countries, much less in other countries. Similarly they do not control budgets for health ministries or foreign aid to implement research results, and may be, by law, prevented from providing assistance with implementation of research results. At best, they can generate data to inform the deliberations of ministers of health, aid officials, international funding organizations, and relevant others, and then try to persuade those parties to implement effective interventions.

Further, because most Phase III trials take years to conduct, policy-makers in developing countries and aid agencies may resist agreements to provide an intervention before they know how beneficial it is, the logistical requirements for implementing and distributing it, and how it compares to other potential interventions. Such cautiousness seems reasonable given the scarce resources available for health delivery.

Sixth, requiring reasonable availability tacitly suggests that the population cannot make its own, autonomous decisions about what benefits are worth the risks of a research trial. In many cases the resources expended on making a drug or vaccine available could be directed to other benefits instead, which the host community might actually prefer. Disregarding the community's view about what constitutes appropriate benefits for them—insisting that a population must benefit in a specific manner—implies a kind of paternalism.

Finally, requiring a prior agreement to supply a proven product at the end of a successful trial can become a "golden handcuff," constraining rather than benefiting the population. If there is a prior agreement to receive a specific drug or vaccine, rather than cash or some other transferable commodity, the prior agreement commits the population to using the specific intervention tested in the trial. (Pharmaceutical companies are likely to provide their own product directly and avoid agreements in which they are required to provide the product of a competitor.) Yet if other, more effective or desirable interventions are developed, the population is unlikely to have the resources to obtain those interventions. Hence prior agreements can actually limit access of the population to appropriate interventions.

Because of these difficulties, the reasonable availability requirement is recognized more in the breech than in its fulfillment; consequently much effort has been devoted to identifying and justifying exceptions.

THE FAIR BENEFITS FRAMEWORK

Certainly, targeted populations in developing countries ought to benefit when clinical research is performed in their communities. Making the results of the research available is one way to provide benefits to a population, but it is not the only way. Hence it is not a necessary condition for ethical research in developing countries, and it should not be imposed unless the developing countries have themselves affirmed it.

This was the consensus of the clinical researchers, bioethicists, and IRB chairs and members from eight African and three Western countries—Egypt, Ghana, Kenya, Malawi, Mali, Nigeria, Tanzania, Uganda, Norway, the United Kingdom, and the United States—who participated in the 2001 Conference on Ethical Aspects of Research in Developing Countries (EARD). As an alternative to reasonable availability, this group proposes the "fair benefits framework."[29]

The fair benefits framework supplements the usual conditions for the ethical conduct of research trials, such as independent review by an institutional review board or research ethics committee and individual informed consent.[30] In particular, it relies on three background principles that are widely accepted as requirements for ethical research. First, the research should have social value: it should address a health problem of the developing country population. Second, the subjects should be selected fairly: the scientific objectives of the research itself, not poverty or vulnerability, must provide a strong justification for conducting the research in a specific population. The subjects might be selected, for example, because the population has a high incidence of the disease being studied or of the transmission rates of infection necessary to evaluate a vaccine. Third, the research must have a favorable risk-benefit ratio: benefits to participants must outweigh the risks, or the net risks must be acceptably low.

To these widely accepted principles, the fair benefits framework adds three further principles, which are specified by fourteen benchmarks (see Table 1):

Principle 1: Fair benefits

There should be a comprehensive delineation of tangible benefits to the research participants and the population from both the conduct and results of the research. These benefits can be of three types: (1) benefits to research participants during the research; (2) benefits to the population during the research; or (3) benefits to the participants and population after completion of the research. It is not necessary to provide each of these types of benefits; the ethical imperative based on the conception of exploitation is only for a fair level of benefits. It would seem fair that as the burdens and risks of the research increase, the benefits should also increase. Similarly, as the benefits to the sponsors, researchers, and others outside the population increase, the benefits to the host population should also increase.

TABLE 1   The Fair Benefits Framework

Principles	Benchmarks for determining whether the principle is honored.
Fair benefits	• **Benefits to participants during the research**
	1) **Health improvement:** Health services that are essential to the conduct of the research will improve the health of the participants.
	2) **Collateral health services:** Health services beyond those essential to the conduct of the research are provided to the participants.
	• **Benefits to participants and population during the research**
	3) **Collateral health services:** Additional health care services are provided to the population.
	4) **Public Health Measures:** There are additional public health measures provided to the population.
	5) **Employment and economic activity:** The research project provides jobs for the local population and stimulates the local economy.
	• **Benefits to population after the research**
	6) **Availability of the intervention:** If proven effective, the intervention should be made available to the population.
	7) **Capacity development:** There are improvements in health care physical infrastructure, training of health care and research personnel, or training of health personnel in research ethics.
	8) **Public health measures:** Additional public health measures provided to the population will have a lasting benefit.[OK?]
	9) **Long-term collaboration:** The particular research trial is part of a long-term research collaboration with the population.
	10) **Financial rewards:** There is a plan to share fairly with the population the financial rewards or intellectual property rights related to the intervention being evaluated.
Collaborative partnership	1) **Free, uncoerced decisionmaking:** The population is capable of making a free, uncoerced decision: it can refuse participation in the research.
	2) **Population support:** When it has understood the nature of the research trial, the risks and benefits to individual subjects, and the benefits to the population, the population decides that it wants the research to proceed.
Transparency	1) **Central repository of benefits agreements:** An independent body creates a publicly accessible repository of all formal and informal benefits agreements.
	2) **Community consultation:** Forums with populations that may be invited to participate in research, informing them about previous benefits agreements.

Because the aim of the fair benefits framework is to avoid exploitation, the population at risk for exploitation is the relevant group to receive benefits and determine their fairness. Indeed, determination of whether the distribution of benefits is fair depends on the level of benefits received by those members of the community who actually participate in the research, for it is they who bear the burdens of the interaction. However, each benefit does not have to accrue solely to the research participants; a benefit could be directed instead to the entire community. For instance, capacity development or enhanced training in ethics review would be provided to the community, and then benefit the participants indirectly. The important question is how much the participants will benefit from these measures.

In addition, the community will likely bear some burdens and impositions of the research because its health care personnel are recruited to staff the research teams, and its physical facilities and social networks are utilized to conduct the study. Thus, to avoid exploitation, consideration of the benefits for the larger community may also be required. However, since exploitation is a characteristic of micro-level transactions, there is no justification for including everybody in an entire region or country in the distribution of benefits (nor in the decisionmaking that is required by the next principle) unless the whole region or country is involved in bearing the burdens of the research and at risk for exploitation.

Principle 2: Collaborative partnership

The population being asked to enroll determines whether a particular array of benefits is sufficient and fair. Currently, there is no shared international standard of fairness; reasonable people disagree.[31] More importantly, only the host population can determine the value of the benefits for itself. Outsiders are likely to be poorly informed about the health, social, and economic context in which the research is being conducted, and they are unlikely to fully appreciate the importance of the proposed benefits to the population.

Furthermore, the population's choice to participate must be free and uncoerced; refusing to participate in the research study must be a realistic option. While there can be controversy about who speaks for the population being asked to enroll, this is a problem that is not unique to the fair benefits framework. Even—or especially—in democratic processes, unanimity of decisions cannot be the standard; disagreement is inherent. But how consensus is determined in the absence of an electoral process is a complex question in democratic theory beyond the scope of this article.

Principle 3: Transparency

Fairness is relative, since it is determined by comparisons with similar interactions. Therefore transparency—like the full information requirement for ideal market transactions—allows comparisons with similar transactions. A population in a developing country is likely to be at a distinct disadvantage relative to the sponsors from the developed country in determining whether a proposed level of benefits is fair. To address these concerns, a publicly accessible repository of all benefits agreements should be established and operated by an independent body, such as the World Health Organization. A central repository permits independent assessment of the fairness of benefits agreements by populations, researchers, governments, and others, such as nongovernmental organizations. There could also be a series of community consultations to make populations in developing countries aware of the terms of the agreements reached in other research projects. Such information will facilitate the development of "case law" standards of fairness that evolve out of a number of agreements.

Together with the three background conditions, these three new principles of the fair benefits framework ensure that: (1) the population has been selected for good scientific reasons, (2) the research poses few net risks to the research participants, (3) there are sufficient benefits to the participants and population, (4) the population is not subject to a coercive choice, (5) the population freely determines whether to participate and whether the level of benefits is fair given the risks of the research, and (6) there is an opportunity for comparative assessments of the fairness of the benefit agreements.

APPLICATION TO THE HEPATITIS A VACCINE CASE

We can compare the reasonable availability requirement with the fair benefits framework in the case of Havrix, an inactivated hepatitis A vaccine that was tested in 1990 among school children from Kamphaeng Phet province in northern Thailand.[32] The study was a collaboration of the Walter Reed Army Institute of Research (in the United States), SmithKline Beecham Biologicals, and Thailand's Ministry of Public Health. Initially, there was a randomized, double-blind Phase II study involving 300 children, primarily family members of physicians and nurses at the Kamphaeng Phet provincial hospital. After a demonstration of safety and of an antibody response that neutralizes hepatitis A, a randomized, double blind Phase

III study with a hepatitis B vaccine control involving 40,000 children, one to sixteen years old, was initiated to assess protection against hepatitis A infection.

The study was conducted in Thailand for several reasons. First, there were increasingly common episodes of hepatitis A infection during adolescence and adulthood, including hepatitis A outbreaks, such as at the National Police Academy in 1988. Second, while hepatitis A transmission was focal, there was a sufficiently high transmission rate—119 per 100,000 population—in rural areas to assess vaccine efficacy. Third, the area had been the site of a prior Japanese encephalitis vaccine study.[33] Ultimately, the Japanese encephalitis vaccine was registered in Thailand in 1988 and included in the Thai mandatory immunization policy in 1992.

Prior to the Phase III study, there was no formal agreement to make Havrix widely available in Thailand. Due to competing vaccination priorities (especially for implementation of hepatitis B vaccine), the cost of a newly developed hepatitis A vaccine, and the available health care budget in Thailand, it was unlikely that Havrix would be included in the foreseeable future in Thailand's national immunization program, in which vaccines are provided to the population at no cost. In addition, SmithKline Beecham Biologicals made no commitment to provide free Havrix to Thailand. However, the company did commit to provide the vaccine to all research participants effective and to pursue Havrix registration in Thailand, enabling the vaccine to be sold in the private market. While there was no promise about what the prices would be for the private market, SmithKline Beecham Biologicals had previously utilized tiered pricing on vaccines. Registration and distribution would enable the Ministry of Public Health to use Havrix to control hepatitis A outbreaks at schools and other institutions. Nevertheless, at the start of the trial, all collaborators recognized that the largest market for Havrix would be travelers from developed countries.

Was the Havrix study ethical? Although all the study participants ultimately received hepatitis A and B vaccines, the study did not fulfill the reasonable availability requirement. There was no prior agreement to provide the vaccine to everyone in Kamphaeng Phet province, and since most Thais would not be able to afford the vaccine, committing to registering and selling it on the private market does not seem to "reasonably available." Thus, by this standard, the trial seems to be unethical.

The fair benefits framework, however, requires a more multifaceted assessment. First, the study seemed to fulfill the background requirements of social value, fair subject selection, and favorable risk-benefit ratio. Hepatitis A was a significant health problem in northern Thailand and recognized as such by the Thai Ministry of Public Health. Although the population in Kamphaeng Phet province was poor, the epidemiology of hepatitis A provided an independent scientific rationale for site selection. The preliminary data indicated that the candidate vaccine had an excellent safety profile and probable protective efficacy, suggesting a highly favorable risk-benefit ratio for participants.

The benefits of the Havrix trial were of several sorts. By design, all 40,000 children in the trial received both hepatitis A and B vaccines. In addition, regional medical services were augmented. The research team contracted with the community pubic health workers to examine all enrolled children absent from school at their homes, to provide necessary care, and, if appropriate, to arrange transfer to the district or provincial hospital.

There were also benefits for the provincial population. Public health stations throughout Kamphaeng Phet province that lacked adequate refrigeration to store vaccines, medicines, and blood specimens received new refrigerators. Similarly, rural health stations lacking reliable access to the existing FM wireless network link with the provincial hospital's consultants were joined to the network. In the six schools that had hepatitis A outbreaks during the study, the research team arranged for inspection of the schools and identification of deficiencies in toilet, hand-washing facilities, and water storage contributing to the outbreak. At each school, the researchers contracted and paid to have recommended improvements implemented. In addition, public health workers were provided with unlimited stocks of disposable syringes and needles, as well as training on measures to reduce the incidence of blood-borne diseases. Hepatitis B vaccinations were provided to all interested government personnel working on the trial, including approximately 2,500 teachers, public health workers, nurses, technicians, and physicians. Since deaths of enrolled research participants were tracked and investigated, the research team identified motor vehicle accidents, especially pedestrians struck by cars, as a major cause of mortality in the province and recommended corrective measures.[34] Finally, the training of Thai researchers and experience in conducting the Havrix trial may have facilitated subsequent research trials, including the current HIV vaccine trials in Thailand.

Regarding the principle of collaborative partnership, there were extensive consultations in Kamphaeng Phet province prior to initiating and conducting the trial. The provincial governor, medical officer, education secretary, and hospital director provided comments before granting their approval. In each of the 146 participating communities, researchers made public presentations about the study and held briefings for interested parents and teachers. Each school appointed a teacher to maintain a liaison with the research team. Parental and community support appeared to be related to the provision of hepatitis B vaccine to all participants, since hepatitis was seen as a major health problem and the children lacked access to the vaccine.

Furthermore, the protocol was reviewed by the Thai Ministry of Public Health's National Ethical Review Committee, as well as by two IRBs in the United States. The Ministry of Public Health appointed an independent committee composed of thirteen senior physicians and ministry officials to monitor the safety and efficacy of the trial. And rejecting the trial appeared to be a genuine option; certainly those Thai scientists who tried hard to prevent it, including by lobbying the National Ethics Review Committee, seemed to think so.

At the time of this trial, there was no central repository of benefits agreements to fulfill the transparency principle. However, the measures taken to benefit the population, including provision of the hepatitis A and B vaccines and registration of Havrix in Thailand, were discussed with the Ministry of Public Health and provincial officials and published.

Did the Havrix study provide fair benefits? Clearly some in Thailand thought not. They argued that the trial did not address a pressing health need in a manner appropriate to the country; instead, they held, it addressed a health interest of the U.S. army. Second, some have alleged there was insufficient technology transfer. In particular, no training was provided to Thai researchers to conduct testing for the antibody to hepatitis A or to develop other laboratory skills. Third, it was claimed that inadequate respect was accorded to the Thai researchers, as none were among the study's principal investigators and none were named in the original protocol (they were simply referred to as "Thai researchers"). Only after protests were they individually identified. The American investigators claim vehemently that this charge is inaccurate. A prominent vaccine researcher summarized the sentiment against Thai participation:

> Journalists in the country have accused the government and medical community of a national betrayal in allowing Thai children to be exploited.... The role of Thailand in rounding up its children for immunization was hardly seen as a meaningful partnership in this research aim. In private, government ministers agreed with this, but the sway of international politics and money was too persuasive.[35]

Many others argued that the benefits to the population of Kamphaeng Phet province were sufficient, especially given the minimal risk of the study. Still others are uncertain. In their view, the level of benefits were not clearly inadequate, but more long-term benefits could

have been provided to the community depending on the level of the sponsors' benefits—in this case, SmithKline Beecham's profits from vaccine sales. To address the uncertainty of how much a company might benefit from drug or vaccine sales, some propose profit-sharing agreements that provide benefits to the community related to the actual profits.

Universal agreement is a naïve and unrealistic goal. The goal is only a consensus in the population to be enrolled in the trial. Consensus on the appropriateness of a research study acknowledges that some disagreement is not only possible but likely, and even a sign of a healthy partnership.[36] In this trial, the national ministry, the provincial governmental and health officials, and the Kamphaeng Phet population seemed supportive.

Further, the dissent focused not on whether the vaccine would be made available to the population if it were proven effective, but on the level of a broad range of burdens and benefits, both to the community and to the sponsors. It is precisely this sort of broad, nuanced, and realistic assessment of the community's interests that is permitted and promoted by the fair benefits framework. Rather than making any one type of benefit into a moral litmus test, the fair benefits framework takes into account all of the various ways the community might benefit from the research.

REFERENCES

1. M. Barry, "Ethical Considerations of Human Investigation in Developing Countries: the AIDS Dilemma," *NEJM* 319 (1988) 1983–86; M. Angell, "Ethical Imperialism? Ethics in International Collaborative Clinical Research," *NEJM* 319 (1988): 1081–83; N.A. Christakas, "The Ethical Design of an AIDS Vaccine Trial in Africa," *Hastings Center Report* 18, no. 3 (1988): 31–37.

2. P. Lurie and S.M. Wolfe, "Unethical Trials of Interventions to Reduce Perinatal Transmission of the Human Immunodeficiency Virus in Developing Countries," *NEJM* 337 (1997): 853–56; M. Angell, "The Ethics of Clinical Research in the Third World," *NEJM* 337 (1997): 847–49; H. Varmus and D. Satcher, "Ethical Complexities of Conducting Research in Developing Countries," *NEJM* 337 (1997): 1003–1005; R. Crouch and J. Arras, "AZT Trials and Tribulations," *Hastings Center Report* 28, no. 6 (1998): 26–34; C. Grady, "Science in the Service of Healing," *Hastings Center Report* 28, no. 6 (1998): 34–38; R.J. Levine, "The 'Best Proven Therapeutic Method' Standard in Clinical Trials in Technologically Developing Countries." *IRB* 20 (1998): 5–9; B.R. Bloom, "The Highest Attainable Standard: Ethical Issues in AIDS Vaccines," *Science* 279 (1998): 186–88.

3. World Medical Association. Declaration of Helsinki, 2000 at www.wma.net/e/policy12-c_e.html; Council for International Organizations of Medical Science, *International Ethical Guidelines for Biomedical Research Involving Human Subjects* (Geneva: CIOMS, 1993); P. Wilmshurst, "Scientific Imperialism: If They Won't Benefit from the Findings, Poor People in the Developing World Shouldn't be Used in Research," *BMJ* 314 (1997): 840–41; P.E. Cleaton-Jones, "An Ethical Dilemma: Availability of Anti-retroviral Therapy after Clinical Trials with HIV Infected Patients are Ended," *BMJ* 314 (1997): 887–88.

4. CIOMS, *International Ethical Guidelines*, 1993.

5. World Medical Association Declaration of Helsinki.

6. Medical Research Council of the United Kingdom, *Interim Guidelines—Research Involving Human Participants in Developing Societies: Ethical Guidelines for MRC-sponsored Studies* (London: MRC, 1999); Joint United National Programme on HIV/AIDS (UNAIDS), *Ethical Considerations in HIV Preventive Vaccine Research* (Geneva: UNAIDS, 2000); National Consensus Conference, *Guidelines for the Conduct of Health Research Involving Human Subjects in Uganda* (Kampala, Uganda: National Consensus Conference, 1997); Medical Research Council of South Africa, *Guidelines on Ethics for Medical Research* (South Africa: Medical Research Council, 1993).

7. L.H. Glantz et al., "Research in Developing Countries: Taking 'Benefit' Seriously," *Hastings Center Report* 28, no. 6 (1998): 38–42; G.J. Annas and M.A. Grodin, "Human Rights and Maternal-Fetal HIV Transmission Prevention Trials in Africa," *American Journal of Public Health* 88 (1998): 560–63.

8. H.T. Shapiro and E.M. Meslin, "Ethical Issues in the Design and Conduct of Clinical Trials in Developing Countries," *NEJM* 345 (2001): 139–42. See also National Bioethics Advisory Commission, *Ethical and Policy Issues in International Research: Clinical Trials in Developing Countries* (Washington D.C.: U.S. Government Printing Office, 2001).

9. Annas and Grodin, "Human Rights and Maternal-Fetal HIV Transmission Prevention Trials in Africa."

10. E.J. Emanuel, D. Wendler, and C. Grady, "What Makes Clinical Research Ethical?" *JAMA* 283 (2000): 2701–711; E.J. Emanuel et al., "What Makes Clinical Research in Developing Countries Ethical? The Benchmarks of Ethical Research," *Journal of Infectious Diseases* 189 (2004): 930–37.

11. Ibid.; R.J. Levine, *Ethical and Regulatory Aspects of Clinical Research*, 2nd Edition (New Haven, Conn.: Yale University Press, 1988).

12. N. Black, "Evidence based policy: proceed with care," *BMJ* 323 (2001): 275–79.

13. Wilmshurst, "Scientific Imperialism," and National Consensus Conference, *Guidelines for the Conduct of Health Research Involving Human Subjects in Uganda*; L.H. Glantz et al., "Research in Developing Countries: Taking "Benefit" Seriously;" G.J. Annas and M.A. Grodin, "Human Rights and Maternal-Fetal HIV Transmission Prevention Trials in Africa."

14. Glantz et al., "Research in Developing Countries."

15. CIOMS, *International Ethical Guidelines for Biomedical Research Involving Human Subjects*, 2nd edition (Geneva: CIOMS, 2002).

16. A. Wertheimer, *Exploitation* (Princeton, N.J.: Princeton University Press, 1999), chapter 1; N.A. Christakis, "The Ethical Design of an AIDS Vaccine Trial in Africa," *Hastings Center Report* 28 (1998): 31–37.

17. Wertheimer, *Exploitation*.

18. A. W. Wood, "Exploitation," *Social Philosophy and Policy* 12 (1995): 135–58.

19. Wertheimer, *Exploitation*.

20. Buchanan, *Ethics, Efficiency and the Market*, p. 87.

21. C. Korsgaard, "The Reasons We Can Share: An Attack on the Distinction Between Agent-relative and Agent-neutral Values," in *Creating the Kingdom of Ends* (New York: Cambridge University Press, 1996).

22. Wertheimer, *Exploitation*.

23. J. Rawls, *A Theory of Justice*, 2nd edition (Cambridge, Mass.: Harvard University Press, DATE).

24. Wertheimer, *Exploitation*.

25. CIOMS, *International Ethical Guidelines for Biomedical Research Involving Human Subjects*.

26. CIOMS, *International Ethical Guidelines for Biomedical Research Involving Human Subjects*, 2nd edition.

27. I. Chalmers, "What is the Prior Probability of a Proposed New Treatment being Superior to Established Treatments?" *BMJ* 314 (1997): 74–75; B. Djulbegovic et al., "The Uncertainty Principle and Industry-Sponsored Research," *Lancet* 356 (2000): 635–38.

28. NBAC, *Ethical and Policy Issues in International Research*.

29. Participants in the 2001 Conference on Ethical Aspects of Research in Developing Countries, "Fair Benefits from Research in Developing Countries," *Science* 298 (2002): 2133–34.

30. Emanuel, Wendler, and Grady, "What Makes Clinical Research Ethical?" and Levine, *Ethical and Regulatory Aspects of Clinical Research*; J. Rawls, *The Law of Peoples* (Cambridge, Mass.: Harvard University Press, 1999).

31. T. Pogge, *World Poverty and Human Rights* (Cambridge, U.K.: Polity Press, 2002), chapters 1 and 4.

32. B.I. Innis et al. "Protection against Hepatitis A by an Inactivated Vaccine," *JAMA* 271 (1994): 1328–34.

33. C. Hoke et al., "Protection against Japanese Encephalitis by Inactivated Vaccines," *NEJM* 319 (1988): 608–614.

34. C.A. Kozik et al., "Causes of Death and Unintentional Injury among School Children in Thailand," *Southeast Asian Journal of Tropical Medicine and Public Health* 30 (1999): 129–35.

35. "Interview with Prof Natth," *Good Clinical Practice Journal* 6, no. 6 (1999): 11.

36. A. Gutmann and D. Thompson, *Democracy and Disagreement* (Cambridge, Mass.: Harvard University Press, 1996).

VULNERABLE POPULATIONS

The Patient as Person: Explorations in Medical Ethics

Paul Ramsey

In 1958 and 1959 the *New England Journal of Medicine* reported a series of experiments performed upon patients and new admittees to the Willowbrook State School, a home for retarded children in Staten Island, New York. These experiments were described as "an attempt to control the high prevalence of infectious hepatitis in an institution for mentally defective patients." The experiments were said to be justified because, under conditions of an existing controlled outbreak of hepatitis in the institution, "knowledge obtained from a series of suitable studies could well lead to its control." In actuality, the experiments were designed to duplicate and confirm the efficacy of gamma globulin in immunization against hepatitis, to develop and improve or improve upon that inoculum, and to learn more about infectious hepatitis in general.

The experiments were justified—doubtless, after a great deal of soul searching—for the following reasons: there was a smoldering epidemic throughout the institution and "it was apparent that most of the patients at Willowbrook were naturally exposed to hepatitis virus"; infectious hepatitis is a much milder disease in children; the strain at Willowbrook was especially mild; only the strain or strains of the virus already disseminated at Willowbrook were used: and only those small and incompetent patients whose parents gave consent were used.

The patient population at Willowbrook was 4478, growing at a rate of one patient a day over a three-year span, or from 10 to 15 new admissions per week. In the first trial the existing population was divided into two groups: one group served as uninoculated controls, and the other group was inoculated with 0.01 ml. of gamma globulin per pound of body weight. Then for a second trial new admittees and those left uninoculated before were again divided: one group served as uninoculated controls and the other was inoculated with 0.06 ml. of gamma globulin per pound of body weight. This proved that Stokes et al. had correctly demonstrated that the larger amount would give significant immunity for up to seven or eight months.

Serious ethical questions may be raised about the trials so far described. No mention is made of any attempt to enlist the adult personnel of the institution, numbering nearly 1,000 including nearly 600 attendants on ward duty, and new additions to the staff, in these studies whose excusing reason was that almost everyone was "naturally" exposed to the Willowbrook virus. Nothing requires that major research into the natural history of hepatitis be first undertaken in children. Experiments have been carried out in the military and with prisoners as subjects. There have been fatalities from the experiments; but surely in all these cases the consent of the volunteers was as valid or better than the proxy consent of these children's "representatives." There would have been no question of the understanding consent that might have been given by the adult personnel at Willowbrook, if significant benefits were expected from studying that virus.

Second, nothing is said that would warrant withholding an inoculation of some degree of known efficacy from part of the population, or for withholding in the first trial less than the full amount of gamma globulin that had served to immunize in previous tests, except the need to test, confirm, and improve the inoculum. That, of course, was a desirable goal; but it does not seem possible to warrant withholding gamma globulin for the reason that is often said to justify controlled trials, namely, that one procedure is *as likely* to succeed as the other.

Third, nothing is said about attempts to control or defeat the low-grade epidemic at Willowbrook by more ordinary, if more costly and less experimental, procedures. Nor is anything said about admitting no more patients until this goal had been accomplished. This was not a massive urban hospital whose teeming population would have to be turned out into the streets, with resulting dangers to themselves and to public health, in order to sanitize the place. Instead, between 200 and 250 patients were housed in each of 18 buildings over approximately 400 acres in a semirural setting of fields, woods, and well-kept, spacious lawns. Clearly it would have been possible to secure other accommodation for new admissions away from the infection, while eradicating the infection at Willowbrook building by building. This might have cost money, and it would certainly have required astute detective work to discover the source of the infection. The doctors determined that the new patients likely were not carrying the infection upon admission, and that it did not arise from the procedures and routine inoculations given them at the time of admission. Why not go further in the search for the source of the epidemic? If this had been an orphanage for normal children or a floor of private patients, instead of a school for mentally defective children, one wonders whether the doctors would so readily have accepted the hepatitis as a "natural" occurrence and even as an opportunity for study.

The next step was to attempt to induce "passive-active immunity" by feeding the virus to patients already protected by gamma globulin. In this attempt to improve the inoculum, permission was obtained from the parents of children from 5 to 10 years of age newly admitted to Willowbrook, who were then isolated from contact with the rest of the institution. All were inoculated with gamma globulin and then divided into two groups: one served as controls while the other group of new patients were fed the Willowbrook virus, obtained from feces, in doses having 50 percent infectivity, i.e., in concentrations estimated to produce hepatitis with jaundice in half the subjects tested. Then twice the

50 percent infectivity was tried. This proved, among other things, that hepatitis has an "alimentary-tract phase" in which it can be transmitted from one person to another while still "inapparent" in the first person. This, doubtless, is exceedingly important information in learning how to control epidemics of infectious hepatitis. The second of the two articles mentioned above describes studies of the incubation period of the virus and of whether pooled serum remained infectious when aged and frozen. Still the small, mentally defective patients who were deliberately fed infectious hepatitis are described as having suffered mildly in most cases: "The liver became enlarged in the majority, occasionally a week or two before the onset of jaundice. Vomiting and anorexia usually lasted only a few days. Most of the children gained weight during the course of hepatitis."

That mild description of what happened to the children who were fed hepatitis (and who continued to be introduced into the unaltered environment of Willowbrook) is itself alarming, since it is now definitely known that cirrhosis of the liver results from infectious hepatitis more frequently than from excessive consumption of alcohol! Now, or in 1958 and 1959, no one knows what may be other serious consequences of contracting infectious hepatitis. Understanding human volunteers were then and are now needed in the study of this disease, although a South American monkey has now successfully been given a form of hepatitis, and can henceforth serve as our ally in its conquest. But not children who cannot consent knowingly. If Peace Corps workers are regularly given gamma globulin before going abroad as a guard against their contracting hepatitis, and are inoculated at intervals thereafter, it seems that this is the least we should do for mentally defective children before they "go abroad" to Willowbrook or other institutions set up for their care.

Discussions pro and con of the Willowbrook experiments that have come to my attention serve only to reinforce the ethical objections that can be raised against what was done simply from a careful analysis of the original articles reporting the research design and findings. In an address at the 1968 Ross Conference on Pediatric Research, Dr. Saul Krugman raised the question, Should vaccine trials be carried out in adult volunteers before subjecting children to similar tests? He answered this question in the negative. The reason adduced was simply that "a vaccine virus trial may be a more hazardous procedure for adults than for children." Medical researchers, of course, are required to minimize the hazards, but not by moving from consenting to unconsenting subjects. This apology clearly shows

that adults and children have become interchangeable in face of the overriding importance of obtaining the research goal. This means that the special moral claims of children for care and protection are forgotten, and especially the claims of children who are most weak and vulnerable. (Krugman's reference to the measles vaccine trials is not to the point.)

The *Medical Tribune* explains that the 16-bed isolation unit set up at Willowbrook served "to protect the study subjects from Willowbrook's other endemic diseases—such as shigellosis, measles, rubella and respiratory and parasitic infections—while exposing them to hepatitis." This presumably compensated for the infection they were given. It is not convincingly shown that the children could by no means, however costly, have been protected from the epidemic of hepatitis. The statement that Willowbrook "had endemic infectious hepatitis and a sufficiently open population so that the disease could never be quieted by exhausting the supply of susceptibles" is at best enigmatic.

Oddly, physicians defending the propriety of the Willowbrook hepatitis project soon begin talking like poorly instructed "natural lawyers"! Dr. Louis Lasagna and Dr. Geoffrey Edsall, for example, find these experiments unobjectionable—both, for the reason stated by Edsall: "the children would apparently incur no greater risk than they were likely to run by nature." In any case, Edsall's examples of parents consenting with a son 17 years of age for him to go to war, and society's agreement with minors that they can drive cars and hurt themselves were entirely beside the point. Dr. David D. Rutstein adheres to a stricter standard in regard to research on infectious hepatitis: "It is not ethical to use human subjects for the growth of a virus for any purpose."

The latter sweeping verdict may depend on knowledge of the effects of viruses on chromasomal difficulties, mongolism, etc., that was not available to the Willowbrook group when their researches were begun thirteen years ago. If so, this is a telling point against appeal to "no discernible risks" as the sole standard applicable to the use of children in medical experimentation. That would lend support to the proposition that we always know that there are unknown and undiscerned risks in the case of an invasion of the fortress of the body—which then can be consented to by an adult in behalf of a child only if it is in the child's behalf medically.

When asked what she told the parents of the subject-children at Willowbrook, Dr. Joan Giles replied, "I explain that there is no vaccine against infectious hepatitis. . . . I also tell them that we can modify the disease with gamma globulin but we can't provide lasting immunity without letting them get the disease." Obviously vaccines giving "lasting immunity" are not the only kinds of vaccine to be used in caring for patients.

Doubtless the studies at Willowbrook resulted in improvement in the vaccine, to the benefit of present and future patients. In September 1966, "a routine program of GG [gamma globulin] administration to every new patient at Willowbrook" was begun. This cut the incidence of icteric hepatitis 80 to 85 percent. Then follows a significant statement in the *Medical Tribune* article: "A similar reduction in the icteric form of the disease has been accomplished among the employees, who began getting routine GG earlier in the study." Not only did the research team (so far as these reports show) fail to consider and adopt the alternative that new admittees to the staff be asked to become volunteers for an investigation that might improve the vaccine against the strand of infectious hepatitis to which they as well as the children were exposed. Instead, the staff was routinely protected earlier than the inmates were! And, as we have seen, there was evidence from the beginning that gamma globulin provided at least some protection. A "modification" of the disease was still an inoculum, even if this provided no lasting immunization and had to be repeated. It is axiomatic to medical ethics that a known remedy or protection—even if not perfect or even if the best exact administration of it has not been proved—should not be withheld from individual patients. It seems to a layman that from the beginning various trials at immunization of all new admittees might have been made, and controlled observation made of their different degrees of effectiveness against "nature" at Willowbrook. This would doubtless have been a longer way round, namely, the "anecdotal" method of investigative treatment that comes off second best in comparison with controlled trials. Yet this seems to be the alternative dictated by our received medical ethics, and the only one expressive of minimal care of the primary patients themselves.

Finally, except for one episode the obtaining of parental consent (on the premise that this is ethically valid) seems to have been very well handled. Wards of the state were not used, though by law the administrator at Willowbrook could have signed consent for them. Only new admittees whose parents were available were entered by proxy consent into the project. Explanation was made to groups of these parents, and they were given time to think about it and consult with their own family physicians. Then late in 1964 Willowbrook was closed to all new admissions because of overcrowding. What then happened can most impartially be described in the words of an article defending the Willowbrook project on medical and ethical grounds:

> Parents who applied for their children to get in were sent a form letter over Dr. Hammond's signature saying that there was no space for new admissions and that their name was being put on a waiting list.
>
> But the hepatitis program, occupying its own space in the institution, continued to admit new patients as each new study group began. "Where do you find new admissions except by canvassing the people who have applied for admission?" Dr. Hammond asked.
>
> So a new batch of form letters went out, saying that there were a few vacancies in the hepatitis research unit if the parents cared to consider volunteering their child for that.
>
> In some instances the second form letter apparently was received as closely as a week after the first letter arrived.

Granting—as I do not—the validity of parental consent to research upon children not in their behalf medically, what sort of consent was that? Surely, the duress upon these parents with children so defective as to require institutionalization was far greater than the duress on prisoners given tobacco or paid or promised parole for their cooperation! I grant that the timing of these events was inadvertent. Since, however, ethics is a matter of criticizing institutions and not only of exculpating or making culprits of individual men, the inadvertence does not matter. This is the strongest possible argument for saying that even if parents have the right to consent to submit the children who are directly and continuously in their care to nonbeneficial medical experimentation, this should not be the rule of practice governing institutions set up for their care.

Such use of captive populations of children for purely experimental purposes ought to be made legally impossible. My view is that this should be stopped by legal acknowledgment of the moral invalidity of parental or legal proxy consent for the child to procedures having no relation to a child's own diagnosis or treatment. If this is not done, canons of loyalty require that the rule of practice (by law, or otherwise) be that children in institutions and not directly under the care of parents or relatives should *never* be used in medical investigations having present pain or discomfort and unknown present and future risks to them, and promising future possible benefits only for others.

The Dangers of Difference

Patricia A. King

It has been sixty years since the beginning of the Tuskegee syphilis experiment and twenty years since its existence was disclosed to the American public. The social and ethical issues that the experiment poses for medicine, particularly for medicine's relationship with African Americans, are still not broadly understood, appreciated, or even remembered.[1] Yet a significant aspect of the Tuskegee experiment's legacy is that in a racist society that incorporates beliefs about the inherent inferiority of African Americans in contrast with the superior status of whites, any attention to the question of differences that may exist is likely to be pursued in a manner that burdens rather than benefits African Americans.

The Tuskegee experiment, which involved approximately 400 males with late-stage, untreated syphilis and approximately 200 controls free of the disease, is by any measure one of the dark pages in the history of American medicine. In this study of the natural course of untreated syphilis, the participants did not give informed consent. Stunningly, when penicillin was subsequently developed as a treatment for syphilis, measures were taken to keep the diseased participants from receiving it.

Obviously, the experiment provides a basis for the exploration of many ethical and social issues in medicine including professional ethics,[2] the limitations of informed consent as a means of protecting research subjects, and the motives and methods used to justify the exploitation of persons who live in conditions of severe economic and social disadvantage. At bottom, however, the Tuskegee experiment is different from other incidents of abuse in clinical research because all the participants were black males. The racism that played a central role in this tragedy continues to infect even our current well-intentioned efforts to reverse the decline in health status of African Americans.[3]

Others have written on the scientific attitudes about race and heredity that flourished at the time that the Tuskegee experiment was conceived.[4] There has always been widespread interest in racial differences between blacks and whites, especially differences that related to sexual matters. These perceived differences have often reinforced and justified differential treatment of blacks and whites, and have done so to the detriment of blacks. Not surprisingly, such assumptions about racial differences provided critical justification for the Tuskegee experiment itself.

Before the experiment began a Norwegian investigator had already undertaken a study of untreated syphilis in whites between 1890 and 1910. Although there had also been a follow-up study of these untreated patients from 1925 to 1927, the original study was abandoned when arsenic therapy became available. In light of the availability of therapy a substantial justification for replicating a study of untreated syphilis was required. The argument that provided critical support for the experiment was that the natural course of untreated syphilis in blacks and whites was not the same.[5] Moreover, it was thought that the differences between blacks and whites were not merely biological but that they extended to psychological and social responses to the disease as well. Syphilis, a sexually transmitted disease, was perceived to be rampant among blacks in part because blacks—unlike whites—were not inclined to seek or continue treatment for syphilis.

THE DILEMMA OF DIFFERENCE

In the context of widespread belief in the racial inferiority of blacks that surrounded the Tuskegee experiment, it should not come as a surprise that the experiment exploited its subjects. Recognizing and taking account of racial differences that have historically been utilized to burden and exploit African Americans poses a dilemma.[6] Even in circumstances where the goal of a scientific study is to benefit a stigmatized group or person, such well-intentioned efforts may nevertheless cause harm. If the racial difference is ignored and all groups or persons are treated similarly, unintended harm may result from the failure to recognize racially correlated factors. Conversely, if differences among groups or persons are recognized and attempts are made to respond to past injustices or special burdens, the effort is likely to reinforce existing negative stereotypes that contributed to the emphasis on racial differences in the first place.

This dilemma about difference is particularly worrisome in medicine. Because medicine is pragmatic, it will recognize racial differences if doing so will promote health goals. As a consequence, potential harms that might result from attention to racial differences tend to be overlooked, minimized, or viewed as problems beyond the purview of medicine.

The question of whether (and how) to take account of racial differences has recently been raised in the context of the current AIDS epidemic. The participation of African Americans in clinical AIDS trials has been disproportionately small in comparison to the numbers of African Americans who have been infected with the Human Immunodeficiency. Because of the possibility that African Americans may respond differently to drugs being developed and tested to combat AIDS,[7] those concerned about the care and treatment of AIDS in the African American community have called for greater participation by African Americans in these trials. Ironically, efforts to address the problem of underrepresentation must cope with the enduring legacy of the Tuskegee experiment—the legacy of suspicion and skepticism toward medicine and its practitioners among African Americans.[8]

In view of the suspicion Tuskegee so justifiably engenders, calls for increased participation by African Americans in clinical trials are worrisome. The question of whether to tolerate racially differentiated AIDS research testing of new innovative therapies, as well as the question of what norms should govern participation by African Americans in clinical research, needs careful and thoughtful attention. A generic examination of the treatment of racial differences in medicine is beyond the scope of this article. However, I will describe briefly what has occurred since disclosure of the Tuskegee experiment to point out the dangers I find lurking in our current policies.

INCLUSION AND EXCLUSION

In part because of public outrage concerning the Tuskegee experiment,[9] comprehensive regulations governing federal research using human subjects were revised and subsequently adopted by most federal agencies.[10] An institutional review board (IRB) must approve clinical research involving human subjects, and IRB approval is made contingent on review of protocols for adequate protection of human subjects in accordance with federal criteria. These criteria require among other things that an IRB ensure that subject selection is "equitable." The regulations further provide that:

"[i]n making this assessment the IRB should take into account the purposes of the research and the setting in which the research will be conducted and should be particularly cognizant of the special problems of research involving vulnerable populations, such as women, mentally disabled persons, or economically or educationally disadvantaged persons."[11]

The language of the regulation makes clear that the concern prompting its adoption was the protection of vulnerable groups from exploitation. The obverse problem—that too much protection might promote the exclusion or underrepresentation of vulnerable groups, including African Americans—was not at issue. However, underinclusion can raise as much of a problem of equity as exploitation.[12]

A 1990 General Accounting office study first documented the extent to which minorities and women were underrepresented in federally funded research. In response, in December 1990 the National Institutes of Health, together with the Alcohol, Drug Abuse and Mental Health Administration, directed that minorities and women be included in study populations, so that research findings can be of benefit to all persons at risk of the disease, disorder or condition under study; special emphasis should be placed on the need for inclusion of minorities and women in studies of diseases, disorders and conditions that disproportionately affect them.[13]

If minorities are not included, a clear and compelling rationale must be submitted.

The new policy clearly attempts to avoid the perils of overprotection, but it raises new concerns. The policy must be clarified and refined if it is to meet the intended goal of ensuring that research findings are of benefit to all. There are at least three reasons for favoring increased representation of African Americans in clinical trials. The first is that there may be biological differences between blacks and whites that might affect the applicability of experimental findings to blacks, but these differences will not be noticed if blacks are not included in sufficient numbers to allow the detection of statistically significant racial differences. The second reason is that race is a reliable index for social conditions such as poor health and nutrition, lack of adequate access to health care, and economic and social disadvantage that might adversely affect potential benefits of new interventions and procedures. If there is indeed a correlation between minority status and these factors, then African Americans and all others with these characteristics will benefit from new information generated by the research. The third reason is that the burdens and benefits of research should be spread across the population regardless of racial or ethnic status.[14] Each of these reasons for urging that representation of minorities be increased has merit. Each of these justifications also raises concern, however, about whether potential benefits will indeed be achieved.

The third justification carries with it the obvious danger that the special needs or problems generated as a result of economic or social conditions associated with minority status may be overlooked and that, as a result, African Americans and other minorities will be further disadvantaged. The other two justifications are problematic and deserve closer examination. They each assume that there are either biological, social, economic, or cultural differences between blacks and whites.

THE WAY OUT OF THE DILEMMA

Understanding how, or indeed whether, race correlates with disease is a very complicated problem. Race itself is a confusing concept with both biological and social connotations. Some doubt whether race has biological significance at all.[15] Even if race is a biological fiction, however, its social significance remains.[16] As Bob Blauner points out, "Race is an essentially political construct, one that translates our tendency to see people in terms of their color or other physical attributes into structures that make it likely that people will act for or against them on such a basis."[17]

In the wake of Tuskegee and, in more recent times, the stigma and discrimination that resulted from screening for sickle cell trait (a genetic condition that occurs with greater frequency among African Americans), researchers have been reluctant to explore associations between race and disease. There is increasing recognition, however, of evidence of heightened resistance or vulnerability to disease along racial lines.[18] Indeed, sickle cell anemia itself substantiates the view that biological differences may exist. Nonetheless, separating myth from reality in determining the cause of disease and poor health status is not easy. Great caution should be exercised in attempting to validate biological differences in susceptibility to disease in light of this society's past experience with biological differences. Moreover, using race as an index for other conditions that might influence health and well-being is also dangerous. Such practices could emphasize social and economic differences that might also lead to stigma and discrimination.

If all the reasons for increasing minority participation in clinical research are flawed, how then can we promote improvement in the health status of African Americans and other minorities through participation in clinical research while simultaneously minimizing the harms that might flow from such participation? Is it possible to work our way out of this dilemma?

An appropriate strategy should have as its starting point the defeasible presumption that blacks and whites are biologically the same with respect to disease and treatment. Presumptions can be overturned of course, and the strategy should recognize the possibility that

biological differences in some contexts are possible. But the presumption of equality acknowledges that historically the greatest harm has come from the willingness to impute biological differences rather than the willingness to overlook them. For some, allowing the presumption to be in any way defeasible is troubling. Yet I do not believe that fear should lead us to ignore the possibility of biologically differentiated responses to disease and treatment, especially when the goal is to achieve medical benefit.

It is well to note at this point the caution sounded by Hans Jonas. He wrote, "of the new experimentation with man, medical is surely the most legitimate; psychological, the most dubious; biological (still to come), the most dangerous."[19] Clearly, priority should be given to exploring the possible social, cultural, and environmental determinants of disease before targeting the study of hypotheses that involve biological differences between blacks and whites. For example, rather than trying to determine whether blacks and whites respond differently to AZT, attention should first be directed to learning whether response to AZT is influenced by social, cultural, or environmental conditions. Only at the point where possible biological differences emerge should hypotheses that explore racial differences be considered.

A finding that blacks and whites are different in some critical aspect need not inevitably lead to increased discrimination or stigma for blacks. If there indeed had been a difference in the effects of untreated syphilis between blacks and whites such information might have been used to promote the health status of blacks. But the Tuskegee experiment stands as a reminder that such favorable outcomes rarely if ever occur. More often, either racist assumptions and stereotypes creep into the study's design, or findings broken down by race become convenient tools to support policies and behavior that further disadvantage those already vulnerable.

REFERENCES

1. For earlier examples of the use of African Americans as experimental subjects see Todd L. Savitt, "The Use of Blacks for Medical Experimentation and Demonstration in the Old South," Journal of Southern History 48, no. 3 (1982): 331–48.

2. David J. Rothman, "Were Tuskegee & Willowbrook 'Studies in Nature'?" Hastings Center Report 12, no. 2 (1982): 5–7.

3. For an in-depth examination of the health status of African Americans see Woodrow Jones, Jr., and Mitchell F. Rice, eds. Health Care Issues in Black America: Policies, Problems, and Prospects (New York: Greenwood Press, 1987).

4. See for example Allan M. Brandt, "Racism and Research: The Case of the Tuskegee Syphilis Study," Hastings Center Report 8, no. 6 (1978): 21–29; and James H. Jones, Bad Blood: The Tuskegee Syphilis Experiment (New York: Free Press, 1981).

5. Jones, Bad Blood, p. 106.

6. Martha Minow, *Making All the Difference: Inclusion, Exclusion, and American Law* (Ithaca, N.Y.: Cornell University Press, 1990)

7. Wafaa El-Sadr and Linnea Capps, "The Challenge of Minority Recruitment in Clinical Trials for AIDS," *JAMA* 267, no. 7 (1992): 954–57.

8. See for example Stephen B. Thomas and Sandra Crouse Quinn, "Public Health Then and Now," *American Journal of Public Health* 81, no. 11 (1991): 1498–1505; Henry C. Chinn, Jr., "Remember Tuskegee," *New York Times*, 29 May 1992.

9. Tuskegee Syphilis Study Ad Hoc Advisory Panel, *Final Report of the Tuskegee Syphilis Study Ad Hoc Advisory Panel* (Washington, D.C.: U.S. Department of Health, Education and Welfare, Public Health Service, 1973).

10. *Federal Policy for the Protection of Human Subjects; Notices and Rules, Federal Register* 56, no. 117 (1991): 28002.

11. 45 Code of Federal Regulations Section 46.111 (a)(3).

12. This problem is discussed in the context of research in prisons in Stephen E. Toulmin, "The National Commission on Human Experimentation: Procedures and Outcomes," in *Scientific Controversies: Case Studies in the Resolution and Closure of Disputes in Science and Technology*, ed. H. Tristram Engelhardt, Jr. and Arthur L. Caplan (New York: Cambridge University Press, 1987), pp. 602–6.

13. National Institutes of Health and Alcohol, Drug Abuse and Mental Health Administration, "Special Instructions to Applicants Using Form PHS 398 Regarding Implementation of the NIH/ADAMHA Policy concerning Inclusion of Women and Minorities in Clinical Research Study Populations," December 1990.

14. Arthur L. Caplan, "Is There a Duty to Serve as a Subject in Biomedical Research?" *IRB: A Review of Human Subjects Research* 6, no. 5 (1984): 1–5.

15. See J. W. Green, *Cultural Awareness in the Human Services* (Englewood Cliffs, NJ.: Prentice-Hall, 1982), p. 59; Bob Blauner, "Talking Past Each Other: Black and White Languages of Race," *American Prospect* 61, no. 10 (1992): 55–64.

16. Patricia A. King, "The Past as Prologue: Race, Class, and Gene Discrimination," in *Using Ethics and Law as Guides*, ed. George J. Annas and Sherman Elias (New York: Oxford University Press, 1992), pp. 94–111.

17. Blauner, "Talking Past Each Other," p. 16.

18. See for example James E. Bowman and Robert F. Murray, Jr., *Genetic Variation and Disorders in People of African Origin* (Baltimore, Md.: Johns Hopkins University Press, 1981); Warren W. Leary, "Uneasy Doctors Add Race-Consciousness to Diagnostic Tools," *New York Times*, 15 September 1990.

19. Hans Jonas, "Philosophical Reflections on Experimenting with Human Subjects," in *Experimentation with Human Subjects*, ed. Paul A. Freund (New York: George Braziller, 1970), p. 1. Recent controversy in genetic research makes Jonas's warning particularly timely. See Daniel Goleman, "New Storm Brews on Whether Crime Has Roots in Genes," *New York Times*, 15 September 1992.

Judging the Past

Allen Buchanan

THE CASE OF THE HUMAN RADIATION EXPERIMENTS

Our reluctance to measure the morality of past practices is more than a nagging problem for moral theorists. The legitimacy of retrospective moral judgment has fundamental implications for how practices and institutions should be viewed, and judged, now.

"It was a different world then." "They weren't as sensitive to these issues as we are nowadays." "You can't judge people of that time by our standards." Such remarks are common. They express a reluctance to make moral judgments about the past—even a conviction that such judgments are invalid. There seems to be a special reluctance to make moral judgments about particular individuals in the past. Even if we are willing to say that what they did was wrong, or that the institutions within which they operated were unjust or corrupt, we may be reluctant to blame them as individuals for doing what they did.

Exactly what is supposed to be wrong or dubious about making retrospective moral judgments is not usually made explicit. If something is wrong about applying current moral standards to past actions, institutions, or persons, we need an account of what that something is. For we do in fact make some retrospective moral judgments with complete confidence. For example, few of us would say that slavery is wrong now but was not wrong a hundred and fifty years ago (unless we mean it was not legally wrong). We believe it was wrong a hundred and fifty years ago, even though it was widely practiced and many people did not see that it was wrong, or at least refused to admit that it was. How can our willingness to make some retrospective moral judgments with confidence be reconciled with the belief that there is something problematic about retrospective moral judgments as such?

This is not just a puzzle for moral theorists. It is an urgent practical question. What position we take on retrospective moral judgment has fundamental implications for what should be done now. If we cannot judge that rights were violated in the past, then we cannot accept arguments for compensation grounded on the assumption that rights were violated.

Something else is at stake: the very possibility of moral progress. If we cannot apply the same moral yardstick to the past and the present, then we cannot say either that there has been or that there has not been moral progress.

THE TASK OF THE ADVISORY COMMITTEE ON HUMAN RADIATION EXPERIMENTATION

The investigation of radiation experiments conducted on human beings under the auspices of several agencies of the federal government between 1944 and 1974 provides a concrete focus for the problem of retrospective moral judgment. The Advisory Committee on Human Radiation Experiments, which was created by President Clinton and which recently published its final report, was asked to evaluate the ethics of these experiments and make recommendations for how to avoid abuses in the future. The committee was also charged with a prior task: to determine what ethics criteria should be used to evaluate the experiments.[1] To answer this question, the committee had to take a stand on the problem of retrospective moral judgment.

Even if it had not been implicated in the committee's formal mandate, the problem of retrospective moral judgment could not have been avoided easily. Although the first revelations of the human radiation experiments evoked confident condemnation in some quarters, some members of the general public and of the press expressed the belief that there would be something inappropriate about blaming those responsible for the experiments. The proper task, rather, was to learn from past mistakes and try to ensure that they did not occur again. This view, I shall argue, mistakenly assumes either that we cannot make valid retrospective moral judgments or that making them is not relevant to the task of minimizing the possibility of future abuses.

Contrary to appearances, there is no distinct problem about the validity of retrospective moral judgments as such. The mere passage of time could not possibly affect the validity of moral judgments. The fact that it has now been fifty years since Hitler tried to destroy the Jews and to enslave the greater part of mankind in no way diminishes the wrongness of his actions. Nor does it reduce his culpability. The validity of these moral judgments will not be affected by the passing of another fifty years, nor a hundred, nor a thousand. So if there is some reason to refrain from making retrospective moral judgments, it must be something other than the mere passage of time.

CULTURAL ETHICAL RELATIVISM

Remarks such as "It was a different world then" and "We can't judge the past by contemporary standards" are revealing. The assumption must be that the validity of moral judgments depends upon their cultural context, and that cultural contexts change over time. In other words, skepticism about retrospective moral judgments is simply a special case of the more general position known as cultural ethical relativism. According to this position, the validity of all moral judgments is culturally relative. This position implies that moral judgments about the past are invalid if they are applied across cultural boundaries.

According to cultural ethical relativism, moral judgments applied across cultural boundaries are invalid because moral judgments can be justified only by reference to shared values, and shared values are found only within a particular culture. We cannot validly apply ethical standards that can be justified only by reference to the shared values of our culture to actions, agents, or institutions in other cultures that do not share those values, whether they are contemporaneous with ours or existed in the past.

Strictly speaking, this position denies that there are any human rights. Human rights, by definition, are rights we have simply by virtue of our humanity, regardless of differences in our cultures, and regardless of when or where we live. The fundamental idea behind human rights is that because of the kind of beings they are, humans are entitled to be treated in certain ways (and not treated in certain ways). Thus, statements about human rights are justified by appeal to the morally relevant features of human beings, all human beings, as such. The implication is that cultural differences among human beings do not and cannot vitiate this justification because it appeals to features that all human beings have in all cultures.

According to the very concept of human rights, the validity of statements about human rights does not depend upon the fact (if it is a fact) that all cultures happen to share certain values by reference to which such statements can be justified. Even if it should turn out that there exists a culture whose values cannot be appealed to to justify the statement that there is a human right not to be tortured, for example, it does not follow that there is no such human right. Whether there is a human right not to be tortured depends only on whether the statement "The right not to be tortured is a human right" can be justified by reference to the morally relevant features of human beings as such, not upon whether all cultures happen to include values that can be invoked in such a justification.

In denying that there are any human rights, cultural ethical relativism not only invalidates retrospective moral judgments about actions or institutions occurring in different cultural contexts, it also implies that some of the most basic moral judgments we make about our own contemporaries are unjustified. We are barred from saying not only that agents in the past, such as Hitler, violated human rights, but also that human rights violations are occurring in the world at the present time. At most we can say that there are actions which most (or perhaps even all) cultures happen to recognize as violations of rights. If those who engage in the actions in question belong to a culture that does not recognize those actions as violations of rights, we cannot even say they are violating anyone's rights, much less that human rights are being violated. At most we can say that according to our culture they are violating rights. Thus, for example, whether we can say that Bosnian Serbs who killed unarmed Muslim prisoners are guilty of violating rights will depend upon whether the cultural values of the killers justify the statement that they violated the rights of those they killed. Even if we conclude that they do, we cannot say that human rights were violated. At most we can say that the Bosnian Serbs did something that happens to be wrong in all cultures, because all cultures happen to have values that justify saying that what they did is wrong. If a culture comes to embrace genocide, then those within it who commit genocide cannot coherently be judged to have committed a wrong, according to cultural ethical relativism. And if genocide is wrong only because it is regarded as such by certain cultures, we cannot say that it is wrong simply by virtue of what human beings as such are entitled to. So we cannot say that there is a human right against genocide.

Presumably, most of us do not believe that we must first determine whether the cultural values of the Bosnian Serbs condemn the killing of prisoners to know that the rights of those who were killed were violated. And presumably, most of us who condemn the killings believe that those who were killed were wronged simply as human beings—that they were treated in ways that human beings as such ought not to be treated. For those of us who believe these things, cultural ethical relativism must be rejected.

Assuming that we do reject this position we cannot then appeal to it to explain why "we cannot judge the past by present standards." Instead, we must consider whether there are other ways in which differences between the present cultural milieu and the milieu in which past actions occurred can invalidate or qualify moral judgments we make about the past. Before exploring these, however, another limitation of cultural ethical relativism is worth emphasizing. Even if we were to accept such relativism it still would not follow that it is "wrong to judge the past by present standards." That would follow only if the past objects of our moral judgment existed in a culture that did not include among its values those values by reference to which we make the moral judgments in question. And notice also how implausible it would be to assume that there are no basic values that are shared across otherwise quite different cultures.

This simple point has great significance for how we ought to evaluate some of the actions that occurred during the human radiation experiments. When we attempt to evaluate these actions, we are not making judgments about an alien culture. It is our culture, American culture, of fifty to twenty years ago. In some cases, those who authorized or conducted the experiments violated very general moral principles that were widely accepted at the time and that we continue to endorse today. Among these are prohibitions against deceit, against harming innocent persons without their consent, against treating persons as mere means, and against exploiting the vulnerable. We regard such principles as so fundamental that we assume, with reason, that they are applicable in any cultural setting in which morality itself has meaning.

To take only one example, all of these very general principles were violated during the course of an experiment conducted under the auspices of the U.S. government at the Fernald School in the late 1940s and early 1950s. With the complicity of the school's highest administrator, physicians tricked the parents of retarded children at the school into giving permission for their children to participate in a "science club." In fact the "science club" was a cover for an experiment in which the children were fed radioisotopes mixed with oatmeal at special "science club breakfasts" (pp. 344–47). Whether the ingestion of the isotopes posed a significant physical risk is perhaps disputable. What is beyond dispute is that these children and their parents were treated as mere means for others' ends, that they were exploited, and that they were chosen for exploitation because their powerlessness made them vulnerable. As one witness before the committee bitterly observed: "They didn't conduct experiments like this at Choate or Andover."

It would be nonsense to suggest that American culture has changed so much in the past few decades that it is inappropriate to apply these very general moral principles to the case of the experiments at the Fernald

School. Changes there have certainly been, but the prohibitions against exploiting the vulnerable, against using persons as mere means, and against manipulating people in deceptive and demeaning ways are hardly new moral insights.

Of course, some might agree that these fundamental principles were accepted in the American culture of a few decades ago, but point to a difference in the cultural context that might be thought to invalidate our condemnation of the Fernald experiments. These and most of the other human radiation experiments occurred in the depths of the Cold War. Even if American culture of that time included these general moral principles, perhaps at the time they were thought to be overridden by the requirement of national security. Indeed, this period was called the Cold War to emphasize the urgency of the situation. And in desperate situations, otherwise compelling moral restraints may be relaxed.

One of the most significant findings of the committee is that the so-called "national security exception" was not in fact invoked to justify any of the morally dubious actions undertaken in any of the human radiation experiments, including those at the Fernald School (p. 793). None of the hundreds of memoranda, transcripts of meetings, and official policy statements reviewed by the committee even imply that the justification for infringing otherwise valid moral principles was that national security considerations overrode them. Extensive and often candid discussions of ethical issues did take place at the highest levels of policymaking, but the national security exception was not invoked. Instead, it was the need to avoid legal liability and public outrage that the participants invoked to justify their deceptions and manipulations.

Furthermore, even if the national security exception had been invoked, it is doubtful that doing so would have provided a valid excuse. The reason for using retarded children at a state school, and for duping them and their parents, was to capitalize on their powerlessness—to avoid the risk of resistance had the truth about the experiment been told and to minimize the risk of exposure that would have existed had better off children been used. The committee found no evidence to support the hypothesis that government officials first sought to conduct the experiments without deception and without singling out a vulnerable group, but then found that the only way to serve vital national security interests was to deceive and exploit the vulnerable. So even if American culture during the period of the radiation experiments included a heightened concern about national security, there is little reason to conclude that this cultural difference removes blame for what was done.

CULTURALLY INDUCED IGNORANCE

There is another way in which a different cultural context in the past might be thought to invalidate retrospective moral judgments. Recognizing it does not commit one to cultural ethical relativism (and hence to the denial that there are human rights). Nor does it require us to swallow the implausible thesis that a few decades can lead to the abandonment of the most basic of general moral principles. Culturally induced ignorance—if it is nonculpable ignorance—can invalidate the moral judgments we make about the behavior of persons in another cultural setting. This ignorance exists when enculturated beliefs and concepts prevent individuals from discerning what they ought to do and is nonculpable when individuals cannot be blamed for not escaping the effects of such ignorance. Where individuals are prevented from discerning what they ought to do because of such nonculpable ignorance, it would be wrong to blame them for the actions they perform as a result of it.

There are two distinct ways in which a person's ability to discern what he ought to do can be impaired by his enculturated beliefs and concepts. First, morally relevant factual information simply may not be available in the culture. Second, the individual, like other members of the culture, may be morally ignorant. Due to his deeply enculturated beliefs and conceptual framework, he may be unable to discern what he ought to do because he is unable to make certain moral distinctions or even to recognize certain individuals as beings with rights, as members of the moral community.

To illustrate how culturally induced factual ignorance can undercut an otherwise valid retrospective moral judgment, consider the following case. Suppose we agree that persons should not be subjected to extremely risky medical experiments without a reasonable prospect of significant benefit to themselves. Suppose also that a scientist working in the 1940s subscribed to this tenet of the ethics of experimentation, but believed that the experiment for which he was recruiting subjects involved only minimal risk. Finally, suppose that his belief about the level of risk, though quite false, was supported by the best scientific evidence of his day, which he had conscientiously studied. Under such conditions we might well conclude that even if the patients' rights were violated, the scientist was not blameworthy. It is not hard to imagine errors of scientific fact that could have lead to wrongful actions in the human radiation experiments. If we, from the vantage point of superior data, believe that certain experiments were too risky, we might conclude that they never should have been performed. Yet if we believe that the best-informed scientific opinion of the day erroneously regarded certain experiments as being of minimal risk, we might also conclude that the scientists conducting them were not culpable. Given what they knew—and all they could have known at the time—they acted responsibly. They were ignorant of morally relevant facts, but their ignorance was nonculpable.

In at least four groups of experiments, however, the advisory committee's research uncovered no basis for arguing that factual error, culturally induced or otherwise, mitigates blame for wrongdoing. As we have already seen, the moral fault in the case of the Fernald School experiments had nothing to do with estimates of risk. Even if it is true that the amounts of radioisotopes given to the children in their "science club breakfasts" posed no significant risk of physical injury, they were treated wrongly nonetheless. The same was true in the plutonium injection experiments conducted at the University of Rochester and at the University of California between 1947 and 1950 and the total body irradiation experiments conducted at the University of Cincinnati Medical Center, which continued for over a decade until 1972 (pp. 243–46, pp. 390–97).

In the experiments at Rochester and California, sick individuals were subjected to radioactive substances without being informed of the nature of the procedure and without being told that the procedure was expected to yield no therapeutic benefit for them. In the case of the total body irradiation experiments, the researchers were aware that the doses being administered were extremely risky and even collected data that they concluded showed that the "treatment" carried a one in four risk of death from suppression of bone marrow production; yet the experiments continued (pp. 385–90). Similarly, although a government study had shown that American uranium workers were subject to dangerous levels of radon, the miners were not informed of the results of the study (pp. 565–75).

In none of these four groups of experiments can it be argued that factual errors that were widespread or uncorrectable at the time invalidate judgments of wrongdoing. So if the different cultural context of these human radiation experiments is to provide a reason why we should not make moral judgments about them, it is not because those who authorized and conducted the experiments were prevented from knowing what they ought and ought not to have done due to factual ignorance that was pervasive in their culture.

Earlier, a distinction was made between culturally induced factual ignorance and culturally induced moral ignorance, and it was noted that both can vitiate judgments of moral blame. Moral ignorance may be a less familiar notion than that of factual ignorance, but it is equally debilitating, and in some cases may be harder to correct.

History provides all too many examples in which the dominant culture of a society recognized that it is wrong to exploit persons or to kill persons wantonly or for trivial reasons, but failed to recognize that certain classes of individuals are persons, and hence that they possess the rights that persons possess. At least some of those thoroughly embued with the ideology of slavery in the antebellum South may have been morally blind in precisely this way, and their culture may have induced this dreadful and debilitating condition. Because they did not recognize blacks as persons, they did not see slavery as a violation of the rights of persons.

As with culturally induced factual ignorance, it is important to distinguish between culpable and nonculpable enculturated moral ignorance. Whether a person's moral ignorance is something for which he is culpable depends chiefly upon whether he had access to corrective beliefs and whether he availed himself of them. In other words, the fact that false beliefs are prevalent in a culture does not mean that they are not remediable. And if they are remediable, we may be blamed for maintaining them. Culpable moral ignorance cannot exculpate one of the wrongs that result from it.

Is there reason to believe that whatever wrongs were done in the course of the radiation experiments were the result of nonculpable, culturally induced moral ignorance? It is not possible here to answer this question with regard to all of the thousands of actions that are grouped together under the heading "the human radiation experiments." Nevertheless, a strong prima facie case can be made that the excuse of nonculpable culturally induced moral ignorance is not plausible in some of the most morally troubling experiments.

Consider again the four groups of experiments described above. In the case of the uranium miners, the excuse of cultural moral blindness would be far-fetched. Nothing in the cultural milieu of the United States in the 1940s and 1950s encouraged the belief that individuals who happened to be miners had no rights or were expendable. (Some of the minors were Native Americans, and strong prejudices existed against this group, but many were not). Moreover, the desperate attempts of the government to suppress disclosure of the study results indicate an awareness of the public outrage that would have followed revelation that the government knew the miners' lives were threatened but did nothing to prevent them from dying.

Nor is there any reason to believe that culturally induced moral ignorance undercuts the judgments by which we condemn the actions at the Fernald School.

It is one thing to say that the retarded have often been discriminated against, perhaps more so in the past than at present. It is another to suggest that cultural biases toward them were so extreme—and so incorrigible—that individuals who violated the most basic moral principles in their treatment of these children are blameless. Moreover, had there been strong cultural agreement that it was permissible to use retarded persons as mere means, there would have been no need to practice such an elaborate deception.

The plutonium and total body irradiation experiments require a more complicated analysis because they were performed in a medical context in which more specialized ethical principles were operative.

THE EVOLVING REQUIREMENT OF CONSENT

Perhaps the most plausible argument for not blaming physicians involved in radiation experiments that we now regard as wrongful is one based on the very plausible premise that the current standard of informed consent was not generally accepted at the time. Here it is important to distinguish between two modes of moral progress: compliance with the same standards may increase over time, or better standards may emerge over time. The fact that moral standards evolve (rather than being replaced instantaneously by entirely different standards) complicates retrospective moral judgment. The evolution of the requirement of informed consent is an excellent example of this complication. It is also directly relevant to our case study, the moral evaluation of the human radiation experiments.

We now recognize that medical treatment requires the informed consent of the patient (if the patient has decisional capacity). For a considerable period prior to the general acceptance of this principle, there was widespread acceptance of the principle that the consent of the patient is necessary. The replacement of the requirement of bare consent with the requirement of informed consent can certainly be viewed as moral progress.

Furthermore, the notion of informed consent itself has undergone a process of refinement and development through common law rulings, through analyses and explanations of these rulings in the legal literature, through philosophical treatments of the key concepts of autonomy and decisional capacity, and through guidelines advanced in reports by government and professional bodies. As a rough generalization, it can be said that the current dominant understanding of informed consent is more complex and more demanding than either the much earlier

requirement of consent or the first interpretations of what constitutes informed consent. If this is the case, then, a question arises: Is it appropriate to judge the actions of physicians in the past by the current standard of informed consent?

There is one reason not to do so. The principle of informed consent is both a principle of the professional ethics of physicians and a legal standard. As such it is an institutional product, or rather the product of the interactions of two institutions, medicine and law. For this reason, the principle of informed consent cannot be lumped together with the very general, commonsense moral prohibitions against deception, against treating persons as mere means, and against exploiting the vulnerable. It would, therefore, be wrong to hold individual physicians to the current, rather refined standard, if the institutions of law and medicine that existed when they acted had not yet developed such a standard.

Having said this, one must hasten to add that in none of the four groups of experiments discussed above was there even bare consent. So at least for these experiments, the fact that there has been progress in the development of the standard of consent is irrelevant.

THE HIPPOCRATIC TENET

Since the time of Hippocrates, it has been a fundamental ethical tenet of the medical profession (at least in the West) that the physician is not to harm his or her patient. Because it is universally acknowledged that even the best medical treatment sometimes involves incidental harms, the "First do no harm" admonition of the Hippocratic corpus is generally and quite reasonably understood to mean that the physician may harm the patient only for therapeutic reasons, that is, only when a significant net benefit to the patient is expected.

Thus, any experiments that physicians subjected their patients to that could be expected to cause harm without compensating therapeutic benefits violated this fundamental tenet of medical ethics. This is precisely what occurred, repeatedly over a ten-year period, in the case of the total body irradiation experiments at the University of Cincinnati Medical Center. Quite apart from whether these experiments also violated the requirement of informed consent, and independently of whether they violated the Nuremburg code (which was accepted by the American Medical Association in 1946), the physicians who conducted them are blameworthy.

WHY WE SHOULD MAKE RETROSPECTIVE MORAL JUDGMENTS

I have argued that there is a moral basis for making judgments of individual and professional culpability regarding some of the human radiation experiments. Even if my argument succeeds, another question remains: Granted that such judgments are valid, ought we to make them? Some might argue that there is nothing to gain from issuing judgments of culpability, that energies should be focused instead on the future—on realistic efforts to ensure that these sorts of wrongs will not occur again.

It would be a grave mistake, however, to assume that the choice is either to make judgments of culpability or to focus on future prevention, as if the two were unconnected. Effective preventive action must include serious efforts to make government officials and biomedical researchers today and in the future accountable for complying with sound ethical principles and procedures for the protection of human subjects. Holding people accountable—and deterring wrongdoing by putting people on notice that they will be held accountable—means specifying what their obligations are and making it clear that they will be judged culpable if they fail to honor those obligations.

Efforts to deter future wrongdoing are likely to be more effective, other things being equal, if individuals know that they personally will be held accountable. If this is not made clear, then individuals operating within complex institutions and organizations may console themselves with the thought that even if "the government" or "the agency" or "the profession" is found blameworthy, no serious consequence will be visited upon them as individuals. Refraining from making judgments of individual culpability about past abuses of human subjects can only feed this dangerous tendency to seek shelter behind the institutional or professional veil.

Perhaps even more importantly, it will be very hard if not impossible to explain and to justify effective proposals for institutional or professional reform without making clear references to particular instances of culpable action performed by identifiable individuals. Unless this is done, the specifics of reform proposals may appear unmotivated or of dubious relevance.

For these reasons, we should make judgments of individual culpability about wrongdoings in the past, if we have sufficient empirical evidence to do so responsibly. What I have argued in this essay is that there is in general no conceptual bar to making judgments of individual culpability about agents in the past. Whether there is sufficient empirical evidence will depend upon the particulars of the case. The herculean research effort mounted by the Advisory Committee on Human Radiation Experimentation supplies a wealth of such evidence.

REFERENCE

1. *Final Report: Advisory Committee on Human Radiation Experiments.* (*Washington, D.C.: Government Printing Office, 1995*). Also available from Oxford University Press.

The Ethics of Paying for Children's Participation in Research

David Wendler, Jonathan E. Rackoff, Ezekiel J. Emanuel, and Christine Grady

Paying for children's participation in research has become relatively common. A review of data from CenterWatch, a clinical trials listing service, suggests that nearly 25% of pediatric trials offer payment.[1] The amount of payment in the studies cited ranged from $25 (to children) for a study of influenza medication to $1500 (to families) for the time and travel involved in a study of medication for psoriasis.

Paying participants of any age remains controversial.[2] Some argue that payment may reduce participants' understanding or the voluntariness of their informed consent.[3] Others argue it may commodify research participation.[4,7] Conversely, *not* paying participants may be unethical: perhaps they should be rewarded for contributing to the social good; perhaps they should share in the profits of research. Although these issues concern paying participants of any age, the current article focuses on the ethics of paying for *children*, persons under 18 years of age who by law cannot consent, to participate in research.

The literature offers minimal and, occasionally, conflicting guidance on paying for children's research participation. The US Federal regulations (45CFR46) offer no guidance, whereas the American Academy of Pediatrics (AAP) argues this practice is consistent with the "traditions and ethics of society," but advocates

Wendler, David. "The Ethics of Paying for Children's Participation in Research," *The Journal of Pediatrics* 141:2 (2002), 166–171. Copyright © 2002. Reprinted by permission of Copyright Clearance Center on behalf of the publisher.

2 safeguards. Parents should receive no more than "a token gesture of appreciation," and payments to children should not be disclosed until the study's end.[5,6] The Institutional Review Board (IRB) at Children's Memorial Hospital in Chicago prohibits direct cash payments and requires that payment for *healthy* children's participation go to the children.[7] More recently, the European Union has prohibited all "incentives or financial inducements" for pediatric research.[8]

To assess these recommendations and develop consistent guidelines, it will first be necessary to develop a general ethical analysis of paying for children's research participation on the basis of 3 key questions: (1) when does payment raise ethical concerns? (2) which types of payment are most worrisome? and (3) what safeguards are needed to address these concerns?

Because children cannot consent, someone else, typically their parents, must decide whether to enroll them in research. Offers of payment raise ethical concerns then, because they have the potential to distort parents' decision-making; the opportunity for financial gain may lead parents to agree to research enrollment they otherwise would have opposed as contrary to their children's interests.

IRB   Intitutional Review Board

Some payments may *unwittingly* distort parents' decision-making. Research enrollment decisions are inherently complex, and the offer of payment may lead parents to unconsciously inflate the benefits and/or minimize the risks of their children's research participation. This possibility seems especially worrisome in the context of pediatric research because the primary decision-makers, typically the child's parents, may benefit financially without having to face the risks. Payment may also entice some parents to *intentionally* take advantage of their role as primary decision-makers, ignoring risks and enrolling children for their own benefit.

Finally, most children have limited experience with money, raising the possibility that payment may distort their decision-making as well. Because parents are the primary decision-makers, distortions of children's decision-making seem less worrisome. Nonetheless, this is a concern, particularly with respect to protocols that require children's "assent" or positive agreement.[9]

TYPE OF PAYMENT FOR RESEARCH PARTICIPATION

To assess the ethical concerns raised by the potential for payment to distort parents' and children's

decision-making, it is critical to differentiate research-related payments into 4 different types:

1. **Reimbursement payments** compensate parents and children for their direct research-related expenses and should be based on the actual costs (eg, transportation, meals, lodging) that families incur.
2. **Compensation payments** compensate parents and children for the time and inconvenience of research participation. Levels of compensation payments should be a function of the demands (clinic visits, hospital stays, research procedures) that research places on families.
3. **Appreciation payments** are bonuses given after children's participation to thank them for their efforts.
4. **Incentive payments** encourage children's research enrollment. Payments may be designed to act as incentives, for instance, when an investigator intentionally reimburses families above their actual costs to encourage enrollment. Payments may also *inadvertently* act as incentives if they unintentionally exceed families' costs and, thereby, act as incentives without being intended as such.

DUE COMPENSATION

The potential for payment to distort parents' or children's decision-making varies across the 4 types of payment. Reimbursement payments repay parents for the direct costs of research participation, ensuring that it is "revenue neutral." For this reason, reimbursement payments should not distort parents' or children's decision-making and seem ethically acceptable. Indeed, it seems IRBs should consider requiring investigators to reimburse parents, particularly when they incur significant direct costs and the research offers little or no potential medical benefit.

Compensation payments are intended to "zero out" the incremental time, burdens, and inconveniences that research participation adds to families' lives, above direct financial outlays. Unfortunately, unlike reimbursement payments, the precise level of compensation needed to "zero out" families' research burdens cannot be determined simply by adding up their actual expenses. Instead, IRBs will have to estimate the point at which compensation payments "zero out" the level of burden that families have in a given protocol. The complexity of this determination introduces the possibility that compensation payments may sometimes inadvertently exceed families' actual burden, providing an incentive for them to enroll in research. The potential for compensation payments to act as inadvertent incentives is increased by the fact that a protocol's level of burden will vary from family to family, with protocols that seem burdensome to some families and innocuous to others.

In practice, investigators will not be able to determine the level of compensation needed to precisely "zero out" different families' burdens. Instead, research institutions should develop standardized levels of compensation for the time children spend in research and the research procedures they undergo. It has been argued that compensation payments for the time *adults* spend in research should be commensurate with wages for unskilled, but essential, jobs.[4] Analogously, compensation payments for the time adolescents spend in research could be based on the minimum wage for teenagers, with children compensated for the time they are engaged in research activities.

To minimize the potential for compensation payments to distort parents' decision-making, they should be directed to the person who bears the burdens of research participation, typically the child. At the same time, some protocols require parents to contribute their own time, for instance, staying with a young child during research procedures. Banning all compensation payments to parents could block families with fewer economic resources from participating in such research. As with children's subjective sense of burden, the monetary value of a given amount of time will vary widely from family to family. To guard against the possibility that adequate compensation for some parents may act as an inadvertent incentive for others, compensation payments to parents should be calibrated to the economic resources of the least well-off families. By analogy to payment for adults who participate as *subjects*, payments to compensate parents who contribute to their children's research participation could be based on minimum wage levels for adults.

When calculated accurately, compensation payments ensure that children and their parents are compensated for the incremental time, burdens, and inconveniences that research participation adds to their lives. Hence, with these payments in place, additional appreciation payments seem unnecessary. In addition, if families learn before enrollment that appreciation payments are being offered, they may inadvertently act as incentives. This suggests the best approach may be to ban additional appreciation payments, provided compensation levels are adequate.

By compensating families for the direct costs and burdens of research participation, reimbursement and compensation payments eliminate the financial obstacles that might keep most families from participating in research. It is hoped, with these obstacles eliminated, that families will decide to enroll in research because they want to help others and/or believe that the research is in the child's best interests. However, in some cases, even altruism and the potential for direct benefit to the child, combined with reimbursement and compensation payments, may not be enough to encourage sufficient enrollment.

This possibility raises the central ethical concern related to pediatric payment: Is it ethical for investigators to offer incentive payments on top of appropriate reimbursement and compensation payments?

BANS ON THE DISCLOSURE OF PAYMENTS

The American Academy of Pediatrics guidelines are meant to ensure that payment is not "part of the reason that a child volunteered or is volunteered for a study" by banning the *disclosure* of payments until the child's participation in research is completed.[6] Although this practice seems to eliminate payment's potential to distort parents' or children's decision to enroll in research, it raises a number of ethical concerns.

It is widely agreed that investigators should disclose the true nature of their research to subjects. Although a practice of nondisclosure does not involve outright deception, it does require investigators to conceal pertinent information and may lead families to the mistaken belief that payment is not being offered. A policy of nondisclosure would also place research teams in an awkward position when families ask whether payment is being offered. Finally, even when research teams observe a strict policy of nondisclosure, families may learn through support networks or webpages that payment is being offered, raising the possibility that payments may act as inadvertent incentives.

BANS ON INCENTIVE PAYMENTS

An alternative approach, advocated by the European Union, is to ban all payments that might act as incentives, eliminating the possibility that incentive payments might distort parents' or children's decision-making. Given the importance of ensuring that families make research decisions consistent with children's interests, such bans seem defensible. But are they desirable?

Improving medical care for children is an important social goal, especially since so many treatments have not been validated for use in children. To the extent incentive payments are needed to recruit enough subjects to complete important research, banning them could hinder attempts to achieve this important social goal. This suggests that instead of banning incentive payments entirely, it makes sense to consider whether there are any alternatives that allow incentive payments, while minimizing their potential to distort parents' or children's decision-making.

MINIMIZING DISTORTED DECISION-MAKING

Payment's potential influence on parents' decision-making can be compared with its potential influence on physicians' decision-making. Physicians' primary interest should be their patient's welfare; parents' primary interest should be their children's welfare. Just as offers of payment may distort physicians' consideration of patients' welfare, they may also distort parents' protection of their children's welfare. Borrowing from guidelines on physician's conflicts of interest suggests that addressing incentive payments' potential to distort decision-making requires minimizing both the *likelihood* of distorted decision-making, and the *magnitude* of its potential harms.

Policies that prohibit all incentives, such as the European Union's, seem to assume that payment should never be offered as a positive reason to enroll children in research because such offers, no matter how small, may distort parents' decision-making. Although understandable, this view seems to overestimate the potential effect of relatively small incentives. For instance, relatively small incentive payments may be enough to convince parents to do things against which they have only a slight disinclination, such as driving their child to a research hospital, but not enough to get them to do things against which they have a stronger disinclination, such as enrolling their children in research that poses undue risks. Unfortunately, there are insufficient empirical data to determine precisely what levels of incentive payments might entice parents to enroll their children in research that is inconsistent with the children's interests. Until such data are developed, IRBs considering whether to approve incentive payments should carefully assess what levels would encourage children's research participation without distorting parents' decision-making. In making these assessments, IRBs might appeal to existing community standards regarding appropriate incentives outside of the research context. For instance, what incentives are considered acceptable to encourage children to shovel snow from an infirm neighbor's sidewalk?

In some cases, IRBs may accept that incentives are needed to ensure sufficient enrollment, but remain concerned that the needed payments may distort parents' or children's decision-making. Presumably, the potential to distort families' decision-making will be negligible when very small incentive payments, such as $10, are offered. Moreover, the magnitude of any harms that result from families' distorted decision-making will be minor when the research poses little or no risks. However, concerns that payment may introduce an undue inducement should be carefully addressed when larger incentive payments are needed, and the research poses more than minor risks. In these cases, IRBs should consider requiring that a child advocate independently assess the appropriateness of the payment levels and families' decisions to enroll. In particular, the independent consultant could assess families' reasons for thinking that participation is consistent with the children's interests, for instance, by asking the children how they feel about the prospect of participating in the research and asking the parents what effect they think the research might have on their child.

Even when incentives do not distort families' decision-making, they may introduce a selection bias by increasing the number of families who enroll in research for the money. In addition, families who enroll in research for monetary gain may be less reliable research participants; they may be less likely to take medications on schedule, report side effects, attend required clinic visits, etc. To minimize payment's potential negative effect on pediatric research, IRBs should approve incentives in addition to reimbursement and compensation payments in limited cases only.

To consider an example, protocols without the potential for "important subject benefit" must obtain the assent of children who are capable of providing it (46.408). This requirement can make it difficult to complete certain minimal risk studies in younger children. For instance, many children 7 years to 11 years old have developed a sense of independence, but do not yet recognize the importance of research. These children may refuse to assent to a research survey or the provision of a saliva sample for biologic testing simply because they would rather be playing with their friends. A $5 incentive payment may be sufficient to encourage such children to give their assent (thus allowing researchers to complete important research) without being large enough to entice children's agreement to a study they recognize as contrary to their interests, such as one that includes procedures they find terrifying.

Finally, in addition to inappropriate inducements to *enroll* children in research, payments may provide an inappropriate inducement to *keep* children in research; parents and children may be unwilling to drop out for fear of losing money. To address this possibility, subjects who become ineligible after enrollment should receive any incentive payments that were offered but not yet delivered, and should receive pro-rated reimbursement and compensation for participation to date.

The *magnitude* of the harms that may result from distorted decision-making depends on the extent to which children thereby are exposed to risks. Current Federal regulations allow children to be enrolled in research when the prospect of direct benefit "justifies" the risks. Children may be enrolled in research that does not offer a compensating potential for direct benefit only when the risks are no greater than a "minor increase" over the risks children face in everyday life (45CFR46.406).

By limiting the risks to which children may be exposed in research that does not offer a compensating potential for direct benefit, the Federal regulations may appear sufficient to address the potential harms of pediatric payment; as long as any "excess" risks are low, even payments that distort parents' decision-making won't lead to serious harm. The problem with relying on the risk guidelines alone is that IRBs must make prospective risk assessments on the basis of the population of children they expect to be enrolled, not the specific children that actually do enroll. Even when IRBs make accurate risk assessments, the research may pose serious "idiosyncratic" risks to certain children. For instance, a brief magnetic resonance imaging scan that poses very low risks to the vast majority of children may pose serious risks to children with a morbid fear of loud noises. Given this possibility, it is important for parents to provide an additional confirmation that research enrollment poses acceptably low risks to their children in particular, yielding an important reason to ensure that payment does not distort their decision-making. To this end, we consider 11 safeguards to minimize the likelihood that payment for pediatric research will distort parents' or children's decision-making. The proposed additional safeguards are grouped by institutional guidelines, IRB review process, and mechanisms for payment.

Institutional guidelines

1. Develop guidelines for all 4 types of payment. Such guidelines should specify standards for reimbursement and compensation payments to avoid variation across similar protocols and minimize the extent to which compensation payments may act as inadvertent incentives. Institutions should consider requiring families to be reimbursed for anything more than minor direct costs. Compensation amounts for children should be determined on the basis of the accepted minimum wage payments for teenagers. Lower payments or nonmonetary forms of compensation are most appropriate for younger children. Guidelines should also consider banning appreciation payments, and allowing incentive payments in limited cases only, with strict limits on incentive amounts.

2. Adopt an explicit policy on advertising payment for children's research participation. These polices should specify the extent to which payment may be included in advertising for pediatric research. Mention of types of payment may be appropriate provided they are not emphasized and risks and burdens are also mentioned. Specific payment amounts should not be included in advertisements for pediatric research.

The IRB review process

3. Require an explicit justification for all incentives. Given the potential for distorted decision-making, the default should be to limit payment to reimbursement and compensation. IRBs should approve payment beyond compensation levels only when it is within institutional limits and there is sufficient justification, for example, when data suggest payment is needed to recruit enough subjects.

4. Allow children to be paid less than adults in identical studies. Recent National Institutes of Health and Food and Drug Administration mandates to encourage children's participation in research may increase the number of children who participate in protocols designed for adults.[10–12] Because fairness recommends likes be treated alike, it may be assumed children should be paid the same as adults for equivalent burdens. However, even when adults and children assume the same level of burdens, they are not equal in other ways. Most importantly, a given amount of payment is likely to exert a greater influence on children's decision-making than adults' decision-making. When such influence could lead to distorted judgment, it seems appropriate, as expressed by most guidelines, to privilege protecting children over treating them like adults.

5. Ensure payment to withdrawn subjects. To minimize the chances that payment provides undue influence to keep children in research, subjects who become ineligible after enrolling should be ensured reimbursement for expenses incurred, compensation for time and burdens to date, and any incentives that were offered but not yet delivered.

6. Consider independent consent assessments in worrisome cases. When compensation or incentive payments may represent an undue inducement to enroll in research that poses more than minor risks, the IRB should consider requiring an independent assessment by a child advocate. The advocate could assess the appropriateness of the level of payment and assess families' decision to enroll. Payment may be acceptable as a positive reason to enroll children in research, provided it does not entice parents or children to enroll in research that conflicts with the child's interests.

7. Develop a general policy on describing payments in consent and assent forms. Payments should be listed in a separate section of the consent and assent forms, not in the benefits section. Compensation payments should be described per unit of time or procedure, not as lump sums. How payment will be handled in the event of early withdrawal or disqualification should be described.

Payment mechanisms

8. Direct compensation payments to the proper party. Payments to compensate for research participation should go to the person who bears the burden, typically the child.

9. Avoid lump sum payments.   Large lump payments, such as $2000, are more enticing than equivalent, pro-rated payments, such as $40 per weekly clinic visit. To address this concern, reimbursement payments should be provided as costs are incurred, and compensation payments should be provided at regular intervals throughout research participation.

10. Consider deferred payments.   Large sums, even when based on participation time and burdens, may distort parents' and children's decision-making. Hence, for protocols that offer large sums, deferred payment mechanisms, such as savings bonds for the child, might be appropriate.

11. Consider noncash payments.   Parents often exercise control over their children's assets. To minimize parents' access to children's payments, gift certificates redeemable at children's stores or the choice of an age-appropriate gift, such as a book, video, or movie pass, could be offered in lieu of money.

Ethical concerns over payment for children's research participation tend to regard all forms of payment as equally suspect. However, payments to reimburse for out-of-pocket expenses and to compensate for research time and burdens are ethically justifiable and should be strongly considered in cases where research-related costs are especially high and there is little or no potential for medical benefit. Although banning all incentive payments beyond reimbursement and compensation is ethically defensible, doing so runs the risk of impeding socially valuable pediatric research. To avoid this cost, small incentive payments may be acceptable when needed to ensure sufficient enrollment in important research.

REFERENCES

1. Center Watch clinical trials listing service. Boston (MA): Center Watch; 2000. Also available at: http://www.centerwatch.com

2. US Department of Health and Human Services, Office of Protection from Research Risks. Protecting human research subjects: IRB guidebook. Washington (DC): 1993.

3. McNeill P. Paying people to participate in research: why not? Bioethics 1997;11:390–6.

4. Dickert N, Grady C. What's the price of a research subject? N Engl J Med 1000;341:198–203.

5. Code of Federal Regulations. Title 45, part 46. October 1, 2001. Available at: http://www.access.gpo.gov/nara/cfr/waisidx_01/45cfr46_01.html.

6. American Academy of Pediatrics. Guidelines for the ethical conduct of studies to evaluate drugs in pediatric populations (RE9503). Pediatrics 1995;95:286–94.

7. Giddling SS, Camp D, Flanagan MH, Kowalski J, Lingl L, Silverman B, et al. A policy regarding research in healthy children. J Pediatr 1993;123:852–5.

8. Directive 2001/10/ec of the European Parliament and of the Council of 4 April 2001 on the approximation of the laws, regulations, and administrative provisions of the Member States relating to the implementation of good clinical practice in the conduct of clinical trials on medicinal products for human use. Article 4(d).

9. Code of Federal Regulations. Title 45, part 46.408(a). Available at: http://www.access.gpo.gov/nara/cfr/waisidx_01/45cfr46_01.html.

10. National Institutes of Health. Policy and guidelines on the inclusion of children as participants in research involving human subjects. NIH Guide Grants Contracts; March 6, 1998. Available at: http://www.nih.gov/grants/guide/notice-ofiles/not98–024.html.

11. Regulations requiring manufacturers to assess the safety and effectiveness of new drugs and biological products in pediatric patients. Docket No. 97N0165, pp66631–72 (FR Doc. 98–31902.

12. Food and Drug Administration. Modernization Act of 1997 (FDAMA-1997), section 505A. Available at: http://www.fda.gov/opacom/7modact.html.

CLINICAL TRIALS

Of Mice But Not Men: Problems of the Randomized Clinical Trial

Samuel Hellman and Deborah S. Hellman

As medicine has become increasingly scientific and less accepting of unsupported opinion or proof by anecdote, the randomized controlled clinical trial has become the standard technique for changing diagnostic or therapeutic methods. The use of this technique creates an ethical dilemma.[1,2] Researchers participating

Hellman, Samuel and Deborah S. Hellman. "Of Mice but Not Men: Problems of the Randomized Clinical Trial," *The New England Journal of Medicine* 324 (May 30, 1991), 1585–1589. Copyright © 1991. Reprinted by permission of Massachusetts Medical Society.

in such studies are required to modify their ethical commitments to individual patients and do serious damage to the concept of the physician as a practicing, empathetic professional who is primarily concerned with each patient as an individual. Researchers using a randomized clinical trial can be described as physician-scientists, a term that expresses the tension between the two roles. The physician, by entering into a relationship with an individual patient, assumes certain obligations, including the commitment always to act in the patient's best interests. As Leon Kass has rightly maintained, "the physician must produce unswervingly the virtues of loyalty and fidelity to his patient."[3] Though the ethical requirements of this relationship have been modified by legal obligations to report wounds of a suspicious nature and certain infectious diseases, these obligations in no way conflict with the central ethical obligation to act in the best interests of the patient medically. Instead, certain nonmedical interests of the patient are preempted by other social concerns.

The role of the scientist is quite different. The clinical scientist is concerned with answering questions—i.e., determining the validity of formally constructed hypotheses. Such scientific information, it is presumed, will benefit humanity in general. The clinical scientist's role has been well described by Dr. Anthony Fauci, director of the National Institute of Allergy and Infectious Diseases, who states the goals of the randomized clinical trial in these words: "It's not to deliver therapy. It's to answer a scientific question so that the drug can be available for everybody once you've established safety and efficacy."[4] The demands of such a study can conflict in a number of ways with the physician's duty to minister to patients. The study may create a false dichotomy in the physician's opinions: according to the premise of the randomized clinical trial, the physician may only know or not know whether a proposed course of treatment represents an improvement; no middle position is permitted. What the physician thinks, suspects, believes, or has a hunch about is assigned to the "not knowing" category, because knowing is defined on the basis of an arbitrary but accepted statistical test performed in a randomized clinical trial. Thus, little credence is given to information gained beforehand in other ways or to information accrued during the trial but without the required statistical degree of assurance that a difference is not due to chance. The randomized clinical trial also prevents the treatment technique from being modified on the basis of the growing knowledge of the physicians during their participation in the trial. Moreover, it limits access to the data as they are collected until specific milestones are achieved. This prevents

physicians from profiting not only from their individual experience, but also from the collective experience of the other participants.

The randomized clinical trial requires doctors to act simultaneously as physicians and as scientists. This puts them in a difficult and sometimes untenable ethical position. The conflicting moral demands arising from the use of the randomized clinical trial reflect the classic conflict between rights-based moral theories and utilitarian ones. The first of these, which depend on the moral theory of Immanuel Kant (and seen more recently in neo-Kantian philosophers, such as John Rawls[5]), asserts that human beings, by virtue of their unique capacity for rational thought, are bearers of dignity. As such, they ought not to be treated merely as means to an end; rather, they must always be treated as ends in themselves. Utilitarianism, by contrast, defines what is right as the greatest good for the greatest number—that is, as social utility. This view, articulated by Jeremy Bentham and John Stuart Mill, requires that pleasures (understood broadly, to include such pleasures as health and well-being) and pains be added together. The morally correct act is the act that produces the most pleasure and the least pain overall.

A classic objection to the utilitarian position is that according to that theory, the distribution of pleasures and pains is of no moral consequence. This element of the theory severely restricts physicians from being utilitarians, or at least from following the theory's dictates. Physicians must care very deeply about the distribution of pain and pleasure, for they have entered into a relationship with one or a number of individual patients. They cannot be indifferent to whether it is these patients or others that suffer for the general benefit of society. Even though society might gain from the suffering of a few, and even though the doctor might believe that such a benefit is worth a given patient's suffering (i.e., that utilitarianism is right in the particular case), the ethical obligation created by the covenant between doctor and patient requires the doctor to see the interests of the individual patient as primary and compelling. In essence, the doctor-patient relationship requires doctors to see their patients as bearers of rights who cannot be merely used for the greater good of humanity.

As Fauci has suggested,[4] the randomized clinical trial routinely asks physicians to sacrifice the interests of their particular patients for the sake of the study and that of the information that it will make available for the benefit of society. This practice is ethically problematic. Consider first the initial formulation of a trial. In particular, consider the case of a disease for which there is no satisfactory therapy—for example, advanced cancer or the acquired immunodeficiency syndrome (AIDS). A new agent that promises more effectiveness is the subject of the study. The control group must be given either an unsatisfactory treatment or a placebo. Even though the therapeutic value of the new agent is unproved, if physicians think that it has promise, are they acting in the best interests of their patients in allowing them to be randomly assigned to the control group? Is persisting in such an assignment consistent with the specific commitments taken on in the doctor-patient relationship? As a result of interactions with patients with AIDS and their advocates, Merigan[6] recently suggested modifications in the design of clinical trials that attempt to deal with the unsatisfactory treatment given to the control group. The view of such activists has been expressed by Rebecca Pringle Smith of Community Research Initiative in New York: "Even if you have a supply of compliant martyrs, trials must have some ethical validity."[4]

If the physician has no opinion about whether the new treatment is acceptable, then random assignment is ethically acceptable, but such lack of enthusiasm for the new treatment does not augur well for either the patient or the study. Alternatively, the treatment may show promise of beneficial results but also present a risk of undesirable complications. When the physician believes that the severity and likelihood of harm and good are evenly balanced, randomization may be ethically acceptable. If the physician has no preference for either treatment (is in a state of equipoise[7,8]), then randomization is acceptable. If, however, he or she believes that the new treatment may be either more or less successful or more or less toxic, the use of randomization is not consistent with fidelity to the patient.

The argument usually used to justify randomization is that it provides, in essence, a critique of the usefulness of the physician's beliefs and opinions, those that have not yet been validated by a randomized clinical trial. As the argument goes, these not-yet-validated beliefs are as likely to be wrong as right. Although physicians are ethically required to provide their patients with the best available treatment, there simply is no best treatment yet known.

The reply to this argument takes two forms. First, and most important, even if this view of the reliability of a physician's opinion is accurate, the ethical constraints of an individual doctor's relationship with a particular patient require the doctor to provide individual care. Although physicians must take pains to make clear the speculative nature of their views, they cannot withhold these views from the patient. The patient asks from the doctor both knowledge and judgment. The relationship established between them rightfully allows patients to

ask for the judgment of their particular physicians, not merely that of the medical profession in general. Second, it may not be true, in fact, that the not-yet-validated beliefs of physicians are as likely to be wrong as right. The greater certainty obtained with a randomized clinical trial is beneficial, but that does not mean that a lesser degree of certainty is without value. Physicians can acquire knowledge through methods other than the randomized clinical trial. Such knowledge, acquired over time and less formally than is required in a randomized clinical trial, may be of great value to a patient.

Even if it is ethically acceptable to begin a study, one often forms an opinion during its course—especially in studies that are impossible to conduct in a truly double-blinded fashion—that makes it ethically problematic to continue. The inability to remain blinded usually occurs in studies of cancer or AIDS, for example, because the therapy is associated by nature with serious side effects. Trials attempt to restrict the physician's access to the data in order to prevent such unblinding. Such restrictions should make physicians eschew the trial, since their ability to act in the patient's best interests will be limited. Even supporters of randomized clinical trials, such as Merigan, agree that interim findings should be presented to patients to ensure that no one receives what seems an inferior treatment.[6] Once physicians have formed a view about the new treatment, can they continue randomization? If random assignment is stopped, the study may be lost and the participation of the previous patients wasted. However, if physicians continue the randomization when they have a definite opinion about the efficacy of the experimental drug, they are not acting in accordance with the requirements of the doctor-patient relationship. Furthermore, as their opinion becomes more firm, stopping the randomization may not be enough. Physicians may be ethically required to treat the patients formerly placed in the control group with the therapy that now seems probably effective. To do so would be faithful to the obligations created by the doctor-patient relationship, but it would destroy the study.

To resolve this dilemma, one might suggest that the patient has abrogated the rights implicit in a doctor-patient relationship by signing an informed-consent form. We argue that such rights cannot be waived or abrogated. They are inalienable. The right to be treated as an individual deserving the physician's best judgment and care, rather than to be used as a means to determine the best treatment for others, is inherent in every person. This right, based on the concept of dignity, cannot be waived. What of altruism, then? Is it not the patient's right to make a sacrifice for the general good? This question must be considered from both positions—that of the patient and that of the physician. Although patients may decide to waive this right, it is not consistent with the role of a physician to ask that they do so. In asking, the doctor acts as a scientist instead. The physician's role here is to propose what he or she believes is best medically for the specific patient, not to suggest participation in a study from which the patient cannot gain. Because the opportunity to help future patients is of potential value to a patient, some would say physicians should not deny it. Although this point has merit, it offers so many opportunities for abuse that we are extremely uncomfortable about accepting it. The responsibilities of physicians are much clearer; they are to minister to the current patient.

Moreover, even if patients could waive this right, it is questionable whether those with terminal illness would be truly able to give voluntary informed consent. Such patients are extremely dependent on both their physicians and the health care system. Aware of this dependence, physicians must not ask for consent, for in such cases the very asking breaches the doctor-patient relationship. Anxious to please their physicians, patients may have difficulty refusing to participate in the trial the physicians describe. The patients may perceive their refusal as damaging to the relationship, whether or not it is so. Such perceptions of coercion affect the decision. Informed-consent forms are difficult to understand, especially for patients under the stress of serious illness for which there is no satisfactory treatment. The forms are usually lengthy, somewhat legalistic, complicated, and confusing, and they hardly bespeak the compassion expected of the medical profession. It is important to remember that those who have studied the doctor-patient relationship have emphasized its empathetic nature.

> [The] relationship between doctor and patient partakes of a peculiar intimacy. It presupposes on the part of the physician not only knowledge of his fellow men but sympathy.... This aspect of the practice of medicine has been designated as the art; yet I wonder whether it should not, most properly, be called the essence.[9]

How is such a view of the relationship consonant with random assignment and informed consent? The Physician's Oath of the World Medical Association affirms the primacy of the deontologic view of patients' rights: "Concern for the interests of the subject must always prevail over the interests of science and society."[10]

Furthermore, a single study is often not considered sufficient. Before a new form of therapy is generally accepted, confirmatory trials must be conducted. How can one conduct such trials ethically unless one is convinced that the first trial was in error? The ethical problems we have discussed are only exacerbated when a completed randomized clinical trial indicates that a given treatment is preferable. Even if the physician believes the initial trial was in error, the physician must indicate to the patient the full results of that trial.

The most common reply to the ethical arguments has been that the alternative is to return to the physician's intuition, to anecdotes, or to both as the basis of medical opinion. We all accept the dangers of such a practice. The argument states that we must therefore accept randomized, controlled clinical trials regardless of their ethical problems because of the great social benefit they make possible, and we salve our conscience with the knowledge that informed consent has been given. This returns us to the conflict between patients' rights and social utility. Some would argue that this tension can be resolved by placing a relative value on each. If the patient's right that is being compromised is not a fundamental right and the social gain is very great, then the study might be justified. When the right is fundamental, however, no amount of social gain, or almost none, will justify its sacrifice. Consider, for example, the experiments on humans done by physicians under the Nazi regime. All would agree that these are unacceptable regardless of the value of the scientific information gained. Some people go so far as to say that no use should be made of the results of those experiments because of the clearly unethical manner in which the data were collected. This extreme example may not seem relevant, but we believe that in its hyperbole it clarifies the fallacy of a utilitarian approach to the physician's relationship with the patient. To consider the utilitarian gain is consistent neither with the physician's role nor with the patient's rights.

It is fallacious to suggest that only the randomized clinical trial can provide valid information or that all information acquired by this technique is valid. Such experimental methods are intended to reduce error and bias and therefore reduce the uncertainty of the result. Uncertainty cannot be eliminated, however. The scientific method is based on increasing probabilities and increasingly refined approximations of truth.[11] Although the randomized clinical trial contributes to these ends, it is neither unique nor perfect. Other techniques may also be useful.[12]

Randomized trials often place physicians in the ethically intolerable position of choosing between the good of the patient and that of society. We urge that such situations be avoided and that other techniques of acquiring clinical information be adopted. For example, concerning trials of treatments for AIDS, Byar et al.[13] have said that "some traditional approaches to the clinical-trials process may be unnecessarily rigid and unsuitable for this disease." In this case, AIDS is not what is so different; rather, the difference is in the presence of AIDS activists, articulate spokespersons for the ethical problems created by the application of the randomized clinical trial to terminal illnesses. Such arguments are equally applicable to advanced cancer and other serious illnesses. Byar et al. agree that there are even circumstances in which uncontrolled clinical trials may be justified: when there is no effective treatment to use as a control, when the prognosis is uniformly poor, and when there is a reasonable expectation of benefit without excessive toxicity. These conditions are usually found in clinical trials of advanced cancer.

The purpose of the randomized clinical trial is to avoid the problems of observer bias and patient selection. It seems to us that techniques might be developed to deal with these issues in other ways. Randomized clinical trials deal with them in a cumbersome and heavy-handed manner, by requiring large numbers of patients in the hope that random assignment will balance the heterogeneous distribution of patients into the different groups. By observing known characteristics of patients, such as age and sex, and distributing them equally between groups, it is thought that unknown factors important in determining outcomes will also be distributed equally. Surely, other techniques can be developed to deal with both observer bias and patient selection. Prospective studies without randomization, but with the evaluation of patients by uninvolved third parties, should remove observer bias. Similar methods have been suggested by Royall.[12] Prospective matched-pair analysis, in which patients are treated in a manner consistent with their physician's views, ought to help ensure equivalence between the groups and thus mitigate the effect of patient selection, at least with regard to known covariates. With regard to unknown covariates, the security would rest, as in randomized trials, in the enrollment of large numbers of patients and in confirmatory studies. This method would not pose ethical difficulties, since patients would receive the treatment recommended by their physician. They would be included in the study by independent observers matching patients with respect to known characteristics, a process that would not affect patient care and that could be performed independently any number of times.

This brief discussion of alternatives to randomized clinical trials is sketchy and incomplete. We wish only to point out that there may be satisfactory alternatives, not to describe and evaluate them completely. Even if randomized clinical trials were much better than any alternative, however, the ethical dilemmas they present may put their use at variance with the primary obligations of the physician. In this regard, Angell cautions, "If this commitment to the patient is attenuated, even for so good a cause as benefits to future patients, the implicit assumptions of the doctor-patient relationship are violated."[14] The risk of such attenuation by the randomized trial is great. The AIDS activists have brought this dramatically to the attention of the academic medical community. Techniques appropriate to the laboratory may not be applicable to humans. We must develop and use alternative methods for acquiring clinical knowledge.

REFERENCES

1. Hellman S. Randomized clinical trials and the doctor-patient relationship: and ethical dilemma. Cancer Clin Trials 1979; 2:189–93.

2. *Idem.* A doctor's dilemma: the doctor-patient relationship in clinical investigation. In: Proceedings of the Fourth National Conference on Human Values and Cancer, New York, March 15–17, 1984. New York: American Cancer Society, 1984:144–6.

3. Kass L. R. Toward a more natural science: biology and human affairs. New York: Free Press, 1985:196.

4. Palca J. AIDS drug trials enter new age. Science 1989; 246:19–21.

5. Rawls J. A theory of justice. Cambridge, Mass.: Belknap Press of Harvard University Press, 1971:183–92, 446–52.

6. Merigan T. C. You *can* teach an old dog new tricks—how AIDS trials are pioneering new strategies. N Engl J Med 1990; 323:1341–3.

7. Freedman B. Equipoise and the ethics of clinical research. N Engl J Med 1987; 317:141–5.

8. Singer P. A, Lantos J. D, Whitington P. F, Broelsch C. E, Siegler M. Equipoise and the ethics of segmental liver transplantation. Clin Res 1988; 36:539–45.

9. Longcope W. T. Methods and medicine. Bull Johns Hopkins Hosp 1932; 50:4–20.

10. Report on medical ethics. World Med Assoc Bull 1949; 1:109, 111.

11. Popper K. The problem of induction. In: Miller D, ed. Popper selections. Princeton, N.J.: Princeton University Press, 1985:101–17.

12. Royall R. M. Ethics and statistics in randomized clinical trials. Stat Sci 1991; 6(1):52–62.

13. Byar D. P, Schoenfeld D. A, Green S. B, et al. Design considerations for AIDS trials. N Engl J Med 1990; 323:1343–8.

14. Angell M. Patients' preferences in randomized clinical trials. N Engl J Med 1984; 310:1385–7.

Women and Underserved Populations: Access to Clinical Trials

Sara Goering

INTRODUCTION

Lack of adequate access to health care for traditionally underserved populations (most notably poor ethnic minorities and women) is tied to a lack of medical research focused on their particular needs. The two problems are intricately related—each feeds on the other. Many of the factors that make access to health care difficult for underserved populations (including, for instance, lack of funding, geographical maldistribution of services, inadequate transportation, and cultural or linguistic differences and discrimination) also make it difficult to involve them as subjects in medical research. Although a majority of these barriers to health care could be overcome by balancing current socioeconomic inequities, a growing body of literature suggests that in at least some instances diseases themselves may be manifested differently among the races and sexes, requiring different kinds or levels of treatment. Thus, socioeconomic reparations alone will not remedy the health problems of underserved ethnic groups and women. Without research to assess the particular needs of these groups, access to the existing health care system might not significantly help them and in some cases could even be harmful....

In this [selection] I will show why restricting medical research to studies done with white, middle-aged men as subjects is inappropriate and unjust. I will point to several examples in which such conduct has led to worrisome results. I will also show how the current justifications for the exclusion of minorities and women in research are based on racism and sexism in the medical establishment, and suggest that steps be taken to remedy this situation. Finally, I will offer a word of caution regarding the segregation of races and sexes in research, for the potential for great benefits is tainted with the possibility of serious costs.

PROBLEMS WITH THE WHITE MALE MODEL

A growing body of literature reveals clinical studies in which ethnic and sex differences have a significant effect on the course and kind of treatment. Simply extrapolating data obtained from white middle-aged men is proving not to be the answer to settling these differences. Although they are an easily accessible population to procure as research subjects, white middle-aged men are not a truly representative population, and the seemingly less accessible populations pay the price of misrepresentation.

Techniques and treatments that have been studied on white middle-aged men in a controlled and closely monitored research environment are then unleashed on the much more diverse general population, most often without the security of the clinical setting. Patients from populations who experience difficulties in getting access to health care may be given a new treatment and never be heard from again, at least not by the same physician. Given that population differences in disease manifestation and treatment do exist, this is a dangerous method of treating underserved populations and may place them in even greater danger than the illness for which they believe they are receiving treatment. In what follows, I will give several examples as evidence of this problem. Clearly, the solution is to target more clinical studies on the particular medical needs of these populations, using members of the groups themselves as subjects.

Thus far, the issue of ethnic and sex differences in disease diagnosis and treatment has been addressed only in obvious cases, such as sickle cell disease among African Americans, Tay-Sachs among Eastern European Jews.... Noteworthy population differences, however, go far beyond these most obvious cases. Consider the following examples.

Studies conducted on white men led the American Heart Association to suggest a diet for all Americans to reduce their cholesterol levels in order to decrease the risk of coronary heart disease. Although they recommended a general reduction in cholesterol intake, they targeted low-density lipoprotein (LDLs) in particular. Further studies, however, have suggested that, although high levels of LDLs are dangerous for men, they are far less threatening for women. In addition, women are much more sensitive to low levels of the so-called good cholesterol, or high-density lipoprotein (HDLs). This means that diets that recommend a general cholesterol reduction are potentially harmful to women.

In another study, African-American men with psychiatric problems traditionally treated with lithium, a drug tested and used successfully on white men, suffered excessive toxic reactions when treated with the drug. It was found that the African-American men as a group had less efficient lithium-sodium countertransport mechanisms than white men. The toxicity of the lithium treatment greatly increased the already high risk of renal failure for the African-American men.

A number of studies have shown that Asian patients react more strongly than whites when treated with popranolol, a beta-blocker that reduces heart rate and blood pressure. While this variation was traditionally accounted for by generalized differences in body size and/or weight, new evidence shows that Asians as a group have a much faster metabolism for popranolol than whites and that a smaller percentage of the dosage is inactivated by plasma protein binding in Asians. On the other hand, data show that African-American hypertensive patients do not respond to beta-blockers as well as whites and that the serum concentration of popranolol is lower in African-American patients than in whites who received identical doses.

While the list of studies showing significant differences between populations goes on, its length is not to be outdone by the number of studies continuing to ignore these findings. For instance, an NIH-funded study on the potential prophylactic effects of aspirin on heart disease was conducted entirely on men, although heart disease is the number one killer of women. One reason cited for the exclusion of women as subjects was the lack of available women physicians. (The study was conducted with physicians as subjects.) Others blame the extra time and money that would have been needed to complete the study to significance. . . .

The lack of women in the subject population of this study made it difficult for many doctors to personally prescribe the courses of action that are publicly suggested by organizations such as the American Heart Association. However, after an uproar about the unknown effects of regular aspirin consumption on women, another study was undertaken with female nurses as subjects, with the conclusion that aspirin does indeed reduce the risk of heart attack for women. The fact that these studies rendered similar results for both sexes should not be too quickly generalized to other disorders and treatments.

Recently, for example, concern has arisen about sex differences in response to HIV infection. In order to be considered for most clinical drug trials for AIDS, a person must exhibit "full-blown" AIDS, which includes a broad spectrum of illnesses related to HIV infections. Until recently, many women did not fit this description because their infections had progressed in a different pattern than that strictly recognized as AIDS, resulting in a new diagnosis, AIDS Related Complex (ARC). If HIV affects men and women differently, resulting in varying groups of infections, we ought not limit our studies to the syndrome as it affects men. In 1993 the Centers for Disease Control revised its classification system for HIV infection, in part to address these concerns.

Craig Svensson has investigated the exclusion of African Americans from clinical drug trials, focusing on studies published in *Clinical Pharmacology and Therapeutics* over a three-year period.[1] He found that only ten of fifty published accounts of new drug trials included any racial data, and even in the study of antihypertensive drugs, an area in which differential racial responses to drug treatments have been well-documented, only about half of the researchers gave racial data. Of the antihypertensive studies that included subjects of different races, only one attempted to determine if there was a race-related response difference. Furthermore, in more than half of the trials in which racial data were available, the percentage of African-American subjects was less than the percentage of African Americans in the community and in the U.S. population. Apparently, African Americans were underrepresented in the clinical trials, and as Svensson notes, this "suggests that insufficient data exist to accurately assess the safety and efficacy of many new drugs in blacks."[2]

JUSTIFICATIONS FOR THE EXCLUSIONS IN CLINICAL TRIALS

How do researchers explain this blatant and seemingly unethical exclusion of ethnic minorities and women in medical research? Their reasoning is varied and extensive, covering problems from financing and recruitment to problems with tight experimental control and subject safety. Svensson's study suggests that many researchers simply have not even considered racial health differences a pertinent issue in their research. In what follows, I will address these so-called justifications and show why none of them is truly substantial, and how most of them can be overcome.

Some of the researchers involved claim that using white middle-aged men is necessary because of the need to maintain tight experimental controls and to avoid confounding factors. Clearly, research done on homogeneous groups yields tighter, more exact results.

Yet this is precisely the problem at hand. The tighter and more exact the results are, the less they can be safely generalized to the population as a whole. Since the population in general is not homogeneous, why should we take data from one of the homogeneous groups within it and apply it to all the other groups? Surely it would be safer and more beneficial to society as a whole to study representative groups from each population sector and thus to obtain tight and exact data specific to each population's distinct needs.

In defense of the exclusion of women in medical research, many researchers claim that the fluctuating hormonal cycles of women serve as confounding factors in clinical studies. However, as Dresser correctly questions, "Why is it female, but not male, hormones that 'complicate' research?"[3] Why is it that white men must serve as the exclusive prototype? In addition, one wonders why, if the menstrual cycles of women may complicate the experimental results, women are then allowed and even encouraged to abide by the results obtained on men—results that take no account of the potential complications? The fact is, women have distinct hormonal cycles, and if complications are a possibility during clinical trials, then they are also a possibility after drug or treatment approval, when women may be taking a new drug outside the safe confines of the clinical setting.

Another excuse for not using women as subjects in clinical trials deals with the possibility that a woman may become pregnant while participating in the research. In such a case, participation in the experiment may cause complications with the pregnancy, miscarriage, or birth defects. This means that, in effect, "In the name of *potential* protection for *potentially* pregnant women and their fetuses, all women have lost the opportunity to improve and extend their lives." This attempted justification ignores the fact that many potential women subjects may be beyond their reproductive years, not sexually active, or simply taking adequate precautions against pregnancy. To preclude all women from participating is to assume that all women are simply walking wombs who are unreliable in their contraceptive practices. This assumption is a bit ridiculous, particularly when some of the women concerned may be elderly cardiac patients who presumably are not planning pregnancies.

Even if we consider only sexually active fertile women who are in their reproductive years, it seems that we really ought to allow these women themselves to make decisions regarding their participation in clinical trials. Most of the women in this group would no doubt prefer to be informed of the risks and hazards as well as the potential benefits, and then to choose whether to participate. We might also ask why sexually active fertile women of reproductive age are excluded while men of the same class are allowed, and in many cases encouraged, to participate. Drugs and other treatments that could potentially damage a woman's reproductive system or a fetus might very well also have a detrimental effect on a man's sperm.

Problems associated with the recruitment of minority and women subjects are also often cited as reasons for their exclusion in clinical trials. There are at least several reasons for recruitment problems. First, these difficulties point to much greater problems within the medical system. For instance, a great disparity exists between the numbers of ethnic minorities and women, as compared to white men, studying in medical schools and working as medical researchers and physicians. Therefore, this common subject pool for medical research is nearly devoid of available nonstandard (white male) subjects. The long-term answer is to get a more diverse population into the profession. In the short term, however, there are other solutions. Clearly, subjects will have to come from outside the medical system, and the solution to their recruitment will have to address the existing obstacles. Poor women, for example, may need help with child care and transportation in order to participate. This will undoubtedly involve extra financial burdens on the researchers and, in the end, on the taxpaying public, but ... potential payoffs are surely worth the associated costs.

Second, widespread distrust of the medical establishment was understandably strengthened after the Tuskegee study (in which African-American men with syphilis were deliberately left untreated in order to study the course of the disease; this study started in the 1930s and was not ended until 1972). Following this study, the National Commission for the Protection of Human Research Subjects of Biomedical and Behavioral Research released the Belmont Report, which warned against "vulnerable subjects ... such as racial minorities ... being continually sought as research subjects" owing to their availability in research-oriented university and public hospitals. The commission was concerned that less advantaged populations would become guinea pigs for treatments that would in the end be more readily available to the more advantaged groups who weren't involved in the risks and discomforts of the research. While this was and remains a serious concern, researchers may have overcompensated, translating it into a policy of complete exclusion of minorities and women from clinical studies. Today we must understand that ethnic minorities and women have much to gain from participation in clinical studies. As long as their participation is carefully controlled and not abused, they will be able to reap benefits that have for too long accrued almost exclusively to white men.

One potential solution to the recruitment problems is to start with community-based research that comes out of minority practices and clinics in underserved areas. Minority populations will presumably be more likely to trust community health care facilities and physicians than more distant and less personal health care providers. This would also alleviate some of the problems of transportation, accessibility, and linguistic or cultural differences and discrimination in the delivery of health care.... However, potential conflicts of interest exist when the provider serves a dual role as researcher and physician.

Finally, there are the inevitable financial difficulties associated with intensified recruitment and more diverse research. These difficulties have been remedied in part by the recent NIH Women's Health Initiative—a ten-year, $500 million study involving three large-scale research projects on women's health issues. This project was launched under the directorship of Bernadine Healy, after several years of NIH guideline revisions regarding the inclusion of women and minorities in research, and a General Accounting Office investigation into the rules, spurred by the Congressional Caucus for Women's Issues. The result is an enormous and lengthy research initiative for women's health issues. Significant financial backing for health issues specific to particular ethnic groups is needed before we can realistically feel that health care equity in clinical studies is being adequately addressed.

CONCLUSION

There are, of course, more problems on the horizon. Acknowledging inherent differences between the races and sexes may inadvertently cause a rise in racism and sexism. It may refuel the fires of the once livid nature/nurture debate, which will bring with it all the misconceptions about superior and inferior genetic abilities associated with eugenics. It may "serve only the interests of those eager to blame the disproportionate share of the burden of poverty and disease borne by minorities on inherent racial traits and genetic defects rather than on societal problems such as poverty, suboptimal health care, or a legacy of racial prejudice."[4] Differences in disease manifestation, treatment, and incidence among population sectors could lead to increases in discrimination and exclusionary hiring practices. Differences between the blood and kidneys of different ethnic groups could lead to white-only or black-only blood banks and organ donor lists, reminiscent of the segregated drinking fountains and restaurants of another era.

On the other hand, failing to acknowledge the differences is also a form of racism, one that is alive and well today, and that is thus perhaps more important than the distant fear. Our society ought to be able to address the inherent differences among its population and embrace them, rather than instinctively labeling them as flaws. As Dresser has said, "Perhaps we have come far enough to recognize such differences without transforming them into tools for maintaining the traditional social hierarchy" (p. 29). The challenge is ours to move forward rather than to stagnate or return to the clearly unjust ways of bygone eras. An ethical medical establishment must ascertain the particular needs of all its patients and must find a way to allow them equity in access to treatment. One of the first steps toward this goal should be the inclusion of nontraditional groups as subjects of medical research.

NOTES

1. C. K. Svensson, "Representation of American Blacks in Clinical Trials of New Drugs," *Journal of the American Medical Association* 261(2) (1989): 263–265.—Ed.

2. Svensson, p. 265—Ed.

3. R. Dresser, "Wanted: Single, White Male for Medical Research," *Hastings Center Report* 22(1) (1992): 24.—Ed.

4. N. Osbourne and M. D. Feit, "The Use of Race in Medical Research," *Journal of the American Medical Association* 267(2) (1992): 275–279.—Ed.

Chapter 5

Health, Normalcy, and the "Abnormal" Patient

Action Alert: September 3rd is "Blog Against the Telethon Day"

Jerry Lewis is the host of the Muscular Dystrophy Association's Annual Telethon, a telethon that occurs every Labor Day to raise funds for cures by using disabled people as poster children. Disabled people protest the telethon because of its outdated, negative portrayal of disabilities. These images that the telethon promotes sticks in people's minds and continually serve as a barrier for disabled people. Disability is not the problem, but rather the attitudes and barriers that society places on us.

A lot of visitors to this site are from outside the disability community and probably don't have any idea why a group like Not Dead Yet would care about the telethon.

It's a complex issue, but here it is as succinctly as I can put it:

There are powerful cultural stereotypes that promote the widespread belief that tragedy, grief, and suffering are inevitable aspects of disability; furthermore, those same stereotypes suggest that those emotions put the blame for those feelings on the disability itself, rather than any social factors such as segregation, isolation, or impoverishment. Thus, according to people who believe those stereotypes, the only "relief" a person with a disability can hope for is a "cure."

Posted by Not Dead Yet at 9:42 AM

Friday, August 31, 2007

http://notdeadyetnewscommentary.blogspot.com/search/label/action%20alert

For many decades now, comedian Jerry Lewis has been held in high regard for doing his annual telethon (the "Jerry Lewis Telethon") to fund muscular dystrophy. As a result of his yearly telethons, Lewis has managed to raise millions of dollars for research into the prevention of this disease. Yet as indicated above, Not Dead Yet (a disability rights activist group) claims that Lewis has exploited and denigrated people with disabilities, characterizing them as needy, pathetic, pitiable characters. Indeed, some members of Not Dead Yet were once "Jerry's Kids," poster children for his telethon, who now find his depictions of them (and other individuals with disabilities) to be negative stereotypes.

Not Dead Yet raises issues that are core to the concerns of this chapter: questions of "normalcy," disability, and discrimination. This activist group rejects the simple assumption that disability results from a biological or medical problem; as they state above, "Disability is not the problem, but rather the attitudes and barriers that society places on us." This raises a number of questions, including What causes a person's disability? Is it a physical lack (such as the lack of hearing or sight)? Is it caused by society, which has failed to accommodate persons with disabilities and has expressed attitudes of disgust and/or contempt toward them? Consider the following case concerning LaKeisha and James Bright, and their decision to have cochlear implant surgery for their deaf baby girl. The Brights, like most nondisabled citizens, treat deafness as a medical problem, as a natural disability, and not as a problem constructed by society.

CASE STUDY: A CHILD'S RIGHT TO AN OPEN FUTURE?

LaKeisha and James Bright became parents a year ago to a beautiful, healthy baby girl. However, after a period of time, the Brights suspected that their daughter could not hear, as loud sounds did not cause her to startle or cry. After a consultation with a specialist, it was determined that their daughter Tonya was deaf. LaKeisha and James are not deaf themselves, although James has a grandfather who was born deaf, and who was raised to lip-read. They have no knowledge of deafness and do not know American Sign Language. Both of them want a child with whom they can communicate, and who can fully participate in their community; they fear that deafness may divide their family and keep Tonya from fully understanding her African heritage.

LaKeisha and James are now considering cochlear implant surgery for Tonya once she is old enough to physically withstand it. They consult with a specialist who informs them that Tonya would make an excellent candidate, and that with cochlear implant surgery, "the sooner, the better." The specialist tells them that with early implants and a good deal of early speech therapy Tonya will learn to speak normally, like any other hearing child. The Brights are determined to have the surgery done on the grounds that they want what is best for their daughter, and that a life without hearing is abnormal and undesirable. They do not want Tonya to suffer unnecessarily with a disability that could be fairly easily eliminated.

In this case the Brights are faced with a difficult decision that no parent wants to encounter: doing invasive surgery on their infant or letting her grow up deaf. While surgery on a young child is never desirable, in this case the risks of a surgical intervention are arguably outweighed by the harms associated with deafness. The question is, however, whether deafness is a disability or simply a difference; and whether it is discriminatory to assume that a life led as a hearing person is qualitatively better than one lived as a deaf person.

One can generally claim that all parents want what is best for their children. The main goal of parenting is to raise children who are healthy, normal, who have a full range of life options, and who will end up being better off than their parents or grandparents. When a child is born with a condition that may interfere with its flourishing, parents must agonize over what to do. Whether the condition is mental or physical, it is understandable that parents want to do anything and everything to eliminate or minimize that condition. Whatever the decision made, the choice is almost always based on a concern for what is best for the child, and what will lead to maximal function and flourishing.

However, as in the case of LaKeisha and James, parental judgments about a child's best interests tend to be based on either (a) the culture's views of what is normal and acceptable, or (b) the parents' own circumstances, values, and beliefs. Accordingly, LaKeisha and James desire a child who will fit within their culture's conception of what is normal and functional and who at the same time will reflect their own circumstances as hearing persons. It is without doubt that families that experience a lack of "fit" between members (some family members deaf, while others hearing; some family members dwarfs while others full height) face particular challenges. Arguably, it is reasonable that parents would wish to have children with whom they can communicate well, to whom they can pass on their cultures and their values. The problem arises when there are conflicts between the individual family and society—when the choices of individual parents may negatively impact groups within society.

Take the Brights, for example. In this scenario the choice is seemingly clear: to elect to do surgery on their infant daughter so that she can be raised to hear and speak. However, activist groups such as Not Dead Yet, the National Association for the Deaf, and individuals from within the Deaf community argue that such choices are not simply private, familial ones; they have a direct impact on the way the deaf are perceived within society and make a clear statement about the disvalue of individuals who may be different. Whatever choice the Brights make, then, it is not so obviously just a parental decision made within the private realm of the family unit; it also has broader social and political implications (Figure 5.1).

Furthermore, some proponents of Deaf culture claim that deafness is not a disability, but rather constitutes a culture with its own unique language (American Sign Language). To be born deaf is a privilege, according to these deaf advocates, and to perform cochlear implant surgery on babies born

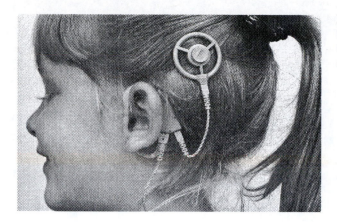

FIGURE 5.1 Components of a cochlear implant, including the transmitter embedded in the scalp and the microphone around the child's ear.

deaf is to thus rob them of the rich culture into which they were born. So rather than being a choice that ensures their daughter Tonya has as many future options as possible, the Brights' decision to have Tonya undergo the surgery is read by some as a form of cultural genocide that leads to the demise of **Deaf culture** and that results in a profound loss to Tonya as well.

As many of the articles in this chapter indicate, there is a growing awareness of the degree to which individuals are discriminated against when they do not fit within the cultural norms of able-bodiedness and/or "normal" physical appearance. Whether one is born deaf, ambiguously sexed so that one is not clearly male or female, physically disabled, or mentally ill, one faces social demands to somehow "fit in" with the rest of society. For individuals born intersex (i.e., neither clearly male nor clearly female), a series of surgeries and treatments are usually recommended to make the infants unambiguously male or female; for those born deaf, cochlear implant surgery can be done in an attempt to remove the deafness; for those suffering mental illness, drug therapies can be used to normalize their mental states; and for those whose physical bodies do not match their gender identities, they can elect to have gender reassignment surgery to allow for a more "normal" social presentation. As critics are now arguing, all of these forms of alteration are rooted in our strict cultural norms that dictate that having a particular kind of body and a particular type of mental function is necessary, and that bodies and mental functions that fall outside these norms are undesirable and should be eliminated. Let us briefly consider how these norms and expectations work, and what they mean for how we treat bodies within both medicine and society.

THE CONSTRAINT OF SOCIAL NORMS

Whether one's body or mental states are considered to be "abnormal" has a great deal to do with how well one meets the cultural standards of what counts as acceptable appearance or behavior.

As some bioethicists have argued, not many individuals have the luxury of being considered completely normal in terms of their appearance or behavior. Our narrow social norm is that of an independent, autonomous, rational agent who is not limited by any physical impediments and who makes optimal choices that are not inhibited by fear, illness, ignorance, or discrimination. While few members of society fit that norm, it prevails nonetheless and serves to inform our opinions and behaviors. Our social attitudes and policies reflect the view that not being able to walk, talk, hear, or speak normally, or being partially or completely dependent on others for help, reduces our human value and our rights. Furthermore, one can be viewed as "abnormal" based on *health* norms; to take a current example, health care professionals and the public are becoming increasingly concerned about the failure of many citizens to achieve a healthy body size, especially as this is occurring in young children (Figure 5.2).

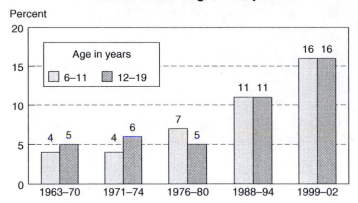

Prevalence of overweight among children and adolescents ages 6–19 years

FIGURE 5.2   Chart on childhood obesity

Note: Excludes pregnant women starting with 1971–74. Pregnancy status not available for 1963–65 and 1966–70. data for 1963–65 are for children 6–11 years of age; data for 1966–70 are for adolescents 12–17 years of age, not 12–19 years.

Source: CDC/NCHS, NHES and NHANES

There is evidence for this view given our attitudes toward aging and old age, toward persons with physical disabilities, and toward those with severe mental illness. As critics like Susan Wendell (later in this chapter) argue, these social norms eventually work against all of us as we are debilitated by events such as illness, accident, or the aging process. The public social realm is not constructed to include individuals who need places to sit or lie down and rest, who cannot climb or walk well, or who need the accommodation of aids like strollers, walkers, or wheelchairs. In effect, our narrow social norms discriminate against all of us in one way or another at different points in our lives. This is true despite statistics indicating that an estimated 38.9 million people in the United States have a disability, or 14.8% of the population age 5 and over.[1]

Bioethicists who accept the able-bodied cultural norm claim that it is not mere discrimination that leads us to alter disabled or atypical bodies. Rather, it is that such bodies are not functional—a biological fact that cannot be ignored—that leads us to alter them. So, for example, it is not discriminatory to claim that paraplegia is a suboptimal state, since legs were intended for walking, and if one cannot walk then one's body is malfunctioning. Similarly, it is not discriminatory toward deaf individuals to claim that deafness is a disability and that it should be eliminated, since deafness represents a dysfunction of one's ears, which are meant for hearing. By considering the normal form and function of body parts, these bioethicists claim that we should intervene to help ensure as much function (or as close to normal function as possible) for those individuals whose body parts are malfunctioning.

THE SOCIAL VERSUS THE MEDICAL MODEL OF DISABILITY

The dispute that arises between bioethicists concerning our bodily norms is rooted in a different view of the causes of disability. For bioethicists who claim that a normal body is one that functions properly, the problem is with individual bodies that behave abnormally, and that need to be fixed or altered. Such critics promote what is called the **medical model of disability,** which holds that bodily malfunction is a medical issue that should be addressed through medical treatment. The emphasis is on fixing the individual's body so that it is as normal as possible in function and appearance; the problem is not seen to have its roots in society.

As one example, consider the situation of actor Christopher Reeve, who in 1995 became paralyzed from the neck down following a riding accident. Reeve, who was 42 years old at the time, was thrown from his horse and landed on his head during the second of three trial events in an equestrian competition. As a result of the accident, he suffered fractures to the top two vertebrae, considered the most serious of cervical injuries, and also damaged his spinal cord (Figure 5.3).

Some bioethicists claimed his disability was purely physical. He could no longer walk because of his severe spinal cord injury, and as a result was rendered physically disabled. Even Reeve himself

FIGURE 5.3 In 1995 actor Christopher Reeve suffered severe spinal cord injury, leaving him paralyzed from the neck down.

saw his disabilities as purely physical in nature. He became a vocal supporter of research into spinal cord injuries, and set it as a personal goal to one day walk again. Reeve was committed to the goal of developing medical treatments to overcome disabling conditions like spinal cord injury, making it possible for victims to return to normal human function. He died on October 11, 2004, at the age of 52 after developing a serious systemic infection during treatment for a pressure wound.

An important feature of the medical model of disability is that it absolves society of responsibility for an individual's inability to fit within the cultural norms. Our norms surrounding the body are based on an understanding of what bioethicist Norman Daniels calls **species-typical functioning.** Valuing walking over the use of wheelchairs expresses a value system that is rooted in the typical function that human beings are supposed to achieve; that using a wheelchair is considered undesirable is reflective of the fact that most people in fact value walking over wheeling. But notice also that the medical model of disability raises a utilitarian question of cost–benefit analysis, since it leads us to ask whether the cost to achieve "species-typical functioning" for an individual is worth the expense. Arguments have been made to the effect that if we pour too many of our resources into treating or curing people who suffer from disabilities, we will be pulling those resources away from other important social goods. In this way, we may be asking whether one individual's life is "worth" the cost to improve that individual's condition when the money could be better spent elsewhere, a kind of crass cost–benefit analysis to which many bioethicists claim a human life should not be submitted.

Those bioethicists, like Susan Wendell, who reject our narrow bodily norms argue instead that what needs to be "fixed" is not the individual bodies that fail to meet the standard, but society itself. Whether or not one can walk or hear or think normally is neither good nor bad; rather, it is how we respond to these differences that really matters. This is the **social model of disability,** which holds that there is nothing inherently disabling about using a wheelchair or being blind; it is how society is constructed that renders someone functional or nonfunctional. For example, spending one's life in a wheelchair is only going to be experienced as a problem insofar as one is unable to access public spaces and social goods. Otherwise, it makes no difference whether one gets around by walking or wheeling. An individual is thus only disabled by a society that does not plan for and accommodate differences in mobility by making it impossible to go to the movies, or hold down a job, or use the public washrooms. As bioethicist Anita Silvers points out, we can get a better sense of how disability is socially constructed if we engage in what she calls historical counterfactualizing.[2] As she claims, we must try to imagine how our social and public world would be set up if most citizens got around by wheeling rather than walking—how our public buildings would be constructed, what kinds of things would be done differently, and what would be considered "normal" function. She points out that once we engage in this thought experiment, we can readily see that what makes persons normal or abnormal, functional or nonfunctional, is the way society is set up from the beginning. It just so happens that our society was constructed around the expectation that one would walk rather than wheel about; there is nothing inherently better about walking. The goal should not be to spend our resources to make everyone ambulatory, but rather to fix society so that it is accessible to people with different forms of mobility.

The argument that disability is socially constructed is supported by statistical evidence concerning the well-being and social participation of individuals with disabilities. According to 2004 statistics from the National Organization on Disability, three times as many individuals with disabilities live in poverty, with incomes less than $15,000, as those without disabilities (26% vs. 9%); only 35% are employed full or part time, compared with 78% of nondisabled individuals; they are twice as likely to drop out of high school (21% vs. 10% of the nondisabled population); they are twice as likely to have inadequate transport (31% vs. 13%); and lack health insurance at much higher rates than the nondisabled. Unsurprisingly, then, the life satisfaction of individuals with disabilities falls far below that of the nondisabled (34% claiming to be "very satisfied" as compared to 61% of the nondisabled community).[3] As critics have pointed out, it is the lack of social support networks and public accommodation for persons with disabilities that create the problems they experience, not their physical or medical conditions.

As we can see, the dispute between bioethicists who hold a social versus a medical model of disability directly relates to the question of how we should deal with disability. According to the medical model, the goal should be to fix as many disabled individuals as possible, spending our resources to minimize the effects of physical impairments on those who suffer from them. In a related vein, we should also dedicate funds to investigating cures for things such as spinal cord injuries and other disabling conditions. The focus is on the underlying physical causes of an individual's malfunction and doing all we can to eliminate that malfunction. For those who endorse the social model of disability, it is both wasteful and offensive to spend our time and money trying to alter individuals' bodies; rather, we should commit our money and efforts toward changing society so that people of all levels and forms of function can fully participate. So, for example, this would mean putting our emphasis on building curb cuts so that people with wheelchairs and walkers can navigate city streets, constructing public transit that is fully accessible to all citizens, and ensuring that housing and public spaces are constructed so that all people can live and socialize within them. For these critics, the more we focus on the medical problem of the individual, the more we marginalize disability and treat individuals as problems, rather than seeing the way their problems are constructed by our society.

This debate over the social versus the medical model of disability is connected in interesting ways to the **Americans with Disabilities Act (ADA),** a piece of legislation that was passed in 1990. The intention of the ADA is to ensure the civil rights of individuals who are living with disabilities, and is of historical significance because it finally recognizes that people with disabilities suffer discrimination and marginalization within society. The legislation covers areas of life such as employment, communication, transportation, access to public services, and access to government resources. As the Preamble to the ADA indicates, approximately 43 million Americans have one or more disabilities (physical and/or mental), a number that is increasing as the population ages. Society has historically isolated and segregated individuals with disabilities, and discrimination continues to be a pervasive problem. Unlike individuals who have experienced discrimination based on their skin color, sex, religion, age, or national origin, individuals who have experienced discrimination based on their disability have not had legal pathways available to redress such discrimination. Finally, discrimination against persons with disabilities has resulted in serious social and economic costs to the individuals and society, an injustice that needs to be corrected by ensuring their equal protection under the law.[4]

Clearly, as supporters of the social model of disability argue, the ADA recognizes the degree to which society discriminates against individuals with disabilities, and it seeks to provide legal redress to those individuals. The emphasis is not on the medical basis for one's disability, as evidenced by the fact that, in the Act, "disability" is defined as: "(A) a physical or mental impairment that substantially limits one or more of the major life activities of such individual; (B) a record of such an impairment; or (C) being regarded as having such impairment."[5]

There is much room for a social understanding of disability within the ADA, given that one must have an impairment that "substantially limits one or more of the major life activities" and that one must be socially "regarded as having such an impairment." These factors are not necessarily medical ones; in fact, the ADA makes clear that how we socially regard the individual is of great importance. Indeed, those who uphold the social model of disability see great promise in the ADA in terms of understanding disability as a socially constructed problem.

However, this has not prevented the courts from defining disability based on narrow medical understandings, and awarding individuals only in cases where there is a medical cause for the disability. As a result, the court cases that have successfully invoked the ADA have been mostly limited to individuals diagnosed with a medical condition. So, for example, someone who petitions using the ADA because he is discriminated against for being short is unlikely to win his case unless he has been medically diagnosed and treated for shortness of stature. Even though a short individual who has not been diagnosed with a medical condition may be equally discriminated against, only the person with a medical history will likely be recognized under the ADA. So despite the promise of the Americans with Disabilities Act to change our thinking about disabilities, it has (to date) rather served to strengthen the view of disability as individual bodily malfunction caused by a medical condition. Thus far, in the courts, the medical model of disability has won out over the social model.

So far we have considered issues surrounding the improvement and normalization of disabled bodies—bodies that function differently from the biological and social norm. There is a separate issue, however, where we encounter the desire to alter or improve bodies that are functional and healthy. In these cases, the individual's body is not dysfunctional and it may not be considered disabled in any serious way. And yet the individual may autonomously request the alteration of his or her body based on his or her own perception that there is something lacking (Figure 5.4).

Or, in cases where the individual is not capable of demanding the alteration, his or her parents or guardians may do so in the best interest of that individual. In these situations, which may include the request for **gender reassignment surgery,** cosmetic surgeries, and circumcision (both male and female), we see the tension between the values of patient autonomy and physician nonmaleficence. It is to this issue that we now turn.

ALTERING THE BODY: TENSIONS BETWEEN AUTONOMY AND NONMALEFICENCE

Imagine that you are a physician presented with a patient who has a healthy functioning male body. Yet your patient tells you that he finds his body loathsome, that it does not match the person inside, and that he wants to feminize himself through gender reassignment surgery. In so doing, he says, he

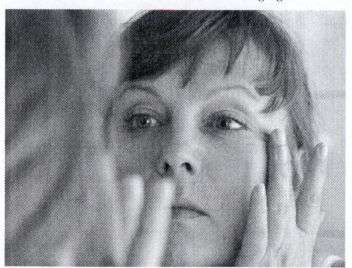

FIGURE 5.4 Western cultural beauty norms lead many women to consider cosmetic alteration.

will achieve his "true self," by allowing his body and gender identity to finally match. As this patient's physician, you are committed to the preservation of patient health and to the principle of nonmaleficence (do no harm). While you acknowledge that your patient is suffering from this lack of fit between sex and gender identity, you also acknowledge the grave harm to which he will be subjected if you recommend gender reassignment surgery for him.

Furthermore, imagine that you are a pediatrician who is sought out by the parents of a little girl with severe mental and physical disabilities. The parents are concerned about doing everything in their power to ensure that their daughter is loved, protected, and included within her familial and social communities. But these parents realize that as their daughter grows and matures into womanhood, the chances increase that she will eventually be institutionalized because they will not be able to care for her. With a concern for doing what is in their daughter's best interests, they consult you to ask about doing a series of interventions to prevent the physical maturing of their daughter's body: surgery to remove her breast buds so that she will not develop breasts at puberty; a hysterectomy to prevent the onset of her menstrual cycle; and growth inhibitors to maintain her small and child-like size. All of these interventions are intended to benefit the child, though they certainly will directly benefit the family members who are taking care of her.

The preceding scenario is no mere thought experiment. In a 2004 Seattle case, the parents of a child known only as "Ashley X" sought and successfully received ethically questionable treatment for their 6½-year-old daughter. Ashley was born in 1997 with severe developmental disabilities due to static encephalopathy; she has not developed beyond the mental age of a 3-month-old infant. The treatment that was done (known as "The Ashley Treatment")[6] included growth attenuation through hormone treatments, hysterectomy, bilateral mastectomy to prevent the development of breasts, and an appendectomy. The rationale for this treatment was a complex blend of physical, psychological, and medical concerns. Her parents wanted to continue to care for her at home; to minimize Ashley's risk of developing bedsores; to prevent the discomfort associated with menstruation; and to also prevent the possibility of pregnancy should she be sexually abused. The appendectomy was performed out of a concern that Ashley might develop appendicitis (a condition that develops in 5% of the population), something that would be difficult to diagnose in Ashley because of her inability to communicate the painful symptoms associated with it. Critics of the treatment were shocked that the physicians involved were willing to perform such invasive surgeries on the healthy body of a 6-year-old child.

In cases such as this, concerns for preventing harm to the individuals may come into conflict with the autonomous wishes of the individuals or their proxy decision-makers. As we can see with the accepted practice of gender reassignment surgery, and with the willingness to perform "The Ashley Treatment," concern for respecting autonomy may outweigh the principle of nonmaleficence if the benefits of doing such surgical alterations are deemed to be weighty enough. In cases of **transsexualism,** if the individual has followed an accepted course in his or her transition (following the Benjamin Standards of Care), then the individual's request for gender reassignment surgery may be fulfilled. According to the Benjamin Standards, there are a number of eligibility criteria that apply to biological males and females: The individual (1) must have reached the legal age of majority; (2) must have undergone 12 months of continuous hormone therapy; (3) must have lived full time for 1 year in the gender to which he or she wishes to be assigned; (4) must understand the costs, length of hospitalization, possible complications, and postsurgical rehabilitation requirements; and (5) must be aware of different competent surgeons who are available.[7] These standards are intended to find the balance between patient autonomy (the request to change sex based on the patient's sense of a "lack of fit" between sex and gender) and nonmaleficence (since the surgeries are permanent and cannot be undone if the patient changes his or her mind).

In the case of Ashley X, the Seattle hospital agreed that Ashley would benefit from the surgeries proposed by her parents, and their request was fulfilled. According to many critics, the willingness to do such surgical interventions at the parents' request indicates both a hypervaluing of parental authority and a devaluing of persons with disabilities. Had the value of nonmaleficence been taken more seriously, since doing invasive surgery on a healthy body is both dangerous and unnecessary, Ashley would not be condemned to a perpetual and undignified physical state of childhood. These critics claim that The Ashley Treatment served her individual family and society more than it served her best interests, and that it will likely act as a precedent for the surgical modifications of other individuals like Ashley who have a mental disability but are otherwise healthy.

Thus, while the values of autonomy and nonmaleficence may come into conflict in cases such as these, we find that the tension is often resolved by emphasizing autonomy over other medical concerns. Yet this is not always the case. In some situations, such as **body identity integrity disorder** (where individuals have a distorted sense of their physical bodies, sometimes feeling that limbs are foreign objects that must be removed) or anorexia nervosa (where an individual starves him- or herself, sometimes to death), we find that even the strongest-stated autonomous desire to have a limb removed or to refuse food is not honored. In these situations, caregivers will usually refuse to adhere to the patient's wishes because of the great harm—including death—that will likely occur.

When considering the intersections between medicine and disability, we can begin to see that medicine not only treats persons with disabilities (and persons with "abnormal" bodies), but that it also *constructs* them as disabled and abnormal. The medical willingness to alter, fix, remove, and improve upon human bodies that do not fit the cultural norm has had devastating impact for many individuals who have been subjected to these medical interventions. Indeed, many of the horror stories told by persons with disabilities and persons born **intersexed** have to do with their treatment within the medical field—repeated surgeries, months spent in hospitals, being paraded about as medical curiosities, and so on. While sometimes these medical interventions can be helpful, beneficent, and even life preserving for some individuals, there are many (like The Ashley Treatment) that raise serious ethical questions about the medical treatment of the "abnormal" body.

Looking Ahead

- Genetic and reproductive technologies will continue to advance, such that it will be increasingly possible to "correct" genetic anomalies and thus attempt to eliminate disabilities (see Chapter 7). We can expect that many couples will elect to use technologies to avoid the birth of babies with disabilities.
- The practice of altering the bodies of severely physically and mentally disabled children will likely continue, and may increase in light of "The Ashley Treatment." Any surgical interventions and/or physical alterations of such children will be justified by the principle of beneficence, or a concern for what is in their best interests.
- The "age boom" that will occur within the next 15–20 years may result in increased attention given to issues of disability and impairment, given the large number of senior citizens who will become disabled. An increasing number of citizens will require walkers, wheelchairs, canes, and other mobility aids, and they may not hear or see well. Society will need to accommodate these differences, since it will be much more difficult to ignore them when the number of disabled citizens rapidly increases.
- Disability may also be spotlighted more as the war ends, and as soldiers who served in Iraq return home in impaired and disabled condition.

Endnotes

1. See http://www.pascenter.org/state_based_stats/state_statistics_2003.php?state=us
2. Anita Silver, David Wasserman, and Mary Mahowald, *Disability, Difference, Discrimination: Perspectives on Justice in Bioethics and Public Policy* (New York: Rowman & Littlefield, 1998), 129–131.
3. See the National Organization on Disability at http://nod.org/index.cfm?fuseaction=page.viewPage&pageID=1430&nodeID=1&FeatureID=1422&redirected=1&CFID=28663953&CFTOKEN=93646472
4. See the full Americans with Disabilities Act at http://www.ada.gov/pubs/ada.htm#Anchor-Sec-49575
5. Ibid.
6. For more information concerning "The Ashley Treatment," see her parents' blog at http://ashleytreatment.spaces.live.com/blog/
7. To access the Harry Benjamin Standards of Care for transsexuals, see http://www.tc.umn.edu/~colem001/hbigda/hstndrd.htm

HEALTH AND NORMALCY

On the Distinction Between Disease and Illness

Christopher Boorse

DISEASE AND ILLNESS

What is the theoretical notion of a disease? An admirable explanation of clinical normality was given thirty years ago by C. Daly King.

> The normal . . . is objectively, and properly, to be defined as that which functions in accordance with its design.

The root idea of this account is that the normal is the natural. The state of an organism is theoretically healthy, i.e. free of disease, insofar as its mode of functioning conforms to the natural design of that kind of organism. Philosophers have, of course, grown repugnant to the idea of natural design since its cooptation by natural-purpose ethics and the so-called argument from design. It is undeniable that the term "natural" is often given an evaluative force. Shakespeare as well as Roman Catholicism is full of such usages, and they survive as well in the strictures of state legislatures against "unnatural acts." But it is no part of biological theory to assume that whàt is natural is desirable, still less the product of divine artifice. Contemporary biology employs a version of the idea of natural design that seems ideal for the analysis of health.

The crucial element in the idea of a biological design is the notion of a natural function. I have argued elsewhere that a function in the biologist's sense is nothing but a standard causal contribution to a goal actually pursued by the organism. Organisms are vast assemblages of systems and subsystems which, in most members of a species, work together harmoniously in such a way as to achieve a hierarchy of goals. Cells are goal-directed toward metabolism, elimination, and mitosis; the heart is goal-directed toward supplying the rest of the body with blood; and the whole organism is goal-directed both to particular activities like eating and moving around and to higher-level goals such as survival and reproduction. The specifically physiological functions of any component are, I think, its species-typical contributions to the apical goals of survival and reproduction. But whatever the correct analysis of function statements, there is no doubt that biological theory is deeply committed to attributing functions to processes in plants and animals. And the single unifying property of all recognized diseases of plants and animals appears to be this: that they interfere with one or more functions typically performed within members of the species.

The account of health thus suggested is in one sense thoroughly Platonic. The health of an organism consists in the performance by each part of its natural function. And as Plato also saw, one of the most interesting features of the analysis is that it applies without alteration to mental health as long as there are standard mental functions. In another way, however, the classical heritage is misleading, for it seems clear that biological function statements are descriptive rather than normative claims. Physiologists obtain their functional doctrines without at any stage having to answer such questions as, What is the function of a man? or to explicate "a good man" on the analogy of "a good knife." Functions are not attributed in this context to the whole organism at all, but only to its parts, and the functions of a part are its causal contributions to empirically given goals. What goals a type of organism in fact pursues, and by what functions it pursues them, can be decided without considering the value of pursuing them. Consequently health in the theoretical sense is an equally value-free concept. The notion required for an analysis of health is not that of a good man or a good shark, but that of a good specimen of a human being or shark.

All of this amounts to saying that the epistemology King suggested for health judgments is, at bottom, a statistical one. The question therefore arises how the functional account avoids our earlier objections to statistical normality. King did explain how to dissolve one version of the paradox of saying that everyone is unhealthy. Clearly all the members of a species can have some disease or other as long as they do not have the same disease. King somewhat grimly compares the

Abridged from Boorse, Christopher. "On the Distinction Between Disease and Illness," *Philosophy and Public Affairs,* 5:1 (1975), 49–68. Excerpt only from section 2, p. 56–62. Copyright © 1975. Reprinted by permission of Blackwell Publishing Ltd.

job of extracting an empirical ideal of health from a set of defective specimens to the job of reconstructing the Norden bombsight from assorted aerial debris. But this answer does not touch universal diseases such as tooth decay. Although King nowhere considers this objection, the natural-design idea nevertheless suggests an answer that I suspect is correct. If what makes a condition a disease is its deviation from the natural functional organization of the species, then in calling tooth decay a disease we are saying that it is not simply in the nature of the species—and we say this because we think of it as mainly due to environmental causes. In general, deficiencies in the functional efficiency of the body are diseases when they are unnatural, and they may be unnatural either by being atypical or by being attributable mainly to the action of a hostile environment. If this explanation is accepted, then the functional account simultaneously avoids the pitfalls of statistical normality and also frees the idea of theoretical health of all normative content.

Theoretical health now turns out to be strictly analogous to the mechanical condition of an artifact. Despite appearances, "perfect mechanical condition" in, say, a 1965 Volkswagen is a descriptive notion. Such an artifact is in perfect mechanical condition when it conforms in all respects to the designer's detailed specifications. Normative interests play a crucial role, of course, in the initial choice of the design. But what the Volkswagen design actually *is* is an empirical matter by the time production begins. Thenceforward a car may be in perfect condition regardless of whether the design is good or bad. If one replaces its stock carburetor with a high-performance part, one may well produce a better car, but one does not produce a Volkswagen in better mechanical condition. Similarly, an automatic camera may function perfectly and take wretched pictures; guided missiles and instruments of torture in perfect mechanical condition may serve execrable ends. Perfect working order is a matter not of the worth of the product but of the conformity of the process to a fixed design. In the case of organisms, of course, the ideal of health must be determined by empirical analysis of the species rather than by the intentions of a designer. But otherwise the parallel seems exact. A person who by mutation acquires a sixth sense, or the ability to regenerate severed limbs, is not thereby healthier than we are. Sixth senses and limb regeneration are not part of the human design, which at any given time, for better or worse, just is what it is.

We have been arguing that health is descriptively definable within medical theory, as intelligence is in

psychological theory or validity in logical theory. Nevertheless medical theory is the basis of medical practice, and medical practice unquestioningly presupposes the value of health. We must therefore ask how the functional view explains this presumption that health is desirable.

In the case of physiological health, there are at least two general reasons why the functional normality that defines it is usually worth having. In the first place, most people do want to pursue the goals with respect to which physiological functions are isolated. Not only do we want to survive and reproduce, but we also want to engage in those particular activities, such as eating and sex, by which these goals are typically achieved. In the second place—and this is surely the main reason the value of physical health seems indisputable—physiological functions tend to contribute to all manner of activities neutrally. Whether it is desirable for one's heart to pump, one's stomach to digest, or one's kidneys to eliminate hardly depends at all on what one wants to do. It follows that essentially all serious physiological diseases will satisfy the first requirement of an illness, namely, undesirability for its bearer.

This explanation of the fit between medical theory and medical practice has the virtue of reminding us that health, though an important value, is conceptually a very limited one. Health is not unconditionally worth promoting, nor is what is worth promoting necessarily health. Although mental-health writers are especially prone to ignore these points, even the constitution of the World Health Organization seems to embody a similar confusion:

> Health is a state of complete physical, mental, and social well-being, and not merely the absence of disease or infirmity.

Unless one is to abandon the physiological paradigm altogether, this definition is far too wide. Health is functional normality, and as such is desirable exactly insofar as it promotes goals one can justify on independent grounds. But there is presumably no intrinsic value in having the functional organization typical of a species if the same goals can be better achieved by other means. A sixth sense, for example, would increase our goal-efficiency without increasing our health; so might the amputation of our legs at the knee and their replacement by a nuclear-powered air-cushion vehicle. Conversely, as we have seen, there is no a priori reason why ordinary diseases cannot contribute to well-being under appropriate circumstances.

In such cases, however, we will be reluctant to describe the person involved as ill, and that is because the term "ill" *does* have a negative evaluation built into it. Here again a comparison between health and other properties will be helpful. Disease and illness are related somewhat as are low intelligence and stupidity, or failure to tell the truth and speaking dishonestly. Sometimes the presumption that intelligence is desirable will fail, as in a discussion of qualifications for a menial job such as washing dishes or assembling auto parts. In such a context a person of low intelligence is unlikely to be described as stupid. Sometimes the presumption that truth should be told will fail, as when the Gestapo inquires about the Jews in your attic. Here the untruthful householder will not be described as speaking dishonestly. And sometimes the presumption that diseases are undesirable will fail, as with alcoholic intoxication or mild rubella intentionally contracted. Here the term "illness" is unlikely to appear despite the presence of disease. One concept of each pair is descriptive; the other adds to the first evaluative content, and so may be withheld where the first applies.

If we supplement this condition of undesirability with two further normative conditions, I believe we have the beginning of a plausible analysis of "illness."

A disease is an *illness* only if it is serious enough to be incapacitating, and therefore is

1. Undesirable for its bearer;
2. A title to special treatment; and
3. A valid excuse for normally criticizable behavior.

The motivation for condition (ii) needs no explanation. As for (iii), the connection between illness and diminished responsibility has often been argued, and I shall mention here only one suggestive point. Our notion of illness belongs to the ordinary conceptual scheme of persons and their actions, and it was developed to apply to physiological diseases. Consequently the relation between persons and their illnesses is conceived on the model of their relation to their bodies. It has often been observed that physiological processes, e.g. digestion or peristalsis, do not usually count as actions of ours at all. By the same token, we are not usually held responsible for the results of such processes when they go wrong, though we may be blamed for failing to take steps to prevent malfunction at some earlier time.

Who is Disabled? Defining Disability

Susan Wendell

The question of how we should define disability is not merely the beginning of an analytic exercise. We encounter the problem of definition as soon as we take an interest in disability. For example, how many people have disabilities? Estimates of the incidence of disability worldwide and within countries vary greatly among the estimators, because not only methods of gathering information about disabilities, but also understandings of what constitutes disability, vary greatly among those gathering the information. Questions of definition arise in countless practical situations, influence social policies, and determine outcomes that profoundly affect the lives of people with disabilities.

Definitions of disability officially accepted by government bureaucracies and social service agencies determine people's legal and practical entitlement to many forms of assistance, where assistance is available. This may include economic help for such purposes as: education, training, and retraining; obtaining equipment, such as wheelchairs for basic mobility or computers for basic communication; modifying a home or a vehicle to enable a person with a disability to use it; hiring assistants to help with bodily maintenance and household tasks; even obtaining medical supplies such as medications and bandages. For people with disabilities who are unemployed, it includes the basic support to buy food and shelter. It also includes eligibility for accessible housing and special forms of transportation, and even for such seemingly minor (but actually major) means of access as a disabled parking sticker.

Wendell, Susan. "Who Is Disabled? Defining Disability," *The Rejected Body: Feminist Philosophical Reflections on Disability,* New York: Routledge (1996). Excerpt p. 11–23. Copyright © 1996. Reprinted by permission of Copyright Clearance Center on behalf of Taylor & Francis Group LLC Books. Abridged from Wendell, Susan. "Who Is Disabled? Defining Disability," The Rejected Body: Feminist Philosophical Reflections on Disability, New York: Routledge (1996). Excerpt p. 11–23. Copyright © 1996. Reprinted by permission of Copyright Clearance Center on behalf of Taylor & Francis Group LLC Books.

Socially accepted definitions of disability determine the recognition of disability by friends, family members, and co-workers. Recognition of a person's disability by the people s/he is closest to is important not only for receiving their help and understanding when it is needed, but for receiving the acknowledgement and confirmation of her/his reality, so essential for keeping a person socially and psychologically anchored in a community. It is not uncommon for friends and even family members to desert a person who has debilitating symptoms that remain undiagnosed. They may insist that the ill person is faking, or mentally ill and unwilling to get appropriate treatment. People whose disability is unrecognized are frequently pressured to keep up a pretense of normality, to continue to work as if nothing were wrong, and/or to undergo unnecessary psychiatric treatment.

Definitions of disability are important to those who are organizing people with disabilities for political purposes, for example, to press for fuller recognition of their rights, for increased accessibility to public places, or for better opportunities to work. There have been struggles within political groups of people with disabilities, especially in recent years, to include more categories of people. For example, people with AIDS and with debilitating chronic illnesses like ME fought within disability groups for the recognition that they too are disabled, share similar needs and struggles, and suffer similar forms of insult, discrimination, distrust, and exclusion.

Definitions of disability affect people's self-identity. Recognizing yourself as disabled and identifying with other people who are disabled and learning about their experiences can all contribute to understanding and interpreting your own experiences, and to knowing that you are not alone with problems that you may have believed were unique to you. But being identified as disabled also carries a significant stigma in most societies and usually forces the person so identified to deal with stereotypes and unrealistic attitudes and expectations that are projected on to her/him as a member of this stigmatized group.

A careful effort to define disability can clarify our conceptions of disability and reveal misconceptions and false stereotypes. For example, for many people the paradigmatic disabled person is a young, healthy, paraplegic man who has been injured in an accident but continues to be athletic, or a young, healthy, professionally successful blind woman who has 'overcome' her handicap with education. In fact, arthritis, rheumatism, heart and respiratory disease, stroke,

Parkinsonism, hypertension, and epilepsy are major causes of disability in Canada, the United States, and Great Britain, and many people with disabilities in these countries are also ill and/or old (Health and Welfare Canada and Statistics Canada 1981; Statistics Canada 1986 and 1991; Pope and Tarlov 1991; LaPlante 1991; Bury 1978).

THE UNITED NATIONS DEFINITIONS

The United Nations definition of disability (UN 1983: I.c. 6–7) is widely used and tends to be favoured by disability activists and other advocates of greater opportunities for people with disabilities (Wright 1983, 10–12; Fine and Asch 1988, 5–6). It offers the following definitions of and distinctions among impairment, disability, and handicap:

"Impairment:

Any loss or abnormality of psychological, physiological, or anatomical structure or function. *Disability:* Any restriction or lack (resulting from an impairment) of ability to perform an activity in the manner or within the range considered normal for a human being. *Handicap:* A disadvantage for a given individual, resulting from an impairment or disability, that limits or prevents the fulfillment of a role that is normal, depending on age, sex, social and cultural factors, for that individual."

Handicap is therefore a function of the relationship between disabled persons and their environment. It occurs when they encounter cultural, physical or social barriers which prevent their access to the various systems of society that are available to other citizens. Thus, handicap is the loss or limitation of opportunities to take part in the life of the community on an equal level with others.(UN 1983: I.c. 6–7)

There are two things I like about the UN definitions. First, they are general enough to include many conditions that are not always recognized by the general public as disabling, for example, debilitating chronic illnesses, such as Crohn's disease, which limit people's activities but do not necessarily cause any immediately observable disability. I shall return to this aspect of the definitions later in this chapter. Second, the definition of *handicap* explicitly recognizes the possibility that the primary causes of a disabled person's inability to do certain things may be social; they may be lack of opportunities, lack of accessibility, lack of services, poverty or discrimination, and they often are. It is this latter aspect of the definitions that makes them appealing to advocates for people with disabilities.

Nevertheless, there are several criticisms I have of the UN definitions that may throw some light on the nature of disability and the problems associated with defining it. First, the definitions of "impairment" and "disability" seem to imply that there is some universal, biologically or medically describable standard of structure, function, and human physical ability. As we shall see, there would be important advantages to employing some universal standards, should we be able to agree on them. Yet surely what are "normal" structure, function, and ability to perform an activity all depend to some degree on the society in which the standards of normality are generated. For example, I, who can walk about half a mile several times a week but not more, am not significantly disabled with respect to walking in my society, where most people are not expected to walk further than that in the course of their daily activities. But in some societies, in Eastern Africa for example, where women normally walk several miles twice a day to obtain water for the household, I would be much more severely disabled. It is not just that I would be considered more disabled in those societies but that I would in fact need constant assistance to carry on the most basic life activities. What is normal ability in urban Western Canada is neither normal nor adequate ability in rural Kenya.

Failure to recognize that standards of structure, function, and ability are socially relative could be dangerous to people with disabilities. If the standards employed are generated by people in highly industrialized societies, many people in less industrialized societies and in rural areas where there are fewer technological resources will be considered non-disabled when they are in fact in need of special assistance to survive and participate in life where they are.

On the other hand, definitions of impairment and disability could be relativized too much to some socieities. If most people in a particular society are chronically undernourished, that society's standards of "normal" functioning might become so low as to mask the widespread disability among its citizens that starvation is causing. Another particularly disturbing example is the genital mutilation of girls. In societies where the majority of people approves of the practice and the vast majority of girls has been mutilated, the girl who has a clitoris (and other external sexual organs, depending on the form of mutilation practiced) is considered abnormal. Yet because genital mutilation often causes severe infections, shock, hemorrhage, and chronic physical and mental health problems, in addition to reducing or destroying some women's capacities for sexual pleasure, I cannot believe that the rest of the world should accept uncritically those societies' standards of normal structure and function for women. To do so seems a betrayal of the girls and women whose lives, health, and sexuality are endangered by mutilation.

Iris Marion Young's statement that "women in sexist society are physically handicapped," and her arguments in support of it present another strong challenge to the idea that culturally relative standards of physical structure, function, and ability should be accepted. Young argues that lack of opportunities and encouragement to develop bodily abilities, rigid standards of feminine bodily comportment, and constant objectification and threat of invasion of their bodies combine to deprive most women in sexist societies of their full physical potential. In these societies, a "normal" woman is expected to lack strength, skills, and the range of movement that "normal" men are expected to possess and that she might have developed had she grown up in a less sexist society. If we accept these standards uncritically, we will tend to overlook the ways that those societies create physical disadvantages for women.

Thus there seem to be problems both in denying the social and cultural relativity of impairment and disability (as used in the UN definitions) and in accepting it. The UN definitions seem to recognize the relativity of standards of ability while attempting to universalize them by using the phrase "in the manner or within the range considered normal for a human being." Unfortunately, that does not amount to a practical recognition of the relativity of disability. A woman in Kenya who can walk only as much as I can will still not be considered disabled with respect to walking, because her ability falls within the worldwide *range* considered normal. Nor does it universalize standards enough to create the basis for criticizing societies whose standards of health and good functioning fall too low for some or all of their members. The standards of such societies could still be seen to fall, by definition, in the "range considered normal for a human being."

Philosopher Ron Amundson suggests that we define disabilities as "the absences of basic personal abilities." (Amundson 1992, 108) "Basic personal abilities" enable us to perform such actions as "moving one's arms, standing, seeing and hearing things in the environment," and also to remain alert for several hours a day and to remain active without unreasonable fatigue. The actions they enable us to perform are "biomedically typical of the human species (suitably relativized to age and perhaps sex)." This is an attractive attempt to universalize the concept of disability via an appeal to common sense (with some additional appeal to biomedical standards). Yet the idea of a basic personal ability seems less clear when we ask, "How well?" or "How much?" How well must one see or hear in order to have the basic personal ability? How long must one be able to stand or how fast must one be able to walk? Is running a basic personal ability? I find myself unable to answer these questions without first asking about the circumstances of the person whose abilities are being discussed. How much ability is basic, like how much ability is normal, seems to depend on how much is necessary to perform the most common tasks of daily living in a particular physical and social environment. For example, far more strength and stamina are necessary to live where there is no water on tap, where it gets cold and there is no central heating, where a fire has to be built every time a meal is cooked, and all the clothes are washed by hand. In such an environment I would be considered a helpless invalid, and indeed I would lack most of the personal abilities I would need.

Appeal to what is biomedically typical of the human species would not seem to help settle the question, since people who are biomedically identical have different personal abilities, and people who have the same personal abilities are biomedically different. Eyeglasses, hearing aids, good prostheses, and other products of medical technology optimize the abilities of some people, while others, who have identical physical conditions but do not have access to the technology, lack the same abilities. People who use strong but completely effective corrective lenses may have the same personal ability to see as people with uncorrected good eyesight; do we want to call them or their seeing biomedically identical? Of course, in asking whether a person is disabled we could consider only whether a person's biology is typical of the human species, but Amundson would not like that, since, as he points out, atypical and even pathological biology is not necessarily disabling, that is, it does not necessarily affect a person's abilities adversely. I think we are stuck with the problem that the question of what abilities are basic, like that of what abilities are normal, is to a significant extent relative to the environment in which the abilities are exercised.

This is not the same point as claiming that a person's physical structure, function, or ability may or may not be *disadvantageous* in a given environment. Like the authors of the UN definitions and others (e.g., see Wright 1983), Amundson distinguishes "disability" from "handicap." He defines "handicap" as "an opportunity loss sustained by an individual resulting from the interaction between that individual's (biomedical) disability and the specific environment in which the individual's opportunities exist."

(Amundson 1992, 111). So, applying this to my most recent example, I might lack most of the basic personal abilities required in my environment, but I still might live quite well, participate actively in my community, and have many valuable opportunities if I could buy the services most people perform for themselves. For reasons I will explain shortly, I like Amundson's definition of "handicap" better than that offered by the United Nations.

Nevertheless, we still need some recognition of the relativity of standards of structure, function, and ability to the customs and conditions of different societies so that what the UN calls "impairment" and "disability" will be concepts that are useful and accurate in identifying those individuals who may need adjustments in their environment or direct assistance in order to survive and participate in their societies. On the other hand, we also need some cross-cultural comparisons and criticism of societies' standards of structure, function, and ability to perform activities. Such comparisons could contribute to raising the standards and, eventually, the levels of health in a society and help to protect people whose ill health or disability might serve the interests of others within their society.

My other criticisms of the UN definitions concern how they define "handicap." Because that definition refers to "a role that is normal, depending on age, sex, social and cultural factors, for that individual," the definitions imply that women can be disabled, but not handicapped, by being unable to do things which are not part of the "normal" roles of women in their societies. Thus, for example, if it is not considered essential to a woman's role in a given society that she be able to read, then a blind woman who is not provided with education in Braille or good alternatives to printed material is not handicapped by that lack of assistance, according to these definitions. In general, where the expectations for women's participation in social and cultural life are considerably lower than they are for men, disabled women's opportunities will be severely constrained, and the UN has, through its own definitions, robbed itself of the ability to criticize the circumstances in which many disabled women live.

Moreover, disability in women often goes unrecognized and rehabilitation of women is often minimal because of the expectation that women need only be able to function well enough to perform household duties (Fine and Asch 1988; Russo and Jansen 1988; Driedger and Gray 1992). On the other hand, because women's unpaid work in the home (and in volunteer activities) is not publicly valued, and because disability is still defined in many places as the inability to earn wages, women's inabilities to perform their traditional unpaid labour often go unrecognized as disability (Reisine and Fifield 1988).

In addition, the UN definitions suggest that we can be disabled, but not handicapped, by the normal process of aging, since although we may lose some ability, we are not "handicapped" unless we cannot fulfill roles that are normal *for our age*. Yet the fates of old people and of people with disabilities tend to be linked in a society because aging is disabling. A society that provides few resources to allow disabled people to participate in its activities will be likely to marginalize all people with disabilities, including the old, and to define the appropriate roles of old people as very limited, thus disadvantaging them. I think the UN should recognize that old people can be handicapped unnecessarily by their societies, but its definitions seem to prevent that recognition.

Realizing that aging is disabling helps non-disabled people to see that people with disabilities are not 'Other,' that they are really themselves at a later time. Unless we die suddenly, we are all disabled eventually. Most of us will live part of our lives with bodies that hurt, that move with difficulty or not at all, that deprive us of activities we once took for granted, or that others take for granted—bodies that make daily life a physical struggle. We need understandings of disability and handicap that do not support a paradigm of humanity as young and healthy. Encouraging everyone to acknowledge, accommodate, and identify with a wide range of physical conditions is ultimately the road to self-acceptance as well as the road to increasing the opportunities of those who are disabled now.

Ron Amundson objects to Norman Daniel's classifying the disabled with the group Daniels calls the "frail elderly," that is, those who, according to Daniels, are experiencing a normal reduction in biomedical functioning associated with aging. Amundson says of this: "To the extent that frailty and opportunity reduction is a natural consequence of aging, classifying disability with age-frailty again falsely depicts handicaps as a natural and expected part of human existence" (Amundson 1992, 115).

I appreciate Amundson's concern that grouping the "frail elderly" together with nonelderly people with disabilities will lead most people to assume that the opportunities of the latter are reduced by nature and not by the failures of society. But I prefer challenging the underlying assumption about what is natural to pressing the distinction between the two groups. It is not obvious to me that the reduction of opportunities experienced by the elderly are any more attributable to nature than the reduction of opportunities experienced by nonelderly people with disabilities. True, there may be many physical feats they will never accomplish again, but this is also true of nonelderly people with disabilities, and it does not imply for either group that their opportunities to do other things must be diminished. In fact, many elderly people who used to take too many limitations on their activities for granted now take advantage of improvements in accessibility, such as ramps and lowered curbs, that were made with nonelderly people with disabilities in mind. I imagine that if we did not construct our environment to fit a *young* adult, non-disabled, male paradigm of humanity, many obstacles to nonelderly people with disabilities would not exist.

When disability is carefully distinguished from the expected frailties of old age, we lose the main benefit of the insight that aging is disabling. That insight enables non-disabled people to realize that they are temporarily non-disabled, and that in turn enables them to see that it is in their own direct interest to structure society so that people with disabilities have good opportunities to participate in every aspect of social life. Therefore, I do not think that for most social and political purposes it is a good idea to make distinctions among disabilities according to whether they were brought on by aging.

WHO DEFINES DISABILITY AND FOR WHAT PURPOSES?

I believe that discussion of how disability *should* be defined is essential for clarifying our understanding of disability and, ultimately, for formulating policies. But defining disability and identifying individuals as disabled are also social practices that involve the unequal exercise of power and have major economic, social, and psychological consequences in some people's lives. To ignore these practices would leave us with an idealized picture of the problems of definition. To understand how the power of definition is exercised and experienced, we have to ask who does the defining in practice, for what purposes and with what consequences for those who are deemed to fit the definitions.

On the subject of defining race, Evelyn Brooks Higginbotham says:

> Like gender and class, then, race must be seen as a social construction predicated upon the recognition of difference and signifying the simultaneous distinguishing and positioning of groups vis-à-vis one another. More than this, race is a highly contested representation of relations of power between social categories by which individuals are identified and identify themselves. The recognition of racial distinctions emanates from and adapts to multiple uses of power in society. Perceived as "natural" and "appropriate," such racial categories are strategically

necessary for the functioning of power in countless institutional and ideological forms, both explicit and subtle.(Higginbotham 1992, 253–54)

Much of what Higginbotham says about race is also true for disability, although the positioning of groups (disabled versus non-disabled, those with acceptable bodies versus those with rejected bodies) and the contesting of representations (e.g., pitiful cripple, inspiring example) are, I think, in earlier stages of development in disability politics than they are in racial politics. Despite the fact that there is sometimes more biological reality underlying distinctions between the non-disabled and the disabled than there is underlying distinctions between races, the belief that 'the disabled' is a biological category is like the belief that 'Black' is a biological category, in that it masks the social functions and injustices that underlie the assignment of people to these groups.

Charlotte Muller (1979, 43) points out that the providers of health care and of benefits and services to people with disabilities generally define who needs their help. This is an important reminder that the power to define is not necessarily in the hands of those who are most affected by the definitions. Later in this book, I will discuss more fully the cognitive authority (Addelson 1983) of medical professionals and bureaucrats to describe us to ourselves and others, and the practical consequences of that authority. Here perhaps it is sufficient to note that there may be important differences between the definitions of disability employed by so-called 'providers' and the definitions of disability employed by people with disabilities. It is in the interest of many providers to define disability narrowly, so that fewer people are seen to be entitled to the benefits they are supposed to provide than if disability were defined more broadly. Many examples of this can be seen when insurance companies are involved as providers; clearly it is in their direct financial interest to define disability as narrowly as they can without risking costly litigation. The multiplicity of providers can create confusion about who is disabled; it is not uncommon for people with disabilities to find themselves fitting some bureaucracies' definitions of disability and not others.

WHO IDENTIFIES HERSELF/HIMSELF AS DISABLED?

It is important to keep in mind that some people who consider themselves disabled are not identified as disabled by everyone else, and that not everyone who is identified by other people as disabled (either for purposes of entitlement, purposes of discrimination, or others) considers herself or himself disabled.

On the one hand, many people who identify themselves as disabled, because their bodies cause them great physical, psychological, and economic struggles are not considered disabled by others because the public and/or the medical profession do not recognize their disabling conditions. These people often long to be perceived as disabled, because society stubbornly continues to expect them to perform as healthy non-disabled people when they cannot, and refuses to acknowledge and support their struggles. For example, pelvic inflammatory disease (PID) causes severe prolonged disability in some women. Women with PID are often given psychiatric diagnoses and have to endure the skepticism of families and friends, in addition to living with intense and unrelenting abdominal pain (Moore 1985).

Of course, no one wants the social stigma associated with disability, but, as I have already pointed out, social recognition of disability determines the practical help a person receives from doctors, government agencies, insurance companies, charity organizations, and often from families and friends. Moreover, if you are correctly identified by others as disabled, your experience of your own body is (at least to some extent) recognized by your society and the people who surround you; denial of their experience is a major source of loneliness, alienation, and despair in people with unrecognized disabilities (Jeffreys 1982). In addition, for many people with disabilities, identity as a person with a disability has a vital political meaning; they are members of a group of people who share the social oppressions of disability and struggle together against them.

On the other hand, there are many reasons for not identifying yourself as disabled, even when other people consider you disabled. First, disability carries a stigma that many people want to avoid, if at all possible. For newly disabled people, and for children with disabilities who have been shielded from knowledge of how most non-disabled people regard people with disabilities, it takes time to absorb the idea that they are members of a stigmatized group. Newly disabled adults may still have the stereotypes of disability that are common among non-disabled people. They may be in the habit of thinking of disability as total, believing that people who are disabled are disabled in all respects. Since they know that they are not themselves disabled in all respects, they may resist identifying themselves as people with disabilities. They may fear, with good reason, that if they identify themselves as disabled, others will see them as wholly disabled and fail to recognize their remaining abilities or, perhaps worse, see their every ability and achievement as 'extraordinary' or 'courageous' (Wright 1983).

For some people, having hoped or expected to recover from accident or injury, or having hoped for a 'cure' since childhood, identifying themselves as disabled may mean giving up on being healthy, or being able to walk, see, or hear (for example, deaf children often expect to grow up into hearing adults), and accepting the prospect of the rest of one's life with the body and abilities one currently has (Wright 1983). Canadian filmmaker Bonnie Klein describes how, sixteen months after a debilitating stroke, she did not accept herself as disabled. Even though she used a wheelchair, she chose "a glamorous cinema with inaccessible bathrooms" for the premier of one of her films (Klein 1992).

For people who identify themselves strongly with their work and fear (or know) that they cannot continue the same work with their new bodies, accepting disability means making a deep change of identity. Barbara Rosenblum, who became ill with cancer in midlife, wrote:

> My work identity runs through my very cellular structure. For me, work is like a religion. I have devoted my life to it. Being a sociologist has been central to my identity and now I am giving that up. I was frightened when I thought of going on disability. Would they write "disabled professor" on my records at the hospital? (Butler and Rosenblum 1991, 63)

Recognizing myself as disabled certainly required that I change my self-identity and adopt a radically new way of thinking about myself. This included accepting the reality (though not the justice) of the stigma of being chronically ill, especially the shame of being unable to do many things that people still expected me to do. It also required reimagining my life with a new, much more limited, and perpetually uncomfortable body, and then reorganizing my work, home, and relationships to make this different life possible. All of this was difficult, but another very important part of changing my identity helped me through the rest. I found that I could make sense of what was happening to me by talking with other people with disabilities and reading books and articles by them. They already knew how the stigma of disability works, and how to live well with illness and physical limitations. In the process of learning what I needed to know from them, I recognized myself as one of them. When I identified myself as a person with a disability, I no longer felt I was struggling alone.

It was easier to identify myself as disabled to myself than it was to identify myself as disabled to others. For me, this was not primarily because I was afraid of the stigma; I had already encountered the most profound

ways that the stigma of chronic illness would affect me. The problem was that when I had recovered enough strength to return to work part-time, I no longer *looked* very ill although I still fought a daily battle with exhaustion, pain, nausea, and dizziness, and I used a cane to keep my balance. I was struggling, and since people could not see that I was struggling, I was constantly explaining to them that I was struggling, that I could no longer do things that I had done before, and that I did not know when or even if I would ever be able to do them again. I simply wanted my friends and the people I worked with to recognize my limitations and to accept, as I had, that they might be permanent, but it is hard to describe the invisible reality of disability to others without feeling that you are constantly complaining and asking for sympathy. Then too, others resisted believing that I might never regain my previous health and ability. They tried to talk me out of attitudes and actions that they saw as "giving up hope" and that I saw as acceptance and rebuilding my life.

In addition, there was another obstacle to identifying myself to others as disabled. Although I felt that the struggles of people with disabilities, especially women with disabilities, were my struggles (and I still do), I also felt a kind of unworthiness to count myself among people with disabilities, because I was so much better off than they were.

I have heard other people with disabilities, some of them in terrible circumstances, say that they do not consider themselves disabled because "others are so much worse off than I am." I think it is sometimes a way of minimizing one's own difficulties in order not to feel frustration, grief, or shame. Or it can be a way of clinging to one's right to pity others, and therefore to feel stronger, healthier, and more 'normal' than them. I think it is sometimes based on the stereotype of disability that pictures people with disabilities as totally disabled, unable to do anything for themselves or others, and therefore in need of charity; as long as they can do anything, people who have this stereotype in mind refuse to think of themselves as disabled out of pride and to avoid charity.

Something else was also bothering me. My reluctance came partly from awe of people who lived with more disabling conditions than mine; after all, I had learned most of what I knew about how to cope from them. It also came from guilt and shame that while I was able-bodied I had barely noticed, and certainly had not begun to understand, the struggles of people with disabilities or the privileges I had because I was not disabled. I realized too how lucky I was to have built a professional life before I became ill that provided not only adequate disability insurance but also the possibility of continuing my work with my new limitations.

Bonnie Klein describes feelings similar to mine, which occurred the first time she attended a meeting of the DisAbled Women's Network, Canada:

> I feel apologetic, illegitimate, because I was not born disabled, and I am not as severely disabled as many other people. I feel guilty about my privileges of class, profession (including my disability pension), and family. I am a newcomer to the disability movement; I have not paid my dues. (Klein 1992, 73)

My own embarrassment and fear of rejection gave way to the reality of shared work, shared experiences, and mutual understanding. When I began teaching a course on women and disability and meeting a lot of women with disabilities, I found that they treated me as one of them, welcomed my contribution to disability movement, and taught me about their lives with great generosity, regardless of the severity of their own disabilities and disadvantages. Although I am still very aware of my privileges, I no longer feel unworthy to call myself a disabled woman.

HEARING

Ethical Issues in Cochlear Implant Surgery: An Exploration into Disease, Disability, and the Best Interests of the Child

Harlan Lane and Michael Grodin

Conventional wisdom in medicine assumes that deaf children have a serious sensory impairment that gives rise to a disability and to social, educational, and linguistic handicaps. From that perspective, childhood deafness should be mitigated or corrected as far as possible. However, the disability construction of deafness has been challenged by deaf communities in the U.S. and abroad for more than a century (Lane 1984).

This article explores the disputed issues in the context of a recent development in the surgical treatment of deaf children—cochlear-implant surgery. It is our thesis that there is something unique about childhood deafness that challenges the value-laden claim that growing up deaf involves a disability and that challenges, therefore, the appropriateness of surgical intervention to mitigate that disability. Since this deaf point of view is less well known and is counterintuitive for many hearing readers, we dwell on it more than the disability construction; however, our aim is not to advocate for either construction but rather to analyze the issues in a way that illuminates broad questions of interest to medical ethicists. Our discussion focuses primarily on the special nature of the deaf community and concerns about tolerance, diversity, and, ultimately, eugenics. While our analysis is theoretical, it has practical significance for contemporary medical (and other social) practices. The fundamental issue we will address

is whether childhood deafness should be treated, even if the interventions were safe and totally effective. If there are significant ethical dilemmas associated even with medical interventions that would provide close to normal hearing, then present practices, which leave the deaf child "severely hearing-impaired," are open to more serious challenge.

CONTEXT

The deaf-world

Some factual information provides the context for the ethical issues. American Sign Language (ASL) is the primary language of an estimated one million Americans (Schein 1989). Scholarly research, particularly in recent decades, has revealed ASL to be a full-fledged natural language, unrelated to English, with a complex grammar and art forms all its own (Valli and Lucas 1995). Research has also shown that the users of the language are members of a tight-knit social structure and share a culture with characteristic customs, values, and attitudes (Lane, Hoffmeister, and Bahan 1996; Padden and Humphries 1988). Hereafter, we will refer to the members of that culture as DEAF and to the culture itself as the DEAF-WORLD; these are glosses of

Abridged from Lane, Harlan and Grodin, Michael. "Ethical Issues in Cochlear Implant Surgery: An Exploration into Disease, Disability, and the Best Interests of the Child," *Kennedy Institute for Ethics Journal,* 7:3 (1997), 231–251. Copyright © 1997. Reprinted by permission of The Johns Hopkins University Press.

the signs in ASL with which those people refer to themselves and their culture, respectively. We also follow DEAF-WORLD practices in referring to children of any age as DEAF who have, for whatever reason, the physical constitution characteristic of this minority—viz., they rely so much more on vision than on hearing that they would communicate most readily in a natural signed language. (The issue is examined further in a later section.) The English terms *deaf, hearing-impaired,* and *deaf community* are commonly used to designate a much larger and more heterogeneous group than the members of the DEAF-WORLD. Most of the estimated 20 million U.S. citizens in this larger group communicate primarily in English or one of the spoken minority languages (Binnie 1994); they do not identify themselves as members of the DEAF-WORLD, nor do they participate in its organizations, profess its values, or behave in accord with its mores; rather, they consider themselves hearing people with a disability.

DEAF people obtain information primarily through vision—they are "visual people." Some, usually the offspring of DEAF parents, start their acculturation to the DEAF-WORLD in infancy; some in childhood, often upon placement in an educational program for DEAF children; and some never. Once acculturated to the DEAF-WORLD, DEAF people know the language, customs, attitudes, values, and the like, of that culture, and they self-identify as DEAF. There is a "ninety percent" rule that captures four important statistics about the DEAF-WORLD: 90 percent of children born to DEAF couples have normal hearing; 90 percent of DEAF people marry another DEAF person; 90 percent of DEAF children have hearing parents; and 90 percent of children who might be candidates for cochlear implants because of their inability to hear even very loud sounds were born that way or became DEAF before age one (Schein 1989; CADS 1992).

Being DEAF is highly valued in DEAF culture. DEAF people who espouse those cultural values are glad they are DEAF, and they reject the suggestion that they have an impairment or a disability. (The ASL sign that translates, roughly, as *disability* does not include being DEAF.) This contrasts with the predominant attitudes of people with disabilities (although there is diversity within both groups). Leaders of the disability rights movement call for ambivalence about their impairment. Individually they want it valued, as a part of who they are; at the same time, as the result of poverty, war, disease, or accident, they ask that we regret the impairment and try to prevent it (Abberley 1987; Lane 1995b). The DEAF-WORLD is not ambivalent; its members characteristically think it is a good thing to be DEAF

and would like to see more of it. Unlike most expectant parents with disabilities, expectant DEAF parents characteristically hope to have children with whom they can share their language, culture, and unique experiences—that is, DEAF children. Whereas people with disabilities seek, above all, better medical care, rehabilitation services, personal assistance services—e.g., help with personal hygiene, dressing, and eating—integration into society at large and independence, DEAF people do not attach particular importance to any of these services. Nor do they have any more concern with autonomy and independent living than people in general; DEAF people cherish interdependence with other DEAF people. Integration of DEAF children into hearing schools and classes is anathema to the DEAF-WORLD. The specialized schools for the DEAF, especially the residential schools, were the setting in which most DEAF adults acquired fluent (manual) language and socialization. It has been those specialized schools and, after graduation, the DEAF clubs with their athletic, literary, political, and social programs that have provided most DEAF people in America, despite their having hearing parents, with the generational continuity that is essential for a rich culture.

What seems to lie at the heart of all these differences between the values of people with disabilities and those of the DEAF is that people with disabilities in the U.S. are acculturated to mainstream American values while DEAF views, although influenced by the hearing culture that engulfs the DEAF-WORLD, are also shaped by the unique culture of the DEAF-WORLD itself. Indeed, the political agenda of the DEAF-WORLD—highlighting such issues as education for DEAF children using the DEAF-WORLD minority language and the provision of interpreters—more closely resembles the agenda of other language minorities than it does the agenda of any group of people with a disability. It may be objected that each disability grouping has its characteristic demands, so that the distinct concerns of culturally DEAF people, and even the fact that they do not see themselves as people with a disability, do not necessarily make it inappropriate to group DEAF people among people with disabilities. However, there is nothing inherent in DEAF people that requires them to be seen as people with disabilities, nor can any reason be given why they must be mistaken about their identity. When there are enough fundamental differences between the two groups, we are at liberty to revise our social construction. The social constructions of several other minority groups—Blacks and Gays, to name two—have shifted over the years in the direction of the group's own self-construction (Lane 1995b).

COCHLEAR IMPLANTS

The latest collision between the disability and cultural constructions of childhood deafness arose in 1990 when, after five years of clinical research trials, the U.S. Food and Drug Administration (FDA) approved surgical implantation of cochlear prostheses in children over the age of two. (The FDA had formerly approved this prosthesis for adolescents over age 12 and adults.) In the wake of the FDA approval, several medical, paramedical, and consumer groups also endorsed the practice; among them, the National Institutes of Health, the American Academy of Otolaryngology/Head and Neck Surgery, the American Speech-Language Hearing Association, and the Cochlear Implant Club International. An estimated 5,000 children in the U.S. and abroad have been surgically implanted with cochlear prostheses of the type approved by the FDA. Numerous national organizations of the DEAF around the world and the World Federation of the Deaf (with 110 member nations) have published position papers opposed to childhood implant surgery.[1] The single most recurrent criticism is that the surgery is unethical. For example, the National Association of the Deaf in the U.S. condemned the FDA decision as "unsound scientifically, procedurally and ethically" (NAD 1991).

In the surgical procedure under dispute, the hospitalized child is placed under general anesthesia for three to four hours. After preliminary surgery, a wire carrying electrodes is inserted into the inner ear. A receiver coil connected to the wire is sutured to the skull and the skin is sewn over it. A small microphone worn on an ear piece picks up sound and sends signals to a speech processor worn on a belt or in a pocket. The processor sends electrical signals to the implanted receiver via a transmitter mounted behind the ear, and those signals stimulate the auditory nerve. The surgery normally is followed by very extensive speech and hearing therapy, administered by speech pathologists, teachers, and, frequently, parents. The research literature shows that the benefit in speech perception obtained by the minority of children, those who lost their hearing after acquiring English—an estimated 3 percent of children with profound hearing losses[2] (CADS 1992)—is similar to that obtained by patients deafened in adulthood: in many cases such children recover substantial ability to recognize words by ear. However, for the estimated 86 percent born with profound hearing losses who must *acquire* spoken language rather than recover some ability to perceive it by ear, the results are different. There has been no case reported in the scientific literature of a child acquiring spoken language as a result of implant surgery, although there are anecdotal reports. Several medical centers around the U.S. have investigated auditory word recognition in such implanted children. Their results converge in revealing that the majority of implanted children who were born DEAF are unable to follow instructions to take the test or get no words correct on the test (without prompting), even after five years of implant use and habilitative therapy (Lane 1995a). A few children do much better, however, for reasons that are unclear.

There is a consensus among audiologists (who evaluate the children's ability to hear speech, provide training, and "fit" the prostheses) and otologists (who perform the surgery) that children with cochlear implants remain "severely hearing-impaired" (see, e.g., Horn, Noza, and Dolitsky 1991; Boothroyd 1993). This leads to a variety of concerns. For example, the decision to have the surgery and habilitation may promote delays in the child's acquisition of ASL and therefore may delay the time when that child has any full language at his or her command. Developmental milestones for signed languages are similar to those for spoken languages, and the later the acquisition of ASL, the poorer its mastery on the average (Petitto 1993; Mayberry and Eichen 1991). If implanted children become fluent neither in English nor in ASL, their intellectual, social, and psychological development may be compromised. However, we wish to explore the ethical dimensions and arguments that arise in the dispute over childhood implants, to point out important considerations in the debate rather than to advocate for or against implant surgery, and to examine what light is shed on this issue by examining parallel cases. For these purposes, it is helpful to consider whether the surgery would be ethical if, contrary to the present facts, implants could deliver close to normal hearing for most implanted children, and the children then proceeded to acquire spoken language.

ETHICAL ISSUES RAISED BY COCHLEAR-IMPLANT SURGERY ON CHILDREN

Parents have an ethical duty to act in the reasonable best interests of their DEAF child, and the surgeons have an ethical obligation to provide their patients, given their consent, with a safe and potentially effective treatment. Both groups see implant surgery as promising at least an increased responsiveness to sound, and in particular to speech. At best, the hope is that surgery will allow the DEAF child to acquire spoken language. That, in turn, would provide the child with easier communication with parents, peers, teachers, and others. Moreover, the child would not be subject to the stigma of being DEAF. With a "perfect implant," the child would acquire English not ASL (assuming the parents are English speakers) and become acculturated to his or her parents' culture and not that of the DEAF-WORLD. If this surgery were performed on a large scale, many children who would have learned ASL and who would have become acculturated to the DEAF-WORLD would not do so. Some 60,000 schoolchildren in the U.S. receive special services for the hearing-impaired, and, with a perfect implant available, most would be candidates for the surgery. Thus, the population of the DEAF-WORLD in the U.S. would decline drastically—although most DEAF children of DEAF parents would presumably continue to enter it. The presently thriving culture would diminish as well, and possibly die. If so, the program of cochlear implantation in children, and the parental decisions that implemented it, would have as one effect the diminution of a minority culture. It would also reinforce the belief that those remaining in the DEAF-WORLD suffer from an impairment, a belief that the DEAF-WORLD finds erroneous and inimical to its interests.

Let us assume then that it is in the best interest of the DEAF child to receive a perfect implant and not in the interest of the DEAF-WORLD for substantial numbers of DEAF children to do so, as that would lead to a diminution of the DEAF-WORLD and its culture. Let us further assume that preservation of minority cultures is a good. We would argue—but will not do so here, for it would take us too far afield—that the variety of humankind and cultures enriches all cultures and contributes to the biological, social, and psychological well-being of humankind. Laws and covenants, such as the United Nations Declaration of the Rights of Persons Belonging to National or Ethnic, Religious and Linguistic Minorities (1992), are founded on a belief in the value of protecting minority cultures. Programs that substantially diminish minority cultures are engaged in ethnocide (Diamond 1970), and may constitute crimes against humanity. The United Nations Convention on the Prevention and Punishment of the Crime of Genocide (1948) defines as genocide "any of the following acts committed with intent to destroy in whole or in part a national, ethnical, racial or religious group, [including] measures intended to prevent births within the group." While surgical programs that implant large numbers of DEAF children do not have as their intent the destruction of DEAF-WORLD culture, both the U.N. Declaration and the Convention express humankind's

interest in preserving and fostering minority languages and cultures and thus, once the minority language and culture of the DEAF-WORLD is recognized, alert us to the conflict of values arising from those surgical programs.

Clearly, there is a tension, then, between concern for the individual DEAF child who would benefit from a perfect implant and concern for the DEAF-WORLD, which would be harmed by the widespread use of implants. Granted that the parents of that child have a primary duty to pursue their child's reasonable best interests, do the hearing parents of the DEAF child also have an obligation to consider the destructive effects on the DEAF-WORLD of parental decisions for childhood implant surgery? If the parents do not have that obligation, does society at large have such an obligation? Consider a different case of tension between concern for the individual and concern for the minority group. How should parents act if they endorse busing for school desegregation in their town but believe that their own child would be adversely affected by being bused? Suppose we respond that parents must, in the end, weigh the consequences for their own child more heavily than those for the minority culture, whether the DEAF-WORLD or African Americans. How would this calculation be affected by recognizing that the DEAF child's physical constitution would otherwise have made him or her a member of the DEAF-WORLD? Does this oblige the parents to place more value on the welfare of that particular minority culture than the value that our common humanity leads us to place on the protection of all minority cultures?

Consider white foster parents who have a Black child and hearing parents who have a DEAF child. Both sets of parents have physical attributes markedly different from their children, and in both cases the children would become members of minority groups different from their parents' culture if no special measures, such as surgery, were undertaken to change that. Are white foster parents of a Black child, then, obliged to consider not only the interests of their town and their Black child in the busing issue but also the views of the Black community? Suppose the white foster parents believe that Black parents might give even more weight than they do to desegregation. Should they allow that to tip the balance in favor of busing their child? In short, does having a child that would normally be a member of a distinct minority culture oblige the child's parents, whether foster or not, to give more weight to acting in the best interests of that minority culture than they would have otherwise? Or is the parents' sole duty the reasonable best interests of their child, leaving to social institutions the responsibility for defending the interests of minority cultures? Relegating the responsibility to society does not provide an entirely satisfactory solution since: (1) hearing parents are members of the larger society to which the responsibility for defending the DEAF-WORLD would be left and (2) if hearing parents elected in large numbers to have their DEAF children surgically implanted, it is hard to see what measures a concerned society might take to ensure the survival of the DEAF-WORLD that would not trammel the primary authority of the parents' decision.

Consider a further case of tension between concern for the individual and for the minority group. Some Black leaders and organizations have condemned transracial adoption practices on the ground, among others, that they promote "cultural genocide" (see Simon and Altstein 1992). This issue is a closer parallel than desegregation to the fundamental interest of the DEAF-WORLD in its very survival in the face of widespread cochlear implantation. Suppose a white couple wishes to adopt a particular Black infant whose quality of life would, let us assume, then improve. Does the couple have an ethical obligation, grounded in the value we place on other cultures, other ways of life, to weigh the negative views of the Black minority since the child they propose to adopt is Black and, even if not yet acculturated to African-American culture, would normally acquire that minority culture if they did not intervene? Suppose that the couple agrees that preservation of Black culture is a good and that the policy of transracial adoption is inimical to that good; is the ethically right course for them to decline to adopt the Black child? Since they are not the child's parents, they would have no preexisting parental obligation to benefit the child. Should they decline to adopt even if there are no Black foster parents available and the child is languishing in an orphanage?

Perhaps the couple will respond that they can satisfy their concern for the Black minority by doing all in their power to raise their child biracially and biculturally. Hearing parents of a DEAF child cannot attempt to resolve the tension in this way since, if their child had a perfect implant, he or she would no longer have the physical constitution that is necessary to be DEAF. Moreover, the parents would have little reason to ensure that their child learns ASL, especially since he or she could never be a full-fledged member of the DEAF-WORLD, which would, in any event, be moribund. Consider instead then, a large-scale program that

resettled in the United States children from a culture whose survival is threatened by war or disease or famine. Would such a program be ethical if it enhanced the lives of the children at the expense of hastening the demise of their culture? If not, should government permit such a program? Should citizens agree to serve as foster parents under those conditions?

The Congress and the courts of the U.S. seem to have held both values dear—the best interests of the child and those of the minority culture—in legislating and adjudicating cases under the Indian Child Welfare Act of 1978. Passed at a time when the survival of Native-American cultures was considered threatened by very high rates of transracial adoption, the act was designed to prevent the undermining of Native-American tribes, stating that "it is the policy of this nation to protect the best interests of Indian children and to promote the stability and security of Indian tribes...." The Supreme Court has ruled that lower courts must consider the best interests of the particular Indian tribe as well as the best interests of the child (Simon and Altstein 1992).

WHICH CHILDREN ARE DEAF?

The extent to which analogies from transracial adoption are helpful in examining the case of DEAF children depends on how we analyze the relationship between the parent and the child. If we see as the defining characteristic of the relationship the biological ties between parent and child, then it is not illuminating for the issue of DEAF children to conclude, for example, that foster parents of a Black child have an obligation to defend the interests of the Black minority. Hearing parents of the DEAF child object that they, unlike foster parents, are the child's biological parents; this child belongs not to another culture but to their own culture. Since it has not yet made any ties to the DEAF-WORLD, they need not be concerned about that world any more than any other person. In contrast, where there are cultures whose members have a characteristic physical constitution, all the children with that constitution tend to be seen as the rightful recipients of that culture to some degree.

Clearly, Black leaders believe that African-American children, for example, have an African-American heritage from the day they are born, regardless of whether they are allowed to take possession of that heritage. Accordingly, the National Association of Black Social Workers came out opposed to transracial adoption on the grounds that it will deprive such children of their heritage. We need not decide at this juncture whether it is more important for these Black children to be adopted as quickly as possible or to take possession of their heritage; the relevant point is whether they do have such a heritage at birth. Likewise, does a visual child—one who relies primarily on vision—however raised, have a DEAF heritage. For members of the DEAF-WORLD, the answer is clearly "yes." They feel a strong bond with that child; they may note that it has "DEAF eyes," and, after all, that the child's life trajectory, given its constitution, will likely cause him or her to become fully acculturated to the DEAF-WORLD. The DEAF child can be deprived of the opportunity to acculturate to that world, as can the Black child or the Native-American child, but the child's potential for acculturation to that world, which is rooted in his or her physical difference, remains, so we consider the child with that difference DEAF, Black, or Native-American right from the start, whether they are in fact able to enter their respective cultures or not. This would explain why adult DEAF, Black, and Native-Americans, for example, feel a strong emotional investment in the welfare of, respectively, DEAF, Black and Native-American children, and identify and empathize with them, even when they are not related to them.

Although some children are DEAF for hereditary reasons, others become DEAF as a sequel to illness prenatally or in childhood. Children in other cultural minorities do not acquire their distinctive physical constitution as a sequel to illness or in childhood, so an examination of the cultural norms for membership in the DEAF-WORLD is particularly interesting. The reasons for which the DEAF constitution arises are irrelevant for those norms, but the constitution itself is essential; hearing children of DEAF adults, called "codas," are not considered DEAF despite their fluency in ASL and acculturation to the DEAF-WORLD, a situation that is perhaps comparable to Caucasians who are occasionally raised in a Native-American culture but are not considered Native-Americans. However, as with other language minorities, the characteristic constitution is important in that it predisposes the person to communicate in the language and thus to participate in the life of the culture (Bahan 1994). If that predisposition is undermined by long acculturation to spoken language and culture, as it would be in a hearing adult who later is deafened, it seems that that person is not considered DEAF on constitutional grounds alone and must acquire signed language fluency and DEAF-WORLD cultural norms before the DEAF-WORLD will view him or her as DEAF.

Consider a contrasting view, namely that children who are so much more reliant on vision than on hearing that they have severe difficulty with oral communication nevertheless start out in mainstream hearing society and become part of the DEAF-WORLD only when they are "placed in that community by their parents or voluntarily decide to enter it" (Cohen 1994, p. 1). From this vantage point, if the child is fitted with the perfect implant early enough, the DEAF-WORLD is utterly irrelevant, and the child should be considered formerly deaf not DEAF. However, we would not say of, for example, Hispanic-American children that they start out in the mainstream society and only become members of the Hispanic minority culture when placed there by their parents or their own decision; rather, we would say that the child "is Hispanic" and has an Hispanic heritage at birth. Is that because Hispanic children normally have Hispanic parents—is it the parents' culture that is criterial in ascribing a cultural heritage to the child? No, since an Hispanic-American infant adopted at any age into an English-speaking foster family is still viewed as an Hispanic-American child. Likewise, a Native-American infant who is transracially adopted is still considered a Native-American child. Suppose an embryo formed by the union of two Native-Americans were implanted in the womb of a Caucasian woman, would the child to which she gave birth be considered Caucasian or Native-American? It seems that the cultural membership ascribed to the child is not based on its parents' culture, but rather on the culture the child would enter given its physical makeup. What makes the DEAF case unique among minorities, and therefore challenging for our ethical reasoning, is that these two criteria—the culture of the parents and the culture that the child's constitution predisposes him to enter—have separated.

THE EUGENICS DISPUTE

DEAF children and the DEAF-WORLD are not the only groups whose interests are affected by a policy authorizing cochlear implantation. The interests of parents, professionals, and the wider society are also at stake. This becomes clearer in the dispute between hearing and DEAF cultural values in the realm of eugenic measures aimed at avoiding the birth of DEAF children in the first place. The underlying reason, we submit, that doctors and parents want cochlear prostheses for DEAF children is that their construction of those children's reality is based on disability. The underlying reason that the DEAF-WORLD is at odds with them is that its cultural construction of the reality of DEAF children is based on the children's potential for sharing the language and culture of the DEAF-WORLD and identifying with it (Lane 1992, 1995b). It follows from the disability construction that being DEAF is not a good thing and that efforts will be undertaken not only to eradicate the underpinning physical difference in the individual child with prosthetic surgery but also to prevent more children with that disability from being born through genetic counseling and genetic engineering. More than half of all children who are DEAF in the U.S. are DEAF for hereditary reasons (Reardon 1992).

The DEAF-WORLD seems to have a favorable view of genetic research and counseling under two conditions. First, some DEAF adults seek genetic counseling when considering a mate, in order to enhance the possibility that they will have DEAF children (Jordan 1991). Second, while DEAF adults welcome the birth of DEAF children, they commonly support measures that would reduce the numbers of DEAF children that are born with what are seen as disabilities in DEAF culture—e.g., motor impairments. However, genetic counseling and research aimed at reducing the numbers of children born simply DEAF and eugenic proposals, such as gene therapy, with that same goal are considered highly unethical (Jordan 1991). The former chairman of a National Institutes of Health planning group recently acknowledged this conflict in an interview with *The New York Times*: "I am dedicated to curing deafness. That puts me on a collision course with those who are culturally deaf. That is interpreted as genocide of the deaf" (Pride in a Silent Language 1993).

If it is unethical for the majority culture to aim to reduce the numbers of children born DEAF because measures intended to prevent births within a cultural group constitute genocide, is it also unethical for a DEAF couple to seek genetic counseling to reduce the chances of having a hearing child? Davis (1997, p. 14) concludes that it is: Even "if Deafness is considered a culture, . . . then deliberately creating a Deaf child who will have only very limited options to move outside of that culture also counts as a moral harm." On the other hand, many members of oppressed cultures put great weight on marrying someone from their own culture so that their child will be a member of that culture— even if marrying outside of the culture would potentially give their child a more open future. What is more ethically disquieting than people coupling to have children like themselves are eugenic social

policies that favor some cultural groups—especially majorities—over others.

Contemporary efforts to regulate childbearing by DEAF people have a long history. Alexander Graham Bell was the leading figure in the last century in efforts to stop DEAF reproduction through model sterilization laws, campaigns to dissuade DEAF adults from marrying and procreating, and efforts to discourage DEAF socializing and education in the company of other DEAF people (Lane 1984). In 1992, Boston University researchers announced that they had identified the "genetic error responsible for the most common type of inherited deafness" (BU Team 1992). The director of the National Institute on Deafness and Other Communication Disorders (NIDCD) called the finding a "major breakthrough that will improve diagnosis and genetic counseling and ultimately lead to substitution therapy or gene transfer therapy" (BU Team 1992, p. 6). Thus a new form of medical eugenics applied to DEAF people was envisioned, in this case by an agency of the U.S. government.

Suppose we say that it is unethical to take measures aimed at reducing the number of births of children who will populate a given language and cultural minority. Once again, a unique property of the DEAF-WORLD probes our ethical reasoning. For not only do most DEAF people have hearing parents, but also some DEAF people, albeit a small percent, acquire the defining physical makeup that leads them into the DEAF-WORLD as a sequel to illness, such as meningitis, and not as a result of heredity. Is there an ethical dilemma in providing prenatal care whose effects are to reduce the likelihood of a hearing parent having a DEAF child? Is it problematic to treat a child for an illness that, untreated, might very well lead to that child becoming DEAF? If we presume that doctors should treat children to avoid their becoming DEAF, then why is it unethical for the doctors to try to avoid DEAF births in the first place by, for example, genetic counseling?

CULTURAL DISAGREEMENTS ON MEDICAL PRACTICE

Mainstream American culture is generally well-disposed to attempts to mitigate disability with high technology, and cochlear implants in particular have been presented in the media as a very positive development (Lane 1994). Many people see such measures aimed at giving a DEAF child hearing as beneficent. However, speech and hearing are not valued in the culture of the

DEAF-WORLD, which resists efforts to inculcate them in DEAF children and adults. Suppose we grant the earlier argument that the DEAF infant is a member of the DEAF-WORLD and therefore that DEAF-WORLD values have standing along with the values of that child's hearing parents. Let us further assume that the implant surgery is not a matter of saving life or of alleviating great suffering. (Although membership in the DEAF-WORLD undoubtedly brings disadvantages as well as advantages, there are countless happy and successful DEAF adults.) Is there a way to choose between the opposing cultural views of what constitutes proper medical practice in this case? Is it unethical for the surgeon in our hearing culture to proceed to operate on the DEAF child? Is it ethical for a plastic surgeon to reduce the Negroid features of a Black child, assuming the operation entails low risk and the parents request it? If the ear surgeon has an ethical obligation to provide prostheses to DEAF children, supposing the surgeon believes them to be a potentially effective treatment, is it unethical for DEAF parents to refuse such a treatment for their DEAF child, as they assuredly do? If it is ethical to change the makeup of a child born DEAF so the child has a makeup more like its hearing parents and considered better in hearing culture, is it ethical to change the makeup of a child born hearing so that the child has a makeup more like its DEAF parents and considered better in DEAF culture?

Consider the argument of some hearing parents who favor implant surgery for their child that the surgical procedure is readily reversible—the external equipment could simply be put aside—so their child could always choose to be DEAF at a later date. Therefore, in approving the surgery, they maintain, they are not choosing for their child, they are creating the conditions that will allow their child to choose. However, with a successful implant it seems likely that most users would not become acculturated to the DEAF-WORLD, so in choosing implant surgery the parents have indeed chosen their child's cultural membership. Moreover, the family's evident embrace of the disability model combined with their child's late, and therefore impaired, mastery of ASL would create further barriers to a true choice. True, given the present imperfect implants, implanted DEAF children are more motivated to acculturate to the DEAF-WORLD, although therapeutic efforts aim to avoid that by favoring speech over ASL and mainstream classes over education with other DEAF children. In seeking to give their children the choice of two worlds, parents may place them in the predicament of many hard-of-hearing children, too hard of hearing to move readily in their parents' hearing culture, but too hearing in their values and communication to move readily in the DEAF-WORLD. It seems as problematic to raise a child in two different "worlds," with two opposed constructions of the child's fundamental nature, as it is to raise a child in two contrasting religions simultaneously, aiming to allow the child to exercise choice later as an adult.

DEAF people live in a hearing society and American society makes special allowance for their fuller participation—allowances such as provision of interpreters, cash payments for disability, special education programs, and more. When the DEAF-WORLD opposes childhood implantation in principle—i.e., presumably, even with perfect implants—does it undermine its moral claim to the provision of interpreters and other special provisions? Indeed, if it insists there is no disability in being culturally DEAF, is it ethical to accept benefits provided under legislation such as the Americans with Disabilities Act? What should any minority do if its means for fuller participation in the society are provided by laws that classify it in ways it opposes? Does the DEAF-WORLD have particular claim on interpreting services since, unlike other non-English speakers, most of its members cannot in principle acquire spoken language? Similarly, does the DEAF-WORLD have a special claim on bilingual education (in English and ASL), which it strongly favors. If so, is the claim flawed that to be culturally DEAF is not to have a disability?

PARENTAL SURROGACY

Parents are given great, but not unlimited, moral and legal authority in the U.S., when it comes to making decisions that affect their children. Not only do parents normally have the reasonable best interests of their children at heart, but also they likely will be affected more than any other adult by their parental decisions, and their children's values as competent adults are likely to resemble their own. However, it is open to question whether a DEAF child's values as an adult will closely resemble those of its hearing parents, and it is arguable whether others do not also have an important stake in the rearing of the child. On the first count, is it ethically troubling that in choosing the implant surgery for their child, hearing parents are making a choice that their child probably would not make if the choice were postponed until the child were old enough to judge? Of course, we cannot be certain that a particular DEAF child would refuse implant surgery if mature enough to express an informed choice, nor can we even be totally certain that the child will enter the DEAF-WORLD.

However, we do know what most people believe who were once DEAF children but are now old enough to make a considered decision, and they are overwhelmingly opposed. Is the parents' surrogacy also weakened by the fact that the surgery promises a solution to their own communicative impasse with their child? It is extremely rare for parents who have a good command of a signed language to consent to cochlear implant surgery for their children.

Finally, the parental commitment to the best interests of the child flows not only from biology but also, as with foster parents, from rearing. Does parental commitment also flow from a genuinely concerned community to which the child will ultimately belong—absent any special intervention? Does a Native-American tribe have parent-like moral authority when it comes to the proper rearing of a transracially adopted child from that tribe? Does the DEAF-WORLD have such authority with respect to the rearing of DEAF children? No one has proposed transferring legal authority from the hearing parents to DEAF adults (Balkany, Hodges, and Goodman 1996, notwithstanding). The question is, rather, how great is the parents' obligation to consider these voices that emanate from a culture more connected with their child than with themselves?

CONCLUSION

This paper has examined some features of the DEAF-WORLD as a paradigm to explore the grounding questions of disease, disability, and what constitutes the best interests of the child. We have shown the parallels and discontinuities of comparing people in the DEAF-WORLD to people in mainstream society who have disabilities. We have raised serious questions about the appropriateness of a disability model and surgery based on that model in view of DEAF people's membership in

a specific cultural group. Ultimately, how we treat this problem will say a great deal about what kind of society we are and the kind of society in which we wish to live. Difference and diversity not only have evolutionary significance but, we would argue, are a major part of what gives life its richness and meaning. We have examined ethical tensions that arise even when positing a perfect cochlear implant, leaving to other fora the debate about burdens and benefits of the present prostheses, which are far from perfect. Ultimately, addressing ethical quandaries surrounding the use of cochlear implants in children will require not only a commitment to continued open and explicit dialogue, but also attention to the requisite concern for the respect and dignity of all who contribute to that discourse.

NOTES

1. Illustrative position papers are available from: National Association of the Deaf, 814 Thayer Avenue, Silver Spring, MD 20910; Les Sourds en Colère, BP 322, 75122 Cedex 03 Paris, France; Canadian Cultural Society of the Deaf, #144, 11337 61 Avenue, Edmonton, Ontario T6H 1M3; Danske Doves Landsforbund, Postboks 704, Fensmarkgade 1, DK 2200 Kobenhavn, Denmark; Sveriges Dovas Riksforbund, PO Box 300, S-79327 Leksand, Sweden; Norges Doveforbund, PO Box 6850, N-0130 Oslo, Norway; Deutscher Gehorenlosenbund, Paradeplatz 3, 2370 Rendsburg, Germany; World Federation of the Deaf, Proceedings of the XII World Congress of the World Federation of the Deaf, Vienna, Austria, 10–15 July 1995; World Federation of the Deaf 13D Chemin du Levant, F-01210 Ferney-Voltaire, France; National Institutes of Health Consensus Development Conference Statement, Cochlear Implants in Adults and Children, 15–17 May 1995: Federal Building, Room 618, 7550 Wisconein Avenue, Bethesda, MD 20892; American Academy of Otolaryngology-Head and Neck Surgery, One Prince Street, Alexandria, VA.

2. Persons with hearing losses termed "profound" require at least 90 dB greater sound pressure level than the norm in order to detect pure tones at selected frequencies. Those with "severe" losses require 70 to 89 dB more. Children with losses that place them in either category routinely receive special class placement and speech, hearing, language, and educational assistance.

Cochlear Implants and the Claims of Culture? A Response to Lane and Grodin

Dena S. Davis

Let me begin by expressing my gratitude to Harlan Lane and Michael Grodin (1997) for their provocative and hard-hitting article. By positing a situation in which cochlear implants are risk-free and effective,

they have constructed the strongest case possible for the use of such implants and thus have challenged themselves to make the most robust and uncompromising argument for the position that DEAF

Davis, Dena. "Cochlear Implants and the Claims of Culture? A Response to Lane and Grodin," *Kennedy Institute for Ethics Journal*, 7:3 (1997), 253–258.Copyright © 1997. Reprinted by permission of The Johns Hopkins University Press.

people are not disabled, but rather are members of a linguistic/cultural minority, and that parents act wrongly when they seek to convert deaf babies into hearing ones.

I will respond under three headings.

IS DEAFNESS A DISABILITY?

I cannot accept the claim that deafness is not to be perceived as a disability. The DEAF-WORLD of which the authors speak has created a rich and unique culture, and I am happy to assent to the claim that that culture is qualitatively, though not quantitatively, equal to that of the hearing world. It also is true that a great deal of what "disables" the deaf in our present world is socially constructed and could be substantially ameliorated by a more caring majority. But there is a difference between valuing the culture that the DEAF-WORLD has built and equating deafness *with* culture.

One of the defining differences between culture and disability is the option that human adults have to choose the extent to which they identify with and participate in their culture. As the authors state, many people who are physically deaf are not members of the DEAF-WORLD. Some hearing people are more at home in the DEAF-WORLD and more fluent in American Sign Language (ASL) than are many deaf people (Cohen 1995). Despite the many positive aspects of the DEAF-WORLD and despite the fact that DEAF and deaf people may, on average, lead lives as happy and productive as those of hearing people, I maintain that the inability to hear is a deficit, a disability, a lack of perfect health. A hearing person has a choice about whether to participate in DEAF culture, by learning ASL, attending social and cultural events, and so on. A nonhearing person, however, is irrevocably cut off from large areas of the hearing world. Even if I were to follow Lane and Grodin's generous example and posit an ideal educational environment for the deaf, most prelingually deafened persons would not be able to communicate effectively orally, with obvious social and vocational consequences. (I can anticipate an obvious response, that hearing people are equally disadvantaged because they can never be fully accepted in the DEAF-WORLD. But if that is true, it is because DEAF people are prejudiced against them, not because they are disabled from learning the necessary skills.)

IS CULTURAL MEMBERSHIP PHYSIOLOGICALLY DETERMINED?

I reject the notion that physical characteristics, hereditary or congenital, constitute cultural membership. Culture, the "body of customary beliefs, social forms, and material traits constituting a distinct complex of tradition of a racial, religious, or social group" (Webster's International Dictionary 1993), is passed on by people, not by genes. A child born into an Ashkenazic Jewish family, for example, partakes of that culture because her parents pass it on to her, *in exactly the same way* as they would pass it on to a child whom they adopted at birth (or as an embryo). Should this couple happen to have both a biological child and an adopted one, they would not consider one child to be "more" Jewish than the other. This is as silly as saying that Madeleine Albright is "really" Jewish. The opposite notion seems to me deeply racist and genetically determinist.

There are, of course, some counterexamples to my claim, as Lane and Grodin point out. In one type of counterexample, one acknowledges that a white couple raising an African-American child has an obligation to give the child a clear and proud sense of her black identity because, whatever they do, the child will be treated by others as a black person and therefore she needs a proud racial identity as a buffer against racism. In another type of counterexample, one might argue that a child with, say, an Italian genetic ancestry should know something about his parents' and grandparents' culture, feel proud of the accomplishments of his ancestors, and so forth. But neither of these arguments fits the situation of a deaf child born to hearing parents. Deaf children who are fitted with perfect cochlear implants will not be treated by others as deaf, and children of hearing parents obviously do not have deaf ancestors.

My point is that even if I were to accept the claim that deafness is a culture rather than a disability and even if there were *no* downsides to being deaf, there is no reason to fault hearing parents who, reasonably enough, prefer to have children who share their language and culture— and those of their siblings—and who do not require huge investments of parental resources to learn sign language, to pay for special schools and equipment, and so on.

PRESERVATION OF MINORITY CULTURES

Lane and Grodin raise the question of whether, since the "preservation of minority cultures is a good," parents have an ethical obligation not to choose cochlear implants for their nonhearing child, because converting their child from deaf—and therefore potentially DEAF—to hearing diminishes the population strength of the DEAF-WORLD. I perceive three arguments against this claim.

First, even if deafness is a culture rather than a disability, I think that the authors are, quite simply, asking too much. Raising a DEAF child well requires an enormous commitment of time, money, and energy. Parents, who usually are not expecting their new baby to be deaf, must learn ASL quickly in order to communicate with their child early so that language is mastered at the appropriate developmental stages. In addition, they may need to pull up stakes and relocate to a community that can offer the appropriate services. If they adopt the DEAF values that the authors describe, integration of their child into hearing schools will be "anathema," and they probably will have to send their child to a residential school at a much earlier age than they would normally contemplate. If cochlear implants in the first year of life present a risk-free alternative, it seems unrealistic to expect parents to choose this enormous burden for reasons unrelated to the welfare of their child. (Especially since, as the authors suggest, it is not wrong to seek to cure such deafness-causing diseases as meningitis even if doing so will reduce the DEAF population.) Furthermore, hearing parents might plausibly worry that they will not be successful in raising a happy and productive DEAF or deaf child; how much simpler, then, from the perspective of the child's own well-being, to choose the implants.

Second, as the authors point out, there are many more "deaf" people than there are "DEAF" people since many "visual" people fail to become successful members of the DEAF-WORLD or choose not to do so. Thus, there is no certainty, perhaps not even a likelihood, that the child in question will make that step, and without that likelihood all of the arguments about not diminishing minority cultures fall flat.

Third, against the authors' positive depiction of the DEAF-WORLD, one needs to think seriously about the limited opportunities that exist for even the most positively acculturated DEAF person. Marriage partners, conversation partners, vocations, and avocations are severely limited. Yes, one can think of cultural minorities about whom the same could be said—e.g., the Amish or very Orthodox Jews—but these children can change their minds as adults and a significant percentage do so. As I have argued elsewhere, every child has a "right to an open future" (Davis 1997; the concept is Joel Feinberg's) in which she can choose her mate, her

vocation, her religion, her reading material, her place of residence, and so forth. Because deafness severely limits the child's future *in an irrevocable fashion*, I cannot agree that parents act wrongly in "curing" a child's deafness.[1] Furthermore, if deafness is not a culture but a disability, then the authors' claim becomes even harder to sustain, even if that disability were the entry ticket to a rich and happy culture.

Against these arguments, the authors suggest that the parents of a deaf child have a special connection to the DEAF-WORLD, which grounds a unique obligation to be concerned for the continuing strength and flourishing of the DEAF population. They suggest that this special concern may be powerful enough to tip the balance when parents are weighing their obligations to the child's best interest against their moral concern for the flourishing of minority cultures. This suggestion seems false. We all have obligations to be concerned about the situation of vulnerable minorities. Those of us in the majority group who have family members in the minority population arguably have a special awareness of the minority situation, but not therefore a unique obligation. It is not, after all, considered a valid moral argument to say, "Why should I care about the flourishing of the DEAF population? No one in my family is DEAF!" Some years ago, when my only child was quite young, I would occasionally—mostly to be provocative— respond to persons who questioned my active commitment to gay rights by saying that, after all, my son had approximately a 10 percent chance of turning out to be gay, and I needed to enhance his chances of having a just and pro-gay society to live in. But in retrospect, that seems nonsensical; now that my child has turned out to be heterosexual, I certainly do not think that I have any less reason to continue my work for gay rights.

In conclusion, I cannot accept the foundational claim that deafness is primarily to be understood as (potential) membership in a cultural and linguistic minority, rather than as a disability. But even if I were to be persuaded to that claim, I do not agree that the needs of that culture for continuing population strength trump a hearing family's plausible assumption that by giving their baby normal hearing, they have increased her chances for a happy life and also for a much more open future.

Like the authors, I end with more questions. By limiting myself to Lane and Grodin's challenge, I have made only a very narrow claim: that hearing parents do not act wrongly when they choose (safe and effective) cochlear implants for a deaf baby. Questions abound for future dialogue: Do hearing parents therefore act wrongly if they *decide against* implants? Ought this to be considered neglect and grounds for the state to step in and insist on implants? What about parents who are deaf or DEAF? Is it wrong for them to choose implants for their children? Wrong for them to refuse implants? Wrong for them to seek genetic counseling to maximize their chances of having deaf children? Wrong for them deliberately to expose themselves to rubella, for example, in order to change a hearing fetus to a deaf one? If we accept the disability premise, these will be tough questions with which to grapple.

The author of this article is hearing.

NOTE

1. Lane and Grodin note that most DEAF adults are opposed to the notion of cochlear implants and infer from that that DEAF children would refuse implant surgery if they were old enough to be consulted. But, of course, in my view, children are not born DEAF, merely deaf. Further, it makes as much sense to ask ordinary hearing people now if they would have wanted implants had they been born deaf as it does to ask DEAF people that question.

THE BODY

"Ambiguous Sex" or Ambivalent Medicine?

Alice Domurat Dreger

ETHICAL ISSUES IN THE TREATMENT OF INTERSEXUALITY

What makes us "female" or "male," "girls" or "boys," "women" or "men"—our chromosomes, our genitalia, how we (and others) are brought up to think about ourselves, or all of the above? One of the first responses to the birth of a child of ambiguous sex by clinicians, and parents, is to seek to "disambiguate" the situation: to assign the newborn's identity as either female or male, surgically modify the child's genitalia to conform believably to that sex identity, and provide other medical treatment (such as hormones) to reinforce the gender decided upon. The assumptions that underly efforts to "normalize" intersexual individuals and the ethics of "treatment" for intersexuality merit closer examination than they generally receive.

A number of events have lately aroused substantial public interest in intersexuality (congenital "ambiguous sex") and "reconstructive" genital surgery. Perhaps the most sensational of these is the recent publication of unexpected longterm outcomes in the classic and well-known "John/Joan" case. "John" was born a typical XY male with a twin brother, but a doctor accidentally ablated John's penis during a circumcision at age eight months. Upon consultation with a team of physicians and sexologists at the Johns Hopkins Hospital (circa 1963) it was decided that given the unfortunate loss of a normal penis John

should be medically reconstructed and raised as a girl—"Joan." Surgeons therefore removed John/Joan's testes and subsequently subjected Joan to further surgical and hormonal treatments in an attempt to make her body look more like a girl's. The team of medical professionals involved also employed substantial psychological counseling to help Joan and the family feel comfortable with Joan's female gender. They believed that Joan and the family would need help adjusting to her new gender, but that full (or near-full) adjustment could be achieved.

For decades, the alleged success of this particular sex reassignment had been widely reported by Hopkins sexologist John Money and others as proof that physicians could essentially create any gender out of any child, so long as the cosmetic alteration was performed early. Money and others repeatedly asserted that "Johns" could be made into "Joans" and "Joans" into "Johns" so long as the genitals looked "right" and everyone agreed to agree on the child's assigned gender. The postulates of this approach are summarized succinctly by Milton Diamond and Keith Sigmundson: "(1) individuals are psychosexually neutral at birth and (2) healthy psychosexual development is dependent on the appearance of the genitals" (p. 298). While not a case of congenital intersexuality, the John/Joan case was nevertheless used by many clinicians who treat intersexuality as proof that in intersex cases the same postulates should hold. The keys seemed to be surgical creation of a believable

Abridged from Dreger, Alice. "Ambiguous Sex–Or Ambivalent Medicine? Ethical Issues in the Treatment of Intersexuality," *Hastings Center Report*, 28:3 (1998), 24–35. Copyright © 1998. Reprinted by permission of The Hastings Center.

sexual anatomy and assurances all around that the child was "really" the assigned gender.

But reports of the success of John/Joan were premature-indeed, they were wrong. Diamond and Sigmundson recently interviewed the person in question, now an adult, and report that Joan had in fact chosen to resume life as John at age fourteen. John, now an adult, is married to a woman and, via adoption, is the father of her children. John and his mother report that in the Joan-years, John was never fully comfortable with a female gender identity. Indeed, Joan actively attempted to resist some of the treatment designed to ensure her female identity; for instance, when prescribed estrogens at age twelve, Joan secretly discarded the feminizing hormones. Depressed and unhappy at fourteen, Joan finally asked her father for the truth, and upon hearing it, "All of a sudden everything clicked. For the first time things made sense, and I understood who and what I was" (p. 300). At his request, John received a mastectomy at age fourteen, and for the next two years underwent several plastic surgery operations aimed at making his genitals look more masculine.

Diamond and Sigmundson are chiefly interested in using this new data to conclude that "the evidence seems overwhelming that normal humans are not psychosocially neutral at birth but are, in keeping with their mammalian heritage, predisposed and biased to interact with environmental, familial, and social forces in either a male or female mode." In other words, sexual nature is not infinitely pliable; biology matters.

In their report, Diamond and Sigmundson also take the opportunity of publication to comment on the problem of the lack of long-term follow-up of cases like these. But what is also troubling is the lack of ethical analysis around cases like this—particularly around cases of the medical treatment of intersexuality, a phenomenon many orders of magnitude more common than traumatic loss of the penis. While there have been some brief discussions of the ethics of deceiving intersex patients (that discussion is reviewed below), the medical treatment of people born intersexed has remained largely ignored by ethicists. Indeed, I can find little discussion in the literature of any of the ethical issues involved in "normalizing" children with allegedly "cosmetically offensive" anatomies. The underlying assumption grounding this silence appears to be that "normalizing" procedures are necessarily thoroughly beneficent and that they present no quandaries. This article seeks to challenge that assumption and to encourage interested parties to reconsider, from an ethical standpoint, the dominant treatment protocols for children and adults with unusual genital anatomy.

Frequency of intersexuality

Aside from the apparent presumption that "normalizing" surgeries are necessarily good, I suspect that ethicists have ignored the question of intersex treatment because like most people they assume the phenomenon of intersexuality to be exceedingly rare. It is not. But how common is it? The answer depends, of course, on how one defines it. Broadly speaking, intersexuality constitutes a range of anatomical conditions in which an individual's anatomy mixes key masculine anatomy with key feminine anatomy. One quickly runs into a problem, however, when trying to define "key" or "essential" feminine and masculine anatomy. In fact, any close study of sexual anatomy results in a loss of faith that there is a simple, "natural" sex distinction that will not break down in the face of certain anatomical, behavioral, or philosophical challenges.

Sometimes the phrase "ambiguous genitalia" is substituted for "intersexuality," but this does not solve the problem of frequency, because we still are left struggling with the question of what should count as "ambiguous." (How small must a baby's penis be before it counts as "ambiguous"?) For our purposes, it is simplest to put the question of frequency pragmatically: How often do physicians find themselves unsure which gender to assign at birth? One 1993 gynecology text estimates that "in approximately 1 in 500 births, the sex is doubtful because of the external genitalia. I am persuaded by more recent, well-documented literature that estimates the number to be roughly 1 in 1,500 live births.

The frequency estimate goes up dramatically, however, if we include all children born with what some physicians consider cosmetically "unacceptable" genitalia. Many technically nonintersexed girls are born with "big" clitorises, and many technically nonintersexed boys are born with hypospadic penises in which the urethral opening is found somewhere other than the very tip of the penis.

Dominant treatment protocols

Contemporary theory, established and disseminated largely via the work of John Money and endorsed by the American Academy of Pediatrics, holds that gender identity arises primarily from psychosocial rearing (nurture), and not directly from biology (nature); that all children must have their gender identity fixed very early in life for a consistent, "successful" gender identity to form; that from very early in life the child's anatomy must match the "standard" anatomy for her or his gender; and that for gender identity to form psychosocially boys primarily require "adequate" penises with no vagina, and girls primarily require a vagina with no easily noticeable phallus.

Note that this theory presumes that these rules must be followed if intersexual children are to achieve successful psychosocial adjustment appropriate to their assigned gender—that is, if they are to act like girls, boys, men, and women are "supposed" to act. The theory also by implication presumes that there are definite acceptable and unacceptable roles for boys, girls, men, and women, and that this approach will achieve successful psychosocial adjustment at least far more often than any other approach.

Many parents, especially those unfamiliar with sex development, are bothered by their children's intersexed genitals and receptive to offers of "normalizing" medical treatments. Many also actively seek guidance about gender assignment and parenting practices. In the United States today, therefore, typically upon the identification of an "ambiguous" or intersexed baby teams of specialists (geneticists, pediatric endocrinologists, pediatric urologists, and so on) are immediately assembled, and these teams of doctors decide to which sex/gender a given child will be assigned. A plethora of technologies are then used to create and maintain that sex in as believable a form as possible, including, typically, surgery on the genitals, and sometimes later also on other "anomalous" parts like breasts in an assigned male; hormone monitoring and treatments to get a "cocktail" that will help and not contradict the decided sex (and that will avoid metabolic dangers); and fostering the conviction among the child's family and community that the child is indeed the sex decided—"psychosocial" rearing of the child according to the norms of the chosen sex. Doctors typically take charge of the first two kinds of activities and hope that the child's family and community will successfully manage the all-critical third.

Clinicians treating intersexuality worry that any confusion about the sexual identity of the child on the part of relatives will be conveyed to the child and result in enormous psychological problems, including potential "dysphoric" states in adolescence and adulthood. In an effort to forestall or end any confusion about the child's sexual identity, clinicians try to see to it that an intersexual's sex/gender identity is permanently decided by specialist doctors within forty-eight hours of birth. With the same goals in mind, many clinicians insist that parents of intersexed newborns be told that their ambiguous child does really have a male or female sex, but that the sex of their child has just not yet "finished" developing, and that the doctors will quickly figure out the "correct" sex and then help "finish" the sexual development.

Because of widespread acceptance of the anatomically strict psychosocial theory of treatment, the practical rules now adopted by most specialists in intersexuality are these: genetic males (children with Y chromosomes) must have "adequate" penises if they are to be assigned the male gender. When a genetic male is judged to have an "adequate" phallus size, surgeons may operate, sometimes repeatedly, to try to make the penis look more "normal." If their penises are determined to be "inadequate" for successful adjustment as males, they are assigned the female gender and reconstructed to look female. (Hence John to Joan.) In cases of intersexed children assigned the female sex/gender, surgeons may "carve a large phallus down into a clitoris" (primarily attempting to make the phallus invisible when standing), "create a vagina using a piece of colon" or other body parts, "mold labia out of what was a penis," remove any testes, and so on.

Meanwhile, genetic females (that is, babies lacking a Y chromosome) born with ambiguous genitalia are declared girls—no matter how masculine their genitalia look. This is done chiefly in the interest of preserving these children's potential feminine reproductive capabilities and in bringing their anatomical appearance and physiological capabilities into line with that reproductive role. Consequently, these children are reconstructed to look female using the same general techniques as those used on genetically male children assigned a female role. Surgeons reduce "enlarged" clitorises so that they will not look "masculine." Vaginas are built or lengthened if necessary, in order to make them big enough to accept average-sized penises. Joined labia are separated, and various other surgical and hormonal treatments are directed at producing a believable and, it is hoped, fertile girl.

What are the limits of acceptability in terms of phalluses? Clitorises—meaning simply phalluses in children labeled female-are frequently considered too big if they exceed one centimeter in length. Pediatric surgeons specializing in treating intersexuality consider "enlarged" clitorises to be "cosmetically offensive" in girls and therefore they subject these clitorises to surgical reduction meant to leave the organs looking more "feminine" and "delicate." Penises—meaning simply phalluses in children labeled male—are often considered too small if the stretched length is less than 2.5 centimeters (about an inch). Consequently, genetically male children born at term "with a stretched penile length less than 2.5 [centimeters] are usually given a female sex assignment."

One of the troubling aspects of these protocols are the asymmetric ways they treat femininity and masculinity. For example, physicians appear to do far more to preserve the reproductive potential of children born with ovaries than that of children born with testes. While genetically male intersexuals often have infertile testes, some men with micropenis may be able to father children if allowed to retain their testes.

Similarly, surgeons seem to demand far more for a penis to count as "successful" than for a vagina to count as such. Indeed, the logic behind the tendency to assign the female gender in cases of intersexuality rests not only on the belief that boys need "adequate" penises, but also upon the opinion among surgeons that "a functional vagina can be constructed in virtually everyone [while] a functional penis is a much more difficult goal." This is true because much is expected of penises, especially by pediatric urologists, and very little of vaginas. For a penis to count as acceptable—"functional"— it must be or have the potential to be big enough to be readily recognizable as a "real" penis. In addition, the "functional" penis is generally expected to have the capability to become erect and flaccid at appropriate times, and to act as the conduit through which urine and semen are expelled, also at appropriate times. The urethral opening is expected to appear at the very tip of the penis. Typically, surgeons also hope to see penises that are "believably" shaped and colored.

Meanwhile, very little is needed for a surgically constructed vagina to count among surgeons as "functional." For a constructed vagina to be considered acceptable by surgeons specializing in intersexuality, it basically just has to be a hole big enough to fit a typical-sized penis. It is not required to be self-lubricating or even to be at all sensitive, and certainly does not need to change shape the way vaginas often do when women are sexually stimulated. So, for example, in a panel discussion of surgeons who treat intersexuality, when one was asked, "How do you define successful intercourse? How many of these girls actually have an orgasm, for example?" a member of the panel responded, "Adequate intercourse is defined as successful vaginal penetration. All that is required is a receptive hole."

Indeed, clinicians treating intersex children often talk about vaginas in these children as the absence of a thing, as a space, a "hole," a place to put something. That is precisely why opinion holds that "a functional vagina can be constructed in virtually everyone" because it is relatively easy to construct an insensitive hole surgically. (It is not always easy to keep them open and uninfected.) The decision to "make" a female is therefore considered relatively fool-proof, while "the assignment of male sex of rearing is inevitably difficult and should only be undertaken by an experienced team" who can determine if a penis will be adequate for "successful" malehood.

The problem of "normality"

The strict conception of "normal" sexual anatomy and normal sex behavior that underlies prevailing treatment protocols is arguably sexist in its asymmetrical treatment of reproductive potential and definitions of anatomical "adequacy." Additionally, as Lee and other critics of intersex treatment have noted, "[d]ecisions of gender assignment and subsequent surgical reconstruction are inseparable from the heterosexual matrix, which does not allow for other sexual practices or sexualities. Even within heterosexuality, a rich array of sexual practices is reduced to vaginal penetration." Not surprisingly, feminists and intersexuals have invariably objected to these presumptions that there is a "right" way to be a male and a "right" way to be a female, and that children who challenge these categories should be reconstructed to fit into (and thereby reinforce) them.

Indeed, beside the important (and too often disregarded) philosophical-political issue of gender roles, there is a more practical one: how does one decide where to put the boundaries on acceptable levels of anatomical variation? Not surprisingly, the definition of genital "normality" in practice appears to vary among physicians. For example, at least one physician has set the minimum length of an "acceptable" penis at 1.5 centimeters.

"Ambiguous" genitalia do not constitute a disease. They simply constitute a failure to fit a particular (and, at present, a particularly demanding) definition of normality. It is true that whenever a baby is born with "ambiguous" genitalia, doctors need to consider the situation a potential medical emergency because intersexuality may signal a potentially serious metabolic problem, namely congenital adrenal hyperplasia (CAH), which primarily involves an electrolyte imbalance and can result in "masculinization" of genetically female fetuses. Treatment of CAH may save a child's life and fertility. At the birth of an intersex child, therefore, adrenogenital syndrome must be quickly diagnosed and treated, or ruled out. Nonetheless, as medical texts advise, "of all the conditions responsible for ambiguous genitalia, congenital adrenal hyperplasia is the only one that is life-threatening in the newborn period," and even in cases of CAH the "ambiguous" genitalia themselves are not deadly.

As with CAH's clear medical issue, doctors now also know that the testes of androgen insensitivity syndrome (AIS) patients have a relatively high rate of becoming cancerous, and therefore AIS needs to be diagnosed as early as possible so that the testes can be carefully watched or removed. However, the genitalia of an androgen-insensitive person are not diseased. Again, while unusual genitalia may signal a present or potential threat to health, in themselves they just look different. As we have seen, because of the perception of a "social emergency" around an intersex birth, clinicians take license to treat nonstandard genitalia as a medical problem requiring prompt correction. But as Suzanne Kessler sums up the situation, intersexuality does not threaten the patient's life; it threatens the patient's culture.

Psychological health and the problem of deception

Clearly, in our often unforgiving culture intersexuality can also threaten the patient's psyche; that recognition is behind the whole treatment approach. Nevertheless, there are two major problems here. First, clinicians treating intersex individuals may be far more concerned with strict definitions of genital normality than intersexuals, their parents, and their acquaintances (including lovers). This is evidenced time and again, for example, in the John/Joan case:

John recalls thinking, from preschool through elementary school, that physicians were more concerned with the appearance of Joan's genitals than was Joan. Her genitals were inspected at each visit to The Johns Hopkins Hospital. She thought they were making a big issue out of nothing, and they gave her no reason to think otherwise. John recalls thinking: "Leave me be and then I'll be fine . . . It's bizarre. My genitals are not bothering me; I don't know why it is bothering you guys so much."

Second, and more basically, it is not self-evident that a psychosocial problem should be handled medically or surgically. We do not attempt to solve the problems many dark-skinned children will face in our nation by lightening their skins. Similarly, Cheryl Chase has posed this interesting question: when a baby is born with a severely disfigured but largely functional arm, ought we quickly remove the arm and replace it with a possibly functional prosthetic, so that the parents and child experience less psychological trauma? While it is true that genitals are more psychically charged than arms, genitals are also more easily and more often kept private, whatever their state.

Why would a physician ever withhold medical and personal historical information from an intersexed patient? Because she or he believes that the truth is too horrible or too complicated for the patient to handle. In a 1988 commentary in the *Hastings Center Report,* Brendan Minogue and Robert Tarszewski argued, for example, that a physician could justifiably withhold information from a sixteen-year-old AIS patient and/or her parents if he believed that the patient and/or family was likely to be incapable of handling the fact that she has testes and an XY chromosomal complement. Indeed, this reasoning appears typical among clinicians treating intersexuality; many continue to believe that talking truthfully with intersexuals and their families will undo all the "positive" effects of the technological efforts aimed at covering up doubts. Thus despite intersexuals' and ethicists' published, repeated objections to deception, in 1995 a medical student was given a cash prize in medical ethics by the Canadian Medical Association for an article specifically advocating deceiving AIS patients (including adults) about the biological facts of their conditions. The prize-winner argued that "physicians who withhold information from AIS patients are not actually lying; they are only deceiving" because they selectively withhold facts about patients' bodies.

But what this reasoning fails to appreciate is that hiding the facts of the condition will not necessarily prevent a patient and family from thinking about it. Indeed, the failure on the part of the doctor and family to talk honestly about the condition is likely only to add to feelings of shame and confusion. One woman with AIS in Britain writes, "Mine was a dark secret kept from all outside the medical profession (family included), but this [should] not [be] an option because it both increases the feelings of freakishness and reinforces the isolation. Similarly, Martha Coventry, a woman who had her "enlarged" clitoris removed by surgeons when she was six, insists that "to be lied to as a child about your own body, to have your life as a sexual being so ignored that you are not even given the decency of an answer to your questions, is to have your heart and soul relentlessly undermined."

Lying to a patient about his or her biological condition can also lead to a patient unintentionally taking unnecessary risks. As a young woman, Sherri Groveman, who has AIS, was told by her doctor that she had "twisted ovaries" and that they had to be removed; in fact, her testes were removed. At the age of twenty; "alone and scared in the stacks of a [medical] library," she discovered the truth of her condition. Then "the pieces finally fit together. But what fell apart was my relationship with both my family and physicians. It was not learning about chromosomes or testes that caused enduring trauma, it was discovering that I had been told lies. I avoided all medical care for the next 18 years. I have severe osteoporosis as a result of a lack of medical attention. This is what lies produce."

Similarly, as B. Diane Kemp—"a social worker with more than 35 years' experience and a woman who has borne androgen insensitivity syndrome for 63 years" notes, "secrecy as a method of handling troubling information is primitive, degrading, and often ineffective. Even when a secret is kept, its existence carries an aura of unease that most people can sense . . . Secrets crippled my life."

Clearly, the notion that deception or selective truthtelling will protect the child, the family, or even the adult intersexual is extraordinarily paternalistic and naive, and, while perhaps well-intentioned, it goes against the dominant trend in medical ethics as those ethics guidelines are applied to other, similar situations. In what other realms are patients regularly not told the medical names for their conditions, even when they ask? As for the idea that physicians should not tell patients what they probably "can't handle," would a physician be justified in using this reasoning to avoid telling a patient she has cancer or AIDS?

In their commentary in the *Hastings Center Report* Sherman Elias and George Annas pointed out that a physician who starts playing with the facts of a patient's condition may well find himself forced to lie or admit prior deception. "Practically," Elias and Annas wrote, "it is unrealistic to believe that [the AIS patient] will not ultimately learn the details of her having testicular syndrome. From the onset it will be difficult to maintain the charade." They also note that without being told the name and details of her condition any consent the AIS patient gives will not truly be "informed." As an attorney Groveman too argues "that informed consent laws mandate that the patient know the truth before physicians remove her testes or reconstruct her vagina."

Informed consent and risk assumption

It is not at all clear if all or even most of the intersex surgeries done today involve what would legally and ethically constitute informed consent. It appears that few intersexuals or their parents are educated, before they give consent, about the anatomically strict psychosocial model employed. The model probably ought to be described to parents as essentially unproven insofar as the theory remains unconfirmed by broad-based, longterm follow-up studies, and is directly challenged by cases like the John/Joan case as well as by ever-mounting "anecdotal" reports from former patients who, disenfranchised and labeled "lost to follow-up" by clinicians, have turned to the popular press and to public protest in order to be heard. Of course, as long as intersex patients are not consistently told the truth of their conditions, there is some question about whether satisfaction can be assessed with integrity in long-term studies.

At a finer level, many of the latest particular cosmetic surgeries being used on intersexed babies and children today remain basically unproven as well, and need to be described as such in consent agreements. For example, a team of surgeons from the Children's Medical Center and George Washington University Medical School has reported that in their preferred form of clitoral "recession" (done to make "big" clitorises look "right"), "the cosmetic effect is excellent" but "late studies with assessment of sexual gratification, orgasm, and general psychological adjustment are unavailable . . , and remain in question. In fact the procedure may result in problems like stenosis, increased risk of infections, loss of feeling, and psychological trauma. (These risks characterize all genital surgeries.)

The growing community of open adult intersexuals understandably question whether anyone should have either her ability to enjoy sex or her physical health risked without personal consent just because she has a clitoris, penis, or vagina that falls outside the standard deviation. Even if we did have statistics that showed that particular procedures "worked" a majority of the time we would have to face the fact that part of the time they would not work, and we need to ask whether that risk ought to be assumed on behalf of another person.

Beyond "monster ethics"

In a 1987 article on the ethics of killing one conjoined twin to save the other, George Annas suggested (but did not advocate) that one way to justify such a procedure would be to take "the monster approach." This approach would hold that conjoined twins are so grotesque, so pathetic, any medical procedure aimed at normalizing them would be morally justified. Unfortunately, the present treatment of intersexuality in the U.S. seems to be deeply informed by the monster approach; ethical guidelines that would be applied in nearly any other medical situation are, in cases of intersexuality, ignored. Patients are lied to; risky procedures are performed without follow-up; consent is not fully informed; autonomy and health are risked because of unproven (and even disproven) fears that atypical anatomy will lead to psychological disaster. Why? Perhaps because sexual anatomy is not treated like the rest of human anatomy, or perhaps because we simply assume that any procedure which "normalizes" an "abnormal" child is merciful. Whatever the reason, the medical treatment of intersexuality and other metabolically benign, cosmetically unusual anatomies needs deep and immediate attention.

While it is easy to condemn the African practice of female genital mutilation as a barbaric custom that violates human rights, we should recognize that in the United States medicine's prevailing response to intersexuality is largely about genital conformity and the "proper" roles of the sexes. Just as we find it necessary to protect the rights and well-being of African girls, we must now consider the hard questions of the rights and well-being of children born intersexed in the United States.

As this paper was in process, the attention paid by the popular media and by physicians to the problems with the dominant clinical protocols increased dramatically, and many more physicians and ethicists have recently come forward to question those protocols. Diamond and Sigmundson have helpfully proposed tentative new "guidelines for dealing with persons with ambiguous genitalia."

As new guidelines are further developed, it will be critical to take seriously two tasks. First, as I have argued above, intersexuals must not be subjected to different ethical standards from other people simply because they are intersexed. Second, the experiences and advice of adult intersexuals must be solicited and taken into consideration. It is incorrect to claim, as I have heard several clinicians do, that the complaints of adult intersexuals are irrelevant because they were subjected to "old, unperfected" surgeries. Clinicians have too often retreated to the mistaken belief that improved treatment technologies (for example, better surgical techniques) will eliminate ethical dilemmas surrounding intersex treatment. There is far more at issue than scar tissue and loss of sensation from unperfected surgeries.

The Ashley Treatment:
Best Interests, Convenience, and Parental Decision-Making

S. Matthew Liao, Julian Savulescu, and Mark Sheehan

The story of Ashley, a nine-year-old from Seattle, has caused a good deal of controversy since it appeared in the *Los Angeles Times* on January 3, 2007.[1] Ashley was born with a condition called static encephalopathy, a severe brain impairment that leaves her unable to walk, talk, eat, sit up, or roll over. According to her doctors, Ashley has reached, and will remain at, the developmental level of a three-month-old.[2]

In 2004, Ashley's parents and the doctors at Seattle's Children's Hospital devised what they called the "Ashley Treatment," which included high-dose estrogen therapy to stunt Ashley's growth, the removal of her uterus via hysterectomy to prevent menstrual discomfort, and the removal of her breast buds to limit the growth of her breasts. Ashley's parents argue that the Ashley Treatment was intended "to improve our daughter's quality of life and not to convenience her caregivers."[3] They also "decided to share our thoughts and experience . . . to help families who might bring similar benefits to their bedridden 'Pillow Angels,'" which means that this treatment has public policy implications.

In the case of incompetent children like Ashley, parents are the custodians of the child's interests and are required to make decisions that protect or promote those interests. Doctors should also offer treatments that are in Ashley's best interests. It would be wrong to offer a treatment that was against the interests of the child but in the parents' (or others') interests. The central questions in medical ethics in relation to this case are: Were these treatments in Ashley's best interests? Do they treat her as a person with dignity and respect, and were they likely to make her life go better?

Ashley's parents argue that they sought the Ashley treatment in order to alleviate Ashley's "discomfort and boredom." Their contention that stunting Ashley's growth was done for sake of improving "our daughter's quality of life and not to convenience her caregivers" is controversial.

According to her parents, keeping Ashley small—at around seventy-five pounds and four feet, five inches tall—means that Ashley can be moved considerably more often, held in their arms, be taken "on trips more frequently," "have more exposure to activities and social gatherings," and "continue to fit in and be bathed in a standard size bathtub." All this serves Ashley's health and well-being because, so the parents argue, "the increase in Ashley's movement results in better blood circulation, GI functioning (including digestion, passing gas), stretching, and motion of her joints," which means that Ashley will be less prone to infections.

Undoubtedly, the parents are right that Ashley will benefit in the manner they have proposed if they can do all these things for her. The claim about the value of small size in a particular social circumstance is certainly not unique. Dwarves have given the same argument as a justification for preferring to have short children. They have argued that parenting dwarves is desirable for them because of their own size and because they have made modifications to their homes and their surroundings to take into account their short stature.[4]

As a general point, it is entirely conceivable that in some natural, social, or psychological circumstances, having a normal body may be a disadvantage. In H.G. Wells' short story "The Country of the Blind," Nunez, a mountaineer in the Andes, falls and comes upon the Country of the Blind. Nunez has normal vision, but in this society of blind people, he is disadvantaged, and he eventually consents to have his eyes removed. Similarly, in a world of loud noise, being able to hear could be a disadvantage. In the case of apotemnophilia—a body dysmorphic disorder in which the patient feels incomplete possessing all four limbs—doctors justify amputation by reasoning that the patient's psychology demands it. In Ashley's case, having a normal-sized body could be a disadvantage. Stunting Ashley's growth may then be in her overall interest, given her likely natural and social circumstances.

Of course, Ashley's parents may have had other motives besides her benefit. Many critics have claimed that what her parents were really after was to make things easier or more convenient for themselves. Convenience may have been at least *part* of their motivation. Her parents could have found ways to take care of Ashley even if she had grown to her normal size of five feet, six inches. They argue that they were already near their limits when lifting Ashley; but if their own convenience was no consideration, they could have augmented their strength by hiring people to help them, or by going to the gym, or by taking steroids, and so on. We are not advocating any of these things; we are asserting only that since the parents *could* have taken these measures, part of the rationale for making Ashley smaller may have been their own convenience.

This said, acting out of the motive to convenience the caregivers or otherwise promote their interests is not necessarily wrong, for two reasons. First, motives may only form part of the justification of the treatment of children. Whether the treatment will benefit or harm them is just as important, and sometimes even more so. Imagine a parent who takes a child with appendicitis to a hospital merely hoping that the child will get admitted so that the parent can get some badly needed sleep. Does this make it wrong to perform an appendectomy? Obviously not. In such a case, the justification of the procedure depends on the interests of the child and not on the motives of the parents (though of course the two can be related).

Second, in any plausible moral theory, moral obligations should typically not be so demanding that one must make enormous sacrifices in order to fulfil them. As Judith Jarvis Thomson observes, "nobody is morally *required* to make large sacrifices, of health, of all other interests and concerns, of all other duties and commitments … in order to keep another person alive."[5] Exactly where the demands of morality stop, especially in the case of parents, is not easy to say. But, arguably, if Ashley's parents have to take steroids, which may have side effects, in order to move Ashley around, or if they will have to impoverish themselves in order to hire additional caregivers, then these alternatives might just be too demanding, and Ashley's parents would not be obligated to pursue them.

Of course, someone might accept that the demands of morality have limits but still question whether stunting Ashley's growth for her caregivers' convenience is justified. Indeed, many are worried that the Ashley Treatment might represent a return to the practices of the eugenics movement and be an affront to human dignity.[6] In particular, it has been asked whether, if it is permissible to stunt Ashley's growth to keep her small, why it is not also permissible surgically to remove her legs to keep her small. Needless to say, it is disturbing to think of a scenario in which severely disabled institutionalized children are subjected to mass surgery and growth-stunting to make the staff's work easier.

These questions raise issues concerning the ethics of body modification. Some forms of plastic surgery are performed on children: "bat ears" are sometimes corrected to prevent a child's being teased, and growth hormone or estrogen treatment is sometimes provided to children predicted to have short or tall stature.[7] However, other forms of body modification that might be allowed in adults are not permitted in children. A Scottish surgeon, Robert Smith, amputated the healthy legs of two patients suffering from apotemnophilia. The patients had received psychiatric and psychological treatment prior to the operation, but did not respond. Both operations were carried out with private funding, and the patients said they were satisfied with the results.[8] But this kind of surgery could not be ethically performed on healthy children because it is not plausibly in their interests, given the risks to, and the stress such an operation would impose on, their bodies. For this reason, surgically removing Ashley's legs just so she would be easier to care for would be unethical.

Giving Ashley estrogen to stunt her growth is obviously controversial but may be justifiable in this circumstance. Imagine that as a part of Ashley's condition, her body would grow to five times the size of other people. She would be enormous. In such a case, it does not seem too objectionable to arrest this kind of development through pharmacological means to allow her to be nursed and cared for, even if this is done partly for the caregivers' convenience. That is, suppose that if her development was not arrested, providing her with decent care would eventually require twenty people. If this is right, the question is not whether development *may* be arrested, but only *when* it may be arrested.

Here it is important to point out that decisions of this kind should be made on a case by case basis, with independent ethical review, such as occurred in this case through a hospital's clinical ethics committee. In general, it is inappropriate for institutions to biologically modify their patients to make them easier to manage, though clearly many demented people are sedated for this purpose. The benefits of being cared for at home by one's family may warrant imposing some burdens on incompetent dependants to enable them to remain at home and to make it possible for care to be delivered there. When the parents' resources are limited, the state, with its greater resources, should not resort to biological modification when the patient's quality of life can be preserved through social services.

The removal of Ashley's uterus and her breast buds is another matter. Ashley's parents argue that a hysterectomy will allow her to avoid the menstrual cycle and the discomforts commonly associated with it, eliminate "any possibility of pregnancy," and also eliminate the possibility "of uterine cancer and other common and often painful complications that cause women later in life to undergo the procedure." We find these arguments debatable.

For starters, it is unclear how much discomfort women suffer from the menstrual cycle, and whether the level of discomfort justifies hysterectomy. Also, even if Ashley will experience some discomfort, it is unclear

why less invasive methods—such as giving Ashley pain killers whenever she experiences cramps—are not sufficient. Furthermore, removing Ashley's uterus may cause her ovaries not to function normally as a result of a compromised supply of blood.[9] This may result in Ashley's ovaries not producing enough of the hormones that would otherwise protect her against serious common diseases such as heart disease and osteoporosis.

Regarding unwanted pregnancies, while this does occur sometimes, the parents' statement gives the impression that sexual abuse is a given to one in Ashley's situation. Also, the parents may be in danger of blaming the victim. Ashley would get pregnant only through sexual abuse, but surely action should be taken against the offenders rather than Ashley. In any case, there are less invasive ways of avoiding pregnancy, such as putting Ashley on birth control pills.

Finally, regarding the possibility of uterine cancer and other painful complications, it seems premature to undertake a preventive measure when no one knows whether the symptoms will ever manifest. Giving Ashley regular health checkups seems to be much more appropriate and less invasive.

According to Ashley's parents, surgically removing Ashley's breast buds is justified because Ashley will not be breastfeeding. In addition, their presence "would only be a source of discomfort to her" because Ashley is likely to have large breasts, and "large breasts are uncomfortable lying down with a bra and even less comfortable without a bra." Moreover, they "impede securing Ashley in her wheelchair, stander, or bath chair, where straps across her chest are needed to support her body weight." Furthermore, removing her breasts also means that she can avoid the possibility of painful fibrocystic growth and breast cancer, which runs in Ashley's family. Finally, according to the parents, large breasts "could 'sexualize' Ashley towards her caregiver, especially when they are touched while she is being moved or handled, inviting the possibility of abuse." Again, we find these arguments problematic. We shall start with the ones that have been addressed previously.

In arguing that the breasts could "sexualize" Ashley, the parents are again in danger of blaming the victim for possible abuse. Moreover, someone might sexually abuse Ashley whether she has breasts or not. The focus should be on the potential sex offenders.

The argument that breasts would make securing Ashley in her wheelchair difficult, and so on, is an argument from convenience. Like the previous argument about size, it depends on how likely the harm to Ashley would be and how great the sacrifice of coping with management would be. Unlike Ashley's height and weight, in this case, it does not seem too demanding to require the parents to look for straps that would be more suitable for a larger breast size. Even if Ashley had been allowed to grow her breasts to their full potential, surely there are disabled persons with similar breast sizes, and their caregivers have apparently been able to use straps that are suitable for them (although the situation may be different when the patient's disability is as grave as Ashley's).

The possibility of painful fibrocystic growth and breast cancer is similar to the risk of uterine cancer; here, too, undertaking a preventive measure when the symptoms have not manifested seems premature. Even in the case of familial breast cancer, such as cancer linked to the genes BRCA 1 and 2, it is still not standard medical practice to offer prophylactic mastectomy to children, even those with a permanent intellectual disability that renders them incompetent. Many would argue that screening is preferable until there is more debate on the justification of prophylactic surgery in incompetent people.

The argument that Ashley does not need her breasts because she will not breastfeed (making her breasts only a "source of discomfort") assumes that the sole function of having breasts is for breastfeeding. Allowing Ashley to develop breasts may enable her to form and complete her gender identity. It is true that gender assignment surgery has been performed on children at birth in cases of intersex conditions,[10] but there is a growing consensus that surgery should be delayed until the child can make his or her own decision about it.[11] Ashley will never (on the evidence provided) be able to decide for herself. But there is a difference between gender assignment and gender *elimination*. Ashley's parents argue that since Ashley has the mental state of a three-month-old, it is more fitting for her to have the body of an infant. They cite the statement of George Dvorsky, a member of the board of directors for the Institute for Ethics and Emerging Technologies, approvingly:

> If the concern has something to do with the girl's dignity being violated, then I have to protest by arguing that the girl lacks the cognitive capacity to experience any sense of indignity. Nor do I believe this is somehow demeaning or undignified to humanity in general; the treatments will endow her with a body that more closely matches her cognitive state—both in terms of her physical size and bodily functioning. The estrogen treatment is not what is grotesque here. Rather, it is the prospect of having a full-grown and fertile woman endowed with the mind of a baby.

This argument implies that anyone with the mind of a baby should have the body of a baby, but there's no reason to think this is true. Indeed, suppose a woman in her forties has such severe dementia that her mental state is reduced to that of a baby; to hold that she should no longer have breasts is absurd.

It is important to remember that surgical procedures like hysterectomy are not without risks. Anaesthetics are occasionally lethal, and the surgical complications can include perforation of the bowel, infection, and occasionally death. All told, drug treatment to stunt growth seems more justifiable than the surgical modifications.

Ashley's case calls to attention the fact that every able person in our society has at least a prima facie duty to provide support and assistance to those who are providing care, not just for the likes of Ashley, but also for all normal children, the elderly, and others in care. Because of their basic, biological need for love, children have a human right to be loved.[12] Successfully discharging the duty to love children requires considerable time and resources. Possibly some parents can successfully discharge this duty using their own resources. But for many others, it can be quite difficult, owing perhaps to the demands of employment or of other family members. However, if the right of children to be loved is a human right, and if the duties that stem from such a human right are applicable to all able persons in appropriate circumstances, then all other able persons in appropriate circumstances have associated duties to help parents discharge their duties to love their children. Such help might mean supporting better child care programs or advocating flexible workplace policies that would make it easier for parents to care for their children. It might also mean paying taxes and voting for policies that would help parents discharge their duties.[13]

This argument can be extended to the case of Ashley and others who require care, such as the elderly. Those who require care, like Ashley, have a fundamental need—and, therefore, a human right—to be cared for; and we, as members of society, have an associated duty to support policies that help their families care for them.

One of the main objections to the Ashley Treatment is that Ashley's disadvantage is socially constructed. If more resources were available for her care, then she could be nursed and cared for in a normal adult size. Those who defend the Ashley Treatment are right to respond that because these resources are not now adequately provided, Ashley's parents may be taking the only option open to them. Indeed, to deny her both the necessary social resources and medical treatment is to doubly harm her. If we as a society believe that it is undignified, as a matter of human rights, for Ashley to undergo these treatments, then we must be prepared to provide her caregivers with enough assistance and support that they would not have to resort to these means. Upholding human dignity comes with a price, and if it is what we should value as a society, then we must be prepared to pay to uphold it.

REFERENCES

1. S. Verhovek, "Parents Defend Decision to Keep Disabled Girl Small," *Los Angeles Times,* January 3, 2007.

2. D. Gunther and D. Diekema, "Attenuating Growth in Children with Profound Developmental Disability: A New Approach to an Old Dilemma," *Archives of Pediatrics and Adolescent Medicine* 160, no. 10 (2006): 1013–17.

3. "The 'Ashley Treatment': Toward a Better Quality of Life for 'Pillow Angels,'" http://ashleytreatment.spaces.live.com/ (accessed February 15, 2007).

4. S. Baruch, D. Kaufman, and K. Hudson, "Genetic Testing of Embryos: Practices and Perspectives of U.S. IVF Clinics," *Fertility and Sterility,* forthcoming.

5. J.J. Thomson, "A Defense of Abortion," in *Ethics in Practice,* ed. by H. LaFollette (Oxford, U.K.: Blackwell, 1997), 69–78, at 77.

6. E. Cohen, "Disability Community Decries 'Ashley Treatment,'" http://www.cnn.com/2007/HEALTH/01/11/ashley.outcry/.

7. P. Louhiala, "How Tall Is Too Tall? On the Ethics of Oestrogen Treatment for Tall Girls," *Journal of Medical Ethics* 33, no. 1 (2007): 48–50.

8. C. Dyer, "Surgeon Amputated Healthy Legs," *British Medical Journal* 320 (2000): 332.

9. C. Garcia and W. Cutler, "Preservation of the Ovary: A Reevaluation," *Fertility and Sterility* 42, no. 4 (1984): 510–14.

10. M. Spriggs and J. Savulescu, "The Ethics of Surgically Assigning Sex for Intersex Infants," in *Cutting to the Core: The Ethics of Contested Surgeries,* ed. D. Benatar (Lanham, Md.: Rowman & Littlefield, forthcoming).

11. S.M. Liao, "The Ethics of Using Genetic Engineering for Sex Selection," *Journal of Medical Ethics* 31 (2005): 116–18.

12. S.M. Liao, "The Right of Children to Be Loved," *Journal of Political Philosophy* 14, no. 4 (2006): 420–40.

13. Strictly, these are prima facie duties: it is an open question whether justice requires this use of limited health resources or some other use that may more efficiently and effectively promote health.

The Ethics of Neonatal Male Circumcision: Helping Parents to Decide

Leslie Cannold

The ethics of male circumcision has received little attention in the bioethical literature. In one of the few considerations of the subject, Michael and David Benatar (2003) investigate whether the practice can be justified by examining whether circumcision constitutes bodily mutilation, whether the absence of the child's informed consent makes it wrong, the nature and strength of the evidence regarding medical harms and benefits, and what moral weight cultural considerations have. The Benatars argue that a moral assessment of neonatal circumcision cannot be made without considering its medical costs and benefits. Having provided a thorough assessment on these grounds,[1] they conclude, on the basis of the evenly weighted evidence for and against the procedure, that it is a discretionary medical matter best left to parents to decide on the basis of their own values.

I agree with the Benatars' conclusion that neonatal circumcision is a decision rightly left in the hands of parents. To demonstrate that it is not, it would be necessary to show that the procedure was mutilation or otherwise threatened the health and safety of a child to a degree necessary to justify a societal override of what both legal and ethical precedents have long held to be both a parent's right and responsibility: to make judgments based on their own values about what is in their child's best interests. The Benatars argue persuasively that neither charge, at least on current evidence, can be sustained.[2]

However, claiming that parents should retain the authority to make decisions for their infant boys about circumcision says little about how parents charged with such a decision ought to make it. Circumcision is an invasive medical procedure, and one function of informed consent is to ensure that patients are protected from harm with regard to such procedures. Because infants cannot themselves consent to circumcision or other medical procedures, parents are charged with giving such consent on their behalf. Ensuring that consent is informed facilitates the fulfillment of their obligation to protect their child's best interests. These interests include the child's present and future physical and psychological health and well-being as well as his stake in becoming an autonomous agent in the future capable of making medical and other important life choices for himself.

In this chapter, I will discuss the range of issues—medical, ethical, social, and religious/cultural—that I believe parents must canvass and weigh up in order to give informed consent to circumcising their neonate.

INFORMED CONSENT AND PROXY DECISION MAKING

The notion of "informed consent" arose to describe decision-making procedures necessary to protect patients and research participants from harm. The U.S. Tuskegee syphilis study and the New Zealand "Unfortunate" cervical cancer experiment are only the most well-known examples of where failure to inform patients about the nature and risks/benefits of medical research or therapy caused serious patient harm. More recently, informed consent has become primarily understood as a means of protecting patient autonomy. If a patient autonomously authorizes her medical practitioner to undertake a particular intervention, then she has given her informed consent. The two important characteristics of a consent that is informed are that it is intentionally given by a patient with "substantial understanding and in substantial absence of control by others" (Beauchamp and Childress 1994, 143).

A proxy decision maker is required when a person lacks, either temporarily or permanently, the competence to consent for herself. In the case of neonates, parents are seen to be the most suitable people to act as proxies because—unless shown otherwise—they are assumed to have their child's best interests at heart. However, because neonates have never been autonomous, parents cannot make the circumcision decision on the basis of what they believe their son *would* want were he competent—a standard of decision making known as *substituted judgment*. Instead, Beauchamp and Childress (1994) argue that parents must make their decisions on the basis of what is in their child's best interests, as assessed by their evaluation of what benefits and burdens the intervention is likely to cause.

The informed consent requirement mitigates the child-patient's risk by obligating medical professionals to ensure parent-proxies have a substantial understanding of the risks and benefits of the procedure and have freely consented to it. At the same time, it provides parents with a clear standard against which their discharge of their duties as proxy medical decision makers can be measured. Indeed, Ford (2001) argues that unless parents' consent for their children to have (nonemergency) medical interventions is fully informed, their decisions lack not just ethical but also legal standing.

So what specific issues must a parent gain a substantial understanding of, and give weight to, in order to make an informed decision about circumcising their neonate? In my view, these include considerations of a medical, ethical, social, and religious/cultural nature.

NEONATAL CIRCUMCISION: PARENTAL MOTIVES, PARENTAL CONSIDERATIONS

Parents have different reasons for considering circumcision for their neonate. For some parents, the question of whether or not to circumcise is a medical one, while for others social concerns (e.g., ensuring their son will look like his dad) are predominant, Historically, circumcision was a religious and cultural ritual, and both the Jewish and Muslim traditions continue to demand parents circumcise their children when young.[3]

These different motives mean that not all parents will or should need to consider all the matters that may be of relevance to the decisions of some. To take the most obvious example, while the religious or cultural beliefs or affiliations may be central to Jewish and Muslim parents, such beliefs and affiliations will not and need not feature in the considerations of parents with no such religious or cultural beliefs or ties. However, some aspects of the circumcision decision should feature in the consideration of all parents. Usually, these have included tangible factors like physical and financial risks, harms, and benefits (Beauchamp and Childress 1989, 171), but can—and insofar as circumcision is concerned, I would argue, should—take in social, psychological, and spiritual risks, benefits, and burdens of the procedure. This means that while requirements for informed consent vary among parents, there exists a minimum suite of considerations which all parents should consider relevant to their child's best interests. Parents must canvass such considerations for them to satisfy their responsibility to make an informed and voluntary decision about neonatal circumcision.

Medical

The position of leading medical organizations in the United States, Canada, New Zealand, and Australia (among others) is that there is no medical indication for routine neonatal circumcision (Circinfo.org 2003; CIRP 2004). Moreover, the review of the medical evidence provided by the Benatars shows that the costs and benefits of circumcision are more or less evenly balanced. How should parents respond to these conclusions, which can be summed up as "there are no medical reasons for or against circumcision"?

Declines in the neonatal circumcision rate in many countries following the medical community's rejection of it as a routine procedure suggest that for many parents such authoritative conclusions about the procedure's lack of *net* medical value will be decisive.[4] However, this will not be the case for all parents. This is because, in keeping with their obligation to make the decision based on their assessment of their own child's best interests, some parents will find, among the costs and benefits of circumcision, something they deem particularly relevant to the decision they make about their child. For instance, parents of a premature baby forced to endure numerous painful medical interventions in the early weeks of his life may see the primary interest of their child as being the avoidance of further unnecessary pain,[5] and reject neonatal circumcision on this basis. Alternatively, a father with a long history of painful urinary tract infections (UTIs) may be extremely concerned to see his son avoid this burden as in infant. Having noted that existing medical evidence shows circumcision can protect against childhood UTIs, he may deem the procedure to be in his child's best interests.[6]

Ethical

Beauchamp and Childress (1994) argue that unless parents can answer the question "What would the patient want in this circumstance?" they are unable to make decisions for their infant according to the "substituted judgment" standard, or in the way they would for their baby son if he had once been competent. It is because the newborn has never been competent, and therefore that there is no basis for a judgment of autonomous choice, that parents must decide for their infants on the basis of their own assessment of their child's best interests.

However, their newborn's current incompetency does not mean that parental concerns about their child's autonomy and privacy should disappear from their considerations about circumcision. This is because most newborns will one day acquire the competency necessary to make autonomous decisions about circumcision and other medical and life issues. Indeed, as Ross has argued, one of the obligations parents have is to "promote their child's growth and development" so they can become such independent autonomous agents (1993, 1).

Anticircumcision literature abounds with anecdotal evidence that some adult men who are unhappy about being circumcised feel angry about the fact that their parents' decision about the circumcision deprived them of the capacity to make their own autonomous choice about the procedure.[7] The quality of data on this question is low.[8] However, there seems enough evidence to suggest that an indeterminate number of men will express dissatisfaction with their circumcised status, and that among these will be men angry about being compelled to live with the consequences of a decision they

had no input into or control over and which they cannot alter, at least not easily or well.[9]

To answer the charge that parents have no right to make the circumcision decision for their neonate (whether the charge is made by a disgruntled adult son circumcised as a neonate or by organized opponents of neonatal circumcision) requires consideration of the validity of reasons parents have for believing that the decision about circumcision must be made when the child is an infant, and therefore by them on their child's behalf. Certainly there are nonemergency medical decisions that parents are justified—on the grounds of the child's best interests—in making before the child is old enough to give his own consent. The question is, is circumcision one of them?

Before answering this question, it is necessary to discuss the question of child competency. Competency, which Beauchamp and Childress define as "the ability to perform a task," is not an all-or-nothing affair in either children or adults. Instead it makes sense to talk about a person's competency to undertake a particular task: in this case, consenting to circumcision. When might a boy obtain the competence to make the circumcision decision himself? The courts, political decision makers, and society at large have devoted attention to the question of when children are competent to decide about weighty medical matters,[10] because of the challenge antichoice activists consistently pose to the validity of the decisions young women make about abortion.[11] In the landmark English *Gillick* case, the judge ruled that children under 16 should be deemed competent to consent to medical treatment when they are capable of making a reasonable assessment of the advantages and disadvantages of the treatment proposed (Devereux 1991). Beauchamp and Childress state the requirements for competence in more detail, but contend similarly that if the child can understand information material to his decision, make a judgment about it in light of his values, intend a certain outcome, and freely communicate his wishes to his doctor, then he is autonomous enough to make the decision by and for himself. While there is not a great deal of evidence available about the validity of children's consent to medical treatment, one survey found that the capacity of most 14-year-olds to give informed consent was indistinguishable from that of adults (Devereux 1991, 300). Thus, it is likely that, somewhere around the age of 14, boys will be competent to decide for themselves about circumcision.

It seems valid for parents to choose circumcision for their neonate when the benefits of the procedure they hope to gain for their child—and which they believe are in his best interest—will be reaped partially or in total prior to the child becoming competent to make the decision himself. Circumcising to protect their infant and young child from UTIs is a good example of this sort of choice. However, the same cannot be said if the claimed medical advantage parents find compelling is likely to be reaped by their child *after* he becomes competent to decide about circumcision himself. The reduction in risk of human immunodeficiency virus (HIV) transmission is a good example of this sort of advantage. If there are no compelling reasons why—in order to serve the child's best interests—parents need to circumcise before the child attains competence, then parents should choose to foster their child's future autonomy by refraining from making the circumcision decision for him. Instead, they should wait until he has attained the capacity to decide for himself, and by so doing preserve what Feinberg (1980) calls the child's right to an "open future."[12]

Social

There are two commonly cited social reasons that parents seek circumcision: the belief that the circumcised penis is easier to keep clean,[13] and a desire for the child to "look like dad" or other male family members.[14]

Hygiene. There is no evidence that the uncircumcised penis poses significantly more difficulties either for parents or, as a boy grows, the child himself, to keep clean. Indeed, in the early years, retraction of the foreskin is contraindicated, making the hygiene requirements of uncircumcised boys identical to those without foreskins. Only as the child grows and can, by himself and with ease, retract the foreskin does this need to be done on a daily basis for cleaning. For most boys, retraction will become possible somewhere between the ages of 5 and 10. The question is, once retractable, are the cleaning requirements of the uncircumcised penis onerous and, if so, does this justify a parents' decision to circumcise?

The claim that the hygiene demands of intact children are more onerous than circumcised ones is highly contestable. Most children have a nightly bath or shower and, when retraction becomes possible, the cleaning process is approximately a 5- to 10-second operation. Given this, it is hard to imagine how either the performing of this task by the parent, or the job parents have to remind the child to do it, could be called onerous (or any more onerous than cleaning, or reminding them to clean, behind their ears!). Thus it seems to me that the belief that hygiene requirements of an uncircumcised

boy are more onerous than those of a circumcised child is a false one—and making a decision to circumcise on the basis of it is inadequately informed. Moreover, the solution of circumcision to the parental problem of hygiene may fall foul of demands for consistency. As one 5-year-old American boy noted in response to his mother's explanation that some parents circumcised their sons because they worried that if they didn't, their boys wouldn't keep clean: "Well, that's dumb, Mom!! What are they gonna do? Cut their butts off, too?!"[15]

In addition, parents who choose circumcision to relieve themselves of the burden of caring for a child with an uncircumcised penis may be acting against their obligation to make the circumcision decision on the basis of their assessment of their child's best interests rather than their own. In instances where there are significant differences in the requirements of caring for a particular child who has or does not have a particular intervention (with one way of proceeding offering outcomes that are significantly less burdensome for parents than others), parents may be able to mount a credible case for or against that intervention on the grounds that their well-being and the child's are interdependent, and therefore what is good for them or the family unit as a whole is, for that reason, also good for the child.[16] However, given the facts about the hygiene requirements of children with foreskins, the circumcision decision clearly doesn't qualify.

Just Like Dad. Logically, there seems no reason for a boy to consider any difference between his penis and that of his dad or other male family members as any more remarkable or significant that any of the myriad of other physical dissimilarities between himself and these others. Further, there seems no evidence that children younger than three notice genitals at all, nor that those older than this take any notice of their or other men's foreskins or—if they do—attribute significance to these differences.[17] My husband is circumcised, but his brother—only four years younger—is not, due to changes in standard Australian hospital practice around the time of their births. Neither man recalls any issue arising over the difference in the look of their members or over the difference between my husband's brother's intact penis and that of their father, who was circumcised. Anecdotal evidence suggests that many adult men are not even sure whether their fathers are or were circumcised. Where children do notice, the meaning they make of the differences they observe seem highly variable. One father tells how his boy was 3 before concluding—his foreskin having retracted of its own accord—that he was "just like Daddy." Daddy, however, was circumcised. The boy is now close to 5, but according to his father is still unaware that he is "different from Daddy" (Ray 1997).

What this suggests is that it may be Dad's or other male relatives' awareness of and anxiety about the difference that motivate parental decisions to circumcise, rather than anticipation of and worry about the child's anxiety on this question. While again, the interactive nature of parent—child relations makes it possible that an anxious father could transmit this anxiety to his son, circumcising in order to rule out this possibility seems a clear case of treating the wrong patient. It would be better to attempt to educate fathers to see the differences in penile appearance between themselves and their sons as just one of the many that do and will continue to mark both their appearances and characters. For in the same way that decisions to circumcise made to ease the perceived hygiene burden of boys with foreskins violate parental obligations to make such choices to foster their sons' best interests, so too do decisions made to ease parental anxieties about bodily differences.

Cultural/religious

A number of religions require circumcision. In Islam there seems to be general agreement that circumcision, while encouraged and widely practiced, is not essential, though in Judaism, circumcision is deemed an essential mark for all males. Those who refuse to mark their children thus or, if they are converts, to be circumcised themselves, will—according to the Torah—be "cut off from their kin."[18] While Jews are increasingly questioning the practice of circumcision, it is fair to say that those who believe there is scriptural justification for not undertaking it and are refusing to do so remain in the minority.[19] Thus, for Jewish parents who believe in the importance of following the biblical injunction to ritually circumcise their son and who want their son to be accepted as a member of the Jewish community, circumcision is—in most instances—required.

What does this mean for Jewish parents seeking to make a decision about circumcision for their son? For devout Jews, a failure to circumcise their infant son would clearly be seen as a dereliction of their duty to foster their child's best interests by ensuring he enters properly—meaning through circumcision on the eighth day of his life—into the covenant with God. However, even for Jews who see the requirement to circumcise neonatally as fatally inconsistent with their other values,[20] or even unjustified on theological

grounds, the best-interest requirement can mean they feel compelled to circumcise anyway. This is because refusing to circumcise their child may lead the Jewish community to which they belong, and the wider Jewish community, to withhold recognition and acceptance of their child as a Jew, to view them as negligent for refusing to circumcise and, consequently, to exclude or marginalize them all.[21] Parents who see Jewish religious beliefs or identity as their child's birthright or valued gift, and themselves as morally obliged to provide such a gift, would be hard-pressed not to see neonatal circumcision to be in their child's best interests.

OBJECTIONS

I have argued that while parents are entitled to make the decision to circumcise their male neonate, they are not without responsibilities in the way they go about making this choice. As proxy decision makers, parents are obliged to give informed consent to the procedure being undertaken and, through doing so, ensure that they only authorize the procedure if it can clearly be shown to be in their particular child's best interests.

Female genital mutilation

What does this account suggest about how parents should approach the issue of female genital mutilation (FGM)? Specifically, if the conclusion that parents' religious or cultural beliefs, or parental desires to retain membership in a religious or cultural community, justify male circumcision, doesn't consistency require that parental authorization of FGM be similarly respected?

The simple answer is no. The entitlement parents have to decide about male circumcision is accorded because the procedure is not one that threatens the child's health or well-being. The same cannot be said of FGM, in which anything from part of the clitoris to the entire external female genital organs are excised, leading to—at a minimum—pain for a woman during urination, sex, and/or childbirth, and in a worst-case scenario, the need for surgical intervention in order for a woman to have sex and to give birth. As well, women who have been victims of traditional FGM are at higher risks of pelvic infections, hemorrhaging, obstructed child labor, HIV infection, and even death (Devine et al. 1999). Comparing traditional forms of FGM to male circumcision, according to one commentator, is like equating ear piercing to penectomy (Coleman 1998, 736).

However, the Benatars (2003) argue that the excision of the clitoral prepuce is "anatomically neither more nor less radical a procedure than removal of the penile foreskin," though they do note that while there is some evidence about the medical value of male circumcision, there is none, at least thus far, about the benefits of removing female preputial tissue. *If* it is true that the excision of the clitoral prepuce is analogous to the removal of the penile foreskin, then they are right to suggest that, should evidence of medical benefits for this procedure be discovered, consistency would require that in instances where cultural reasons suffice for undertaking the latter, they should also justify the former. Certainly, I would agree with them that where cultural reasons justify neonatal male circumcision, they would also justify the sort of clitoral "nicking" procedure proposed in the Seattle compromise.[22]

One parent or two? How many parents constitute consent?

I have argued that the only justification for state interference in parents' medical decisions about their children is when those decisions can clearly be shown to threaten the child's health or safety. But what of instances where parents disagree about whether a particular intervention is in their child's best interests? Specifically, when parents disagree about circumcision, is it justified for the state to intervene and, if so, to what end?

Recently, some anticircumcision activists have begun lobbying for legislation requiring doctors to obtain consent from *both* a child's parents before circumcising their neonate. In Australia, the call for two-parent consent followed a case where an Egyptian father circumcised his two children, ages 5 and 9, against their Australian Aboriginal mother's wishes. The police prosecuted the man for assault, but newspaper reports often failed to reveal that the charges were not grounded in his pursuit of circumcision without his wife's consent, but because a Family Court order existed that specifically prohibited the boy's father from harming them during contact visits.[23] It is hard to escape the feeling that those pursuing such legal change are doing so in order to increase the difficulty parents face in circumcising their child, rather than to protect the best interests of children. While anticircumcision activists would, of course, argue that making it harder for parents to choose circumcision is in the best interests of all male children, acting to whittle away the freedom of parents to make their own informed decisions on the matter is contrary to the ethical and legal requirements of the circumcision decision, which are that parents have the right and responsibility to choose for their own child on the basis of what they believe to be in their particular child's best interests.

However, when parents fail to resolve disagreements about matters of critical importance to the child's health and welfare—and here I would include circumcision—they invite state interference (typically in the form of the Family Court) to examine the evidence and make a ruling. The idea that is at work here, affirmed in numerous U.S. court decisions over the years, is that there is a subjective element to the determination of what constitutes a child's best interests. Indeed, it is this subjective element that has led the courts to leave decisions in which the child's health and safety are not at issue to the parents for them to make according to their own values. But where parents cannot agree about serious matters, there is no alternative—and courts should not hesitate—to step in and produce a "trumping" third-party judgment about what is "best."[24]

In one such case, the objection of a secular English mother to the circumcision of her five-year-old son by his religious father was upheld on the basis that she was primarily raising the boy and doing so in a secular fashion, thereby making circumcision against his best interests. The father appealed the case, but lost.[25] However, the court noted that while circumcision was among a "small group" of "important decisions" that requires the consent of both parents, disagreement between parents about such matters would be settled by the courts on the basis of judgments on the individual facts of a case about what constituted a particular child's best interests.[26] Such rulings in other words, do not and should not be understood to be passing blanket judgments on circumcision, but rather to be applying the best-interest test in the absence of an agreement between parents about how to do so. Such an approach suggests that the state has the same responsibility as parents to ensure they gain a substantial understanding of the issues involved in order that it can make an informed and voluntary decision about whether the procedure will serve the particular child's best interests.

CONCLUSION

While parents are legally and ethically responsible for decisions regarding neonatal circumcision, this does not mean they lack responsibilities in regard to their decision. Parents are required to make decisions about the procedure in a substantially informed and voluntary manner, and at a minimum to consider the medical and ethical implications of the procedure for their child. An examination of the full range of motives for parental decisions to circumcise reveals that only some medical and religious or cultural ones seem to meet the requirement that such decisions be made to further the best interest of the child, are not based on false beliefs, and fulfill the ethical requirement that parents assume the decision for their incompetent child only when the benefits they see to be in their child's best interests are to be reaped prior to the child becoming competent to make the decision himself.

NOTES

I am indebted to Neil Levy and Stephen Clarke for helpful comments on earlier drafts.

1. The Benatars consider the issues of neonatal operative and postoperative pain; surgical complications of the procedure; and the relative risks of penile cancer, urinary tract infections, STDs, HIV, plamosis, and paraphimosis in circumcised and uncircumcised boys. They also look at the evidence for claims that genital hygiene is increased in circumcised men relative to those who have not been circumcised, as are the chances of female partners avoiding cervical cancer.

2. One possible counter to this conclusion would be if it could be conclusively demonstrated that circumcision consistently and significantly reduced male sexual pleasure. In this instance, an argument may be able to be made that the procedure does seriously threaten a child's health and safety and so does constitute an unjustified assault on their person. However, as the Benatars rightly note, there is little objective information about the impact of circumcision on male sexuality, and what does exist is contradictory (with some studies saying circumcision has no impact on male sexual pleasure, others concluding it does, while still others report less sexual dysfunction in circumcised males and a preference for circumcised men among female partners) (Laumann, Masi et al. 1997; Masters and Johnson 1966). As a consequence of this uncertainty, I have left the matter of sexual pleasure to one side of this discussion.

3. The Jewish prescription is for ritual circumcision eight days after the child's birth unless the child is unhealthy, in which case the procedure is prohibited. The Islamist tradition is more flexible. While the preferred time is the seventh day after birth, circumcision can be carried out up to 40 days after the child is born or thereafter until the age of 7 years, depending upon the child's health and circumstances (Islam Online 2004).

4. Patel (1966) argues that where medical practitioners opposed the procedure, approximately 20 percent of neonate boys will be circumcised at the insistence of their parents. It is possible, however, that such figures will vary on a country-by-country basis, with rates likely to be higher, regardless of medical attitudes, in countries with long cultural/religious histories of the practice and lower in those without.

5. Few dispute the ability of newborns to experience pain, or that circumcision—the actual procedure and its aftermath—causes it. While interventions deemed to be effective in relieving the pain of circumcision and the aftermath are available, they are not always used, and disagreement exists about ease of administration, risks involved in use in newborns, and the amount of pain caused by the interventions themselves (Benatar and Benatar 2003, 36–37).

6. The Benatars' (2003) review of the evidence led them to suggest circumcision provides a "small but real" benefit of lowering the incidence of UTIs.

7. Circumcision Information Australia notes that they have "received many complaints from adult men who are unhappy about having been circumcised as infants or children. . . . Only the owner of the penis has the right to decide if he would like its appearance, structure and function altered by circumcision or any other needless procedure." Or as one man on the British anticircumcision website Norm.UK.org put it, "I've never expressed my outrage to anyone before, but I do know that the realisation in my late teens that I had had a very important bit of me removed unnecessarily at someone's whim, had a profound effect on me."

8. The one study of psychological consequences reported in the literature was done by Hammond (1999). Among the 546 men he surveyed, he found circumcised men reported "emotional distress, manifesting as intrusive thoughts about one's circumcision, included feelings of mutilation (60%), low self-esteem/inferiority to intact men (50%), genital dysmorphia (55%), rage (52%), resentment/depression (59%), violation (46%), or parental betrayal (30%)." However, the recruitment method of the survey, from among men who had contacted anticircumcision organizations, raises serious questions about the applicability of the findings to the general population of circumcised men.

9. There are men who attempt to reconstruct their foreskin using both surgical and nonsurgical methods. For surgical methods, see Greer, Mohl et al. 1982; Penn 1963; and Goodwin 1990. For nonsurgical, see Bigelow 1995.

10. By age 3 or so, most children are competent to make minor medical decisions like whether or not they want a bandage for a skinned knee. The medical decisions we are discussing here are on the other end of the weightiness scale and therefore require a higher level of competence.

11. My claim here is not that antichoice activists pursue these issues in the court because of sincere concern about the competence of young women to consent to abortion: parental notification/consent laws are a well-established prong of antichoice strategy designed to reduce the incidence of abortion through the creation of all possible legal, bureaucratic, and practical obstacles to women obtaining the procedure "on the ground." All I am arguing here is that when these laws have been challenged, one of the main issues the courts have examined, is the competence of the young woman to consent to her own medical treatment: a competence that—if universal—would render such "squeal" laws an unjustified invasion of the woman's entitlement to privacy and/or autonomy. See Puzella 1997 on U.S. law and Devereux 1991 for the situation in the United Kingdom and Australia.

12. One counter to this argument is the contention that neonatal circumcision is a less risky/painful procedure than circumcision done on an older child or adult. However, it seems to me that unless conclusive evidence that this was the case could be presented, which my reading of the current literature suggests it cannot, this argument must fail. Another objection, suggested by Parfit's (1984) example of a man about to undergo painful surgery, might be that even if the pain of circumcision in adulthood is *less* than that experienced by an infant, parents may feel it better to get this pain over with in infancy when the child won't remember it, rather than leave it in the future as pain *to be* experienced and remembered. However, the comparison between past/future benefits (including the experience of pain and memory of that experience) is false because it presumes what is at issue: whether the child, once an adult, will choose circumcision. While it certainly could be the case that an uncircumcised child who decides when he becomes competent that he wants circumcision might resent his parent's failure to have made the choice for him when he was a child because his pain would have

been in the past and he would be unable to recollect it, the uncircumcised child who does not wish to be circumcised would not appreciate his parent's decision because even though his pain is in the past and he doesn't recall it, he has been left with the unwanted outcome of their decision: circumcision.

13. Hygiene has both health and social dimensions. Failing to bathe, for instance, may leave you more open to infection, but also makes you smell unpleasant to others. After some consideration, I have decided to describe hygiene as a social consideration because the medical literature does not describe smegma, the creamy yellow sebaceous material that is secreted by the glans and often accumulates in clumps under the foreskin, as a medical problem nor suggest that it indirectly causes any medical problems, little less those that would indicate circumcision. See Simpson 1998.

14. See, for example, Dickey 2002.

15. From http://www.mothersagainstcirc.org/easy.htm.

16. Such discussions arise in discussions of the legitimacy of parents allowing their minor children to become organ donors for relatives. Some experts contend that parents should be allowed to make such proxy decisions about organ donation for their incompetent child grounded not only in the donor child's best interests but to further the best interests of the family as a whole. See Morley 2002.

17. Freud theorized that somewhere between the ages of 3 and 6, boys become enamored with their mothers and fear castration by their fathers for this love interest and their newfound interest in masturbation. However, Freud's claim is that what boys notice at this age is the difference between their own genitals and those of girls (whom they see as castrated), not differences between their foreskin status and those of other men. Thus, leaving aside the question of the validity of Freudian theory on this point, it is not relevant to the claims I am making here.

18. The relevant passage, from Genesis 17, reads as follows: "As for you, you and your offspring to come throughout the ages shall keep my covenant. Such shall be the covenant between me and you and your offspring to follow, which you shall keep: Every male among you shall be circumcised. You shall circumcise the flesh of your foreskin and that shall be the sign of the covenant between me and you. And throughout the generations every male among you shall be circumcised at the age of eight days . . . . Thus shall my covenant be marked in your flesh as an everlasting pact. And if any male who is uncircumcised fails to circumcise the flesh of his foreskin, that person shall be cut off from his kin. He has broken my covenant."

19. For the religious justifications for not circumcising, see Goldman 1998 and Moss 1991. However, while there is no doubt that a growing number of Jews are rejecting the practice, even Goldman acknowledges that Jewish parents who don't circumcise are in the minority (see Clemente 1998).

20. Jewish parents with feminist beliefs, for instance, can find the practice offensive or unnecessary, given the lack of a similar ceremony by which girls are welcomed into the Jewish community and a sanctified relationship with God. Indeed, in some Jewish communities, alternate nonsurgical ceremonial practices are being developed to serve these purposes for both boy and girl babies (see, for example, Karsenty 1988).

21. I note here that an uncircumcised Jew is still considered a Jew and therefore I am speaking of a social withholding of recognition and acceptance rather than a legal one.

22. The "Seattle compromise" was a procedure developed by a medical center attempting to manage requests from immigrant Somalian mothers to have their daughters circumcised. The procedure, which would have appeased some mothers, was designed to draw blood but not cause any lasting damage to the child's genitals. See Coleman 1998.

There is one important disanalogy between FGM and male circumcision, which is that while FGM is a cultural practice intended to inhibit and/or control the female body and female sexuality, male circumcision is intended as a ritual of inclusion designed to welcome men—and only men—into a special relationship with God. Coleman (1998), a supporter of the Seattle compromise, sees the patriarchal underpinnings of the practice—its essential aim to ensure the physical and cultural domination of women—as the reason why Americanization of the immigrants who practice it will and should lead to it withering away in a few generations (the compromise representing a "transitional" measure). However, I am unable to see how the patriarchal nature of FGM as against circumcision provides grounds for altering my conclusions about the range and limits of parental freedom to choose FGM, clitoral nicking, or male circumcision for their children.

23. For an account of the case by an anticircumcision group, and several newspaper articles in which it was reported, see CIRP 2004.

24. U.S. courts have gone even further than this. In *Bellotti* v. *Baird*, the Supreme Court accorded itself the right to authorize a young woman's abortion, even in cases where one or both parents have refused consent and the woman is deemed incompetent to consent herself, when it believes the procedure is in her best interests. The implied view of such judgments seems to be that in the absence of agreement between parents or between a parent and (older) child about what is in the child's best interests, the courts must and will decide. See Lurvey 1990 and Puzella 1997.

25. Re J (child's religious upbringing and circumcision). Jane Maynard Barrister, Family Court. I FCR 307 [2000].

26. One of the judges, Dame Elizabeth Butler-Sloss P., argued that a small group of important decisions included sterilization and the change of a child's surname.

Beauty Under the Knife: A Feminist Appraisal of Cosmetic Surgery

Rosemarie Tong and Hilde Lindemann

While roughly two-thirds of the plastic and reconstructive surgery done in the United States today is performed for therapeutic reasons, the other third is performed for aesthetic or cosmetic reasons to enhance one's appearance. As might be expected, however, the line between therapeutic and cosmetic surgery is blurred (Dibacco 1994). For burn victims, accident victims, or victims of violence, for example, the goal is not only to replace damaged tissue and to repair damaged body parts but also to give the patient

---

an acceptable appearance. Nevertheless, there is a difference between undergoing rhinoplasty to relieve one's breathing problems and having the surgery to improve one's already acceptable appearance.

Cosmetic surgery is, like most surgery, somewhat risky. In fact, the American Society of Plastic and Reconstructive Surgeons (ASPRS) publishes a pamphlet on cosmetic surgery, the contents of which could easily raise doubts in potential patients' minds about the wisdom of elective procedures. Not only does this ASPRS pamphlet discuss possibilities such as infection, bleeding, blood clots, scarring, and adverse reactions to anesthesia but it also notes, for example, that liposuction can trigger a shock-inducing excessive loss of fluid and that face-lifts can cause injury to the nerves that control facial muscles. The same pamphlet indicates that breast augmentation surgery is also not without risk: it can result in conditions ranging from tightening and hardening of scar tissue around the implant to the rupturing of the implant (ASPRS 1993, 3).

In addition to entailing some risks, most cosmetic procedures are relatively expensive and not covered by health insurance unless they are performed for a therapeutic purpose. Liposuction, for instance, costs anywhere from $2,600 to $10,000, and its cousin, the tummy tuck costs around $8,000 For breast augmentation, surgical fees alone (not counting anesthesia, operating room facilities, and other related expenses) run between $3,000 and $7,000. Compared to some cosmetic procedures, however, such one-time expenses might seem like a bargain. Many women are advised to get their first face-lift at the age of 40 and to pay anywhere from $5,500 to $14,500 every 5 to 15 years thereafter to have surgery repeated. Similarly, collagen injections usually last only a few months to one year and cost around $375 each time.[1]

Given its risks and costs, many people simply assume that only the rich and famous go in for cosmetic surgery. This commonsense assumption proves to be a false one, however. Almost 70 percent of the people who elect to have cosmetic surgery have family incomes of less than $40,000 per year.[2] Ordinary people—hairdressers, grocery store clerks, and secretaries—as well as movie stars, millionaires, and models are willing to spend a considerable portion of their incomes redesigning their bodies, particularly their faces.

TRADITIONAL FEMINIST CRITICISMS OF COSMETIC SURGERY

From roughly 1975 to 1995, many feminists opposed cosmetic surgery on the grounds that the practice reinforced the oppressive power relation that goes by the name of gender. For the most part, these feminists did not object to therapeutic plastic and reconstructive surgery aimed at removing or repairing the kind of birth defects and developmental abnormalities that cause people to avert their eyes from someone. Nor was their quarrel with surgery whose purpose was to remove or repair acquired deformities, including those resulting from trauma (domestic violence) or disease (breast cancer). Rather, their objection was to the use of plastic and reconstructive surgery for nonmedical purposes, specifically for the purpose of making women look younger and more beautiful.

The fact that many men also underwent cosmetic surgery for nonmedical purposes did not convince the feminists described above that the practice was gender neutral (Devine 1995). Although some men were pressured to get chin, eye, and/or nose jobs in order to look leaner and meaner at the workplace, most men found that they could get by in life—indeed, do very well—without ever visiting a cosmetic surgeon's office. However, the same could not be said for most women, in Kathryn Pauly Morgan's estimation. She claimed that with few exceptions, cosmetic surgery is required for women in ways that it is not required for men.

> As cosmetic surgery becomes increasingly normalized through the concept of female "make-over" that is translated into columns and articles in the print media or made into nationwide television shows directed at female viewers, as the "success stories" are invited on the talk shows along with their "makers," and as surgically transformed women enter the Miss America pageants, women who refuse to submit to the knives and to the needles, to the anesthetics and the bandages, will come to be seen as deviant in one way or another. Women who refuse to use these technologies are already becoming stigmatized as "unliberated," not caring about their appearance (a sign of disturbed gender identity and low self-esteem according to various health-care professionals), as "refusing to be all that they could be" or as "granola-heads."(Morgan 1991, 40)

Sandra Lee Bartky added to Morgan's observations some insightful remarks about how U.S. society in particular uses women's body image to control women's behavior. She wrote:

> Women are no longer required to be chaste or modest, to restrict their sphere of activity to the home, or even to realize their properly feminine destiny in maternity. Normative femininity [that is, the rules for being a good woman] is coming more and more to be centered on woman's body—not its duties and obligations or even its capacity to bear children, but its sexuality, more precisely, its presumed heterosexuality and its appearance. . . . The woman who checks her makeup half a dozen times a day to see if her foundation has caked or her mascara has

run, who worries that the wind or the rain may spoil her hairdo, who looks frequently to see if her stockings have bagged at the ankle, or who, feeling fat, monitors everything she eats, has become, just as surely as the inmate of Panopticon, a self-policing subject, a self committed to a relentless self-surveillance. This self-surveillance is a form of obedience to patriarchy. (Bartky 1990, 81)

An additional issue that troubled feminists throughout the 1970s, 1980s, and early 1990s was that of who performs most of the cosmetic surgeries in the United States. Although more women are choosing dermatology or plastic and reconstructive surgery as their specialty in medical school, their numbers are relatively small in comparison to the men who make the same choice. The preponderance of U.S. board-certified plastic and reconstructive surgeons are men, and despite the fact that men have cosmetic surgery too, most of those who elect it are female. This situation reaffirms an existing hierarchy of women going to men in positions of authority for appraisal and correction of their "flawed" bodies. It also reaffirms a social given, in that women's choices are seen to be more legitimate when supported by or carried out in concert with men, as the male perspective is seen as more rational and authoritative.

Over and beyond Morgan's "Women and the Knife" and Bartky's "Foucault, Femininity, and the Modernization of Patriarchal Power," other well-known examples of feminist disapproval of cosmetic surgery throughout the last few decades include Naomi Wolf's *The Beauty Myth*, Susan Bordo's *Unbearable Weight*, and Elizabeth Haiken's *Venus Envy*. Their position regarding cosmetic surgery, and more generally the female body and its place in society, was that the tyranny of slenderness and youthful appearance symbolized by this surgery is a negative and harmful aspect of American and Western culture.

For Wolf, cosmetic surgery is an example of the "institutionalized forms of power working in concert to force women into extreme beauty practices."[3] As she saw it, women's need throughout the world, (and particularly in developed Western nations) to be beautiful, and the forms that this need takes, is "the result of nothing more exalted than the need in today's power structure, economy, and culture to mount a counteroffensive against women" (Wolf 1991, 13). In addition, women's beauty serves as the foundation of women's identity and leaves them "vulnerable to outside approval" and vulnerable to the need for increasingly invasive ways to stay beautiful (14). Specifically regarding cosmetic surgery, Wolf stated that it is a market that has been created not because of an actual need for the surgery, but for surgeons to make money and as a way of keeping women politically and socially immobilized as they squander time worrying about their perceived "flaws"—time that could be spent on pursuing and achieving educational and occupational goals. As she put it, "Modern cosmetic surgeons have a direct financial interest in a social role for women that requires them to feel ugly" (223).

Noting that women's success depends on their good looks to a far greater degree than men's success does, many feminists in the 1970s, 1980s, and 1990s acknowledged that it was not illogical for the average woman to reason that if "dressing for success" made sense, then so did cosmetic surgery for success. In the estimation of Bordo (1993, 20), women who reasoned in this way were "neither dupes nor critics of sexist culture" but simply individuals who wanted to do well in it. They elected cosmetic surgery not because they were "passively taken in by media norms" but precisely because they had "correctly discerned that these norms shape the perceptions and desires of potential lovers and employers." Far from being embarrassed by their decision to undergo cosmetic surgery, Bordo noted, many of these women regarded themselves as feminists. They viewed themselves as strong women who could "play the game" exceedingly well and use their bodies to achieve their goals.

To be sure, feminists like Morgan, Bartky, Wolf, and Bordo very much doubted that women who deliberately behave in ways that bolster patriarchy can, in good conscience, call themselves feminists. As they saw it, *true* feminists are committed to *resisting* the imperatives of sexist culture. Specifically, they are committed to helping women see the extent to which women are controlled by socially constructed ideals about female beauty—ideals that, because they are overall unattainable, make women feel perpetually badly about themselves, no matter how successful they are in the domestic realm or in the workplace. Bartky provided the telling example of the successful singer Dinah Shore to bolster the claim that no woman is impervious to the force of the Beauty Myth. She quoted Shore:

One of the many things men don't understand about women is the extent to which our self-esteem depends on how we feel we look at any given moment—and how much we yearn for a compliment, at any age. If I had just won the Nobel Peace Prize but felt my hair looked awful, I would not be glowing with self-assurance when I entered the room. (Bartky 1990, 33)

EMERGING REASSESSMENTS OF COSMETIC SURGERY: WHAT DO WOMEN THEMSELVES SAY?

Among the issues about resistance that feminist critics of cosmetic surgery in the 1970s, 1980s, and 1990s never resolved was *how much* resistance to the forces of beauty was required for "true" feminists. Was it enough to resist seriously risky, invasive, and extensive cosmetic surgery elected solely for the purpose of remaining attractive in the eyes of men? Or did one also have to resist relatively risk-free and minor cosmetic surgeries (for example, aggressive skin treatments) elected mainly for the purpose of having clean and healthy-looking skin? Indeed, was one required to resist any and all beautifying or anti-aging products and procedures for fear of reinforcing the view that unless a woman was young and beautiful she was of little value?

Taken to its extreme—that is, to the point of deliberately making one's self ugly to defy the Beauty Myth—most women, including most feminists, came to the conclusion that true feminism was accommodating enough to embrace women who liked "looking good," dressing up, wearing makeup, and even getting a "nip and tuck" here and there. Beginning in the early 1990s, feminists became less interested in telling women what they had to do in order to be free and happy and more interested in simply listening to what women themselves say about their struggles to be free and happy. As Suzanne Fraser put it, it is necessary to examine "the range of ways in which women speak of their motives and their feelings about themselves. . . . Generalizations about motives are untenable" (2003, 3). She, Debra Gimlin, and Kathy Davis have all conducted empirical studies of how women who have undergone cosmetic surgery speak about it, both before and after the procedure.

In listening to women who choose cosmetic surgery, Gimlin found a sharp contrast between what they saw themselves as doing and what theorists took them to be doing. In her 2002 article "Cosmetic Surgery: Paying for Your Beauty," Gimlin wrote:

> Cosmetic surgery stands, for many theorists and social critics, as the ultimate invasion of the human body for the sake of physical beauty. It epitomizes the astounding lengths to which contemporary women will go to obtain bodies that meet current ideals of attractiveness. As such, plastic surgery is perceived by many to be qualitatively different from aerobics, hair styling, or even dieting. In this view, cosmetic surgery is not about controlling one's own body but is instead an activity so extreme, so invasive that it can only be interpreted as subjugation. (95)

In this view, the women who undergo cosmetic surgery are reproducing "some of the worst aspects of the beauty culture, not so much through the act of the surgery itself as through their ideological efforts to restore appearance as an indicator of character." After having listened to what women themselves say about why they opted for surgery, however, Gimlin rejects the social critics' position. "I am not convinced," she writes, "that reducing facial wrinkles is somehow less 'real' than dyeing hair from gray to brown or even that eye surgery or rhinoplasty is somehow less authentic than a decision to have straight rather than curly hair" (107).

Gimlin found that many women who elected cosmetic surgery were quite able to control their need for it. The women she interviewed were not addicted to cosmetic surgery. None of them were like the often-interviewed women who have had one surgery after another so that they could achieve their goal of looking exactly like the doll Barbie: wasp-waisted, full-breasted, and blonde. And none of them thought that cosmetic surgery could or should entirely transform their appearance. On the contrary, the women with whom Gimlin spoke seemed content to use cosmetic surgery to address a particular "flaw" rather than to attain some sort of ideal beauty. They stressed that they did not get surgery to please others but to please themselves or to approximate more closely their own vision of themselves (96, 106–7).

Significantly, in a book just as full of interviews as Gimlin's, Kathy Davis concurs with Gimlin's observations repeatedly. As she puts it in her 1995 *Reshaping the Female Body: The Dilemma of Cosmetic Surgery* (3–5), "Cosmetic surgery was clearly more complicated than I had imagined. I had previously associated it either with well-to-do American housewives who were bored with their suburban lives and wanted to have a face-lift or with the celebrity 'surgical junkies' who couldn't seem to stop remaking their bodies," not feminist friends who understood the dangers and the cultural implications of cosmetic surgery. Davis reveals to her readers how she was initially thrown when her friend, who, as she puts it, is "critical of the suffering women have to endure because their bodies do not meet the normative requirements of feminine beauty," nevertheless decided to have cosmetic surgery "*for herself*" (emphasis in original). She confesses that, for a while, she doubted whether her friend was a feminist at all; but she gradually concluded that for her friend, cosmetic surgery made good sense. Her friend was having the surgery to please herself and cosmetic surgery was giving her the opportunity "to renegotiate her relationship to her body and through her body to the world around her." Davis's friend experienced herself not as "just a body" that had to conform to others' expectations, but as "a subject with a body" that she could use to express herself to others. If one can change one's ways of thinking, why cannot one change one's way of looking?

Gimlin and Davis concede that in obtaining a face-lift, a woman might not be delighting herself but simply doing the best she can in an environment that is sexist, ageist, and deeply moralistic about physical appearance. One of the women Gimlin interviews supports this point when she discusses getting cosmetic surgery to deal with "pressures in 'the workfield.'" As this woman explained, "Despite the fact that we have laws against age discrimination, employers do find ways of getting around it. I know women my age who do not get jobs or are relieved of jobs because of age" (2002, 100). Davis likewise emphasizes that many of the women who get cosmetic surgery are, perhaps, "exercising power under conditions which are not of one's own making. In the context of limited possibilities for action, cosmetic surgery can be a way for an individual woman to give shape to her life by reshaping her body. . . . For a woman whose suffering has gone beyond a certain point, cosmetic surgery can become a matter of justice—the only fair thing to do" (1995, 163).

Davis usefully suggests that cosmetic surgery might be seen as "a dilemma rather than a form of self-inflicted subordination" and that in this way we can "understand what makes it both desirable *and* problematic for so many women" (180, emphasis in original). To see it this way is to recognize that here, as in so many other aspects of their lives, women are faced with a double bind. To ignore the norms that gender imposes on women's appearance is costly: it can play a role in the loss of a promotion, how seriously one is taken in the workplace or elsewhere, and the level of one's income. On the other hand, to conform to the norms of gender helps to perpetuate them, which can also play a role in the loss of a promotion, how seriously one is taken in the workplace or elsewhere, and the level of one's income. Given the damned-if-I-do, damned-if-I-don't nature of the decision to undergo cosmetic surgery and the complicated feelings and beliefs many women have about their bodies, Davis concludes that "a concern for the complexity of women's desire to have cosmetic surgery makes it difficult to come up with either a blanket rejection or a gratifying resolution to the problems of cosmetic surgery" (181).

EMERGING FEMINIST THEORIES ON COSMETIC SURGERY: HONORING WHAT WOMEN WANT

"The emphasis on feminine beauty," Ann J. Cahill observes in a recent article, "is a controlling force in women's lives, and the fact that some individual women claim to be choosing aspects of beautification independently does not necessarily contradict its role in perpetuating sexual inequality. In a word, then, pleasure in feminine beautification can neither be dismissed outright nor uncritically endorsed" (2003, 43). Instead, Cahill urges us to acknowledge that practices aimed at enhancing women's appearance involve "negotiation among a variety of discourses and imperatives" (51).

Cahill argues that for different women there are different limits to beautification, and the question is whether "participation in socially demanded forms of beautification necessarily" hinders "women's ability to function as equal, autonomous beings" (42). At different points in time and in different settings, a woman who beautifies herself in a variety of ways can both experience "a social lessening of her agency" and find that involving herself in certain beautification processes (going to a hair or nail salon) has strengthened the bonds between herself and other women (60).

There is a subversive element to female beautification, in that some women can use the time that they work to beautify themselves or have others beautify them as a time to bond with other women and to improve and build upon female relationships. Indeed, in her study of older women's conversations in beauty parlors, Frida Furman (1997) finds that important ties of friendship and community are forged during these rituals of beautification. Cahill notes that there are "pleasures" when "feminine beautification" is "more than an attempt to overcome or answer the lack associated with the feminine body by a patriarchal society" (2003, 46). She speaks of "specific ways in which beautification practices can create a communal experience that furthers feminist aims," noting that "the time devoted to the process of beautification indicates not its oppressive nature but its potential for feminist agency" (43, 52).

For Cahill, beautification generally and cosmetic surgery specifically become problematic only when they stop being useful to a woman's independence, freedom, and autonomy. As with many feminists of the new millennium, Cahill seems more comfortable with women beautifying themselves to suit social norms and cultural expectations as well as themselves than were feminists writing in the 1970s, 1980s, and 1990s. The fact that a woman uses makeup, has cosmetic surgery, wears sexually provocative clothes, or sells her sexual services is no longer taken as a sure sign that she has demeaned, diminished, or otherwise objectified herself. It has come to seem possible that, on the contrary, such a woman pairs the "trappings of traditional femininity or sexuality" with "demonstrations of strength or power" (Bailey 2002, 145).

The danger, of course, is that contemporary understandings of these matters could fail to take seriously the idea that gender *requires* women to be preoccupied with their looks and femininity. Amy Richards, coauthor of *Manifesta: Young Women, Feminism, and the Future,* stated in an interview: "I don't think these women are saying 'I'm going to be female, going to be objectified, going to wear sexy clothes and so on and be part of the backlash against feminism.' I think they're saying, 'I'm going to do all these things because I want to embrace my femininity'" (Bailey 2002, 144). It is easy, when participating in practices of beautification, to lose sight of the fact that femininity is a social construction working to the systemic advantage of men and the systemic disadvantage of women. To "sound female" and carry oneself in feminine ways requires constant, habitual self-monitoring. There are daily, costly, time-consuming activities involved in being a woman: a feminine body "must constantly reassure its audience by a willing demonstration of difference, even when one does not exist in nature" (Brownmiller 1984, 15).

The dangers notwithstanding, Ann Braithwaite reminds us that 2005 is a very different time from 1975. As she puts it:

> An engagement with . . . practices of seemingly traditional femininity does not necessarily carry the same meanings for young women today or for the culture they live in that they might have to earlier feminist periods, and thus cannot be the point upon which to write off specific cultural practices as somehow apolitical and therefore "post-" or "anti-" feminist.(2002, 340)

For Cathryn Bailey, the fact that younger feminists are focusing on their femininity is "a wake-up call for older feminists that what appears, from one perspective, to be conformist, may, from another perspective, have subversive potential. . . . We cannot assess the meaning of younger women's actions and attitudes without recognizing that the backdrop against which their actions are performed is, in many cases, significantly different" (2002, 145).

Marcelle Karp and Debbie Stoller likewise argue that "the trappings of femininity could be used to make a sexual statement that was powerful, rather than passive" (1999, 45):

> Unlike our feminist foremothers, who claimed that makeup was the opiate of the misses, we're positively prochoice when it comes to matters of feminine display. We're well aware . . . of the beauty myth that's working to keep women obscene and not heard, but we just don't think that transvestites should have all the fun. . . . We love our lipstick, have a passion for polish, and, adore this armor that we call "fashion." To us, it's fun, it's feminine, and, in the particular way we flaunt it, it's definitely feminist.(47)

Jennifer Baumgardner and Amy Richards echo these sentiments in *Manifesta*. As they explain, "The cultural and social weapons that had been identified (rightly so) in the Second Wave as instruments of oppression—women as sex objects, fascist fashion, pornographic materials—are no longer being exclusively wielded against women and are sometimes wielded by women" (2000, 141). They believe that women in general are much more conscious of the ways in which their bodies are used against them and that they often put these bodies and the stereotypes to their own uses, to gain their own power.

Even if gender requires women to look young and beautiful to a far greater degree than it requires men to look good, and even if it punishes women for "letting themselves go," some women nonetheless might choose cosmetic surgery not because they or others feel they are worth nothing without it, nor because they fear that they might lose their husbands or jobs, but simply because they would like to look better than they do. Others, rightly supposing that it is easier to change one's physical appearance than to shift entrenched social attitudes and topple unjust power systems, might prefer the surgery to nastier forms of discrimination. In our deeply gendered society, a woman cannot know whether her decision to undergo cosmetic surgery will really further her own or other women's interests in freedom and well-being (Bartky 1990, 62). All that she can do is ponder the matter from a feminist political and ethical point of view and hope that, on balance, her decision to use cosmetic surgery will not frustrate her own or other women's ability to live well and fully.

NOTES

1. See, for example, prices advertised at the San Francisco Plastic Surgery and Laser Center, http://www.sfcosmeticsurgery.com/costs/index.htm, or the Liposuction Cosmetic Surgery Center, http://www.liposuction-cosmetic-surgery.com/costs.htm. Statistics for 2003 (the most recent year for which they are available) are kept by the American Society of Plastic and Reconstructive Surgeons and can be viewed at http://www.plasticsurgery.org/public_education/2003statistics.cfm.
2. American Society of Plastic and Reconstructive Surgeons, statistics for 2003.
3. Wolf, quoted in Fraser 2003, 100.

Food Marketing and Childhood Obesity—A Matter of Policy

Marion Nestle

Everyone knows that American children are becoming fatter, but not everyone agrees on the cause. Many of today's children routinely consume more calories than they expend in physical activity, but this imbalance results from many recent changes in home, school, and neighborhood environments. Concerned about the health and economic costs of childhood obesity, in 2004 Congress asked the Centers for Disease Control and Prevention to examine one potential cause—the marketing of foods directly to children. The result is a new Institute of Medicine (IOM) study, *Food Marketing to Children and Youth: Threat or Opportunity*,[1] that provides a chilling account of how this practice affects children's health. Food marketing, the IOM says, intentionally targets children who are too young to distinguish advertising from truth and induces them to eat high-calorie, low-nutrient (but highly profitable) "junk" foods; companies succeed so well in this effort that business-as-usual cannot be allowed to continue.

Since the late 1970s, obesity rates have more than doubled among children 6 to 11 years of age and more than tripled among those 12 to 19 years of age. As one consequence, type 2 diabetes mellitus is no longer rare in pediatric practice.[2] The IOM states its first conclusion politely: the diets of American children are "in need of improvement." As its report makes clear, this is a gross understatement: at least 30 percent of the calories in the average child's diet derive from sweets, soft drinks, salty snacks, and fast food. Soft drinks account for more than 10 percent of the caloric intake, representing a doubling since 1980. According to the U.S. Department of Agriculture, even babies consume measurable quantities of soft drinks, and pediatricians say it is not unusual for overweight children to consume 1200 to 2000 calories per day from soft drinks alone.

Is food marketing responsible? The IOM analyzes the results of 123 published, peer-reviewed studies addressing links between food marketing and children's preferences, requests, consumption, and adiposity. Despite Talmudic parsing of the limitations of the research, the IOM finds that the preponderance of evidence supports the links. Marketing strongly influences children's food preferences, requests, and consumption. The idea that some forms of marketing increase the risk of obesity, says the IOM, "cannot be rejected."

The IOM conducted its study under a considerable handicap. Companies would not provide proprietary information, because the IOM is required to make public all documents it uses. The report reveals why companies insist on keeping such research private. It lists numerous firms that conduct marketing research focused even on preschool children, using methods—photography, ethnography, focus groups—in an Orwellian-sounding fashion to elucidate the psychological underpinnings of children's food choices, "kid archetypes," the "psyche of mothers as the family gatekeeper," and "parent-child dyads of information." As the IOM documents, this enterprise is breathtaking in its comprehensive and unabashed effort to provide a research basis for exploiting the suggestibility of young children. Although marketers justify appeals to children as "training" in consumer culture, as free speech, and as good for business, they are not selling just any consumer product: they are selling junk foods to children who would be better off not eating them.

American children spend nearly $30 billion of their own money annually on such foods, and companies design products to tap this market. Since 1994, U.S. companies have introduced about 600 new children's food products; half of them have been candies or chewing gums, and another fourth are other types of sweets or salty snacks. Only one fourth are more healthful items, such as baby foods, bread products, and bottled waters. Companies support sales of "kids' foods," with marketing budgets totaling an estimated $10 billion annually.[1,3] Kellogg spent $22.2 million just on media advertising to promote 139.8 million dollars' worth of Cheez-It crackers in 2004, but these figures are dwarfed by McDonald's $528.8 million expenditure to support $24.4 billion in sales.

Marketing to children is hardly new, but recent methods are far more intense and pervasive. Television still predominates, but the balance is shifting to product placements in toys, games, educational materials, songs, and movies; character licensing and celebrity endorsements; and less visible "stealth" campaigns involving word of mouth, cellular-telephone text messages, and the Internet. All aim to teach children to recognize brands and pester their parents to buy them. The IOM notes that by two years of age, most children can recognize products in supermarkets and ask for them by name.

Nestle, Marion. "Food Marketing and Childhood Obesity—A Matter of Policy," *New England Journal of Medicine*, 354:24 (June 15, 2006), 2527–2529. Copyright © 2006. Reprinted by permission of Massachusetts Medical Society.

But the most insidious purpose of marketing is to persuade children to eat foods made "just for them"—not what adults are eating. Some campaigns aim to convince children that they know more about what they are "supposed to" eat than their parents do. Marketers explicitly attempt to undermine family decisions about food choices by convincing children that they, not adults, should control those choices.[4] Indeed, children now routinely report that they, and not their parents, decide what to eat.

The IOM concludes that its data establish a "need and an opportunity [to]... turn food and beverage marketing forces toward better diets for American children and youth." This will be no small task. Junk foods are major sources of revenue for food companies. In response to threats of lawsuits and legislation, companies are scrambling to support health and exercise programs, to announce policies renouncing advertising directed at children under certain ages, and to make their products appear more healthful. Hence: vitamin-enriched candy, whole-grain chocolate cereals, and trans fatfree salty snacks. Yet candies, soft drinks, and snack foods remain the most heavily promoted products.[1]

Companies, says the IOM, must do better. At the moment, their efforts—and those of government agencies—to promote more healthful foods "remain far short of their full potential." If the industry does not change its practices voluntarily, "Congress should enact legislation mandating the shift." Strong words, but the IOM can only advise. Others, however, can act. In January 2006, advocacy groups announced a Massachusetts lawsuit to enjoin Kellogg and Viacom, owner of the Nickelodeon television network, from promoting junk foods to children.[5] Dozens of state legislatures have introduced bills to curb food marketing, and parent and advocacy groups are demanding bans on food marketing in schools.

Such efforts may push U.S. policies in the direction of those of at least 50 other countries that regulate television advertising aimed at children. Australia, for example, bans food advertisements meant for children younger than 14 years of age; the Netherlands bans advertisements for sweets to those younger than 12; and Sweden bans the use of cartoon characters to promote foods to children younger than 12. Although such actions have not eliminated childhood obesity—rates in these countries are increasing, although they remain lower than the U.S. rate—they may help to slow current trends. In contrast, U.S. regulations apply only to time: commercials may take up to 12 minutes per hour during weekdays but "only" 10.5 minutes per hour on weekends.

The IOM report provides plenty of evidence to support additional policy actions. Worth serious consideration, I believe, are restrictions or bans on the use of cartoon characters, celebrity endorsements, health claims on food packages, stealth marketing, and marketing in schools, along with federal actions that promote media literacy, better school meals, and consumption of fruits and vegetables. Without further changes in society, such actions may not be enough to prevent childhood obesity, but they should make it much easier for parents—and health care providers—to encourage children to eat more healthfully.

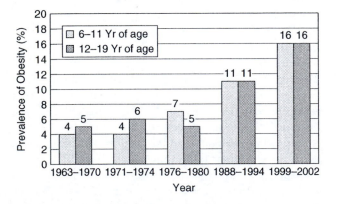

Percentages of U.S. children and teenagers who were obese.

Data from the IOM report[1]

NOTES

1. McGinnis JM, Gootman JA, Kraak VI, eds. Food marketing to children and youth: threat or opportunity? Washington, D.C.: National Academies Press, 2006.

2. Koplan JP, Liverman CT, Kraak VI, eds. Preventing childhood obesity: health in the balance. Washington, D.C.: National Academies Press, 2005.

3. California Pan-Ethnic Health Network, Consumers Union. Out of balance: marketing of soda, candy, snacks and fast foods drowns out healthful messages. San Francisco: Consumers Union, September 2005. (Accessed May 25, 2006, at http://www.consumersunion.org/pdf/OutofBalance.pdf.)

4. Pestering parents: how food companies market obesity to children. Washington, D.C.: Center for Science in the Public Interest, November 2003. (Accessec May 25, 2006, at http://www.cspinet.org/new/200311101.html.)

5. Parents and advocates will sue Viacom & Kellogg, Press release of the Center for Science in the Public Interest, Washington, D.C., January 18, 2006. (Accessed May 25, 2006, at http://www.cspinet.org/new/200601181.print.html.)

SEXUAL IDENTITY

Do Ask, Do Tell

Jennifer E. Potter

As a consequence of bias and ignorance within the medical profession, lesbians and gay men frequently receive suboptimal health care. Knowledge of each patient's sexual orientation and behaviors is critical for the development of a productive therapeutic relationship, accurate risk assessment, and the provision of pertinent preventive counseling. However, clinicians often forget to ask about this information, and many lesbians and gay men are reticent to reveal the truth. I present vignettes from my personal experiences as a lesbian patient and doctor to illustrate the importance of creating an environment in which such disclosure can occur and to portray the challenges and rewards of coming out as a gay physician.

I juggle many hats in my life: mother, partner, doctor, and educator. Like all my female colleagues, my experiences as a daughter, sister, patient, and student have influenced my approach to each of these roles. But I am also lesbian, and this fact has shaped my life profoundly. It underlies my decision to become a primary care doctor; select women's health as an area of clinical expertise; and commit myself especially to improving the lives of lesbians, gay men, and people from other minority groups.

It is a challenge to be lesbian in our society. People assume that a young woman is straight, will marry, can get pregnant if she is sexually active, and will have children. This progression is "normal." Anything else is different and may be perceived as abnormal, wrong, or bad. Historical and continuing records of harassment, assaults, and homicides against lesbians and gay men abound. The medical profession itself has viewed homosexuality as a disorder; aversion techniques, hormone administration, shock treatment, castration, and even lobotomy have been used as purported "treatments".[1] I feel fortunate that I have never been the target of clearly overt actions because of my sexual orientation.

Insidious effects of prejudice affect my life deeply, however. Imagine how it feels to hear yet another gay joke or to open the paper to confront yet another anti-gay news story. Examples include the U.S. military's "don't ask, don't tell" policy, repeated referenda that limit the civil rights of lesbians and gay men (even compared with other minority groups), and the opposition of many religious organizations. Many lesbians and gay men find it difficult to avoid internalizing some of these homophobic attitudes. As a consequence, shame and fear are common emotions, and we are more likely to be isolated; engage in risky behaviors; suffer from stress-related health conditions, substance abuse, or depression; and attempt suicide.[2]

Finding help is not easy. It is hard to trust other people, even health professionals, when one anticipates disapproval. Doctors share the same biases as the rest of society and are frequently ignorant about lesbian and gay health issues. I have often been disappointed with the medical care I have received; several examples from my experience as a lesbian patient are illustrative.

As a teenager, I reacted to the emergence of attraction to other girls with a jumble of conflicting feelings: excitement, fear, fascination, and horror. When I tried to broach the topic cautiously with my family doctor, he laughed and said, "Don't worry about that; it's just a phase a lot of girls go through." He meant to reassure me, but his comment trivialized and dismissed me instead. An important opportunity was missed to explore and validate my feelings.

By age 15, I was overwhelmed and isolated and made a suicidal gesture that might have had grave consequences. The psychiatrist to whom I was referred believed that same-sex attraction was a sign of stunted psychological development. His attitude perpetuated my notion that something was wrong with me; I stifled exploration of my identity during 2 ensuing years of therapy. I eventually found the support I needed when I met a lesbian couple who listened to me, encouraged me to be myself, and demonstrated that it was possible both to be lesbian and to pursue the goals I wanted in life—a committed relationship, a family, diverse friends, and a deeply challenging and rewarding career.

In college, I consulted a physician for evaluation of vaginal symptoms. She asked if I was sexually active (yes), whether I was using contraception (no), and whether I was trying to conceive (no). Before I had a chance to explain, she began to talk about birth control options and the importance of using condoms to prevent sexually transmitted diseases. At that point, I was too embarrassed to reveal my lesbianism. I never did ask the question that was on my mind ("Could I infect my lover?") and left, uncomfortable, with an absurd prescription for the pill. Her immediate assumption that I was straight and my reticence to reveal the truth prevented the development of a productive doctor—patient relationship and resulted in inappropriate care.

Later in life, when I disclosed my lesbianism to a new internist, she told me that my risk for cervical cancer was so low that I did not need to have regular Papanicolaou smears. This advice was incorrect. She assumed that my sexual relationships were exclusively lesbian and that the chief cause of cervical cancer, human papillomavirus, cannot be transmitted by woman-to-woman sexual contact. However, sexual identity cannot be equated with sexual behavior. Some lesbians are celibate, many have male partners, and some have partners of both sexes. Moreover, emerging evidence suggests that several genital infections can be acquired during lesbian sexual activity.[3] A detailed sexual history is necessary to understand the situation of each patient, ascertain risks for sexually transmitted diseases, and provide pertinent medical counseling.

As a result of my experiences with doctors who did not know how to communicate effectively, I became interested in ways to break down barriers that prevent gay and other minority patients from obtaining good care. I joined a lesbian and gay speaker's bureau and told my story to students at local high schools, colleges, and medical schools. I believe I helped to enlighten others and demolish some stereotypes. Then, after considering teaching, nursing, psychology, and medicine, I decided that my best course of action was to become a physician.

The medical establishment was an inhospitable place for gay trainees in the 1980s. As recommended by my premedical advisor, I concealed my lesbianism during the medical school application process; I question whether I would have received my "Welcome to the Harvard family" letter if I had been more forthright. Once a trainee, I faced all the challenges that every medical student and resident encounters: trying to master a huge body of knowledge, accepting the enormous responsibility of caring for people, learning to function with aplomb in emergency situations, and competing with others for advancement. In addition, I had to cope with tacit and overt advice that my lesbianism would be tolerated only as long as I kept quiet about it.

Ambivalence about being open is a problem that heterosexual persons can barely comprehend. It arises because of a continuing lack of acceptance of gays by most of the population and the fact that homosexuality is invisible, unlike the minority status of people with different skin color or language. As a consequence, disclosure is a choice left to each gay person.

On the face of it, maintaining silence makes almost everyone happy. I can interact with others without fear of prejudice, and people are spared the discomfort of responding to a sensitive proclamation. But invisibility has many downsides. Self-respect is difficult to preserve when one lies by omission. Silence implies acceptance that, as a member of a minority group, I have nothing valuable to contribute—that I am a "minus." If I selectively omit mention of involvement in activities that could identify me as gay, I cannot highlight all of my accomplishments. If I attend professional social gatherings alone, I miss the opportunity to introduce my partner of 23 years, show our example of a long-term relationship, and provide everyone with a chance to build acceptance.

Secrecy leads to isolation. Whenever I encounter new and unfamiliar situations, I am tempted to watch, wait, and figure out the lay of the land before revealing my lesbianism. Although this strategy feels safe, it produces loneliness. A subculture of lesbians and gay men exists through which clandestine identification takes place. But when secrecy is the paramount mode of operation, people are reluctant to gather together because of guilt by association. Silence limits opportunities for friendship, support, and professional collaboration not only with other lesbians and gay men but also with sympathetic people from the mainstream who share my values and goals.

Secrecy also requires an enormous expenditure of energy. Staying "in the closet" is not a passive process; constant vigilance is required to steer conversations away from personal issues. Of course, people sometimes ask directly whether I am in a relationship. If I deny that I am involved, I enter a vicious cycle of deception. If I admit to having a partner but try to conceal her sex, I have to take great care to avoid the pronouns "she" and "her" in subsequent discussion. Such behavior wastes a great deal of energy that could be channeled productively.

When I remain silent, people make assumptions about me that can be very awkward, especially if they later realize that their beliefs were wrong. When I started to practice medicine, many of my colleagues assumed that I was single because I did not talk about a boyfriend or husband or wear a wedding ring. Some concluded that I was an "old maid by choice"—a woman who had subjugated family to career. Others assumed that I was available, so I had to decline advances. When I became pregnant, nearly everyone assumed that I was married. In a particularly embarrassing moment, the chief of a major service told me in a public forum that he thought he knew my husband!

I have gradually learned that it is advantageous to be open about my sexual orientation. Disclosure is empowering: It allows me to be myself, integrate my public and private lives, voice my opinions, celebrate all of my achievements, and work passionately to increase tolerance and acceptance. I know that I deserve respect and recognize that I serve as an important role model.

Coming out is a process that never ends. Every time I meet someone new, I must decide if, how, and when I will reveal my sexual orientation. I find it simplest to be candid with colleagues from the start, but this approach can be awkward with patients, because it is considered inappropriate to mention intimate personal details in the context of a professional relationship. However, every doctor—patient interaction is built on trust, and I believe strongly that I have an obligation to be honest. Patients often ask me personal questions about my family and how I balance home life and career. Up-front disclosure of my sexual orientation avoids embarrassing people who might otherwise assume that I am straight and ask about my "marriage" or "husband" and allows patients who feel uncomfortable having a lesbian as their physician to choose a different doctor.

In general, I try to communicate who I am nonverbally, by displaying pictures of my family and having gayfriendly posters and health literature in my office. I developed and use an intake form that is inclusive of alternative lifestyles and avoids the designations "single," "married," "divorced," and "widowed." My name is listed in a lesbian and gay health guide, I give talks to lay audiences on lesbian and gay health issues, and I volunteer free health screening for lesbians and other minority groups in the community. I have also developed and teach a curriculum on lesbian and gay health to medical students and residents as well as to peers at continuing medical education conferences. When I am asked directly about my private life, I answer truthfully.

Reactions to my openness have been mixed, but my experiences coming out as a lesbian health professional have been rewarding overall. When I decided to coordinate a lesbian and gay student group in medical school, I had to identify myself to the administration in order to apply for funding and take the risk of being seen posting notices about group activities. Some flyers were defaced, presumably by other medical students, and I once saw one being removed by a dean. I tried to channel my anger into eloquence and gave a talk to my classmates. Although a few ignored me subsequently and one student began to pray for me every morning before class began, the posters were no longer disturbed and attendance at group-sponsored educational events increased.

Later, as a resident in the early AIDS era, I encountered numerous examples of homophobia in the hospital. There were many antigay jokes; some implied that gay men were getting what they deserved. Some of my peers refused to shake hands with gay patients or put on gowns and gloves before entering their rooms. My coming out stopped the jokes, at least in my presence, and seemed to result in more humane behavior toward people with AIDS-related illnesses.

Over the years, I have received a few lectures on the ills of homosexuality and even a letter stating that people like me should not be permitted to become doctors. However, several gay patients have told me that my visibility enabled them to find me and finally receive the understanding and support they craved. My openness has also allowed gay medical students and residents to identify me as a role model and mentor, and many of my straight colleagues and patients have thanked me for the opportunity to examine their assumptions and biases about gay people.

Somewhat to my surprise, my openness has not harmed my clinical practice. On the contrary, I have many referrals from medical colleagues and hospital administrators who want me to care for their wives and daughters, and I was recognized by *Boston Magazine* as a top internist for women in the February 2001 issue. Coming out has also afforded me some novel professional opportunities. I believe that my openness during an era of emphasis on cultural competence was a factor in my appointment to the Beth Israel Deaconess Hospital Board of Trustees. Likewise, my willingness to speak out has resulted in invitations to participate in a panel discussion on lesbian and gay health at the Massachusetts Department of Public Health and to serve on an advisory board to the American Cancer Society.

Despite these successes, much work still needs to be done. In recent years, Harvard Medical School has taken steps to diversify the racial and ethnic composition of its student body and to increase tolerance and acceptance of its gay community by sponsoring town meeting discussions. However, few minority faculty members have been promoted to leadership positions, and consequently, many of my values and those of minority colleagues remain poorly represented. I strive to promote further institutional change by being visible and voicing my questions and concerns.

A professor at my institution once warned that it is a mistake to "ghetto-ize" one's career in women's health. I take issue with this statement. I believe that my work is not only legitimate but of critical value. My talents include an instinctive ability to understand and empower patients from highly diverse backgrounds and a gift for changing the attitudes and behaviors of medical students and doctors. My work requires courage and resilience, and I believe that the outcomes are as important as the results of basic science research and clinical trials. Challenging clinicians' stereotypes and increasing the sensitivity with which they communicate with people from different cultures will benefit all of their present and future patients. I am proud to be a lesbian physician and educator.

REFERENCES

1. Miller N. Out of the Past: Gay and Lesbian History from 1869 to the Present. New York: Vintage Books; 1995.
2. Dean L. Meyer IH, Robinson K, Sell RL, Sember R, Silenzio VMB, et al. Lesbian, gay, bisexual, and transgender health: findings and concerns. Journal of the Gay and Lesbian Medical Association. 2000;4:101–51.
3. Diamant AL, Lever J. Schuster M. Lesbians' sexual activities and efforts to reduce risks for sexually transmitted disease. Journal of the Gay and Lesbian Medical Association. 2000;4:41–8.

Transsexualism and Gender Reassignment Surgery

Heather Draper and Neil Evans

The term *transsexual* is applied to people whose "gender identity is incongruent with their anatomical sex" (Herman-Jeglinska 2002, 527), that is, they believe themselves to be trapped in a body that is of the opposite sex to the one they believe themselves to be.[1] Gender reassignment surgery (GReS)[2] in conjunction with hormone therapy—particularly for male-to-female (MF) transsexuals—has been the treatment of choice (for both individuals and their doctors) for many decades now. Transsexualism has been recognized as a psychiatric classification (DSM IV [1994] 302.85) since 1980. The surgery is obviously very radical: genitalia are removed and replaced with reconstructed genitalia, breasts are removed or implants given, and vocal chords, along with teeth, noses, lips, and so forth may be altered to align them with the appearance of the desired sex. The surgical process is generally—but not always—spread over a series of months, and the hormone therapy will continue for life.

Clearly, such radical—some might say mutilating—surgery would be difficult to justify, even with the consent of the patient, without certainty about the following: that the patient's assertion is real rather than delusional (or put another way, that transsexualism is a genuine condition); that the therapy is effective; that the therapy is the only means of resolving the patient's problems; and, finally that the correct diagnosis has been reached. After all, healthy, functioning organs are removed and replaced by largely dysfunctional ones, and loss of spontaneous reproductive capacity is also inevitable.[3] Yet there remains controversy about whether transsexualism is a genuine condition, and there can therefore be no certainty that this is the best way of resolving the patient's problem. There is no compelling evidence about the effectiveness of the therapy of choice; and mistakes in diagnosis—assuming the possibility of correct diagnosis—are made with disastrous consequences for those who wrongly receive the surgery (Batty 2004). Yet around 5,000 GReSs have already been performed in the United Kingdom and the leading U.K. clinic plans to perform around 150 more of these in 2005 at a cost of at least £3000 each (Batty 2004), though the total cost facing a health authority is likely to be considerably more than this.[4]

Ethical debate about transsexualism was reignited in Australia in 2004 when the Family Court of Australia gave permission for a 13-year-old girl to begin hormone therapy as a prelude to possible reassignment surgery when she reached the age of majority.[5] Some of the debate seems to have been caused by a misunderstanding of the effects of the treatment, namely, that it was thought to have included the surgery itself or to be permanent in nature—which was not the case. Nonetheless, the concern of many commentators centered on whether it was right to give treatment to a minor for a condition of uncertain validity. Although it is arguably permissible not to interfere with an adult's decision to do something that seems grossly harmful from another's point of view, it seems even more contestable to facilitate the same process in a minor. Spriggs (2004) noted, however, that the court decision "was not about giving in to the unstable preferences of an immature person," but was rather about determining how best to accommodate her development needs.

It is interesting to note that our reactions to issues tangentially related to the question of whether transsexualism is an actual medical disorder illustrate how important it is to decide this issue. For instance, objections to transsexuals taking part in competitive sports, or to becoming fellows of the all-woman Newnham College at Cambridge University, or to having their birth certificates or passports reissued, all come back to the issue of whether such women or men are really what they claim to be or are only ever surgically reconstructed versions of their original selves.

In this chapter we will explore some of the reasons GReS is contested surgery and offer some suggestions for how, given these constraints, the surgery should be conducted.

THE CASE OF SAM HASHIMI/SAMANTHA KANE/CHARLES KANE

The case of Sam Hashimi gained wide publicity in the United Kingdom during 2004, largely as a result of his own dealings with the media. Hashimi came to the United Kingdom as a student when he was 17. His first brush with publicity was in 1990 when, as a wealthy property developer, he made an unsuccessful takeover bid for a Sheffield football club. It is unclear from his various and inconsistent accounts whether he wrongly considered himself to be a transsexual as a result of losing his money, wife, and family or whether he always knew he was a transsexual. What is known is that Sam Hashimi became Samantha Kane during 1997.

As Samantha, Kane (1998) wrote a book about her experiences as an MF transsexual and, according to a subsequent documentary[6] also regained her wealth, though not her children's affections. Between 2003 and 2004 she was on a list of 12 patients whom colleagues of leading gender reassignment specialist Russell Reid claimed had been wrongly diagnosed and operated on. Reid was referred to the General Medical Council by these colleagues, and Kane made it known that she intended to sue him. The BBC documentary about Kane concerned his experiences as a wrongly diagnosed transsexual, which included following him through some of his therapies to be changed back to a man—Charles Kane.

Kane's case is unusual to the extent that Kane has been prepared to be a more public figure.[7] There are other reported instances, particularly of MF transsexuals seeking to get their surgery reversed.[8] The number of MF transsexuals seeking reversal is still only a small minority of all cases. The prevalence of MF requests for reversal probably reflects the fact that there appears to be somewhere between four and eight times more MF transsexuals than FM (female-to-male) ones (Raymond 1979, 24).

It is important to be sure about what such cases actually show. On the one hand, they have been used by critics of the whole notion of transsexualism to support the claim that it is a condition created by psychiatrists. On the other, all they may show is that doctors need to be extremely cautious in making a diagnosis and adhering to accepted guidelines before agreeing to perform surgery. For those concerned, undertaking surgery has left them suspended in a tragic limbo between male and female. It would be foolhardy in the extreme to assume that mistakes in diagnosis never occur, even in areas of medicine where there is absolutely no controversy about the condition misdiagnosed. However, when scalpels for hire undertake GReS, on the basis of only a short interview or basic physical appearance, it is unsurprising that mistakes—by both doctor and patient—are made.

Adhering to the strict guidelines, however, might not be acceptable to some transsexuals. Standard practice is for transsexuals to have at least three months of psychotherapy before beginning hormone therapy, and then to live as a member of their proclaimed sex for at least one year, full time and publicly—before undergoing any surgery (Harry Benjamin International Gender Dysphoria Association 2001). Given that transsexuals may wait for several years or even decades before presenting for help, a further wait can be frustrating. From the clinician's point of view, given that all there is to go on is the patient's sincere belief and ability to convince, the waiting period is an opportunity to be convinced over time, particularly when for a substantial period of this time the patient must experience the possible challenge to his/her beliefs of going public and facing the consequences in terms of negotiating new relationships with family, friends, and work colleagues. The waiting period is, then, also a test of resolve. However, from the point of view of the transsexual, particularly given that biomedical ethics and patient expectations are driven by patient autonomy and rights, this period can be viewed as unacceptably paternalistic. Let's return to the Kane documentary for a moment.

In this documentary, Kane is followed as he rather impulsively buys a boat. As the documentary continues, it becomes clear that Kane has no experience with boats (including how to navigate one as well as basic knowledge like how to start the engines). He is impatient with the bureaucracy surrounding boat sales and eventually begins to realize that he may not have bought the right boat, though he retains his image of himself with the boat that motivated the purchase. Our point here is that he was free to purchase this rather costly boat, and no one would dream of considering anyone negligent in having sold it to him. Even if we speculate that the agent "saw him coming" and was a tad unscrupulous in not ensuring that the boat fitted his needs, it would be difficult to argue that the agent had a duty not to sell the boat, or even to probe too deeply into what Kane needed most. Indeed, Kane might have been justifiably annoyed as a consumer having his judgment questioned if he was unwilling to seek advice in the first place. So, given that transsexuals themselves have a clear idea of what they want—even Kane, we must suppose, or else we would have also to question his current change of heart and subsequent surgery—then how can the waiting period be justified, especially when the patient is willing and perfectly able to pay for the surgery he or she wants?

The answer to this problem could be thought to lie in the difference between medicine and boat selling. Doctors have duties because health is of fundamental importance. Medicine, it has been claimed, is more than the mere gratification of a patient's preferences or the granting to patients of what makes them happy (Kass 1981). It is objective to the extent that the "state of an organism is theoretically healthy, i.e. free from disease, insofar as its mode of functioning conforms to the natural design of that kind of organism" (Boorse 1991, 57). Thus, the doctors' duty is based not just on the importance of promoting or restoring health but also on a shared understanding of what health is. And this returns us to the issue of whether transsexualism is a legitimate concern for medicine, and by implication a genuinely medical problem.

THE EXTENT TO WHICH TRANSSEXUALISM IS A MEDICAL/SURGICAL PROBLEM

In the treatment of transsexualism, there is a convergence of three very different medical specialties: psychiatry, medicine, and surgery. The initial assessment, supervision, and monitoring falls to the psychiatrist; the patient is then referred to an endocrinologist, who takes responsibility for hormone and other therapies while a surgeon performs bodily reconstruction. This co-operation of specialties would appear to endorse the place of transsexualism within a medical model of

disease or illness, but in each case there is a considerable divergence from normal practice in order to incorporate an ontological acceptance of transsexualism. We will focus particularly on psychiatry and surgery.

It is not unusual for psychiatrists to treat people who make claims that apparently challenge reality. For instance, in anorexia they would work on a woman's perception of herself as fat and try to realign her view of herself with the reality of her extreme thinness. Where transsexualism is unusual in psychiatry is that it is up to the patient to convince the psychiatrist that her view of herself, despite the "reality" of her body, is the correct one.[9] Thus, unlike the person with anorexia, the transsexual does not deny the facts of her male body: she is not trying to assert that her male penis is in fact a clitoris. Instead, she is arguing that it *ought* to be a clitoris. The transsexual's claim is based on some inner and unseen self that contradicts the facts about the external self. If there is a delusion operating here, then it is not a delusion about external appearances but about an inner self. In this respect, transsexualism is more like body dysmorphia.

In simple terms, then, in transsexualism the psychiatrist seeks to be convinced by the patient's view of reality, rather than the patient being convinced by the psychiatrist's, and it is only possible for the psychiatrist to be convinced if he has subscribed to the view that there *is* such a thing as transsexualism. Thus, the convincing that needs to be done centers around the sincerity and/or strength of the patient's own conviction, as measured against the psychiatrist's experience (either at first or second hand) with other transsexuals and their psychiatric histories. One aspect of this is the extent to which the patient is suffering as a result of her condition, which may take the form of suicidal tendencies, extreme unhappiness, and being unable to function socially (work, interact with family and friends, and so forth).

There are differing views about how transsexualism came to be accepted as a psychiatric condition. Hart and Wellings (2002) suggest that medical interest in the whole spectrum of human sexual behavior has its origins in the post-Victorian era where efforts were made to value the individual and his own suffering and to destigmatize certain individuals. Then there was the influence of the sexologists in particular, such as Havelock Ellis, who were part of medicine's general expansion into areas that had not traditionally been viewed as part of its remit. Out of such expansion medicine incorporated such human behaviors as masturbation, homosexuality, transvestism, and transsexuality. Finally, there was a general improvement in surgical techniques and discoveries in medicine (such as those related to hormones) that made treatment a possibility, though left the notion of transsexualism open to the same charge as other conditions that arose during the expansion of the medical boundaries, namely, that conditions of health or unhealthiness are related more to the possibility of "cure" than to concepts of health per se (infertility could be another example here).

From the point of view of psychiatry, however, another general criticism is that the treatments on offer alter the *body* when the condition itself seems to have its origins in the *mind*. Of course, much of modern psychiatric practice involves altering the body, primarily the brain, using chemicals. So perhaps the challenge should be rephrased: if, as some psychiatrists hypothesize, transsexualism is caused by some malfunction in the wiring in the brain during fetal development, and if drugs were developed that could make good this wiring, would the treatment of preference continue to be the realignment of the body with the beliefs of the individual, or would it be to realign the perception with the body? Restoring the wiring to working order would be to cure transsexualism, whereas GReS concentrates only on the symptoms and thus could be argued to produce surgically constructed men and women (Raymond 1979, xvi n 5); put even more strongly, GReS turns "men into fake women and women into fake men" (Szasz 1980, 86–87).

Ironically, to argue that, given the choice, we should opt to treat the brain, and therefore the perception of the transsexual, suggests that the perception of the transsexual is actually a false one, which in turn undermines not the sincerity of the transsexuals claim but the truth of the claim, and therefore the validity of GReS. This does not mean that performing GReS is wrong: it could still be argued to be a pragmatic response to extreme suffering using what is currently available. So the current situation could be characterized in terms of what we can do technically determining treatment, which in turn determines diagnosis. If we accept that what is currently happening is a pragmatic approach, rather than one that accepts the truth of what is claimed, it makes sense for psychiatrists to base a referral for radical surgery on proof of the extreme unhappiness of the patient and evidence that they are sincere in the beliefs about their gender and steadfast in their resolve to seek surgery. The extreme unhappiness might justify surgery within the current model of medical ethics, where no intervention should be given unless the harms outweigh the benefits. Thus surgery can be considered worthwhile on balance,

even if the condition does not actually exist in quite the way that the transsexual believes.

Turning to surgery, this same on-balance justification could be employed, even though it could be contested when measured against the normal practice of surgery. Normally a surgeon would expect to remove or repair only diseased tissue, organs, or limbs, yet this is not what is happening in GreS where healthy, but undesired, organs are removed. However, there are other departures from normal practice that still fit comfortably with the surgical model, for instance, surgical sterilization or removal of healthy tissue for transplantation into another person. The "fit" seems to depend both on the acceptability to the surgeon of the existence of the condition and how extreme it is. Thus, removal of a healthy kidney for transplantation purposes is acceptable, but removal of a healthy heart would not be; likewise, GReS seems to be acceptable, while, in the United Kingdom at least, few surgeons would be comfortable removing two or more limbs in the case of body dysmorphia.

We have already looked at the question of how plausible the whole notion of transsexualism is, and clearly any surgeon performing the surgery must be prepared either to accept that transsexualism is a genuine condition or accept the "on balance justified" argument. But there are a series of other interrelated issues that arise for the surgeon. The first is how effective surgery is likely to be, since if it is not very effective this would affect the "on balance" judgment. Next is the question of whether the results have to be plausible—whether, for instance, the MF transsexual will pass readily as a woman. Finally there is the question of whether the surgery should be aimed solely at reconstruction or if it is necessary for the surgeon to create for the transsexual the woman or man he/she desires to become— the "ideal" or "perfect" man or woman.

There are two senses in which GReS can be judged to be effective or not: there is technical success, judged totally in terms of the surgical procedures, and success in terms of whether the patient feels better or more balanced as a result of having their gender reassigned. While the latter is in part dependant on the former, what is important from the point of view of the justification for performing the surgery is the latter: the surgery could be a success locally but fail in terms of the global project of improving the patient's quality of life. There is conflicting evidence of success taken globally. While there are papers purporting to have illustrated success, the Aggressive Research Intelligence Facility (ARIF) of the University of Birmingham, England, does not consider that the issue of effectiveness can be settled on the basis of the evidence currently available.[10] Moreover, there is much less evidence relating to FM transsexuals than to MF transsexuals. This is in part due to the smaller numbers but could also be due to a reluctance of FM transsexuals to draw any kind of attention to themselves (Raymond 1979, xxii). Lack of *conclusive* evidence of effectiveness does not, however, mean that it is not effective—especially as, in the current economic climate, it is not sufficient to show that an intervention is effective; it must also be *more* effective than other interventions in a randomized control trial. As ARIF observes, a trial aiming to randomize transsexuals in trial arms that would include psychotherapy only or doing nothing only as well as GReS are unlikely to recruit sufficient, if any, participants.

What we do know from retrospective research is that two factors seem to point to greater overall success. The first of these is the age at which surgery is performed (Lawrence 2003, 300) and the age at onset of the feelings of being a transsexual. The older one is, in each case, the less likely one is to be satisfied post-surgery. The second is the extent to which the surgery is unproblematic or successful in its own right. This brings in the two further related issues mentioned above: plausibility and conformity to desires.

The job of the surgeon here is to reassign gender, but for gender reassignment to be successful, it must also be plausible. The MF should be able to pass as a woman and the FM as a man, one aspect of which is being able to attract sexual attention[11] from genetic men/women rather than reconstructed men/women, irrespective of sexual orientation. This might depend on physical characteristics that are not very amenable to surgical correction such as height and build. If the success of the surgery is based at least in part on how plausible the results are likely to be, then plausibility is likely, consciously or unconsciously, to become one criterion in the assessment of the suitability of transsexuals for GReS. This may, however, undermine other aspects of the assessment, such as testing the sincerity of the patient's belief or the resolve to continue.[12]

Plausibility is, however, quite a different goal from the one that the transsexual might set for him/herself. Many transsexuals seek not just to change sex but to end up as a conventionally attractive member of the opposite sex. The desire to be physically attractive is common, but in terms of GReS what might otherwise be classed as a cosmetic effect appears more fundamental. So, for instance, a typical MF transsexual is likely to want to be and appear to be more feminine than an average genetic woman

(Herman-Jeglinska 2002). Bound up with the conviction that he is truly female may be the desire to be an attractive female conforming to cultural norms of female beauty such as prettiness, thinness, femininity, desirability to the opposite sex, demureness, and provocativeness. For the transsexual, this means that cosmetic surgery might not be viewed as an optional extra to the GReS but part and parcel of changing gender. This can lead to differing expectations of what counts as success between the patients and their surgeons.

The surgeons could be defended for arguing that their role is to reassign sex, and so while they might not oppose cosmetic surgery in principle, they might argue that requests for what they perceive as cosmetic surgery should be judged alongside other (i.e., non-transsexual) patients' requests for enhancement and perhaps would not be available using public funds. Perhaps, then, all the surgeon contracts to do is to make a constructed woman/man rather than an *attractive* constructed woman/man.

This is important when considering how well a surgeon can be said to have done her job, or in a worst-case scenario, whether she can be considered negligent or to have in some other way failed her patient. Thus there might be two standards against which the surgery can be judged: the objective assessment of whether the surgery was carried out with due care (for example, avoiding unnecessary scarring, employing modern techniques competently, and so on), and the subjective judgment of the patient about whether the surgery has made her the kind of woman she wanted to be as opposed to simply making her a woman. We would argue that it is in the former that the duty of the surgeon lies, but this is not straightforward.

A transsexual person can be thought of, along with all others, as existing through three dimensions of the self: past, present, and future. The past self for the transsexual is the suffering self, the self that existed from earlier times as an isolated, estranged, unhappy, and dispossessed misfit. This past self often contemplated suicide and eventually sought medical help to alleviate the distress. The present self (now diagnosed as a transsexual) is a self on a journey, a transitional self moving forward. Nothing for this person is permanent because everything else in life is on hold, awaiting surgery. It is the future self exclusively that matters. It is the female self that is achieved following surgery that is the self that will know fulfillment, happiness, and recognition. This future self is to be revealed when all the surgical bandages are removed and she stands in front of a mirror for herself and all others to see. This is the moment of realization and of completion. This is the moment that life will begin for the first time and unhappiness will become a thing of the past.

In her autobiography *Conundrum,* Jan Morris writes of her response when she looked at herself in the mirror following surgery. Her physical appearance at last corresponded to the inner feelings that she had possessed for so long. In turn her new physicality impacted upon her inner experience in a way that was pleasing to her.

> It is not merely the loss of androgens that has made me more retiring, more ready to be led, more passive: the removal of the sex organs themselves has contributed; for there was to the presence of the penis something positive, thrusting and muscular. My body was then made to push and to initiate and it is now made to yield and accept and the outside change has had its inner consequences.(1974, 141)

This comment seems to demonstrate Morris's desire to conform to stereotypical views of femininity and the way in which surgery, especially as a result of the removal of the penis, accomplished this.

These divisions of the self are not absolute, as they coexist and overlap but they provide a useful way of clarifying goals and concerns. To which self does the surgeon and psychiatrist owe a duty of care? Is it to the past suffering self—in which case, the motivation for performing GReS becomes one of alleviating and not creating further suffering? Or is it to the present self for whom surgery becomes a means or *the* means of achieving realization? Or is it to the future self—in which case, the surgeon may be agreeing to create a future self that brings about the dreams and wishes of the transsexual that include being sculpted into an attractive as well as plausible woman.

The pre-op transsexual has an unusually heavy investment in her future self. It could be argued that she is almost exclusively investing in her future self. Such investment is inherently problematic, though not only does it lead to a truncated appreciation of the present life but it also carries with it the increased possibility that such investment will fail to bring the hoped-for returns (as it does for anyone living primarily in the future). To exclusively focus upon a future self in the belief that realizing that self will be the equivalent of entering the Promised Land is first to nurture false beliefs and second to create a condition in which disillusionment is a real possibility.

Thus, from this perspective, the transsexual may feel that it is legitimate to hold the surgeon responsible for any failure to make her an attractive woman because it is the surgeon who is constructing her as a woman. A genetic woman may regard herself as unattractive but, adverse incidents aside, has no one to blame for

this. It seems to us, then, vital that it be made clear to the transsexual from the outset that the purpose of the surgery is to reassign gender and not to make an ideal (according to the patient) woman.

PROCEEDING WITH TREATMENT

What we have established so far is that although there could be grounds for suspecting that transsexualism is not a genuine condition in the sense that someone of one gender *is* trapped inside the body of the opposite gender, there are grounds for treating those that suffer as a result of their transsexual beliefs with GReS as a pragmatic response to an otherwise insoluble and debilitating condition. This justification is based on surgery being of benefit to the patient *on balance*. However, such a justification must require certain safeguards and precautions.

We have noted that in order to make a diagnosis, a psychiatrist has to be convinced of the sincerity of the transsexual's beliefs, and that in order to refer the patient for GReS, there must also be certainty about the resolve of the patient both to publicly live as a member of the opposite gender—with all the consequences that will flow for relationships with family, friends, and work colleagues—and to face repeated surgical procedures. It is clear from the Harry Benjamin guidelines that not all transsexuals require GReS; some are content with hormone therapy only, some do not even wish to live as a member of the opposite sex. Likewise, not all transsexuals want to undergo a complete gender reassignment: some FM transsexuals, while happy to live as a male, do not want to undergo penile construction but are content to go only as far as having breasts, ovaries, and uterus removed. So even though there is a sense in which, as we have explained, the possibility of GReS has facilitated the emergence of a diagnosis of transsexualism, this does not mean that GReS naturally follows from diagnosis. Thus, psychiatrists have an obligation to explore with the patient what is required for her to live a more balanced life. This is an unsurprising conclusion in the age of informed consent. However, if we also recall that the justification for surgery is an on balance one, it is arguable that psychiatrists should be trying first and foremost to assess how *little* intervention is necessary to improve the patient's quality of life, rather than simply assessing whether they are informed about and prepared for the consequences of GReS.

Against this background and notwithstanding the arguments already outlined in relation to paternalism, the Harry Benjamin guidelines on both eligibility and readiness for GReS criteria are not just prudent in terms of defending negligence claims, but an ethical requirement. These require that the patient has reached the age of majority, has received hormone therapy for at least 12 months, has had 12 months successful *continuous* real-life experience (as opposed to real-life tests) of living as a member of the opposite sex, and has demonstrated progress in consolidating a gender identity and also that the continuous real-life experience has had an overall positive effect on his/her mental health. Although psychotherapy is not a requirement, given the criteria and the need for assessment, a therapeutic relationship of at least 12 months' standing seems to be built into the guidelines. Moreover, it seems to us that those seeking a reversal of GReS, too, should meet the same criteria. The Harry Benjamin guidelines also recommend long-term follow-up, though it is difficult to see how the psychiatrist can ensure the patient's cooperation with this.

One moot point is the extent to which the transsexual is obliged to take account the affects of her decision on her family members, particularly children who are still minors. Clearly, no self-respecting psychiatrist would fail to discuss these with her patient. But exploring how a patient will cope with and manage upheaval is different from asking whether the patient is entitled to visit such upheaval on others, especially minor children. What we are seeking to challenge here is one of the precepts of modern psychotherapy, namely, that everyone *deserves* to be happy. Of course, this is not just an issue for transsexual parents; it is also an issue for would-be separating parents or indeed all parents. It is difficult to judge what the balance ought to be between self-fulfillment and our obligations to our children. We do not have time here for an extensive consideration of the issues; we merely want to raise the possibility that transsexuals have obligations to others as well as themselves and to suggest that these obligations also warrant serious ethical, as opposed to psychiatric, consideration. This might commit a transsexual to never having GReS or it might be the case that GReS can be delayed, giving weight to the obligations of the existing person as well of those of the future person they would like to become. Those advocating publicly funded GReS must also be aware that as well as committing public funds to the immediate and long-term treatment of the transsexual person, they may also be committing funds to the immediate and long-term care of her family. Likewise, those who consider that GReS paid for by the patient herself raises fewer ethical concerns should consider whether the transsexual should also commit to fund the health care of any dependants affected by her decisions.

Returning to the actual surgery, what are the obligations of the surgeon? Surgeons are not merely technicians; if they want to remain members of the medical profession, they have to abide by professional standards, and this means being more than surgically competent. The treatment of transsexuals is a team effort involving psychiatrists, endocrinologists, and surgeons. The psychiatrist takes the lead role in the diagnosis and assessment of the patient, and it is not unreasonable for the surgeon and endocrinologist to depend upon the psychiatrist's judgment. But this should not be an uncritical trust. As professionals, they must also be satisfied both ontologically and in terms of individual patients that intervention is necessary. This means that they should not be treating any patients who are not under the care of a psychiatrist (one who has experience of transsexualism) and they should not treat any patient who has not fulfilled the Harry Benjamin criteria of eligibility and readiness. While the surgeon cannot also be expected to undertake a psychiatric assessment, she can be expected to satisfy herself that such an assessment has been made by at least one, if not two, suitably qualified psychiatrists.

Further than this, the surgeon also has an obligation to ensure that her expectations for the surgery are in line with those of the patient. Based on our previous discussion, and again in line with conventional thinking about consent, this may involve explicit discussion with the patient about what can be realistically achieved with GReS and possibly later with cosmetic surgery.

A surgeon performing GReS cannot be held responsible for not constructing an attractive male or female, only for not performing with due skill and competence, but such a surgeon could be held responsible for holding out false promise or for not ensuring that the patient has realistic expectations of what they will look like when the bandages are removed and the scars heal.

NONMEDICAL ETHICS ISSUES

In this chapter, we have concentrated on GReS as a contested form of surgery in the context of medical ethics. To close, we would like to mention some aspects of transsexualism and GReS that we do not have time to explore in detail.

First, we have not explored the nature of gender and its social construction. Historically, gender was thought of as coexistent with the sex of the body and thus was essentially dimorphic. Male characteristics were assumed to belong to the male body and vice versa. However, as a result of the gradual medicalization of human sexual behavior (as discussed above), John Money (1955) was able to introduce a concept of gender that owed its origin to the linguistic nature of the term and served as a way of distinguishing between feminine and masculine *character* traits and those that are *biological*. Thus a way was open to construct notions of gender that were independent of bodily considerations. This in turn had consequences for medicine with regard to the legitimacy of transsexualism as a medical condition and for feminism in its attempts to eradicate sexual and gender dimorphism as an expression of masculine and paternalistic power dynamics. Without such a distinction between gender and sex, the concept of transsexualism would have been impossible.

Second, we tried to show how GReS is contestable from within a mainstream view of medical ethics. But there are other ways of exploring what the concept of transsexualism means, how we should respond to it and its implications for society. Janice Raymond (1979), for instance, writes about the implications for feminism of accepting the concept of MF transsexualism and GReS and welcoming what she terms "she-males" within feminism. In the preface to the *Transsexual Empire*, she warns:

> What goes unrecognised, consciously or unconsciously, by women who accept such transsexuals as women and as lesbian feminists is that their masculine behaviour is disguised by the castration of the male "member." Loss of a penis, however, does not mean the loss of an ability to penetrate women—women's identities, women's spirits, women's sexuality . . . the transsexually constructed lesbian-feminist not only colonizes female bodies but appropriates a feminist "soul." (xix)

Finally, we have not addressed the legal and social issues that greatly perplex postoperative transsexuals. Although some governments do have policies to ensure that transsexuals have equal rights in terms of access to health care resources, employment protection, and other social benefits,[13] there remain certain sticking points, particularly related to the changing of birth certificates and the right to marry. Concerns have also been raised about the extent to which transsexualism can be accommodated within sporting competitions as the combination of different sex and gender might give postoperative transsexual competitors an unfair advantage over genetic men or women.

NOTES

1. The ICD-10 judged transsexualism according to three criteria: "1. The desire to live and be accepted as a member of the opposite sex, usually accompanied by the wish to make his or her body as congruent as possible with the preferred sex though surgery and hormone treatment; 2. The transsexual identity has been persistent for at least two years; 3. The disorder is not a symptom of another mental disorder or chromosomal abnormality" (Harry Benjamin International Gender Dysphoria Association 2001).

2. Sometimes also referred to as "sex reassignment surgery" or "sex-change operation."

3. Gametes can be stored, but it is difficult to see how useful they would be given that most transsexuals claim also to be heterosexual.

4. The Suffolk Health Authority (1994) estimated this to be in the region of £50,000 more than 10 years ago.

5. *Re Alex: hormonal treatment for gender identity dysphoria* [2004] FamCA 297.

6. BBC1, "Make Me a Man Again," October 19, 2004.

7. Charles Kane is now reported to be writing a new book, *Back on Mars from a Long Trip to Venus*.

8. See, for instance, Batty 2004.

9. The assumption here is not that all transsexuals are male to female; the designation of "she," etc., is used simply for reasons of style.

10. The available evidence reviewed and their reasons can be found online at http://www.arif.bham.ac.uk/Requests/g/genderreass.htm.

11. Which is not be the same thing as being generally sexually attractive, that is, conventionally beautiful or handsome.

12. Batty (2004) suggests that there is too much emphasis on plausibility in the history of those who consider that their surgery was a mistake.

13. For a summary of the British government policy, see http://www.dca.gov.uk/constitution/transsex/policy.htm.

MENTAL HEALTH CARE

Surreptitious Prescribing in Psychiatric Practice

Peter Whitty and Pat Devitt

Throughout medicine, and particularly in psychiatry, treatment nonadherence by patients remains one of our greatest challenges. Estimated rates of nonadherence among all psychiatric patient groups range between 20 and 50 percent, and this figure rises as high as 70 to 80 percent among patients with schizophrenia (1).

Whitty, Peter and Pat Devitt. "Surreptitious Prescribing in Psychiatric Practice," *Psychiatric Services*, 56 (2005), 481–483. Copyright © 2005. Reprinted by permission of American Psychiatric Association.

Treatment nonadherence is associated with poor outcomes for patients with schizophrenia, and efforts aimed at improving adherence have provided mixed results (2). In one study, compliance therapy, based on motivational interviewing, improved medication adherence, attitudes to treatment, and insight at six months (3). However, a similar study did not replicate these findings (4). A recent review concluded that current clinical interventions to improve adherence, such as psychoeducation and pre-discharge contracts, need frequent repetition and are unlikely on their own to improve medication adherence among patients with schizophrenia (5).

To improve the care of patients with severe mental illness, clinicians and family members sometimes resort to concealing medications in food or drink—a practice referred to as surreptitious prescribing. In this paper we describe advantages and disadvantages of surreptitious prescribing in the context of community psychiatric service. We also examine its legal and ethical aspects and present guidelines for clinicians who are considering the surreptitious prescribing of medications.

SURREPTITIOUS PRESCRIBING

Surreptitious prescribing is the practice of supplying a prescription to a family member or health care professional of a patient and knowing that the medication will likely be concealed in food or drink and administered to the unknowing patient. Most clinicians can recall scenarios in which medication was administered in such fashion. Medical treatment is often given without consent in emergency or life-threatening situations (6). In pediatric circles there is a precedent for drugs being administered surreptitiously, a practice accepted by both clinicians and parents (7).

Although this practice is not well described in the psychiatric literature (8), it is, nevertheless, more common than one might imagine. In one study of 50 elderly patients, 79 percent received their medication surreptitiously (8). For patients with dementia this figure was 94 percent (8). In a survey of 21 psychiatrists, 38 percent admitted to having participated in surreptitious prescribing (6). However, this figure is likely to underestimate true practice, because many respondents felt uncomfortable on direct questioning about admitting to deceiving their patients. Fear of professional censure results in minimal discussion or recording in patients' case notes, which serves to compound the atmosphere of secrecy and suspicion (9,10).

Advantages

Surreptitious prescribing has a number of potential advantages in treating patients suffering from severe mental illness. Serious clinical risks and substantial costs are associated with delay in treating patients with acute psychiatric illness (11). The toxic effects of untreated psychosis are also well documented (12,13). Delaying psychiatric treatment among such patients is associated with increased morbidity and poorer outcomes in terms of prolonged individual suffering, increased risk of self-destructive behavior, deterioration of the therapeutic alliance, and increased physical assaults by the patient. Additionally, delay in initiating treatment of patients with acute psychiatric illness can lead to the demoralization of health care professionals and redirection of limited clinical resources to nontherapeutic activities. Surreptitious prescribing raises the possibility of intervening at an earlier stage before relapse and the need for certification and admission to the hospital.

Surreptitious prescribing can also prevent the need to repeatedly restrain and forcibly administer injections to patients. Family and caregivers often find this form of prescribing more satisfying, because it may also reduce the need for certification and the use of seclusion and restraint. In the case of patients with dementia who forget to take medication because of cognitive decline, restraint can be viewed as a cruel substitute for surreptitious administration (14).

A significant evidence base exists for family involvement in the management of psychotic illness (15,16), and surreptitious prescribing could be viewed as willingness of the family to be more involved in a patient's care.

Disadvantages

Prescribing surreptitiously runs the risk of denying the patient the opportunity of gaining insight. In some cases, insight improves only after recurrent relapses with the realization by the patient of the relationship between nonadherence and relapse. Surreptitious prescribing may serve to reinforce the patient's view that illness is not present and that he or she does not require treatment. The practice may also discourage patients from availing themselves of psychiatric treatment, because some may perceive surreptitious prescribing as granting too paternalistic a role to psychiatrists. Furthermore, some people may view surreptitious prescribing as a cheap means of managing inadequate staffing levels and thus encouraging untidy practice. Surreptitious prescribing also runs the risk of overlooking research and not improving our understanding of why patients are noncompliant in the first place. Patient, doctor, medication, and illness factors are associated with poor compliance, and ultimately our goal should be to better understand the reasons behind noncompliance and address these reasons before resorting to surreptitious prescribing.

Legal and ethical issues

Many of the disadvantages of surreptitious prescribing are related to legal and ethical issues. The major risk for clinicians who prescribe medication surreptitiously is that they are in effect taking the law into their own hands. One must question whether this form of prescribing in psychiatric care is necessary or legally defensible given the legal methods for involuntary committing and treating patients—involuntary hospital admission, outpatient commitment, and appointment of a guardian—that are outlined in mental health legislation. Furthermore, antipsychotic medications are associated with well documented side-effects, including extrapyramidal movements and sudden death in some circumstances.

Malpractice suits against doctors and health facilities and product liability suits against manufacturers of antipsychotic drugs have taken place in the United States and Canada among patients who developed tardive dyskinesia as a result of taking antipsychotic drugs. Certain jurisdictions believe that a doctor who proceeds without consent will be liable for trespass, assault, or battery. This view is in keeping with the 2000 guidelines of the Royal College of Psychiatrists and stands regardless of whether the doctor believed that what he or she did was good for the patient (17). In such cases the doctor could be prosecuted as an accomplice to battery.

The use of surreptitious prescribing for a patient lacking mental competence is a key issue. Mental competence reflects the ability of a patient to evidence a choice, understand the given information, appreciate or believe its content, and reason about the given information (18). In cases in which a patient has competence to consent to or to refuse treatment the clinician should proceed with the wishes of the patient. Lack of mental competence qualifies a patient in most jurisdictions for detention and enforced treatment under mental health legislation. One alternative might be to prescribe medication surreptitiously; however, this places the determination of competence solely with the clinician.

A further limitation of surreptitious prescribing is the legal implication of a relative acting as the proxy decision maker for a patient without mental competence. This legality varies across countries. For example, in the United Kingdom relatives do not have such powers (except in Scotland), and decisions need to be made in the patient's best interests. However, we are unaware of any jurisdictions where a proxy can make a decision for a competent patient, except young children.

From an ethical point of view, surreptitious prescribing could be viewed as a form of misuse of power and a breach of the trust in the doctor-patient relationship from the patient's perspective, as the patient is unaware of treatment received. The involvement of relatives and caregivers in the process also raises the issue of breach in confidentiality. These factors may result in irreversible damage to the therapeutic relationship in some cases. Although some may view surreptitious prescribing as a deprivation of the rights of the patient, it is also worth remembering that, paradoxically, withholding medication necessary to effectively treat mental illnesses could also be viewed as a deprivation of the patient's rights.

GUIDELINES

The most critical aspect of surreptitious prescribing relates to the legal implications involved. For this reason the clinician must assess the competence of the patient to give informed consent on an ongoing basis, because competence may vary over the course of a psychotic illness in conjunction with insight. Even competent patients with dementia may lack competence during an episode of delirium and regain it with resolution of the acute confusional state. If the patient regains mental competence as a result of medication administered surreptitiously, the clinician has a duty to involve the patient in future treatment decisions. In such cases, advance directives may help with the decision process, because the patient could conceivably give informed consent to the clinician at a time when he or she is deemed mentally competent, and the clinician could proceed with surreptitious prescribing when the patient is considered to lack competence. While weighing the advantages and disadvantages of surreptitious prescribing, the clinician must also consider the clinical implications of withholding treatment from such patients. Obtaining a second opinion from a colleague or the local ethics committee could reduce the legal and ethical dilemmas.

The involvement of family members and other caregivers is essential, and all potential benefits and risks of surreptitious prescribing should be explained in advance to the family and caregivers. It is also advisable to obtain the family's consent in writing. Furthermore, the family's motivation must be well-intentioned and not based on a desire to tranquilize and quiet an ill relative. Before proceeding the clinician should have a documented history of recurrent relapses secondary to medication nonadherence. All factors associated with nonadherence should also be examined, and every intervention as a means to improving adherence should be exhausted. These efforts include providing psychoeducation, avoiding polypharmacy, minimizing or treating side effects when possible, improving social and family support, and ensuring good quality of service provision and delivery of care. Furthermore, surreptitious prescribing should not be considered as a means of managing staff shortages.

The paramount principle is ensuring the well-being of a patient who lacks the competence to give informed consent. It is likely that no single rule can be applied to all cases, and any decision should respect the patient's viewpoint and also that of the family or caregivers who are integral in maintaining the patient's good health. The final decision is likely to be multidisciplinary, involving all health care professionals involved in the patient's care.

REFERENCES

1. Breen R, Thornhill JT: Noncompliance with medication for psychiatric disorders: reasons and remedies. CNS Drugs 9:457–471, 1998
2. Adams SG Jr, Howe JT: Predicting medication compliance in a psychotic population. Journal of Nervous Mental Disease 181: 558–560, 1993
3. Kemp R, Kirov G, Everitt, et al: Randomised controlled trial of compliance therapy: 18-month follow-up. British Journal of Psychiatry 172:413–419, 1998
4. O'Donnell C, Donohoe G, Sharkey L. et al: Compliance therapy: a randomised controlled trial in schizophrenia. British Medical Journal 327:834–836, 2003
5. Zygmunt A, Olfson M, Boyer CA, et al: Interventions to improve medication adherence in schizophrenia. American Journal of Psychiatry 159:1653–1664, 2002
6. Valmana A, Rutherford J: Suspension of nurse who gave drug on consultant's instructions: over a third of psychiatrists had given a drug surreptitiously or lied about a drug. British Medical Journal 314:300, 1997
7. Griffith D. Bell A: Commentary: treatment was not unethical. British Medical Journal 313:1250, 1996
8. Treloar A, Beats B, Philpot M: A pill in the sandwich: covert medication in food and drink. Journal of the Royal Society of Medicine 93:408–411, 2000
9. Kellet J. A nurse is suspended. British Medical Journal 313:1249–1251, 1996
10. Welsh S. Deahl M: Covert medication—ever ethically justifiable? Psychiatric Bulletin 26:123–126, 2002
11. Kelly M. Dunbar S, Gray JE, et al: Treatment delays for involuntary psychiatric patients associated with reviews of treatment capacity. Canadian Journal of Psychiatry 47:181–185, 2002
12. Loebel AD, Lieberman JA, Alvir JMJ, et al: Duration of psychosis and outcome in first-episode schizophrenia. American Journal of Psychiatry 149:1183–1188, 1992
13. Norman R, Malla A: Duration of untreated psychosis: a critical examination of the concept and its importance. Psychological Medicine 31:381–400, 2001
14. Treolar A, Philpot M, Beats B: Concealing medication patients' food. Lancet 357:62–64, 2001
15. Sellwood W, Tarrier N, Quinn J, et al: The family and compliance in schizophrenia: the influence of clinical variables, relatives' knowledge and expressed emotion. Psychological Medicine 33:91–96, 2003
16. Pilling S, Bebbington P, Knipers E, et al: Psychological treatments in schizophrenia: I. Meta-analysis of family intervention and cognitive behaviour therapy. Psychological Medicine 32:763–782, 2002
17. Good psychiatric practice, Council Report CR83. London, Royal College of Psychiatrists, 2000
18. Grisso T, Appelbaum PS: Assessing Competence to Consent to Treatment: A Guide for Physicians and Other Health Professionals. Oxford University Press, 1998

Chapter 6

Beginning of Life

FIGURE 6.1 If you could increase the chance of reproducing beautiful children, and thus giving them an advantage in society, would you?

The photo above presents what is considered to be a classically beautiful woman (Figure 6.1). This standard of beauty is held in such high regard that many people are willing to pay a great deal of money to achieve it, whether for themselves or for their offspring. Some entrepreneurs have capitalized on this demand to provide services that offer (or purport to offer) a shot at being beautiful, or having beautiful children.

The *ron's angels* website is one such entrepreneurial venture. The site advertises male and female models who are auctioning off their eggs and sperm, commonly at the rate of $25,000 and up. According to the website:

Beauty is its own reward. This is the first society to truly comprehend how important beautiful genes are to our evolution. Just watch television and you will see that we are only interested in looking at beautiful people . . . . The act of creating better looking, or in some organisms, more disease resistant, offspring has been taking place for hundreds of years . . . . If you could increase the chance of reproducing beautiful children, and thus giving them an advantage in society, would you?

While the website may seem to overemphasize the importance of beauty to happiness and success in life, and it may overemphasize parents' desire to have beautiful children, there is clearly a market for such ideas. In keeping with the attitude expressed by the *ron's angels* website, many parents do, indeed, pay a premium for the eggs and sperm of individuals who are perceived to be beautiful, or athletic, or intellectually gifted. This is one direction in which the new technologies are taking us, such that some ethicists claim parents are now in pursuit of the "custom made" or "perfect" baby.

CASE STUDY: THE PROBLEM OF MULTIPLE EMBRYOS

Susan Smith is a 32-year-old woman who has been seeking to get pregnant for the past 2 years. She and her husband, Rob, have a 3-year-old daughter named Kayla. After Kayla turned a year old, Susan and Rob decided that they wanted to try for their second baby. But a year later, Susan was still not pregnant.

Susan and Rob are a working-class Idaho couple with a very small, but comfortable, home. Rob is a construction worker and Susan is a nurse practitioner. Together they earn enough money to get by, though sometimes money is tight. They love their daughter Kayla, and shower her with attention. It is their hope to provide Kayla with a brother or sister, and to have a second child to love.

The Smiths seek medical help in trying to achieve a pregnancy. Susan's physician, Dr. Scott, recommends a course of fertility drugs that may help her to conceive. The drug would cause Susan to hyperovulate by producing a large number of eggs in each monthly cycle; the hope is that at least one of the eggs would be fertilized during sexual intercourse, but it is a possibility, the doctor warns, that Susan might conceive more than one embryo through this process. Susan and Rob are willing to take this risk and, since they can't afford **in vitro fertilization (IVF)** services, they decide to go ahead with the more affordable option of trying the fertility drugs.

Only a couple of months after taking the fertility drugs, Susan discovers that she is pregnant. But at her first routine prenatal checkup, Dr. Scott suspects that Susan might be carrying multiple embryos. He refers Susan to a reproductive specialist for an ultrasound and follow-up care.

The specialist talks to Susan and Rob and explains that Susan is carrying five embryos, a situation caused by the fertility drugs. Since Susan's body was hyperstimulated to release several eggs in her cycle, it was a high likelihood that such a large number of embryos might result. The specialist explains that, given the complications Susan suffered during her first pregnancy with Kayla, and given the large number of embryos that Susan is carrying, it is a strong possibility that she will miscarry the pregnancy. The specialist is worried about health risks for Susan, and the likely bad outcomes for her embryos. He recommends that Susan reduce her embryos to two, which would significantly lower her risks and would greatly improve the chances that they will develop normally *in utero*.

The procedure, called selective reduction, is not something that Susan and Rob want to consider. They are religious people, and believe that each of their embryos has an equal right to life. Susan does not want to violate her religious beliefs by selectively reducing her embryos; but nor does she want to risk her health, her life, or her babies' lives by continuing on with five embryos/fetuses. The specialist tells them that some women have successfully gestated and birthed multiple fetuses (like Nadya Suleman, who successfully carried eight fetuses to term), but that in most cases the pregnancy ends in disaster.

This case raises several important issues that relate to the beginning of life. As with any issue that involves the potential death of embryos or fetuses (including abortion, stem cell research, selective reduction of multiple embryos, sex selection, or IVF) one must consider the moral status of the embryo/fetus, and whether that status warrants the same protection that is extended to legal and moral persons. Susan and Rob are religious people who believe that their embryos each have an equal right to life: so the question of selectively reducing them raises deep concerns about the right to life. If they believe that their embryos do, indeed, have full moral rights that equal any other person, then it would be morally wrong to eliminate three of them. On the other hand, the Smiths knew that in using the fertility drugs they were taking a great risk of conceiving multiples, so their religious commitments may ultimately come second to other concerns, such as protecting the safety of Susan and the remaining embryos.

From a utilitarian perspective, couples like the Smiths must consider the physical, emotional, financial, and other harms that would be associated with carrying to term a multiple pregnancy. In this instance, Susan could very well risk her life and that of the five embryos; she could leave her daughter Kayla without a mother; and even if the pregnancy were to be successfully brought to term, the resulting babies could suffer serious physical and cognitive complications. The couple would have to contend with an unexpectedly large family, which requires financial resources that they simply do not have. And Susan and Rob must consider the physical and emotional stresses of rearing five newborns, a challenge that very few parents are able to meet.

One could certainly claim that Susan and Rob's physician is partly to blame for this moral dilemma. Dr. Scott was willing to allow the couple to take the risk of using fertility drugs, even knowing the physical risk to Susan and knowing the dilemma in which this might place the couple with regard to their religious commitment. There are steps Dr. Scott could have taken to prevent this situation from occurring. For example, if a physician detects through ultrasound that a woman has produced a large number of eggs in one cycle, the patient could be warned to avoid intercourse to prevent multiple conceptions. One might argue from a principle of nonmaleficence that physicians have an obligation to counsel female patients not to conceive when there is evidence that they have hyperovulated. For couples who are without the resources to use IVF and other costly reproductive interventions, the use of fertility drugs is their best hope to achieve a pregnancy; fertility drugs have come to be known as the "poor person's" reproductive technology. It may therefore be incumbent on reproductive specialists to take a very cautious approach, even in cases where patients are eager to access drugs and technologies to achieve a pregnancy.

The use of reproductive technologies to achieve pregnancies is on the rise. Many couples who cannot afford the high cost of reproductive techniques such as IVF elect to use fertility drugs. Indeed, the cost of IVF services can run into tens of thousands of dollars, depending on how complicated the procedures get and how many cycles a couple attempts in order to achieve a pregnancy. These new technologies raise a host of questions that go beyond concerns for the moral status of the fetus, but also include concerns about respect for human life.

ABORTION

Perhaps one of the most vexing and persistent bioethical issues is the debate surrounding abortion. Despite the decades that have passed since the landmark case *Roe v. Wade,* and despite the number of abortions that are performed in the United States each year (in 2005, 1.21 million[1]), the killing of the embryo/fetus through abortion is still one of the most strongly debated topics in bioethics.

The term "abortion" includes a variety of practices and procedures, including the use of RU-486 (or mifepristone, which brings on a woman's menstrual cycle and causes the implanted embryo to be expelled); the morning-after pill (which is taken as an emergency contraceptive, preventing the blastocyst from implanting in the uterine wall); and surgical abortions such as dilation and curettage (D&C), which involves the dilation of a woman's uterus and scraping of the uterine wall; dilation and evacuation (D&E), which suctions rather than scrapes the fetus out of the woman's uterus; and intact dilation and extraction (IDX), which is only used in late abortion. After partially delivering the developing fetus, the physician punctures its skull to suction out the brain and then crushes the fetus's skull to enable the woman to expel it through the birth canal. IDX abortions are only done in cases of serious need, since the procedure is harmful to both the fetus and the woman carrying it.

Abortion has been legal in the United States since the Supreme Court ruling on *Roe v. Wade* that was handed down on January 23, 1973.[2] In their ruling, the Chief Justices struck down a restrictive Texas law that allowed abortion only to save a woman's life: under all other circumstances, abortion was a criminal offense that was punishable by imprisonment. Since most other states had abortion laws that were very similar to those in Texas, the ruling served in effect to decriminalize abortion in the United States. While the decision did not result in unlimited access to abortion, it did strictly limit the extent to which each state can restrict abortion services for women.

The Court used the traditional division of pregnancy into "trimesters" as a guide for the degree to which states can interfere with a woman's access to abortion. During the first trimester (the first 12 weeks of pregnancy), women have full abortion access, free from state intervention. In the second trimester (from weeks 12 to 24), states may only place restrictions on abortion that serve to protect the health and safety of the pregnant woman. During the final trimester (weeks 24 to 36), states may restrict a woman's access to abortion in ways that do not violate her own health and safety. This right to restrict abortion is based on a concern for the late-term fetus, which may be capable of surviving on its own outside the woman's uterus.

One might wonder what circumstances would prompt a woman's request for an abortion. The circumstances can vary greatly, and here we offer a few examples of the grounds on which women seek them. The reasons that women feel they need abortions are as various as the women requesting them, since no two persons' social situations are identical. But generally speaking, women seek abortions in cases where they have been raped and become pregnant as a result; in cases where the continuation of the pregnancy will result in the woman's death; in cases where genetic counseling indicates the probability that a woman will produce a child with severe disabilities; and in cases where a woman is unmarried, or married but unable to afford another child. In some cases, a woman's emotional, psychological, or physical health is at stake; and sometimes it is for the health of the family unit that the abortion is requested.

The moral approach one takes to abortion depends heavily on one's view of the moral status of the fetus. We discuss that issue in the section that follows. But first, let's consider the different positions on abortion. The moral views on abortion include conservative, moderate, liberal, pro-choice feminist, and pro-life feminist approaches. Many of these views are presented in the articles we have included in this chapter. Conservative approaches to abortion argue that the right to life begins at the moment of conception and that abortion is rarely, if ever, justified. Moderate approaches take the view that abortion is sometimes justified, but that not all choices to abort are morally acceptable. Liberal approaches deny that the fetus has full moral status, and argue that the fetus lacks a right to life because it lacks the characteristics that would make it a person. Feminist positions on the abortion debate differ sharply from traditional approaches in that, rather than arguing the issue of the moral status of the fetus, they concern themselves with the social, political, and economic factors that lead women to choose abortion, and the need for social supports that would allow women to carry wanted fetuses to term. An emphasis on social justice and the subordination of vulnerable parties is at the core of feminist approaches to abortion. Pro-life and pro-choice feminist positions differ in that pro-life feminists raise their concerns for social justice and oppression in connection to fetuses, arguing that women are morally wrong to abuse their power to oppress fetuses (a subordinated group) by aborting them. Pro-choice feminists deny that fetuses are an oppressed group, and instead focus on the needs, desires, and contexts of the women who request abortion services. Clearly, there are a variety of positions on the abortion debate, and each position has a different lens through which it views the practice of abortion. Relevant to each position, from conservative to feminist, is a view on the moral status of the embryo/fetus.

THE MORAL STATUS OF THE EMBRYO/FETUS

At the heart of the abortion debate, and of any practice that results in the death of the embryo/fetus (including stem cell research, genetic testing, reproductive technologies, and sex selection), is a dispute over their moral status. According to some views, from the moment of conception each human being has a full moral right to life. Some adherents hold this view for religious reasons: Since God gave us life, it is up to God alone to determine when a life should end. Others hold this view based on an argument from probabilities: Once egg and sperm have joined, the probability that a baby will be born is very high if the pregnancy is not interrupted.[3] Still others reason that there is no clear ground on which to determine when full moral status should be accorded to the fetus, so the only sensible point at which to do so is the moment of conception, which avoids any arbitrary line-drawing concerning when a human fetus gains full moral rights.

Those who deny that the embryo/fetus has a full right to life base their position on the fact that an early embryo or fetus in no way resembles individuals to whom we accord full moral rights. The issue for these critics is **personhood,** and the particular features that make a human being a person. While those who refuse to award the embryo/fetus full moral status do not deny that it is a human being (after all, a human embryo/fetus has a human genetic code), they do claim that it lacks personhood. To have personhood, or to be a person, means to have a number of characteristics that the fetus clearly lacks, such as the capacity to reason, to differentiate oneself from others, to communicate, to have a sense of a past and a future, and so on. Embryos and fetuses—even very late-term fetuses—lack these capacities, and cannot be said to exhibit them in any way.

The problem is that, beyond embryos and fetuses, newborns can also be said to be non-persons because they lack all of the essential characteristics that make one a person. If we link a being's moral rights to its capacity to exhibit personhood, then there is a broad range of human beings who are excluded from being accorded full moral rights, including the embryo/fetus, babies and young children, those with severe mental impairment, patients in a persistent vegetative state, and older adults with advanced Alzheimer's disease. None of the individuals in these categories has the capacity to reason, to communicate, to differentiate self from other, or to have a sense of the past or the future. So the issue of personhood raises thorny questions concerning a large range of human beings, and the kind of treatment that is due to them.

One might ask why the moral status of the embryo/fetus is so important to the abortion debate. The answer is that—at least, according to many bioethicists—we cannot solve the problem of abortion if we are not clear in our use of categories. One of the most important categories is moral status: whether or not the embryo/fetus has the right to be treated on a par with every other human person. So far we have not achieved agreement on this issue. Conservatives accord full moral rights to the embryo/fetus from the moment of conception, while some liberals would not confer moral rights until well after birth. The disagreement is not simply one of moral belief; it is also a metaphysical difference concerning views of what it means to be a person, and whether or not our lives are God-given.

If one is to accept the view that personhood determines a being's moral rights, then does that mean we may do anything we want to those human beings who are not persons? No. There are other grounds for protecting such individuals from being abused, violated, or used as means to an end. One reason for protecting them is because they are extremely vulnerable parties, and any decent society protects its most weak and vulnerable from being exploited. Another reason for protecting them is because to use and abuse vulnerable human beings—even if they are not persons—reflects badly on the rest of the human community. It makes a terrible statement about the kinds of persons we are if we take advantage of the weak and vulnerable; we may, then, have very strong reasons for treating these parties with respect, even if they are not persons with full moral rights. Finally, the respectful treatment of human embryos/fetuses may be grounded in the fact that they are human beings with the *potential* for personhood. Unlike the other cases we mentioned of the severely mentally disabled, the patient in a persistent vegetative state, or the older adults with severe Alzheimer's disease, the embryo/fetus has the potential to be a person through its continued development. In claiming that the embryo/fetus is not a person, then, critics are not claiming that anything and everything can be done to it: on the contrary, there are respectful and disrespectful ways to treat nonpersons and potential persons.

While the moral status of the embryo/fetus, and the issue of personhood, relates in obvious ways to the abortion debate, it also has implications for the practice of **assisted reproductive technologies (ART).** These technologies involve a variety of procedures for achieving pregnancy, and often involve as a side effect the destruction of embryos or the killing of fetuses. Let's turn now to consider the practice of ART.

ASSISTED REPRODUCTIVE TECHNOLOGIES

The category of "assisted reproductive technologies" (ART) is broad and includes a wide variety of practices and procedures to assist a woman (or a couple) in achieving a pregnancy. Some of the practices that are placed under the umbrella of ART include in vitro fertilization (IVF), commercial surrogacy, artificial insemination by donor (AID), sex selection, egg and sperm vending, and the use of fertility drugs. What these different practices share in common is that individuals who seek them out are having difficulty conceiving a child without assistance (usually at least 6 months of attempting pregnancy without success), they are only accessed through experts (doctors, lawyers, fertility clinics), they involve some degree of financial cost, and they rely on some kind of technological intervention.

The promise of assisted reproductive technologies came to the public's attention with the birth of Louise Brown on July 25, 1978. Louise was born in England, and made headlines because she was the first IVF baby ever born. Her birth raised a series of questions concerning the safety and morality of scientifically intervening in the natural process of reproduction. Many critics predicted a very bad outcome for Louise; they thought she would likely exhibit some kind of defect as a result of having been conceived in a petri dish; yet none of the dire predictions have come true. Today, Louise is living a happy and flourishing life, she has become a mother herself, and she has not suffered any negative health effects from the IVF that brought her into existence.

Still, the development of ART has resulted in some highly morally questionable practices. Some critics refer to practices that fall under the umbrella of ART as occurring within the "wild west" of medicine, where there has been little opportunity for research and testing to ensure the safety and reliability of procedures, and where there is little governmental and legal oversight. Indeed, there have been important moments since the development of these technologies where we see that the technologies have outstripped ethics and the law. One such moment involves the case of Mary Sue Davis and Junior Davis.[4]

In 1988, nine ova were taken from Mary Sue Davis and fertilized with the sperm of her husband, Junior Davis. Two of the resulting embryos were placed in Mary Sue's uterus, but no pregnancy resulted. The seven remaining embryos were frozen for possible future attempts at pregnancy.

Months later, the couple divorced. A legal dispute arose over the disposition of the frozen embryos. Mary Sue sought the right to have them implanted in her uterus; Junior Davis objected on the grounds that he had a "right not to be a parent." In the initial judgment, it was determined that the fetuses were persons with an interest in being born to their mother, and that Mary Sue had the right to implant them. The judge vested interest of the embryos in Mary Sue.

Junior Davis appealed, and the appeal court overturned the previous decision. It was determined that there is a right to procreate and a right not to procreate, and that in this case Junior had a "constitutionally protected right not to beget a child where no pregnancy has taken place." The decision in this case supported the idea that people have a right to retain control over their gametes, even after they have been removed by choice from their bodies. The case also served to equalize men's and women's reproductive freedoms, treating them as if they are equivalent—although some critics have pointed out the undesirability of doing so, because women by necessity put in a great deal more time and effort, and take greater risks in reproduction and the use of reproductive technologies.

This case exemplifies the kinds of moral problems that have arisen with the practice of ART. The moral and legal problems are going to continue, as increasing numbers of couples seek assisted reproductive technologies in order to fulfill their dreams of having a family. Currently, the average cost for a complete IVF cycle in the United States is about $10,000 plus medications. Some clinics may charge as much as $15,000–25,000 for a complete cycle. Couples are willing to shoulder a great financial burden in the hopes of having their own biological children.

The desire to have children that are one's genetic relations is what drives the ART industry. Certainly it is a preference that has been strongly supported within society, and within the courts. People often comment that a child looks like her mother or father; and the courts have awarded custody and made dispositional decisions based on biological connections to offspring. Social parenting—the responsibility for loving and raising a child, genetic connections aside—has been given a lower status to concerns for maintaining genetic links.

The case of Mary Sue and Junior Davis highlights a general concern surrounding the way we treat the "materials" that result from reproductive technologies. The couple had undergone IVF treatment and, in order to make future IVF cycles less stressful and onerous for Mary Sue, they had frozen seven embryos for future use. While less common in 1988, the **cryopreservation** of human embryos is now a standard part of IVF treatment, and most couples that undergo IVF do elect to freeze "spare" embryos. Indeed, recent statistics indicate that there are close to a half million frozen embryos in the United States sitting in storage. Many IVF clinics are in a quandary about what to do with these embryos, because they are the property of the couple who underwent the IVF cycles, and because those couples are reluctant to simply destroy them.

The various practices that are part of ART return us to the issue of the moral status of the embryo/fetus. Some critics of these technologies object to them on the grounds that they result in the killing or death of the embryo/fetus. For example, the practice of IVF involves selecting out only the best embryos that are likely to successfully implant; any that appear defective are destroyed. Since only a certain number of embryos are returned to the woman's uterus for implantation, the rest end up being cryopreserved, which often results in their destruction through the freezing and thawing process. Beyond IVF, other practices like sex selection and commercial surrogacy involve the destruction of the embryo/fetus, since sex selection involves using ultrasound technology to determine the sex of the fetus, and then terminating the pregnancy if it is found that the fetus is not a boy (or occasionally a girl), and commercial surrogacy may involve IVF treatments, which result in the destruction of the embryo/fetus.

Sex selection is becoming more common both as part of other reproductive technologies (such as IVF) and on its own. While many couples do not seek ART with the specific purpose of sex selection in mind, it can become an option as a side effect of the technology. For example, couples who use IVF may elect to use **preimplantation genetic diagnosis** to determine the genetic health and viability of their embryos, and through this process they may learn the sex of the created embryos. Couples may then select for the sex of their infants based on preferences for the number of boys or girls they wish to have. However, sex selection is often used as a stand-alone technology to determine and select for a child of the "right" sex. In many cultures there is still a strong preference for boys, since raising girls entails extreme cost (as in the case of dowries in some countries wherein the parents of a bride are expected to provide money and/or gifts to the groom's family when the young woman is accepted into the groom's family). As a way of avoiding the birth of a girl, some couples seek ultrasound or use genetic testing as a cover for finding out the sex of their embryos/fetuses. If they discover that they are carrying a girl, couples may abort their pregnancies to try again for the desired males. Couples may also use sex selection for purposes of family balance or sex complementarity, fulfilling the desire to have the experience of raising both male and female children.

Clearly, this practice returns us to the controversial practice of abortion, since as of yet we have no developed pre-conception technologies that can reliably ensure the birth of a child of the desired sex. While there has been much interest in developing sperm sorting techniques to allow couples the choice of sex, this technology is still far from perfect. In the meantime, those who strongly desire a child of a particular sex must abort the embryo/fetus they are carrying and try again. The current practice of sex selective abortion thus raises the age-old problem of whether it is killing a person with a right to life. But it also troubles ethicists because it involves the practice of killing an otherwise *wanted* embryo/fetus.

Unlike abortions that are done because the pregnancy itself is not desired—for reasons of rape, ill health of the mother or fetus, or economic or psychological burdens—sex selective abortion involves the abortion of a pregnancy that may have been sought out and desired, and that would have been carried to term but for the "wrong" sex of the embryo/fetus. Critics find this troubling, even if they may accept abortion in general, because it implies not just that *a* pregnancy is undesirable but that *this* pregnancy is undesirable. Parents are being given increasing power over the selection and production of their offspring in ways that may be troubling and problematic. Feminists, too, have criticized the sexist practice of sex selection to eliminate unwanted girl babies, resulting in what is coming to be known as a "lost generation of girls" in some countries.

In cases in which it is difficult or impossible for a woman to carry a pregnancy to term, she and her husband may elect to hire a surrogate to do it for her. This practice, known as commercial surrogacy (or contract motherhood), is expensive and as a result is restricted to those who have the financial means. Costs vary, but may include paying for the surrogate's time and expenses, paying for the services of a third-party broker that brings the couple together with the surrogate, and paying for the cost of IVF or donor insemination that is part of the pregnancy process.

Commercial surrogacy contracts involve a couple hiring a woman either (1) to undergo IVF using the commissioning couple's sperm and egg, creating embryos that are implanted in the surrogate for gestation (known as "gestational surrogacy," since the resulting infant is not genetically connected to the commercial surrogate); or (2) to undergo artificial insemination by donor (AID) to become pregnant using the surrogate's egg and the commissioning male's sperm (known as "traditional surrogacy"). Many couples who can afford it prefer gestational surrogacy because it allows them to be the genetic parents to the resulting child, and it reduces the likelihood that they will lose the child in a court battle should the surrogate change her mind.

It is not uncommon at the point of birth for commercial surrogates to change their minds about giving up the babies they gestated for 9 months. Even though surrogacy brokers and centers for surrogate parenting require that potential surrogates have previously gestated and given birth to their own children, this does not guarantee that the women will not become attached to the embryos/fetuses growing inside their bodies. Indeed, consider the infamous case of Mary Beth Whitehead, a surrogate who changed her mind and petitioned the courts to keep the baby that resulted, even though she contracted with William and Elizabeth Stern to give up the baby at birth. This was the first commercial surrogacy case to be disputed within the courts, and as a result it was the topic of much discussion in the media.[5]

William Stern was a 40-year-old biochemist and his wife Elizabeth Stern was a 40-year-old pediatrician suffering the effects of multiple sclerosis. Due to the risks involved with any attempt by Elizabeth to get pregnant, the couple contacted the Infertility Center of New York to arrange for a commercial surrogate—a woman who would carry a baby to term and give it over to the Sterns to raise as their child. The couple lived in New Jersey.

The Infertility Center had the Sterns contact Mary Beth Whitehead, a young married woman with two children. Whitehead was artificially inseminated with William Stern's sperm; they agreed that she would carry the fetus to term for a fee of $10,000 and give it up to the Sterns at birth.

After giving birth to the baby (a little girl whom Whitehead named Sara), Whitehead felt she could not go through with the arrangement. The Sterns could not accept this, and sought a temporary court order to get custody of the baby, whom they named Melissa. Knowing that her baby was going to be apprehended, Whitehead fled the state with "Sara" and the rest of her family. The police tracked down the Whiteheads and recovered the baby.

Since William and Elizabeth Stern only had temporary legal custody of Melissa/Sara, both parties appealed to the New Jersey court to determine permanent custody for the baby. Judge Harvey R. Sorkow granted full legal custody to the Sterns, ruling that surrogacy arrangements are contractually binding.

Mary Beth Whitehead appealed to the New Jersey Supreme Court. The Sorkow decision was overruled on the grounds that surrogacy goes against public policy and is equivalent to baby selling under New Jersey adoption laws. The placement of Melissa/Sara was finally decided based on the principle of "best interest of the child"; it was determined that the child would have the best life options with the Sterns. Whitehead was granted occasional visitation rights with Melissa.

As this case indicates, the practice of commercial surrogacy is fraught with ethical, legal, and social concerns, including the following questions: Who are the "true" parents of the child that is a product of a surrogacy contract—the woman who gestates it for 9 months, the couple who commission the birth of the baby, or the person(s) who donate their sperm or eggs to the creation of the infant? How should the child's "best interests" be determined in cases where custody is disputed? Is a commercial surrogacy contract tantamount to baby selling, or is it better understood as a payment for a woman's time and trouble to carry the fetus to term? While commercial surrogacy has continued as a practice since the Whitehead and Stern case, the questions concerning the practice have not gone away. Indeed, the practice has spread to the international market, raising even more complex questions concerning the ethics of reproductive "tourism," as more affluent couples from wealthy nations travel to poor countries to receive reproductive services.

The practice of ART has resulted in a sharp increase in the number of multiple embryos/fetuses a woman will carry in a single pregnancy. Indeed, statistics indicate that the incidence of triplet births in the United States quadrupled between 1981 and 1997 (Figure 6.2).[6] When women assume the risk of carrying multiple embryos/fetuses to term, the result is often a preterm delivery in which the premature neonates are extremely compromised. So the practice of ART also raises concerns about the treatment of premature and severely premature neonates .

Medical practitioners sometimes attempt to sustain the lives of fetuses that are born as early as 22 weeks' gestation. Statistically, an infant born at 22 weeks' gestation has little to no hope of surviving; by 23 weeks its chances improve slightly, although there is every likelihood that if the infant survives at all it will have several, and severe, physical and cognitive disabilities. Between 24 and 26 weeks' gestation

**Rate of Triplet and Other Higher-Order Multiple Births —
United States, 1980–2003**

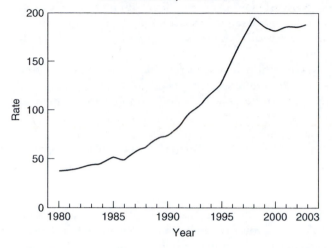

FIGURE 6.2   Triplet and other high-order multiple births.

the fetus' chances of being saved improve, with better statistical outcomes for neonates at 25 and 26 weeks gestation. However, the most recent research shows that of children born under 26 weeks' gestation, 46% suffered moderate to severe disabilities, including cerebral palsy, blindness, deafness, and low intelligence. Only 1 in 10 severely premature neonates does not wind up disabled in some way.[7]

Much has been written on the ethics of treating babies of very low birth weight (less than 1,500 grams). As suggested above, the concern focuses on the number of weeks that the fetus has been gestated prior to birth. Generally speaking, babies born weighing less than 1,500 grams lack much of what is needed to survive. Their skin is as thin as tissue, making it dangerous to touch and handle them for medical treatment; they cannot maintain a steady body temperature; their major organs have not developed sufficiently to enable them to work effectively; and babies born preterm often have not yet developed the surfactant necessary for proper lung function. This raises serious ethical questions at the beginning of life for these tiny human beings (Figure 6.3).

First, one must consider principles of beneficence and nonmaleficence in treating these premature (and sometimes severely premature) neonates. We must be very clear what ends we hope to achieve in aggressively treating these infants. At the earlier end of the spectrum, treatment is almost always futile, and results in an accumulation of harm to both the neonate and its parents. The care is invasive, painful,

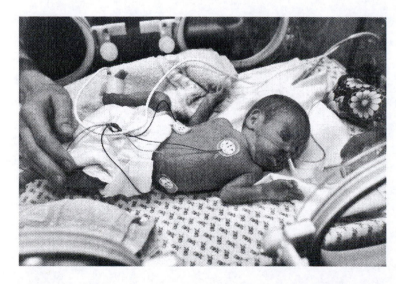

FIGURE 6.3   The ability to treat extremely premature infants leads to serious ethical questions when the costs are prohibitive and their survival rates are very low.

and costly, often running into hundreds of thousands of dollars and leaving families bankrupt and ruptured. So one must ask what good can come from aggressive treatment. As the odds for successful outcomes increase (beyond 26 weeks' gestation), so do the reasons in favor of aggressively intervening to save the life. Thus, if the Smiths were to decide to carry the pregnancy to term, they would have to face the certainty that their babies would be born prematurely, with all the risks and potential harms that entails. ART is, indeed, a mixed blessing for infertile couples.

We would be remiss not to mention the broader ethical questions relating to ART that are raised by feminists, gays and lesbians, and African Americans. Presently, ART is practiced within fertility clinics that are privately owned and operated. In the United States, these private clinics are largely free to determine those individuals they will accept as potential clients. The use of ART by postmenopausal and other non-traditional women (including single women, women with disabilities, and lesbians) is generally not supported by these clinics, although some will do so when their main concern is company profits (Figure 6.4).

Many fertility clinics are dedicated to the norm of the traditional nuclear family, and as a result only accept heterosexual married couples for treatment. Similarly, as critics point out, a series of court cases over the past 20 years have been decided in favor of biological parents such that our legal understanding of what it means to be a parent comes down to one's genetic connection to a child and/or one's marital status. Through the practices of many fertility clinics and the decisions handed down in many court cases, we see the attempt to maintain the traditional conception of the nuclear family: the father's right to his offspring, the importance of one's genetic connection to offspring, and the moral rightness of the heterosexual, two-parent norm.

Feminists, gays and lesbians, and African American scholars have criticized the practice of ART for this attempt to maintain the norm of the heterosexual married family. As race theorists point out, reproductive technologies have also been used to encourage and allow the production of white babies in particular; the production of more (and multiple) black babies is not considered desirable. This claim is supported by the fact that the state has singled out poor black women for prosecution in cases where women have been addicted to drugs or alcohol during pregnancy, and that it has encouraged young black women to take long-lasting contraceptives (like the controversial Norplant) by offering it free to individuals living in poor areas of the United States where African Americans happen to be the prevalent population.

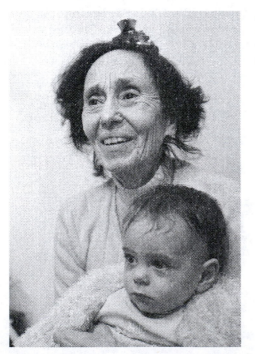

FIGURE 6.4   Adriana Iliescu, 67, holds her one year old daughter in her arms. Iliescu used donor egg and sperm to conceive, and is one of the oldest women in the world to give birth.

   Feminists and gay/lesbian critics point out that ART largely serves the interests of men and the nuclear family, although some indicate the ways in which the technologies are being used to the benefit of gay and lesbian couples. A growing number of gays and lesbians are accessing ART in the clinic (or making private arrangements for reproductive assistance) in order to form their own families. Lesbian couples may use artificial insemination to achieve pregnancies without the need for a male partner; and some gay couples have sought out commercial surrogates to carry babies that the couples then adopt at birth. Thus, despite the attempt to limit ART to the traditional patriarchal family, we see it being used to allow for the formation of nontraditional families, such as families headed by gay and lesbian couples, and families where the mothers are beyond the age of menopause, but have used IVF to allow the gestation and birth of their own offspring. However, despite this broadened use of ART, we still see few African American families accessing it when they experience problems with infertility.

Looking Ahead

- Given the current state of abortion practices, assisted reproductive technologies, and views on the moral status of the embryo/fetus, it is possible to predict some likely future directions that will be taken at the beginning of life. First, one could imagine the erosion of women's abortion rights given the ability to save fetuses at an increasingly earlier gestational age. It is more difficult to justify abortion if, at the same time, hospitals are trying to save the lives of babies that are born prematurely. And furthermore, it will be more difficult to justify killing the fetus if it is possible to abort it and have it adopted by another couple or if a preservational abortion could be done that allows the fetus to survive the abortion process. One can predict that advancements in treatment of severely premature neonates will have an effect on the way we view and treat fetuses in the abortion context, although skeptics claim that there is a gestational age (prior to 22 weeks) beyond which it will be impossible to save the fetus.

- In the future we will likely see the development of **ectogenesis,** or the development of the "glass uterus." There is much interest and excitement in the possibility that gestation of embryos/fetuses could occur outside the uterus. The technology may be desired for different reasons: so that women who want children but do not want the experience of pregnancy can have that option, and so that it would be possible to complete the gestation of aborted fetuses outside a woman's body. Researchers in Japan and other countries have been trying to advance research into ectogenesis, and it is likely that we will see the results in years to come.

- Given the desire on the part of many couples to be able to determine the sex of their babies, but given the reluctance to abort embryos/fetuses of the wrong sex, there is a strong likelihood that the process of **sperm sorting** will be perfected such that individuals will be able to pay for the privilege of selecting the sex of their offspring prior to conception. Such a technology would likely be used by couples who desire a child of a particular sex, but who refuse to do sex selective abortions. It would also likely be used by couples that suffer from male- or female-linked genetic disorders, allowing them to reproduce without inflicting the genetic disease upon their offspring. And of course, the technology would prove beneficial to those individuals from cultures that already practice sex selection, but currently use ultrasound and other technologies after the point of pregnancy to determine the sex of their fetuses.

- The practice of reproductive travel and tourism will become increasingly common as wealthier couples from developed countries travel to developing countries to receive reproductive treatments and services. There are great cost savings to these couples, who may select from services such as "IVF holidays," egg vending, and commercial surrogacy, to name a few. In response to this likely increase in reproductive tourism, we will see concerns raised regarding the exploitation and potential abuse of poor women in developing countries whose reproductive "services" are being purchased.

Endnotes

1. See the Guttmacher Institute at http://www.guttmacher.org/pubs/fb_induced_abortion.html [Accessed on June 17, 2008]

2. For details on the *Roe v. Wade* case, see Roe v. Wade, 410 U.S. 113 (1973)

3. See John T. Noonan Jr., "An Almost Absolute Value in History," *The Morality of Abortion: Legal and Historical Perspectives,* ed. John T. Noonan, Jr. (Cambridge, MA: Harvard University Press, 1970).

4. For the decision in the *Davis v. Davis* case, see Davis v. Davis, 842 S.W.2d 588, 597 (Tenn. 1992).

5. See *In the Matter of Baby M.,* 109 N.J. 396 (1988)

6. See the Centers for Disease Control and Prevention study at http://www.cdc.gov/MMWR/preview/mmwrhtml/mm4924a4.htm.

7. M.C. Allen, P.K. Donohue, and A.E. Dusman, "The Limit of Viability—Neonatal Outcome of Infants Born at 22 to 25 Weeks' Gestation," *New England Journal of Medicine,* 329:22 (1993).

ABORTION

Why Abortion is Immoral

Don Marquis

The view that abortion is, with rare exceptions, seriously immoral has received little support in the recent philosophical literature. No doubt most philosophers affiliated with secular institutions of higher education believe that the anti-abortion position is either a symptom of irrational religious dogma or a conclusion generated by seriously confused philosophical argument. The purpose of this essay is to undermine this general belief. This essay sets out an argument that purports to show, as well as any argument in ethics can show, that abortion is, except possibly in rare cases, seriously immoral, that it is in the same moral category as killing an innocent adult human being.

This essay will neglect issues of great importance to a complete ethics of abortion. Some anti-abortionists will allow that certain abortions, such as abortion before implantation or abortion when the life of a woman is threatened by a pregnancy or abortion after rape, may be morally permissible. This essay will not explore the casuistry of these hard cases. The purpose of this essay is to develop a general argument for the claim that the overwhelming majority of deliberate abortions are seriously immoral.

I.

A necessary condition of resolving the abortion controversy is a more theoretical account of the wrongness of killing. After all, if we merely believe, but do not understand, why killing adult human beings such as ourselves is wrong, how could we conceivably show that abortion is either immoral or permissible?

II.

In order to develop such an account, we can start from the following unproblematic assumption concerning our own case: it is wrong to kill *us*. Why is it wrong? Some answers can be easily eliminated. It might be said that what makes killing us wrong is that a killing brutalizes the one who kills. But the brutalization consists of being inured to the performance of an act that is hideously immoral; hence, the brutalization does not explain the immorality. It might be said that what

makes killing us wrong is the great loss others would experience due to our absence. Although such hubris is understandable, such an explanation does not account for the wrongness of killing hermits, or those whose lives are relatively independent and whose friends find it easy to make new friends.

A more obvious answer is better. What primarily makes killing wrong is neither its effect on the murderer nor its effect on the victim's friends and relatives, but its effect on the victim. The loss of one's life is one of the greatest losses one can suffer. The loss of one's life deprives one of all the experiences, activities, projects, and enjoyments that would otherwise have constituted one's future. Therefore, killing someone is wrong, primarily because the killing inflicts (one of) the greatest possible losses on the victim. To describe this as the loss of life can be misleading, however. The change in my biological state does not by itself make killing me wrong. The effect of the loss of my biological life is the loss to me of all those activities, projects, experiences, and enjoyments which would otherwise have constituted my future personal life. These activities, projects, experiences, and enjoyments are either valuable for their own sakes or are means to something else that is valuable for its own sake. Some parts of my future are not valued by me now, but will come to be valued by me as I grow older and as my values and capacities change. When I am killed, I am deprived both of what I now value which would have been part of my future personal life, but also what I would come to value. Therefore, when I die, I am deprived of all of the value of my future. Inflicting this loss on me is ultimately what makes killing me wrong. This being the case, it would seem that what makes killing *any* adult human being prima facie seriously wrong is the loss of his or her future.

How should this rudimentary theory of the wrongness of killing be evaluated? It cannot be faulted for deriving an 'ought' from an 'is', for it does not. The analysis assumes that killing me (or you, reader) is prima facie seriously wrong. The point of the analysis is to establish which natural property ultimately explains the wrongness of the killing, given that it is wrong. A natural property will ultimately explain the wrongness of killing, only if (1) the explanation fits with our intuitions about the matter and (2) there is no other natural property that

Abridged from Marquis, Don. "Why Abortion is Immoral," *Journal of Philosophy* 86:4 (April 1989), 183, 189–194, 201–202. Copyright © 1989. Reprinted by The Journal of Philosophy and the author.

provides the basis for a better explanation of the wrongness of killing. This analysis rests on the intuition that what makes killing a particular human or animal wrong is what it does to that particular human or animal. What makes killing wrong is some natural effect or other of the killing. Some would deny this. For instance, a divine-command theorist in ethics would deny it. Surely this denial is, however, one of those features of divine—command theory which renders it so implausible.

The claim that what makes killing wrong is the loss of the victim's future is directly supported by two considerations. In the first place, this theory explains why we regard killing as one of the worst of crimes. Killing is especially wrong, because it deprives the victim of more than perhaps any other crime. In the second place, people with AIDS or cancer who know they are dying believe, of course, that dying is a very bad thing for them. They believe that the loss of a future to them that they would otherwise have experienced is what makes their premature death a very bad thing for them. A better theory of the wrongness of killing would require a different natural property associated with killing which better fits with the attitudes of the dying. What could it be?

The view that what makes killing wrong is the loss to the victim of the value of the victim's future gains additional support when some of its implications are examined. In the first place, it is incompatible with the view that it is wrong to kill only beings who are biologically human. It is possible that there exists a different species from another planet whose members have a future like ours. Since having a future like that is what makes killing someone wrong, this theory entails that it would be wrong to kill members of such a species. Hence, this theory is opposed to the claim that only life that is biologically human has great moral worth, a claim which many anti-abortionists have seemed to adopt. This opposition, which this theory has in common with personhood theories, seems to be a merit of the theory.

In the second place, the claim that the loss of one's future is the wrong-making feature of one's being killed entails the possibility that the futures of some actual nonhuman mammals on our own planet are sufficiently like ours that it is seriously wrong to kill them also. Whether some animals do have the same right to life as human beings depends on adding to the account of the wrongness of killing some additional account of just what it is about my future or the futures of other adult human beings which makes it wrong to kill us. No such additional account will be offered in this essay. Undoubtedly, the provision of such an account would be a very difficult matter. Undoubtedly, any such account would

be quite controversial. Hence, it surely should not reflect badly on this sketch of an elementary theory of the wrongness of killing that it is indeterminate with respect to some very difficult issues regarding animal rights.

In the third place, the claim that the loss of one's future is the wrong-making feature of one's being killed does not entail, as sanctity of human life theories do, that active euthanasia is wrong. Persons who are severely and incurably ill, who face a future of pain and despair, and who wish to die will not have suffered a loss if they are killed. It is, strictly speaking, the value of a human's future which makes killing wrong in this theory. This being so, killing does not necessarily wrong some persons who are sick and dying. Of course, there may be other reasons for a prohibition of active euthanasia, but that is another matter. Sanctity-of-human-life theories seem to hold that active euthanasia is seriously wrong even in an individual case where there seems to be good reason for it independently of public policy considerations. This consequence is most implausible, and it is a plus for the claim that the loss of a future of value is what makes killing wrong that it does not share this consequence.

In the fourth place, the account of the wrongness of killing defended in this essay does straightforwardly entail that it is prima facie seriously wrong to kill children and infants, for we do presume that they have futures of value. Since we do believe that it is wrong to kill defenseless little babies, it is important that a theory of the wrongness of killing easily account for this. Personhood theories of the wrongness of killing, on the other hand, cannot straightforwardly account for the wrongness of killing infants and young children. Hence, such theories must add special ad hoc accounts of the wrongness of killing the young. The plausibility of such ad hoc theories seems to be a function of how desperately one wants such theories to work. The claim that the primary wrong-making feature of a killing is the loss to the victim of the value of its future accounts for the wrongness of killing young children and infants directly; it makes the wrongness of such acts as obvious as we actually think it is. This is a further merit of this theory. Accordingly, it seems that this value of a future-like-ours theory of the wrongness of killing shares strengths of both sanctity-of-life and personhood accounts while avoiding weaknesses of both. In addition, it meshes with a central intuition concerning what makes killing wrong.

The claim that the primary wrong-making feature of a killing is the loss to the victim of the value of its future has obvious consequences for the ethics of abortion. The future of a standard fetus includes a set of experiences, projects, activities, and such which are identical with the futures of adult human beings and are identical with the futures of young children. Since the reason that is sufficient to explain why it is wrong to kill human beings after the time of birth is a reason that also applies to fetuses, it follows that abortion is prima facie seriously morally wrong.

This argument does not rely on the invalid inference that, since it is wrong to kill persons, it is wrong to kill potential persons also. The category that is morally central to this analysis is the category of having a valuable future like ours; it is not the category of personhood. The argument to the conclusion that abortion is prima facie seriously morally wrong proceeded independently of the notion of person or potential person or any equivalent. Someone may wish to start with this analysis in terms of the value of a human future, conclude that abortion is, except perhaps in rare circumstances, seriously morally wrong, infer that fetuses have the right to life, and then call fetuses "persons" as a result of their having the right to life. Clearly, in this case, the category of person is being used to state the *conclusion* of the analysis rather than to generate the *argument* of the analysis.

The structure of this anti-abortion argument can be both illuminated and defended by comparing it to what appears to be the best argument for the wrongness of the wanton infliction of pain on animals. This latter argument is based on the assumption that it is prima facie wrong to inflict pain on me (or you, reader). What is the natural property associated with the infliction of pain which makes such infliction wrong? The obvious answer seems to be that the infliction of pain causes suffering and that suffering is a misfortune. The suffering caused by the infliction of pain is what makes the wanton infliction of pain on me wrong. The wanton infliction of pain on other adult humans causes suffering. The wanton infliction of pain on animals causes suffering. Since causing suffering is what makes the wanton infliction of pain wrong and since the wanton infliction of pain on animals causes suffering, it follows that the wanton infliction of pain on animals is wrong.

This argument for the wrongness of the wanton infliction of pain on animals shares a number of structural features with the argument for the serious prima facie wrongness of abortion. Both arguments start with an obvious assumption concerning what it is wrong to do to me (or you, reader). Both then look for the characteristic or the consequence of the wrong action which makes the action wrong. Both recognize that the wrong-making feature of these immoral actions is a property of actions sometimes directed at individuals other than postnatal human beings. If the structure of the argument for the wrongness of the wanton infliction of pain on animals is sound, then the structure of the argument for the prima facie serious wrongness of abortion is also sound, for the structure of the two arguments is the same. The structure common to both is the key to the explanation of how the wrongness of abortion can be demonstrated without recourse to the category of person. In neither argument is that category crucial . . . .

Of course, this value of a future-like-ours argument, if sound, shows only that abortion is prima facie wrong, not that it is wrong in any and all circumstances. Since the loss of the future to a standard fetus, if killed, is, however, at least as great a loss as the loss of the future to a standard adult human being who is killed, abortion, like ordinary killing, could be justified only by the most compelling reasons. The loss of one's life is almost the greatest misfortune that can happen to one. Presumably abortion could be justified in some circumstances, only if the loss consequent on failing to abort would be at least as great. Accordingly, morally permissible abortions will be rare indeed unless, perhaps, they occur so early in pregnancy that a fetus is not yet definitely an individual. Hence, this argument should be taken as showing that abortion is presumptively very seriously wrong, where the presumption is very strong—as strong as the presumption that killing another adult human being is wrong.

In this essay, it has been argued that the correct ethic of the wrongness of killing can be extended to fetal life and used to show that there is a strong presumption that any abortion is morally impermissible. If the ethic of killing adopted here entails, however, that contraception is also seriously immoral, then there would appear to be a difficulty with the analysis of this essay.

But this analysis does not entail that contraception is wrong. Of course, contraception prevents the actualization of a possible future of value. Hence, it follows from the claim that futures of value should be maximized that contraception is prima facie immoral. This obligation to maximize does not exist, however; furthermore, nothing in the ethics of killing in this paper entails that it does. The ethics of killing in this essay would entail that contraception is wrong only if something were denied a human future of value by contraception. Nothing at all is denied such a future by contraception, however.

Candidates for a subject of harm by contraception fall into four categories: (1) some sperm or other, (2) some ovum or other, (3) a sperm and an ovum separately, and (4) a sperm and an ovum together. Assigning the harm to some sperm is utterly arbitrary, for no reason can be given for making a sperm the subject of harm rather than an ovum. Assigning the harm to some ovum is utterly arbitrary, for no reason can be given for making an ovum the subject of harm rather than a sperm. One might attempt to avoid these problems by insisting that contraception deprives both the sperm and the ovum separately of a valuable future like ours. On this alternative, too many futures are lost. Contraception was supposed to be wrong, because it deprived us of one future of value, not two. One might attempt to avoid this problem by holding that contraception deprives the combination of sperm and ovum of a valuable future like ours. But here the definite article misleads. At the time of contraception, there are hundreds of millions of sperm, one (released) ovum and millions of possible combinations of all of these. There is no actual combination at all. Is the subject of the loss to be a merely possible combination? Which one? This alternative does not yield an actual subject of harm either. Accordingly, the immorality of contraception is not entailed by the loss of a future-like-ours argument simply because there is no nonarbitrarily identifiable subject of the loss in the case of contraception.

III.

The purpose of this essay has been to set out an argument for the serious presumptive wrongness of abortion subject to the assumption that the moral permissibility of abortion stands or falls on the moral status of the fetus. Since a fetus possesses a property, the possession of which in adult human beings is sufficient to make killing an adult human being wrong, abortion is wrong. This way of dealing with the problem of abortion seems superior to other approaches to the ethics of abortion, because it rests on an ethics of killing which is close to self-evident, because the crucial morally relevant property clearly applies to fetuses, and because the argument avoids the usual equivocations on 'human life', 'human being', or 'person'. The argument rests neither on religious claims nor on Papal dogma. It is not subject to the objection of "speciesism." Its soundness is compatible with the moral permissibility of euthanasia and contraception. It deals with our intuitions concerning young children.

Finally, this analysis can be viewed as resolving a standard problem—indeed, *the* standard problem—concerning the ethics of abortion. Clearly, it is wrong to kill adult human beings. Clearly, it is not wrong to end the life of some arbitrarily chosen single human cell. Fetuses seem to be like arbitrarily chosen human cells in some respects and like adult humans in other respects. The problem of the ethics of abortion is the problem of determining the fetal property that settles this moral controversy. The thesis of this essay is that the problem of the ethics of abortion, so understood, is solvable.

A Defense of Abortion

Judith Jarvis Thomson

Most opposition to abortion relies on the premise that the fetus is a human being, a person, from the moment of conception. The premise is argued for, but, as I think, not well. Take, for example, the most common argument. We are asked to notice that the development of a human being from conception through birth into childhood is continuous; then it is said that to draw a line, to choose a point in this development and say "before this point the thing is not a person, after this point it is a person" is to make an arbitrary choice, a choice for which in the nature of things no good reason can be given. It is concluded that the fetus is, or anyway that we had better say it is, a person from the moment of conception. But this conclusion does not follow. Similar things might be said about the development of an acorn into an oak tree, and it does not follow that acorns are oak trees, or that we had better say they are. Arguments of this form are sometimes called "slippery slope arguments"—the phrase is perhaps self-explanatory—and it is dismaying that opponents of abortion rely on them so heavily and uncritically.

I am inclined to agree, however, that the prospects for "drawing a line" in the development of the fetus look dim. I am inclined to think also that we shall probably have to agree that the fetus has already become a human person well before birth. Indeed, it comes as a surprise when one first learns how early in its life it begins to acquire human characteristics. By the tenth week, for

---

Abridged from Thomson, Judith Jarvis. "A Defense of Abortion" *Philosophy and Public Affairs,* 1:1 (1971), 47–50, 54–66 (excerpts). Copyright © 1971. Reprinted by permission of Blackwell Publishing Ltd.

example, it already has a face, arms and legs, fingers and toes; it has internal organs, and brain activity is detectable. On the other hand, I think that the premise is false, that the fetus is not a person from the moment of conception. A newly fertilized ovum, a newly implanted clump of cells, is no more a person than an acorn is an oak tree. But I shall not discuss any of this. For it seems to me to be of great interest to ask what happens if, for the sake of argument, we allow the premise. How, precisely, are we supposed to get from there to the conclusion that abortion is morally impermissible? Opponents of abortion commonly spend most of their time establishing that the fetus is a person, and hardly anytime explaining the step from there to the impermissibility of abortion. Perhaps they think the step too simple and obvious to require much comment. Or perhaps instead they are simply being economical in argument. Many of those who defend abortion rely on the premise that the fetus is not a person, but only a bit of tissue that will become a person at birth; and why pay out more arguments than you have to? Whatever the explanation, I suggest that the step they take is neither easy nor obvious, that it calls for closer examination than it is commonly given, and that when we do give it this closer examination we shall feel inclined to reject it.

I propose, then, that we grant that the fetus is a person from the moment of conception. How does the argument go from here? Something like this, I take it. Every person has a right to life. So the fetus has a right to life. No doubt the mother has a right to decide what shall happen in and to her body; everyone would grant that. But surely a person's right to life is stronger and more stringent than the mother's right to decide what happens in and to her body, and so outweighs it. So the fetus may not be killed; an abortion may not be performed.

It sounds plausible. But now let me ask you to imagine this. You wake up in the morning and find yourself back to back in bed with an unconscious violinist. A famous unconscious violinist. He has been found to have a fatal kidney ailment, and the Society of Music Lovers has canvassed all the available medical records and found that you alone have the right blood type to help. They have therefore kidnapped you, and last night the violinist's circulatory system was plugged into yours, so that your kidneys can be used to extract poisons from his blood as well as your own. The director of the hospital now tells you, "Look, we're sorry the Society of Music Lovers did this to you—we would never have permitted it if we had known. But still, they did it, and the violinist is now plugged into you. To unplug you would be to kill him. But never mind, it's only for nine months. By then

he will have recovered from his ailment, and can safely be unplugged from you." Is it morally incumbent on you to accede to this situation? No doubt it would be very nice of you if you did, a great kindness. But do you have to accede to it? What if it were not nine months, but nine years? Or longer still? What if the director of the hospital says. "Tough luck. I agree, but now you've got to stay in bed, with the violinist plugged into you, for the rest of your life. Because remember this. All persons have a right to life, and violinists are persons. Granted you have a right to decide what happens in and to your body, but a person's right to life outweighs your right to decide what happens in and to your body. So you cannot ever be unplugged from him." I imagine you would regard this as outrageous, which suggests that something really is wrong with that plausible-sounding argument I mentioned a moment ago.

In this case, of course, you were kidnapped, you didn't volunteer for the operation that plugged the violinist into your kidneys. Can those who oppose abortion on the ground I mentioned make an exception for a pregnancy due to rape? Certainly. They can say that persons have a right to life only if they didn't come into existence because of rape; or they can say that all persons have a right to life, but that some have less of a right to life than others, in particular, that those who came into existence because of rape have less. But these statements have a rather unpleasant sound. Surely the question of whether you have a right to life at all, or how much of it you have, shouldn't turn on the question of whether or not you are a product of a rape. And in fact the people who oppose abortion on the ground I mentioned do not make this distinction, and hence do not make an exception in case of rape.

Nor do they make an exception for a case in which the mother has to spend the nine months of her pregnancy in bed. They would agree that would be a great pity, and hard on the mother; but all the same, all persons have a right to life, the fetus is a person, and so on. I suspect, in fact, that they would not make an exception for a case in which, miraculously enough, the pregnancy went on for nine years, or even the rest of the mother's life.

Some won't even make an exception for a case in which continuation of the pregnancy is likely to shorten the mother's life; they regard abortion as impermissible even to save the mother's life. Such cases are nowadays very rare, and many opponents of abortion do not accept this extreme view.

Where the mother's life is not at stake, the argument I mentioned at the outset seems to have a much stronger pull. "Everyone has a right to life, so the unborn person has a right to life." And isn't the child's right to life weightier than anything other than the mother's own right to life, which she might put forward as ground for an abortion?

This argument treats the right to life as if it were unproblematic. It is not, and this seems to me to be precisely the source of the mistake.

For we should now, at long last, ask what it comes to, to have a right to life. In some views having a right to life includes having a right to be given at least the bare minimum one needs for continued life. But suppose that what in fact IS the bare minimum a man needs for continued life is something he has no right at all to be given? If I am sick unto death, and the only thing that will save my life is the touch of Henry Fonda's cool hand on my fevered brow, then all the same, I have no right to be given the touch of Henry Fonda's cool hand on my fevered brow. It would be frightfully nice of him to fly in from the West Coast to provide it. It would be less nice, though no doubt well meant, if my friends flew out to the West Coast and brought Henry Fonda back with them. But I have no right at all against anybody that he should do this for me. Or again, to return to the story I told earlier, the fact that for continued life the violinist needs the continued use of your kidneys does not establish that he has a right to be given the continued use of your kidneys. He certainly has no right against you that you should give him continued use of your kidneys. For nobody has any right to use your kidneys unless you give him this right—if you do allow him to go on using your kidneys, this is a kindness on your part, and not something he can claim from you as his due. Nor has he any right against anybody else that they should give him continued use of your kidneys. Certainly he had no right against the Society of Music Lovers that they should plug him into you in the first place. And if you now start to unplug yourself, having learned that you will otherwise have to spend nine years in bed with him, there is nobody in the world who must try to prevent you, in order to see to it that he is given some thing he has a right to be given.

Some people are rather stricter about the right to life. In their view, it does not include the right to be given anything, but amounts to, and only to, the right not to be killed by anybody. But here a related difficulty arises. If everybody is to refrain from killing that violinist, then everybody must refrain from doing a great many different sorts of things. Everybody must refrain from slitting his throat, everybody must refrain from shooting him—and everybody must refrain from unplugging you from him. But does he have a right against everybody that they shall refrain from unplugging you from him? To refrain from doing this is to allow him to continue to use your kidneys. It could be argued that he has a right against us that we should allow him to continue to use your kidneys. That is, while he had no right against us that we should give him the use of your kidneys, it might be argued that he anyway has a right against us that we shall not now intervene and deprive him of the use of your kidneys. I shall come back to third-party interventions later. But certainly the violinist has no right against you that you shall allow him to continue to use your kidneys. As I said, if you do allow him to use them, it is a kindness on your part, and not something you owe him.

The difficulty I point to here is not peculiar to the right to life. It reappears in connection with all the other natural rights, and it is something which an adequate account of rights must deal with. For present purposes it is enough just to draw attention to it. But I would stress that I am not arguing that people do not have a right to life—quite to the contrary, it seems to me that the primary control we must place on the acceptability of an account of rights is that it should turn out in that account to be a truth that all persons have a right to life. I am arguing only that having a right to life does not guarantee having either a right to be given the use of or a right to be allowed continued use of another person's body—even if one needs it for life itself. So the right to life will not serve the opponents of abortion in the very simple and clear way in which they seem to have thought it would.

There is another way to bring out the difficulty. In the most ordinary sort of case, to deprive someone of what he has a right to is to treat him unjustly. Suppose a boy and his small brother are jointly given a box of chocolates for Christmas. If the older boy takes the box and refuses to give his brother any of the chocolates, he is unjust to him, for the brother has been given a right to half of them. But suppose that, having learned that otherwise it means nine years in bed with that violinist, you unplug yourself from him. You surely are not being unjust to him, for you gave him no right to use your kidneys, and no one else can have given him any such right. But we have to notice that in unplugging yourself, you are killing him; and violinists, like everybody else, have a right to life, and thus in the view we were considering just now, the right not to be killed. So here you do what he supposedly has a right you shall not do, but you do not act unjustly to him in doing it.

The emendation which may be made at this point is this: the right to life consists not in the right not to be killed, but rather in the right not to be killed unjustly. This runs a risk of circularity, but never mind: it would enable us to square the fact that the violinist has a right to life with the fact that you do not act unjustly toward him in unplugging yourself, thereby killing him. For if you do not kill him unjustly, you do not violate his right to life, and so it is no wonder you do him no injustice.

But if this emendation is accepted, the gap in the argument against abortion stares us plainly in the face: it is by no means enough to show that the fetus is a person, and to remind us that all persons have a right to life—we need to be shown also that killing the fetus violates its right to life, i.e., that abortion is unjust killing. And is it?

I suppose we may take it as a datum that in a case of pregnancy due to rape the mother has not given the unborn person a right to the use of her body for food and shelter. Indeed, in what pregnancy could it be supposed that the mother has given the unborn person such a right? It is not as if there are unborn persons drifting about the world, to whom a woman who wants a child says "I invite you in."

But it might be argued that there are other ways one can have acquired a right to the use of another person's body than by having been invited to use it by that person. Suppose a woman voluntarily indulges in intercourse, knowing of the chance it will issue in pregnancy, and then she does become pregnant; is she not in part responsible for the presence, in fact the very existence, of the unborn person inside? No doubt she did not invite it in. But doesn't her partial responsibility for its being there itself give it a right to the use of her body? If so, then her aborting it would be more like the boys taking away the chocolates, and less like your unplugging yourself from the violinist—doing so would be depriving it of what it does have a right to, and thus would be doing it an injustice.

And then, too, it might be asked whether or not she can kill it even to save her own life: If she voluntarily called it into existence, how can she now kill it, even in self-defense?

The first thing to be said about this is that it is something new. Opponents of abortion have been so concerned to make out the independence of the fetus, in order to establish that it has a right to life, just as its mother does, that they have tended to overlook the possible support they might gain from making out that the fetus is dependent on the mother, in order to establish that she has a special kind of responsibility for it, a responsibility that gives it rights against her which are not possessed by any independent person—such as an ailing violinist who is a stranger to her.

On the other hand, this argument would give the unborn person a right to its mother's body only if her pregnancy resulted from a voluntary act, undertaken in full knowledge of the chance a pregnancy might result from it. It would leave out entirely the unborn person whose existence is due to rape. Pending the availability of some further argument, then, we would be left with the conclusion that unborn persons whose existence is due to rape have no right to the use of their mothers' bodies, and thus that aborting them is not depriving them of anything they have a right to and hence is not unjust killing.

And we should also notice that it is not at all plain that this argument really does go even as far as it purports to. For there are cases and cases, and the details make a difference. If the room is stuffy, and I therefore open a window to air it, and a burglar climbs in, it would be absurd to say, "Ah, now he can stay, she's given him a right to the use of her house—for she is partially responsible for his presence there, having voluntarily done what enabled him to get in, in full knowledge that there are such things as burglars, and that burglars burgle." It would be still more absurd to say this if I had had bars installed outside my windows, precisely to prevent burglars from getting in, and a burglar got in only because of a defect in the bars. It remains equally absurd if we imagine it is not a burglar who climbs in, but an innocent person who blunders or falls in. Again, suppose it were like this: people-seeds drift about in the air like pollen, and if you open your windows, one may drift in and take root in your carpets or upholstery. You don't want children, so you fix up your windows with fine mesh screens, the very best you can buy. As can happen, however, and on very, very rare occasions does happen, one of the screens is defective, and a seed drifts in and takes root. Does the person-plant who now develops have a right to the use of your house? Surely not—despite the fact that you voluntarily opened your windows, you knowingly kept carpets and upholstered furniture, and you knew that screens were sometimes defective. Someone may argue that you are responsible for its rooting, that it does have a right to your house, because after all you could have lived out your life with bare floors and furniture, or with sealed windows and doors. But this won't do—for by the same token anyone can avoid a pregnancy due to rape by having a hysterectomy, or anyway by never leaving home without a (reliable!) army.

It seems to me that the argument we are looking at can establish at most that there are some cases in which the unborn person has a right to the use of its mother's body, and therefore some cases in which abortion is unjust killing. There is room for much discussion and argument as to precisely which, if any. But I think we should sidestep this issue and leave it open, for at any rate the argument certainly does not establish that all abortion is unjust killing.

There is room for yet another argument here, however. We surely must all grant that there may be cases in which it would be morally indecent to detach a person from your body at the cost of his life. Suppose you learn that what the violinist needs is not nine years of your life, but only one hour: all you need do to save his life is to spend one hour in that bed with him. Suppose also that letting him use your kidneys for that one hour would not affect your health in the slightest. Admittedly you were kidnapped. Admittedly you did not give anyone permission to plug him into you. Nevertheless it seems to me plain you ought to allow him to use your kidneys for that hour—it would be indecent to refuse.

Again, suppose pregnancy lasted only an hour, and constituted no threat to life or health. And suppose that a woman becomes pregnant as a result of rape. Admittedly she did not voluntarily do anything to bring about the existence of a child. Admittedly she did nothing at all which would give the unborn person a right to the use of her body. All the same it might well be said, as in the newly amended violinist story, that she ought to allow it to remain for that hour—that it would be indecent of her to refuse.

Now some people are inclined to use the term "right" in such a way that it follows from the fact that you ought to allow a person to use your body for the hour he needs, that he has a right to use your body for the hour he needs, even though he has not been given that right by any person or act. They may say that it follows also that if you refuse, you act unjustly toward him. This use of the term is perhaps so common that it cannot be called wrong; nevertheless it seems to me to be an unfortunate loosening of what we would do better to keep a tight rein on. Suppose that box of chocolates I mentioned earlier had not been given to both boys jointly, but was given only to the older boy. There he sits stolidly eating his way through the box, his small brother watching enviously. Here we are likely to say, "You ought not to be so mean. You ought to give your brother some of those chocolates." My own view is that it just does not follow from the truth of this that the brother has any right to any of the chocolates. If the boy refuses to give his brother any he is greedy, stingy, callous—but not unjust. I suppose that the people I have in mind will say it does follow that

the brother has a right to some of the chocolates, and thus that the boy does act unjustly if he refuses to give his brother any. But the effect of saying this is to obscure what we should keep distinct, namely the difference between the boy's refusal in this case and the boy's refusal in the earlier case, in which the box was given to both boys jointly, and in which the small brother thus had what was from any point of view clear title to half.

A further objection to so using the term "right" that from the fact that A ought to do a thing for B it follows that R has a right against A that A do it for him, is that it is going to make the question of whether or not a man has a right to a thing turn on how easy it is to provide him with it; and this seems not merely unfortunate, but morally unacceptable. Take the case of Henry Fonda again. I said earlier that I had no right to the touch of his cool hand on my fevered brow even though I needed it to save my life. I said it would be frightfully nice of him to fly in from the West Coast to provide me with it, but that I had no right against him that he should do so. But suppose he isn't on the West Coast. Suppose he has only to walk across the room, place a hand briefly on my brow—and lo, my life is saved. Then surely he ought to do it—it would be indecent to refuse. Is it to be said, "Ah, well, it follows that in this case she has a right to the touch of his hand on her brow, and so it would be an injustice in him to refuse"? So that I have a right to it when it is easy for him to provide it, though no right when it's hard? It's rather a shocking idea that anyone's rights should fade away and disappear as it gets harder and harder to accord them to him.

So my own view is that even though you ought to let the violinist use your kidneys for the one hour he needs, we should not conclude that he has a right to do so— we should say that if you refuse, you are, like the boy who owns all the chocolates and will give none away, self-centered and callous, indecent in fact, but not unjust. And similarly, that even supposing a case in which a woman pregnant due to rape ought to allow the unborn person to use her body for the hour he needs, we should not conclude that he has a right to do so; we should say that she is self-centered, callous, indecent, but not unjust, if she refuses. The complaints are no less grave; they are just different. However, there is no need to insist on this point. If anyone does wish to deduce "he has a right" from "you ought," then all the same he must surely grant that there are cases in which it is not morally required of you that you allow that violinist to use your kidneys, and in which he does not have a right to use them, and in which you do not do him an injustice if you refuse. And so also for mother and unborn child. Except in such cases as the unborn person has a right to demand it—and we were leaving open the possibility that there may be such cases—nobody is morally required to make large sacrifices, of health, of all other interests and concerns, of all other duties and commitments, for nine years, or even for nine months, in order to keep another person alive.

We have in fact to distinguish between two kinds of Samaritan: the Good Samaritan and what we might call the Minimally Decent Samaritan. The story of the Good Samaritan, you will remember, goes like this:

> A certain man went down from Jerusalem to Jericho, and fell among thieves, which stripped him of his raiment, and wounded him, and departed, leaving him half dead.
>
> And by chance there came down a certain priest that way: and when he saw him, he passed by on the other side.
>
> And likewise a Levite, when he was at the place, came and looked on him, and passed by on the other side.
>
> But a certain Samaritan, as he journeyed, came where he was, and when he saw him he had compassion on him.
>
> And went to him, and bound up his wounds, pouring in oil and wine, and set him on his own beast, and brought him to an inn, and took care of him.
>
> And on the morrow, when he departed, he took out two pence, and gave them to the host, and said unto him, "Take care of him; and whatsoever thou spendest more, when I come again, I will repay thee." (Luke 10:30–35)

The Good Samaritan went out of his way, at some cost to himself, to help one in need of it. We are not told what the options were, that is, whether or not the priest and the Levite could have helped by doing less than the Good Samaritan did, but assuming they could have, then the fact they did nothing at all shows they were not even Minimally Decent Samaritans, not because they were not Samaritans, but because they were not even minimally decent.

These things are a matter of degree, of course, but there is a difference, and it comes out perhaps most clearly in the story of Kitty Genovese, who, as you will remember, was murdered while thirty-eight people watched or listened, and did nothing at all to help her. A Good Samaritan would have rushed out to give direct assistance against the murderer. Or perhaps we had better allow that it would have been a Splendid Samaritan who did this, on the ground that it would have involved a risk of death for himself. But the thirty-eight not only did not do this, they did not even trouble to pick up a phone to call the police. Minimally Decent Samaritanism would call for doing at least that, and their not having done it was monstrous.

After telling the story of the Good Samaritan, Jesus said, "Go, and do thou likewise." Perhaps he meant that we are morally required to act as the Good Samaritan did. Perhaps he was urging people to do more than is morally required of them. At all events it seems plain that it was not morally required of any of the thirty-eight that he rush out to give direct assistance at the risk of his own life, and that it is not morally required of anyone that he give long stretches of his life—nine years or nine months—to sustaining the life of a person who has no special right (we were leaving open the possibility of this) to demand it.

Indeed, with one rather striking class of exceptions, no one in any country in the world is legally required to do anywhere near as much as this for anyone else. The class of exceptions is obvious. My main concern here is not the state of the law in respect to abortion, but it is worth drawing attention to the fact that in no state in this country is any man compelled by law to be even a Minimally Recent Samaritan to any person; there is no law under which charges could be brought against the thirty eight who stood by while Kitty Genovese died. By contrast, in most states in this country women are compelled by law to be not merely Minimally Decent Samaritans, but Good Samaritans to unborn persons inside them. This doesn't by itself settle anything one way or the other, because it may well be argued that there should be laws in this country as there are in many European countries—compelling at least Minimally Decent Samaritanism. But it does show that there is a gross injustice in the existing state of the law. And it shows also that the groups currently working against liberalization of abortion laws, in fact working toward having it declared unconstitutional for a state to permit abortion, had better start working for the adoption of Good Samaritan laws generally, or earn the charge that they are acting in bad faith.

I should think, myself, that Minimally Decent Samaritan laws would be one thing, Good Samaritan laws quite another, and in fact highly improper. But we are not here concerned with the law. What we should ask is not whether anybody should be compelled by law to be a Good Samaritan, but whether we must accede to a situation in which somebody is being compelled—by nature, perhaps—to be a Good Samaritan. We have, in other words, to look now at third-party interventions. I have been arguing that no person is morally required to make large sacrifices to sustain the life of another who has no right to demand them, and this even where the sacrifices do not include life itself; we are not morally required to be Good Samaritans or anyway Very

Good Samaritans to one another. But what if a man cannot extricate himself from such a situation? What if he appeals to us to extricate him? It seems to me plain that there are cases in which we can, cases in which a Good Samaritan would extricate him. There you are, you were kidnapped, and nine years in bed with that violinist lie ahead of you. You have your own life to lead. You are sorry, but you simply cannot see giving up so much of your life to the sustaining of his. You cannot extricate yourself, and ask us to do so. I should have thought that—in light of his having no right to the use of your body—it was obvious that we do not have to accede to your being forced to give up so much. We can do what you ask. There is no injustice to the violinist in our doing so.

Following the lead of the opponents of abortion, I have throughout been speaking of the fetus merely as a person, and what I have been asking is whether or not the argument we began with, which proceeds only from the fetus's being a person, really does establish its conclusion. I have argued that it does not.

But of course there are arguments and arguments, and it may be said that I have simply fastened on the wrong one. It may be said that what is important is not merely the fact that the fetus is a person, but that it is a person for whom the woman has a special kind of responsibility issuing from the fact that she is its mother. And it might be argued that all my analogies are therefore irrelevant—for you do not have that special kind of responsibility for that violinist; Henry Fonda does not have that special kind of responsibility for me. And our attention might be drawn to the fact that men and women both are compelled by law to provide support for their children.

I have in effect dealt (briefly) with this argument in section 4 above; but a (still briefer) recapitulation now may be in order. Surely we do not have any such "special responsibility" for a person unless we have assumed it, explicitly or implicitly. If a set of parents do not try to prevent pregnancy, do not obtain an abortion, but rather take it home with them, then they have assumed responsibility for it, they have given it rights, and they cannot now withdraw support from it at the cost of its life because they now find it difficult to go on providing for it. But if they have taken all reasonable precautions against having a child, they do not simply by virtue of their biological relationship to the child who comes into existence have a special responsibility for it. They may wish to assume responsibility for it, or they may not wish to. And I am suggesting that if assuming responsibility for it would require large sacrifices, then they may

refuse. A Good Samaritan would not refuse—or anyway, a Splendid Samaritan, if the sacrifices that had to be made were enormous. But then so would a Good Samaritan assume responsibility for that violinist; so would Henry Fonda, if he is a Good Samaritan, fly in from the West Coast and assume responsibility for me.

My argument will be found unsatisfactory on two counts by many of those who want to regard abortion as morally permissible. First, while I do argue that abortion is not impermissible, I do not argue that it is always permissible. There may well be cases in which carrying the child to term requires only Minimally Decent Samaritanism of the mother, and this is a standard we must not fall below. I am inclined to think it a merit of my account precisely that it does not give a general yes or a general no. It allows for and supports our sense that, for example, a sick and desperately frightened fourteen-year-old schoolgirl, pregnant due to rape, may of course choose abortion, and that any law which rules this out is an insane law. And it also allows for and supports our sense that in other cases resort to abortion is even positively indecent. It would be indecent in the woman to request an abortion, and indecent in a doctor to perform it, if she is in her seventh month, and wants the abortion just to avoid the nuisance of postponing a trip abroad. The very fact that the arguments I have been drawing attention to treat all cases of abortion, or even all cases of abortion in which the mother's life is not at stake, as morally on a par ought to have made them suspect at the outset.

Second, while I am arguing for the permissibility of abortion in some cases, I am not arguing for the right to secure the death of the unborn child. It is easy to confuse these two things in that up to a certain point in the life of the fetus it is not able to survive outside the mother's body; hence removing it from her body guarantees its death. But they are importantly different. I have argued that you are not morally required to spend nine months in bed, sustaining the life of that violinist, but to say this is by no means to say that if, when you unplug yourself, there is a miracle and he survives, you then have a right to turn round and slit his throat. You may detach yourself even if this costs him his life; you have no right to be guaranteed his death, by some other means, if unplugging yourself does not kill him. There are some people who will feel dissatisfied by this feature of my argument. A woman may be utterly devastated by the thought of a child, a bit of herself, put out for adoption and never seen or heard of again. She may therefore want not merely that the child be detached from her, but more, that it die. Some opponents of abortion are inclined to regard this as beneath contempt—thereby showing insensitivity to what is surely a powerful source of despair. All the same, I agree that the desire for the child's death is not one which anybody may gratify, should it turn out to be possible to detach the child alive.

At this place, however, it should be remembered that we have only been pretending throughout that the fetus is a human being from the moment of conception. A very early abortion is surely not the killing of a person, and so is not dealt with by anything I have said here.

On the Moral and Legal Status of Abortion

Mary Anne Warren

The question which we must answer in order to produce a satisfactory solution to the problem of the moral status of abortion is this: How are we to define the moral community, the set of beings with full and equal moral rights, such that we can decide whether a human fetus is a member of this community or not? What sort of entity, exactly, has the inalienable rights to life, liberty, and the pursuit of happiness? Jefferson attributed these rights to all *men,* and it may or may not be fair to suggest that he intended to attribute them *only* to men. Perhaps he ought to have attributed them to all human beings. If so, then we arrive, first, at the problem of defining what makes a being human, and second, at the equally vital question namely, What reason is there for identifying the moral community with the set of all human beings, in whatever way we have chosen to define that term?

ON THE DEFINITION OF "HUMAN"

One reason why this vital second question is so frequently overlooked in the debate over the moral status of abortion is that the term "human" has two distinct, but not often distinguished, senses. This fact results in a slide of meaning, which serves to conceal the fallaciousness of the traditional argument that since (1) it is wrong to kill innocent human beings, and (2) fetuses are innocent human beings, then (3) it is wrong to kill fetuses. For if "human" is used in the same sense in both (1) and (2) then, whichever of the two senses is meant, one of these premises is question-begging. And if it is used in two different senses, then of course the conclusion doesn't follow.

Thus, (1) is a self-evident moral truth, and avoids begging the question about abortion, only if "human being" is used to mean something like "a full-fledged member of the moral community." (It may or may not also be meant to refer exclusively to members of the species *Homo sapiens.*) We may call this the *moral* sense of "human." It is not to be confused with what we will call the *genetic* sense, i.e., the sense in which any member of the species is a human being, and no member of any other species could be. If (1) is acceptable only if the moral sense is intended, (2) is non-question-begging only if what is intended is the genetic sense.

In "Deciding Who Is Human," Noonan argues for the classification of fetuses with human beings by pointing to the presence of the full genetic code, and the potential capacity for rational thought. It is clear that what he needs to show, for his version of the traditional argument to be valid, is that fetuses are human in the moral sense, the sense in which it is analytically true that all human beings have full moral rights. But, in the absence of any argument showing that whatever is genetically human is also morally human, and he gives none, nothing more than genetic humanity can be demonstrated by the presence of the human genetic code. And, as we will see, the *potential* capacity for rational thought can at most show that an entity has the potential for *becoming* human in the moral sense.

DEFINING THE MORAL COMMUNITY

Can it be established that genetic humanity is sufficient for moral humanity? I think that there are very good reasons for not defining the moral community in this way. I would like to suggest an alternative way of defining the moral community, which I will argue for only to the extent of explaining why it is, or should be, self-evident. The suggestion is simply that the moral community consists of all and only *people,* rather than all and only human beings; and probably the best way

Abridged from "On the Moral and Legal Status of Abortion" by Mary Ann Warren, The Monist, 57:1 (January 1973). Copyright © 1973 *The Monist: An International Quarterly Journal of General Philosophical Inquiry,* Peru, Illinois, 61354. Reprinted by permission.

of demonstrating its self-evidence is by considering the concept of personhood, to see what sorts of entity are and are not persons, and what the decision that a being is or is not a person implies about its moral rights.

What moral characteristics entitle an entity to be considered a person? This is obviously not the place to attempt a complete analysis of the concept of personhood, but we do not need such a fully adequate analysis just to determine whether and why a fetus is or isn't a person. All we need is a rough and approximate list of the most basic criteria of personhood, and some idea of which, or how many, of these an entity must satisfy in order to properly be considered a person.

In searching for such criteria, it is useful to look beyond the set of people with whom we are acquainted, and ask how we would decide whether a totally alien being was a person or not. (For we have no right to assume that genetic humanity is necessary for personhood.) Imagine a space traveler who lands on an unknown planet and encounters a race of beings utterly unlike any he has ever seen or heard of. If he wants to be sure of behaving morally toward these beings, he has to somehow decide whether they are people, and hence have full moral rights, or whether they are the sort of thing which he need not feel guilty about treating as, for example, a source of food.

How should he go about making this decision? If he has some anthropological background he might look for such things as religion, art, and the manufacturing of tools, weapons, or shelters, since these factors have been used to distinguish our human from our prehuman ancestors, in what seems to be closer to the moral than the genetic sense of "human." And no doubt he would be right to consider the presence of such factors as good evidence that the alien beings were people, and morally human. It would, however, be overly anthropocentric of him to take the absence of these things as adequate evidence that they were not, since we can imagine people who have progressed beyond, or evolved without ever developing, these cultural characteristics.

I suggest that the traits which are most central to the concept of personhood, or humanity in the moral sense, are, very roughly, the following:

1. Consciousness (of objects and events external and/or internal to the being), and in particular the capacity to feel pain;
2. Reasoning (the *developed* capacity to solve new and relatively complex problems);
3. Self-motivated activity (activity which is relatively independent of either genetic or direct external control);

4. The capacity to communicate, by whatever means, messages of an indefinite variety of types, that is, not just with an indefinite number of possible contents, but on indefinitely many possible topics;
5. The presence of self-concepts, and self-awareness, either individual or racial, or both.

Admittedly, there are apt to be a great many problems involved in formulating precise definitions of these criteria, let alone in developing universally valid behavioral criteria for deciding when they apply. But I will assume that both we and our explorer know approximately what (1)–(5) mean, and that he is also able to determine whether or not they apply. How, then, should he use his findings to decide whether or not the alien beings are people? We needn't suppose that an entity must have *all* of these attributes to be properly considered a person; (1) and (2) alone may well be sufficient for personhood, and quite probably (1)–(3) are sufficient. Neither do we need to insist that any one of these criteria is *necessary* for personhood, although once again (1) and (2) look like fairly good candidates for necessary conditions, as does (3), if "activity" is construed so as to include the activity of reasoning.

All we need to claim, to demonstrate that a fetus is not a person, is that any being which satisfies *none* of (1)–(5) is certainly not a person. I consider this claim to be so obvious that I think anyone who denied it, and claimed that a being which satisfied none of (1)–(5) was a person all the same, would thereby demonstrate that he had no notion at all of what a person is—perhaps because he had confused the concept of a person with that of genetic humanity. If the opponents of abortion were to deny the appropriateness of these five criteria, I do not know what further arguments would convince them. We would probably have to admit that our conceptual schemes were indeed irreconcilably different, and that our dispute could not be settled objectively.

I do not expect this to happen, however, since I think that the concept of a person is one which is very nearly universal (to people), and that it is common to both proabortionists and antiabortionists, even though neither group has fully realized the relevance of this concept to the resolution of their dispute. Furthermore, I think that on reflection even the antiabortionists ought to agree not only that (1)–(5) are central to the concept of personhood, but also that it is a part of this concept that all and only people have full moral rights. The concept of a person is in part a moral concept; once we have admitted that *x* is a person we have recognized, even if we have not agreed to respect, *x*'s right to be treated as a member of the moral community. It is true that the claim that *x* is a *human being* is more commonly voiced as part of an appeal to treat *x* decently than is the claim that *x* is a person, but this is either because "human being" is here used in the sense which implies person-hood, or because the genetic and moral senses of "human" have been confused.

Now if (1)–(5) are indeed the primary criteria of personhood, then it is clear that genetic humanity is neither necessary nor sufficient for establishing that an entity is a person. Some human beings are not people, and there may well be people who are not human beings. A man or woman whose consciousness has been permanently obliterated but who remains alive is a human being which is no longer a person; defective human beings, with no appreciable mental capacity, are not and presumably never will be people; and a fetus is a human being which is not yet a person, and which therefore cannot coherently be said to have full moral rights. Citizens of the next century should be prepared to recognize highly advanced, self-aware robots or computers, should such be developed, and intelligent inhabitants of other worlds, should such be found, as people in the fullest sense, and to respect their moral rights. But to ascribe full moral rights to an entity which is not a person is as absurd as to ascribe moral obligations and responsibilities to such an entity.

FETAL DEVELOPMENT AND THE RIGHT TO LIFE

Two problems arise in the application of these suggestions for the definition of the moral community to the determination of the precise moral status of a human fetus. Given that the paradigm example of a person is a normal adult being, then (1) How like this paradigm, in particular how far advanced since conception, does a human being need to be before it begins to have a right to life by virtue, not of being fully a person as of yet, but of being *like* a person? and (2) To what extent, if any, does the fact that a fetus has the *potential* for becoming a person endow it with some of the same rights? Each of these questions requires some comment.

In answering the first question, we need not attempt a detailed consideration of the moral rights of organisms which are not developed enough, aware enough, intelligent enough, etc., to be considered people, but which resemble people in some respects. It does seem reasonable to suggest that the more like a person, in the relevant aspects, a being is, the stronger is the case for regarding it as having a right to life, and indeed the stronger its right to life is. Thus we ought to take seriously the suggestion that, insofar as "the human individual develops biologically in a continuous fashion . . . the rights of a human person might develop in the same way." But we must keep in mind that the attributes which are relevant in determining whether or not an entity is enough like a person to be regarded as having some of the same moral rights are no different from those which are relevant to determining whether or not it is fully a person—i.e., are not different from (1)–(5)—and that being genetically human, or having recognizably human facial and other physical features, or detectable brain activity, or the capacity to survive outside the uterus, are simply not among these relevant attributes.

Thus it is clear that even though a seven- or eight-month fetus has features which make it apt to arouse in us almost the same powerful protective instinct as is commonly aroused by a small infant, nevertheless it is not significantly more personlike than is a very small embryo. It is *somewhat* more personlike; it can apparently feel and respond to pain, and it may even have a rudimentary form of consciousness, insofar as its brain is quite active. Nevertheless, it seems safe to say that it is not fully conscious, in the way that an infant of a few months is, and that it cannot reason, or communicate messages of indefinitely many sorts, does not engage in self-motivated activity, and has no self-awareness. Thus, in the *relevant* respects, a fetus, even a fully developed one, is considerably less personlike than is the average mature mammal, indeed the average fish. And I think that a rational person must conclude that if the right to life of a fetus is to be based upon its resemblance to a person, then it cannot be said to have any more right to life than, let us say, a newborn guppy (which also seems to be capable of feeling pain), and that a right of that magnitude could never override a woman's right to obtain an abortion, at any stage of her pregnancy.

There may, of course, be other arguments in favor of placing legal limits upon the stage of pregnancy in which an abortion may be performed. Given the relative safety of the new techniques of artificially inducing labor during the third trimester, the danger to the woman's life or health is no longer such an argument. Neither is the fact that people tend to respond to the thought of abortion in the later stages of pregnancy with emotional repulsion, since mere emotional responses cannot take the place of moral reasoning in determining what ought to be permitted. Nor, finally, is the frequently heard argument that legalizing abortion, especially late in the pregnancy, may erode the level of respect for human life, leading, perhaps to an increase in unjustified euthanasia and other crimes. For this threat, if it is a threat, can be better met by educating people to the kinds of moral distinctions which we are making here than by limiting access to abortion (which limitation may, in its disregard for the rights of women, be just as damaging to the level of respect for human rights).

Thus, since the fact that even a fully developed fetus is not personlike enough to have any significant right to life on the basis of its person-likeness shows that no legal restrictions upon the stage of pregnancy in which an abortion may be performed can be justified on the grounds that we should protect the rights of the older fetus; and since there is no other apparent justification for such restrictions, we may conclude that they are entirely unjustified. Whether or not it would be *indecent* (whatever that means) for a woman in her seventh month to obtain an abortion just to avoid having to postpone a trip to Europe, it would not, in itself, be *immoral,* and therefore it ought to be permitted.

POTENTIAL PERSONHOOD AND THE RIGHT TO LIFE

We have seen that a fetus does not resemble a person in any way which can support the claim that it has even some of the same rights. But what about its *potential,* the fact that if nurtured and allowed to develop naturally it will very probably become a person? Doesn't that alone give it at least some right to life? It is hard to deny that the fact that an entity is a potential person is a strong prima facie reason for not destroying it; but we need not conclude from this that a potential person has a right to life, by virtue of that potential. It may be that our feeling that it is better, other things being equal, not to destroy a potential person is better explained by the fact that potential people are still (felt to be) an invaluable resource, not to be lightly squandered. Surely, if every speck of dust were a potential person, we would be much less apt to conclude that every potential person has a right to become actual.

Still, we do not need to insist that a potential person has no right to life whatever. There may well be something immoral, and not just imprudent, about wantonly destroying potential people, when doing so isn't necessary to protect anyone's rights. But even if a potential person does have some prima facie right to life, such a right could not possibly outweigh the right of a woman to obtain an abortion, since the rights of any actual person invariably outweigh those of any potential person, whenever the two conflict. Since this may not be immediately obvious in the case of a human fetus, let us look at another case.

Suppose that our space explorer falls into the hands of an alien culture, whose scientists decide to create a few hundred thousand or more human beings, by breaking his body into its component cells, and using these to create fully developed human beings, with, of course, his genetic code. We may imagine that each of these newly created men will have all of the original man's abilities, skills, knowledge, and so on, and also have an individual self-concept, in short that each of them will be a bona fide (though hardly unique) person. Imagine that the whole project will take only seconds, and that its chances of success are extremely high, and that our explorer knows all of this, and also knows that these people will be treated fairly. I maintain that in such a situation he would have every right to escape if he could, and thus to deprive all of these potential people of their potential lives; for his right to life outweighs all of theirs together, in spite of the fact that they are all genetically human, all innocent, and all have a very high probability of becoming people very soon, if only he refrains from action.

Indeed, I think he would have a right to escape even if it were not his life which the alien scientists planned to take, but only a year of his freedom, or, indeed, only a day. Nor would he be obligated to stay if he had gotten captured (thus bringing all these people-potentials into existence) because of his own carelessness, or even if he had done so deliberately, knowing the consequences. Regardless of how he got captured, he is not morally obligated to remain in captivity for *any* period of time for the sake of permitting any number of potential people to come into actuality, so great is the margin by which one actual person's right to liberty outweighs whatever rights to life even a hundred thousand potential people have. And it seems reasonable to conclude that the rights of a woman will outweigh by a similar margin whatever right to life a fetus may have by virtue of its potential personhood.

Thus, neither a fetus's resemblance to a person, nor its potential for becoming a person provides any basis whatever for the claim that it has any significant right to life. Consequently, a woman's right to protect her health, happiness, freedom, and even her life, by terminating an unwanted pregnancy will always override whatever right to life it may be appropriate to ascribe to a fetus, even a fully developed one. And thus, in the absence of any overwhelming social need for every possible child, the laws which restrict the right to an abortion, or limit the period of pregnancy during which an abortion may be performed, are a wholly unjustified violation of a woman's most basic moral and constitutional rights.

POSTSCRIPT ON INFANTICIDE

Since the publication of this [essay], many people have written to point out that my argument appears to justify not only abortion, but infanticide as well. For a new-born infant is not significantly more personlike than an advanced fetus, and consequently it would seem that if the destruction of the latter is permissible so too must be that of the former. Inasmuch as most people, regardless of how they feel about the morality of abortion, consider infanticide a form of murder, this might appear to represent a serious flaw in my argument.

Now, if I am right in holding that it is only people who have a full-fledged right to life, and who can be murdered, and if the criteria of personhood are as I have described them, then it obviously follows that killing a new-born infant isn't murder. It does *not* follow, however, that infanticide is permissible, for two reasons. In the first place, it would be wrong, at least in this country and in this period of history, and other things being equal, to kill a new-born infant, because even if its parents do not want it and would not suffer from its destruction, there are other people who would like to have it, and would, in all probability, be deprived of a great deal of pleasure by its destruction. Thus, infanticide is wrong for reasons analogous to those which make it wrong to wantonly destroy natural resources, or great works of art.

Secondly, most people, at least in this country, value infants and would much prefer that they be preserved, even if foster parents are not immediately available. Most of us would rather be taxed to support orphanages than allow unwanted infants to be destroyed. So long as there are people who want an infant preserved, and who are willing and able to provide the means of caring for it, under reasonably humane conditions, it is, *certeris paribus*, wrong to destroy it.

But, it might be replied, if this argument shows that infanticide is wrong, at least at this time and in this country, doesn't it also show that abortion is wrong? After all, many people value fetuses, are disturbed by their destruction, and would much prefer that they be preserved, even at some cost to themselves. Furthermore, as a potential source of pleasure to some foster family, a fetus is just as valuable as an infant. There is, however, a crucial difference between the two cases: so long as the fetus is unborn, its preservation, contrary to the wishes of the pregnant woman, violates her rights to freedom, happiness, and selfdetermination. Her rights override the rights of those who would like the fetus preserved, just as if someone's life or limb is threatened by a wild animal, his right to protect himself by destroying the animal overrides the rights of those who would prefer that the animal not be harmed.

The minute the infant is born, however, its preservation no longer violates any of its mother's rights, even if she wants it destroyed, because she is free to put it up for adoption. Consequently, while the moment of birth does not mark any sharp discontinuity in the degree to which an infant possesses the right to life, it does mark the end of its mother's right to determine its fate. Indeed, if abortion could be performed without killing the fetus, she would never possess the right to have the fetus destroyed, for the same reasons that she has no right to have an infant destroyed.

On the other hand, it follows from my argument that when an unwanted or defective infant is born into a society which cannot afford and/or is not willing to care for it, then its destruction is permissible. This conclusion will, no doubt, strike many people as heartless and immoral; but remember that the very existence of people who feel this way, and who are willing and able to provide care for unwanted infants, is reason enough to conclude that they should be preserved.

Abortion, Intimacy, and the Duty to Gestate

Margaret Olivia Little

1. INTRODUCTION: THE METHOD QUESTION

It is often said that the public debate on abortion, in addition to being politically intractable, is too crude: any reasoning proffered (as opposed to the more usual fist-pounding) fails to capture the subtleties and ambivalences that suffuse the issue. And indeed, anyone who has tussled with the issue in good faith should agree it is a thorny issue. In part, this is because the topic is plain old hard: it touches on an enormous number of complex and recondite subjects, requiring

Abridged from Little, Margaret Olivia. "Abortion, Intimacy, and the Duty to Gestate," *Ethical Theory and Moral Practice* 2:3 (September 1999), 295–312. Copyright © 1999. Reprinted by permission of Copyright Clearance Center on behalf of the publisher.

us to juggle bundles of distinctions that are themselves points of contention in morality and law. But evaluative questions about abortion are not just hard in the way a complex math or public policy question is hard. They are hard because *even* careful and clear-headed application of the usual tools seems to yield analyses that feel orthogonal to the subject. There is something about abortion that is not captured however carefully we parse counterexamples or track down the implications of traditional classifications.

I want to argue that this is no accident. The topics that abortion touches on, including motherhood and intimacy, and again vulnerability and responsibility, are amongst those least explored by mainstream theory. Most profoundly of all, abortion is about a kind of interconnection that our inherited theories are particularly ill-suited to address.

Under mainstream political theory, it turns out, the *very notion of a person* is someone physically separate from others. But abortion deals with a situation marked by a particular, and particularly thorough-going, kind of physical intertwinement. This means that the fetus, the gestating woman, and their relationship do not fit ready-made categories; the question we're being asked to address falls outside of our theory's comfort zone.

Let me put it more bluntly. The central figures in the abortion drama—fetus, gestating woman, and their relationship—are left out of the conceptual paradigm. When we reason about them, we appeal to analogies that are at best awkward, at worst dangerous, but always distorting, for we are trying to analogize to classifications that have at their root the denial of the situation we confront. And again, when entertaining the possibility that the fetus is a person, we have no way of acknowledging the kind of relationship that holds between the pregnant woman and this person: it turns up in the literature as either a relationship between strangers or with the woman dubbed a ready-made mother who is blithely assigned responsibilities of a kind and level unmatched by any other citizen.

A question of method thus shadows all discussions of abortion, whether acknowledged or not. Abortion asks us to face the morality and politics of intertwinement and enmeshment with a conceptual framework that is, to say the least, poorly suited to the task. A tradition that imagines persons as physically separate might be expected not to do well when analyzing situations in which persons *aren't* as it imagines them. And this is, in fact, precisely what we find.

To be pregnant is to be *inhabited*. It is to be *occupied*. It is to be in a state of physical *intimacy* of a particularly thorough-going nature. The fetus intrudes on the body massively; whatever medical risks one faces or avoids, the brute fact remains that the fetus shifts and alters the very physical boundaries of the woman's self. To mandate continuation of gestation is, quite simply, to force continuation of such occupation. To mandate that the woman remain pregnant is to mandate that she remain in a state of physical intertwinement against her consent. The fetus, of course, is innocent of mal-intent, indeed, of any intent; but the complaint here is not with the fetus, it is with the state. The complaint is with the idea of forcing a woman to be in a state of physical intimacy with and occupation by this unwitting entity. For, unwitting or not, it still intertwines and intrudes on her body; and whatever the state's beneficent motives for protecting the interests of the fetus, it matters that the method used for that protection involves forcing others to have another entity live inside them.

If the conversations I've had with people are any indication, the protest will be immediate: this description demeans the meaningfulness and fulfillment of pregnancy. For many women, gestating their babies is experienced not as an intrusion but as wonderful and loving enmeshment; the intimacies involved (if not all the physical symptoms) are cherished. Indeed, not being able to become pregnant or to sustain pregnancy is a deep misery to many women. The picture above, it will be objected, expresses a distorted and, indeed, hostile picture of the relationship involved in gestation.

But this is to miss the point *completely*. I know all too well how wonderful and meaningful pregnancy can be: my own stood as a wonderful contrast to the stories of difficulty above; and the intimacy of the experience was one of the aspects that meant the most to me. But mine was a *willing* gestation—a gestation under consent. Just as sexual intercourse can be a joy under consent and a violation without it, gestation can be a beautiful experience with it and a harmful one without it. To think that the above concern insults the meaningfulness of pregnancy is simply to misunderstand the point. We don't impugn how meaningful it is to have willing sex when we protest against a rape; the fact that sexual intercourse can be wonderful doesn't mean we would think it appropriate for the state to conscript people into serving as prostitutes. Or, as Andrew Koppelman puts it, "Plantation slavery obviously cannot be justified on the grounds that many people find gardening deeply satisfying, but the objection is really no better than that".

2. MORALITY AND INTIMATE DUTIES

The matter of lived urgency to so many women, of course, is not so much whether they should have a legal right to abort, but whether and when it is moral to *exercise* that right. In my experience, mainstream discussions of this question are disturbingly off-base. To be asked to gestate is to be asked to share one's very body—and likely, by the end, one's heart. To gestate is to be engaged in an *intimacy* of deep proportions. The ethical issues salient to questions of intimate actions, though, have been almost universally ignored in traditional philosophy.

A good example can be found in discussions that urge gestation under the rubric of beneficence. It is certainly true that there can be profoundly strong reasons of beneficence to gestate a fetus—reasons that can be acute even before one thinks the fetus is a person. But the literature discussing the point has a curiously abstract quality to it. It isn't just that the many possible countervailing reasons for declining this "opportunity to assist" are summarily dispensed with reminders that the duty is "merely prima facie." It's that the qualitative differences between gestating and giving money to Oxfam, say, or again between gestation and soldierly heroism, are ignored. There are special facets to a decision about charity when the beneficence is a matter of sharing one's body, heart, and soul, not just one's pocketbook or general energies, when the sacrifice contemplated is measured, not in degrees of risk, but in degrees of *intertwinement*. Illumination on these facets will not be found in discussions of volunteering at homeless shelters or falling on grenades in foxholes (if anything, we need examples from, say, sexual ethics or the morality of foster care). What we need in thinking about abortion is a moral approach that does justice to the ethics of intimacy; what we have is a moral approach that rarely uses the word.

Gestation, I've claimed, is an intimacy of the first order—it is even more intimate than donating an organ, for it involves an intertwinement and on-going occupation. This means, on the above approach, that a responsibility to gestate does not arise merely from the fact of being in biological relationship with the fetus: pregnant women do not have an automatic, role-based moral duty to gestate. But this doesn't mean that pregnancy is not a moral moment. For one thing, just as there are mild virtues of openness to relationship, it is a general virtue to be welcoming of germinating human life that comes one's way (a virtue that is perfectly consistent with using birth control—one may try one's best to avoid guests and yet think

it a virtue to welcome them if they show up on your doorstep). More importantly, the biological substrate of being connected to the child in one's belly grounds a special claim of openness to further relationship. What this virtue demands depends on context: in particular, like the virtue of welcome, what the virtue of openness asks of us depends on what *space*—material, psychic, emotional—we have in our lives (a theme deeply embedded in how women talk of the decision of whether or not to abort). One may have good reasons to dig deep and open the door; one may have good reasons to decline if there is little room at the table.

What I now want to suggest is that this framework of relationship ethics helps to make sense of what can otherwise seem to be rather puzzling features of certain intuitions about the moral responsibilities of gestation. More specifically, it can help to capture and to make sense of the fact that intuitions about the moral responsibility to gestate are, at one and the same time, *varied, urgently felt,* and curiously *underdetermined*. For if responsibilities to share one's body turn on the specifics of the lived relationship at hand, the lived relationship accompanying gestation is itself varied, urgently felt, and curiously underdetermined. Let me explain.

Just as women differ in their conceptions of the fetus's status, they differ in how they conceptualize the relationship they are in with that fetus. Some women feel from the start that they are in a special personal relationship with the growing fetus. They conceptualize themselves as a mother, thickly construed, in relationship with an entity that is "their child," whatever the further metaphysical details. The structure of their psyche has already shifted, the fetus's welfare is inextricably bound with their own, and it is unthinkable not to gestate—or it would, at the least, take enormously weighty reasons to refuse. For others, the sense of relationship grows, as most personal relationships do, slowly: the pregnancy begins as mere biological relationship but, as the day-to-day preoccupations of decisions involving the welfare of another (of mediating what she eats, how she sleeps) accumulate, she finds herself in personal relationship. For other women, the relationship is never one of motherhood thickly construed: she is simply in biological relationship with a germinating human organism. For still others, the sense of relationship shifts throughout pregnancy: a conception of motherhood is tried on, then dispatched, or arrives fully formed out of the blue.

For purposes of the woman's *integrity,* her conception is determinative. Her own sense of what type of reasons she would need to end a pregnancy is in large part a function of how she understands the particular relationship she is experiencing in gestating (including its other relatum). For a woman one who conceives of herself as already intertwined as mother, and the fetus as her child, it would take reasons approaching life and death to decline gestating; for one who conceives of herself as in a biological relationship with burgeoning life, lesser reasons will suffice.

From an external or objective perspective, though, it is very difficult to get a foothold on what expectations and claims we might press on behalf of the fetus—to determine, as it were, which woman's conception is correct. And this, crucially, is not just because it's hard to garner evidence, but because there *isn't* much to determine what the relationship is. The problem is not just that one of its members is unconscious. Relationship-based responsibilities can exist towards those who are unconscious: if one's mother lies in a coma, part of what one owes her flows from the relationship. But in this case, we can (if we are sufficiently close to the details) assess what in particular the mother might be owed because there *has been* a full-blooded lived relationship: what particular expectations it would be reasonable to hold on the mother's behalf, as it were, would be grounded in that history—the shared experiences, the texture of the emotional connections, the parties' subjective conceptions, that filled in and defined the relationship. With gestation, though, it is hard to determine what reasonable expectations we might press on behalf of the fetus; and this is because there simply *is* little to the relationship, *as* a relationship, other than the biological substrate and the woman's experience and conception of it.

Now mentioning the woman's conception of the pregnancy and fetus makes many people nervous. It can sound as though we are ceding far too much power to her subjective experience (as do some crude conventionalists, according to whom the woman's view of the fetus determines its metaphysical and normative status). But the claim here is not that the woman's assessment of the pregnancy determines the fetus's status and hence gives her some absolute dominion (as though she could permissibly torture the fetus if only she regards it as an object) any more than parents' sense of their relationship with a newborn determines whether they may smother it. The point here is a specific and contained one. Not everything about one's moral duties to fetuses (or again to newborns) trades on personal relationship. There are all sorts of duties that have nothing to do with those particulars. But some responsibilities, including, I've urged, responsibilities of gestation, do. The only claim about the woman's conception is that it's the only thing we have, other than mere biology, to tell whether there is a personal relationship extant and what its textures are like. We might say that her conception is largely determinative of what the relationship is, and that her moral responsibilities follow its suit; or—better, I think—we may simply say that there is too little going on for there to be a fact of the matter of what responsibilities are objectively owed.

This analysis captures a sort of moral Catch-22 that seems to me accurate to the experience, and the morality, of gestation. I have said that the ethics of relationships encompasses more than the moral expectations that flow from an extant relationship: it includes considerations about when one ought to enter or to be open to entering relationships. I pointed out that, with personal relationships, such claims are not claims to a relationship itself, but claims that the other be open to the relationship, open to taking measures and activities that leave its development possible. But with the fetus, of course, what you would need to do to leave open the possibility of developing a personal relationship is precisely what you have no special responsibility to provide until you have entered the relationship: the use and occupation of your body. By its biological connection, the fetus has a claim to the woman's openness toward a thicker relationship; but until such a thicker relationship exists, it has no strong claim to the intimacy involved in bodily gestation.

One of the most common reasons women seek abortions is that they do not have room in their life just then to be a mother, but they know if they continue the pregnancy they will not be able to give up the child. What has seemed paradoxical (and indeed ethically confused) to many strikes me as a perfectly sensible, and often wise, appreciation of the different moral contours involved with entering, existing in, and exiting relationships. One may decline to enter a relationship that, once extant, changes the contours of your psyche such that you couldn't leave it; and one may have reasons morally adequate to declining a relationship that would not be adequate to refusing the sacrifices legitimately expected of those in it.

ETHICAL DILEMMAS IN THE CARE OF PREGNANT WOMEN

Punishing Drug Addicts Who Have Babies: Women of Color, Equality, and the Right of Privacy

Dorothy E. Roberts

I. INTRODUCTION

A growing number of women across the country have been charged with criminal offenses after giving birth to babies who test positive for drugs. The majority of these women, like Jennifer Johnson, are poor and black. Most are addicted to crack cocaine. The prosecution of drug-addicted mothers is part of an alarming trend toward greater state intervention into the lives of pregnant women under the rationale of protecting the fetuses from harm. This intervention has included compulsory medical treatment, greater restrictions on abortion, and increased supervision of pregnant women's conduct.

Such government intrusion is particularly harsh for poor women of color. They are the least likely to obtain adequate prenatal care, the most vulnerable to government monitoring, and the least able to conform to the white, middle-class standard of motherhood. They are therefore the primary targets of government control.

The prosecution of drug-addicted mothers involves two fundamental tensions. First, punishing a woman for using drugs during pregnancy pits the state's interest in protecting the future health of a child against the mother's interest in autonomy over her reproductive life—interests that until recently had not been thought to be in conflict. Second, such prosecutions represent one of two possible responses to the problem of drug-exposed babies. The government may choose either to help women have healthy pregnancies or to punish women for their prenatal conduct. Although it might seem that the state could pursue both of these avenues at once, the two responses are ultimately irreconcilable. Far from deterring injurious drug use, prosecution of drug-addicted mothers in fact deters pregnant women from using available health and counseling services, because it causes women to fear that, if they seek help, they could be reported to government authorities and charged with a crime. Moreover, prosecution blinds the public to the possibility of nonpunitive solutions and to the inadequacy of the nonpunitive solutions that are currently available.

The debate between those who favor protecting the rights of the fetus and those who favor protecting the rights of the mother has been extensively waged in the literature. This article does not repeat the theoretical arguments for and against state intervention. Rather, it suggests that both sides of the debate have largely overlooked a critical aspect of government prosecution of drug-addicted mothers. Can we determine the legality of the prosecutions simply by weighing the state's abstract interest in the fetus against the mother's abstract interest in autonomy? Can we determine whether the prosecutions are fair simply by deciding the duties a pregnant woman owes to her fetus and then assessing whether the defendant has met them? Can we determine the constitutionality of the government's actions without considering the race of the women being singled out for prosecution?

Before deciding whether the state's interest in preventing harm to the fetus justifies criminal sanctions against the mother, we must first understand the mother's competing perspective and the reasons for the state's choice of a punitive response. This article seeks to illuminate the current debate by examining the experiences of the class of women who are primarily affected—poor black women.

Providing the perspective of poor black women offers two advantages. First, examining legal issues from the viewpoint of those whom they affect most helps to uncover the real reasons for state action and to explain the real harms that it causes. It exposes the way in which the prosecutions deny poor black women a facet of their humanity by punishing their reproductive choices. The government's choice of a punitive response perpetuates the historical devaluation of black women as mothers. Viewing the legal issues from the experiential standpoint of the defendants enhances our understanding of the constitutional dimensions of the state's conduct.

Second, examining the constraints on poor black women's reproductive choices expands our understanding of reproductive freedom in particular and of the right of privacy in general. Much of the literature discussing reproductive freedom has adopted a white

Abridged from Roberts, Dorothy. "Punishing Drug Addicts Who Have Babies: Women of Color, Equality, and the Right of Privacy," *Harvard Law Review*, Vol. 104 (1991), 124–55.

middle-class perspective, which focuses narrowly on abortion rights. The feminist critique of privacy doctrine has also neglected many of the concerns of poor women of color.

My analysis presumes that black women experience various forms of oppression simultaneously, as a complex interaction of race, gender, and class that is more than the sum of its parts. It is impossible to isolate any one of the components of this oppression or to separate the experiences that are attributable to one component from experiences attributable to the others. The prosecution of drug-addicted mothers cannot be explained as simply an issue of gender inequality. Poor black women have been selected for punishment as a result of an inseparable combination of their gender, race, and economic status. Their devaluation as mothers, which underlies the prosecutions, has its roots in the unique experience of slavery and has been perpetuated by complex social forces . . . .

This article advances an account of the constitutionality of prosecutions of drug-addicted mothers which explicitly considers the experiences of poor black women. The constitutional arguments are based on theories both of racial equality and of the right of privacy. I argue that punishing drug addicts who choose to carry their pregnancies to term unconstitutionally burdens the right to autonomy over reproductive decisions. Violation of poor black women's reproductive rights helps to perpetuate a racist hierarchy in our society. The prosecutions thus impose a standard of motherhood that is offensive to principles of both equality and privacy. This article provides insight into the particular and urgent struggle of women of color for reproductive freedom. Further, I intend my constitutional critique of the prosecutions to demonstrate the advantages of a discourse that combines elements of racial equality and privacy theories in advocating the reproductive rights of women of color . . . .

A. The disproportionate impact on poor black women

Poor black women bear the brunt of prosecutors' punitive approach. These women are the primary targets of prosecutors, not because they are more likely to be guilty of fetal abuse, but because they are black and poor. Poor women, who are disproportionately black, are in closer contact with government agencies, and their drug use is therefore more likely to be detected. Black women are also more likely to be reported to government authorities, in part because of the racist attitudes of health care professionals. Finally, their failure to meet society's image of the ideal mother makes their prosecution more acceptable.

To charge drug-addicted mothers with crimes, the state must be able to identify those who use drugs during pregnancy. Because poor women are generally under greater government supervision—through their associations with public hospitals, welfare agencies, and probation officers—their drug use is more likely to be detected and reported. Hospital screening practices result in disproportionate reporting of poor black women. The government's main source of information about prenatal drug use is hospitals' reporting of positive infant toxicologies to child welfare authorities. This testing is implemented almost exclusively by hospitals serving poor minority communities. Private physicians who serve more affluent women perform less of this screening for two reasons: they have a financial stake both in retaining their patients' business and securing referrals from them, and they are socially more like their patients.

Hospitals administer drug tests in a manner that further discriminates against poor black women. One common criterion triggering an infant toxicology screen is the mother's failure to obtain prenatal care, a factor that correlates strongly with race and income. Worse still, many hospitals have no formal screening procedures, relying solely on the suspicions of health care professionals. This discretion allows doctors and hospital staff to perform tests based on their stereotyped assumptions about drug addicts.

Health care professionals are much more likely to report black women's drug use to government authorities than they are similar drug use by their wealthy white patients. A study recently reported in the *New England Journal of Medicine* demonstrated this racial bias in the reporting of maternal drug use. Researchers studied the results of toxicologic tests of pregnant women who received prenatal care in public health clinics and in private obstetrical offices in Pinellas County, Florida. Substance abuse by pregnant women did not correlate substantively with racial or economic categories, nor was there any significant difference between public clinics and private offices. Despite similar rates of substance abuse, however, black women were ten times more likely than whites to be reported to public health authorities for substance abuse during pregnancy. Although several possible explanations can account for this disparate reporting, both public health facilities and private doctors are more inclined to turn in pregnant black women who use drugs than pregnant white women who use drugs.

It is also significant that, out of the universe of material conduct that can injure a fetus, prosecutors have focused on crack use. The selection of crack addiction for punishment can be justified neither by the number of addicts nor the extent of the harm to the fetuses. Excessive alcohol consumption during pregnancy, for example, can cause severe fetal injury, and marijuana use may also adversely affect the unborn. The incidence of both these types of substance abuse is high as well. In addition, prosecutors do not always base their claims on actual harm to the child; rather, they base it on the mere delivery of crack by the mother. Although different forms of substance abuse prevail among pregnant women of various socioeconomic levels and racial and ethnic backgrounds, inner-city black communities have the highest concentrations of crack addicts. Therefore, selecting crack abuse as the primary fetal harm to be punished has a discriminatory impact that cannot be medically justified.

Focusing on black crack addicts rather than on other perpetrators of fetal harms serves two broader social purposes. First, prosecution of these pregnant women serves to degrade women whom society views as undeserving to be mothers and to discourage them from having children. If prosecutors had instead chosen to prosecute affluent women addicted to alcohol or prescription medication, the policy of criminalizing prenatal conduct very likely would have suffered a hasty demise. Society is much more willing to condone the punishment of poor women of color who fail to meet the middle-class ideal of motherhood.

In addition to legitimizing fetal rights enforcement, the prosecution of crack-addicted mothers diverts public attention from social ills such as poverty, racism, and a misguided national health policy—implying instead that shamefully high black infant death rates are caused by the bad acts of individual mothers. Poor black mothers thus become the scapegoats for the black community's ill health. Punishing them assuages any guilt the nation might feel at the plight of an underclass with infant mortality at rates higher than those in some less developed countries. Making criminals of black mothers apparently helps to relieve the nation of the burden of creating a health care system that ensures healthy babies for all its citizens.

For a variety of reasons, then, an informed appraisal of the competing interests involved in the prosecutions must take account of the race of the women affected.

II. PROSECUTING DRUG ADDICTS AS PUNISHMENT FOR HAVING BABIES

It is important to recognize at the outset that the prosecutions are based in part on a woman's pregnancy and not on her illegal drug use alone. Prosecutors charge these defendants not with drug use but with child abuse or drug distribution—crimes that relate to their pregnancy. Moreover, pregnant women receive harsher sentences than do drug-addicted men or women who are not pregnant.

The unlawful nature of drug use must not be allowed to confuse the basis of the crimes at issue. The legal rationale underlying the prosecutions does not depend on the illegality of drug use. Harm to the fetus is the crux of the government's legal theory. Criminal charges have been brought against women for conduct that is legal but is alleged to have harmed the fetus.

When a drug-addicted woman becomes pregnant, she has only one realistic avenue to escape criminal charges—abortion. Thus, she is penalized for choosing to have the baby rather than choosing to have an abortion. In this way, the state's punitive action may coerce women to have abortions rather than risk being charged with a crime. Thus, it is the choice of carrying a pregnancy to term that is being penalized.

There is also good reason to question the government's justification for the prosecutions—the concern for the welfare of potential children. I have already discussed the selectivity of the prosecutions with respect to poor black women. This focus on the conduct of one group of women weakens the state's rationale for the prosecutions.

The history of overwhelming state neglect of black children casts further doubt on its professed concern for the welfare of the fetus. When a society has always closed its eyes to the inadequacy of prenatal care available to poor black women, its current expression of interest in the health of unborn black children must be viewed with suspicion. The most telling evidence of the state's disregard of black children is the high rate of infant death in the black community. In 1987, the mortality rate for black infants in the United States was 17.9 deaths per thousand births—more than twice the figure of 8.6 for white infants. In New York City, while infant mortality rates in upper- and middle-income areas were generally less than 9 per thousand in 1986, the rates exceeded 19 in the poor black communities of the South Bronx and Bedford-Stuyvesant and reached 27.6 in Central Harlem.

The main reason for these high mortality rates is inadequate prenatal care. Most poor black women face financial and other barriers to receiving proper care during pregnancy. In 1986, only half of all pregnant black women in the United States received adequate prenatal care. It appears that in the eighties, black women's access to prenatal care has actually declined. The government has chosen to punish poor black women rather than to provide the means for them to have healthy children.

The cruelty of this punitive response is heightened by the lack of available drug treatment services for pregnant drug addicts. Protecting the welfare of drug addicts' children requires, among other things, adequate facilities for the mother's drug treatment. Yet a drug addict's pregnancy serves as an obstacle to obtaining this treatment. Treatment centers either refuse to treat pregnant women or are effectively closed to them, because the centers are ill-equipped to meet the needs of pregnant addicts. Most hospitals and programs that treat addiction exclude pregnant women because their babies are more likely to be born with health problems requiring expensive care. Program directors also feel that treating pregnant addicts is worth neither the increased cost nor the risk of tort liability.

Moreover, there are several barriers to pregnant women who seek to use centers that will accept them. Drug treatment programs are generally based on male-oriented models that are not geared to the needs of women. The lack of accommodations for children is perhaps the most significant obstacle to treatment. Most outpatient clinics do not provide child care, and many residential treatment programs do not admit children. Furthermore, treatment programs have traditionally failed to provide the comprehensive services that women need, including prenatal and gynecological care, contraceptive counseling, appropriate job training, and counseling for sexual and physical abuse. Predominantly male staffs and clients are often hostile to female clients and employ a confrontational style of therapy that makes many women uncomfortable. Moreover, long waiting lists make treatment useless for women who need help during the limited duration of their pregnancies.

Finally, and perhaps most important, ample evidence reveals that prosecuting addicted mothers may not achieve the government's asserted goal of healthier pregnancies; indeed, such prosecutions will probably lead to the opposite result. Pregnant addicts who seek help from public hospitals and clinics are the ones most often reported to government authorities. The threat of prosecution based on this reporting forces women to remain anonymous and thus has the reverse effect of deterring pregnant drug addicts from seeking treatment. For this reason, the government's decision to punish drug-addicted mothers is irreconcilable with the goal of helping them.

Pregnancy may be a time when women are most motivated to seek treatment for drug addiction and to make positive lifestyle changes. The government should capitalize on this opportunity by encouraging drug-addicted women to seek help and by providing them with comprehensive treatment. Punishing pregnant women who use drugs only exacerbates the causes of addiction—poverty, lack of self-esteem, and hopelessness. Perversely, this makes it more likely that poor black women's children—the asserted beneficiaries of the prosecutions—will suffer from the same hardships....

III. CONCLUSION

Our understanding of the prosecutions of drug-addicted mothers must include the perspective of the women whom they most directly affect. The prosecutions arise in a particular historical and political context that has constrained reproductive choice for poor women of color. The state's decision to punish drug-addicted mothers rather than to help them stems from the poverty and race of the defendants and from society's denial of their full dignity as human beings. Viewing the issue from their vantage point reveals that the prosecutions punish for having babies women whose motherhood has historically been devalued.

A policy that attempts to protect fetuses by denying the humanity of their mothers will inevitably fail. We must question such a policy's true concern for the dignity of the fetus, just as we question the motives of the slave owner who protected the unborn slave child while whipping his pregnant mother. Although the master attempted to separate the mother and fetus for his commercial ends, their fates were inextricably intertwined. The tragedy of crack babies is initially a tragedy of crack-addicted mothers: both are part of a larger tragedy of a community that is suffering a host of indignities, including, significantly, the denial of equal respect for its women's reproductive decisions.

It is only by affirming the personhood and equality of poor women of color that the survival of their future generations will be ensured. The first principle of the government's response to the crisis of drug-exposed babies should be the recognition of their mothers' worth and entitlement to autonomy over their reproductive lives. A commitment to guaranteeing these fundamental rights of poor women of color, rather than punishing them, is the true solution to the problem of unhealthy babies.

The Rights of "Unborn Children" and the Value of Pregnant Women

Howard Minkoff and Lynn M. Paltrow

A quarter century after the "International Year of the Child," we now seem to be in the era of the "Unborn Child." Partly this is because of medical advances: highly refined imaging techniques have made the fetus more visually accessible to parents. In good measure, however, the new era is a product of political shifts. In 2004, President Bush signed into law the Unborn Victims of Violence Act, which makes it a separate federal offense to bring about the death or bodily injury of a "child in utero" while committing certain crimes, and recognizes everything from a zygote to a fetus as an independent "victim" with legal rights distinct from the woman who has been harmed. In 2002, the Department of Health and Human Services adopted new regulations expanding the definition of "child" in the State Children's Health Insurance Program "so that a State may elect to make individuals in the period between conception and birth eligible for coverage." Finally, Senator Brownback and thirty-one cosponsors have proposed the Unborn Child Pain Awareness Act, a scientifically dubious piece of legislation that would require physicians performing the exceedingly rare abortions after twenty weeks to inform pregnant women of "the option of choosing to have anesthesia or other pain-reducing drug or drugs administered directly to the pain-capable unborn child."

The legislative focus on the unborn is aimed at women who choose abortion, but it may also have adverse consequences for women who choose not to have an abortion, and it challenges a central tenet of human rights—namely, that no person can be required to submit to state enforced surgery for the benefit of another.

The historical context of fetal rights legislation should make the most fervent proponents of fetal rights—pregnant women—wary. Often, in the past, expansions of fetal rights have been purchased through the diminution of pregnant women's rights. The fetal "right" to protection from environmental toxins cost pregnant women the right to good jobs: for nearly ten years before the U.S. Supreme Court ruled against such polices in 1991, companies used "fetal protection" policies as a basis for prohibiting fertile women from taking high-paying blue collar jobs that might expose them to lead. The fetal "right" to health

and life has cost women their bodily integrity (women have been forced to undergo cesarean sections or blood transfusion), their liberty (women have been imprisoned for risking harm to a fetus through alcohol or drug use), and in some cases their lives (a court-ordered cesarean section probably accelerated the death in 1987 of Angela Carder, who had a recurrance of bone cancer that had metastasized to her lung). The fetal "right" not to be exposed to pharmaceutical agents has cost pregnant women their right to participate in drug trials that held out their only hope of cure from lethal illnesses. The vehicle for these infringements on pregnant women's rights has been third parties' assertions that they, rather than the mother, have the authority to speak for the fetus in securing these newly defined rights. For example, employers have argued for the right to speak for the fetus in determining when a work environment is inappropriate for the fetus. In mandating cesarean section, the courts have apparently concluded that the judiciary is better positioned to speak for the fetus and that a competent but dying mother's wishes to refuse surgery are no longer worthy of consideration. Most recently, a state's attorney has taken up the cudgel for the fetus by charging a woman with murder for her refusal to consent to a cesarean section.

It is within the context of these attempts to wrest the right to speak for the fetus from mothers that legislation that will expand the rights of the fetus—such as the Unborn Victims of Violence Act—must be considered. The act makes the injury or death of a fetus during commission of a crime a federal offense, the punishment for which "is the same as the punishment . . . for that conduct had that injury or death occurred to the unborn child's mother."[1] As written, the law appears unambiguously to immunize pregnant women against legal jeopardy should any act of theirs result in fetal harm: "Nothing in this section shall be construed to permit the prosecution . . . of any woman with respect to her unborn child." But similar statutory guarantees proffered in the past have not been decisive. In 1970 the California Legislature created the crime of "fetal murder" and specifically excluded the conduct of the pregnant woman herself, but women who suffered stillbirths were nevertheless prosecuted under the statute. The prosecutor explained that "The fetal murder law was never intended to protect pregnant women from assault by third parties which results in death of the fetus. The purpose was to protect the unborn child from murder."[2]

In Missouri cases, a woman who admitted to smoking marijuana once while pregnant and a pregnant woman who tested positive for cocaine were charged with criminal child endangerment on the basis of a statute that declares the rights of the unborn—yet also includes an explicit exception for the pregnant woman herself in language strikingly similar to that used in the Unborn Victims Act ("nothing in this section shall be interpreted as creating a cause of action against a woman for indirectly harming her unborn child by failing to properly care for herself"[3]). The state argued that this language did not preclude prosecution of the pregnant women because "the pregnant woman is not in a different position than a third-party who injures the unborn child" and because her drug use "'directly' endangered the unborn child."[4]

Even if the historical record did not contain these examples of a legislative bait and switch, the principles codified by the new federal statute would be worrisome. When laws create parity between harming pregnant women and harming members "of the species Homo sapiens" of any gestational age (as the Unborn Victims of Violence Act specifies), they establish symmetry between the rights of pregnant women and those of fetuses. In so doing, they suggest a need to balance rights when those rights appear to conflict with each other, and potentially to subordinate the rights of the women to those of the fetus. But to take this stance is not merely to elevate the rights of the unborn to parity with those of born individuals. It is in fact to grant them rights previously denied to born individuals: courts have allowed forced surgery to benefit the unborn, but have precluded forced surgery to benefit born persons. In 1978 Robert McFall sought a court order to force his cousin David Shimp, the only known compatible donor, to submit to a transplant. The court declined, explaining: "For our law to compel the Defendant to submit to an intrusion of his body would change every concept and principle upon which our society is founded. To do so would defeat the sanctity of the individual and would impose a rule which would know no limits."[5]

The Unborn Child Pain Awareness Act is yet another example of a law focused on the fetus that devalues pregnant women and children and sets the stage for further erosion of their human rights. It mandates that prior to elective terminations, physicians deliver a precisely worded, though scientifically questionable, monologue that details the purported pain felt by the fetus and allows for fetal pain management. In so doing, it introduces two damaging concepts. First, it makes women and abortion providers a unique class, excluded from the standard medical model in which counseling is provided by a physician who uses professional judgment to determine what a reasonable individual would need in order to make an informed choice about a procedure. Instead, legislators' judgment is substituted for a physician's determination of the appropriate content of counseling.

Second, it elevates the rights of the midtrimester fetus beyond those of term fetuses, as well as those of its born siblings. Congress has never mandated that mothers be told that there may be fetal pain associated with fetal scalp electrodes or forceps deliveries. Nor have doctors been compelled to speak to the pain that accompanies circumcision or, for that matter, numerous medical conditions for which people are prevented from receiving adequate palliative care. Indeed, there is no federal law scripting counseling about the pain that could accompany any procedure to any child, or indeed any person, after birth. Society has generally relied on professionals to exercise medical judgment in crafting the content of counseling, and on medical societies to assure that counseling evolves as science progresses.

While support for fetal rights laws is now *de rigueur* among politicians, there is apparently no similar mandate to address the social issues that truly threaten pregnant women and victimize their fetuses. Although states increasingly are seeking ways to arrest and punish women who won't undergo recommended surgery or who are unable to find drug rehabilitation programs that properly treat pregnant women and families, no means have been found to guarantee paid maternity leave or to proffer more than quite limited employment protections from discrimination for women when they are pregnant. Many of our nation's tax and social security policies, rather than bolstering women's social standing, help to ensure mothers' economic vulnerability. Hence, the opposition to the Unborn Victims of Violence Act from some activists must be recognized as the logical consequence of years of having mothers beatified in words and vilified in deeds.

These arguments should not be misconstrued as evidence of a "maternal-fetal" conflict. Unless stripped of their rights, pregnant women will continue to be the most powerful advocates for the wellbeing of unborn children. Clashes between the rights of mothers and their fetuses are used as Trojan horses by those who would undermine the protections written into law by *Roe*. Proponents of the right-to-life agenda recognize that when fetal rights expand, the right to abortion will inevitably contract. Furthermore, the responsibilities of physicians in this environment are clear and are grounded in the principles of professionalism—primacy of patient welfare, patient autonomy, and social justice.[6] Those principles require that patients' needs be placed before any "societal pressures" and that "patients' decisions about their care must be paramount."[7] These words are bright line guideposts for clinicians who may at times feel caught in a balancing act. Whether the counterclaim to a pregnant woman's right to autonomy is a societal demand for drug test results obtained in labor, an administrator's request to get a court order to supersede an informed woman's choice, or a colleague's plea to consider fetal interests more forcefully, these principles remind us that no other concern should dilute physicians' commitment to the pregnant woman.[8]

The argument that women should not lose their civil and human rights upon becoming pregnant is predicated neither on the denial of the concept that an obstetrician has two patients, nor on the acceptance of any set position in the insoluble debate as to when life begins. The courts have provided direction for those dealing with the competing interests of two patients, even if one were to concede that the fetus in this regard is vested with rights equal to that of a born person. A physician who had both Robert McFall (potential marrow recipient) and David Shimp (potential donor) as patients may well have shared the judge's belief that Shimp's refusal to donate his marrow, and thereby to condemn McFall to death, was "morally reprehensible." But the clinician would ultimately have to be guided by the judge's decision to vouchsafe David Shimp's sanctity as an individual. Pregnancy does not diminish that sanctity or elevate the rights of the fetus beyond that of Robert McFall or any other born person. Thus, while the obstetrician's commitment to his "other" patient (the fetus) should be unstinting, it should be so only to a limit set by those, to quote Justice Blackman, "who conceive, bear, support, and raise them."[9] To do otherwise would be to recruit the medical community into complicity with those who would erode the rights of women in the misguided belief that one can champion the health of children by devaluing the rights of their mothers.

NOTES

1. 18 U.S.C. s.1841(a)(2)(A).

2. *Jaurigue v. California,* Reporter's Transcript, Hearing August 21, 1992, Case No. 18988, Justice Court Cr. No. 23611, Sup. Court of California for the County of San Benito, Honorable Donald Chapman, Judge, p. 2823.

3. *Missouri v. Smith,* Jackson County Circuit Court, No. CR2000–00964 (June 23, 2000).

4. *Missouri v. Smith,* Jackson County Circuit Court, Case No. CR2000–00964, State's Response to Motion to Dismiss the Indictment (Aug 10, 2002) at 2.

5. *McFall v. Shimp,* 10 Pa. D.&C. 3d 90 (Allegheny Cty. 1978).

6. ABIM Foundation, American Board of Internal Medicine, ACP-ASIM Foundation, American College of Physicians-American Society of Internal Medicine, European Federation of Internal Medicine, "Medical Professionalism in the New Millennium: A Physician Charter," *Annals of Internal Medicine* 136, no. 3 (2002): 243–46.

7. Ibid.

8. ACOG Committee on Ethics, "Maternal Decision Making, Ethics, and the Law," *Obstetrics & Gynecology* 106 (2005): 1127–37.

9. *Int'l Union v. Johnson Controls, Inc.,* 499 U.S. 197–206 (1991).

The Right Not to Know HIV-Test Results

Marleen Temmerman, Jackoniah Ndinya-Achola

SUMMARY

Large numbers of pregnant women in Africa have been invited to participate in studies on HIV infection. Study protocols adhere to guidelines on voluntary participation after pre-test and post-test counselling and informed consent; nevertheless, women may consent because they have been asked to do so without fully understanding the implications of being tested for HIV.

Our studies in Nairobi, Kenya, show that most women tested after giving informed consent did not actively request their results, less than one third informed their partner, and violence against women because of a positive HIV-antibody test was common. It is important to have carefully designed protocols

Temmerman, Marleen, and Ndinya-Achola, Jackoniah. "The Right Not to Know HIV-Test Results," *Lancet,* 345:955 (June 10, 1995), 969–970. Copyright © 1995. Reprinted by permission of Copyright Clearance Center on behalf of Elsevier, Inc.

weighing the benefits against the potential harms for women participating in a study.

Even after having consented to HIV testing, women should have the right not to be told their result.

INTRODUCTION

The number of women of reproductive age in Africa infected with HIV is increasing rapidly, and for almost a decade, studies of perinatal HIV transmission have been undertaken. These studies are based on voluntary participation after informed consent and counselling before and after the test. The aims of counselling women with positive tests are to help them cope with the disease and prepare for the future, to reduce risk behaviour, and to enable women to make informed choices about reproductive health issues. However, little is known about the effectiveness of counselling pregnant women. We report here some effects on women of being told they are HIV positive in perinatal transmission studies in Kenya.

PATIENTS AND METHODS

As part of a study examining the effect of maternal HIV infection on pregnancy outcome in Nairobi, 7893 pregnant women from two ante-natal clinics were tested for HIV infection between January, 1989, and March, 1992, according to a protocol approved by the National AIDS Control Programme in Kenya. The methods and results of these studies have been described.[1-3] All pregnant women were invited to participate in the study after a group information session on HIV and other sexually transmitted diseases (STDs), which was given by a study nurse.

Blood was obtained for HIV-1 and syphilis antibodies after individual counselling and informed consent, as recommended by the World Health Organization.[4,5] Counselling after a positive test was provided by a trained counsellor, and women were encouraged to visit the clinic at any time for further support. The effect of HIV infection on their own lives and the lives of their families was discussed. Emphasis was placed on information about heterosexual transmission, potential impact of future pregnancies on the woman's health, on the risk of perinatal transmission, and the high mortality of infected children. Women were advised to inform their partner of their HIV status, and to bring their partner to the clinic for further counselling. A free supply of condoms was offered as well as a choice of all

family planning methods currently used in Kenya. The overall HIV-1 seroprevalence was 8.5% (672/7893).

RESULTS

During the first two years of the study, 5274 women were tested for HIV and given an appointment one week later to collect their results. Over 90% of women returned to the clinic as instructed and were given their test result. 324 women were HIV positive and invited to participate in a study of HIV infection and pregnancy outcome. More than 25% dropped out immediately before counselling could be provided and never returned to the clinic. Out of 243 women invited to participate and counselled on at least two occasions, only 66 (27.2%) communicated the test result to their partner, of whom 21 showed up with their partner to be tested and counselled. 5 (23.8%) of these partners were HIV seronegative.

11 women were chased away from their house or replaced by another wife, 7 were beaten up, and 1 committed suicide. Most of these women (13 out of 19) had informed their partner as instructed by the research staff.

Alarmed by the violence against women as a consequence of their being identified as HIV positive, we changed our policy on counselling. For the last year of the study we continued providing information on HIV and STDs to pregnant women waiting at the ante-natal clinic, but after the blood test we did not give them an appointment for collection of results. Instead we told the patients they could come in at any time during the morning and ask for their results, or they could collect them at the next pre-natal visit.

Only 109 out of 311 (35%) women with a positive test during the third year of the study ever called for the result or asked at subsequent pre-natal visits. Of the 9 partners who came to the clinic, 2 were seronegative. Violence related to the HIV testing was reported by 6 women. Throughout the study, the results of the blood test were requested at equal rates by HIV-seropositive and HIV-seronegative women, suggesting that this population did not consider themselves at special risk.

DISCUSSION

These findings suggest that most women in this situation consent to testing if asked by someone they trust—in this case a medically trained person who is supposed to know what is best for them. Thus, if an appointment to return to the clinic was given, they kept it because they were told to; not necessarily because they wanted to know the test result. When free to inquire only if they wanted to, the majority of these women (202/311, 65%) did not. This attitude could be due to many reasons, including fear, ignorance, or reluctance to face additional burdens in life.

Our results also show that being enrolled in a study of perinatal HIV transmission is not always harmless for the women involved, who are often blamed for bringing AIDS or other diseases into the family. There is not much we can offer African women once we have told them the bad news: there is no zidovudine or any other medication available—neither for herself nor for preventing transmission to her child. The child is at high risk of being infected and there is no safe alternative to breastfeeding in most settings. Hence, the options for women who know they are HIV positive are either trying to cope with this extra burden silently or sharing the information with their partner at the risk of violence and/or divorce, and hence the breaking up of a family unit. The violence reported is probably an underestimate because we were not able to follow-up women in their communities and homes; our data only reflect spontaneous reports by women or their relatives.

Over 80% of our patients were married women in a stable relationship. Thus, the spread of the HIV epidemic may not be influenced by educating this group about the risks of transmission. Our findings are similar to those of previous studies in Nairobi in which 37% of HIV-infected pregnant women informed their partner,[6] and in Kinshasa where only 2% of women brought their partner for testing and counselling. Also, knowledge of HIV-antibody status combined with an understanding of the risk of HIV transmission and possible adverse effects on health did not have a major impact on women's attitudes or subsequent childbearing.[5–9] This is not surprising given the strong pressure on women to bear children and the partner's lack of participation in HIV counselling.

Perinatal transmission and intervention studies should be carefully designed and women carefully selected after counselling. Even after agreeing to be tested, potential participants should be given the chance not to be informed on the test result and should have the right not to know. Before undertaking a new study, investigators should weigh the benefits of the study for women involved against possible risks such as increased violence and loss of security.

REFERENCES

1. Temmerman M, Chomba EN, Ndinya-Achola J, Plummer FA, Coppens M, Piot P. Maternal HIV-1 infection and pregnancy outcome. Obstet Gynecol 1994; 83: 495–501.
2. Temmerman M, Nyongo A, Bwayo J, Fransen K, Coppens M, Piot P. Risk factors for mother-to-child transmission of HIV-1 infection. Am J Obstet Gynecol (in press).
3. Temmerman M, Mohamed Ali F, Ndinya-Achola JO, Moses S, Plummer FA, Piot P. Rapid spread of both HIV-1 and syphilis among antenatal women in Nairobi, Kenya. AIDS 1992; 6:1181–85.
4. World Health Organization: Guidelines for counselling about HIV infection and disease. WHO AIDS Series 8. Geneva: WHO; 1990.
5. World Health Organization: Report on the consultation on partner notification for preventing HIV transmission. Geneva: WHO/GPA; 1989 (WHO/GPA/ESR/8.92).
6. Temmerman M, Moses S, Kiragu D, Fusallah S, Wamola I, Plot P. Impact of post-partum counselling of HIV infected women on their subsequent reproductive behaviour. AIDS Care 1990; 2; 247–52.
7. Heyward WL, Batter VL, Malulu M, et al. Impact of HIV counselling and testing among child-bearing women in Kinshasa, Zaire. AIDS 1993; 7: 1633–37.
8. Allen S, Serufilira A, Gruber V, et al. Pregnancy and contraception use among Rwandan women after HIV testing and counselling. Am J Public Health 1993; 83: 705–10.
9. Ryder RW, Batter VL, Nsuami M, et al. Fertility rates in 238 HIV-1 seropositive women in Zaire followed for 3 years post-partum. AIDS 1991; 5: 1521–27.

MEDICAL CONTROL OF PREGNANCY AND CHILDBIRTH

Decision-Making about Caesarean Delivery

R.B. Kalish, L.B. McCullough, F.A. Chervenak

There is a fundamental but unrecognised flaw in current thinking about caesarean delivery. Modern obstetrics teaching dictates that a caesarean delivery is either medically indicated or not—ie, elective or on demand. Accepted indications include placenta praevia and cephalopelvic disproportion. We propose a rethinking that challenges the idea that all indications for caesarean delivery can be reliably categorised binomially. A grey area exists that has a larger effect on modern-day obstetrics than most people think.

Kalish, R.B., L.B. McCullough and F.A. Chervenak. "Decision-making about caesarean delivery," *Lancet* 367:9514 (2006), 883–5. Copyright © 2006. Reprinted by permission of Copyright Clearance Center on behalf of Elsevier, Inc.

Discussion of elective caesarean delivery has been revitalised. Published work has examined the right of pregnant women to choose the mode of delivery, whether or not there is an accepted medical indication.[1-3] Scientific evidence about the safety and potential benefits of elective caesarean delivery has been accumulating. Obstetricians worldwide have identified the idea of caesarean delivery on maternal request as a contemporary ethical controversy.[1,4] The US National Institute of Child Health and Human Development is convening an expert consensus meeting on March 27–29, 2006, to discuss this topic.[5]

The issue of caesarean delivery by patient's request is not solely limited to the antepartum period. One of every eight intrapartum caesarean deliveries has some clinical element of maternal or clinical choice.[6] The time has come to fully assess the subtle, but real, factors that alter decision-making about caesarean delivery by both doctor and patient.

Appropriate use of medical interventions should be based on evidence of benefits and risks. Some caesarean deliveries are clearly medically indicated—ie, cases with good evidence that caesarean delivery decreases risks to the mother and fetus compared with vaginal delivery. However, the scarcity of data that such benefits exist means increased uncertainty about the best mode of delivery. For example, for years, breech fetuses were routinely delivered vaginally, because this procedure was deemed safe for the fetus and mother. However, because findings have challenged the notion that vaginal breech delivery is as safe as caesarean delivery,[7] most obstetricians have abandoned this breech delivery. Another example is vaginal birth after previous caesarean delivery. Although this practice became common in the 1990s and was thought to improve obstetric outcomes, evidence has pointed to the fact that there might be real, albeit rare, outcomes of such an approach, and alternatives—ie, repeat caesarean delivery—have become more acceptable.[8]

Two important questions arise. First, when there is real clinical uncertainty about the benefits and risks of caesarean section, how should obstetricians form their judgments? Second, how should they present the choice to the patient? Traditionally, obstetricians have based clinical judgment on beneficence—ie, the ethical obligation to do good for patients by the medically best alternative. However, beneficence-based clinical judgment is not dichotomous; it admits of justified variation when evidence lends support to more than one alternative as reasonable.

How should decision-making proceed when the clinical situation proves to have more than one reasonable management option with an incremental increased risk to either the neonate or mother depending on the path chosen? Who should decide how much risk is worth taking? Should the patient be given any role in the decision-making? Traditionally, the answer to the last question has been no, other than to obtain consent to authorise the chosen clinical management. Obstetricians should engage in evidence-based decision-making with patients to implement an important implication of patients' autonomy: when there is real uncertainty about clinical benefits and risks of reasonable alternatives, competent adult patients should be given the opportunity to make their own decisions about how to manage such uncertainty. Kypros Nicolaides and colleagues[9] recently showed that patients can responsibly make such evidence-based decisions in first-trimester risk assessment. Adopting such a strategy will help to prevent unjustifiable paternalism and provide a more appropriate model of medical decision-making when level of risk is high and certainty is low.[10]

Historically, this important role for patients' autonomy has not been well appreciated and, hence, has been largely absent from obstetric thinking. Even in countries such as Brazil, where caesarean rates in private hospitals approach 80–90%, this high rate is not a reflection of maternal choice or autonomy, and a woman's role in the rise in caesarean rates is overemphasised, with doctor's preference being a more realistic explanation.[11]

In cases with the highest levels of evidence, such as placenta praevia or breech presentation, caesarean delivery can be confidently recommended. However, when data are less certain, for example in the use of mid-forceps or allowing a prolonged second stage of labour, the pregnant woman should be given prominence in the decision-making process. The doctor is obligated to take time to provide her with information and advice, elicit her values, explore her concerns and emotional and social needs, and work with her to make a thoughtful decision. The decision should ultimately come from the patient, who will live with the outcomes of her choice.

The current obstetric notion of indicated versus non-indicated caesarean delivery is generally simple-minded. However, it is dominant in major obstetric textbooks and peer-reviewed work.[4,12–14] None of the major textbooks mentions evidence-based decision-making by patients about caesarean section, even when no clear evidence of benefit of vaginal versus caesarean delivery exists.

Decision about caesarean delivery should rigorously adhere to the requirements of professional integrity. Of special concern is the potential for bias in evaluating evidence that is introduced by the obstetrician's economic self-interest. There is a potent source of bias in the context of self-referral for surgical procedures, which is the standard for caesarean delivery, unlike most other surgical procedures.

We caution against a misreading of patients' autonomy. Doctors' medical expertise and authority should not be marshalled to convince a woman to choose caesarean delivery. Respect for patients' autonomy should not be used as an excuse to undertake more caesarean sections for reasons such as a doctor's convenience. Through an organisational culture of beneficence and patients' autonomy, guided by rigorous peer review, a true and just obstetric ideal can be born.

NOTES

1. Minkoff H, Chervenak FA. Elective primary caesarean delivery. *N Engl J Med* 2003; **348:** 946–50.

2. Hannah ME. Planned elective caesarean section: a reasonable choice for some women? *CMAJ* 2004; **170:** 813–14.

3. Anderson GM. Making sense of rising caesarean section rates. *BMJ* 2004; **329:** 696–97.

4. Schenker JG, Cain JM. FIGO committee report: FIGO Committee for the Ethical Aspects of Human Reproduction and Women's Health. *Int J Gynaecol Obstet* 1999; **64:** 317–22.

5. Department of Health and Human Services, National Institutes of Health. State-of-the-Science Conference: cesarean delivery on maternal request. *Fed Regist* 2006; **71:** 5346–47.

6. Kalish RB, McCullough L, Gupta M, Thaler HT, Chervenak FA. Intrapartum elective cesarean delivery: a previously unrecognized clinical entity. *Obstet Gynecol* 2004; **103:** 1137–41.

7. Hannah ME, Hannah WJ, Hodnett ED, et al. Outcomes at 3 months after planned cesarean vs planned vaginal delivery for breech presentation at term: the international randomized Term Breech Trial. *JAMA* 2002; **287:** 1822–31.

8. Landon MB, Hauth JC, Leveno KJ, et al. Maternal and perinatal outcomes associated with a trial of labor after prior cesarean delivery. *N Engl J Med* 2004; **351:** 2581–89.

9. Nicolaides KH, Chervenak FA, McCullough LB, Avgidou K, Papageorghiou A. Evidence-based obstetric ethics and informed decision-making by pregnant women about invasive diagnosis after first-trimester assessment of risk for trisomy 21. *Am J Obstet Gynecol* 2005; **193:** 322–26.

10. Whitney SN, McGuire AL, McCullough LB. A typology of shared decision making, informed consent, and simple consent. *Ann Intern Med* 2004; **140:** 54–59.

11. Osis MJ, Padua KS, Duarte GA, Souza TR, Faundes A. The opinion of Brazilian women regarding vaginal labor and cesarean section. *Int J Gynaecol Obstet* 2001; **75**(suppl 1): 559–66.

12. Creasy RK, Resnik R. Maternal-fetal medicine, 5th edn. Philadelphia: Saunders, 2004.

13. Cunningham FG, Gant NF, Leveno KJ, Gilstrap LC, Hauth JC, Wenstrom KD. William's obstetrics, 21st edn. New York: McGraw-Hill, 2001.

14. James DK, Steer PJ, Weiner CP, Gonik B. High risk pregnancy: management options, 3rd edn. Philadelphia: Saunders, 2006.

Women's Reproductive Autonomy: Medicalisation and Beyond

Laura Purdy

Nothing would advance women's welfare more than respecting their reproductive autonomy. This statement presupposes autonomy's prerequisites, such as decent health care, education, and alternative ways of supporting themselves. By reproductive autonomy, I mean the power to decide when, if at all, to have children; also, many—but not all—of the choices relevant to reproduction. I focus here on decisions about whether and when to have children. Women should also generally determine how their pregnancy will be carried out and how the birth will happen. New technologies are, however, continually raising new questions, and reproduction both requires and affects others (children, men, society at large); many issues therefore must be examined on a case by case basis. Reproductive autonomy thus has much in common with Robertson's notion of procreative liberty, but is not identical with it.[1] The desirability of women's reproductive autonomy is in part derived from the more general benefits of reproductive

Purdy, Laura. "Women's Reproductive Autonomy: Medicalisation and Beyond," *Journal of Medical Ethics,* 32:5 (May 2006), 287–291. Copyright © 2006. Reprinted by permission of Rightslink on behalf of BMJ Publishing Group Ltd.

autonomy recognised by many writers in the liberal tradition. (See—for example—work by Joel Feinberg, John Robertson, and John Harris.) Such autonomy is particularly important for women, however, because reproduction still takes place in women's bodies, and because they are generally expected to take primary responsibility for child rearing. The need to locate women's autonomy within this broader liberal context has led to a critical rethinking of the concept of autonomy, including a need to focus on options excluded from those among which subjects may choose.[2]

In 2005, the factors that influence women's reproductive autonomy most strongly are poverty, and belief systems that devalue such autonomy. Ensuring that every woman had the prerequisites for practising basic reproductive autonomy would take only a fraction of the world's resources: but that autonomy is a low priority for most societies, or is anathema to their belief systems altogether. So poverty and anti-autonomy belief systems work together to deny women control over their lives. Although lack of access to the prerequisites for exercising autonomy is often a result of anti-autonomy belief systems, it can also be a consequence of racism or limitless greed.

Belief systems that devalue women's reproductive autonomy are widespread. They are more or less explicit, and are based on a variety of religious and philosophical ideas. Most influential in Western societies are probably the biblical sources that depict women's origin in Adam's rib as a mark of their subservient nature. Also hugely influential is the Aristotelian elaboration of that nature as lacking elements of rationality, particularly those elements that legitimise individual purposes (as opposed to group function). There is, however, no shortage of other belief systems alleged to justify the subordination of women's autonomy—where such justification is thought to be needed at all.

This situation is doubly sad because women's reproductive autonomy is not only intrinsically valuable for women, but also instrumentally valuable for the welfare of all humankind. This point was finally recognised internationally at the 1994 population conference in Cairo where it was reasserted that only by providing women with the prerequisites for autonomy, including the prospect of security and fulfilment with few or no children, is there any hope of meeting basic human needs.[3] The conference concluded that investment in health, education, and women's empowerment is necessary to reduce the birthrate. Naturally, population issues are

complicated, and a decent life for all will never be possible without much greater political and economic equality. However, not only are such changes not on the horizon in 2005, but population growth must still slow if human needs are to be met sustainably. Such a slowing of population growth would also free up women's energy to tackle the monumental social and political problems facing humankind.

Moreover, the overall turn to the right in the last twenty years of the twentieth century is seriously eroding previous progress toward women's reproductive autonomy. In the US members of that right wing movement adopted the traditional social views of the religious segment of society they courted. The history is somewhat different in each country, particularly Muslim countries, although each appears to have had similar outcomes with respect to women's reproductive autonomy. Most disturbingly, these various movements to the right of the political spectrum have once again put in question the desirability of both women's autonomy and the more general appreciation of reproductive autonomy with which it is allied. This is not to say that such reproductive autonomy was previously universally accepted, but it was (in the US and some other countries) implicit in the reigning liberal paradigm and the activist judicial elaboration of that paradigm.

This paper does not attempt to update the arguments for women's reproductive autonomy: it takes for granted the moral and practical necessity of such autonomy, and digs deeper into the question of what such a commitment might entail.

UNFINISHED BUSINESS

The liberal paradigm was theoretically committed to women's reproductive autonomy. But to many feminists, that commitment looked shallow and all too readily forgotten when conflicting interests arose. See for example, John Robertson's work.[1] Despite his allegiance to what many see as an extreme position, procreative liberty, and despite a much more woman friendly approach than many writers in reproductive ethics, he compromises women's interests at crucial junctures. Feminists—those who seek justice for women—have most reliably sought to protect and expand their reproductive autonomy, and a large and excellent feminist literature on reproduction, including its politics, and its legal and sociological contexts now exists. For a more detailed discussion of the concept of feminism see my paper in *Health Care Analysis*.[4]

Nevertheless, there is further ground to be covered. Sweeping legal decisions (both legislation and court judgments), and the day to day interactions between patients and healthcare providers have received substantial popular and scholarly scrutiny. However, somewhat less attention has been directed toward the mid-level policy making that, at least in the US and Canada, plays a significant role in shaping women's options. Other critically important dimensions of reproductive autonomy are also in need of further work. For example, for an eye opening treatment of the way race alters the politics of reproductive autonomy see the book by Dorothy Roberts.[5] Also, I believe that even feminists have failed to focus sufficiently on the pronatalism and other cultural factors that can lead women to unwittingly make reproductive decisions that may not be in their own interest. The influence of other critically important elements of the overall context, such as mid-level policies, is especially noticeable given the relatively liberal constitutional frameworks within which abortion decisions are to be made in those countries. In both the US and Canada— for example, policies established by professional societies and individual hospitals greatly affect women's reproductive autonomy. Consider how abortion access, as defined by *Roe* (and subsequent Supreme Court cases), has been sculpted by such policies. *Roe* announced that in the first trimester, a decision to abort was between a woman and her doctor. Although feminists have quite rightly objected to the medical paternalism implicit in this standard, for some women this has meant in practice that abortion is available to them on demand, without further restrictions imposed by states. However, subsequent Supreme Court decisions opened the way for numerous restrictions (such as required counselling, twenty-four hour waiting periods, and special requirements for minors seeking abortions) imposed by particular states. Later in pregnancy, states could regulate abortion with an eye to women's health (in the second trimester) or out of respect for fetal life (in the third trimester). Yet most US hospitals developed policies prohibiting abortions after a given number of weeks, some do not offer abortion at any stage of pregnancy, and many training programmes have deleted abortion from ob/gyn requirements or do not offer such training at all. So abortions are now unavailable in most US counties. Violence against abortion clinics has also reduced the number of practitioners willing to provide abortions. Likewise, in Canada, although abortion has been decriminalised for some fifteen years, professional societies and individual hospitals have stepped into what they saw as a regulatory vacuum to restrict women's access to abortion. Inappropriate medicalisation can be a major factor in subtly altering (or even erasing altogether) women's voices. Such medicalisation has been a cornerstone of feminist critiques of health care. At the core of these critiques is the claim that it reduces "political, personal, and social issues to medical problems, thereby giving scientific experts the power to 'solve' them within the constraints of medical practice".[6] "Medicalisation" has sometimes been construed as requiring that women (and other common targets of medicalisation, such as gay men) refrain from attempting to get medical help for their bodily conditions: but that conclusion begs the question whether recourse to medicine necessarily leads to harmful loss of control.[7-10] Another central question is whether this loss of control is embedded in the concept of medicalisation so that it cannot be used to refer to properly autonomous health care. At least some feminists believe it must be possible to develop health services that are respectful of women's interests and choices.[7] The difficulty is in noticing where women's say is insidiously appropriated (whether intentionally or unintentionally), and then showing why (and how) to reframe issues so as to restore their autonomy.

Unfortunately, women's loss of control is so longstanding and so central to so many cultures that recognising it can be difficult. Almost everyone, for example, now agrees that involuntary sterilisation policies that have targeted disadvantaged girls and women were morally impermissible. But less obviously coercive policies adopted by physicians that limited access to sterilisation for more privileged women were equally unjustifiable. Women seeking sterilisation were subjected to various limits based on their age and number of children. Who were physicians to decide how women should live their lives? Investigating the possible answers begins to lay bare the illicit connections between conceptions of women's nature and health.[i]

No doubt there are dozens or even hundreds of similar examples to which historians could point.

People—even feminists—now tend to take it for granted that (where reproductive autonomy is the professed goal) policies have been cleaned up so as to advance that goal. It is therefore something of a shock to uncover new pockets of medicalisation, such as the pregnancy reduction policy I was asked to evaluate as the bioethicist on the ob/gyn ethics committee at a large teaching hospital in 1998. Despite the hospital's

---

[i]For discussion of this point see my contribution to *Feminism and Bioethics: Beyond Reproduction.*[11]

overall goal of patient autonomy (a goal enshrined in provincial law), women had no choice at all. In fact, the policy incorporated multiple, often inconsistent strands, like a twisted rock face where a region's geological history is displayed.

The 1989 policy (reaffirmed by another committee in 1993) stated that although triplets could be reduced to twins, twins would not be reduced to singletons. Interestingly, the policy was introduced about the time that, in the wake of the state's inability to convict Henry Morgenthaler for performing abortions, abortion became legally unregulated in Canada. Thus abortion was no longer a criminal offence. In the United States, although various legislative and judicial bodies had been eating away at *Roe v Wade* almost since its inception in 1973, women's negative right to first trimester abortions was also legally protected. That is, it was in principle illegal to interfere with a woman's right to choose to abort, although there was no positive duty to provide her with the material resources necessary to carry out her decision. Furthermore, there were in 1989 strong pro-choice movements and highly articulate defences of that position in the philosophical literature and elsewhere.

At issue was a narrow question: is there a morally relevant difference between reducing a pregnancy from triplets to twins, and reducing twins to a singleton? The answer to this question is clear: the motive, method, and consequences of the acts are the same; nor does a twin fetus suddenly sprout rights lacking in a triplet fetus. Given this point, it is contradictory to reject reduction to a singleton if reduction to twins is offered. However, both the existence of the 1989 policy and the reception of my analysis and conclusion revealed how easily decision making in the clinical environment can be detached from its philosophical and political roots. Indeed, the argumentation about the procedure was so disconnected from abortion issues that reduction did not seem to be about abortion at all, yet both hospital policy and the objections to my position were shot through with unstated assumptions about abortion.

THE MEDICAL CONTEXT

Ovulation induction and in vitro fertilisation, fertility treatments that have come to be widely used in developed nations since the 1970s, have greatly increased the incidence of multiple pregnancy. Ovarian stimulation may cause many eggs to ripen simultaneously; if a woman then has intercourse, several may be fertilised.

This is what happened in the recent widely publicised cases of septuplets and octuplets. Attempts to increase the success rate of IVF may also lead physicians to place many embryos in a woman's uterus.[ii]

Women are designed, however, to carry one fetus at a time, and the more fetuses, the more risky the pregnancy, both for the woman herself and for the fetuses. Where there is more than one fetus women are more likely to develop serious health problems; they are also more likely to lose the entire pregnancy. The more fetuses she carries, the greater the risk that some or all of the babies will die, or will suffer from serious disability.

Recent studies comparing the number of fetuses with pregnancy outcomes show that the best outcomes are for singleton pregnancies. According to some indicators, twin pregnancies have somewhat worse outcomes, and triplets still worse ones. Thus it is slightly riskier to be born a twin than a singleton, and still riskier to be born a triplet. The outcomes get rapidly worse with quadruplets and beyond.

Reduction—aborting one or more of the fetuses—was introduced as a way to mitigate the consequences of such higher order multiple pregnancies (so called "supertwins"), reducing risk. However, reduction itself carries about an eight percent chance of losing the whole pregnancy, although it appears that this figure is somewhat unreliable because of small samples and lack of information about the "natural" rate of pregnancy loss in these circumstances.

The main impetus for reduction seems to have been to diminish the risks inherent in pregnancies involving more than four fetuses. Yet the statistics also show some benefit in reducing three to two, and further benefit in reducing two to one. The risk reduction at each step is small, but noticeable. The statistics here vary with the study consulted. Recent studies underline the increased risk, both to women and their offspring. For instance: "maternal mortality is sevenfold greater in multiple pregnancies than in singletons, perinatal mortality rates are fourfold higher for twins and sixfold higher for triplets".[12] Another article states that: "in France, between 1986 and 1998, triplets represented 5.6% of all the IVF babies, but accounted for 30% of the high prematurity (<33 weeks), 11% of SGA, and 15% of the perinatal mortality. For twins, the rates were respectively 37, 52, 55, and 54%."[13] Regardless of the statistics, my central point holds: moral decisions of this sort cannot be deduced from *any* set of statistics.

[ii]For discussion of these issues contact the author to see my unpublished paper, Could there be a right not to be born an octuplet.

THE POLICY

Given this medical context, one might well be curious about the reasoning that led to the current policy. The policy seemed to focus almost entirely on risk: the risks of having triplets were regarded as sufficient to justify the risk of reduction, but not the risks of having twins.

However, this use of statistics hides a raft of important issues. First, as with all risk issues, the data do not tell you what to do. One might argue either way here:

- a) the risk of twins is less than with triplets, so reduction is no longer justifiable on medical grounds, or
- b) if the risk of twins is greater than for a singleton, then reduction is justifiable.

Deciding which direction to go requires further argument.

Secondly, the undiscriminating use of the word "risk" obscures more than it informs here. On the one hand it masks quite different kinds of risk—with quite different burdens—as well as differences in who bear them. Thus subtracting the risk of pregnancy loss from the risk inherent in a given multiple does not make sense, even though it may be treated as a simple piece of mathematics. The moral and emotional issues raised by losing all your fetuses are quite different from those raised by having one or more children with serious disability. Also, taking risks with your own health is different from risking the life or health of your fetuses or children.

On the other hand, and still more importantly, we live in a pluralistic world, and different players will evaluate these outcomes quite differently. Some women—even women who are undergoing fertility treatments—may prefer to risk losing a particular pregnancy rather than to risk the welfare of the fetuses that would be born; others may judge that it is preferable to try to protect the lives of all their fetuses, even if some or all might be disabled. Likewise, some women whose own health is more at risk from a multiple pregnancy might prefer risking the lives of the fetuses rather than their own health, although other women might prefer the reverse. The point here is that it should be up to women—not doctors or hospitals—to choose which possible outcomes they prefer.

It should also be noticed that if this were any other procedure, the case would need no argument. In the US and Canada, paternalism was officially rejected years ago, replaced with a contractual model of the physician/patient relationship requiring physicians to lay out for patients the possible consequences of various alternative treatments, and to let patients decide what to do, based on their own values. In the absence of the kind of statutory requirements common elsewhere in the world, this reduction policy appears to be left over from the 1930s, not 1993. This paradigm of informed consent also increases the burden of proof on any statutory regulation that limits women's reproductive liberty—or any regulation that limits patient choice.

How could such a policy escape notice for so long? The answer seems to be obvious: unacknowledged, but very much present, is the spectre of abortion politics. The premise underlying this particular document is clearly a "moderate" position on abortion.

Why a moderate position? Because the policy accepts abortion in some cases (triplets to twins) but holds that abortion cannot be justified in others where the case is judged less compelling (twins to singleton). Making such distinctions is the hallmark of moderate positions. A conservative position would deny, and a radical position would accept, reduction no matter the number of fetuses. The arguments about risk purport to provide moral justification for the distinction made here between permissible and impermissible reductions.

Because the abortion premise is unstated, however, the argumentation and conclusion appear to be purely medical matters, the right course to be determined by risk computation. If the premise were stated, however, reduction would be set into its proper context—namely, the abortion context. That context would have raised the question of women's autonomy, which was never mentioned in the document.

ADDITIONAL CLINICAL CONSIDERATIONS

The medical literature on reduction, and the policy alluded to, raise three more general issues that might bear on policy decisions of this sort: resource allocation, responsibility, and women's emotional wellbeing.

Resource allocation loomed large in our ob/gyn ethics committee's discussion of hospital policy. In Ontario, public funding of IVF was then available only on a limited basis, and there were long waiting lines. Some members of the committee argued that where a woman had used substantial social resources getting pregnant, it would be unjust to offer reduction for twins because if they lost the pregnancy and returned for further fertility treatments, treatment would be still further delayed for those waiting in line. Since success rates drop as women age, some on the list might thus be deprived of any hope of a genetically related baby.

As an adherent of quite an egalitarian notion of justice, I would agree that, other things being equal, a woman who foolishly endangers a pregnancy achieved under such conditions might reasonably be denied further fertility services. The rub, of course, is the definition of "foolish". Preferring a singleton to twins is not foolish, however, as I will argue shortly.

Moreover, it is interesting to compare this objection to the reduction of twins with policies then in force in other departments of the same hospital. When transplant fails—for example, in some circumstances, the transplant programme does second, third, and sometimes even fourth retransplants, even where doing so means that others on the waiting list will undoubtedly die. In short, once a relationship is established with a given patient, he or she can be given priority even if others suffer as a result. Whether one thinks this transplant policy is justifiable or not—and there are good reasons for doubting that it is—this divergence is psychologically interesting. One might well wonder whether sexist assumptions play any role here, given that IVF patients are all women.

In addition, no one raised the fact that twins are likely to use more medical resources than singletons, and that, with respect to some indicators, the risks for twins are closer to the risks for triplets than to the risks for a singleton. Surely *those* resources are as relevant to the discussion as the resources required for fertility services. Perhaps the compartmentalisation of hospital services hid that point from the members of our committee.

Another objection to providing reduction of twins was that patients know infertility treatment might lead to a twin pregnancy, and so they should accept twins. This is a new twist on the old rejection of abortion based on the view that if women have sex so too should they be prepared for babies. However, society applies the more general principle upon which this objection is based—that it can never be morally appropriate to attempt to prevent undesirable consequences of actions—very inconsistently: other values such as concern for welfare determine where it does not hold. In any case, this position proves too much as it would also justify refusing to reduce any multiple pregnancy.

Last but not least, there was resistance to reduction based on beliefs about women's emotional wellbeing. There is evidence that women find reduction emotionally painful, which is not surprising given that they are in fertility programmes to become pregnant. A study by Berkowitz *et al* shows that more than 65% of such women recalled acute feelings of emotional pain, stress, and fear during the procedure; 70% mourned for the lost fetuses, and their grieving lasted on average 3.2 months. Furthermore, 37% of the patients experienced an anniversary grief reaction, and although persistent depressive symptoms were generally mild, 17.6% reported lingering moderately severe feelings of guilt and sadness, and moderate levels of anger. Despite these mixed reactions, however, 93% said they would undertake the procedure again.[14] These statistics underline the importance of counselling before and after any such procedure: but using them to deny women reduction would be seriously paternalistic. It also ignores the possibility that women who are refused reduction may have their lives significantly altered for the worse in ways they would not have chosen if given the opportunity.

SETTING REDUCTION IN THE ABORTION CONTEXT

Analysing the medical objections to reduction of twins thus shows that they are by no means the merely technical calculations that appear to lead so inexorably to a policy that precludes choice on the part of women.

I have hinted at some of the reasons why women should not be denied reduction of twins. First, the disaggregation of "risk" reveals the necessity for making choices involving legitimate differences in values. Second, the autonomy model of informed consent requires women to have choices about their treatment and precludes healthcare providers from making paternalistic decisions about their welfare. Thirdly, sexist assumptions may lead to unjustifiable inconsistencies in hospital policies about resource allocation that disadvantage infertile women.

Why has decision making about reduction tended to ignore these issues? I believe that the answer is, at least in part, because the medical environment focuses on pregnancy as a medical condition that is relieved by birth. But pregnancy and birth are not just—or even primarily—a medical matter: they are about shaping a life and creating a family.

I suspect that most people would concede that being presented with three new babies at a time would stretch the financial and personal resources of almost any family. The image of two new babies is, however, far less likely to trigger this kind of sympathy or understanding. After all, the average family with children has at least two of them, so the financial and personal burdens of twins might seem less daunting. Perhaps it is a bit much for both to come at once, but that is surely a relatively trivial difference.

Is it so trivial? For women in less than optimal circumstances, it certainly is not. Many families are living on the financial edge, and statistics suggest that the double shift for women is still common as many men are still not sharing domestic chores equally. Even for women in optimal circumstances, having twins rather than a single child (perhaps followed a few years later by another) can vastly change options. Many of the most desirable jobs are still designed for those with undemanding family commitments, and that second baby might deprive a woman of a position she could do brilliantly with just one baby, but not two. It is hardly up to third parties to rule on the importance of such considerations.

CONCLUSION

Reproductive autonomy takes these answers seriously, and they need to be reflected in relevant policy.

So we need to be much more attentive to the way policies such as the one I describe here can stealthily limit women's autonomy, without making the kind of waves more public limits do.

Naturally, this work is necessary, but not sufficient, to ensure women's reproductive autonomy. Removing external limits on decision making simply creates opportunities for genuine autonomy. Far more work needs to be done to help women surmount the

internalised constraints on their choices arising from such cultural factors as pronatalism, geneticism, and sexism. Some informed consent theorists are grappling with those issues, but they must be left for another day.

REFERENCES

1. Robertson J. *Children of choice: freedom and the new reproductive technologies.* Princeton: Princeton University Press, 1994.
2. Mackenzie C, Stoljar N, eds. *Relational autonomy: feminist perspectives on autonomy, agency, and the social self.* Oxford: Oxford University Press, 2000.
3. United Nations International Conference on Population and Development. Cairo, Egypt, Sept 5–13, 1994. www.iisd.ca/cairo.html [accessed 9 Sept 2005].
4. Purdy L. What feminism can do for bioethics. *Health care anal* 2001;**9**:117–32.
5. Roberts D. *Killing the black body: race, reproduction, and the meaning of liberty.* New York: Pantheon, 1997.
6. Sawicki J. Disciplining mothers: feminists and the new reproductive technologies. *Disciplining Foucault: feminism, power, and the body.* New York: Routledge, 1991:67–94.
7. Riessman CK. Women and medicalisation: a new perspective. *Soc Policy* 1983;**14**:3–18.
8. Morgan K. Contested bodies, contested knowledges: women, health, and the politics of medicalisation. In: Sherwin S, eds. *The politics of women's health: exploring agency and autonomy.* Philadelphia: Temple University Press, 1998:83–121.
9. Purdy L. Medicalisation, medical necessity, and feminist medicine. *Bioethics* 2001;**15**:248–61.
10. Garry A. Medicine and medicalisation: a response to Purdy. *Bioethics* 2001;**15**:261–9.
11. Purdy L, A feminist view of health. In: Wolf SM, eds. *Feminism and bioethics: beyond reproduction.* Oxford: Oxford University Press, 1996:163–83.
12. Wimalsundra RC, Trew G, Fisk NM. Reducing the incidence of twins and triplets. *Best Prac Res Clin Obstet Gynaecol* 2003;**17**:309–29.
13. ESHRE Task Force on Ethics and Law. Ethical issues related to multiple pregnancies in medically assisted procreation. *Hum Reprod* 2003;**18**:1976–9.
14. Berkowitz RL, Lynch L, Stone J, *et al.* The current status of multifetal pregnancy reduction. *Am J Obstet Gyncol* 1996;**174**:1265–72.

Ethical Issues in the Delivery Room: Resuscitation of Extremely Low Birth Weight Infants

Mary Ann Wilder

Baby Girl L was born at 23 3/7 weeks gestational age (GA) with a birth weight of 480 g. The parents had numerous conferences with the neonatologists and were well informed about the morbidity and mortality

at this GA. The parents requested that everything be done for their baby, and aggressive resuscitation in the delivery room and life support in the neonatal intensive care unit (NICU) were performed. During this

Wilder, Mary Ann. "Ethical Issues in the Delivery Room: Resuscitation of Extremely Low Birth Weight Infants," *Journal of Perinatal & Neonatal Nursing,* 14:2 (2000), 44–57. Copyright © 2000. Reprinted by permission of Lippincott Williams & Wilkins.

time, numerous ethical issues became apparent with the health care team members and other parents in the NICU. The following ethical issues and questions were identified.

- Who determines whether an infant at the limits of viability between 22 and 24 weeks GA should be resuscitated?
- What if parents demand or object to the resuscitation and do they have the right both morally and legally?
- What if the neonatologist, nurses, and other health care team members object?
- What happens when parents, physicians, nurses, and other health care team members disagree about resuscitation?

This article summarizes outcome data of extremely immature infants, defines some problems of decision making in the delivery room, identifies several ethical principles, and describes three approaches to the question of resuscitation in the delivery room. Nurses need to be an integral part of the decision making process. They need to understand the ethical principles involved in choosing the right option and the impact of their personal morals and ethical beliefs on that decision.

BACKGROUND

The neonatal team attending high-risk deliveries is often faced with difficult ethical decisions that must be made at a moment's notice. One of these is whether or not to perform aggressive cardiopulmonary resuscitation on extremely premature infants of 22–24 weeks GA in the delivery room. The persistent conflict among those who challenge the appropriateness of aggressive resuscitation measures for these infants and those who initiate such treatment has been a source of ongoing concern for physicians, nurses, parents, judges, and policy makers. Oftentimes, the delivery room decision to not resuscitate is made rapidly, without full knowledge of the infant's physical condition and future potential and occasionally without appropriate consultation with the family. Infants with a GA of 22–24 weeks are unlikely to survive and are often left with neurodevelopmental problems.[1] According to Muraskas et al. at Loyola University Medical Center, neonatal survival rates from 1990–1994 were 19% at about 22–23 weeks GA and 63% at about 25–25 weeks GA.[2] Some of the neurodevelopmental problems included cerebral palsy, blindness, deafness, severe hypotonia, and developmental delays.[3] Nevertheless, many physicians offer intensive care treatment for such infants and many parents

request it. The main issue is whether to not aggressively resuscitate infants of 22–24 weeks-estimated GA in the delivery room. We also look at some of the ethical considerations involved in these decisions.

According to the current medical definition of viability, the fetus must be sufficiently advanced to survive and develop outside the womb into an infant, even though this survival may require extraordinary medical intervention including life support.[4] During the past three decades, we have seen the use of advanced biomedical knowledge, technology, and pharmacology lowering the limits of viability, increasing survival but with little decrease in morbidity statistics.[4–8] At the lower limits of viability, there are no criteria observable at birth that can tell us which liveborn infant is capable of long-term survival and which one is not. Kraybill[1] defines a zone of uncertain viability between 22 and 25 completed weeks of gestation with a corresponding birth weight between 400 and 600 g. The definition of this zone of uncertain viability is "below which long-term survival is presently impossible and above which, given appropriate intensive care, survival is reasonably possible, although not assured."[4(p207)] According to Jakobi and colleagues, the viability of an infant is not only dependent on his or her biologic potential but also on the biomedical technological capacity and the expertise of the local NICU.[5] Whether to provide and how long to continue intensive treatment of newborn infants in this zone is a difficult moral and ethical issue for parents, physicians, and nurses for whom their care is entrusted.

REPORTED OUTCOMES OF EXTREMELY LOW BIRTH WEIGHT INFANTS

In 1994, Synnes[6] reported a 16% survival rate for 23 weeks gestation. In 1998, Battin reported survival statistics of 0% for below 23 weeks, 5% for 23 + weeks, 45% for 24 weeks, 60% for 25 weeks, and 81% for 26 weeks (Fig. 1).[7] The appropriateness of initiating resuscitation in the United States for infants born below 24 weeks GA is widely debated.[2] Hack[3] published data to suggest that our increasingly aggressive approach to extremely low birth weight (ELBW) infants resulted in both a prolongation of the dying process and an increase in the incidence of moderate to severe handicaps. Campbell[8] suggested that the rise in the number of extremely immature infants who survive with some degree of disability raises the question of whether the vigorous technology of intensive care,

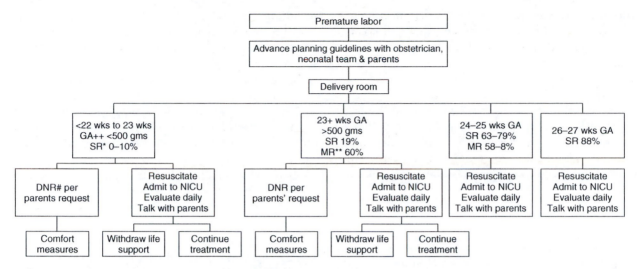

FIGURE 1   Resuscitation decisions for the 22–27 wk GA infant, *SR = survival rate, **MR = morbidity rate, #DNR = do not resusciate, and ++GA = gestational age.

which inevitably inflicts distress in the short term, produces more harm than benefit for the infant in the long term.

RESUSCITATION DECISIONS BASED ON GA

Whether to resuscitate and initiate intensive care for ELBW infants is a momentous question. Both decisions to resuscitate and not to resuscitate may have significant and profound consequences. Failure to resuscitate promptly an infant who is judged incorrectly to be nonviable may increase the risk of permanent disability if the child survives. Conversely, the resuscitation and continued intensive treatment of an infant who is not sufficiently mature to be capable of survival without life support systems are distressing to parents and health care members, wasteful of scarce resources, and may be inhumane to the infant. Yet such decisions must often be made within minutes of birth.[9]

Judgments concerning the developmental status or organ specific disabilities are made within this short time period. These decisions are based on limited knowledge. Limited time and knowledge not withstanding, the actions taken in the delivery room can irrevocably determine the future physical and psychological constitution of the newborn. The child who is transferred to the NICU is not merely a result of the natural lottery of life but has been altered by delivery room interventions. However, we must think about whether we should sustain life just to maintain a biologic process or hope for a meaningful quality of life. According to

Penticuff's research, nurses seem to be more involved in dilemma resolution activities when they perceive themselves to be very concerned about the ethical aspects of specific clinical situations.[10] However, many nurses may be aware of the more common ethical principles but may be unaware of how to implement them.

Ethical principles

Ethics is defined "as the study of rational processes for determining the most morally desirable courses of action in view of conflicting moral choices."[11(p550)] Ethical decisions often have to be made when the right choice is not obvious and when all available options may seem reasonable depending on one's particular point of view. When real choices exist between possible courses of action, there is an ethical dilemma. The individual beliefs and values of not only the patient and family members but also the health care providers involved in caring for the infant may influence the decisions. The ways in which a person views the preservation of life, the avoidance of death, and the relief of pain and suffering will have an effect on the choices they make when faced with an ethical dilemma. Religious beliefs, cultural views of life and death, and opinions about science and technology also influence decision making.[11-13] When we take all the issues and factors into consideration, it is apparent that when decisions must be made about initiation or termination of life-supporting therapy, there is often no clearly right or clearly wrong choice.

The ethical questions and concerns surrounding treatment of infants at the threshold of viability relate to the ethical principles of beneficence, nonmalificence, quality of life, best interests and legal rights, autonomy, justice, and futility. It is often difficult for neonatal and perinatal nurses to implement these principles in the face of advancing biomedical and technical knowledge.

The principle of beneficence dictates that all medical decisions must be made so as to do good for the patient and provide treatment whenever possible.[4] But for some infants, it can be argued that it is difficult for physicians to determine whether their actions will benefit or harm the infant. Mahowald[12] wrote:

> With regard to each infant beneficence entails concern for both immediate and long range needs; these are often inseparable from consideration of the family and social supports upon which the child depends. In certain tragic circumstances, this principle entails recognition of the fact that caring extends beyond curing and affirmation of the right to die as part of an individual's right to life.[12(p82)]

Beneficence. The principle of beneficence includes not only the importance of preserving life, but also the realization that sometimes not to preserve life is in the best interest of and consistent with the wishes of the patient. Medical treatment for the infant is not mandated if it is not medically indicated, it merely prolongs the process of dying, it is futile, it fails to ameliorate all of the patient's life-threatening conditions and is virtually futile and under the circumstances inhumane.[9]

Nonmaleficence. The principle of nonmaleficence requires that health care practitioners must also do "no harm" to their patients.[4] Although some neonatal intensive care has unintended and undesirable consequences, the physician and nurses are obligated to ensure that the good outweighs the harm. But there is not general agreement on which neonatal outcomes should be considered good and which harmful. Certain outcomes are regarded as acceptable by some but are considered unacceptable by others. The use of advanced technology for the intended purpose of extending and saving life is considered to be good; however, when this technology merely prolongs dying or when quality of life is poor, a controversy between beneficence and nonmaleficence occurs.[14] Where should the line be drawn? The nature of nonmaleficence, or doing no harm, when applied to the treatment of preterm neonates, has quality-of-life implications that may introduce conflict into our obligation of autonomy, respect for persons and beneficence.[15]

Quality-of-life. The quality-of-life issue focuses on social worth and is measured by its degree of benefit or burden to others, primarily parents and society.[16] It suggests that life has value and the potential to be meaningful and worthwhile and embodies the moral nature of personhood. If we deny personhood status to the newborn infant on the basis of inability to be rational or self-conscious then, in simple terms, we are eradicating the infant's equality and rights. Although the notion of a right is a very subjective and controversial concept, the right to life can be neither singular nor absolute, particularly if the judged value of preserving life at all costs outweighs the suffering that implementing treatment may cause.[17]

Legal rights. An infant at birth in the United States has full legal rights. However, these legal rights do not mean that all treatment must be provided.[18] The best interest of an infant is generally acknowledged to be the one acceptable criterion by which to arrive at a morally justified treatment decision.[9] For instance, in the Hastings Center Report, "Imperiled Newborns," it is asserted "for the large majority of infants (the best interests) standard is applicable and should be used determining whether life-sustaining treatment should be administered."[19(p14)] A necessary condition for a newborn to have best interest is to have interests. A newborn can have as other individuals do, an interest not to be wronged that is not to be used solely as a means to satisfy someone else's ends; the infant may also have interests in being fed, caressed or kept warm. The newborn is not self-conscious, not future oriented and cannot be said to have an interest in his or her own future existence. Brody also argues for consideration of the interests of family members, particularly when the benefit to the infant is questionable and where life-saving treatment imposes severe burdens on the family.[20]

Infant's best interest. The infant's best interest is legally and ethically primary and should be weighed over the family's well-being or societal concerns. However, there is considerable discussion in the literature about the need to include the family's interests when making life and death decisions regarding severely compromised infants who may be a significant burden.[4,9,20–24] The American Academy of Pediatrics, in its guidelines on forgoing life-sustaining medical treatment, states that "society generally presumes that parents should exercise the right to refuse medical treatment when nonautonomous children cannot do so for themselves."[25(p167)]

Autonomy. The principle of individual autonomy states that the patient has the right to make decisions regarding his/her medical care.[11] The physicians, nurses, and other health care team members must provide all of the information necessary for the patient to make informed decisions. For this to happen, patients must be capable of understanding a certain amount of scientific information and be willing to ask questions about what they do not fully understand. Infants cannot express or exercise the right to autonomy, thus medical decision making becomes the responsibility of surrogates, which may include the parents, legal guardians, medical teams, hospital ethics committees, or the courts.[11] Paris and others have addressed the currently recognized limits of parental autonomy in providing surrogate decisions.[4,24,26]

Occasionally, parental interests may conflict with the best interests of the infant. According to Peabody,[27] this may include the desire for a perfect child, inability or unwillingness to accept a child with neurodevelopmental delay, fear of financial burdens, fear of impact on stability of a family and other individual cultural beliefs and values. This could result in a refusal of lifesaving treatment, which may or may not be in the infant's best interest. Parents can also demand continuation of futile, aggressive care that may be painful and induce suffering for reasons not part of an infant-centered consideration. Obviously there is a potential for conflict of interest. Peabody states that any surrogate decision maker for health care choices must give fully informed consent or refusal under the same rigorous requirements as demanded by the informed consent doctrine for the patient-doctor relationship when the patient is competent.[27] These concepts must include full disclosure of the benefits and risks of all reasonable alternatives. The parents must demonstrate comprehension and understanding of these concepts and their choice must be voluntary. Many have argued that those who bear the burden of a decision ought to have the major role in making it.[27] It seems that the best interests standard for the infant must include full involvement of the parents and a commitment on the part of society to provide the resources that will allow the family to make decisions that are truly in the infant's best interests without creating an undue burden on them.[28] Recently the American Academy of Pediatrics recommended that in regarding the prognosis of the ELBW infant, it is essential to inform prospective parents concerning the expectation for infant outcome.[29] Decisions made before delivery may be altered depending on the condition of the infant at birth, especially the postnatal GA assessment and the infant's response to resuscitation and stabilization. When the decision is made not to resuscitate or to discontinue treatment, the family should be allowed to hold, touch and interact with their infant both before and after death. Physicians and nurses should provide the family with all available data along with an explanation of the risks incurred by the various management options and potential outcome. This information allows the family to make an appropriate decision for their infant. However, we must be aware of the fact that mothers really need to comprehend the medical facts presented to them while receiving treatment for premature labor and other family members may be under a great deal of stress.

Futility. Parental refusal of a recommended and definitely efficacious therapy for a critically ill child does not relieve the physicians and nurses from an ethical duty to advocate for that treatment for the child.[28] This is particularly true if parental refusal of treatment puts the child at significant and imminent risk of harm. These obligations support the duty of the physician and nurse who advocate for the infant's best interest. Sometimes physicians and nurses may seek to override parental views and beliefs through an ethics committee mediation or court intervention. The physician's obligations to the infant may result in the recommendation to withhold or withdraw treatment and allow the infant to die when the prognosis worsens and the iatrogenic burden increases.[28] Sanders et al, found that more than 70% of neonatologists were not willing to resuscitate infants less than 23 weeks GA in the delivery room.[30] They also found that 90% considered nonintervention or compassionate care appropriate for infants born at <23 weeks GA.[27] As GA increased, neonatologists provided more aggressive treatment.

Justice. The principle of justice directs a sense of fairness to all and that all infants should receive equal consideration in matters of medical care. Justice implies that scarce resources should be allocated for the maximum common good and not be consumed by a favorite majority. The issue of how scarce and expensive medical resources are distributed has challenged the medical profession for decades. Some critics believe that too much money is being spent in trying to save infants who are not likely to gain sufficient benefits and may have extremely bad outcomes.[23] Rea states that for a health care provision to be effective, it must have the desired outcome without incurring a higher cost than necessary.[31] We provide maximal intensive care for sick infants but minimal support to families who provide a lifetime of care to a child with a disability. To discriminate against sick neonates for political reasons is inconsistent with the principle of justice.[15]

The mean NICU stay for nonsurvivors is less than 8 days, which suggests that resource allocation for non-survivors is comparatively small.[7] Meadow et al. found that approximately 80% of ELBW infant deaths occurred in the first three days of life and that once the infant survived to day of life four, the likelihood of sur-vival was 81%.[1] Survival no longer depended on birth weight, but on the severity of the illness. Consequently, medical resources allocated to nonsurvivors remained low and independent of birth weight. This formulation lends significance to the reasonableness of physicians in offering neonatal intensive care to ELBW infants with unlikely prospects for survival and of parents and surro-gate decision makers in requesting/assenting to it.[1]

The Child Abuse Amendments of 1984 defined a new category of child neglect called "medical neglect."[4] This is defined as the withholding of medically indicated treatment from disabled infants with life-threatening conditions.[4] Extremely immature infants may or may not fall in this category, although they are at risk for a later disability. In this amendment there are two excep-tions to the requirement that medically indicated treat-ment always be given to ELBW infants. The first exception is when provision of such treatment would merely prolong dying, not be effective in relieving or correcting all of the infant's life-threatening condi-tions, or otherwise be futile in terms of survival of the infant. The second exception is when that provision of treatment would be futile and under the circum-stances, inhumane.[4] Two other provisions of the Child Abuse Amendments are consistent with provisional intensive care for all. These are the requirements that appropriate nutrition, hydration, and medications always be provided, and the suggestion that withholding or withdrawing of treatment is under the responsibility of a multidisciplinary institutional committee.[4] In the event that parents are not acting in the best interest of their infant, or have made a decision in which the infant's life is at stake, the paternalistic power of the state, or "*parents patriae*" may be exercised to override parental choices pertaining to treatment given to their infant. A judge may authorize treatment to proceed despite the lack of parental consent. The best interests of the child represents the legal standard most judges apply in the light of evidence they hear before deciding

to interrupt parental authority.[21] When parents withhold consent to the treatment of a premature infant, a care-giver may perform the following action:

1. Acquiesce to the parental decision not to treat (includ-ing refusal of intubation, use of surfactant, resuscita-tion, etc.), and allow the infant to live or die naturally without the application of medical technology.
2. Go to the court for treatment authorization to set aside parental control and custody of the infant. The court can also charge the parents with child neglect or aban-donment as state and federal law provides.
3. Treat over objection, realizing that by so doing they may have created the elements of a legally noted claim for battery or other grounds for a personal injury action.[21]
4. Seek ethics committee advice and guidance. However, in a study done by Catlin, 91% of the physicians stated that the legal system had no effect on their care of infants.[32]

Treatments that offer no benefit and serve to pro-long the dying process are considered futile and should not be employed.[9] A variety of treatments are available today as a consequence of technological and pharmacological developments. These choices gener-ate dilemmas for health care personnel and parents as to if and when we should implement them. Heroic measures or extraordinary means of support may be overused. The term extraordinary refers to therapy that is futile and if used would not offer a reasonable hope of benefit.[17] The perception of futility is central to the gray zone of viability. Persisting with painful and expensive treatment that is futile can be seen as caus-ing harm.[25] However, parents may view even one chance in a million as worth taking. Physicians and nurses often say that treatment is futile because a good outcome is extremely unlikely. The burden of the ill-ness looms large. Health care team members at the bedside may be acutely aware of the child abuse legis-lation that addresses treatment that is virtually futile and under the circumstances inhumane. Thus it is understandable that parents and health care members might disagree about futility.

Suggested recommendations

In attempting to decide whether to resuscitate ELBW infants in the delivery room, there are three recom-mendations often discussed in the literature. Before delivery, the ideal situation is to have a plan in place with knowledgeable parents and the entire team in agreement. However, until the infant is delivered, we still cannot be 100% sure of the birth weight, GA, and physiological condition. Clinically, many nurses may not be familiar with the various recommendations cited in the various journals. When you are the nurse in the delivery room or the admitting nurse in the NICU, the question often arises as to why we resuscitated this 22–24 week GA infant, but in another infant we didn't. How and why are these decisions made? In Penticuff's discussion of nurse advocacy and infant suffering in the NICU, she stated that nurses had experienced significant emotional distress when they believed that the management therapies being used resulted in infant suffering without proportional benefit.[33] The following recommendations with their ethical considerations may provide an understanding as to why some ELBW infants are resuscitated and some are not.

The first recommendation favors fully aggressive support to all infants, regardless of GA and birth weight, with full support until death or severe devastation of the individual is certain. This gives every infant a chance or right to live. It respects the infant as a person and gives him/her the right to medical care and treatment. It provides for the aggressive use of the most modern technology and research applications, which may be futile, harmful, beneficial, lifesaving or prolong inevitable death. It has total disregard for cost. It may not serve the infant's best interests especially in regard to pain and suffering. It offers little to no parental autonomy in deciding treatment issues. It is life at all costs. If this is added to the belief that it is wrong to withdraw life support, it may result in a stalemate that is agonizing to the parents and psychologically destructive to the NICU team.[4] What should we think about when a 22-week GA infant is born into this NICU approach and the parents have requested no resuscitation? At this point in time the survival for infants of this GA is about 0%, therefore the outcome will be the same with or without treatment. The infant may not survive initial resuscitation or will spend a short time in the NICU. How will these parents feel about the aggressive, painful, futile treatment given to their infant against their wishes?

The second recommendation draws a line at a certain level of risks of mortality and morbidity and treats only infants above this level. This approach seeks to define by GA, birth weight, and possible other criteria such as Apgar score a group of infants for whom the probability of survival is very low as judged from current data. The ability to determine GA and fetal weight accurately is problematic since third trimester ultrasound may be accurate + or − two weeks.[34] Therefore, while expecting a 22-week GA infant, a postnatal assessment may reveal a 20- to 24-week GA infant. Thus, our estimated survival rate can be from 0% to 63%.[4] This

lack of accuracy adds a major element of uncertainty to ante-natal counseling and decision making. In the United States, there are no specific recommendations for the resuscitation of infants at the limit of viability. Arbitrary limits depending on the NICU and obstetrician vary from 23 weeks to 24 weeks GA and a birth weight of 500 g. It is interesting to note that the Japanese Eugenic Protection Act defined the limits of viability to 22 completed weeks of gestation and reported a survival rate of 28% at 22 to 23 weeks.[35] In Sweden, the limit of viability for this approach is 25 weeks GA and 800 g.[27] Infants whose survival probabilities are judged to be below these limits are given supportive care (warmth, feedings, oxygen), but intensive care (mechanical ventilation, life supporting drugs, etc.) is not provided. However, cases exist about infants thought to be nonviable being "put aside" in the delivery room only to be discovered later on to be breathing. During this period of neglect, infants may have suffered hypoxia and acidosis, increasing the risk of damage to the central nervous system and the probability of permanent disability if they survive.[4]

Also, if the infant is not resuscitated, the parental instinct to support the life of a newborn cannot be acted upon, and the parents may carry longstanding misgivings about the failure to try to help the infant survive. This approach is just in providing similar treatment or withholding of treatment to similar infants. It is socially aware in its hesitancy to provide intensive care to infants with a high risk of neurodevelopmental disability and a very uncertain benefit. It is aware of the benefit/burden ratio as viewed from both the infant's and parent's best interests. It is financially responsible in reserving health care resources for a higher cost effectiveness ratio. It also accepts that it will fail to save some lives who would be individually, socially, and economically worthy.[27] Hoerster agrees with this approach at 28 weeks GA and stated that if we do not draw a line there may be a risk of a slippery-slope that might lead to a situation where the lives of infants with survival interest are threatened.[36] However, the survival rate for infants 24 to 25 weeks GA has been reported to be 63%.[4] If we use this approach and draw an arbitrary line of viability based on a certain GA, are we to allow all these potential individuals below this line to have no chance at life?

In the case of MacDonald v. Milleville an infant male was born at 23 3/7 weeks GA 670 g and Apgars of 3 at 1 minute and 5 at 6 minutes. After ten minutes of ambu-bagging on 100% oxygen the heart rate was 40–60 and resuscitative efforts were discontinued. The infant was given to the parents to hold and comfort. Approximately one hour later, nurses heard a faint cry and the heart rate was 130. Parents requested everything be done for their infant even though the physician informed them of the risks and possible morbidity. The infant had a stormy neonatal course with respiratory distress syndrome, bronchopulmonary dysplasia, patent ductus arterious, necrotizing enteropolitis, retinopathy of prematurity, Grade III intraventricular hemorrhage, peripentricular leukomalacia, and numerous other problems.[37] The infant was discharged at 6 months of age. At 8 years of age his developmental age was 5 months and he suffered from severe brain injury. The physician and hospital were sued for medical malpractice. Failure to provide resuscitation was considered negligent behavior and contributed to the anoxic brain damage. Also, the doctor ending the attempts at resuscitation without the parents' authorization violated the principle of autonomy. However in 1989, between 8% and 15% of infants born at 23 weeks GA survived and, of those survivors, only 2% escaped severe abnormalities.[37,38] Data suggested that if an extremely low birth weight infant fails to respond to aggressive resuscitative measures by 10 minutes of age, most neonatologists would stop.[37] After a 2-week trial, the jury found the doctor had no obligation to seek parental authorization to end a failed attempt at resuscitation. Further, the physician's actions with regard to the resuscitation did not violate the standard of care. His professional duty to the infant was to cease ineffective therapies (futile) and shift his approach to the care and comfort of a dying infant.[37]

The third recommendation is called the individualized prognostic strategy or provisional intensive care for all. It uses statistical outcomes as baseline background data. Each infant with a reasonable chance for survival defined as 23 weeks, 500 grams in the US, is aggressively resuscitated in the delivery room unless there is prior clear agreement with the parents to withhold treatment.[4,34] At this point the infant's response to initial treatment is evaluated and initial aggressive neonatal intensive care is instituted if resuscitation is successful. A trial of intensive care for at least 2 days would be encouraged, because during that interval the future course often becomes more predictable.[4] Premature delivery often occurs without much advance warning. Even given adequate time, prenatal discussions are often hampered by imprecise knowledge about the infant's maturity, size and condition. Maternal anxiety, pain and medication may limit comprehension of the data presented to the mother prior to birth.

It is often a matter of practical necessity therefore that final decisions are postponed until after the infant has been born. This provisional intensive care for all provides a means of preserving options. This approach responds to parental instincts to support life and provides a proper role for parents in decision making. With more information available, the physicians, nurses, health care team members, and family can discuss treatment options. This approach allows for parental autonomy with informed consent based on medically, ethically, and legally sound treatment options. It allows for more than one possible outcome and more than one choice. The benefit/burden ratio is initially uncertain but can be assessed with more time. This approach respects the infant's right to life and medical treatment and is in his/her best interests. However, there is always the potential abuse of parental informed consent due to failure to disclose all the risks and benefits and all reasonable alternatives. Often, the medical team biases will come into play and may not be in the best interest of both the family and infant (Table 1).

In the Messenger case, Baby M. was born at 25 weeks GA. Parents were counseled that the mortality rate was 50–70% and the incidence of intraventricular hemorrhage was 20–40%. Parents requested no resuscitation in the delivery room. Parents were informed of a 'wait and see' approach in this NICU and that if, once intubated, the infant took a downward course, life-sustaining therapies would be discontinued. The infant was born and weighed 780 grams, hypotonic, cyanotic, intubated, ventilated, and admitted to the NICU by the physician's assistant. The father questioned the decision to resuscitate and wanted the infant extubated. The neonatologist informed the parents about further evaluation before withdrawing life support. The father later extubated his infant and placed him in his mother's arms where he died. The father was brought to trial and the jury found his action "neither grossly negligent nor a breach of his legal duty to provide proper medical treatment for his son."[21] According to Paris, parents do not have the sole right to refuse medical treatment for their infant. It is the child's best interests that are to be the focus and goal of treatment decisions.[26] In this case the outcome was unknown and some might challenge the accuracy of data given to the parents on survival rates and morbidity rates. However, did the information given to the parents warrant a predelivery decision to withhold resuscitation and aggressive life support? These statistics were more than sufficient evidence of the disproportionate burden that awaited this child to justify a decision to withhold resuscitation.

TABLE 1   Resuscitation Approaches and Their Ethical Issues

No resuscitation	Resuscitate all	Resuscitate and evaluate
Based on criteria	Aggressive support to all	Initial aggressive support
Fails in infant's right to life	Right to life	Right to life
Justice for some	Justice for all	Justice for all
Fails to save some lives	Lifesaving	Lifesaving
In infant's best interest?	In infant's best interest?	In infant's best interest?
Financially responsible	Disregard for costs	Initial minimal cost
Respects parental autonomy	No parental autonomy	Parental autonomy
Time for informed decisions?	Futile treatment?	Time for informed decisions
Provides for improved quality of life based on morbidity	Quality of life issues	Quality of life issues
	Harmful?	Time for ethics committee
	Life at all costs	
	Psychologically destructive to NICU team and parents	

The management in the delivery room of ELBW infants at 22–26 weeks gestation involves difficult choices for parents, physicians, nurse practitioners, nurses, and other members of the health care team. The current state of knowledge permits only a rough assessment of prognosis, and these infants should not be denied the benefit of medical care because of arbitrary viewpoints. It is not reasonable or likely to be successful to offer resuscitation to babies born at 20–22 weeks GA if the parents agree and the infant is born in very poor condition. Oftentimes, the infant may be vigorous at birth and resuscitation is done only to have the infant not survive in the NICU. Infants 23–24 weeks GA or more should be resuscitated initially and further assessed with possible withdrawal of support later on depending on the complications involved. Various statistics are now being reported on the survival of 22–23 week GA infants. This continues to remain a very gray area. However, erring on the side of life is in general an appropriate principle, even though in individual cases some people may see prolongation of a hopeless existence as the greater tragedy. According to Battin, the infant will either survive or not in 3 to 8 days.[7] The burden of decisions of 'what if' would be avoided on all concerned. There would still be a slight prolongation of possible futile treatment, pain, and emotional suffering but at least everyone tried and gave the infant the best possible chance to live. Guilt, anger, and the potential for litigation may be minimized with this approach. Often parents have commented on the death of their premature infant as "at least we all did everything possible."

There is never a complete right or wrong answer in an ethical dilemma, otherwise no dilemma exists. As research and technology advances occur, resuscitation and neonatal intensive care may be more successful in lower GA infants. We must be aware of these future ethical dilemmas and evaluate our own professional judgment based on our personal ethical beliefs.

REFERENCES

1. Meadow W, Reimshisel T, Lantos J. Birthweight specific mortality for ELBW infants vanishes by four days of life: Epidemiology and ethics in the neonatal intensive care unit. *Pediatrics.* 1996;97:636–643.

2. Muraskas T, Marshall P, Tomich P, Myers T, Gianopoulos J, Thomasma D. Neonatal viability in the 1990's: Held hostage by technology. *Cambridge Q Healthcare Ethics.* 1999;8:160–172.

3. Hack M, Fanaroff A. Outcomes of children of extremely low birthweight and gestational age in the 1990's. *Early Human Dev.* 1999;53:193–218.

4. Kraybill E. Ethical issues in the care of extremely low birth weight infants. *Semin Perinatol.* 1998;22(3):207–215.

5. Jakobi P, Weissman A, Paldi E. The extremely low birthweight infant: the twenty-first century dilemma. *Am J Perinatol.* 1993;10:155–159.

6. Synnes A, Ling E, Whitfield M, et al. Perinatal outcomes of a large cohort of extremely low gestational age infants (twenty-three to twenty eight completed weeks of gestation). *J Pediatr.* 1994;125(6):952–960.

7. Battin M, Ling E, Whitfield M, Mackinnon M, Effer S. Has the outcome for extremely low gestational age (ELGA) infants improved following recent advances in neonatal intensive care? *Am J Perinatol.* 1998;15(8):469–477.

8. Campbell A, McHaffie H. Prolonging life and allowing death: infants. *J Med Ethics.* 1995;21:339–344.

9. Stevenson D, Goldworth A. Ethical dilemmas in the delivery room. *Semin Perinatol.* 1998;22(3):198–206.

10. Penticuff JH, Walden M. Influence of practice environment and nurse characteristics on perinatal nurses responses to ethical dilemmas. *Nurs Res.* 2000;49(2):64–72.

11. Aloan C, Hill T. *Respiratory Care of the Newborn.* 2nd ed. Philadelphia: Lippincott; 1997.

12. Mahowald M. Ethical decisions in neonatal intensive care. In: Younger S, ed. *Human Values in Critical Care Medicine.* New York: Praeger; 1986.

13. Catalano J. *Ethical and Legal Aspects of Nursing.* Springhouse, PA: Springhouse; 1991.

14. Avery GB. The morality of drastic intervention. In: Avery GB, Fletcher MA, MacDonald M, eds. *Neonatology: Pathophysiology and Management of the Newborn.* 4th ed. Philadelphia: Lippincott; 1994.

15. Jones V. Professional and ethical issues in neonatal nursing: making choices. *J Neonatal Nurs.* 1997;3(5):23–27.

16. Kenner C, Lott J, Flandermeyer A. *Comprehensive Neonatal Nursing.* Philadelphia: W.B. Saunders; 1998.

17. Harms D, Giordano J. Ethical issues in highrisk infant care. *Iss Comprehen Pediatr Nurs.* 1990;13:1–14.

18. Snyder R. End of life decisions at the beginning of life. *Medicine Law.* 1996;15:283–289.

19. Caplan A, Cohen CB. Imperiled newborns. *Hastings Ctr Rep.* 1987;17:14.

20. Brody H. In the best interests. *Hastings Ctr Rep.* 1988;18:37–38.

21. Pinkerton J, Finnerty J, Lombardo P, et al. Parental rights at the birth of a near-viable infant: Conflicting perspectives. *Am J Obstet Gynecol.* 1997;177:283–290.

22. Pierce S. Neonatal intensive care. Decision making in the face of prognostic uncertainly. *Nurs Clin North Am.* 1998;33(2):287–297.

23. Munson R. *Intervention and Reflection: Basic Issues in Medical Ethics*—5th ed. Belmont, CA: Wadsworth Publishing; 1996.

24. Hammerman C, Kornbluth E, Lavie O, Zadka P, Aboulafia Y, Eidelman A. Decision making in the critically ill neonate: cultural background vs. individual life experiences. *J Med Ethics.* 1997;23:164–169.

25. Avery G. Futility considerations in the neonatal intensive care unit. *Semin Perinatol.* 1998;22(3):216–222.

26. Paris J, Bell A. Guarantee my child will be "normal" or stop all treatment. *J Perinatol.* 1993;13(6):469–472.

27. Peabody J, Martin G. From how small is too small to how much is too much. Ethical issues at the limits of neonatal viability. *Clin Perinatol.* 1996;23(3):473–489.

28. Fleischman A, Chervenak F, McCullough L. The physician's moral obligations to the pregnant woman, the fetus, and the child. *Semin Perinatol.* 1998;22(3):184–188.

29. American Academy of Pediatrics. Perinatal care at the threshold of viability. *Pediatrics.* 1995;96(5):974–976.

30. Sanders M, Donohue P, Oberdorf M, Rosenkrantz T, Allen M. Perceptions of the limit of viability: neonatologists' attitudes toward extremely preterm infants. *J Perinatol.* 1995;15(6):494–502.

31. Rea J. The very preterm baby and health service rationing. *Br J Midwifery.* 1995;3:425–427.

32. Catlin A. Physicians' neonatal resuscitation of extremely low-birth-weight preterm infants. Image: *J Nurs Sch.* 1999;31(3):269–275.

33. Penticuff JH. Infant suffering and nurse advocacy in neonatal intensive care. *Nurs Clin North Am.* 1989;24(4):987–997.

34. Boyle R, Kattwinkel J. Ethical issues surrounding resuscitation. *Clin Perinatol.* 1999;26(3):779–793.

35. Oishi M, Nichida H, Sasaki T. Japanese experience with micropremies weighing less than 600 grams born between 1984 to 1993. *Pediatrics.* 1997;99:1–5.

36. Hoerster N. *Newborns and the Right to Life.* Oxford, England: Blakewell Publishers Ltd; 1997.

37. Paris J, Goldsmith J, Cimperman M. Resuscitation of a micropremie: the case of MacDonald v. Milleville. *J Perinatol.* 1998; 18(4):302–305.

38. Paris J, Schreiber M. Parental discretion in refusal of treatment for newborns. A real but limited right. *Clin Perinatol.* 1996;23(3):573–580.

ASSISTED REPRODUCTIVE TECHNOLOGIES

Payment for Egg Donation and Surrogacy

Bonnie Steinbock

Both payment for egg donation and payment for surrogacy raise ethical issues. I will address only egg donation, for two reasons. First, more has been written about surrogacy than about egg donation. Second, and more important, the two practices raise very different ethical issues. Surrogacy, or contract pregnancy as some prefer to call it, involves giving birth to a child and then waiving one's rights to custody of that child. In a few well-publicized cases, surrogates have changed their minds and attempted to keep the children. This has never, to my knowledge, occurred with egg donation. This is because there is a huge psychological and emotional difference between giving someone else your egg to gestate and deliver a baby, and gestating and delivering a baby yourself and then giving that baby to someone else. Indeed, in most cases, the egg donor does not even know if a child resulted from her donation. While a donor certainly should think about how she will feel about the possibility that there will be a child, or children, genetically linked to her out there in the world, she does not have to contemplate surrendering a child to

Steinbock, Bonnie. "Payment for Egg Donation and Surrogacy," *The Mount Sinai Journal of Medicine,* 71:4 (September 2004), 255–265. Copyright © 2004. Reprinted by permission of John Wiley & Sons, Inc.

whom she has given birth. Additionally, a child born from a surrogate arrangement may feel abandoned by the biological mother, just as an adopted child often does. The feelings of rejection by such children are likely to be compounded by the recognition that the birth mothers conceived them and relinquished them for money. It is implausible that a child conceived through egg donation would feel the same way. Finally, whatever may be wrong with commercial egg donation, it cannot plausibly be characterized as "baby selling."

A TERMINOLOGICAL POINT: "DONORS" VS. "VENDORS"

Some view the term "commercial egg donation" as an oxymoron. Thomas Murray (1) writes, "Despite the repeated reference to 'donors' of both ovum and sperm, paying individuals for their biological products makes them vendors, not donors." He recommends that the term "AID" (artificial insemination by donor) should really be "AIV" (artificial insemination by vendor). In response, some maintain that paying gamete providers does not make them vendors, because they are not being paid for a product, but are being compensated for their time, inconvenience, and risk. I will have more to say about this later. In the meantime, I continue to use the term "donation" even when referring to the commercial enterprise, not because I want to prejudge the question of whether payment is for the product or compensation, still less to prejudge the question of moral acceptability, but simply because it is accepted usage.

LAW AND MORALITY

One important distinction is between the legality and the morality of egg donation. While legality and morality are not entirely separate, and arguments for making something illegal are often moral arguments, the two often raise different issues. In Germany, Norway, Sweden, and Japan, the use of donor eggs is illegal (2). It is unlikely that egg donation could be banned in the United States, because such a ban would probably violate the constitutional right to privacy (3). What about banning payments to egg donors? In Canada, there is proposed legislation to ban the "buying and selling of eggs, sperm and embryos, including their exchange for goods, services or other benefits...." The Minister of Health adds (4), "This prohibition will come into force over a period of time to ease the transition from the current commercial system to an altruistic system."

Legislation in the United States banning payment to egg donors might not withstand constitutional scrutiny. It would depend on whether or not banning payment is viewed as an undue restriction on procreative liberty. The point I am making is that even if there are serious moral objections to commercial egg donation, there could be constitutional barriers to making it illegal.

When the topic is the morality of a controversial practice, an important question is whether it is morally permissible. However, this is not the only question we can ask. Margaret Little characterizes moral permissibility as "the thinnest moral assessment." Writing about abortion, Little (5) says, "...many of our deepest struggles with the morality of abortion concern much more textured questions about its placement on the scales of *decency, respectfulness,* and *responsibility*. It is one thing to decide that an abortion was permissible, quite another to decide that it was *honorable;* one thing to decide that an abortion was impermissible, quite another to decide that it was *monstrous*." So even if paying egg donors is morally permissible, it does not follow that it is desirable, praiseworthy, or decent.

The practice of commercial egg donation has come under severe criticism, but before examining the ethics of paying donors, we need to see if there is something intrinsically wrong about donating one's gametes to others for the purposes of reproduction, even in the absence of any payment.

NONCOMMERCIAL GAMETE DONATION

The Roman Catholic Church opposes gamete (ovum or sperm) donation because of its views on the unity of sexual intercourse and procreation. Sexual intercourse without openness to procreation is wrong, the Church claims (hence its opposition to birth control), but equally so is procreation without sexual intercourse (hence its opposition to most forms of assisted reproduction). Even the "simple case" of *in vitro* fertilization (IVF), where the husband and wife provide the gametes and the resulting embryos are implanted in the wife's uterus, is impermissible, according to Catholic teaching. The wrong is compounded in gamete donation, as the introduction of "a third party" violates the unity of marriage. In addition, according to the Rev. Albert Moraczewski, egg donation is demeaning to women, "A donor woman is not really being treated as a person," he said. "Whether she is paid or acts out of kindness, her egg is being used, so she is not fully treated as a person whose reproductive capacity should be expressed as a result of the love of her husband" (6).

But why is egg donation demeaning? Presumably blood donation is not demeaning, and does not fail to treat the donor as a person. What is the difference? The answer, according to the Vatican, is that egg donation involves a wrongful use of reproductive capacity. But then to characterize egg donation as demeaning is not to give a reason why it is wrong; rather, egg donation is demeaning because it is wrong. To see egg donation as demeaning, one must accept the principle that reproductive capacity should be exercised only through a sexual act in the context of a loving marriage. And that principle is justified by the supposedly indissolvable unity of sex, love and procreation. There is nothing inconsistent or incoherent in this view, but it is unlikely to be persuasive to non-Catholics who accept contraception or assisted reproduction.

A different objection to gamete, specifically sperm, donation comes from Daniel Callahan. AID is "fundamentally wrong," according to Callahan, because a sperm donor is a father, who has all the duties of any other biological father, including rearing responsibilities. Sperm donation, according to Callahan, is as irresponsible as abandoning a woman when she becomes pregnant. He writes (7):

> The only difference between the male who impregnates a woman in the course of sexual liaison and then disappears, and the man who is asked to disappear voluntarily after providing sperm, is that the latter kind of irresponsibility is, so to speak, licensed and legitimated. Indeed, it is treated as a kindly, beneficent action. The effect on the child is of course absolutely identical—an unknown, absent father.

Certainly, it is true that the child born from sperm donation does not know his or her genetic father. But it is not true that these children are fatherless, as is true of most children whose fathers abandon their mothers. They do have fathers—the men who are raising them. Why, one may ask, is it irresponsible to enable an infertile man, who wants very much to parent a child, to become a father? Sperm donors, it may be said, do not evade or abandon their obligations, as do men who abandon women they have impregnated, but rather transfer their rearing rights and duties to others. These others may be men or they may be single women or lesbian couples, who are increasingly using sperm donation. Is it wrong to donate sperm if the resulting child will grow up in a fatherless home? Is this an abandonment of one's responsibility as a father? In my view, this depends on whether the child can be expected to have a reasonably good life. There is evidence that children in single-parent households are at a disadvantage (since

it is usually more stressful to raise a child on one's own), but growing up in a lesbian family does not appear to have a negative impact on quality of parenting or children's psychological development (8). Many lesbian mothers attempt to mitigate the disadvantages of not having a father by making sure that there are other men in their child's life.

David Benatar (9) acknowledges that "gamete donation is not a unilateral abandonment of responsibility," but rather a transference of responsibility. Nevertheless, Benatar thinks that the responsibility of child rearing is one that should not be transferred, that doing so shows a lack of moral seriousness. Certainly, transferring child-rearing responsibilities without much thought is reprehensible; one thinks of Rousseau, who took five illegitimate children he had with his mistress to an orphanage. But is that what gamete donors do? Sperm and ova are not, after all, children. In my opinion, gamete donors do not give others their children to raise. Rather, they enable people who very much want to have children of their own to do so by providing them with genetic material. A woman who does not have eggs can still experience gestation, birth, and lactation, giving her a biological, if not genetic, connection to her child. In addition, if her husband's sperm is used, he will also have a biological connection to the child.

THE NEED FOR EGG DONATION

Egg donation began in the early 1980s; the first pregnancy using this technique was reported in Australia in 1983 (2). Ovum donation is offered to women with three types of reproductive problems. Women in the first group lack functioning ovaries. Those in the second group have no detectable ovarian failure, but they do not achieve pregnancy through IVF. These include women for whom ovarian retrieval is unsuccessful and those who cannot undergo egg retrieval, usually because scarring or endometriosis prevents access to the ovaries. A third group of women use donated eggs for genetic reasons.

When egg donation was first introduced, the eggs came from either close friends or relatives, in a practice known as "known donation," or they came from women who were undergoing IVF themselves. Because the number of eggs retrieved exceeded the number of embryos that could be safely implanted, women undergoing IVF often had extra eggs, which they were often willing to make available for donation. This source greatly diminished when it became possible to freeze embryos (egg freezing is still experimental). Another source of eggs was from patients undergoing tubal ligation (6). However, the demand for donors soon outstripped these sources and programs began to recruit women from the public at large through advertising. Thus, commerical egg donation came into being.

The main reason for the increasing demand for egg donors is that, for some women, using an egg donor significantly improves their chances of becoming pregnant. "An infertile woman using her own eggs for *in vitro* fertilization has about a 15 to 20 percent chance of becoming pregnant, less if her ovaries are scarred by infection or endometriosis or are simply too old to function effectively. With an egg donor, her chances of bearing a child shoot up to 30 or even 40 percent" (10). The older the woman, the greater are her chances of becoming pregnant if she uses donor eggs. According to one article (11), "a 44-year-old woman attempting IVF with her own eggs at Pacific Fertility has a 3.5 percent chance of becoming pregnant. If that same woman uses a donor egg from a younger woman, her chances of giving birth are 50 percent." For some women, therefore, egg donation provides the only realistic option for having a child.

WHAT IS INVOLVED IN EGG DONATION?

The process is very time-consuming. First, the prospective donor must be accepted into a program; this may involve several visits. She will undergo physical and gynecological examinations, blood and urine tests, and a psychological examination, and participate in discussions of the responsibilities involved in becoming a donor. Because eggs cannot be frozen (or "banked"), the actual donation cycle will not occur unless the prospective donor is accepted, is matched with a recipient, and has given her consent.

The following is typical of the medical process undergone by donors. First, the donor may take a prescribed medication for one or more weeks to temporarily stop her ovaries' normal functioning. This makes it easier to control her response to fertility drugs which will be used later in the cycle. She will be given an injection by the physician or instructed in how to inject the medication daily at home. The medications may cause hot flashes, vaginal dryness, fatigue, sleep problems, body aches, mood swings, breast tenderness, headache and visual disturbances.

Next, medications must be injected over a period of about 10 days to stimulate her ovaries to mature a number of eggs (typically 25–30) for retrieval. Frequent early morning transvaginal ultrasound examinations and blood tests (about every 2–3 days) are needed to monitor the donor's response to the drugs, and adjust the dose as needed. While using injectable fertility drugs, the donor may experience mood swings, breast tenderness, enlarged ovaries and bloating. Occasionally, these medications result in ovarian hyperstimulation syndrome, in which the ovaries swell and fluid builds up in the abdominal cavity. If the hyperstimulation is mild, it will recede after the donor's next menstrual period. If the hyperstimulation is moderate, careful monitoring, bed rest, and pain medication may be necessary. Severe hyperstimulation is infrequent, but may cause serious medical complications, such as blood clots, kidney failure, fluid accumulation in the lungs, and shock. This condition can be life-threatening. Severe hyperstimulation occurs in about 1–10% of IVF cycles. It may result in one or both of the donor's ovaries having to be removed.

The mature eggs are removed from the ovaries in a minor surgical procedure called "transvaginal ovarian aspiration." It is usually done in the physician's office. First, the donor will be given painkillers or put under intravenous sedation. Then, the physician inserts a needle through the vagina to aspirate the eggs out of the follicles. According to one description, "The procedure takes 15 to 60 minutes and, except for grogginess and some mild pelvic discomfort, there should be no aftereffects (12)." Some may experience more than mild pelvic discomfort: one egg donor described it (on a website for donors) as "feeling like somebody punched you in the stomach." Many donors find the actual retrieval less unpleasant than the side effects from the drugs.

WHY DO WOMEN WANT TO DONATE?

Given the rigors of egg donation, why would a woman who was not undergoing IVF or tubal ligation be willing to undergo egg donation for strangers? Some donors are curious about their own bodies and fertility. They want to know if their eggs are "good" (10). Some have a personal reason for helping, such as having friends or relatives who have struggled with infertility or have undergone miscarriages. Others are attracted by the idea of giving "the gift of life," as the advertisements for egg donors put it. One donor explained it as follows, on a donor website: "I can't even describe how it felt to know that in some small way I helped this couple achieve a huge dream in their life." But while most egg donors are motivated in part by altruistic considerations, most women would not be egg donors for strangers without financial compensation. Many say that egg donation would be impossible if they were not compensated for lost work time, transportation, daycare costs, and the like. However, most donors think that reimbursement for pecuniary expenses alone is not enough. They think that it is only fair that they should receive reasonable compensation for what they go through in order to provide eggs: the inconvenience, burden, and medical risk they have endured.

HOW MUCH PAYMENT?

Compensation has been increasing rapidly over the years. In the mid-1980s, egg donors were paid only about $250 per cycle. Today, the payment is usually between $1,500 and $3,000—depending on the location of the clinic. In an effort to attract donors, some clinics offer substantially more. In 1998, Brooklyn IVF raised its donor compensation from $2,500 to $5,000 per cycle to keep pace with St. Barnabas Medical Center in nearby Livingston, New Jersey. "It's obvious why we had to do it," says Susan Lobel, Brooklyn IVF's assistant director. "Most New York area IVF programs have followed suit" (13).

Donors with particular attributes, such as enrollment in an Ivy League college, high SAT scores, physical attractiveness, or athletic or musical ability have allegedly been offered far larger sums. "The International Fertility Center in Indianapolis, Indiana, for instance, places ads in the *Daily Princetonian* offering Princeton women as much as $35,000 per cycle. The National Fertility Registry, which, like many egg brokerages, features an online catalogue for couples to browse in, advertises $35,000 to $50,000 for Ivy League eggs" (13). In March 2000, an ad appeared in *The Daily Californian* (the campus newspaper for the University of California, Berkeley), which read, "Special Egg Donor Needed," and listed the following criteria for a "preferred donor": "height approximately 5'6", Caucasian, S.A.T. score around 1250 or high A.C.T., college student or graduate under 30, no genetic medical issues." The compensation was listed as $80,000 "paid to you and/or the charity of your choice." In addition, all related expenses would be paid. Extra compensation was available for someone especially gifted in athletics, science/mathematics or music.

Perhaps the most well-known instance of commercial egg donation is Ron Harris's web site, www.ronsangels .com, which offered models as egg donors, "auctioning their ova via the Internet to would-be parents willing to pay up to $150,000 in hopes of having a beautiful child" (14). A subsequent story suggested that the "egg auction" might just be a publicity stunt to attract

people to an erotic web site, a claim that a spokesman for Mr. Harris denied (15). Some infertility experts maintain that the ads offering large sums of money for special donors are not genuine offers, but rather a "bait and switch" tactic to recruit donors. Donors who respond are told that the ad has been filled, but that there are other recipients (offering substantially less money) seeking donors. *The Daily Californian* ad mentioned above specifically stated, "This ad is being placed for a particular client and is not soliciting eggs for a donor bank." I recently e-mailed the International Infertility Center in Indianapolis, asking them if the fee of $35,000 mentioned in the news report was actually paid to anyone. They responded that the "high-profile client" on whose behalf they had advertised did not find an ovum donor meeting the requirements, and so no ovum donor was compensated $35,000 for a cycle. I have not been able to discover if any "special donors" have received the sums in the ads.

Most people would distinguish between reasonable compensation and offering $30,000 or more to special donors. What explains the negative reaction most people experience when learning of these huge offers? Perhaps we think that people who are so intent on getting superior eggs (or "designer genes") will be incompetent parents. Instead of anticipating having a child to love, it seems that the couple is focusing on the traits their child will have. They are not satisfied with having a healthy child, which is the reason for genetic screening of donors. Nor is their aim simply to have children who resemble them, something that adoptive parents also usually want. These are reasonable requests, whereas seeking donors from Ivy League schools, with high SATs and athletic ability, indicates something else. The placers of these ads want, and are willing to pay huge sums to get, a "superior" child, and this seems inconsistent with an ideal of unconditional parental love and acceptance.

Moreover, anyone who thinks that it is possible to guarantee that a child will be brilliant, athletic, musically talented, or even blond haired and blue eyed, is likely to be disappointed. According to several prominent geneticists writing in *The New Republic* "despite what your high school biology teacher told you, Mendelian rules do not apply even to eye color or hair color" (16). Even genetic diseases widely considered to follow Mendelian rules, like sickle-cell anemia, may be more or less severe, due to the interaction with other genes in the genome. Predicting or determining nondisease-related traits like intelligence, athletic ability, or musical talent is even less likely, as there are probably thousands of genes that play a role. Finally, the interaction of genes and the environment makes it very difficult to know in advance what phenotypic traits an individual will have. This is not to deny that traits like intelligence or athletic ability have a genetic component, but only to say that they cannot be guaranteed by the choice of an egg donor (who, after all, only provides half the genes). We may well worry about the welfare of a child who fails to live up to parental expectations, after the parents have spent all that money.

The welfare of offspring is a legitimate concern, despite philosophical worries over how to conceptualize it (17). If commercial egg donation led to poor parenting or had adverse effects on the parent-child relationship, that would be an important moral objection. Yet such an objection might not justify the conclusion that the buying and selling of eggs is morally impermissible, still less that it should be legally banned. For we do not think that procreation is morally permissible only for ideal parents. Nevertheless, concern about effects on parenting and the parent-child relationship fall under the heading of "thick" moral assessments, and may be legitimate.

On the other hand, it is possible that couples who place the ads understand that they cannot determine their children's traits and that they do not have false expectations. Nevertheless, they might say, they want to give their child an advantage, a better chance at traits likely to help the child in life. It is not that they can only love a tall, brilliant, athletic child, they might say, but rather than they are well aware how advantageous such traits can be. Why, they might ask, if they have the money to spend, should they not use it to give their child the best chance in life? Indeed, some have argued that prospective parents are morally required to have the best child they can (18).

The Human Fertilization and Embryology Authority (HFEA) in the U.K. cited "the physical and psychological well-being of children born from egg donation" as a reason to ban all payments, not just large ones, to egg donors. According to one member of HFEA (19), "Children produced by egg donation could be adversely affected psychologically if they knew that payment had been made as part of their creation." This seems not only speculative, but implausible. Children may be psychologically harmed if they sense that their parents' love is contingent on their having certain traits, but why would a child be psychologically harmed by learning that the woman who provided the egg from which he or she was conceived received payment? It seems to me that this concern stems from an inappropriate analogy with commercial surrogacy. Children might well be

upset to learn that their biological mothers gave them away for money, but it seems implausible that any child would have similar feelings about an egg donor. This being the case, it is hard to see why children would be affected by whether donors were paid or not.

Another moral objection to these ads is that they are elitist and violate a principle of equality. There is something offensive in the idea that the eggs of Princeton women are worth $50,000, while the eggs of women at Brooklyn College are worth only $5,000. (John Arras has jokingly suggested that perhaps *US News & World Report* should include how much their coeds can get for their eggs in their rankings of colleges [personal communication].) Yet it is not clear why we should be offended at the difference in the price put on eggs if we are not offended by differences in employment opportunities or salary.

Some people are disturbed not only by the payment of large sums to egg donors, but by any payment at all. Commercial egg donation is criticized on the grounds that this "commodifies" the human body or "commodifies" reproduction.

COMMODIFICATION

To commodify something is to give it a market price. That in itself is not a bad thing. We could not buy our groceries or clothes or the morning paper if they did not have a market price. If some things should not be commodified, we need a rationale for this. This is not always forthcoming. As the guest editors of a recent special issue on commodification in the *Kennedy Institute of Ethics Journal* say (20), "Unfortunately, a great deal of the talk about 'commodification' has been clumsy and sloppy. The term has been used as a magic bullet, as if saying, 'But that's commodification!' is the same as having made an argument."

The challenge is to distinguish legitimate activities in which the human body or its abilities are used, from those thought to be illegitimate. As Ruth Macklin has put it (21), "Every service in our economy is sold: academics sell their minds; athletes sell their bodies . . . . If a pretty actress can sell her appearance and skill for television, why should a fecund woman be denied the ability to sell her eggs? Why is one more demeaning than the other?"

Those who tend to oppose commodification typically portray those who are skeptical about its moral wrongness as being enamored of the market, of thinking that freedom of choice is the only or the most important moral value. They say, "... there are some categories of human activities that should not be for sale (22)." But this, even if true, is unhelpful. We want to know *what* things and activities should not be for sale and *why?* Michael Walzer gives voting as an example of a market exchange that should be blocked. Citizens may not sell their votes or vote a certain way for a price (23). This is so even if the exchange is fully voluntary and even if it makes both parties better off. The reason why votes may not be sold is that this conflicts with the rationale for having the institution of voting in the first place. Voting is intended to express the will of the people in a democracy. Democracy is subverted if votes can be bought.

What we want, then, is a similarly persuasive rationale for the wrongness of selling human body parts. Suzanne Holland attempts to give one. She writes (24):

> For many of us, our sense of the dignity of humanity is fundamentally disturbed by the suggestion that that which bears the marks of personhood can somehow be equated with property. We do not wish to have certain aspects of that which we associate with our personhood sold off on the market for whatever the market will bear.

Eggs should not be seen as property, according to Holland, because the human body is "inalienable." But what does this mean? To call rights "inalienable" is to say that they cannot be taken away from us, though Joel Feinberg has argued that we can waive them (25). If calling the human body "inalienable" means that others cannot use my body or body parts without my permission, that is undeniable. But why does this imply that I may not sell my gametes? If "inalienable" just means "may not be treated like property," then Holland has not given a reason why eggs are not property, but rather a tautology.

The fact that something is a human body part does not make it obviously wrong to sell it. In the novel *Little Women*, Jo sells her hair to raise money for her father, who is serving as a chaplain in the Union Army. Surely that was not morally wrong of Jo, nor demeaning to her. Indeed, her willingness to part with "her one beauty" is an unselfish and noble gesture. If selling one's hair is morally permissible, but selling one's gametes is not, what is the moral difference?

It might be thought that I am missing an obvious point. Selling one's hair is not wrong because hair is unrelated to sex and reproduction. Selling one's eggs is akin to selling one's body in prostitution, and "we all know" that prostitution is wrong. Actually, prostitutes do not literally sell their bodies, since they do not relinquish control. It is more accurate to say that they rent them

out, or rather that they perform sexual acts in exchange for money. Most of us believe that this is wrong, but this belief may be due in part to sexual puritanism. Perhaps the distaste we feel for prostitution stems (at least in part) from the way prostitutes have typically been regarded in patriarchal societies—as women of no value, undeserving of respect. Imagine a world in which those who provided sexual services were treated with as much respect as psychotherapists, trainers, and masseurs are in our society. It might be that, under such conditions, prostitution would not be as degrading. But even if this argument is invalid, there is a vast personal difference between these two types of "selling," and there is no obvious reason why paying egg donors is incompatible with treating them with respect.

There are two more reasons why selling eggs might be wrong. Providing eggs is both painful and risky. Perhaps offering money to women will lead them to take undue risks, opening up the potential for coercion or exploitation. In addition, some argue that payment for eggs inserts the values of the market into the family. I will consider these objections in turn.

THE POTENTIAL FOR COERCION OR EXPLOITATION

In its report on *Assisted Reproductive Technologies,* the New York State Task Force made the following recommendation (2):

> Gametes and embryos should not be bought and sold, but gamete and embryo donors should be offered compensation for the time and inconvenience associated with donation. Payments to egg donors should not be so high as to become coercive or so low that they provide inadequate reimbursement for time and inconvenience.

Can offering large sums of money for eggs be seen as coercive? That depends on the theory of coercion that one adopts (26). In one theory, to coerce is to make a threat: do this or I will make you worse off. The classic example is the highwayman who says, "Your money or your life." Clearly, potential egg donors are not coerced in this sense, no matter how much money is offered to them. They can turn down the offer and be no worse off than they were.

Perhaps this is too narrow a view of coercion. Perhaps there can be "coercive offers" as well as threats. Consider the following example:

The Lecherous Millionaire: Betty's child will die without expensive surgery, which is not covered by her insurance. Alan, a millionaire, offers to pay for the surgery if Betty will have sex with him.

Alan is not threatening Betty. He will not harm her if she refuses. Yet there is a very real sense in which she has "no choice," and for this reason we might see the offer as coercive. But even if this is true, and there can be "coercive offers," does this apply to egg donation? It might, if the money were offered to terribly poor women whose lives, or the lives of their children, depended on their donating eggs. A woman whose only choice was to give away her eggs or see her child die of starvation might well be seen as the victim of coercion. However, poor women are not usually sought out as egg donors. Typical egg donors are middle-class, often professional, young women. It is simply not true to say that they have no choice but to sell their eggs.

Very large offers of money could be quite tempting to any woman, not just those in desperate need of money. But, as Wertheimer points out, offers are not coercive just because they are tempting. And they are not coercive because they are so good that it would be irrational to refuse. It is not coercive to offer someone a great job at double the salary she is currently earning (27).

However, if offers of large sums of money are not coercive, they may still be criticized as being "undue inducements." Offering "too much" money may be an attempt to manipulate women into becoming donors. The lure of financial gain may lead them to discount the risks to themselves and to make decisions they will later regret. To take advantage of this is a form of exploitation.

It might be argued that we should not attempt to protect adults from irrational assessments or choices they will later regret, because this is paternalistic. However, paternalism involves preventing people from doing what they want on the grounds that this is in their best interest. It is not paternalistic to refrain from taking advantage of someone's susceptibility to temptation.

Some people have tried to meet the charge of commodification by distinguishing between compensating egg donors for their time, risk, and inconvenience, and payment for their eggs. This distinction has been challenged by several commentators, including Ruth Macklin, who writes (21), "If there is something suspect about commodifying human reproductive products, it is similarly suspect to commodify human reproductive services." However, I think there are two reasons to distinguish between payment for time, risk, and inconvenience, and payment for eggs. First, if payment is viewed as compensation for the burdens of egg retrieval, then large payments based on the donor's college, height, or SAT scores would be unjustified. It

is as burdensome for a SUNY-Albany student as it is for a Princeton student to go through the egg retrieval process. Additionally, if payment is compensation for the donor's time, risk, and burden, then donors would be compensated regardless of the number or quality of eggs retrieved, whereas this makes no sense if payment is for the product (eggs). Despite Macklin's rejection of the product/service distinction, she makes precisely this recommendation.

If excessive payments exploit donors, so do payments that are too low. Justice would seem to require that the women who go through the rigors of egg retrieval be fairly compensated. Why are only egg donors expected to act altruistically, when everyone else involved in egg donation receives payment? In light of the sacrifices of time, risk, and burden that egg donors make, it seems only fair that they receive enough money to make the sacrifice worthwhile.

OTHER WORRIES ABOUT EXPLOITATION

Concerns about the exploitation of egg donors are not limited to payment issues. When the New York State Task Force on Life and the Law completed its report on assisted reproductive technologies (2), one of its findings was that there were serious omissions in the process of gaining informed consent of egg donors. Donors did not always know how strenuous donation would be, or how much time it would take. They often had only the vaguest idea about who would pay their expenses, should there be medical complications stemming from donation. In one study, researchers were told by a number of women that all of their follow-up care was provided free of charge, but two women were billed for medical expenses for follow-up care and medical complications even though both were promised that the clinic would cover these costs:

> One woman was promised follow-up care prior to donating, but after the donation, that care was denied. She sought out her own personal physician for a sonogram and had to pay hundreds of dollars out of pocket because she was uninsured at the time. (28)

Another woman fainted at work while taking hormonal injections. She had muscle spasms and started to convulse, and had to stay overnight in the hospital. "The clinic denied that her condition was related to the donation and refused to pay for her hospitalization. She is currently fighting with her own health insurance and worker's compensation over the $3500 bill" (28).

One of the most significant sources of conflict in egg donation is the pressure on health care providers to hyperstimulate the donor to produce the maximum number of oocytes. The more eggs, the better the recipient's chances at implantation, but the greater the danger to the donor of suffering from hyperstimulation syndrome (28). One donor who testified before the advisory committee to the New York State Task Force on Life and the Law revealed that one of her cycles had been stopped, but she had no idea that this was due to excessive stimulation, which had posed health risks to her. She thought that the reason so many eggs had been retrieved was that she was "super-fertile." One of the fertility doctors on the committee said that it was not uncommon for clinics to "flatter" donors in this way, to get them to be repeat donors. Such deceptive treatment of donors is, in my view, a greater source of exploitation, and an area of greater moral concern, than offering payment.

Altruistic egg donation would not necessarily be immune from exploitation. In fact, the true risks and burdens of egg donation might be less likely to be revealed in a voluntary system than in a carefully regulated commercial market, if only because the counseling and screening of donors costs money. Yet altruism can be an appropriate factor. When egg donation imposes little or no extra burden, as in the case of women who are undergoing IVF themselves or women having tubal ligations, there is less reason to compensate women for donating. Altruism in such cases is morally appropriate, as is the case with blood donation, which also involves minimal time and risk. The greater the burdens and risks, the less appropriate is the expectation of altruistic donation.

For some critics, it is not concerns about vulnerable donors that lie at the heart of their objections to commercial egg donation, but rather the effects on the families that are created, and ultimately on society at large.

THREATS TO FAMILIES

Tom Murray writes (1):

> New reproductive technologies are a challenge to our notions of family because they expose what has been at the core of the family to the vicissitudes of the market. At the heart of our often vague concerns about the impact of new reproductive technologies, such as those about the purchase of human eggs, is our sense that they threaten somehow what is valuable about families.

While Murray acknowledges that even noncommercial gamete donation raises "morally relevant difficulties" (presumably those raised by Callahan [7] and Benatar

[9], as well as the issue of the introduction of "a third party" into the marital relationship), he thinks it likely that these difficulties are outweighed by the good of creating new parent-child relationships. It is payment that Murray finds morally objectionable. He writes (1):

> If you believe that markets, the values markets exemplify, and the relationships that typify market interactions, celebrate human freedom, and that such freedom is the preeminent good, then none of this should bother you. If, however, you regard families as a sphere distinct from the marketplace, a sphere whose place in human flourishing requires that it be kept free of destructive incursions by the values of the market, paying gamete providers should trouble you.

I think we would all agree that families should be protected from destructive incursions by the values of the market—but which incursions are destructive? Presumably it is okay to pay the people who care for our children: day care workers, nannies, and babysitters. These transactions, supposedly, do not commercialize families. Also, presumably, there is nothing wrong with paying those who provide fertility treatment: doctors, nurses, receptionists, lawyers, and genetics counselors. So what is it about paying gamete providers that is threatening to families? Murray does not say. One can agree with his view (1) that "thinking of children as property, and of family life as essentially a series of commercial transactions, is a grievous distortion," but it is unclear what this has to do with paying gamete donors. Eggs are not children, and buying eggs (or even embryos) is not buying children. Still less is it clear why reasonable compensation to egg providers should turn family life into a series of commercial transactions.

INCOMPLETE COMMODIFICATION: A REASONABLE COMPROMISE

Is there room for compromise between those who prefer an altruistic system of egg donation and those who think that egg donors should be paid? Suzanne Holland suggests we take an approach she calls "incomplete commodification" (24):

> With respect to gamete donors, an incompletely commodified approach could recognize that donors are contributing to something that can be seen as a social and personal good (remedying infertility), even as they deserve a degree of compensation that constitutes neither a financial burden ([if they are paid] too little) nor a [temptation to undergo] health risk ([if paid] too much). I see no reason not to follow the suggestion of [the] ASRM [American Society for Reproductive Medicine] and cap

egg donor compensation at $5000.... Allowing some compensation, but capping it at $5000, would reduce the competition for eggs and perhaps curb the lure of advertising that is targeted to college students in need of "easy money."

Not everyone agrees that $5,000 is appropriate compensation. Mark V. Sauer, a reproductive endocrinologist at Columbia-Presbyterian Medical Center, was "shocked" by the decision of St. Barnabas to double compensation from the community standard of $2,500 to $5,000 per cycle: "Even if one considers the time spent in traveling to the local office and waiting for an ultrasound exam to be 'work,' donors now will be earning in excess of $300 per hour. I find it hard to believe that anyone thinks this 'reasonable compensation' according to the recommendations of the Ethics Committee of the American Society for Reproductive Medicine" (29). However, Sauer's figure apparently takes into consideration only the number of hours spent traveling to and waiting at the clinic, together with the time required for the procedure. It does not consider compensation for risk or discomfort, or the time that some donors will have to take off from work or classes due to side effects from the drugs they must take. When these factors are considered, reimbursement of $5,000 may not be an "indecent proposal." Perhaps if, like Sauer, doctors are worried that (29) "most importantly, and most unfortunately, these expenses will have to be passed on directly to our patients, who are already spending considerable sums of money to seek this procedure," they might consider reducing their fees.

If compensation were completely banned, few women would agree to be egg donors. Very little egg donation would occur, and this would be unfortunate for those women who cannot have babies any other way. This is part of the justification for paying egg donors; the other part has to do with treating donors fairly. At the same time, legitimate concerns about the psychological welfare of the offspring created, and the potential for exploitation of donors, speaks to the need to limit payments to amounts that are reasonable and fair.

REFERENCES

1. Murray TH. New reproductive technologies and the family, In: Cohen CB, editor. New ways of making babies: the case of egg donation. Bloomington (IN) and Indianapolis (IN): Indiana University Press; 1996. pp. 51–69.

2. Assisted reproductive technologies: analysis and recommendations for public policy. New York. The New York State Task Force on Life and the Law; 1998. p. 237.

3. Bonnicksen AL. Private and public policy alternatives in oocyte donation. In: Cohen CB, editor. New ways of making babies, the case of egg donation. Bloomington (IN) and Indianapolis (IN): Indiana University Press; 1996. pp. 156–174.

4. Executive summary. New reproductive and genetic technologies: setting boundaries, enhancing health. Jun 1996 p. 7; Health Canada (last updated 2002–02–07).

5. Little MO. The morality of abortion. In: Wellman C, Frey R, editors. Companion to applied ethics. Oxford (UK). Blackwell; 2003.

6. Brozan N. Babies from donated eggs; growing use stirs questions. N Y Times 1988 Jan 18, Sect. A.1.

7. Callahan D. Bioethics and fatherhood Utah Law Rev 1992; 3:735–746.

8. Golombok S, Tasker F, Murray C. Children raised in fatherless families from infancy: family relationships and the socioemotional development of children of lesbian and single heterosexual mothers. J Child Psychol Psychiatry 1997; 38(7):783–791.

9. Benatar D. The unbearable lightness of bringing into being. J Applied Phil 1999; 16(2):173–180.

10. Jones M. Donating your eggs. Glamour 1996 Jul p. 169.

11. Belkin L. Pregnant with complications, N Y Times Mag 1997 Oct 26, p. 38.

12. Aronson, D. et al. Resolving infertility: understanding the options and choosing solutions when you want to have a baby. New York: Harper Resource; 1999.

13. Lopez KJ. Egg heads: young women in need of cash are increasingly deciding to sell their bodies. National Review 1998 Sept 1, 50(16) 26.

14. Goldberg C. On web, models auction their eggs to bidders for beautiful children. N Y Times 1999 Oct 23; Sect. A:11.

15. Goldberg C. Egg auction on internet is drawing high scrutiny. N Y Times 1999 Oct 26; Sect. A:26.

16. Collins F, Weiss L, Hudson K. Heredity and humanity. The New Republic 2001 Jun 25, p. 27.

17. Buchanan A, Brock DW, Daniels N, Wikler D. From chance to choice: genetics and justice. Cambridge (UK): Cambridge University Press; 2000.

18. Savulescu J. Procreative beneficence: why we should select the best children. Bioethics 2001; 15(5–6):413–426.

19. Johnson MH. The culture of unpaid and voluntary egg donation should be strengthened. BMJ 1997; 314:1401–1402.

20. Davis DS, Holland S. Introduction. Kennedy Inst Ethics J 2001; 11(3):219.

21. Macklin R. What is wrong with commodification? In: Cohen CB. editor. New ways of making babies: the case of egg donation. Bloomington (IN) and Indianapolis (IN): Indiana University Press; 1996. pp. 106–121.

22. Ketchum SA. Selling babies and selling bodies. Hypatia 1989;4(3):116–127.

23. Walzer M. Spheres of justice. New York: Basic Books; 1983.

24. Holland S. Contested commodities at both ends of life: buying and selling gametes, embryos, and body tissues. Kennedy Inst Ethics J 2001; 11(3):263–284.

25. Feinberg J. Voluntary euthanasia and the inalienable right to life. Phil and Pub Aff 1978; 7(2):93–123.

26. Wertheimer A. Coercion. Princeton (NJ): Princeton University Press; 1987.

27. Wertheimer A. Exploitation. Princeton (NJ): Princeton University Press; 1996.

28. Kalfoglou AL, Geller G. Navigating conflict of interest in oocyte donation: an analysis of donors' experiences. Womens Health Issues 2000; 10(5):226–239.

29. Sauer MV. Indecent proposal: $5,000 is not "reasonable compensation" for oocyte donors [editorial]. Fertil Steril 1999; 71(1):7–8.

The Myth of the Gendered Chromosome: Sex Selection and the Social Interest

Victoria Seavilleklein and Susan Sherwin

Sex selection technologies have become increasingly prevalent and accessible. We can find them advertised widely across the Internet and discussed in the popular media—an entry for "sex selection services" on Google generated 859,000 sites in April 2004. The available services fall into three main types: (1) preconception sperm sorting followed either by intrauterine insemination of selected sperm (IUI) or by in vitro fertilization (IVF); (2) preimplantation genetic diagnosis (PGD), by which embryos created by IVF are tested and only those of the desired sex are transferred to the woman's uterus; and (3) prenatal testing of fetuses through ultrasound or chromosomal analysis, followed by selective abortion of fetuses detected to be of the undesired sex.[1]

Our aim in this paper is twofold: (1) to explore the problematic relationship between what is advertised (gender selection) and what is really being offered (sex selection via chromosome selection), and (2) to explore the moral responsibilities of fertility experts who promote and entrench false and troubling expectations about the connections between biological (chromosomal) status and the social category of gender through their participation in ambiguously described "sex selection" practices. We will discuss some of the problems that emerge from the conflation of biological categories of sex with social categories of gender in the context of these reproductive services, paying particular attention to the ways in which medicalized approaches to gender in sex selection obscure the reality of such phenomena as intersexuality, transsexuality, and homosexuality and, more generally, perpetuate harmful stereotypes that attach to traditional conceptualizations of gender. Consequently, we will argue that sex selection practices are so potentially harmful to the social interest that their prohibition by governments is warranted and even morally required.

To be clear about the practices we are criticizing, here is a brief review of the actual services available. Depending on the techniques that are used, sperm sorting can be the simplest, least invasive, and, therefore, least expensive option. This procedure involves the provision of sperm (collected through male masturbation), which is then subjected to mechanical, chemical, or light-based techniques to separate sperm according to

whether they carry X or Y chromosomes. Once the sperm are sorted, a pregnancy can be sought in a variety of different ways. The least medicalized method is for the sperm of the desired sex to be delivered to the partner's vagina through intrauterine insemination (IUI), where drugs may be used to induce ovulation. If this procedure is unsuccessful (or looks unfavorable), in vitro fertilization (IVF), possibly including intracytoplasmic sperm injection (ICSI), may be used. IVF involves artificial stimulation of the woman's ovaries, careful monitoring, surgical removal of the eggs, and fertilization of the eggs in vitro; in cases of a low sperm count or sperm of poor quality, ICSI may be used for fertilization purposes. Fertilized embryos are then transferred back to the womb or frozen for later use.

Although IUI represents the safest, lowest technology option (especially when drugs are not used for ovulation), IVF (and/or ICSI) is invasive, expensive, and carries serious risks of harm to the women involved, the children who are produced through its use, and the relationships of the contracting couples. Whichever method is used to procure a pregnancy, however, whether the eventual child produced will be of the desired sex is uncertain. There are a variety of different methods by which sperm are sorted and there is little available scientific evidence as to the actual success rates of different approaches.

Preimplantation genetic diagnosis is a second type of sex selection technology that also involves the use of in vitro fertilization. Instead of introducing sorted sperm prior to fertilization, however, the harvested eggs are allowed to develop to the eight-cell stage; at that point, it is possible to extract a cell to analyze its chromosomal makeup. Embryos can then be sorted into male and female groupings and only those with the desired sex chromosomes will be transferred to the woman's womb (or frozen for later use). In contrast to other sperm-sorting techniques, this procedure has the distinct advantage of removing virtually all uncertainty regarding the sex chromosomes, but, again, it involves the serious physical and psychosocial risks that are associated with IVF.

Alternatively, it is possible to initiate a pregnancy and then make use of various types of prenatal testing (ultrasound, amniocentesis, or chorionic villi sampling) to

Seavilleklein, Victoria and Susan Sherwin. "The Myth of the Gendered Chromosome: Sex Selection and the Social Interest," *Cambridge Quarterly of Health Care Ethics*, 6:1 (2007), 7–19. Copyright © 2007. Reprinted by permission of Cambridge University Press.

determine the chromosomal sex of the developing fetus. If abortion is legal within the jurisdiction, the woman can then abort the fetus if it is the "wrong" sex. If there are multiple fetuses, a frequent occurrence when women use assisted reproduction technologies, they may choose to selectively terminate some fetuses; sex is often used as the basis for choice in such circumstances. Interestingly, in countries where abortion is legal (such as it is in Canada), prenatal testing and selective abortion would still be permitted even if legislation were to prohibit preconception sex selection. However, although women are able to obtain prenatal information about the likely sex of their fetus in most medical facilities in Canada, the information may not be available until well into the second trimester, and most doctors refuse to perform abortions so far into a pregnancy unless there are strong medical indications (i.e., risk of serious illness to the pregnant woman or the resulting child).

Ever since these technologies became available, there has been vigorous debate in the literature as to the legitimacy of using the powers of reproductive and genetic medicine for sex selection purposes, especially because the most reliable forms of sex selection technology involve prenatal testing (and now PGD) and selective abortion (or discarding) of fetuses (embryos) that happen to be of the undesired sex. Many feminists who have fought hard for women's unfettered "right to choose" abortion find themselves distressed to think that some women would terminate wanted pregnancies solely on the basis of the sex of the child.

The ethical battle lines quickly formed. On one side were the defenders of procreative liberty, led by their standard-bearer, John Robertson.[2] According to Robertson and others in this camp, procreation is a matter so near and dear to the hearts and plans of most people that it is a serious violation of individual liberty for the state to act in any way that restricts personal choice in this area. Proponents of procreative liberty may dislike the idea of parents choosing to abort perfectly healthy fetuses for the sake of some individual preference regarding the child's sex, but they believe a far graver harm is at stake if the state tries to intervene and restrict patient (or client) access to relatively safe interventions that promise to increase personal choice and control in the sphere of reproduction.

In opposition, particularly to the forms of sex selection that involve destruction of embryos or fetuses, we find, not surprisingly, the various conservative factions that oppose all forms of abortion; indeed, many conservatives have felt vindicated in their opposition to allowing choice on abortion by the idea that, once available,

women will choose such a "trivial" reason to terminate a pregnancy. In the case of sex selection, however, conservatives are not alone. As noted above, many feminists have also expressed deep reservations about the practice. They observe that, worldwide, the vast majority of people seeking sex selection technologies do so to produce male rather than female children. In the overwhelming number of cases, the technology is used to destroy female fetuses to facilitate another pregnancy that might turn out to be male. This is no mere coincidence in the view of feminists. Rather, it is an expression of cultural prejudices against girls and women, a sex so devalued that it is often judged better that a child not be born than it be born female. It seems that legitimizing such prejudices by treating them as appropriate targets for medical intervention is likely to deepen, rather than lessen, their impact. Although most feminists have been reluctant to authorize state intervention in women's hard-won right to choose abortion for any reason, many have proposed that restrictions be put in place regarding disclosure of fetal sex to discourage the practice of selectively aborting female fetuses.[3]

Rather than get caught up in the abortion debates, we will concentrate on the new technological options that occur outside of women's bodies, namely, sperm sorting before conception and PGD before implantation; restrictions on either or both of these technologies leave intact women's right to choose abortion. We believe that there is still plenty of reason for concern about the proliferation of these options. We fear that if these practices become accepted as familiar, even routine (or at least acceptable) options in reproduction, the social message that it is normal to try to control the sex of one's offspring will be enacted again and again.[4] Prospective parents will observe the morally accepted use of valuable and limited medical time and expertise being directed at the goal of controlling the sex of each child and take that as confirmation that this is a common and appropriate way to create families.

At present, there is little evidence that most North Americans are interested in avoiding the birth of female children.[5] The defenders of procreative liberty take this information as evidence that we have nothing to fear about allowing a practice of sex selection, because there is unlikely to be wholesale slaughter of female fetuses in most Western nations. They point out that the major reason people in the West report wanting access to sex selection technologies is to promote "family balance" by which they mean having both male and female offspring in roughly equal numbers. In other words, at least in the West, sex selection technology will be used not to ensure procreation of children of a single sex, but to counteract the possibility that any particular family will have children of only one sex when they would prefer some of each. Hence, it appears just as likely that it will be used to generate the birth of girls as boys. This, they assume, is a "gender-neutral" application, because it seems that it will apply approximately equally to male and to female fetuses. These are empirical claims that we suspect cannot be known in advance of the general availability and social acceptance of the techniques. However, it is worth nothing that most people, when pressed, believe that an ideal family would involve a boy born first and a girl second.[6] Because the average number of children per woman in Cananda is only 1.50,[7] we can only wonder how many parents using sex selection techniques would get around to having the girl. But we will not challenge the empirical assumptions of the defenders of procreative liberty here.

Our worry addresses the pervasive and harmful gender norms that are being reinforced when the practice of selecting the sex of one's (next) child is legitimized. If we look to the advertisements for the companies marketing these technologies, we can readily see that they are promoting a simple equation: that predetermining the sex of a child is concomitant with predetermining its gender. The Fertility Institutes advertises, for example, that "It has been known for many years that the gender of a pregnancy is determined by the sex chromosome carried by the sperm."[8] Similarly, Sydney IVF states that PGD as a means of sex selection ensures that "couples can now be almost certain that their child will be the gender they request."[9] Technologies designed to ensure that babies have the chromosomes of a particular sex (or rather, that they do not have the chromosomes of the unwanted sex) are clearly being marketed as offering children of specific genders. These companies are using "sex" and "gender" interchangeably despite the fact that "sex" is traditionally used to refer to biological sex and "gender" to one's social identification with one sex or the other. Although we use the terms according to these traditional definitions for the sake of clarity, it is important to notice that both of these definitions are open to challenge and that our arguments here further undermine the possibility of a clear definition of either term or a clear distinction between the two.

The emphasis placed on "family balancing" in Western arguments in support of sex selection technologies also suggests that what is desired by families seeking these techniques is not primarily a child with different genitals but a child who conforms to the opposite gender role to the children they already have. The fact that couples are willing to pay thousands of dollars for sex selection services and spend the time, effort, and emotional energy, not to mention facing the physical risks, associated with sex selection procedures indicates a strong belief that important differences attach to having a child of one sex rather than the other. This belief is not adequately captured by differences in physiological sex and can only be explained in terms of assumptions about the different social roles, including behaviors, interests, and practices, that are considered appropriate for boys and men and for girls and women. In other words, part of what is expected from sex selection techniques is a child that will conform to assumed (and desired) gender roles.

Implicit in these gender expectations, we suspect, is likely to be conformity to a desired sexual orientation. Anne Bolin observes that there are four gender markers: physiological sex, gender identity, social identity, and sexual orientation.[10] Indeed, in Western society, where heterosexuality has been dominant historically, gender roles appear to be formed dichotomously from heterosexual ideals.[11] On the one hand, men have traditionally been regarded as more aggressive and more rational than women and as the economic providers for the family. Many women, on the other hand, have struggled against their historical description as more emotional than men and, hence, more suited to caretaking positions (e.g., of children and of the home) because these characterizations have served to exclude women from the workforce and the political arena and forced them to be economically dependent on men. Although expectations about the dichotomous roles of men and women are becoming less rigid in many parts of the world, they have not disappeared.

In fact, the relationship between sexual orientation and gender expectations seems to be dialectical: each is framed by assumptions about the dichotomous nature of the other. Underlying the choice for a baby girl, then, is very likely an unexamined presumption that their daughter will eventually get married and have children or, for a boy, that their son will eventually find a nice girl to settle down with. Indeed, where there is confusion regarding the sex of a child, the concern that the child will grow up to be homosexual is often expressed as a dominant concern by mothers.[12] Sex selection for the purposes of "family balancing" is not a simple matter of balancing chromosomes, therefore, but reflects an acceptance of socially entrenched gender and sexuality norms and stereotypes.

Clearly, then, sex selection, whether by sperm sorting or PGD, is not a guarantor of gender, with all the complexities that gender entails. The implicit (or explicit) gender promises of fertility clinics cannot be relied on because all that can be "virtually guaranteed" in the implantation of PGD embryos (and the nonguaranteed promises of sperm sorting) is that the resultant child will have the desired sex chromosomes; there can be no guarantees that the gender role the child comes to identify with will correlate with the sex of his or her chromosomes, especially as he or she grows up. Although parents may attempt to raise their child in conformity with a certain gender role, as the child passes through adolescence and into adulthood, his or her gender identity—defined as one's psychological or emotional identification as male or female—may diverge from his or her sex of rearing. Experience with intersexuals, transsexuals, and transvestites, for example, has shown that there is no simple one-to-one correlation between sex and gender. In intersexuality, chromosomal sex is not even sufficient for determining physiological sex, let alone gender. What, we must ask, will be the response of parents who have gone to a great deal of time, trouble, and expense to ensure a baby of a chosen gender if that child ends up failing to meet standard gender norms or rejects the prescribed gender identity entirely? Will medicine continue to play an active role in trying to ensure conformity?

It is clear, though seldom publicly discussed, that children do not always develop gender identities that match the gender roles in which they were raised. "Tomboys," for example, may conform more to the male gender role than the female stereotype would typically allow, whereas "sissies" may resemble female gender norms more than stereotypical male behavior. Despite these modest deviations, however, children who display such behaviors are still mostly accepted in society—especially because it is commonly assumed that they will "outgrow" these tendencies after puberty. Other forms of behavior that deviate more significantly from traditional gender roles are less accepted in society. Many transvestites, for instance, obtain a great deal of pleasure from conforming to the gender role of the opposite sex in the form of cross-dressing. This phenomenon covers a wide range of behaviors from wearing a few items of clothing to full-scale impersonation, either in jest or as an expression of personal identity.[13] Although explanations for why people cross-dress are various, they include the erotic sensation gained by cross-dressing and a desire to experience the gender identity of the opposite sex.

Most transsexuals—a condition that was originally recognized as an extreme version of transvestism[14]— typically never feel comfortable with the gender role prescribed by their physiological sex and many choose to live the gender experiences associated with the opposite sex.[15] Because gender identity is considered fixed in adulthood[16] and begins to develop long before then, the most desirable option that many transsexuals feel is available to them is to surgically and hormonally alter their body so that it matches their gender identity. The fact that people with ordinary (i.e., nonpathological) physiologies feel the need to go through drastic surgical interventions, including lifelong hormone therapy and the control of secondary sex characteristics, so their bodies match their gender identities indicates that chromosomal sex is not the sole determining factor for gender.

Sexual orientation also seems to develop independently of both sex and gender identity in many cases.[17] Homosexuals and bisexuals, for example, generally have ordinary physiologies and "matching" gender identities; what distinguishes them from their heterosexual peers is that they feel erotic attraction toward members of the same sex. Transvestism has been associated with homosexuality and with both homosexuality and heterosexuality at different times in its history and in different cultures. Studies carried out on male transvestites between 1972 and 1988 found that by far the majority was heterosexual, although some had occasional homosexual contact.[18] Intersexuals, who challenge traditional categories of sex by exhibiting physiological characteristics of both sexes, have been known to form successful relationships both with members of the opposite sex to the one to which they were assigned and with members of the same sex, or to be bisexual; many are disinterested in forming any kind of sexual relationship. The case of transsexuals is complicated further because they can be regarded as heterosexual after receiving sex reversal surgery or they can be attracted to members of the sex to which they just changed. Although proving a lack of homosexual orientation is often a condition for being approved for sex reversal surgery, there is some awareness of male to female transsexuals specifically adopting lesbian identities.[19] In light of the complex relations between sex, gender, and orientation, it is naïve to assume that there is a smooth and predictable connection among these traits, especially one that can be predetermined by chromosomes.

Furthermore, it is not even guaranteed that chromosomal constitution predetermines physiological sex. Although in the majority of births, a quick genital inspection can determine the sex of the infant, this is not always the case. In approximately 1.7% of live births,[20] the external genitalia of the baby are ambiguous with regard to sex, and a medical team, usually consisting of a urologist, a geneticist, and a pediatric endocrinologist,[21] is needed to determine the sex assignment of the child. Because gonads produce hormones that govern the development of the internal sex organs and the external genitalia, any variation in gonadal formation, enzymatic error, hormone inhibition, or lack of receptor for the hormones can result in a variety of intersex conditions wherein the gonadal sex, chromosomal sex, genital sex, hormonal sex, and apparent sex may not match.[22] In cases of complete androgen insensitivity syndrome (AIS), for example, where the body lacks the receptors for the androgen hormones, the person may look female in every way and identify herself as a female, and yet be a chromosomal and gonadal male.

Not even the correlation between chromosomal sex and genetic sex is automatic, although it is extremely rare for them to come apart. Genetic sex is determined by the genetic sequencing that governs testicular development, thought to be the SRY gene. Although this gene is usually found on the Y chromosome, it may be found on a different chromosome and sometimes even on the X chromosome. Such an individual would have an XX karyotype despite having testes and a male apparent sex. It is possible, therefore, for even genetic sex to fail to reflect chromosomal sex.[23]

The medical field has been involved in the identification and medical control of "deviations" from stereotypical gender ideals for more than a century. Surgical interventions to "normalize" the genitalia of intersexuals have been undertaken since the 1950s, including myriad procedures such as vaginoplasty, peotomy, castration, hysterectomy, clitorectomy, hypospadias surgery, mastectomy, and penile reconstruction, many of which require repeated surgeries. Hormonal therapy usually begins just before or at puberty, to be continued throughout the individual's life. These interventions are all performed with the motivation of helping the child develop a stable gender identity and live a "normal" and well-adjusted life as a girl/woman or as a boy/man. Similar procedures are followed in sex reversal surgeries for transsexuals, who also began to receive medical treatment of their bodies in the second half of the 20th century; although the condition was regarded as pathological prior to this time, the only available "treatment" was psychiatric. Before being approved for the surgery, transsexuals must pass a sexological examination, a full psychiatric examination, prove that they are not homosexual,[24] and pass a "real-life test" in which they must live as a member of the opposite sex for 2 years. Notably, when sex reversal surgeries were first performed, doctors did not think they were truly changing the sex but only the secondary sex characteristics with the motivation of making the individual better "socially adjusted."[25]

Transvestism and homosexuality have also been heavily pathologized. In the 18th and 19th centuries both were considered to be "crimes against nature"; they later became defined as mental disorders in the *Diagnostic and Statistical Manual* (DSM) of the American Psychiatric Association. Whereas transvestism remains recorded in the DSM IV as a sexually deviant behavior (along with such activities as pedophilia, exhibitionism, and voyeurism), homosexuality was removed in 1973, possibly due to the fact that it has been more closely studied than transvestism and because homosexuals are better politically organized than transvestites. Homosexuality is still regarded by some people as a "disease" to be cured, however, and therefore remains in the sights of the medical field. Various physiological bases for homosexuality have been proposed over the years, including a difference in brain size between homosexuals and heterosexuals, but none have ever been proven. The most recent—and, arguably, the most insidious—attention directed toward homosexuality is in efforts to find a homosexual "gene"; such chromosomal association would allow prospective parents to select against the "condition" in prenatal testing and in PGD.

Given the history of medical involvement with phenomena such as homosexuality, transsexuality, and intersexuality, the medical establishment should be well aware of the fact that there are significant variations in the combinations of sex, gender, and sexual orientations in the human population. Practitioners should also be aware that medicine, historically, has not always been successful in "normalizing" everyone to fit heterosexual gender norms, with the possible exception of transsexuals. Homosexuals rally against judgments that they are abnormal or deviant and they are currently struggling to be recognized as equals in law and in society. Members of the intersex community have also taken the initiative in recent years to speak out against the medical treatment that they received, usually as infants and therefore without their consent.[26] The heartache, anger, and sense of injustice in their stories should serve as a warning that it is not possible to fit everyone into stereotypical sex/gender roles.

It is important to recognize that none of these forms of classification is itself straightforward. Even on their own, gender, sexuality, and even sex do not fit neatly into two exhaustive and complementary categories; each admits of variations and gradations. When sex, gender, and sexuality are interpreted as simple dualisms, each side of the traditional pair carries with it problematic stereotypes. Feminists have routinely challenged these traditional conceptions and objected to the behavioral expectations they generate on the grounds that such interpretations are deeply entwined with patterns of gender and sexuality oppression.[27] Efforts to find coherence among dichotomous categories (such as sex and gender) when they are individually messy and problematic tend to compound and magnify the problems of each concept on its own. Hence, the presumed correlation between sex and gender promoted by fertility clinics masks a wealth of social and political debate as well as conceptual confusion, which ought to be carefully reflected on instead of brushed under the carpet by marketing campaigns for sex selection services.

The provision of sex selection services by the medical field is therefore socially, ethically, and morally problematic because it involves accepting simplistic notions of sex, gender, and the connection between them when each of these categories has been demonstrated repeatedly to be far from clear. Using the terms "sex selection" and "gender selection" interchangeably, as do so many fertility clinics, is not only misleading but may well be harmful to society, to individuals who do not fit well within the available dichotomous categories, and to children produced through sex selection techniques. The assumption that gender is easily characterized and reducible to sex is problematic for society in the sense that it may serve to make people in general less tolerant of diversity; this intolerance can have a significant impact on matters of social justice.[28] Those who fall outside accepted gender norms, for instance those with any of the phenomena of difference discussed in this essay, are often stigmatized by virtue of this difference, which can to various degrees affect their self-worth, self-confidence, psychological stability, bodily comfort, personal safety, and personal relationships.

Promises that sex selection will "virtually guarantee" the gender of choice may also make parental acceptance of children who do not fit traditional gender norms particularly difficult, which can only negatively impact the children produced by these technologies. Although having a child who reveals that she is a homosexual or a transsexual may create strain in many families—and the occurrence of intersexuality is particularly difficult to cope with because it must be faced immediately upon birth[29]—we suspect that these disclosures will be particularly challenging for parents who have gone to extreme lengths to produce a child who conforms to a specific gender ideal. Parental expectations that gender identity

and sexual orientation will reflect the stereotype of the desired sex may also place increased burdens on the child to conform and increased punishment for a failure to do so. Although these considerations are at a further distance from the original reliance on sex selection services, the expectations encouraged from the procedure—and, in particular, the way in which they are marketed—may become entrenched such that they continue to have an impact throughout the life of the child.

The widespread social understanding of sex as determining gender suggests that the problem is not likely to be removed even if advertisers could be persuaded to resist the temptation to promise "gender selection" when they are in fact selling choice of sex chromosomes. Despite the wording, prospective parents would still be likely to assume that by choosing a male or a female child they are choosing one of two possible genders. These cultural expectations are deeply entrenched and are surely being reinforced by the growing market in sex selection services. Why else would prospective parents go to the trouble, risk, and expense of such services unless they had certain expectations about the difference attached to having a child of a particular sex?

Moreover, because the traditional expectations that attach to standard gender norms—which are uncritically promoted by sex selection technologies—are implicated in existing patterns of gender and sexuality oppression, they are problematic even for those who do seem to fit within their traditional boundaries. Gender expectations have historically been used to restrict the life prospects of men and, especially, of women; the entrenchment of such expectations can only serve to perpetuate this limitation of life choices even for those who seem to conform to traditional conceptualizations of sex and gender.

Of course, the problems of assuming dichotomous categories of sex, gender, and sexuality, and the harms attached to pervasive social efforts to enforce "gender-appropriate" behaviors that rest on these assumptions long predate the availability of sex selection services. These attitudes and problems are deeply entrenched within prevailing social norms. Our argument is not that the marketing of sex selection services is the source of such expectations but that it accepts them unquestioningly and provides them with a scientific and medical veneer that makes them appear biologically based and unproblematic. The continuous focus on conformity to gender stereotypes that is supported by the implied correlation between sex and gender in sex selection bypasses urgent questions about whether the dichotomy on which our gender stereotypes are based is even desirable.[30]

Thus, the serious ethical implications involved in the use and promotion of sex selection services cannot be overlooked. It is morally irresponsible to promise delivery of a child of a chosen gender when that is clearly beyond the power of reproductive technology. In addition, there are social concerns about the ways in which these technologies entrench social expectations about the virtual correlation between sex and gender and reinforce without question traditional gender role expectations. The variations and combinations of types of sex, gender identities, and sexual orientations discussed in this essay should sound warning bells to enthusiastic supporters of sex selection services, to parents who wish to make use of this technology, and to champions of social justice.

What, then, is to be done? We can make efforts to educate individual consumers about the problematic assumptions underlying these technologies, even though education about the complexities of gender as a social construct is likely to be difficult to digest and act on within a marketplace promising a technological fix to all sorts of gender hopes and dreams. As well, we can—and should—try to educate fertility experts about their moral and professional responsibilities to avoid participating in, and thereby legitimating and perpetuating, desires for access to these technologies on the part of consumers. Professional societies for physicians engaged in fertility treatments should take a moral stand opposing such activities on the part of their members.[31]

Nonetheless, change in societal understanding of sex and gender is unlikely to be achieved simply by appeal to individual actors. Until society does revise its understanding of the complex and diverse nature of sex, gender, and sexuality, there will be many reasons for individuals to choose to participate in the existing social patterns and stereotypes. Therefore, it is important to seek change at the level of policy as well where prohibitions on sex selection services can be enforced more readily on behalf of the social interest, especially where the social interest conflicts with individual preferences. Hence, we encourage more governments to take the choice out of the hands of individual consumers and practitioners through restrictive legislation, such as that introduced in Canada. We believe the arguments regarding the social and personal hazards of conflating gender with chromosomal sex, together with society's interest in social justice, are weighty enough to justify legislative efforts to prohibit sex selection and to belie its portrayal as a simple expression of reproductive freedom.

NOTES

1. Infanticide is also a form of sex selection that is practiced throughout the world in areas where ultrasounds to determine fetal sex are not accessible.

2. Robertson J.A. *Children of Choice*. Princeton, NJ: Princeton University Press; 1994.

3. See, for example, Wertz DC, Fletcher JC. Sex selection through prenatal diagnosis: A feminist critique. In: Bequaert Holmes H, Purdy LM, eds. *Feminist Perspectives in Medical Ethics*. Bloomington: Indiana University Press; 1992.

4. Results from surveys show that 25%–35% of parents or prospective parents in the United States would choose to use sex selection services if they were available. Microsort alone, a technology involving the separation of sperm using a modified flow cytometer, is predicted to have a market in the United States of $200 to $400 million per year. Wadman M. So you want a girl? *Fortune;* 2001;143(19 Feb):174–79.

5. See Royal Commission on New Reproductive Technologies, *Proceed with Care. Final Report of the Royal Commission on New Reproductive Technologies,* chap. 28. Ottawa. Canada Communications Group; 1993.

6. See Robertson JA. Preconception gender selection. *American Journal of Bioethics* 2001;1(1): 2–9.

7. This figure is for women in Canada aged 15–49 in 2002, according to Statistics Canada. Canada's fertility rate falls in the middle of the rates of other nations around the world, with Italy, Japan, and Germany having slightly lower fertility rates and the United States, Australia, the United Kingdom, and France having slightly higher rates.

8. *Fertility Evaluation and Procedures: Scientific Understanding*. Los Angeles: The Fertility Institutes. Available at http://www.fertility-docs.com/fertility_gender.phtml; last accessed 3 Oct 2006.

9. Sidney IVF. *How is sex selection done at SIVF?* Sidney, Australia: SIVF. During the publication process, the page was removed from SIVF's website as a result of new Australian ethical guidelines recommending against sex selection services being performed for nonmedical reasons. While publicly disagreeing with the moral reasons given in the guidelines, SIVF has halted its sex selection services. The original webpage can still be viewed at http://web.archive.org/web/20041015078938/http://www.sivf.com.au/ss_how.htm; last accessed 3 Oct 2006.

10. Polin A. Transforming transvestism and transsexualism: Polarity, politics, and gender. In: Bullough B, Bullough VL, Elias J, eds. *Gender Blending*. New York: Prometheus Books; 1997:26.

11. McKinnon C. *Feminism Unmodified: Discourses on Life and Law*. Cambridge, Mass: Harvard University Press; 1987:50. In other societies, there is acceptance of a third gender, such as the *guevedoche* in the Dominican Republic, the *hijra* in India, and the *kwolu-aatmwal* in the highlands of Papua New Guinea. Nataf Z. Whatever I feel [pseudo-hermaphroditism]. *New Internationalist* 1998;300(April):22–25.

12. Weiss M. Fence sitters: Parents' reactions to sexual ambiguities in their newborn children. *Semiotica* 1995;107:33–50.

13. Bullough V, Bullough B. *Cross-Dressing, Sex, and Gender*. Philadelphia: University of Pennsylvania Press; 1993: ii.

14. King D. *The Transvestite and the Transsexual*. Avebury, UK: Ashgate Publishing Ltd.; 1993, esp. chapter 2.

15. Some studies posit that the number of male to female transsexuals is about 1 in 100,000 and of female to male transsexuals is about 1 in 130,000; Eichler M. Sex change operations: The last

butwark of the double standard. In Nelson ED, Robinson BW, eds. *Gender in the 1990s: Images, Realities, and Issues.* Nelson, Canada: International Thomson Publishing; 1995:30. Bullough and Bullough, however, estimate that the incidence of transsexuality is approximately 1:50,000 in both men and women; see note 14, Bullough, Bullough 1993:314.

16. Wilson B, Reiner W. Management of intersex: A shifting paradigm. In: Dreger AD, ed. *Intersex in the Age of Ethics.* Hagerstown, Md. University Publishing Group, Inc.; 1999:121.

17. Milton Diamond argues, for example, that sexual orientation is partially predisposed prenatally and develops independently of sex of rearing and the appearance of the genitals; see Diamond M. Sexual identity and sexual orientation in children with traumatized or ambiguous genitalia. *The Journal of Sex Research* 19974(2):199–211.

18. See note 14, Bullough, Bullough 1993:294.

19. Pauly I. Gender identity and sexual orientation. In: Denny D, ed. *Current Concepts in Transgender Identity.* New York: Garland Publishing, Inc.; 1998:237–48.

20. Blackless M, Charuvastra A, Fausto-Sterling A, Luzanne K, Lee E. How sexually dimorphic are we? Review and synthesis. *American Journal of Human Biology* 2000;12:161.

21. See note 17, Wilson, Reiner 1999:123.

22. For a comprehensive survey of all the variations from the dichotomous ideal of male and female, see note 21, Blackless et al. 2000.

23. They might also have an X0 karyotype, where "0" marks the absence of the second chromosome; see note 17, Wilson, Reiner 1999:120.

24. The motivation for this requirement seems to be that the transsexual must "truly" fit the gender role of the opposite sex, namely being attached to members of the opposite sex (post-surgery) in a heterosexual relationship. If an individual is homosexual, there would be no need to undergo the surgery because they can engage in sexual activity without it.

25. See note 15, King 1993:51–8.

26. See, for example, the autobiographical accounts in Dreger AD, ed. *Intersex in the Age of Ethics.* Hagerstown, MD: University Publishing Group, 1999; and in Carlisle D. *Human Sex Change and Sex Reversal.* New York: Edwin Mellen Press; 1998. Visit also the web site of the Intersex Society of North America at http://www.isna.org and the web site of the United Kingdom Intersex Association at http://www.ukia.co.uk/voices/index.htm.

27. See, for example, Frye M. The necessity of differences: Constructing a positive category of women. *Signs* 1996;21(4):991–1010; Bartky SL. *Femininity and Domination: Studies in the Phenomenology of Oppression.* New York: Routledge; 1990; Butler J. *Gender Trouble: Feminism and the Subversion of Identity.* New York: Routledge; 1990.

28. In Nazi Germany, for example, homosexuals were the second largest group targeted after the Jews, and it is estimated that more than 220,000 were killed; see McNeill JJ. *The Church and the Homosexual.* Kansas City: Sheed Andrews and McMeel Inc.; 1976:82.

29. A cross-cultural, long term study by Meira Weiss shows that parents of newborns are much more likely to reject a baby with external defects than internal ones. Because of the importance of sex in categorizing a child, ambiguity of sexual genitalia is particularly traumatic; see note 13, Weiss 1995:37.

30. Many feminists argue, for example, that heterosexism perpetuated by ideals of the traditional family, has been associated historically with spousal violence, child abuse, rape, inequality of domestic chores, and the perpetuation of male dominance. The effects on women as a result of this patriarchal structure include the physical and emotional separation of women from other women, exploited labor in the home and in childbearing, forced sexual submission, and the exclusion from cultural and professional pursuits. Gender roles based on this model, therefore, may not be worth perpetuating. See Seaville V. *Catholicism and the Moral Status of Homosexuality.* Master's thesis. Calgary, Alberta. University of Calgary; 2002:99.

31. For example, the Society of Obstetricians and Gynaecologists of Canada has taken this stance.

May Doctors Refuse Infertility Treatments to Gay Patients?

Jacob M. Appel

One of the most sacrosanct principles of medical practice in the United States is that physicians have a right to choose their own patients as long as the patient is not in a medical emergency. During the 1980s, a minority of health care professionals invoked this prerogative in refusing to treat AIDS patients.[1] More recently, doctors incensed over malpractice premiums have refused to care for lawyers and their family members.[2] However, this sort of physician autonomy is not without certain limits—most notably the restrictions found in various federal and state civil rights statutes. No physician or hospital receiving government funding, including Medicare and Medicaid, may discriminate against potential patients on the basis of race, color, religion, or national origin,[3] and many states have expanded these protections to cover gender and sexual orientation. What remains unclear is whether physicians with bona fide religious objections to treating certain patients are exempt from these proscriptions. A California case, currently on appeal before a state court, may soon decide the matter.[4]

Appel, Jacob M. "May Doctors Refuse Infertility Treatments to Gay Patients" *Hastings Center Report*, 36:4 (2006), 20–21. Copyright © 2006. Reprinted by permission of The Hastings Center.

The plaintiff in the case, Guadalupe T. Benitez, is a thirty-three-year-old medical assistant currently living with a same-sex partner in suburban San Diego.[5] She received infertility treatments at the North Coast Women's Care Medical Group starting in August 1999 and running until July 2000, when her physicians, Christine Brody and Douglas Fenton, refused to continue treating her because of her sexual orientation. According to Benitez, Dr. Brody told her that she had "religious-based objections to treating homosexuals to help them conceive children by artificial insemination," while Dr. Fenton refused to authorize a refill of her prescription for the fertility drug Clomid on the same grounds.[6] In response, Benitez filed suit under California's Unruh Civil Rights Act, charging illegal discrimination on the basis of sexual orientation.[7] The case gained widespread attention when the California Medical Association, historically friendly to gay rights, backed the two Christian physicians in their claim that their freedom of religion under the federal and state constitutions trumped the requirements of the state statute.[8] It is the CMA's position that such claims should be addressed on a case-by-case basis, rather than by a blanket rule.

The controversy in *Benitez v. NCWC* stands at the nexus of two competing approaches to the issue of "conscience" exemptions. On the one hand, most states have statutes that shield medical students and physicians from having to perform procedures, such as abortion and sterilization, to which they object on religious or moral grounds. Several public policy reasons are advanced for these "conscience" clauses: First, highly qualified physicians, forced to compromise their sincerely held religious beliefs, might leave the field of medicine entirely, and similarly, some prospective physicians might choose to pursue other career paths instead. Second, physicians who object to a particular procedure are not in a position to provide the level of emotional and moral support that their patients have a right to expect. In contrast, our society seems highly unwilling to tolerate physicians who refuse or limit service to an entire class of patients, even when they act out of sincere religious beliefs. It is highly unlikely that any court would permit an Orthodox Jewish physician to provide separate waiting rooms for men and women, or allow a Muslim physician to require all female patients to wear head coverings.[9] The Benitez case, however, presents an instance where both an objection to a specific procedure and to a general class of patients overlap. The physicians at NCWC are unwilling to perform a specific procedure on a general class of patients.

Two further concerns in many "conscience" cases are the impact of an exemption on the overall availability of the procedure and the social stigma and discomfort associated with being refused care. What makes the Benitez case highly unusual is that neither of these issues alone appears to justify the denial of a conscience exemption to the health care providers. There is no evidence that discrimination against gays and lesbians at fertility clinics is widespread—this appears to be the only such instance to have arisen in California, and in fact, Benitez quickly found another physician willing to perform the procedure and thereafter gave birth to a son.[10]

Nor does it appear likely that prospective patients will suffer a great deal of embarrassment by allowing a few physicians to opt out. This contrasts significantly with the case of a pharmacist who refuses to fill a birth control prescription. Filling a prescription is an incidental matter to which most women give minimal thought—and which they may need to repeat often and quickly in a variety of geographic locales. Not knowing whether a particular pharmacy fills such prescriptions is the sort of disruptive uncertainty liable to inconvenience many women and even to deter some from seeking contraceptives. In contrast, a patient pursuing fertility treatments might well do considerably more research when choosing a provider. Here, unlike in the pharmacy setting, it is hard to imagine prospective patients walking in off the street for care. If any physicians opting out of performing certain procedures on certain patients publicize their decisions adequately, it appears unlikely that prospective patients will be highly inconvenienced.[11] They will simply go elsewhere.

Finally, it is worth considering whether doctors should be held to the same standards as other providers of public services and public accommodations. The nature of the doctor-patient relationship is fundamentally more intimate than the sorts of interactions that occur between landlords and tenants or innkeepers and guests. (The question does arise as to whether IVF offered to a fertile patient is "health care" or merely a straightforward business deal, but that intriguing question lies beyond the scope of this essay.) One might argue that, as in this case, having physicians with strongly held biases express their views openly would actually do a service to prospective patients—presumably giving them a chance to avoid such providers. In contrast, few patients would want the care of a doctor who greeted them with smiles but secret disapproval. The situation here is further complicated because physicians engaged in fertility treatments often make personal judgments about who will be a fit parent. They often feel a responsibility to the child they are bringing into the world, as well as the parent.[12] No other situation in the business world seems analogous.

That is not to say that Ms. Benitez shouldn't prevail. Rather, it is to argue that if she should prevail, she should do so because we as a society refuse to tolerate medical discrimination against gays and lesbians in all circumstances as a matter of principle—not because allowing a religious exception to the civil rights statutes will have a significant impact on the health care that they receive. This case pits two incompatible forms of "liberty" against each other. The California appellate court would do well to frame its opinion in terms of such principles, rather than getting bogged down in extraneous questions of health care access.

NOTES

1. "When Doctors Refuse To Treat AIDS," (editorial) *New York Times* (August 3, 1987). The AMA has since issued a policy statement against this practice, see AMA Policy Statement on Potential Patients (E10.5) at http://www.ama-assn.org/apps/pf_new/pf_online?f_n=browse&doc=policyfiles/HnE/E-10.05.HTM&&s_r-&st_p-&nth-l&prev_pol=policyfiles/HnE/E9.132.HTM&nxt_pol=policyfiles/HnE/E-10.01.HTM&. In addition, the First Circuit Court of Appeals in *Abbott v. Bragdon* found that AIDS was a disability under the Americans with Disabilities Act and that medical professionals could not discriminate against AIDS patients. 107 F. 3d. 934.

2. L. Parker, "Medical Malpractice Battle Gets Personal," *USA Today* (June 14, 2004).

3. Civil Rights Act of 1964 (Public Law—880–352 88th Congress—H.R. 7152).

4. *Benitez v. North Coast Women's Care Medical Group, Inc.*, 106 Cal. App. 4th 978 (2003).

5. G. Moran, "Maternal Wish, Doctors' Faith at Odds in Court," *The San Diego Union-Tribune* (August 7, 2005).

6. *Benitez v. North Coast Women's Care Medical Group, Inc.*

7. Unruh Civil Rights Act, California Civil Code, Sections 51–51.3. Although the UCRA did not historically apply to gays and lesbians, the California Supreme Court extended protections to registered domestic partners in *Koebke v. Bernardo Heights Country Club*, 05 C.D.O.S. 6731.

8. M. McKee, "When Friends Become Enemies," *The Recorder* 129, no. 118 (2005): 1. Drs. Brody and Fenton also argue that they discriminated based upon martial status rather than sexual orientation per se; they also refuse fertility treatment to single heterosexual women on the same religious grounds.

9. Single-gender waiting rooms and religious dress codes for patients are prevalent in many nations and have been tolerated in both Canada and Europe.

10. Moran, "Maternal Wish." The Benitez case is further complicated because Ms. Benitez's second physician was an off-plan provider not covered by her insurance, initially forcing her to pay for her procedure out of pocket (although her plan subsequently made an exception for her). This unfortunate circumstance could be remedied by legislation requiring all health care plans to include at least one provider willing to perform such procedures regardless of the patient's sexual orientation, so it is not determinative for the larger principles at stake in the case.

11. Some evidence suggests that Drs. Brody and Fenton failed to make full disclosure in this case.

12. W. Buchanan, "Doctor and Patient Both Say Their Liberty Was Violated," *The San Francisco Chronicle* (July 29, 2005).

Navigating Race in the Market for Human Gametes

Hawley Fogg-Davis

Since the first successful birth resulting from in vitro fertilization in 1978, ethicists have debated a wide spectrum of moral questions raised by IVF, including concerns about economic exploitation, profiteering, health effects on women's bodies, interference with traditional family norms, and children's welfare.[1] Yet these discussions rarely, if ever, address the racially selective use of reproductive technologies. Legal scholar Dorothy Roberts has documented a racial disparity in access to and use of reproductive technologies, pointing out that even though black women experience infertility at higher rates than white women, white women are twice as likely as black women to use reproductive technologies.[2] But no one has yet explored the production and reproduction of racial meanings *within* this newfangled market.

How do descriptive and prescriptive notions of race affect the economic behavior of those who possess the financial means, time, and cultural capital to pursue assisted reproduction? Conversely, how do the racial choices of gamete consumers shape contemporary notions of race?[3] Are whites, who comprise the overwhelming majority of gamete consumers, morally justified in choosing the gametes of a white donor?[4] Is same-race preference among black or other nonwhite gamete shoppers morally different from same-race

Fogg-Davis, Hawley. "Navigating Race in the Market for Gametes" *Hastings Center Report*, 31:5 (2001), 13–21. Copyright © 2001. Reprinted by permission of Rowman & Littlefield.

preference among whites? Do cross-racial choices, such as a white couple's request for an Asian American egg donor, amount to benign or invidious racial discrimination? In sum, what role, if any, should race play in the selection and purchase of human reproductive tissue?

Race-based gamete selection raises two major, linked ethical issues. One is the harm that racial stereotyping causes to individuals, and the second is the public awareness that racial stereotyping is an accepted feature of this largely unregulated market.[5] Choosing a donor according to racial classification is based on racial stereotypes of what that donor is like, and of what a child produced using that person's gametes will be like, as well as the gamete consumer's own racial self-concept and racial aspirations. Race-gamete selection is tied to race-based desires in family formation. The dangerous subtext, or subliminal message, conveyed by race-based gamete choice is that a child created using the gametes donated by a racially designated person ought to adopt a race-specific cultural disposition, and develop his or her self-concept within those parameters. The net result is the constriction of individual freedom in forging one's identity.

Negative social repercussions also flow from this process of racial sorting. Naomi Zack argues that the white American family has historically been and continues to be "a publicly sanctioned private institution for breeding white people."[6] Race-specific gamete shopping underscores and extends Zack's point.

Assisted reproduction, as the name suggests, brings reproductive decisionmaking into public view. Racial choices made in this arena publicly reinforce and make explicit the routine use of racial discrimination in the choice of a partner for procreative sexual intercourse. It is not so much that the former is morally worse than the latter. Both operate on the level of racial stereotype, prejudging and weeding out certain individuals based at least partly on their ascribed race.

The unique problem of racial choice in the gamete market lies in *how* interpersonal racial choices are expressed. Noncoital reproduction requires people to articulate a race-based reproductive choice that usually remains unspoken in coital reproduction. The price tag attached to these racial reproductive choices enhances the publicity of the stereotyping.

Explicit racial selectivity in the gamete market has the potential to uncover submerged racial biases that permeate the U.S. social terrain. But if we unearth these racial desires only to ignore them, thereby affirming them by default, then we end up sanctioning stereotypes of race-based familial structure. The fact that racially coded donor profiles exist and can be viewed by the public makes this practice part of our public consciousness. Hence, race-based donor choices are inextricably tied to public notions of the normative role that race ought to play in family formation.

My argument against this mode of racial stereotyping is not based in color blindness or a call for abolishing racial categories. Race can and should be a source of self-identification, and to some extent group identification, but it should never be overwhelming or fixed. What is needed, instead, is a way for individuals to mediate or navigate over the course of their lives between the racial categories ascribed to them and their own racial self-identification.

I call this theoretical concept "racial navigation." Racial navigation recognizes the practical need for individuals living in a race-conscious society to acknowledge the social and political weight of racial categories, while urging individuals to resist passively absorbing these expectations into their self-concepts. My objective is to maximize human freedom under the existential pressure of racial categories. While racial navigation begins at the personal level, I intend for it to guide interpersonal conduct in the market for human gametes and beyond.[7] Before delving into the theoretical underpinnings of racial navigation, and demonstrating how it might mitigate the perpetuation of racial stereotypes in the gamete market, I want first to give a brief overview of how race is marketed in the business of paid gamete donation.

THE RACIAL MARKETING OF HUMAN GAMETES

The U.S. fertility treatment business is a booming, multibillion-dollar industry. With infertility rates on the rise,[8] the number of clinics offering IVF has risen sharply since the mid-1980s to approximately 330 nationwide.[9] Largely unregulated, these clinics compete fiercely with each other for a market of approximately 2.1 million infertile married couples.[10] Only a small percentage of these couples are likely to pursue IVF, donor insemination, or other assisted reproductive technologies.[11] And those who do pursue assisted reproduction have to be wealthy enough to afford fertility services such as IVF, which costs an average of $7,800 per cycle.[12] In discussing her finding that white women are twice as likely as black women to use reproductive technologies,[13] Roberts suggests that the disparity may "stem from a complex interplay of financial barriers, cultural preferences, and more deliberate professional manipulation" (p. 253).

Roberts argues that most blacks de-emphasize the role of genetics in both familial and community membership, as well as in the process of personal identity. Whereas many whites have historically gone to extraordinary and absurd lengths to guard against the "pollution" of a white "blood-line" by either avoiding interracial sexual relationships or evading the consequences of such relationships, Roberts notes a general attitude of acceptance of *mélange* within black families and extended kin networks:

> The notion of racial purity is foreign to Black folks. Our communities, neighborhoods, and families are a rich mixture of languages, accents, and traditions, as well as features, colors, and textures. Black life has a personal and cultural hybrid character. There is often a melange of physical features—skin and eye color, hair texture, sizes, and shapes—within a single family. We are used to "throwbacks"—a pale, blond child born into a dark-skinned family, who inherited stray genes from a distant white ancestor . . . . We cannot expect our children to look just like us (p. 263).

Even though prejudice against dark skin color and "African" physical features has existed within black communities since slavery, Roberts maintains, "sharing genetic traits seems less critical to Black identity than to white identity" (p. 263).

It is important to distinguish between *genetic traits* and *genetic ties*. Genetic traits refer, in the case of physical race, to the *physical expression* of genes inherited from biological parents. This genetic inheritance includes recessive genes—genes that are not physically expressed—and this (among other factors[14]) makes it possible for children to have physical characteristics that differ from those of their biological parents. A genetic tie, on the other hand, refers to the simple fact of sharing genes with another person, a biological relative. Although having a genetic tie to someone often means sharing genetic traits, the two are conceptually distinct. You and I may share the genetic trait of big ears and have no genetic tie. Likewise, genetically tethered sisters may share very few genetic traits. Roberts is right to point out that black Americans tend to de-emphasize genetic traits when it comes to determining who is black. Acceptance of *mélange* among African Americans is a practical response to the prior white American existential claim that any person with a black family member (a black genetic tie, not a black genetic trait) cannot be a white person.[15]

Genetic ties are another matter. While it is true that blacks have been more likely than whites to

develop kin networks among nongenetically related individuals, it is not clear that contemporary black Americans deemphasize the value of genetic ties to the extent Roberts implies.[16] Given the syncretic and hybrid nature of black cultural practices, which Roberts concedes, particularly the deceptively simple aspiration to be an American,[17] it seems unlikely that we can exempt blacks entirely from the widespread, culturally based desire to have one's "blood-line" perpetuated *vis á vis* genetically related children.

Racial disparity in the fertility services market more likely stems from economic disparities between blacks and whites, professional manipulation, and historically based fears of technological intervention with reproduction.[18] Whatever the reasons for racial disparity among fertility consumers, the fact remains that most of them are white, middle and upper class, married couples. The expressed and anticipated demands of these individuals shape the contours of today's gamete market.

Racial category is the primary criterion used by those interested in buying human eggs and sperm for the purposes of donor insemination and IVF. Race is also often prominent in private advertisements soliciting egg and sperm donors; it is the first category on the donor lists of most fertility clinics, many of which are publicly accessible via the Internet.[19] Donor lists include various details about the people who have contracted with the clinic to sell their gametes. Objective facts such as blood type, height, weight, and eye color are listed alongside more subjective "facts" such as hair texture, ethnic origin, skin tone, and tanning ability. Self-reported skills, accomplishments, and boasts—like years of education and athletic and musical talent—find a place on the screen or page next to the donor's favorite color, foods, and hobbies. At the California Cryobank in Beverly Hills, a gamete shopper can even judge donors' responses to the quintessential question, "Where do you see yourself in five years?" Donor profiles increasingly bulge with information that ranges from vital health information to genetically irrelevant details such as a donor's self-reported life goals. And the "more is better" trend in donor profile information is likely to continue, in step with the elusive quest for a comprehensive picture of the genetic material with which the consumers of this human tissue will attempt to create a baby.

The California Cryobank offers an online donor catalog where the serious and curious alike can pore over an extensive grid of one hundred and seventy-two sperm donors.[20] Of these donors, 146 are listed as Caucasian, fifteen as Other, nine as Black/African

American, and sixteen as Asian. In addition to "racial group," each donor's profile contains an abbreviated statement of "ethnic origin." Most of the Caucasian donors list multiple ethnic origins; many claim three and four different ethnicities. For example, donor 993 describes himself as Caucasian and of Irish, Russian, English, and French descent. All but one of the Asian donors describe themselves as mono-ethnic—as, for example, Korean or Filipino. Almost every African American donor describes himself as ethnically African American. Two black donors describe themselves as Nigerian, and one self-identifies as African American and Ethiopian. The "racial group" of Other contains an eclectic array of ethnic "mixes"—German and Chinese, Pacific Islander, and African American—as well as the singular "ethnic origins" of Mexican and East Indian. Donors are further subdivided by their "skin tones," which range from fair to medium to olive to dark.

The above donor catalog highlights the idiosyncratic and *ad hoc* use of racial classification in U.S. society. From the very moment we try to place individuals into racial boxes we discover that the center cannot hold and things very rapidly fall apart. Why do members of the Caucasian group typically have multiple ethnic origins while members of the African American/Black racial group almost universally have an ethnic origin equivalent to their racial group? How does one really distinguish between an olive complexioned Caucasian man and an "Other" who describes himself as Italian and African American with fair skin? Should the staff of California Cryobank decide what racial box to check, or should each individual donor have the freedom to describe his racial identity using language that transcends the sperm bank's racial boxes? And how are racial descriptions of sperm donors related to the consumer's goal of creating a baby?

RACE-BASED SOCIAL ONTOLOGY

Answering this last question requires inquiry into the meaning of race in our current social ontology. Charles Mills defines social ontology as "the basic struts and girders of social reality," "analogous to the way 'metaphysics' *simpliciter* refers to the deep structure of reality as a whole."[21] This deep structure is not, in Mills's view, metaphysical. Instead, racial categories are devised, maintained, and revised through political decisions. Mills defines racial constructivism in the following way: "The intersubjectivist agreement in moral and scientific constructivism is a hypothetical agreement of all

under *epistemically* idealized conditions. Racial constructitivism, by contrast, involves actual agreement of some under conditions where the constraints are not epistemic (getting at the truth) but *political* (establishing and maintaining privilege)" (p. 48). In this sense, race is not metaphysical, but a "*contingently* deep reality that structures our particular social universe, having a social objectivity and causal significance that arise out of *our* particular history" (p. 48).

Such inquiry is not limited to individual acts of racism. Instead, Mills and others point to a more insidious kind of racial hierarchy that has been built over a series of political decisions. Structural racism refers to official and unofficial social policies that invidiously affect the lives of nonwhites but cannot be traced to the actions of specific individuals.[22] I do not share Derrick Bell's pessimism that structural racism is permanent.[23] Indeed, the contours of U.S. structural racism have changed over time from chattel slavery to *de jure* segregation to our present circumstance, and this last stop will not be our final destination. As Michael Banton reminds us, the meaning of race has shifted significantly over the last three centuries throughout the globe, and will continue to change in the future.[24]

But change is slow. Racial classification continues to be a source of social hierarchy, a mark of civic standing, cultural development, beauty, intelligence, and subordination. All of us engage this drama. The weight of structural racism on individual lives is felt in the memoir of Toi Derricotte, a light skinned black woman who is often perceived as white. Derricotte explores her own racism against darker skinned blacks, and her action and inaction in the face of racist comments from white neighbors, colleagues, and cab drivers and others who believe her to be one of "them."[25] Proof that white skin continues to expand one's social and economic opportunities is brought into sharp focus by Derricotte's experience of shopping for a house in a wealthy and predominately white suburb of New York City. "I had decided not to take my husband with me to the real estate offices because when I had, since he is recognizably black, we had been shown houses in entirely different neighborhoods, mostly all-black . . . At night, under cover of darkness, I would take him back to circle the houses that I had seen and I would describe the insides" (p. 13).

As a form of structural racism, housing discrimination has been resistant to antidiscrimination policies and law, which the Supreme Court has interpreted to require evidence of discriminatory intent or purpose. Ultimately, housing discrimination supports a social value that many Americans subscribe to, but rarely express out loud: the right to live in a race-specific neighborhood, a preference that is often translated into the economic right to maintain one's property value. Where one lives greatly affects one's social status, as does the racial composition of one's family portrait; the two are connected, as Derricotte's decision not to introduce her husband to the real estate agent illustrates. Though racial discrimination in housing and gamete markets are different in many respects, both imply a greater degree of intimacy than public accommodations such as hotels, theatres, and restaurants. There is a strong presumption in favor of individual autonomy when it comes to decisions that affect who one must interact with on the home front.

John Robertson argues for an expansive notion of what he terms "procreative liberty" in the market for reproductive technologies. On Robertson's view, "individuals should be free to use these techniques or not as they choose, without government restriction, unless strong justification for limiting them can be established" (p. 4). Such justification is "seldom present," and is limited to preventing women from using their reproductive capacity for nonreproductive ends such as producing fetal tissue for research and transplant.[26] He discusses the ethical conflicts arising from "quality control measures" that use technologies to screen out and select for genetic characteristics, but he avoids the subject of race completely. Ironically, the following statement could support my concern about racial stereotyping if Robertson considered race-based procreative choices a kind of "quality control": "Quality control measures may in practice not be optional for many women, and may place unrealistic expectations on children who are born after prenatal screening" (p. 11).

I agree with Robertson that government should not restrict racial discrimination in the gamete market, but disagree with his decision to shield these choices from moral investigation. Concern for individual freedom should motivate inquiry into the ways that a race-driven market in human reproductive tissue is likely to constrain personal identity expression. Robertson fails to acknowledge this possibility because he restricts his notion of individual liberty to the freedom to make procreative choices in a free economic market. As with many libertarian arguments, the status quo becomes ground zero, and little or no attempt is made to dig below its surface.[27]

Ground zero consists of a socially diffuse system of racial classification that threatens to trap individuals in racial stereotypes. Like gamete shoppers who create the demand for racially labeled donors, the suburban real estate agent automatically associated Derricotte's white phenotype with a certain set of cultural practices and behaviors that were then aligned with racially coded neighborhoods. Robin Kelley and others have criticized this tendency to treat "culture" and "behavior" as synonyms.[28] Culture describes a set of available practices and artifacts that have evolved over time and will continue to change. Individuals respond to cultural menus in different ways, and they should be encouraged in this personal expression.[29] Individual cultural choices and personal behavior among residents of predominately black urban neighborhoods, for example, are not monolithic. Kelley reminds us that "By conceiving black urban culture in the singular, interpreters unwittingly reduce their subjects to cardboard typologies who fit neatly into their own definition of the 'underclass' and render invisible a wide array of complex cultural forms."[30]

NAVIGATING BETWEEN RACIAL IMPOSITION AND RACIAL SELF-IDENTIFICATION

It is this varied response to the imposition of racial classification that is missing from the racial menus of fertility clinics trading in gametes. If consumer demand is rooted solely in a visual, third person conception of race, then the California Cryobank and other fertility clinics will tailor their business strategies to satisfy that racial demand. But racial identification also involves a cognitive dimension, as Robert Gooding-Williams points out.[31] This cognitive dimension creates psychological space for the ongoing process of racial navigation. Racial navigation describes the activity of fending off simplistic and rigid notions of racial identity both in one's self-understanding and in the perception of others. It is a normative theoretical tool available to all living in a system of racial classification. Racial navigation recognizes the practical and strategic need to make sense of oneself within a social ontology of racial categories, to see oneself through the eyes of others in order to challenge that imposition and create new racial meanings for oneself.[32] There is no endpoint for racial navigation. The goal is to create and sustain a fluid self-concept that recognizes the existential weight of racial categories but does not accept them as adequate descriptions of human beings.

Again, racial navigation is made possible by the cognitive dimension of racial meaning. A person may look white, but know herself to be black based on the social convention that any one with one black ancestor is classified as black. The seeming paradox of being a "white black woman," as law professor Judy Scales-Trent describes herself, is made possible by this rule of hypodescent.[33] Gooding-Williams illuminates this notion by distinguishing between *being black* and *being a black person*.[34] Being black is a third person identification that entails being classified by others as visually black or cognitively black—that is, black according to the social convention of hypodescent. Being a black person, on the other hand, is a first person identity that refers to a person's decision to navigate between these two levels of personal and social meaning, to "make choices, to formulate plans, to express concerns, etc. in light of one's identification of oneself as black" (p. 23). When a black person passes for white she understands herself to be engaged in an act of (willful or unintentional) deception, and everyone knows that such deception is possible.[35]

So being seen or thought of as black, according to the social rule of hypodescent, is "a necessary but not sufficient condition of being a black person" (p. 58). To become a black person one must actively incorporate the fact that one has been designated as black into one's self-concept. A person who is visibly and cognitively designated as white, but who decides to affect certain stereotypical black cultural practices, thus thinking of himself as a black person, can never become a black person since he has failed the first criterion of being socially "seen" as black. The derogatory term "whigger," popular in the mid-1990s, conveys the artificiality, even offensiveness, of the white suburban youth who listens to rap music incessantly and mimics black urban slang.[36] "Whiggers" do not challenge racial stereotypes because their participation in black cultural forms is typically fleeting and no one believes them to be "really" black. Individuals who do satisfy the first criterion of being black can either absorb the racial expectations of others (stereotypes) or challenge the flatness of racial imposition by personalizing their black identities. As Gooding-Williams notes, those identified by others as being black can and often do express their black personhood in an infinite number of ways.

BARRIERS TO RACIAL NAVIGATION IN THE GAMETE MARKET

It is not impossible for racial navigation to begin after racially coded gametes have been bought. But the unexamined use of race to choose gamete donors makes it less likely that people will question third person racial meanings in their self-concepts, family interactions, and social behavior. And even if racial navigation is jumpstarted after the point of purchase, there is still the lingering damage of the initial racial restriction imposed on market actors, as well as the race-based expectations for children born using donated gametes. Racially organized gamete markets will have profound negative personal and social consequences even if the participants start to navigate racial meanings after they exit the market.

First person views of race fall out of the gamete market altogether. Sperm and egg donors are classified according to a third person view of race for the specific purpose of satisfying race-specific consumer demand. A fertility clinic's business success depends on its staff seeing a prospective donor's racial classification through the eyes of actual and potential customers. At the California Cryobank a client can pay an additional fee for the services of a matching counselor who tries to make an even more precise "match" between the genetic traits desired by the consumer and the genetic traits of particular donors. The PBS Frontline documentary, "Making Babies," showed a matching counselor scrutinizing a sperm donor's photograph while describing his physical features to a client over the telephone.

When counselors examine a donor's profile they find a third person account of that donor's racial identification. They must then shift perspective and attempt to see the donor's racial identification and more pointedly his racial traits through the eyes of the shopper with his or her racial desires. The result is a kind of third person racial identification "once removed." During the economic transaction, the donor's first person sense of racial self recedes further and further into the background, as the idea of race becomes packaged as a genetic commodity that can be detached from particular persons for the purpose of economic trade. In turning race into a genetic commodity, these market forces obliterate, or at least seriously erode, the donor's first person sense of racial self. The absence of first person expression of racial identity is critical because first person views mitigate the binding effects of racial classification, and serve as a break on our will to confine people to racial boxes.

One might argue that first person accounts of racial identity are present in the gamete market in the form of the copious "personal" information contained in donor profiles. The demand for extensive donor profiles might signal that consumers want to know what *sort* of Korean-American a sperm donor is, that they are interested in looking beyond the first column of donors' ascribed race. This is a step toward racial navigation, but the additional information in these donor files is too general to establish the robust sense of first person, raced identity that I have in mind. Donors respond to questions like whether they are athletic, what their career goals entail, their favorite color, and such. They are not asked to give an account of how they have responded to the imposition of race. I am not suggesting that this question should be added to donor questionnaires. The enormity of such an existential question, and the expectation that one's answer will change over time, makes it impossible to answer in a paragraph on a form. I am suggesting, however, that gamete shoppers consider the motivation behind their race-based choices for sperm and ova in the first place.

MOTIVATIONS AND CONSEQUENCES

Whites overwhelmingly demand "white" gametes, as evidenced by the fact that 85 percent of the donors "hired" by California Cryobank are identified as "Caucasian." When people buy gametes according to the racial classification of the donor, they are saying that race is heritable and relevant to their vision of family structure. They are saying that a person's gametes are transmitters of racial meaning that can and should be selectively transmitted to "their" child, through the use of reproductive technologies.[37] The idea that race is a bundle of heritable characteristics such that "all members of these races share certain traits and tendencies with each other that they do not share with members of any other race" is what K. Anthony Appiah calls *racialism*.[38] The racial classification of gametes in the fertility market can be described as *genetic* racialism—the false belief that human genetic tissue transmits specific racial traits and tendencies to future human beings.

So far I haven't said much about the difference between racialism and racism. I've discussed the infusion of our social ontology with a powerful system of racial classification, and I've ventured into the controversial territory of structural racism, suggesting that these two concepts frame the individual actions of gamete shoppers. But I need to address the question of individual racial motivation more directly. Are the consumer demands of gamete shoppers racist? Racism connotes intent to harm someone or some group of people based solely or primarily on racial classification.

Do white gamete shoppers *intend* to inflict racially invidious harm when they satisfy their desire for a white family through the purchase of a white donor's gametes? Are nonwhite gamete shoppers racist when they choose gametes from donors who share their own racial classification? What of the person who picks a donor of a racial category different from his own?

Appiah draws a distinction between racialism and racism. For him, racialism is false but not necessarily racist. Racialism is "a cognitive rather than a moral problem" (p. 13). In order for racialism to be racist the racial classifier must attach some moral significance to racial demarcation. But Appiah's position errs in two respects. First, the distinction between racialism and racism is not very helpful in excavating the morality of racial choice in the gamete market because there is no reliable way of gauging whether or not a racial choice has become a "moral problem." The distinction relies on a bright line between motivation and consequence that does not make much of a moral difference. Racialism, no matter how well intentioned, is always poised to cause moral difficulty in the form of racial stereotyping. This constant threat is precisely why racial navigation calls for constant vigilance.

The second problem concerns Appiah's claim that racialism is false, and that racial categories should be abolished because of the restrictions they exert on personal lives: "it is not that there is *one* way that blacks should behave, but that there are proper black modes of behavior. These notions provide loose norms or models, which play a role in shaping the life plans of those who make these collective identities central to their individual identities; of the identities of those who fly under these banners."[39] Though Appiah recognizes and appreciates the recuperative value that racial self-identification can have in the form of, for instance, black power counter-narratives, he urges us to move beyond racialism as a long-term goal (p. 614). Based on this reasoning, I suspect Appiah would advocate the removal of racial classification from gamete donor lists altogether.

I agree with Appiah that racialism places restrictions on the expression and life plans of individuals. Indeed, my notion of racial navigation is consistent with Appiah's plea for us to treat the personal dimensions of ourselves as "not too tightly scripted," "not too constrained by the demands and expectations of others" (p. 614). But I am more confident than Appiah that such personal life-scripts can and do thrive in the midst of racial expectations. I suppose my goals are more short term, and therefore geared more toward coping with the social reality of race. Racial categories will remain a prominent feature of our social world for the foreseeable future, and will carry expectations for those whom they describe. We can change the expectations, but we cannot jettison racial categories altogether. My hope in applying racial navigation to the gamete market is that the racial sorting of gamete donors might come to mean something different, something less determinate, than it does now. For the racial expectations that parents have for their children affect the identity developments of both children and parents, as well as the broader social norms regarding the role that race should play in family life. The motivations of individual gamete consumers, whatever their race, are morally interesting only insofar as they reinforce a narrow set of racial expectations.

Naomi Zack shares my consequentialist position that no significant moral difference exists between racialism and racism in the construction of family life. There simply is no escaping the fact that human breeding is "a selective practice invented and reinforced within cultures."[40] A white identity is achieved by looking at one's genealogy and finding no black genetic ties. Here, again, the distinction between genetic ties and genetic traits is critical, since many white people exhibit "black" genetic traits. Thus a white person's preference for a white donor as a means to having a white child perpetuates the exclusionary proposition that white families are racially pure. The desire for a white family results in "tightly scripted" identity narratives that limit the life opportunities for everyone.

COPING WITH RACIAL CATEGORIES

Binding racial narratives are of course not unique to the practice of paid gamete donation. The mixture of science with the desire for a racially specific family does, however, exacerbate this general social problem. The new reproductive technologies expose familial racial expectations in a public and systematic way. As Stephen Gould observes, people often turn to science to confirm their racial prejudices, with the effect that these prejudices drive scientific research and the social use of new technologies.[41] The negative consequence is that people will feel more justified in holding race-specific views about family formation.

Zack and Appiah's philosophical arguments against racialism are sound, but their rejection of racial categories is not practical, and therefore not helpful in making today's gamete market more racially just. Philosophers interested in bioethics need to offer some direction on how to cope with racial categories in the here and now instead of turning to utopian visions of a world without race. The most we can do to alleviate the cruelty of racial categories today and in the future is to find ways to maximize human agency under racial constraint in the hopes of breaking the stereotypes that feed personal and social race-based harm. This flexibility in light of racial imposition is the purpose of racial navigation, which aims to mediate between the racial expectations of others and one's own path.

I am not proposing that breaking racial stereotypes through examples of varied racial response is all that is needed to fight the invidious effects of racialism in the gamete market and beyond. But racial navigation is a vital piece of the puzzle. Laws can and should set the parameters for our social conduct, but law cannot (nor should it try to) reach into the realm of human intimacy. That domain is for us to grapple with in our own hearts and minds. We have a moral responsibility to question the racial meanings swirling around in our social ontology because these racial meanings shape and constrict our self-understandings, and by extension, our family plans.

REFERENCES

1. J.A. Robertson, *Children of Choice; Freedom and the New Reproductive Technologies* (Princeton: Princeton University Press, 1994).

2. In 1995, the National Survey of Family Growth found that 10.5 percent of African American women were infertile, compared to 6.4 percent of white women. Seven percent of Hispanic women were infertile, and "other" women experienced infertility at a rate of 13.6 percent. "Fertility, Family Planning, and Women's Health: New Data From the 1995 National Survey of Family Growth," *U.S. Dept. of Health and Human Services.* High rates of infertility among black women may be linked to "untreated chlamydia and gonorrhea, STDs that can lead to pelvic inflammatory disease; nutritional deficiencies; complications of childbirth and abortion; and environmental and workplace hazards"; D. Roberts, *Killing the Black Body: Race, Reproduction, and the Meaning of Liberty* (New York: Random House, 577), pp. 251–52.

3. In this article I focus on economic transaction involving sperm and ova, but the race-based selection and "hiring" of surrogate and gestational mothers also raises ethical concerns. As with paid gamete "donation," the reinforcement of racial stereotype is of concern, but issues of economic exploitation that entangle race and class status present additional moral worries.

4. The term "donor" continues to be used to describe individuals who are in fact paid in exchange for their gametes. "Donor" attributes altruistic motives to the sellers of gametes even when financial gain is the only or overriding factor expressed. See R. Mead, "Eggs for Sale," *The New Yorker* (9 August 1999).

5. Doctors must be licensed to perform fertility therapies such as in vitro fertilization and gamete intrafallopian transfer, and clinics must report their success rates to the Centers for Disease Control. The American Society of Reproductive Medicine recommends guidelines and ethical standards but physicians are not legally obligated to follow their recommendations.

6. N. Zack, *Race and Mixed Race* (Philadelphia: Temple University Press, 1993), p. 40.

7. I develop the concept of racial navigation in the context of the lingering public debate over transracial adoption in the book *The Ethics of Transracial Adoption* (Ithaca: Cornell University Press, forthcoming 2001).

8. In 1988, 12 percent of U.S. women of childbearing age sought professional advice regarding infertility (medical advice, tests, drugs, surgery, or assisted reproductive technologies). This number grew to 15 percent in 1995. See ref. 2, "Fertility, Family Planning, and Women's Health." Sperm counts in U.S. men have decreased annually from 1938 to 1996 at a rate of about 1.5 percent. *The National Institutes of Health,* "Environmental Health Perspectives," November 1997.

9. http://news.mpr.org/features/199711/21_smiths_fertility/part3/sectionI.shtml.

10. See ref. 8, "Fertility, Family Planning, and Women's Health.

11. <http://news.mpr.org/features/199711/20_smiths_fertility/part3/>

12. This cost covers the entire process from the initial consultation to the actual transfer. "American Society for Reproductive Medicine," 1995; see website for the American Society for Reproductive Medicine, Patient FAQ.

13. See ref. 2, Roberts, *Killing the Back Body,* p. 251.

14. These other factors include the inter-generational "grand shuffling of the genetic deck," which "gives each gene slightly different properties and is one reason children differ from their parents." N. Wade, "Earliest Divorce Case: X and Y Chromosomes." *New York Times* (29 October 1999).

15. For a historical overview of the "one drop rule" see J.F. Davis, *Who Is Black? One Nation's Definition* (University Park, Penn. The Pennsylvania State University Press, 1991).

16. For a discussion of extended kin networks in black communities see C. Stack *All Our Kin: Strategies for Survival In a Black Community* (New York: Harper and Row; 1974).

17. Orlando Patterson contends that African Americans are a diverse group and "very American." They are a hard-working disproportionately God-fearing, law-abiding group of people who share the same dreams as their fellow citizens, love and cherish the land of their birth with equal fervor, contribute to its cultural, military, and political glory and global triumph our of all proportion to their numbers, and, to every dispassionate observer, are in their values, habits, ideals, and ways of living among the most 'American' of Americans.' *The Ordeal of Integration* (New York: Civitas, 1997), p. 171.

18. Dorothy Roberts documents the sterilization abuse of black women that ironically increased with the demise of Jim Crowism. Physicians at state institutions often performed hysterectomies on poor black women without their consent. Roberts also details the recent efforts to require the injection of Norplant and Depo-Provera as a condition to receiving welfare benefits. See ref. 2, Roberts, *Killing the Black Body,* p. 4.

19. Although my Internet search of fertility clinics offering sperm and egg donation was not exhaustive, every site I visited used race as the primary sorting category. Not all clinics make their donor lists available to the public, and some require registration with the clinic as a precondition to viewing donor lists.

20. Available at http://db.orn.com/cryobank/cryo.fm.

21. C. Mills, *Blackness Visible* (Ithaca Cornell University Press, 1998), p. 44.

22. What I term "structural racism" is similar to what Kwame Ture and Charles Hamilton call "institutional racism." I prefer the former because it denotes a meta-physical as well as physical rendering of racial hierarchy. K. Ture and C. Hamilton *Black Power: The Politics of Liberation* (New York Random House, 1992, 1967), p. 4.

23. D. Bell *Faces at the Bottom of the Well: The Permanance of Racism* (New York: Basic Books, 1992).

24. M. Banton, "The Idiom of Race: A Critique of Presentism," in *Theories of Race and Racism,* ed. I. Black and J. Solomons (New York: Routledge, 2000).

25. T. Derricotte, *The Black Notebooks: An Interior Journey* (New York: W.W. Norton, 1997); see *Village of Arlington Heights v. Metropolitan Hous. Dev. Corp.,* 429 U.S. 252 (1977).

26. See ref. 1, Robertson, *Children of Choice,* p. 20.

27. For example, R. Posner, *Sex and Reason* (Cambridge, Mass.: Harvard University Press, 1992).

28. R.D.G. Kelley, *Yo' Mama's DisFunktional! Fighting the Culture Wars in Urban America* (Boston: Beacon Press, 1997), p. 16.

29. For example, W. Kymlicka's argument in favor of "contexts of choice" in *Liberalism, Community and Culture* (New York: Oxford University Press, 1989).

30. See ref. 28, Kelley, *Yo Mama's DisFunktional!* p. 17.

31. R. Gooding-Williams, "Race, Multiculturalism and Democracy," *Constellations* 5, no. 1 (1998): 23.

32. The strategic value of racial self-awareness is tangible in the domain of antidiscrimination laws and policies that attempt to correct for race-based disadvantage. This critique of colorblindness is found in the body of work that has been dubbed Critical Race Theory. For a thorough overview of the scholarly activist movement see the introduction to K. Crenshaw et al., eds., *Critical Race Theory: The Key Writings That Made the Movement* (New York: New Press, 1996).

33. J. Scales-Trent, *Notes of a White Black Woman* (University Park, Penn.: Pennsylvania State University Press, 1995).

34. See ref. 31, Gooding-Williams, "Race, Multiculturalism and Democracy," p. 23.

35. For example, A Piper, "Passing for White, Passing for Black," *Transition,* 58 (1992): 4–32.

36. For an excellent example of contemporary "whiggers" see the film, "Black and White."

37. The issue of parental rights and obligations of genetic and social parents is not a settled matter. Ethical and legal issues become especially controversial when the custody or ownership of embryos is at stake.

38. A. Appiah, *In My Father's House* (New York: Oxford, 1992), p. 13.

39. A. Appiah, "Racial Identity and Racial Identification," in *Theories of Race and Racism,* ed. L. Black and J. Solomons (New York: Routledge, 2000), p. 613.

40. See ref. 6, Zack. *Race and Mixed Race,* p. 40.

41. S.J. Gould, *The Mismeasure of Man* (New York: Norton, 1981).

Souls on Ice:
America's Human Embryo Glut and the Unbearable Lightness of Almost Being

Liza Mundy

Janis Elspas is a mother of four. Unlike most parents, she had three of her children simultaneously. The nine-year-old triplets were born in 1997 after Elspas underwent a series of in vitro fertilization treatments for infertility. Her oldest child, 10, is the happy result of a prior IVF treatment round. Elspas worked hard to get her children, and is grateful to have them. But four, thanks very much, are plenty. The problem is that Elspas also has 14 embryos left over from the treatment that produced her 10-year-old. The embryos are stored in liquid nitrogen at a California frozen storage facility—she is not entirely sure where—while Elspas and her husband ponder what to do with them.

Give them away to another couple, to gestate and bear? Her own children's full biological siblings—raised in a different family? Donate them to scientific research? Let them . . . finally . . . lapse? It is, she and her husband find, an intractable problem, one for which there is no satisfactory answer. So what they have done—thus far—is nothing. Nothing that is, but agonize.

"I don't have the heart to thaw them," says Elspas, who works as media relations director for a multi-birth networking group called the Triplet Connection. "But then again, I don't have the will to do something with them."

Elspas is by no means alone, either in having frozen human embryos she and her husband must eventually figure out what to do with, or in the moral paralysis she feels, surveying the landscape of available choices. In fact, she is part of an explosively growing group. In 2002, the Society for Assisted Reproductive Technology—the research arm for U.S. fertility doctors—decided to find out how many unused embryos had accumulated in the nation's 430 fertility clinics. The RAND consulting group, hired to do a head count, concluded that 400,000 frozen embryos existed—a staggering number, twice as large as previous estimates. Given that hundreds of thousands of IVF treatment rounds have since been performed, it seems fair to estimate that by now the number of embryos in limbo in the United States alone is closer to half a million.

This embryo glut is forcing many people to reconsider whatever they thought about issues such as life and death and choice and reproductive freedom. It's a dilemma that has been quietly building: The first American IVF baby was born in 1981, less than a decade after *Roe v. Wade* was decided. Thanks in part to *Roe*, fertility medicine in this country developed in an atmosphere of considerable reproductive freedom (read: very little government oversight), meaning, among other things, that responsibility for embryo disposition rests squarely with patients. The number of IVF rounds, or "cycles," has grown to the point that in 2003 about 123,000 cycles were performed, to help some of the estimated 1 in 7 American couples who have difficulty conceiving naturally. Early on, it proved relatively easy to freeze a lab-created human embryo—which unlike, say, hamburger meat, can be frozen, and thawed, and refrozen, and thawed, and then used. (To be precise, the technical term is "preembryo," or "conceptus"; a fertilized egg is not considered an embryo until about two weeks of development, and IVF embryos are frozen well before this point.) Over time—as fertility drugs have gotten more powerful and lab procedures more efficient—it has become possible to coax more and more embryos into being during the average cycle. Moreover, as doctors transfer fewer embryos back into patients, in an effort to reduce multiple births, more of the embryos made are subsequently frozen.

And so, far from going away, the accumulation of human embryos is likely to grow, and grow, and grow. And in growing, the embryo overstock is likely to change—or at least complicate—the way we collectively think about human life at its earliest stages, and morally what is the right thing to do with it. At some point, embryos may alter or even explode the reproductive landscape: It is IVF embryos, after all, that are at the center of the nation's stem cell debate, which itself has prompted a new national conversation about life and reproductive liberty, creating new alliances as well as schisms. In 2001, as one of his first major domestic policy decisions, George W. Bush banned federal funding for labs developing new stem cell lines using leftover IVF embryos; then in May 2005, the U.S. House of Representatives passed a bill approving funding for stem cell research using these same embryos, setting the stage for an eventual conservative showdown. In the course of this debate, embryos have emerged as another tool for truly hardline conservatives looking for new ways to beat back abortion rights. Like "fetal rights" laws that seemingly protect unborn children from acts of homicide, "embryo rights" are being waved about as a weapon in the assault on abortion rights, as anti-abortion lawmakers talk about seizing control over frozen embryo stores; limiting the creation of new embryos; or both.

But the impact of the embryo is also taking place on a more subtle and personal level. The glut's very existence illuminates how the newest reproductive technologies are complicating questions about life; issues that many people thought they had resolved are being revived and reconsidered, in a different emotional context. As with ultrasound technology—which permits parents to visualize a fetus in utero—IVF allows many patients to form an emotional attachment to a form of human life that is very early, it's true, but still life, and still human. People bond with photos of three-day-old, eight-cell embryos. They ardently wish for them to grow into children. The experience can be transforming: "I was like, 'I created these things, I feel a sense of responsibility for them,'" is how one IVF patient put it. Describing herself as staunchly pro-choice, this patient found that she could not rest until she located a person—actually, two people—willing to bring her excess embryos to term. The presence of embryos for whom (for which?) they feel a certain undefined moral responsibility presents tens of thousands of Americans with a dilemma for which nothing—nothing—has prepared them.

A new demographic is wrestling with questions initially posed by contraception and abortion. A world away from the exigencies, mitigating circumstances, and carefully honed ideologies that have grown up in and around U.S. abortion clinics, it is people like Janis Elspas who are being called upon to think, hard, about when life begins, and when it is—or is not right to terminate it. They are in this position, ironically enough, not because they don't want a family, but precisely because they do. Among the nation's growing ranks of IVF patients, deciding the fate of frozen embryos is known as the "disposition decision," and it is one of the hardest decisions patients face, so unexpectedly problematic that many decide, in the end, to punt, a choice that is only going to make the glut bigger, the moral problem more looming and unresolved.

"ARE THEY PEOPLE? AREN'T THEY PEOPLE?"

To show just how difficult embryo disposition can be: Dr. Robert Nachtigall, a veteran San Francisco reproductive endocrinologist, directed a study of patients who had conceived using IVF together with egg donation, another rapidly growing niche of fertility medicine. As Nachtigall and his colleagues at the University of California-San Francisco were interviewing these parents, they were struck by comments made, separately, by several couples.

Hard as it was deciding whether to go ahead with egg donation, these parents said, it was harder still deciding the fate of their leftover embryos.

"Until recently, I don't know if any of us were aware of the scope of the embryo dilemma," Nachtigall told colleagues at the 2005 annual meeting held by the American Society for Reproductive Medicine (ASRM), the trade group for fertility doctors. Struck by these unprompted revelations, he and fellow researchers decided to do a new study, this one looking explicitly at the way patients think about their unused, iced-down embryos. The study was published in 2005 in the journal *Fertility and Sterility*. Strikingly, Nachtigall found that even in one of the bluest regions of the country, which is to say, among people living in and around San Francisco, few were able to view a three-day-old laboratory embryo with anything like detachment. "Parents variously conceptualized frozen embryos as biological tissue, living entities, 'virtual' children having interests that must be considered and protected, siblings of their living children, genetic or psychological 'insurance policies,' and symbolic reminders of their past infertility," his report noted. Many seemed afflicted by a kind of *Chinatown* syndrome, thinking of them simultaneously as: Children! Tissue! Children! Tissue!

An earlier study, conducted by psychologist Susan Klock and colleagues at the Northwestern University School of Medicine, found that many patients begin IVF with some notion about how they will dispose of surplus embryos. (The choices come down to five: use them; donate them for research; donate them to another infertile person; freeze them indefinitely; or have them thawed, that is, quietly disposed of.) What Klock also reported was that many couples found their thinking transformed once treatment was over. More than half the couples who had planned to dispose of their embryos decided, instead, to use them, or donate them. Conversely, seven of the eight couples who had planned to donate them to research decided to use them, or dispose of them. Nearly all who had planned to donate their embryos to another couple found that, when push came to shove, they could not relinquish their potential genetic offspring. In short: Almost all reconsidered, not in any way that could be neatly summarized. All in all, 71 percent changed their minds about what to do. Also striking: Only about half of patients with embryos stored for more than three years could be located. The rest were incommunicado.

Nachtigall's study elaborated on these findings. Couples, he found, were confused yet deeply affected by the responsibility of deciding what to do with their embryos. They wanted to do the right thing. All of the 58 couples in his study had children as a result of treatment, so they knew, well, what even three-day-old embryos can and do grow into. (Nachtigall is currently studying a much larger sample of couples, where both egg and sperm come from the parents. It should answer the question of whether couples who use donor eggs are in any way distinct in their thinking about embryos.) "Some saw them as biological material, but most recognized the potential for life," Nachtigall told colleagues at the ASRM meeting. "For many couples, it seems there is no good decision; yet they still take it seriously morally."

For virtually all patients, he found, the disposition decision was torturous, the end result unpredictable. "Nothing feels right," he reported patients telling him. "They literally don't know what the right, the good, the moral thing is." In the fluid process of making a decision—any decision—some try to talk themselves into a clinical detachment. "Little lives, that's how I thought about them," said one woman. "But you have to switch gears and think, 'They're not lives, they're cells. They're science.' That's kind of what I had to switch to." Others were not able to make that switch, thinking of their embryos as almost sentient. "My husband talked about donating them to research, but there is some concern that this would not be a peaceful way to go," said one woman. Another said, "You start saying to yourself, 'Every one of these is potentially a life.'"

Many were troubled, Nachtigall said, by the notion of donating embryos to research or to another couple, and thereby losing control over their fate and well-being; they seemed to feel a parental obligation to protect their embryos. "I couldn't give my children to someone else to raise, and I couldn't give these embryos to someone else to bear," said one woman. Another woman described her embryos as a psychic insurance policy, providing "intangible solace" against the fundamental parental terror that an existing child might die. "What if [my daughter] got leukemia?" said yet another, who considered her frozen embryos a potential source of treatment. A patient put the same notion more bluntly: "You have the idea that in a warehouse somewhere there's replacement part should yours get lost, or there is something wrong with them."

For others, embryos carried a price tag that made them seem like a consumer good; a few parents considered destroying them to be a "waste" of all the money spent on treatment.

"You weigh what's best," Nachtigall quoted one parent as saying, but what's best is not, often, clear. This parent continued: "Are they people? Aren't they people? In part of my mind, they're potential people, but the point is, it seems odd to me to keep them frozen forever. It seems like not facing the issue." A patient who had decided to donate embryos for research said, "We've agreed that it's the right thing for us to do, but the final step is to get the forms notarized, and we haven't done it. I will honestly say that it will be a day of mourning."

For those couples who did reach a decision, the resolution came as a great relief, bringing with it, his report noted, "a profound sense of completeness and resolution."

Nachtigall also found that patients sometimes disposed of embryos in novel ways that fell short of actual plug pulling. In a version of the rhythm method of contraception, he learned, some patients (though none of the ones in his study) solved their dilemma through the laborious—and expensive—process of having leftover embryos transferred into the woman's uterus at a time in her monthly cycle when implantation would be unlikely. Others buried embryos. Still others could not bring themselves to dispose of them at all. "We'll have a couple more pregnancies and we'll just grow the whole lot," one father told Nachtigall and his team.

Of the 58 couples Nachtigall and his group interviewed, the average couple had seven frozen embryos in storage. The average embryo had been in storage for four years. Even after that much time had elapsed, 72 percent had not decided what to do, and a number echoed the words of one patient: "We can't talk about it." The embryos keep alive the question of whether to have more children, a topic on which many spouses disagree. "I still have six in the bank," said one woman, who had not given up the idea of bearing them. "They call to me. I hate to talk about it. But they call to me." Her words are reminiscent of a comment made by the singer Celine Dion, who, after undergoing IVF in 2001, later said, in describing her plans for a second child: "This frozen embryo that is in New York is my child waiting to be brought to life."

It should be noted that the confusion felt by parents is shared by the minds who guide American jurisprudence. As University of Wisconsin law professor and bioethicist Alta Charo pointed out at the 2005 ASRM meeting, the embryo issue tends to emerge as a point of dispute in divorce cases. Tracing the confused path of judicial decision-making, Charo offered one situation in which a Tennessee court ruled frozen embryos to be potential children, or effectively so, and—in the court's traditional role of acting in the best interests of children in custody suits—awarded a batch of disputed embryos to the parent who intended to bring them to term. That decision was reversed by a second court, which chose to treat the embryos as property and proposed dividing them, like furniture, between the ex-spouses. But the state's Supreme Court ultimately awarded the embryos to the spouse who did not intend to use them. In general, Charo said, courts tend to this latter approach: They take pains to avoid situations where one person will bring the embryos to term against the wishes of the ex-partner, privileging the right not to procreate over the desire to do so.

For the most part, courts often do regard embryos as property, but property with an elevated moral status, "like pets, or natural resources, or pieces of art," as Charo put it. In Louisiana, however, embryos have been designated as "juridical persons." "No one knows what this means," Charo said, comparing the status of Louisiana embryos to that formerly assigned to slaves: not fully human under the law, but deserving of some rights. One thing "juridical person" does mean is that in Louisiana, fertility clinics are forbidden to dispose of embryos. They are directed to act in the best interests of the embryos, whatever that may be: a kind of guardian *ad litem* of the embryo.

Similarly, the federal government, in its role as regulator, has found the embryo a slippery creature to define. In 2002, the U.S. Department of Health and Human Services began distributing grants to groups willing to raise public awareness about what the Bush administration likes to call "embryo adoption." Also known as "embryo donation," this is a process whereby embryos are relinquished by whoever created them and handed over to another couple, or person. In most states, this is essentially a property transfer, not an adoption, and advocates for the infertile, as well as old-line reproductive rights groups, fear the use of the word "adoption" is one more attempt to confer humanhood on the embryo, a backdoor anti-abortion sally. They are right: To dramatize his opposition to federal funding for stem cell research, Bush in May 2005 posed with a group of "Snowflakes" babies, children who started life as leftover IVF embryos and were donated to other couples, thanks to the brokerage of an explicitly Christian, explicitly pro-life embryo adoption group called Snowflakes.

Inconveniently for the president, at that very moment the U.S. Food and Drug Administration was in the process of categorizing the human embryo as biological tissue, thereby putting into effect strict disease-testing requirements that would make embryo adoption, or donation, impossible. Clinics feared they would need to close down their donation programs. At the last moment, an exemption for embryos was carved out, and embryo donations were permitted to go forward. The infertility lobby was delighted and a little smug, not just because doctors and patients' groups support embryo donation (which they do), but because "tissue" remains the designation conferred on embryos by the FDA. Like abortion rights groups, the infertility field likes this designation, which helps preserve for it total reproductive freedom by encouraging the notion of the embryo as a multicelled clump of tissue.

But the idea of potential personhood has clearly been implanted, so to speak; human embryos are going to continue to be a political battleground as anti-abortion advocates include them in the umbrella concept of "pre-born life." During last year's stem cell debate, then-House Majority Leader Tom DeLay referred to embryos as "living, distinct human beings," while a conservative columnist referred to them as "microscopic Americans." The president calls them "nascent human life." As *Slate*'s Will Saletan has pointed out, pro-life lawmakers periodically threaten all-out war on the reproductive liberty enjoyed by IVF patients; Republican Rep. Chris Smith of New Jersey hinted at this when he said, "The public policy we craft should ensure that the best interests of newly created human life is protected." Senator Sam Brownback (R-Kan.) has suggested that the government should limit the number of embryos created to one or two per IVF cycle.

Unnerved, advocacy groups for the infertile and those who serve them called a press conference in

2005, where Sean Tipton, spokesman for ASRM, said that "patients control and make the decision about what happens with those embryos, and that's the way it is now, and it's important that that's the way it stays." The problem is that many patients do view embryos as nascent human life and, paralyzed by this thought, cannot decide how to decide.

It's an issue that affects anybody with an interest in reproductive issues—which is to say, pretty much every American. Some think that the embryo glut may offer the next serious challenge to *Roe*. "For the moment couples still have dispositional control, but I predict that that is going to be challenged very soon," Alta Charo said at the 2005 meeting, speaking to doctors and fertility clinic staffers. Arguing that pro-life advocates can taste "total victory" after "an ongoing nibble-at-the-edges battle" involving state-house measures like informed consent and mandatory waiting periods, Charo predicted that somewhere, soon, "some obscure legislature" will propose to seize control of frozen embryos, the measure will be challenged, and the ensuing lawsuit will end up in the U.S. Supreme Court. Traditionally, she pointed out, abortion rights involves weighing the interests of the woman against those of the fetus, and up to now the woman's interests have been considered paramount. But now the interests of the embryo, or fetus, or potential child, can be separated out. This, she said, is a watershed development.

For those who want to test the core of *Roe v. Wade,* Charo told the fertility specialists, "you guys are the perfect opportunity to separate the question of embryos and best interests, and the woman's right to direct her body. You take a law like Louisiana's, saying that personhood begins at conception, and that you cannot discard embryos. Now the Supreme Court has the ability to look at the status of the embryo, not as compared with the woman's right to control what she wants to do with her body. There is no bodily interest. It's entirely possible that the first real challenge to *Roe* will be looking at the embryo in isolation. The question about discard is very, very important. This will be where they start their litigation strategy, to chip away at *Roe.*"

It should be pointed out, however, that even anti-abortion conservatives are not united in their ideas about the embryo and whether it has rights, or best interests, or even the potential for life. Once a person contemplates an embryo—really looks at it, under a microscope or in a photograph—his or her opinion is often changed, and not in any consistent or predictable

direction. This is true for pro-choice and pro-life alike. While researching a book on assisted reproduction and its impact, I interviewed California Rep. Dana Rohrabacher, a reliably anti-abortion Republican member of the House. Rohrabacher was one of some 50 Republicans who defied the president by voting in favor of federal funding for stem cell research using surplus IVF embryos. For Rohrabacher it was not abstract: He and his wife, Rhonda, went through IVF treatment and have triplets as a result.

Going through that process, Rohrabacher told me, fundamentally changed his thinking about life and its origins. "For a long time I've been pro-life, and I still consider myself to be pro-life," he reflected, sitting on the front porch of his Huntington Beach bungalow, which, inside, had been taken over by the demands of triplet care. "I have done a lot of soul-searching but also a lot of rethinking about reality, and what's going on here, and I have come to the conclusion that I'm . . . first, I'm still pro-life. But I always said that life begins at conception. But . . . I was always predicating that on the idea that life begins at conception when conception begins in a woman's body."

Now, Rohrabacher realizes, conception can take place outside the human body. That, for him, is a meaningful difference. The crux of the matter: Is the embryo in the womb, or is it in a lab? "I don't think that the potential for human life exists in a human embryo until it's implanted in a human body. So you are not destroying a human life by basically not using a fertilized egg. These are not potential human lives until they are implanted in a body. Left alone, they will not become a human being. When they are implanted in a female body, they have a chance to become a human being, so I still would be opposed to abortion."

"PEOPLE DO NOT WANT TO INHERIT EMBRYOS"

Less examined has been the fact that the embryo glut presents an immediate and pressing problem for the very people who helped create it: fertility doctors. In clinics around the country, doctors are at their wits' end trying to figure out what to do with embryos that have fallen, willy-nilly, under their moral, medical, and, possibly, legal purview. The way this happens is: When patients agree to have embryos frozen, they sign forms stating what should be done with the embryos should the patients divorce, disappear, or stop paying storage fees. After treatment has concluded, many patients eventually do stop paying, disappear, move, leave no forwarding address. In such cases, doctors are, at a certain point, technically free to dispose of abandoned embryos. But many are reluctant to take that step. They are terrified that at some point a patient will come back and sue them for—well, for something.

"Nobody does it [destroys abandoned embryos]," says Alan DeCherney, the editor of *Fertility and Sterility* and a reproductive endocrinologist who is now at the National Institutes of Health. "It's a hot topic. People think the risk of holding them is less than the risk of destroying them."

And the risk of holding them is considerable. "I have tons of embryos, and I can't track down the owners," said one Los Angeles doctor, Vicken Sahakian of the Pacific Fertility Center, sitting in his posh Wilshire Boulevard office. Sahakian practically had his head in his hands, thinking about all those embryos. "It's one of the main problems I have. I have thousands of embryos from patients who have been through this program for, what, 10-, 12-plus years, changing addresses, and never called back, never paid storage fees—you can't track them down." Sahakian does the best he can to whittle down his own embryo glut; he runs a strong embryo donation program, encouraging couples to donate embryos to other patients and handling the logistics. He has also hired a collection agency to try to track down patients and force them to make a resolution. His "biggest nightmare," he said, is that he will be unable to sell his practice when he is ready to retire, because no doctor will want to buy a practice that comes with a closetful of unclaimed embryos and the vague, terrible responsibility they entail. "The person buying it does not want to buy the embryos. That's the rule," he said. "People do not want to inherit embryos. So what do you do with them? I have embryos that have been here since 1992."

The overages have grown to such proportions that companies now exist, solely, to manage embryo inventory. Back in 1990, Russell Bierbaum, who at the time worked for a sperm bank, had a vision of the future, and what he saw was: lots and lots of frozen embryos. So he founded a company called ReproTech, which can be hired to assume and maintain doctors' embryo inventory, as well as handle transport, a tricky process in and of itself. (What box do you fill out, exactly, on the FedEx form? "Warning: Contains microscopic Americans"?) It took a while for the idea to come to fruition, he says, but now business is booming: He has two facilities, in Minnesota and Florida, and is constantly adding new storage tanks. Bierbaum

prefers to assume responsibility for embryos soon after their creation. His employees stay in touch with patients, keeping addresses current, periodically calling to say hello and review the options. In a few instances, he says, he will take over abandoned embryos and attempt to track patients down. It is therefore people like ReproTech staff members— rather than, say, ministers or psychologists—who often are the ones discussing, with patients, fundamental questions touching on birth and death and life and reproduction, all the essential questions of humanity. "We end up being the counselors without the credentials," acknowledges Bierbaum, "just answering the questions, being available."

It's hard to know how, exactly, the embryo overstock will go away. The RAND study found that only about 3 percent of unused embryos have been slated to be donated for research. In England, unused embryos are destroyed after five years, though this government policy did not occur without controversy; the first time embryos were set to be destroyed, a group of pro-life advocates staged protests. The deadline was extended, but eventually the embryos were destroyed. Other countries, such as Germany and Italy, forbid the freezing of embryos. In those countries, every embryo made must be implanted. Both of these ideas are of course anathema to American fertility advocacy groups and to the medical field, because it would open the door to that dreaded phenomenon, governmental control over human life and its disposition.

So what are we going to do with our embryo glut? Robert Nachtigall believes that with better patient counseling and logistical co-ordination between fertility clinics and research labs, many more unused embryos could be directed toward stem cell research, and that many patients would be happy to know that their embryos are being used to find a cure for afflictions such as Parkinson's disease and juvenile diabetes.

"I think it's a mistake to call it a glut," says Nachtigall. "I mean, these embryos are created in a process as hundreds of thousands of couples attempt to overcome infertility, and their presence is perhaps an unanticipated side effect of the use of advanced reproductive technology. But there is nothing inherently negative or wrong about their existence, and as we turn our attention to them, we may find that indeed they could be a tremendous resource for science, the country, and for mankind, for that matter."

The problem is, few fertility clinics counsel patients about disposition, at least not at any length; and because of the ban on federal funding, few labs can receive human embryos for research. Nor has the fertility profession served itself or its patients entirely well, encouraging the idea that embryos are multicelled clumps of tissue. They *are* multicelled clumps of tissue, it's true, but they are also more complicated and more emotionally fraught. One of the powerful findings of Nachtigall's study was how isolated patients felt in making the disposition decision; how they longed for counseling, advice, some sort of out-loud moral conversation between people who had been through, and thought through, the same issues. Whether the reproductive rights community might ever hold such a grand, collective conversation seems unlikely, in this charged political atmosphere. But it would be useful, to put it mildly.

Meanwhile, the technology itself is so new that nobody knows what the expiration date on embryos might be. Might all these embryos become nonviable and nonproblematic? Unlikely. Recently, a San Francisco woman gave birth using an embryo that had been frozen for 13 years. So patients like Janis Elspas continue to agonize over their aging embryonic stores. An Orthodox Jew, Elspas believes her religion would permit her to quietly terminate what are, basically, little more than fertilized eggs. "But considering all the pain and suffering we went through to get those embryos, I still consider it the destruction of a God-given gift."

After weighing all the options, and rejecting them, one patient says wryly, but a little wearily: "Maybe when I die, they'll just bury my embryos with me."

Chapter **7**

Genetic Technologies

Bulls Ship Curry to Knicks

Deerfield, Ill. (AP) – The Bulls dealt center Eddy Curry to the Knicks on Monday, ending a contentious negotiation in which Chicago insisted the restricted free agent take a DNA test over a heart problem . . .

The Bulls had insisted that Curry take a DNA test to determine whether he's susceptible to a potentially fatal heart problem. Curry, who missed the final 13 games of the regular season and the playoffs after experiencing an irregular heartbeat, balked, saying it violated his privacy.

"I would never put a player on the floor in a Chicago Bulls uniform if I didn't do everything in my power to find out all the information that was available," Paxson [Bulls general manager] said. "You can debate genetic testing 'til you're blue in the face. But from what I know, from what I've learned over the last six months, that test could have helped us determine the best course of action." . . .

Several prominent cardiologists cleared Curry to play, but Barry Maron, a world-renowned specialist in hypertrophic cardiomyopathy, suggested the DNA test. Paxson has said he understands the privacy issues involved but insisted the Bulls do not have an ulterior motive; they simply do not want a situation similar to those of former Boston Celtics guard Reggie Lewis or Loyola Marymount star Hank Gathers—players with hypertrophic cardiomyopathy who collapsed and died.

Paxson, speaking during the team's media day, told reporters the Bulls had offered Curry $400,000 annually for the next 50 years if he failed the genetic test.

"So he would have an above average lifestyle that would put him in a position that most other people aren't in," Paxson said. "Our intention through that whole process was to show him that we did care about him and that we were concerned about his well-being."

(The Associated Press, October 3, 2005)

The availability of genetic technologies changed the life and the career of Eddy Curry, a professional basketball player. Because he refused to undergo a genetic test, his team traded him. His team's general manager insisted that they asked him to take the genetic test because they "care about him" and are "concerned about his well-being." Curry said that taking the test would violate his privacy. Both parties seem to be committed to moral values, to doing what is right.

Lots of questions arise here that take us into the thick of the debate over genetic technologies. We know that there are genetic diseases, that is, diseases that tend to run in families, that can be inherited from our parents. For some of these diseases there are treatments or cures whereas for others there are not. Sometimes there are tests that can identify these genetic diseases. Should we take the tests or not? There is also research focused on using genetic technologies to treat or cure diseases. Should we use these technologies or not? What if in the course of developing these life-saving treatments we must destroy embryos—is that morally permissible? Genetic technologies can be used to determine the sex and health status of embryos/fetuses. Is it acceptable to use this information to choose a certain sort of child? In Eddy Curry's case, when he refused to take the genetic test and share the results with his employer, there were consequences; he was traded to another team. Is it acceptable for employers to require genetic tests of their employees? Are they allowed to fire or to refuse insurance coverage to an employee who refuses to take a genetic test? Consider the case of Gloria Spinelli who must also make a decision about genetic testing.

CASE STUDY: GLORIA'S DECISION

This has been a rough year for Gloria Spinelli, age 45. She was diagnosed with an early stage of breast cancer. She was not overly surprised by the diagnosis since her mother and two aunts had also had breast cancer. She underwent successful lumpectomy surgery and chemotherapy treatment and now was feeling well. Her family, including her husband, two daughters, aged 10 and 12, and two sisters, have rallied around her. Meanwhile, her doctor refers Gloria to a genetics specialist in his practice.

The genetic counselor suggests that Gloria could be tested to see whether she carries one of the known breast cancer genes, BRCA 1 and BRCA 2. Someone who has the BRCA 1 or BRCA 2 gene has a greater probability of developing breast cancer (a 36–85% likelihood of developing cancer versus the 13% likelihood of a woman without either of the genes[1]). The counselor points out that these two genes are responsible for only a small percentage of breast cancer cases and that having one of these genes puts a person at increased risk for breast cancer but does not mean that the person will necessarily develop breast cancer.[2] Gloria's mother, surviving aunts, and sisters could be invited to consider genetic testing. According to the counselor, the advantages of testing include knowing the specific genetic reason for their breast cancer and in the sisters' cases knowing whether they have inherited one of these genes. If they have, then there are treatment options they could consider such as frequent mammography screening, dietary changes, or prophylactic mastectomy.

Gloria doesn't see any reason for her to be tested given that she already contracted the disease. She feels that her mother and surviving aunts would also see no value in the test, although she is willing to speak to her sisters about it. However, she would like to have her daughters tested to know if they are at any special risk.

GENETICS

Before we take up Gloria's case, it may be helpful to recall some basic facts of genetics. The human genome (genetic makeup) consists of 23 pairs of chromosomes. A female has 22 pairs of chromosomes plus two X chromosomes, one inherited from each parent. A male has 22 pairs of chromosomes plus an X chromosome from his mother and a Y chromosome from his father. Together these chromosomes probably contain between 30,000 and 40,000 genes.[3] The nucleus of every cell in a person's body (except for sperm or egg cells) contains two copies of each gene, one inherited from each parent. The DNA (deoxyribonucleic acid) that makes up these genes and chromosomes is a double-stranded helix, a long series of nucleotides that code for certain proteins. Most genes have at least two variations, called alleles; therefore, a child may inherit either one of the two alleles from each parent. In 2000, the first rough draft of the map of the human genome was completed so that we now know approximately where on the chromosomes certain genes sit.

Some diseases and conditions are associated with certain genes or certain chromosomes. For instance, Down syndrome results from an extra copy of chromosome 21 (three copies are present instead of the usual two). Hemophilia results from mutations on the X chromosome. If a parent has an unusual gene, say one that is much larger than the typical gene or is missing some part of the gene, then the child stands a 50% risk of inheriting that gene (Figure 7.1).

Some diseases or conditions result if there is one "bad" copy of a gene (e.g., Huntington's disease), whereas other diseases and conditions happen only if there are two "bad" copies of a gene (e.g., Tay-Sachs disease).

All cells contain genes and chromosomes but some of the most accessible cells from which to extract DNA are the cells in blood and skin. There is DNA in both **somatic cells** (the differentiated cells of a person's body) and in **germ-line cells** (the reproductive cells, namely egg and sperm, that can go on to become the next generation).

A mistake in a gene can have several consequences. Sometimes a mistake in one gene is enough to cause a disease. If you have this mistaken gene you have or will develop this disease. Other times, in cases where it takes two "bad" copies of a gene to cause a disease, a person with one bad copy of the gene has no symptoms of the disease, but he is called a "carrier" of the disease because he can still pass on the "bad" copy of the gene to his descendents (Figure 7.2).

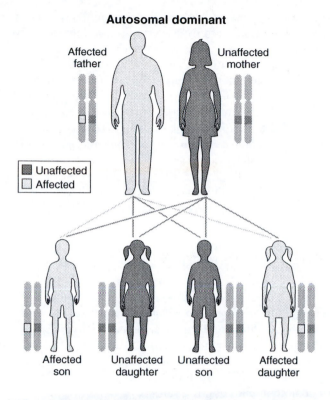

Autosomal dominant

Affected father

Unaffected mother

Unaffected
Affected

Affected son

Unaffected daughter

Unaffected son

Affected daughter

FIGURE 7.1   Diagram of affected father passing on mutation.

And at still other times, a mutation (mistake) in a gene causes no symptoms or problems that we have yet identified. Scientists are at work trying to determine what each gene does.

There is a lot of interest in determining how genes relate to personality traits, intelligence, and susceptibility to addiction. For example, people ask whether genes are responsible for making a

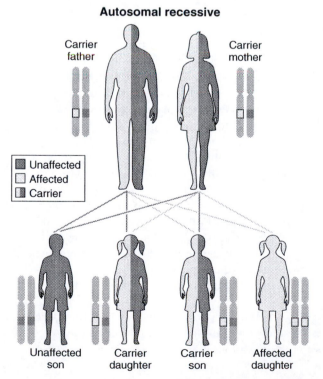

Autosomal recessive

Carrier father

Carrier mother

Unaffected
Affected
Carrier

Unaffected son

Carrier daughter

Carrier son

Affected daughter

FIGURE 7.2   Diagram of carrier father passing on mutation.

person shy or smart or gay or alcoholic. These personality characteristics or states are likely so complex that there are no simple genetic explanations for them. But given everything we have learned about genes so far, there may very well be some genetic influence or component to these traits.

As discussed, some genes are responsible for certain conditions or diseases. Having the gene means you will have the disease. This role for genes is called **genetic determinism,** namely, the view that genes control human lives. In the early years of genetics, this was the popular view. Many believed that our genes make us who we are. But now that view has been shown to be false. For one thing, we have discovered that there is no one-to-one relationship between all genes and all diseases. Some diseases are caused by several genes working together. In some cases genes do not inevitably cause disease but rather they raise the likelihood of developing certain diseases. These genes indicate a predisposition toward a certain disease. For instance, in Gloria's case the BRCA 1 or BRCA 2 gene would mean her odds of developing cancer were substantially higher than a woman who does not have either of these genes. At other times, it is genes in combination with environmental and lifestyle factors that raise the odds in favor of certain people contracting certain diseases.

GENETIC TECHNOLOGIES: FOR WHOM?

Now, armed with this background information, let us move into the realm of bioethics. First, whose DNA, whose genes and chromosomes, can be analyzed? The answer is everyone's, in other words, any being or person for whom there is a sample of DNA, including adults, children, and embryos/fetuses. We can do genetic screening on symptomatic individuals (those who have symptoms) and on presymptomatic individuals (those with no symptoms). This means that we can test embryos/fetuses for diseases that they will have from birth or for diseases that they will not get until late in life. Parents could then decide to abort embryos/fetuses who will suffer from a genetic disease or if they are using *in vitro* fertilization procedures, they could select embryos/fetuses who are free from a genetic disease.

Some think it is a good thing to be able to select certain embryos/fetuses (and reject others) based on the quality of life they will have as children or as adults. These ethicists, like Laura Purdy in the article included in this chapter, argue that it is wrong to knowingly risk harming a child by possibly passing on to him or her a horrific genetic disease. For reasons of nonmaleficence and beneficence, parents-to-be may have a duty to use genetic screening themselves or to test an embryo/fetus to avoid subjecting a child to great pain or harm. Some maintain that children have a right to a "minimally satisfying life" (Laura Purdy) or to an "open future" (Dena Davis) or, viewed from the other side, that parents-to-be have duties to provide for their children a minimally satisfying life that offers opportunities for growth and choice. It may be morally necessary to do genetic testing in order for parents to fulfill these duties or honor these rights and so to avoid harm to future generations.

Others think that using genetic testing to select certain embryos or fetuses and reject others is taking reproductive freedom too far. They argue that it is not up to us to "play God" and choose who will live or whose life is worth living. They point out that any judgment about what kind of life is worth living is highly subjective and arbitrary and is likely to be unduly influenced by social pressures and expectations. For example, while we as outsiders may judge that a life with cystic fibrosis or Huntington's disease is not worth living, those who have the disease or face the certainty of developing the disease may feel quite differently. Life may be preferable to no life, even if the life in question is short or is burdened by symptoms of disease. Some, such as Erik Parens and Adrienne Asch,[4] have also pointed out that selecting embryos/fetuses that are free from disease and impairments over those that suffer from disease and impairments is disrespectful to those currently living with diseases and impairments. It sends a message of disapproval and expresses contempt for those with diseases and disabilities. This disability rights critique of using genetic testing on embryos/fetuses considers the negative impact of such testing on others in the community.

Returning to Gloria's case, recall that she was especially interested in having her daughters tested for the BRCA 1 and BRCA 2 genes. This raises the issue of whether minor children should undergo genetic testing at their parents' request. Obviously, minor children cannot make their own medical decisions so

FIGURE 7.3   A bride and groom are married at an orthodox Jewish wedding. Before the wedding, they had undergone genetic testing which determined that their offspring would never be at risk for Tay-Sachs disease.

there is concern about their autonomy and well-being when they cannot consent for themselves. Many professional organizations urge caution or are opposed to genetic testing of asymptomatic children for adult-onset conditions.[5] It is thought to be better to wait until the child is older and can decide for him or her self. However, a 2005 study showed that clinical geneticists in the U.S., Canada, UK, Australia, and New Zealand have tested minor children for diseases for which there is no treatment, usually Huntington's disease, a fatal, late-onset neurological disease.[6] From the 301 responses to the survey, there were 49 cases of such testing. In 22 cases the minor child was under 14 years of age. The results of the test were disclosed to only two children. In the remaining 27 cases, the minor child was "mature" (over age 14) and the results were disclosed to all but one child. Parents (and their children's doctors) in these cases must have believed there was some value in obtaining genetic information about these children. In spite of the moral reasons against such testing, it is evident that parents like Gloria sometimes request genetic testing for their children.

We can promote genetic testing to individuals or to groups. Since genetic diseases and conditions are family diseases, many of them are more common in certain ethnic or cultural or geographically close groups than others. So someone of African descent is at greater risk of sickle cell anemia than someone from the general population. Similarly, someone of European descent is at greater risk of cystic fibrosis and a person of Ashkenazi Jewish descent stands a greater risk of inheriting Tay-Sachs disease (Figure 7.3). It might be viewed then as beneficial to highlight these genetic differences and to recommend or even require testing of the members of these ethnic groups. On the other hand, to target ethnic groups because of genetic differences may be viewed as racial stereotyping, ethnic discrimination, or genocide.

Genetic technologies are also expensive. The genetic test for BRCA 1 costs between $750 and $2,750.[7] Many insurance companies do not cover the costs for genetic tests and so Gloria may have to pay "out of pocket" for these tests for her daughters. Perhaps her sisters are not as financially secure as Gloria. It may be impossible for them to come up with the money to pay for the test. For now at least, genetic tests and whatever forms of genetic therapies or technologies are developed can be used only by the wealthy. For the foreseeable future, genetic technologies will not be available to the poor or to those who are medically underserved. Thus, there is an economic issue and a serious moral issue relating to justice and equality in considering who may use or benefit from genetic technologies.

GENETIC TECHNOLOGIES: WHY?

Why might we be interested in genetic knowledge about ourselves or someone else? What is the value of having this information? There appear to be four distinguishable answers to this question. The first answer is that genetic information, perhaps like all information, is inherently valuable. It is better to know than not to know. This reasoning may be based in Kantian theory. An individual can perhaps only act in a fully autonomous way when all the information relevant to making good choices is available. If important facts about the length and quality of your future life are available, you may need to have that information in order to act in a self-determining, autonomous way.

There are also utilitarian reasons at work here. The argument would go: Suppose you are at risk of inheriting a deadly, adult-onset genetic disease. The disease occurs if only one "bad" gene is inherited from either parent. One of your parents died from the disease and hence you have a 50% risk of getting the disease. If you know you will not get the disease, you can forego worrying about it or risking passing it on to your children. If you find out you will eventually contract the disease, you can make plans for your future care, live your life fully now, and avoid having children. Either way, the argument goes, there are more good consequences that result from knowing whether one will inherit a genetic disease than from not knowing.

However, this argument has not persuaded everyone. In a famous case, Nancy Wexler decided that for her it was better not to know she might have inherited a fatal genetic illness.

In 1978, Nancy Wexler's mother died from Huntington's disease (HD). Symptoms begin when a person is in his or her mid-30s or mid-40s. The disease is manifest first in small twitches, clumsiness, and awkward movements, but over 20 years it leads to mental deterioration and involuntary muscle spasms, and ultimately to death. Her father, Milton Wexler, founded an organization to promote research into the disease.

Research began by collecting DNA samples from families that included both people with HD and people without HD. In 1981, Nancy Wexler traveled to Lake Maracaibo in Venezuela where there is a high incidence of HD to collect more DNA samples (Figure 7.4).

In 1983, a team at Massachusetts General Hospital found a "genetic marker" for the disease. They found a genetic pattern that was characteristic of those with HD and absent in those without HD. It consisted of extra genetic material, of a segment of DNA repeated many more times than in the DNA of a person without HD. Finally, in 1993, the gene itself was discovered on chromosome 4. After years of assuming that she and her sister would take a test for HD when it became available, in the end Nancy did not take the test. She and her sister understood that if either tested positive it would destroy their father.[8]

Nancy Wexler is not alone in having made the decision not to know. Many at risk for HD choose not to be tested. In one study, letters were sent to 137 people at 50% risk of developing HD informing them of the availability of free presymptomatic testing. After 2 years, only 13 people (9.5%) had requested testing.[9] It is likely that one important factor in deciding whether the information from the HD test is valuable is that there is no cure or effective treatment for the disease.

This leads to a second reason why genetic information may be valuable to people. There might be some therapeutic value to the information. We can see that this may be true in Gloria's case. The information of her own status regarding the BRCA 1 and 2 genes may be irrelevant to her because

FIGURE 7.4 Nancy Wexler working with Huntington's disease patient in Venezuela.

she already has the disease. But information about her daughters' status or her sisters' status could be valuable. There may be precautions that can be taken, such as more frequent mammogram screenings, lifestyle changes, or even prophylactic mastectomy. In the case of many genetic diseases, there are treatments that can be given to control or minimize the development of the disease. The best example of this is the genetic disease known as phenylketonuria, or PKU. In most states in the United States, newborns are screened for this disease before leaving the hospital. By switching to a special diet the worst symptoms of the disease (including mental retardation) can be completely avoided.

This reason does more than support the value of genetic information. It also argues in favor of genetic interventions. That is, if we could rearrange someone's DNA, say add a missing gene or delete a mutation, then we could improve the person's health or longevity. Perhaps the strongest argument for genetic technologies is this therapeutic one. Fixing people's genetic makeup seems to hold out great promise. It would allow us to repair the DNA of not only existing adults but also of embryos/fetuses who at present can only be aborted or "selected against." We might even be able to completely eradicate a genetic disease by repairing the DNA of germ-line cells. Then all subsequent generations would be free from the disease. To date, the only success stories for gene therapy have involved cases where children were supplied with genes they were missing either intravenously or by nasal mist. We do not know yet how to delete or repair genes.

The first gene therapy trial began in 1990 with the treatment of a young girl, Ashanti DeSilva, who had SCID (severe combined immunodeficiency). Some of her white blood cells were extracted, mixed with a genetically modified retrovirus that carried a normal copy of the gene she lacked, then returned to her bloodstream by injection. The virus then transferred the normal gene to her white blood cells by infecting the cells. This treatment was successful in her case, although most of the gene therapy trials from 1990 to 1999 were unsuccessful.[10] In 1999, a young man named Jesse Gelsinger who had a mild form of a genetic disease that affected his liver died after volunteering to participate in a gene therapy trial. The virus carrying the corrected genes into his body caused an immune response that led to his death.[11] So the hopes for gene therapy have been largely unrealized so far.

A third reason why there is so much interest in genetic technologies is that some people hope to be able to use them for "enhancement" purposes. Rather than focusing on the therapy implications of genetic technologies (treatment of disease), these people stress the enhancement implications of them (improvement of life). Genetic technologies may help people become smarter, more athletic, more beautiful, happier, and live longer. Scientists may learn how to turn off or slow down aging genes and speed up or supplement muscle-producing genes or genes that influence intelligence. Some would argue that we already use genetics to enhance our lives when athletes take genetically produced human growth hormone and parents-to-be select sperm and egg donors who are Nobel prize winners or top fashion models. The more we know about how genes function, the more we may be inclined to "tweak" ourselves and our children. But what could be wrong with this? Isn't it natural that people want to improve their lives and give their children every advantage for a better life?

But maybe there is a difference between improving one's life through hard work and improving one's life through adding or subtracting genes. If wealthy people can choose embryos that have the genes for intelligence, blue eyes, and height, it might mean that those of different social classes would differ not only economically but also in intelligence and appearance. There might be parental peer pressure that would lead a parent-to-be to genetically select whatever society deems to be the "right" traits for a child. A society might be mistaken in valuing athletic prowess over artistic creativity. It is not clear that a world in which everyone was stronger, taller, and blue-eyed would be a better world. Thus, our interest in bettering ourselves, if extended to genetic enhancement technologies, raises issues of human nature, justice, autonomy, the ends of science and medicine, the **commodification** of children, and ultimately **eugenics.**

A fourth reason why genetic testing in particular may be valuable is that employers or insurers may find that the information gained helps them make prudent decisions about hiring or insuring. Utility is the main value at stake here. If an employer could require genetic testing of his or her future hires, the employer could determine who will get HD, who is at higher risk for breast cancer, and so on. The company could then hire the "healthier" workers, those likely to have a longer work life. Wouldn't this be economically reasonable? Yes, in one sense, from the company's viewpoint, it might maximize the good for the most people to screen future employees this way. But the well-being of individuals and their rights to privacy and nondiscrimination make this company policy look unacceptable. There is also the scientific point that most and probably all of us are at increased risk because of genetics for some diseases. It doesn't seem fair to treat those at risk for the diseases for which we have tests as "unhealthy" while others at risk for diseases for which we have no tests are considered "healthy."

According to a survey conducted by the Genetics and Public Policy Center at Johns Hopkins University in 2007, 81% of Americans are against allowing employers to use genetic tests to make hiring or promotion decisions and 85% oppose allowing health insurance companies to use genetic tests to determine who to insure or how much to charge.[12] In 2005, IBM publicly promised that it would not use genetic screening in the workplace.[13] Finally, in 2008, the U.S. Senate and the U.S. House both passed the Genetic Information Non-Discrimination Act (GINA) that prevents employers from using genetic tests to hire, fire, or promote and prohibits insurance companies from using such tests to set premiums or determine enrollment eligibility. Thus, while genetic information or genetic technologies may be of some benefit to employers and insurers, there are also moral reasons not to make such information available to them.

GENETIC TECHNOLOGIES: WHAT?

Finally, let us consider the various ways that genetic technologies can be used. One of the primary ways, as in Gloria's case, is genetic testing whereby individuals or groups may determine whether or not they have inherited, have a heightened risk of developing, or are carriers of certain diseases. Genetic therapy is a second way that genetic technologies may be used. Scientists hope that genetic therapies will provide more complete cures for disease and even "personalized medicine" where we will be able to determine which treatment is most effective for those of a particular genetic makeup. Genetic therapies may also be used to enhance and improve human lives. But much of the contemporary discussion regarding genetic technologies focuses on the techniques and the possibilities of cloning and stem cell research.

Cloning refers to the creation of an exact genetic copy of a cell or embryo. The process happens naturally in the case of identical twins. But genetic technologies have developed other ways of producing genetically identical cells. Scientists can take a donor egg cell, remove the nucleus, and insert a nucleus from one of a person's own somatic cells. Via an electric current, this egg then continues to develop as a genetic duplicate of the donated cell nucleus.

There are two ways in which such developing cells might be used. In **therapeutic cloning** the goal is to be able to generate cells, tissues, and even organs that are genetically identical to the somatic cell donor's own cells, tissues, or organs. If this person needed a bone marrow donation, a skin graft, or a kidney, then we would be able to grow a perfect fit, a spare part that brings no risk of rejection. In **reproductive cloning,** the aim is to bring to life an offspring who is genetically identical to the somatic cell donor. This is precisely what occurred with Dolly the sheep in 1996. In fact, there are companies that offer to provide "gene banking" services to pet owners who want to store their beloved pets' DNA for future reproductive cloning.[14] Curiously, the biological parents of a reproductive clone are neither the somatic cell donor nor the egg donor but the parents of the now replicated somatic cell donor!

Embryonic stem cell research is a second, much-debated use of genetic technologies. Stem cells are cells that exist naturally in the human body. They are cells that produce other cells. Embryonic stem cells (that come from early embryos at approximately 4 days after fertilization) have the unique property of being toti-potent, that is, the cells are so young that they are not yet differentiated into skin, muscle, or other cells. Embryonic stem cells (ESC) can become any kind of cells. Research scientists are hopeful that ESC could be used to treat diseases and conditions such as spinal cord injuries, Parkinson's disease, and so on.

But ESC research is morally controversial. In 2001, President George W. Bush declared that no federal funds could be used to create embryos for ESC research and that only ESC research projects on the existing stem cell lines could apply for federal funding. His reason, and the reason many individuals and groups are opposed to ESC research, is that early embryos are destroyed (killed) in the process of harvesting the stem cells. Some think these early embryos do not have moral status and so there is no harm in using them for research. But at least in the United States there has been significant concern expressed over the destruction of human embryos and hence scientists have been looking for other ways to recover stem cells. In November 2007, there were reports of the success of "direct reprogramming"—a procedure that turns ordinary skin cells into cells with the properties of embryonic stem cells.[15] If successful and proven safe, this kind of ESC research would for many be morally preferable because it would no longer involve destroying early embryos. But in a recent development, in March 2009, President Barack Obama abolished the Bush-era restraints and decided to allow federally funded scientists to use new embryonic stem cells for research.

Genetic technologies hold great promise as ways to fight disease and improve lives but there is still a great deal we do not understand about what genes do and how to manipulate them. In addition to these scientific difficulties, there are moral questions about what technologies we should use, who ought to use them, and what reasons are good reasons for using them. The readings that follow will help us to reflect on questions like these.

Looking Ahead

- We can expect that genetic testing will become available for many more genetic conditions and illnesses. While today genetic testing is used primarily to diagnose serious and debilitating conditions, in the future genetic tests will be able to reveal nonharmful conditions as well. Tests will be able to be performed at home, hence avoiding the need for counseling. Parents will have their newborn babies tested so that they will be able to create environments and take steps to avoid having their children develop certain diseases. Young people will be able to test themselves for genes related to lung capacity and muscle development in order to determine the likelihood of their becoming professional athletes. Department store cosmetic counters will offer clients a quick genetic test for genetic markers relevant to skin health. Then they will develop a face cream especially suited to what is present or lacking in the client's skin cells.[16]
- People will adopt genetic therapies and enhancement medicines in hopes of avoiding the symptoms of old age and giving themselves an advantage. Gene doping will become a problem in Olympic, professional, and even amateur athletics. We will have to figure out ways to screen athletes to determine whether they have used genetic supplements. Older people will make use of anti-aging genetic treatments in order to live longer and better. People with impairments will find human growth hormone and other genetic therapies useful. There will be increased pressure on those who are different or disabled to take advantage of therapies that would help them "fit in." More genetic therapies will be started *in utero* so that a child's condition can be improved before birth. There will be more genetic treatments for common diseases and conditions, such as chronic ear infections and sinus infections. Once a genetic therapy is discovered for a particular disease, say sickle cell anemia, there will be pressure to use the therapy on germ-line cells so that the disease can be eliminated entirely from future generations. Stem cells will continue to be a focus of scientific and medical research. Scientists will learn how to turn genes off and on. This means that genetic mutations need not be removed from a cell but can simply be silenced. Researchers will develop better and safer ways to reprogram somatic differentiated cells into toti-potent stem cells. Patients will then be able to have some of their own skin or kidney or other cells reprogrammed and reimplanted without any fear of rejection. Because of this ability to regrow new tissues and organs, there will be dramatic advances in medical treatment.
- Some people will clone their pets. Parents who have a child with a genetic disease or impairment will ask to clone their child, minus the genes causing the impairment, in order to give birth to another child who can then be the perfect bone marrow, tissue, or organ donor.

Endnotes

1. See "Genetic Testing for BRCA 1 and BRCA 2: It's Your Choice" at the National Cancer Institute (http://www.cancer.gov/cancertopics/factsheet/Risk/BRCA) [Accessed on April 20, 2008].

2. Ibid.

3. Julia Richards and Scott Hawley, *The Human Genome, A User's Guide,* 2nd ed. (Amsterdam: Elsevier, 2005), 303.

4. Erik Parens and Adrienne Asch, "The Disability Rights Critique of Prenatal Genetic Testing: Reflections and Recommendations," *Hastings Center Report* 29:5 (1999), S1–S22.

5. See, for example, the American Academy of Pediatrics Policy "Ethical Issues with Genetic Testing in Pediatrics" (http://aappolicy.aappublications.org/cgi/content/full/pediatrics%3b107/6/1451 [Accessed on April 20, 2008]), the American Medical Association, Code of Ethics, Genetic Testing of Children (http://www.ama-assn.org/apps/pf_new/pf_online?f_n=browse&doc=policyfiles/HnE/E-2.138.HTM) [Accessed on April 20, 2008], and the State of New York Department of Health (http://www.health.state.ny.us/press/releases/2001/genetics.htm) [Accessed on April 20, 2008].

6. Rony E. Duncan, et al., "An International Survey of Predictive Genetic Testing in Children for Adult Onset Conditions," *Genetics in Medicine* 7:6 (2005), 390–396. See also A.R. Bradbury et al., "Parental Disclosure of Genetic Test Results to Young Adults, Adolescents and Children," *Journal of Clinical Oncology* 23:16S (meeting abstract) (2005), 1016; Sara Hammer Riordan and Lois J. Loescher, "Medical Students' Attitudes Toward Genetic Testing of Minors," *Genetic Testing* 10:1 (2006), 68–73.

7. Gregory E. Pence, *Medical Ethics: Accounts of the Cases that Shaped and Define Medical Ethics,* 5th ed. (New York: McGraw-Hill, 2008), 326.

8. As reported to Diane Sawyer on *60 Minutes* in May 1987.

9. Kimberly A. Quaid and Michael Morris, "Reluctance to Undergo Predictive Testing: The Case of Huntington Disease," *American Journal of Medical Genetics* 45:1 (1993), 41–45.

10. William Klug and Michael Cummings, *Concepts of Genetics,* 7th ed., (Upper Saddle River: Prentice Hall, 2003), 533.

11. Sheryl Gay Stolberg, "The biotech death of Jesse Gelsinger," *New York Times Magazine* (November 28, 1999).

12. See the testimony of Kathy Hudson, PhD, Director, Genetics and Public Policy Center, Johns Hopkins University, before the House Energy and Commerce Committee, Subcommittee on Health (http://www.dnapolicy.org/resources/HudsonE&CTestimony3.7.07writtenfinal.pdf) [Accessed on April 21, 2008].

13. See http://www.businessweek.com/technology/content/oct2005/tc20051011_9733_tc024.htm [Accessed on April 21, 2008].

14. See http://www.perpetuate.net/ [Accessed on April 21, 2008] and http://www.viagen.com/en/our-services/preserving-your-pets/ [Accessed on April 21, 2008].

15. See http://www.nytimes.com/2007/06/06/science/06cnd-cell.html?_r=1&oref=slogin [Accessed on April 21, 2008].

16. According to this testimony in 2003, this is already happening: http://www4.od.nih.gov/oba/SACGHS/meetings/June2003/Presentations/Juengst_t.pdf [Accessed on April 21, 2008].

TESTING AND SCREENING

Genetic Dilemmas and the Child's Right to an Open Future

Dena S. Davis

The profession of genetic counseling is strongly characterized by a respect for patient autonomy that is greater than in almost any other area of medicine. When moral challenges arise in the clinical practice of genetics, they tend to be understood as conflicts between the obligation to respect patient autonomy and other ethical norms, such as doing good and avoiding harm. Thus, a typical counseling dilemma exists when a person who has been tested and found to be carrying the gene for Tay-Sachs disease refuses to share that information with siblings and other relatives despite the clear benefits to them of having that knowledge, or when a family member declines to participate in a testing protocol necessary to help another member discover his or her genetic status.

This way of looking at moral issues in genetic counseling often leaves both the counselors and commentators frustrated, for two reasons. First, by elevating respect for patient autonomy above all other values, it may be difficult to give proper weight to other factors, such as human suffering. Second, by privileging patient autonomy and by defining the patient as the person or couple who has come for counseling, there seems no "space" in which to give proper attention to the moral claims of the future child who is the endpoint of many counseling interactions.

These difficulties have been highlighted of late by the surfacing of a new kind of genetic counseling request: parents with certain disabilities who seek help in trying to assure that they will have a child who shares their disability. The two reported instances are in families affected by achondroplasia (dwarfism) and by hereditary deafness. This essay will focus on deafness.

Such requests are understandably troubling to genetic counselors. Deeply committed to the principle of giving clients value-free information with which to make their own choices, most counselors nonetheless make certain assumptions about health and disability—for example, that it is preferable to be a hearing person rather than a deaf person. Thus, counselors typically talk of the "risk" of having a child with a particular genetic condition. Counselors may have learned (sometimes with great difficulty) to respect clients' decisions not to find out if their fetus has a certain condition or not to abort a fetus which carries a genetic disability. But to respect a parental value system that not only favors what most of us consider to be a disability, but actively expresses that preference by attempting to have a child with the condition, is "the ultimate test of nondirective counseling."[1]

To describe the challenge primarily as one that pits beneficence (concern for the child's quality of life) against autonomy (concern for the parents' right to decide about these matters) makes for obvious difficulties. These are two very different values, and comparing and weighing them invites the proverbial analogy of "apples and oranges." After all, the perennial critique of a principle-based ethics is that it offers few suggestions for ranking principles when duties conflict. Further, beneficence and respect for autonomy are values that will always exist in some tension within genetic counseling. For all the reasons I list below, counselors are committed to the primacy of patient autonomy and therefore to nondirective counseling. But surely, most or all of them are drawn to the field because they want to help people avoid or at least mitigate suffering.

Faced with the ethical challenge of parents who wish to ensure children who have a disability, I suggest a different way to look at this problem. Thinking this problem through in the way I suggest will shed light on some related topics in genetics as well, such as sex selection. I propose that, rather than conceiving this as a conflict between autonomy and beneficence, we recast it as a conflict between parental autonomy and the child's future autonomy: what Joel Feinberg has called "the child's right to an open future."

NEW CHALLENGES

The Code of Ethics of the National Society of Genetic Counselors states that its members strive to:

- Respect their clients' beliefs, cultural traditions, inclinations, circumstances, and feelings.
- Enable their clients to make informed independent decisions, free of coercion, by providing or illuminating the necessary facts and clarifying the alternatives and anticipated consequences.[2]

Considering the uncertain and stochastic nature of genetic counseling, and especially in light of the difficulty physicians experience in sharing uncertainty with patients, it is remarkable that medical geneticists have hewed so strongly to an ethic of patient autonomy. This phenomenon can be explained by at least five factors: the desire to disassociate themselves as strongly as possible from the discredited eugenics movement;[3] an equally strong desire to avoid the label of "abortionist," a realistic fear if counselors are perceived as advocates for abortion of genetically damaged fetuses;[4] the fact that few treatments are available for genetic diseases (p. 29); an awareness of the intensely private nature of reproductive decisions; and the fact that genetic decisions can have major consequences for entire families.[5] As one counselor was quoted, "I am not going to be taking that baby home—they will."[6]

The commitment to patient autonomy faces new challenges with the advances arising from the Human Genome Project. The example of hereditary deafness is reported by Walter E. Nance, who writes:

> It turns out that some deaf couples feel threatened by the prospect of having a hearing child and would actually prefer to have a deaf child. The knowledge that we will soon acquire [due to the Human Genome Project] will, of course, provide us with the technology that could be used to assist such couples in achieving their goals. This, in turn, could lead to the ultimate test of nondirective counseling. Does adherence to the concept of nondirective counseling actually require that we assist such a couple in terminating a pregnancy with a hearing child or is this nonsense?[7]

Several issues must be unpacked here. First, I question Nance's depiction of deaf parents as feeling "threatened" by the prospect of a hearing child. From Nance's own depiction of the deaf people he encounters, it is at least as likely that deaf parents feel that a deaf child would fit into their family better, especially if the parents themselves are "deaf of deaf" or if they already have one or more deaf children. Or perhaps the parents feel that Deafness (I use the capital "D," as Deaf people do, to signify Deafness as a culture) is an asset—tough at times but worthwhile in the end—like belonging to a racial or religious minority.

Second, I want to avoid the issue of abortion by discussing the issue of "deliberately producing a deaf child" as distinct from the question of achieving that end by aborting a hearing fetus. The latter topic is important, but it falls outside the purview of this paper. I will focus on the scenario where a deaf child is produced without recourse to abortion. We can imagine a situation in the near future where eggs or sperm can be scrutinized for the relevant trait before fertilization, or the present situation in which preimplantation genetic diagnosis after in vitro fertilization allows specialists to examine the genetic makeup of the very early embryo before it is implanted.

Imagine a Deaf couple approaching a genetic counselor. The couple's goals are to learn more about the cause(s) of their own deafness, and, if possible, to maximize the chance that any pregnancy they embark upon will result in a Deaf child. Let us suppose that the couple falls into the 50 percent of clients whose Deafness has a genetic origin.[8] The genetic counselor who adheres strictly to the tenets of client autonomy will respond by helping the couple to explore the ways in which they can achieve their goal: a Deaf baby. But as Nance's depiction of this scenario suggests, the counselor may well feel extremely uneasy about her role here. It is one thing to support a couple's decision to take their chances and "let Nature take its course," but to treat as a goal what is commonly considered to be a risk may be more pressure than the value-neutral ethos can bear. What is needed is a principled argument against such assistance. This refusal need not rise to a legal prohibition, but could become part of the ethical norms and standard of care for the counseling profession.[9]

The path I see out of this dilemma relies on two steps. First, we remind ourselves why client autonomy is such a powerful norm in genetic counseling. Clients come to genetic counselors with questions that are simultaneously of the greatest magnitude and of the greatest intimacy. Clients not only have the right to bring their own values to bear on these questions, but in the end they must do so because they—and their children—will live with the consequences. As the President's Commission said in its 1983 report on Screening and Counseling for Genetic Conditions:

> The silence of the law on many areas of individual choice reflects the value this country places on pluralism. Nowhere is the need for freedom to pursue divergent conceptions of the good more deeply felt than in decisions concerning reproduction. It would be a cruel irony, therefore, if technological advances undertaken in the name of providing information to expand the range of individual choices resulted in unanticipated social pressures to pursue a particular course of action. Someone who feels compelled to undergo screening or to make particular reproductive choices at the urging of health care professionals or others or as a result of implicit social pressure is deprived of the choice-enhancing benefits of the new advances. The Commission recommends that those who counsel patients and those who educate the public about genetics should not only emphasize the importance of preserving choice but also do their utmost to safeguard the choices of those they serve.[10]

Now let us take this value of respect for autonomy and put it on both sides of the dilemma. Why is it morally problematic to seek to produce a child who is deaf? Being deaf does not cause one physical pain or shorten one's life span, two obvious conditions which it would be prima facie immoral to produce in another person. Deaf people might (or might not) be less happy on average than hearing people, but that is arguably a function of societal prejudice. The primary argument against deliberately seeking to produce deaf children is that it violates the child's own autonomy and narrows the scope of her choices when she grows up; in other words, it violates her right to an "open future."

THE CHILD'S RIGHT TO AN OPEN FUTURE

Joel Feinberg begins his discussion of children's rights by noticing that rights can ordinarily be divided into four kinds. First, there are rights that adults and children have in common (the right not to be killed, for example). Then, there are rights that are generally possessed only by children (or by "childlike" adults). These "dependency-rights," as Feinberg calls them, derive from the child's dependence on others for such basics as food, shelter, and protection. Third, there are rights that can only be exercised by adults (or at least by children approaching adulthood), for example, the free exercise of religion. Finally, there are rights that Feinberg calls "rights-in-trust," rights which are to be "saved for the child until he is an adult." These rights can be violated by adults now, in ways that cut off the possibility that the child, when it achieves adulthood, can exercise them. A striking example is the right to reproduce. A young child cannot physically exercise that right, and a teenager might lack the legal and moral grounds on which to assert such a right. But clearly the child, when he or she attains adulthood, will have that right, and therefore the child now has the right not to be sterilized, so that the child may exercise that right in the future. Rights in this category include a long list: virtually all the important rights we believe adults have, but which must be protected now to be exercised later. Grouped together, they constitute what Feinberg calls "the child's right to an open future."[11]

Feinberg illustrates this concept with two examples. The first is that of the Jehovah's Witness child who needs a blood transfusion to save his life but whose parents object on religious grounds. In this case, the parents' right to act upon their religious beliefs and to raise their family within the religion of their choice conflicts with the child's right to live to adulthood and to make his own life-or-death decisions. As the Supreme Court said in another (and less defensible) case involving Jehovah's Witnesses:

Parents may be free to become martyrs themselves. But it does not follow that they are free in identical circumstances to make martyrs of their children before they have reached the age of full and legal discretion when they can make that decision for themselves.[12]

The second example is more controversial. In 1972, in a famous Supreme Court case, a group of Old Order Amish argued that they should be exempt from Wisconsin's requirement that all children attend school until they are either sixteen years old or graduate from high school.[13] The Amish didn't have to send their children to public school, of course; they were free to create a private school of their own liking. But they framed the issue in the starkest manner: to send their children to any school, past eighth grade, would be antithetical to their religion and their way of life, and might even result in the death of their culture.

The case was framed as a freedom of religion claim on the one hand, and the state's right to insist on an educated citizenry on the other. And within that frame, the Amish won. First, they were able to persuade the Court that sending their children to school after eighth grade would potentially destroy their community, because it

takes them away from their community, physically and emotionally, during the crucial and formative adolescent period. During this period, the children must acquire Amish attitudes favoring manual work and self-reliance and the specific skills needed to perform the adult role of an Amish farmer or housewife. In the Amish belief higher learning tends to develop values they reject as influences that alienate man from God. (p. 211)

Second, the Amish argued that the state's concerns—that children be prepared to participate in the political and economic life of the state—did not apply in this case. The Court listened favorably to expert witnesses who explained that the Amish system of home-based vocational training—learning from your parent—worked well for that community, that the community itself was prosperous, and that few Amish were likely to end up unemployed. The Court said:

the value of all education must be assessed in terms of its capacity to prepare the child for life . . . It is one thing to say that compulsory education for a year or two beyond the eighth grade may be necessary when its goal is the preparation of the child for life in modern society as the majority live, but it is quite another if the goal of education can be viewed as the preparation of the child for life in the separated agrarian community that is the keystone of the Amish faith. (p. 222)

What only a few justices saw was that the children themselves were largely ignored in this argument. The Amish wanted to preserve their way of life. The state of Wisconsin wanted to make sure that its citizens could vote wisely and make a living. No justice squarely faced the question of whether the liberal democratic state owes all its citizens, especially children, a right to a basic education that can serve as a building block if the child decides later in life that she wishes to become an astronaut, a playwright, or perhaps to join the army. As we constantly hear from politicians and educators, without a high school diploma one's future is virtually closed. By denying them a high school education or its equivalent, parents are virtually ensuring that their children will remain housewives and agricultural laborers. Even if the children agree, is that a choice parents ought to be allowed to make for them?

From my perspective, the case was decided wrongly. If Wisconsin had good reasons for settling on high school graduation or age sixteen as the legal minimum to which children are entitled, then I think that the Amish children were entitled to that minimum as well, despite their parents' objections. In deciding the issue primarily on grounds that the Amish were not likely to create problems for the state if allowed to keep their children out of school, the Court reflected a rather minimalist form of liberalism. In fact, the abiding interest of this case for many political philosophers lies in the deep conflict it highlights between two different concepts of liberalism: commitment to autonomy and commitment to diversity. William Galston, for example, argues that:

> A standard liberal view (or hope) is that these two principles go together and complement one another; the exercise of autonomy yields diversity, while the fact of diversity protects and nourishes autonomy. By contrast, my . . . view is that these principles do not always, perhaps even do not usually, cohere, that in practice, they point in quite different directions in currently disputed areas such as education . . . Specifically: the decision to throw state power behind the promotion of individual autonomy can weaken or undermine individuals and groups that do not and cannot organize their affairs in accordance with that principle without undermining the deepest sources of their identity.[14]

Galston claims that "properly understood, liberalism is about the protection of diversity, not the valorization of choice . . . To place an ideal of autonomous choice . . . at the core of liberalism is in fact to narrow the range of possibilities available within liberal societies" (p. 523).

One can see this conflict quite sharply if one returns to the work of John Stuart Mill. On the one hand, there is probably no philosopher who gives more weight to the value of individual choice than does Mill. In *On Liberty,* he claims that the very measure of a human being is the extent to which he makes life choices for himself, free of societal pressure:

> The human faculties of perception, judgment, discriminative feeling, mental activity, and even moral preference, are exercised only in making a choice. He who does anything because it is the custom makes no choice.[15]

Mill would abhor a situation like that of the Amish communities in *Yoder,* which unabashedly want to give their children as few choices as possible. But, on the other hand, it is clear from both common sense and from Mill's own statements that in order for people to have choices about the pattern of their lives (and to be inspired to create new patterns) there must be more than one type of community available to them. To quote Mill again, "There is no reason that all human existence should be constructed on some one or some small number of patterns" (p. 64). As we look at the last three centuries of American history, we see what an important role different community "patterns" have played, from the Shakers to the Mormons to Bronson Alcott's Fruitlands to the communal experiments of the 1960s. If those patterns are to exhibit the full range of human endeavor and experiment, they must include communities that are distinctly anti-liberal. Not only does the panoply of widely different communities enrich our culture, but it also provides a welcome for those who do not fit into the mainstream. As Mill says, "A man cannot get a coat or pair of shoes to fit him unless they are either made to his measure, or he has a whole warehouseful to choose from; and is it easier to fit him with a life than with a coat[?]" (p. 64). Some of us are geniuses who make our lives to "fit our measure," others are happy enough to fit into the mainstream, but for others, the availability of a "warehouseful" of choices increases the possibility of finding a good fit. And for some, a good fit means an authoritarian community based on tradition, where one is freed from the necessity of choice. Thus Galston is correct in pointing to the paradox: if the goal of a liberal democracy is to actively promote something like the greatest number of choices for the greatest number of individuals, this seems to entail hostility toward narrow-choice communities like the Amish. But if the Amish, because of that hostility, fail to flourish, there will be fewer choices available to all.

The compromise I promote is that a liberal state must tolerate even those communities most unsympathetic to the liberal value of individual choice. However, this tolerance must exist within a limiting context, which is the right of individuals to choose which communities they wish to join and to leave if they have a mind to. Even Galston begins with the presumption that society must "defend . . . the liberty not to be coerced into, or trapped within, ways of life. Accordingly, the state must safeguard the ability of individuals to shift allegiances and cross boundaries."[16] Thus, I argue that the autonomy of the individual is ethically prior to the autonomy of the group. Both ideals have powerful claims on us, but when group rights would extinguish the abilities of the individuals within them to make their own life choices, then the liberal state must support the individual against the group. This is especially crucial when the individual at issue is a child, who is particularly vulnerable to adult coercion and therefore has particular claims on our protection.

Unfortunately, it is precisely where children are concerned that groups are understandably most jealous of their prerogatives to guide and make decisions. The Amish are an example of a group guarding its ability to shape the lives of its children; Deaf parents wishing to ensure Deaf children are an example of families pursuing the same goals. Of course, groups and families ought to—in fact, they must—strive to shape the values and lives of the children in their care, not to do so leads to social and individual pathology. But when that shaping takes the form of a radically narrow range of choices available to the child when she grows up, when it impinges substantially on the child's right to an open future, then liberalism requires us to intervene to support the child's future ability to make her own choices about which of the many diverse visions of life she wishes to embrace.

But I concede one problem with this point of view. As a liberal who believes that the state should not dictate notions of "the good life," Feinberg believes that the state must be neutral about the goals of education, skewing the question neither in favor of the Amish lifestyle nor in favor of the "modern," technological life most Americans accept. The goal of education is to allow the child to make up its own mind from the widest array of options; the best education is the one which gives the child the most open future. A neutral decision would assume only that education should equip the child with the knowledge and skills that will help him choose whichever sort of life best fits his native endowment and matured disposition. It should send him out into the adult world with as many open opportunities as possible, thus maximizing his chances for self-fulfillment.[17]

The problem here is that an education which gave a child this array of choices would quite possibly make it impossible for her to choose to remain Old Order Amish. Her "native endowment and matured disposition" might now have taken her away from the kind of personality and habits that would make Amish life pleasant. Even if she envies the peace, warmth, and security that a life of tradition offers, she may find it impossible to turn her back on "the world," and return to her lost innocence. To quote the Amish, she may have failed irreversibly to "acquire Amish attitudes" during "the crucial and formative adolescent period." This problem raises two issues. First, those of us who would make arguments based on the child's right to an open future need to be clear and appropriately humble about what we are offering. Insisting on a child's right to a high school education may open a future wider than she otherwise could have dreamed, but it also may foreclose one possible future: as a contented member of the Amish community. Second, if the Amish are correct in saying that taking their children out of school at grade eight is crucial for the child's development into a member of the Amish community, then there is no "impartial" stance for the state to take. The state may well be impartial about whether the "better life" is to be found within or without the Amish community, but it cannot act in an impartial fashion. Both forcing the parents to send their children to school or exempting them from the requirement has likely consequences for the child's continued existence within the community when she grows up and is able to make a choice. Feinberg seeks to avoid this second problem by claiming that the neutral state would act to

> let all influences . . . work equally on the child, to open up all possibilities to him without itself influencing him toward one or another of these. In that way, it can be hoped that the chief determining factor in the grown child's choice of a vocation and life-style will be his own governing values, talents and propensities. (pp. 134–35)

The problem with this is that, as I understand the Amish way of life, being Amish is precisely not to make one's life choices on the basis of one's own "talents and propensities," but to subordinate those individual leanings to the traditions of the group. If one discovers within oneself a strong passion and talent for jazz dancing one ought to suppress it, not nurture it.

IS CREATING A DEAF CHILD A MORAL HARM?

Now, as we return to the example of the couple who wish to ensure that they bear only deaf children, we have to confront two distinctly different issues. The first is, in what sense is it ever possible to do harm by giving birth to a child who would otherwise not have been born at all? The second is whether being deaf rather than hearing is in fact a harm.

The first issue has been well rehearsed elsewhere.[18] The problem is, how can it be said that one has harmed a child by bringing it into the world with a disability, when the only other choice was for the child not to have existed at all? In the case of a child whose life is arguably not worth living, one can say that life itself is a cruelty to the child. But when a child is born in less than ideal circumstances, or is partially disabled in ways that do not entail tremendous suffering, there seems no way to argue that the child herself has been harmed. This may appear to entail the conclusion, counter to our common moral sense, that therefore no harm has been done. "A wrong action must be bad for someone, but [a] choice to create [a] child with its handicap is bad for no one."[19]

All commentators agree that there is no purely logical way out of what Dan Brock calls the "wrongful handicap" conundrum (p. 272). However, most commentators also agree that one can still support a moral critique of the parents' decision. Bonnie Steinbock and Ron McClamrock argue for a principle of "parental responsibility" by which being a good parent entails refraining from bringing a child into the world when one cannot give it "even a decent chance at a good life."[20] Brock, following Parfit, distinguishes same person from same number choices. In same person choices, the same person exists in each of the alternative courses of action the agent chooses, but the person may exist more or less harmed. In same number choices, "the choice affects who, which child, will exist."[21] Brock claims that moral harms can exist in both instances, despite the fact that in same number choices the moral harm cannot be tied to a specific person. Brock generates the following principle:

> Individuals are morally required not to let any possible child . . . for whose welfare they are responsible experience serious suffering or limited opportunity if they can act so that, without imposing substantial burdens or costs on themselves or others, any alternative possible child . . . for whose welfare they would be responsible will not experience serious suffering or limited opportunity. (pp. 272–73)

While agreeing with Brock, Steinbock, and others, I locate the moral harm differently, at least with respect to disabled persons wishing to reproduce themselves in the form of a disabled child. Deliberately creating a child who will be forced irreversibly into the parents' notion of "the good life" violates the Kantian principle of

treating each person as an end in herself and never as a means only. All parenthood exists as a balance between fulfillment of parental hopes and values and the individual flowering of the actual child in his or her own direction. The decision to have a child is never made for the sake of the child—for no child then exists. We choose to have children for myriad reasons, but before the child is conceived those reasons can only be self-regarding. The child is a means to our ends: a certain kind of joy and pride, continuing the family name, fulfilling religious or societal expectations, and so on. But morally the child is first and foremost an end in herself. Good parenthood requires a balance between having a child for our own sakes and being open to the moral reality that the child will exist for her own sake, with her own talents and weaknesses, propensities and interests, and with her own life to make. Parental practices that close exits virtually forever are insufficiently attentive to the child as end in herself. By closing off the child's right to an open future, they define the child as an entity who exists to fulfill parental hopes and dreams, not her own.

Having evaded the snares of the wrongful handicap conundrum, we must tackle the second problem: is being deaf a harm? At first glance, this might appear as a silly question. Ethically, we would certainly include destroying someone's hearing under the rubric of "harm"; legally, one could undoubtedly receive compensation if one were rendered deaf through someone else's negligence. Many Deaf people, however, have recently been claiming that Deafness is better understood as a cultural identity than as a disability. Particularly in the wake of the Deaf President Now revolution at Gallaudet University in 1988, Deaf people have been asserting their claims not merely to equal access (through increased technology) but also to equal respect as a cultural minority. As one (hearing) reporter noted:

> So strong is the feeling of cultural solidarity that many deaf parents cheer on discovering that their baby is deaf. Pondering such a scene, a hearing person can experience a kind of vertigo. The surprise is not simply the unfamiliarity of the views; it is that, as in a surrealist painting, jarring notions are presented as if they were commonplace.[22]

From this perspective, the use of cochlear implants to enable deaf children to hear, or the abortion of deaf fetuses, is characterized as "genocide."[23] Deaf pride advocates point out that as Deaf people they lack the ability to hear, but they also have many positive gains: a cohesive community, a rich cultural heritage built around the various residential schools, a growing body of drama, poetry, and other artistic traditions, and, of course, what makes all this possible, American Sign Language.[24] Roslyn Rosen, the president of the National Association of the Deaf, is Deaf, the daughter of Deaf parents, and the mother of Deaf children. "I'm happy with who I am," she says, "and I don't want to be 'fixed.' Would an Italian-American rather be a WASP? In our society everyone agrees that whites have an easier time than blacks. But do you think a black person would undergo operations to become white?"[25]

On the other side of the argument is evidence that deafness is a very serious disability. Deaf people have incomes thirty to forty percent below the national average.[26] The state of education for the deaf is unacceptable by anyone's standards; the typical deaf student graduates from high school unable to read a newspaper.[27]

However, one could also point to the lower incomes and inadequate state of education among some racial and ethnic minorities in our country, a situation we do not (or at least ought not) try to ameliorate by eradicating minorities. Deaf advocates often cite the work of Nora Ellen Groce, whose oral history of Martha's Vineyard, *Everyone Here Spoke Sign Language,* tells a fascinating story. For over two hundred years, ending in the middle of the twentieth century, the Vineyard experienced a degree of hereditary deafness exponentially higher than that of the mainland. Although the number of deaf people was low in noncomparative terms (one in 155), the result was a community in which deaf people participated fully in the political and social life of the island, had an economic prosperity on par with their neighbors, and communicated easily with the hearing population, for "everyone here spoke sign language." So endemic was sign language for the general population of the island that hearing islanders often exploited its unique properties even in the absence of deaf people. Old-timers told Groce stories of spouses communicating through sign language when they were outdoors and did not want to raise their voices against the wind. Or men might turn away and finish a "dirty" joke in sign when a woman walked into the general store. At church, deaf parishioners gave their testimony in sign.

As one Deaf activist said, in a comment that could have been directly related to the Vineyard experience, "When Gorbachev visited the U.S., he used an interpreter to talk to the President. Was Gorbachev disabled?"[28] Further, one might argue that, since it is impossible to eradicate deafness completely even if that were a worthy goal, the cause of deaf equality is better served when parents who are proud to be Deaf deliberately have Deaf children who augment and strengthen the existing population. Many of the problems that deaf people experience are the result of being born, without advance warning, to hearing parents. When there is no reason to anticipate the birth of a deaf child, it is often months or years before the child is correctly diagnosed. Meanwhile, she is growing up in a world devoid of language, unable even to communicate with her parents. When the diagnosis is made, her parents first must deal with the emotional shock, and then sort through the plethora of conflicting advice on how best to raise and educate their child. Most probably, they have never met anyone who is deaf. If they choose the route recommended by most Deaf activists and raise their child with sign language, it will take the parents years to learn the language. Meanwhile, their child has missed out on the crucial development of language at the developmentally appropriate time, a lack that is associated with poor reading skills and other problems later (p. 43).

Further, even the most accepting of hearing parents often feel locked in conflict with the Deaf community over who knows what is best for their child. If Deafness truly is a culture rather than a disability, then raising a deaf child is somewhat like white parents trying to raise a black child in contemporary America (with a background chorus of black activists telling them that they can't possibly make a good job of it!). Residential schools, for example, which can be part of the family culture for a Deaf couple, can be seen by hearing parents as Dickensian nightmares or, worse, as a "cultlike" experience in which their children will be lost to them forever.

By contrast, deaf children born to Deaf parents learn language (sign) at the same age as hearing children. They are welcomed into their families and inculcated into Deaf culture in the same way as any other children. Perhaps for these reasons, by all accounts the Deaf of Deaf are the acknowledged leaders of the Deaf Pride movement, and the academic crème de la crème. In evaluating the choice parents make who deliberately ensure that they have Deaf children, we must remember that the statistics and descriptions of deaf life in America are largely reflective of the experience of deaf children born to hearing parents, who make up the vast majority of deaf people today.

But if Deafness is a culture rather than a disability, it is an exceedingly narrow one. One factor that does not seem clear is the extent to which children raised with American Sign Language as their first language ever will be completely comfortable with the written word. (Sign language itself has no written analogue and has a completely different grammatical structure from English.) At present, the conflicted and politicized state of education for the deaf, along with the many hours spent (some would say "wasted") on attempting to teach deaf children oral skills, makes it impossible to know what is to blame for the dismal reading and writing skills of the average deaf person. Some deaf children who are raised with sign language from birth do become skilled readers. But there is reason to question whether a deaf child may have very limited access to the wealth of literature, drama, and poetry that liberals would like to consider every child's birthright.

Although Deaf activists rightly show how many occupations are open to them with only minor technological adjustments, the range of occupations will always be inherently limited. It is not likely that the world will become as Martha's Vineyard, where everyone knew sign. A prelingually deafened person not only cannot hear, but in most instances cannot speak well enough to be understood. This narrow choice of vocation is not only a harm in its own sake but also is likely to continue to lead to lower standards of living. (Certainly one reason why the Vineyard deaf were as prosperous as their neighbors was that farming and fishing were just about the only occupations available.)

EITHER WAY, A MORAL HARM

If deafness is considered a disability, one that substantially narrows a child's career, marriage, and cultural options in the future, then deliberately creating a deaf child counts as a moral harm. If Deafness is considered a culture, as Deaf activists would have us agree, then deliberately creating a Deaf child who will have only very limited options to move outside of that culture, also counts as a moral harm. A decision, made before a child is even born, that confines her forever to a narrow group of people and a limited choice of careers, so violates the child's right to an open future that no genetic counseling team should acquiesce in it. The very value of autonomy that grounds the ethics of genetic counseling should preclude assisting parents in a project that so dramatically narrows the autonomy of the child to be.

CODA

Although I rest my case at this point, I want to sketch out some further ramifications of my argument. Are there other, less obvious, ways in which genetic knowledge and manipulation can interfere with the child's right to an open future?

The notion of the child's right to an open future can help in confronting the question of whether to test children for adult-onset genetic diseases, for example Huntington disease.[29] It is well known that the vast majority of adults at risk for Huntington disease choose not to be tested. However, it is not uncommon for parents to request that their children be tested; their goals may be to set their minds at rest, to plan for the future, and so on. On one account, parental authority to make medical decisions suggests that clinicians should accede to these requests (after proper counseling about possible risks). A better account, in my opinion, protects the child's right to an open future by preserving into adulthood his own choice to decide whether his life is better lived with that knowledge or without.[30]

Finally, a provocative argument can be made that sex selection can be deleterious to the child's right to an open future. I am ignoring here all the more obvious arguments against sex selection, even when accomplished without abortion. Rather, I suspect that parents who choose the sex of their offspring are more likely to have gender-specific expectations for those children, expectations that subtly limit the child's own individual flowering. The more we are able to control our children's characteristics (and the more time, energy, and money we invest in the outcome), the more invested we will become in our hopes and dreams for them. It is easy to sympathize with some of the reasons why parents might want to ensure a girl or boy. People who already have one or two children of one sex can hardly be faulted for wanting to "balance" their families by having one of each. And yet, this ought to be discouraged. If I spent a great deal of time and energy to get a boy in the hope of having a football player in the family, I think I would be less likely to accept it with good grace if the boy hated sports and spent all his spare time at the piano. If I insisted on having a girl because I believed that as a grandparent I would be more likely to have close contact with the children of a daughter than of a son, I think I would find it much harder to raise a girl who saw motherhood as a choice rather than as a foregone conclusion. Parents whose preferences are compelling enough for them to take active steps to control the outcome, must, logically, be committed to certain strong gender-role expectations. If they want a girl that badly, whether they are hoping for a Miss America or the next Catherine McKinnon, they are likely to make it difficult for the actual child to resist their expectations and to follow her own bent.

REFERENCES

1. Walter E. Nance, "Parables," in *Prescribing Our Future: Ethical Challenges in Genetic Counseling*, ed. Dianne M. Bartels, Bonnie S. LeRoy, and Arthur L. Caplan, (New York: Aldine De Gruyter, 1993), p. 92.

2. National Society of Genetic Counselors, Code of Ethics, reprinted in *Prescribing Our Future*, pp. 169–71.

3. James R. Sorenson, "Genetic Counseling: Values that have Mattered," *Prescribing Our Future*, p. 11; Arthur L. Caplan. "The Ethics of Genetic Counseling." *Prescribing Our Future*, p. 161.

4. Charles Bosk, "Workplace Ideology," *Prescribing Our Future*, pp. 27–28.

5. Dianne M. Bartels, "Preface," *Prescribing Our Future*, pp. ix-xiii.

6. Barbara Katz Rothman; *The Tentative Pregnancy: Prenatal Diagnosis and the Future of Motherhood* (New York: Viking Press, 1986), p. 41.

7. Nance, "Parables," p. 92.

8. D. Lindhout, P.G. Frets, and M.C. Niermeijer, "Approaches to Genetic Counseling," *Annals of the New York Academy of Sciences* 630 (1991): 223–29, at 224.

9. Jeffrey R. Botkin, "Fetal Privacy and Confidentiality," *Hastings Center Report* 25, no. 3 (1995): 32–39.

10. President's Commission for the Study of Ethical Problems in Biomedical and Behavioral Research. *Screening and Counseling for Genetic Conditions: A Report on the Ethical, Social and Legal Implications of Genetic Screening, Counseling, and Education Programs* (Washington, D.C.: Government Printing Office, 1983), p. 56.

11. Joel Feinberg, "The Child's Right to an Open Future," in *Whose Child? Children's Rights, Parental Authority, and State Power*, ed. William Aiken and Hugh LaFollette (Totowa, N.J.: Littlefield, Adams & Co., 1980), pp. 124–53.

12. Prince v. Massachusetts, 321 U.S. 158 (1944), at 170.

13. Wisconsin v. Yoder, 406 U.S. 205 (1972).

14. William Galston, "Two Concepts of Liberalism," *Ethics* 105, no. 3 (1995): 516–34, at 521.

15. John Stuart Mill, *On Liberty* (New York: W. W. Norton, 1975), p. 55.

16. Galston, "Two Concepts of Liberalism," p. 522.

17. Feinberg, *The Child's Right*, pp. 134–35.

18. Cynthia Cohen, "'Give Me Children or I Shall Die!' New Reproductive Technologies and Harm to Children," *Hastings Center Report* 26, no. 2 (1996): 19–29.

19. Dan Brock, "The Non-Identity Problem and Genetic Harms," *Bioethics* 9, no. 3/4 (1995): 269–75, at 271.

20. Bonnie Steinbock and Ron McClamrock, "When Is Birth Unfair to the Child?" *Hastings Center Report* 24, no. 6 (1994): 15–21, at p. 17.

21. Brock, "The Non-Identity Problem," p. 272.

22. Edward Dolnick, "Deafness as Culture," *The Atlantic Monthly* 272/3 (1993): 37–53.

23. Amy Elizabeth Brusky, "Making Decisions for Deaf Children Regarding Cochlear Implants: The Legal Ramifications of Recognizing Deafness as a Culture Rather than a Disability," *Wisconsin Law Review* (1995): 235–70.

24. John B. Christiansen, "Sociological Implications of Hearing Loss," *Annals of the New York Academy of Science* 630 (1991): 230–35.

25. Dolnick, "Deafness as Culture," p. 38.

26. Nora Ellen Groce, *Everyone Here Spoke Sign Language: Hereditary Deafness on Martha's Vineyard* (Cambridge: Harvard University Press, 1985), p. 85.

27. Andrew Solomon, "Defiantly Deaf," *New York Times Magazine*, 28 August 1994: 40–45 et passim.

28. Dolnick, "Deafness as Culture," p. 43.

29. I am grateful to Thomas H. Murray and Ronald M. Green for bringing this topic to my attention.

30. "The Genetic Testing of Children," *Journal of Medical Genetics* 31 (1994): 785–97.

Genetics and Reproductive Risk: Can Having Children Be Immoral?

Laura M. Purdy

Is it morally permissible for me to have children?[1] A decision to procreate is surely one of the most significant decisions a person can make. So it would seem that it ought not to be made without some moral soul-searching.

There are many reasons why one might hesitate to bring children into this world if one is concerned about their welfare. Some are rather general, like the deteriorating environment or the prospect of poverty. Others have a narrower focus, like continuing civil war in Ireland, or the lack of essential social support for childrearing persons in the United States. Still others may be relevant only to individuals at risk of passing harmful diseases to their offspring.

There are many causes of misery in this world, and most of them are unrelated to genetic disease. In the general scheme of things, human misery is most efficiently reduced by concentrating on noxious social and political arrangements. Nonetheless, we shouldn't ignore preventable harm just because it is confined to a relatively small corner of life. So the question arises: can it be wrong to have a child because of genetic risk factors?[2]

Unsurprisingly, most of the debate about this issue has focused on prenatal screening and abortion: much useful information about a given fetus can be made available by recourse to prenatal testing. This fact has meant that moral questions about reproduction have become entwined with abortion politics, to the detriment of both. The abortion connection has made it especially difficult to think about whether it is wrong to prevent a child from coming into being since doing so might involve what many people see as wrongful killing; yet there is no necessary link between the two.

Clearly, the existence of genetically compromised children can be prevented not only by aborting already existing fetuses but also by preventing conception in the first place. Worse yet, many discussions simply assume a particular view of abortion, without any recognition of other possible positions and the difference they make in how people understand the issues. For example, those who object to aborting fetuses with genetic problems often argue that doing so would undermine our conviction that all humans are in some important sense equal.[3] However, this position rests on the assumption that conception marks the point at which humans are endowed with a right to life. So aborting fetuses with genetic problems looks morally the same as killing "imperfect" people without their consent.

This position raises two separate issues. One pertains to the legitimacy of different views on abortion. Despite the conviction of many abortion activists to the contrary, I believe that ethically respectable views can be found on different sides of the debate, including one that sees fetuses as developing humans without any serious moral claim on continued life. There is no space here to address the details, and doing so would be once again to fall into the trap of letting the abortion question swallow up all others. Fortunately, this issue need not be resolved here. However, opponents of abortion need to face the fact that many thoughtful individuals do not *see* fetuses as moral persons. It follows that their reasoning process and hence the implications of their decisions are radically different from those envisioned by opponents of prenatal screening and abortion. So where the latter see genetic abortion as murdering people who just don't measure up, the former see it as a way to prevent the development of persons who are more likely to live miserable lives. This is consistent with a world view that values persons equally and holds that each deserves high quality life. Some of those who object to genetic abortion appear to be oblivious to these psychological and logical facts. It follows that the nightmare scenarios they paint for us are beside the point: many people simply do not share the assumptions that make them plausible.

How are these points relevant to my discussion? My primary concern here is to argue that conception can sometimes be morally wrong on grounds of genetic risk, although this judgment will not apply to those who accept the moral legitimacy of abortion and are willing to employ prenatal screening and selective abortion. If my case is solid, then those who oppose abortion must be especially careful not to conceive in certain cases, as they are, of course, free to follow their conscience about abortion. Those like myself who do not see abortion as murder have more ways to prevent birth.

HUNTINGTON'S DISEASE

There is always some possibility that reproduction will result in a child with a serious disease or handicap. Genetic counselors can help individuals determine whether they are at unusual risk and, as the Human Genome Project rolls on, their knowledge will increase by quantum leaps. As this knowledge becomes available, I believe we ought to use it to determine whether possible children are at risk *before* they are conceived.

I want in this paper to defend the thesis that it is morally wrong to reproduce when we know there is a high risk of transmitting a serious disease or defect. This thesis holds that some reproductive acts are wrong, and my argument puts the burden of proof on those who disagree with it to show why its conclusions can be overridden. Hence it denies that people should be free to reproduce mindless of the consequences.[4] However, as moral argument, it should be taken as a proposal for further debate and discussion. It is not, by itself, an argument in favor of legal prohibitions of reproduction.[5]

There is a huge range of genetic diseases. Some are quickly lethal; others kill more slowly, if at all. Some are mainly physical, some mainly mental; others impair both kinds of function. Some interfere tremendously with normal functioning, others less. Some are painful, some are not. There seems to be considerable agreement that rapidly lethal diseases, especially those, like Tay-Sachs, accompanied by painful deterioration, should be prevented even at the cost of abortion. Conversely, there seems to be substantial agreement that relatively trivial problems, especially cosmetic ones, would not be legitimate grounds for abortion.[6] In short, there are cases ranging from low risk of mild disease or disability to high risk of serious disease or disability. Although it is difficult to decide where the duty to refrain from procreation becomes compelling, I believe that there are some clear cases. I have chosen to focus on Huntington's disease to illustrate the kinds of concrete issues such decisions entail. However, the arguments presented here are also relevant to many other genetic diseases.[7]

The symptoms of Huntington's disease usually begin between the ages of thirty and fifty. It happens this way:

> Onset is insidious. Personality changes (obstinacy, moodiness, lack of initiative) frequently antedate or accompany the involuntary choreic movements. These usually appear first in the face, neck, and arms, and are jerky, irregular, and stretching in character. Contractions of the facial muscles result in grimaces, those of the respiratory muscles, lips, and tongue lead to hesitating, explosive speech. Irregular movements of the trunk are present; the gait is

shuffling and dancing. Tendon reflexes are increased. . . . Some patients display a fatuous euphoria; others are spiteful, irascible, destructive, and violent. Paranoid reactions are common. Poverty of thought and impairment of attention, memory, and judgment occur. As the disease progresses, walking becomes impossible, swallowing difficult, and dementia profound. Suicide is not uncommon.[8]

The illness lasts about fifteen years, terminating in death.

Huntington's disease is an autosomal dominant disease, meaning that it is caused by a single defective gene located on a non-sex chromosome. It is passed from one generation to the next via affected individuals. Each child of such an affected person has a fifty percent risk of inheriting the gene and thus of eventually developing the disease, even if he or she was born before the parent's disease was evident.[9]

Until recently, Huntington's disease was especially problematic because most affected individuals did not know whether they had the gene for the disease until well into their childbearing years. So they had to decide about childbearing before knowing whether they could transmit the disease or not. If, in time, they did not develop symptoms of the disease, then their children could know they were not at risk for the disease. If unfortunately they did develop symptoms, then each of their children could know there was a fifty percent chance that they, too, had inherited the gene. In both cases, the children faced a period of prolonged anxiety as to whether they would develop the disease. Then, in the 1980s, thanks in part to an energetic campaign by Nancy Wexler, a genetic marker was found that, in certain circumstances, could tell people with a relatively high degree of probability whether or not they had the gene for the disease.[10] Finally, in March 1993, the defective gene itself was discovered.[11] Now individuals can find out whether they carry the gene for the disease, and prenatal screening can tell us whether a given fetus has inherited it. These technological developments change the moral scene substantially.

How serious are the risks involved in Huntington's disease? Geneticists often think a ten percent risk is high.[12] But risk assessment also depends on what is at stake: the worse the possible outcome the more undesirable an otherwise small risk seems. In medicine, as elsewhere, people may regard the same result quite differently. But for devastating diseases like Huntington's this part of the judgment should be unproblematic: no one wants a loved one to suffer in this way.[13]

There may still be considerable disagreement about the acceptability of a given risk. So it would be difficult

in many circumstances to say how we should respond to a particular risk. Nevertheless, there are good grounds for a conservative approach, for it is reasonable to take special precautions to avoid very bad consequences, even if the risk is small. But the possible consequences here *are* very bad: a child who may inherit Huntington's disease has a much greater than average chance of being subjected to severe and prolonged suffering. And it is one thing to risk one's own welfare, but quite another to do so for others and without their consent.

Is this judgment about Huntington's disease really defensible? People appear to have quite different opinions. Optimists argue that a child born into a family afflicted with Huntington's disease has a reasonable chance of living a satisfactory life. After all, even children born of an afflicted parent still have a fifty percent chance of escaping the disease. And even if afflicted themselves, such people will probably enjoy some thirty years of healthy life before symptoms appear. It is also possible, although not at all likely, that some might not mind the symptoms caused by the disease. Optimists can point to diseased persons who have lived fruitful lives, as well as those who seem genuinely glad to be alive. One is Rick Donohue, a sufferer from the Joseph family disease. "You know, if my mom hadn't had me, I wouldn't be here for the life I have had. So there is a good possibility I will have children."[14] Optimists therefore conclude that it would be a shame if these persons had not lived.

Pessimists concede some of these facts, but take a less sanguine view of them. They think a fifty percent risk of serious disease like Huntington's appallingly high. They suspect that many children born into afflicted families are liable to spend their youth in dreadful anticipation and fear of the disease. They point out that Rick Donohue is still young, and has not experienced the full horror of his sickness. It is also well-known that some young persons have such a dilated sense of time that they can hardly envision themselves at thirty or forty, so the prospect of pain at that age is unreal to them.[15]

More empirical research on the psychology and life history of sufferers and potential sufferers is clearly needed to decide whether optimists or pessimists have a more accurate picture of the experiences of individuals at risk. But given that some will surely realize pessimists' worst fears, it seems unfair to conclude that the pleasures of those who deal with the situation simply cancel out the suffering of those others when that suffering could be avoided altogether.

I think that these points indicate that the morality of procreation in situations like this demands further investigation. I propose to do this by looking first at the position of the possible child, then at that of the potential parent.

POSSIBLE CHILDREN AND POTENTIAL PARENTS

The first task in treating the problem from the child's point of view is to find a way of referring to possible future offspring without seeming to confer some sort of morally significant existence upon them. I will follow the convention of calling children who might be born in the future but who are not now conceived "possible" children, offspring, individuals, or persons.

Now, what claims about children or possible children are relevant to the morality of childbearing in the circumstances being considered? Of primary importance is the judgment that we ought to try to provide every child with something like a minimally satisfying life. I am not altogether sure how best to formulate this standard but I want clearly to reject the view that it is morally permissible to conceive individuals so long as we do not expect them to be so miserable that they wish they were dead.[16] I believe that this kind of moral minimalism is thoroughly unsatisfactory and that not many people would really want to live in a world where it was the prevailing standard. Its lure is that it puts few demands on us, but its price is the scant attention it pays to human well-being.

How might the judgment that we have a duty to try to provide a minimally satisfying life for our children be justified? It could, I think, be derived fairly straightforwardly from either utilitarian or contractarian theories of justice, although there is no space here for discussion of the details. The net result of such analysis would be the conclusion that neglecting this duty would create unnecessary unhappiness or unfair disadvantage for some persons.

Of course, this line of reasoning confronts us with the need to spell out what is meant by "minimally satisfying" and what a standard based on this concept would require of us. Conceptions of a minimally satisfying life vary tremendously among societies and also within them. *De rigeur* in some circles are private music lessons and trips to Europe, while in others providing eight years of schooling is a major accomplishment. But there is no need to consider this complication at length here since we are concerned only with health as a prerequisite for a minimally satisfying life. Thus, as we draw out what such a standard might require of

us, it seems reasonable to retreat to the more limited claim that parents should try to ensure something like normal health for their children. It might be thought that even this moderate claim is unsatisfactory since in some places debilitating conditions are the norm, but one could circumvent this objection by saying that parents ought to try to provide for their children health normal for that culture, even though it may be inadequate if measured by some outside standard.[17] This conservative position would still justify efforts to avoid the birth of children at risk for Huntington's disease and other serious genetic diseases in virtually all societies.[18]

This view is reinforced by the following considerations. Given that possible children do not presently exist as actual individuals, they do not have a right to be brought into existence, and hence no one is maltreated by measures to avoid the conception of a possible person. Therefore, the conservative course that avoids the conception of those who would not be expected to enjoy a minimally satisfying life is at present the only fair course of action. The alternative is a laissez-faire approach which brings into existence the lucky, but only at the expense of the unlucky. Notice that attempting to avoid the creation of the unlucky does not necessarily lead to *fewer* people being brought into being; the question boils down to taking steps to bring those with better prospects into existence, instead of those with worse ones.

I have so far argued that if people with Huntington's disease are unlikely to live minimally satisfying lives, then those who might pass it on should not have genetically related children. This is consonant with the principle the greater the danger of serious problems, the stronger the duty to avoid them. But this principle is in conflict with what people think of as the right to reproduce. How might one decide which should take precedence?

Expecting people to forego having genetically related children might seem to demand too great a sacrifice of them. But before reaching that conclusion we need to ask what is really at stake. One reason for wanting children is to experience family life, including love, companionship, watching kids grow, sharing their pains and triumphs, and helping to form members of the next generation. Other reasons emphasize the validation of parents as individuals within a continuous family line, children as a source of immortality, or perhaps even the gratification of producing partial replicas of oneself. Children may also be desired in an effort to prove that one is an adult, to try to cement a marriage, or to benefit parents economically.

Are there alternative ways of satisfying these desires? Adoption or new reproductive technologies can fulfill many of them without passing on known genetic defects. Replacements for sperm have been available for many years via artificial insemination by donor. More recently, egg donation, sometimes in combination with contract pregnancy,[19] has been used to provide eggs for women who prefer not to use their own. Eventually it may be possible to clone individual humans, although that now seems a long way off. All of these approaches to avoiding the use of particular genetic material are controversial and have generated much debate. I believe that tenable moral versions of each do exist.[20]

None of these methods permits people to extend both genetic lines, or realize the desire for immortality or for children who resemble both parents; nor is it clear that such alternatives will necessarily succeed in proving that one is an adult, cementing a marriage, or providing economic benefits. Yet, many people feel these desires strongly. Now, I am sympathetic to William James's dictum regarding desires: "Take any demand, however slight, which any creature, however weak, may make. Ought it not, for its own sole sake to be satisfied? If not, prove why not."[21] Thus a world where more desires are satisfied is generally better than one where fewer are. However, not all desires can be legitimately satisfied since, as James suggests, there may be good reasons—such as the conflict of duty and desire—why some should be overruled.

Fortunately, further scrutiny of the situation reveals that there are good reasons why people should attempt—with appropriate social support—to talk themselves out of the desires in question or to consider novel ways of fulfilling them. Wanting to see the genetic line continued is not particularly rational when it brings a sinister legacy of illness and death. The desire for immortality cannot really be satisfied anyway, and people need to face the fact that what really matters is how they behave in their own lifetime. And finally, the desire for children who physically resemble one is understandable, but basically narcissistic, and its fulfillment cannot be guaranteed even by normal reproduction. There are other ways of proving one is an adult, and other ways of cementing marriages—children don't necessarily do either. Children, especially prematurely ill children, may not provide the expected economic benefits anyway. Non-genetically related children may also provide benefits similar to those that would have been provided by genetically related ones, and expected economic benefit is, in many cases, a morally questionable reason for having children.

Before the advent of reliable genetic testing, the options of people in Huntington's families were cruelly limited. On the one hand, they could have children, but at the risk of eventual crippling illness and death for them. On the other, they could refrain from childbearing, sparing their possible children from significant risk of inheriting this disease, perhaps frustrating intense desires to procreate—only to discover, in some cases, that their sacrifice was unnecessary because they did not develop the disease. Or they could attempt to adopt or try new reproductive approaches.

Reliable genetic testing has opened up new possibilities. Those at risk who wish to have children can get tested. If they test positive, they know their possible children are at risk. Those who are opposed to abortion must be especially careful to avoid conception if they are to behave responsibly. Those not opposed to abortion can responsibly conceive children, but only if they are willing to test each fetus and abort those who carry the gene. If individuals at risk test negative, they are home free.

What about those who cannot face the test for themselves? They can do prenatal testing and abort fetuses who carry the defective gene. A clearly positive test also implies that the parent is affected, although negative tests do not rule out that possibility. Prenatal testing can thus bring knowledge that enables one to avoid passing the disease to others, but only, in some cases, at the cost of coming to know with certainty that one will indeed develop the disease. This situation raises with peculiar force the question of whether parental responsibility requires people to get tested.

Some people think that we should recognize a right "not to know." It seems to me that such a right could be defended only where ignorance does not put others at serious risk. So if people are prepared to forgo genetically related children, they need not get tested. But if they want genetically related children then they must do whatever is necessary to ensure that affected babies are not the result. There is, after all, something inconsistent about the claim that one has a right to be shielded from the truth, even if the price is to risk inflicting on one's children the same dread disease one cannot even face in oneself.

In sum, until we can be assured that Huntington's disease does not prevent people from living a minimally satisfying life, individuals at risk for the disease have a moral duty to try not to bring affected babies into this world. There are now enough options available so that this duty needn't frustrate their reasonable desires. Society has a corresponding duty to facilitate moral behavior on the part of individuals. Such support ranges from the narrow and concrete (like making sure that medical testing and counseling is available to all) to the more general social environment that guarantees that all pregnancies are voluntary, that pronatalism is eradicated, and that women are treated with respect regardless of the reproductive options they choose.

NOTES

1. This paper is loosely based on "Genetic Diseases: Can Having Children Be Immoral?" originally published in *Genetics Now*, ed. John L. Buckley (Washington, DC: University Press of America, 1978) and subsequently anthologized in a number of medical ethics texts. Thanks to Thomas Mappes and David DeGrazia for their helpful suggestions about updating the paper.

2. I focus on genetic considerations, although with the advent of AIDS the scope of the general question here could be expanded. There are two reasons for sticking to this relatively narrow formulation. One is that dealing with a smaller chunk of the problem may help us think more clearly, while realizing that some conclusions may nonetheless be relevant to the larger problem. The other is the peculiar capacity of some genetic problems to affect ever more individuals in the future.

3. For example, see Leon Kass, "Implications of Prenatal Diagnosis for the Human Right to Live," *Ethical Issues in Human Genetics*, eds. Bruce Hilton et al. (New York: Plenum Press, 1973).

4. This is, of course, a very broad thesis. I defend an even broader version in "Loving Future People," *Reproduction, Ethics and the Law*, ed. Joan Callahan (Bloomington: Indiana University Press, forthcoming).

5. Why would we want to resist legal enforcement of every moral conclusion? First, legal action has many costs, costs not necessarily worth paying in particular cases. Second, legal enforcement would tend to take the matter in question out of the realm of debate and treat it as settled. But in many cases, especially where mores or technology are rapidly evolving, we don't want that to happen. Third, legal enforcement would undermine individual freedom and decision-making capacity. In some cases, the ends envisioned are important enough to warrant putting up with these disadvantages, but that remains to be shown in each case.

6. Those who do not see fetuses as moral persons with a right to life may nonetheless hold that abortion is justifiable in these cases. I argue at some length elsewhere that lesser defects can cause great suffering. Once we are clear that there is nothing discriminatory about failing to conceive particular possible individuals, it makes sense, other things being equal to avoid the prospect of such pain if we can. Naturally, other things rarely are equal. In the first place, many problems go undiscovered until a baby is born. Secondly, there are often substantial costs associated with screening programs. Thirdly, although women should be encouraged to consider the moral dimensions of routine pregnancy; we do not want it to be so fraught with tension that it becomes a miserable experience. (See "Loving Future People.")

7. It should be noted that failing to conceive a single individual can affect many lives: in 1916, nine hundred and sixty-two cases could be traced from six seventeenth-century arrivals in America. See Gordon Rattray Taylor, *The Biological Time Bomb* (New York, 1968), p. 176.

8. *The Merck Manual* (Rathway, N. J.: Merck, 1972), pp. 1363, 1346. We now know that the age of onset and severity of the disease is related to the number of abnormal replications of the glutamine code on the abnormal gene. See Andrew Revkin, "Hunting Down Huntington's," *Discover*, December 1993, p. 108.

9. Hyrnie Gordon, "Genetic Counseling," *JAMA*, Vol. 217, no. 9 (August 30, 1971), p. 1346.

10. See Revkin, "Hunting Down Huntington's," pp. 99–108.

11. "Gene for Huntington's Disease Discovered," *Human Genome News*, Vol. 5, no. 1 (May 1993), p. 5.

12. Charles Smith, Susan Holloway, and Alan E. H. Emery, "Individuals at Risk in Families—Genetic Disease," *Journal of Medical Genetics*, Vol. 8 (1971), p. 453.

13. To try to separate the issue of the gravity of the disease from the existence of a given individual, compare this situation with how we would assess a parent who neglected to vaccinate an existing child against a hypothetical viral version of Huntington's.

14. The *New York Times*, September 30, 1975, p. 1, col. 6. The Joseph family disease is similar to Huntington's disease except that the symptoms start appearing in the twenties. Rick Donohue was in his early twenties at the time he made this statement.

15. I have talked to college students who believe that they will have lived fully and be ready to die at those ages. It is astonishing how one's perspective changes over time, and how ages that one once asssociated with senility and physical collapse come to seem the prime of human life.

16. The view I am rejecting has been forcefully articulated by Derek Parfit, *Reasons and Persons* (Oxford: Oxford University Press, 1984). For more discussion, see "Loving Future People."

17. I have some qualms about this response since I fear that some human groups are so badly off that it might still be wrong for them to procreate, even if that would mean great changes in their cultures. But this is a complicated issue that needs its own investigation.

18. Again, a troubling exception might be the isolated Venezuelan group Nancy Wexler found where, because of inbreeding, a large portion of the population is affected by Huntington's. See Revkin, "Hunting Down Huntington's."

19. Or surrogacy, as it has been popularly known. I think that "contract pregnancy" is more accurate and more respectful of women. Eggs can be provided either by a woman who also gestates the fetus or by a third party.

20. The most powerful objections to new reproductive technologies and arrangements concern possible bad consequences for women. However, I do not think that the arguments against them on these grounds have yet shown the dangers to be as great as some believe. So although it is perhaps true that new reproductive technologies and arrangements shouldn't be used lightly, avoiding the conceptions discussed here is well worth the risk. For a series of viewpoints on this issue, including my own "Another Look at Contract Pregnancy," See Helen B. Holmes, *Issues in Reproductive Technology 1: An Anthology* (New York: Garland Press, 1992).

21. *Essays in Pragmatism*, ed. A. Castell (New York: 1948), p. 73.

Using Preimplantation Genetic Diagnosis to Save a Sibling: The Story of Molly and Adam Nash[1]

Bonnie Steinbock

Molly Nash was born on July 4, 1994 with multiple birth defects due to Fanconi anemia, a deadly genetic disease that causes bone marrow failure, eventually resulting in leukemia and other forms of cancer. Her best chance for survival was a bone marrow transplant from a perfectly matched sibling donor. Lisa and Jack Nash had considered having another child, not as a source of bone marrow but because they very much wanted another child. They had decided against it because there was a one-in-four chance that the infant would have the same illness as Molly, and aborting an affected fetus was not an option Mrs. Nash would consider. Then they learned about preimplantation genetic diagnosis (PGD), which would enable them to screen embryos for the disease, and implant only the healthy ones. Moreover, the embryos could also be tested to find which ones shared Molly's tissue type. The baby would be not only disease-free, but could also provide bone marrow to Molly. Moreover, because blood cells saved from the baby's umbilical cord and placenta could be used, there would be no need to extract the bone marrow from the baby's body, a procedure which is both painful and carries some risk.

The odds of producing an embryo that is disease-free, a perfect match, and capable of initiating a pregnancy are daunting. In January 1999, Lisa Nash produced 12 eggs, 2 of which were healthy matches. She became pregnant, but miscarried. In June she produced only four eggs, one of which was a match, but she did not become pregnant. In September, she produced eight eggs, only one of which was a healthy match, but again she did not become pregnant. Molly was getting sicker and her physician recommended proceeding with a transplant from a nonrelated donor, although the odds that such a transplant would work were virtually nil. The Nashes decided to try a different IVF clinic, one known for being more aggressive. Lisa's hormone regimen was changed and in December 1999, 24 eggs were retrieved. Only one was a match, but this time she became pregnant. She was confined to bed to prevent a miscarriage. On August 29, 2000, after 52 hours of labor (Lisa resisted a cesarean section because more cord blood could be collected during a vaginal birth), Adam Nash was delivered by C-section. In October 2000, doctors at Fairview-University Hospital in Minneapolis, which specializes in bone marrow transplants for children with Fanconi anemia, successfully transferred tissue from Adam's umbilical cord into Molly's body. Molly, by all accounts, is doing very well. She is back at school, or rather a visiting teacher, who must wear a mask during lessons, comes to her home. She takes ballet lessons. Her transplant did not cure her of Fanconi anemia, but merely prevented her developing leukemia. She is likely to suffer Fanconi's other complications, particularly cancers of the mouth and neck, but that is far off in the future.

Adam Nash was not unique in being conceived to save a sibling. Ten years earlier, another couple, Abe and Mary Ayala, decided to have Abe's vasectomy reversed, in the hopes that Mary would become pregnant with a child who could be a bone marrow donor for their daughter, Anissa, aged 17, who had been diagnosed with leukemia. Surprisingly, the reversal worked and Mary, aged 42, became pregnant. Moreover, the baby, Marissa Eve, born on April 3, 1990, turned out to be a compatible donor. At the time, the reaction from medical ethicists was generally negative. Philip Boyle, an associate at the Hastings Center, said, "It's troublesome, to say the least. It's outrageous that people would go to this length." Alexander Capron, professor of law and medicine at the University of Southern California, suggested that having a baby to save another child was ethically unacceptable because it violated the Kantian principle that persons are never to be used solely as a means to another person's ends. Others, however, challenged the view that Marissa was being used as a means only, or that she was not given the respect due to persons. The crucial thing, they argued, was that her parents and siblings intended to love the new addition to the family as much as her older brother and sister, whether or not she could donate bone marrow. The risk to Marissa was minimal; indeed, if Anissa already had a baby sister with compatible marrow, no one would have questioned using the infant as a donor. Why should the moral situation be different if the choice is to create a child in the hopes that she will be a donor?

Unlike the Ayalas, who thought they had completed their family, the Nashes wanted another child. When they were told that the same technique that could prevent the birth of a child with Fanconi might also identify a compatible donor for Molly, they jumped at the chance. As Mrs. Nash put it, "You could say it was an added perk to have Adam be the right bone marrow type, which would not hurt him in the least and would save Molly's life. We didn't have to think twice about it."[2]

Are there ethical objections to what the Nashes did? Some oppose PGD even for its ordinary use, to prevent the birth of a child with a serious disability.[3] Others do not oppose PGD in principle, but think that it should not be used to save the lives of existing children. One concern is that the parents of fatally ill children will be unable to refuse to go through IVF if it is presented as their only chance for saving their child. Furthermore, not every story of a Fanconi child has the happy ending afforded the Nash family. Some women go through cycle after cycle of IVF, only to fail to produce a compatible embryo, or to suffer repeated miscarriages.[4] It may be argued that this is not a choice that doctors should offer desperate parents, given that the odds of success are relatively low. At the same time, many women choose to undergo the rigors of IVF to have babies. If it is not unethical to give them this choice, is it unethical to give them the chance to save their child's life, if they are fully informed about the burdens and risks, and the odds of success?

Some ethicists object to the idea of having a baby for "spare parts." Clearly it would be wrong to create a baby for spare parts if that would be harmful to the child. One could not create a baby for his heart or lungs or even kidney. In what sense has Adam Nash been harmed? He owes his very existence to the fact that he was a perfect match for Molly. Of course, many embryos were discarded and this is considered immoral by those who view preimplantation embryos as tiny children. This, however, is not an objection to using PGD to create donors, but to PGD generally, and indeed to all of IVF.

Finally, many are profoundly disturbed by the possibility of "having babies to spec," of choosing who will be born based on their genetic characteristics. "If we can screen an embryo for tissue type, won't we one day screen for eye color or intelligence?"[5] Some ethicists fear that the use of PGD to get compatible donors today will lead to a world in which parents will be able to select their children's physical, mental, and emotional traits. From one perspective, PGD offers parents of desperately ill children the hope of a miracle. From another, it opens the door to "genetic engineering" and a new eugenics.

NOTES

1. Much of the factual material in this case study comes from Lisa Belkin, "The Made-to-Order Savior," *The New York Times Magazine*, July 1, 2001.
2. Denise Grady, "Son Conceived to Provide Blood Cells for Daughter," *The New York Times*, October 4, 2000, A24.
3. See Adrienne Asch, "Prenatal Diagnosis and Selective Abortion: A Challenge to Practice and Policy," *American Journal of Public Health*, Vol. 89, no. 11 (November 1999): 1649–1657. In this volume, pp. 523–533. Though Asch does not specifically discuss PGD, her objections to selective abortion extend to embryo selection and discard as well.
4. See Belkin, *op. cit.*
5. *Ibid.*

Predictive Genetic Testing in Young People for Adult-Onset Conditions: Where is the Empirical Evidence?

R.E. Duncan and M.B. Delatycki

There are polarized views concerning the issue of predictive genetic testing in young people. Some perceive such testing as too potentially harmful to allow. Others perceive it as an opportunity for the promotion of benefit, an opportunity even for the prevention of harm. Both views are based on logical argument, but what of the empirical evidence that is required for informing this theoretical debate?

In this article, we review the discourse concerning predictive genetic testing in young people, focusing specifically on predictive genetic tests for adult-onset severe conditions, for which no prevention or treatment exists. Examples of these are tests for Huntington's disease (HD) or autosomal dominant spinocerebellar ataxia undertaken in asymptomatic individuals. We describe the arguments used to oppose such testing in

Duncan, R. E. and M. B. Delatycki, "Predictive Genetic Testing in Young People for Adult-Onset Conditions: Where is the Empirical Evidence?" *Clinical Genetics* 69 (2006), 8–16. Copyright © 2006. Reproduced with permission of Blackwell Publishing Ltd.

young people and those lending support. We then look to empirical research in the hope of finding evidence to resolve these issues but find little. Finally, we concentrate on why empirical evidence is so lacking and how the debate can be advanced.

Throughout the article, we use the terms 'medical benefit' and 'non-medical benefit' (or 'medical reasons' and 'non-medical reasons') to distinguish between different motivations for predictive genetic testing. When using the term 'medical benefit', we refer to clinical benefits only. That is, a predictive genetic test creates medical benefit when knowledge of gene status is able to assist in either preventing or treating the condition, altering clinical outcome. When using the term 'non-medical benefit', we refer to the range of psychosocial benefits that predictive genetic testing may create, such as decreased uncertainty or a greater ability to plan for the future—that is, benefits of testing that do not alter disease progression or outcome but have the potential to impact positively on the individual's life nonetheless.

GUIDELINES CONCERNING TESTING IN YOUNG PEOPLE

The first guidelines concerning this issue were those published by the International Huntington Association and the World Federation of Neurology in relation to predictive testing for HD[1,2]. These made an explicit recommendation that testing should not be provided to those under the age of 18 years. Subsequently, International Human Genetic Societies have published similar guidelines[3-6]. These guidelines purport that when medical benefit is not an outcome, testing should be deferred until young people are autonomous and able to make a competent decision about testing themselves. Existing guidelines remain somewhat elusive about the ways in which competence should be assessed and the capacities necessary for making an informed decision about predictive genetic testing.

WHAT IS SO DIFFERENT ABOUT YOUNG PEOPLE?

The existence of guidelines that specifically relate to young people highlights the fact that issues concerning young people are often separated from those involving adults in discussions about predictive genetic testing. There are both cognitive and psychosocial justifications for this separation. In relation to cognitive development,

young people gradually acquire knowledge, and the ability to interpret this knowledge, as they mature. This can create greater vulnerability in relation to predictive genetic testing. For example, if cognition has not reached an appropriate capacity, decision-making ability and the ability to perceive long-term impacts of genetic testing may not be sufficient. For even younger children, reduced, albeit age-appropriate, cognitive capacity may mean that they attribute their future illness to bad behaviour, perceiving it as punishment[7,8].

Psychosocially, there are several additional reasons for the separation of young people from adults. There are specific developmental processes that occur during adolescence, and there are theoretical reasons to suggest that predictive testing may impact specifically upon these. For example, adolescence is a time when self-identity is being formulated and strengthened[9]. Other developmental processes of adolescence include the establishment of peer relations and the gradual shift to independence[9]. Adolescence is also often a time where young people engage in their first intimate relationships[9]. These developmental processes are relatively specific to adolescence, and therefore predictive genetic testing at this time may have impacts that are different from those that occur when adults are tested. Some of these processes extend to younger children, for example, the emergence of a unique self-identity, which involves the realization of one's own motivations, behaviours, values, opinions and desires. The establishment of peer relations and the development of specific relationships within the family also begin in young children. The fact that young people are still dependent on their parents constitutes another important difference between young people and adults. For example, the emotional state of parents, who may themselves be affected by the familial condition, can also impact upon young people.

DISTINGUISHING BETWEEN IMMATURE AND MATURE YOUNG PEOPLE

When talking about young people, it is necessary to make a distinction between immature and mature individuals. When referring to immature young people, we refer to young people who do not possess cognitive capacities that allow them to appreciate the implications of predictive testing. When referring to mature young people, we refer to young people who are able to engage in discussions about genetics and predictive genetic tests. Of particular importance here is the ability to perceive long-term implications of these tests.

Because both cognitive and psychological capacities vary greatly between individuals, we are not comfortable with providing a specific age range to associate with the terms 'immature' and 'mature'.

In this article, we are primarily concerned with mature young people only—that is, those for whom an informed decision about predictive genetic testing is possible. When relaying the current discourse concerning predictive genetic testing in young people, we do consider arguments relating to both mature and immature young people. However, the conclusions we draw about provision of predictive genetic tests to young people relate solely to mature young people.

We acknowledge that the difficulty here is not defining such categories but rather identifying means to distinguish 'immature' young people from 'mature' young people. This task must be carried out by individual clinicians who base their decisions on real knowledge of the young person presenting to them and the family dynamics that surround this person. However, we argue that clinicians must seriously consider the possibility that mature young people may be much younger than 18 years of age.

OBJECTIONS TO PREDICTIVE GENETIC TESTING IN YOUNG PEOPLE

Many arguments used to oppose testing in young people focus specifically on immature young people. The most common of these relate to the ethical principle of autonomy, arguing that immature young people should not undergo testing because they lose the opportunity to then make an autonomous decision about testing as an adult. Testing of young people, it is argued, is only acceptable when young people are directly involved in the decision[10-12]. This argument is often supported by the finding that the majority of adults at risk of HD choose not to undergo testing[13]. Arguments about autonomy are frequently summarized as assertions about a child's right to 'an open future'[14].

Concerns about confidentiality have also been used as justifications for not testing immature young people. It is argued that when young people undergo testing, they are not granted the same degree of confidentiality that adults receive, due to the disclosure of results to young people's parents[13,15,16].

Potential psychological harm is yet another concern. Authors suggest that young people may blame themselves for a 'bad' result, causing guilt[7,8]. Objections have also related to the potential for misunderstanding of the genetic information that is imparted. It is argued that parents may not be able to convey accurate information to their children concerning genetic risks[7].

Several concerns about predictive genetic testing in young people relate to mature young people also. It is argued that changes in the self-concept may occur, where a gene-positive result (indicating an increased risk) may lead to feelings of unworthiness, disrupting the normal identification processes with peers[7,17]. Concerns also exist around feelings of inadequacy that may develop, causing young people to become afraid of relationships and even to believe that they are 'unmarriageable'[11].

Fears about the decision-making process that leads young people or their parents to request testing pose additional reasons for concern. Young people's requests for testing may reflect their parents' wishes more than their own. In extreme cases, parents may even coerce their children into testing.

Concerns about potential harm to the parent–child relationship have featured prominently in the literature. It is argued that parents may alter the expectations they have of their child, forcing children to grow up in a world of limited horizons[17,18]. Much has also been written about 'vulnerable child syndrome', where children are overprotected and restricted in childhood activities[18,19]. Some authors worry that parents may react to the threatened loss of their child by emotionally distancing themselves[7]. It has also been suggested that parents may spend less resources, both physical and emotional, on a child who tests gene-positive[11]. Children may even be affected indirectly if parents suffer from guilt[11,18].

Family dynamics are the source of further concerns, specifically the bonds between siblings. It is argued that testing may divide siblings who previously shared a 'bond of risk'[8]. It has also been suggested that if one sibling receives a predictive test result, other siblings may develop a false belief that they are then at an increased or decreased risk[17]. Additional concerns also relate to the broader family. For example, 'bonds of risk' may be altered between parents and children or even with more distant relatives.

Fears of potential stigmatization and discrimination are also commonly raised. These concerns relate to both insurance, such as health, life and disability insurance, and employment discrimination[11]. Insurance companies generally refuse to issue life insurance to adults who have received a gene-positive result but do offer insurance, albeit at increased rates, to adults who are at risk but have not yet been tested[20]. Thus, if young people are tested under the age of 18 years and receive a gene-positive test result, there is a possibility that they

TABLE 1   Arguments Used to Oppose Predictive Genetic Testing in Young People

Testing immature young people removes their right to make a decision about testing as an autonomous adult.

When young people are tested, confidentiality is breached because parents are informed of the test result.

Parents may alter their expectations of a child who receives a gene-positive result.

Harm to the parent—child relationship may occur, especially if parents experience anxiety or guilt.

Young people may blame themselves for a gene-positive result, viewing it as punishment.

Young people may misunderstand the genetic information that is conveyed to them.

If one sibling has information about his or her gene status, other siblings may inappropriately believe that they are at higher or lower risk than they are.

Children may develop an altered self-concept, identifying themselves as a 'carrier of a gene mutation' and feeling unworthy or unmarriageable.

Children who test gene-positive may have difficulty obtaining life insurance as adults.

will not be able to obtain life insurance once they are adults.

Table 1 presents the arguments used to oppose predictive genetic testing in young people.

SUPPORT FOR PREDICTIVE GENETIC TESTING IN YOUNG PEOPLE

Much of the literature supporting testing in young people focuses upon the existence of young people who are competent to make a decision about testing themselves[21–24]. Arguments are made in favour of the 'emancipated minor' who is treated as an adult by law with respect to medical decisions[17]. It is suggested that if young people's values and identity appear coherent, their requests for testing should be satisfied.

Several authors also argue that allowing young people to make decisions about testing will promote benefits. It is suggested that respecting young people's decisions about testing will empower them to feel like active participants in their health, as opposed to powerless victims of their genes[23]. It has also been proposed that allowing young people to be involved in such decisions will promote the development of their autonomy[24–27].

It has been argued that genetic information is of great use to mature young people wishing to pursue life plans[23], in that such information could be used to inform reproductive decisions, career choices, financial plans and end-of-life decisions[25]. Advantages such as more opportunity to prepare psychologically have also been highlighted[28].

Support for testing young people often focuses on the harm that could result if testing is not performed. Concerns relating to the depression and anguish that may develop in the face of uncertainty have also been noted[27]. It has been argued that too little attention has been paid to the psychological harms that may be caused by withholding genetic testing[29].

There have also been a number of arguments specifically in favour of testing immature young people. It has been argued that testing immature young people may benefit them by helping them to incorporate their gene status into their identity[18,29]. Early testing may also result in better psychosocial adjustment, as life plans are yet to be firmly established[25]. Some argue that adults who were not tested as children lose their right to be tested as children and therefore the potential benefits of growing up with that information[28]. Parents may also benefit from an early diagnosis in their children, as they can adjust and plan the disclosure of news to their children[19]. It is argued that testing may also facilitate openness in the family, creating a healthier environment[15,19]. Reduction of uncertainty and anxiety is yet another proposed benefit of testing[25].

Support for testing of immature young people often revolves around parental rights[8,24,27]. It is argued that the desires of parents should be satisfied, out of deference to the fact that parents bear primary responsibility for their children[24]. Arguments opposing paternalism have also been made[24,25,27].

Table 2 presents the arguments used to support predictive genetic testing in young people.

WHAT DOES EMPIRICAL EVIDENCE TELL US?

At such an impasse in theoretical debate, there is a need to consult empirical evidence. Unfortunately, only two studies have been reported describing the effects of predictive genetic testing in young people for non-medical reasons. One of these is a case study involving a 5-year-old girl who underwent genetic testing for a

TABLE 2   Arguments Used to Support Predictive Genetic Testing in Young People

Mature young people can be competent, and therefore these competent individuals should have access to testing.

Knowledge of gene status can help young people plan for their future.

Testing helps increase young people's sense of themselves as active participants in their lives, rather than powerless victims of their genes, helping to promote autonomy.

Not providing testing could cause psychological harm.

Early knowledge of gene status may help parents prepare their children.

Parents bear primary responsibility for their children and should therefore be afforded the right to make a decision about whether or not to have their children tested.

It is paternalistic not to allow testing.

Testing early allows that genetic status to be incorporated into the child's self-identity and to prepare psychologically.

Testing facilitates openness in the family.

familial hepatic nuclear factor-1α mutation underlying maturity-onset diabetes of the young (MODY)[30,31], while the other reports clinicians' descriptions of tests they provided to young people for non-medical reasons[32]. MODY can present under the age of 18 years, and hence the appropriateness of including tests for MODY in this review is debatable, but given the extreme lack of empirical evidence, we refer to it briefly.

The case study relating to MODY relates to a 5-year-old girl being tested pre-symptomatically after her 11-year-old symptomatic sister was found to have a hepatic nuclear factor-1α mutation[30,31]. The test was performed because of a parental desire to reduce uncertainty in the context of the family. In-depth interviews were conducted with the parents and both children and a range of professionals involved in the case. Interviews were conducted prior to the test and 6 weeks after receipt of the gene-positive result. Following the receipt of a gene-positive result, the father reported feeling 'a bit guilty' and that it was his fault that his daughter had received a gene-positive test result but noted that this was short lived, lasting no more than a day. The mother described that although she felt initially disappointed by her daughter's gene-positive test result, the 'nagging feeling' at the back of her mind had ceased. Several of the professionals interviewed noted that the couple looked more relaxed and confident after the test. The mother confirmed this observation, stating that she was certain that they had made the right decision in deciding to have their daughter tested. The father noted that 'now we know the results, the suspense has gone'. It seemed that both parents were aware of the importance of treating their daughter normally.

The study reporting clinicians' descriptions of cases in which they provided predictive genetic tests to young people was an international survey[32]. The primary aim of this survey was to document descriptive examples of the occurrence of genetic testing in young people for non-medical reasons, in the countries where guidelines exist. Some insights into the outcomes of testing were described by clinicians. From 49 reports of predictive testing in minors, there were no catastrophic events such as suicide, attempted suicide or psychiatric hospitalization reported. There were two adverse events that occurred for mature young people who were tested: anxiety about other family members and initial rebellion. There were several reports of beneficial outcomes of testing, such as the ability to better concentrate on school and the incorporation of knowledge into future plans. An additional important finding was that three sets of parents who had information about the gene-positive status in their immature children experienced adverse events related to whether and when they would inform their children of this knowledge[32].

The only other empirical evidence available about predictive testing in young people concerns tests for familial adenomatous polyposis (FAP) that were performed for medical reasons, as preventative treatment exists. Although the motivation for testing in these cases is therefore different from those we are primarily concerned with, the fact that these tests were performed for medical reasons theoretically should not remove the potential for harm or benefit.

There are four articles that have reported the effects of predictive genetic testing in young people for FAP [33–36]. The first was a case study involving a couple who had both their 2-year-old and 4-year-old daughters tested[33]. The couple was interviewed prior to testing, 2 weeks after testing and again 15 months after testing. It was reported that for this couple, the experience of testing their children was a valuable one. However, no follow-up was reported on if and when the children were informed of the test results and how this impacted on them.

The second study assessed the psychological effects of predictive genetic testing in 41 young people who were tested for FAP, as well as their parents[34]. Children and parents were assessed prior to testing and 3 months after receiving the test result. It was found that mean scores for depression, anxiety and behavioural problems in the young people remained within the normal range after testing. Parents' depression scores also remained within the normal limits after testing.

The third study assessed anxiety and distress levels of 60 young people who were tested for FAP and compared these with the same measures in 148 adults who were also tested[35]. It was found that young people who received a gene-positive result displayed anxiety and distress levels within the normal range, while 43% of adults receiving a gene-positive result displayed clinically significant anxiety levels.

The fourth study assessed symptoms of depression, anxiety and behavioural problems in 48 young people who were tested for FAP and assessed levels of depression in their parents[36]. Assessments were performed prior to testing and 3, 12 and 23–55 months after testing. This study reported no clinically significant changes in the mean psychological test scores of either the children who were tested or their parents. However, there were subclinical increases in depression in the group of children who tested gene-positive and also had a gene-positive sibling. Several individual children who tested gene-negative and had a gene-positive sibling also demonstrated clinical elevations in anxiety.

In brief, the empirical evidence relating to testing young people for FAP indicates that generally young people cope well with information about their genetic status. However, it is not possible to generalize these data to predictive genetic testing in young people for non-medical reasons.

HOLES IN THE EXISTING LITERATURE

There is a severe lack of empirical evidence available about the impacts of offering predictive genetic tests to young people for adult-onset conditions that cannot be prevented or treated. Given that the debate about such testing emerged more than 15 years ago, this is somewhat surprising[37].

FILLING THE HOLES: WHY IS IT SO DIFFICULT?

Calls for more research into the effects of predictive genetic testing in young people have been made numerous times[5,6,21–24,38,39]. Such testing is occurring in young people for non-medical reasons in several countries, despite the recommendations in current guidelines against this[32]. Why then is there such a lack of empirical evidence?

There are four possible reasons: (i) such tests are rarely performed; (ii) such tests are generally 'one-off' cases in a clinical setting and are therefore not assessed in the same way that they would be as part of a research study; (iii) clinicians involved in the provision of tests to young people are placed in a potentially vulnerable position and (iv) there is an absence of a single, leading group to coordinate such research.

Given the recommendations made in existing guidelines, it could be assumed that the current lack of empirical evidence has been brought about by the fact that clinicians are following existing guidelines. That is, the lack of empirical evidence reflects a lack of such test provision. However, recent evidence now indicates that although such testing is rare, tests are being provided in several countries around the world[32]. Even so, this evidence also indicates that it is much more common for clinicians to refuse such testing than to perform it[32]. Given that similar test uptake in adults has been shown to be much lower than that originally predicted, it is likely that demand for testing young people will also remain low[13].

Almost all of the tests that are provided to young people for non-medical reasons are isolated cases performed in the clinical setting. This makes large-scale research efforts increasingly difficult, as the only way that outcomes of such testing can be studied is through an international, multicentre collaboration.

Coordination of research into many individual tests across several international centres requires a level of knowledge and interest in researching these outcomes. In order to involve clinicians in a common goal, they must perceive a need for such research, be inspired enough to collaborate and have the resources to devote to the pursuit. Clinicians may only ever provide a predictive genetic test to a young person once during their career. It is a challenge therefore to reach these individuals, before they even perceive a need to be reached.

Research into the impacts of predictive genetic testing in young people therefore requires the cooperation of clinicians who provide these tests. In other words, clinicians providing tests to young people must be willing to 'offer this decision up' for scrutiny, in the knowledge that they have acted in conflict with current recommendations. This position is a vulnerable one, and even with the strictest measures for ensuring anonymity, this may prevent clinicians from taking part in a research study and drawing attention to such cases when they occur.

Finally, the absence of a single, leading group to coordinate such research provides an immense barrier to research into the outcomes of predictive genetic testing in young people. There must be a leader in such a pursuit so that interest can be aroused, groups can be coordinated, research protocols can be provided and results can be analysed and published. Significant funding needs to be made available to coordinate such a study.

CONCLUSION: A WAY FORWARD

The outcomes of predictive testing in adults for severe genetic conditions have been thoroughly studied. Where testing is performed in the setting of a protocol with pre-test and post-test counselling, there has not been the rate of negative consequences that some had predicted, prior to the availability of such testing[40–46].

There are now strong arguments to suggest that some mature young people will benefit from predictive genetic testing for adult-onset conditions. In fact, there are strong arguments to suggest that not offering testing in some of these cases may cause harm. More importantly, there is evidence that such tests are currently being performed in several countries[32]. It is therefore appropriate to now proceed in a manner similar to that employed when predictive genetic testing for HD first became available to adults. Testing should be offered in selected cases to mature minors who request testing themselves. This should be performed as part of an international, multicentre research protocol. The inclusion of counselling in any testing protocol is vital. However, while counselling is considered important in avoiding adverse effects of testing, how much and what type of counselling is effective is unknown and also warrants research.

In order to move forward in the quest for empirical research concerning the effects of predictive genetic testing in young people, a specific research protocol is required—that is, a means to carry out such research that can be shared by researchers internationally. There are several options for such a protocol, and both qualitative and quantitative methodology should be employed. Qualitative research methods will minimize initial assumptions about the likely impacts of testing young people, leaving room for new conceptions to emerge. It is important that in the first instance, outcomes are explored widely in order to learn of the range of ways in which such testing may affect young people. Potential qualitative research methods include in-depth interviews with young people who have undergone

predictive genetic tests, surveys that incorporate open-ended questions or a standard format for clinicians to write up case studies. Given the need for international research, qualitative interviews could even be conducted over the telephone by one core group of researchers.

Standardized quantitative measures should also be utilized. These may incorporate questionnaires specifically concerning predictive genetic testing, or they may take advantage of the already existing validated psychological instruments, such as measures of depression and anxiety. The qualitative phase should inform the specific outcomes that are measured by quantitative methodologies.

These standardized measures used to assess the impact of testing in young people must include both harmful and beneficial outcome measures. Until now, there has been a trend to measure only the harmful consequences of predictive genetic testing in young people, in order to either support or refute assertions about potential harm in current literature. However, if a realistic and balanced understanding of the ways in which a predictive genetic test may influence the life of a young person is to be achieved, a range of both positive and negative outcomes need to be researched. These measures need to be administered before testing occurs and then again several times after testing.

A leader is now required in the field of predictive genetic testing in young people. This leading group will coordinate research internationally, so that in the rare event that clinicians decide to provide young people with a predictive genetic test for an adult-onset severe condition, they do so in the knowledge that there is a need to research the outcomes, a protocol in place to do this and a group of expert researchers to provide guidance. Only in this way will informed, evidence-based decisions about predictive genetic testing in minors for adult-onset severe conditions be possible.

We do not believe that the provision of predictive genetic tests to mature young people who request them is unethical. Existing guidelines purport a prohibitive stance regarding testing of young people which, initially, was entirely appropriate until more evidence became available. When little evidence is available, it is much easier to ethically justify acts of omission, where no harm can be caused, than acts of commission, where harm may be caused. However, as evidence accumulates concerning testing of adults for non-medical reasons, and evidence begins to emerge concerning testing of young people, such a prohibitive stance becomes more difficult to justify. Ethics is not only about non-maleficence but also about beneficence. Importantly, failing to promote benefits can also cause harm. Arguments exist to contradict existing guidelines, emerging evidence indicates that young people cope well with information about their gene status, and there is now evidence that testing of young people is occurring in several countries. Therefore, we believe that it is unethical not to research the outcomes of tests that are provided and that future arguments and policy should be based upon empirical evidence.

REFERENCES

1. International Huntington Association and the World Federation of Neurology Research Group on Huntington's Chorea. Ethical issues policy statement on Huntington's disease molecular genetics predictive test. J Med Genet 1990: 27: 34–38.

2. International Huntington Association and the World Federation of Neurology Research Group on Huntington's Chorea. Guidelines for the molecular genetics predictive test in Huntington's disease. J Med Genet 1994: 31: 555–559.

3. Clarke A. The genetic testing of children. Working Party of the Clinical Genetics Society (UK). J Med Genet 1994: 31: 785–797.

4. American Society of Human Genetics Board of Directors, American College of Medical Genetics Board of Directors. Points to consider: ethical, legal and psychosocial implications of genetic testing in children and adolescents. Am J Hum Genet 1995: 57: 1233–1241.

5. European Society of Human Genetics. Provision of genetic services in Europe: current practices and issues. 2001 [retrieved from http://www.eshg.org/ESHGgeneticservicesrec.pdf].

6. Human Genetics Society of Australasia. Predictive testing in children and adolescents: Human Genetics Society of Australasia. 2003 [retrieved from http://www.bgsa.com.au/].

7. Fanos JH. Developmental tasks of childhood and adolescence: implications for genetic testing, Am J Med Genet 1997: 71 (1): 22–28.

8. Meiser B, Gleeson MA, Tucker KM. Psychological impact of genetic testing for adult-onset disorders: an update for clinicians. Med J Aust 2000: 172: 126–129.

9. Rice FP, Dolgin KG. The adolescent: development, relationships, and culture, 11th edn. Boston: Allyn and Bacon, 2005.

10. Hoffmann DE, Wulfsberg EA. Testing children for genetic predispositions: is it in their best interest? J Law Med Ethics 1995: 23 (4): 331–344.

11. Holland J. Should parents be permitted to authorize genetic testing for their children? Fam Law Q 1997: 31 (2): 321–353.

12. Bloch M, Hayden MR. Opinion: predictive testing for Huntington disease in childhood: challenges and implications. Am J Hum Genet 1990: 46: 1–4.

13. Clarke A, Flinter F. The genetic testing of children: a clinical perspective. In: The troubled helix: social and psychological implications of the new human genetics (Marteau T, Richards M, eds). Cambridge: Cambridge University Press, 1996: 164–176.

14. Davis DS. Genetic dilemmas and the child's right to an open future. Rutgers Law J 1997: 28: 549–592.

15. Fryer A. Genetic testing of children. Arch Dis Child 1995: 73 (2): 97–99.

16. Fryer A. Inappropriate genetic testing of children. Arch Dis Child 2000: 83 (4): 283–285.

17. Wertz DC, Fanos JH, Reilly PR. Genetic testing for children and adolescents. Who decides? JAMA 1994: 272 (11): 875–881.

18. Ross LF, Moon MR. Ethical issues in genetic testing of children. Arch Pediatr Adolesc Med 2000: 154 (9): 873–879.

19. Lessick M, Faux S. Implications of genetic testing of children and adolescents. Holist Nurs Pract 1998: 12 (3): 38–46.

20. Australian Law Reform Commission, Australian Government. Essentially yours: the protection of human genetic information in Australia. 1996 [retrieved from http://www.austlii.edu.au/au/other/alrc/publications/reports/96/].

21. Geller G. Weighing burdens and benefits rather than competence. BMJ 1999: 318: 1066.

22. Dickenson DL. Can children and young people consent to be tested for adult onset genetic disorders? BMJ 1999: 318: 1063–1066.

23. Elger BS, Harding TW. Testing adolescents for a hereditary breast cancer gene (BRCA1). Arch Pediatr Adolesc Med 2000: 154 (2): 113–119.

24. Clayton EW. Genetic testing in children. J Med Philos 1997: 22 (3): 233–251.

25. Savulescu J. Predictive genetic testing in children. Med J Aust 2001: 175 (7): 379–381.

26. Robertson S, Savulescu J. Is there a case in favour of predictive genetic testing in young children? Bioethics 2001: 15 (1): 22–49.

27. Sharpe NF. Presymptomatic testing for Huntingtons disease: is there a duty to test those under the age of 18 years? Am J Med Genet 1993: 46: 250–253.

28. Michie S. Predictive testing in children: paternalism or empiricism? In: The troubled helix: social and psychological implications of the new human genetics (Marteau T, Richards M, eds). Cambridge: Cambridge University Press, 1996: 177–186.

29. Binedell J, Soldan JR, Scourfield J, Harper PS. Huntington's disease predictive testing: the case for an assessment approach to requests from adolescents. J Med Genet 1996: 33 (11): 912–918.

30. Shepherd M, Hattersley AT, Sparkes AC. Predictive genetic testing in diabetes: a case study of multiple perspectives. Qual Health Res 2000: 10 (2): 242–259.

31. Shepherd M. Ellis I, Ahmad AM et al. Predictive genetic testing in maturity-onset diabetes of the young (MODY). Diabet Med 2001: 18 (5): 417–421.

32. Duncan RE, Savulescu J, Gillam L, Williamson R, Delatycki MB. An international survey of predictive genetic testing in children for adult onset conditions. Genet Med 2005: 7 (6): 390–396.

33. Michie S, McDonald V, Bobrow M, McKeown C, Marteau T. Parents responses to predictive genetic testing in their children—report of a single case study. J Med Genet 1996: 33 (4): 313–318.

34. Codori AM, Petersen GM, Boyd PA, Brandt J, Giardiello FM. Genetic testing for cancer in children. Short-term psychological effect. Arch Pediatr Adolesc Med 1996: 150 (11): 1131–1138.

35. Michie S, Bobrow M, Marteau TM. Predictive genetic testing in children and adults: a study of emotional impact. J Med Genet 2001: 38 (8): 519–526.

36. Codori AM, Zawacki KL, Petersen GM et al. Genetic testing for hereditary colorectal cancer in children: longterm psychological effects. Am J Med Genet 2003: 116A (2): 117–128.

37. Harper PS, Clarke A. Should we test children for 'adult' genetic diseases? Lancet 1990: 335 (8699): 1205–1206.

38. Hanson JW, Thomson EJ. Genetic testing in children: ethical and social points to consider. Pediatr Ann 2000: 29 (5): 285–292.

39. Duncan RE. Predictive genetic testing in young people: when is it appropriate? J Paediatr Child Health 2004: 40: 593–595.

40. Craufurd D, Harris R. Ethics of predictive testing for Huntington's chorea: the need for more information. BMJ 1986: 293: 249–251.

41. Hayden MR. Predictive testing for Huntington disease: are we ready for widespread community implementation? Am J Med Genet 1991: 40: 515–517.

42. Bundey S. Few psychological consequences of presymptomatic testing for Huntington disease. Lancet 1997: 349 (9044): 4.

43. Marteau T, Croyle RT. Psychological responses to genetic testing. BMJ 1998: 316: 693–696.

44. Shaw C, Abrams K, Marteau TM. Psychological impact of predicting individuals' risks of illness: a systematic review. Soc Sci Med 1999: 49: 1571–1598.

45. Horowitz MJ, Field NP, Zanko A, Donnelly EF, Epstein C, Longo F. Psychological impact of news of genetic risk for Huntington disease. Am J Med Genet 2001: 103: 188–192.

46. Almqvist E, Brinkman R, Wiggins S, Hayden M. Psychological consequences and predictors of adverse events in the first 5 years after predictive testing for Huntington's disease. Clin Genet 2003: 64 (4): 300–309.

GENETIC KNOWLEDGE

The Right Not to Know: An Autonomy Based Approach

R. Andorno

The claim for a "right not to know" might sound strange. Over the last decades it has been strongly stressed that the patient has the right to be informed about the risks and benefits of a treatment or intervention and, on this basis, to consent—or not—to them. Having affirmed the patient's "right to know" as a fundamental ethical and legal principle, we are now faced with the apparently opposite demand. This takes place particularly in the field of genetics: as the predictive power of genetic tests increases, more and more people come to know that they are at risk from a serious disease with no real chance of reducing that risk or of obtaining an effective treatment. To illustrate the problem, let us consider the following examples:

- Barbara, a 35 year old woman and mother of two children, has a family history of breast cancer. Urged by her relatives, she decided to undergo the BCRA1/2 testing. If Barbara has the mutation, she has 80% risk of developing breast cancer. Three days later, depressed by the difficult decisions she would have to make in case the mutation was found, she asked the doctor not to inform her about the test results.
- Peter, a 29 year old married man, is invited to participate in a research study about the mutations that may cause Alzheimer's disease (the most common cause of dementia) because a member of his family has been diagnosed with this disorder. DNA samples will be coded, but the unit's director will keep a confidential list of the names of each participant. Although this is a research study and not a clinical genetic test, the laboratory offers Peter the opportunity to be informed about the result of the analysis, in case it indicates the presence of a mutation. This information may be helpful in predicting his risk of developing Alzheimer's disease or of having children with this disorder. However,

Peter does not want to know the results and therefore does not sign the request to be informed.

Far from being purely academic, both scenarios happen in the daily routine of genetic testing and research. In order to understand the refusal of Anne and Peter to have access to their genetic information, one has to consider that the burden of knowledge may become unbearable for them, leading to a severe psychological depression and having a negative impact on their family life and on their social relationships in general. For many people, the discovery that they have a genetic condition that places them at a high risk of suffering certain untreatable diseases could so depress them that the quality, joy, and purpose of their lives would literally evaporate.[1] Now, in such situations, "it may not be justifiable to take away hope from a person by exposing them to knowledge they do not want".[2] Therefore, it seems reasonable to allow these people to choose not to receive that potentially harmful information and to continue their lives in peace.

This paper argues that "autonomy", understood in a wide sense, provides a theoretical basis for a right not to know one's genetic status. The discussion will focus on predictive testing of adults, and not on other types of genetic testing (diagnostic testing, preimplantation genetic diagnosis, prenatal testing, and newborn screening), which raise other specific ethical issues. It is also worth mentioning here that, although the interest in not knowing may be greater in the case of single gene disorders (when a particular mutation is causally sufficient for a disease to occur) than in polygenic disorders, it is not the purpose of this paper to enter into a detailed discussion of the issues raised by each type of genetic testing. Rather, what is intended is to provide a broad philosophical and legal analysis of the debate regarding the right not to know one's genetic status.

After summarising the objections made against the right not to know (1), it will be recalled that various recent ethical and legal instruments explicitly recognise this claim (2). Then, this paper will attempt to respond to those objections (3), and will suggest some conditions that should be fulfilled for the exercise of the right not to know (4).

OBJECTIONS TO THE RIGHT NOT TO KNOW

Several criticisms have been formulated against the formal recognition of a right not to know one's genetic status. The main practical objection is that this right is not feasible because, in order to decide not to receive some information, the person should previously be informed of the possibility of having a particular health risk. Now, this is precisely what the individual wanted to avoid.[3,4]

A most fundamental objection is that, according to a long and well established philosophical tradition, knowledge is always good in itself and therefore a "right to remain in ignorance" appears as a contradiction; that is, as an irrational attitude, which is incompatible with the notion of "right".[5,6] Let us recall that, according to Aristotle "all men by nature desire to know" and this desire is one of the features that distinguishes humans from other animals.[7] The Enlightenment's philosophers considered also human progress in direct connection with an increasing access to knowledge. In the words of Kant, "Sapere aude!" ("Have courage to use your own understanding!") was indeed the motto of the Enlightenment.[8] Adopting this latter perspective, a contemporary philosopher acidly criticises the recent international recognition of the right not to know as "directly opposed to human rights philosophy and to ethics".[9]

The right not to know would be also contrary to the recent evolution of the doctor-patient relationship, which tends to abandon the old paternalism that allowed the doctor not to tell the truth to the patient. Moreover, the claim not to know would be contrary to the doctor's "duty to disclose" risks to patients. Therefore such a claim would represent a return to a paternalistic attitude given that it puts people in a state of ignorance, depriving them of choice.[10] For the same reason, the right not to know is criticised as being opposed to patients' *autonomy*, given that the exercise of autonomy depends on the ability to understand relevant information and only on this basis to consent to treatment.[11]

Another objection refers to the value of solidarity and responsibility for others: the individual who chooses not to know his or her genetic status—thereby putting him or herself in a position of being unable to disclose that vital information to family members—could be said to be acting against solidarity. The same thing could be said about an individual who refuses to participate in a population screening programme because of a claimed right not to know.[12]

ETHICAL AND LEGAL RECOGNITION OF THE RIGHT NOT TO KNOW

In spite of the criticisms levelled against it, the right not to know has been explicitly recognised by various recent ethical and legal instruments relating to biomedical issues. The most impressive examples are probably the European *Convention on Human Rights and Biomedicine* and the UNESCO *Universal Declaration on the Human Genome and Human Rights,* both adopted in 1997. Article 10.2 of the European Convention states: "Everyone is entitled to know any information collected about his or her health. However, the wishes of individuals not to be so informed shall be observed". The Explanatory Report to the Convention justifies the right not to know by saying that "patients may have their own reasons for not wishing to know about certain aspects of their health".[13]

Similarly, the UNESCO Declaration on the Human Genome provides (in Article 5c) that: "The right of every individual to decide whether or not to be informed of the results of genetic examination and the resulting consequences should be respected".

Other important international ethical guidelines also explicitly recognise the right not to know. According to the "Declaration on the Rights of the Patient" adopted by the World Medical Association in 1981 and amended in 1995, "the patient has the right not to be informed on his/her explicit request, unless required for the protection of another person's life" (Article 7d).[14] The WHO "Guidelines on Ethical Issues in Medical Genetics and the Provision of Genetic Services" (1997) states that "the wish of individuals and families not to know genetic information, including test results, should be respected, except in testing of newborn babies or children for treatable conditions" (see table 7 in these Guidelines).

It is important to note that in all the aforementioned international instruments, an explicit choice is necessary for the functioning of the right not to know: the European Convention refers to an individual's "wishes"; the UNESCO Declaration mentions the individual's "decision"; the WMA Declaration points out the necessity of an "explicit request" of the patient; the WHO Guidelines mention the "wishes" of individuals and their families.

At the national level, the right not to know is recognised by the French Law on Patients' Rights, adopted in March 2002: "everyone has the right to be informed on his/her health status.... The person's will to remain ignorant of diagnostic and prognostic information should be respected, except when third parties are exposed to a risk of transmission" (Article 1111–2. Public Health Code). Similar provisions can be found in the Dutch Medical Treatment Act of 1994 (Civil Code, Article 449), the Belgian Patient's Rights Act of 2002 (Article 6), and the Hungarian Health Act of 1997 (Section 14.1).

In the United Kingdom, the former Human Genetics Advisory Commission (HGAC) recommended in its July 1999 report that "an individual's 'right not to know' their genetic constitution should be upheld".[15] More recently, the current Human Genetics Commission (HGC) concluded in its report on the use of personal genetic data that "people have an 'entitlement not to know' genetic information about themselves".[16]

THE RIGHT NOT TO KNOW: AN EXPRESSION OF "AUTONOMY"

The main thesis of this paper is that the claim for not knowing one's genetic status, far from being contrary to *autonomy*—understood as an individual's self determination—may be indeed considered a legitimate expression of this basic bioethical principle. In other words, the choice of not knowing the results of genetic tests does not fall into a paternalistic attitude because the challenge to medical paternalism is precisely based on the idea that people should be free to make their own choices with respect to information. If we understand autonomy in this wider sense, then the decision not to know should be, at least in principle, as fully respected as the decision to know.[17,18]

Thus, the possibility to choose not to know the results of genetic tests may constitute an *enhancement of autonomy*, because the decision to know or not to know is not taken out of the hands of the patient by the doctor. Precisely with this broad understanding of autonomy, the right not to know is widely recognised, for example, by the German legal literature as a part of the "right to informational self determination" ("Recht auf informationelle Selbstbestimmung").[19,20]

In addition to this, let us not forget that there is not an absolute "duty to disclose" information to patients, neither on legal nor on ethical grounds. On the contrary, it is the responsibility of the healthcare professional to assess the amount of information an individual wants and is able to deal with at a particular time.[21]

If this understanding of autonomy is correct, it can be argued that the theoretical foundation of the right not to know lies on the respect for individual *autonomy,* even if the ultimate foundation of this right is the individual's *interest in not being psychologically harmed*. Both grounds are indeed situated at a different level. Autonomy is the immediate source of the right not to know, but what is in the end protected is the psychological integrity of the person. Certainly, patients do not need to prove the harmful effects of genetic information, because each of them is entitled to recognise what information may be psychologically harmful. In any case, the recognition of the potentially negative effect of genetic information allows us to better understand what the right not to know tends to protect and what, ultimately, justifies this claim. We deal here with nothing more than the oldest principle of medical ethics: "first, do not harm" (*Primum non nocere*), which is formulated in modern times in the so called "principle of non-maleficence" that certainly includes patient's psychological integrity.[22]

The criticism that the right not to know is contrary to the requirement of informed consent seems misplaced. The right to remain in ignorance about one's genetic make up should not be mistaken for a *waiver* of informed consent. In the exercise of a waiver, a patient voluntarily relinquishes the right to an informed consent and relieves the physician from the obligation to inform. It seems to be a consensus among ethicists that the acceptance of waivers of consent is a dangerous practice.[23] But in the case of the right not to know the informed consent exists, insofar as the person is perfectly aware that he or she will be submitted to a genetic test that may indicate the risk of developing a disease. In this case, the individual just refuses to be informed of the test outcome. Thus, the ignorance does not concern the *medical practice* itself, for which a valid informed consent has been given, but only its *result*. Consequently, the individual does not receive any particular medical treatment on the basis of ignorance. A different situation may arise in the emerging area of pharmacogenetics. What if a patient arguing the right not to know refuses the test that can determine if a particular drug may have an adverse effect and in spite of that demands the medicine? In such a case the pharmacogenetic test, as far as it has been proved to be effective, should perhaps be considered as a part of the treatment itself. Therefore, it would be a breach of the physician's duty of care to prescribe a drug for a patient who intends to use it without the test having been performed. In other words, in the absence of the test, the requirement of informed consent for the treatment would not be met. This conclusion is especially valid because information about drug response could hardly be considered contrary to the patient's interests.

What about the argument that the right not to know is intrinsically not feasible because its exercise always requires a previous knowledge? Certainly, for the exercise of this right the person should have, at least, a general and abstract knowledge of the risk. We know that we are all at risk of developing genetic diseases, particularly when we have a family history of a particular genetic condition. But some risks may be so remote in our perception as to seem virtually inconceivable. In contrast, a genetic testing, which may determine individuals likely to suffer from a serious disorder or even the certainty that the disease will emerge (in the case of a single gene disorder), makes those vague concerns look much more real. This is precisely why an individual's refusal to know the results of genetic tests might make sense.

One has to recognise however that the refusal to be informed about one's genetic status may in some cases be problematic, because genetic information is not only an individual, but also a family affair. Tests results may alert family members about a serious risk, giving them the opportunity of changing their life plans, or eventually of preventing or treating a disease. The familial nature of genetic information has even led some ethicists to argue that the concept of "genetic privacy" is a contradiction in terms.[24] In any case, the question is: how can the right not to know be harmonised with the potential interest of a patient's relative in knowing?

As it has already been pointed out, some legal and ethical regulations try to give an answer to this difficult dilemma: the right not to know (like most rights) is *not absolute* because its exercise is conditioned by the fact that *there is no risk of serious harm to other persons*.[25–27] That means that the disclosure to family members, if ever, could be accepted as an exceptional measure, as long as two conditions are fulfilled: firstly, the disclosure is necessary for avoiding a serious harm to them; secondly, some reasonable form of cure or therapy is available. However, we should not forget that we are dealing with unsolicited genetic information. We are indeed not sure that relatives really want to receive such information. This is why we should be extremely prudent before any unsolicited approach is made.

Those "other persons" that the exercise of the right not to know should not harm could be society in general. Public health interests may in particular circumstances justify limitations on the right to ignore one's genetic make up as they may justify limitations to confidentiality, for instance, in the case of infectious diseases.[28] Surely, the circumstances in which the right not to know and confidentiality can be breached in the interest of public health should be well defined by law. Particularly important in this context are population genetic screening programmes, which can contribute to the prevention of genetic diseases. For example, potential parents could be alerted to the risks they may take if they marry and have children with a person who also carries the genetic trait. However, such programmes face significant challenges in terms of informed consent, privacy, and risks of stigmatisation of ethnic groups. In addition, there is the fear that public screening programmes could encourage eugenic practices, like systematic abortion of affected fetuses.[29] In summary, we have to make a substantial effort in this area to ensure an adequate balance between the respect for individuals' rights and the benefits of using genetic information for the common good of society.

THE WISH OF NOT KNOWING SHOULD BE EXPLICIT

Graeme Laurie has argued that, in addition to "autonomy", the right not to know might be based on a particular form of *spatial privacy*, the so called "psychological spatial privacy", which encompasses separateness of the individual's psyche. This aspect of spatial privacy tends to safeguard *one's own sense of the self* and to provide a larger protection of the interest in not knowing than simple *choice*, especially in those cases in which no explicit choice has been made.[30–32]

Laurie's concern is perfectly understandable: it is true that even if no wish has been expressed, the interest in not knowing can also be compromised by unsolicited revelations of genetic information. This circumstance leads the author to advocate a "prima facie" respect for the interest in not knowing, even in absence of an explicit choice.[33] This means, in practice, an *inversion of the burden of proof*: it is not the person interested in not knowing who should express his or her wish but, on the contrary, it is the individual who intends to disclose the information who, before any disclosure, should be sure that some special conditions are fulfilled (for example, the availability of a cure, the severity of the condition, the nature of the testing, and the question of how the individual might react if exposed to unwarranted information).[34,35] Therefore, this position "places the onus of justifying disclosure firmly on the shoulders of those who would do so".[36]

The appeal to privacy in order to call for an attitude of prudence in the disclosure of genetic information is fully justified, especially when there are doubts about the patient's will. Moreover, the "privacy approach" provides an insightful explanation of what is at stake in this issue. It is true that when there is no previously expressed wish in respect of the information, the potential interference is primarily with the spatial privacy interests—or let's say, with the psychological integrity—of the individuals in question, rather than with their autonomy per se.[37]

However, what is difficult to accept in Laurie's view is the assumption that those individuals who have not made any explicit choice of not knowing their genetic status (which means almost everybody) want to ignore it. In the case of competent patients, this assumption can hardly be harmonised with their "right to know", as well as with the "duty to inform" that, in principle, the health-care professional has towards them. Both competing rights—to know and not to know—cannot be the rule. Surely, to determine which right should prevail will depend on the circumstances of each case, but law and ethics need *rules* to operate in a coherent manner; and the rule in this field is that patients have a right to know their health status. This is why it seems that the right not to know may only be accepted as an *exception,* at least with regard to competent persons. The situation is probably different in the testing of minors, in which case genetic tests for adult onset genetic disorders should perhaps be simply banned, particularly when no cure is possible.[38]

In brief, therefore, the argument of this paper is that the right not to know cannot be *presumed,* but should be "activated" by the explicit will of the person.[39] Let us recall that, for those cases in which the interest in not knowing seems clear, but no explicit choice has been made, we already have the concept of "therapeutic privilege", which allows physicians to withhold information if, based on sound medical judgement, they believe that divulging the information would be harmful to a depressed or unstable patient, especially when there is currently no effective treatment.[40,41] But this is different to recognising a "right" not to know, because the violation of a "right" (in this case, by disclosure of the unsolicited information) means that the professional could eventually incur civil liability. Now, such a serious consequence in cases in which patients had not expressed their interest in not knowing seems a step too far.

Thus, the exercise of an autonomous choice seems necessary for the functioning of the right not to know, because it is impossible to determine a priori the wish of the patient. Precisely one of the particularities of this right consists in the fact that it almost entirely depends on the subjective perceptions of the individual, who is, in fact, the best interpreter of his or her best interest. It should be noted that the problem of genetic tests is raised not so much by the information itself (which is neutral) but by the *effect* that that information may have on the person who has been tested. That effect varies greatly from individual to individual. This is why the previous informed consent should be as comprehensive as possible, in order to know in advance the patient's interests and possible fears.

One could argue that this autonomy based approach is unrealistic, because it ignores the fact that people are not always free to decide according to their real interests.[42] For instance, various forms of coercion, in a more or less subtle way, may lead individuals to choose to know their genetic make up, when in fact they would prefer to ignore it. The most obvious example is the requirement of genetic tests as a condition of employment or insurance. Nevertheless, the factual possibility of coercion in certain circumstances is not per se a sufficient reason to deny people the right to self determination regarding genetic information. It is true that coercion may happen in the field of genetic testing, but it may happen in all areas of clinical and research activities as well. If we consider that the likelihood of coercion is very high in certain circumstances, what we can do (as many ethical guidelines suggest) is simply to prohibit the requirement of genetic tests by insurance companies or employers and the requirement to disclose results of any previously undertaken genetic tests. Or at least we can put additional safeguards in place to ensure that people are free from coercion and are not exposed to unjustified discrimination. However, the risk of coercion should not lead us to deny that competent people, with appropriate genetic counselling, are in principle able to decide whether they want to know their genetic status or not.

Do third parties like patients' relatives have a right not to know? In this case one has to recognise that such a right is even difficult to conceive. Firstly, for a practical reason: how can patients' relatives exercise this right, if they probably even ignore that a family member has been tested?[43] Moreover, against *whom* would they have this right? Against the doctor who, having tried to help them, disclosed that information? Against the family member who was tested and had revealed, for example at a family gathering, that he or she is at risk of a genetic illness? Would such a general "right not to know" not be a serious obstacle to confidence within the family? In addition to this, how can doctors assume that patients' relatives do not have interest in knowing genetic information, which may be extremely important to them? Certainly, doctors should in principle avoid disclosing information about patients to individuals with whom they do not have any professional relationship. Healthcare professionals have a duty of confidentiality towards their patients. But if in a particular case a doctor considers in good faith that he or she is morally obliged to disclose that information to patients' relatives—for example, because a reasonable treatment or preventive measure is available—it would be an exaggeration to make him or her legally responsible on the basis of a supposed "right not to know" of those individuals. On the other hand, if there is no treatment or preventive measure for the disease, it is hard to imagine why healthcare professionals would be so interested in disclosing genetic information to patients' relatives. If such a thing could come to happen, the doctor would be violating without justification his or her professional duties. However, we do not need to postulate that third parties have a "right not to know" their genetic make up, which would be an excessively strong argument, in order to protect them from unjustified invasions of their privacy.

One could theoretically imagine a solution to this complex dilemma with the creation of a "public register"—similar to those that exist for organ donation—where people can express in advance their wish to know or not know their genetic status. Of course, those who do not register a refusal would not be automatically presumed to be interested in knowing their genetic make up. The only purpose of such a register would be to give people a means to specify in advance their preferences concerning genetic information and, at the same time, to facilitate the task of doctors, who could consult the register before making any unsolicited disclosures. Nevertheless, for the moment we are still very far from a general solution of this kind. Therefore, it seems that at present the right not to know can only operate within the doctor-patient relationship and as the result of an explicit choice made in that context. In summary, "autonomy"—that is, explicit will—is the best guarantee that we do not make a mistake in deciding for others whether they have an interest in knowing their genetic status or not.

CONCLUSION

The increasing access to genetic information leads law makers to recognise new rights in order to protect confidentiality and privacy of people. The "right not to know"

is one of them. This claim is based on individuals' autonomy and on their interest in not being psychologically harmed by the results of genetic tests. Such a right, as an exception to both the patient's "right to know" and the doctor's "duty to inform", needs to be "activated" by the explicit will of the patient. In addition, this right has two characteristics: firstly, it can only operate in the context of the doctor-patient relationship; secondly, it is a relative right, in the sense that it may be restricted when disclosure to the individual is necessary in order to avoid serious harm to third parties, especially family members, which means that some form of prevention or treatment is available.

REFERENCES

1. Wachbroit R. Disowning knowledge: issues in genetic testing. *Philosophy and Public Policy Quarterly* 1996;3/4. http://www.puaf.umd.edu/IPPP/rw.htm (accessed 16 April 2004).

2. Chadwick R. The philosophy of the right to know and the right not to know. In Chadwick R, Levitt M, Shickle D, eds. *The right to know and the right not to know.* Aldershot: Ashgate, 1997:18.

3. Wertz DC, Fletcher JC. Privacy and disclosure in medical genetics examined in an ethics of care. *Bioethics* 1991;5:212–32.

4. Romeo-Casabona CM. Human rights issues in research on medical genetics. In: *Ethics and Human Genetics,* Strasbourg: Council of Europe Editions, 1994:167–74.

5. Ost D. The 'right' not to know. *The Journal of Medicine and Philosophy* 1984;3:301–12.

6. Harris J, Keywood K. Ignorance, information and autonomy. *Theoretical Medicine and Bioethics* 2001;22:415–36.

7. Aristotle. *Metaphysics.* Oxford: Clarendon Press, 1958:1.

8. Kant I. *What is Enlightenment?* In Beck LW, ed. *Kant on History.* Indianapolis: Bobbs-Merrill Press, 1963:3.

9. Hottois G. A philosophical and critical analysis of the European Convention of Bioethics. *Journal of Medicine and Philosophy* 2000;2:133–46.

10. Canellopoulou Bottis M. Comment on a view favouring ignorance of genetic information: confidentiality, autonomy, beneficence and the right not to know. *European Journal of Health Law* 2000;2:185–91.

11. See reference 6:418–19.

12. See reference 2:20.

13. Council of Europe. *Explanatory Report to the Convention on Human Rights and Biomedicine.* Strasbourg: Council of Europe, 1997: paragraph 67. http://www.coe.int/bioethics (accessed 16 April 2004).

14. World Medical Association. *Declaration of the Rights of the Patient* ("Lisbon Declaration"), 1981 (amended 1995). http://www.wma.net/e/policy.html (accessed 16 April 2004).

15. UK Human Genetics Advisory Commission. *The implications of genetic testing for employment,* July 1999, point 3.19. http://www.dah.gov.uk/hgac/ (accessed 16 April 2004).

16. UK Human Genetics Commission. *Inside information—balancing interests in the use of personal genetic data.* May 2002:14. http://www.hgc.gov.uk/business_publications.htm (accessed 16 April 2004).

17. See reference 1.

18. Husted J. Autonomy and a right not to know. In Chadwick R, Levitt M, Shickle D, eds. *The right to know and the right not to know.* Aldershol: Ashgate, 1997:55–68.

19. Wiese G. Gibt es ein Recht auf Nichtwissen? [Is there a right not to know?]. In Jayme E, *et al*, eds. *Festschrift für Hubert Niederländer.* Heidelberg: Carl Winter/Universitätsverlag, 1991:475–88.

20. Taupitz J. Das Recht auf Nichtwissen [The right not to know]. In Hanau P. Lorenz E, Matthes H, eds. *Festschrift für Günther Wiese,* Neuwied, Luchterhand Verlag, 1998: 583–602.

21. British Medical Association. *Human genetics. Choice and responsibility.* Oxford: Oxford University Press, 1998:86–88.

22. Beauchamp TL, Childress JF. *Principles of biomedical ethics,* 5th edn. New York: Oxford University Press, 2001:117.

23. See reference 22:93.

24. Sommerville A, English V. Genetic privacy: orthodoxy or oxymoron? *J Med Ethics* 1999;25:144–50.

25. See reference 13, paragraph 70.

26. See reference 14, article 7d.

27. See reference 16:48.

28. Council of Europe. *Convention on Human Rights and Biomedicine.* Article 26.

29. Hoedemaekers R, ten Have H. Geneticization: The Cyprus Paradigm. *Journal of Medicine and Philosophy* 1998; 23:274–87.

30. Laurie G. In defence of ignorance: genetic information and the right not to know. *European Journal of Health Law* 1999;6:119–32.

31. Laurie G. Protecting and promoting privacy in an uncertain world: further defences of ignorance and the right not to know. *European Journal of Health Law* 2000;7:185–91.

32. Laurie G. Challenging medical-legal norms. The role of autonomy, confidentiality, and privacy in protecting individual and familial group rights in genetic information. *The Journal of Legal Medicine* 2001;22:1–54.

33. See reference 30:127.

34. See reference 30:128–9.

35. Laurie G, *et al. Genetic databases. Assessing the benefits and the impact on human & patient rights.* Report for Consultation to the WHO. Geneva, WHO, May 2001, Recommendation 16.

36. Laurie G. *Genetic privacy. A challenge to medico-legal norms.* Cambridge: Cambridge University Press, 2002:259.

37. See reference 36:210.

38. McLean S. The genetic testing of children: some legal and ethical concerns. In Clarke A, ed. *The genetic testing of children.* Oxford: Bios, 1998:17–26.

39. See reference 20:592.

40. Council of Europe. *Convention on Human Rights and Biomedicine.* Article 10.3.

41. See reference 22:84

42. See reference 36:209.

43. See reference 10:179.

Genetic Links, Family Ties, and Social Bonds: Rights and Responsibilities in the Face of Genetic Knowledge

Rosamond Rhodes

I. INTRODUCTION

An old adage tells us that blood is thicker than water. The message of the saying is that blood ties carry moral weight. A thoughtful person might wonder how to act on that advice. It had been assumed that hereditary similarities gave those of the same blood common characteristics and, hence, special responsibilities to each other. So, before modern genetics we might have considered which of our familial relations count as blood. How thick are our responsibilities to blood? And, how thin are our responsibilities to water?

Knowledge of genetics, however, complicates the message that we might previously have drawn from the saying. Since learning that all living organisms have 80% of their DNA in common, that apes differ from humans in only 2% of their DNA, and that humans differ from one another by less than .1% of their DNA, the concept of blood ties becomes much more complicated. We still need to learn which social bonds involve thick

responsibilities and which ties demand less of us. As we get a clearer picture of our genetic similarities and differences, we also need to find out more about the bearing of our genetic links on our ethical obligations.

The particular genetic knowledge questions that I shall address turn attention to another set of issues. Instead of looking at the responsibilities professionals or institutions have to individuals, I will take up the question of what responsibilities individuals have to one another. In other words, I want to examine a different set of questions about genetic knowledge. I am interested in whether individuals have a moral right to pursue their own goals without contributing to society's knowledge of population genetics, without adding to their family's genetic history, and without discovering genetic information about themselves and their offspring. These questions are not dramatically distinct from other personal decisions. The point of this discussion is rather to demonstrate the similarity that may be obscured by dazzling new technology and to point a way

Abridged from Rhodes, Rosamond. "Genetic Links, Family Ties, and Social Bonds: Rights and Responsibilities in the Face of Genetic Knowledge," *Journal of Medicine and Philosophy* 23: 1 (1998), 10–30. Copyright © 1998. Reprinted by permission of Oxford University Press.

toward structuring our thinking about these novel circumstances in terms of traditional moral frameworks.

To approach these questions of personal decision making in the face of new genetic technology we will have to examine the presumed right to genetic ignorance and its relation to rights of privacy. We will also need an account of why the various social bonds have different strengths and why more or less demanding obligations attach to them. Certainly an analysis of these issues will have implications for the mainstream discussion of professional and institutional responsibilities with respect to genetic knowledge. I leave those extrapolations for other discussions. I offer four cases to help us focus on the issues I have identified, the cases of Tom, Dick, Harry, and Harriette.

II. CLINICAL CASES

A. Case I - Tom

Human DNA contains 6 billion base pairs. An average gene contains about 2,000 base pairs. Our approximately 100,000 genes contain about 200,000,000 basepairs of DNA. DNA is a double helix molecule of strands of just four bases, adenosine, thymine, guanine, and cytosine, referred to by their abbreviations ATCG. The genetic code is carried by triplets of these nucleotides, sequences of three bases. Only a small portion of the genetic sequences of DNA is related to our particular recognizable characteristics.

By studying families with a history of Huntington disease, however, geneticists have learned that 40 or more CAG repeats identify a person who will develop the disease. Even though the typical small number of repeats is not associated with any identifiable trait, or phenotype, an expanded number of repeats is associated with this adult onset degenerative nervous system disorder. When a parent has the disease there is a 50% chance of a child inheriting it. And when the genetic marker is inherited, if the person does not die early from some other cause, Huntington will eventually develop.

Population studies of Huntington disease have not been undertaken. Without studying the general population no one knows whether there are individuals who have long CAG repeats and no familial history of the disease. No one knows whether long CAG repeats without a family history are indications of the disease. As the technology for genetic blueprints approaches our grasp, it becomes easy to imagine that population information about the phenotypic implications of long CAG repeats could be significant to people who might have them.

Tom's family has no history of Huntington disease. If researchers were to undertake a population study to learn more about the genetics of Huntington disease should Tom volunteer to be a research subject and allow his cheek to be swabbed for collection of genetic material? Does he owe this debt to his fellows? Tom is reluctant to learn anything about himself that might give him cause to worry. Could his reluctance justify refusing to participate?

B. Case 2 - Dick

Dick has been diagnosed with Marfan syndrome, an inherited disorder of the connective tissue. People with this syndrome are very tall and typically have heart and eye defects. Dick's cousin, Martha, is tall but it is not clear whether she too has Marfan syndrome. Martha understands that Marfan syndrome is a dominant genetic disorder, so that she would have a 50% chance of having a child with this disorder if she has the mutation causing Marfan syndrome.

She and her husband have consulted a genetic counselor because they want to have children but would want to avoid having children with this problem. The counselor explains that while the gene for Marfan syndrome has been fully mapped and cloned, each family has its own specific familial mutation. Searching for the specific mutation in the DNA of Martha's family will involve a lengthy and expensive process. A better alternative would be a linkage study to discover the pattern of this family's co-inheritence of variations in neighboring genes with the Marfan mutation. Genes that are close to one another on a chromosome tend to be inherited together. By collecting genetic samples from close relatives and comparing the patterns of linked genes, geneticists are able to identify a familial pattern and associate it with the genetic defect. Future fetuses can then be screened for the identified genetic pattern.

Martha's mother has average stature and so does her only sister. But her father, who died in a car accident, and his brother were both tall. Martha's uncle Henry has agreed to provide a blood sample for the linkage study. Martha has also asked Dick, Uncle Henry's only child, to participate in the linkage study. Does Dick have a moral responsibility to allow himself to be tested?

C. Case 3 - Harry

After three years of deterioration and suffering, Harry's father died of Huntington disease at age 49. When his father was diagnosed all of the immediate family were invited to participate in a genetic counselling session.

Harry, who was 22 years old at the time, learned that this degenerative disease of the basal ganglia is physically and mentally disabling and that he has a one in two chance of developing it. Because the number of CAG repeats tends to increase in the offspring of affected males, and because more CAG repeats indicates earlier onset of the disease, if he has inherited the genotype Harry is likely to be afflicted earlier than his father was. Although Harry's brother was tested for the genetic marker and found to be unaffected, Harry has refused the test saying that he does not want to know.

Harry and Sally have fallen in love. They want to marry and have a family. Does Harry have a moral right not to know whether he has a long CAG repeat?

D. Case 4 - Harriette

Harriette's sister had a child who died of Tay-Sachs disease after a brief and agonizing life. Harriette's family as well as her husband's are part of a community that is known to have a significant number of Tay-Sachs disease carriers. Harriette wants to have children and she knows that Tay-Sachs is a recessive inherited disease. She knows that she and her husband could be tested and learn whether their offspring might have the disease. She and her husband have discussed the situation and decided not to be tested. Harriette says that she does not want the information to affect her choice. She has decided to take whatever she gets.

Does Harriette have the moral right to act in ignorance? Is it ethically permissible for her to take this chance for her child? If she should have one affected child, would it be her moral right to have another?

III. A RIGHT TO GENETIC IGNORANCE

When we hear the phrase, "a right not to know," it does not sound like something that we should obviously challenge. Hearing it applied in the medical context might even sound acceptable. Imagine the patient saying to his doctor, "If you find something terrible, do what you have to but I do not want to know." It is not hard to imagine the doctor justifying going along with the patient's request by maintaining that "the patient has a right not to know." However, when we begin to examine the supposed right not to know we cannot fail to notice a stark contrast to our ordinary moral thinking. This discrepancy invites us to challenge the ethical status of the right not to know.

A television commercial shows a blindfolded man test driving a car so that he can fairly assess the smoothness of its ride. That man behind the wheel might later decide that he prefers driving blindfolded. When he does not see what is in front of him he does not have to take those obstacles into account: his decision-making is simplified and he is freed from a host of troubling concerns. Even though we might sympathize with his motives, we would, nevertheless, find the prospect of his driving blindfolded totally ridiculous and morally unacceptable to such an extreme as to be not worth considering. Obviously, driving a car without being able to see where you are going puts the property and lives of others in danger. No one has the right to do that. In other words, anyone who gets behind the wheel of a car is obliged to pay careful attention to his surroundings. If he is obliged to know his situation when he is driving, he has no right to choose to be in ignorance when he drives.

This is the line of reasoning that supports negligence law. Even when people can honestly assert that they were ignorant of the hazards posed by their action or some possibly dangerous circumstance involving their property, they are still held liable for consequent harms. They are liable because they have an obligation to know: they have no right not to know.

The eighteenth-century philosopher, Immanuel Kant, is the most acknowledged source of our appreciation of the ethical significance of respect for autonomy. It seems fitting and prudent, therefore, to turn to his writings for support in what may appear, at first glance, as an attack on autonomy. We can appreciate the general form of the argument against a right not to be informed by looking at a short essay by Kant. The essay I have in mind is 'On a supposed right to tell lies from benevolent motives,' published in 1797. There Kant recounts the situation of someone planning a murder asking you if your friend, his intended victim, is in your house when you had previously observed your friend entering. According to my reading of this controversial essay, Kant argues that benevolence cannot justify lying to the murderer because you cannot know whether your lie will accomplish good or actually harm the intended victim who might have already left the house unobserved. On the other hand, you will know with certainty that your lying will undermine our general reliance on veracity and that would do "wrong to men in general". In other words, those who believe that benevolence justifies this lie are mistaken because, according to Kant's argument, concern for benevolence justifies not lying. Regardless of whether you are willing to accept Kant's conclusion in his case, the form of the argument, that benevolence cannot justify lying because benevolence is the ground for not lying, is compelling. As I see it, the argument is actually more persuasive when applied to the supposed right to genetic ignorance.

Those who have argued for a right not to know genetic information about themselves have grounded their argument on the right to have one's autonomous choices respected. Following Kant's model, I want to argue that respect for autonomy actually leads to the opposite conclusion, the obligation to pursue genetic knowledge.

Through the active history of the American bioethics movement, the principle of respect for autonomy has been a cornerstone for bioethics argument. It has supported the consensus for a strong commitment to confidentiality, sustained arguments for informed consent in research, and upheld arguments for truth-telling and patient self-determination, particularly in decisions about withholding and withdrawing treatment. Respect for autonomy entails regarding others as capable of making choices for themselves that reflect their own values and commitments. It is, in part, because we recognize that people could have good reasons for not wanting to share personal medical information with everyone that we have to respect patient confidentiality. It is because we recognize that a host of personal commitments and a personal attitude toward risk can impact on judgments about whether to participate in a research protocol that we require informed consent in human experimentation. It is because people can have good reasons for making different choices about their medical treatments that patients need to have information about their medical condition and the alternative treatments . Clearly, having information has been recognized as essential for making choices. Any piece of information might change a person's choice and lead her to pursue a different course than she might have without the information or with different information. So, because it allows others to make choices according to their own lights, health care providers are ethically obligated to make available the information that may be relevant to the patient. The reason for providing information in the typical medical context is that the patient is presumed to be an autonomous agent. Without the relevant information, the patient cannot make autonomous choices. From my point of view as an individual autonomous agent (as opposed to the point of view of some professional inside or policy-maker outside of the medical context who might be inclined to limit my autonomy) when I choose to remain ignorant of relevant information, I am choosing to leave whatever happens to chance. I am following a path without autonomy. Now, if autonomy is the ground for my right to determine my own course, it cannot also be the ground for not determining my own course. If autonomy justifies my right to knowledge, it cannot also justify my refusing to be informed. I may not be aware of the moral implications of ceding autonomy by insisting on genetic ignorance, but the ramifications are there, nevertheless.

From a Kantian perspective, autonomy is the essence of what morality requires of me. The core content of my duty is self-determination. To say this in another way, I need to appreciate that my ethical obligation is to rule myself, that is, to be a just ruler over my own actions. As sovereign over myself I am obligated to make thoughtful and informed decisions without being swayed by irrational emotions, including my fear of knowing significant genetic facts about myself. When I recognize that I am ethically required to be autonomous, I must also see that, since autonomous action requires being informed of what a reasonable person would want to know under the circumstance, I am ethically required to be informed. So, if I have an obligation to learn what I can, when genetic information is likely to make a significant difference in my decisions and when the relevant information is obtainable with reasonable effort, I have no right to remain ignorant. From the recognition of my own autonomy, I have a duty to be informed. I have no right to remain ignorant.

Another example from Kant can be explicated to make the point about genetic ignorance in a different way. In this example from the *Foundations of the Metaphysics of Morals* Kant proves that it is immoral to make a promise with the intention of breaking it. According to his case someone who is in need of money procures a loan by promising to repay it, while knowing that he will not be able to return the money. Again Kant uses a consistency proof to show that making a promise without intending to keep it is immoral. The borrower relies upon the institution of promising to secure his loan, but unless people fulfilled their promises no one would trust another to meet a pledge of future performance.

Taking a broad view of promising, any commitment that we undertake with respect to another is some sort of promise that carries a moral responsibility to do one's part. My commitment to look after my sister's children while she goes off on a business trip certainly counts as a promise, but so does getting behind the wheel to drive a car, and developing a friendship. Drawing on this inclusive view of promises, we can see that I would have been immoral to have said that I would babysit for my niece and nephew if I had no intention of ever spending time with them. I would have unethically treated others who use the roads if I had started off in my car with no intention of keeping my eyes wide open and focused on what was in front of me. I would have failed in my obligations to my friend if I had accepted the benefits of her friendship without ever being willing to do my part in return. From this Kantian perspective we recognize that human interactions are crammed with undertakings that implicitly require performance by those who take on the responsibilities that define those undertakings.

Sometimes being able to satisfy a responsibility turns on some bit of knowledge that I could easily know. I would be morally culpable to undertake the obligation without first attempting to ascertain whether I had a reasonable chance of meeting that obligation. If I borrowed some cash and gave you a check in return without looking up my balance at the back of the same checkbook, I should be counted as blameworthy for my failure to repay my debt by the promised date. It is a small step to recognize that the same reasoning could apply to genetic knowledge. When I believe that meeting an obligation to another turns on genetic knowledge that is easy to obtain, I should not undertake the obligation until I have first learned that I am likely to be able to do what I have committed myself to doing.

I need to support the institution of promise keeping because I also rely upon others to keep their commitments to me. I should also keep my promises because I have given others a reason to rely on me. Unless I try to obtain pivotal information before undertaking commitments, I am likely to find myself having made promises that I cannot keep. Had it not been for my reluctance to be informed, I would not have been in the situation of violating the moral command against breaking promises.

IV. TOM, DICK, HARRY, AND HARRIETTE

In the same way, when we face a choice between alternative actions and when the choice turns on genetic knowledge, preserving our autonomy requires that we pursue the information. And, when we have to decide whether to assume an obligation and when the decision even in part turns on genetic knowledge, we have a moral duty to pursue that information. These strong conclusions have implications for Tom, Dick, Harry, and Harriette. None of them can claim a right to genetic ignorance. Because there is no right to genetic ignorance Tom cannot use it as a ground for refusing to participate in the population study and Dick cannot use it as a reason for not helping his cousin Martha. And as for Harry and Harriette, because they are on the brink of making important decisions that involve commitments to others, there is at least a *prima facie* reason for maintaining that they are ethically obligated to learn crucial genetic facts about themselves.

Harry is considering marriage and fatherhood but he knows that he has a 50% chance of developing Huntington disease. Because marriage and fatherhood are essentially commitments to others, he has the duty to learn whether he is likely to be able to meet these responsibilities to his future wife and children. If he worried that he might develop the disease and seriously tried to take his duties into account while still refusing genetic tests, he would be likely to make different decisions than he would have made in the face of knowledge. For example, knowing that he was not going to develop Huntington disease might free him to take a job in Australia that would allow him better opportunities for career advancement and the development of his talents. Knowing that he was going to develop the disease might lead him to accept a less promising job that would allow him to remain geographically close to Sally's family. Taking a farsighted view of his situation allows us to imagine that his trying to second guess what he ought to do while considering two dramatically different scenarios could lead him to do what he might otherwise have seen as wrong. His informed assessment could lead him to a different conclusion.

Harriette is considering motherhood. She knows that she may have a chance as high as one in four of having a child with Tay-Sachs disease. She and her husband have agreed to forego testing and she expresses a willingness to undertake responsibility for any children they should have. If neither she nor her husband carry the trait, or even if only one of them carries the trait, they are worrying for nothing and making choices in light of that concern that may be inappropriate for their actual situation. On the other hand, if they were to have the genetic testing and learn that they were both carriers they could consider their reproductive choices in that light.

The analysis of the presumed right to genetic ignorance has taken us some way in discerning the rights and responsibilities of genetic knowledge. Exploring the thickness of social ties may take us some steps farther in understanding more about what the individuals in our cases owe to others.

V. SOCIAL BONDS

Looking at DNA does allow us dramatically to see how much alike we all are and which individuals are most similar. If genetic similarity were the source of our moral relationships, genetic maps could identify our most similar sibling, or even some distant DNA matching stranger, as the one to whom we owed the most. But if anyone maintained that we had different degrees of responsibilities to different siblings it is not likely that they would attribute that distinction to our degrees of genetic matching. More likely reasons would be related to the intimacy and dependency of our previous relationship, or the strength of our feelings, or the history of our interactions, or something about our relative wherewithal and neediness. These reasons, however, point to social relations, not blood or genes, as relevant features for moral responsibility. Furthermore, the genetically closest matching stranger has less of a moral claim on us than many others because of the absence of a previous relationship and the lack of history of interacting. Blood alone does not tell the story of our moral responsibility to one another. The bonds that have moral weight and give us thick responsibilities to one another typically include a social component.

Although many philosophers have taken a simple view of human relationships and morality and argued that we owe the same to everyone, the cases we are considering suggest a need for a richer account of moral responsibility. For some insight into the complexities of social bonds, allow me to go back farther into the history of ethics. Aristotle discusses justice and friendship as an apportionment of rights, responsibilities, and things between individuals.

Taken together these Aristotelian conclusions can provide some additional guidance for resolving our cases. First, they express the moral stance that we owe something to everyone. Second, they outline a collection of distinct considerations that we need to accord some weight and take into account in the assessment of our duties to others.

1. Family relationships count.
2. Social relationships count.
3. The history of a relationship counts.
4. The particulars of the relationship and situation count.

With this much guidance in hand, let us return to the cases and see if we can make more headway in identifying the ethical duties of Tom, Dick, Harry, and Harriette. These considerations should be seen as *prima facie* duties that must be taken into account in moral deliberation. They could, however, be out-weighed by other considerations that may be relevant to the particular case.

VI. CASE DISCUSSION

Because we have duties to our fellows, *Tom* has a responsibility to participate in the population study. What is being asked of him requires little effort, minuscule discomfort, and no physical risk. Yet, the information to be gained by the study could have a significant impact on the well-being and decisions of others. Because the information can be a significant good to them and because we are morally required to render service to our brethren, Tom has a duty to participate in the study.

Similarly, *Dick* is obligated to provide a blood sample for a family linkage study. His familial relationship with Martha is closer than his bond with a stranger, so it would be more terrible to ignore her need than it would be to ignore a stranger's. Compassionate concern for Martha who wants to have a child who is unaffected by Marfan syndrome should incline him to cooperate. If Dick had been particularly close lifelong friends with his cousin, or if Martha had been his sister, he might have even stronger moral reasons for trying to be of service. On the other hand, if the cousins had minimal contact in their childhood, and if they had not even spoken to one another in the past decade, his responsibility might be somewhat diminished.

Dick's case is particularly interesting because it is only his blood ties to Martha that give him an obligation to participate in the linkage study. No one else can do it for her and no one else could take his place. Dick's case makes the point that we have some of our responsibilities because of our unique ability to help, others only because of our biological ties. So morality is not entirely constructed out of socially created links. Adoption would be another relevant example. A birth mother can relinquish all of her social rights and duties to her child and the adopting parents can take them all on. But the birth mother cannot transfer her biological responsibilities. Perhaps this insight calls for collecting a blood sample from the birth mother when the child is given up for adoption so that it could provide the genetic information that her child might need from her later in life.

We have already discussed some of the issues relating to *Harry's* obligation to pursue genetic knowledge. In addition, his "fuller friendship" with Sally gives her a special claim on him. Their social relationship gives them mutual responsibilities to treat one another as partners. To use the language of feminist philosopher, Patricia Mann, they have a mutual responsibility to recognize and support one another's "social agency," which, according to Mann, is associated with "motivation, responsibility, and expectation of recognition or reward". For Harry this involves acknowledging Sally's motivation with respect to entering a marriage, the responsibilities it would entail for her, and the rewards she would anticipate and how all of that might be impacted by his developing Huntington disease. Recognizing her agency would require him to inform her of his chance of developing Huntington disease, to discuss the alternatives relating to marriage and reproduction with her as a genuine partner, and to support her agency in whatever choice she should make for herself with respect to their future.

Harry's standing with respect to his future children raises another set of concerns. What duties does he undertake when he chooses to become a father? Is there some way that he can meet his obligations to his child if he becomes disabled and dies before the child matures?

And as for *Harriette's* case, a lurking issue of family ties involves informing other family members about their risk for having an affected child. Was Harriette's sister obligated to inform her siblings that she had an affected child? If she were estranged from the others and lived on the other side of the country would she be bound to tell? We know that families do keep secrets. Yet, because the impact of this disease is so devastating to the affected child and the entire household, and because family relations seem to carry some moral weight, and because we should care about the projects of close friends as well as strangers, there seem to be sufficient reasons for claiming that Harriette's sister should inform her siblings regardless of their present social relationship.

The most troubling issue of family bonds related to this case, however, turns on whether there are some children who are better off not being born. A Tay-Sachs baby appears normal for the first few months. Then, between the fourth and eighth month of life, the nerves begin to be affected by a fatty substance that accumulates in the cells. The child becomes blind, deaf, unable to swallow. The muscles atrophy, response to the environment dwindles, and the relentless deterioration continues until the child is totally debilitated and develops uncontrollable seizures. Death from pneumonia or infection usually occurs between age five and eight. Are there some lives that parents have no right to create?

VII. CONCLUSION

The arguments we have considered have led to some strong and perhaps surprising conclusions. The clearest conclusion is that no one has a moral right to genetic ignorance. The other noteworthy conclusion is that moral responsibility depends on a variety of factors including blood ties, social relationships, the history of an interaction, and particular features of the situation and the individuals involved.

These conclusions have obvious and forceful implications for the individuals who may have reasons for considering genetic services. They are also significant for geneticists and genetic counselors in that they present good reasons for taking a certain view on what would be right for their patients and clients to choose. However, I need to caution that my line of argument does not go so far as to over-ride the genetics community's well-modulated commitment to non-directive counseling. A vivid imagination can allow us to see that in spite of the arguments against a right to genetic ignorance, in some unusual situation a rational person could have good reasons for making another choice.

Keeping Pace with the Times—The Genetic Information Nondiscrimination Act of 2008

Kathy L. Hudson, M.K. Holohan, and Francis S. Collins

Laws and institutions must go hand in hand with the progress of the human mind. As that becomes more developed, more enlightened, as new discoveries are made, new truths disclosed, and manners and opinions change with the change of circumstances, institutions must advance also, and keep pace with the times.

—*Thomas Jefferson, July 12, 1810*

When the first federal legislation to prevent the misuse of genetic information was introduced in 1995, many in the health care, research, and policy communities considered the measure to be forward looking. Others called it premature. After all, scientists were just getting ready to start the sequencing of the human genome. Only about 300 genetic tests were available, most of them for rare diseases and usually performed in research settings.

Yet, anticipating an explosion in the clinical relevance of genetic testing and sensing Americans' growing concern that their genetic information could be used against them by health insurers and in the workplace, we

---

Hudson, Kathy L., M. K. Holohan, and Francis S. Collins, "Keeping Pace with the Times—The Genetic Information Nondiscrimination Act of 2008," *The New England Journal of Medicine* 358:25 (June 19, 2008) 2661–2663. Copyright © 2008 by Massachusetts Medical Society. All rights reserved.

and many others became convinced that reforms were needed as soon as possible.[1,2] Little did we know that "as soon as possible" would mean a 13-year legislative saga that culminated on May 21, 2008, with President George W. Bush's signing of the Genetic Information Nondiscrimination Act (GINA) of 2008. At last, the United States has a federal law that protects consumers from discrimination by health insurers and employers on the basis of genetic information (see box).

In the years between GINA's inception and its enactment, genomic information has grown exponentially, revolutionizing nearly all areas of biomedical research and, many believe, promising an eventual transformation of health care. Researchers completed the reference sequence of the human genome in April 2003 and went on to produce a map of human genetic variation that has greatly accelerated the search for genes involved in susceptibility to common diseases. Genetic tests now encompass more than 1500 conditions, with most of the growth in the area of common diseases. With many of these tests becoming available in the clinic and some even being offered directly to consumers, GINA's protections could no longer be dismissed as premature; they were rapidly coming to seem essential to Americans' ability to make the most of the much-anticipated era of personalized medicine.

Quick Guide to GINA

WHAT GINA DOES

Prohibits group and individual health insurers from using a person's genetic information in determining eligibility or premiums

Prohibits an insurer from requesting or requiring that a person undergo a genetic test

Prohibits employers from using a person's genetic information in making employment decisions such as hiring, firing, job assignments, or any other terms of employment

Prohibits employers from requesting, requiring, or purchasing genetic information about persons or their family members

Will be enforced by the Department of Health and Human Services, the Department of Labor, and the Department of Treasury, along with the Equal Opportunity Employment Commission; remedies for violations include corrective action and monetary penalties

WHAT GINA DOES NOT DO

Does not prevent health care providers from recommending genetic tests to their patients

Does not mandate coverage for any particular test or treatment

Does not prohibit medical underwriting based on current health status

Does not cover life, disability, or long-term-care insurance

Does not apply to members of the military

KEY TERMS

"Genetic information" includes information about:
> A person's genetic tests
> Genetic tests of a person's family members (up to and including fourth-degree relatives)
> Any manifestation of a disease or disorder in a family member
> Participation of a person or family member in research that includes genetic testing, counseling, or education

"Genetic tests" refers to tests that assess genotypes, mutations, or chromosomal changes

Examples of protected tests are:
> Tests for *BRCA1/BRCA2* (breast cancer) or *HNPCC* (colon cancer) mutations
> Classifications of genetic properties of an existing tumor to help determine therapy
> Tests for Huntington's disease mutations
> Carrier screening for disorders such as cystic fibrosis, sickle cell anemia, spinal muscular atrophy, and the fragile X syndrome

Routine tests such as complete blood counts, cholesterol tests, and liver-function tests are not protected under GINA

Still, in a policy system that may be better suited to responding to crises than promoting prevention, legislators are rarely in an optimal position to act on the potential effects of emerging technologies. Thanks to the efforts of key lawmakers, their staffs, and advocates such as the Coalition for Genetic Fairness, GINA eventually garnered overwhelming bipartisan support in the current Congress. One silver lining of GINA's slow progress through Congress is the many opportunities it offered to educate policymakers about the potential of genomic medicine and the challenges that must be addressed if we are to realize that potential.

"GINA is the first major new civil rights bill of the new century," said Senator Edward Kennedy (D-MA), who cosponsored GINA in the Senate with Senator Olympia Snowe (R-ME). "Discrimination in health insurance and the fear of potential discrimination threaten both society's ability to use new genetic technologies to improve human health and the ability to conduct the very research we need to understand, treat, and prevent genetic disease," said Kennedy.

To be sure, some protections existed before GINA. The Health Insurance Portability and Accountability Act of 1996, for example, provided some restrictions on the use of genetic information in setting premiums and determining eligibility for benefits in group health plans. GINA, however, will strengthen those safeguards by limiting insurers' ability to use genetic information to raise rates for an entire group and by extending protections to individual health insurance plans. Also, before GINA's passage, many states had enacted laws against genetic discrimination, which varied widely in their scope and degree of protection. GINA now sets a nationwide level of protection but does not preempt state laws that provide even broader safeguards.

Despite the historic protections provided by GINA, we acknowledge that the law is not perfect and does not go as far as many organizations and families had wished. Originally, some had hoped to include protection for people in whom a genetic illness has been diagnosed—not just those whose tests show a genetic susceptibility to disease. Such a provision, however, had two important flaws, one economic and one ethical. First, it would have caused a severe disruption in the individual health insurance market in the United States, which currently underwrites on the basis of diagnosed diseases. Second, it would be fundamentally unjust to treat people with genetic diseases differently from those whose diseases are nongenetic or have unknown causes. In the end, lawmakers settled on protecting genetic information that could predict future disease, along with the genetic test results of people who are already affected by a genetic disease.

Along with the benefits it provides to individuals, the new law should have positive effects on the fields of clinical research and health care delivery. Studies have shown the "fear factor" to be a major obstacle to patients' participation in research studies that involve the collection of genetic information. Fear of genetic discrimination has also put a damper on patients' willingness to consider genetic tests recommended by their health care providers or to have the results of such tests included in their medical records.[3] It must be emphasized that GINA does not in any way limit the ability of health care professionals to do what they are currently doing: they may still use their clinical judgment to decide whether or not to recommend genetic testing to patients under their care.

"This bill unlocks the great promise of the Human Genome Project by alleviating the most common fear about genetic testing," said Representative Judy Biggert (R-IL), who cosponsored GINA in the House with its leading proponent, Representative Louise Slaughter (D-NY). "It will accelerate research . . . and allow Americans to finally realize the benefits and health care savings offered by gene-based medicine," noted Biggert.

Now that the President has signed GINA, federal agencies must write the implementing regulations that will provide detailed guidance for health insurers and employers about how to comply with the new law. The health insurance regulations will take effect 12 months from now, and the employment regulations 6 months after that. However, it will take much more than sound regulations to ensure that we reap the full benefits of GINA. We need to make certain that health care professionals and patients understand the new protections—and, equally important, that clinical researchers, research administrators, institutional review boards, and research participants are fully informed about the new law and its implications. Such educational efforts are daunting, given the decentralized nature of our systems of health care delivery and protection of human subjects.

Although safeguarding genetic information from misuse by health insurers and employers is a key prerequisite to more individualized approaches to medicine, many other critical challenges remain. First and foremost, we need to ensure that genetic tests are safe, reliable, and marketed in a clear and truthful manner. There are important gaps in the oversight of genetic tests, and multiple advisory groups have called for regulatory reform to ensure the analytic and clinical validity of genetic tests.[4,5] Clearly, our country's substantial investment and innovation in genetic science ought to be matched by innovation in regulation.

Finally, we need to look carefully at other areas of our society in which it might be tempting to use—or misuse—genetic information. GINA addresses only employment and health insurance, not life insurance, disability insurance, or long-term-care insurance. This is not the result of an oversight: a strategic decision was made early on to recognize the very distinct markets, social purposes, risks of adverse selection, and bodies of relevant law governing these types of insurance. It may well be time for a thoughtful evaluation of these other realms that are likely to be touched by the swift advance of genomic science.

NOTES

1. Hudson KL, Rothenberg KH, Andrews LB, Kahn MJ, Collins FS. Genetic discrimination and health insurance: an urgent need for reform. Science 1995;270:391–3.
2. Rothenberg K, Fuller B, Rothstein M, et al. Genetic information and the workplace: legislative approaches and policy changes. Science 1997;275:1755–7.
3. Hudson KL. Prohibiting genetic discrimination. N Engl J Med 2007;356:2021–3.
4. *Idem.* Genetic testing oversight. Science 2006;313:1853.
5. U.S. system of oversight of genetic testing: a response to the charge of the Secretary of Health and Human Services. Bethesda, MD: Secretary's Advisory Committee on Genetics, Health, and Society, April 2008. (Accessed May 27, 2008, at http://www4.od.nih.gov/oba/SACGHS/reports/SACGHS_oversight_report.pdf.)

THERAPY AND ENHANCEMENT

Questions about Some Uses of Genetic Engineering

Jonathan Glover

Let us now turn to the question of what, if anything, we should do in the field of human genetic engineering.

The positive-negative distinction

We are not yet able to cure disorders by genetic engineering. But we do sometimes respond to disorders by adopting eugenic policies, at least in voluntary form. Genetic counselling is one instance, as applied to those thought likely to have such disorders as Huntington's chorea. This is a particularly appalling inherited disorder, involving brain degeneration, leading to mental decline and lack of control over movement. It does not normally come on until middle age, by which time many of its victims would in the normal course of things have had children. Huntington's chorea is caused by a dominant gene, so those who find that one of the parents has it have themselves a 50 per cent chance of developing it. If they do have it, each of their children will in turn have a 50 per cent chance of the disease. The risks are so high and the disorder so bad that the potential parents often decide not to have children, and are often given advice to this effect by doctors and others.

Another eugenic response to disorders is involved in screening-programmes for pregnant women. When tests pick up such defects as Down's syndrome (mongolism) or spina bifida, the mother is given the possibility of an abortion. The screening-programmes are eugenic because part of their point is to reduce the incidence of severe genetic abnormality in the population.

These two eugenic policies come in at different stages: before conception and during pregnancy. For this reason the screening-programme is more controversial, because it raises the issue of abortion. Those who are sympathetic to abortion, and who think it would be good to eliminate these disorders will be sympathetic to the programme. Those who think abortion is no different from killing a fully developed human are obviously likely to oppose the programme. But they are likely to feel that elimination of the disorders would be a good thing, even if not an adequate justification for killing. Unless they also disapprove of contraception, they are likely to support the genetic-counselling policy in the case of Huntington's chorea.

Few people object to the use of eugenic policies to eliminate disorders, unless those policies have additional features which are objectionable. Most of us are resistant to the use of compulsion, and those who oppose abortion will object to screening-programmes. But apart from these other moral objections, we do not object to the use of eugenic policies against disease. We do not object to advising those likely to have

Huntington's chorea not to have children, as neither compulsion nor killing is involved. Those of us who take this view have no objection to altering the genetic composition of the next generation, where this alteration consists in reducing the incidence of defects.

If it were possible to use genetic engineering to correct defects, say at the foetal stage, it is hard to see how those of us who are prepared to use the eugenic measure just mentioned could object. In both cases, it would be pure gain. The couple, one of whom may develop Huntington's chorea, can have a child if they want, knowing that any abnormality will be eliminated. Those sympathetic to abortion will agree that cure is preferable. And those opposed to abortion prefer babies to be born without handicap. It is hard to think of any objection to using genetic engineering to eliminate defects, and there is a clear and strong case for its use.

But accepting the case for eliminating genetic mistakes does not entail accepting other uses of genetic engineering. The elimination of defects is often called "negative" genetic engineering. Going beyond this, to bring about improvements in normal people, is by contrast "positive" engineering. (The same distinction can be made for eugenics.)

The positive-negative distinction is not in all cases completely sharp. Some conditions are genetic disorders whose identification raises little problem. Huntington's chorea or spina bifida are genetic "mistakes" in a way that cannot seriously be disputed. But with other conditions, the boundary between a defective state and normality may be more blurred. If there is a genetic disposition towards depressive illness, this seems a defect, whose elimination would be part of negative genetic engineering. Suppose the genetic disposition to depression involves the production of lower levels of an enzyme than are produced in normal people. The negative programme is to correct the genetic fault so that the enzyme level is within the range found in normal people. But suppose that within "normal" people also, there are variations in the enzyme level, which correlate with ordinary differences in [the] tendency to be cheerful or depressed. Is there a sharp boundary between "clinical" depression and the depression sometimes felt by those diagnosed as "normal"? Is it clear that a sharp distinction can be drawn between raising someone's enzyme level so that it falls within the normal range and raising someone else's level from the bottom of the normal range to the top?

The positive-negative distinction is sometimes a blurred one, but often we can at least roughly see where it should be drawn. If there is a rough and ready distinction, the question is: how important is it? Should we go on from accepting negative engineering to accepting positive programmes, or should we say that the line between the two is the limit of what is morally acceptable?

There is no doubt that positive programmes arouse the strongest feelings on both sides. On the one hand, many respond to positive genetic engineering or positive eugenics with Professor Tinbergen's thought "I find it morally reprehensible and presumptuous for anybody to put himself forward as a judge of the qualities for which we should breed" [*Guardian*, 5 March, 1980].

But other people have held just as strongly that positive policies are the way to make the future of mankind better than the past. Many years ago H. J. Muller expressed this hope:

> And so we foresee the history of life divided into three main phases. In the long preparatory phase it was the helpless creature of its environment, and natural selection gradually ground it into human shape. In the second—our own short transitional phase—it reaches out at the immediate environment, shaking, shaping and grinding to suit the form, the requirements, the wishes, and the whims of man. And in the long third phase, it will reach down into the secret places of the great universe of its own nature, and by aid of its ever growing intelligence and cooperation, shape itself into an increasingly sublime creation—a being beside which the mythical divinities of the past will seem more and more ridiculous, and which setting its own marvellous inner powers against the brute Goliath of the suns and the planets, challenges them to contest.

The case for positive engineering is not helped by adopting the tones of the mad scientist in a horror film. But behind the rhetoric is a serious point. If we decide on a positive programme to change our nature, this will be a central moment in our history, and the transformation might be beneficial to a degree we can now scarcely imagine. The question is: how are we to weigh this possibility against Tinbergen's objection, and against other objections and doubts?

For the rest of this discussion, I shall assume that, subject to adequate safeguards against things going wrong, negative genetic engineering is acceptable. The issue is positive engineering. I shall also assume that we can ignore problems about whether positive engineering will be technically possible. Suppose we have the power to choose people's genetic characteristics. Once we have eliminated genetic defects, what, if anything, should we do with this power? . . .

The view that overall improvement is unlikely or impossible

There is one doubt about the workability of schemes of genetic improvement which is so widespread that it would be perverse to ignore it. This is the view that, in any genetic alteration, there are no gains without compensating losses. On this view, if we bring about a genetically based improvement, such as higher intelligence, we are bound to pay a price somewhere else: perhaps the more intelligent people will have less resistance to disease, or will be less physically agile. If correct, this might so undermine the practicability of applying eugenics or genetic engineering that it would be hardly worth discussing the values involved in such programmes.

This view perhaps depends on some idea that natural selection is so efficient that, in terms of gene survival, we must already be as efficient as it is possible to be. If it were possible to push up intelligence without weakening some other part of the system, natural selection would already have done so. But this is a naive version of evolutionary theory. In real evolutionary theory, far from the genetic status quo always being the best possible for a given environment, some mutations turn out to be advantageous, and this is the origin of evolutionary progress. If natural mutations can be beneficial without a compensating loss, why should artificially induced ones not be so too?

It should also be noticed that there are two different ideas of what counts as a gain or a loss. From the point of view of evolutionary progress, gains and losses are simply advantages and disadvantages from the point of view of gene survival. But we are not compelled to take this view. If we could engineer a genetic change in some people which would have the effect of making them musical prodigies but also sterile, this would be a hopeless gene in terms of survival, but this need not force us, or the musical prodigies themselves, to think of the changes as for the worse. It depends on how we rate musical ability as against having children, and evolutionary survival does not dictate priorities here.

The view that gains and losses are tied up with each other need not depend on the dogma that natural selection *must* have created the best of all possible sets of genes. A more cautiously empirical version of the claim says there is a tendency for gains to be accompanied by losses. John Maynard Smith, in his paper on "Eugenics and Utopia," takes this kind of "broad balance" view and runs it the other way, suggesting, as an argument in defence of medicine, that any loss of genetic resistance to disease is likely to be a good thing: "The reason for this is that in evolution, as in other fields, one seldom gets something for nothing. Genes which confer disease-resistance are likely to have harmful effects in other ways: this is certainly true of the gene for sickle-cell anaemia and may be a general rule. If so, absence of selection in favour of disease-resistance may be eugenic."

It is important that different characteristics may turn out to be genetically linked in ways we do not yet realize.

In our present state of knowledge, engineering for some improvement might easily bring some unpredicted but genetically linked disadvantage. But we do not have to accept that there will in general be a broad balance, so that there is a presumption that any gain will be accompanied by a compensating loss (or Maynard Smith's version that we can expect a compensating gain for any loss). The reason is that what counts as a gain or loss varies in different contexts. Take Maynard Smith's example of sickle-cell anaemia. The reason why sickle-cell anaemia is widespread in Africa is that it is genetically linked with resistance to malaria. Those who are heterozygous (who inherit one sickle-cell gene and one normal gene) are resistant to malaria, while those who are homozygous (whose genes are both sickle-cell) get sickle-cell anaemia. If we use genetic engineering to knock out sickle-cell anaemia where malaria is common, we will pay the price of having more malaria. But when we eradicate malaria, the gain will not involve this loss. Because losses are relative to context, any generalization about the impossibility of overall improvements is dubious.

The family and our descendants

Unlike various compulsory eugenic policies, genetic engineering need not involve any interference with decisions by couples to have children together, or with their decisions about how many children to have. And let us suppose that genetically engineered babies grow in the mother's womb in the normal way, so that her relationship to the child is not threatened in the way it might be if the laboratory or the hospital were substituted for the womb. The cruder threats to family relationships are eliminated.

It may be suggested that there is a more subtle threat. Parents like to identify with their children. We are often pleased to see some of our own characteristics in our children. Perhaps this is partly a kind of vanity, and no doubt sometimes we project on to our children similarities that are not really there. But, when the similarities do exist, they help the parents and children to understand and sympathize with each other. If genetic engineering resulted in children fairly different from their parents, this might make their relationship have problems.

There is something to this objection, but it is easy to exaggerate. Obviously, children who were like Midwich cuckoos, or comic-book Martians, would not be easy to identify with. But genetic engineering need not move in such sudden jerks. The changes would have to be detectable to be worth bringing about, but there seems no reason why large changes in appearance, or an unbridgeable psychological gulf, should be created in any one generation. We bring about environmental changes which make children different from their parents, as when the first generation of children in a remote place are given schooling and made literate. This may cause some problems in families, but it is not usually thought a decisive objection. It is not clear that genetically induced changes of similar magnitude are any more objectionable.

A related objection concerns our attitude to our remoter descendants. We like to think of our descendants stretching on for many generations. Perhaps this is in part an immortality substitute. We hope they will to some extent be like us, and that, if they think of us, they will do so with sympathy and approval. Perhaps these hopes about the future of mankind are relatively unimportant to us. But, even if we mind about them a lot, they are unrealistic in the very long term. Genetic engineering would make our descendants less like us, but this would only speed up the natural rate of change. Natural mutations and selective pressures make it unlikely that in a few million years our descendants will be physically or mentally much like us. So what genetic engineering threatens here is probably doomed anyway....

Risks and mistakes

Although mixing different species and cloning are often prominent in people's thoughts about genetic engineering, they are relatively marginal issues. This is partly because there may be no strong reasons in favour of either. Our purposes might be realized more readily by improvements to a single species, whether another or our own, or by the creation of quite new types of organism, than by mixing different species. And it is not clear what advantage cloning batches of people might have, to outweigh the drawbacks. This is not to be dogmatic that species mixing and cloning could never be useful, but to say that the likelihood of other techniques being much more prominent makes it a pity to become fixated on the issues raised by these ones. And some of the most serious objections to positive genetic engineering have wider application than to these rather special cases. One of these wider objections is that serious risks may be involved.

Some of the risks are already part of the public debate because of current work on recombinant DNA. The danger is of producing harmful organisms that would escape from our control. The work obviously should take place, if at all, only with adequate safeguards against such a disaster. The problem is deciding what we should count as adequate safeguards. I have nothing to contribute to this problem here. If it can be dealt with satisfactorily, we will perhaps move on to genetic engineering of people. And this introduces another dimension of risk. We

may produce unintended results, either because our techniques turn out to be less finely tuned than we thought, or because different characteristics are found to be genetically linked in unexpected ways.

If we produce a group of people who turn out worse than expected, we will have to live with them. Perhaps we would aim for producing people who were especially imaginative and creative, and only too late find we had produced people who were also very violent and aggressive. This kind of mistake might not only be disastrous, but also very hard to "correct" in subsequent generations. For when we suggested sterilization to the people we had produced, or else corrective genetic engineering for *their* offspring, we might find them hard to persuade. They might like the way they were, and reject, in characteristically violent fashion, our explanation that they were a mistake.

The possibility of an irreversible disaster is a strong deterrent. It is enough to make some people think we should rule out genetic engineering altogether, and to make others think that, while negative engineering is perhaps acceptable, we should rule out positive engineering. The thought behind this second position is that the benefits from negative engineering are clearer, and that, because its aims are more modest, disastrous mistakes are less likely.

The risk of disasters provides at least a reason for saying that, if we do adopt a policy of human genetic engineering, we ought to do so with extreme caution. We should alter genes only where we have strong reasons for thinking the risk of disaster is very small, and where the benefit is great enough to justify the risk. (The problems of deciding when this is so are familiar from the nuclear power debate.) This "principle of caution" is less strong than one ruling out all positive engineering, and allows room for the possibility that the dangers may turn out to be very remote, or that greater risks of a different kind are involved in *not* using positive engineering. These possibilities correspond to one view of the facts in the nuclear power debate. Unless with genetic engineering we think we can already rule out such possibilities, the argument from risk provides more justification for the principle of caution than for the stronger ban on all positive engineering....

DECISIONS

Some of the strongest objections to positive engineering are not about specialized applications or about risks. They are about the decisions involved. The central line of thought is that we should not start playing God by redesigning the human race. The suggestion is that there is no group (such as scientists, doctors, public officials, or politicians) who can be entrusted with decisions about what sort of people there should be. And it is also doubted whether we could have any adequate grounds for basing such decisions on one set of values rather than another. . . .

1. Not playing God

Suppose we could use genetic engineering to raise the average IQ by fifteen points. (I mention, only to ignore, the boring objection that the average IQ is always by definition 100.) Should we do this? Objectors to positive engineering say we should not. This is not because the present average is preferable to a higher one. We do not think that, if it were naturally fifteen points higher, we ought to bring it down to the present level. The objection is to our playing God by deciding what the level should be.

On one view of the world, the objection is relatively straightforward. On this view, there really is a God, who has a plan for the world which will be disrupted if we stray outside the boundaries assigned to us. (It is *relatively* straightforward: there would still be the problem of knowing where the boundaries came. If genetic engineering disrupts the programme, how do we know that medicine and education do not?)

The objection to playing God has a much wider appeal than to those who literally believe in a divine plan. But, outside such a context, it is unclear what the objection comes to. If we have a Darwinian view, according to which features of our nature have been selected for their contribution to gene survival, it is not blasphemous, or obviously disastrous, to start to control the process in the light of our own values. We may value other qualities in people, in preference to those which have been most conducive to gene survival.

The prohibition on playing God is obscure. If it tells us not to interfere with natural selection at all, this rules out medicine, and most other environmental and social changes. If it only forbids interference with natural selection by the direct alteration of genes, this rules out negative as well as positive genetic engineering. If these interpretations are too restrictive, the ban on positive engineering seems to need some explanation. If we can make positive changes at the environmental level, and negative changes at the genetic level, why should we not make positive changes at the genetic level? What makes this policy, but not the others, objectionably God-like?

Perhaps the most plausible reply to these questions rests on a general objection to any group of people trying to plan too closely what human life should be like. Even if it is hard to distinguish in principle between the use of genetic and environmental means, genetic changes are likely to differ in degree from most environmental ones. Genetic alterations may be more drastic or less reversible, and so they can be seen as the extreme case of an objectionably God-like policy by which some people set out to plan the lives of others.

This objection can be reinforced by imagining the possible results of a programme of positive engineering, where the decisions about the desired improvements were taken by scientists. Judging by the literature written by scientists on this topic, great prominence would be given to intelligence. But can we be sure that enough weight would be given to other desirable qualities? And do things seem better if for scientists we substitute doctors, politicians or civil servants? Or some committee containing businessmen, trade unionists, academics, lawyers and a clergyman?

What seems worrying here is the circumscribing of potential human development. The present genetic lottery throws up a vast range of characteristics, good and bad, in all sorts of combinations. The group of people controlling a positive engineering policy would inevitably have limited horizons, and we are right to worry that the limitations of their outlook might become the boundaries of human variety. The drawbacks would be like those of town-planning or dog-breeding, but with more important consequences.

When the objection to playing God is separated from the idea that intervening in this aspect of the natural world is a kind of blasphemy, it is a protest against a particular group of people, necessarily fallible and limited, taking decisions so important to our future. This protest may be on grounds of the bad consequences, such as loss of variety of people, that would come from the imaginative limits of those taking the decisions. Or it may be an expression of opposition to such concentration of power, perhaps with the thought: 'What right have *they* to decide what kinds of people there should be?' Can these problems be side-stepped?

2. The genetic supermarket

Robert Nozick is critical of the assumption that positive engineering has to involve any centralized decision about desirable qualities: "Many biologists tend to think the problem is one of *design*, of specifying the best types of persons so that biologists can proceed to produce them. Thus they worry over what sort(s) of person there is to be and who will control this process. They do not tend to think, perhaps because it diminishes the importance of their role, of a system in which they run a "genetic supermarket," meeting the individual specifications (within certain moral limits) of prospective parents. Nor do they think of seeing what limited number of types of persons people's choices would converge upon, if indeed there would be any such convergence. This supermarket system has the great virtue that it involves no centralized decision fixing the future human type(s)."

This idea of letting parents choose their children's characteristics is in many ways an improvement on decisions being taken by some centralized body. It seems less likely to reduce human variety, and could even increase it, if genetic engineering makes new combinations of characteristics available. (But we should be cautious here. Parental choice is not a guarantee of genetic variety, as the influence of fashion or of shared values might make for a small number of types on which choices would converge.)

To those sympathetic to one kind of liberalism, Nozick's proposal will seem more attractive than centralized decisions. On this approach to politics, it is wrong for the authorities to institutionalize any religious or other outlook as the official one of the society. To a liberal of this kind, a good society is one which tolerates and encourages a wide diversity of ideals of the good life. Anyone with these sympathies will be suspicious of centralized decisions about what sort of people should form the next generation. But some parental decisions would be disturbing. If parents chose characteristics likely to make their children unhappy, or likely to reduce their abilities, we might feel that the children should be protected against this. (Imagine parents belonging to some extreme religious sect, who wanted their children to have a religious symbol as a physical mark on their face, and who wanted them to be unable to read, as a protection against their faith being corrupted.) Those of us who support restrictions protecting children from parental harm after birth (laws against cruelty, and compulsion on parents to allow their children to be educated and to have necessary medical treatment) are likely to support protecting children from being harmed by their parents' genetic choices.

No doubt the boundaries here will be difficult to draw. We already find it difficult to strike a satisfactory balance between protection of children and parental freedom to choose the kind of upbringing their children should have. But it is hard to accept that society should set no limits to the genetic choices parents can make for their children. Nozick recognizes this when he says the genetic supermarket should meet the specifications of parents "within certain moral limits." So, if the supermarket came into existence, some centralized policy, even if only the restrictive one of ruling out certain choices harmful to the children, should exist. It would be a political decision where the limits should be set.

There may also be a case for other centralized restrictions on parental choice, as well as those aimed at preventing harm to the individual people being designed. The genetic supermarket might have more oblique bad effects. An imbalance in the ratio between the sexes could result. Or parents might think their children would be more successful if they were more thrusting, competitive and selfish. If enough parents acted on this thought, other parents with different values might feel forced into making similar choices to prevent their own children being too greatly disadvantaged. Unregulated individual decisions could lead to shifts of this kind, with outcomes unwanted by most of those who contribute to them. If a majority favour a roughly equal ratio between the sexes, or a population of relatively uncompetitive people, they may feel justified in supporting restrictions on what parents can choose. (This is an application to the case of genetic engineering of a point familiar in other contexts, that unrestricted individual choices can add up to a total outcome which most people think worse than what would result from some regulation.)

Nozick recognizes that there may be cases of this sort. He considers the case of avoiding a sexual imbalance and says that "a government could require that genetic manipulation be carried on so as to fit a certain ratio." He clearly prefers to avoid governmental intervention of this kind, and, while admitting that the desired result would be harder to obtain in a purely libertarian system, suggests possible strategies for doing so. He says: "Either parents would subscribe to an information service monitoring the recent births and so know which sex was in shorter supply (and hence would be more in demand in later life), thus adjusting their activities, or interested individuals would contribute to a charity that offers bonuses to maintain the ratios, or the ratio would leave 1:1, with new family and social patterns developing." The proposals for avoiding the sexual imbalance without central regulation are not reassuring. Information about likely prospects for marriage or sexual partnership might not be decisive for parents' choices. And, since those most likely to be "interested individuals" would be in the age group being genetically engineered, it is not clear that the charity would be given donations adequate for its job.

If the libertarian methods failed, we would have the choice between allowing a sexual imbalance or imposing some system of social regulation. Those who dislike central decisions favouring one sort of person over others might accept regulation here, on the grounds that neither sex is being given preference: the aim is rough equality of numbers.

But what about the other sort of case, where the working of the genetic supermarket leads to a general change unwelcome to those who contribute to it? Can we defend regulation to prevent a shift towards a more selfish and competitive population as merely being the preservation of a certain ratio between characteristics? Or have we crossed the boundary, and allowed a centralized decision favouring some characteristics over others? The location of the boundary is obscure. One view would be that the sex-ratio case is acceptable because the desired ratio is equality of numbers. On another view, the acceptability derives from the fact that the present ratio is to be preserved. (In this second view, preserving altruism would be acceptable, so long as no attempt was made to raise the proportion of altruistic people in the population. But is *this* boundary an easy one to defend?)

If positive genetic engineering does become a reality, we may be unable to avoid some of the decisions being taken at a social level. Or rather, we could avoid this, but only at what seems an unacceptable cost, either to the particular people being designed, or to their generation as a whole. And, even if the social decisions are only restrictive, it is implausible to claim that they are all quite free of any taint of preference for some characteristics over others. But, although this suggests that we should not be doctrinaire in our support of the liberal view, it does not show that the view has to be abandoned altogether. We may still think that social decisions in favour of one type of person rather than another should be few, even if the consequences of excluding them altogether are unacceptable. A genetic supermarket, modified by some central regulation, may still be better than a system of purely central decisions. The liberal value is not obliterated because it may sometimes be compromised for the sake of other things we care about.

3. A mixed system

The genetic supermarket provides a partial answer to the objection about the limited outlook of those who would take the decisions. The choices need not be concentrated in the hands of a small number of people. The genetic supermarket should not operate in a completely unregulated way, and so some centralized decisions would have to be taken about the restrictions that should be imposed. One system that would answer many of the anxieties about centralized decision-making would be to limit the power of the decision-makers to one of veto. They would then only check departures from the natural genetic lottery, and so the power to bring about changes would not be given to them, but spread through the whole population of potential parents. Let us call this combination of parental initiative and central veto a "mixed system." If positive genetic engineering does come about, we can imagine the argument between supporters of a mixed system and supporters of other decision-making systems being central to the political theory of the twenty-first century, parallel to the place occupied in the nineteenth and twentieth centuries by the debate over control of the economy.

My own sympathies are with the view that, if positive genetic engineering is introduced, this mixed system is in general likely to be the best one for making decisions. I do not want to argue for an absolutely inviolable commitment to this, as it could be that some centralized decision for genetic change was the only way of securing a huge benefit or avoiding a great catastrophe. But, subject to this reservation, the dangers of concentrating the decision-making create a strong presumption in favour of a mixed system rather than one in which initiatives come from the centre. And, if a mixed system was introduced, there would have to be a great deal of political argument over what kinds of restrictions on the supermarket should be imposed. Twenty-first-century elections may be about issues rather deeper than economics.

If this mixed system eliminates the anxiety about genetic changes being introduced by a few powerful people with limited horizons, there is a more general unease which it does not remove. May not the limitations of one generation of parents also prove disastrous? And, underlying this, is the problem of what values parents should appeal to in making their choices. How can we be confident that it is better for one sort of person to be born than another?

4. Values

The dangers of such decisions, even spread through all prospective parents, seem to me very real. We are swayed by fashion. We do not know the limitations of our own outlook. There are human qualities whose value we may not appreciate. A generation of parents might opt heavily for their children having physical or intellectual abilities and skills. We might leave out a sense of humour. Or we might not notice how important to us is some other quality, such as emotional warmth. So we might not be disturbed in advance by the possible impact of the genetic changes on such a quality. And, without really wanting to do so, we might stumble into producing people with a deep coldness. This possibility seems one of the worst imaginable. It is just one of the many horrors that could be blundered into by our lack of foresight in operating the mixed system. Because such disasters are a real danger, there is a case against positive genetic engineering, even when the changes do not result from centralized decisions. But this case, resting as it does on the risk of disaster, supports a principle of caution rather than a total ban. We have to ask the question whether there are benefits sufficiently great and sufficiently probable to outweigh the risks.

But perhaps the deepest resistance, even to a mixed system, is not based on risks, but on a more general problem about values. Could the parents ever be justified in choosing, according to some set of values, to create one sort of person rather than another?

Is it sometimes better for us to create one sort of person rather than another? We say "yes" when it is a question of eliminating genetic defects. And we say "yes" if we think that encouraging some qualities rather than others should be an aim of the upbringing and education we give our children. Any inclination to say "no" in the context of positive genetic engineering must lay great stress on the two relevant boundaries. The positive-negative boundary is needed to mark off the supposedly unacceptable positive policies from the acceptable elimination of defects. And the genes-environment boundary is needed to mark off positive engineering from acceptable positive aims of educational policies. But it is not clear that confidence in the importance of these boundaries is justified....

Gene Therapy: What has been Achieved after 25 Years?
Successes and Failures in a New Field of Medicine

Sheldon Krimsky

In the 1980s, somatic cell human gene therapy (HGT) was considered so promising to some that several clinical investigators were willing to risk their reputations and leave the country to experiment on desperate human subjects in ways that would have violated U.S. guidelines.[1] The media coverage of HGT focused on the most dramatic cases, typically, the potential to reverse the course of an inherited, life threatening or life limiting genetic disorder. The idea that we were not complete prisoners of our diseased genes was a powerful metaphor for human transcendence over the lottery of our genome. It took another decade before the National Institutes of Health established guidelines and set up an advisory committee process to carry out case-by-case reviews of human gene therapy experimental protocols. The first U.S. approved clinical trial for somatic cell gene transfer in humans took place in 1990.

The prospects of HGT were viewed through two lenses. Some scientists claimed that HGT would revolutionize medical therapies and that it introduces an entirely new dimension for tackling the recalcitrant disorders brought on by gene mutations. Others saw HGT as part of a continuum of drug therapies—a form of molecular medicine. In this case, the drugs were delivered in the form of DNA directly into cells, rather than indirectly through the bloodstream. The DNA codes for the production of the therapeutic proteins to be made by the machinery of the cell. In 1995, a special advisory panel to the NIH described somatic cell human gene therapy as follows:

> Somatic gene therapy is a logical and natural progression in the application of fundamental biomedical science to medicine and offers extraordinary potential, in the long-term for the management and correction of human disease, including inherited and acquired disorders, cancer, and AIDS.[2]

However, the same panel warned that the putative revolutionary benefits of HGT were being oversold:

> Overselling of the results of laboratory and clinical studies by investigators and their sponsors—be they academic, federal, or industrial—has led to the mistaken and widespread perception that gene therapy is further developed and more successful than it really is.[3]

In 2004, I supervised a study by Christine Crofts, a sociology doctoral student at Boston College who was interested in investigating the research infrastructure developing around human gene therapy. When she completed her inquiry, we co-authored a paper that was

---

published in the February 2005 issue of *Human Gene Therapy,* from which some of the data cited in this article are derived.[4] We were interested in discovering whether there were any successful human applications of somatic cell gene therapy, the level of government funding it receives, the number of clinical trials that have been undertaken, the amount of support coming from the private sector, and the production of intellectual property resulting from the research in this topic.

We learned that a sizable cottage industry of research and development activities had grown around the prospects of somatic cell gene therapy and that, despite very limited clinical success, this infrastructure of activities has only expanded since 1990. The late New York University sociologist of science Dorothy Nelkin wrote in 1996 that the history of gene therapy has been an "upside down" affair where "conceptual advances [have] become widely accepted and firmly established as medical principle before even a simple clinical instance of clinical efficacy has been demonstrated."[5] The disciplinary and commercial activity that has grown around HGT is a strong indicator that scientists were highly confident that a major breakthrough would occur in this area of research.

While most of the science media has focused on the role of somatic cell gene transfer for inherited diseases, we found that only ten percent of all the clinical trials funded in 2004 were directed at individuals with diseases resulting from monogenic traits. Ironically, the majority of trials were directed at cancer, a disease (or complex of diseases) that is not, in most cases, associated with germ line gene mutations. Sixty-six percent of the gene therapy clinical trials in 2004 were for cancer-related diseases, where the theory of oncogenes was intriguing, but unrelated in any direct way to HGT. Rather, it relies on an interesting set of experiments described below. In any case, the cumulative pattern of clinical trials gives similar results. From 1990 through 2004, the National Institutes of Health Recombinant DNA Advisory Committee reviewed 590 human gene therapy protocols. Seventy-one percent of the trials were for cancer, ten percent were directed at monogenic diseases, seven percent for infectious diseases, and twelve percent for other diseases and disorders.

By 2004, the number of gene-therapy trials approved worldwide was 888. The countries with the highest number of approved HGT trials were the United States with 613, United Kingdom with 96 and Germany with 53.[6]

What is it about HGT that has attracted so much attention among cancer researchers? First, experimentation with HGT techniques for cancer has an advantage over trials for monogenic diseases because there are so many more cases of cancer. This means the chance of recruiting people into a clinical trial is much greater. Second, the funding levels for cancer research are significantly higher than those for monogenic diseases.

These reasons aside, it seemed that there still must have been some reasonable hypotheses about how HGT could be used in cancer therapy to justify the attention it had received. We found four main strategies for using HGT in cancer treatment. They all involve the delivery of genes into cells either in vitro (before the genetically altered cells are delivered into humans) or in vivo (by the use of delivery mechanisms that get the genes into the appropriate cells in the human subject).

For example, there is the transfer of drug-resistant genes into non-cancer cells to protect them from the cell-toxicity of chemotherapy agents. The strategy here is to protect all the neighboring cells except the target cells from the chemotherapy. This would permit the use of higher levels of the locally-directed chemotherapy agent.

A second strategy is the targeting of tumor cells with genes encoding enzymes that activate a toxin that kills the cell. Without the toxin, neighboring cells would not be affected by the chemotherapy agent.

Third, on the assumption that tumor suppressor genes (TSGs) can prevent the growth of tumors, scientists are looking at the use of somatic cell gene transfer to enhance or restore the function of TSGs in the relevant cells that are tumorigenic.

A fourth strategy is to increase the proliferation of cell populations in the immune system that have anti-tumorigenic properties.

These strategies are all based on the unconfirmed hypothesis that genes can be transported into target cells stably and safely, and that the transported genes will encode the correct proteins, and that the amount of protein production will be sufficient for the task.

MONOGENIC PROSPECTS

Clinical gene transfer protocols for inherited monogenic disorders have been approved for: adenosine deaminase deficiency, alpha-1-antitrypsin deficiency, chronic granulomatous disease, Canavan disease, cystic fibrosis, familial-hypercholesterolemia, Fanconi's anemia, Gaucher disease, Hunter syndrome, ornithine transcarbamylase deficiency (OTC), and severe combined immunodeficiencies syndrome (SCIDS).

Eighteen-year-old Jesse Gelsinger died in 1999 after he was recruited into an experimental gene therapy trial at the University of Pennsylvania. The purpose of the trial was for the clinical team to gain some understanding of how HGT might contribute in helping to treat infants with Jesse's genetic disorder, OTC. People with this disorder cannot break down ammonia, a natural byproduct of protein metabolism. Jesse was able to stay alive with a strict diet and large amounts of medication. Jesse's death resulted in a short period of retrenchment and soul searching about the prospects and dangers of HGT, but research activity in the field bounced back fairly rapidly. All the indicators we could find illustrated a field undergoing sustained growth—even without an unambiguously marketable product or therapy.

There were 159 NIH grants that had the term "gene therapy" in the title or abstract in 1990, and the number rose steadily until 1996, when 629 were approved. In 1997, the number of grants more than doubled to 1335. The number peaked at 1985 in 2001, and dropped to 1599 in 2003.

The commercial aspect of HGT was also developing quite robustly toward the turn of the century. From 1990 through 1996 there were thirty gene therapy-related U.S. patents issued. In 1997, 49 patents were issued. By 2002 and 2003, 131 and 125 gene therapy patents were issued respectively. The total patent count from 1990 through 2003 is 759.

Many companies dedicated to gene therapy began forming around 1990. Over a period of thirteen years 151 companies have been formed. A review of Medline between 1990 and 2003 shows a dramatic annual rise in gene therapy research articles, from 177 published in 1990 to 1666 published in 2003. In that same period, nine journals dedicated to HGT were founded.[7]

SUCCESS?

The one application of HGT reported as successful in the primary medical literature is its use to treat a class of genetic diseases known as severe combined immunodeficiency syndrome (SCIDS), which is considered fatal without bone marrow transplants. In 1990, two girls with severe cases of SCIDS underwent the first approved gene therapy treatments in the United States. They are now college students, but still receive regular injections to bolster their immune system.[8]

The first announcement of unambiguously successful treatments came in 2002 when the results of ten French children treated by somatic cell gene therapy were reported.[9] The favorable outcome was mixed, however,

with news that three of the children contracted leukemia from the retrovirus used to carry the genes into the cells—an effect known as "insertional mutagenesis."[10]

Some scientists believe they can minimize the risks of leukemia because they have discovered the particular combination of genes that gave rise to it.[11] Others speak of the HGT trial as a guarded success because, while iatrogenic leukemia is a serious complication, they believe it has a good treatment record, whereas untreated SCIDS has a much higher mortality rate. In December 2004, *The Lancet* reported the successful treatment of four children with X-linked SCIDS, ranging in age from four to thirty-three months. All patients were doing well after treatment and exhibited varying degrees of recovery of immunological cell numbers and immune function. Doctors were able to discontinue immunoglobulin replacement therapy for two patients eighteen and twenty-one months after HGT treatment. Also, unlike with the French children, there were no major complications reported in the British patients. The UK study concluded: "Gene Therapy is an effective treatment for SCID-X1 and for adenosine-deaminase-deficient SCID. Our findings suggest superior reconstitution and lower morbidity and mortality than with mismatched bone-marrow transplantation."[12] Scientists from Italy and Israel reported successful treatments of two SCIDS patients who now live normal lives and have been taken off enzyme replacement therapy.[13]

As of January 2005, 17 out of 18 SCIDS patients treated by an ex-vivo retroviral mediated gene transfer "had their immunodeficiencies corrected with clear and sustained clinical benefits."[14] While the positive responses to HGT treatment for 17 SCIDS patients is a welcome and dramatic outcome, there remain a host of unknowns and concerns.

In the past, human gene therapy researchers in the United States violated federal rules when they failed to report unexpected adverse events associated with the therapy. Fewer than five percent of the serious adverse events were reported. There are uncorroborated allegations that six unreported deaths may be attributable to HGT.

Questions remain over whether the therapeutic gene will eventually stop being expressed and whether the benefit from the HGT, namely the reconstitution of the immune system in the case of SCIDS, will be temporary or permanent.

There are concerns that there will be more cases of leukemia from HGT. One recent publication in which no cases of "insertional mutagenesis" were observed remained cautious: "This risk cannot be clearly defined. At latest analysis we have not observed any evidence of clinically manifest insertional mutagenesis, although our follow-up is short in comparison. Slight differences in protocols...might affect the risk, but we do not believe this possibility to be likely."[15]

Some patients still required prophylactic medication after somatic cell gene therapy. Other risks of HGT are beginning to be reported in primate studies that may complicate the risk benefit assessment.[16]

Notwithstanding the remarkable successes in the activation of a nonfunctional immune system, at least partially for the 17 SCID patients, HGT remains in its infancy and is regularly oversold to the media and to the venture capital community. Until the leukemia problem can be eliminated, it is unlikely that HGT will be adopted as "standard of care" for SCIDS patients. Moreover, the message we get is that HGT will cure "defective genes" and make people whole again. In reality most of the HGT research has been brought under the umbrella of oncology and has less to do with repairing "defective genes" than with delivering drugs to treat individuals who have suffered damage to the genes in their somatic cells.

REFERENCES

1. In July 1980, Martin Cline, a biomedical scientist at UCLA transplanted cells genetically altered in vitro into the bone marrow of two women with an inherited blood disease called beta thalassemia major. One woman was a 16 year old from Italy and a second was a 21 year old from Israel. See, Sheldon Krimsky, Biotechnics and Society, New York: Praeger, 1991, pp. 164–165.

2. Stuart H. Orkin and Arno G. Motulsky. Report and Recommendations of the Panel to Assess the NIH Investment in Research on Gene Therapy. December 7, 1995, p. 1. <http://www.nih.gov/news/panelrep.html>

3. Ibid., p. 2

4. Christine Crofts and Sheldon Krimsky. Emergence of a Scientific and Commercial R&D Infrastructure for Human Gene Therapy. *Human Gene Therapy* (February 2005).

5. Dorothy Nelkin. Covering Gene Therapy: Beware the Hype. *The Quill* 84:34–36 (1996).

6. M. Cavazzana-Calvo, A. Thrasher, and F. Mavilio. The Future of Gene Therapy. *Nature* 427:779–781 (February 26, 2004).

7. The journals are: *Human Gene Therapy, Cancer Gene Therapy, Gene Therapy, Journal of Gene Medicine, Genes and Immunity, Gene Therapy and Regulation, Current Gene Therapy, Gene Vaccines and Therapy,* and *Molecular Therapy.*

8. Robert Cooke. On the eve of medical history. *Newsday* January 18, 2005.

9. S. Hacein-Bay Abina, F. Le Deist, F. Carlier. Sustained correction of X-linked severe combined immunodeficiency by ex vivo gene therapy. *NEJM* 346:1185–93 (2002).

10. S. Hacein-Bay Abina, C. Von Kalle, M. Schmidt et al. A serious adverse event after successful gene-therapy for X-linked severe combined immunodeficiency *NEJM* 348:255–56 (2003).

11. U.P. Dave, N.A. Jenkins, and N.G. Copeland. Gene therapy insertional mutagenesis insights. *Science* 303:333 (January 16, 2004).

12. A. Aluti, S. Slavin, M. Aker et al. Correction of ADA-SCID by stem cell gene therapy combined with nonmyeloabiative conditioning. *Science* 296:2187 (June 28, 2002).

13. Ibid. 2410–2413

14. Editorial. Efficacy of gene therapy for SCID is being confirmed. *The Lancet* 364:2155 (December 18/25, 2004).

15. H.B. Gaspcr, K.I. Parsley, S. Howe et al. Gene therapy of X-linked several combined immunodeficiency by use of pseudo-typed gammaretroviral vector. *The Lancet* 364:2181–2187 (December 18/24, 2004), p. 2186.

16. G. Gau, C. Lebherz, D.J. Welner et al. Erythropoietin gene therapy leads to autoimmune anemia in macaques. *Blood* 103:3300–3302 (May 1, 2004).

Enhancement Technologies and Identity Ethics

Carl Elliott

In the late 1960s, the pharmaceutical company Sandoz began marketing a new "major tranquilizer" called Serentil. The ad for Serentil read: "The newcomer in town who *can't* make friends. The organization man who *can't* adjust to altered status within his company. The woman who *can't* get along with her new daughter-in-law. The executive who *can't* accept retirement." These problems often make people anxious and tense. But Serentil can help. In large, capital letters at the top of the ad was the slogan, "For the anxiety that comes from not fitting in."

The Serentil ad was not a success. In fact, the FDA forced Sandoz to withdraw it and publish a correction. The mistake Sandoz made was not that of offering Serentil as a medical fix for social problems. Their mistake was making the offer so explicit. Sandoz did not try to redefine the social problem into a medical problem, did not use medical language, and did not hide behind technical-sounding diagnostic labels. They just said it out loud, for everyone to hear; here is a drug that will make misfits feel less anxious about not fitting in. And so all the American buttons were pushed: it's a crutch, it's a chemical lobotomy, it will suck away Yankee initiative and erode the work ethic. The FDA forced Sandoz to issue a correction stating that, contrary to its earlier ad, Serentil was useful only in "certain disease states." Sandoz did not intend Serentil to be used for "everyday anxiety situations encountered in the normal course of living."

The debate over the Serentil ad followed what has become a familiar pattern. Doctors begin using a new drug or surgical procedure that looks as much like a cosmetic intervention—or "enhancement technology"—as a proper medical treatment. This new technology promises to take the edge off of some sharply uncomfortable aspect of American social life (social stigma, childhood teasing, occupational stress, sexual inadequacy, racial discrimination, or suburban alienation). The technology takes off spectacularly, after which comes round after endless round of self-flagellation about social conformity, dependence, and treating social problems with pills. For a while there are the usual symptoms of public hand-wringing—anxious editorials, dispassionate debates in medical journals, an occasional congressional hearing or governmental task force; and then the issue takes a nose-dive into obscurity. The technology is either consigned to the history books, like Miltown (a minor tranquilizer of the 1950s that no one remembers anymore) or accepted as part of ordinary life in America, like acne creams and diet drugs. Occasionally controversy will resurface for air a few years later, the way a public outcry over Ritalin emerged two decades after the initial Ritalin scare in the 1970s, but more often it is simply forgotten, except for the occasional physician who is old enough to recall what we used to worry about back in the old days. Cosmetic surgery, Valium, Ritalin, Prozac, Paxil, steroids, gene therapy, growth hormone, Viagra, Botox: all have their days in the headlines, and each time, the same debates are rehearsed. *Brave New World* is invoked: self-reliance and bootstrap-pulling are encouraged: slavish conformity to the opinions of others is roundly deplored. "We have created in America a culture of drugs. We have produced an environment in which people come naturally to expect that they can take a pill for every problem—that they can find satisfaction and health and happiness in a handful of tablets or a few grains of powder." The speaker? Richard Nixon.

Bioethicists and clinicians began to worry about enhancement technologies with the development of gene therapy in the late 1980s. Gene therapy refers to the prospect of treating genetic illnesses by manipulating genetic material. The first human gene therapy protocols were aimed at a metabolic disease called ADA (adenosine deaminase) deficiency, which results in a compromised immune system. Many gene therapy enthusiasts saw the ADA deficiency protocol as a first step toward treating genetic diseases that are far more

common, like cystic fibrosis. Yet many of those same enthusiasts were troubled by the prospect of eugenics, or the effort to improve human beings by altering their genetic condition. So a bright line was drawn between genetic "treatment," which was seen as ethically acceptable, and genetic "enhancement," which was not. Other writers have clung to this distinction as a way of determining not just which technologies we ought to have worries about, but which technologies that health services should fund: medically necessary "treatments" should be funded, while "enhancements" should not. And so the distinction between enhancement and treatment seems to be one that we are stuck with. Bioethicists now use the term "enhancement technologies" to designate a variety of drugs and procedures that are employed by doctors not just to control illness, but also to improve human capacities or characteristics. They range from psychoactive drugs (Ritalin, Prozac, Paxil) to surgical procedures (liposuction, breast augmentation, limb-lengthening surgery) to so-called "lifestyle drugs" (Viagra, Botox, Propecia).

Not too long ago I gave a talk on enhancement technologies to an audience of doctors at a local hospital. During the question and answer session, a medical student asked me what I thought about the dangers of cultural conformity. The danger that most people seem to see with things like cosmetic surgery and genetic enhancement, he said, is that the American people will use the technologies to conform to a narrow, restricted cultural ideal. Everyone will want to be young, white, thin, smart, athletic, and good-looking in a very conventional, Hollywood sort of way. But he thought this fear was unrealistic, even absurd. Take his case, for example. He wore an earring, and his hair was pulled back in a ponytail. This made him stand out among his medical school classmates, he explained, but he liked it that way. In his view, there would always be people like him in America: people who wanted to stretch the limits of the conventional, who thrived on being different, who resisted cultural norms. America is a country of individualists. Conformity is the last thing we need to worry about.

It wasn't hard to see why he felt this way. In the sea of middle-aged white coats and suits that surrounded him, his earring looked like an act of rebellion. Yet if we had been talking not in a hospital auditorium but on the street a few blocks away, his outfit would have been passé. Standing outside the Condom Kingdom or Saint Sabrina's Parlor in Purgatory, where every second passerby is wearing dreadlocks, neck tattoos and a tongue stud, he would have been far more likely to turn heads on the street wearing a blue blazer and a tie. He knew this, of course, but he was still able to see his appearance as a kind of existential act, a strike against conformity. He wasn't like those conservative, bow-tied Midwestern guys in loafers. He was a rebel and an outsider. He didn't care what other people thought. He wore an earring.

What you see when you look at America just may make all the difference to the way you approach the debate over enhancement technologies. Is America a country of rebels or a country of social conformists? A land of Huck Finns or a land of George Babbitts? Perhaps, as Tocqueville thought, it is both. Tocqueville believed that social conformity and social rebellion are merely different sides of the same coin. Both are consequences of the American preoccupation with the opinions of other Americans. This, he thought, is because Americans are so disdainful of authority and tradition. Americans don't look to their ancestors for guidance, and they don't see any obvious signs of superiority in their contemporaries, so they are "constantly brought back to their own judgment as the most apparent and accessible form of truth." But Tocqueville also saw how this aspiration to self-sufficiency easily slides into social conformity. If you can't look up to any external authority to tell you what to think and how to act, then you are constantly looking over your shoulder at your peers. Authority is replaced by public opinion. "When the public governs," writes Tocqueville, "all men feel the value of public goodwill, and all try to win it by gaining the esteem and affection of those among whom they must live."

Tocqueville put his finger on a tension that lies at the heart of the way Americans think about enhancement technologies. People who see America as a land of rebels are worried about individual rights being taken away: They are ever vigilant of the government, the law, the schools, and the churches depriving us of the right to do with our bodies what we wish. They may not be particularly interested in breast augmentation themselves, may have no use for Propecia or Botox or Viagra, but they want nobody telling them what they can't have. People who see America as a land of social conformists, on the other hand, worry what people will do with these individual rights once they are guaranteed. They worry about a homogeneous cultural landscape, stripped of character and diversity, where everyone dreams the same dreams and aspires to identical futures. Both visions have some truth to them, of course. You can look at America and see a country of rebels and visionaries and lost souls: Wyatt Earp on his horse, Travis Bickle in his taxi, Charlie Parker improvising solos in a lonely hotel room. But you can also look at America and see a very different place. Some people look at America and

see a land of generic shopping malls and chain restaurants, of fashion slaves and social strivers, of religious fanatics committing mass suicide like lemmings going over a cliff. You can look at America and see 240 million people watching cable TV in their basements.

ENHANCEMENT

The term "enhancement" was originally intended to suggest a contrast with treatment, but the distinction between treatment and enhancement has proven too elastic to be of much use. In psychiatry, this elasticity is probably inevitable. The lines between social anxiety disorder and shyness, depression and sadness, and attention deficit-hyperactivity disorder and restless absentmindedness are very fuzzy (and if truth be told, somewhat arbitrarily drawn). Yet even for physical interventions, the line between treatment and enhancement is no longer clear. Synthetic growth hormone for ordinary short children may look like a straightforward enhancement, but it can also be characterized as a treatment for psychological suffering. Pediatricians have argued that extremely short children (especially boys) are stigmatized—that they are teased and humiliated as kids, that they have a harder time attracting partners and making money as adults, that they suffer from low self-esteem—and that short stature is, as one researcher put it in a review article, a "disability." The same could be said for the psychological suffering caused by small breasts, crooked teeth, balding heads or wrinkled skin. If a condition causes people to suffer, and that suffering can be addressed by doctors, then it will not be much of a stretch to characterize that condition as an illness or a disability.

The phrase "enhancement technology" also suggests a certain uniformity of purpose. Some interventions fit neatly into this descriptive box—performance-enhancing drugs for athletes, for instance. But others seem rather different. They look less like treatments or enhancements than like ways for people to shape their identities. How should we describe the man who gets sex-reassignment surgery to become a woman, the shy graduate student who uses Paxil to become more outgoing, or the businessman who gets rhinoplasty to make his nose look "less Jewish"? These people are not seeking enhancement so much as self-transformation. What bioethicists call "enhancement technologies" may actually be tools for working on the soul.

The physician-novelist Walker Percy anticipated this thirty years ago. Percy's third novel, *Love in the Ruins,* is about an alcoholic psychiatrist and ex-mental patient named Thomas More. More invents an instrument called The Ontological Lapsometer—or as he calls it, a "stethoscope of the human soul." With the Ontological Lapsometer, More can diagnose and treat existential problems. If patients are alienated or anxious or lonely, a quick temporal lobe massage with the Lapsometer will put them right. And they are not just blissfully anesthetized after a treatment with the Lapsometer. They are fulfilled. They feel like themselves. Their lost and alienated lives have meaning again.

Love in the Ruins was published 15 years prior to the development of antidepressants like Prozac. Yet many of Tom More's patients share the same complaints as today's antidepressant users, and the Ontological Lapsometer works in much the same way. When More uses the language of neurochemistry to describe the spiritual ailments of the late modern age, he sounds very much like the biological psychiatrists who inhabit contemporary university medical centers. Where More speaks of pineal selfhood and red nucleus activity, biological psychiatrists speak of dopamine and serotonin transmission. Where More talks about measuring "perturbations of the soul" through electronic micro-circuitry, biological psychiatrists talk about measuring depression and anxiety with standardized interviews and diagnostic instruments. Where More speaks of a pineal massage with the Ontological Lapsometer, psychiatrists speak of a 6-week course of Selective Serotonin Reuptake Inhibitors. All of which work, at least on occasion. Put a shy, anxious woman on Paxil and she may become outgoing and confident. Put a sexually obsessed man on Celexa and his obsessions may disappear. Give More's alienated patients a pineal massage with the Lapsometer and soon they are back to work, healthy and happy and fulfilled.

If a drug or procedure really does make you feel fulfilled and authentically yourself, what's wrong with that? Perhaps nothing at all. But Percy has a much darker view. At one point Tom More is approached by Art Immelman, who wants to buy the rights to the Lapsometer and market it for the drug industry. He tells More, "Doc, we're dedicated to the freedom of the individual to choose his own destiny and develop his own potential." Art Immelman, of course, is the devil.

In 1971, when *Love in the Ruins* was published, the figure of Art Immelman looked like satire. No longer. Prescription pharmaceuticals have been transformed into items of mass consumption. In 2000, according to the National Institute of Health Care Management, antidepressants were the most profitable class of drugs in America. They are advertised in magazine and web ads with slogans like "The Zoloft Saturday," "Paxil . . . Your life is waiting!" or "I got my playfulness back" with Effexor. Eli Lilly markets ProzacWeekly with cut-out newspaper coupons. A thriving black market for lifestyle drugs has emerged on the Internet, while cosmetic surgery has never been more popular than it is now. ABC even produces a cosmetic surgery reality show called "Extreme Makeover." In 1999, the U.S. pharmaceutical industry spent $13.9 billion in promotions. In 2000, it spent $2.4 billion solely on direct-to-consumer advertising, mainly television ads. This represents a remarkable tenfold increase since 1996. GlaxoSmithKline spent more money advertising Paxil than Nike spent advertising its top shoes.

Yet there is often a striking contrast between private conversation about enhancement technologies and the broader public discussion. In public, for example, everyone seems to be officially anti-Prozac. Feminists ask me why doctors prescribe Prozac more often for women than for men. Undergraduates worry that Prozac might give their classmates a competitive edge. Philosophy professors argue that Prozac would make people shallow and uncreative. Germans object that Prozac is not a natural substance. Americans say that Prozac is a crutch. Most people seem to feel that Prozac is creating some version of what the historian David Rothman called, in a *New Republic* cover story, "shiny, happy people."

In private, though, people have started to seek me out and tell me their Prozac stories. They have tried Prozac and hated it; they have tried Prozac and it changed their life; they have tried Prozac and can't see what the big deal is. It has begun to seem as if everyone I know is on Prozac, or has been on Prozac, or is considering taking Prozac, and all of them want to get my opinion. Most of all, they want me to try Prozac myself. "How can you write about it if you've never even tried it?" I can see their point. Still, it strikes me as a strange way to talk about a prescription drug. These people are oddly insistent. It was as if we were back in high school, and they were trying to get me to smoke a joint.

People who look at America from abroad often marvel at the enthusiasm with which Americans use enhancement technologies. I can see why. It is a jolt to discover the rates at which Americans use Ritalin or Prozac or Botox. But "enthusiasm" is probably the wrong word to describe the way Americans feel about enhancement technologies. If this is enthusiasm, it is the enthusiasm of a diver on the high platform, who has to talk himself into taking the plunge. Unlike Nixon, I don't think that Americans expect happiness in a handful of tablets. We take the tablets, but we brood about it.

We try to hide the tablets from our friends. We worry that taking them is a sign of weakness. We try to convince our friends to take them too. We fret that if we don't take them, others will outshine us. We take the tablets, but they leave a bitter taste in our mouths.

Why? In those tablets are a mix of all the American wishes and lusts and fears: the drive to self-improvement, the search for fulfillment, the desire to show that there are second acts in American lives: yet a mix diluted by nagging anxieties about social conformity, about getting too much too easily, about phoniness and self-deception and shallow pleasure. This is not a story from *Brave New World*. It is not even a story of enhancement. It is a story of flop sweat, sleepless nights and the sting of casual insults. It is less a story about trying to get ahead than about the terror of being left behind, and the humiliation of crossing the finish line dead last, while the crowd points at you and laughs. You can still refuse to use enhancement technologies, of course—you might be the last woman in America who does not dye her gray hair, the last man who refuses to work out at the gym—but even that publicly announces something to other Americans about who you are and what you value. This is all part of the logic of consumer culture. You cannot simply opt out of the system and expect nobody to notice how much you weigh.

THE WAY WE LIVE NOW

Why here, why now? On one level, the answer seems obvious: because the technology has arrived. If you are anxious and lonely and a drug can fix it, why stay anxious and lonely? If you are unhappy with your body and surgery can fix it, why stay unhappy? The market moves to fill a demand for happiness as efficiently as it moves to fill a demand for spark plugs or toggle bolts. It is on a deeper level that the question of enhancement technologies becomes more puzzling. What has made the ground for these technologies so fertile? The sheer variety of technologies on display is remarkable. Some people want their legs lengthened, while others want them amputated. Black folks rub themselves with cream to make their skin lighter, while white folks broil in tanning parlors to make their skin darker. Blushing men get endoscopic surgery to reduce blood flow above the neck, while elderly men take Viagra to increase blood flow below the belt. Each technology has its own rationale, its own cultural niche, a distinct population of users, and an appeal that often waxes or wanes with changes in fashion or the state of scientific knowledge. But do they have

anything in common? Is there anything about the way we live now that helps to explain their popularity?

The "self that struggles to realize itself," as the philosopher Michael Walzer puts it, has become a familiar notion to most people living in the West today. We tend to see ourselves as the managers of life projects that we map out, organize, make choices about, perhaps compare with other possible projects, and ultimately live out to completion. From late adolescence onwards, we are expected to make important decisions about what to do for a living, where to live, whether to marry and have children, all with the sense that these decisions will contribute to the success or failure of our projects. Yet as Walzer points out, there is nothing natural or inevitable about this way of conceptualizing a life. Not everyone in the West today will think of their lives as planned projects, and most people at most times in history have probably thought of their lives differently. Marriages are arranged; educational choices are fixed; gods are tyrannical or absent. A life might be spontaneous, rather than planned; its shape might be given to us, rather than created. The shapes of lives can be determined not by the demands of personal values or self-fulfillment but by those of God, family, social station, caste or one's ancestors.

But we are the inheritors of a cultural tradition, rooted mainly in the 18th century, in which the meaning and significance of a human life have become bound up with our individual identities. Many of us living in the late modern age don't expect to find the meaning of our lives by looking to God, truth or any other external moral framework. And we don't think of our identities as fixed entities, determined by their place in a social hierarchy and ratified by God and nature. We expect (and are expected) to generate an identity for ourselves through the choices we make. A successful life depends on the generation of a successful identity.

Generating an identity is not a purely individual project, of course. Charles Horton Cooley articulated this nicely at the beginning of the twentieth century with his notion of the "looking glass self." As the metaphor suggests. Cooley thought that our sense of ourselves is formed (at least in part) by our social reflection. Cooley thought the looking glass self had three elements: the imagination of the way we appear to others. the imagination of their judgments about us, and some sort of reaction to that judgment—pride if we're lucky, mortification if we're not. Especially interesting to Cooley was the way that the private self was supported by this social reflection. "In the days of witchcraft," Cooley wrote, "it used to be believed that if one person secretly made a waxen image of another and stuck pins in the image, its counterpart would suffer tortures, and that if the image was melted the person would die." So it is with the private self and its social reflection. Dress up the image and the person prospers; melt the image and the person melts as well.

One way to understand enhancement technologies is to see them as representative of two strands of this ethic of individual identity. One strand of this ethic, as Anthony Appiah has observed, we have inherited from romanticism. This strand stresses the importance of self-discovery, or finding oneself. We all have authentic selves, and to live a valuable life we must look inward to discover who we are. The other strand, more familiar from existentialism, stresses the importance of self-creation. We are the sole authors of our lives, and the success or failure of those lives depends on what we make of them. Neither strand is complete, of course. The romantic picture overlooks the role of individual effort and creativity (the self that stands admiringly in front of the looking glass, practicing his smile and styling his hair), while the existential strand overlooks the dependence of the self on the social structures in which it is located (the looking glass itself). But both play familiar parts in the culture of contemporary individualism.

What is striking about the language people use to describe enhancement technologies is not just that they see these technologies as a way to shape their identities, which we might expect from the existentialist picture of the self. They also describe them as a way of finding or revealing their true selves. This description fits more closely with the romantic picture. Even as people undergo the most dramatic transformations imaginable—from wallflower to party girl on Paxil, from bookworm to musclehead on steroids—they describe the transformation as a matter of becoming their true selves. Samuel Fussell, an editor turned bodybuilder, writes that the reason he began taking anabolic steroids was that "I was so uncomfortable not being me." A melancholy divorcee tells psychiatrist Peter Kramer that she only feels like herself on Prozac. NFL running back Ricky Williams tells the press that on Paxil, he can act like "the real Ricky Williams." Amputee wannabes—candidates for healthy limb amputations—often compare themselves to transsexuals who are trapped in the wrong bodies. One person seeking amputation of his healthy leg told a BBC interviewer that his leg "is a wrongness, it's not a part of who I am." In each case, the "true self" is the one produced by medical technology.

Walzer's notion of life as a project suggests both individual responsibility and moral uncertainty. If I am the planner and manager of my life, then I am at least partly responsible for its success or failure. Thus the lure of enhancement technologies: as tools to produce a better, more successful project. Yet if my life is a project, what exactly is the purpose of the project? How do I tell a successful project from a failure? Aristotle (for example) could write confidently about the good life for human beings because he was confident about what the purpose of being a human being was. Just as a knife has a purpose, so human beings have a purpose; just as the qualities that make for a good knife are those that help the knife slice, whittle and chop, the qualities that make a human being better are those that help us better fulfill our purpose as human beings.

Our problem is that most of us don't have Aristotle's confidence about the purpose of human life. Good knives cut, that much we can see, but what does a good human being do, and how will we know when we are doing it? Is there even such a thing as a single, universal human purpose? Not if we believe what we are told by the culture that surrounds us. From philosophy courses and therapy sessions to magazines and movies, we are told that questions of purpose vary from one person to the next: that, in fact, a large part of our life project is to discover our own individual purpose and develop it to its fullest. This leaves us with unanswered questions not just about what kinds of lives are better or worse but about the criteria by which such judgments are made. Is it better to be a successful bail bondsman or a second-rate novelist? On what yardstick do we compare the lives of Reform Jews, high church Episcopalians and California Wiccans? Where exactly should the choices we make about our lives be anchored?

Many people today believe that the success or failure of a life has something to do with the idea of self-fulfillment. We may not know exactly what a successful life is, but we have a pretty good suspicion that it has something to do with being fulfilled—or at the very least, that an unfulfilled life runs the risk of failure. In the name of fulfillment people quit their jobs in human resources and real estate to become poets and potters, leave their dermatology practices to do medical mission work in Bangladesh, even divorce their husbands or wives (the marriage was adequate, but it was not fulfilling). Women leave their children in day care because they believe that they will be more fulfilled with a career: they leave their jobs because they believe that it will be more fulfilling to stay home with the kids. Fulfillment has a strong moral strand to it—many people feel as if they *ought* to pursue a career, that they *ought* to leave a loveless marriage— but its parameters are vague and indeterminate. How exactly do I know if I am fulfilled? Fulfillment looks a little like being in love, a little like a successful spiritual quest; it is a state centered largely on individual psychic well-being. If I am alienated, depressed, or anxious, I can't be completely fulfilled.

If I am not fulfilled, I am missing out on what life can offer. Life is a short, sweet ride, and I am spending it all in the station. The problem is that there is no great, overarching metric for self-fulfillment, no master schedule that we can look up at and say, "Yes, I've missed the train." So we look desperately to experts for instructions—counselors, psychiatrists, advice columnists, self-help writers, life coaches, even professional ethicists. We read the ads on the wall for cosmetic dentistry, and we look nervously at the people standing next to us in line. Does she know something that I don't? Is she more fulfilled? How does my psychic well-being compare to hers?

The very nature of psychic well-being makes these comparisons both relentless and inconclusive. In *The Philosophical Investigations,* Ludwig Wittgenstein imagines a kind of philosophical game. "Suppose everyone had a box with something in it: we call it a 'beetle,'" writes Wittgenstein. "No one can look into anyone else's box, and everyone says he knows what a beetle is by looking only at *his* beetle." It would be quite possible, Wittgenstein points out, for each person to have something different in his box. It would even be possible for the contents of the boxes to be constantly changing. In fact, it would even be possible for all the boxes to be empty—and still the players could successfully use the term "beetle" to talk about the contents of their boxes. There need not be any actual beetles in the boxes for the game to be played.

Wittgenstein's beetle box game makes an important point about the words we use to describe our inner lives—words such as "pain," "depression," "anxiety," "fulfillment" and so on. Like the word "beetle" in Wittgenstein's game, which does not refer to an insect but rather gets its meaning from the rules of the beetle-box game, words such as "depression" or "fulfillment" get their meanings not from the inner mental states they describe, but from the larger context in which they are used. We learn how to use these words not by looking inward and naming what we find there, but by taking part in the game. The players do not all need to be experiencing the same thing in order for the words to make sense. I say I am fulfilled, you say you are fulfilled, we both understand what the other means—yet this does not mean that our inner psychic states are the same. We can all talk about our "beetles" yet all have different things in our boxes.

To see why this matters, imagine a slightly different version of Wittgenstein's beetle-box game. In this version of the game each player still has access only to his or her box, the contents of which are called "beetle." But now some new players can win the game by persuading others that the "beetles" in their boxes are inferior. These players develop an entirely new vocabulary to describe and explain "beetles," the purpose of which is to distinguish between the quality of various "beetles." Because nobody can look into the box of another player, nobody has any way to compare his or her "beetle" to that of another player. But because of what they are being told by the new players, the players now have reason to suspect that their "beetles" could be inferior. So they begin to worry. How does my "beetle" measure up? Is my "beetle" healthy? Would I be happier with a different "beetle"?

The reason the new players in this game can successfully sow the seeds of doubt about "beetles," of course, is the fact that no player can look into another player's box. And this is precisely the reason it is possible to successfully market so many ways of improving psychic well-being, from psychoactive drugs and cosmetic surgery to self-help books and advice columns. If I never know for certain whether the quality of my experience matches up to yours, I am always susceptible to the suggestion that it could be improved. This is why I look so closely at the ads for Paxil and Viagra, read magazine articles about personal fitness and performance anxiety, and scan the shelves at Border's for books about depression, attention deficit disorder and the 12-step method for achieving spiritual success. My inner life could be better; I could be more fulfilled; I could be psychologically healthier, if I could only find the right intervention.

In other times and places, success or failure in a life might have been determined by fixed and agreed-upon standards. You displeased the ancestors; you shamed your family; you did not accept Jesus Christ as your personal savior. You arrived late to the station, and the train left without you. But our situation today is different—not for everyone, of course, but for many of us. We have gotten on the train, but we don't know who is driving it, or where, some point off in the far distance, the tracks are leading. The other passengers are smiling, they look happy, yet underneath this façade of good cheer and philosophical certainty, a demon keeps whispering in our ears: "What if I have gotten it all wrong? What if I have boarded the wrong train?"

Tocqueville hinted at this worry over 150 years ago when he wrote about American "restlessness in the midst of abundance." Behind all the admirable energy of American life Tocqueville saw a kind of grim relentlessness. We build houses to pass our old age, Tocqueville wrote, and then sell them before the roof is on; we clear fields, and then leave it to others to gather the harvest; we take up a profession, and then leave it to take up another one or go into politics. Americans frantically pursue prosperity, and when we finally get it, we are tormented by the worry that we might have gotten it quicker. An American on vacation, Tocqueville marveled, "will travel five hundred miles in a few days as a distraction from his happiness."

Tocqueville may well have been right about American restlessness, but it took another Frenchman, the surrealist painter Phillipe Soupault, to put his finger on the form that it has taken today. According to Soupault, Americans see the pursuit of happiness not just as a right, as the Declaration of Independence states, but as a strange sort of duty. In the United States,

he wrote, "one is always in danger of entrapment by what appears on the surface to be a happy civilization. There is a sort of obligation to be happy." Humans are born to be happy, and if they are not, something has gone wrong. As Soupault puts it, "Whoever is unhappy is suspect." Substitute self-fulfillment for happiness and you get something of the ethic that motivates the desire for enhancement technologies. Once self-fulfillment is hitched to the success of a human life, it comes perilously close to an obligation—not an obligation to God, country or family, but an obligation to the self. We are compelled to pursue fulfillment through enhancement technologies not in order to get ahead of others, but to make sure that we have lived our lives to the fullest. The train has left the station and we don't know where it is going. The least we can do is be sure we are making good time.

Gene Doping:
Will Athletes Go for the Ultimate High?

Christen Brownlee

In 1998, the press jumped on H. Lee Sweeney's first study showing that gene therapy could enhance mouse muscle. Soon, the calls and e-mails started flowing in, first as a trickle, then as if from a fire hose. They're still coming, Sweeney says. Some people beg him to reverse their muscle degeneration caused by disease or aging. However, about half of the calls and e-mails come from healthy individuals—professional power lifters, sprinters, and weekend wannabe athletes of all stripes. They want bigger, higher-performing muscles. One caller offered $100,000 for muscle enhancement, and a high school football coach asked Sweeney to treat his whole team.

The requests from healthy athletes "really caught me off guard," says Sweeney, a physiology professor at the University of Pennsylvania in Philadelphia. His goal had been to stave off the muscle wasting that comes with muscle dystrophy and just plain aging.

Now, Sweeney finds himself in the middle of what could become the sports world's next serious dilemma: Should gene enhancement, or doping, be permissible for athletes attempting to improve their performance? And if not, how can it be prevented?

Gene doping could someday provide extra copies of genes that offer a competitive advantage, such as those that increase muscle mass, blood production, or endurance. The products of gene doping would be

proteins similar, if not identical, to the body's versions and would therefore be less detectable in an athlete than are performance-enhancing drugs such as steroids and insulin. Consequently, rules against gene doping might be difficult to enforce.

Heading off what they see as an inevitable problem for the future, the Montreal-based World Anti-Doping Agency (WADA), which works with Olympic officials to prevent athletes from using performance-boosting drugs, already has banned genetic enhancement.

Some researchers predict that gene doping might become a problem as early as the next summer Olympics, in 2008. "Gene doping is going to happen because technology is going to ripen in the gene therapy setting," says Ted Friedmann, director of the Human Gene Therapy Program at the University of California, San Diego and a consultant for WADA. "Of course, it's going to be too tempting for athletes to avoid."

NATURAL HEALING, BABY

The roots of gene doping lie in gene therapy, the decades-old idea of inserting genes into the body's cells to correct genetic flaws that cause diseases such as juvenile diabetes, hemophilia, and cystic fibrosis. Although simple in concept, gene therapy has been tricky to carry out reliably in patients. Scientists can count only one success: a 2000 study that cured nine French infants of severe combined immune deficiency, also known as "bubble-boy syndrome" (SN: 4/29/00, p. 277: Available to subscribers at http://www.sciencenews.org/articles/20000429/fob3.asp). Even then, two of these patients developed leukemia 2 years later, a mystery that scientists have yet to fully explain.

Some biologists currently are developing new methods to introduce target genes into cells by using electricity, chemicals, or pressure. But for now, researchers typically infect cells with a virus, nature's mastermind at getting foreign genetic material past stringent cellular defenses.

The viruses that scientists have modified for use in gene therapy are vastly different from those that circulate in nature. Researchers pare down the viruses' genetic code, trimming away the genetic material that enables the agents to cause disease. They retain only the genes associated with the proteins making up a virus' outer coat.

Such stripped-down viruses can transform cells into factories that churn out empty shells, "like hollow M&Ms," said James Mason, director of the Gene Therapy Vector Laboratory at the Institute for Medical Research in Long Island, N.Y. Then, researchers paste a human gene—such as one for a blood-clotting protein that a patient lacks—within the virus' remaining genetic sequence to craft a vector that shuttles a therapeutic gene into the patient's cells.

The original idea behind gene therapy was to replace a missing or damaged gene, thereby providing an essential substance that the patient had been lacking. Many scientists have taken this initial concept one step further, says Sweeney. Instead of simply supplying a copy of a missing gene, he and others realized that gene therapy could also fortify muscle, bones, and other tissue at the first signs of disease or aging. This approach could slow the progress of muscle wasting from aging or diseases, such as muscular dystrophy and osteoporosis, he says.

It's not a big technical leap from gene therapy to gene doping. "The sorts of things you'd want to do to help make muscle stronger or repair itself better in a diseased or old person would also make a healthy young person's muscles stronger and repair faster," Sweeney says.

According to Thomas Murray, president of the Hastings Center in Garrison, N.Y., and chairman of WADA's ethics panel, gene doping crosses an ethical line. The traditional draw of athletics, he says, is the combination of an athlete's natural talents with complementary virtues such as determination and discipline.

"What's chilling about the prospect of gene doping is that it arguably changes a person's natural abilities," Murray says. "It violates our understanding of what should make for success in sports."

MIGHTY MICE

When his work attracted athletes' attention, Sweeney had been focused on the problem of muscle-mass depletion that occurs with aging. He and his colleagues had noted that when a protein called insulin growth factor 1, or IGF-1, interacts with cells on the outside of muscle fibers, the muscles grow. The researchers reasoned that if they could insert the gene responsible for making IGF-1 inside muscle cells, those cells would then proliferate and increase the muscle's size.

To test this idea, Sweeney's group injected a virus carrying the gene for IGF-1 into the leg muscles of mice and then monitored the animals. The scientists found that when the mice became senior citizens, at about 20 months of age, the animals retained the muscle strength and speed of their early adult days.

After that promising start, the researchers made an even more startling observation. Young mice injected with the gene grew stronger and more muscular, even without exercise. In a later study, Sweeney noticed that rats' strength could be boosted further by a training regimen in which the animals climbed ladders after weights had been tied to their tails.

The genetic and physiological modifications that led to these "Schwarzenegger mice," as they became known in news reports, could prove intriguing to weight lifters, wrestlers, and other athletes whose sports hinge primarily on strength.

Another set of experiments, by scientists at the Salk Institute in San Diego, produced mouse muscles that just keep going without fatiguing. This result has obvious implications for long-distance swimmers, runners, and others for whom endurance is pivotal. Ronald Evans and his colleagues had started out with the intention of engineering mice that stay trim. To do this, the researchers inserted genes that code for a fat-burning protein called PPAR-delta.

The mice that resulted stayed slender, even when fed a high-fat diet, but also developed an unusually large number of slow-twitch muscle fibers, the type the body relies on during extended exertion. "This change produced the 'marathon mouse,' able to run twice the distance of its normal littermate," Evans says.

Genetic engineering differs from gene therapy in many ways, including that the genetic modifications are passed on to offspring. However, Evans predicts that eventually gene therapy could similarly enhance endurance.

LETHAL LEGACY

Sweeney has developed a stock response to athletes who contact him. "I basically say this is experimental. It's in animals, and even if I had it available to give to humans, it has to go through clinical trials to make sure it's safe," he says.

Ascertaining the safety of gene therapy—and its gene-doping offshoot—couldn't be more important to Jim Wilson, a professor of medicine at the University of Pennsylvania in Philadelphia. He presided over the clinical trial in which 18-year-old Jesse Gelsinger died in 1999 after suffering a massive immune reaction to the virus used to deliver a target gene.

In a recent study designed to test the effectiveness of several viral vectors, Wilson discovered another deadly result. He and his colleagues injected macaque monkeys with different strains of the same virus that carried a gene for making erythropoietin (EPO), a protein that signals bone marrow to produce red blood cells. EPO is manufactured for patients with anemia resulting from kidney failure. It is also used as a doping agent among athletes because with bonus red blood cells, the body can absorb extra power-generating oxygen. Wilson chose EPO because it's easy to detect.

In his experiment, as expected, the high concentrations of EPO produced so many red blood cells that the macaques' blood thickened into sludge. As they had done in previous experiments, the researchers remedied this by drawing blood from the primates at regular intervals to thin the remaining blood enough to circulate properly. But as the experiment wore on, Wilson's team noticed an unusual response in some of the macaques. Rather than remaining at high concentrations, EPO concentrations in these animals' blood plummeted, leading to severe anemia.

After autopsying these monkeys, Wilson and his colleagues came to a troubling conclusion: The animals' immune systems had cleared out not only EPO produced by the inserted gene but also the macaques' natural EPO.

Wilson notes that unpredictable results such as these are common in the field of gene therapy, which is why the strategy is still experimental.

"[Gene therapy's] potential to treat disease is substantial, but we're now in a phase where we're still working on the technology," Wilson says. "We ought to pay attention to these kinds of immune responses not only for EPO but for other kinds of gene therapy." In other words, athletes who try gene doping could find themselves dead rather than in the winners circle.

UNETHICAL ADVANTAGES

Despite the dangers now inherent in gene therapy, some researchers worry that unprincipled scientists will inevitably gene dope unscrupulous athletes. "You have to remember that most of these athletes are very young, in their twenties, and so they have feelings of invincibility," says Olivier Rabin, scientific director of WADA.

The financial reward that accompanies athletic success adds to the incentive to try an untested procedure. "There's so much money in sports today, and when you see what a national title or gold medal around your neck will bring in your life, some are mentally ready to bear the risks," Rabin says.

He reports that, besides working with legislators and athletes, WADA is encouraging scientists to develop tests that could catch gene-doped competitors. Some researchers have feared that because an inserted gene's products can be extremely similar to the body's natural chemicals, routinely snagging rogue athletes could prove impossible. The only way to test for gene doping, some surmised, would be to biopsy muscles or other tissues into which gene vectors had been injected. The biopsy would require a surgical procedure right before competition.

However, a new study published in the September *Molecular Therapy* raises the likelihood that a test might be possible. A team led by Françoise Lasne and Philippe Moullier at the National Anti-Doping Laboratory in Chatenay-Malabry, France, found that monkeys doped with the gene for EPO by muscle injections produced a protein slightly different from their native EPO. These small differences could, in part, underlie the disastrous immune response that Wilson's team observed in some of the macaques in their study.

Although the scientists aren't sure why the doped EPO is different, they suspect that cells in various tissues might not make the same modifications to the protein after it is produced. Kidney cells normally produce EPO, but in response to the gene doping, muscle manufactured it too. Distinctive modifications by these organs eventually might provide a basis for detecting EPO from gene doping.

Someday, says ethicist Murray, gene doping might become widespread and even acceptable in all sports, making such tests unnecessary. But he and other experts don't expect that to happen anytime soon.

"When we think about the meaning of sports, these days, it's about natural talents and virtues," he says. "I can't tell you what your grandchildren and great grandchildren will believe, but I hope that there will still be meaning in perfecting natural abilities."

REFERENCES

Barton-Davis, E.R. and H.L. Sweeney. 1998. Viral mediated expression of insulin-like growth factor I blocks the aging-related loss of skeletal muscle function. *Proceedings of the National Academy of Sciences* 95(Dec. 22): 15603–15607. Available at http://www.pnas.org/cgi/content/full/95/26/15603.

Gao, G. and J.M. Wilson. 2004. Erythropoietin gene therapy leads to autoimmune anemia in macaques. *Blood* 103(May 1): 3300–3302. Abstract available at http://www.bloodjournal.org/cgi/content/abstract/103/9/3300.

Lasne, F., P. Moullier, *et al.* 2004. "Genetic doping" with erythropoietin cDNA in primate muscle is detectable. *Molecular Therapy* 10(September):409–410. Abstract available at http://dx.doi.org/10.1016/j.ymthe.2004.07.024.

Wang, Y.-X. and R.M. Evans. 2004. Regulation of muscle fiber type and running endurance by PPAR-delta. *PLOS Biology* 2(October): 1532–1539. Available at http://dx.doi.org/10.1371/journal.pbio.0020294.

STEM CELLS

Declaration on the Production and the Scientific and Therapeutic Use of Human Embryonic Stem Cells

Pontifical Academy for Life

. . .

Given the nature of this article, the key ethical problems implied by these new technologies are presented briefly, with an indication of the responses which emerge from a careful consideration of the human subject from the moment of conception. It is this consideration which underlies the position affirmed and put forth by the Magisterium of the Church.

The *first ethical problem,* which is fundamental, can be formulated thus: *Is it morally licit to produce and/or use living human embryos for the preparation of ES cells?*

The answer is negative, for the following reasons:

1. On the basis of a complete biological analysis, the living human embryo is—from the moment of the union of the gametes—a *human subject* with a well defined identity, which from that point begins its own *coordinated, continuous and gradual development,* such that at no later stage can it be considered as a simple mass of cells.

2. From this it follows that as a "*human individual*" it has the *right* to its own life; and therefore every intervention which is not in favour of the embryo is an act which violates that right. Moral theology has always taught that in the case of "*jus certum tertii*" the system of probabilism does not apply.

3. Therefore, the ablation of the inner cell mass (ICM) of the blastocyst, which critically and irremediably damages the human embryo, curtailing its development, is a *gravely immoral* act and consequently is *gravely illicit.*

4. *No end believed to be good,* such as the use of stem cells for the preparation of other differentiated cells to be used in what look to be promising therapeutic procedures, *can justify an intervention of this kind.* A good end does not make right an action which in itself is wrong.

5. For Catholics, this position is explicitly confirmed by the Magisterium of the Church which, in the Encyclical *Evangelium Vitae,* with reference to the Instruction *Donum Vitae* of the Congregation for the Doctrine of the Faith, affirms: "The Church has always taught and continues to teach that the result of human procreation, from the first moment of its existence, must be guaranteed that unconditional respect which is morally due to the human being in his or her totality and unity in body and spirit: The human being is to be respected and treated as a person from the moment of conception; and therefore from that same moment his rights as a person must be recognized, among which in the first place is the inviolable right of every innocent human being to life."

The *second ethical problem* can be formulated thus: *Is it morally licit to engage in so-called "therapeutic cloning"*

Pontifical Academy for Life. "Declaration on the Production and the Scientific and Therapeutic Use of Human Embryonic Stem Cells," Vatican City, August 25, 2000. Reprinted by permission of The Pontifical Academy for Life.

by producing cloned human embryos and then destroying them in order to produce ES cells?

The answer is negative, for the following reason: Every type of therapeutic cloning, which implies producing human embryos and then destroying them in order to obtain stem cells, is illicit; for there is present the ethical problem examined above, which can only be answered in the negative.

The **third ethical problem** can be formulated thus: *Is it morally licit to use ES cells, and the differentiated cells obtained from them, which are supplied by other researchers or are commercially obtainable?*

The answer is negative, since: prescinding from the participation—formal or otherwise—in the morally illicit intention of the principal agent, the case in question entails a proximate material cooperation in the production and manipulation of human embryos on the part of those producing or supplying them.

In conclusion, it is not hard to see the seriousness and gravity of the ethical problem posed by the desire to extend to the field of human research the production and/or use of human embryos, even from an humanitarian perspective.

The possibility, now confirmed, of using **adult stem cells** to attain the same goals as would be sought with embryonic stem cells—even if many further steps in both areas are necessary before clear and conclusive results are obtained—indicates that adult stem cells represent a more reasonable and human method for making correct and sound progress in this new field of research and in the therapeutic applications which it promises. These applications are undoubtedly a source of great hope for a significant number of suffering people.

Morals and Primordials

Louis M. Guenin

What may we do with a human embryo? On this moral question hinges the fate of embryonic stem cell research. To defeat such research, opponents appeal to the premise that killing an embryo is always wrong. Before we may pronounce the verdict of any moral view—including our own—we must look beyond slogans and ascertain that view's fundamental principles. Thereafter comes the task of identifying and rigorously scrutinizing arguments. Upon close study of principles and arguments, it becomes plain that embryonic stem cell research gains moral approval even within views that might be presumed to oppose such research.

Embryonic stem cells are derived from blastocysts at about day 5 of gestation, the window of opportunity for obtaining pluripotent cells that can be grown without differentiating. Let us define as an "epidosembryo" (after the Greek *epidosis* for a beneficence to the common weal) a human embryo that (i) was created in vitro in an assisted reproduction procedure, (ii) remained in storage after completion of all intrauterine transfers requested by the mother, and (iii) has departed parental control according to instructions to the attending physician that the embryo shall be given to research and that there shall not occur any transfer to a uterus, or ex vivo nurture beyond a number of weeks specified in the instructions, of either the embryo or any totipotent cell taken from the embryo. Let us assume that we owe great respect to any human embryo and to any possible person into which an embryo may develop. For the reasons explained below, I claim that experiments with epidosembryos are permissible at least for embryos that are less than 2 weeks old.

The argument for epidosembryo research is as follows. Outside a uterus, an embryo cannot long survive. When a fertility patient decides against intrauterine transfer of an embryo, that embryo's developmental potential fails of enablement. Donor instructions governing an epidosembryo allow nothing but research. Hence no possible person corresponds to an epidosembryo. Nor has the epidosembryo preferences that could be frustrated or sentience by which it could suffer. Nothing can be gained for an epidosembryo by arranging that it perish as waste rather than perish in aid of others. We have a duty, when our means allow, to aid those who suffer. If we spurn epidosembryo research, not one more baby is likely to be born. If we conduct research, we may relieve suffering. Therefore epidosembryo research is permissible and praiseworthy. Such research includes studies of embryos themselves, from which we may learn how birth defects occur, and studies of stem cells with their distinctive therapeutic promise.

Epidosembryo donors turn statistical accident to good. Fertility clinicians recover and fertilize about a dozen eggs per patient; given the mortality rate of fertilized eggs (zygotes), any fewer fertilizations would fail to optimize chances of pregnancy. Once a patient has given birth to all the children that she wants, unused embryos usually perish as waste. (Under U.K. law, an embryo ordinarily may be stored for only 5 years.) Whereas if given to research, a single embryo will yield a cell line long sustaining a stem cell investigator's work.

The foregoing argument differs from the utilitarian argument with which scientists often defend embryonic stem cell research. Utilitarianism commands us to maximize the sum of individual utilities. A utilitarian may predict greater aggregate utility from performing research than from forgoing it. This argument may convince confirmed utilitarians who imagine a calculation of aggregate utility, but doubtless only them. In the absence of interpersonally comparable utility measures, we cannot meaningfully sum utilities across a population. Given intense preferences about an issue of life and death, we cannot put much store in a computational argument that lacks the computation. For many nonutilitarians, paramount moral principles supersede the maximization of any welfare index.

I now turn to two presumptive opponents of embryo research. We shall find that these views, when fully assembled, support epidosembryo research. Less strict views not mentioned below also join in support of such research. According to the views within this broad universe of support, if a government thwarts epidosembryo research, it does a disservice to the cause of morality.

The first presumptive opponent is Kantianism. That each of us possesses a dignity above price is an intellectual legacy from Kant. According to Kant, we should never treat humanity simply as a means, but always as an end. Embryo experimentation uses embryos solely as means. But for Kant, the basis of dignity is autonomous reason; humanity includes only rational beings. Embryos are not rational. In general, Kant holds that as rational beings we should act on those maxims that, without contradicting ourselves, we can will as universal laws. That a woman may decide against intrauterine transfer and donate an epidosembryo is such a universalizable maxim. We also have a duty of beneficence. We cannot decline to will that aid be given those in need if we wish it to be given us should we be in need. As soon as we imagine ourselves in the place of those who suffer in ways that epidosembryo research could prevent, we are impelled to the universalizable maxim that we should foster that research. This implies a duty to foster such research.

The second presumptive opponent is Catholicism. The Greeks and Romans routinely killed slaves and barbarians; the Spartans abandoned infants to the elements. Against these and later assaults, the Catholic church has championed human life. Against abortion the church now asserts two doctrines: (i) the sanctity of life, the belief that human life is a sacred gift of God that we must respect, and (ii) zygotic personhood, the thesis that fertilization suffices to create a new person. Held inconsistent with the sanctity of life are destruction of embryos and (as departures from God's manner of giving life and as a path to eugenics) in vitro fertilization, intrauterine transfer, and embryo cryopreservation. Given that in vitro fertilizations nonetheless occur, we must decide what to do with epidosembryos. It seems difficult to deny that relieving widespread suffering is morally better than destroying embryos at no gain. One who opposes abortion may further promote life by endorsing research on epidosembryos. Donors of epidosembryos give fresh voice to esteem for life.

Zygotic personhood, which does collide with embryo research, is an implausible contradiction of the Catholic church's magisterium for most of its history. Until 1869, the church followed Aristotle's view that not until at least day 40 does an embryo develop sufficient human form to acquire an intellectual soul, that which distinguishes human from beast (*Historia Animalium* 583b). Until then, said Aquinas, "conception is not completed." Aristotle believed that form and matter correspond, a view known as "hylomorphism," from which it follows that a being without a brain cannot house an intellectual soul. Hence the wrongfulness of abortion was said to vary with time of gestation. Pope Innocent III in 1211 settled on quickening (at 12 to 16 weeks) as the time of ensoulment. In 1869, Pope Pius IX, without mentioning time of gestation, listed those procuring abortions among the excommunicated. This was read to imply zygotic personhood. Recently in *Donum Vitae* (1987), the church has conceded that personhood is a philosophical question, and so we search its texts for an argument for zygotic personhood. Scripture is silent. We find in *Declarato de Abortu Procurato* (1974) that the church argues for zygotic personhood by identifying a person with a genome. But the magisterium cannot maintain this materialist thesis, this radical genetic reductionism, without contradicting its belief in mind and soul. And even for materialists, only a being capable of consciousness can be a person for purposes of the duty not to kill.

In any case, the matter comes to rest on one necessary condition of personhood. Until day 14, the possibility of monozygotic twinning (and recombination) remains. That is, until day 14, identity of an individual is not established. "No entity," said the philosopher W. V. Quine, "without identity."

At the foundation of Christianity lies the second greatest of the commandments—that one love one's neighbor as oneself—as well as the Golden Rule, a form of which appears in virtually every moral view since Confucius, and the call to charity. These precepts require us to imagine ourselves possessing the preferences of those who suffer. Concerning medicine, the Catholic church teaches in *Declarato de Abortu Procurato* that "in the outpouring of Christian generosity and charity every form of assistance should be developed."

Many moral views also urge justice in the distribution of resources. To exclude publicly funded scientists from embryonic stem cell research serves only to constrain progress while privatizing it. If we give away the public store by abstaining from public research, we may wake up to find patentees controlling most of the transplantable cell types. The poor will likely be the losers. And if the government does not permit public scientists to derive cells, we may be forsaking, for no moral gain, the benefit of innovations in cell derivation.

We honor human life by probing our moral views to their foundations. There we find a common conclusion. It is virtuous to eliminate suffering in actual lives when we may do so at no cost in potential lives. In this work of mercy, scientists form the vanguard. They also respect human life who toil to relieve its afflictions.

Alternative Sources of Stem Cells

Bonnie Steinbock

Embryonic stem cell research pits the promise of curing devastating diseases and saving lives against the destruction of human life at its earliest stages. To circumvent this moral dilemma, the President's Council on Bioethics recently published a white paper, *Alternative Sources of Human Pluripotent Stem Cells,*[1] that examines four ways human pluripotent cells might be derived without killing human embryos.

The effort to find such alternatives demonstrates a welcome recognition of the potential benefit of ESC research—sometimes dismissed as mere "hype" by its opponents. The White Paper is no "white wash": the scientific and ethical obstacles to finding acceptable alternatives are clearly laid out, and the diversity of opinion among the Council members is honestly acknowledged. Given the deep moral or religious opposition to destroying human embryos, the attempt to find alternative sources of human pluripotent cells is clearly worthwhile. The question, however, remains: can this be done, and at what cost?

DERIVING STEM CELLS FROM DEAD EMBRYOS

The first proposal is based on an analogy with organ donation: just as it is ethically acceptable to remove organs from no-longer-living developed human beings, it should be equally acceptable to remove stem cells from no-longer-living human embryos. Using the traditional definition of death as the irreversible loss of the integrated functioning of an organism as a whole, Donald Landry and Howard Zucker of the Columbia University College of Physicians and Surgeons suggested in a proposal to the council that the embryo is properly considered "organismically dead" when it has irreversibly lost the capacity for continued and integrated cellular division, growth, and differentiation.

A central question raised by the proposal and taken up in the white paper is whether the concept of organismic death—the death of an organism as a whole—can meaningfully be applied to organisms at the very beginning of life, when they are composed of a few undifferentiated cells. Moreover, even if the concept can be applied, determining that an embryo has died is more difficult than it is for an adult. An embryo has no integrating organs: no brain to be "brain-dead," no heart to cease beating and circulating blood. The problem is compounded by the fact that, in order for stem cells to be derived, the arrested embryos must contain at least some viable cells that retain normal developmental potential and that can be induced to resume dividing. But if these cells can resume dividing under certain conditions, has the embryo in fact died?

Janet Rowley, a member of the President's Council, raises a different objection. She notes that part of the proposal involves observing thawed IVF embryos to see which ones have undergone spontaneous cleavage arrest and are thus "organismically dead." However, not all the thawed embryos will be dead; about half will continue to grow and divide. What will happen to these healthy embryos? They will be allowed to die while "scientists struggle to recoup a few living cells from the dead embryos!" She finds "totally baffling" the notion that it is ethically sound to let healthy embryos die rather than use them to try to develop cell lines that could benefit sick and dying patients.

NONHARMFUL BIOPSY

The second proposal is based on the idea that stem cell lines might be derived from single cells extracted from early embryos in ways that do not destroy the embryo, which could then be used for reproduction. The impetus for this proposal comes from preimplantation genetic diagnosis, in which one or two cells are removed from an embryo created through IVF. (The cells are then tested for genetic disease.) More than 1,000 babies have been born worldwide after PGD, with apparently no ill effects. However, in the absence of long-term safety studies, it is not possible to determine conclusively that embryo biopsy is safe for the future child.

The justification for PGD, with its unknown long-term risks, is that it enables at-risk couples to have their own biological child free from a specific genetic disease. By contrast, in this proposal, a healthy embryo would be subjected to biopsy procedures to extract stem cells for research. The President's Council concluded that we should not impose risks on living embryos destined to become children for the sake of getting stem cells for research. And even if the biopsied embryo and the resulting child were not physically harmed, the council suggested that there might be a strong moral argument against biopsy on the grounds that the embryo is being treated merely as a means to another's ends.

There are several objections that could be made here. First, it could be argued that the embryo is being treated merely as a means to another's ends in both PGD and embryonic stem cell research. In embryo biopsy for the purpose of PGD, the purpose of the procedure is to further the reproductive goals of the prospective parents. In embryo biopsy for the derivation of stem cells, the purpose is to further the scientific goals of researchers and society as a whole. If one is ethically acceptable, why not the other? Second, what is the moral objection to subjecting the embryo to biopsy if there is no physical risk either to the embryo or to the future child? On this line of argument, it would be unacceptable ever to use children in research that posed no risk to them, which seems implausible. Finally, one may question whether the Kantian prohibition against treating other persons merely as means to one's ends can be applied to very early embryos. To treat other persons as "ends in themselves" is to take their ends—that is, their interests, goals, and projects—seriously. I would argue that undifferentiated clusters of a few cells do not have interests, goals, or projects, and thus cannot be the subjects of Kantian respect for persons. Of course, some argue that embryos do have interests. Since the embryo is the same individual as the person into which it develops, it therefore has *that* individual's interests. However, prior to the development of the primitive streak (the precursor of the nervous system), the embryo can become two or more people, making any identification between the early embryo and the later person impossible. Moreover, even if the later person and the embryo are one and the same individual, this identification is possible only if there is or could be a later person. This is not the case for nonviable IVF embryos and probably not for cloned embryos.[2]

ALTERED NUCLEAR TRANSPLANTATION

The third proposal comes from William Hurlbut, a member of the President's Council, who proposes creating a "biological artifact," lacking the moral status of a human embryo, from which pluripotent stem cells could be derived. He points out that sometimes in natural reproduction, an embryo cannot develop due to the lack of certain essential elements. Hurlbut's proposal attempts to mimic these natural examples using a technique he calls "altered nuclear transfer." ANT is based on the technique of somatic cell nuclear transfer—cloning—with one modification: some developmental genes in the somatic cell nucleus would be silenced prior to transfer to the enucleated oocyte. To ensure that the stem cells taken from the artifact were usable, the missing genes would be reinserted after the cells were extracted.

Since ANT is as yet untested experimentally (even in animals), no one knows whether it would work. Somatic cell nuclear transfer has proven difficult enough; *altered* nuclear transfer, which inserts a defective nucleus into the egg cell, seems likely to be still harder. ANT is complex, technically challenging, and not even testable without time-consuming experiments involving substantial investment of precious resources. As a result, it could set back the progress of embryonic stem cell research considerably. As Michael Gazzaniga, also a member of the President's Council, expressed it in an appendix to the White Paper: "Why delay what we know works with this sideshow?" Another source of opposition comes from those who think it is unethical to create embryo-like entities and then intentionally modify them to prevent them from developing into human embryos. Robert Lanza of Advanced Cell Technologies told *Science* magazine, "I think this is an abuse of cloning technology. It will be a sad day when scientists use genetic manipulation to deliberately create crippled embryos to please the Church."[3]

DEDIFFERENTIATION

The fourth proposal is to reprogram differentiated somatic cells so as to restore to them the pluripotency of ES cells. Whether this could work is anyone's guess: new scientific advances and technological innovation would be needed. The council found this to be ethically the most attractive proposal because it involves neither the creation nor the destruction of human embryos. Individual somatic cells have no special moral status, nor would they if they were returned to a pluripotent stage. However, a potential ethical problem looms if the technique returned the cells beyond pluripotency to totipotency. Since a totipotent cell can develop into a complete organism, it could be considered an embryo.

In his appendix, Michael Gazzaniga describes the distinction between pluripotent and totipotent cells as arbitrary. He writes, "Winding the clock back on a developed somatic cell and to stop it at a critical point is supposed to be void of ethical issues while letting a cell grow forward to just before the same point as with SCNT is not ethical?" This objection presumably means that there is no ethical difference between stopping the dedifferentiation process before the cell can become an embryo, on the one hand, and creating a cloned embryo and then destroying it, on the other. However, for those who think that the human embryo has a special moral status, the difference is like that between birth control (which prevents cells from forming a human being) and abortion (which kills an existing human being).

If it were easy to come up with an alternative source of ES cells, there would be no question that this should be done, if only for political reasons. However, an easy alternative is not on the horizon; there are serious scientific and ethical objections to all four proposals. The question is whether it is ethically imperative to overcome these objections. That question in turn depends on the moral status of the very early embryo. If these few undifferentiated cells are people, like you or me, then research that kills them cannot be justified, no matter how promising. But are they people? Most Americans, from a variety of ethical and religious traditions, do not view them this way. In light of this, there seems little reason why costly, technically challenging, and time-consuming proposals to find alternatives must be pursued, especially when their pursuit may delay potentially lifesaving research.

NOTES

1. The President's Council on Bioethics, *Alternative Sources of Human Pluripotent Stem Cells* (Washington, D.C.: President's Council on Bioethics, 2005).

2. See R. Jaenisch, "Human Cloning: The Science and Ethics of Nuclear Transplantation," *New England Journal of Medicine* 351 (2004): 2787–91.

3. C. Holden and G. Vogel, "Cell Biology: A Technical Fix for an Ethical Bind?" *Science* 306 (2004): 2174–76, at 2174.

HUMAN CLONING

Cloning of Human Beings

Leon R. Kass

Mr. Chairman, Members of the Commission.

I am deeply grateful for the opportunity to present some of my thoughts about the ethics of human cloning, by which I mean precisely—the production of cloned human beings. This topic has occupied me off and on for over 30 years; it was the subject of one of my first publications in bioethics 25 years ago. Since that time, we have in some sense been softened up to the idea of human cloning—through movies, cartoons, jokes, and intermittent commentary in the mass media, occasionally serious, more often lighthearted. We have become accustomed to new practices in human reproduction—in vitro fertilization, embryo manipulation, and surrogate pregnancy—and, in animal biotechnology, to transgenic animals and a burgeoning science of genetic engineering. Changes in the broader culture

Kass, Leon. "Cloning of Human Beings," Testimony presented to the National Bioethics Advisory Commission, March 14, 1997, Washington, D.C.

make it now more difficult to express a common, respectful understanding of sexuality, procreation, nascent life, and the meaning of motherhood, fatherhood, and the links between the generations. In a world whose once-given natural boundaries are blurred by technological change and whose moral boundaries are seemingly up for grabs, it is, I believe, much more difficult than it once was to make persuasive the still compelling case against human cloning. As Raskolnikov put it, "Man gets used to everything—the beast!"

Therefore, the first thing of which I want to persuade you is not to be complacent about what is here at issue. Human cloning, though in some respects continuous with previous reproductive technologies, also represents something radically new, both in itself and in its easily foreseeable consequences. The stakes here are very high indeed. Let me exaggerate, but in the direction of the truth: You have been asked to give advice on nothing less than whether human procreation is going to remain human, whether children are going to be made rather than begotten, and whether it is a good thing, humanly speaking, to say yes to the road which leads (at best) to the dehumanized rationality of Brave New World. If I could persuade you of nothing else, it would be this: What we have here is not business as usual, to be fretted about for a while but finally to be given our seal of approval, not least because it appears to be inevitable. Rise to the occasion, address the subject in all its profundity, and advise as if the future of our humanity may hang in the balance.

"Offensive." "Grotesque." "Revolting." "Repugnant." "Repulsive." These are the words most commonly heard these days regarding the prospect of human cloning. Such reactions one hears both from the man or woman in the street and from the intellectuals, from believers and atheists, from humanists and scientists. Even Dolly's creator, Dr. Wilmot, has said he "would find it offensive" to clone a human being. People are repelled by many aspects of human cloning: The prospect of mass production of human beings, with large clones of lookalikes, compromised in their individuality; the idea of father-son or mother-daughter twins; the bizarre prospects of a woman giving birth to a genetic copy of herself, her spouse, or even her deceased father or mother; the creation of embryonic genetic duplicates of oneself, to be frozen away in case of later need for homologous organ transplantation; the narcissism of those who would clone themselves, the arrogance of others who think they know who deserves to be cloned or which genotype any child-to-be should be thrilled to receive; the Frankensteinian hubris to create human life and increasingly to control its destiny; man playing at being God. Almost no one

sees any compelling reason for human cloning; almost everyone anticipates its possible misuses and abuses. Many feel oppressed by the sense that there is nothing we can do to prevent it from happening. This makes the prospect all the more revolting.

Revulsion is surely not an argument, and some of yesterday's repugnances are today calmly accepted. But in crucial cases, repugnance is often the emotional bearer of deep wisdom, beyond reason's power fully to articulate it. Can anyone really give an argument fully adequate to the horror which is father-daughter incest (even with consent) or having sex with animals or eating human flesh, or even just raping or murdering another human being? Would anyone's failure to give full rational justification for his revulsion at these practices make that revulsion ethically suspect? Not at all. In my view, our repugnance at human cloning belongs in this category. We are repelled by the prospect of cloning human beings not because of the strangeness or novelty of the undertaking, but because we intuit and feel, immediately and without argument, the violation of things we rightfully hold dear. I doubt very much whether I can give the proper rational voice to this horror, but in the remarks that follow I will try. But please consider seriously that this may be one of those instances about which the heart has its reasons that reason cannot adequately know.

I will raise four kinds of objections: the ethics of experimentation; identity and individuality; fabrication and manufacture; despotism and the violation of what it means to have children.

First, any attempt to clone a human being would constitute an unethical experiment upon the resulting child-to-be. As the animal experiments indicate, there is grave risk of mishaps and deformities. Moreover, one cannot presume a future cloned child's consent to be a clone, even a healthy one. Thus, we cannot ethically get to know even whether or not human cloning is feasible.

I understand, of course, the philosophical difficulty of trying to compare life with defects against nonexistence. But common sense tells us that it is irrelevant. It is surely true that people can harm and even maim children in the very act of conceiving them, say, by paternal transmission of the HIV virus or maternal transmission of heroin dependence. To do so intentionally, or even negligently, is inexcusable and clearly unethical.

Second, cloning creates serious issues of identity and individuality. The cloned person may experience concerns about his distinctive identity not only because he will be in genotype and appearance identical to another human being, but, in this case, it will be to a twin who might be his "father" or "mother"—if one can still call them that. What would be the psychic burdens of being the "child" or "parent" of your twin? Moreover, the cloned individual will be saddled with a genotype that has already lived. He will not be fully a surprise to the world: people are likely always to compare his performances in life with that of his alter ego. True, his nurture and circumstance in life will be different; genotype is not exactly destiny. But one must also expect parental and other efforts to shape this new life after the original—or at least to view the child with the original version firmly in mind. For why else did they clone from the star basketball player, mathematician, and beauty queen—or even dear old Dad—in the first place?

Genetic distinctiveness not only symbolizes the uniqueness of each human life and the independence of its parents that each human child rightfully attains. It can also be an important support for living a worthy and dignified life. Such arguments apply with great force to any large-scale replication of human individuals. But they are, in my view, sufficient to rebut even the first attempts to clone a human being. One must never forget that these are human beings upon whom our eugenic or merely playful fantasies are to be enacted.

Third, human cloning would represent a giant step toward turning begetting into making, procreation into manufacture (literally, something "hand made"), a process already begun with in vitro fertilization and genetic testing of embryos. With cloning, not only is the process in hand, but the total genetic blueprint of the cloned individual is selected and determined by the human artisans. To be sure, subsequent development is still according to natural processes; and the resulting children will still be recognizably human. But we here would be taking a major step into making man himself simply another one of the man-made things. Human nature becomes merely the last part of nature to succumb to the technological project, which turns all of nature into raw material at human disposal, to be homogenized by our rationalized technique according to the subjective prejudices of the day.

How does begetting differ from making? In natural procreation, we two human beings come together, complementarily male and female, to give existence to another being who is formed, exactly as we were, by what we are—living, hence perishable, hence aspiringly erotic human beings. But in clonal reproduction, and in the more advanced forms of manufacture to which it leads, we give existence to a being not by what we are but by what we intend and design. As with any product of our making, no matter how excellent, the artificer stands above it, not as an equal but as a superior, transcending it by his will and creative prowess. Scientists who clone

animals make it perfectly clear that they are engaged in instrumental making; the animals are, from the start, designed as means to serve rational human purpose. In human cloning, scientists and prospective "parents" would be adopting the same technocratic mentality to human children: human children would be their artifacts. Such an arrangement is profoundly dehumanizing, no matter how good the product. Mass-scale cloning of the same individual makes the point vividly; but the violation of human equality, freedom, and dignity are present even in a single planned clone.

Finally, and perhaps most important, the practice of human cloning by nuclear transfer—like other anticipated forms of genetic engineering of the next generation—would enshrine and aggravate a profound and mischief-making misunderstanding of the meaning of having children and of the parent-child relationship. When a couple now chooses to procreate, the partners are saying yes to the emergence of new life in its novelty, are saying yes not only to having a child but also, tacitly, to having whatever child this child turns out to be. Whether we know it or not, we are thereby also saying yes to our own finitude and mortality, to the necessity of our replacement and the limits of our control. In this ubiquitous way of nature, to say yes to the future by procreating means precisely that we are relinquishing our grip, even as we thereby take up our own share in what we hope will be the immortality of human life and the human species. This means that our children are not our children: They are not our property, they are not our possessions. Neither are they supposed to live our lives for us, or anyone else's life but their own. To be sure, we seek to guide them on their way, imparting to them not just life but nurture, love, and a way of life; to be sure, they bear our hopes that they will surpass us in goodness and happiness, enabling us in small measure to transcend our own limitations. But their genetic distinctiveness and independence is the natural foreshadowing of the deep truth that they have their own and never-before-enacted life to live. Though sprung from a past, they take an uncharted course into the future.

Much mischief is already done by parents who try to live vicariously through their children; children are sometimes compelled to fulfill the broken dreams of unhappy parents; John Doe, Jr. or the III is under the burden of having to live up to his forebear's name. But in cloning, such overbearing parents take at the start a decisive step which contradicts the entire meaning of the open and forward-looking nature of parent-child relations. The child is given a genotype that has already lived, with full expectation that this blueprint of a past life ought to be controlling of the life that is to come.

Cloning is inherently despotic, for it seeks to make one's children or someone else's children after one's own image (or an image of one's choosing) and their future according to one's will. In some cases, the despotism may be mild and benevolent, in others, mischievous and downright tyrannical. But despotism—the control of another through one's will—it will unavoidably be.

What then should we do? We should declare human cloning deeply unethical in itself and dangerous in its likely consequences. In so doing, we shall have the backing of the overwhelming majority not only of our fellow Americans, but of the human race—including, I believe, most practicing scientists. Next, we should do all that we can to prevent human cloning from happening, by an international legal ban if possible, by a unilateral national ban, at a minimum. Scientists can, of course, secretly undertake to violate such a law, but they will at least be deterred by not being able to stand up proudly to claim the credit for their technological bravado and success. Such a ban on human cloning will not harm the progress of basic genetic science and technology; on the contrary, it will reassure the public that scientists are happy to proceed without violating the deep ethical norms and intuitions of the human community.

The President has given this Commission a glorious opportunity. In a truly unprecedented way, you can strike a blow for the human control of the technological project, for wisdom, prudence, and human dignity. The prospect of human cloning, so repulsive to contemplate, in fact provides the occasion—as well as the urgent necessity—of deciding whether we shall be slaves of unregulated progress, and ultimately its artifacts, or whether we shall remain free human beings who guide our technique toward the enhancement of human dignity. To seize the occasion, we—you—must, as the late Paul Ramsey said, "raise the ethical questions with a serious and not a frivolous conscience. A man of frivolous conscience announces that there are ethical quandaries ahead that we must urgently consider before the future catches up with us. By this he often means that we need to devise a new ethics that will provide the rationalization for doing in the future what men are bound to do because of new actions and interventions science will have made possible. In contrast a man of serious conscience means to say in raising urgent ethical questions that there may be some things that men should never do. The good things that men do can be made complete only by the things they refuse to do."

Reproductive Cloning Combined with Genetic Modification

C. Strong

It has been argued that the use of cloning by infertile couples to have genetically related children would be ethically justifiable.[1] It has also been suggested that lesbian or gay couples might wish to use cloning as a way to have genetically related children.[2] This article explores the ethics of using cloning combined with genetic modification to produce genetically related children. A caveat should be stated at the outset, however. Cloning research in animals has shown that a high percentage of cloned embryos do not successfully implant or gestate, presumably because of genetic abnormalities. There have also been reports of cloned animal fetuses and offspring with serious congenital malformations.[3] Clearly, the risks to offspring constitute a conclusive argument against human reproductive cloning at this time. In the future, however, it is possible that our technology will permit cloning with no more risk to offspring than that involved in natural procreation. For the sake of argument, let us assume that cloning technology has advanced to that point, opening the way to address other pros and cons

of human reproductive cloning. Similarly, developing the technology to perform genetic modifications safely in humans is likely to be difficult. Whether the complications involved can be overcome remains uncertain. Nevertheless, there is no good reason to rule out the possibility that, given enough time, researchers will surmount the obstacles.

It could be objected that cloning combined with genetic modification is too speculative and futuristic to deserve our attention. In reply, this objection overlooks the fact that currently there is a vigorous worldwide debate on the ethics of human cloning. It is relevant to that ongoing debate to argue, as I shall do in this article, that technological advances in cloning and genetic modification can thoroughly undermine many of the main objections to human reproductive cloning. Discussing futuristic scenarios can be worth while when doing so casts new light on current debates.

Most of the main objections to human reproductive cloning are based on the claim that these children would lack genetic uniqueness. It is alleged that this would harm the children,[4,5] fail to treat them with respect,[6–8] harm society,[6,9] and violate human dignity.[10] In response, it has been argued that it is a mistake to believe that children who have the same nuclear DNA as someone else will lack uniqueness.[11] For one thing, the imprinting of a child's DNA could differ from that of his or her progenitor (the person who is the source of his or her nuclear DNA), resulting in phenotypic differences even though they have the same nuclear DNA.[12] Even if the imprinting is the same, the child will be exposed to different uterine and social environments compared with the progenitor.[13,14] Divergent social environments are expected to result in different attitudes, goals, and life choices. Moreover, cloning does not duplicate the brain. As the brain develops in a growing child, neural connections are made in response to environmental stimuli. Different stimuli result in different patterns of connections.[15,16] The child's brain will vary in many ways from that of the progenitor.

Despite these persuasive arguments, opponents of cloning continue to put forward the objections based on lack of uniqueness. An example is Leon Kass and the President's Council on Bioethics, who have continued to propound these objections even after the publication of the responses mentioned above.[5,11,13–16] Although it seems reasonable to hold that these challenges by Kass and others have been met satisfactorily, it is possible to put forward additional considerations against their objections based on lack of uniqueness. Specifically, it can be pointed out that in the future it may be possible to combine cloning with genetic modification so that the child would have a unique set of nuclear genes. Scientific advances may enable us to add and delete genes in an individual human cell. Let us again assume, for the sake of argument, that such modifications could be carried out safely. Cloning could be performed using a cell nucleus from one member of an infertile couple. This could be followed by gene replacements in the preembryo, giving the child characteristics different from the parent whose nucleus was used. Alternatively, gene replacements could be carried out on the cell nucleus prior to cloning. Examples of modifications could include changes in hair colour, eye colour, or skin complexion. Health related changes could also be made, such as replacing genes that cause infertility or susceptibilities to disease. The modifications need not involve attempts at non-disease genetic enhancement, such as improved intelligence or increased height, but could have as their primary aim the creation of a genetically related child with a unique set of nuclear genes. In this type of scenario, the objection based on lack of uniqueness would

no longer be applicable. Not only would there be phenotypic uniqueness, which presumably would be present even if there were identical nuclear DNA, but there would also be nuclear DNA uniqueness. The child would not be a clone, but the techniques used would include the cloning of cells, presumably by somatic cell nuclear transfer. In this article, I consider the ethical permissibility of using cloning combined with genetic modification to create genetically related children when this frequent objection to cloning is taken out of the picture.

Another possible feature of the envisioned scenario is that the genetic modification could aim to give the child a nuclear DNA relationship to both members of an infertile couple. The member of the couple whose cell nucleus is used for cloning would contribute most of the genes that the child would have. The genetic modifications that would accompany the cloning could aim to duplicate certain selected genetic characteristics of the other member of the couple, such as hair or eye colour. The child would possess nuclear genetic characteristics of both parents. The use of cloning combined with genetic modification could therefore be attractive to some infertile couples because it would enable both members to have a nuclear DNA relationship to the child.

Given the assumption that genetic modification is possible, it could be asked whether the future infertility cases we are considering could be cured by gene therapy. If so, there would be no need for cloning as a method for helping infertile couples to have genetically related children. In reply, if gene therapy for infertility were possible, some couples would probably prefer that approach. However, not all causes of infertility will be remediable by adding or deleting genes. Some couples are infertile because the woman's ovaries have been surgically removed; for others, advancing age diminishes the capacity of ova to become fertilised. Non-genetic factors such as environmental toxins, radiation, or testicular trauma are believed to be responsible for some cases of infertility.[17–19] Other cases could be multifactorial, with both genetic and environmental causes. Moreover, there may be a period in the future when gene insertion and deletion is possible, but not all of the genetic causes of infertility are known. Putting aside infertility cases, there would still be an issue concerning the use of cloning and genetic modification to allow lesbian and gay couples to have genetically related children.

Whether cloning combined with genetic modification in the scenarios being considered is ethically justifiable involves the following question: which has greater weight, the procreative freedom of couples in these scenarios, or the arguments against cloning combined with genetic modification? First I shall address this question in the context of infertile couples, and then consider the issue as it relates to lesbian and gay couples.

INFERTILE COUPLES

Why should the freedom of infertile couples to use cloning and genetic modification be valued? Given that the main reason under consideration for using such technology is to have genetically related children, we need to ask what reasons can be given to value the having of genetically related children. A strategy for exploring this question is to consider reasons that can be given for valuing genetically related children in the ordinary scenario in which couples beget by sexual intercourse and raise the children who are born. There is widespread agreement that procreative freedom in this ordinary scenario deserves respect and protection. If reasons for valuing freedom to procreate in the ordinary scenario are also applicable to the freedom to have genetically related children by cloning combined with genetic modification, that would constitute an important reason to respect freedom in the latter scenario.

Elsewhere I identified a number of reasons worthy of consideration that help to explain why persons find it meaningful to have genetically related children in the ordinary scenario.[20] Because I have discussed these reasons in detail, including the application of several of them to cloning without genetic modification,[1] I shall not repeat these here. Rather, I shall comment briefly on the applicability of these reasons to cloning combined with genetic modification. It will suffice to focus on two of the reasons. First, having a genetic child in the ordinary scenario may be valued by some, in part, because it involves participation in the creation of a child. Similarly, in the case of cloning and genetic modification, one can envision several ways in which both members of an infertile couple could participate in the creation of a child. The member who provides a cell nucleus for cloning would participate by contributing most of the genes for the child. This would involve a physical transfer in which chromosomes from that person's body would be in the initial pre-embryonic cell of the offspring. Moreover, the genetic modifications could aim to duplicate some of the nuclear genes of the other member of the couple, thereby allowing that member to participate genetically in the creation of the child. Although this may not involve the physical transfer of this member's genes, there would still be a genetic connection in the sense that certain chosen genes would be duplicated. Those genes would be identified, perhaps sequenced, and this information would be

used in carrying out the genetic modification. In addition, regardless of whose cell nucleus is used for nuclear transfer, if the woman is capable of producing ova, she could have a genetic connection by providing mitochondrial DNA to the child. Moreover, if she is capable of gestating, she could participate by gestating and giving birth to the child.

Secondly, having genetic children in the ordinary scenario could be meaningful to a couple in part because they regard it as an affirmation of mutual love and acceptance. It can be a deep expression of acceptance to say to another, in effect: "I want your genes to contribute to the genetic makeup of my child." In such a context, there may be an anticipation that the bond between the couple will grow stronger because of children in common to whom each has a genetic relationship. A similar affirmation of mutual love is possible when combining cloning and genetic modification. The couple create a child who has genetic characteristics of both members. Although infertility denies them the ability to contribute equally to the genetic makeup of the child, at least they have a method by which each can make a genetic contribution. In addition, when the man's cell nucleus is used and the woman gestates, the child comes forth from their two bodies.

In discussing these reasons, I do not mean to imply that one ought to desire genetic offspring, or that one ought to desire cloning combined with genetic modification as a way to have genetically related children. Rather, the point is that the desire for genetic children—and hence the desire for cloning combined with genetic alteration in the scenarios being considered—could be supported by reasons that deserve consideration. Although not everyone in the infertile couple's situation would want to pursue these methods, some might. These reasons help to explain why the freedom to use cloning combined with genetic modification to create a child with a genetic relationship to both members should be valued.

OBJECTIONS TO CLONING COMBINED WITH GENETIC MODIFICATION

In the type of scenario we are considering, the objection based on lack of genetic uniqueness does not apply. However, there are other objections that could be raised against cloning combined with genetic modification.

High genetic similarity to one parent

An objection could focus on the fact that the child would be very similar genetically to the parent whose cell nucleus is used. Because of this close genetic similarity, there could be a tendency for that parent's life to be regarded as a standard to be met or exceeded by the child. If the child feels pressured to accept that standard, this may be a significant impediment to freedom in directing his or her own life.

In reply, this objection is similar to that to cloning based on lack of uniqueness, in that it is based on the view that genes determine who we are. As I argued above, even if there is identical nuclear DNA, one would expect significant differences between the child and the progenitor because of environmental influences. Similarly, when there is less than full duplication of genes, one would expect important differences. Moreover, parents' lives are often held up as standards, even in the absence of cloning and genetic modification. This can be either bad or good for a child, depending on how it is handled. It has the potential to inhibit as well as to promote development of the child's talents, abilities, and autonomy. Similarly, giving a role model or standard to a child created through cloning combined with genetic modification is not necessarily bad. It depends on how the standard is regarded and used by the parents. If it is used in a loving and nurturing manner, it can help children to develop their autonomy, rather than inhibit it.

If there is a concern that some parents could have rigid expectations concerning what their child should accomplish, or might otherwise set inappropriate standards, this topic could be addressed in preconception counselling. Psychological counselling is already widely accepted in preparing infertile couples for various non-coital reproductive methods, such as surrogate motherhood and donor insemination. Couples planning to use cloning combined with genetic modification could be counselled about the psychological dimensions of this method of procreation, including a possible tendency to assume, erroneously, that a close genetic similarity will determine the life path that the child will follow.

Objectification of children

Another objection is that cloning combined with genetic modification would transform babymaking into a process similar to manufacturing. Children would become products made according to specification. This would objectify children and adversely affect parental attitudes toward children and other aspects of parent–child relationships.[21,22] This argument arises from reflection on what it would be like if there were a widespread practice of designing the genetic characteristics of our children. The designing envisioned includes enhancing offspring's non-disease characteristics, such as height, intelligence, and body build; it is especially these types of genetic manipulations that raise concerns about undesirable changes in the attitudes and expectations of parents toward their children.

However, a reply can be made. Although these are important concerns, their bearing on the cases being considered is at best indirect. These cases do not involve efforts to enhance non-disease characteristics. They do not aim to make the child smarter, taller, stronger, or faster. Rather they aim to create a child who is genetically related to both members of a couple and who has unique genes. Thus, the concerns expressed above that are specific to trying to improve the child's abilities do not directly apply. The claim that the genetic modification in question would objectify the child is also weakened by the fact that a purpose of the modification is to give the child his or her own unique set of nuclear genes.

It could be objected that permitting genetic modification to create a child who is genetically related and genetically unique would set a precedent for other types of genetic modifications, including enhancement of non-disease characteristics. If we permit the former, it could be argued, it becomes more difficult to prevent the latter. One can reply to this objection without taking a position on the desirability of permitting enhancement of non-disease characteristics. The reply need only point out that, as the objection assumes, we can distinguish between cases that involve enhancement of non-disease characteristics and those that do not. Given that we can make this distinction, we can adopt policies that deal with these various types of genetic modification in different ways, if we choose to do so. If there were a plausible concern that a widespread practice of genetic non-disease enhancement would be harmful, there would be a middle ground that could be taken. Cloning combined with genetic modification could be restricted to a relatively small number of cases, such as those in which these techniques are the only way to produce genetically related children. In addition, the modifications could be restricted, if it were reasonably considered important to do so, to those that aim to give the child unique nuclear DNA and a genetic relationship to both members of a couple.

LESBIAN COUPLES

It has been suggested that lesbian couples might want to use cloning to have children.[2] Cloning could be attractive to some lesbian couples because it avoids third-party collaboration. Some might prefer to avoid the social complications that can arise when a semen donor who is known to them is involved; and some may prefer not to use anonymous semen donors because the child might later desire to meet the genetic father, a desire that could not be fulfilled. Taking it a step further, cloning combined with genetic modification could be requested by some lesbian couples because it not only avoids the use of sperm donors but permits them to have a child who has genetic characteristics of both of them and who has a unique set of nuclear genes.

Most of the reasons that make procreation meaningful to heterosexual couples in the ordinary scenario would be applicable to the use of cloning combined with genetic modification by lesbian couples. For example, this technique would permit the couple to participate more fully in the creation of a person. One member of the couple could provide the nuclear genes, and the other could provide the ovum with its associated mitochondrial genes. Genetic modification could duplicate selected genes of the member who does not provide the cell nucleus. Either member could participate by gestating and giving birth to the child. The fact that both members contribute genes to the child could also be meaningful to the couple as an affirmation of mutual love and acceptance.

The objections that have been raised against reproductive cloning combined with genetic modification, which were discussed above, could be raised in the context of such procreative methods being used by lesbian couples. However, the responses that were discussed above would again be applicable, and therefore the objections are also unsuccessful in this context.

Putting aside concerns about cloning, some have objected to any type of assisted reproduction for lesbian couples. One issue is that children raised in lesbian households will become homosexual themselves. Other versions of the objection claim that these children would be harmed by various factors associated with being raised by lesbians, including social stigma, the lack of a male role model, and the lower incomes of women compared with men. In reply, several points can be made. First, the objection makes the mistake of assuming that being homosexual is inherently harmful, as opposed to being a condition in which harms arise because of the prejudices of others. This assumption seems itself to reflect a prejudice against homosexuals. Secondly, the claim that the children produced would have an increased tendency to become homosexual is not confirmed by the evidence. A number of studies have supported the conclusion that there is no increased incidence of homosexuality in children raised by lesbians in comparison with children raised in heterosexual households.[23,24] Thirdly, even if the various purported harms were to happen, it would be a mistake to think that their likely occurrence would make it unethical to create the child. The problem is that the objection focuses exclusively on harms to the child, without consideration of benefits to the child. It makes this mistake because it overlooks the fact that without the procreation in question the child would not exist. If one holds that lesbians bringing a child into existence can harm the child, then one must also hold that lesbians bringing a child into being can benefit the child. It would be arbitrary to make one claim but deny the other. In assessing this objection, we need to consider the benefits as well as the harms. There would be benefits; after all, the procreation would give the child a life. Life generally is a good thing. Presumably the child would have many good experiences associated with being alive, and it is reasonable to expect that the benefits are going to outweigh the harms—that the child would have a good life on balance. If the child benefits on balance, then no wrong is done in creating him or her, at least as far as harms and benefits are concerned.

Perhaps it will be objected that procreation by lesbians is wrong because some harms will occur to the child, although admittedly not a net harm. However, the assertion that it is wrong to create children who will experience harms, although not a net harm, leads to unacceptable conclusions. We would have to say, for example, that it is wrong for fertile minority couples who are subject to discrimination to have children because the children would suffer harms caused by discrimination. Surely, this would be an incorrect conclusion. The objection amounts to saying that it is wrong to reproduce when some ideal of freedom from harm cannot be satisfied. However, there is no obligation to have children only if their lives will be free from harm, as this counterexample illustrates.

GAY COUPLES

It has been pointed out that gay couples might wish to use cloning as a means of having children.[2] However, the main arguments that have been put forward supporting the ethical permissibility of infertile couples and lesbian couples using cloning without genetic modification would not be applicable to gay couples. Those arguments rest on the fact that there are scenarios in which the aims of cloning by infertile and lesbian couples would be to have a child who is genetically related to one member of the couple and to avoid third-party collaborative repro-duction.[1,25] For gay couples, it would be possible to cre-ate a child genetically related to one member by means other than cloning, assuming individual fertility. For example, sperm from one of the men could be combined with a donor egg, and a resulting pre-embryo could be implanted in a woman willing to bear the child. The avail-ability of this alternative raises the question of why a gay couple would want to use cloning. The reason could not be to avoid third-party collaborative reproduction because that is not possible; cloning a gay man would require an ovum donor and a surrogate mother. Therefore, the pur-pose of cloning without genetic modification, in the case of gay couples, would not be to have a child who is genet-ically related to one member of the couple while avoid-ing third-party collaborative reproduction.

When cloning is combined with genetic modifica-tion, however, a new rationale becomes available for gay couples—to have a child who shares genetic char-acteristics of both members of the couple. Several of the reasons that make procreation meaningful to het-erosexual couples in the ordinary scenario would apply to the use of cloning combined with genetic modifica-tion by gay couples. It would enable both members to participate in the creation of a person. One member would provide nuclear genes and genetic modifications could duplicate selected genes of the other member. Creating a child with genetic similarities to both could also be meaningful to a couple as an expression of mutual love and acceptance. In addition, this would be a means towards the experiences of child rearing. These considerations suggest that the reproductive free-dom of gay couples to use cloning combined with genetic modification deserves respect because it can be based on some of the same reasons that make repro-ductive freedom generally worth protecting. The objec-tions to lesbian couples having children could also be raised against gay couples having children. However, those objections again fail, for the same reasons.

CONCLUSION

In conclusion, I have argued that cloning combined with certain types of genetic modifications can be eth-ically justifiable when carried out by infertile, lesbian, or gay couples as a means to have children with a genetic relationship to both members of the couple. My focus on these types of cases should not be taken to imply that there are no other types of scenario in which cloning combined with genetic modification would be ethically justifiable.

REFERENCES

1. Strong C. Cloning and infertility. *Camb Q Healthc Ethics* 1998;**7:**279–93.
2. Murphy T. Entitlement to cloning. *Camb Q Healthc Ethics* 1999;**8:**364–8.
3. National Academy of Sciences. *Scientific and medical aspects of human reproductive cloning.* Washington, DC: National Academy Press, 2002:11–12,39–42.
4. Holm S. A life in the shadow: one reason why we should not clone humans. *Camb Q Healthc Ethics* 1998;**7:**160–2.
5. President's Council on Bioethics. Human cloning and human dignity: an ethical inquiry. Washington, DC, 2002:102–4, 110–11, http://www.bioethics.gov (accessed 30 Mar 2005).
6. National Bioethics Advisory Commission. Cloning human beings. Rockville, MD, 1997:66–72. http://www.georgetown.edu/research/nrcbl/nbac/pubs.html (accessed 30 Mar 2005).
7. Williamson R. Human reproductive cloning is unethical because it undermines autonomy: commentary on Savulescu. *J Med Ethics* 1999;**25:**96–7.
8. Shuster E. Human cloning: category, dignity, and the role of bioethics. *Bioethics* 2003;**17:**517–25.
9. Massey JB, Slayden S, Shapiro DM, *et al.* Unnatural deeds do breed unnatural troubles (Macbeth: Act v, Scene 1) [letter]. *Fertil Steril* 2001;**76:**1083–4.
10. Häyry M. Philosophical arguments for and against human reproductive cloning. *Bioethics* 2003;**17:**447–59.
11. Lewontin R. The confusion over cloning. In: McGee G, ed. *The human cloning debate.* Berkeley, CA: Berkeley Hills Books, 2000:154–69.
12. Simpson JL. Toward scientific discussion of human reproduc-tive cloning. *Reprod Biomed Online* 2003;**7:**10–11.
13. Gould SJ. Dolly's fashion and Louis's passion. In: Pence GE, ed. *Flesh of my flesh: the ethics of cloning humans.* Lanham, MD: Rowman and Littlefield, 1998:101–10.
14. Harris J. *Clones, genes, and immortality.* Oxford: Oxford University Press, 1998:27–8.
15. Eisenberg L. Would cloned humans really be like sheep? *N Engl J Med* 1999;**340:**471–5.
16. Johnson G. Soul searching. In: Nussbaum MC, Sunstein CR, eds. *Clones and clones: facts and fantasies about human cloning.* New York, NY: Norton, 1998:67–70.
17. Kenkel S, Rolf C, Nieschlag E. Occupational risks for male fer-tility: an analysis of patients attending a tertiary referral centre. *Int J Androl* 2001;**24:**318–26.
18. Howell S, Shalet S. Fertility preservation and management of gonadal failure associated with lymphoma therapy. *Curr Oncol Rep* 2002;**4:**443–52.
19. Nolten WE, Vioska SP, Korenman SG, *et al.* Association of ele-vated estradiol with remote testicular trauma in young infertile men. *Fertil Steril* 1994;**62:**143–9.
20. Strong C. *Ethics in reproductive and perinatal medicine: a new frame-work.* New Haven, CT: Yale University Press, 1997:18–22.
21. Botkin JR. Prenatal screening: professional standards and the limits of parental choice. *Obstet Gynecol* 1990;**75:**875–80.
22. Strong C. Tomorrow's prenatal genetic testing: should we test for "minor" diseases? *Arch Fam Med* 1993;**2:**1187–93.
23. Tasker F, Golombok S. Adults raised as children in lesbian fam-ilies. *Am J Orthopsychiatry* 1995;**65:**203–15.
24. Golombok S, Spencer A, Rutter M. Children in lesbian and sin-gle-parent households: psychosexual and psychiatric appraisal. *J Child Psychol Psychiatry* 1983;**24:**551–72.
25. Strong C. Clone alone. *Camb Q Healthc Ethics* 2002;**11:**76–82.

Chapter 8

Organ Donation and Transplantation

"To Remember Me"

The day will come when my body will lie upon a white sheet neatly tucked under four corners of a mattress located in a hospital; busily occupied with the living and the dying. At a certain moment a doctor will determine that my brain has ceased to function and that, for all intents and purposes, my life has stopped.

When that happens, do not attempt to instill artificial life into my body by the use of a machine. And don't call this my deathbed. Let it be called the bed of life, and let my body be taken from it to help others lead fuller lives.

Give my sight to the man who has never seen a sunrise, a baby's face or love in the eyes of a woman.

Give my heart to a person whose own heart has caused nothing but endless days of pain.

Give my blood to the teenager who was pulled from the wreckage of his car, so that he might live to see his grandchildren play.

Give my kidneys to the one who depends on a machine to exist from week to week.

Take my bones, every muscle, every fiber and nerve in my body and find a way to make a crippled child walk.

Explore every corner of my brain.

Take my cells, if necessary, and let them grow so that, someday a speechless boy will shout at the crack of a bat and a deaf girl will hear the sound of rain against her window.

Burn what is left of me and scatter the ashes to the winds to help the flowers grow.

If you must bury something, let it be my faults, my weakness and all prejudice against my fellow man.

Give my sins to the devil.

Give my soul to God.

If, by chance, you wish to remember me, do it with a kind deed or word to someone who needs you. If you do all I have asked, I will live forever.

Robert N. Test[1]

"To Remember Me" by Robert Noel Test, 1976.

The narrator of the poem views his death as a chance to further the lives of others. He reminds us of the many ways that the bodies of the dead can give life and improve life for those who are incapacitated and suffering. But how should we think about the organs that we collect from donors and give to recipients? Are they products, commodities, gifts, possessions, society's resources, or something else? The poem reminds us that organs become available for transplant usually because someone has died. While one family rejoices in the availability of the heart, another grieves for the one who no longer needs the heart. Inevitably, discussions about the transplantation of organs take place in the context of a community, where some people have resources, organs, tissues, and so on, and other people need those resources.

The poem also highlights how valuable these transplantable organs are. Each organ for transplant is truly a prize; he or she who obtains it receives the "gift of life." Many of those who wait for an organ die before one becomes available. Who should be the lucky recipients—those who can pay for it, those who have waited the longest for it, those who are citizens of the country where the organ becomes available, those who have been chosen by the donor or the donor's family, or others for different reasons?

Several points must be noted before turning to moral problems related to the transplantation of organs. First, there are various types of organs and tissues that can be donated. Some of them can be donated by a **living donor** (kidney, liver lobe, lung lobe, etc.) whereas others can only come from a **dead donor** (heart, lungs, pancreas, etc.). Some body parts that can be donated are renewable resources, such as sperm and blood. Others, such as kidneys and liver lobes, are nonrenewable organs. As we think about the morality of harvesting organs, we should expect that different kinds of moral considerations will be required depending on whether we are referring to easily given, renewable blood or bone marrow donations, more invasive kidney donations, or heart donations from deceased donors. Second, one of the scientific facts that used to drive any discussion of organ transplantation was the risk that the patient's body might treat the transplanted organ as foreign material and so reject it. Hence, organs from close relatives were more successfully transplanted. In the last few years, there have been vast improvements in immunosuppressive drugs and thus the risk of rejection has been reduced. But "matching factors" are still important considerations. There are also concerns about the long-term side effects of the immunosuppressive drugs, so these risks must be measured. Finally, in most countries, including the United States, it is illegal to sell organs. In Iran, however, it is legal to sell a kidney.[2] A 2007 report from the World Health Organization lists the following countries as places where kidneys are reportedly sold: Bolivia, Brazil, Iraq, Israel, Peru, the Republic of Moldova, and Turkey.[3] Although India banned organ sales in 1994, the Voluntary Health Association of India estimates that about 2,000 Indians sell a kidney every year (Figure 8.1).[4]

The first successful organ transplant took place in 1954. It was a kidney transplant between identical twins and it was performed by Dr. Joseph Murray at Peter Bent Brigham Hospital in Massachusetts.[5] The first successful heart transplant was performed in 1967 by Dr. Christiaan Barnard in South Africa. The recipient lived 18 days. In a 1968 heart transplant, the recipient lived 19 months and Mrs. Dorothy Fisher, who received a heart transplant in 1969, was Barnard's longest surviving recipient, living 24 years with the transplanted heart.[6]

In the United States, the policies regarding organ transplantation, including organ matching and placement, are developed and carried out by the **United Network for Organ Sharing (UNOS).** In May 2008, there were 99,134 candidates on the waiting lists for organs. In 2007, 28,355 transplants took place and 14,399 people were donors.[7] These numbers show that many more people need organ transplants than receive them because there are simply not enough donors.

Other issues related to organ transplantation are raised by the following statistics from the American Heart Association.[8] In 2006, there were 2,192 heart transplants performed in the United States. As the graph shows, the majority of these heart transplant patients were male (74.2%) and most of them were also white (68.4%) (Figure 8.2). Perhaps there are medical or scientific reasons why most heart transplants go to white men—reasons related to diagnosis, prognosis, matching factors, size of donor heart, and so on, but there may also be social reasons such as insurance coverage, access to appropriate care, or discrimination.

In this chapter, the readings focus on issues pertaining to scarcity and **allocation,** the acquisition of organs, the topic of living donors, and the allocation of organs. That is, we consider how and from

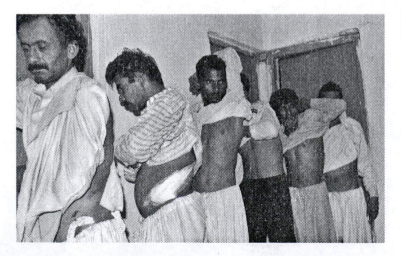

FIGURE 8.1 Men in Pakistan who have sold their kidneys.

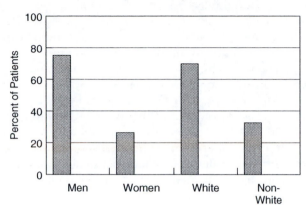

U.S. Heart Transplant Patients

FIGURE 8.2   Chart of U.S. heart transplants.

whom organs for transplant should be collected and how and to whom organs for transplant should be distributed. Here is a case that raises both types of issues.

CASE STUDY: WILFRED'S DILEMMA

Wilfred is a 35-year-old machinist who was forced to take medical retirement last year when he was diagnosed with polycystic kidney disease. At the time he knew nothing about the disease. It is a genetic disease that one of Wilfred's biological parents must have suffered from, however, because Wilfred was adopted as an infant, he never knew them.

Wilfred's condition has worsened and he needs a kidney transplant. His physician has added Wilfred's name to the waiting list at the regional organ bank. It is unclear how quickly he will get a kidney.

Meanwhile, Wilfred has been searching for his biological parents, in part to determine whether he has any siblings who might be willing to donate a healthy kidney to him.

A friend has also talked to Wilfred about the possibility of obtaining a kidney overseas where people who have money can obtain organs more easily. According to the friend, there are good hospitals in other countries where one can receive an organ transplant for a fraction of the cost of the same transplant in the United States. Wilfred believes that he has enough money and is strong enough to travel. He has made contact online with a hospital in Iran willing to perform the transplant.

On the other hand, Wilfred's adoptive parents are opposed to his search for his biological siblings. They think that the time is not right, it is too emotionally burdensome, for Wilfred to discover his biological family now when he is so ill. They think that since no siblings have reached out to Wilfred before that he is going to suffer greatly in discovering either that he has no siblings or that they will not donate an organ to him.

Wilfred's physician is opposed to the idea of having the transplant done overseas. He is worried about the quality of care, the support system available to the patient, and the burdens of international travel.

SCARCITY OF RESOURCES

Any discussion of scarce resources takes place in the context of the principle or value of justice. While other values are also relevant—for example, autonomy and beneficence—it is justice that is most central. Justice concerns what is owed or deserved, what a person has a moral claim or right to, or fairness. Justice is at issue both when we acquire organs for transplant and when we make decisions about who will receive the collected organs. Some ways of acquiring organs may be unjust, for example, kidnapping people and forcibly taking their organs. These unjust methods of acquiring organs may of course also violate other values such as respect for persons, autonomy, and nonmaleficence. In considering how to justly pass out organs to recipients, we are concerned with what is called **distributive justice.** Distributive justice has to do with the allocation or passing out of resources, of society's benefits and burdens. So welfare benefits are passed out to certain citizens just as are tax burdens. Some principle of justice must be adopted that determines who deserves to receive the benefits and who must shoulder the burdens. Issues of distributive justice are especially pressing when resources are limited. If there is not enough of the social benefit to distribute it equally to all, then inevitably there are questions regarding who should receive the benefit. When the benefit is life-saving, the fact that not all can be provided with the benefit is tragic. Minimally, it is crucial to adopt the best possible—that is, the morally best—principle of justice.

Moral theories recommend different principles of distribution. For utilitarian theory, a just allocation of resources means focusing on bringing about the greatest good for the greatest number of people. It looks at outcomes and would likely award organ transplants to the people who would benefit most from the organs or those who if saved would probably benefit others or society. Deontological theories, such as Kant's, emphasize the dignity of each and every person and their right not to be treated as simply a means to another's end. Such a theory would probably favor a more egalitarian system of distributing limited resources, such as a lottery or a waiting list. Care theories that put relationships first might prefer a system that allows individuals to decide for themselves to whom to give their organs and tissues. This disagreement about how to proceed justly in allocating organs brings us back to one of our earlier questions. Should organs be classified as society's resources or as individuals' personal possessions?

There is no simple answer to this question. Individual countries and the world community as a whole have struggled with how to best handle scarce medical resources. Moral considerations are important—respect for persons, efforts to benefit others, and the fair treatment of all persons. But practical considerations count as well—for example, who can pay for the scarce resource or necessary procedures and who is lucky enough to find a willing donor. The policies governing the acquisition and distribution of scarce organs have changed over time and will continue to change as our technological abilities improve and as we assess the consequences of our current policies.

ACQUIRING ORGANS

Abstract questions about scarce resources and just policies do not help Wilfred. He of course wants to live and to do that he needs a kidney. As a U.S. citizen, he has two main, but not exclusive, choices. He can have his name added to a waiting list (or several waiting lists) and be patient until a kidney becomes available from a dead or living donor. Or, he can take a more active approach and pursue a living donor transplant. To find a living donor, he can ask his relatives or friends to consider donating a kidney to him, he can advertise to find a willing donor, or he can travel to a foreign country where kidneys are more readily available (Figure 8.3). In our case, Wilfred is pursuing both options, although both choices raise some ethical concerns.

Consider first the "dead donor" option. Under the umbrella of UNOS, there are 63 regional organ banks that handle the work of educating the public about organ donation, collecting organs, and maintaining waiting lists for organs. A person with a medical need for an organ is added to the waiting list and advances up the waiting list as those before him get organs, die, or are no longer good candidates for transplants. In addition to "seniority," time spent on the waiting list, other factors count as well, such as matching factors (blood type, antigen). Extra points, which move a person up the waiting list, are also assigned to children and to those who have donated an organ.[9]

FIGURE 8.3   Billboard sign looking for a liver donor.

This waiting list system takes into account beneficence (who would benefit most from the organ) and equality (all are subject to the same criteria and wait their turn). But still several kinds of ethical concerns arise. One such concern is that patients may obtain organs more quickly in some areas of the country than in others. Patients have also found that it is possible to be enrolled on multiple waiting lists. This may increase their odds of getting an organ. But this requires mobility and the financial resources to travel and to have several doctors in different locations. The waiting list system may thus privilege those who live in certain geographical areas or those with resources. Finally, given the earlier statistic on how many heart transplant recipients are male and white, people question whether there is equal access to the waiting list. Are all patients treated equally in being considered for organs?

Wilfred might decide instead to try to find a living donor himself. At least it offers the promise of quicker access to a kidney. He can perhaps track down his biological relatives or appeal to friends to donate. Even if his family members or friends are not good matches for him, a hospital may be able to construct a **"paired exchange."** Here Wilfred's friend or family member donates to another patient while that patient's friend or family member donates to Wilfred. On the other hand, some people in Wilfred's situation have put their appeal for an organ on a billboard or presented it on a talk show television program. Others have used a private website, MatchingDonors.com, to post their stories and to wait for donors to step forward. In 2004, Bob Hickey was the first to receive a kidney transplant from a donor, Robert Smitty, in a match that was worked out on the Internet (Figure 8.4).

Wilfred has a number of choices to make in his pursuit of a kidney. He may not be considering all of the moral issues related to these choices, but we ought to consider them. The readings to follow will consider these and more. We need many more organs than we currently have and one way to address this is to find a way to increase the supply of organs. Perhaps we could pay people for their organs (but then are we preying on the poor, exerting undue pressure, or commodifying people?). Or, we could offer financial incentives such as forgiveness of medical expenses or tax benefits to those who donate (but doesn't this still target those of modest means and lead us to think of human body parts as "things"?). We could assume that people are willing to donate their organs ("presumed consent") unless they explicitly refuse to donate (but does this violate their autonomy?). A new method for retrieving organs, known as the **Pittsburgh protocol,** allows that patients (or their representatives) who have decided to withdraw life support systems can be approached for consent to having their organs removed once their hearts stop beating. These

FIGURE 8.4   Bob Hickey and Robert Smitty.

"non-heart-beating donors" have their organs taken at least 2 minutes after their hearts have ceased beating (the Institute of Medicine recommends waiting 5 minutes), even though they may not be brain-dead yet (but does this violate nonmaleficence by rushing their deaths?). Another controversial procedure involves administering drugs that preserve organs to patients who die in the emergency room or while being transported to the hospital. This gives the medical team more time to approach the family for permission to take the organs (but does it violate the patient's dignity by treating her as a means to another's good?).

ALLOCATING ORGANS

In the early 1960s the first effective kidney dialysis machines became available. In Seattle, Washington, Swedish Hospital agreed to cover the cost of the treatments for the first patients. Many more people applied to receive treatment than there were machines available. So began what came to be known as the "God Committee." This committee, composed of seven laypeople assisted by two physicians, deliberated and decided who would receive the life-saving treatment. Because there were no medical alternatives at the time, they decided who would have a chance at a longer life and who would die. Assuming that many applicants had an equal need for dialysis—they would die without it—the question is then what other criteria count in deciding who to save. Should married people be saved over single people, people with "important" jobs over people with "ordinary" jobs, or should names be chosen by chance or lottery? This issue of how to spend scarce medical resources such as organs forces us to assess how we weigh individual human lives.

In at least one way the work of the "God Committee" was unusual. In the beginning, it did not have to factor in financial considerations. In reality, in a society where some people have insurance or can otherwise pay for their medical treatment while others cannot, it is impossible to distribute scarce organs without some consideration of financial consequences. But even apart from financial factors, in order to allocate organs we must think about "differences."

Some people are old; some are young. Some are smokers or alcoholics while others are not. Some of those who need organs are requesting a second transplant while others are awaiting their first transplant. The problem is in deciding what differences are relevant, that is, what differences count. Is it "ageism" (akin to racism and sexism) if younger people are preferred for transplants over older people, or can we all agree that use of the "age" difference is justified?

In 1987, Daniel Callahan in *Setting Limits* argued for the idea of a "natural lifespan." Medical resources should be used to enable people to achieve this natural lifespan, but beyond that no one has a right to expect or demand their lives be saved. In part his argument for an age criterion is financial, based on the excessive costs of medical care for the very elderly. But in part his argument is also philosophical. A society should spend the bulk of its resources in enabling people to achieve this natural lifespan. Once a person has accomplished that they only have the right to basic health care or to health care aimed at the relief of suffering.

In 1995, baseball legend Mickey Mantle, a recovered alcoholic, received a liver transplant after only a day or two on the waiting list. This decision was later defended based on his medical need and on priority given to regional candidates. Critics worried about whether his celebrity status was a factor, whether recovered alcoholics ought to have the same chance to receive a liver as nonalcoholics, and whether local candidates should be preferred over more distant candidates. In 1998 the Department of Health and Human Services mandated that liver transplants must be allocated nationally, not regionally. While this system ensures equal access to the organ, some have voiced that it may compromise organ donation programs in that people are especially motivated to donate when they can help their neighbors or address local needs for organs.

Finally, since organs and tissues are donated by individuals or their surrogates, there is the value of autonomy to consider. Autonomy concerns can affect not only the acquisition of organs but also the distribution of organs. **Directed donation** occurs when an organ donor specifies to whom the organ will go. This kind of allocating may bypass the national waiting list system. As we said earlier in Wilfred's case, he may seek out a willing donor who directs that Wilfred be the one to receive his organ. Often this is a good thing—when, for instance, a family member is willing to donate to a relative or a neighbor to a friend. But there may be some negative consequences in allowing donors to handpick who gets their organs. For example, it may be that if Wilfred's friend picks Wilfred to receive his kidney, he has acted contrary to justice and utility. Others on the waiting list may need his kidney more than Wilfred and may be better matches for it. Wilfred's friend may allow his familiarity with Wilfred to cloud whatever duty he may have to act fairly and realize the greatest good. Also, if it is his autonomy as a donor that reigns supreme in these transactions, then would it be acceptable for him to insist that his organs go only to white people or only to men? We might come across a potential donor who wants to pick the future recipient of her organs based on certain characteristics, such as race, gender, age, or lifestyle choices. Does a donor have the right to make choices that others might consider racist, sexist, or unjust?

As you can see, there are still many moral questions pertaining to organ transplantation that are unresolved. The readings explore these issues further.

Looking Ahead

- Research continues on facial transplants for those with serious burns or other disfigurements. In 2005, a French woman received the first partial face transplant in which donor skin, muscle, tissues, arteries, and veins were used to replace the damaged bottom half of her face. She has slowly gained control over her facial expressions and has signed a movie contract to tell her story.[10]
- Scientists specializing in regenerative medicine will grow human organs from a patient's own cells and private companies will market and sell patients perfect organ replacements. This will revolutionize transplant medicine because it will eliminate the risk that a donated organ will be rejected and it will eliminate the current waiting list for organs. Already in a clinical trial in Philadelphia, a patient is getting a bladder transplant with an organ built from the patient's own cells. The patient's cells were grown in the lab and then attached to a biodegradable bladder-shaped scaffold. Eight weeks later the scaffold was infused with millions of bladder cells. It was transplanted into the patient and once the scaffold dissolves, what will be left is a new bladder. Other clinical trials in process are working on growing new limbs, new esophageal tissue, and new arteries.[11]
- Medical tourism will be a growth industry. More wealthy and even middle-class citizens of first-world countries will travel to developing countries for organ transplants. James Payne from Florida is one such example. He needed a liver transplant but was told by his Florida hospital that they could not do the transplant for several months and that the cost would be $450,000. Instead, he and his wife bought plane tickets to India and had the transplant done at one of New Delhi's premier hospitals for $58,000, which included their 10-week stay in the hospital.[12] On the other hand, the ethical worry is that impoverished people in developing countries will continue to be coerced or pressured into giving up their own organs or the organs of their loved ones.

Endnotes

1. See http://www.journeyofhearts.org/kirstimd/remember.htm [Accessed on August 30, 2008].
2. See http://news.bbc.co.uk/2/hi/programmes/this_world/6090468.stm [Accessed on April 7, 2008].
3. See http://www.who.int/bulletin/volumes/85/12/06-039370/en/#R19 [Accessed on April 7, 2008].
4. See http://news.bbc.co.uk/1/hi/health/2224554.stm [Accessed on April 7, 2008].
5. See http://nobelprize.org/nobel_prizes/medicine/laureates/1990/press.html [Accessed on April 7, 2008].
6. See http://en.wikipedia.org/wiki/Christiaan_Barnard [Accessed on April 7, 2008].
7. See http://www.unos.org/ [Accessed on May 1, 2008] and http://www.optn.org/latestData/rptData.asp [Accessed on May 1, 2008].
8. See http://www.americanheart.org/presenter.jhtml?identifier=4588 [Accessed on May 21, 2008].
9. See http://www.unos.org/PoliciesandBylaws2/policies/pdfs/policy_7.pdf [Accessed on May 21, 2008].
10. See these articles: http://news.bbc.co.uk/1/hi/health/4484728.stm; http://www.washingtonpost.com/wp-dyn/content/article/2007/12/12/AR2007121202012.html and http://abcnews.go.com/Health/Cosmetic/story?id=1386491 [Accessed on April 7, 2008].
11. Wyatt Andrews, "Medicine's Cutting Edge: Re-Growing Organs," CBSNews.com (March 23, 2008), http://www.cbsnews.com/stories/2008/03/22/sunday/main3960219.shtml?source=search_story [Accessed on April 6, 2008].
12. Laurie Goering, "For Big Surgery, Delhi is Dealing," *Chicago Tribune* (March 28, 2008).

SCARCITY AND ALLOCATION

The Allocation of Exotic Medical Lifesaving Therapy

Nicholas Rescher

I. THE PROBLEM

Technological progress has in recent years transformed the limits of the possible in medical therapy. However, the elevated state of sophistication of modern medical technology has brought the economists' classic problem of scarcity in its wake as an unfortunate side product. The enormously sophisticated and complex equipment and the highly trained teams of experts requisite for its utilization are scarce resources in relation to potential demand. The administrators of the great medical institutions that preside over these scarce resources thus come to be faced increasingly with the awesome choice: *Whose life to save?*

A (somewhat hypothetical) paradigm example of this problem may be sketched within the following set of definitive assumptions: We suppose that persons in some particular medically morbid condition are "mortally afflicted": It is virtually certain that they will die within a short time period (say ninety days). We assume that some very complex course of treatment (e.g., a heart transplant) represents a substantial probability of life prolongation for persons in this mortally afflicted condition. We assume that the facilities available in terms of human resources, mechanical instrumentalities, and requisite materials (e.g., hearts in the case of a heart transplant) make it possible to give a certain treatment—this "exotic (medical) lifesaving therapy," or ELT for short—to a certain, relatively small number of people. And finally we assume that a substantially greater pool of people in the mortally afflicted condition is at hand. The problem then may be formulated as follows: How is one to select within the pool of afflicted patients the ones to be given the ELT treatment in question; how to select those "whose lives are to be saved"? Faced with many candidates for an ELT process that can be made available to only a few, doctors and medical administrators confront the decision of who is to be given a chance at survival and who is, in effect, to be condemned to die.

As has already been implied, the "heroic" variety of spare-part surgery can pretty well be assimilated to this paradigm. One can foresee the time when heart transplantation, for example, will have become pretty much a routine medical procedure, albeit on a very limited basis, since a cardiac surgeon with the technical competence to transplant hearts can operate at best a rather small number of times each week and the elaborate facilities for such operations will most probably exist on a modest scale. Moreover, in "spare-part" surgery there is always the problem of availability of the "spare parts" themselves. A report in one British newspaper gives the following picture: "Of the 150,000 who die of heart disease each year [in the U.K.], Mr. Donald Longmore, research surgeon at the National Heart Hospital [in London] estimates that 22,000 might be eligible for heart surgery. Another 30,000 would need heart and lung transplants. But there are probably only between 7,000 and 14,000 potential donors a year." Envisaging this situation in which at the very most something like one in four heart-malfunction victims can be saved, we clearly confront a problem in ELT allocation.

A perhaps even more drastic case in point is afforded by long-term haemodialysis, an ongoing process by which a complex device—an "artificial kidney machine"—is used periodically in cases of chronic renal failure to substitute for a non-functional kidney in "cleaning" potential poisons from the blood. Only a few major institutions have chronic haemodialysis units, whose complex operation is an extremely expensive proposition. For the present and the foreseeable future the situation is that "the number of places available for chronic haemodialysis is hopelessly inadequate."

The traditional medical ethos has insulated the physician against facing the very existence of this problem. When swearing the Hippocratic Oath, he commits himself to work for the benefit of the sick in "whatsoever house I enter." In taking this stance, the physician substantially renounces the explicit choice of saving certain lives rather than others. Of course, doctors have always in fact had to face such choices on the battlefield or in times of disaster, but there the issue had to be resolved hurriedly, under pressure, and in circumstances in which the very nature of the case effectively precluded calm deliberation by the decision maker as well as criticism by others. In sharp contrast, however, cases of the type we have postulated in the present discussion arise predictably, and represent choices to be made deliberately and "in cold blood."

It is, to begin with, appropriate to remark that this problem is not fundamentally a medical problem. For when there are sufficiently many afflicted candidates for ELT then—so we may assume—there will also be more than enough for whom the purely medical grounds for ELT allocation are decisively strong in any individual case, and just about equally strong throughout the group. But in this circumstance a selection of some afflicted patients over and against others cannot *ex hypothesi* be made on the basis of purely medical considerations.

The selection problem, as we have said, is in substantial measure not a medical one. It is a problem *for* medical men, which must somehow be solved by them, but that does not make it a medical issue—any more than the problem of hospital building is a medical issue. As a problem it belongs to the category of philosophical problems—specifically a problem of moral philosophy or ethics. Structurally, it bears a substantial kinship with those issues in this field that revolve about the notorious whom-to-save-on-the-lifeboat and whom-to-throw-to-the-wolves-pursuing-the-sled questions. But whereas questions of this just-indicated sort are artificial, hypothetical, and far-fetched, the ELT issue poses a *genuine* policy question for the responsible administrators in medical institutions, indeed a question that threatens to become commonplace in the foreseeable future.

Now what the medical administrator needs to have, and what the philosopher is presumably *ex officio* in a position to help in providing, is a body of *rational guidelines* for making choices in these literally life-or-death situations. This is an issue in which many interested parties have a substantial stake, including the responsible decision maker who wants to satisfy his conscience that he is acting in a reasonable way. Moreover, the family and associates of the man who is turned away—to say nothing of the man himself—have the right to an acceptable explanation. And indeed even the general public wants to know that what is being done is fitting and proper. All of these interested parties are entitled to insist that a reasonable code of operating principles provides a defensible rationale for making the life-and-death choices involved in ELT.

II. THE TWO TYPES OF CRITERIA

Two distinguishable types of criteria are bound up in the issue of making ELT choices. We shall call these *Criteria of Inclusion* and *Criteria of Comparison*,

respectively. The distinction at issue here requires some explanation. We can think of the selection as being made by a two-stage process: (1) the selection from among all possible candidates (by a suitable screening process) of a group to be taken under serious consideration as candidates for therapy, and then (2) the actual singling out, within this group, of the particular individuals to whom therapy is to be given. Thus the first process narrows down the range of comparative choice by eliminating *en bloc* whole categories of potential candidates. The second process calls for a more refined, case-by-case comparison of those candidates that remain. By means of the first set of criteria one forms a selection group; by means of the second set, an actual selection is made within this group.

Thus what we shall call a "selection system" for the choice of patients to receive therapy of the ELT type will consist of criteria of these two kinds. Such a system will be acceptable only when the reasonableness of its component criteria can be established.

III. ESSENTIAL FEATURES OF AN ACCEPTABLE ELT SELECTION SYSTEM

To qualify as reasonable, an ELT selection must meet two important "regulative" requirements: it must be *simple* enough to be readily intelligible, and it must be *plausible,* that is, patently reasonable in a way that can be apprehended easily and without involving ramified subtleties. Those medical administrators responsible for ELT choices must follow a modus operandi that virtually all the people involved can readily understand to be acceptable (at a reasonable level of generality, at any rate). Appearances are critically important here. It is not enough that the choice be made in a *justifiable* way; it must be possible for people—*plain* people—to "see" (i.e., understand without elaborate teaching or indoctrination) that *it is justified,* insofar as any mode of procedure can be justified in cases of this sort.

One "constitutive" requirement is obviously an essential feature of a reasonable selection system: all of its component criteria—those of inclusion and those of comparison alike—must be reasonable in the sense of being *rationally defensible*. The ramifications of this requirement call for detailed consideration. But one of its aspects should be noted without further ado: it must be *fair*—it must treat relevantly like cases alike, leaving no room for "influence" or favoritism, etc.

IV. THE BASIC SCREENING STAGE: CRITERIA OF INCLUSION (AND EXCLUSION)

Three sorts of considerations are prominent among the plausible criteria of inclusion/exclusion at the basic screening stage: the constituency factor, the progress-of-science factor, and the prospect-of-success factor.

A. The constituency factor

It is a "fact of life" that ELT can be available only in the institutional setting of a hospital or medical institute or the like. Such institutions generally have normal clientele boundaries. A veterans' hospital will not concern itself primarily with treating nonveterans, a children's hospital cannot be expected to accommodate the "senior citizen," an army hospital can regard college professors as outside its sphere. Sometimes the boundaries are geographic—a state hospital may admit only residents of a certain state. (There are, of course, indefensible constituency principles—say race or religion, party membership, or ability to pay; and there are cases of borderline legitimacy, e.g., sex.) A medical institution is justified in considering for ELT only persons within its own constituency, provided this constituency is constituted upon a defensible basis. Thus the haemodialysis selection committee in Seattle "agreed to consider only those applications who were residents of the state of Washington. . . . They justified this stand on the grounds that since the basic research . . . had been done at . . . a state-supported institution—the people whose taxes had paid for the research should be its first beneficiaries."

While thus insisting that constituency considerations represent a valid and legitimate factor in ELT selection, I do feel there is much to be said for minimizing their role in life-or-death cases. Indeed a refusal to recognize them at all is a significant part of medical tradition, going back to the very oath of Hippocrates. They represent a departure from the ideal arising with the institutionalization of medicine, moving it away from its original status as an art practiced by an individual practitioner.

B. The progress-of-science factor

The needs of medical research can provide a second valid principle of inclusion. The research interests of the medical staff in relation to the specific nature of the cases at issue is a significant consideration. It may be important for the progress of medical science—and thus of potential benefit to many persons in the future—to determine how effective the ELT at issue is with diabetics or persons over sixty or with a negative RH factor. Considerations of this sort represent another type of legitimate factor in ELT selection.

A very definitely *borderline* case under this head would revolve around the question of a patient's willingness to pay, not in monetary terms, but in offering himself as an experimental subject, say by contracting to return at designated times for a series of tests substantially unrelated to his own health, but yielding data of importance to medical knowledge in general.

C. The prospect-of-success factor

It may be that while the ELT at issue is not without *some* effectiveness in general, it has been established to be highly effective only with patients in certain specific categories (e.g., females under forty of a specific blood type). This difference in effectiveness—in the absolute or in the probability of success—is (we assume) so marked as to constitute virtually a difference in kind rather than in degree. In this case, it would be perfectly legitimate to adopt the general rule of making the ELT at issue available only or primarily to persons in this substantial-promise-of-success category. (It is on grounds of this sort that young children and persons over fifty are generally ruled out as candidates for haemodialysis.)

***

We have maintained that the three factors of constituency, progress of science, and prospect of success represent legitimate criteria of inclusion for ELT selection. But it remains to examine the considerations which legitimate them. The legitimating factors are in the final analysis practical or pragmatic in nature. From the practical angle it is advantageous—indeed to some extent necessary—that the arrangements governing medical institutions should embody certain constituency principles. It makes good pragmatic and utilitarian sense that progress-of-science considerations should be operative here. And, finally, the practical aspect is reinforced by a whole host of other considerations—including moral ones—in supporting the prospect-of-success criterion. The workings of each of these factors are of course conditioned by the ever-present element of limited availability. They are operative only in this context, that is, prospect of success is a legitimate consideration at all only because we are dealing with a situation of scarcity.

V. THE FINAL SELECTION STAGE: CRITERIA OF SELECTION

Five sorts of elements must, as we see it, figure primarily among the plausible criteria of selection that are to be brought to bear in further screening the group constituted after application of the criteria of inclusion: the relative-likelihood-of-success factor, the life-expectancy factor, the family role factor, the potential-contributions factor, and the services-rendered factor. The first two represent the *biomedical* aspect, the second three the *social* aspect.

A. The relative-likelihood-of-success factor

It is clear that the relative likelihood of success is a legitimate and appropriate factor in making a selection within the group of qualified patients that are to receive ELT. This is obviously one of the considerations that must count very significantly in a reasonable selection procedure.

The present criterion is of course closely related to item *C* of the preceding section. There we were concerned with prospect-of-success considerations categorically and *en bloc*. Here at present they come into play in a particularized case-by-case comparison among individuals. If the therapy at issue is not a once-and-for-all proposition and requires ongoing treatment, cognate considerations must be brought in. Thus, for example, in the case of a chronic ELT procedure such as haemodialysis it would clearly make sense to give priority to patients with a potentially reversible condition (who would thus need treatment for only a fraction of their remaining lives).

B. The life-expectancy factor

Even if the ELT is "successful" in the patient's case he may, considering his age and/or other aspects of his general medical condition, look forward to only a very short probable future life. This is obviously another factor that must be taken into account.

C. The family role factor

A person's life is a thing of importance not only to himself but to others—friends, associates, neighbors, colleagues, etc. But his (or her) relationship to his immediate family is a thing of unique intimacy and significance. The nature of his relationship to his wife, children, and parents, and the issue of their financial and psychological dependence upon him, are obviously matters that deserve to be given weight in the ELT selection process. Other things being anything like equal, the mother of minor children must take priority over the middle-aged bachelor.

D. The potential future-contributions factor (prospective service)

In "choosing to save" one life rather than another, "the society," through the mediation of the particular medical institution in question—which should certainly look upon itself as a trustee for the social interest—is clearly warranted in considering the likely pattern of future *services to be rendered* by the patient (adequate recovery assumed), considering his age, talent, training, and past record of performance. In its allocations of ELT, society "invests" a scarce resource in one person as against another and is thus entitled to look to the probable prospective "return" on its investment.

It may well be that a thoroughly egalitarian society is reluctant to put someone's social contribution into the scale in situations of the sort at issue. One popular article states that "the most difficult standard would be the candidate's value to society," and goes on to quote someone who said: "You can't just pick a brilliant painter over a laborer. The average citizen would be quickly eliminated." But what if it were not a brilliant painter but a brilliant surgeon or medical researcher that was at issue? One wonders if the author of the *obiter dictum* that one "can't just pick" would still feel equally sure of his ground. In any case, the fact that the standard is difficult to apply is certainly no reason for not attempting to apply it. The problem of ELT selection is inevitably burdened with difficult standards.

Some might feel that in assessing a patient's value to society one should ask not only who if permitted to continue living can make the greatest contribution to society in some creative or constructive way, but also who by dying would leave behind the greatest burden on society in assuming the discharge of their residual responsibilities. Certainly the philosophical utilitarian would give equal weight to both these considerations. Just here is where I would part ways with orthodox utilitarianism. For—though this is not the place to do so—I should be prepared to argue that a civilized society has an obligation to promote the furtherance of positive achievements in cultural and related areas even if this means the assumption of certain added burdens.

E. The past services-rendered factor (retrospective service)

A person's services to another person or group have always been taken to constitute a valid basis for a claim upon this person or group—of course a moral and not necessarily a legal claim. Society's obligation for the recognition and reward of services rendered—an obligation whose discharge is also very possibly conducive to self-interest in the long run—is thus another factor to be taken into account. This should be viewed as a morally necessary correlative of the previously considered factor of *prospective* service. It would be morally indefensible of society in effect to say: "Never mind about services you rendered yesterday—it is only the services to be rendered tomorrow that will count with us today." We live in very future-oriented times, constantly preoccupied in a distinctly utilitarian way with future satisfactions. And this disinclines us to give much recognition to past services. But parity considerations of the sort just adduced indicate that such recognition should be given *on grounds of equity*. No doubt a justification for giving weight to services rendered can also be attempted along utilitarian lines. ("The reward of past services rendered spurs people on to greater future efforts and is thus socially advantageous in the long-run future.") In saying that past services should be counted "on grounds of equity"—rather than "on grounds of utility"—I take the view that even if this utilitarian defense could somehow be shown to be fallacious, I should still be prepared to maintain the propriety of taking services rendered into account. The position does not rest on a utilitarian basis and so would not collapse with the removal of such a basis.

***

As we have said, these five factors fall into three groups: the biomedical factors *A* and *B,* the familial factor *C,* and the social factors *D* and *E*. With items *A* and *B* the need for a detailed analysis of the medical considerations comes to the fore. The age of the patient, his medical history, his physical and psychological condition, his specific disease, etc., will all need to be taken into exact account. These biomedical factors represent technical issues: they call for the physicians' expert judgment and the medical statisticians' hard data. And they are ethically uncontroversial factors—their legitimacy and appropriateness are evident from the very nature of the case.

Greater problems arise with the familial and social factors. They involve intangibles that are difficult to judge. How is one to develop subcriteria for weighing the relative social contributions of (say) an architect or a librarian or a mother of young children? And they involve highly problematic issues. (For example, should good moral character be rated a plus and bad a minus in judging services rendered?) And there is something strikingly unpleasant in grappling with issues of this sort for people brought up in times greatly inclined towards maxims of the type "Judge not!" and "Live and let live!" All the same, in the situation that concerns us here such distasteful problems must be faced, since a failure to choose to save some is tantamount to sentencing all.

Unpleasant choices are intrinsic to the problem of ELT selection; they are of the very essence of the matter.

***

But is reference to all these factors indeed inevitable? The justification for taking account of the medical factors is pretty obvious. But why should the social aspect of services rendered and to be rendered be taken into account at all? The answer is that they must be taken into account not from the *medical* but from the *ethical* point of view. Despite disagreement on many fundamental issues, moral philosophers of the present day are pretty well in consensus that the justification of human actions is to be sought largely and primarily—if not exclusively—in the principles of utility and of justice. But utility requires reference of services to be rendered and justice calls for a recognition of services that have been rendered. Moral considerations would thus demand recognition of these two factors. (This, of course, still leaves open the question of whether the point of view provides a valid basis of action: Why base one's actions upon moral principles?—or, to put it bluntly—Why be moral? The present paper is, however, hardly the place to grapple with so fundamental an issue, which has been canvassed in the literature of philosophical ethics since Plato.)

VI. MORE THAN MEDICAL ISSUES ARE INVOLVED

An active controversy has of late sprung up in medical circles over the question of whether non-physician laymen should be given a role in ELT selection (in the specific context of chronic haemodialysis). One physician writes: "I think that the assessment of the candidates should be made by a senior doctor on the [dialysis] unit, but I am sure that it would be helpful to him—both in sharing responsibility and in avoiding personal pressure—if a small unnamed group of people [presumably including laymen] officially made the final decision. I visualize the doctor bringing the data to the group, explaining the points in relation to each case, and obtaining their approval of his order of priority."

Essentially this procedure of a selection committee of laymen has for some years been in use in one of the most publicized chronic dialysis units, that of the Swedish Hospital of Seattle, Washington. Many physicians are apparently reluctant to see the choice of allocation of medical therapy pass out of strictly medical hands. Thus in a recent symposium on the "Selection of Patients for Haemodialysis," Dr. Ralph Shakman writes: "Who is to implement the selection? In my opinion it must ultimately be the responsibility of the consultants in charge of the renal units . . . I can see no reason for delegating this responsibility to lay persons. Surely the latter would be better employed if they could be persuaded to devote their time and energy to raise more and more money for us to spend on our patients." Other contributors to this symposium strike much the same note. Dr. F. M. Parsons writes: "In an attempt to overcome . . . difficulties in selection some have advocated introducing certain specified lay people into the discussions. Is it wise? I doubt whether a committee of this type can adjudicate as satisfactorily as two medical colleagues, particularly as successful therapy involves close cooperation between doctor and patient." And Dr. M. A. Wilson writes in the same symposium: "The suggestion has been made that lay panels should select individuals for dialysis from among a group who are medically suitable. Though this would relieve the doctor-in-charge of a heavy load of responsibility, it would place the burden on those who have no personal knowledge and have to base their judgments on medical or social reports. I do not believe this would result in better decisions for the group or improve the doctor-patient relationship in individual cases."

But no amount of flag waving about the doctor's facing up to his responsibility—or prostrations before the idol of the doctor-patient relationship and reluctance to admit laymen into the sacred precincts of the conference chambers of medical consultations—can obscure the essential fact that ELT selection is not a wholly medical problem. When there are more than enough places in an ELT program to accommodate all who need it, then it will clearly be a medical question to decide who does have the need and which among these would successfully respond. But when an admitted gross insufficiency of places exists, when there are ten or fifty or one hundred highly eligible candidates for each place in the program, then it is unrealistic to take the view that purely medical criteria can furnish a sufficient basis for selection. The question of ELT selection becomes serious as a phenomenon of scale—because, as more candidates present themselves, strictly medical factors are increasingly less adequate as a selection criterion precisely because by numerical category-crowding there will be more and more cases whose "status is much the same" so far as purely medical considerations go.

The ELT selection problem clearly poses issues that transcend the medical sphere because—in the nature of the case—many residual issues remain to be dealt with once *all* of the medical questions have been faced. Because of this there is good reason why laymen as well as physicians should be involved in the selection process. Once the medical considerations have been brought to bear, fundamental social issues remain to be resolved. The instrumentalities of ELT have been created through

the social investment of scarce resources, and the interests of the society deserve to play a role in their utilization. As representatives of their social interests, lay opinions should function to complement and supplement medical views once the proper arena of medical considerations is left behind. Those physicians who have urged the presence of lay members on selection panels can, from this point of view, be recognized as having seen the issue in proper perspective.

One physician has argued against lay representation on selection panels for haemodialysis as follows: "If the doctor advises dialysis and the lay panel refuses, the patient will regard this as a death sentence passed by an anonymous court from which he has no right of appeal." But this drawback is not specific to the use of a lay panel. Rather, it is a feature inherent in every *selection* procedure, regardless of whether the selection is done by the head doctor of the unit, by a panel of physicians, etc. No matter who does the selecting among patients recommended for dialysis, the feelings of the patient who has been rejected (and knows it) can be expected to be much the same, provided that he recognizes the actual nature of the choice (and is not deceived by the possibly convenient but ultimately poisonous fiction that because the selection was made by physicians it was made entirely on medical grounds).

In summary, then, the question of ELT selection would appear to be one that is in its very nature heavily laden with issues of medical research, practice, and administration. But it will not be a question that can be resolved on solely medical grounds. Strictly social issues of justice and utility will invariably arise in this area—questions going outside the medical area in whose resolution medical laymen can and should play a substantial role.

VII. THE INHERENT IMPERFECTION (NON-OPTIMALITY) OF ANY SELECTION SYSTEM

Our discussion to this point of the design of a selection system for ELT has left a gap that is a very fundamental and serious omission. We have argued that five factors must be taken into substantial and explicit account:

A. *Relative likelihood of success.*   Is the chance of the treatment's being "successful" to be rated as high, good, average, etc.?

B. *Expectancy of future life.*   Assuming the "success" of the treatment, how much longer does the patient stand a good chance (75 per cent or better) of living—considering his age and general condition?

C. *Family role.*   To what extent does the patient have responsibilities to others in his immediate family?

D. *Social contributions rendered.*   Are the patient's past services to his society outstanding, substantial, average, etc.?

E. *Social contributions to be rendered.*   Considering his age, talents, training, and past record of performance, is there a substantial probability that the patient will—*adequate recovery being assumed*—render in the future services to his society that can be characterized as outstanding, substantial, average, etc.?

This list is clearly insufficient for the construction of a reasonable selection system, since that would require not only *that these factors be taken into account* (somehow or other), but—going beyond this—would specify *a specific set of procedures for taking account of them.* The specific procedures that would constitute such a system would have to take account of the inter-relationship of these factors (e.g., *B* and *E*), and to set out exact guidelines as to the relevant weight that is to be given to each of them. This is something our discussion has not as yet considered.

In fact, I should want to maintain that there is no such thing here as a single rationally superior selection system. The position of affairs seems to me to be something like this: (1) It is necessary (for reasons already canvassed) to *have* a system, and to have a system that is rationally defensible, and (2) to be rationally defensible, this system must take the factors *A–E* into substantial and explicit account. But (3) the exact manner in which a rationally defensible system takes account of these factors cannot be fixed in any one specific way on the basis of general considerations. Any of the variety of ways that give *A–E* "their due" will be acceptable and viable. One cannot hope to find within this range of workable systems some one that is *optimal* in relation to the alternatives. There is no one system that does "the (uniquely) best"—only a variety of systems that do "as well as one can expect to do" in cases of this sort.

The situation is structurally very much akin to that of rules of partition of an estate among the relations of a decedent. It is important *that there be* such rules. And it is reasonable that spouse, children, parents, siblings, etc., be taken account of in these rules. But the question of the exact method of division—say that when the decedent has neither living spouse nor living children then his estate is to be divided, dividing 60 per cent between parents, 40 per cent between siblings versus dividing 90 per cent between parents, 10 per cent between siblings—cannot be settled on the basis of any general abstract considerations of reasonableness. Within broad limits, a *variety* of resolutions are all perfectly acceptable—so that no one procedure can justifiably be regarded as "the (uniquely) best" because it is superior to all others.

VIII. A POSSIBLE BASIS FOR A REASONABLE SELECTION SYSTEM

Having said that there is no such thing as *the optimal* selection system for ELT, I want now to sketch out the broad features of what I would regard as *one acceptable system.*

The basis for the system would be a point rating. The scoring here at issue would give roughly equal weight to the medical considerations (*A* and *B*) in comparison with the extramedical considerations (*C* = family role, *D* = services rendered, and *E* = services to be rendered), also giving roughly equal weight to the three items involved here (*C*, *D*, and *E*). The result of such a scoring procedure would provide the essential *starting point* of our ELT selection mechanism. I deliberately say "starting point" because it seems to me that one should not follow the results of this scoring in an *automatic* way. I would propose that the actual selection should only be guided but not actually be dictated by this scoring procedure, along lines now to be explained.

IX. THE DESIRABILITY OF INTRODUCING AN ELEMENT OF CHANCE

The detailed procedure I would propose—not of course as optimal (for reasons we have seen), but as eminently acceptable—would combine the scoring procedure just discussed with an element of chance. The resulting selection system would function as follows:

1. First the criteria of inclusion of Section IV above would be applied to constitute a *first phase selection group*—which (we shall suppose) is substantially larger than the number *n* of persons who can actually be accommodated with ELT.

2. Next the criteria of selection of Section V are brought to bear via a scoring procedure of the type described in Section VIII. On this basis a *second phase selection group* is constituted which is only *somewhat* larger—say by a third or a half—than the critical number *n* at issue.

3. If this second phase selection group is relatively homogeneous as regards rating by the scoring procedure—that is, if there are no really major disparities within this group (as would be likely if the initial group was significantly larger than *n*)—then the final selection is made by *random* selection of *n* persons from within this group.

This introduction of the element of chance—in what could be dramatized as a "lottery of life and death"—must be justified. The fact is that such a procedure would bring with it three substantial advantages.

First, as we have argued above (in Section VII), any acceptable selection system is inherently non-optimal. The introduction of the element of chance prevents the results that life-and-death choices are made by the automatic application of an admittedly imperfect selection method.

Second, a recourse to chance would doubtless make matters easier for the rejected patient and those who have a specific interest in him. It would surely be quite hard for them to accept his exclusion by relatively mechanical application of objective criteria in whose implementation subjective judgment is involved. But the circumstances of life have conditioned us to accept the workings of chance and to tolerate the element of luck (good or bad): human life is an inherently contingent process. Nobody, after all, has an absolute right to ELT—but most of us would feel that we have "every bit as much right" to it as anyone else in significantly similar circumstances. The introduction of the element of chance assures a like handling of like cases over the widest possible area that seems reasonable in the circumstances.

Third (and perhaps least), such a recourse to random selection does much to relieve the administrators of the selection system of the awesome burden of ultimate and absolute responsibility.

These three considerations would seem to build up a substantial case for introducing the element of chance into the mechanism of the system for ELT selection in a way limited and circumscribed by other weightier considerations, along some such lines as those set forth above.

It should be recognized that this injection of *man-made* chance supplements the element of *natural* chance that is present inevitably and in any case (apart from the role of chance in singling out certain persons as victims for the affliction at issue). As F. M. Parsons has observed: "any vacancies [in an ELT program—specifically haemodialysis] will be filled immediately by the first suitable patients, even though their claims for therapy may subsequently prove less than those of other patients refused later." Life is a chancy business and even the most rational of human arrangements can cover this over to a very limited extent at best.

Ethics and the Allocation of Organs for Transplantation

James F. Childress

A quarter of a century ago, in my second year of teaching at the University of Virginia, I began to explore the emerging field of biomedical ethics through a seminar on "Artificial and Transplanted Organs," which included both faculty and students from law, medicine, and the humanities. My paper for the seminar was entitled "Who Shall Live When Not All Can Live?" This experience drew me into biomedical ethics, because of the complex mix of ethical, legal, and medical issues and the fruitfulness of interdisciplinary and interprofessional dialogue.

Several of the major problems confronting that seminar have persisted, often in altered form. In the area of organ transplantation, two significant issues continue to require society's attention: (1) how can the organ supply be increased, and (2) how should the available organs be allocated? I want to make a few points about ethical criteria in the allocation of donated organs, as a way to indicate some directions for organ allocation policies in the twenty-first century. I will focus on the second question because I believe that a tremendous and ever-widening gap will persist between the need for transplantable organs and the supply of human cadaveric organs.

COMMUNITY OWNERSHIP OF DONATED ORGANS AND PUBLIC PARTICIPATION

Since the mid-1980s, the operative conception of the ownership of donated organs has shifted, with major implications for the procedures used to formulate policies for organ allocation. As vice-chair of the federal Task Force on Organ Transplantation in the mid-1980s, I did not immediately realize that debates about allocation policies often reflected different conceptions of the ownership of donated organs. More specifically, organ allocation policies largely presupposed that donated organs belonged to, or were under the dispositional authority of, transplant surgeons, with only limited public accountability. However, the Task Force (1986) held that donated organs belong to the community, and that transplant professionals are only trustees and stewards of those organs for the community's welfare. This conception of ownership implies that the public should participate in setting the criteria for organ allocation.

According to Jeffrey Prottas (1994), another member of the Task Force, these shifts represent the "socialization" of organ transplantation. Although professional dominance, through knowledge and power, continues in the United Network for Organ Sharing (UNOS)—the national organ procurement and transplantation network that was established in the late 1980s—that dominance is now more circumscribed and accountable, particularly because UNOS, in developing any allocation policy, has to respond "to public criticisms with public answers." Not only is organ allocation policy now in the public domain—and thus a matter of public ethics rather than medical ethics—the terms of the debate have changed, as Prottas further notes, so that equity must be considered along with efficiency.

BALANCING SEVERAL ETHICAL PRINCIPLES OR VALUES

The main ethical criteria for organ allocation express principles that are prominent in the major competing theories of justice, particularly libertarian, egalitarian, utilitarian, and communitarian theories. The principles of liberty, equality, utility, and community all play important roles, and organ allocation policies often seek to *balance* these competing principles, which frequently are specified or circumscribed—for instance, utility is specified as *medical utility.* Just or equitable policies are found in the process of balancing.

UNOS (1994) attempts to develop an equitable organ allocation system in light of a "set of basic principles" and "specific measurable objectives" that have been derived from these principles. It uses the metaphor of "balance" for its efforts to relate these different principles and objectives. For instance, it holds that balancing requires that "equal consideration" be given to both medical utility and to justice, so that neither can be ranked a priori over the other. However, it may not be possible to "give equal weight to [both] medical utility

and justice" (UNOS 1994, p. 123) because trade-offs appear to be unavoidable in many policies and are consistent with the metaphor of balancing.

MEDICAL UTILITY AND EQUALITY

Medical utility—maximizing the welfare of patients suffering from end-stage organ failure—includes, at a minimum, attention to the factors that influence both graft and patient survival, as well as to patient needs for transplantable organs. In kidney transplantation, the scientific and ethical debate about medical utility often focuses on tissue matching, especially in view of available immunosuppressive medications. This technical debate influences judgments about the conditions under which kidneys should be shared outside their community of origin. For example, since cyclosporine is nephrotoxic, many argue that a donated kidney needs to be transplanted quickly in order to increase the chances of successful transplantation. A donated kidney can be used more quickly if it is used locally rather than shipped elsewhere.

It is essential to determine which degrees of tissue matching really make a significant difference in transplantation outcomes over time. It is also morally imperative to monitor tissue matching to determine if it has unjustified discriminatory effects, for example, against blacks and other minorities. If such discriminatory effects emerge and persist, it may be necessary to sacrifice some probability of success in order to take affirmative action to protect blacks and other minorities. A 1994 UNOS decision decreases the emphasis on tissue match and gives more priority to time on the waiting list, apparently without reducing successful outcomes.

According to the Council on Ethical and Judicial Affairs of the American Medical Association (1995), allocation policies for organs (and other scarce resources) should depart from equal opportunity mechanisms, such as time on the waiting list, *only* where there are *very substantial differences* in such factors as probability of success. Of course, there is debate about when differences between patients are very substantial. Specifically, the AMA Council contends that, in the absence of conclusive evidence on the importance of HLA matching in ensuring a successful graft, it may not be justifiable to give priority for a kidney to one patient over another merely because of his or her "marginally higher chance of a successful graft." However, while the AMA Council suggests that a 10 percent higher chance of successful graft survival is only "marginally higher," others might view it as substantially higher because of its possible impact on the patient's welfare as well as the patient's possible need for retransplantation and thus for another kidney from the scarce donor pool.

EQUAL OPPORTUNITY AND TIME ON THE WAITING LIST

Queuing is sometimes a favored criterion in microallocation because it appears to be objective and impersonal, but it is actually justified by appealing to values such as equal opportunity. Nevertheless, both practical and ethical problems emerge. For instance, it is not always easy to determine when a patient entered the waiting list. While time of entry to the UNOS list is currently used, critics note that physicians can manipulate this criterion—for example, by putting patients on the list for a kidney transplant before they become dialysis dependent.

The fairness of queuing (as well as of randomization) also depends in part on background conditions—for example, some people may not seek care as early as others because of limited financial resources and insurance, while others may receive inadequate medical advice about how early to seek transplantation. Even though some of the inequities in access to organ transplants appear to occur at the point of admission to waiting lists, such decisions have been left entirely in the hands of the transplant teams. In the absence of consistent criteria, patients are put on the waiting list at various stages in their development of end-stage organ failure as well as with various probabilities of successful outcome—e.g., some centers would not have listed Mickey Mantle as a transplant candidate. UNOS is now considering whether to establish minimum standards for admission to waiting lists.

INTO THE NEXT CENTURY

In conclusion, I want to underline several important themes for debates about organ allocation into the next century. First, it will not be possible, I believe, to reverse the conception of the ownership of donated organs that has shaped many organ allocation policies over the last decade. Barring major changes in the methods of organ procurement, the community will continue to be viewed as the owner of donated organs, with the implication that transplant professionals

serve as trustees and stewards of those organs, and that organ allocation policies must be formulated with public as well as professional input.

Second, I affirm the moral relevance of several moral principles or values in organ allocation, as well as the common metaphor of balancing. Even though it is not always possible to give each principle or value "equal weight" at every point in time, "an allocation system based upon any one factor would result in injustice" (UNOS 1994, p. 36).

Third, the process of balancing principles and values over time in organ allocation policies rightly involves public participation, justification, and accountability, which need to be extended to admission to the waiting list. There are important "moral connections" between organ procurement and organ allocation. Organs are donated by and for the public, and the public, as the owner of donated organs, should play an important role in setting the criteria for their allocation and distribution. Furthermore, confidence in the justice of policies of organ allocation and distribution appears to be an important condition for the public's willingness to donate cadaveric organs.

Fourth, balancing principles and values occurs over time so that UNOS can, quite legitimately, change the weights or points it assigns to different factors in allocation, in light of significant public principles and values and empirical evidence about the effects of existing allocation policies. In more general terms, as Guido Calabresi and Philip Bobbitt noted years ago in *Tragic Choices* (1977), a society often has to reaffirm a principle or value that it has neglected or downplayed in previous policies, and this process continues over time. The proper balance often can only be achieved over time, rather than at a single point in time.

REFERENCES

Calabresi, Guido, and Bobbitt, Philip. 1997. *Tragic Choices*. New York: Norton.

Council on Ethical and Judicial Affairs, American Medical Association. 1995. Ethical Considerations in the Allocation of Organs and Other Scarce Medical Resources Among Patients. *Archives of Internal Medicine* 155: 29–45.

Prottas, Jeffrey M. 1994. *The Most Useful Gift: Altruism and the Public Policy of Organ Transplants*. San Francisco: Jossey-Bass Publishers.

Task Force on Organ Transplantation. 1986. *Organ Transplantation: Issues and Recommendations*. Rockville, MD: Office of Organ Transplantation, Health Resource and Service Administration, U.S. Department of Health and Human Services.

UNOS. United Network for Organ Sharing. 1994. Statement of Principles and Objectives of Organ Allocation. *UNOS Update* 10 (August): 20–38.

Measured Fairness, Situated Justice: Feminist Reflections on Health Care Rationing

James Lindemann Nelson

Bioethical analyses of allocation issues have proceeded in a manner largely detached from feminist reflections on power, privilege, and justice; what little feminist analysis of health care justice issues exists has not, in general, closely examined the terms of mainstream debate. The disengagement between these discourses is regrettable, and in this essay, I aim to set two leading themes in contemporary discussion of rationing into dialogue with feminist-inspired ideas.

One such theme concerns the development of a theory of rationing. It is widely believed now that even the best arguments supporting the claim that there is a right to health care are not able to determine just how much and what kind of health care people are entitled to by virtue of that right, as distribution simply on the basis of need is either impossible (since the need is in principle unlimited) or is itself unjust (since the attempt to provide care on the basis of need would undermine the provision of other goods to which claims of right can be made). Work by Frances Kamm, Norman Daniels, and Dan Brock, among others, is bringing to a new level of sophistication discussion of how goods that are scarce and valuable can be distributed most defensibly. Their writing has made more precise our grasp of the questions whose answers seem essential to a respectable theory of rationing.

The second theme is a dubiousness about the whole project of building a theory of rationing. It argues that there can be no such generally defensible theory; rather, distinct communities must bring their own conceptions of the good to bear on decisions about the allocation of rare and valuable resources. Justice in the distribution of health care will mean one thing to Orthodox Jews, something else to mainstream yuppies, and yet something else, perhaps, to lesbians trying to create more women-centered spaces and institutions in their lives. Several writers have explored variations on this theme, notably H. Tristram Engelhardt, Jr. and Ezekiel Emanuel.

These two themes in rationing—the one constructive, the other skeptical—seem mutually disengaged, and surely, they are both disengaged from feminism. In this essay, I will argue that each has something to say to the other and that feminism has something to say to both.

MEASURING FAIRNESS: TOWARD A THEORY OF RATIONING

Recent work on rationing theory is characterized by a process of excavating and examining relevant, fine-grained considerations that reveal the true complexity of the task of fully understanding and assessing our moral commitments as we set rationing priorities. For example, in puzzling over who should receive scarce, potentially life-extending organs, one might on this approach begin by imagining two transplant candidates, Kay and Marie, each, say, age 35, each with an equally good chance of enjoying a five-year graft survival, each of whom has been waiting an equally long time, and each of whom faces an imminent death without the transplant. Suppose an organ for which they are equally well matched becomes available. This example is a paradigm case of a rationing decision, but it might seem to be a relatively easy one, since the costs and benefits on either side seem to cancel each other out. Fairness is the crucial concern, and so there is a strong inclination to randomize by flipping a coin or something of that sort. Now imagine that Kay will not benefit as much as Marie—perhaps, for some reason, her graft is not expected to last more than three years. Should that change our response? Now suppose that Kay is five years younger than Marie. Is that relevant? Would it be relevant if she were only 15, a full 20 years younger? Complicate the situation still further by imagining that Marie's need is more pressing; she will die sooner for want of the organ than will Kay, although there is no guarantee that Kay will survive until another suitable organ presents itself.

Should we decide which person receives the organ according to which option generates the most life-years saved? Are nonconsequentialist considerations relevant here? Should we ignore these differences, and stick with the coin flip? Perhaps we should roll a six-sided die, with Marie's name on four faces and Kay's on two—or vice versa.[1]

Frances Kamm (1993) in particular has pursued such questions with relentless thoroughness. She has attracted new attention to a variety of considerations important to rationing theory, including;

Distinguishing among various dimensions of the notion of need.   Kamm points out that "to say that someone to some degree needs [some scarce resource] is to say that he will in some way be badly off without it. But there are different ways of being badly off".[2] This is a crucial observation, given the intuitive plausibility of the principle "to each according to her needs" in rationing decisions. Imagine two patients vying for the last available ICU bed. Is the needier patient the more fragile of the two, the one who is likelier to die if her admission is delayed? Or is the needier patient the younger of the two, the one who, were she to die, would have had less life overall?

Distinguishing between urgency and need.   Urgency denotes how soon one will become badly off for want of a good. In the distribution of organs, for example, current policy responds to urgency at the expense of the age dimension of need outlined above, namely, the younger patient who (arguably) most needs not to be badly off in the relevant respect. And even within the category of urgency, a further distinction can be drawn between a dimension of time (how *soon* one will be badly off) and a dimension of quality (how *badly off* one will be soon).

Distinguishing various dimensions of the notion of outcome.   Along with determining which individuals are the neediest, we also need to know how a "good outcome" should be understood. Should we attempt to determine not merely, say, the number of life-years saved by one intervention or policy rather than another, but also the quality of those years, either as experienced by the patient herself, or by others? Should any quality of life that seems acceptable to the person whose life it is count equally? If so, and if therefore we should not prefer a candidate who, say, would likely achieve some significant accomplishment over a candidate who would not, can we then prefer a candidate who would likely live for ten years over one who would have an equal likelihood of living only five? Why can we maximize the good of years of life, but not the good of what is done with those years?

Identifying and sorting out other potentially relevant factors.   Imagine we have to choose between saving two people. If we save person A, we also (somehow) can prevent a third person from undergoing a significant loss—say, the loss of an arm. However, if we save person B, the third party will lose her arm. Intuitively, this would seem to provide us with a good reason for favoring person A, if not absolutely, then at least by weighing the odds of rescue in her favor. Yet imagine a case in which a single man and a mother with five dependent children are candidates for the last ICU bed. Is the suffering of the children a "tie breaker" in the same way that the extra arm might be?[3]

Kamm's contribution toward a theory of rationing involves eliciting intuitive responses to these and many other different scenarios and then attempting to gather the responses under unifying principles. She allows that perhaps only a few people will have intuitions about her cases and their variations that seem reliable to them. Still, those few people will be the "natural source of data" about the principles that give rise to these responses. She thinks it likely that, on sufficient reflection, these clear-headed, thoughtful, and sensitive people will tend to reach similar responses about the cases. Deep disagreement seems for her to be a phenomenon most often encountered at the level of theoretical justification; at the level of action and policy, she opines, there will be much more agreement. It seems plain that Kamm hopes that even pluralism at the theoretical level will be constrained by sufficiently sensitive and disciplined reflection on a sufficiently wide range of cases, thereby generating powerful and plausible principles.

Kamm's work has been particularly distinctive, powerful, and influential, so it seems appropriate to ask whether her methods and conclusions reflect an approach to a theory of rationing that should trouble feminists. There is reason to think so. At the level of methodology, for example, many feminists are dubious about moral theories that rely heavily on hypotheticals in an attempt to determine what is "required by reason"; to do so without careful attention to the influence of the historical and social forms in which reason makes itself manifest misconstrues reason's nature.[4] Many feminists also place a good deal of emphasis on ethical reasoning, not only as a situated, but also as a collaborative enterprise—an endeavor that can be seen as part of our attempt to forge viable forms of community in ways that are "transparent" about their values, their fidelity in living up to them, and their historical specificity.

A related concern stems from what I take to be a widely shared feminist suspicion (indeed, widely shared on the left generally) about the use of intuition in moral reasoning. This concern arises from the conviction that our moral intuitions emerge (at least in no negligible degree) from the circumstances of our socialization, and those circumstances are, virtually without exception, shot through with misogynist and otherwise unacceptable practices of action, policy, and thought. Thus, even if the distinctions that Kamm identifies are reasonable ones to draw when thinking about equitable distribution in conditions of scarcity, our intuitive responses to these distinctions are likely to reflect a bias against women, as well as other biases. This is just as much the case if the consensus that Kamm seems to expect were actually to emerge; feminists have had just as much reason to be suspicious of the general run of agreement about action and policy as of disagreement about theory. Answers can be as dubious as questions.

More concrete grounds for these suspicions emerge when we consider some of Kamm's conclusions about questions relevant to rationing, particularly those concerning the concept of need. For example, in discussing ways of understanding the relationship between age and neediness, she writes:

> First we consider how much life a person should have (given the biological limits of length and quality of human life). Then we get the figures for how much each person has already had of this ideal. The degree of neediness is determined by comparing how far away from the ideal each person is, given how much they have had.

She goes on to imagine that a reasonable life span is 70 years and considers the relative neediness of A, who is 10, and B, who is 20. The ratio is 60 versus 50, so A will be 1 1/5 as needy as B. Other things equal, A gets the preference. But suppose A is male and B female. Then using the same ideal life span for both is plainly not correct. More accurately figured, the ratio is 60 versus something like 58, a very much closer call. In many instances involving resource allocation decisions between women and men, this difference could be decisive; indeed, it invites us to see gender as a generally relevant consideration within a theory of rationing life-extending goods.

Another, more complex way in which Kamm's view may invite feminist concern stems from the doctrine that one ought to consider need only in terms of what is from the potential recipient's point of view "adequate conscious life" rather than in terms of "hedonic or structural goods." What Kamm call "hedonic goods" are those whose value is a matter of the amount of pleasure or happiness they produce. "Structural" or "formal goods," on the other hand, refer to achievements whose value is not exhausted by the pleasure or happiness they yield. It does not matter, then, how much one gets out of life (so long as it's better than nothing) or what one has achieved. Eyebrows will go up at the consequence Kamm draws from this view:

> This standard of need will, in a sense, favor men over women, at least in our society. That is, men will have more achievements to their credit earlier than women (though not if we include reproduction and the raising of children as achievements). If absence of formal goods is not a criterion for need, women may die more frequently than men without the nonreproductive formal goods to their credit.

Kamm's point is that even though women lack equal opportunity for significant "public accomplishment" and so tend to be less well off than men, that sort of disadvantage is not relevant to fair allocation of lifesaving resources.

If gender itself does not count as a formal or structural feature of a life, it is surely strongly correlated with formal goods, including the good of the respect due persons. Even if we assumed achievement to be constant among genders, women in general might "need more not to die" for want of their obtaining this important good. So it becomes very important to understand why, on Kamm's view, the provision of social resources for health care ought not to be sensitive to the extent to which women are needier in this respect.

Kamm develops a doctrine that is related to Michael Walzer's "spheres of justice" idea to account for her intuitions here. In health care allocation, she notes, we are concerned with promoting not just any kind of good, but goods that are relevant to the aim of saving lives by medical means. Completing significant projects, defending children from psychological stress, or presumably enjoying certain formal goods, such as equal respect, are not part of that sphere and therefore are not relevant to decision making concerning health care resources. For this reason (among others), the single mother of five should not receive any priority over the single man without dependents. If, however, that mysterious extra arm could be salvaged if we saved the mother, but not the single man, this would be a relevant consideration, since health care counts preserving limbs among the goods that pertain to its sphere. The idea here is that "adequate conscious life" is a correct understanding of the kind of good the absence of which creates medically relevant need, whereas "formal or structural goods" are not, since adequate conscious life pertains to the sphere of health care in a way that, say, compensating for previous injustice does not. But in completely setting aside "structural" features of life, as Kamm does, we lose any sense of the contextual features that form peoples' lives and well-being and that may even contribute to their health status. We also lose sight of the fact that what kind of health care society provides is itself an expression of what that society values.

Consider, for example, women suffering from anorexia nervosa. Mary Mahowald (1992), among others, has argued that this sometimes lethal illness is a more or less direct result of pressures on girls and women resulting from the way society constructs gender. Assuming this is so, is it then appropriate to give some priority in allocation of research or therapeutic resources to those who suffer from this disease? Kamm might reply that the causal circumstances of contracting a disease are not relevant to making distributive decisions—if two people are equally needy, if their need is equally urgent, and if treatment promises equal outcomes, the fact that the one's health problem arises from a third party's malice, while the other's is simply a matter of physical bad luck, seems beside the point.

It may be important to keep in mind, however, not just what is being distributed, but who is doing the distributing. If a private individual is facing questions about how to distribute her private resources for others' health care needs, perhaps it is inappropriate for her to take such matters as the causal circumstances of the disease into account. But if we are talking about how to direct social subventions for health care, we find ourselves willy-nilly in two spheres at once: health care provision and social policymaking. We are simultaneously responding to health care needs and making a statement about the kind of society we think we ought to be creating.

Recall that we have assumed that the casual circumstances of anorexia stem not from nature, nor from individual agency, but from a malignant social structure. As anorexia is revealed to be a social as well as a medical problem, so to speak, it may be appropriate to accord girls and women suffering from the condition some preference in allocation. To do so would be a way of acknowledging that society accepts responsibility for trying to dismantle misogyny and to use its medical resources to counter the kinds of sicknesses that stem from social ills.[5]

Allowing spheres to interpenetrate in this fashion may seem to open up a set of allocation considerations that are paralyzingly complex. Presumably conditions other than anorexia can be traced to social malignancies, and determining how to rank the bad physical effects of sexism, racism, and classism may be so daunting as to drive us back into the safety of impermeable spheres. But the entire spheres approach is questionable. Walzer's work has been criticized precisely because it lacks the resources to recognize and respond to endemic and deeply seated evils such as misogyny. Certain goods, Walzer thinks, "cluster together" because of the meanings those goods have been socially assigned. "Social assignments of meaning," however, are surely suspect from a feminist perspective; they are often part of an ideology that hides the subordinate status of women, making it seem natural rather than deeply problematic. Kamm's adoption of the spheres approach, then, may have incorrectly leveled the playing field concerning expenditures between women and men. Whether our intuitions concerning certain allocation decisions match hers or not, why should we accept that the goal of socially supported health care interventions

is simply to extend life or enhance health? Why not use those social resources allocated to health care in ways that promote not only health, but justice?

To make the feminist analysis yet more concrete, consider that there is a possible (and to my mind, plausible) feminist slant on health care allocation that would highlight the fact that health care is in many ways an extremely inefficient way of achieving the kinds of goods that it targets. ICU beds and organ transplants, the kinds of tangible, solid goods that seem immediately most amenable to a Kamm-style analysis, reflect a high-tech orientation in medicine that arguably expends many more life years than it saves, at least in terms of opportunity costs. If we accept the moral intuitions that give rise to such a high-tech orientation, or the spheres approach that accounts for them, we do not allow ourselves to see as pertinent the kind of searching questions that we should be asking about the justice of the deep structure of the health care system.

SITUATING JUSTICE: CAN THERE BE A THEORY OF RATIONING?

Yet even if there are good grounds for doubt about some of Kamm's particular conclusions, the questions that she and other rationing theorists have identified seem squarely relevant to the broader inquiry. To invoke Norman Daniels's four famous rationing questions: Just who are the worst off with respect to some good, and what priority should they be accorded in its distribution? How should we weigh patterns of distribution designed to achieve the best overall outcome with the value of giving each potential beneficiary a fair chance of receiving the benefit? How can we properly compare policies that yield small benefits to many with those that yield large benefits to a few? And how should we proceed to answer these questions if we are unsuccessful at developing a theory that provides determinate answers that attract consensus?

This is the skeptic's cue. Pluralism in matters of health care distribution is not likely to go away anytime soon, nor is it likely to be overcome by theory building—at least, not theory building that aspires to be universally accepted. Perhaps, as Engelhardt and Emanuel have suggested, the best we can do is to allow people emerging from specific moral traditions to develop their own answers to the challenges of rationing.

Ezekiel Emanuel has developed this notion at considerable length. He argues that, contrary to received opinion, what generates bioethical problems is not medicine's expanding technological power, but rather the fact that medicine is embedded in a political system whose allegiance is to a liberal political philosophy, characterized by its avowal of neutrality with respect to contending conceptions of the good life. To resolve medical ethical problems—and, *a fortiori*, problems about the just allocation of health care resources—we need a richer conception of what a good life is. Only against such a backdrop will we be able to resolve questions concerning the kinds and intensities of health care to provide and, one supposes, the kinds of principles to which we should appeal in determining how to deal with scarcity.

Emanuel's technique, broadly speaking, is to show that the best accounts liberals can give of why there is a moral claim to some reasonable amount of health care—that is to say, Rawlsian/Daniels-type accounts relying on the ideas of health as a primary good and of rights to a species-typical opportunity range—seriously underdetermine what health care should be provided at public expense and what health care withheld. He describes four plausible priority schemes for health care delivery. The first is, roughly, the current system—pull out all the stops to extend life, but put chronic or palliative care decidedly on the back burner; the second eliminates lifesaving care for the elderly, but provides resources for caring for chronic disabilities of the old; the third favors providing treatment for conditions that can be cured or at least greatly ameliorated such that patients have a real chance at independent, autonomous living (those needing long-term nursing care, for example, need not apply); the fourth makes services available or withholds them as a function of their overall cost-effectiveness, such that the young and potentially productive do well, and the elderly and expensive do not.

The argumentative resources open to "liberal legislators" are insufficient for resolving this indeterminacy. What is needed to serve as a nonarbitrary basis for choice is a conception of what it is in life that one should strive for and what it is one should avoid, of what our most attractive opportunities are and our gravest dangers—in short, a conception of the good.

Yet given the persistence of pluralism, how can any such conception be made effective in a way that does not seem arbitrary and unjust to those who do not share the favored view? Emanuel's response is to call for the establishment of relatively small communities consisting of people who share a view of the good. These communities will exist together in a federation; the federation will be governed by certain principles of the right, which will ensure basic freedoms. Within those constraints, however, the communities will get to work out their own destinies.

With respect to matters of health care, this comes down to the construction of "community health programs," or CHPs, which consist of about 20,000 people each. These communities would, for example, agree on how to make decisions for members should they become incompetent. They would also determine the overall slant that the community would take concerning what kind of health care should be guaranteed to all and what kind might not be available.

CHPs could be exclusive. A lesbian CHP, to use an example of Emanuel's, would have the authority to exclude men, even if they were willing to espouse and abide by the conception of the good that expressed itself in the community's health care plan. Within such a lesbian CHP, then, women united by a rich conception of the good, to which they had not only an intellectual but a personal, historical, and perhaps constitutive relationship, could tailor their health care (and, of course, other aspects of their joint lives) in a way that resisted both the blatant and the subtle forms of heterosexism. In particular, they could craft a theory of rationing that contained thoughtful responses to Daniels's four questions.

There are, of course, other, less ambitious responses to an ineradicable pluralism concerning distributive justice. We might respond to the challenge of the questions identified by Kamm and Daniels purely procedurally; we might merely vote on different possible schemes for allocating health care and accept the verdict. What would be amiss with that?

Emanuel notes that advocates of different schemes of "truly" basic health care services do not simply articulate their scheme and then urge voting. "Instead people argue about which scheme is more just and worthy". In other words, a premature turn to pure majority rule may result in a system of health care allocation that violates important convictions concerning the appropriate resolution of the kinds of problems Kamm and Daniels have identified, as well as other morally relevant concerns. Emanuel inspires an alternative thought: rather than resolving the form of a just allocation system democratically across the country as a whole, why not do it in terms of the CHPs of which he writes? In these programs, then, the form and scope of the health care system would reflect, in general, the sense of the good espoused by those who will receive the care and, in particular, would reflect answers to questions posed by the need to ration that might be thought to gain coherence and authority in that they stem from intuitions nourished by distinct, shared conceptions of the good.

While Emanuel's proposal attracts the kind of practical criticism that all radical ideas tend to garner—i.e., how could we ensure that there would be both the normative and geographic proximity necessary for his vision of community life?—the idea of specialized CHPs might at first blush seem a feminist's dream, enough so as to motivate real effort to overcome the practical problems. The proposal seems to embody a way of dealing with the "dilemmas of difference" to which feminist theorists have been highly sensitive in recent years; it accommodates the differences within, as well as among, feminists. For example, one also can imagine CHPs for nonlesbian feminists; for feminists who identify primarily with heterosexually married, or bisexual, or transsexual peers; for feminists of color; and so forth. But there are in principle problems with this approach, as well—ones that should particularly concern feminists. As Marilyn Friedman has noted:

> The practices and traditions of numerous communities are exploitative and oppressive toward many of their own members. This problem is of special relevance to women. Feminist theory is rooted in a recognition of the need for change in all the traditions and practices which show gender differentiation; many of these are located in just the sorts of communities invoked by communitarians, for example, family practices and national political traditions.

Not all communities, that is to say, will be communities of lesbians qua lesbians or of feminists qua feminists of whatever stripe. In addition to (or rather than) being feminists, lesbians are also Conservative Jews or Orthodox Catholics or Mennonites, Latina or African-American or Polynesian, lawyers or air traffic controllers or dental hygienists. In what communities will they find themselves most deeply embedded? With what resources will they be able to recognize and dismantle the understandings of gender that hinder their lives in those communities?

Friedman is not altogether answered by citing either the general allegiance to constraints of the right that Emanuel's liberal communitarianism would require, nor by the fact that, to some extent, membership in various communities is a matter of the choice of potential members (anyone can leave any CHP and, once in, one cannot be excluded). For feminism's aspirations are not limited simply to creating nonsexist communities in which women (and others) may choose to reside; feminism wants to challenge and restructure what it sees as a virtually ubiquitous feature of all human communities—i.e., that to one extent or another, they construct gender in ways that subject women (and others) to disrespect and serious suffering.

Still, as I have already hinted, there might be some conditions under which feminists might be less skeptical of at the idea of CHPs, at least as a progressive step toward a more just society. There is nothing to prevent feminists who identify with other groups from being active in their nonfeminist CHPs, responding to their community's dominant ideology with what Hilde Lindemann Nelson has called "counterstories"—i.e., narratives of resistance and insubordination expressed in terms that are drawn from the community's own conception of the good. At the same time, explicitly feminist communities might allow feminist theory to grow in important ways. This "unity of theory and practice" theme is, of course, not a new insight from the perspective of feminist theory. But recalling it does suggest a way in which some version of the Emanuel scheme might be attractive to feminists, including feminists concerned with the structure of health care delivery.

So it seems that both the quest for a theory of rationing and the idea that such theories are best worked out within communities that share some appreciable degree of normative coherence might be "starters" from the point of view of working out a feminist vision of justice in the allocation of scarce health care resources.

A FEMINIST SKETCH OF MEASURED FAIRNESS, SITUATED JUSTICE

In his *Hastings Center Report* review of Emanuel's *The Ends of Human Life,* Daniels claimed that his four rationing questions represented as much of a challenge to communitarians as to liberals. But that remains to be seen. Indeed, what is easily the most thoughtful and thorough attempt to answer the questions—Kamm's work—itself draws on intuitions that do not seem strictly liberal. Recall her allusion to the spheres approach: Walzer is widely regarded as providing an alternative to liberalism, as appropriate principles for distribution emerge not out of neutrality about the good, but from specific, concrete notions of the "social meanings" of various kinds of goods.

It seems likely that liberalism will not so much develop a widely convincing theory of rationing that answers the four questions, as it will develop a process of rationing that leaves as much of the substantive issues to individual decision making and interest group lobbying. This kind of approach is not known for its sensitivity to fine distinctions and is notorious for producing logjams, at worst, and incrementalism, at best.

The interests of women and other people who lack social power are not liable to be in good hands. Still, it remains a worthwhile question whether the CHP vision will do better. Will the values around which the CHP members cluster be sufficiently rich to yield an adequately sophisticated theory of rationing? Not in every case, perhaps; even some CHPs might have to fall back on proceduralism. But feminism provides an interesting alternative to this rather glum prospect, in part because of its degree of normative depth.

In the majority of its incarnations, at least, feminism is not inclined to regard existing institutions as worth preserving without good reason to regard them as serving aims that promote the welfare and dignity of women. It is skeptical of the social "given," vigilant in safeguarding the interests of women and other marginalized people, and tends to be anti-hierarchical. It shares common human concerns about health as a good and is very concerned about equity in distributing means to attain or defend that good. But feminism is not inclined to see the processes and structures we have erected in order to pursue those goals as particularly hallowed. All this might well be reflected in the ways feminist communities both respond to and refine the questions and methodology that have emerged in the effort to refine our understanding of rationing.

Feminist CHPs might then become laboratories for conceptions of health and health care that might not only answer well to the self-understandings and moral sensibilities within those communities, but at the same time demonstrate ways of arranging matters in a way that replenishes an awareness of possibilities that other communities and the wider polity might draw from. Graphic, practical demonstration of how those conceptions play out may have tremendous rhetorical force. It is, I think, unrealistic to believe that the form of a community's health program stems solely, or even primarily, from its notion of the human good, no matter how articulated and coherent that might be. A community's grasp of its own best impulses may be weak; it may suffer from fears about the unknown, individual selfishness, disinclination to change, and the interaction of calcified social structures and calcified imaginations. Some of these occluding forces may respond best not simply to argument, but to what might be called witness. While feminists should not resign their view that the discursive force of their critiques should be felt generally across communities and social institutions, the opportunity to develop both a theory of feminist allocative ethics and the practice of such an ethical vision is one that should be carefully considered.

NOTES

1. This idea is inspired by Brock (1988).
2. Kamm's own discussion is focused on organs for transplant, but she does in fact say that "the word 'resource' or 'procedure' could be used most everywhere 'organ transplant' occurs or is implied" (Kamm, 1993, p. 233).
3. In addition to the distinctions whose significance she expressly considers, Kamm allows that there may be other relevant considerations—for example, whether personal contributions to one's illness should alter allocation decisions. She clearly thinks that any such further factors should be considered in the mode she has been using and should take account of the results already reached.
4. Among others, Lynn Hankinson Nelson (1990), Donna Haraway (1988), Sandra Harding (1986, 1991), and Lorraine Code (1991) have developed this notion.
5. While Kamm allows that personal responsibility for illness might be relevant, she does not discuss social responsibility for illness.

ACQUIRING ORGANS

Limiting Financial Disincentives in Live Organ Donation: A Rational Solution to the Kidney Shortage

R. S. Gaston, G. M. Danovitch, R. A. Epstein, J. P. Kahn, A. J. Matas and M. A. Schnitzler

INTRODUCTION

Fifty years ago, no effective treatment existed for end-stage renal disease (ESRD). Now, dialysis and transplantation are widely available, and almost all Americans with Stage 5 chronic kidney disease (CKD) are customarily offered renal replacement therapy. Current data indicate that transplantation affords not only better quality of life, but also increases longevity compared to dialysis. The prospect of improved outcomes has encouraged

Abridged from Gaston, R.S.; Danovitch, G.M.; Epstein, R.A.; Kahn, J.P.; Matas, A.J.; and M.A. Schnitzler. "Limiting Financial Disincentives in Live Organ Donation: A Rational Solution to the Kidney Shortage," *American Journal of Transplantation* 6 (2006), 2548–2555 (excerpts). Copyright © 2006. Reprinted by permission of Blackwell Publishing Ltd.

more and more CKD patients to seek transplantation. However, now that transplants work most of the time, we lack kidneys for the majority of candidates.

In an ideal world, increased demand would have been met by an increase in the number of donors. This has not occurred; the gap between demand and supply of deceased donor (DD) kidneys has widened, and, while absolute growth in the number of living donors (LDs) appears dramatic, it in reality reflects only growth in need. In 2005 fewer than 15% of the 70 000 Americans seeking transplants obtained them. It is estimated that by 2010, the waiting list will contain over 100 000 names, with many more acceptable candidates never referred. Despite ample evidence that transplants are most beneficial when performed early in the course of CKD therapy, waiting times, already 5–10 years in some parts of the country, are lengthening, a development that ensures the morbidities that accumulate during chronic dialysis will be amply expressed in those ultimately receiving transplants. An even more ominous comparison is of annual death rates on the waiting list that over 4 years have increased by 23% (from 6.3% to 8.2%). Although, recent years have witnessed modest increases in the number of DD kidneys, their average age has also steadily increased (because of a reduction in traumatic deaths), raising new issues of organ quality. In truth, if all potential DDs in the United States became actual donors, there would still be a substantial organ deficit. While the kidney shortage in the United States is not a novel issue, the sheer magnitude of its current scope and implication for patients mandates that remedies be pursued with renewed vigor.

Indeed, the present situation is already generating responses that are similar to those observed with severe shortages in other sectors of the economy. There is an increased willingness to use kidneys whose features may be less than ideal (expanded criteria donors); desperate individuals make public solicitations for directed donations; and some now attempt to go outside the controlled national system to obtain organs from questionable sources. At the same time, given increasing reliance on LDs, our responsibility to accurately inform them of and protect them from risk as much as possible is growing; proceedings from a recent international conference regarding care of the live donor highlights those responsibilities and defines potential deficiencies in the current American system, particularly regarding long-term follow-up. Calls for greater government regulation are increasing.

Against this backdrop, our group (the authors, composed of individuals from differing backgrounds—economics, law, medicine and philosophy) came together of our own accord to discuss new approaches that might increase the number of live kidney donors, with a particular focus on the role financial incentives might play as part of a practical, rather than theoretical, solution. Our effort grew out of mutual frustration with the growing organ shortage and observation that years of discussion had failed to generate broad-based action. The authors hold widely divergent opinions regarding the propriety of market-based approaches to increase organ availability. However, we quickly agreed that the current U.S. system, based on presumptions of pure altruism, fails to fully reckon the risks (financial and physical) assumed by LDs, and makes no provision to compensate for those risks. Though we, as other interested parties, continue to disagree as to the ideal approach, the proposal presented herein establishes a middle ground between those of us who favor market mechanisms (chiefly payment) and those who maintain that payment for organs raises significant ethical concerns and may ultimately stifle the positive altruistic attributes underlying current policy. Until now, the restriction against provision of 'valuable consideration' codified in the National Organ Transplant Act of 1984, P.L. 58–507 (NOTA, Table 1) has been interpreted as precluding most any form of donor compensation. However, we believe the key components of our proposal are not only consistent with NOTA, but are a necessary step in U.S. implementation of evolving worldwide standards regarding LDs and recent recommendations of the Amsterdam Forum on Care of the Live Donor.

ELIMINATING THE ORGAN SHORTAGE

There are only two ways to eliminate the organ shortage. The first is to reduce demand. Criteria for transplantation could be made restrictive enough that similar numbers of patients are listed and transplanted each year. Defining stricter limits would, however, create numerous ethical issues regarding priority. Some might term such an approach as a 'straw man', a change so absurd as to be unworthy of consideration. However, credible proposals are already circulating that would promote allocation of DD kidneys to younger, healthier patients. Nowhere else in American medicine are health professionals required to make such Faustian decisions, and no precedent exists for their making.

The only other solution is to increase the supply of transplantable kidneys. Accordingly, a recent Institute of Medicine (IOM) report recommends substantially increased efforts to enhance recovery of organs from DDs. However, given the limitations noted above, and

TABLE 1   Pertinent Passages from Section 301 of National Organ Transplant Act

301. Prohibition of organ purchases	
(a) Prohibition.	It shall be unlawful for any person to knowingly acquire, receive or otherwise transfer any human organ for valuable consideration for use in human transplantation if the transfer affects interstate commerce.
(b) Penalties.	Any person who violates subsection (a) of this section shall be fined not more than $50 000 or imprisoned not more than 5 years, or both.
(c) Definitions.	For purposes of subsection (a) of this section:
	(1) The term 'human organ' means the human (including fetal) kidney, liver, heart, lung, pancreas, bone marrow, cornea, eye, bone and skin or any subpart thereof and any other human organ (or any subpart thereof, including that derived from a fetus) specified by the Secretary of Health and Human Services.
	(2) The term 'valuable consideration' does not include the reasonable payments associated with the removal, transportation, implantation, processing, preservation, quality control and storage of a human organ or the expenses of travel, housing and lost wages incurred by the donor of a human organ in connection with the donation of the organ.
	(3) The term 'interstate commerce' has the meaning prescribed for it by section 321(b) of Title 21.

the near-term unlikelihood of xenografting, we believe the only way to substantially change the dynamic of the current impasse in kidney transplantation is an increase in the number of LDs. Our proposal, which does not address the shortage in transplantable hearts or livers, should be viewed as complementary to, not a substitute for, ongoing efforts (such as the Organ Donation Breakthrough Collaborative) to increase the number of DDs.

ECONOMIC BENEFITS OF KIDNEY TRANSPLANTATION

The financial benefits of a successful kidney transplant are enormous, to both recipient and society. In a recent article, Matas and Schnitzler calculated that a single LD transplant saved taxpayers a minimum of $94 000 over the average lifespan of the allograft compared to the cost of maintenance dialysis. This estimate did not include savings associated with reducing the size of and duration of time spent on the waiting list. Nor did it include the impact of improved quality of life in the recipient, which clearly has financial implications as well. In a different context, two economists, Murphy and Topel, estimated that increases in longevity and health since 1970 produced aggregate gains of $2.6 trillion per year, with men at age 50 gaining $350 000 per year in additional satisfaction, and women of that age about $180 000. While one might quarrel with these figures, a quality of life improvement of $50 000 per year per patient (of transplant vs.

dialysis) looks to be very conservative, bringing the total economic benefit of an average LD kidney transplant, with anticipated half-life of at least 10 years, to well over $500 000.

RISKS OF DONOR NEPHRECTOMY

The perioperative mortality (0.03%) and morbidity (<2%) associated with kidney donation are well documented. However, the short- and long-term health and social impacts of donor nephrectomy remain relatively undefined, owing in part to the paucity of long-term follow-up studies, the most comprehensive of which are from Western Europe. While it is known that some American donors eventually develop CKD themselves, long-term medical risk associated with donor nephrectomy cannot be accurately assessed in this country due to the patchwork access to health care afforded donors at this time.

Several studies have documented the impact of nephrectomy on a donor's subsequent quality of life. Although most donors look back at the event favorably, some do not, especially when perioperative complications occured or the recipient had a bad clinical outcome. Financial implications of donor nephrectomy are even less well defined. Hiller and colleagues found 70% of 61 LDs to have expressed socioeconomic concerns before making the decision to donate. Of these, 29% worried about financial ramifications of time missed from work, 10% about childcare, 2% about job security and another 2% about future health insurance coverage. Prospective donors who did not ultimately donate reported similar concerns. Estimates of out of pocket expenses associated with donation range from $550 to $20 000. Exact quantitation of the number of potential donors ultimately dissuaded from proceeding by financial concerns is not available, although a recent survey indicates it may be as high as 40%.

A NEW PROPOSAL

In order to address the issues outlined above, our group made several assumptions, most of which are evidence based. First, although circumstances have changed over the past half century, risks associated with donor nephrectomy remain ethically justifiable and medically acceptable. Second, the outcome of LD transplants (patient and graft survival) is better than that of DD transplants; results with allografts from unrelated living donors (LURD) are equivalent to the those attained with related donors. Third, under current policy in the United States, donor interests remain unprotected relative to current Western standards: risk cannot be quantitated (particularly among ethnic minorities) and LDs are not adequately shielded from financial and health consequences associated with nephrectomy. Fourth, notwithstanding NOTA, there is sustained ethical opposition to the use of an open or unregulated market in LD organs. Fifth, recent programs enacted nationally and locally reflect general agreement not to allow financial disincentives to impede donation.

Details of the proposal

We propose LDs be provided an inalienable package of benefits that would not enrich anyone (provide valuable consideration) but rather is designed to leave the donor as well off (fiscally and physically) as before donation. The goal of this proposal is to protect donors from uncompensated risks of death, bodily injury, loss of capacity or financial dislocation, and in so doing, encourage more potential donors to pursue their altruistic impulses. While we would expand compensation beyond what currently is accepted by many in the field, we also cap the total amount at levels far below what proponents of open markets would prefer. We acknowledge that any package of benefits would increase the overall cost of LD transplants; however, these increased costs are more than offset by savings resulting from decreased utilization of long-term dialysis. Specific details of the proposed donor benefits package, including cost projections, are outlined in Table 2. In our cost estimates, a fixed amount was chosen to avoid the complexity of individualization based on income or family circumstance.

First, to cover the small but real mortality risk, we propose a 1-year term life insurance policy of $1 000 000, to be adjusted for inflation. The choice of that figure is less than the $6 000 000 amount that is often used in the valuation of human lives, but is still substantial and would help any affected family over a serious financial hurdle. This term life insurance would be in addition to already existing private coverage, and its spirit is in keeping with the well-intentioned but poorly subscribed voluntary life insurance benefit currently offered through the Southeastern Organ Procurement Foundation (SEOPF).

Second, to offset any increased risk of medical complications after donation, we propose health insurance for long-term medical care. To avoid duplication, it would be integrated with other forms of coverage already in place for individual donors, and would consist of a supplemental, nontransferable policy to cover any shortfall that might occur. The simplest way to implement this aspect of the package would be to make all donors Medicare eligible from the time of donation (median age: 40 years) until they reach 65 years of age or otherwise qualify. This component would ensure that all donors have access to long-term follow-up, making

TABLE 2   Proposed Benefits and Estimated Costs

One-year-term life insurance policy:	$1300–$3300
Death benefit equal to $1 000 000	
Health insurance:	$15 000–$20 000
Medicare as primary or secondary insurer from donation until age 65 years or otherwise eligible	
Reimbursement of out-of-pocket expenses/lost wages related to donor evaluation and/ or nephrectomy	$2225–$4500
Compensation for inconvenience, anxiety, and/or pain	$5000
$5000 cash or $10 000 tax deduction	
Total cost estimate per achieved donor	$23 525–$32 800

outcomes relatively easy to track even without creation of a new donor registry. The impact of nephrectomy on long-term donor health in this country could at last be reliably determined.

Third, we would include reasonable sums to reimburse travel and lost wages associated with time off work, during both the evaluation and perioperative phases. Potential donors incur these expenses deliberately for the benefit of others, and should not be subject to the vagaries of individual employers. This component differs from coverage offered under workers' compensation and disability programs, which often require waiting periods before compensation is awarded.

Fourth, we recognize that kidney donation involves inconvenience, pain and anxiety that starts before and lasts beyond the operation, as with any significant surgical procedure. We believe that either a tax deduction of $10 000 or a nontaxable lump sum payment of $5000 would be an appropriate offset for this inconvenience. As a group, we could not agree on which of these options is best. In general, we favored a tax deduction, but recognized it would be of no benefit to the significant proportion of the population that does not pay income taxes. As a compromise, we propose both be offered, allowing the donor to decide.

Estimated costs and funding of the proposal

The cost (in premiums) of life insurance is fundamentally derived from the actuarial expectation of loss. Perioperative mortality has been estimated at 0.03%. If we assume that an additional 0.1% of donors die because of donation, then the expected cost of the $1 000 000 payment per death would be $1300 per donor. A higher donor-associated death rate of 0.3% would bring the total to $3300 per donor.

Medicare coverage costs can be estimated from the current median donor age (40 years) and the realization that all citizens become eligible for coverage at age 65. Thus on average, 25 years of additional eligibility would be required. Modifying Center for Medicare and Medicaid Services (CMS) estimates of the cost of 30 years of coverage for disabled beneficiaries, one may derive a projected cost of $18 124 per donor (range of $15 000–20 000/donor). Since many donors already have private insurance, and donors represent an extremely healthy segment of the general population, actual costs are likely to be much less.

The costs of travel and lost wages can be estimated from reports in the literature. Johnson and colleagues,

in a survey of former donors, reported mean personal expenses (travel, lost wages and other costs) of $579. Nonetheless, a wide range of personal expenses was reported ($0–$20 000). At the University of Alabama at Birmingham, 1003 potential donors were evaluated between 2001 and 2004, and 622 LD transplants were performed, indicating that 38% of evaluated donors never proceeded to nephrectomy. These persons also lost wages and costs of travel, and should be included in this part of the compensation package. Thus, the total actual and prospective donor personal costs from these historical studies ranges from $724 to $1449 per achieved donor. If our proposal is implemented, we presume that the availability of compensation for travel and lost wages would lead to an increased pool of potential donors taking time off work and traveling greater distances. Therefore, we triple the historical estimates and assume the average figure for travel, lost wages and personal expenses would range from $2225 to $4500 per achieved donor. Due to disparity across income categories, a fixed sum might be the simplest and most equitable approach to deal with this issue.

Finally, adding a $5000 direct payment (or a $10 000 tax deduction) to these costs for loss of amenities and anxiety produces a range for the cost of our proposal of $23 525–$32 800 per donor. While at first glance expensive, it is far less than—and easily offset by—the estimated $94 000 savings to the health care system generated by the average LD kidney, and approximately half the cost of a single year on dialysis ($58 000). Using the midpoint of our range to calculate the financial implications of our proposal indicates that each newly generated donor produces a net financial benefit (to payers and society) of at least $66 000.

Funding sources for this proposal should be readily available via the Medicare ESRD program administered by CMS. To offset costs of the proposal, including making benefits available to currently uncompensated donors, the number of donors must increase proportionately beyond the 6647 individuals who donated kidneys in 2004. For the program to be cost neutral to CMS, an additional 2800 donors per year are required, a 43% increase. Given data that 25–40% of potential donors may be dissuaded by financial concerns (see above), such an increase seems quite plausible. The shift of funds from one modality of kidney treatment to another places no additional burdens on the public treasury, and therefore does not require a separate appropriation. The improved outcomes (including quality of life) for patients in the Medicare ESRD program compellingly support such a proposal.

Some may object to the proposal as offering benefits more attractive to the less affluent than the well-off, with a potential for significant exploitation of poorer Americans. However, the scope of the package we advocate serves only to bring donor compensation in this country in line with current Western standards, with donor care covered under national health insurance in most countries, and insurance against death, disability and financial dislocation in some. It is difficult to view this proposal as materially enriching anyone enough to coerce an otherwise unwarranted decision to donate. Nonetheless, its implementation would require oversight of subsequent impact on different segments of society. A sensible first step might be a pilot project, with resulting information enabling all interested parties to ascertain the overall risks and benefits.

FINAL REFLECTIONS

Currently, the debate regarding utilization of financial incentives to promote organ donation is highly polarized between advocates and opponents. Proposals ranging from reimbursed expenses to fully unregulated free markets in kidneys have been eloquently debated in philosophical and medical forums. In the meantime, we continue to abandon donors into the vagaries of the American healthcare system, largely unaware of what lies ahead in their lives, even as the waiting list grows ever lengthier. While we recognize the benefits to society at large of dynamic intellectual exchange, our proposal tries to go beyond lamentation and abstract discussion to a workable compromise that promotes the interests of everyone involved.

We in no way wish to minimize the enormous sacrifices of previous live donors. But we think the shift in social circumstances that has brought about an increased demand for kidneys—without a commensurate increase in supply—requires exploration of approaches that

might have seemed outlandish in 1984 when NOTA was implemented. Well-intentioned attempts to preserve a pure altruism, while noble, fail to recognize the true cost to donors and our responsibility to ensure donor safety, not to mention the scope of unmet needs in desperately ill patients, even as they have all increased over time.

As acknowledged in the recent IOM report, new approaches are necessary. We believe our proposal to be ethically consistent with the IOM mandate. It would compensate donors for the real costs incurred by their endeavor without exploiting those potential donors whose circumstances might cause them to be blinded by overt financial offers for their organs. Market proponents must recognize the validity of longstanding tradition and current mores: in Western society organ selling within established markets has always been subject to deep aversion, as reflected in NOTA's sharp restriction on the types of valuable consideration allowed. Organ selling may or may not be ethically defensible, but it is not practical. Market opponents, however, must concede not all financial incentives will invariably corrupt the system; there need be no slippery slope to exploitation and social decay. What principle are we defending by basing solutions to the unconscionable kidney shortage solely on assumptions that an ever greater number of persons will continue to accept uncompensated risk of bodily harm or financial disruption?

The authors understand this proposal, by staking middle ground, may be alienated from natural constituencies on both sides of the organ markets debate. Nonetheless, we believe compensating donor risk in the fashion we propose, or something akin to it, is not only an acceptable alternative to the current impasse, but also the right thing to do. We hope that from the controversy this paper generates will emerge open consideration, then further refinement, and, ultimately, implementation of policy change of potentially great benefit to patients and society.

An "Opting In" Paradigm for Kidney Transplantation

David Steinberg

AN "OPTING IN" PARADIGM FOR KIDNEY TRANSPLANTATION

We rely on live kidney donors because there are insufficient deceased donations. Is there a defensible paradigm that might bring the supply of cadaveric kidneys closer

to demand and lessen the need for live donations? I will suggest one that responds to the unfairness inherent in the existence of "organ takers" and "organ givers" and also takes into account reciprocity and concern for the welfare of the group. This paradigm, which I will refer to as "opting in," is based on utility and fairness.

Abridged from Steinberg, David. "An 'Opting In' Paradigm for Kidney Transplantation," *The American Journal of Bioethics* 4:4 (2004), 4–14. Copyright © 2004. Reprinted by permission of Copyright Clearance Center on behalf of the publisher.

Utility

Although conceptual difficulties exist in calculating the net benefit of kidney transplantation, organs are transplanted because we believe that organ transplantation increases the total medical good. The dominant reason for kidney transplantation is utilitarian. Although some people may suffer because of transplantation, overall it is considered beneficial for the group. The starting premise in any justification of organ transplantation should be unabashedly utilitarian because that is the dominant motivating force.

"Opting in" and fairness

The current system of kidney allocation based on need combined with organ procurement based on voluntary donation has failed to satisfy the demand for kidneys. This failure has spawned discussion of plans to provide a financial incentive for kidney donation, an approach that would unfairly separate "organ givers" and "organ takers" by economic status. In some parts of the world payment for organs has already become common practice. In China organs are taken from executed prisoners, most often without their consent—a practice that might in part be responsible for the large number of executions in China.

An alternate approach would preferentially distribute organs to people who have previously agreed to donate an organ. Currently, organ allocation considerations are essentially restricted to the time frame that begins after it is known who needs a kidney and who is an available and eligible donor. The process could begin earlier, at a time when potential recipients and potential donors are healthy and it is unknown who will need a kidney and who will be able to donate one—a time when, as noted by the late philosopher John Rawls, as far as our individual fate is concerned, we act behind "a veil of ignorance."

Planning at this point could avoid the unfair separation of persons into "organ givers" and "organ takers." Jarvis has used the judgmental but colorful phrase "free riders," for people who would accept an organ if they needed one but would not donate one themselves and advocates that only those who have previously identified themselves as potential organ donors be allowed to receive organs. Eaton favors a similar but less draconian social contract. She would not exclude "free riders" as organ recipients but would penalize them for their "uncharitable views." If there were equally needy recipients, the "free rider" would lose out; no one would be forced to donate their organs, but those who refuse would have to accept the practical consequences of being discriminated against in the allocation of organs.

Gubenats and Kliemt suggested a "solidarity rule" that would provide a nonmonetary incentive to donate. People who, prior to developing a disease, declare a willingness to donate their organs would be given priority in organ allocation. Kleinman and Lowy called for an advance directive organ registry. All persons over age 18 would voluntarily provide their advance directive to a central registry, agreeing to donate their organs at death. Those who registered would get priority in organ allocation. Daar similarly called for giving people who have signed a donor card preference to encourage "enlightened self-interest."

A pool of citizens who are potentially either organ donors or recipients, depending on their fate, exists in several countries, including Belgium, Spain, Norway, Italy, Switzerland, Denmark, and Austria. These pools have been created using minor variations on a doctrine often referred to as "presumed consent." Citizens are assumed to be organ donors unless they have specifically "opted out" and made it known they do not want to be an organ donor. Of note, in Belgium less than 2% of the population has "opted out." So-called "presumed consent" laws are similar to "opting in" programs because they both create a pool of citizens who, when they die, are destined to become organ donors. There is no preferential treatment given to members of the "presumed consent" pool, but they all benefit because the pool increases the likelihood a kidney would be available for anyone who needed one. Although fairness is better served when a citizenry that is willing to take an organ is also willing to give an organ, the prime motivation for systems of presumed consent is utilitarian. In Belgium and Spain there has been an increase in organ supply despite a decrease in potential donors.

A system of "presumed consent" with the opportunity to "opt out" would probably be unacceptable in the United States because of concerns over individual freedom. Veatch notes that a variety of surveys indicate no empirical basis for presuming consent, which leaves many "presumed consent" laws tantamount to the "routine salvaging" of organs. Laws that presume consent have been claimed to be at odds with Western liberalism because they place the state in a position of primacy over the individual. By forcing individuals to protect themselves from government-supported violations of their bodily integrity, "presumed consent" laws, despite the opportunity to "opt out," would create the perception that individual liberty was compromised. This would not be the case in systems based on voluntarily "opting in."

Veatch has proposed a system of "required response." People would be asked in a variety of settings to state whether they did or did not want to be an organ donor; they could also state they did not know whether they wanted to be an organ donor. Veatch suggests posing this question on the application for a driver's license that would be considered incomplete without an answer. He also suggests that the question be asked on income tax returns, though he doesn't propose a penalty for failure to respond. Veatch's attempts to get people to confront the question of whether they will donate their organs would likely make more organs available. However, I suspect the end result would be better if those requests were coupled with significant incentives.

A system that offered preference in organ allocation to those who chose to "opt in" would be a very attractive form of organ insurance. You would not be presumed to be a kidney donor until you voluntarily "opted in" and agreed to donate a kidney. If you became ill, you would more quickly receive an organ that would substantially improve the quality of your life or save your life, and at the minimal cost of promising to donate your organs after you die, have no use for them, and can no longer suffer. It is an opportunity a rational person should willingly accept as very attractive.

An "opting in" kidney transplantation system comes with a significant moral cost. Medical care based on factors other than need is problematic, especially if failure to "opt in" is considered morally blameworthy. Criminals and our enemies in mortal combat are entitled to medical care. Patients who brought on their illness because they smoked or drank too much are entitled to medical care. The unavailability of medical care, including transplants, for those in need simply because they lack money or cannot afford health insurance is deplorable. Gillon notes the important moral tradition in medicine that treatment should be given on the basis of medical need and "scarce resources should not be prioritized on the basis of a patient's blame-worthiness." I am sympathetic to Gillon's concern that if we discriminate against the sick who are considered blameworthy because they did not choose to "opt in," then what other fault might next be used to deny health care.

Organ allocation based on factors other than need currently exists. UNOS lists waiting patients only for transplant centers that are part of UNOS. Geography is a determining factor because organs are first distributed within a specific geographic region. Patients are denied transplants because they lack insurance or adequate funds. UNOS gives preference to prior organ donors by assigning four points to a person who has previously donated a vital organ or a segment of a vital organ within

the United States. The distribution of healthcare based on factors other than need requires justification. In the case of an "opting in" organ transplantation system, justification would be based on the promise of making more organs available for transplantation, with an increase in overall health and a diminished requirement for living donors; nonetheless, we should acknowledge this moral transgression with regret and be reluctant to repeat it in other situations. Unfortunately, whatever mechanism is chosen to reduce the scarcity of kidneys will entail compromise. Criticisms of an "opting in" system should be evaluated in comparison with other options for increasing organ availability or maintaining the status quo of extreme organ scarcity.

An "opting in" system avoids many of the moral problems associated with living organ donation. One inequity would be resolved because the entity assuming risk—the members of the "opting in" pool—would also be the entity that incurred the benefit. Because everyone in the pool is potentially both an "organ giver" and an "organ taker," that unfair distinction would disappear, and within the pool there would be no "free riders." The conundrum of when altruism is appropriate would become irrelevant because those who donate a kidney would get something in return: the promise of a lesser wait for a kidney were they fated to need one. Autonomy would be respected because entrance to the transplantation pool would be voluntary. Each member could make risk/benefit calculations according to individual values before they joined the pool. Members of the pool would be expressing solidarity with each other, though with a greater degree of self-interest than the altruistic stranger.

PRINCIPLES OF AN "OPTING IN" PROGRAM

The details of an "opting in" system for deceased organ donation would have to be devised by a panel with technical expertise; nonetheless, some basic principles can be defined:

1. The "opting in" pool should be integrated with the current UNOS waiting list until it becomes sufficiently large—if it ever does—to be self-sufficient and meet the needs of its members. The absolute number of retrievable organs in an "opting in" system will be limited because the number of eligible deceased donors is limited.

2. The definition(s) of death used would have to be precisely stated because some people would not "opt in" if they considered the definition(s) of death used unacceptable. For example, brain death might be an unacceptable criterion for Orthodox Jews.

3. The preference given to those who "opt in" should be sufficient to motivate people to join the pool; initially

it should probably be credited in the form of added allocation points.

4. A relatively simple means should be devised to determine that everyone entering the pool is at a reasonably equal and low risk for needing a kidney. For example, a person who did not choose to join the pool until they developed diabetes, hypertension, or proteinuria should not be permitted to join, because they are significantly more likely to need a kidney. The need to join while you are healthy should encourage more healthy people to join the "opting in" pool lest they wait until they develop a problem and are no longer eligible for the benefits of being in the pool. Healthy people who have signed organ donor cards under the current voluntary system should be given the option of joining the "opting in" pool. Religious objection to either the definition of death employed or organ procurement from the dead should not be a common problem; however, some adjustment should be made to lessen discrimination against potential organ recipients who were unable to join the "opting in" pool because of established religious views. Similar concessions should be made for children and for adults unable to join the pool because they are not capable of decision making.

5. There should be a central registry, possibly at UNOS, where their social security numbers would identify those who "opt in." All deaths would warrant a mandatory check against this listing. Organs would automatically be retrieved from those who had "opted in" and were eligible donors at the time of death. Legislation would be needed to prevent reneging by the next of kin. Although the sensibilities of the next of kin warrant respect, greater respect should be given to the declared wishes of the deceased who have "opted in"; also, this program wouldn't work if the next of kin could renege. Legislation that would violate the sanctity of the dead body for organ retrieval would not greatly differ in nature from laws that require an autopsy under certain circumstances and should be acceptable.

6. Anyone in the "opting in" pool who subsequently becomes ineligible as a donor because of illness will retain their preference points.

7. To the extent reasonable, people on the UNOS waiting list who do not have "opting in" preference points should not be allowed to die or suffer permanent disability. A kidney should not go to someone with "opting in" preference points who is able to survive without a kidney if there is an alternate recipient who will otherwise die. The greater the disadvantage of not joining the pool, the more likely it is that the pool will successfully recruit members; at the same time, regretfully, nonmembers will suffer more. However, if the "opting in" pool is successful and the total number of available organs increases, total suffering and organ waiting lists will decrease. Experience and trial-and-error adjustments will be required to fine-tune the program.

8. People who have "opted in" are guaranteed to become organ donors. The identity of people who have "opted in" should either be hidden or the medical profession must clearly state they will receive optimal medical treatment and their families will not be encouraged to withdraw treatment because of any ulterior motives. Joining the "opting in" pool should not be perceived as a hazard to your health.

9. People who "opt in" should agree to donate all salvageable organs, and preference programs for the allocation of organs other than kidneys should also be developed.

Arguments could be made to justify an "opting in" organ transplantation pool for live kidney donation. However, retrieving a kidney from a live donor would remain undesirable. At this time, I would restrict "opting in" programs to deceased organ donation.

CONCLUSION

Ideally, everyone should agree to donate their salvageable organs at death. Since that has not happened, an "opting in" program becomes a reasonable option. Although an "opting in" program mimics altruism, it is based on enlightened self-interest. The emotions that foster reciprocal altruism have been conserved in nature because they confer an evolutionary survival advantage. Cultural evolution works faster than genetic evolution and can be used to take advantage of the lessons of nature. An "opting in" policy, despite being rooted in enlightened self-interest, would be a cultural meme that simulates reciprocal altruism. If an "opting in" program is successful it might ironically, by demonstrating the utilitarian value of reciprocal altruism, promote the attitude that self-interest sometimes requires the perception that we are all part of a common humanity.

Conscription of Cadaveric Organs for Transplantation: Let's at Least Talk About It

Aaron Spital and Charles A. Erin

Among patients with end-stage renal disease (ESRD), those who receive kidney transplants enjoy a better quality and longer duration of life compared with those who are treated with dialysis.[1] Renal transplantation is also less costly than dialysis.[2] Clearly then, from the point of view of both the patient and society, renal

Spital, Aaron and Charles A. Erin. "Conscription of Cadaveric Organs for Transplantation: Let's at Least Talk About It," *American Journal of Kidney Diseases* 39:3 (2002), 611–615. Copyright © 2002. With permission from Elsevier.

transplantation is the best therapy for ESRD. For patients with irreversible failure of other vital organs, transplantation, which now has high success rates,[3] offers the only hope for long-term survival.

Unfortunately, the ability to deliver this medical miracle is limited by a severe shortage of transplantable organs. In most developed countries, the rate at which people with end-stage organ disease (ESOD) are being added to transplant waiting lists greatly exceeds the rate at which organs are being donated.[4,5] This has led to long and steadily lengthening lists of potential recipients waiting and hoping for organs to become available for life-saving transplants. For example, in the United States, as of June 2001, almost 77,000 people were registered on the national transplant waiting list.[6] The result is a tragic situation in which people with ESOD are dying not because modern medicine does not know how to treat them, but rather because we have been unable to procure enough organs for all who need them. Compounding this tragedy is the fact that many usable organs are being buried instead of being transplanted because of the relatively low efficiency of cadaveric organ procurement (the major source of transplantable organs).[7,8]

If we are to remedy this tragic situation we need to ask what is wrong with our current system for procuring cadaveric organs for transplantation and what can we do to improve it? To answer these questions, we need to briefly review the procurement systems currently in use.

PROBLEMS WITH CURRENT CADAVERIC ORGAN PROCUREMENT SYSTEMS AND PROPOSED IMPROVEMENTS

Cadaveric organ procurement now involves three basic steps: (1) identification of a potential organ donor; (2) maintaining the potential donor in good physiological condition to preserve organ function; and (3) obtaining consent to remove organs for transplantation, usually from the family, after brain death has been declared. (To our knowledge, all developed countries require consent before organs can be removed from recently deceased individuals.) While failure at any of these steps will result in donor loss, the major barrier to procurement is failure to obtain consent.[4,8–10]

Two systems for obtaining consent are currently in place.[4,11] Some countries, including the United Kingdom, Canada, and the United States, practice so-called "opting-in." This requires explicit consent from the decedent before death or from the decedent's family after death; in practice, the decision is almost always

made by the family, because even when a donor card or other similar document is available, very few centers will honor it without permission from the next of kin.[12] Many other European countries follow an "opting-out" approach in which the organs of recently deceased people may be removed for transplantation unless the decedent has voiced her objection premortem or her family objects at the time of her death. This system is also called (erroneously, we believe) "presumed consent."[13] It should be noted that most countries with presumed consent laws still consult with and honor the wishes of the family before removing organs from recently deceased individuals.[4,14]

It is not our purpose here to argue the relative merits of these two approaches but rather to point out that under both systems many life-saving organs are lost because of family refusal. For example, in the United States, despite great efforts to increase consent rates, about 50% of families say no when asked for permission to remove organs from recently deceased loved ones.[8,10] Similar results were reported in a recent study from France (an opting-out country).[9] Clearly, if the consent barrier could be eliminated, many more organs for transplantation would become available.

Several proposals designed to increase consent rates have been suggested. These include providing financial[15,16] or nonfinancial incentives (such as priority status for transplantation for people agreeing to donate after death),[17] and mandated choice, which would require every adult to make a binding decision for him or herself regarding posthumous organ donation.[18] The envisioned benefits of these approaches have been discussed in the literature. But despite growing interest in them, especially financial incentives, all are controversial and have been sharply criticized.[19–22] Furthermore, it is highly unlikely that any of them would approach the 100% efficiency of cadaveric organ procurement that patients with ESOD so desperately need. However, there is another alternative that would likely achieve this seemingly unreachable goal but which is rarely mentioned in reviews of this subject[5,23,24]—conscription of all usable cadaveric organs.

A PROPOSAL FOR CONSCRIPTION OF CADAVERIC ORGANS

Under conscription, all usable organs would be removed from recently deceased people and made available for transplantation; consent would be neither required nor requested and, with the possible exception of people with religious objections, opting-out would not be possible.[25,26] No doubt this proposal will initially evoke shock, mockery, and even outrage among those who believe that consent is an absolute requirement for cadaveric organ procurement. But the ethical basis for this widely held view is far from clear. Indeed, perhaps because the idea that consent is necessary has been so readily accepted as a given, few authors have seen the need to justify this point of view.[27] We believe that this is a mistake. We will argue that careful consideration of the relevant issues will show that consent for cadaveric organ removal is not ethically required and that conscription is actually preferable. This conclusion is based on an assessment of the envisioned advantages and disadvantages of conscription of cadaveric organs.

Advantages of conscription of cadaveric organs for transplantation

The most important advantage of conscription is that the number of cadaveric organs made available to patients with ESOD would increase dramatically. No longer would large numbers of precious life-saving organs be buried or burned instead of transplanted because, under conscription, the efficiency of cadaveric organ procurement would approach 100%. From the point of view of efficiency, no other approach to organ procurement can even come close. As a result of the increased number of transplantable organs that conscription would provide, the lives of many more people with ESOD would be improved and extended.

Another advantage to conscription is that it is simpler and less costly than other approaches to organ procurement.[15] Under conscription there would be no need to convince people to donate their organs, no need to train requestors to obtain and document informed consent, no need for donor registries, no need for complex regulatory mechanisms that would be required to avoid abuses under plans for financial incentives, and no need to spend resources to induce people to participate.

A third advantage to conscription is that because consultation with the family would no longer occur, this plan would eliminate the added stress that uncomfortable staff members and devastated families now experience when confronting the possibility of organ donation. And the current need to seek some form of family approval often results in delays that can jeopardize the quality of organs. Obviously, this would not occur under conscription.

A final advantage of conscription is that it satisfies the ethical principle of distributive justice, which refers to fair and equitable distribution of benefits and burdens.[28] Under conscription all people would share the burden of providing organs after death and all would stand to benefit should the need arise. This contrasts with current procurement systems in which people can choose not to donate their organs and yet compete equally for an organ with more generous people who choose to give. And in contrast to proposals for financial incentives, there would be no risk of exploitation of the poor for the benefit of the rich.

Disadvantages of conscription of cadaveric organs and responses to them

A major concern about conscription of cadaveric organs is that it violates the ethical principle of respect for individual autonomy. However, it makes little sense to speak of autonomy of a dead person.[29,30] As Jonsen[30] points out, "consent is ethically important because it manifests and protects the moral autonomy of persons . . . [and] it is a barrier to exploitation and harm. These purposes are no longer relevant to the cadaver which has no autonomy and cannot be harmed." On the other hand, it has been argued that people have critical interests[31] that persist after death,[32] and Childress[33] asserts that "people can be wronged even when they are not harmed (e.g., by having their will thwarted after their deaths) . . . " We are not convinced that this is true,[13,34] but even if it is, as will soon be discussed, this concern is not sufficient to reject conscription.

Another disadvantage of conscription is that it may harm the interests of surviving family members who are opposed to organ procurement. Many people have strong feelings about how the body of a recently deceased loved one should be handled. And as Boddington[35] points out, "So much does the death of a group member affect those still alive, and so heavily imbued with spiritual, religious, and cultural significance are the rituals of death in human societies, that there are good grounds for respecting claims of the group [i.e., the family] for autonomy over these matters."

It appears then that conscription has the potential to harm families and perhaps "wrong" the decedent. It may therefore violate the ethical principle of non-maleficence which states that one should not intentionally inflict harm.[28] However, it is important to remember that this principle is not absolute and may be justifiably overridden when the expected benefit of an action exceeds the harm inflicted.[28] In our view, this would apply to conscription of cadaveric organs for transplantation. However strong are the interests of the family, and even if there are individual interests that survive after death, it is hard to see how they could possibly be as important as the lives of desperately ill patients with ESOD who will die without an organ transplant. Preservation of life is perhaps the paramount principle of medical ethics.[36] Consistent with this view, Jonsen[30] argues, "respecting the former beliefs of the decedent or observing cultural practices about burial, while important, would seem to yield before the significant value of therapy for those suffering from serious illness." On this point Harris[32] is even stronger: "If we can save or prolong the lives of living people and can only do so at the expense of the sensibilities of others, it seems clear to me that we should. For the alternative involves the equivalent of sacrificing people's lives so that others will simply *feel* better or not feel so bad, and this seems nothing short of outrageous." And consider that a military draft is widely accepted during wartime even though the death of a young son would be much more painful for families than would the drafting of organs from a relative who is already dead.[11,26]

A final concern about conscription of cadaveric organs is that it would generate outrage among the public. While initially there probably would be public resistance to this plan, some authors believe it might not be as great as one might think.[27] Furthermore, we and others[32] believe that eventually people would get used to the idea, especially once they realize that everyone stands to benefit from the practice. Support for this prediction comes from the observation that there already exist widely accepted coercive practices that require participation of all citizens regardless of their wishes. These include forced taxation, a military draft in wartime, mandatory autopsy in cases of suspected foul play, and required vaccination of children attending public schools.[26] But even if the public remained opposed to conscription, this would still not be a sufficient reason for abandoning the plan. As already alluded to, the state may act coercively in order to protect itself and the lives of its constituents. As noted by Silver,[26] "Even if the Court were to conclude that an individual's decision regarding the disposition of her dead body is protected by the right of privacy, it would likely uphold the proposed organ draft on the ground that it promotes a state interest of sufficient importance to warrant an intrusion into constitutionally protected decisionmaking. State interests in obtaining evidence and in public health already override the individual's 'liberty' to be disposed of as she pleases. Surely, state interests in preserving life are more important than these other state interests and the invasion no more severe."

The possibility of religious objection is a sensitive and important issue. But it should be noted that even the protection of religious interests is not absolute.[25] For example, these interests are not sufficient to prevent compulsory autopsy. Are not the reasons for conscription of cadaveric organs at least as compelling as those for autopsy?

A FINAL ARGUMENT SUPPORTING CONSCRIPTION OF CADAVERIC ORGANS FOR TRANSPLANTATION

Peters[17] and others claim that consenting to posthumous organ removal should not be considered an act of charity but rather "a moral duty of substantial stringency." Peters[17] argues that because there is no risk of harming cadavers, and because their organs may be life-saving, posthumous organ donation is an example of an easy rescue of an endangered person. Based on this reasoning, he concludes that everyone is "under a moral obligation to *now* explicitly consent to the posthumous taking of his or her own organs for this lifesaving purpose."[17] Unfortunately, left to their own devices, not enough people meet this obligation. Conscription of cadaveric organs could then be justified as necessary to ensure that all citizens do what they should have done on their own but did not. "Good Samaritan" laws provide precedent for this approach.

CONCLUSION

The severe shortage of organs is the major barrier to transplantation today and the situation is growing steadily worse. This crisis has led many workers in the field to propose and try new approaches in the hope of improving the efficiency of cadaveric organ procurement. All of them are beset by logistical and ethical problems, but only conscription can achieve an efficiency rate that approaches 100%. Because the stakes are so high we should aim for nothing less. A strong burden of proof falls upon those who would oppose conscription to justify why any non–life-threatening interest should be given greater weight than those of patients with ESOD, many of whom will continue to die unless conscription of cadaveric organs becomes routine. If we can conscript young men into the military at the risk of losing their lives in the name of protecting the welfare of our citizens, then surely we can conscript organs from cadavers that cannot be harmed for the same purpose. No doubt there will be many people who do not agree, but before rejecting the idea out of hand, let's at least talk about it.

REFERENCES

1. Wolfe RA, Ashby VB, Milford EL, et al: Comparison of mortality in all patients on dialysis, patients on dialysis awaiting transplantation, and recipients of a first cadaveric transplant. N Engl J Med 341:1725–1730, 1999

2. US Renal Data System: Excerpts From the USRDS 2000 Annual Data Report: Atlas of End-Stage Renal Disease in the United States. Am J Kidney Dis 36:S163–S176, 2000 (suppl 2)

3. Lin HM, Kauffman M, McBride MA, et al: Center-specific graft and patient survival rates. 1997 United Network for Organ Sharing (UNOS) Report. JAMA 280:1153–1160, 1998.

4. Cohen B, Wight C: A European perspective on organ procurement. Transplantation 68:985–990, 1999

5. Hou S: Expanding the kidney donor pool: Ethical and medical considerations. Kidney Int 58:1820–1836, 2000

6. www.unos.org/Newsroom/critdata_main.htm

7. Evans RW, Orians CE, Ascher NL: The potential supply of organ donors. An assessment of the efficiency of organ procurement in the United States. JAMA 267:239–246, 1992

8. Gortmaker SL, Beasley CL, Brigham LE, et al: Organ donor potential and performance: Size and nature of the organ donor shortfall. Crit Care Med 24:432–439, 1996

9. Durand-Zaleski J, Waissman R, Lang P, Weil B, Foury M, Bonnet F: Nonprocurement of transplantable organs in a tertiary care hospital. Transplantation 62:1224–1229, 1996

10. Siminoff LA, Arnold RM, Caplin AL, Virnig BA, Seltzer DL: Public policy governing organ and tissue procurement in the United States. Ann Intern Med 123:10–17, 1995

11. Spital A: Obtaining consent for organ donation: What are our options? Balliere's Clin Anaesth 13:179–193, 1999

12. Wendler D, Dickert N: The consent process for cadaveric organ procurement, How does it work? How can it be improved? JAMA 285:329–333, 2001

13. Erin CA: Presumed consent, contracting out, and conscription of the dead. BSHI 36:4–7, 1999

14. Matesanz R: Cadaveric organ donation: Comparison of legislation in various countries of Europe. Nephrol Dial Transplant 13:1632–1635, 1998

15. Barnett AH, Kaserman DL: The shortage of organs for transplantation: Exploring the alternatives. Issues Law Med 9:117–137, 1993

16. Council on Ethical and Judicial Affairs, American Medical Association. Financial incentives for organ procurement. Ethical aspects of future contracts for cadaveric donors. Arch Intern Med 155:581–589, 1995

17. Peters DA: A unified approach to organ donor recruitment, organ procurement, and distribution. J Law Health 3:157–3187, 1989–90

18. Spital A: Mandated choice for organ donation. Time to give it a try. Ann Intern Med 125:66–69, 1996

19. Dossetor J: Kidney vending: "Yes!" or "No!" Am J Kidney Dis 35:1002–1018, 2000

20. Klassen AC, Klassen DK: Who are the donors in organ donation? The family's perspective in mandated choice. Ann Intern Med 125:70–73, 1996

21. Menikoff J: Organ swapping. Hastings Center Report 29:28–33, 1999

22. Gillon R: On giving preference to prior volunteers when allocating organs for transplantation. J Med Ethics 21:195–196, 1995

23. Gridelli B, Remuzzi G: Strategies for making more organs available for transplantation. N Engl J Med 343:404–410, 2000

24. Hauptman PJ, O'Connor KJ: Procurement and allocation of solid organs for transplantation. N Engl J Med 336:422–431, 1997

25. Compulsory removal of cadaver organs. Columbia Law Rev 69:693–705, 1979

26. Silver T: The case for a post-mortem organ draft and a proposed model organ draft act. Boston Univ Law Rev 68:681–728, 1988

27. Emson HE: The ethics of human cadaver organ transplantation: A biologist's viewpoint. J Med Ethics 13:124–126, 1987

28. Beauchamp TL, Childress JF: Principles of Biomedical Ethics (ed 4). Oxford, UK, Oxford University Press, 1994, pp. 194, 327

29. Murray TH, Youngner SJ: Organ salvage policies. A need for better data and more insightful ethics. JAMA 272:814–815, 1994

30. Jonsen AR: Transplantation of fetal tissue: An ethicist's viewpoint. Clin Res 36:215–219, 1988

31. Dworkin R: Life's Dominion: An Argument About Abortion and Euthanasia. London, UK, Harper Collins, 1993, pp. 199–213

32. Harris J: Wonderwoman and Superman. The Ethics of Human Biotechnology. Oxford, UK, Oxford University Press, 1992, pp. 100–103

33. Childress JF: Ethical criteria for procuring and distributing organs for transplantation. J Health Politics Policy Law 14:87–113, 1989

34. Erin CA: Some comments on the ethics of consent to the use of ovarian tissue from aborted fetuses and dead women, in Harris J, Holm S (eds): The Future of Human Reproduction. Ethics, Choice, and Regulation. Oxford, UK, Clarendon, 1998, pp. 162–175

35. Boddington P: Organ donation after death—Should I decide, or should my family? J Appl Philosophy 15:69–81, 1998

36. Dukeminier J, Sanders D: Organ transplantation: A proposal for routine salvaging of cadaver organs. N Engl J Med 279:413–419, 1968

"An Ignoble Form of Cannibalism": Reflections on the Pittsburgh Protocol for Procuring Organs from Non-Heart-Beating Cadavers

Renée C. Fox

In August, I flew to Paris to participate in a Controversy Plenary Session at the XIVth International Congress of the Transplantation Society on the topic: "Regulated Commercialism of Vital Organ Donation: A Necessity?" My assignment was to speak to the "con" side of the issue in question—namely, the proposal to provide financial incentives for organ donation by creating a market system (particularly a futures market) in transplanting cadaver organs.[1]

Fox, Renée C. "'An Ignoble Form of Cannibalism': Reflections on the Pittsburgh Protocol for Procuring Organs from Non-Heart-Beating Cadavers," *Kennedy Institute of Ethics Journal* 3:2 (1993), 231–239. Copyright © 1993 by The Johns Hopkins University Press. Reprinted by permission of The Johns Hopkins University Press.

Two months before my trip to Paris, I read a letter to the editor in *The New England Journal of Medicine* reporting on the transplantation of the kidneys of a 28-year old man who committed suicide by carbon monoxide poisoning. There is a shortage of organs available for transplantation, the authors of the letter went on to say, and since "[c]arbon monoxide poisoning is a leading cause of accidental death and suicide" in the United States (3500 deaths per year), "the routine rejection of donors" in this state "can have a considerable effect on the pool of cadaveric donors." The "excellent outcome" of their own experience with the transplantation of two such kidneys, the letter-writers claimed, "suggests that patients with carbon monoxide poisoning can be accepted as kidney donors provided that their renal function is adequate at the time of donation" (Hébert et al. 1992).

And now, in October, two months after my brief trip to Paris, I find myself at the University of Pittsburgh Medical Center (UPMC), contributing to a meeting organized around a protocol to procure organs for donation from so-called "non-heart-beating cadavers."

All three of these events are examples of what I view as the worrisome, zeal-ridden strategies for augmenting the number of donated organs that are presently being considered by the medical profession. Catalyzed by the conviction that there is a severe, even tragic shortage of organs available for transplantation that can and must be alleviated, the escalating search for organs is premised on the uncritical, "not-totally rational beliefs that transplantation is an unequivocally and unconditionally good way of sustaining lives; [and] that the more organs proffered, procured, and transplanted, the better . . ." (Fox 1993, p. 55). Within this driven framework, the Pittsburgh protocol is the most elaborately macabre scheme for obtaining organs that I have encountered. It borders on ghoulishness. I do not consider it either medically acceptable or morally permissible. Even if it were, this proposal would be unlikely to lead to a substantial increase in non-living donors or in transplantable organs.

In a number of ways, I am as medically perplexed as I am profoundly disturbed by the protocol. Why, I wonder, is it structured around the concept of "non-heart-beating cadavers"? According to the Uniform Determination of Death Act, "An individual who has sustained either (1) irreversible cessation of circulatory or respiratory functions, or (2) irreversible cessation of all functions of the entire brain, including the brain stem, is dead." Death can still be determined according to the more traditional criteria that denote permanent loss of heart and lung function. These grounds have not been supplanted by "brain death" standards. Isn't a "non-heart-beating cadaver," then,

simply someone who has been pronounced dead on the basis of long established cardiopulmonary criteria? Why is there felt a need to underscore the fact that the individual declared dead on this basis does not have a beating heart? (Or, for that matter, why the insistence on invoking the term "cadaver" in this connection?)

Is this vocabulary intended to signal that the prospective donor is *really* dead, in the face of doubts about it? Does the terminology contain a cryptic reference to the fact that protocol requires no more than two minutes of electrocardiographic indicators of ventricular fibrillation, electrical asystole, or electromechanical dissociation for "the diagnosis of death" to be made, instead of the six to seven minutes that physicians are expected to observe, for example, at the Hospital of the University of Pennsylvania (the academic medical center with which I am most familiar)?

Are the physicians who coined and use the phrase "non-heart-beating cadaver" emphasizing this partly to give them confidence that even if they waited more than two minutes, the patient/donor's heart would not beat again? Or are they so young, or so medically inexperienced in all but organ transplantation work that they have rarely pronounced death in the traditional way, and therefore feel uneasy about it? (Since having to deal with "heart-beating cadavers" in the context of transplants has been a source of considerable stress for intensive care unit medical and nursing personnel, it would be rather ironic if cessation of the heartbeat were now considered to be perturbing as well.)

Why did the drafters and supporters of this protocol feel compelled to state and restate that "organs will not be procured until after the patient is declared dead," and that "no organs may be procured until death is certified"? Rather than assuring the reader that this is indeed the case, it raises the very spectre that it attempts to dispel: Was initiating organ procurement before the pronouncement of death seriously contemplated? And is shortening the timing of electrocardiographic criteria for certifying death to two minutes a technologically sophisticated way of disguising the fact that organ procurement does in fact begin before the patient/donor is unambiguously and irreversibly dead? In this respect (and others), there is a disquieting, "doth protest too much" quality to what the principles, procedures, and guidelines of the protocol declare.

These concerns are enhanced for me by what I regard as one of the most puzzling and fundamental medical questions that this organ procurement plan evokes: What is galvanizing this frenetic process? Under the proposed new policy, in a collective effort to keep warm ischemia time of organs to a minimum, doctors and nurses put death on an accelerated time clock, and then race frantically to beat that clock. It is on their urgent commitment to saving every second that they can, after the death of the patient/donor is pronounced, that they base and justify transporting that person to the operating room while he or she is still alive, putting in a femoral line, and doing skin preparations and sterile draping for the procurement surgery prior to that individual's death in an enclave of the hospital inaccessible to his or her family or clinical caretakers.

But is all of this really necessary? Is the viability of every transplantable organ and tissue equally vulnerable to prolonged ischemia, or is it particularly the heart and the liver that are subject to this eventuality? Aren't there ways in which the hospital could work on quickening the movement of the patient/donor from the intensive care unit to the operating room as soon as he (she) is pronounced dead? How many more organs would be damaged or perish if the donor were not already in the operating room when death occurred, or if the insertion of a femoral line, surgical skin care, and draping were done post-mortem?

These are vital questions of more than medical and technical import, because in the name of retrieving as many transplantable organs and tissues as possible from non-living donors, the "planned terminal management" scheme outlined in the Pittsburgh protocol subjects patient/donors to inhumane and irreverent deaths, increases the suffering of their families, and exposes the nursing and medical personnel involved to new forms of emotional and existential strain.

To begin with, although the guidelines affirm and re-affirm that the dying patient/donors will receive comforting medication, especially sedating narcotic drugs, these statements are repeatedly accompanied, qualified, and counterbalanced by references to steps that must and will be taken to ensure that the drugs given will not have the "unintentional," "secondary," or "double effect" of unduly "hastening," or "causing" these patients' deaths. Translated from the convoluted language in which it is expressed, what the drafters of the document are saying is that they do not want to kill, or appear to be killing patients in order to get their organs. Rather than incurring this risk or accusation, these patients will be given less, and/or less continuous, medication than they would ordinarily receive for comfort at this stage in the dying process if they were not candidate organ donors.

This is horrifyingly apparent when one reads that patient/donors' "recovery of cognition (awareness)" is one of the criteria used for verifying that they are "not receiving substantially more medication than needed to provide comfort." This means that it is only after such

a patient/donor "wakes up," and thereby "adequately indicates the reversal of sedation," that more comfort medication will be administered. How much and what kind of additional pain and terror will this dying patient experience under these circumstances, in order to assuage the medical team's and the hospital's "concern," as they put it, that "when the life support is withdrawn, the high level of drugs rather than the underlying condition will be the cause of the patient's death"?

In this connection, one of the disconcerting and eerie side-effects of the use of the term "patient" in the protocol to include the "surrogate of a patient who lacks decision making capacity" is that it gives the misleading impression that a considerable number of patient/donors will be conscious and lucid enough for a sufficiently long period of time to meet and discuss with a member of the Ethics Consultation Service, and then review the 10-point informed consent procedure with the intensive care physician before personally signing the consent form, and at some unspecified later time, lapsing into unconsciousness. This impression is reinforced by the passing reference to "conscious patients who clearly can sense discomfort (e.g. patients with amyotrophic lateral sclerosis") in the "Specific Guidelines and Corresponding Rationale" section of the protocol.

In any case, whatever the state of consciousness of the patient/donor may be when the process of withdrawing life support begins, the protocol contains no guarantee that this will be done exactly as it would if the critically ill person were not a prospective donor or, to quote the protocol again, "in a sequence and rate that best serves the patient," his or her "comfort" and "autonomy." In what order will the different types of life support be removed? Will those decisions be unconsciously, if not intentionally influenced by the physician's desire to protect and preserve the patient/donors' organs for transplantation? A survey questionnaire-based study of "how physicians decide to withdraw life support in critically ill patients," conducted by Drs. Nicholas A. Christakis and David A. Asch found that "in a wide variety of clinical situations," internists have "significant and strong preferences regarding the specific form of life support withdrawn. The order of preference, from most likely to least likely to withdraw, [was] as follows: blood products, hemodialysis, intravenous vasopressors, total parenteral nutrition, antibiotics, mechanical ventilation, tube feedings, and intravenous fluids."[2] Are these the preferences that will guide the procedures followed by the Pittsburgh team? And if their process of withdrawing life support from prospective "non-heart-beating" donors differs from the way it is done with other critically ill patients, will this subvert the primary goal of these physicianly decisions—that of allowing patients to die as humanely as possible?

In the end, the protocol leaves open the gruesome possibility that after obtaining consent, and transporting the patient to the operating room for the withdrawal of life support, the pronouncement of death, and the procurement surgery, the decision may be made by the "responsible transplantation surgeon" that the ischemia has been too prolonged for the organs to be utilized. Not only may the organ procurement surgery be canceled under these circumstances, but according to the protocol, "the designated ICU physician may also decide to return the patient to the ICU." In what state will this patient be? What will happen to him or her next? How will the family, or for that matter, the ICU staff, be able to cope with this fearful turn of events? The more intently one examines the details of this plan, the more ghastly it seems.

If asked to identify what is most dreadful about it, I would single out the desolate, profanely "high tech" death that the patient/donor dies, beneath operating room lights, amidst masked, gowned, and gloved strangers, who have prepared his (her) body for the eviscerating surgery that will follow.

This contrasts sharply with the procedures that the nursing and medical staff responsible for the care of hospitalized, non-donor patients try to follow when they sense that an imminent death is approaching. Under the best of circumstances, if the patient's next of kin are not present in the hospital, they are contacted, and given time to arrive for a bedside visit with the patient before death is pronounced. Immediately thereafter, nurses who have taken care of the patient begin post-mortem care—washing and positioning the patient's body, removing whatever signs of suffering from it they can, and also cleaning the room to make things presentable for family viewing. Usually it is not until relatives have "witnessed death in their loved one," if they wish to do so, "and said goodbye," that the nurses cover the patient's hands and face with a plastic shroud, and relinquish the body to escort personnel for transport to the morgue (Wolf 1988, pp. 136–39).[3]

Under the Pittsburgh protocol, however, the dying patient/donor is sped away to the operating room, where he (she) is isolated from family, and where life support is withdrawn, and death is pronounced. The patient literally "dies on the operating table"—one of the most traumatic experiences that surgeons, surgical nurses, and anesthesiologists can undergo. Although in this organ donor context the patient's death is not due either to surgery or its failure, the association is there nonetheless, along with a powerful sacrificial meaning—all the more so because it is on the same patient and table that the operating room team performs organ

procurement surgery. I surmise that the room then becomes the site for the patient/donor's post-mortem care, given by the nurses under the supervision of the Pittsburgh Transplant Foundation. "The procedure for organ procurement, cleaning the body, and transfer to the morgue is to be conducted with respect and sensitivity to the deceased and his/her surrogate," the protocol states; but how respectful and sensitive can this process be if it separates patient and family from one another throughout the entire trajectory?

Furthermore, situating the sequence of events in the operating room symbolically contaminates it in ways that could be profoundly disquieting to the surgical team (I would predict especially to the nurses). I would not be surprised if the surgical staff felt a strong aversion to doing other procedures in the room and on the table where donors die, have their organs taken from them, and where their bodies are readied for the morgue. Rituals to repurify the setting in which these acts took place might be needed to make the situation more tolerable for the staff—providing that one felt it morally justified to implement this plan, which I do not.

What the protocol asks of donors, their families, and caretakers goes so far beyond the pale of the medically decent, morally allowable, and spiritually acceptable that it strains credulity. Certainly it did mine. Now that I am more sure, however, that I understand its provisions and implications, I would never consent to becoming such a "non-heart-beating cadaver" organ donor myself, or to having a member of my family or anyone else for whom I was responsible do so. And if I were a health care professional, I would avail myself of an option that the protocol offers: that of refusing "to participate in the procedures," because "such participation [would be] against [my] personal, ethical [and] religious beliefs." For, in my view, the kind of "rational mutilation of the body"[4] and "death by protocol"[5] that are involved here desecrate what is sacred about human bodily life and bodily death, and brings us close to the foreboding image once invoked by the theologian Paul Ramsey (1970, pp. 208–9): the reduction of persons to "an ensemble of . . . interchangeable . . . spare parts" in which "everyone [becomes] a useful precadaver."

But how can one account for the fact that after what has been described as almost four years of deliberation and review by various experts and groups, both from within and outside of the UPMC, involving "more than 100 individuals," this protocol and the organ donor policy that it delineates were "approved according to university and hospital procedures" (DeVita and Snyder 1993)? Several factors appear to have converged to bring this about: The magnitude and scope of the UPMC's transplant program, where on average a transplant is performed every 12 hours in one of its three hospitals, and more types of organ transplants are done than in any other institution in the world; the exceptionally large number of its personnel directly involved in transplantation-related activities or in the care of critically ill patients; and the ways in which the daily professional rounds of the Center's staff continually expose them to the need for donor organs, and to the many very sick individuals and their families awaiting them. The mixture of ardor about transplantation, familiarity with the procedure, identification with prospective organ recipients, and desperation about the shortage of organs that these conditions have engendered seem to have eroded respect for the significance of the willingness of patients and their families to donate organs, and decreased awareness of the sacred trust with which medical professionals who receive and utilize these "gifts of life" are invested. Despite the extensive efforts that were made to develop an ethical policy for organ procurement from non-heart-beating donors, a worrisomely earnest, generalized inability to recognize or actively respond to what is wrong with the protocol that has resulted from this process prevails in the Pittsburgh Medical Center milieu.

Physician-philosopher Leon R. Kass (1992, p. 73) has referred to organ procurement and transplantation as a "noble form of cannibalism." For the reasons that I have set forth in these reflections, I regard this Pittsburgh version as an *ignoble* form of medically rationalized cannibalism that should be prohibited.

NOTES

1. This Plenary Session, moderated by Ronald D. Guttman, took place on August 19, 1992. Lloyd Cohen, a jurist, presented the argument for the "Pro" side of the question.

2. I would like to thank Nicholas Christakis for illuminating and helping me to think through what I found to be the troubling withdrawal of life support and the administration of comfort medication issues that the Pittsburgh protocol presents.

3. For everything I know about "the nursing ritual of post-mortem care" and its meaning for nurses, other hospital personnel, and patient's families, I am beholden to Zane Robinson Wolf.

4. This concept is formulated and developed by sociologist Jonathan B. Imber of Wellesley College in an as-yet unpublished paper, "The Kinds of Death We Have: Reflections on Autopsy and Public Trust in the Medical Profession."

5. I am indebted to Albert Yan (1992)—a fourth-year medical student at the University of Pennsylvania, and Trustee and Former Editor-in-Chief of the *American Journal of Ethics and Medicine*—for this insightful image.

REFERENCES

Christakis, Nicholas A., and Asch, David A. How Do Physicians Decide Which Forms of Life Support to Withdraw? University of Pennsylvania. Unpublished paper.

DeVita, Michael A., and Snyder, James V. 1993. Development of the University of Pittsburgh Medical Center Policy for the Care of Terminally Ill Patients Who May Become Organ Donors after Death Following the Removal of Life Support. *Kennedy Institute of Ethics Journal* 3: 131–43.

Fox, Renée C. 1993. Regulated Commercialism of Vital Organ Donation: A Necessity? (Con). *Transplantation Proceedings* 25: 55–57.

Hébert, Marie-Josée; Boucher, Anne; Beaucage, Giles; et al. 1992. Transplantation of Kidneys From a Donor With Carbon Monoxide Poisoning. *New England Journal of Medicine* 326: 1571.

Kass, Leon R. 1992. Organs For Sale? Propriety, Property, and the Price of Progress. *The Public Interest* 107 (Spring): 65–86.

Ramsey, Paul. 1970. *The Patient As Person: Explorations in Medical Ethics.* New Haven: Yale University Press.

Wolf, Zane Robinson. 1988. *Nurses' Work, The Sacred and The Profane.* Philadelphia: University of Pennsylvania Press.

Yan, Albert. 1992. Insiders' Observations on Today's Medical Students. Presentation at the Workshop on "The Medical Students of Today and Tomorrow," organized by the Medical College of Pennsylvania and The Acadia Institute for the Study of Medicine, Science, and Society, Bar Harbor, Maine. 12–13 October, at the Medical College of Pennsylvania, Philadelphia.

LIVING DONORS

The Ethics of Organ Donation by Living Donors

Robert D. Truog

Most organs for transplantation come from cadavers, but as these have failed to meet the growing need for organs, attention has turned to organs from living donors. Organ donation by living donors presents a unique ethical dilemma, in that physicians must risk the life of a healthy person to save or improve the life

Truog, Robert D. "The Ethics of Organ Donation by Living Donors," *New England Journal of Medicine* 353:5 (2005), 444–446. Copyright © 2005. Reprinted by permission of Massachusetts Medical Society.

of a patient. Transplantation surgeons have therefore been cautious in tapping this source. As surgical techniques and outcomes have improved, however, this practice has slowly expanded. Today, according to the United Network for Organ Sharing (UNOS), almost half of all kidney donors in the United States are living. In 2004, living organ donors also provided a lobe of the liver in approximately 320 cases and a lobe of a lung in approximately 15 cases.

Three categories of donation by living persons can be distinguished: directed donation to a loved one or friend; nondirected donation, in which the donor gives an organ to the general pool to be transplanted into the recipient at the top of the waiting list; and directed donation to a stranger, whereby donors choose to give to a specific person with whom they have no prior emotional connection.

Each type of donation prompts distinct ethical concerns. With directed donation to loved ones or friends, worries arise about the intense pressure that can be put on people to donate, leading those who are reluctant to do so to feel coerced. In these cases, transplantation programs are typically willing to identify a plausible medical excuse, so that the person can bow out gracefully.[1] Equally important, however, are situations in which people feel compelled to donate regardless of the consequences to themselves. In one instance, both parents of a child who was dying of respiratory failure insisted on donating lobes of their lungs in a desperate but unsuccessful attempt to save her life.[2] Such a sense of compulsion is not unusual. In cases like these, simply obtaining the informed consent of the relative is insufficient—physicians are obligated to prevent people from making potentially life-threatening sacrifices unless the chance of success is proportionately large.

Nondirected donation raises different ethical concerns. The radical altruism that motivates a person to make a potentially life-threatening sacrifice for a stranger calls for careful scrutiny. One recent case involved a man who seemed pathologically obsessed with giving away everything, from his money to his organs, saying that doing so was "as much a necessity as food, water, and air."[3] After donating one kidney to a stranger, he wondered how he might give away all his other organs in a dramatic suicide. Other psychologically suspect motivations need to be ruled out as well. Is the person trying to compensate for depression or low self-esteem, seeking media attention, or harboring hopes of becoming involved in the life of the recipient? Transplantation teams have an obligation to assess potential donors in all these

dimensions and prohibit donations that arouse serious concern.[1]

Directed donation to a stranger raises similar ethical questions with a few additional wrinkles. This type of donation usually occurs when a patient advertises for an organ publicly, on television or billboards or over the Internet. Such advertising is not illegal, but it has been strongly discouraged by the transplantation community. Two central objections are that the practice is unfair and that it threatens the view that an organ is a "gift of life," not a commodity to be bought and sold.

Some argue that just as we have a right to donate to the political parties and charities of our choice, so should we be able to choose to whom to give our organs. In practice, however, this means that those who have the most compelling stories and the means to advertise their plight tend to be the ones who get the organs—rather than those most in need. This strikes some ethicists as unfair. Unlike monetary gifts, they argue, organ transplantation requires the involvement of social structures and institutions, such as transplantation teams and hospitals. Hence, the argument goes, these donations are legitimately subject to societal requirements of fairness, and transplantation centers should refuse to permit the allocation of organs on the basis of anything but morally relevant criteria.[4]

The most ethically problematic cases are those in which the recipient is chosen on the basis of race, religion, or ethnic group. In one case, for example, the family of a brain-dead Florida man agreed to donate his organs—but insisted that because of the man's racist beliefs, the recipients must be white. Although the organs were allocated accordingly, Florida subsequently passed a law prohibiting patients or families from placing such restrictions on donation.[5]

Even when the motives for choosing a recipient may be unethical, however, there might be reasons for allowing the donation to proceed. Consider a case that was discussed at a recent public forum hosted by Harvard Medical School's Division of Medical Ethics: a Jewish man in New York learned of a Jewish child in Los Angeles who needed a kidney transplant. The man wanted to help someone of his own faith and decided he was willing to donate a kidney to help this particular child. Despite his discriminatory preference, one might view the donation as permissible, since at least some patients would benefit (the child would receive a kidney, and those below her on the waiting list would move up one notch) and no one would be harmed (those above the girl on the waiting list would not receive the kidney under any circumstances, because the man would not give it to them). Whether directed donation to strangers violates standards of fairness is thus controversial. But if it is permitted, it will be very difficult to prohibit discriminatory preferences, since donors can simply specify that the organ must go to a particular person, without saying why.

The other substantial cause for concern about this type of donation is its potential for making possible the buying and selling of organs. These practices are strictly prohibited by law, yet they seem to be an inherent risk in directed donations to strangers. Wealthy patients in need and healthy donors looking for a quick fix to their financial problems will always be able to find ways around even the most earnest attempts to prevent money from changing hands.

Despite these concerns, efforts to direct organ donations to strangers are not new, dating back at least to the celebrated 1982 case of Jamie Fiske, whose father successfully mounted a nationwide appeal for someone to donate a liver to her. Today, many such solicitations are transmitted over the Internet, where, when the practice was relatively limited, organ solicitation was managed quietly, on a case-by-case basis, by individual transplantation centers. All this changed, however, with the emergence in 2004 of MatchingDonors.com (as discussed by Steinbrook in this issue of the *Journal,* pages 441–444). This Web site currently claims to have more than 2100 registered potential donors and to have brokered 12 transplantations, with about 20 more recipient–donor pairs matched and awaiting surgery.

Although the business conducted on this organization's Web site does not raise any fundamental ethical issues not already posed by other methods of solicitation, it does introduce a new degree of visibility that increases the magnitude of the issue. Will competing commercial Web sites begin to emerge? How will these sites be held accountable? Dr. Jeremiah Lowney, the medical director of MatchingDonors.com, recently argued that just as a dating service could not be held responsible for a bad date, his Web site has no responsibility for the outcomes of its matches. Furthermore, the Web site has no mechanism for ensuring the quality of the information it provides about transplantation and donation by living persons or for checking the accuracy of information submitted by potential donors and recipients.

Given the life-or-death consequences of the procedure, organ donation should not be governed by the ethics of caveat emptor. Nevertheless, MatchingDonors.com has clearly identified a need, and if this need is not met by a service that can address the ethical challenges, the vacuum will be filled by other enterprises. Entrepreneurs commonly open up useful new markets and services that must eventually become subject to rigorous standards and regulations.

The solicitation of organs over the Internet is probably here to stay, but it will require higher standards of responsibility and accountability than are currently in place. UNOS has more than 20 years of experience in managing the cadaveric-donor pool and is in a good position to extend its jurisdiction to include donation by living donors. The organization recently considered the topic of solicitation and decided not to pursue building a Web site similar to that of MatchingDonors .com but, instead, to provide educational information for anyone who is willing to be a living donor of a kidney and to develop a nationwide mechanism for allocating organs for nondirected donation by living donors.

This effort, however, does not go far enough. The proposal does not address directed donation and leaves many critical aspects of donation by living donors to the transplantation centers. Organ transplantation is big business, and each center is highly motivated to expand its share of the pie. They therefore have intolerable conflicts of interest when it comes to regulating themselves. Instead, UNOS should be charged with standardizing the process for evaluating potential donors, ensuring that independent advocates are assigned to help donors make an informed choice, developing mechanisms to deal with potential injury or death to the donor, setting standards for both directed and nondirected donation, and prohibiting transplantation when the chance of success is insufficient to justify the risks. Comprehensive oversight is necessary if the ethical pitfalls are to be adequately addressed.

NOTES

1. Abecassis M, Adams M, Adams P, et al. Consensus statement on the live organ donor. JAMA 2000;284:2919–26.
2. Kolata G. Lungs from parents fail to save girl, 9, and doctors assess ethics. New York Times May 20, 1991:A11.
3. Parker I. The gift: Zell Kravinsky gave away millions: but somehow it wasn't enough. The New Yorker, August 2, 2004:54–63.
4. Kluge E-HW. Designated organ donation: private choice in social context. Hastings Cent Rep 1989;19(5):10–6.
5. Veatch RM. Transplantation ethics. Washington, D.C.: Georgetown University Press, 2000.

Organs.com: New Commercially Brokered Organ Transfers Raise Questions

Arthur Caplan

On October 20, 2004, surgeons removed a kidney from Robert Smitty and transplanted it into Robert Hickey, a fifty-eight-year-old physician with renal failure, at Denver's Presbyterian/St Luke's Medical Center. Hickey had paid MatchingDonors.com, a commercial website, a $295 monthly fee to have his need for a kidney advertised on the website. Smitty, a thirty-two-year-old sometime photographer from Chattanooga, Tennessee, had found Hickey on the MatchingDonors.com website. He is the first person in the United States known to have arranged an organ donation to a stranger using a commercial company as middleman.

The media paid a lot of attention to the Smitty/Hickey transplant, and much of it was very positive. They were fascinated with the scenario of those dying of organ failure turning to the Internet to save themselves. Good Samaritans in cyberspace could learn about those in need, weigh their respective plights, and select a fortunate supplicant to save. Unfortunately, this first case did not have the happy ending the media had envisioned.

On October 28, 2004, Robert Smitty became the first person involved in an organ transfer brokered by a commercial Website to land in jail. Smitty had failed to pay his child support and, partly as a result of the media attention that the transplant generated, was arrested and jailed upon his return to Tennessee. Suspicion that he had sold his kidney was and remains rampant.

The story of Robert Smitty's kidney highlights the need to find ways to allow those waiting for transplants to locate living persons who want to donate an organ to a complete stranger. In contrast to cadaver donation, a national system for bringing donors and recipients together does not exist. Smitty's story also highlights the absolute lack of any oversight for this new form of organ donation.

In 1997, there were no documented instances of absolute strangers donating organs. By 2003, there were dozens of such cases, and the numbers continue to grow, as does the number of sites on the Web "brokering" organs. So what is wrong with giving those who need organs a chance to find them?

The practice of soliciting strangers for organ donation is fundamentally unfair. Those who can pay middlemen to publicize their plight will have greater access to potential lifesaving transplants. Moreover, those who for whatever reason are not as "attractive" as other potential recipients will not fare well in a begging competition.

The Web is not a haven for the forthright. In matters of mating and mortgages, which dominate Internet brokerage, lying abounds. The same dearth of honesty complicates the use of the Internet to match kidneys or lobes of liver.

Also, the prospects for coercion and extortion in the wild and wooly Web are staggering. As Smitty's example reminds us, for every truly generous person who wishes to help a complete stranger, plenty of people see the redundancy of their kidneys or the regenerative power of their livers as quick tickets out of debt or the fast route to the good life. Unregulated brokerage of organs on the Internet could mean that organ sales will flourish, with the highest bidders faring the best.

Still, there are those who defend the rights of private citizens to communicate with one another in order to broker whatever arrangements they wish with respect to their body parts. But even if the line between altruism and commerce is allowed to grow fuzzy, there are other challenges to be addressed.

The transplant centers that perform these operations have a duty not only to care for those on their waiting lists, but also to protect the health and dignity of those from whom organs are extracted. Yet there are no agreed-upon protocols for the management of strangers seeking to give organs. Should such persons have to undergo a psychological evaluation to insure that they are competent? If so, who should do that exam? Should everyone be assigned a donor advocate who has no direct interest in whether someone actually becomes a source of an organ, and, if so, who should that be?

No protocols govern how long a stranger who wants to donate should have to wait; what to do if someone changes his or her mind at the last minute; who will pay if a donor dies or is injured; what role if any a potential donor's family should play; or what medical criteria should govern donor eligibility. Perhaps most disturbingly, there is no consensus among transplant centers regarding the degree of contact, either before or after surgery, that should be permitted between those making organs available and those who need them. Like adoption, a case can be made for either "open" or "closed" organ donation, but to date no policies have been established.

I can think of no ethical reason why a healthy, informed person cannot rationally decide to give another person a kidney or a lobe of liver or lung. But commercially brokered Internet matching between strangers does not appear to protect the interests of either donors or recipients.

Child Organ Donation, Family Autonomy, and Intimate Attachments

Lynn A. Jansen

What standard or principle should guide decision-making concerning the permissibility of allowing children to be organ donors? For a long time, it has been widely assumed that the best interest of the child is the appropriate standard. But recently, several critics have charged that this standard fails to give due weight to the interests of the family and the intimate relationships that the family makes possible. This article reviews and rejects both the best-interest standard (as it has been traditionally conceived) and the alternative standard recommended by the critics. I then propose a new standard to help parents, healthcare professionals, and judges decide when it is and is not permissible for children to serve as organ donors. This new standard modifies and broadens the best-interest standard to allow it to account adequately for the contribution that intimate relationships make to the well-being of children.

DEFINING THE FOCAL CASES

Before proceeding, I will simplify the discussion by drawing a distinction and making two assumptions. Doing so will allow me to sidestep some important complications that would need to be addressed in a full treatment of child organ donation, but it will enable me to focus the discussion more precisely on the issues that I want to address here. The distinction I wish to draw concerns the degree of risk that the organ donation poses to the donor. I shall distinguish between donations that involve only a minor risk to the donor and donations that involve a significant increase over minor risk to the donor. Examples of the former include the donation of a pint of blood or bone marrow. Examples of the latter include the donation of a kidney. Unlike the former donations, the donation of a kidney poses a substantial risk to the developing capacities of the child, and, as such, it is considerably more difficult to justify. For this reason, it is necessary to keep this distinction in mind.

The first assumption I make is that the prospective child organ donor does not actively dissent to the proposed organ donation. Active dissent does not occur if the child either consents to the organ donation or is too young to consent or dissent. If a child donor does actively dissent to being an organ donor, it will become considerably more difficult to justify the organ donation. My second assumption is that at least one parent of the child who is a prospective organ donor consents to the donation. If neither parent consents to the organ donation, I assume that the donation would not be justified.

This distinction and these two assumptions enable me to define two focal cases:

1. a child who wants to be an organ donor (or at least does not actively dissent to being one), who has at least one parent who consents to the donation, and who is considering an organ donation that involves only a minor risk to the donor

2. a child who wants to be an organ donor (or at least does not actively dissent to being one), who has at least one parent who consents to the donation, and who is considering an organ donation that involves a significant increase over minor risk to the donor

With respect to these two focal cases, I seek to identify the standard that should guide decisionmaking concerning the permissibility of child organ donation. If such a standard can be identified for these focal cases, then it should prove useful in thinking about nonfocal cases. But, at least in this article, I do not attempt to extend the analysis to these nonfocal cases.

THE BEST-INTEREST PRINCIPLE

Many have thought that, in these focal cases, as well as in other cases, the standard that should govern decisionmaking concerning child organ donation is one that appeals to the best interests of the child organ donor. According to this standard, to justify organ donation it must be demonstrated that the organ donation is in the best interests of the donor. Otherwise, the organ donation is ethically impermissible. This standard, which I refer to as the *best-interest principle,* has been routinely invoked by the courts. To take just one example, *in re Richardson—1973,* a Louisiana appeals court held that, in spite of the consent of his parents, it would be impermissible to allow a retarded minor to donate a kidney to save the life of his sister. As a justification for this ruling, the court maintained that the donation was not in the retarded minor's best interest. In many other court decisions, some of which have ruled to permit the organ donation in question, the best-interest principle has loomed large.

Despite its appeal, however, this standard is often difficult to apply. It is often unclear what interests of the donor should be taken into account when considering what is in his or her best interests. On this matter, it is often assumed that the psychological interests of the donor are relevant, but it is far from clear how these can be assessed in anything but a very speculative manner. How, for example, should the psychological anguish a prospective donor would suffer if he did not donate be balanced against the known health risks that the donation poses to his well-being?

But this practical difficulty with applying the best-interest principle is not a good reason for rejecting it. Any general standard for assessing the ethical permissibility of child organ donation requires sensitive judgment to be applied properly. There are, however, two more compelling reasons why this standard is questionable. First, the standard does not take into account the value of intimate relationships between children and potential organ recipients. As it has been traditionally conceived, the best-interest principle directs decisionmakers "to focus on the individual's self-regarding interests, not upon his or her alleged interests in the good of others." This narrow construal of the best interests of the child discounts one important class of benefits—namely, the benefits the child receives when he or she makes a contribution to the welfare of another person to whom he or she stands in an intimate relationship.

I will discuss these benefits in more detail later. My point here is that the best-interest principle (as it has been traditionally conceived) does not permit decisionmakers to consider all the relevant benefits. It directs them to consider only one class of benefits—those associated with the self-regarding interests of the donor. Although this class of benefits is obviously very important, it does not include all the benefits relevant to a consideration of the ethical permissibility of child organ donations.

This point is strengthened by a second one. Parents who have more than one child have obligations to further the interests of each one. These obligations can sometimes come into conflict. Suppose, for example, that the best interests of a child would be set back by requiring him to do something that is necessary to advance the best interests of his sister. Here, if the parents are to act on the best-interest principle, they need to know whether to further his best interests or those of his sister. Further suppose that the issue at stake concerns the need for one child to make an organ donation to the other. Now, if it is claimed that parents must always look out for the best interests of the child who would be serving as the organ donor, then we need to be given some reason why this is the case. This reason cannot appeal to the obligation parents have to promote the best interests of their children, because this obligation fails to discriminate between the organ donor and the recipient when both are children of the parents.

This example demonstrates that the best-interest principle cannot stand alone. It must be supplemented by a further ethical principle that requires parents to balance fairly the competing obligations they owe to their children. I shall not propose such a fairness principle here. I mention the need for such a principle for the purpose of underscoring a simple but important truth. Values other than those associated with the best interests of the child organ donor are relevant to judgments about the ethical permissibility of child organ donation. These other values need to be taken into account. Once we do this, however, we will need either to leave the best-interest principle behind or modify it considerably.

THE INTRAFAMILIAL PRINCIPLE

This has motivated some to look for a different standard for assessing the ethical permissibility of child organ donation. One such standard was suggested by the court in *Nathan v. Farinelli.* In this case (which involved kidney donation from one child to a sibling), the court ruled that permissible child organ donation does not require that the donor's best interests are served by doing so; rather all that is required is that the donor's parents make an informed decision about the matter that takes into account all the relevant benefits and risks. The court's decision, however, does not grant unlimited discretion to the parents. The judgment in this case was premised on the assumption that child organ donation is only permissible between family members, and, in particular, between siblings. Accordingly, the ruling in *Nathan v. Farinelli* would not justify a child donating an organ to a family friend or to a stranger, even if the parents of the child wanted her to do this and even if they took into account all the relevant benefits and risks of her doing so.

This suggests a reasonably clear standard for assessing the ethical permissibility of child organ donation, one that I refer to as the *intrafamilial principle*. This principle holds that child organ donation is ethically permissible if it satisfies two necessary conditions: (1) that the parents of the child donor have considered all the relevant benefits and risks of the donation and have consented to it, and (2) that the recipient of the donated organ is a family member of the donor. This principle can be qualified and supplemented in various ways. For example, it may be held that if the parents' decision to consent, even if it is based on a consideration of all the relevant benefits and risks, is patently unreasonable, then the child organ donation should not take place. Alternatively, it may be held that, in some cases of child organ donation, a further condition must be met for the donation to be justified. In case 2 examples, for instance, it may be thought that the child donor's consent is necessary for the donation to be ethically permissible. Notwithstanding these complications, the intrafamilial principle is a clear alternative to the best-interest principle. Moreover, it does not suffer from the defects of the best-interest principle noted previously. That is, in considering the full range of benefits and risks, the parents of a prospective child organ donor can give appropriate weight to his interests in the well-being of other family members. Nor does this principle direct parents to treat one of their children unfairly so as to promote the best interests of another. In considering the full range of benefits and risks, they can give appropriate weight to the possibly competing interests of the siblings of the child who is a prospective organ donor.

Still, despite these attractions, the intrafamilial principle runs into some serious problems of its own. An adequate ethical standard for assessing the permissibility of child organ donation must not only provide a means for identifying the class of persons to whom a child organ donor could (permissibly) donate his or her organs, but it must also provide guidance as to when these donations would be ethically appropriate. I argue that the intrafamilial principle fails to provide appropriate guidance on this crucial issue.

To see why, we must specify more concretely what is meant by "the full range of benefits and risks" that the parents must consider. If these concern only the best interests of the child organ donor, then the intrafamilial principle is indistinguishable from the best-interest principle. But proponents of the intrafamilial principle do not, of course, intend to restrict the meaning of this phrase in this way. Rather, they argue that under

certain circumstances parents should be able to "trade off" the well-being of one child to promote family goals and objectives. According to Lainie Friedman Ross, for example, because "families can have interests that are not reducible to the interests and needs of particular members, parents must be allowed to make intrafamilial trade-offs." Call this the *trade-off idea*.

I argue that the trade-off idea is misguided. Although it gives content to the intrafamilial principle, it should be rejected because it is based on an ethically suspect conception of the family. It must be noted, however, that the rejection of the trade-off idea does not imply that the state should intervene to prevent families from acting on it.

The justification of state intervention raises additional considerations.

Bearing this in mind, what is wrong with the trade-off idea? It will be useful here to distinguish two possibilities. In the first, the overall interests of the child organ donor are set back for the good of the family understood as a collective unit. In the second, the interests of the child organ donor are advanced by the donation. This could occur because the child may benefit from helping a family member, and this benefit may outweigh the cost to him of the organ donation. The trade-off idea fails to distinguish these possibilities. But when proponents of the intrafamilial principle claim that "families can have interests that are not reducible to the interests and needs of particular members" they strongly suggest that the first possibility is what they have in mind. This is a mistake. It unnecessarily reifies the family, making it look as if it has purposes and goals of its own that stand over and above the purposes and goals of individuals within it. This obscures a true and important fact about family members—namely, that, although they share interests and concerns, they also have interests and concerns of their own that can and often do come into conflict with the interests and concerns of other family members.

This is why this understanding of the family is ethically suspect. It may be objected at this point that, when the family as a whole benefits, each member of the family benefits as well. But notice that, to the extent that this is true, we have moved from the first possibility to the second. As I explain in the next section, the second possibility does not require us to accept the trade-off idea. If the child organ donor will himself benefit from the donation, then his interests are not being traded off to benefit the family as a whole.

A second problem confronts the intrafamilial principle as well. As discussed, this principle restricts child organ donation to family members of the organ donor. But it is not clear how the family or the boundaries of the family should be defined. These problems have arisen in cases that have come, or may someday come, before the courts. By looking at a couple of these cases, I argue that we have reason to reject the intrafamilial principle in favor of another principle, one that captures its good insights but does not suffer from its problems.

HARD CASES

One case that poses a problem for the intrafamilial principle came before the Illinois courts in 1990. It concerned bone-marrow testing and harvesting procedures between 3-year-old twins and their 12-year-old half-brother, who was suffering from mixed lineage leukemia. The twins' mother, Nancy Curran, refused to consent to the twins being tested to serve as bone marrow donors for their half brother, whereas the twins' father, Tamas Bosze, believed that the testing should take place. The dispute between the parents of the twins ended up in court, and eventually the Illinois Supreme Court ruled in favor of Curran. The twins' half-brother died, having never received the bone marrow donation that he needed.

This case raises many interesting issues, but two in particular bear importantly on the plausibility of the intrafamilial principle. The first is that, in this case, the parents of the prospective child organ donors disagreed among themselves about what ought to be done. When this occurs, the intrafamilial principle runs into problems, for the principle vests decision-making authority with the family. It does not specify who should have decisionmaking authority when family members—in particular, parents—disagree among themselves. The second issue concerns the relationship that must obtain between two people for them to be considered family members for the purposes of applying the intrafamilial principle. In this case, the twins were biologically related to their half-brother, but he did not live with them and they barely knew him. To apply the intrafamilial principle, we must know whether a genetic or biological relationship between donor and recipient is sufficient or whether some kind of emotional relationship is also required.

In deciding for Curran, the Illinois Supreme Court argued that an "existing close relationship between the donor and recipient" must be present for the donation to be permissible. Finding no such close relationship in this case, it ruled in Curran's favor. I believe that the court was correct in this judgment. The existence of a close emotional relationship between donor and recipient is more important than their genetic relationship. However, when it is thought through, this point, as I discuss in the next section, pulls us beyond the intrafamilial principle.

THE INTIMATE ATTACHMENT PRINCIPLE

I now propose a third principle—the *intimate attachment principle*—for determining the ethical permissibility of child organ donation. This principle builds on the good insight behind the intrafamilial principle. It holds that child organ donation is only permissible if it meets the following condition: There must exist an intimate attachment between the child donor and the recipient. This intimate attachment usually exists between biological family members, but it does not always exist, as *Curran v. Bosze* illustrates. More importantly, intimate attachments can exist between children and other persons who are not related to them. Thus, in principle at least, the intimate attachment principle can justify child organ donation to recipients outside the family.

What, then, is an intimate attachment between persons—in particular, between a child and another person? The key element in such an attachment is that the well-being of the child is, in some way, inextricably bound up with the well-being of the person to whom he or she has an attachment. As one writer described it, an intimate attachment is a relationship "in which one shares one's self with one or more others." When such an attachment is present, the child's well-being will diminish significantly if this person dies.

There are, of course, different ways in which a child's well-being can be bound up with the well-being of another person. Consider the case of a child's parent. Children obviously have a strong interest in the continued survival of their parents. Their emotional development, as well as their physical support, clearly are at stake. For this reason, I believe that child organ donations to their parents could, where medically appropriate, be justified. Children can also form intimate attachments with siblings and close friends. In the *Curran* case, the court held that the prospective child organ donors did not have a "close existing relationship" with their half-brother. As I said, I believe this was a correct ruling; but it should be clear that "close existing relationships" can obtain between friends as well as siblings. Given this obvious fact, to restrict child organ donation to siblings would be arbitrary. So long as the child organ donation would be medically appropriate, I see no reason why children should not be permitted to donate organs to close friends.

Admittedly, the notion of an intimate attachment and the corresponding notion of a child's well-being bound up with another are not precise ideas. Reasonable people will sometimes disagree over whether such an attachment exists in a given case. This, however, is to be expected. I am not proposing an algorithm for determining when each and every prospective donation would be ethically permissible. More modestly, I am proposing a standard or principle to help guide or direct thinking on this matter. It is also true that the notion of an intimate attachment is no more imprecise than the notion of the child's (self-regarding) best interest, which, as we have seen, has been the dominant principle relied on by the courts.

Indeed, as I suggested earlier, the intimate attachment principle can be understood as an extension of the best-interest principle. When an intimate attachment exists between a child organ donor and a prospective recipient, then the well-being of the former is bound up with the latter. This makes it possible for the organ donation to serve the best interests of both the donor and the recipient. When this occurs, it follows that the best-interest principle, properly understood, should favor the donation. For reasons that are not entirely clear, proponents of the best-interest principle have been inclined to maintain that only the self-regarding interests of the child donor should be considered. This has made their principle vulnerable to the objection that it is based on an atomistic conception of the well-being of children, one that fails to give due weight to the interests they have in forming and maintaining intimate relations with others. This objection is well founded. It is the good point behind the intrafamilial principle. But the proper response to this objection is not to abandon the best-interest principle in favor of the intrafamilial principle. Rather, we should retain the best-interest principle and withdraw the claim that it is only the self-regarding interests of the child that are to be counted in the calculation of his or her best interests. In proposing and recommending the intimate attachment principle,

I am arguing, in effect, that we need to broaden our understanding of the best interests of the child organ donor.

CONCLUSION

According to the intimate attachment principle, child organ donations are ethically permissible if there exists an attachment between the child donor and the recipient such that the well-being of the former depends, in part at least, on the well-being of the latter. The application of this principle to real-world cases leaves much room for debate. To what degree, for example, must the child donor's well-being depend on the recipient's well-being for there to exist an intimate attachment? And how should we verify that an intimate attachment exists when there is doubt on the matter? Despite these hard questions, however, the intimate attachment principle provides a clear and compelling standard for assessing the ethical permissibility of child organ donation. It refines the best-interest principle and captures what is valuable in the intra-familial principle. When an intimate attachment exists between a child donor and a recipient, the interests of the child donor will be furthered by the donation. And, given that intimate attachments usually exist between family members, the intimate attachment principle will generally not conflict with family autonomy. Although it captures what is valuable in both of these other principles, however, the intimate attachment principle goes beyond them and provides a stronger justification for child organ donation. This justification, if taken seriously, would have important implications for current practice. The intimate attachment principle broadens the scope of permissible child organ donation. If the argument of this paper is correct, the range of ethically permissible child organ donations is significantly broader than is currently thought.

ALLOCATING ORGANS

The Prostitute, the Playboy, and the Poet: Rationing Schemes for Organ Transplantation

George J. Annas

In the public debate about the availability of heart and liver transplants, the issue of rationing on a massive scale has been credibly raised for the first time in United

States medical care. In an era of scarce resources, the eventual arrival of such a discussion was, of course, inevitable.[1] Unless we decide to ban heart and liver

Annas, George J. "The Prostitute, The Playboy, and the Poet: Rationing Schemes for Organ Transplantation," *American Journal of Public Health* 75:2 (1985), 187–189. Copyright © 1985. Reprinted by permission of American Public Health Association.

transplantation, or make them available to everyone, some rationing scheme must be used to choose among potential transplant candidates. The debate has existed throughout the history of medical ethics. Traditionally it has been stated as a choice between saving one of two patients, both of whom require the immediate assistance of the only available physician to survive.

National attention was focused on decisions regarding the rationing of kidney dialysis machines when they were first used on a limited basis in the late 1960s. As one commentator described the debate within the medical profession:

> "Shall machines or organs go to the sickest, or to the ones with most promise of recovery; on a first-come, first-served basis; to the most 'valuable' patient (based on wealth, education, position, what?); to the one with the most dependents; to women and children first; to those who can pay; to whom? Or should lots be cast, impersonally and uncritically?"[2]

In Seattle, Washington, an anonymous screening committee was set up to pick who among competing candidates would receive the life-saving technology. One lay member of the screening committee is quoted as saying:

> "The choices were hard ... I remember voting against a young woman who was a known prostitute. I found I couldn't vote for her, rather than another candidate, a young wife and mother. I also voted against a young man who, until he learned he had renal failure, had been a ne'er do-well, a real playboy. He promised he would reform his character, go back to school, and so on, if only he were selected for treatment. But I felt I'd lived long enough to know that a person like that won't really do what he was promising at the time."[3]

When the biases and selection criteria of the committee were made public, there was a general negative reaction against this type of arbitrary device. Two experts reacted to the "numbing accounts of how close to the surface lie the prejudices and mindless cliches that pollute the committee's deliberations," by concluding that the committee was "measuring persons in accordance with its own middle-class values." The committee process, they noted, ruled out "creative nonconformists" and made the Pacific Northwest "no place for a Henry David Thoreau with bad kidneys."[4]

To avoid having to make such explicit, arbitrary, "social worth" determinations, the Congress, in 1972, enacted legislation that provided federal funds for virtually all kidney dialysis and kidney transplantation procedures in the United States.[5] This decision, however, simply served to postpone the time when identical decisions will have to be made about candidates for heart and liver transplantation in a society that does not provide sufficient financial and medical resources to provide all "suitable" candidates with the operation.

There are four major approaches to rationing scarce medical resources: the market approach; the selection committee approach; the lottery approach; and the "customary" approach.[1]

THE MARKET APPROACH

The market approach would provide an organ to everyone who could pay for it with their own funds or private insurance. It puts a very high value on individual rights, and a very low value on equality and fairness. It has properly been criticized on a number of bases, including that the transplant technologies have been developed and are supported with public funds, that medical resources used for transplantation will not be available for higher priority care, and that financial success alone is an insufficient justification for demanding a medical procedure. Most telling is its complete lack of concern for fairness and equity.[6]

A "bake sale" or charity approach that requires the less financially fortunate to make public appeals for funding is demeaning to the individuals involved, and to society as a whole. Rationing by financial ability says we do not believe in equality, but believe that a price can and should be placed on human life and that it should be paid by the individual whose life is at stake. Neither belief is tolerable in a society in which income is inequitably distributed.

THE COMMITTEE SELECTION PROCESS

The Seattle Selection Committee is a model of the committee process. Ethics Committees set up in some hospitals to decide whether or not certain handicapped newborn infants should be given medical care may represent another.[7] These committees have developed because it was seen as unworkable or unwise to explicitly set forth the criteria on which selection decisions would be made. But only two results are possible, as Professor Guido Calabrezi has pointed out: either a pattern of decision-making will develop or it will not. If a pattern does develop (e.g., in Seattle, the imposition of middle-class values), then it can be articulated and those decision "rules" codified and used directly, without resort to the committee. If a pattern does not develop, the committee is vulnerable to the charge that it is acting arbitrarily, or dishonestly, and therefore cannot be permitted to continue to make such important decisions.[1]

In the end, public designation of a committee to make selection decisions on vague criteria will fail because it too closely involves the state and all members of society in explicitly preferring specific individuals over others, and in devaluing the interests those others have in living. It thus directly undermines, as surely as the market system does, society's view of equality and the value of human life.

THE LOTTERY APPROACH

The lottery approach is the ultimate equalizer which puts equality ahead of every other value. This makes it extremely attractive, since all comers have an equal chance at selection regardless of race, color, creed, or financial status. On the other hand, it offends our notions of efficiency and fairness since it makes *no* distinctions among such things as the strength of the desires of the candidates, their potential survival, and their quality of life. In this sense it is a mindless method of trying to solve society's dilemma which is caused by its unwillingness or inability to spend enough resources to make a lottery unnecessary. By making this macro spending decision evident to all, it also undermines society's view of the pricelessness of human life. A first-come, first-served system is a type of natural lottery since referral to a transplant program is generally random in time. Nonetheless, higher income groups have quicker access to referral networks and thus have an inherent advantage over the poor in a strict first-come, first-served system.[8,9]

THE CUSTOMARY APPROACH

Society has traditionally attempted to avoid explicitly recognizing that we are making a choice not to save individual lives because it is too expensive to do so. As long as such decisions are not explicitly acknowledged, they can be tolerated by society. For example, until recently there was said to be a general understanding among general practitioners in Britain that individuals over age 55 suffering from end-stage kidney disease not be referred for dialysis or transplant. In 1984, however, this unwritten practice became highly publicized, with figures that showed a rate of new cases of end-stage kidney disease treated in Britain at 40 per million (versus the US figure of 80 per million) resulting in 1500–3000 "unnecessary deaths" annually.[10] This has, predictably,

led to movements to enlarge the National Health Service budget to expand dialysis services to meet this need, a more socially acceptable solution than permitting the now publicly recognized situation to continue.

In the US, the customary approach permits individual physicians to select their patients on the basis of medical criteria or clinical suitability. This, however, contains much hidden social worth criteria. For example, one criterion, common in the transplant literature, requires an individual to have sufficient family support for successful aftercare. This discriminates against individuals without families and those who have become alienated from their families. The criterion may be relevant, but it is hardly medical.

Similar observations can be made about medical criteria that include IQ, mental illness, criminal records, employment, indigency, alcoholism, drug addiction, or geographical location. Age is perhaps more difficult, since it may be impressionistically related to outcome. But it is not medically logical to assume that an individual who is 49 years old is necessarily a better medical candidate for a transplant than one who is 50 years old. Unless specific examination of the characteristics of older persons that make them less desirable candidates is undertaken, such a cut off is arbitrary, and thus devalues the lives of older citizens. The same can be said of blanket exclusions of alcoholics and drug addicts.

In short, the customary approach has one great advantage for society and one great disadvantage: it gives us the illusion that we do not have to make choices; but the cost is mass deception, and when this deception is uncovered, we must deal with it either by universal entitlement or by choosing another method of patient selection.

A COMBINATION OF APPROACHES

A socially acceptable approach must be fair, efficient, and reflective of important social values. The most important values at stake in organ transplantation are fairness itself, equity in the sense of equality, and the value of life. To promote efficiency, it is important that no one receive a transplant unless they want one and are likely to obtain significant benefit from it in the sense of years of life at a reasonable level of functioning.

Accordingly, it is appropriate for there to be an initial screening process that is based *exclusively* on medical criteria designed to measure the probability of a successful transplant, i.e., one in which the patient survives for at least a number of years and is rehabilitated. There is room in medical criteria for social worth judgments, but there is probably no way to avoid this completely. For example, it has been noted that "in many respects social and medical criteria are inextricably intertwined" and that therefore medical criteria might "exclude the poor and disadvantaged because health and socioeconomic status are highly interdependent."[11] Roger Evans gives an example. In the End Stage Renal Disease Program, "those of lower socioeconomic status are likely to have multiple comorbid health conditions such as diabetes, hepatitis, and hypertension" making them both less desirable candidates and more expensive to treat.[11]

To prevent the gulf between the haves and have nots from widening, we must make every reasonable attempt to develop medical criteria that are objective and independent of social worth categories. One minimal way to approach this is to require that medical screening be reviewed and approved by an ethics committee with significant public representation, filed with a public agency, and made readily available to the public for comment. In the event that more than one hospital in a state or region is offering a particular transplant service, it would be most fair and efficient for the individual hospitals to perform the initial medical screening themselves (based on the uniform, objective criteria), but to have all subsequent non-medical selection done by a method approved by a single selection committee composed of representatives of all hospitals engaged in the particular transplant procedure, as well as significant representation of the public at large.

As this implies, after the medical screening is performed, there may be more acceptable candidates in the "pool" than there are organs or surgical teams to go around. Selection among waiting candidates will then be necessary. This situation occurs now in kidney transplantion, but since the organ matching is much more sophisticated than in hearts and livers (permitting much more precise matching of organ and recipient), and since dialysis permits individuals to wait almost indefinitely for an organ without risking death, the situations are not close enough to permit use of the same matching criteria. On the other hand, to the extent that organs are specifically tissue- and size-matched and fairly distributed to the best matched candidate, the organ distribution system itself will resemble a natural lottery.

When a pool of acceptable candidates is developed, a decision about who gets the next available, suitable organ must be made. We must choose between using a conscious, value-laden, social worth selection criterion (including a committee to make the actual choice), or some type of random device. In view of the unacceptability and arbitrariness of social worth criteria being applied, implicitly or explicitly, by committee, this method is neither viable nor proper. On the other hand, strict adherence to a lottery might create a situation where an individual who has only a one-in-four chance of living five years with a transplant (but who could survive another six months without one) would get an organ before an individual who could survive as long or longer, but who will die within days or hours if he or she is not immediately transplanted. Accordingly, the most reasonable approach seems to be to allocate organs on a first-come, first-served basis to members of the pool but permit individuals to "jump" the queue if the second level selection committee believes they are in immediate danger of death (but still have a reasonable prospect for long-term survival with a transplant) and the person who would otherwise get the organ can survive long enough to be reasonably assured that he or she will be able to get another organ.

The first-come, first-served method of basic selection (after a medical screen) seems the preferred method because it most closely approximates the randomness of a straight lottery without the obviousness of making equity the only promoted value. Some unfairness is introduced by the fact that the more wealthy and medically astute will likely get into the pool first, and thus be ahead in line, but this advantage should decrease sharply as public awareness of the system grows. The possibility of unfairness is also inherent in permitting individuals to jump the queue, but some flexibility needs to be retained in the system to permit it to respond to reasonable contingencies.

We will have to face the fact that should the resources devoted to organ transplantation be limited (as they are now and are likely to be in the future), at some point it is likely that significant numbers of individuals will die in the pool waiting for a transplant. Three things can be done to avoid this: 1) medical criteria can be made stricter, perhaps by adding a more rigorous notion of "quality" of life to longevity and prospects for rehabilitation; 2) resources devoted to transplantation and organ procurement can be increased; or 3) individuals can be persuaded not to attempt to join the pool.

Of these three options, only the third has the promise of both conserving resources and promoting autonomy. While most persons medically eligible for a transplant would probably want one, some would not—at least if they understood all that was involved, including the need for a lifetime commitment to daily immunosuppression medications, and periodic medical monitoring for rejection symptoms.

Accordingly, it makes public policy sense to publicize the risks and side effects of transplantation, and to require careful explanations of the procedure be given to prospective patients *before* they undergo medical screening. It is likely that by the time patients come to the transplant center they have made up their minds and would do almost anything to get the transplant. Nonetheless, if there are patients who, when confronted with all the facts, would voluntarily elect not to proceed, we enhance both their own freedom and the efficiency and cost-effectiveness of the transplantation system by screening them out as early as possible.

CONCLUSION

Choices among patients that seem to condemn some to death and give others an opportunity to survive will always be tragic. Society has developed a number of mechanisms to make such decisions more acceptable by camouflaging them. In an era of scarce resources and conscious cost containment, such mechanisms will become public, and they will be usable only if they are fair and efficient. If they are not so perceived, we will shift from one mechanism to another in an effort to continue the illusion that tragic choices really don't have to be made, and that we can simultaneously move toward equity of access, quality of services, and cost containment without any challenges to our values. Along with the prostitute, the playboy, and the poet, we all need to be involved in the development of an access model to extreme and expensive medical technologies with which we can live.

REFERENCES

1. Calabresi G, Bobbitt P: *Tragic Choices.* New York: Norton, 1978.
2. Fletcher J: Our shameful waste of human tissue. *In:* Cutler DR (ed): The Religious Situation. Boston: Beacon Press, 1969; 223–252.
3. Quoted in Fox R, Swazey J: The Courage to Fail. Chicago: Univ of Chicago Press, 1974; 232.
4. Sanders & Dukeminier: Medical advance and legal lag: hemodialysis and kidney transplantation. UCLA L Rev 1968; 15:357.
5. Rettig RA: The policy debate on patient care financing for victims of end stage renal disease. Law & Contemporary Problems 1976; 40:196.
6. President's Commission for the Study of Ethical Problems in Medicine: *Securing Access to Health Care.* US Govt Printing Office, 1983; 25.
7. Annas GJ: Ethics committees on neonatal care: substantive protection or procedural diversion? Am J Public Health 1984; 74:843–845.
8. Bayer R: Justice and health care in an era of cost containment: allocating scarce medical resources. Soc Responsibility 1984; 9:37–52.
9. Annas GJ: Allocation of artificial hearts in the year 2002: *Minerva v National Health Agency.* Am J Law Med 1977; 3:59–76.
10. Commentary: UK's poor record in treatment of renal failure. Lancet July 7, 1984; 53.
11. Evans R: Health care technology and the inevitability of resource allocation and rationing decisions, Part II. JAMA 1983; 249:2208, 2217.

What "Race" Cannot Tell Us about Access to Kidney Transplantation

Elisa J. Gordon

Despite a growing awareness within American biomedicine and bioethics that the social category "race" is of limited use in describing patients,[1,2] some fields of medicine continue to use it interchangeably with, or instead of, the term "ethnicity." Doing so reflects the assumption that social categories have a basis in physiology.

In this paper I critique the use of "race" as it is used by researchers and bioethicists writing about "racial" differences in access to kidney transplantation. The use of "race" reflects scientifically inaccurate assumptions about the biological bases of social problems and thus limits our understanding and resolution of the bioethical dilemma of potential inequalities in transplantation. By no means does deconstruction of "race" imply that inequitable access to transplantation does not exist. Rather, this paper identifies the limits of biological criteria and proposes other more useful criteria for documenting inequities in access to transplantation.

ETHNICITY AND "RACE"

The terms "ethnicity" and "race" are each cultural constructions of social identity.[3,4] This means that historical and cultural notions of social identity, not biological criteria, inform the mechanisms for identifying who belongs to particular "races" or ethnic groups and what meanings are attributed to persons so categorized. An "ethnic group" is usually defined in anthropology in cultural terms:

> A self-perceived inclusion of those who hold in common a set of traditions not shared by others with whom they are in contact. Such traditions typically include "folk" religious beliefs and practices, language, a sense of historical continuity, and common ancestry or place of origin. (p. 18)[5]

"Race" popularly refers to membership in socially defined groups that purportedly share some specific biological traits, notably skin color.[6] Both the nonbiological and biological criteria that are used to identify "races" are arbitrary. For example, the racial categories in the United States are applied to people from different: geographic regions (e.g., Asians); languages (e.g., Hispanic); religions (e.g., Jews); and putative skin color (white, red, yellow, brown).[7,8]

When investigators set out to examine the relationship between ethnicity and/or "race" and a bioethics issue such as access to transplantation, the intent should be to find out whether people engage in similar behaviors because of their shared worldview or social circumstances. The intent should not be to assess whether groups of people with a common identity tend to act in certain ways because of some inherently shared biological characteristic, like one's genetic makeup. Yet this very notion underlies much contemporary research using "race" or ethnicity.

The variable "race" is problem laden because there is no scientific basis for racial categories. As the renowned geneticist Richard Lewontin notes, any human population of the world shares 93% of all genetic material.[9] There is greater genetic variation within putative "races" than between them. "Races" do not empirically exist because not one set of phenotypic or genetic traits is consistent within or distinctive of any group called a "race."

PROBLEMS IN ACCESS TO KIDNEY TRANSPLANTATION

Access to transplantation occurs through several steps: (1) patients decide whether to seek a transplant; (2) nephrologists decide whether to refer patients to a transplant center; (3) transplant professionals decide whether to place patients on the national transplant waiting list; and (4) kidneys are allocated to patients according to the United Network

for Organ Sharing (UNOS) point system.[10] UNOS accords patients points on the basis of their: human leukocyte antigen (HLA) matches with the donor, waiting time, blood type, and sensitization to past antigens, among others.[11] HLAs are important because the greater number of matches, the better probability of a patient obtaining a kidney and of patient and kidney survival.

The clinical literature reports consistently that African American or "black" patients face greater difficulty obtaining kidney transplants than "whites" in terms of: (1) time from renal failure to transplant; (2) time from renal failure to wait listing; and (3) time from wait listing to transplantation.[12-14] Although "blacks" make up over 33% of the end-stage renal disease (ESRD) population, they receive only 21% of the transplants.[15] "Blacks" were found to be only 55% as likely as "whites" to receive a kidney transplant when controlling for sex, income, and size of referring dialysis unit.[16] "Blacks" thus wait almost twice as long as "whites" for their first transplant.[17]

Inequity appears in all stages of the process of gaining access to transplantation. This in itself is legitimately alarming. However, it is even more unsettling when biological reasons are given to explain this observation. Literature frequently concludes that the "race"-based differential is due primarily to the biological factors of blood type and HLAs.[18,19]

Transplant investigators have explained these biological differences by putative "race" primarily in terms of HLAs, which are the main components of immunological tolerance to foreign organs. Clinicians have found that many HLAs are more common in some human populations than others. The variation of HLAs among humans poses a problem for organ donation and, consequently, access to transplantation. Clinicians contend that HLAs commonly found in the organ-donor population, which is predominantly "white," are not found in the "black" organ-recipient population. According to transplant professionals, the reasons "blacks" have difficulty obtaining access to cadaver donor kidneys are that, for "blacks," "white" kidneys do not work as well as "black" kidneys in terms of patient and graft survival,[20] and, for historical and cultural reasons, too few "blacks" donate kidneys.[21] This perspective on HLAs and "race" is suspect, especially because immunosuppressant drugs are becoming advanced enough to compensate for HLA mismatches.[22] More likely, it is nonmedical factors that prevent access to transplants by "blacks," including nonreferral to transplant centers[23] and less consideration as transplant candidates than "whites."[24]

KEY ASSUMPTIONS
IN THE TRANSPLANT LITERATURE

The clinical transplant literature maintains several assumptions about "race" that impede a full understanding of problems in access to transplantation and ways to resolve them. The main assumption is that "races" represent biologically distinct groups of people. This assumption becomes apparent when studies compare the HLA patterns within putative "races." As mentioned earlier, it is common for clinicians and researchers to identify HLAs as specific to racial groups: "blacks" are believed to have different types of HLAs than "whites."[25,26] For example, investigators report that only 20% of "blacks" share antigens often found among the "Caucasian" donor population.[27] Another study claimed that one antigen, HLA-D, is found in 56% of "blacks" whereas it is found in 98% of "whites" (p. 3872).[28] Transplant professionals thus consider the large absence of HLA-D in "blacks" as a trend for "blackness" although this fingerprint describes only 44% of the people they refer to as "black." In contrast, a workshop titled "African American Histocompatibility," which sought to find "a better definition of HLA antigens in African Americans," contended that "more than any other group, African Americans have a high frequency of difficult-to-define specificities and a high level of diversity."[29] Regardless of the evidence for HLA diversity within African Americans, transplant professionals continue to consider this group distinct from "whites" and continue to assume that "races" can be distinguished by immunology.

As a related problem, the use of HLAs to compare "races" becomes a tool for a subtle form of denigration when the HLA count in "whites" is used as the baseline so that "blacks" are easily viewed as the nonstandard group. This hidden bias is disclosed when researchers unwittingly ask, "What percent of 'blacks' share HLAs found within the 'white' population?" instead of asking, "What percent of 'whites' share HLAs found within the 'black' population?"

There is no legitimate account for differences in HLAs between putative "races." Geneticists explain commonalities among groups as a factor of genetic clines.[30] Certain genetic material is shared at a higher frequency in some populations than in others. This finding makes sense when people have a long history of intragroup reproduction. However, this explanation is less applicable in geographic regions where genetic mixing occurs. Virtually all American "blacks" or African Americans are part European and some have Native American ancestry.[31,32] Conversely, most Southern "whites" who can trace many generations in the United States, have West African and Native American ancestry.[33,34] Although mixing occurred as a result of the historical conditions of slavery—for example, invasion, and rape, and voluntary culture contact or "transculturalization,"[35]—transplant studies still assume a correspondence between clines and "race."

Four major problems exist with the assumption commonly made about "race" and HLAs in transplant research. First, transplant studies fail to account for the possibility of racial mixing in terms of HLAs. Studies do not use variables to represent people with mixed heritages when statistically tracking their HLAs. By this omission, transplant studies reify distinct racial differences and thus present meaningless results. Transplant centers often classify patients' "race" according to UNOS's national registry whereby "white," "black," and "Hispanic" are listed, but the category of "multiracial" is absent.

Another problem is that although some humans may have higher frequencies of certain HLAs than others, transplant professionals and bioethics studies identify people's "race" according to U.S. notions of phenotype, an arbitrary identifier of "race." Phenotype refers to observable characteristics of an organism resulting from genetic makeup and environmental factors. Americans commonly label people who are actually of mixed ancestry as "black."[36] Anthropologist Faye Harrison suggests that this kind of labeling is a cultural practice derived from a history of prejudice that remains largely at an unconscious level. She terms the practice the "one drop rule." She observes repeatedly that in the United States even a small percent of African American "blood" means that someone will be identified as "black," regardless of appearance, culture, and genetics.[37]

Although determining the HLAs of a kidney donor and recipient is done in a blinded manner, determining their social identity is usually not blinded. Instead it is culturally based, such that people's attributions of ethnicity or "race" are grounded in cultural meanings and interpreted through social interaction. Because of the high variability in phenotype and genotype within putative "races," it is impossible for researchers to consistently identify whether recipients or donors are "black" or "white." This means that transplant studies examining racial differences are likely to report erroneous statistics about transplant allocation and outcome among putative "races."

A third key problem with using racial categories is that transplant studies routinely interchange and thus confuse the concepts of "race" and ethnicity. For instance, it is rarely clear whether the terms "black" and "African American" are being used to denote race or ethnicity, especially when both are used within the same article.[38] These terms are used often in contrast to "white" and "Caucasian" and sometimes "European American," as if any of these were scientifically meaningful racial or ethnic categories. Investigators rarely make an effort to denote ethnicity. In a paper reviewing "racial" disparities in access to transplantation, one table reads, "Patients Who Underwent Cadaver Renal Transplantation or Were Placed on a Waiting List, According to Race or Ethnic Group and Location." The table fails to denote whether the "blacks," "whites," "Hispanics," "Asians," and "other" listed in the table were "races" or ethnic groups.[39] Categorizations that conflate ethnic groups with "race" prevent comparisons to be made on an appropriate theoretical level in that they erroneously confuse biology with a whole range of dynamic behaviors, beliefs, and values.

A fourth problem is that by categorizing patient subjects into "racial" and ethnic groups, transplant and bioethics studies fail to operationalize their variables. Consequently, it is not clear how subjects are relegated to various social groups. For example, whereas some studies compare "white" to "nonwhite" patients,[40] others compare "black" to "nonblack" patients,[41] and most commonly, studies compare only "whites" to "blacks," thereby eliminating from analysis all other ethnic groups, or even "races" for that matter.[42] These and other studies fail to identify the parameters for inclusion in their classification schema.

The implications of this methodological problem are multifold. Whereas the categories "white" or even "European American" are assumed to reflect a putatively homogeneous group of people, many different ethnic groups are comprised with these headings. The use of ethnic categories is only appropriate if one can show cultural similarities among group members. Assessing ethnic identity may be even more difficult to do for those not trained in cultural analysis. Researchers thus generally rely on simple visual characteristics or phenotyping to identify patients' "race." The failure to operationalize key variables results in essentializing conclusions in the transplant and bioethics literatures that assume that all people who appear to belong to a social group are alike in their HLAs or clines. Anthropologists use the term "essentializing" to refer to the assumption that people who share a culture, nationality, sex, or putative "race" will think and act in similar ways that are purportedly unique to that group.

Granted, such categories are not the inventions of transplant researchers who use them. These categories appear on preexisting forms created by government bureaucrats, clinic administrators, and insurers. As well, there are political motivations for employing traditional categories of social identity, such as "race"—notably, to document the presence or absence of discrimination. Yet researchers are not passive in the construction of "race"; they perpetuate the use of these categories and the sense of their reality. Moreover, using arbitrary and/or unknown criteria for classifying subjects prevents the replication of studies, a hallmark of scientific research.

SUGGESTIONS FOR FUTURE RESEARCH

Given that "race" is an unscientific category, bioethicists and scientists should be very cautious about using this variable because of its potential for prejudice and wrongful conclusions. The only exception might be for studies that are designed specifically to examine the cultural construction of social identity. Justifications for continuing to use "race" to reveal discrimination in the absence of more definitive measures[43] raise the same four problems relating to race and HLA as discussed above. Despite good intentions, bioethicists and other scholars using "race" as a research variable must acknowledge its conceptual and methodological limitations. Given its limitations, we are left with an imperfect solution—of being unable to make refined distinctions.

There is much debate about whether to keep or eliminate the term "race" in research. Whereas some argue that the use of linguistic terminology that differentiates groups has historically resulted in egregious forms of discrimination,[44] others contend that, as a socioculturally constructed reality, "race" is useful for describing groups historically and currently facing oppression.[45] Despite different theoretical approaches, many scholars generally concur that funds for healthcare and research be allocated in terms of medical need but not in terms of "racial" characteristics.[46,47]

We must therefore rethink how to test for potential inequalities in transplant access. I recommend that investigators and policymakers focus their attention on socioeconomic status or position (SES) as a key factor in access to healthcare. In the United States, SES and ethnicity are largely interrelated.[48] Existing measures of SES,[49] which vary in their combinations of education, occupation, and income, enable investigators to more accurately assess inequalities in who is receiving transplants. SES has been used effectively in one study to show that patients' SES is related to nephrologists' encouragement to get a transplant.[50] In another, income was reported to explain most "racial" differences in latter steps in transplant access.[51]

The problem with only using SES is that it fails to account for people's lived experience of racial discrimination in the United States. Even if members of groups, such as African Americans, have a high SES, they may experience discrimination in other domains of life.[52] Discrimination is a subtle social and cultural process, not only economic.[53] Developing measures that account for experiences of discrimination is necessary because such experiences inform values and attitudes toward health, morality, and ethical decisionmaking. For instance, due to the Tuskegee syphilis study and other injustices, many African Americans are distrustful of the healthcare system and are consequently less likely to use it.[54] Epidemiologist Nancy Krieger contends that scholars can "raise the scientific standard" in studies of "race/ethnicity" by "improv[ing] measures of noneconomic (interpersonal and structural) and economic manifestations of racial discrimination and use them jointly to analyze health outcomes, including racial/ethnic disparities in health" (p. 213).[55]

Bioethicists should become attuned to the value systems of patients, families, and clinicians and to broader sociocultural and political contexts that generate and perpetuate discrimination. Although Medicare sought to eliminate discrimination by the ability to pay for kidney transplantation, cultural and socioeconomic factors continue to influence patients' access to transplantation and scholars' interpretation of it. Scholars would do well to account for the relationship between SES and experiences of discrimination in studies that evaluate whether social justice is attained in healthcare generally and in the science and practice of organ transplantation in particular.

NOTES

1. Witzig P. The medicalization of race: scientific legitimization of a flawed social construct. *Annals of Internal Medicine* 1996;125(8):675–9.

2. Hahn RA. The state of federal health statistics on racial and ethnic groups. *JAMA* 1992;267(2):268–71.

3. Montagu A. *Man's Most Dangerous Myth: The Fallacy of Race,* 5th ed. New York: Oxford University Press, 1974 (1942).

4. Gaines AD. Race and racism. In: Reich WT, ed. *The Encyclopedia of Bioethics.* New York: Macmillan, 1995:2189–201.

5. De Vos G. Ethnic pluralism: conflict and accommodation. In: De Vos G, Romanucci-Ross L, eds. *Ethnic Identity: Creation, Conflict,* *and Accommodation,* 3rd ed. Walnut Creek, Calif.: Altamira Press, 1995:15–47.

6. Watts E. The biological race concept and diseases of modern man. In: Rothschild H, ed. *Biocultural Aspects of Disease.* New York: Academic Press, 1981:3–23.

7. See note 4, Gaines 1995.

8. See note 6, Watts 1981.

9. Krieger N, Bassett M. The health of black folk: disease, class, and ideology in science. In: Harding S, ed. *The "Racial" Economy of Science.* Bloomington: Indiana University Press, 1993:161–9.

10. Alexander GC, Sehgal A. Barriers to cadaveric renal transplantation among blacks, women, and the poor. *JAMA* 1998;280:1–5.

11. Startzl TE, Shapiro R, Teperman L. The point system for organ distribution. *Transplantation Proceedings* 1989;21(3):3432–6.

12. Kjellstrand CM. Age, sex, and race inequalities in renal transplantation. *Archives of Internal Medicine* 1988;148:1305–9.

13. Eggers PW. Racial differences in access to kidney transplantation. *Health Care Financing Review* 1995;17(2):89–103.

14. Kallich JD, Adams JL, Barton PL, Spritzer KL. Access to cadaveric kidney transplantation. RAND/UCLA Center for Policy Research in Health Care Financing. Prepared for Health Care Financing Administration and the Assistant to the Secretary for Planning and Evaluation. MR-202-HCFA. 1993.

15. See note 13, Eggers 1995.

16. Held PJ, Pauly MV, Bovbjerg RR, Newmann J, Salvatierra O. Access to kidney transplantation: has the United States eliminated income and racial differences? *Archives of Internal Medicine* 1988;148:2594–600.

17. Sanfilippo FP, Vaughn WK, Peters TG, Shield CF, Adams PL, Lorber MI, Williams GM. Factors affecting the waiting time of cadaveric kidney transplant candidates in the United States. *JAMA* 1992;267(2):247–52.

18. See note 14, Kallich, Adams, Barton, Spritzer 1993.

19. Kasiske BL, Neylan JF, Riggio RR, Danovitch GM, Kahana L, Alexander SR, White MG. The effect of race on access and outcome in transplantation. *New England Journal of Medicine* 1991;324(5):302–7.

20. Opeltz G, Wujciak T, Schwarz V, Back D, Mytillineos J, Scherer S. Collaborative transplant study analysis of graft survival in blacks. *Transplantation Proceedings* 1993;25(4):2443–5.

21. Callender CO, Bayton JA, Yeager C, Clark JE. Attitudes among blacks toward donating kidneys for transplantation: a pilot project. *JAMA* 1982;74(8):807–9.

22. van Rood JJ, Lagaaij EL, Doxiadis I, Roelen D, Persijn G, Claas F. Permissible mismatches, acceptable mismatches, and tolerance: new trends in decision making. In: Terasaki P, Cecka J, eds. *Clinical Transplants.* Los Angeles: UCLA Tissue Typing Laboratory, 1993:285–92.

23. Garg PP, Frick KD, Diener-West M, Powe NR. Effect of the ownership of dialysis facilities on patients' survival and referral for transplantation. *New England Journal of Medicine* 1999;341(22):1653–60.

24. Soucie JM, Neylan JF, McClellan W. Race and sex differences in the identification of candidates for renal transplantation. *American Journal of Kidney Diseases* 1992;19(5):414–9.

25. See note 20, Opeltz, Wujciak, Schwarz, Back, Mytillineos, Scherer 1993.

26. Lazda VA. The impact of HLA frequency differences in races on the access to optimally HLA-matched cadaver renal transplants. *Transplantation* 1992;53(2):352–7.

27. Lazda VA, Blaesing ME. Is allocation of kidneys on basis of HLA match equitable in multiracial populations? *Transplantation Proceedings* 1989;21(1):1415–6.

28. Johnson AH, Rosen-Bronson S, Hurley CK. Heterogeneity of the HLA-D region in American blacks. *Transplantation Proceedings* 1989;21(6):3872–3.

29. Johnson AH. Introduction to the African American histocompatibility workshop: goals and overview. *Transplantation Proceedings* 1993;25(4):2398.

30. Livingstone FB. On the nonexistence of human races. In: Harding S, ed. *The "Racial" Economy of Science*. Bloomington: Indiana University Press, 1993 (1964):133–41.

31. See note 4, Gaines 1995.

32. Cavalli-Sforza LL, Menozzi P, Piazza A. *The History and Geography of Human Genes*. Princeton, N.J.: Princeton University Press, 1994.

33. See note 4, Gaines 1995.

34. See note 32, Cavalli-Sforza, Menozzi, Piazza 1994.

35. Washburn WE. American Indians, white and black: the phenomenon of transculturalization. In: Hallowell AI, ed. *Contributions to Anthropology*. Chicago: University of Chicago Press, 1976 (1963):498–529.

36. Harrison FV. The persistent power of "race" in the cultural and political economy of racism. *Annual Review of Anthropology* 1995;24:47–74.

37. Reed E, Cohen DJ, Barr ML, Ho E, Reemtsma K, Rose EA, et al. Effect of recipient gender and race on heart and kidney allograft survival. *Transplantation Proceedings* 1992;24(6):2670–1.

38. Shapiro R, McCauley J, Scantlebury V, Woods H, Irish W, McMichael J, et al. Effect of recipient race on waiting time for renal transplantation at the University of Pittsburgh. *Transplantation Proceedings* 1993;25(4):2458–9.

39. See note 19, Kasiske, Neylan, Riggio, Danovitch, Kahana, Alexander, White 1991.

40. See note 12, Kjellstrand 1988.

41. See note 38, Shapiro, McCauley, Scantlebury, Woods, Irish, McMichael, et al. 1993.

42. See note 17, Sanfilippo, Vaughn, Peters, Shield, Adams, Lorber, Williams 1992.

43. Krieger N. Refiguring "race": epidemiology, racialized biology, and biological expressions of race relations. *International Journal of Health Services* 2000;30(1):211–6.

44. Baker R. Minority distrust of medicine: a historical perspective. *Mount Sinai Journal of Medicine* 1999;66(4):212–22.

45. See note 43, Krieger 2000.

46. See note 43, Krieger 2000.

47. See note 44, Baker 1999.

48. Dressler WM. Health in the African American community: accounting for health inequalities. *Medical Anthropology Quarterly* 1993;7(4):325–45.

49. Krieger N, Williams DR, Moss NE. Measuring social class in U.S. public health research: concepts, methodologies, and guidelines. *Annual Review of Public Health* 1997;18:341–78.

50. Gordon EJ, Sehgal A. Patient-nephrologist discussions about kidney transplantation as a treatment option. *Advances in Renal Replacement Therapy* 2000;7(2):1–7.

51. Ozminkowski RJ, White AJ, Hassol A, Murphy M. Minimizing racial disparity regarding receipt of a cadaver kidney transplant. *American Journal of Kidney Diseases* 1997;30(6):749–59.

52. Twine FW. Brown skinned white girls: class, culture and the construction of white identity in suburban communities. *Gender, Place, and Culture* 1996;3(2):205–24.

53. Essed P. *Everyday Racism*. Newbury Park, Calif.: Sage Publications, 1991.

54. Dula A. African American suspicion of the healthcare system is justified: what do we do about it? *Cambridge Quarterly of Healthcare Ethics* 1994;3:347–57.

55. See note 43, Krieger 2000.

Racist Organ Donors and Saving Lives

T.M. Wilkinson

In a British case, in 1998, a man's relatives stipulated that his organs were to go only to someone who was white (defined, on the form they annotated, as 'non-ethnic'). There was no protocol to deal with a case like this and the relatively junior officials involved were unsure what to do, so the offer was in effect accepted and the man's liver and two kidneys were used for transplant. The recipients were white but would, apparently, have received the organs anyway even if the condition had not been attached. The consultant who transplanted the liver stated that the recipient would have died within 24 hours without the transplant. When the case became public, the government and the panel of inquiry it set up to report on the case categorically condemned the decision to accept the conditional offer.[1]

It looks like a hard task to decide whether the racist conditional offer should have been accepted, and whether subsequent offers should be. As the British Panel pointed out, a life was saved in that case only because the offer was accepted. Saving lives seems a very powerful reason to accept the offer. Fairness, justice, and rejecting racism seem like powerful reasons against. It is rather surprising then that the British government and its panel should have been so confident in rejecting it, and it is also rather surprising that the topic has not provoked much philosophical debate. The problem is not unique to Britain and

---

[1]For the details of the case, see the Department of Health UK. 2000. *Report of the Panel. An Investigation into Conditional Organ Donation.*

as we shall see in this paper, it raises difficult issues that not only cry out for philosophical discussion, but have been fruitfully discussed in political philosophy.[2]

It is not hard to decide in this case whether the racist or his relatives were right to set the condition. Their motive was clearly indefensible, some mix of hatred and contempt for the lives of people they thought not of their own race. There is nothing to be said for such a motive. The hard question is whether, given that the conditional offer has been made, it should be accepted. Startlingly, the British Panel did not make this distinction at the crucial moment when they argued against acceptance. They said: 'to attach any condition to a donation is unacceptable, because it offends against the fundamental principle that organs are donated altruistically and should go to patients in greatest need. The Panel considers that racist conditions are completely abhorrent . . .'[3] We know that the racist condition is wrong and that the donor is offending against a principle, but how is that relevant to the question of whether the racist's offer should be accepted? The Panel does not say.[4]

Partly to avoid confusions like the British Panel's, it is useful to have a separate term to mark the difference between conditionally donating and accepting. I propose 'conditional allocation' to cover the practice of accepting conditionally donated organs and abiding by the condition. The topic of conditional allocation is rather broader than the racist case that is the focus of this paper. People might want to attach different conditions, such as directing that the organs go to a child, or to a co-religionist, or to a group that usually has less access to organs (like blacks in the US, or Maori in New Zealand).[5] These conditions would be less objectionable if they were not based on hatred or contempt for anyone and it is quite consistent to endorse acceptance of some conditional donations and not others. Some, however—like the British Panel—say they oppose the acceptance of any conditions. (The Panel did not consider the currently-sanctioned practice of live conditional donation within families.)

In this paper, I argue that under certain conditions, including those that obtained in the British case, even racist offers should be accepted. This is the hardest case for me to defend, because no one will want to defend the motive. If I can make my case here, then this will carry over to a considerable degree to other, less objectionable, conditions.

The racist case does, of course, have the special feature of involving racism and the paper does have to discuss objections to racism specifically. There are many things wrong with racism: the unjust effects on people's opportunities, the expressions of hatred or contempt, the corrosive effects on social relations, the bad effects on people's attitudes towards themselves, and so on. Moreover, these wrongs can figure in different ways in different moral theories—consequentialist, deontological, or whatever. As far as these moral theories are concerned, I hope to avoid presupposing any in particular. As far as the evils of racism are concerned, I hope that the paper captures adequately what it is that people think would be wrong with accepting racist conditional donations, although I try to show that they should change their minds. I also hope that the arguments in the racist case would apply, perhaps with some changes, to other conditional allocations.

Let us make some simplifications. First, assume that in cases of cadaveric transplantation, the dead person wanted the condition and that the relatives agree with it. This avoids the complication of considering a duty of relatives to carry out wishes they do not endorse. Second, assume that the organs are needed to save lives. Transplanted organs sometimes improve the quality of lives rather than save them, and I think the arguments I develop cover those improvements too, but it is lifesaving I concentrate on here. Third, assume that the alternative to conditional allocation is refusing the condition *and not using the organs*. Thus assume that overt conscription or false promises to honour conditions are ruled out, for instance by people's rights over their bodies or by good public policy. Fourth, assume that people do not have rights that would be infringed on if their conditional offers were rejected by the transplant services. Thus if someone wants to donate conditionally, I assume that the transplant services do not have a correlative duty to carry out the person's wish even if there is a potential recipient willing to fulfil the would-be donor's condition.

[2]One of the few philosophically-detailed discussions is Robert Veatch. 2000. *Transplantation Ethics.* Washington DC: Georgetown University Press: ch. 25. He provides some details of cases in the US too.

[3]Department of Health, *op. cit.* note 1, p. 25.

[4]For more detailed criticism of the Panel's reasoning, see T.M. Wilkinson. What's Not Wrong with Conditional Organ Donation? *J Med Ethics* 2003; 29.

[5]Wayne Arnason is sympathetic to a form of conditional allocation of kidneys where potential black donors are encouraged to donate by being told that the organs they donate are more likely to go to blacks, and the UNOS criteria for allocation are changed so that this is indeed so. See W. Arnason. Directed Donation: the relevance of race. *Hastings Cent Rep* 1991; 21.

These assumptions might not be ethically correct, but they do describe the practice in many jurisdictions.[6]

With these assumptions in place, I am in a position to state the main claim of this paper: conditional allocation, even in the racist case, is justified if it will save at least one life without reducing anyone's access to organs. The bulk of the paper concentrates on defending this claim against these objections: (i) that the good that might come about through conditional allocation does so through wrongful complicity in the racist's wrongdoing; (ii) that conditional allocation symbolizes support for racism; and (iii) that conditional allocation is unjust or unfair and is, for that reason, impermissible.

The claim that conditional allocation is justified if it would save at least one life without reducing anyone else's access states a sufficient and not a necessary condition. What if conditional allocation does reduce someone's access? The final section, on conditional allocation as a policy, considers this possibility and argues that, even then, conditional allocation could be justified.

COMPLICITY

One way to think about the topic of conditional allocation is to see it as about the ethics of doing good through involvement in wrongdoing. The racist unquestionably does wrong in setting the condition. Would it be wrong to accept that condition even to do a great deal of good?

Here is a handy list—attributed to Bob Wachbroit[7]—of ways in which one becomes wrongfully involved in evil: doing the bad thing oneself; directly encouraging others to do evil; indirectly encouraging others, e.g. by widening the acceptance of the evil; and appearing to endorse or legitimize the wrongful deed. The second two are dealt with later in the sections on Shifting Patterns and Symbols of Racism. The first two, doing the bad thing oneself or directly encouraging others, appear not to arise here—the transplant services do not themselves donate organs with racist conditions and they should actively discourage those who would like to. But one might say that the transplant services are complicit in the racist's act. After all, they have to check whether the recipients fulfil the racist's condition, and it may well be thought that this is itself a racist act.[8]

In deciding how bad it is to do what the racist asks, it might be significant that what the transplant services would be doing if they were to comply is not intrinsically wrong. Unlike, say, murdering someone, transplanting organs or checking patients' race or ethnicity are not the kinds of acts that are even prima facie wrong in themselves. (Hospitals legitimately check ethnicity for all sorts of reasons.) So the objection would have to be something like this: the involvement in wrongdoing comes from furthering the wrongful ends.

Furthering wrongful ends might be wrong, but it need not be. If a bank robber orders a teller at gunpoint to fill a bag with money, the teller who complies does not thereby become wrongfully complicit through furthering the wrongdoer's ends. To condemn conditional allocation requires more of a reason than that it furthers wrongful ends, since some furthering is not wrongful. Thus, pending any further reason and the later discussion of widening acceptance of evil or endorsing it, we should not say that the transplant services become wrongfully involved in evil by accepting the racist condition. At least, we should not say this on the strength of Wachbroit's list of ways of being involved.

I am not sure, however, that the list fully captures the unease one might feel about doing good with what one has acquired only through someone else's wrongdoing. One might, say, feel uneasy at using stolen property to save lives even when one is not wrongfully involved in any of the ways on the list. (Assume the property cannot be returned to the rightful owner.) But perhaps one need not feel uneasy in the case of the racist donor given that the donor has, plausibly, not violated anyone's rights in making the offer, but merely wrongfully exercised his own right to donate or withhold his organs. At any rate, we have yet to find a reason to regard conditional allocation as implicating the transplant services in the racist's wrongdoing.

SYMBOLS OF RACISM

We are considering accepting a conditional donation if it would save at least one life without costing anyone else access to organs. But why should access to organs be the only relevant consideration? What about third parties, whether transplant candidates or not, and in

---

[6]I give some argument for these assumptions about the absence of a right to donate in Individual and Family Decisions About Organ Donation. *J Appl Philos* 2007; 24.

[7]See Ronald M. Green. 2001. *The Human Embryo Research Debates.* New York: Oxford University Press: 146.

[8]Paul Snowdon suggested this objection.

particular those in the group the racist wanted barred from receiving his organs? Would conditional allocation make it harder for them to have a sense of self-worth?[9] If so, then acceptance would be bad for some. And should not the transplant service avoid appearing to support racism and ensure that justice is seen to be done?

These ideas are about appearances and they are the foundation for an objection to racial conditional allocation that is independent of whether it really is unjust, appearances aside, or is likely to have bad effects on patterns of donation. One way to put the objection is to say that conditional allocation would have symbolically harmful effects. Crucially, whether it does have these effects depends not on the intentions of the transplant services, but on how their actions are perceived. The questions for this section are whether there must be a conflict between avoiding symbolic harm and saving lives and, if so, how it should be resolved.

Let us have some illustrations of the force and limits of an appeal to symbolic harm. In his defence of levelling down egalitarianism, Jonathan Wolff considers the hypothetical case of the mayor of a town in the Southern US who thinks it better to close down a swimming pool than to leave one for whites only.[10] Wolff stipulates that blacks really would be no worse off for the pool's existence and that whites would be better off (he stipulates away any sense of solidarity that whites might wish to express and any resentment by blacks).[11] Nonetheless, Wolff thinks there is a good and probably sufficient reason to close the pool, and that is to avoid symbolizing support for racism. I agree with Wolff's judgement.

Consider, on the other hand, this case, from the film *Die Hard 3*. Early in this film, the Bruce Willis character parades through Harlem wearing little besides a billboard that says 'I Hate Niggers', and he does this with the encouragement of the police. He wears the billboard because of a credible threat to explode a bomb in a public place unless he does. The intuitive reaction in this case is that his wearing the billboard is not to be condemned for its symbolic support for racism. One explanation might be that it is a little precious to worry about symbols in such circumstances but, significantly, one might also think that wearing the billboard does not really symbolize support for racism. Once the facts are explained, people might see this as a case where

the state has no choice given the importance of saving innocent lives and, because it has no choice, no racism is symbolized. By contrast, allowing the whites-only swimming pool would symbolize support for racism precisely because the benefits are so trivial.

We might wonder whether conditional allocation is more like the billboard than the swimming pool. If saving lives is weighty enough to prevent conditional allocation even counting as a symbol of support for racism, there is no trade off. Lives can be saved at no cost in symbolic harm. Difficulties arise if conditional allocation would symbolize support because then there is an apparent conflict of value between saving lives and avoiding symbolic harm. Conflicts of value are usually tricky so the first hope is either to avoid the conflict or to minimize it.

First, there might be at least some cases where there is no need to trade off symbolic benefits against lives. Because what is symbolized depends on how it is interpreted, it is possible that acceptance of the racist offer could be symbolic in one set of circumstances and not in another. It is significant, as he himself says, that Wolff sets his swimming pool example in the Southern United States, and that it is blacks who are discriminated against. Given its long history of anti-black racism, a whites-only swimming pool could not fail to be highly symbolic of injustice, and the mayor's approval be construed as political support for racism. As Wolff says, it would not be symbolic of support for discrimination if the law required, for genuine public health reasons, that people with red hair not be allowed to use the pool.[12] The lesson we can draw is that how far acceptance of the racist's offer would be construed as symbolic support would depend on where it happened and which race it would be directed against. If, for instance, the conditional donation occurred in the Southern United States and required that someone black receive the organ, acceptance of the offer would presumably be less symbolic of support for racism than if it were an anti-black offer.

The point here is that there might be circumstances when accepting the offer does not symbolize support for racism, in which case refusing symbolic support, however important, would not be a reason against accepting the offer. In other cases, such as where a society is itself irredeemably racist, it might add no *extra* symbolic harm to allocate conditionally and save lives

---

[9]As an anonymous referee put it.

[10]Jonathan Wolff, 2001. Levelling Down. In *Challenges to democracy: the PSA yearbook 2000*. Keith Dowding, James Hughes, and Helen Margetts, eds. Basingstoke: Palgrave.

[11]Ibid: 27, 28, 30–31.

[12]Ibid: 30–31.

and so again avoiding symbolic harm would not be a reason against accepting the offer. The most difficult choice might be where a society has been racist and the state has until recently been thoroughly implicated in this, and where to allow a conditional allocation would jeopardize its sincere efforts at reform.

Second, the state could try to counteract any symbolic support for racism. It could accept conditional offers, publicly deplore the racist motives behind them, while setting out the reasons for accepting them nonetheless, and simultaneously announce an increase in funding for transplant or other services for the discriminated-against group. My purpose here is not to say that these specific suggestions are a good idea but to point out that symbols can be changed, and that there may well be ways of preventing acceptance of racist offers from symbolizing racism. Furthermore, by policy or accident, it might be that the policy is not widely known, and while this would not stop it being a symbol, it would reduce its bad effects.

The aim so far has been to avoid or minimize the conflict between saving lives and avoiding symbolic harms. This has to be the most desirable outcome, for who could deny that they are both valuable? But suppose there are circumstances where the conflict is unavoidable. How should the trade-off be handled? I take it that avoiding symbolic harms cannot have overriding value—there must be some number of lives that would outweigh some level of symbolic harm. More plausibly, one might hold that saving lives has overriding priority.[13] Thus we should save lives whatever the symbolic harms, and conditional allocation could not then be ruled out by symbolic considerations. This may well be correct, but it is not obviously correct. It is often pointed out that we are willing to give up lives for the sake of relatively trivial benefits. James Griffin gives the example of roadside trees in France, which make driving both more pleasurable and more hazardous.[14] The trees come at the price of extra lives lost, but we do not jump to the conclusion that the government should cut them down. Perhaps avoiding symbolic support for racism would also be worth the expected cost in lives.

Whether trading off is the right approach to the value of life in the case of the trees or conditional allocation is too large a subject to go into here. But even if it is, it would not follow that conditional allocation should be ruled out on the grounds that lives saved are outweighed by symbolic considerations. This is because it might be unfair to expect those in need of organs (and their nearest and dearest) to bear the entire cost of symbolic commitments to anti-racism.[15]

To be a sufficient objection to conditional allocation, the argument would have to show that conditional allocation really would cause symbolic harm, that it would do this to a degree large enough to outweigh the value of saving lives, and that it would be reasonable to impose the costs of rejecting conditional allocation on those already very badly off, that is, those in need of lifesaving organs. I cannot show that there are no circumstances in which this objection could succeed, but I hope to have shown that it is unclear that there are any, and there are at least some circumstances in which the objection does not work. Most importantly, there may be ways in which we can save lives without symbolizing support for racism, and those who care about both should try hard to find them.

JUSTICE AND FAIRNESS

One of the major arguments against permitting conditional allocation is that it would be unjust. It might be unjust because it leads to the allocation of organs according to morally irrelevant criteria, like race, or because it permits some to jump the existing queue, or for these and some other reasons. The injustice argument is the subject of the next two sections. These arguments are supposed to rule out conditional allocation even on the assumptions that it improves access for some without reducing it for anyone else and has no further morally bad effects on someone's well-being, such as reducing their sense of self-worth. On these assumptions, rejecting conditional allocation would be levelling down—making some worse off with no gain for others. To justify this, one would have to show both that justice really does require levelling down in this case and that avoiding this injustice overrides the saving of life. These claims are open to question.

---

[13]This seems to be Joel Feinberg's view in 'Sentiment and Sentimentality in Practical Ethics', from J. Feinberg. 1992. *Freedom and Fulfilment,* Princeton NJ: Princeton University Press: 120–121.

[14]James Griffin. 1986. *Well-Being,* Oxford: Clarendon Press: 171.

[15]The point about fairness applies even more strongly to the idea that we should reject conditional allocation in order to promote anti-racism in society. Why should only a few non-volunteers have to sacrifice their lives to this cause when the costs could be spread much more fairly by adopting some other method of promotion? We can ask a similar question of those who think that we should display solidarity with the discriminated-against group by turning down the racist's offer. For the transplant services to turn the offer down does not seem that solidaristic when they are not the ones who will bear the costs.

There has, in recent years, been a great deal written on the topic of levelling down, usually in the context of discussions of egalitarian justice.[16] Some of those opposed to egalitarianism have argued that it is an error to value directly the relation of equality between people. They say that equality is not good in itself because it is not good for anyone.[17] Those who have replied have usually tried to argue that it is a mistake to think that what is of moral importance must be limited to what would be good or bad for people. They have been less concerned to show that equality is one of the things that is of moral importance and still less have they argued that its importance would be great enough to justify levelling down.[18] Egalitarians in political philosophy have not generally gone beyond claiming that equality makes levelling down in *one way better,* as opposed to being *all-things-considered better,* than an unequal world where some are better off and none worse off. The position that levelling down is all-things-considered better is a minority one even among those sympathetic to equality in political philosophy.

My purpose here is not to convince by sheer weight of numbers, but to point out that those who would like to reject conditional allocation even when it levels down should at least realize that they have a job on their hands. It is rather disappointing, then, that they have said so little in defence of their view. In one of the few major philosophical articles devoted to the topic, Robert Veatch rejects conditional allocation on the basis of what he calls 'true egalitarianism', which seems to be a view about fairness.[19] He realizes that this view requires the claim that fairness is more important than beneficence, understood here to require saving lives, but he does not defend that claim. Instead he takes the rejection of conditional allocation as a datum and works back from that to a criticism of Rawlsian maximin justice. But whatever the answer to the question of whether conditional allocation should be rejected, the answer is certainly not a datum or, in Rawlsian jargon, a considered moral judgement. There is simply too little consensus and too much to be said on both sides to make it that.

In the rest of this section, I want to avoid simply asserting the counter intuition that fairness should yield to saving lives, decidedly plausible though it seems to me. Ideally, we could proceed by taking the fairness argument against conditional allocation and subjecting it to detailed scrutiny, but since the argument has not been made in detail, this is not possible. However, I think we can say that part of what the critics have in mind is that conditional allocation would be wrong because it would violate the principle of formal justice that says that like cases should be treated alike.[20]

Notoriously, treating like cases alike leaves open what should count as a like case but, if it is ever clear, it is surely so in circumstances where one gives an organ to one person and not a similarly placed other simply on grounds of race. This is a powerful objection to conditional allocation and it might be this more than anything that leads to the sense that conditional allocation poses a genuine dilemma, in that something of value is lost however it is resolved. Nonetheless, I hope to cast doubt on the scope of the formal justice objection to make it at least unclear that it applies to conditional allocation (in which case, it would not after all create a genuine dilemma). I shall also comment on the weight of the objection, in the light of the earlier remarks about levelling down.

First, then, the doubts about the scope. Who is it who is acting unjustly? One might say, at a minimum, that the racist donor is, but even that is unclear. The donor acts wrongly, but I doubt that he acts contrary to principles of formal justice because I doubt that those principles apply to him in his role as donor. As far as his property is concerned, for instance, he does not have to dispose of it in his will in accordance with treating like cases alike. If he were to direct that his organs were to go to a loved one, we would not think this formally unjust, whereas we certainly would if a judge or professor gave especial preference in sentencing or marking papers to someone she loved. How he disposes of his organs is not a matter for formal justice. What, though, of the public transplant services—should they not follow principles of formal justice in allocating organs? They should for organs that have been donated without conditions so, unlike in the case of the donor, principles of formal justice do apply to them. But it is unclear that

---

[16]See, for example, Derek Parfit. 2000. Equality or Priority? In *The Ideal of Equality.* M. Clayton and A. Williams, eds. Basingstoke. Macmillan; Larry Temkin, 1993. *Inequality.* Oxford; Clarendon Press: ch. 9; John Broome. 1991. *Weighing Goods.* Oxford: Basil Blackwell: ch. 9.

[17]Joseph Raz. 1986. *The Morality of Freedom.* Oxford: Clarendon Press: ch. 9; Harry Frankfurt. 1998. *The Importance of What We Care About.* Cambridge: Cambridge University Press: ch. 11.

[18]Temkin, *op. cit.* note 16, p. 282. As we saw earlier, Wolff was willing to tolerate levelling down in the limited circumstances of swimming pools.

[19]Robert Veatch *op. cit.* note 2.

[20]This is not the place to make grand claims in moral and political philosophy, so let me say that one way to think of formal justice is as a subset of justice, itself a subset of morality. For one account, see John Rawls. 1999. *A Theory of Justice* Rev. Ed. Oxford: Oxford University Press: sec. 10.

they apply when organs have been donated with conditions. The organs are not then freely available for allocation. To be sure, it might be said that the transplant service should turn them down on the grounds that, if they were to accept them, they would violate formal justice. But why should we believe that? The state does not even come into conflict with principles of formal justice when it upholds, through enforcing property rights, a private disposition of property that is not itself in accordance with those principles. To take a second example, public universities are thought by many not to violate principles of formal justice when administering privately-donated scholarships for students from, say, a particular city or religion, although they would violate them if they were to use public funds in this way.[21] The desired conclusion is that formal justice, however important, may not be compromised by conditional allocation.

I am less confident of the conclusion about the scope of formal justice than I am in concluding that its weight is not enough to justify levelling down in cases involving access to organs. Where formal justice is held to be of great importance, it is rarely tested by considering situations in which it would be very bad for some and good for no one. The exception is in punishment, where giving similar punishments might indeed be bad for someone and good for no one else. But punishment is a special case where, if levelling down is justified, it is on the grounds that offenders deserve to be punished.[22] In cases like access to organs, where, we can assume, no one deserves to be badly off, the challenge for those who would reject conditional allocation as formally unjust is to think up parallel cases where we are inclined to uphold formal justice at comparable expense for the innocent and with gain to none.

While conditional allocation has not been shown to be ruled out by formal justice, there is clearly more to justice than formal principles. In the next section, I consider an idea of fairness in a more substantial sense to try to show, at the least, that conditional allocation should not be rejected because it is unfair.

SAVING LIVES AND FAIRNESS

An obvious objection to conditional allocation is that it is unfair. Whether this is a good objection depends on what fairness requires and its weight, and neither of these is obvious. In this section, I aim to show that fairness is not the basis of a good objection to conditional allocation. I do this by comparing conditional allocation with the wider practice of organ transplantation under conditions of scarcity. Bearing in mind that there is always a shortage of organs for transplant, so that not all who need them will get them, what does fairness have to say about the practice of transplantation? There are three possible views: that fairness forbids the practice, requires the practice, and neither forbids nor requires but permits the practice.

It might be argued that, given the shortage of organs, the practice of transplantation is unfair because some will receive a benefit that others, with equally strong claims, will not. Just as parents might withhold their only sweet rather than give it to one child and not the other, so perhaps organs should not be allocated when not all can receive them. This would be a case of levelling down in the name of fairness. (Although parents will realize that there are good reasons besides fairness to avoid giving the sweet to only one of one's children.)

I assume that no one would want to ban organ transplants in conditions of scarcity on the ground that not everyone who needs it can get it. So what of the fairness argument against transplantation? If one thinks there is something unfair about transplantation, but that it should nonetheless be permitted, then the explanation is presumably that saving lives can beat fairness. One could not then argue against conditional allocation on the grounds that fairness always beats saving lives. Alternatively, one might have a different view of fairness.

One might believe that fairness requires organ transplants. There are two plausible reasons for this. Suppose fairness is taken comparatively: whether one is treated unfairly depends on how one is treated relative to others. In that case, it is plausible to argue that there is an inequality between those who need transplanted organs and the vast mass of healthy people who do not, and that it would be unfair to those who need organs not to give them when available so that they can be closer in health to the healthy. A non-comparative interpretation of fairness might say: people who need transplants have claims of needs. It is unfair not to satisfy those claims when one could do so without thereby failing to satisfy anyone else's claims. These both seem like good fairness arguments for transplantation.

These fairness arguments for transplantation also support permitting conditional allocation, on the

---

[21]These examples show that Eike-Henner Kluge is making a false inference when he says that organs must be allocated in accordance with justice and equality because organ donation occurs in a social context. The conclusion might be correct, but the argument has missing premises. See E-H. Kluge. Designated Donation: Private Choice in Social Context. *Hastings Cent Rep* 1989; 19.

[22]See the saints and sinners example in Temkin, *op. cit.* note 16, pp. 273–276.

usual assumptions about its worsening no one's position. If conditional allocation were rejected, those who could have received the conditionally donated organ would be treated unfairly both comparatively and non-comparatively. This leaves it open that fairness is divided against itself in the case of conditional allocation. Compared with rejecting the racist's offer, conditional allocation might be in one way unfair, in a comparative sense, because some do worse than others because of their race, while it is in other ways fairer, because of the reduction in the inequality between the healthy and the sick (comparative) and because some of the sick do better (non-comparative).

The conclusion at this stage can be put as a dilemma: either transplantation is unfair, in which case lifesaving beats unfairness and there is no fairness argument yet for banning conditional allocation; or transplantation is required by fairness, in which case conditional allocation is at least not obviously unfair and is still required by lifesaving. What now of the position that transplantation in conditions of scarcity is neither fair nor unfair but, if it is going to happen, it has to be done fairly? It could then be said that conditional allocation is unfair while transplantation need not be.

One argument might be that when two people have equal claims on one organ, there should be a fair procedure for choosing between them, such as a random choice.[23] Whoever wins gets the organ, so there is no waste, and the loser has not been treated unfairly. But it would be unfair if the person not getting the organ were denied on racist grounds. Hence one can justify transplantation in conditions of scarcity without justifying conditional allocation.

The trouble with this argument is that it envisages a situation where lifesaving and fairness do not conflict. It is not a case of levelling down because the organ is not wasted. To be a test case of levelling down, suppose, for some reason, the results of the fair procedure cannot be acted on. (Perhaps the winner under the fair procedure has just had dinner and cannot be safely operated on right now, when the organ must be used.) It is hard to see that the organ should be wasted even though not allocated in accordance with the fair procedure.

Another argument might be that the excess demand for organs can be managed fairly by having a fair queue.

With a fair queue, transplantation under conditions of scarcity is not unfair, but conditional allocation would be because it would permit some to jump the queue. But the reasons for thinking that queue-jumping is unfair do not clearly tell against conditional allocation. Suppose the queue is fair in the sense that it is based on a fixed rule, and does not admit of discretion or bias. In other words, the fairness involved is the fairness of following a fixed procedure. This is a thin form of fairness and need not condemn conditional allocation since it could be made a fixed rule that conditionally donated organs will be accepted. Suppose there are substantive criteria of fairness that should determine the way in which the queue is organized. Thus it might be unfair to permit queue-jumping because the queue is organized fairly, say because it requires that people wait the same time for organs. The trouble with this kind of argument, for those who are not radicals about constructing queues, is that it would condemn as unfair the queuing method in most countries. In general, the criteria for their queues are a mix of fairness, urgency, and capacity to benefit. The final placings can be described either as trading off fairness against other criteria, like lifesaving, or as using a view of fairness that includes lifesaving, but either way the criteria that justify queues do not clearly condemn conditional allocation.[24]

There is one further argument to show that fairness could not unconditionally defeat conditional allocation. What would be unfair if conditional donations were accepted and the organs used only in those cases when they went to the persons who would have received them had the donation been unconditional? Who then would be treated unfairly? Everyone receives what she would have done had the donation been unconditional, and this is no accident: accepting the conditional donation was itself conditional on no one being unfairly passed over. Of course, the organs would be wasted in those cases where the conditional donation does not coincide with the unconditional donation, something I have argued against in the paper. But how could those who think wastage is justified by fairness continue to think so in the limited cases where conditional allocation does not cause anyone to be treated unfairly?

---

[23]A point made by the anonymous referee.

[24]Some critics of HLA-matching for kidneys in the US, which has the by-product of making it harder for African-Americans to receive cadaveric kidneys for transplant, object on the mixed grounds that (1) HLA-matching is not as efficient as it is made out to be and (2) equity is not given enough weight. See Arnason, *op. cit.* note 5 and Robert Gaston et al. 1998. Racial Equity in Renal Transplantation: The Disparate Impact of HLA-Based Allocation. In *The ethics of organ transplants.* A. Caplan and D. Ceolho eds. Amherst NY: Prometheus Books. Whatever the merits of the criticism of US practice, even these critics believe that efficiency, in the sense of getting more years of benefit, should be a major consideration in allocation.

These two sections on justice and fairness were rather complicated and a summary may help. The question is whether conditional allocation should be ruled out on the grounds that it is unjust or unfair. To say so requires showing that it is unjust or unfair, and that this outweighs saving lives. I complained that critics of conditional allocation had not shown either of those in any detailed way. Having said that, I considered and rejected an objection to conditional allocation from formal justice: it was not clearly formally unjust and anyway formal injustice has not been shown to be decisively bad. Then, to try to find out how fairness might apply to conditional allocation, I considered fairness in relation to the practice of transplanting organs when there are not enough for all who need them. The conclusion is that, on the assumption that the practice is at least morally permissible, either fairness must yield to lifesaving, in which case it should have to yield in the case of conditional allocation too, or fairness requires lifesaving, in which case it may well permit conditional allocation when this is the only way to save lives without reducing anyone's access to organs. There are currently, then, no good arguments from justice or fairness that would justify banning conditional allocation that costs no one access to organs.

SHIFTING PATTERNS OF DONATION, AND SPECULATION

The assumption throughout has been that conditional allocation would improve access to organs for some at no cost in access to organs for anyone else. In this final section, we see that this assumption might not be correct if conditional allocation is made a policy, and we consider what follows if conditional allocation would be bad for some.

A natural worry about a policy of conditional allocation is that it could have bad effects on the patterns or levels of donation, making it harder for some groups to get access to organs or even reducing the overall number of donations. It is not hard to imagine how bad effects might occur. Perhaps people who would have donated unconditionally instead would attach conditions. Perhaps people who would have donated instead refuse to donate at all out of disgust at the policy

of conditional allocation. On the other hand, it is not hard to imagine how conditional allocation might have better effects than no conditional allocation. Perhaps people who would not have donated at all would donate if they could attach conditions (as happened in the British case). This might benefit even those discriminated against, since a conditional donation could shrink the pool of competitors for other organs. Perhaps some conditions may cancel out others, if blacks conditionally donated to blacks and whites to whites. Perhaps people would interpret the refusal to allow conditional allocation as indicating that there is no real shortage of organs and then withhold their own.

Significantly, these are all mere stories. Working out what would happen under various policies of conditional allocation requires empirical investigation. This investigation is beyond me but, until it happens, speculation about the wider effects of conditional allocation provides no reasons for or against it.[25] It could be better or it could be worse than the alternatives. Still, without pre-empting the results of any such investigation, it is worth noting that a) the effects are likely to be different in different times and places and b) the effects on wider patterns of donation may well be negligible, especially if the policy is not widely known. It is also worth mentioning that some of the effects might be altered by various modifications of policy. One suggestion—there might be others—is to use the pool of unconditional donations as a float to prevent unequal access. Thus if a racist refuses to donate to blacks, his offer would be accepted but the next organ from the pool of unconditionally donated organs would go to a black.[26]

Even if we knew the effects of a policy of conditional allocation on levels and patterns of donation, this would not settle questions about its justifiability. We would also need some way to evaluate these effects.[27] If the effects were to save lives without reducing anyone else's access, then, so I have argued, conditional allocation would be justified. If the effects were to reduce access for everyone, then conditional allocation would pretty clearly be a mistake. But there are other possibilities.

Compare two situations that might arise from accepting conditional donations. Suppose there are two groups, whites and blacks, and let the numbers refer to organs available for each group. Compare two possible

---

[25]But for a recent attempt to go beyond speculation, see Aaron Spital. Should people who donate a kidney to a stranger be permitted to choose their recipients? Views of the United States public. *Transplantation* 2003: 76. Spital argues that his results, based on telephone interviews with the general public, suggest that conditional allocation should not be permitted in the case of kidneys donated by living non-relatives in the US, with the exception of conditional donations to children.

[26]Paul Brown suggested this to me.

[27]In practice, we would also need a decision procedure to handle probabilities.

outcomes of conditional allocation against a baseline of refusing conditional donations.

> No conditional allocation: Whites 90, Blacks 15
> Outcome 1: Whites 100, Blacks 10
> Outcome 2: Whites 94, Blacks 15.

One might well object to Outcome 1, when compared with the baseline, on the grounds that it reduces the access of blacks to organs. But this objection does not apply to Outcome 2: blacks' access to organs is not reduced and whites' access is greater compared with the baseline of no conditional allocation.

How conditional allocation should be evaluated in the light of these two distributions depends upon the significance attached to saving the greatest number of lives, to preserving or promoting access for groups, and to not worsening the position of individuals. To explain, a principle of saving the greatest number would recommend conditional allocation even if the result was Outcome 1, that is, blacks do worse. A principle that showed concern for access for groups as well as saving lives would say that conditional allocation is justified if Outcome 2 is the result.[28]

That still leaves it open that, if conditional allocation were adopted, individual members of a group would do worse. The policy might change the timing of donations causing some to miss out even though others from their group subsequently got organs they would not otherwise have had. It might be enough to say to those who lose out when others from their group gain that a policy that saves more lives without reducing the access of any group is prospectively in everyone's interests, and consequently justified.

These sketchy remarks obviously do little justice to difficult topics in moral and political philosophy: whether the greater number should be saved, whether group inequality is morally significant over and above individual inequality, and under what conditions sacrifices can legitimately be imposed on some. There is certainly scope for a critic to develop further arguments against conditional allocation as a policy. But let me repeat the main claim of this paper: conditional allocation is justified if it saves the life of at least one without reducing anyone's access to organs, and restate that this is a sufficient condition. Whether it is also a necessary condition depends on whether it is permissible to impose sacrifices on some. As for what the effects of conditional allocation actually would be, that is a matter for empirical investigation and, until there has been one, speculative appeals to the wider effects do not make a case for or against conditional allocation.

CONCLUSION

There is a simple argument to permit conditional allocation—that it saves some people's lives without costing others their access to organs. The first few sections of this paper considered ways in which one might argue that conditional allocation should nonetheless be rejected. I criticised the claim that the transplant services would be wrongly complicit in the racist's immoral action. The paper then discussed the arguments that permitting conditional allocation would symbolize support for racism, and the main aims were to show that this need not happen and to cast doubt on its weight compared with saving lives. The next two sections considered arguments from justice. One raised doubts about the scope and weight of an argument from formal justice. The other was concerned with the alleged clash of fairness and lifesaving. It argued that either they may not clash—and hence there is no clear unfairness argument against conditional allocation—or that, if they did, lifesaving would win—and hence conditional allocation should be permitted even if unfair. The final section considered conditional allocation as a policy. It separated questions about what the effects would be from their evaluation. For various reasons, this section was unavoidably inconclusive, except in reaffirming that there are circumstances in which conditional allocation would be justified.

The final objection I want to consider is to the overall strategy of the paper. This is the objection that the paper employs a divide and rule strategy. It considers complicity, symbolic considerations, justice, and public policy separately and argues that each on its own is not enough to defeat the reason for conditional allocation, saving lives. But, the objection continues, perhaps these reasons are individually weak but would be strong enough in combination.

On the whole, the divide and rule objection misunderstands the strategy of this paper. Usually, I have tried to show not that lifesaving outweighs other reasons but that there are no reasons to be outweighed. For instance, I say that on all but levelling down conceptions of justice, conditional allocation is not unjust, and that even on levelling down conceptions, it may not be unjust. And I say that symbolic considerations need not conflict with lifesaving through conditional allocation. However, by its very nature, an investigation like this paper's is somewhat open-ended. One cannot, for example, prove that there could never be conflicting considerations of justice or symbolism, so it is in the abstract possible that

---

[28]Thus the British Panel do not give themselves a hard enough time when, in par. 6.5, they interpret their opposition as holding that the increase in the supply of organs is the overriding principle. One does not have to say that to permit conditional allocation.

these could combine to defeat the case for conditional allocation. But it is up to an opponent to turn that abstract possibility into something concrete. Pending that, I stand by the main claim: conditional allocation is justified when it would save the life of at least one person without reducing anyone's access to organs.

Are Alcoholics Less Deserving of Liver Transplants?

Daniel Brudney

As many studies show, Americans tend to think that an illness has a morally weaker claim to medical care when it is caused by personal conduct that is known to put health at risk. More specifically, many Americans believe that health-risky conduct can make for a significantly weaker claim to scarce medical resources. According to one study, for example, "respondents were 10 to 17 times more likely to allocate liver transplants or asthma treatment to patients they deemed not responsible for their illnesses than to patients they deemed responsible for their conditions." My goal in this essay is to see if there are conditions under which this belief may be justified. I want to see where—if anywhere—this belief touches defensible moral ground.

Broadly speaking, one could examine two different issues. When, if ever, is it morally appropriate to make some agents pay at least part of the extra cost of medical care for illness that is due to their voluntary, health-risky conduct? And when, if ever, is it morally appropriate to make it more difficult to gain access to medical resources—and so in effect sometimes to deny access—for illness that is due to an agent's voluntary, health-risky conduct?

The question of when to impose financial costs on health-risky conduct is important, and will become increasingly so as we learn more about our own role in our own ailments. However, rather than try to find criteria for when it would be proper to impose financial costs on agents—a task likely to be burdened by citizens' conflicting beliefs about which activities have significant social value—I will focus on the perhaps more dramatic issue of when voluntary conduct should trigger a lesser claim to medical resources. As my paradigm example, I will look at alcoholics and liver transplants. This sort of case is widespread and presents comparatively few epistemic problems—it occurs reasonably frequently, and frequently it is sufficiently clear that the patient's liver disease is in fact due to drinking.

My analysis will suggest that there are indeed conditions under which it would be justified to give an alcoholic a lesser claim to a transplant, but that at present very few cases would satisfy those conditions. I don't want to blink the fact that when those conditions are satisfied, my claim is that we are justified in putting a desperately ill person in an even graver medical position on the ground that his past conduct was morally lacking. This may seem to border on the cruel, yet in some cases it will be justified. Nevertheless, the central claim of this essay is that in the great majority of cases, at least at present, it will *not* be justified.

An agent's conduct can make him morally vulnerable only if that conduct is in fact voluntary. Throughout, my analysis assumes that the conduct in question is sufficiently voluntary. I leave to others the task of determining what that amounts to.

CONDUCT AND RESPONSIBILITY

Let's take Jane as our first example. Let's assume that her long-term drinking was sufficiently voluntary (whatever we decide that means). And assume, too, that it is sufficiently clear that her drinking ruined her liver. It might be urged, now, that Jane should bear the consequences of her conduct, meaning that she should be penalized by moving her lower down on the waiting list for liver transplants. This claim has in fact been made by a number of writers. I quote from Walter Glannon's formulation:

> [The alcoholic] will have a weaker claim to receive a liver than someone whose end-stage liver failure is beyond his control and thus contracted through no fault of his own....[The] moral judgment of lower or higher priority for claims to medical treatment ...[is made] on grounds of the control of their behavior which they reasonably can be expected to exercise. This control makes them either more or less responsible for their condition and in turn determines the strength of their claims to receive treatment.

Robert Veatch asserts something similar: "[I]f one is free to engage in these risky behaviors," he writes, "one must be prepared to take the consequences, even if that should happen to result in a lower position on the organ waiting list."

Here, then, is the principle that Glannon and Veatch advocate, which I will just call "the Principle":

> An agent is responsible for knowingly, voluntarily, and repeatedly engaging in easily avoidable conduct that might significantly contribute to that agent's needing a scarce, lifesaving resource. An agent who is responsible for such conduct may legitimately be given a weaker claim on scarce, lifesaving resources if her need for such resources is due to such conduct.

The point of "knowingly" and "voluntarily" should be clear even if the standards for knowing enough or being sufficiently voluntary may sometimes be disputable. I include "repeatedly" because it is not clear whether it is suspect to engage in a few instances of health-risky conduct. A decent life is likely to involve some health risks, and it might be thought that penalties for risky conduct should begin beyond a threshold of "normal" or "acceptable" risky conduct. We might even think that a very occasional step over that threshold should be ignored, that each of us should get a mulligan or two of this kind. Our model cases, then, will be those of conduct repeated over a long period of time. This ties into the "easily avoidable" condition. It is but a small crimp in one's lifestyle not to do unprotected class five rock climbs every weekend or to drink until the bar closes four times a week for a decade.

It is important to note that the Principle does not assert that drinking is *malum in se*. Its focus is on the consequences of Jane's conduct, not on whether that conduct was intrinsically good or bad. If drinking did not destroy livers, Jane's drinking would not trigger the Principle. Moreover, we should not confuse the question of whether an agent is responsible for her medical condition with the quite separate question of what institutions should do. That Jane is responsible for her condition does not, of itself, entail any specific institutional response.

Assume now that Jane asks to be put on the transplant list. Assume that, medically speaking, her chance of successful surgery and good long-term outcome is the same as that of many of the nonalcoholics on the list. Of course, in real life a large number of factors will go into ranking Jane versus other candidates. Our question is whether Jane's place on the list should be affected by a particular consideration—namely, the fact that she brought her liver disease on herself. The Principle says, Yes, it should.

DEATH IS DIFFERENT

Jane has brought her liver disease on herself. As Elizabeth Anderson has pointed out, however, we do not necessarily abandon those who have brought their ills on themselves. Suppose Paul is starving to death in the street. He is in this condition because he made foolish investments and refused several job offers. My car is filled with bread, mine to disburse as I wish. Clearly, I should give Paul bread. Clearly, I have an obligation to do so.

The Principle holds that the reason to put Jane lower on the transplant list, and so perhaps to deny her an opportunity for a longer life, is that she has brought her disease on herself. The question is why this is *sufficient* reason to dramatically increase Jane's chance of dying. The answer is not that Jane's conduct has been so intrinsically immoral as to deserve death. If that were the answer, then Jane would not receive a liver even if she were the only claimant—and no one has suggested *that*. It seems odd to impose a drastic consequence for not-intrinsically-immoral conduct. Dramatically increasing the likelihood that Jane will die does not seem a proportional response to her drinking.

It is true that life sometimes imposes draconian penalties for our missteps, even our minor ones. Suppose I fail to look as I cross the street and am hit by a car—killed or crippled. Even if the accident was due to my own carelessness, the consequence is wildly disproportionate. Still, one might say that's how the world works. Yet it needn't be how our public institutions work. It is important to remember that at issue are the decisions of institutions, specifically of institutions directly or indirectly supported by the public purse. The choice of which consequences they impose is up to us. And that decision should not be hostage to the thought that life is unfair.

WHAT KIND OF JUSTICE?

But what of Jack, the person displaced if Jane goes on the list? Surely his need is relevant. Consider a transplant list of ten people in need of a liver. Assume that all are serious candidates in the sense both of desperately needing one *and* of having a good chance of long-term success with one. Suppose both Jane and Jack are candidates for the #1 slot and are essentially equal candidates, except that Jane's liver disease is due to her alcoholism. By whatever other criteria you choose, assume that each is a better candidate than Roy, the #3 candidate—but that Roy is still a *good* candidate for a transplant. If the sanction against Jane is merely the tiebreaker sanction, then Jack goes to #1 and Jane to #2. But had Jane not ruined her liver by her voluntary conduct, Roy would instead be at #2, and so on with the remainder of the list. And of course, if enough livers do not become available, this might mean death for Roy (or for someone else lower down the list). So now—to return to the question of the moral weight of Jane's drinking—the tiebreaker sanction might seem too weak. Shouldn't Jane be put *further* down the list? Shouldn't the fact that she ruined her own liver mean that she should go behind candidates who, measured by other criteria, are worse candidates than Jane but are still viable and, but for the fact that Jane ruined her liver, would be closer to getting a new liver and at least a chance for a longer life?

From one angle, penalizing Jane with the only penalty available seems grossly out of proportion to her conduct; from another, it seems unfair to others not to put them (or at least many of them) before Jane. We are pulled both ways.

It is time to ask what kind of question the transplant question is. Let's go through some possibilities.

Is the issue one of *retributive* justice? Well, with retributive justice, an offender is punished—retribution is exacted—because the offender has done something bad to someone else. But let's assume that so far, Jane's drinking has harmed only Jane and done nothing bad to anyone else. This must be kept in mind when asking whether, in light of her voluntary conduct, an alcoholic is deserving of the potential death sentence that being put well down the transplant list might involve. The issue of harm to others is relevant, but the harm in question is the harm that would occur *if* we transplant Jane, not any harm that Jane has caused *prior* to a transplant.

Is the issue one of *compensatory* justice? Does it concern compensation for a harm done to someone? But again, Jane's drinking, taken by itself, has harmed no one but Jane.

Is the issue one of *distributive* justice? In a sense, it is. There is a scarce good to be distributed, and we are determining what considerations establish stronger or weaker claims. So we might be looking for a justifiable distributive policy to handle this case.

Consider, then, a distributive policy to be applied to future cases. Such a policy would penalize alcoholics, putting them lower on the transplant list. The thought is this: the knowledge that they will be put lower on the list will deter some people from excessive drinking and so from ruining their livers, thus reducing the overall demand for donor livers and so saving lives. One might be skeptical about the likely efficacy of such a policy, of course, but put that aside. In principle, such a policy might be defensible. Still, it would be unfair to apply it to current alcoholics. The proposed policy is supposed

to induce people in the future—once the policy is in effect—to drink less. But obviously it can have no incentive effect for Jane, who has already ruined her liver.

Of course, many things that institutions do involve retroactive consequences. Perhaps I have invested in Acme Tool and Dye because I expected to receive a tax break for doing so. Before I can recoup my investment, the government repeals the tax break and my money is lost. Nevertheless, I have no basis for complaint. That is how public policy works. By contrast, however, when the severe sanctions of the criminal law are at stake, we think things should be different. When the consequences are prison or execution, we think citizens should be put on clear, advance notice. There should be no retroactive penal sanction.

Here, the severity of the consequences to be imposed on Jane is relevant. Her situation does not involve the criminal law, but the impact of penalizing her with respect to the transplant list could turn out be as harsh as any consequence that the criminal law imposes. This is crucial. Although the distribution of a scarce resource—donor livers—makes the case seem to be one of distributive justice, the imposition of a severe sanction for the agent's conduct turns the institutional response into something analogous to the treatment of a criminal. Despite the fact that Jane has done nothing intrinsically immoral, the institutional decision is functionally equivalent to an instance of punishment. And if that is the case, then fairness requires adequate notice to Jane.

I want to belabor this point. If the institutionally mandated consequences to Jane were minor, the issue might be different. What would in effect count as a retroactive penalty might be permissible. But when, as here, the institutionally imposed consequences are very grave, the case seems sufficiently analogous to punishment that considerations relevant to fairness in punishing need to be brought to bear.

Now, some readers may balk at the term "punishment." One doesn't want to see medical institutions in a punitive role. And the analogy is admittedly imperfect. Most importantly, and in contrast to the criminal law, there is no thought of sanctioning Jane as an end in itself. If there are enough livers for all, Jane gets one. On the other hand, we must acknowledge the gravity of what might be done to Jane via the procedures of a publicly funded medical institution. If, in purely medical terms, Jane is no worse a candidate than Jack, but she is to go lower down the transplant list due to her past voluntary conduct, then we are in fact judging that her conduct has been sufficiently morally problematic to warrant imposing a grave, possibly fatal consequence on her. This sort of institutional action should surely trigger at least some of the usual safeguards surrounding punishment. Adequate notice is the most obvious one.

Conceding this point, we might decide to make the proposed policy applicable only to future cases. We could make it purely prospective. Moreover, suppose we promulgate it widely, educating children in schools, buying television ads, putting signs in every bar and labels on every bottle. Imagine that in five or ten years an alcoholic comes to us with a ruined liver. Would it *then* be appropriate to put her further down the transplant list?

Perhaps—on the premise that our new policy has an adequate justification. As noted, one justification might be that given such a policy, some people will drink less and not ruin their livers, and so, on balance, there will be a smaller gap between the supply and demand for livers.

However, there is also another relevant consideration. Maybe Jane is simply less *deserving* of that last available liver than Jack. After all, she has brought her disease on herself. Quite apart from other issues, one might think that makes a moral difference.

In fact, it does make a moral difference, but only in a particular context. Suppose livers were plentiful and cheap (perhaps a well-functioning artificial liver has been invented). In that context, helping Jane would hurt no one. No issue of comparative desert would arise. But that is not our context. In our world, helping Jane often means hurting Jack. And that prompts the thought that Jane is less deserving.

Yet even here, a condition must be met before this thought can be justified, and that condition goes beyond the Principle's focus on the fact that Jane's conduct has been voluntary. *Jane must also have known or be culpable for not knowing certain things*—namely, that if she destroys her liver, she will need a transplant, that donor livers are scarce, and that providing her with a liver will deny one to someone else, and so make that person's death more likely.

Imagine case 1, in which Jane is nonculpably ignorant of the potential consequences of her drinking for others such as Jack. She knows the likely impact of her drinking on herself, but she does not know and is not culpable for not knowing about transplant lists and organ shortages. In case 1, Jane is nonculpably ignorant of the fact that her conduct could have negative consequences for anyone but herself. From her perspective, her conduct is entirely self-regarding. In case 1, Jane does not knowingly create a situation in which saving her life might mean death for Jack. Here, Jane neither intends to harm anyone nor displays negligence with respect to her conduct's impact on others. On the stipulated premise, her conduct is not morally suspect, and so she is not morally deserving of what, by any standard, counts as severe punishment.

By contrast, in case 2, Jane is aware of the likely consequences for others of her drinking. She knows that what she does might create a state of affairs in which she will live only if someone else does not. In case 2, her readiness to drink away her liver can plausibly be seen as expressing a callous disregard for the well-being of whoever will *not* receive a liver should she receive one. Knowingly to drink away one's liver and then to ask for a transplant is to act with reckless disregard for the consequences of your conduct for another person's life chances. To do *that* is in fact highly immoral.

The basis for thinking Jane less deserving of a liver, then, is not merely that she is responsible for her voluntary conduct. That is a necessary but not a sufficient condition. When information has been adequately distributed, Jane's voluntary conduct becomes a form of callous disregard for and indifference to others' dire needs. The harm of her conduct is negligently to make herself a competitor for a scarce, lifesaving resource. Under those circumstances, it is appropriate for a publicly funded institution to judge that Jane is morally less deserving than Jack of receiving that last liver. This is where the widespread belief from which we started does touch defensible ground.

The situation might be thought similar to other forms of negligence. If I drive recklessly but no one is hurt and I am not caught, I have acted immorally but I am lucky and go unsanctioned. If Jane negligently drinks away her liver but an available donor liver has no other claimant, then Jane, too, has acted immorally but is lucky and goes unsanctioned. The thought behind imposing the sanction when we must choose between Jack and case 2 Jane is that she, not he, should be the person vulnerable to luck.

THE CONDITIONS OF SANCTION

So there are circumstances under which it is proper to impose a severe sanction on Jane—but those circumstances must obtain. Jane must know (or ought to know) basic facts about liver scarcity and transplant lists. And it may be a long time before such knowledge is sufficiently widespread that this condition is satisfied, at least for a first transplant. This is the key point. Case 2 Jane's conduct is, morally speaking, highly suspect—but we can say this *only* of case 2 Jane. And hers is, at least at the moment, a rare condition.

For now, the practical outcome of my analysis is something like this: Anyone who is currently a candidate for a first liver transplant due to her own health-risky conduct probably did not know enough (nonculpably) soon enough about donor lists and so forth to count as having negligently disregarded her conduct's consequences for others. But I assume that the process of receiving a transplant is educative, and, in any event, it could be made educative. We could then assume that thereafter the agent knew enough or ought to have known enough. Thus if she comes to need a second transplant because of subsequent voluntary, health-risky conduct, it would be proper to sanction her by putting her lower, perhaps much lower, on the transplant list. Indeed, I think that anyone who has received a transplant, regardless of the original cause of his liver disease, can be assumed thereafter to know enough that subsequent voluntary, health-risky conduct, perhaps including noncompliance with postoperative treatment, makes that person morally vulnerable.

Many issues remain to be explored. For instance, how does the act/omission distinction apply here? That is, is there a morally significant difference between causing one's illness and not preventing it? Consider Allen, whose liver disease is due to a repeated failure to get an easily available and medically recommended hepatitis B shot. If he knew of transplant shortages and so forth,

is he as culpable as case 2 Jane, so that he should also be sanctioned on the transplant list?

Moreover, on my analysis, there will be a question about the process for determining that the agent did or should have had the requisite knowledge. If the justification for a severe sanction bears on claims about what the agent knew or should have known, then there must be an adequate basis for those claims. Having already had a transplant is a useful proxy here. But in the longer term, some other standard for determining what the agent knew or should have known must be worked out.

I leave such issues for another day. My claim here is that there are circumstances under which we may justifiably make it significantly less likely that an agent will obtain a scarce, lifesaving resource—namely, if the agent has engaged in conduct that *deliberately* or *negligently* puts her in competition for the resource in question with others who have *not* engaged in conduct that deliberately or negligently puts them in competition for the resource in question. So there could come a time when we could rightly say that due to their voluntary, health-risky conduct, some agents are less deserving than others of receiving a scarce, lifesaving resource. However, except in rare cases, that time is not now.

Should Age Determine Who Gets a Kidney Transplant?

Judith Graham

If someone needs a kidney transplant today, it doesn't matter if she's 25 or 60 years old. What counts is how long she has spent waiting for a suitable organ to become available.

That would change under a controversial new proposal by the nation's organ transplant network that was unveiled Thursday in Dallas. The plan would give kidneys to patients who would live longest after a transplant, not those who have languished longest on waiting lists.

The goal is to make sure organs go to patients who can get the most benefit from a kidney transplant, extending more peoples' lives. But experts worry that older patients would be far less likely to get transplants if the plan is adopted.

"The thought is, if one person can live 15 years after a kidney transplant and another person can live five years, the organ should go to the person who lives the longest," said Dolph Chianchiano, vice president of health policy for the National Kidney Foundation.

The change would apply only to kidneys from deceased donors; organs from living donors wouldn't be affected.

The proposal, which may be altered and would not take effect until December at the earliest, comes from the Organ Procurement and Transplantation Network, which oversees all transplants in the U.S., and the agency that runs it, the United Network for Organ Sharing.

It would assess the benefit of a kidney transplant by estimating "extra years lived"—how long a patient with failing kidneys might expect to survive after a transplant versus how long the same patient might live on dialysis treatment.

Under this system, younger patients who haven't suffered the effects of age and attendant medical deterioration would be favored over patients in their 50s and above. Chances for a transplant also would get worse for older people with Type 2 diabetes, an increasingly common cause of kidney failure and source of medical complications such as hypertension and heart disease.

The change strikes some transplant experts and patients as unfair and potentially dangerous.

"How do you tell a 55-year-old: Too bad, you're too old, you're not getting a kidney because your life expectancy isn't that of a 35-year-old?" said Dr. Michael Abecassis, chief of organ transplantation at Northwestern's Feinberg School of Medicine. "How's the AARP going to react to that?"

"I don't have problems with trying to maximize this valuable resource—kidneys—which are in such short supply today," said Jack Fassnacht, 51, a Chicago lawyer with polycystic kidney disease who has had two transplants. "But I don't like the idea of suggesting the life of a 30-something has more value than the life of a 50-something. That just doesn't seem fair to me."

The change risks undermining public trust in the nation's transplant system, which depends on a reputation for treating all people equally and impartially, Abecassis said. If trust is compromised, fewer people may be willing to donate organs, aggravating a widening mismatch between demand for kidneys and supply.

But the current system for distributing kidneys has problems too. People with the most urgent medical needs often are not at the top of waiting lists. Increasingly, those spots are occupied by elderly individuals with underlying medical conditions such as heart disease or hypertension, who may not survive long under any circumstances.

That raises the prospect of a 75-year-old getting called by his hospital—we've found a match!—and rushing to receive a kidney from a 28-year-old killed in an auto accident. If the man lives only three more years, some wonder if that is a good use of the organ, especially when kidneys are in such short supply and the waiting lists so long.

Inequalities also occur in the current system because the supply of kidneys, the demand for organs and the availability of medical services vary by location, said Dr. Michael Shapiro, chief of transplantation at Hackensack University Medical Center in New Jersey.

For instance, the wait for a kidney is about 8 to 10 years in New York City but only 2 years in Albany, N.Y., Shapiro said. Waits in Chicago have reached about 5 years, according to several surgeons.

Data released at the Dallas meeting suggest transplant patients in the U.S. would live an extra 11,457 years under the new allocation scheme because more people would receive kidneys that would last longer.

"I think there are advantages to this approach.... Now that [this number] is on the table, it's hard for me to go back and say we shouldn't try to achieve this," said Dr. Mark Stegall, chief of transplantation surgery at the Mayo Clinic.

Stegall headed the study group that prepared the proposal for the Organ Procurement and Transplantation Network, which has government authority to oversee transplants.

He emphasized that the proposal hadn't been finalized. Preliminary plans call for several more meetings this year and a public comment period after a formal proposal is issued.

"Many of us feel there has not been enough discussion along the way in the development of this proposal and would like to see a much more robust public debate," said Dr. J. Richard Thistlethwaite, a transplant surgeon and professor at the University of Chicago. "People don't understand the implications of what's being suggested."

Thistlethwaite said he is uncomfortable with the value judgments he believes are inherent in the proposed system, particularly the emphasis on duration of life over quality of life. "How can we judge who's more deserving and whose life we value the most?" he said. "Where do we draw the line?"

It's a question also being asked by Norma Knowles, 38, a kidney recipient who lives in Columbia, Mo. Knowles, a social worker who works in a dialysis center, has polycystic kidney disease, as do her father and brother and as did her late uncle.

Eight years after a cousin donated a kidney to Knowles, it failed. Knowles went back on the transplant waiting list in July. To survive, this mother of four children administers dialysis to herself for three hours every night.

"Who's to say an older person's five years of life are any less important than a younger person's nine years?" she said. "The length of time doesn't necessarily determine what's best, and we have no right to judge. That's playing God and people aren't going to like it."

Chapter 9

Aging

The Old Fools

What do they think has happened, the old fools,
To make them like this? Do they somehow suppose
It's more grown-up when your mouth hangs open and drools,
And you keep pissing on yourself, and can't remember
Who called this morning? Or that, if they only chose,
They could alter things back to when they danced all night,
Or went to their wedding, or sloped arms some September?
Or do they fancy there's really been no change,
And they've always behaved as if they were crippled or tight,
Or sat through days of thin continuous dreaming
Watching light move? If they don't (and they can't), it's strange:
Why aren't they screaming?

Perhaps being old is having lighted rooms
Inside your head, and people in them, acting
People you know, yet can't quite name; each looms
Like a deep loss restored, from known doors turning,
Setting down a lamp, smiling from a stair, extracting
A known book from the shelves; or sometimes only
The rooms themselves, chairs and a fire burning,
The blown bush at the window, or the sun's
Faint friendliness on the wall some lonely
Rain-ceased midsummer evening. That is where they live:
Not here and now, but where all happened once.
This is why they give

At death, you break up: the bits that were you
Start speeding away from each other for ever
With no one to see. It's only oblivion, true:
We had it before, but then it was going to end,
And it was all the time merging with a unique endeavour
To bring to bloom the million-petaled flower
Of being here. Next time you can't pretend
There'll be anything else. And these are the first signs:
Not knowing how, not hearing who, the power
Of choosing gone. Their looks show that they're for it:
Ash hair, toad hands, prune face dried into lines –
How can they ignore it?

An air of baffled absence, trying to be there
Yet being here. For the rooms grow farther, leaving
Incompetent cold, the constant wear and tear
Of taken breath, and them crouching below
Extinction's alp, the old fools, never perceiving
How near it is. This must be what keeps them quiet:
The peak that stays in view wherever we go
For them is rising ground. Can they never tell
What is dragging them back, and how it will end? Not at night?
Not when the strangers come? Never, throughout
The whole hideous, inverted childhood? Well,
We shall find out.

Philip Larkin, 1988

This poem expresses a certain existential angst associated with growing old and losing one's memory. Larkin wrote the poem during the time that his mother was in a nursing home. The poem explores the conflicted feelings of disgust and tenderness, terror and compassion brought on by being faced with the decay and death of a beloved parent. It offers a clear-eyed look at the inevitability of our own demise. Larkin poignantly links birth to death by pointing to the oblivion experienced at each end: The oblivion associated with birth, which is temporary, and the oblivion of old age and death wherein, as he puts it, "you can't pretend/There'll be anything else."

Larkin's poem reminds us of how much our identities are associated with our minds; that the human condition is wrapped up with the power of choosing. The loss of self recounted in "The Old Fools" is marked by "the power/Of choosing gone." This is certainly a significant theme in bioethics, as patient autonomy—the ability to make choices for oneself—is widely held to be that which makes one worthy of respect. With the onslaught of Alzheimer's disease and severe dementia, argue some bioethicists, comes the loss of the persons we once were, raising difficult questions of how persons in such situations should be treated.

CASE STUDY: AN AFFAIR OF THE DEMENTED

Mrs. O'Brien, 75 years old, is a widow of 10 years and is diagnosed as being mildly demented. Mr. Jackson, 73 years old, is a widower of 12 years and is mild-to-moderately demented. Both are residents of a nursing home. Mr. Jackson has been in the facility for 5 years; Mrs. O'Brien moved in just five months ago.

Shortly after her arrival, Mr. Jackson and Mrs. O'Brien struck up a friendship. That friendship soon progressed into a sexual relationship. Mr. Jackson frequently accompanies Mrs. O'Brien around the facility—to meals, to the day room, etc.—and frequently wants to spend the night with her. They relate to one another the way they related to their marriage partners, with Mr. Jackson taking the lead, guiding Mrs. O'Brien around, and "taking care" of her in ways that are somewhat overbearing. Mrs. O'Brien, however, accepts and even welcomes the attention and care, especially since her marriage followed the same pattern.

He is under the impression that she is his deceased wife. Mrs. O'Brien, however, recognizes that he is not her husband, but she nevertheless welcomes the relationship and gets somewhat agitated when staff removes Mr. Jackson from her room.

Mr. Jackson's two children are accepting, even pleased, with their father's newfound relationship. Mrs. O'Brien's two children, however, are appalled and are complaining to the nursing home about how their mother is being abused and the nursing home is not providing proper care. They are also upset that the staff is letting their mother engage in a relationship with Mr. Jackson that, in their opinion, she would never *normally* consent to. As they put it, "Our mother was always faithful to our father, and would never be with another man." A couple of the staff members who provide care for Mrs. O'Brien are also opposed to the relationship. They complain that Mr. Jackson gets in their way, and that the mornings after he has spent the night, Mrs. O'Brien's dementia is exacerbated by the decreased sleep. On the other hand, some staff members find that the relationship has a positive effect on these residents, and that trying to keep them apart requires a Herculean effort that only results in agitation and upset.[1]

As this case suggests, many of the sorts of ethical issues that arise in connection with older adults are not of the high-tech, urgent nature that we find in the **acute care** setting. On the contrary, care for older adults largely concerns **chronic care** issues, such as those that arise in nursing homes or skilled nursing facilities. The case of Mr. Jackson and Mrs. O'Brien is just one example. While it clearly does not represent a life or death issue, it certainly relates to issues of quality of life (for the couple, the other residents of the nursing home, the staff, and the adult children of Mr. Jackson and Mrs. O'Brien) and to patient autonomy (Figure 9.1).

This case also represents the very common problem of dementia or **Alzheimer's disease** in the long-term care setting. According to the Alzheimer's Association, there are currently 5 million people living with Alzheimer's disease in the United States; every 72 seconds, someone develops the disease, and by the middle of the century one person will develop the disease every 33 seconds.[2] Almost half of all persons 85 years and older have Alzheimer's disease.[3]

The situation in which we find Mr. Jackson and Mrs. O'Brien is not unusual, then, given the prevalence of dementia and/or Alzheimer's disease within nursing homes. Persons with Alzheimer's disease tend to lose their inhibitions, especially concerning sexual matters; it is commonplace for nursing home residents to develop relationships, including sexual ones, with their peers. Justice Sandra Day O'Connor found herself in a similar situation with her husband after he developed Alzheimer's disease and was moved to an Alzheimer's ward at a long-term care facility: In his deep dementia, he developed a relationship with another Alzheimer's patient who was living at the same institution. O'Connor went public with her husband's situation to raise awareness surrounding the care of persons with Alzheimer's. Rather than being upset by this newfound relationship, she was relieved to see her husband of 55 years so content. Similarly, the ethical issues surrounding Mr. Jackson and Mrs. O'Brien's

FIGURE 9.1   This elderly woman is just one of 5 million people currently living with Alzheimer's disease in the United States.

relationship involve concerns for both their own health and well-being, and that of the staff, other residents, and their adult children.

First, consider the question of whether this relationship serves the good of Mr. Jackson and Mrs. O'Brien. It would seem that in one respect both partners are benefited by the human contact and personal attention they derive from the relationship. Both of them are happier and more content such that depression is no longer a concern. On the negative side, however, the pair becomes agitated if the staff attempts to separate them for sleeping purposes; and it seems that Mrs. O'Brien suffers somewhat from lack of sleep due to the physical nature of her relationship with Mr. Jackson, and their desire to sleep together each night. Weighing against allowing the relationship to continue, then, is a concern that it might have some negative impact on Mrs. O'Brien's alertness and clarity of mind.

This affair also raises questions concerning the interests of the other nursing home residents. One might argue that the rules of a nursing home are in place to protect and serve *all* the residents, even if some individuals might be benefited by breaking them. Thus, from a Kantian perspective, even if this couple is not harmed by their relationship, allowing it to continue could very well violate the rights and interests of other residents of the home. For example, if the sleeping quarters are shared then the other women sharing Mrs. O'Brien's space may be disturbed by the nightly sleepovers. Mr. Jackson's possessiveness concerning Mrs. O'Brien could have a negative impact on the relations between the residents, creating relationships of inclusion and exclusion. So even barring any negative outcomes for the couple, the duty to follow the rules may prevail.

With regard to the staff of the nursing home, there is a division in their responses to the relationship between Mr. Jackson and Mrs. O'Brien. Some of the staff is disgruntled because they find the affair inconvenient and even problematic in accomplishing Mrs. O'Brien's care. When Mr. Jackson is in the bed with her they find it difficult to get access to do her care; and some of the staff find it difficult to deal with Mrs. O'Brien when she is sleep deprived and mentally confused. Yet other staff members are happy that the couple have one another for companionship and support, and welcome the liason. The problem, then, is which staff members' wishes should be adhered to: those who want an end to the relationship, or those who want to see it continue?

But perhaps an even more difficult ethical issue arises in connection with the couples' adult children. Mr. Jackson's children are delighted with the match, and express their pleasure that their father has a new love interest; but Mrs. O'Brien's children are horrified, claiming that if their mother were in her "right mind" she would never consent to such a relationship. Though the children are certainly connected to and concerned about their mother, one might wonder how much their wishes should be taken into consideration, given the little time they actually spend at the home with their mother. One solution might be to separate Mr. Jackson and Mrs. O'Brien while her children are visiting her at the home, thus allowing them to visit their mother without the upset of seeing her with another man.

If, however, issues of **dementia** are present, we might question the degree to which either party can truly consent to the relationship. Mr. Jackson has confused Mrs. O'Brien with his deceased wife, so he is not appreciating her as a unique individual. While Mrs. O'Brien may suffer dementia to a lesser degree, her children claim that she would never consent to such a relationship under normal circumstances. It may be the case that her prior values and wishes as a person without dementia should be protected over the newly developed desires and interests of the demented Mrs. O'Brien.

Thus, while the issues raised by the "affair of the demented" are not life threatening or urgent, they do raise important questions about patients with compromised decisional capacity, the duty to adhere to institutional values and rules, and the rights of families to make decisions for their elderly and/or demented members. The essays in this chapter relate to these issues and go beyond to consider other questions, such as the ethics of life-extending technologies, aging and the goals of medicine, and concerns regarding the care expectations for older adults that fall almost entirely upon women.

AGING AND THE GOALS OF MEDICINE

We are currently experiencing what some commentators have called an "age boom," given the rise in the number of citizens over age 65 (Figure 9.2). According to the Centers for Disease Control (CDC), "The number of persons aged ≥65 years is expected to increase from approximately 35 million in 2000 to an estimated 71 million in 2030, and the number of persons aged ≥80 years is expected to increase from 9.3 million in 2000 to 19.5 million in 2030."[4]

This aging population can be largely attributed to two main factors: a decline in fertility and a 20-year increase in the life span during the second half of the 20th century. With so many aging and aged citizens, we must address the question of how we will provide a decent level of health care for a frail and elderly population, and which sorts of treatments and procedures should be provided.

Within the past couple of decades bioethicists have strongly debated the issue of **rationing** health care services to older adults. Supporters of rationing argue that it is irrational and wasteful to allocate scarce, high-tech health care resources (such as heart surgeries, pacemakers, transplants, kidney dialysis, and

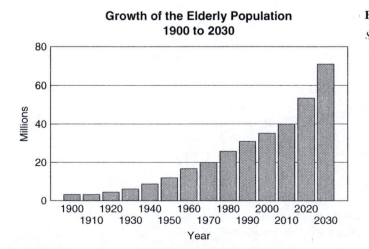

Growth of the Elderly Population 1900 to 2030

FIGURE 9.2   Growth in elderly population.

Source: U.S. Bureau of the Census

other life-extending treatments) to citizens who may not be healthy enough to benefit from the interventions, and who, in receiving such care, will deny the younger population their chance at receiving it. Rather than foolishly avoiding the inevitability of death, the argument goes, we should recognize that there is an end point to our lives at which aggressive, expensive, life-extending medical interventions are not warranted. Instead, we should graciously embrace old age and death, and place our health care resources into life-improving care for older adults (providing things such as canes and walkers, cataract surgeries, hearing aids, hip replacement surgeries, and other life-improving treatments).

Yet critics of such rationing argue that it is both ageist and sexist. It is ageist to assume that simply because someone has reached the age of 75 or more years, he or she is "not worth" the health care expenditures, and that he or she cannot benefit from the allocated care. Certainly as the average life span increases to 90 or even 100 years of age, it is more difficult to claim that, at 75 years of age, one is close to death and has completed all his or her life projects and goals. As the life span increases, so will our expectations and goals; it will become increasingly unlikely that one will see him- or herself as being advanced in age if he or she is likely to live another 20 years and has unfinished life projects, such as traveling or witnessing the birth of one's great-grandchildren. But in addition, feminist critics have claimed that rationing care to older adults results in unintended sexism, since the oldest-old population is largely made up of women. Statistics indicate that women outlive men in the United States such that within the age group of 80 and over, women overwhelmingly outnumber men.[5] Thus, to limit care to that group of oldest-old citizens is to limit care to women; and, as Nora Kizer Bell argues in her article in this chapter, such limits have serious gender implications.

Whether we agree that it is desirable or reasonable to ration care to older adults in particular, one thing is clear: We will have to make difficult decisions concerning the provision of health care to our elderly citizens and consider what our aims and purposes are in allocating health care resources to the aged. But perhaps even more urgently, we will need to determine how we will meet the increasing demands for caregiving that are sure to accompany an aging population.

CAREGIVING FOR OLDER ADULTS AND THE EXPLOITATION OF WOMEN'S CARE WORK

The medical and personal care of individuals in the privacy of their homes—a practice known as **home health care**—has been on the rise over the past two decades. This practice, which commonly involves the care of older adults by women, is riddled with ethical problems, especially within the current social and political climate (Figure 9.3). Home care came on the scene just as health care services were being reduced, and as questions were being raised about how much health care society can afford to commit

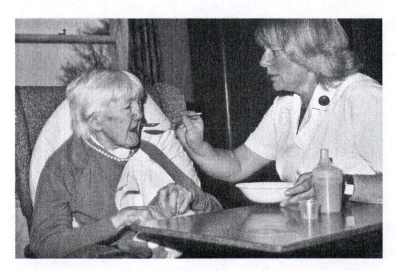

FIGURE 9.3 A nurse feeds an elderly woman who has severe Arthritis of the hands.

to older adults, and when it is morally just to limit care. Home care has been deemed a cost-saving, efficient care paradigm, thus justifying the deinstitutionalization movement that limits hospital or nursing home care by sending patients home as quickly as possible.

The informal provision of home health care is the foundation for home health services. Since patients are sent home from the hospital "sicker and quicker," and formal home care services are generally provided for only 60 days after discharge from a hospital, this means that a great deal of care-taking falls upon families themselves. Home health services have also faced recent serious cutbacks, meaning that families must become more resourceful in finding means to provide care for their dependent family members. As one expert notes, "Currently the average caregiver is a 45-year-old married woman of the 'sandwich generation' caught between the demands of children at home and aging parents."[6] Usually, the "resourcefulness" requires female family members to take leave from their paid employment in order to be available as familial caretakers; the result of such leaves can often be financially devastating to families, since women's employment is no longer supplemental.

There are also serious health costs for elderly women caring for spouses who have been hospitalized for serious illness; a recent *New England Journal of Medicine* study shows that elderly caregivers (both male and female) are at increased risk of dying prematurely, especially in the first few months after their loved ones are sent home from hospital. The study indicates that the health risks were highest when the spouse's hospitalization was for a chronic and disabling illness like congestive heart failure or dementia.[7] So clearly, the costs of caregiving (done largely by women) is not only economic, but also health related.

On November 5, 1994, Ronald Reagan publicly disclosed the fact that he had recently been diagnosed with Alzheimer's disease, and that he was exiting public life (Figure 9.4). In one section of his letter, Reagan stated:

> Unfortunately, as Alzheimer's Disease progresses, the family often bears a heavy burden. I only wish there was some way I could spare Nancy from this painful experience. When the time comes I am confident that with your help she will face it with faith and courage.[8]

Reagan's letter points to the fact that no matter what station of life they occupy, women take responsibility for the care burden associated with ill or dying family members. Nancy Reagan was no exception, and cared at home for her husband until the day he died.

FIGURE 9.4 Ronald Reagan, the 40th President of the United States, and his wife Nancy. Reagan developed Alzheimer's disease in his 80s.

Home care services are required in our current social context, given that home is where individuals clearly want to be. Since home care is rooted in the private sphere of the home, and care work historically has been construed as "women's work," the provision of home care has fallen almost exclusively on women, both as unpaid family members and as formal, paid caretakers. As Martha Holstein's article in this chapter argues, it is unjust to allow the lion's share of care work to fall on women's shoulders. We must, therefore, find other ways of providing caregiving services to older adults that do not exploit women. There are interesting cross-cultural questions concerning how and whether caregiving will be completed that are also addressed in this chapter.

AUTONOMY AND LONG-TERM CARE

Autonomy, captured in ideas of negative liberty and noninterference, has a particular appeal to Americans, who are raised on the belief that all people have the right to live as they choose. Feminist moral theorists (and some gerontologists) have been critical of this focus, especially in the realm of health care. Autonomy is a formative notion on which North American culture and our system of health care delivery is largely based. Indeed, it has become the foundational principle of health care. Consider, for example, the **Patient Bill of Rights** that hangs above virtually every hospital admissions desk across the country. The visible posting of this bill serves to indicate hospitals' serious commitment to patient autonomy and to reassure patients that their autonomy will be respected. Such a preoccupation with autonomy obscures the fact that we ultimately lack control over aging, illness, disability, suffering, and death. To admit this lack of autonomy is to admit that the human condition is beyond our control; to relinquish autonomy is to acknowledge our deep vulnerability, especially as we age.

Furthermore, this preoccupation with autonomy relates to independence, since a person's independence and her ability to live independently of others is symbolic of her autonomy. Dependence has been associated with weakness, incapacity, neediness, and a lack of dignity; insofar as individuals are able to resist dependency, they are able to maintain their dignity and self-respect. But this strong emphasis on autonomy as independence has had a very negative impact on aging and aged persons, who find themselves increasingly in need of assistance to bathe, go to the bathroom, dress, eat, and get about. It is seen to be shameful and embarrassing to admit that you can no longer perform all these tasks unassisted, and as a result many older adults will refuse for as long as possible to ask for help; instead, they struggle or simply go without their baths or meals rather than ask for assistance.

So the principle of autonomy is arguably of little use when we are considering people of advanced age, who cannot maintain the facade of being independent and self-sufficient. In addition, though, the principle is not helpful within the context that a large number of older adults find themselves: nursing homes or assisted-living centers. As George Agich points out in his article included in this chapter, the conditions of old age and the living conditions one finds in long-term care facilities are not conducive to the principle of autonomy as it has traditionally been understood. We need to rethink autonomy, how we understand it, and the ways in which it applies to older adults, in order to ensure that those in long-term care facilities are not harmed by it.

Given the increasing number of aging and aged people who are suffering from Alzheimer's disease, we can further appreciate the inappropriateness of applying a principle of autonomy to older adults in long-term care facilities. It makes no sense to talk about the autonomy of individuals (like Mr. Jackson or Mrs. O'Brien) if those individuals are not capable of clearly understanding their situations or identifying their needs. Indeed, some bioethicists argue not only that an elderly patient with Alzheimer's disease lacks autonomy, but that when determining what we should do with or for such a patient, we should only consider his or her wishes prior to developing Alzheimer's. In other words, some bioethicists think that the wishes of an older adult with moderate to severe dementia should not be adhered to; rather, we should consider what that individual wanted as his or her previously rational, autonomous self. If, for example, an older woman writes an **advance directive** after an initial diagnosis of Alzheimer's disease, and in it she indicates that she does not want to be kept alive once she reaches a state of moderate to deep dementia, then those wishes should prevail even if the woman becomes happily demented and seems to quite enjoy her life. According to this argument, the advance directive serves as a statement of the woman's reasoned values, and should apply even if she experiences her dementia in a pleasant and happy state. Critics of this view, however, claim that it would be wrong to hold the happily demented woman to the wishes of her previously rational self. The individual who wrote the advance directive cannot project herself into the future to understand how she might experience her dementia; thus, to hold the current happily demented self to the wishes of the previous self is, in a very real sense, to allow a different person to govern the interests of the woman with dementia. This debate is taken up in articles included within this chapter.

Given the American hypervaluing of autonomy and independence, the cultural fear of death and dying, and the advanced state of medical technology and medical science, it is unsurprising that we find within the United States a fascination with the possibility of extending human life. Ethical debates surround the attempt to unlock the secret to extended human life. Some scientists claim that the day is not far off when humans could live for as long as 150 years or more. Some scientists support a **"programmed" theory of aging,** arguing that aging is regulated over the life span by one's biological clock: regulation depends on changes in gene expression that affect the systems responsible for repair, maintenance, and defense responses. Others who assume a **damage-based theory of aging** claim that it is the result of cumulative damage to living organisms that is caused by the environment.[9] Whatever the cause of aging, science may be able to slow down the aging process and even produce therapies that would reverse it. The prospects of human longevity raise arguments, pro and con, concerning the advisability of pursuing this goal. Proponents of longevity claim that for individuals who experience their lives as good, more life is necessarily better, and being denied their lives through death is necessarily bad. But those who defend the natural human life span worry that, among other things, the push for anti-aging technology expresses contempt for aging and old age, and that pursuing these technologies will only result in harm to older adults.

Looking Ahead

- Scientists will continue to pursue the goal of human longevity, looking for ways to allow human beings to live for 120–150 years. The study of nanotechnology will allow scientists to determine ways to extend human life while still allowing one to live a vibrant, active lifestyle.
- An aging crisis will hit most developed countries by the year 2025, as the "baby boom" generation comes into advanced age. With lower birth rates in recent generations, and concerns about Social Security and Medicare for older adults, the ability to find, provide, and pay for decent care in the home and community will become exceedingly difficult. Service jobs, such as a home health aide, will not draw new employees unless a change occurs in how such (female) workers are treated and paid.
- With the aging population and the medical problems caused by dementia and Alzheimer's disease, concerted efforts will be made to find a treatment to slow down or stop the progression of the disease. We will have the ability to prevent Alzheimer's disease (by taking certain vitamins, for example) and to slow down its progress, thus improving the health status of many older adults.

Endnotes

1. This case was written and kindly shared by Mark Waymack, Department of Philosophy, Loyola University of Chicago.
2. See http://www.alz.org/alzheimers_disease_facts_figures.asp [Accessed on May 7, 2008].
3. See http://www.alz.org/national/documents/report_alzfactsfigures2007.pdf
4. See the Centers for Disease Control at http://www.cdc.gov/MMWR/preview/mmwrhtml/mm5206a2.htm.
5. See the U.S. Census Bureau at http://www.census.gov/PressRelease/www/releases/archives/facts_for_features_special_editions/003897.html [Accessed on May 9, 2008].
6. Cleda Meyer, "Coping with Caregiver Strain: When the Patient is Your Parent," *Kansas Nurse* (October 2000).
7. Richard Schulz and Scott R. Beach, "Caregivng as a Risk Factor for Mortality," *Journal of the American Medical Association,* 282 (1999), 2215–2219.
8. Ronald Reagan's full letter to the public is available online at http://en.wikipedia,org/wiki/Ronald_Reagan's_Alzheimer's_letter. [Accessed on May 8, 2008].
9. For information concerning why we age, see http://www.senescence.info/theories.html. [Accessed on May 9, 2008]

AGING AND THE ENDS OF MEDICINE

Limiting Health Care for the Old

Daniel Callahan

In October 1986, Dr. Thomas Starzl of Presbyterian University Hospital in Pittsburgh successfully transplanted a liver into a 76-year-old woman, thereby extending to the elderly patient the most technologically sophisticated and expensive kind of medical treatment available (the typical cost of such an option is more than $200,000). Not long after that, Congress brought organ transplants under Medicare coverage, thus guaranteeing an even greater range of this form of lifesaving care for older age groups.

That is, on its face, the kind of medical progress we usually hail: a triumph of medical technology and a newfound benefit provided by an established health care program. However, at the same time those events were taking place, a government campaign for cost containment was under way, with a special focus on health care to the aged under Medicare. It is not hard to understand why. In 1980, people over age 65—11% of the population—accounted for 29% of the total American health care expenditures of $219.4 billion. By 1986, the elderly accounted for 31% of the total expenditures of $450 billion. Annual Medicare costs are projected to rise from $75 billion in 1986 to $114 billion by the year 2000, and that is in current, not inflated, dollars.

Is it sensible, in the face of the rapidly increasing burden of the health care costs for the elderly, to press forward with new and expensive ways of extending their lives? Is it possible even to hope to control costs while simultaneously supporting innovative research, which generates new ways to spend money? Those are now unavoidable questions. Medicare costs rise at an extraordinary pace, fueled by an increasing number and proportion of the elderly. The fastest-growing age group in the United States is comprised of those over age 85, increasing at a rate of about 10% every two years. By the year 2040, it has been projected, the elderly will represent 21% of the population and consume 45% of all health care expenditures. How can costs of that magnitude be borne?

Anyone who works closely with the elderly recognizes that the present Medicare and Medicaid programs are grossly inadequate in meeting their real and full needs. The system fails most notably in providing decent long-term care and medical care that does not constitute a heavy out-of-pocket drain. Members of minority groups and single or widowed women are particularly disadvantaged. How will it be possible, then, to provide the growing number of elderly with even present levels of care, much less to rid the system of its inadequacies and inequities, and, at the same time, add expensive new technologies?

The straight answer is that it will be impossible to do all those things and, worse still, it may be harmful even to try. It may be so because of the economic burden that would be imposed on younger age groups, and because of the requisite skewing of national priorities too heavily toward health care. However, that suggests to both young and old that the key to a happy old age is good health care, which may not be true.

In the past few years, three additional concerns about health care for the aged have surfaced. First, an increasingly large share of health care is going to the elderly rather than to youth. The Federal government, for instance, spends six times as much providing health benefits and other social services to those over 65 as it does to those under 18. Also, as the demographer Samuel Preston observed in a provocative address to the Population Association of America in 1984, "Transfers from the working-age population to the elderly are also transfers away from children, since the working ages bear far more responsibility for childrearing than do the elderly."

Preston's address had an immediate impact. The mainline senior citizen advocacy groups accused Preston of fomenting a war between the generations, but the speech also stimulated Minnesota Senator David Durenberger and others to found Americans for Generational Equity (AGE) to promote debate about the burden on future generations, particularly the Baby Boom cohort, of "our major social insurance programs." Preston's speech and the founding of AGE signaled the outbreak of a struggle over what has come to be called "intergenerational equity," which is now gaining momentum.

The second concern is that the elderly, in dying, consume a disproportionate share of health care costs. Stanford University economist Victor Fuchs notes:

> At present, the United States spends about 1 percent of the gross national product on health care for elderly persons who are in their last year of life. . . . One of the biggest challenges facing policy makers for the rest of this century will be how to strike an appropriate balance between care for the [elderly] dying and health services for the rest of the population.

The third issue is summed up in an observation by Dr. Jerome Avorn of the Harvard Medical School, who wrote in *Daedalus,* "With the exception of the birth-control pill, [most] of the medical-technology interventions developed since the 1950s have their most widespread impact on people who are past their fifties—the further past their fifties, the greater the impact." Many of the techniques in question were not intended for use on the elderly. Kidney dialysis, for example, was developed for those between the ages of 15 and 45. Now some 30% of its recipients are over 65.

The validity of those concerns has been vigorously challenged, as has the more general assertion that some form of rationing of health care for the elderly might become necessary. To the charge that old people receive a disproportionate share of resources, the response has been that assistance to them helps every age group: It relieves the young of the burden of care that would otherwise have to bear for elderly parents and, since those young will eventually become old, promises them similar care when they need it. There is no guarantee, moreover, that any cutback in health care for the elderly would result in a transfer of the savings directly to the young. Also, some ask, "Why should we contemplate restricting care for the elderly when we wastefully spend hundreds of millions on an inflated defense budget?"

The assertion that too large a share of funds goes to extending the lives of elderly people who are terminally ill hardly proves that it is an unjust or unreasonable amount. They are, after all, the most in need. As some important studies have shown, it is exceedingly difficult to know that someone is dying; the most expensive patients, it turns out, are those who were expected to live but died. That most new technologies benefit the old more than the young is logical: most of the killer diseases of the young have now been conquered.

There is little incentive for politicians to think about, much less talk about, limits on health care for the aged. As John Rother, director of legislation for the American Association of Retired Persons, has observed, "I think anyone who wasn't a champion of the aged is no longer in Congress." Perhaps also, as Guido Calabresi, dean of the Yale Law School, and his colleague Philip Bobbitt observed in their thoughtful 1978 book *Tragic Choices,* when we are forced to make painful allocation choices, "Evasion, disguise, temporizing . . . [and] averting our eyes enables us to save some lives even when we will not save all."

I believe that we must face this highly troubling issue. Rationing of health care under Medicare is already a fact of life, though rarely labeled as such. The requirement that Medicare recipients pay the first $520 of hospital care costs, the cutoff of reimbursement for care after 60 days, and the failure to cover long-term care are nothing other than allocation and cost-saving devices. As sensitive as it was to the senior citizen vote, the Reagan Administration agreed only grudgingly to support catastrophic health care coverage for the elderly (a benefit that will not help very many of them), and it expressed its opposition to the version of the bill recently passed by the house. Any administration is bound to be far more resistant to long-term health care coverage.

However, there are reasons other than the economics to think about health care for the elderly. The coming economic crisis provides a much needed opportunity to ask some deeper questions. Just what is it that we want medicine to do for us as we age? Other cultures have believed that aging should be accepted, and that it should be, in part, a time of preparation for death. Our culture seems increasingly to dispute that view, preferring instead, it often seems, to think of aging as hardly more than another disease, to be fought and rejected. Which view is correct?

Let me interject my own opinion. The future goal of medical science should be to improve the quality of old people's lives, not to lengthen them. In its long-standing ambition to forestall death, medicine has reached its last frontier in the care of the aged. Of course, children and young adults still die of maladies that are open to potential cure, but the highest proportion of the dying (70%) are over 65. If death is ever to be humbled, that is where endless work remains to be done, but however tempting the challenge of that last frontier, medicine should restrain itself. To do otherwise would mean neglecting the needs of other age groups and of the old themselves.

Our culture has worked hard to redefine old age as a time of liberation, not decline, a time of travel, of new ventures in education and self-discovery, of the ever-accessible tennis court or golf course, and of delightfully periodic but thankfully brief visits from well behaved grandchildren. That is, to be sure, an idealized picture, but it arouses hopes that spur medicine to wage an aggressive war against the infirmities of old age. As we have seen, the costs of such a war would be prohibitive. No matter how much is spent, the ultimate problem will still remain: people will grow old and die. Worse still, by pretending that old age can be turned into a kind of endless middle age, we rob it of meaning and significance for the elderly.

There is a plausible alternative: a fresh vision of what it means to live a decently long and adequate life, what might be called a "natural lifespan." Earlier generations accepted the idea that there was a natural lifespan—the biblical norm of three score and ten captures that notion (even though, in fact, that was a much longer lifespan than was typical in ancient times). It is an idea well worth reconsidering, and would provide us with a meaningful and realizable goal. Modern medicine and biology have done much, however, to wean us from that kind of thinking. They have insinuated the belief that the average lifespan is not a natural fact at all, but instead one that is strictly dependent on the state of medical knowledge and skill. Also, there is much to that belief as a statistical fact: The average life expectancy continues to increase, with no end in sight.

However, that is not what I think we ought to mean by a natural lifespan. We need a notion of a full life that is based on some deeper understanding of human needs and possibilities, not on the state of medical technology or its potential. We should think of a natural lifespan as the achievement of a life that is sufficiently long to take advantage of those opportunities life typically offers and that we ordinarily regard as its prime benefits—loving and "living," raising a family, engaging in work that is satisfying, reading, thinking, cherishing our friends and families. People differ on what might be a full natural lifespan; my view is that it can be achieved by the late 70s or early 80s.

A longer life does not guarantee a better life. No matter how long medicine enables people to live, death at any time—at age 90 or 100 or 110—would frustrate some possibility, some as-yet-unrealized goal. The easily preventable death of a young child is an outrage. Death from an incurable disease of someone in the prime of young adulthood is a tragedy. However, death at an old age, after a long and full life, is simply sad, but it is a part of life itself.

As it confronts aging, medicine should have as its specific goals the averting of premature death, that is, death prior to the completion of a natural lifespan, and thereafter, the relief of suffering. It should pursue those goals so that the elderly can finish out their years with as little needless pain as possible—and with as much vitality as can be generated in contributing to the welfare of younger age groups and to the community of which they are a part. Above all, the elderly need to have a sense of the meaning and significance of their stage in life, one that is not dependent on economic productivity or physical vigor.

What would medicine oriented toward the relief of suffering rather than the deliberate extension of life be

like? We do not have a clear answer to that question, so long standing, central, and persistent has been medicine's preoccupation with the struggle against death. However, the hospice movement is providing us with much guidance. It has learned how to distinguish between the relief of suffering and the lengthening of life. Greater control by elderly persons over their own dying—and particularly an enforceable right to refuse aggressive life-extending treatment—is a minimal goal.

What does this have to do with the rising cost of health care for the elderly? Everything. The indefinite extension of life combined with an insatiable ambition to improve the health of the elderly is a recipe for monomania and bottomless spending. It fails to put health in its proper place as only one among many human goods. It fails to accept aging and death as part of the human condition. It fails to present to younger generations a model of wise stewardship.

How might we devise a plan to limit the costs of health care for the aged under public entitlement programs that is fair, humane, and sensitive to their special requirements and dignity? Let me suggest three principles to undergird a quest for limits. First, government has a duty, based on our collective social obligations, to help people live out a natural lifespan, but not to help medically extend life beyond that point. Second, government is obliged to develop under its research subsidies, and to pay for, under its entitlement programs, only the kind and degree of life-extending technology necessary for medicine to achieve and serve the aim of a natural lifespan. Third, beyond the point of a natural lifespan, government should provide only the means necessary for the relief of suffering, not those for life-extending technology.

A system based on those principles would not immediately bring down the cost of care of the elderly; it would add cost, but it would set in place the beginning of a new understanding of old age, one that would admit of eventual stabilization and limits. The elderly will not be served by a belief that only a lack of resources, better financing mechanisms, or political power stands between them and the limitations of their bodies. The good of younger age groups will not be served by inspiring in them a desire to live to an old age that maintains the vitality of youth indefinitely, as if old age were nothing but a sign that medicine has failed in its mission. The future of our society will not be served by allowing expenditures on health care for the elderly to escalate endlessly and uncontrollably, fueled by the false altruistic belief that anything less is to deny the elderly their dignity. Nor will it be aided by the pervasive kind of self-serving argument that urges the young to support such a crusade because they will eventually benefit from it also.

We require, instead, an understanding of the process of aging and death that looks to our obligation to the young and to the future, that recognizes the necessity of limits and the acceptance of decline and death, and that values the old for their age and not for their continuing youthful vitality. In the name of accepting the elderly and repudiating discrimination against them, we have succeeded mainly in pretending that, with enough will and money, the unpleasant part of old age can be abolished. In the name of medical progress, we have carried out a relentless war against death and decline, failing to ask in any probing way if that will give us a better society for all.

What Setting Limits May Mean:
A Feminist Critique of Daniel Callahan's *Setting Limits*

Nora K. Bell

In his recent and controversial book, *Setting Limits,* Daniel Callahan has put forth a provocative thesis: that "intergenerational equity." might require us to rethink some of the traditional goals of medicine as they affect care that is provided to the elderly. Specifically, Callahan suggests that the increasing numbers of the elderly, coupled with medicine's increased technological capabilities, create the potential within medicine for "an unending medical struggle against aging and death" that is, perhaps, not properly one of medicine's "deepest ends" or goals.

As Callahan states, his "first and most fundamental" purpose in writing *Setting Limits* is to:

> stimulate a public discussion of the future of health care for the aged. . . . My approach will not generally be a pleasing one. It puts to one side the kind of relentless optimism that has been the mainstay of medical advancement and its economic underpinning. It rejects the conceit that we can have anything we want if we put our minds to it and are willing to pay for it. . . . This book, by contrast, is a call for limits, . . . for a willingness to ask once again how we might creatively and honorably accept aging and death when we become old, not always struggle to overcome them. (1987, 23–24)

On its face, Callahan's aim in this book is one for which I have a great deal of sympathy. I have been present in the ICU when a ninety-two-year-old woman with terminal metastatic cancer is intubated repeatedly each time she extubates herself. I have argued in favor of the "validity" of giving effect to a living will that was executed in a state other than the one in which the elderly patient finds herself hospitalized. I, myself, have argued that the prolongation of life, or the forestalling of death, can be a "false goal" of medicine. I agree that one's quality of life is not necessarily a function of the length of one's life, and I, too, worry about "creeping medical immortality."

But I am more worried about setting involuntary limits. If age becomes a limiting factor, as Dr. Callahan suggests it should, apart from the obvious consequences to which many before me have taken objection, there is yet another consequence that I feel must not be overlooked. The limits that will be set will be limits that affect women more drastically than they affect men. The so-called "frontier" of old age extends endlessly for many more women than it does men.

My objective in writing this essay, therefore, is to examine the implications of Callahan's thesis for elderly women.

RECONSTRUCTING THE ENDS OF AGING

The elderly are currently the heaviest users of health services, and the great bulk of those services is spent in "forestalling death" and in "warehousing" persons until their deaths. In fact, these facts represent part of the challenge society would face in setting limits.

When one looks closely at the data, however, what one very quickly discovers is that there are many more elderly women than there are elderly men, and these older women are poorer, more apt to live alone, and less likely to have informal social and personal supports than their male counterparts. Furthermore, a disproportionate number of nursing home patients are women. Older *women,* therefore, are more likely to make the heaviest demand on health care resources.[1]

Relying on data supporting the above, albeit with hardly any emphasis on how the data speak to gender-related issues, Callahan moves to his second agenda in *Setting Limits,* namely, proposing "a different way of providing care than is commonly considered: that of using age as a specific criterion for the allocation and limitation of health care" (1987, 23). In this section of his book Callahan "reconstructs the ends of aging" and advances

Bell, Nora Kizer. "What Setting Limits May Mean: A Feminist Critique of Daniel Callahan's *Setting Limits,*" *The Other Within Us: Feminist Explorations of Women and Aging,* ed. Marilyn Pearsall, Boulder: Westview Press (1997), 151–159. Copyright © 1997. Reprinted by permission of Westview Press, a member of Perseus Book Group.

his thesis that age should be a limiting factor in the provision of health services: that upon reaching the end of a "natural life span" further medical intervention should be acknowledged as inappropriate.

Callahan proposes a new conception of life and the natural end of one's life in old age, a conception that focuses on the fact that one's life on the whole has had numerous and bountiful experiences whose richness in old age now suggests completeness. Such a conception (or definition) of life makes no evaluative claims about the experiences by which one's life is so defined. Rather, Callahan is offering what he considers to be a *biographical* definition of life; there comes a time when the biography is complete, even though there might be many more pages one could write.

> For the lifelong reader there will still be many old books not read, and a constant stream of new books to be read. For the painter, there will be an infinite number of further possibilities, as there will be for one who enjoys investing in the stock market, understanding nature, watching scientific and other knowledge being discovered, growing a garden, observing the sunset, enjoying music, and taking walks. In that sense, however, life's possibilities will never be exhausted;... Yet even if we will lose such possibilities by death in old age, we will on the whole already have had ample time to know the pleasures of such things. (Callahan, 1987, 67)

Callahan insists that "[t]he pattern I want to note is a familiar one in most cultures, including our own: the belief that death at the end of a long and full life is not an evil, that indeed there is something fitting and orderly about it" (65). The natural end to a long and full life, i.e., the correlative to the "natural life span," is what he calls a "tolerable death": (1) a death that occurs when one has accomplished most of what life has to offer, (2) a death that occurs when one has fulfilled one's obligations to all those to whom one has responsibilities, and (3) a death that no longer offends or engenders rage and despair at human finitude (66).

For Callahan, the end of the aging process is not properly spent, therefore, "warring" against the diseases that accompany longevity. The goal of geriatric medicine is not to seek new ways to predict or prevent late-onset genetic disease; it is not to define "premature" death as a function of state-of-the-art medicine at any given moment; it is not to seek "just a little longer life"; it is not to practice opportunistic medicine or to imagine medicine as providing the fountain of youth. Rather, so that one may experience the natural end of a life, the goal is to put aside the allures that medicine offers for staving off old age. On Callahan's view, society should seek to impose limits on health care for the elderly so

that the richness and fullness of old age aren't lost, and so that old age isn't villified by our fight against it.

OLD AGE IN NEW TIMES

Although Callahan's analyses of social purpose and age, "natural life span" and "tolerable death," and the obligations of the young to the very old (and the old to the young and to the future) are themselves philosophically engaging, and although one could focus on the arguments he advances for giving up certain of medicine's "beloved ideas," it is more to the point to examine the question he poses when he articulates his final goal in urging that society set limits on the provision of medical care to the aged.

The question, as he frames it, is: "What would it mean in practice to have a health policy for the aged of the kind that I propose?" (1987, 23).

Unfortunately, serious problems underlie what Callahan ultimately suggests as his answer, problems that, despite his compassionate and thoughtful insight, redound negatively against his thesis.

In "Old Age in New Times" (the final chapter of *Setting Limits*), Callahan argues for moving beyond the decade-old agenda of anti-ageism to his newer agenda. Callahan is not deeply worried about anti-ageist platforms of health care reform that were based on analyses of the "troubled and horrible lot" of the elderly (Butler, 1975); he acknowledges that there may still be items from that agenda that need to be addressed (although he doesn't tell us what they are). However, he sees the focus on abuses and "unmet basic needs" of the elderly as outmoded, as leading us to seek to extend the outer bounds of medicine's capabilities. Rather, what Callahan wants the reader to adopt as a new focus is captured in his distinction between tragedy, outrage and sadness:

> It is a tragedy when life ends prematurely even though it is possible to save that life, and when old age is full of burdens even though resources are available to relieve them. It is an outrage when, through selfishness, discrimination, or culpable indifference, the elderly are denied what they need and deserve. But it is only a sadness, an ineradicable part of life itself, when after a long and full life a person ages and dies.... It is wise to want to banish the tragedy and the outrage, but not the sadness. (1987, 204)

As Callahan himself argues, on the very next page, one must seek to discern the proper ends of medicine and of aging "in a larger moral and social context" (205). Yet it is precisely that caveat that Callahan seems to have ignored. Setting limits on health care provision in the ways that Callahan suggests may in some cases still be properly described as a "tragedy" and an "outrage."

TOLERABLE OR TRAGIC DEATHS?

Nowhere in the final chapters of *Setting Limits* does Callahan take note of the implications of his thesis for women, or of the special plight of women among the aged (except to mention that women are burdened more than men in being caregivers for sick and aging parents). Nowhere does he discuss whether there might be differences in the definition of "natural life span" or one's perception of a "tolerable death" that are gender-relative. Nowhere does he discuss the fact that the limits he suggests imposing may have tragic consequences for women.

On my view, however, these are the very consequences of setting limits that need to be examined more carefully. In what follows, I would like to offer such an examination by looking more closely at Callahan's three-part definition of what counts as a tolerable death.

First: a tolerable death is one that occurs when an individual has accomplished most of what life has to offer.

Callahan's biographical definition of life fails to take adequate note of the differences in the biographies of men and women. To believe that it is desirable to adopt the use of an age standard suggests that a woman's life should be viewed as completed earlier in her biological chronology than it actually is, that is, when procreation, childrearing, housekeeping and the maintaining of conjugal relationships are complete. The argument in favor of believing that there is an appropriate time in a person's biography for claiming that her life could be considered full strikes me as advancing recognized forms of male bias: both a general *devaluation of women's concerns and an indifference to a woman's "life possibilities" apart from her abasement into more servile positions.* (That is not to say that I couldn't agree that one's life from a certain point forward might not be worth living or might itself be intolerable.)

Why shouldn't one believe, as James Childress (1984) has suggested, that the use of an age standard seems to symbolize a willingness on our part to abandon older female persons and exclude them from communal care?[2] Furthermore, as Childress seems to believe, the use of an age criterion for determining how to allocate health care resources seems to manifest society's perception that youth is valuable and advanced age, particularly advanced female age, has less worth. The testimony of older persons, especially older women, who profess to believe that they are willing, and maybe even morally obliged, to let a younger person (say, a child or a grandchild) live in their stead is less evidence in favor of accepting the argument than it is evidence confirming society's devaluation of older persons and advancing age. Besides, willingness on the part of some older persons to elect to forego certain resources or experiences in favor of giving them to younger persons does not imply that a standard for accomplishing that should be *imposed*. Unless Childress' claim about the use of an age criterion is true, i.e., unless we really do believe that youth is more valuable, why should it be obvious that we should prefer to limit resources to older persons in favor of allocating to younger persons? Why shouldn't we believe that electing such a standard makes women's deaths premature? Why isn't it obvious that women's old age is full of burdens? Is it obvious that there *aren't* resources available to relieve them?

Callahan's biographical definition of life seems to measure a person's life by the notion of a "range of experiences" without taking note of any qualitative measure of those experiences. This understanding of measuring one's life seems counterintuitive. It doesn't seem enough to say that the range of a person's experiences, or the range of her exposure to resources, is greater in virtue of her having lived longer. Surely the quality of those experiences or of those resources colors them in a way that cannot be ignored. For that reason, it seems culpable indifference to fail to count the quality of those experiences as significant.

Insofar as women have historically been disadvantaged with respect to their achievements, their interests, their economic, social and political status, and their sexuality, many would argue that the quality of their life experiences has been so low that with respect to the first criterion of what counts as a tolerable death, Callahan's definition begs the question.

This brings me to the second part of Callahan's definition:

A tolerable death is one that occurs when one has fulfilled one's obligations to all those to whom one has responsibilities.

Women are beginning to enter the paid labor force in substantial numbers, but in spite of their economic emergence, women continue to be in disadvantaged positions in the market place both in terms of the wages they command and the jobs open to them. As human capital, women are valued less highly than men (Bergmann, 1986).

This can be viewed as a natural consequence of the fact that "[i]n the past, women's place in the economy was an assignment to sole responsibility for the care of the children, and to housework and other works that could efficiently be combined in the home with child care. Men were given sole responsibility for earning money, and exempted from taking a share in "women's work"' (Bergmann, 1986, 7). The importance assigned to earning money, among other things, helped contribute to devaluing "women's work." Reskin and Hartmann (1986) and others delineate some of the kinds of work that have been so devalued, among them: *caring work* (child care and nursing care, for example), *consumption work* (all those tasks involved in purchasing goods and services), *kin work* (tasks involved in keeping up with family birthdays, weddings, funerals, and simply "keeping in touch"), *invisible work* (housework, cooking, sewing, washing, ironing, for example). A further indication of the lack of value attached to such work is found in the fact that government and industry have been slow to move to "industrialize" child care and housework, making it even harder for women (especially single mothers) to compete effectively in the job market (Bergmann, 1986, 275–298).[3]

Because of the value attached to providing for another *financially,* women's responsibilities to others continue in large part to be described as consisting in caring work, kin work, consumption work and other forms of so-called "invisible work." It is easy to imagine someone arguing that a woman who is single, or who outlives her spouse, or whose children are independent has outlived her usefulness and her obligations. Furthermore, because women live longer than men and have been in the work force a shorter period of time than men, and hence have contributed less to public funds and have limited provisions of their own for their old age, women could also be perceived as undeservedly requiring more in the way of others' responsibilities *to* them.

As the largest and poorest population of the elderly, it is women who will make the heaviest demands on public monies for health care. It is the older woman who will have the greatest need for increased social and nonfinancial forms of support. It is she who will be society's greatest burden, and it is she for whom limits will be set.

This "larger social and moral context" is of vast importance in evaluating the thesis in *Setting Limits.* Setting limits is much more complex than it appears on the surface. For his part, Callahan acknowledges that an age standard has "symbolic significance" when its use is colored by its context or by the rationale articulated for its use (1987, 169). He also acknowledges that death is a tragedy and an outrage if it comes on the heels of one's having been denied what one needs through discrimination or indifference (1987, 204).

A death is tolerable when it no longer offends or engenders rage and despair:

Of course, I don't pretend to believe that Callahan is interested in dealing women out. If anything, his argument is one that I have heard many so-called senior citizens express almost as eloquently themselves. And I do agree that we have to be sensible about utilizing medical resources, especially in cases where they aren't likely to benefit the recipient or alter an inevitably bad outcome. I acknowledge that we are fast approaching a time in our history when the largest segment of our population, our largest special interest lobby, if you will, is the aging and the elderly. However, I can't agree with Callahan's claim that the age standard which he offers would have a use transformed from its present use, a use that "affirms" and does not denigrate old age (1987, 170).

On the contrary, I want to argue that there is tremendous symbolic significance for women in adopting an age standard, a significance that derives from and is colored by woman's social and moral history.

Honoring a "natural life span" could mean believing that a natural life normally ends in the mid-70s (the life expectancy for males), and in accepting that age standard, Callahan-style policy makers might adopt measures that preclude women from receiving essential services at the ends of our (longer) lives.

Among the items left over from the "old" anti-ageism agenda, the widespread problem of elder abuse and neglect should generate outrage. A University of Massachusetts study suggests that there are six times as many cases of abuse of the elderly as are actually reported (Elder Abuse, 1988). Abuse, neglect, and exploitation include failing to provide the ill and the fragile with minimal medical care, medication, and hospitalization. In a book of this scope, one wonders why this problem isn't given more prominence.

Again because of their numbers, women constitute the majority of those affected by abuse and neglect. When I worry about setting limits, I worry about the attitudes engendered by promulgation of the belief that there is an age beyond which one is getting more than her fair share.

Callahan's argument seems to rest on the presumption that there is little value in providing certain health services to persons who have reached the end of full and natural lives. I protest that presumption because "natural life span" and "tolerable death" are not gender neutral. Providing health services to the very old has been devalued, in part because medical intervention can dehumanize the natural end to one's natural life span. I wonder if that absence of value is not also due in large measure to the fact that there are few male competitors for these services. Couldn't we believe that, like other items in women's social history, when men move to evaluate something that is peculiarly the province of women, it then becomes *devalued?*

Given this social and moral context, woman's old age is not affirmed by setting limits; it is made invisible. Given this context, the deaths of older women *will* engender rage and despair. Given this context, appealing to an age standard will make the deaths of women premature in the fullest sense of the word. Not only will their deaths be sad, they will be a tragedy and an outrage.

NOTES

1. Older women now outnumber older men three to two. This represents a dramatic increase from 1960, when the ratio of elderly men to elderly women was five to four. Furthermore, the ratio changes markedly with increased age. The 1984 census found only 40 men for every 100 women at age 85, but 81 men for every 100 women between the ages of 65 and 69. By the year 2050, the projected life expectancy for females will reach 83.6 years as contrasted with a life expectancy for males of 79.8 years.

   The gender ratios are important for the further reason that they indicate that more women than men will be living alone in old age. Although more than one-third of all elderly disabled men living in their communities were cared for by their wives, only one in ten elderly disabled women were cared for by their husbands (Special Committee on Aging, 1985).

   An obvious concern, and the concern that underlies Callahan's interest in examining medicine's goals for an aging society, is that the projected increase in the size of the older population implies correlative increases in the demand for health care resources and the provision of services to the elderly. In addition, elderly persons are more likely than other adults to be poor.

   Moreover, the economic statistics are especially grim for elderly women. According to a study published in 1985 by the United States Senate's Special Committee on Aging, of those persons between the ages of 65 and 69, white males had a median income of $12,180 per year as compared to a median income of $5,599 for elderly women. Because they live longer than their male counterparts, elderly women average a longer period of retirement than elderly men and must, therefore, rely on private and public sources of income longer than elderly men. Not surprisingly, nearly three-quarters of the population of the elderly poor are women (1985, 2).

   Although at present only about five percent of the elderly live in nursing homes, close to seventy-five percent of all nursing home residents have no spouse and are institutionalized because they have health problems that significantly limit their ability to care for themselves. Not surprisingly, a disproportionate number (74.6 percent) of nursing home patients are very old, white, female, and without spouse (Special Committee on Aging, 1985).

   The economic implications of an aging population are obvious. If limits are not set, Callahan predicts that health care expenditures for the elderly will exceed $200 billion by the year 2000. By 2040, he predicts that pension and health programs will account for 14.5 percent of the GNP and 60.4 percent of the Federal budget, respectively (1987, 228).

2. Childress does not make this argument with respect to older women in particular. He makes it with respect to all older persons.

3. Furthermore, some social changes designed to benefit women economically have actually worked to their detriment. "No-fault divorce looked like a civilized way for equal adults to deal with marital incompatibility. [Yet] its implementation has cut adrift millions of middle-aged and elderly housewives who had every right to believe they had been guaranteed a comfortable home for life. Well-meaning efforts to reform welfare failed miserably to lead single mothers out of poverty" (Bergmann, 1986, 300).

ETHICAL ISSUES IN LONG TERM CARE

Reassessing Autonomy in Long-Term Care

George J. Agich

The realities of long-term care call for a refurbished, concrete concept of autonomy that systematically attends to the history and development of persons and takes account of the experiences of daily living.

Long-term care is an increasingly important subject for bioethical reflection and analysis, yet when viewed through the spectacles of autonomy, the pivotal concept of much bioethical theory, the realities of long-term care seem paradoxical to say the least.[1] The most striking feature of long-term care is that adult individuals suffering from diseases and illnesses of being old experience a compromised vigor and ability to function that requires regular care ranging from help in activities of daily living such as housework, food preparation, and hygiene to highly skilled nursing and medical care. Elders requiring long-term care generally exhibit functional disabilities that frequently bring with them vulnerabilities as well. They exhibit various kinds of dependencies and not the independence so prized by the traditional view of autonomy that stresses values of independence and rational free choice.

Traditional treatments of autonomy simply abstract from actual examples of finite human autonomy and contexts of choice and focus instead on idealizations of autonomous action and choice. As Onora O'Neill has pointed out:

> The limitations of actual human autonomy aren't taken as constraints on working out the determinate implications with respect to autonomy in actual contexts, but often as aberrations from ideally autonomous choosing. The rhetoric of the liberal tradition shows this clearly. Although it is accepted that we are discussing the autonomy of "finite rational beings," finitude of all sorts is constantly forgotten in favor of loftier and more abstract perspectives.[2]

In short, a concrete concept of autonomy is needed if it is to play a significant analytical and practical role in long-term care.

The abstract liberal concept of autonomy has its proper place in the legal/political sphere, where protection of individuals from tyranny and oppression by powerful others is rightly defended, but not in the moral life, where a fuller conception is required, one that acknowledges the essential social nature of human development and recognizes dependence as a nonaccidental feature of the human condition. Such a concept would systematically attend to the history and development of persons and take the experiences of daily living into account; it would view individuals concretely and see choice as a problem of positively providing options that are meaningful for concrete individuals rather than as an issue of removing obstacles to choice or impediments to action. Such a refurbished concept would offer important advantages for capturing the ethical complexities of long-term care.

AUTONOMY AS INDEPENDENCE

As conceived in the western liberal tradition, autonomy focuses on independence of action, speech, and thought. The ideals implicit in this concept include independence and self-determination, the ability to make rational and free decisions, and the ability to identify accurately one's desires and to assess what constitutes one's own best interest. So construed, autonomy supports a broad set of rights that provide the normative basis from which tyranny, oppression, and even the benevolent use of power over vulnerable individuals have been opposed. These features are certainly defensible and need to be preserved, but we

must critically acknowledge that the underlying idea of independence that has come to dominate our understanding of autonomy is an idealization entangled in the historical roots of this tradition in seventeenth-century political and legal debates. Thus, we should not expect a fully adequate picture of what autonomy means in those heterogeneous circumstances that comprise the moral life from this important, but limited context. Unfortunately, this limited orientation has enjoyed a central place not only in academic ethical discourse, but public discourse as well.

According to this view, to be a person is by definition to be capable of free and rational choice; such abilities provide the ethical foundation for the expression of uniquely individual beliefs, desires, preferences, and values. So long as these individual beliefs and desires do not directly cause harm to others, anything goes. Furthermore, decision-making is regarded as a rational process that can ultimately be understood or explained in terms of decision theory. Communicative interactions between individuals are thought to involve primarily the exchange of information. An outgrowth and obvious example of this point is the stress placed on information disclosure in the legal doctrine of informed consent, a stress that tends to make informed consent an event rather than a process.[3]

The attitudes and beliefs associated with this view engender a variety of secondary defenses against dependency: a denial of need, hostility toward helpers even in the face of disabilities that require assistance from others, contempt for the real or imagined weakness of others, and, in some cases, an inflated self-image. This culturally determined aversion to dependence has been termed "counterdependency," an aversion to dependency of all sorts.[4] As a result, Americans frequently look with dread on the thought of dependence and go to great costs to maintain independent lifestyles.[5]

Given the prominence of this cultural attitude in American society, it is not surprising that one common approach to the ethics of long-term care involves focusing on various mechanisms designed to provide elders with specific rights to enable them to resist unwanted interference from others. This approach takes many forms, including attention to the rights of the elderly to certain information (such as provided in preadmission agreements utilized by growing numbers of nursing homes and required by some state regulatory agencies), the access of elders to ombudsmen or advocacy reviews, or the use of formal surrogate decision-making procedures, especially in cases involving withholding or withdrawing life-sustaining treatments. These developments have been widely defended and supported by reference to the ideals of autonomy, yet focusing on procedural protections attests to the fact that even the staunchest proponents of this view recognize that the theory must accommodate in some way the realities of impaired decision-making capacity that are an ineliminable feature of long-term care. Beyond procedural protections, however, this view provides little practical guidance in clarifying the degree and kind of autonomy actually present.

Criticizing the scope and central thrust of the liberal concept of autonomy does not commit one to an outright rejection of the liberal theory. A version of the liberal view-itself admittedly more complex than this brief discussion acknowledges-can be defended along the lines marked out by Charles Larmore in his Patterns of Moral Complexity. In Larmore's view, the liberal theory is defensible, but properly restricted to the political/legal sphere; it does not need to be uncritically extended into the realm of ethics.[6] A fuller account of the nature of autonomous moral agency would include a framework for interpreting what autonomy concretely means and for articulating the essential historical and social nature of persons by taking seriously the concrete developmental aspects of becoming and being a person,[7] as well as the phenomenological reality of being an agent in the world of everyday life without embracing the notion that the ultimate source of value or authority is tradition or community.

ACTUAL AUTONOMY AND IDEAL AUTONOMY

One difficulty with focusing on actual autonomy is the rather messy incompleteness and uncertainty that this phenomenon presents when compared with ideal autonomy. We are forced to say something definite about when specific expressions of autonomy are genuine and when they are spurious or misleading. We cannot simply rely on hypothetical examples of ideally autonomous action or choice, that is, action or choice taken as ideally rational and free, but rather must identify specific concrete conditions or features that contribute to or mark out an action or choice as autonomous. The problem is that autonomy is developmentally and socially conditioned, so that determinate expressions of autonomy will be unique and contextually situated, thus precluding adequate formulation in abstract terms. Instead, a phenomenologically accurate, concrete assessment is required. In point of fact, the task is less difficult than it may first appear if we seriously attend to the core meaning of autonomy itself.

"Autonomy" literally means "self-rule," that is, behavior that is spontaneous and self-initiated; such behavior is regarded as action in the sense that it manifests intentionality. Human action, in turn, can be regarded as free if the individual agent can identify with the elements from which it flows; an action (or choice) is unfree or coerced if the agent cannot identify with or dissociates herself from the elements that generate or prompt the action.[8] This means that the ability reflexively to identify with the constituents of an action is logically prior to freedom and that autonomy is best understood on the basis of the possession of an identity or of a self having a particular determinate nature and character. Expressions of autonomy are thus the playing out of who the individual is as well as who the individual is becoming; the field or stage for such "playing out" is the social world of everyday life.

Because autonomous individuals are situated in concrete social situations, choice is always contextual. To do x means that y is forgone. There are always costs associated with any choice. Making explicit choices or decisions, however, is not the central feature of our lives, most of which are spent acting in habitual, taken-for-granted ways that are not experienced as the result of express decisionmaking. Such actions might be seen as unfree on the traditional view of autonomy, but they are truly free or unfree to the extent that they are consistent with one's self-identity or not. In other words, an individual is autonomous insofar as she is who she is, insofar as one's actions exhibit a developed pattern. But since individuals are never fully formed, but are always dynamically in the process of development, "who an individual is" is always an open question. In the daily course of living that question is suspended or set aside as a conscious issue, but that does not mean that the matter is ever really closed.

Self-identity is not something that one discovers as an uncharted island in the middle of a sea, but rather is something that is made by individuals in the very course of their living. Existential crises or life transitions are clearly paradigmatic ways in which questions such as "who am I?" or "in what do I believe?" come to the fore. Sickness, too, frequently forces an examination of what is so commonly termed one's "values." In point of fact, however, in daily life we seem to proceed oblivious to our own spontaneity and freedom. Thus, to speak of individuals as autonomous requires that we pay attention to the kinds of things with which they properly identify in their lives. Saying this is to expand on the slogan "respect for persons" in a way that reflects the concrete reality of human existence. To respect persons properly requires that we attend to their concrete individuality, to their affective and personal experiences; we need to learn how to acknowledge their habits and identifications.

Frithjof Bergmann has nicely articulated the central elements of such a situated or contextual concept of autonomy:

> For those without identity freedom is indeed "absolute independence." They, it is true, must "go against everything" in order to be free. But this is not the case for all those who do not share in this extreme condition. The greater the extent to which they do identify with something, the less is the complete isolation perquisite to their being free. To put the point paradoxically: "dependency" on something does not in any way diminish one's degree of freedom as long as one truly identifies with the thing on which one is "dependent." If I am in harmony with something—if in fact it is me—(and that is the point of talking about "identification")—then I need not be isolated from it, and need not be protected from it, to be "free." The demand for freedom takes the form of an insistence on total independence only for those who lack identity. For all others the claim is not compelled to this extreme—and yet, in terms of freedom, they have not been compromised and do not receive less.[9]

Thus, not only is tolerance of diversity of choice and taste a necessary adjunct of respecting liberty, but so is acknowledging the irreducible individuality of concrete expressions of autonomy in those individuals not always able to manifest ideally rational and reflective free choice.

AUTONOMY IN LONG-TERM CARE

Culturally defined perceptions that autonomy means independence lead to the attitude of counterdependency in which elders feel obligated to avoid anything that appears to involve dependence; society for its part supports this behavior by institutional arrangements that assure that the full price of independence is paid. The lack of adequate home care services and support, including insurance, for instance, often makes illness or disability an all or none choice: either one accepts full dependency in hospital or nursing home or one struggles with the functional disabilities associated with the illnesses of being old without adequate help until disaster arrives. Long-term care, however, does not always involve institutional living arrangements and such arrangements need not mean passivity for elders.

Long-term care of all sorts, including home care services, is required precisely because individuals experience to some degree an actual loss of functions that we associate with a full sense of developed adult autonomy. They lose various abilities to act in the world and so require more than usual amounts and kinds of support and care from others. Our society displays profound ambivalence about this situation in that we seem to want these individuals to deny their need for care—in short, we want to support their individual right to noninterference even at great personal cost—and yet we recognize that individuals who cannot care for themselves and who place undue burdens on family members require specialized professional care.

Consistent with our society's concern for the right of noninterference, however, is the development of efforts to secure institutionalized patients' rights to noninterference by even benevolently motivated health care professionals, family, or friends. Unfortunately, this adversarial orientation does not adequately capture the mundane ethical reality of either autonomy or long-term care. A contextual account is wanted that attends to the phenomenon of actual rather than ideal autonomy.

The implications for long-term care of this turn to actual autonomy are important. Respect for autonomy cannot mean that caregivers are primarily and absolutely precluded from influencing the decisions of elders. To be exposed to influence as such is not to be enslaved. In fact, we need to acknowledge that the relationship between the receiver of care and the caregiver is far more complicated, especially in long-term care, than the usual model implies.[10] The operating paradigm, however, seems to assume that because the health professional is in a position of power and authority, the patient must be protected by an insulating fabric of rights or else the bogeyman of paternalism will appear. In long-term care, especially when care is provided by family or by professionals in the patient's home, the situation is likely to be reversed, that is, the elder retains significant power and independence, and so the application of the ideal view of autonomy as avoidance of paternalism seems too easy and too simplistic.

Some observers have properly pointed out that what are frequently alleged to be cases of paternalism in health care are actually cases of communication failure on the part of the health professional; health professionals are more frequently "guilty" of beneficence toward patients than paternalism, in the strict sense that patient decisions are overridden in favor of health professionals' view of patients' best interests.[11] Also, it needs to be stressed that the personal relationships that develop between elders and caregivers in long-term care contexts may be more ethically relevant than the professional power or authority that the criticism of paternalism seeks to curb.

Focusing on actual autonomy raises at least two questions regarding long-term care. First, are the choices actually afforded individuals in long-term care the kind that are meaningful or worth making? Even when individuals are afforded an array of choices, autonomy may not be significantly enhanced because the choices available may not be meaningful for the individuals involved. Put simply, choice that enhances autonomy is choice that is meaningful for individuals and allows them to express and develop their own individuality. If such is not the case, then the true sense of autonomy of persons is not enhanced.

Consider, for example, the kinds of choices typically afforded individuals in nursing homes. There are choices regarding limited outings, the use of special services such as hair dressing or participation in structured social and recreational activities such as bingo, or choosing when and what to eat, with whom to associate, or "permission" to ask or not ask staff for help. No matter how extensive this list is, one can and should ask whether it includes alternatives that are meaningful, that preserve and enhance patients' unique individuality and identity. If the actual choices afforded individuals in nursing homes are not experienced by those individuals as meaningful, and other "choices" that are meaningful are discouraged and not enhanced—and that is an empirical matter to be determined on a case-by-case basis—then serious questions arise regarding how autonomy is being respected in these circumstances.

Being able to identify with one's choices is a prerequisite for true autonomy. There are choices individuals can be forced to make that diminish the integrity and self-worth of the person. The seventy-five-year-old woman whose own health is deteriorating must make choices regarding the care of her seventy-eight-year-old husband who has suffered a stroke and is now bedridden. Similarly, the husband must choose institutionalization or watch as his own care literally consumes his wife. The family of such a couple, too, must struggle with equally difficult choices. Do they take the couple into their households for care? Do they break up the couple and arrange for different care for each of their parents? Sometimes, the cost to self for the elder in agreeing to move in with children is too great not because the elder fears dependency and prizes independence, but because the elder cannot identify with a choice that imposes

burdens on children and means the loss of friends and familiar surroundings.

The psychological consequence of this point is evident everywhere in long-term care. Nonidentification characteristically carries with it a sense of "passivity." As Bergmann notes,

> Once the subject structures his experience in a certain way, he has to feel passive, but the sense of passivity in turn reinforces the nonidentification: the self that is overwhelmed at every moment withdraws still further.[12]

Thus, the phenomena of withdrawal and generalized depression often seen among institutionalized elderly may partly be traceable to the existentially tragic choices that the elder is forced to make, or to an abject lack of meaningful choice currently available in our society for impaired elders. From the point of view of actual autonomy, we should see the psychological sequelae of choice, the problems of adapting to new circumstances, as factors that are ethically significant.

If the conscious exercise of choice typically comprises only a small span of our lives, then questions about the style of life and the structure and organization of long-term care become important. For example, is the life available in long-term care something with which the elder can identify, not only through explicit choice but passively and reflexively? Raising this question suggests that a different metaphor of autonomy is appropriate to the new focus on actual autonomy.

Autonomy is not best understood, as in the traditional view, in terms of a model of explicit decisionmaking nodes along a narrow path, such as the decision to institutionalize or to initiate skilled care. Instead, actual autonomy is more complex and clearly less neat. For the most part, there are no well-defined paths or hallways in which one is regularly confronted by a range of options amenable to rational decisionmaking; a more apt metaphor would be an open field with no clearly defined alternatives. Patterns exist, but they are subject to change; they evolve over time. Rather than emerging relatively rarely in conflicts involving rational choice, actual autonomy is always present, though sometimes submerged from view as individuals go about their daily lives. It is because autonomy is always present that it is so difficult to bring into view.

Actual autonomy is utterly ordinary and unremarkable most of the time. Thus, the proper understanding of autonomy involves appreciating how individuals are interconnected and how persons develop in terms of historical and social circumstance. Autonomy is just as significantly present in the acquisition of habits of action and thought (which are as much socially derived as they are individually and uniquely determined) as in clear instances of reflective, deliberative decisionmaking. For this reason, conditions that foster or thwart the development and expression of individuality and self are more significant than the phenomenon of explicit, conscious choice.

One condition central to long-term care is the fact that elders are more likely than younger persons to experience functional disabilities as the result of chronic illnesses.[13] These are often measured in empirical studies by the number of days lost from housework, school, or work, or days spent in bed, but functional disabilities also preclude performing actions that are meaningful or important for individuals. The concept of functional ability measures the impact of an illness or impairment on the individual and on the individual's ability to engage and interact meaningfully in the social world, rather than focusing on the presence or absence of disease. Indeed, some have noted that "the loss or impairment of the ability to perform such basic daily functions as shopping or bathing strikes at what the elderly value most—independent living."[14] "Independent living," however, should not be interpreted as reinstating the concepts of independence and noninterference, but rather as indicating the ability to perform those normal functions of daily living that define the individual's own sense of self-worth and identity.

That loss of function is an important concern is supported by the literature that notes a lack of association in the minds of the elderly between health and the presence of chronic illness or disability.[15] In some studies, 68 percent of noninstitutionalized elderly report their health as excellent or good despite the fact that 85 percent have at least one chronic illness and 47 percent have some functional disability.[16] These findings suggest that individuals experience themselves as healthy if they maintain functional ability even in the face of chronic disease. It would be a mistake, however, to assume that functional ability is important as an end; rather, functional abilities are important not because they are coincident with independence, but because they instrumentally define the sense of self and self-worth of the individuals in question. The account of autonomy just offered helps to explain this.

Maintaining a sense of autonomous well-being is consistent with dependencies on medication or professional care if those dependencies help to maintain a sense of functional integrity in the areas of life that individuals value. Dependencies do not conflict with autonomy if individuals can still maintain a sufficiently adequate range of identifications to sustain their own sense of integrity and worth. Functional ability, then, has to be understood in terms of concrete individuals, not abstractly as general abilities that define independence as a good in itself.

The paradigm case of an actually autonomous person and a liberal nonautonomous person would be a wheel-chair-bound individual assisted by others in various activities of daily living. At the same time, this person is devoted to the cause of Food for Peace (FFP). What this woman can do for FFP is limited, yet she identifies strongly with it. She stuffs envelopes twice a week for the local chapter and rejoices when she sees a television feature on FFP's projects. She has visitors from FFP. Her choices are meaningful in the context of her identifications with FFP. She does not care whether she has her bath at 6:00 a.m. on Thursday or at 2:00 on Friday. Not all choices matter to her, just those that are meaningful in terms of her participatory identification in a larger social context.[17]

A similar and more familiar case would be the intense involvement of an elder with her grandchildren or hobby or commitment to a favorite sports team. The inability to shop or leave the home or institution may be far less significant for such an individual than the ability to entertain her family, pursue her hobby, or watch her team compete on television. The central point is that such matters cannot be determined generally, but only specifically. After all, the core sense of respecting autonomy involves treating individuals as unique individuals, rather than simply as members of a class.

It is possible for health professionals or other care-givers to interact with elders in long-term care such that the professional does not take over the care of the patient, but rather gives the patient's own care back to herself authentically.[18] "Giving the patient's own care back to herself authentically" does not mean that the patient is expected to regain independent functioning or take over her own physical care, but that the care-giver support the patient's own unique identifications and sense of self or values as health care needs are met.

Care-giving relationships involve all kinds of social interactions during the course of which the patient's sense of satisfaction and self-worth can either be enhanced or thwarted. Truly to care for another, one must allow the other to experience the world meaningfully; that means affording "choices" with which the person can genuinely identify and acknowledging his or her sense of self in the course of the myriad interactions that comprise long-term care. This conclusion points us away from an ethics that focuses on what Laurence

McCullough and Stephen Wear have termed "four-alarm cases"—on intractable problems or issues arising in dramatic and conflictual contexts—and toward the mundane attitudes and behaviors of caregivers and elders themselves.[19] These concerns are sometimes denigrated as being merely psychological or psychosocial concerns best left for specialists in these areas; yet helping individuals to flourish, even in the context of long-term care, is an activity that deserves serious ethical reflection. Failure to appreciate this point encourages the view that concern for autonomy must restrictively focus on specific dramatic problems and issues rather than the mundane, interstitial features of long-term care. That view, I have argued, is basically mistaken.

Robert Kastenbaum has observed that in long-term care,

> We often see the clinical ambience minus the clinical benefits. The person who is a patient only temporarily can adjust to the unfamiliar and unlovely hospital routines knowing that this is only an interlude. Some comfort and individuality is sacrificed; however, in fair return the person receives state-of-the-art medical and nursing care. By contrast, the geriatric milieu is a long-term or permanent arrangement for many people, and the clinical ambience is not counterbalanced by superb care. Perhaps the most infuriating note from the standpoint of the patient is the attitude that "this is all for your own good." It is not—and everybody knows it.20
> Kastenbaum argues that the necessary goal for a clinical milieu is "making the world right again."

Frail and impaired older persons experience many sorrows, losses, fears, and frustrations in addition to physical ailments and disabilities. Certainly, a therapeutic environment must provide treatments that can help prevent discomfort and help individuals maintain a level of integrated functioning. But there must be a broader environment that is conducive to health besides the episodic medical treatments that are now provided. In effect, geriatric practice must attend to what Hans Selye has termed "the syndrome of just being sick,"[21] the pervasive sense that things are just "not right." Besides specific disabilities and pains, there is a sense of the world gone awry, a pervasive sense of loss or what might be simply termed "existential despair." Kastenbaum argues that the "just being sick" syndrome can be countered effectively by a milieu that accentuates the positive, namely one that develops a systematic and encompassing framework of positive expectations on the part of everyone involved. Clarifying the components of such a milieu would be one way to operationalize concern for autonomy. To do that, however, requires that the concept of autonomy be refurbished along the lines suggested above.

THE PRACTICAL PURSUIT OF AUTONOMY

Respecting the autonomy of persons in long-term care entails a commitment to identifying and establishing conditions that encourage individuals to face the adversity and threats to self inevitable as a result of the disability and illness that bring elders to long-term care in the first place. Respecting autonomy requires attending to those things with which individuals can truly and significantly identify. Elders must be treated as individuals, as unique persons with identifiable personal histories so far as that is possible. Even when such identifications are difficult to assess, as in cases of severe memory deficits associated with Alzheimer's disease, patients frequently respond, albeit minimally and in deficient ways, to direct contact with caregivers and others. Thus, long-term care can provide positive messages and hope even in the face of serious impairments. Hope does not have to portend recovery, as is frequently assumed in the medical context; rather, hope refers to the prospect of meaningful experience together with others at those times when one most needs comfort and companionship.

The practical pursuit of autonomy varies depending on the context and the different moral agents involved; nonetheless, ethical analysis can still suggest some general guidelines to inform the efforts of long-term care practice. These guidelines include not accepting loss of autonomy and dignity as a normal fate of aging, and challenging accepted beliefs that loss of autonomy is a universal and ineliminable feature in the frail elderly. We must recognize that dependencies may be induced by institutional settings that erode autonomy by robbing individuals of their most basic identifications, and that essential differences between acute care and long-term care should point to the need for the latter to develop a different commitment to enhance the values and identifications of patients, and, finally, that autonomy should not be dealt with as a "problem" reactively, but as an integral and essential aspect of caring for patients.[22]

Focusing on actual autonomy brings ethical reflection to bear on the mundane, interstitial reality of long-term care rather than on idealized crises or problems. A natural consequence of this shift in focus is the awareness that "giving" a frail elder a range of choices or "letting" an elder choose may be ethically less compelling than helping the elder to live in the face of frailty, loss, and ultimately death. So many of the problems that ideal autonomy so aptly addresses seem to arise just because caregivers fail to care in a responsive and responsible fashion. Actual autonomy thus helps to reveal the concrete and complex ethical features of long-term care that are otherwise transparent to the traditional concept of autonomy.

REFERENCES

1. See Gerald Dworkin's discussion of the paradoxes of autonomy in *The Theory and Practice of Autonomy* (Cambridge: Cambridge University Press, 1988), 3–20.

2. Onora O'Neill, "Paternalism and Partial Autonomy," *Journal of Medical Ethics* 10 (1984), 175.

3. Charles W. Lidz et al., "Two Models of Implementing the Idea of Informed Consent," *Archives of Internal Medicine* 148 (June 1988), 1385–89.

4. For a full discussion of this concept see Andrew Joseph Christiansen, "*Autonomy and Dependence in OM Age: An Ethical Analysis*" (Yale University Doctoral Dissertation, 1982), 37–128.

5. Christiansen, "*Autonomy,*" provides an excellent summary of these cultural attitudes and their negative implications for the ethics of long-term care. See also Phillip Clater, *The Pursuit of Loneliness* (Boston: Beacon Press, 1970), 1–28, and Margaret Clar, "Cultural Values and Dependency in Later Life," in *Aging and Modernization,* Donald O. Cowgill and Lowell D. Holmes, eds. (New York: Meredith Corporation, 1972), 263–74.

6. Charles E. Larmore, *Patterns of Moral Complexity* (Cambridge: Cambridge University Press: 1987), 40–85.

7. Lawrence Haworth, *Autonomy: An Essay in Philosophical Psychology and Ethics* (New Haven: Yale University Press, 1986). See also Mary B. Mahowald, "Against Paternalism: A Developmental View," *Philosophy Research Archives* (1980), 6, No. 1386; and "Sex-Role Stereotypes in Medicine," *Hypatia 2* (Summer 1987), 21–38.

8. Frithjof Bergmann, *On Being Free* (Notre Dame, IN: University of Notre Dame Press, 1977), 37.

9. Bergmann, *On Being Free,* 48. Mill, too, insisted that individuals require different conditions for their development: "The same things which are helps to one person toward the cultivation of his higher nature are hindrances to another. The same mode of life is a healthy excitement to one, keeping all his faculties of action and enjoyment in their best order, which to another it is a distracting burden which suspends or crashes all internal life" (On Liberty [Indianapolis, IN: Hackett Publishing Co., 1978], 65).

10. Two helpful critical treatments of the typical model are Andrew Jameton, "In the Borderlands of Autonomy: Responsibility in Long-Term Care Facilities," *The Gerontologist 28,* Supplement (June 1988), 18–23; and Harry R. Moody, "From Informed Consent to Negotiated Consent," *The Gerontologist 28,* Supplement (June 1988), 64–70.

11. David C. Thomasma, "Freedom, Dependency, and the Care of the Very Old," *Journal of the American Geriatrics Society* 31 (December 1984), 911–12; and Caroline Whitbeck, "Why the Attention to Paternalism in Medical Ethics?" *Journal of Health Politics, Polity and Law* 10 (1985), 181–87.

12. Bergmann, *On Being Free,* 47.

13. L. Fredman and S.G. Hynes, "An Epidemiologic Profile of the Elderly," in *Aging and Public Health,* H.T. Phillips and S.A. Gaylord, eds. (New York: Springer, 1985), 1–41.

14. C.C. Pegels, *Health. Care and the Elderly* (Rockville, MD: Aspen Publishing Company, 1981), 5.

15. K.E Ferraro, "Self-Ratings of Health Among the Old and the Old Old," *Journal of Health and Social Behavior* 20 (1980), 377–83, anti G.G. Fillenbaum, "Social Context and Self-Assessments of Health Among the Elderly," *Journal of Health and Social Behavior* 20 (1979), 44–51.

16. B. Filner and T.F. Williams, "Health Promotion for the Elderly: Reducing Functional Dependency" in *Healthy People: The Surgeon General's Report on Health Promotion and Disease Prevention: Background Papers* (Washington, D.C.: U.S. Government Printing Office, 1979), 367–86; and M.G. Kovar, "Health of the Elderly and the Use of Health Services," *Public Health Report* 92 (1977), 9–19. See also, L.W. Butler and P.W. Newacheck, "Health and Social Factors Relevant to Long-Term Care Policy," in *Policy Options in Long-Term Care,* J. Meltzer, F. Farrow, and H. Richman, eds. (Chicago: University of Chicago Press, 1981), 38–77; L. Cluff, "Chronic Disease, Function and the Quality of Care," *Journal of Chronic Disease* 34 (1981), 299–304.

17. This example comes from an anonymous reviewer of an earlier draft of this paper. I use it with thanks.

18. George J. Agich, "The Question of Technology in Medicine," in *Phenomenology and the Understanding of Human Destiny,* Stephen Skousgaard, ed. (Washington, D.C.: Advanced Research in Phenomenology and The University Press of America, 1981), 8587.

19. Laurence McCullough and Stephen Wear, "Respect for Autonomy and Medical Paternalism Reconsidered," *Theoretical Medicine* 6 (October 1985), 294–308.

20. Robert Kastenbaum, "Can the Clinical Milieu Be Therapeutic?" in *Aging and Milieu: Environmental Perspectives on Growing Old,* Graham D. Rowles and Russell J. Ohta, eds. (New York: Academic Press, 1983), 11.

21. Hans Seyle, *The Stress of Life* (New York: McGraw-Hill, 1956), 79.

22. Bart J. Collopy, The Conceptually Problematic Status of Autonomy, Unpublished study prepared for The Retirement Research Foundation, December 1986, pp. 204–208; see also Bart J. Collopy, "Autonomy in Long Term Care: Some Crucial Distinctions," *The Geromologist* 28, Suppl. (1988), 10–17.

Home Care, Women, and Aging: A Case Study of Injustice

Martha Holstein

Home care provides a lens through which to view complex relationships between cultural assumptions, public policy, and private lives. These interactions result in practices that raise questions about care, justice, and welfare rights, the relationship of women (and other "informal" carers) to the state, complex meanings of autonomy, especially in conditions of dependency, and the gendered nature of work. Home care illuminates the gender and class injustices that are historically endemic to American social welfare policy.

Women who provide care to elderly people at home are profoundly affected by policy choices, with their

Holstein, Martha. "Home Care, Women, and Aging: A Case Study of Injustice," *Mother Time: Women, Aging, and Ethics,* ed. Margaret Urban Walker, New York: Rowman & Littlefield (1999), 227–244. Copyright © 1999. Reprinted by permission of Rowman & Littlefield.

generally unarticulated normative assumptions, and by cultural factors. Family caregivers, paid and unpaid, are overwhelmingly female. Wives, daughters, and daughters-in-law, who assume major responsibility for caregiving in the home, are rarely able to relinquish tasks they find onerous; they do not have the resources to purchase help while publicly funded benefits have strict—and low—income ceilings.[1] Paid aides, who are most often themselves economically and socially disadvantaged, generally earn minimum wages and rarely receive benefits; yet few have alternative opportunities to earn a livelihood. Predictably, the shortage of home care workers in many parts of the country will make it a ripe placement for "welfare-to-work" women. Thus, caregiving, rendered with or without pay, falls most heavily on lower-income women who often care for other low-income women. Caregiving's strong gender and class biases (which often map onto race) are rooted in the political and moral economy and the cultural values that have prevailed in American life.

Yet women who provide such care are also subjects of their own lives and so interpret and negotiate external claims in different ways. For this reason, understanding relationships among policy, culture, ideology, and personal biography can suggest how change might evolve. To see how and why certain patterns of responsibility have come to dominate thinking and action, while identifying locations for change, is a contribution that feminist work can make toward healing the world. By examining how structural and cultural forces occasion the inequalities that are so evident in home care, scholars and activists can challenge the status quo created by the dominant social, economic, and political system. We can ask if the often unexamined presuppositions of the system are anti-ethical.[2]

In this chapter, I will both describe and explain the path to the present—why and how women, especially low-income women, were placed in the situation of having to meet seemingly unlimited caregiving demands. The political and moral economy of aging provides the overarching conceptual framework while contemporary moral values, including the emphasis on autonomy, rights, independence, family, and privacy play vital supporting roles. I will suggest ways to think about caregiving that mitigate the disadvantages and isolation of younger and older women who already are often marginal in terms of income and social location. To do so, however, will require cultural, social, and policy shifts. It will require recognizing that caregiving, whether paid or unpaid, is not primarily the responsibility of women; reconceptualizing notions of dependence, independence, autonomy, and related terms; challenging current relationships among family, government, and the labor market that affect the social construction of caregiving;[3] redefining cultural norms; and dissociating caregiving from "social norms and power relations that contribute to women's subordinate status."[4]

HOME AS A "SITE" OF CARE

Caregiving is essential if older people with mental or physical disabilities are to remain at home, where they clearly want to be, especially given the options available. Visit any nursing home and you will find that even patients seriously affected by dementing illnesses plead for home. Home has powerful emotional and symbolic meanings. It connotes family, security, comfort, treasured memories, and even "independence." If one is home, then one is not fully "sick."[5] Implicit norms about independence, autonomy, and productivity reinforce the lure of home. Infused with these values, older people resist encroaching dependencies that arise from chronic illness. Threats to biographical continuity, to dignity, and to a sense of worthiness and competence as adult men and women, become particularly difficult to remedy when popular cultural norms do not speak to dignity or autonomy within the context of dependency.

The operative language of "formal" home care elevates client autonomy, self-determination, and independence as central tenets and features of a powerful belief system. In this milieu, however, these words have a highly individualistic tone that makes it difficult to account for the relational aspects of autonomy that are writ graphically in conditions of dependency. Achieving autonomy or self-determination in common home care situations is inherently a social process—a fact that the language, articulated values, and practices of home care conceal. If autonomy's social and relational character is not accounted for in home care situations, then preserving the elder's autonomy, when he or she cannot manage alone, can negate the very same possibility for the caregiver. Important value conflicts and threats to the identity of both the giver and the receiver of care may emerge. Since respecting an elder's self-determined wish to stay at home may require many extra hands, often at a considerable cost, and since it is unlikely that public spending will increase, the one expandable component of that cost is the "informal" care provided by family members, especially women. Yet, what women do is not counted as a cost.

Staying at "home" may mean staying in someone else's home—one's daughter's or daughter-in-law's—where there are established routines with which the elder is unfamiliar and that he or she may interrupt. And the home, instead of being a place of security and privacy, becomes a "new healthcare marketplace that depends on self care and women's domestic work."[6] So the emotional connotations of home often exist in the realm of ideology or imagination rather than in the experienced world of the older person and her caregiver. In this way, home is often a site of contestation; a recent book by Arlie Hochschild suggests that people often work for long hours not because they must but rather because work is more pleasant, more fun than the demands of home.[7] Despite that common reality, older people find home to be a good place; it is where most of us seek comfort, refuge, and safety. The task, as I see it, is to discover how to support the sacred meanings of home in ways that neither harm nor trump all other social values. It may mean alternatives to home that we have not yet even imagined. When I return to this theme in the conclusion, I will suggest that we picture autonomy, but also responsibility and sacrifice, for care receivers and care givers, stereoscopically, so that their similar but not identical needs are within sight simultaneously.

WHO ARE THE CAREGIVERS?

The most common caregivers are spouses, but gender-neutral language masks an important gender distinction. Demography may not be destiny, but the longer lives of women and the relatively older ages of men at marriage mean that men have spouses to care for them while women are likely to be widows. Most seemingly objectivist accounts of home care lose sight of this particular genderized quality, that access to spouses as carers almost invariably depends on marital status. Most people who receive care at home from *nonspouses* are women.

Three-quarters of unpaid caregivers live with the care recipient, and the majority give care for an average of four hours a day. For some caregivers, their responsibilities at home equal that of a full-time job.[8] Such caregiving often lasts for years. Women represent 70 percent of all caregivers[9] and 77 percent of children giving care. Almost one-third of all caregivers of frail elderly persons are adult daughters; while sons also provide care, they generally assume instrumental and time-flexible tasks like paying bills or mowing the lawn. Daughters shoulder tasks that keep them on call 24 hours a day, with little or no assistance, while sons typically get help from their wives. Paid services may also be distributed unequally—men caring for elderly spouses or parents seem to obtain more paid in-home services than their female counterparts.[10] "The daughters of working-class elderly people are bearing the brunt of informal care in the community."[11] In practice, daughters reduce work, while men reduce caregiving, and as a result, daughters are more likely than sons to perceive caregiving as stressful. As I shall discuss below, other important consequences, particularly economic ones, flow from caregiving responsibilities, and these consequences also affect men and women unequally.

This picture belies the oft-quoted assumption that families abandon their elders. Families take care of their elders, often at great cost to themselves. Older people see their children or other relatives frequently, and that contact generally translates into assistance during times of crises.[12] As important, because the vast majority of older people manage quite well on their own, many also provide personal help and financial support to their children and grandchildren. In the occasionally rancorous and politicized debate about "intergenerational equity" it is easy to lose sight of the two-way nature of support. The invisibility of elder-to-younger care, once again, has to do with the distinction between public and private. Social Security and Medicare are visible intergenerational transfers of public resources; grandparents paying for the grandchildren's summer camp or providing regular child care are private and hence unseen. This fact suggests the dangers of forcing a false division between public and private. When the media and other commentators blame the old for their putative greed, they are ignoring their very real contributions, albeit in the private sphere.

In yet another way, it is easy to forget how elders, even those with seriously disabling conditions, try not to burden their children or grandchildren, often endangering themselves in the process. Translating cultural messages about independence into their own lives, older women are often reluctant to ask for the help they might need. Older women, for example, seek to "conform to the cultural injunction . . . that they do not impose burdens on their children . . . [they] wish to behave in accordance with norms of self-reliance and individualism."[13]

MAKING CONNECTIONS: THE PUBLIC, PRIVATE, POLITICAL, AND PERSONAL

Public policy seeks to "balance the responsibility of individuals, families, and the state" in meeting human needs.[14] While it rests on normative assumptions—how society should be ordered, what values ought to be enhanced, who owes what to whom—these are seldom articulated. But even if stated, these assumptions rarely move beyond platitudes—quite a contrast to their powerfully felt effects. For most of American history, what has become late-twentieth-century rhetoric was reality—government was small and provided few services to anyone. Necessarily, the balance of responsibility rested with individuals and families; this balance made home the taken-for-granted site of care for the ill, the frail, and the dying, but also for those just coming into the world. With few alternatives, women, often joined in unspoken bonds of mutual assistance, were central participants in these fundamental dramas of human life.[15]

Today, despite the exponential growth in medical and even social services, women still perform home care services. Considered as essentially domestic labor, the reality of hands-on, long-term homemaker services matches neither the postacute model that Medicare supports nor the strong ethos of self-care and familism that historically has interpreted public charity as both demoralizing and a largely mythical excuse for families to relinquish their responsibilities. To the legislators and administrators who designed Medicare (enacted in 1965), social services for a dependent population seemed a luxury. Who, some legislators asked, would not like to have his bed made or his meals prepared?[16] Ironically, one suspects that these skeptical legislators neither made their own beds nor prepared their own meals. The invisible work that contributes to and creates the conditions of privilege is largely ignored, unexamined, and undervalued. The norm supporting such a policy choice seems quite clear—someone will (should) be available to cook, clean, and so on, for people unable to do it for themselves, and therefore such caregiving responsibilities, with few exceptions, are not a public responsibility.

Hands-on supportive services were thus left to the residual "welfare," or needs-based, sector of the welfare state. As such they carried the historical baggage associated with notions of deservingness, as defined by the culturally elite, and paternalism. Rarely asking potential or current beneficiaries to define their needs,[17] the designers of welfare programs assume that need is fundamentally apolitical, objective, and easily ascertainable through responses to questions on a standard needs-assessment form or through simple analysis of what interventions would benefit a client. Foucault, in contrast, calls attention to need as a "political instrument, meticulously prepared, calculated, and used."[18] Whoever gets to define some condition as a

need also defines the remedy proposed. This permits the enclaving of certain needs so that they never enter the political sphere. The late philosopher Judith Shklar put it boldly: If one is not asked about how one feels about the arrangements that control one's life, one is reduced to a zero.[19] Taking this welfare state mentality to task, Michael Ignatieff, in his elegant and moving meditation on human need, reminds us that "it is because money cannot buy the human gestures which confer respect, nor rights guarantee them as entitlements, that any decent society requires a public discourse about the needs of the human person."[20]

Welfare benefits also lack the seemingly invincible status (at least until recently) of a program like Social Security, an "earned" benefit closely linked to "productive" employment, that is, a worthy activity in the public sphere. In the moral economy, services provided at home—presumably unskilled and domesticated in nature—are not something that society "owes" to its oldest members and their families as we "owe" retirement benefits, via Social Security, to those who contributed to the nation's economic productivity. Reassurance that one will be cared for so as not to burden one's children too greatly and that one's dignity will be honored despite dependencies is not, in the contemporary moral economy, a social obligation, that is, a burden that the prevailing market economy ought to assume. The moral limits on a market economy, historically envisioned as a constraint to exploitation and oppression, are today quite narrow. This parsimony translates into a long-term care policy grounded in free care provided by women. The generally marginal social and economic status of older women in our society compounds the problem. They rarely have the power to speak authoritatively about the issues that affect their lives. It is in this arena that public home care has had to carve out its acceptable place.

Operationally, this approach to long-term care policy disadvantages women economically both in the short and long term. Spouses providing care often must use up accumulated savings and other resources at a time in their own lives when they have little or no ability to recoup; yet the government does not calculate the actual out-of-pocket costs of such caregiving when it calculates overall costs. Caregiving also harms women's economic future. The work-retirement system currently in place rests on male models. Many older women do not have the consecutive work histories or jobs that offer retirement benefits, conditions that make the system work for men. Caregiving women either reduce the hours they work for pay, rearrange their work schedules, take time off without pay (the option available to them under the

Family and Maternal Leave Act of 1993), or quit their jobs to resolve conflicts between work and caregiving. "Women who take early retirement or otherwise modify their employment to provide care not only lose wages and wage-related benefits, but also jeopardize their own sources of income for their later years."[21] Social Security benefits, private pensions, and the opportunity to accrue retirement savings, for example, are negatively affected by the "drop-out" years when women earn no income and receive no Social Security credits. The work that women do at home, whether for children, spouses, or elderly family members, is a public good, often supportive of economic growth. But rather than also bringing her economic benefits, it has a negative affect. This factor rarely receives attention outside of feminist circles. Productivity, long associated with a paycheck, ignores the productive roles that women, including elderly women, play in supporting the publicly valued productivity of others.[22]

In the last quarter century, hospital cost-containment efforts, supported by renewed ideological commitments to traditional gender roles and a vigorous preference for private rather than public provision of services, accelerated demands on unpaid women caregivers.[23] Since the introduction of Diagnostic Related Groups (DRGs) in the mid-1980s, for example, women increased by twenty-one million days the amount of care they provided. "The sandwich generation of women of all ages are being asked to make great sacrifices of their own time, employment, income, and health to achieve . . . *cost savings* for the government."[24] For policymakers, whose primary interest was cutting government expenditures, caregiving by families was a bonanza—it simultaneously saved money and supported traditional "family values." The women who would provide the bulk of care to patients discharged from hospitals in the subacute phase of an illness had few advocates with power to shape public action, a graphic example of how the distribution of power betokens the actual distribution of resources.

In the 1990s, legislative action in the area of home care increased. Initially Medicaid waiver programs gave states new options. Some states responded with their own community care programs for poor elders who cannot bathe, or dress, or cook, or shop. while the primary goal was cost containment, the language of choice and the humanitarian end of keeping people out of nursing homes supported program development. As a result, many states now screen patients before admitting them to nursing homes and offer an array of services to allow them to stay at home. As with other publicly funded programs, these community care options are struggling to provide as much care as possible to as many people as possible with limited resources. Agencies are thus grappling with timeless questions—breadth versus depth of services and how to use the informal caregiver.

In some states and in some situations, consumer-directed care allows lower-income older adults to hire family members as their caregivers. While not relieving the intensity of the caregiving experience, this option eases somewhat the financial hardships that often result when women leave the workforce to provide care. The low pay attached to home care services, however, hardly remedies the loss of income from most other jobs. Paying relatives for home care also keeps the state at arm's distance from the care-giving situation; state officials then express concern about the adequacy and quality of the care rendered, which can become problematic (conversation with Jean Blaser, Illinois Department on Aging, February 17, 1998). Once public dollars enter the equation, issues of quality assume a different dimension than when families provided the care for free. The most dramatic examples, of course, are indications of abuse or neglect, a particularly problematic concern when older adults do not want to implicate their relatives and would rather risk abuse than be placed in a nursing home (which they see as their only alternative).

Caregiving by women has thus become the unarticulated cornerstone of American long-term care policy, a vivid example of historian Linda Gordon's observation that the effects of policy are determined as much by what it omits as what it addresses.[25] American social welfare policy assumes a residual function in caring for people with mental or physical disabilities; public services meet some needs that families cannot. Families come first, and life in families is private, outside the scope of government. Such primacy and privacy are taken to be normative; therefore, government is justified in staying away. As a result, there has been little incentive to examine—with intent to modify—the ideological and structural conditions that exacerbate the difficulties implicit in the caregiving experience. With few important exceptions,[26] recent attention to caregiving "burden," while unmasking the extent of caring practices, has tended to focus on individual remedies (support groups, education, more "help" for the caregiver, and recently, pay for such caregiving), which renders invisible this burden's structural and cultural roots and obscures the profound economic and other consequences that many women experience.

In sum, policy and its omissions can explain why home care has become primarily a family responsibility. The gendered nature of the labor market offers some suggestion as to why "family" most often means women. Cultural values and assumptions, even ideologies, also support women's primary responsibility for caregiving. These values and assumptions enter into conventional moral understandings about accountabilities and responsibilities.[27] Because they are often internalized and taken as given, they are rarely exposed to analysis. Women's moral perceptions and judgments—what they demand of themselves, how they define their "oughts," what they expect of others—are so shaped by these cultural forces that insight into the situation is often elusive. Both the care giver and the care receiver, in different ways, experience the pressures of cultural norms and ideals that encourage them to live "up to certain standards that define what it means to be a person of worth."[28] They, and in this case lower-income women in particular, do this at considerable cost to themselves and with few opportunities to define those conditions. The pressure is compounded by the sheer weight of responsibility and sorrow that many daughters and sons, no matter their income status, feel as they watch their parents become increasingly disabled.

PATTERNS OF CAREGIVING: WHO IS RESPONSIBLE FOR WHOM AND WHY?

Several factors profoundly direct the gendered nature of caregiving. Most salient are the inner experiences and intentionality of women, the ideology of familism and the way this ideology has historically rendered invisible intrafamily oppression and injustice, the assigning of men and women to separate spheres (the public and the private) for much of American history, and the configuration of the labor market. That women tend to be clustered in low-wage occupations, for example, makes it a matter of simple logic—natural and necessary—that if someone needs to leave work to provide care it will be the woman. The consequences are not innocuous; one result, as noted above, is a lifetime loss of earnings that can significantly affect her own late-life possibilities.

Since women have historically been defined as wives and mothers their role as caregivers for elderly family members seems fully naturalized; what is "natural" does not require examination.[29] Familism's prescriptive assumptions about the "natural" and "right" position of women constrains women's actions and results in economic gender-based inequities across the life span.[30] It also creates, in many families, gender injustices without sources of remedy, since locating such caregiving in the protected private realm guarantees, by virtue of

invisibility, noninterference. Only in cases of reported elder abuse (or child abuse) do caregiving activities within the family come under public scrutiny. And because women's work in the home has often been hidden, a taken-for-granted aspect of daily life, the added responsibilities that come from caregiving for the elderly are also obscured by their seemingly commonplace nature. If our proverbial legislator did not notice that his meals appeared with no apparent effort on his part, then why would he notice that many women prepared meals for their immediate family and then rushed over to the mother's home to make sure that she was properly fed? He would have few ways of understanding the moral value of that act, its implications for gender inequality across the life course, or her anger at this inequality, because he would not have noticed it in the first place. If he sees her at all, perhaps it is as a person *choosing* to act in this way since his range of moral concepts leaves no space for encumbrances that women rarely see as choices. As Diana Meyers so tellingly points out, "insofar as a culture's rules of moral salience occlude dependency, many moral concerns will be denigrated, and the needs of dependents marginalized."[31] Just recently, the *New York Times* quoted a case worker describing a reluctant welfare-to-work client as someone who just stayed home all day and did nothing (except, that is, take care of her three small children).

Women themselves commonly accept these responsibilities with their physical, emotional, and financial costs as "just the way it is," and because resistance has too high a price. They may also experience them as desirable. Personal experience and public ideology become entangled for both care giver and care receiver. To not provide care is to render oneself vulnerable to negative judgment not only by others but by one's own internalized acceptance of cultural norms. Many older women, recognizing their socially devalued status within the family and in society, are reluctant to ask for what they need.[32] Even older women and their caregivers, who have some resources, are often unwilling to buy services. Internalizing the ideology of familism, women see families as the proper givers of care and as closed systems in which outsiders have no place;[33] to seek outside help also means acknowledging that these women cannot cope. Thus, older women simultaneously "take comfort" in having daughters and recall their own sense of obligation to their mothers in the past, while worrying about the burden they place on these same daughters and feeling shame that they do not exemplify cultural ideals of independence and self-sufficiency.

Familism, reborn in the new rhetoric of family values, not only assumes that family care is naturally superior to other forms of care but it also assumes that someone—most probably the woman—not only *is* at home but *ought to be* there with enough free time to provide a full panoply of services to the person needing them. This picture fails to take into account the decline in the birth rate, the delay in the age of parenthood (so that women are likely to have children at home while they are providing eldercare), the increase in divorce, and the creation of blended families. Perhaps most important, the picture ignores women's increased labor force participation, an increase so dramatic since the onset of World War II that it has become one of the defining features of twentieth-century America.[34] That this picture has little connection to reality has not significantly modified the value structure that supports it.

As a result of the apparent naturalness of the caregiving role, families develop patterns of caregiving over time in which expectations are established, and reputations imputed.[35] Families adopt these commitments in different ways. In some cases, the negotiating terms are tacit; everyone expects that one or more individuals will undertake certain responsibilities; once it occurs, they rarely revisit that expectation and since commitments build up over time, individuals cannot easily withdraw or renegotiate moral boundaries. Even when they try, situational factors make it more difficult for some people than others to redraw boundaries; for example, women and people within a parent-child relationship have a more difficult time than men having their excuses for not providing care accepted. Men, with the "excuse" of their "own" family, for example, are often relieved of the commitments that women assume. Work outside the home also provides an excuse for men that is unavailable to women who do not work outside the home; yet even women who hold jobs can rarely use the excuse of work. For a reason to be acceptable, others must see it as morally praiseworthy. The way it has evolved, women have fewer morally acceptable excuses for not providing care than men and so become the obvious carers *without* need for discussion.[36] "These shared assumptions about families, obligations and gender can be understood as the key ingredients in the ideological context in which women find themselves."[37] Mothers and daughters each play out culturally validated rules for morally praiseworthy behavior, often at a serious price to themselves, but with few options. Women know that "pride" derives from exemplifying in their own lives normative expectations.[38] Women—especially daughters—have difficulties establishing limits for the care they provide.

A woman friend, arriving home after a frantic day at work, described an agitated phone call she received from her mother moments later. Her mother wanted her to drive thirty miles to move her car for her. "She was never good to me; yet, now I feel guilty whenever I set limits to the demands I let her place on me. She's not a very nice person, but I keep hoping that she'll change so that before she dies we can have the relationship we never had" (conversation, September 1990). This middle-aged lawyer's internal landscape resembles a battlefield where rage, reluctant love, and dreams of the mythic mother-daughter relationship war with each other. The wisdom of friends—to remember you are doing the best that you can—the advice she would give if she were in their shoes, registers but moderates the turmoil only momentarily. She describes the anxiety she feels when her mother does not answer the phone. Has she fallen and broken a hip? Had a heart attack? Is she lying on the kitchen floor unattended for hours? In seeking to set limits, women's own wishes and aspirations take second place to husbands or children or work as alternative commitments.[39] Setting limits is especially difficult for women who do not work outside the home or who are single and childless.

While the reasons that woman offer for giving care, especially to parents, vary considerably (filial responsibility and reciprocity are not necessarily the dominant themes), a feature of almost all caregivers is the inexorable feeling of necessity—If not me, then who? Their experiences, while stressful psychologically, cannot be singularly captured in the language of stress. Nor can they be reduced to specific tasks. Rather the experiences of caregiving translate into generalized ways of being, of fairly constant anxiety, relentless tiredness, and an urgent need to protect the parent's dignity and maintain his or her sense of self. Caregivers describe feeling powerless because they can change little or nothing, an encompassing sense of responsibility for their parents' lives, and a deep need not to alter previously established relationships. They wish to preserve a sense of maternal omnipotence, and so hide the care they are giving because they do not want to demean their mothers, yet still want to receive praise for what they are doing. While one external observer is often quick to proclaim the woman as a "saint" (conversation, May 1996), thereby relieving society of responsibility to change her situation, another is as likely to wonder why she does that sort of activity.

A society that extols the virtues of independence, views old people with dread, and seeks to distance itself from fundamental life events will disparage as unhealthy women who devote themselves to nursing sick and dying elderly people. A major problem for women is that they are simultaneously encouraged to provide care and condemned for doing so. . . . Caregivers, like mothers, are simultaneously sentimentalized and devalued.[40]

The downside of such treasured values as family, independence, and privacy becomes patently obvious in the context of home care. The perceived obligation to care, one of the unchosen obligations that Annette Baier and other feminist writers describe, clearly places these values in conflict and challenges a rationally self-interested chooser model of moral agency.[41] Many women are emotionally and ideologically attuned to accepting the caregiving role; they find the tasks of caregiving deeply satisfying. The work they do is personal, often demanding, repetitive, mundane, and laden with emotion. Yet it allows them to honor the often inchoate and unspoken sense that this is something that they must do and that others expect of them.[42] More communal values that recognize dependencies and mutual vulnerabilities better articulate what is morally necessary for care at home. A critical sociocultural task is to uncover and create sources of assistance to sustain women so that they are less alone and less at risk economically. The adage "the personal is the political" can be a point of departure for women trying to understand their conflicting feelings, their needs and wants for taking care and being free, for being cared for, secure, but also valued and dignified.

CONCLUSION

Care giving and receiving can reflect unspoken patterns of love and affection that importantly affect, even transform, each participant. In the best caregiving situations, care givers and care receivers affirm each other as persons of worth while care receivers come to recognize that the care giver is reliable and accountable. For all the tales of elder abuse, there are also stories of the dying mother surprising her caregiving daughter with a birthday party, stories where that same mother develops dubious errands so her daughter can get out of the house for a little while, where she continues her vital involvement with caregiving friends by offering pointed advice, political commentary, and reflections on the afterlife.[43]

The moral worlds of care giver and care receiver, in these situations of excellence, transcend tasks—cleaning and dressing, for example—and open up opportunities for growth, forgiveness, and friendship, all morally noteworthy. Psychologist Tom Kitwood once sagely observed, "A psychology of morality will be very much concerned with what people do to one another in the minutiae of everyday life, often without explicit awareness, and almost always without involving conscious moral dilemmas."[44] One task, as we think about the mutualities that

inhere in care giving and care receiving is to imagine more caregiving situations that have the opportunity to be exemplary. Instead what one often encounters is frayed nerves and rather grim physical conditions.

Margaret Urban Walker reminds us that while morality is fundamentally interpersonal, it is constrained and made intelligible by background understandings about what people are supposed to do, expect, and understand.[45] In home care, especially in its most quotidian aspects, we see how people make sense of responsibility in terms of identities, relationships, and values; home care also shows how the phenomenological world is molded by more impersonal forces like race, class, and gender that the political economy explicates. To generate a different world of home care would then call for transformations in the background conditions and in the policy arena. Based on interviews with thirty-two women between the ages of 35 and 85, Jane Aronson notes that if

> the broad social context were one that valued older people, communicated entitlement to needed supports and provided for individual and collective sharing of their provision, Mrs. E. S.'s low spirits and sense of jeopardy might have been much less. If straightforward statements of need were easily speakable, she would not have had to fend off shame, and Mrs. A. C. and her mother would not have had to preserve pride at the cost of denying real need. Mrs. P. S. would have struggled less if prevailing ideologies made possible a wider sharing of responsibility for the care of others, instead of singling her out as an unmarried daughter and pressing her into a caregiving position.[46]

Older women and their female caregivers are particularly vulnerable to cultural messages that might not grip men with equal power. To return to our proverbial legislator, while incontinence and other physical losses may embarrass him, he is not a stranger to receiving care that his privilege has always brought him. The fear of being a burden might be a less familiar emotion to him than to his wife, although some men experience great satisfaction in caring for their spouse—in a sense it offers them a way to "pay back" for the caring they have received.

Much of the material on the stress and burden of caregiving that dominates the gerontological literature focuses on documentation and recommendations for alleviating stress on a personal level through education and counseling and perhaps through additional formal supports. Caregiver support groups can certainly play an important role in helping caregivers cope with their emotions, but they are an unlikely path to resistance unless they begin to unravel the structural and cultural sources of the difficulty and help caregivers renegotiate their response to these external forces. But even that is not enough; serious work on cultural transformation must accompany political work to alter policies. The professional social work and the ethics and aging literatures emphasize elder self-determination and autonomy. Yet, until and unless elders and their caregivers are viewed simultaneously in a relational context, it will be impossible to generate more responsive ways to give care to those who need it without creating patterns of self-sacrifice that neither the older nor younger women deem desirable.

So much of what occurs in caregiving relationships is tacit. Caregivers accept responsibilities because it is what they expect of themselves and it seems to be what others expect of them. These patterns of responsibility and accountability, in Margaret Urban Walker's terms, are not developed collaboratively; instead they reflect how women internalize but also resist cultural impositions, ideological suppositions about family and gender, and impoverished policy responses in the context of their own lives. Jane Aronson says "motivated to reduce feelings of guilt and shame, women implicitly suppress assertion of their own needs, so that the broad pattern of care of old people goes unchallenged—rather it is sustained and reproduced."[47] Encouraging heterodox moral perceptions to flourish as the foundation for identifying wrongful treatment is a good starting place for women, both old and young.[48]

Simultaneously, researchers, scholars, practitioners, and others can ask different questions about caregiving. They can ask not only how to provide support to informal caregivers or protect the self-determined wishes of older clients (which are necessarily influenced by how they perceive their deservingness as older women) but also how to modify those cultural constraints that serve as mechanisms of social control, and how to enrich the options for secure care that policy and economic change can offer. They could ask what it would take to dissociate care from the social norms and power relationships that contribute to women's subordination.[49]

A new language of needs and the creation of proper forums for discussion of needs from the perspective of recipients and care providers are starting places; they can open possibilities previously unnoticed. These public conversations can generate a new language that can situate notions like dignity, self-respect, and cultural inclusion within the context of relationships of dependency. "Without the light of language," Michael Ignatieff observed, "we risk becoming strangers to our better selves."[50] We need to find a way for "positive" heterodox emotions, like compassion, to reenter our public conversation.[51] Such reentry can evoke a commitment to action by opening us to the suffering of others and accepting that our reactions to such suffering are fundamentally moral. Alertness to how the normative assumptions that support politics and policy and the power of ideology and culture become manifest in "ordinary" lives can become the foundation for a sustained ethical analysis of how background conditions mediate life's possibilities and reinforce conditions of inequality.

NOTES

1. Emily Abel, *Who Cares for the Elderly? Public Policy and the Experience of Adult Daughters* (Philadelphia: Temple University Press, 1991).
2. Mario Fabri dos Anjos, "Bioethics in a Liberationist Key," in *A Matter of Principle? Ferment in U.S. Bioethics,* ed. Edwin Dubose, Ron Hamel, and Laurence O'Connell (Valley Forge, Pa.: Trinity Press International, 1994).
3. Nancy Hooyman and Judith Gonyea, *Feminist Perspectives on Family Care: Policies for Gender Justice* (Thousand Oaks, Calif.: Sage, 1995).
4. Emily Abel, "Representations of Caregiving by Margaret Forster, Mary Gordon, and Doris Lessing," *Research on Aging* 17, no. 1 (1995): 63.
5. Baila Miller, *Role of the Family in Homecare,* unpublished manuscript.
6. Nona Glazer, "The Home As Workshop: Women and Amateur Nurses and Medical Care Providers," *Gender and Society* 4 (1990): 479–99.
7. Arlie Hochschild, *The Time Bind: When Work Becomes Home and Home Becomes Work* (New York: Holt, 1997).
8. C. Feldblum, "Home Health Care for the Elderly: Programs, Problems, and Potentials," *Harvard Journal of Legislation* 22 (1985): 194–254. Cited in Terry Arendell and Carroll L. Estes, "Older Women in the Post-Reagan Era," in *Critical Perspectives on Aging: The Political and Moral Economy of Growing Old,* ed. Meredith Minkler and Carroll L. Estes (Amityville, N.Y.: Baywood, 1991), 209–26.
9. Robyn Stone, G. L. Cafferata, and J. Sangl, "Caregivers of the Frail Elderly: A National Profile," *The Gerontologist* 27 (1987): 616–26.
10. Abel, *Who Cares for the Elderly?*
11. Alan Walker, "Care for Elderly People: A Conflict between Women and the State," in *A Labour of Love: Women, Work and Caring,* ed. Janet Finch and D. Groves (London: Routledge and Kegan Paul, 1983), 124.
12. Abel, *Who Cares for the Elderly?*
13. Jane Aronson, "Women's Perspectives on Informal Care of the Elderly: Public Ideology and Personal Experience of Giving and Receiving Care," *Ageing and Society* 10 (1990): 61–84.
14. Philip Clark, "Public Policy in the United States and Canada: Individualism, Familial Obligation, and Collective Responsibility in the Care of the Elderly," in *The Remainder of Their Days: Domestic Policy and Older Families in the United States and Canada,* ed. Jon Hendricks and Carolyn Rosenthal (New York: Garland, 1993), 13.
15. Abel, *Who Cares for the Elderly?*
16. Joanna Weinberg, "Caregiving, Age, and Class in the Skeleton of the Welfare State: And Jill Came Tumbling After," in *Critical Gerontology: Perspectives from Moral and Political Economy,* ed. Meredith Minkler and Carroll L. Estes (Amityville, N.Y.: Baywood, 1998); Nona Glazer, "The Home as Workshop: Women as amateur Nurses and Medical Care Providers," *Gender and Society* 4 (1990): 479–99.

17. See Nancy Fraser's *Unruly Practices* (New York: Routledge, 1989) for an interesting and important discussion of needs negotiation.

18. Michel Foucault, *Discipline and Punish: The Birth of the Prison*, tr. Alan Sheridan (New York: Random House 1979), 26.

19. Judith Shklar, *The Faces of Injustice* (New Haven: Yale University Press, 1990).

20. Michael Ignatieff, *The Needs of Strangers: An Essay on Privacy, Solidarity, and the Politics of Being Human* (New York: Penguin Books, 1984), 13.

21. Arendell and Estes, "Older Women in the Post-Reagan Era."

22. Walker, "Care for Elderly People," 124.

23. Arendell and Estes, "Older Women in the Post-Reagan Era."

24. Carroll L. Estes and Elizabeth A. Binney, "Toward a Transformation of Health and Aging Policy," *International Journal of Health Services* 18, no. 1 (1988): 69–82.

25. Linda Gordon, "The New Feminist Scholarship on the Welfare State," in *Women, the State, and Welfare*, ed. Linda Gordon (Madison: University of Wisconsin Press, 1990), 9–35.

26. Two fine examples of attending to the structural origins of caregiver burden are Suzanne England, Sharon Keigher, Baila Miller, and Nathan Linsk, "Community Care Policies and Gender Justice," in *Critical Perspectives on Aging*; Nancy Hooyman and Judith Gonyea, *Feminist Perspectives on Family Care: Policies for Gender Justice* (Thousand Oaks, Calif.: Sage, 1995).

27. Margaret Urban Walker, *Moral Understandings: A Feminist Study in Ethics* (New York: Routledge, 1998).

28. Donald Moon, "The Moral Basis of the Democratic Welfare State," in *Democracy and the Welfare State*, ed. Amy Gutmann (Princeton: Princeton University Press, 1988), 32.

29. See Janet Finch and Jennifer Mason, *Negotiating Family Responsibilities* (London: Routledge, 1993), for a careful analysis, based on interviews, of how women internalize these cultural values.

30. Hooyman and Gonyea, *Feminist Perspectives on Family Care*, 112; Susan Moller Okin, *Justice, Gender, and the Family* (New York: Basic Books, 1989).

31. Diana Tietjens Meyers, "Emotion and Heterodox Moral Perception: An Essay in Moral Social Psychology," in *Feminists*

Rethink the Self, ed. Diana Tietjens Meyers (Boulder: Westview, 1997), 200.

32. Aronson, "Women's Perspectives on Informal Care of the Elderly."

33. Miller, Role of the Family in Home Care.

34. Walker, "Care for Elderly People."

35. Finch and Mason, *Negotiating Family Responsibilities*.

36. Finch and Mason, *Negotiating Family Responsibilities*.

37. Walker, "Care for Elderly People," 67.

38. Aronson, "Women's Perspectives on Informal Care of the Elderly."

39. Aronson, "Women's Perspectives on Informal Care of the Elderly."

40. Abel, "Representations of Caregiving," 62; Abel, *Who Cares for the Elderly?* 8.

41. Annette Baier, *Postures of the Mind: Essays on Mind and Morals* (Minneapolis: University of Minnesota Press, 1985); see Meyers, ed., *Feminists Rethink the Self*, for a number of thoughtful essays that touch upon the theme of women's experiences that include many of such relational obligations.

42. Finch and Mason, *Negotiating Family Responsibilities*.

43. I speak here of Laurie Shields, the cofounder (with Tish Sommers) of the Older Women's League and one of my heroines. It was to me that she offered a very wise guidance, in the form of a novel she gave me as a Christmas present shortly before she died.

44. Tom Kitwood, "The Dialectics of Dementia: With Particular Reference to Alzheimer's Disease," *Ageing and Society* 10 (1990): 177–96.

45. Walker, *Moral Understandings*.

46. Aronson, "Women's Perspectives on Informal Care of the Elderly," 77.

47. Aronson, "Women's Perspectives on Informal Care of the Elderly."

48. Meyers, "Emotion and Heterodox Moral Perception."

49. Abel, "Representations of Caregiving."

50. Ignatieff, *The Needs of Strangers*, 142.

51. Meyers, "*Emotion and Heterodox Moral Perception.*"

Will Families Support Their Elders? Answers from Across Cultures

Sik Hung Ng

When life was short, people carried on working to support themselves (and others) until they dropped. When only a handful of the population could survive beyond working age, they posed no unbearable burden to the rest of society. But times have changed. The postwar baby boomers can expect to live well beyond the retirement age (usually but not always at 65), and their children and grandchildren will live even longer. The older sector of the population (those over age 65) has increased in both absolute numbers and as a proportion of the general population, and the trend will accelerate for the next twenty years and beyond. In short, the age wave is already upon a large part of today's world, giving new urgency to the age-old question: Who will support the old?

In principle, there are four possible answers to the question: the state, the seniors themselves, a third party, or, sadly, no one. The first three, of course, are not mutually exclusive but can be combined in varying proportions. Let us take a look at history. In ancient

Rome and Greece, seniors themselves were the answer (Parkin 1998). A rugged individualism underlined this type of self-support, best captured in the words of Cicero in 44 B.C.: "Old age will only be respected if it fights for itself, maintains its own rights, avoids dependence on anyone, and asserts control over its own to the last breath" (Parkin 1998, p. 38). Despite the rugged individualism and contrary to the stereotype of elder neglect in western countries, family support, encouraged by Christianity, has long been in place alongside self-support (Hashimoto and Kendig 1992).

In ancient China, where interdependent familial relations between the young and the old prevailed over individualism and the quest for personal independence, seniors were supported by a third party comprising primarily younger family members. In all three places cited, the state moralized about family obligations without entering into a formal support system as a provider. The latter development came about only after the turn of the twentieth century.

The social welfare era as we know it is relatively new by historical standards, and it is already coming to a close in the United States (since Reagan), the United Kingdom (since Margaret Thatcher), New Zealand (since Douglas) and China (since market reforms in the 1980s), to name but a few. In New Zealand, for example, a married couple's superannuation entitlement declined from 89 percent of the national average wage in 1986 to 67 percent in 1997. The retrenchment of state support is partly a response to the ageist perception, rightly or wrongly, of the increasing number of longer-living pensioners as an economically unsustainable and ideologically undesirable burden on the state. This retrenchment will inevitably cause a shift in income-maintenance and health care responsibilities from the state back to seniors themselves or a third party, such as family members. The pendulum of change is on its way back to ancient times.

But if the state finds it economically unaffordable to support seniors and ideologically uncomfortable even if it were able to, would the situation be any easier for seniors and third parties? Clearly the question has multiple facets. Some of the crucial facets have to do with the wealth of the nation, ideology, workforce participation, and demography. More than that, the senior rights movement in the United States has clearly demonstrated that political processes, issues of intergenerational equity, and societal ageism are also intimately involved (Powell, Williamson, and Branco 1996). Ageism in the workplace has meant that older workers who stay on past the traditional retirement age are being looked at

suspiciously as having passed their prime or as selfishly hanging on to their jobs at the expense of younger (and more deserving?) workers. The cumulative effect due to insecurity of work income in old age and reduced pension is that seniors may find it harder and harder to remain self-sufficient or independent. Without belittling the resourcefulness of seniors to take care of themselves, there is a need to explore support from third parties. In this chapter, because of the traditional importance of family support, I focus on families as a source of support and review cross-cultural studies that have made use of the traditional Chinese concept of filial piety.

FAMILY SUPPORT

Largely as a result of industrialization and urbanization, most families living in urban areas today are monogenerational except when parents have dependent children living with them. Fragmentation of the dual or multigenerational family structure calls into question the viability of the family to function as a central element in the informal support system for elderly family members.

A further complication is the increasing number of reconstituted or blended families made up of individuals from two or more previous marriages. From the point of view of the children, their "parents" now comprise a biological parent and a stepparent who live with them, but also a biological parent who does not. Are they supposed to support all three in their old age? Research in this new and important area yields complex results indicating a fluid situation affected not only by kinship and genetic ties but also legal considerations and the quality of interpersonal relationships (Coleman and Ganong 1997; Ganong and Coleman 1998; Ganong et al. 1998).

Concurrent with those family changes, age peers have become the focal point of social life outside the family and have largely displaced older family members as the principal reference group (Chudacoff 1989). The resultant generational gap raises serious questions about the willingness of younger family members to support family elders.

A big difference between family support and support from the formal system is the nature of social-emotional relations that mediate the provision and uptake of support. Family support is provided out of a sense of obligation that goes back to childhood attachment bonds, whereas support from the formal system is more of a job or a vocation, whether it is performed by professionals (e.g., doctors, nurses, police officers), semi-professionals (e.g., home carers) or bureaucrats (e.g., pension officers). Family transactions occur in a particular social-emotional relationship that is highly personal and relatively long-lasting. On the downside, the personal nature of family relationship may make exit from the relationship difficult, and as a result, it creates strain on younger family members who have to provide long-term support year in and year out. Financially, such long-term support may bankrupt the young; support in other areas of need such as disabilities, nursing care, or mental deficits can be just as crippling if it too is long term without a break. The strain gets worse, and exit from it more difficult, if the younger family members are providing the support under emotional blackmail. It takes courage out of years of endurance and suffering to call on support from the formal system. For family elders depending on the particular family relationships, there is the possibility of unmet expectations and, just as bad if not worse, feigned support aimed at inheritance or asset stripping and even outright abuse.

Despite those shortcomings and risks, family support remains irreplaceable amid the ebb and flow of institutionalized care, deinstitutionalization, and community care, whether it is in the United States (Litwak 1985), China (Mok and Xiong 1998), Hong Kong (Chow 2001), or New Zealand (Prime Ministerial Task Force on Positive Ageing 1997). Within the family, younger family members (adult children and their spouses) remain an important group of caregivers, second only after the elder's spouse but ahead of friends and neighbors. Hashimoto and Kendig (1992, p. 3) sum up the overall situation this way: "As people move through their lives in a changing world, it is principally through families that they receive and provide support to those who came before them, and those who follow after them. The importance of family support has been recognized further given that the Welfare State has not solved the health and welfare problems in the industrial countries."

Thus, it behooves researchers to understand support for elders by younger family members, its strengths and weaknesses, or the lack of it as the case may be. Crucially, researchers need to develop conceptual models for differentiating various aspects of support. The family, as an element of the third party, can provide particular aspects of support but not others, whereas other third-party elements, such as neighbors, friends, and community care, may play various complementary roles (Litwak 1985).

In a major work on family function and change, Kagitcibasi (1989) distinguished between material and emotional support ("interdependencies"). In principle, families may be high on both types of interdependencies (pattern X), low on both (pattern Z), or high on one and low on the other. Pattern Z is often taken to be the destiny of Western technological societies. This stereotype about family change is in fact a myth. "The main shift in the world" is not from X to Z, but from X to a pattern that retains emotional support as the main form of family interdependence.

In a discussion of family support in India, Gore (1992) made a similar distinction between material and emotional support, but also reminded us that a fully supportive family would also provide its elders with "meaningful familial roles" (p. 269). If elders can take part in caring for and bringing up their grandchildren, in housework, in contributing to the household income, and contributing in other ways, and be recognized and valued for such roles, they would feel as if they were an integral part of the family instead of being bored or emotionally estranged. Sadly, such familial roles may be the first to disappear when the family support system begins to break down as a result of residential separation and changing ideas about child rearing. Further "atrophy" in family support, according to Gore's (1992) hypothesis, would lead to a decline in emotional and in material support, in that order. This hypothetical order, admittedly speculative, is interesting in that it reverses the order in Kagitcibasi (1989).

If Gore's hypothetical order of family atrophy is valid, in which material support remains the last bastion of family support even after the break-down of familial roles and emotional support, there would be some basis of success for the social policy of shifting material support from the state to the family. This may well be true in countries such as India. Indeed, a survey reported by Esterman and Andrews (1992) showed that in Fiji, the Republic of Korea, Malaysia, and the Philippines, the family remained the major source of income for as many as 40 to 70 percent of elders. Kagitcibasi's (1989) observation, on the other hand, would question the practicality of a social policy that tries to ask the family to provide for family elders' material well-being. Instead, social policy should be based on what is available: the willingness of family members to engage in emotional support for their elders, and on this basis try to mobilize families to enhance elders' quality of life and intergenerational linking. The dilemma is that the emotional function may suffer under the pressure of a social policy change that now attempts to revive the family as a viable social unit to provide material support for elders at a time when younger family members, having grown accustomed to cradle-to-grave state provisions, may not accept material support for elders as one of their filial obligations. This brings us to research on younger people's acceptance of filial obligations toward elderly family members.

FILIAL PIETY

From a social policy perspective, it would be important to know how strongly family members believe they should fulfill particular filial obligations that have implications for government spending. These obligations are mostly material in nature, especially those relating to income maintenance and health care, that is, to assist financially and look after family elders (Binstock 1991; Gunn 1986; Hudson 1997). But emotional bonds and respect (or the lack thereof) often have an impact on these decisions and are important to the psychosocial well-being of elders, so it is important to widen the scope of research on filial obligations to cover emotional bonds and respect.

A wider perspective for thinking about filial obligations is the Confucian ethic of familial relations that covers mutual obligations between spouses, between generations (parents and children), and among members within the same generations (siblings). It is a highly elaborated code of human ethics that would, like the biblical and other religious teachings on familial obligations, provide a useful framework for thinking about the topic. In the Confucian ethic of familial obligations, primary significance has traditionally been accorded to the parent-child component, which comprises parental obligations toward their children and, reciprocally, children's obligations toward their parents. The latter, commonly known as filial piety, is regarded developmentally as the first, or the root, of all virtues (Hwang 1999; Yue 1995). It incorporates material obligations such as finance and caregiving, but more than that, it calls for (and also proscribes) a range of attitudinal and social-interactional obligations. Importantly, it extols the cultivation of a genuine reverence for elders and a concern for family honor as the motivating force behind all filial obligations. It is this attitude of reverence, more so than the fulfillment of material obligations, that distinguishes human filial piety from the humanitarian caring of one's pets. The following excerpt taken from the Analects, the most reliable source of Confucius's teachings, makes plain the point: "Tzu-yu asked about filial piety. Confucius said, 'Filial piety nowadays means to be able to support one's parents. But we support even dogs and horses. If there is no feeling of reverence, wherein lies the difference?'" (translated by Chan 1963, p. 23).

As Kim (2000) has pointed out, when interpreting an ancient text or teaching such as Confucian filial piety for social scientific research, one should go beyond mechanical translation to tease out the meaning of the text in psychological terms and scrutinize its contemporary relevance. In psychological terms, the prime value of the filial piety concept is that it captures the motivational force, emotions, and intergenerational reciprocity that underlie the support of one's own aging parents or grandparents. Nonfilial motivations and considerations, such as charity, pecuniary rewards, and vocational commitments, are less relevant to the family, although they are likely to be more applicable than filial piety to formal and community care.

Recent research has identified several attitudinal and social-interactional elements of Confucian filial piety in addition to finance and caregiving. The most common of these are respect for older family members, pleasing and making them happy, maintaining contact with them, and listening patiently to (or obeying) them (e.g., Gallois et al. 1999; Ng, Loong, Liu, and Weatherall 2000). Other filial elements relating to ancestral worship and continuation of the family line, though important in traditional societies, are generally regarded as less applicable to contemporary times and are seldom included in research (see Ho 1996; Sung 1995).

Relevant studies have shown that the six material, attitudinal, and social-interactional obligations were moderately intercorrelated (Gallois 1998; Gallois et al. 1996), suggesting that filial piety, thus measured, is a unitary concept. However, this does not necessarily imply that support for all six obligations is uniformly high or uniformly low. Instead, it is likely that some obligations are more or less strongly supported than others. Variation across obligations provides important descriptive information on how individuals hierarchically order filial obligations; equally, it facilitates the testing and developing of theoretical ideas about filial obligations for comparisons between and within cultures.

HIERARCHY OF FILIAL OBLIGATIONS

In a study by Ng et al. (2000), about 100 European and 100 Chinese families in New Zealand were sampled. From each family, between one and two middle-aged parents and between one and two children completed a questionnaire containing the six filial obligations (to be answered on a five-point scale). Overall, both ethnic groups said they would support rather than not support the six obligations. However, because of the possible effect of social desirability, one can never be sure of the actual level of support. Hence, it would be more meaningful to interpret the results in terms of their relative ranks than in terms of absolute ratings. Across both ethnic groups, the same hierarchy of obligations emerged, with obedience and financial support at the bottom, care and to please in the middle, and respect and social contact at the top. In broad terms, this hierarchy is similar to that found in Beijing (Yue and Ng 1999) and several other cities around Pacific Rim countries (Gallois et al. 1999).

As obedience has been shown in studies of human values to be one of the least favored values (Chinese Cultural Connection 1987; Ng et al. 1982), any obligation that is as low as obedience, in this case financial support, can be interpreted as out of favor with people. Social-emotional support, by contrast, enjoys much greater support, particularly in the case of respect and social contact. Thus, there is self-report evidence in support of Kagitcibasi's (1989) thesis that families have opted out of material support for elders while retaining social-emotional support. The separation between material and social-emotional support, as we shall see, is stronger in Western than in Eastern cultures.

So far only the order of filial obligations within the hierarchy has been discussed, leaving out the steepness of the hierarchy or the degree of separation among the various obligations. Ng et al. (2000) reported an interesting difference in hierarchical steepness between Chinese and European New Zealanders (see Figure 10.1). Chinese had a relatively flat hierarchy, suggesting that the six elements of filial piety were still relatively intact for

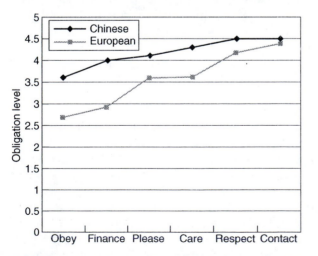

FIGURE 10.1   Obligations Toward Older Parents by Chinese and Europeans.

them. The cross-cultural difference in the steepness of the hierarchy, after ruling out statistically the possibility of acquiescence on the part of Chinese respondents, was due to Europeans' giving a significantly lower endorsement of all obligations except for social contact. In particular, Europeans were much less enthused than Chinese about financial support, obedience, and caregiving. In the light of this more finely grained finding, Kagitcibasi's (1989) thesis needs to be revised to allow for a greater degree in the retention of material obligations. It is noteworthy that even with the development of social welfare provisions in the People's Republic of China, family members are still required by law to support their family elders who are financially unable to provide for themselves (Constitution of the People's Republic of China 1982, Chapter 2, Article 49). This reflects the deeply rooted sense of financial obligation toward elders among Chinese, and possibly also among overseas Chinese. In England (whose legal system has been closely followed in New Zealand), neither financial nor caregiving responsibilities are enjoined by law (Twigg and Grand 1998).

CORRELATES OF FILIAL OBLIGATIONS

Ethnic and cultural, demographic, and psychological variables are three major categories of correlate of filial piety. *Ethnicity* correlates with filial obligations in the direction of a stronger sense of family obligations for Chinese than for European New Zealanders (Ng et al. 2000). This ethnic difference is especially marked with regard to financial support, caregiving, and obedience. A study in the United States comparing Chinese, Japanese, and Korean Americans found that insofar as services and emotional support for elders are concerned, Koreans are the most pious of the three (Masako 1997). These two studies are concerned with comparisons of ethnic groups living in the same country, within either New Zealand or the United States.

Cross-country comparisons from a major Pacific Rim project revealed a pattern similar to that found in the work by Ng and associates (2000). In this Pacific Rim survey, college students from eight nations or regions were asked, among other questions, to indicate how much they would agree or disagree that young adults should fulfil the six family obligations (Gallois 1998). The results showed a systematic East-West difference between Hong Kong, Japan, the Philippines, and South Korea on the one hand, and Australia, Canada, New Zealand, and the United States on the other. Compared to Western respondents, East Asian respondents more strongly endorsed financial support, caregiving, respect, and to please, the same as that found between Chinese and Europeans in New Zealand. For social contact, Western students were more supportive than East Asian students (whereas Chinese and Europeans in New Zealand did not differ significantly on this). Obedience was not asked in the survey, but instead, "listen patiently to elders" was. On this last item, the comparison favored the West.

Several *demographic* variables have been looked at for possible correlations with filial obligations. In the study by Ng and associates (2000), generational gaps between respondent and elders and the age of respondents were found to have a strong bearing on filial obligations. The bigger the generational gap was, the weaker were the obligations. That is, middle-aged respondents' felt obligations were weaker toward their aging grandparents (bigger generational gap) than toward their aging parents (smaller generational gap); and similarly for younger respondents. Second, the older the respondents, the stronger were their felt obligations. In other words, middle-aged parents were more pious than their children. Third, contrary to gender stereotypes, females were not stronger (or weaker) than males in felt obligations. The age and gender findings contradict an American study that found an inverse age effect (felt obligations were stronger among young adult than middle-aged respondents) and a main effect of gender in favor of females (Stein et al. 1998). The differences between the two studies may be a reflection of true differences between the two countries, but this possibility remains to be tested because the two studies also differ significantly in their methodologies. For example, whereas the family was used as the unit of sampling in Ng and associates' study (2000), unrelated individuals were sampled in Stein and associates' study (1998).

Various *psychological* correlates of filial piety have been identified in research. Many of these have been reviewed by Ho (1996) and integrated under the theoretical constructs of *authoritarian moralism* and *cognitive conservatism*. In a recent study, Zhang and Bond (1998) compared the powers of universal personality traits (derived from the West) and indigenous Chinese ones in predicting filial piety among Chinese college students. Among the five factors of the universal Five Factor Inventory, Neuroticism and Openness significantly predicted filial piety. Beyond that, the indigenous personality traits of Harmony and Renqing (relational orientation) significantly improved the prediction of filial piety.

Another recent study revealed an interesting relationship between filial obligations and group-based social identity. Liu, Ng, Weatherall, and Loong (2000) obtained two separate measures of identity for their New Zealand Chinese respondents—one relating to their identification with Chinese and another relating to their identification with New Zealand, their adopted country. Chinese identity, not surprisingly, was positively correlated with filial obligations. For New Zealand identity, a similarly positive correlation with filial obligation also emerged. When a strong New Zealand identity was combined with a strong Chinese identity, adherence to filial piety was stronger still. It was only when respondents had neither a strong Chinese nor New Zealand identity would they disavow filial piety.

The identity results suggest that a strong sense of identity is more important than its particular content for the development of filial piety. In the context of Chinese immigrants, this means that both the retention of a Chinese identity and the acquisition of a New Zealand identity are compatible with filial piety. There are two Chinese sayings that capture these two identities well: "fallen leaves return to their roots" and "grow your roots where you stand." Through the former, immigrants achieve a strong sense of identity by reuniting with and reaffirming their cultural heritage; through the latter they achieve a similarly meaningful sense of identity by putting down their roots where they currently live. Either way, immigrants have a psychological home to belong to and from which they can feel secure enough to respect elders, maintain social contact with them, look after them, and so on.

CONCLUSION

There is evidence from the research that filial obligations now mean first and foremost respect for and maintaining social contact with older family members. The other four obligations, including health care and financial assistance, are of moderate importance only, although they are still relatively high in Asian cultures, especially among Koreans. One of the implications is that the all-too-popular myths about the East and the West—that elders in Eastern cultures are well looked after by their families, whereas those in the West are abandoned by their families—are grossly exaggerated. Another implication is that social policy that aims at encouraging families to take on material obligations does not have enough motivational support from younger family members. In Asian cultures, the policy may capitalize on the relatively high level of avowed support for material obligations; even then, the depth of *genuine* motivation to provide material support remains uncertain as the results of the New Zealand

Chinese have shown (support for financial obligation is only as high as the willingness to obey elders, which can be interpreted as being low). Worse, such a policy runs the risk of straining family relations. As Szinovacz and Ekerdt (1996, p. 391) have put it, "When aging parents are not economically beholden to the wealth of their children and can maintain independent households, intergenerational relationships can be founded on sentiment and affection that are uncomplicated by financial obligation and the strain it engenders. Voluntary emotional bonds, rather than material duty, can tie older people with their adult children and grandchildren."

If a community or country can develop in the direction that Szinovacz and Ekerdt (1996) propose, the burden of filial piety would be lighter and its practice more focused on what younger family members are already most willing to do: respect and maintain social contact with family elders. These attitudinal, social-interactional, and communicative supports (Coupland, Coupland, and Giles 1991; Ng 1998; Nussbaum et al. 1996) are just as valuable as material supports for elders to age well (Rowe and Kahn 1998). Equally, those supports and the satisfying experience of providing them would promote intergenerational solidarity and healthy mutual respect. What better way is there to reduce ageism against the old by the young, or the young by the old?

The concept of filial piety, stripped of its feudal and patriarchic overtones, can offer a useful way of looking at family support for elders. The concept is broad and for this reason can free up research beyond the narrow focus of material support. It grounds the motivational force of filial obligations in the bonding among members of a social group who partake in everyday life for years and share a common identity.

Our knowledge about the development of filial piety is extremely limited. The various correlates of it, reviewed above, suggest that cultural-political processes, socialization processes, and identification processes are involved. Given this, advances in research can best come through multidisciplinary research across nations and across subcultures within nations. As aging is rapidly becoming an issue of global concern, this calls for international cooperation in research and in the dissemination of knowledge.

REFERENCES

Binstock R. H. (1991). Aging, politics, and public policy. In B. B. Hess and E. W. Markson (Eds.), *Growing old in America* (4th ed., pp. 325–340). New Brunswick, NJ: Transaction Publishers.

Chan, W.-T. (1963). *A source book in Chinese philosophy.* Princeton, NJ: Princeton University Press.

Chinese Cultural Connection (1987). Chinese values and the search for culture-free dimensions of culture. *Journal Cross-Culture Psychology, 18,* 143–164.

Chow, W. S. (2001). The practice of filial piety among the Chinese in Hong Kong. In I. Chi, N. L. Chappell, and J. Lubben (Eds.), *Elderly Chinese in Pacific Rim countries: Social support and interaction* (pp. 125–136), Kong: Hong Kong University Press.

Chudacoff, H. P. (1989). *How old are you?* New Jersey: Princeton.

Coleman, M., and Ganong, L. (1997). Beliefs about women's intergenerational family obligations to provide support before and after divorce and remarriage. *Journal of Marriage and the Family, 59,* 165–176.

Coupland, N., Coupland, J., and Giles, H. (1991). *Language, society and the elderly.* Oxford: Blackwell.

Esterman, A., and Andrews, G. R. (1992). Southeast Asia and the Pacific: A comparison of older people in four countries. In H. L. Kendig, A. Hashimoto, and L. C. Coppard (Eds.), *Family support for the elderly: The international experience* (pp. 271–289). Oxford: Oxford University Press.

Gallois, C. (1998). Intergenerational communication and respect of older people around the Pacific Rim. In S. H. Ng. A. Weatherall, J. H. Liu, and C. S. F. Loong (Eds.), *Ages ahead: Promoting intergenerational relationships* (pp. 112–128). Wellington: Victoria University Press.

Gallois, C., Giles, H., Ota, H., Pierson, H. D., Ng, S. H., Lim, T. S., Maher, J., Somera, L., Ryan, E. B., and Harwood, J. (1999). Intergenerational communication across the Pacific Rim: The impact of filial piety. In J.-C. Lasry, J. Adair, and K. Dion (Eds.), *Latest contributions to cross-cultural psychology* (pp. 192–211). Lisse, Netherlands: Swets and Zeitlinger B. V.

Ganong, L., and Coleman M. (1998). Attitudes regarding filial responsibilities to help elderly divorced parents and stepparents. *Journal of Aging Studies, 12,* 271–290.

Ganong, L., Coleman, M., McDaniel, A. R, and Killian, T. (1998). Attitudes regarding obligations to assist an older parent or stepparent following late remarriage. *Journal of Marriage and the Family, 60,* 595–610.

Gore, M. S. (1992). Family support to elderly people: The Indian situation. In H. L. Kendig, A. Hashimoto, and L. C. Coppard (Eds.), *Family support for the elderly: The international experience* (pp. 260–270). Oxford: Oxford University Press.

Gunn, P. A. (1986). Legislating filial piety. The Australian experience. *Ageing and Society, 6,* 135–167.

Hashimoto, A., and Kendig, H. L. (1992). Aging in international perspective. In H. L. Kendig, A. Hashimoto, and L. C. Coppard (Eds.), *Family support for the elderly: The international experience* (pp. 3–14). Oxford: Oxford University Press.

Ho, D. Y.-F. (1996). Filial piety and its psychological consequences. In M. H. Bond (Ed.), *The handbook of Chinese psychology* (pp. 155–165). Hong Kong: Oxford University Press.

Hudson, R. P. (1997). The history and place of age-based public policy. In R. B. Hudson (Eds.), *The future of age-based public policy* (pp. 1–22). Baltimore, MD: John Hopkins University Press.

Hwang, K-K. (1999). Filial piety and loyalty: Two types of social identification in Confucianism. *Asian Journal of Social Psychology, 2,* 163–183.

Kagitcibasi, C. (1989). Family and socialization in cross-cultural perspective: A model for change. *Nebraska Symposium on Motivation, 37,* 135–200.

Kim, U. (2000). Indigenous, cultural, and cross-cultural psychology: A theoretical, conceptual, and epistemological analysis. *Asian Journal of Social Psychology, 3,* 265–287.

Litwak, E. (1985). *Helping the elderly: Complementary roles of informal networks and formal system.* New York: Guilford Press.

Liu, J. H., Ng, S. H., Weatherall, A., and Loong, C. S. F. (2000). Filial piety, acculturation, and inter-generational communication among New Zealand Chinese. *Basic and Applied Social Psychology, 22,* 213–223.

Masako, I. K. (1997). Intergenerational relationships among Chinese, Japanese, and Korean Americans. *Family Relations, 46,* 23–32.

Mok, B. H., and Xiong, Y. (1998). Community care for urban elderly in an aging society: A theoretical exploration of the linkage between the family, the community and the government. *Hong Kong Journal of Gerontology, 12,* 8–16.

Ng, S. H. (1998). Social psychology in an ageing world: Ageism and intergenerational relations. *Asian Journal of Social Psychology, 1,* 99–116.

Ng, S. H., Akhtar Hossain, A. B. M., Ball, P., Bond, M. H., Hayashi, K, Lim, S. P., O'Driscoll, M. P., Sinha, D., and Yang, K. S. (1982). Human values in nine countries. In R. Rath, H. S. Asthana, D. Sinha, and J. B. P. Sinha (Eds.), *Diversity and unity in cross-cultural psychology* (pp. 196–205). Lisse: Swets and Zeitlinger B. V.

Ng, S. H., Liu, J. H., Wiatherall, A., and Loong, C. S. F. (1998). Intergenerational relationships in the Chinese community. In S. H. Ng, A. Weatherall, J. H. Liu, and C. S. F. Loong (Eds.), *Ages ahead: Promoting intergenerational relationships* (pp. 85–104). Wellington: Victoria University Press.

Ng, S. H., Loong, C. S. F., Liu, J. H., and Weatherall, A. 2000. Will the young support the old? An individual- and family-level study of filial obligations in two New Zealand cultures. *Asian Journal of Social Psychology, 3,* 163–182.

Nussbaum, J. F., Hummert, M. L., Williams, A., and Harwood. (1996). Communication and older elders. In B. R. Burleson (Ed.), *Communication yearbook* (Vol. 19, pp. 1–47). Thousand Oaks, CA: Page.

Parkin, T. G. (1998). Ageing in antiquity Status and participation. In P. Johnson and P. Thane (Eds.), *Old age from antique to post-modernity* (pp. 19–42). London: Routledge.

Powell, L. A., Williamson, J. B., and Branco, K. J. (Eds.), (1996). *The senior rights movement: Framing the policy debate in America.* New York: Twayne.

Prime Ministerial Task Force on Positive Ageing. (1997). *Facing the future.* Wellington: Department of Prime Minister.

Rowe, J. W., and Khan, R. L. (1998). *Successful aging.* New York: Pantheon Books.

Stein, C. H., Wemmerus, V. A., Ward, M., Gaines, M. E., and Jewell, T. C. (1998). "Because they're my parents": An intergenerational study of felt obligations and parental caregiving. *Journal of Marriage and the Family, 60,* 611–622.

Sung, K.-T. (1995). Measures and dimensions of filial piety in Korea. *Gerontologist, 35,* 240–247.

Szinovacz, M., and Ekerdt, D. J. (1996). Families and retirement. In R. Blieszner and V. H. Bedford (Eds.), *Aging and the family: Theory and research* (pp. 375–400). Westport, CT: Praeger.

Twigg, J., and Grand, A. (1998). Contrasting legal conceptions of family obligation and financial reciprocity in the support of older people: France and England. *Ageing and Society, 18,* 131–146.

Yue, Q. P. (1995). Filial piety and modernization. In J. Qiao and N. G. Pan (Eds.), *Chinese concepts and behavior* (pp. 123–136). Tianjin, China: Tianjin People's Press.

Yue, X., and Ng, S. H. (1999). Filial obligations and expectations in China: Current views from young and old people in Beijing. *Asian Journal of Social Psychology, 2,* 215–226.

Zhang, J., and Bond, M. H. (1998). Personality and filial piety among college students in two Chinese societies: The added value of indigenous constructs. *Journal of Cross Cultural Psychology, 29,* 402–417.

Elder Abuse, Ethics, and Context

John Hardwig

I. INTRODUCTION

For me, the pivotal moment in the conference on "Violence, Neglect, and the Elderly" came fairly early. I find myself returning over and over to a story that Margaret Hudson told to illustrate her claim that elder abuse is not always a bad person doing horrible things. Often, it is a good person stuck in an intolerable situation.

The story was about an elderly man struggling to care for his wife who was a victim of Alzheimer's. She had taken to wandering at night as well as during the day. As a result, she needed constant supervision— 24 hours/day, 7 days/week. Her husband had no relief from this task; he was on the verge of physical collapse. One night in desperation he tied his wife to her bed. He then slept soundly for the first time in days and did not hear anything until she hit the floor.

A memorable story—it moved others in the audience, as well. But it was an aside in terms of Hudson's analysis. Her argument was not affected in any important way by her story; it is not even included in the written text of her talk.[1] She told the story only to make it clear that she is not insensitive to the problems facing caregivers who end up doing things that we might label abuse.

Still, we can wonder whether Hudson is sensitive enough. If she searches for a common meaning of the term "elder abuse" and in so doing effectively ignores the plight of caregivers, we can rightfully begin to wonder whether she is attentive enough to their problems. One wonders, for example, why the scenarios around which Hudson's research is organized say nothing about the situation of the caregivers and the impact that giving care makes on their own lives. Presumably, Hudson thinks that the situation of caregivers is irrelevant to what is or is not elder abuse. She invites all of us to think so, too.

Hudson is not alone in this; she is in the mainstream. The entire conference was well within the accepted paradigm in this respect. We all pretty much ignored the problems facing caregivers. We alluded to them from time to time, but our analyses were not importantly affected by concerns for abusive caregivers. Their problems were dismissed with an occasional aside that someone—the government, perhaps—should do something more to support those caring for the elderly.

It might seem perfectly appropriate that we ignored the situation of abusive caregivers—after all, we were gathered to advocate for victims of elder abuse, not for their abusers. But I will argue that we cannot get even so far as a definition of elder abuse without considering much more carefully the context in which the abuse occurs. The context must, of course, also be taken into consideration in proposing interventions into cases of possible elder abuse.

II. THE DEFINITION OF ABUSE AND THE SITUATION OF THE CAREGIVER

Is elder abuse wrong? That seems an odd question. Surely, if we can agree on nothing else, we can at least agree that elder abuse is bad, wrong, deplorable, and ought to stop. What could be clearer? The strangeness of the question—Is elder abuse wrong?—suggests that abuse (and neglect, as well) are inextricably moral notions. Other, equally strange statements point to the same conclusion. Do the following statements make sense? "Abusing his wife was the right thing to do in that situation." "Her obligation was clear and it was to neglect her mother." "His father was abused, but he was treated fairly."

The notions of elder abuse (and neglect) seem to rest squarely on the idea that the abused person has been wrongfully treated. Thus, too, the powerful feelings of revulsion when we contemplate the topic; we do not have similarly intense feelings of revulsion or outrage about old people in other harsh or unfortunate circumstances, no matter how harmful the result. But if the concept of abuse implies wrongful treatment, we cannot ascertain whether an elderly person is being abused until we know what is morally acceptable and what is wrongful treatment. We will first need an account of what the moral obligations of a caregiver to an elderly person are. Wrongful treatment occurs when moral obligations are not met.

Still, we may hesitate to embrace the conclusion that abuse is essentially a moral concept. Right and wrong, good and bad, moral and immoral are all very messy concepts. It is notoriously difficult to get agreement about moral concepts. If we hesitate, we might get some help

from Thomas Murray.[2] During the final presentation of the conference, Murray distinguished three senses of "abuse" or "neglect"—the purely descriptive or objective, the moral, and the legal. If that distinction holds, we would be able to say that abuse in the moral sense is, indeed, an inextricably moral notion, but there is another, objective sense of abuse not dependent on moral notions.

But we cannot avoid the nasty problems of ethics by simply sticking to an objective definition. In the first place, we have just been wondering whether there really is a purely descriptive sense of a term like "abuse." But even if there is, it will not do the work we need. A purely descriptive or "objective" definition of elder abuse would be morally neutral; as such, it would not enable us to draw any conclusions about whether the activity so described is right or wrong, unjustified or perfectly appropriate. For that, we need a moral sense of the term.

The justification for legal intervention also rests on the moral definition of the term. Our strong sense of family privacy would shield a family from any intervention not wanted by all members of the family, unless someone is being wrongfully treated.

For these reasons, I will focus on the moral sense of elder abuse and elder neglect. I will cast my argument in terms of elder abuse, though it applies to elder neglect, as well. I will argue that elder abuse is a very contextual matter, heavily dependent on precisely what the conference ignored—the situation of the caregiver. Consequently, we need a very thick description of a case in order to tell whether or not something is elder abuse.

Let us return to Hudson's example. Is tying your demented wife to her bed elder abuse? That seems an easy question to answer. Of course! Surely any time anyone ties an elderly, demented person in her bed, it is elder abuse! Hudson also thinks it is clearly abuse—otherwise this narrative could not illustrate her point that people who abuse the elderly are often stuck in intolerable situations. I assume Hudson will find that most Americans agree.

But we still need to ask, what should the husband have done? Maybe he should have handcuffed her in bed. Would that have been better? With the 20/20 vision of hindsight, we might agree that it would have been. And it might have been better yet if he had used one of those restraints that many seem to believe should be entirely eliminated from nursing homes. Presumably, though, the husband had neither on hand—these are not common household tools. With the wisdom of hindsight, we might also think he should have anticipated this problem a month earlier, installed a lock on his wife's bedroom door, and locked her in her room each night when he went to bed.

Notice that we are tempted to call all of these alternatives elder abuse. Still, we cannot simultaneously recommend them to the husband and also say that they are elder abuse in the moral sense. If the most sensitive and humane option available to the husband was to restrain his demented wife in her bed or lock her in her room at night, then doing so cannot be elder abuse, not in the moral sense.

Now let us imagine a modified version of Hudson's case. The husband is a wealthy man. He can easily afford to hire round-the-clock care for his demented wife. He is well rested, for even if his wife becomes obstreperous in the middle of the night, it does not bother him—he sleeps in another wing of the house. Nevertheless, he ties his wife in her bed out of sheer malice or because he simply does not want to pay for someone to look after her. In that case, we have elder abuse. Given that scenario, what the husband did is clearly wrong and blameworthy.

Elder abuse in the moral sense can be identified only with the help of a thick description of the case, including many features of the situation of the caregiver. To ascertain whether an act is or is not elder abuse, we will need to know who cares for the "victim" and why, how long the caregiver has been providing care, what alternatives are available for giving care, what opportunities for relief the caregiver has, the physical and emotional reserves of this caregiver, the kinship relationship (if any) between caregiver and "victim," and much more.

It is worthwhile to pause here to note that the preceding arguments about the situation of the husband/caregiver can be extended to institutions and the paid caregivers who work in them. In his paper, Ben Rich pointed to many kinds of abuse of the elderly in nursing homes.[3] But I found elements of his discussion similarly unattuned to the situation of the caregivers. Granted, the situation of the staff of a nursing home is rarely even remotely as desperate as that of the husband in Hudson's story. If nothing else, you work your shift and then you can leave the whole situation.

Still, even in the setting of a nursing home, context is relevant to identifying elder abuse in the moral sense. If the demented residents of a nursing home are being sedated or physically restrained so that the staff can sit and gossip in the staff lounge, that is abuse. But if the staffing is very thin and there are so many things that must be attended to, perhaps restraining a resident or locking her in her room is the best, most fair, most humane thing the staff can do. I see no way to eliminate the situation of the caregivers—whether institutional or family—from a discussion of what elder abuse is.

The need to consider the situation of the caregivers reveals what I take to be a major difficulty in Hudson's research program. The scenarios she gives her respondents to test their intuitions about elder abuse are far too incomplete. Her respondents cannot or should not judge whether the activities she describes are abusive in any sense that is incompatible with their being the right thing to do. I suspect that what Hudson's respondents are doing is imaginatively filling in the needed details and then judging a much richer picture they have constructed, not simply the one-sentence description that Hudson has given them. When Hudson finds significant disagreement among her respondents, one major reason for this disagreement may well be that they are imagining different case scenarios. The agreement Hudson finds could also be spurious because people may be giving the same answer about what are really different imagined scenarios.

III. PRINCIPLES FOR CONTEXTUALIZING OBLIGATION OF CAREGIVERS

Because the situation of the caregivers is relevant to judgments of abuse in the moral sense, we will not be able to come up with many, if any, actions which will always be elder abuse. (The only examples I can think of rest on a description of the action that is already pejorative, e.g., beating, drugging.) But it does not follow that there are no moral principles to help guide us in defining the moral concept of elder abuse. Some of these principles will be principles that point to morally relevant features of the caregiver's situation and her relationship to the elderly person she cares for.

It is these principles to which I wish to call attention. They tend to be forgotten. They certainly were forgotten at our conference. We tend to focus on the problems of dependent old people. When we do so, caregivers fade from view or are conceptualized as "problems" (abusers or neglecters), as "family support," or as "family resources" for providing care for an elderly person. This is especially true if we see ourselves as advocates for the elderly.

What, then, are the moral principles for defining a caregiver's obligations to the family member she cares for?

1. Ought implies can. No one is obligated to do more than she can. Consequently, the care an elderly person should receive from her caregiver depends on the caregiver's resources—mental, emotional, physical, social, familial, and economic. However,

2. Can does not imply ought. No one is obligated, except for a very short time, to do "all they can" for someone else, not even for a member of her family. To think someone is so obligated is to treat that person as a mere means to the ends of that family member.

3. Often, It is WRONG to do all you can for an elderly person, even if that is what you want to do. Virtually everyone has other, conflicting obligations which must also be met. If nothing else, there are usually other family members whose needs and interests must be considered. Thus, a woman with children may well owe her mother less care than one who has no children; indeed, a woman who pays little attention to her children because she wants to give the best possible care to her mother is doing something wrong (even if she cannot be said to be abusing or neglecting them). Moreover, if an elderly person must be ignored, or even restricted or restrained so that time and attention can be devoted to fulfilling the caregiver's other obligations, it will sometimes be right to do so (providing other, more suitable alternatives are not available).

It may be possible to define a minimal level of care due to any member of one's family within the limits defined by these three principles. If there is enough food so that everyone can eat, old persons should be fed; if there is enough money to heat the house, an old person should also sleep in a heated room. But even this minimal level of care is conditioned by these three principles: If there is not enough for everyone to eat, it may be wrong to feed the elderly. Moreover, this is a minimal, even rudimentary level of care. Once a minimal level of care is being given, additional principles come into play to help determine whether a less minimalistic level of care is morally required.

4. The wants and interests of caregivers are also relevant to defining the limits of their moral responsibilities to the elderly. This follows from the moral principle that no one is to be treated as a mere means for satisfying other people's ends. Thus, although "what is best for the elderly person" and "what the elderly person wants (or would have wanted)" are always relevant considerations, they are not by themselves sufficient to determine what should be done.[4] Family caregivers have lives of their own. Increases and decreases in the quality of life of the caregiver are just as important to moral judgment as changes in the quality of life of the dependent elderly. Appropriate care must be determined on the basis of fairness to all members of the family.[5]

Some have admitted that fairness to all is the appropriate standard when someone is being cared for at home, but they argue that the wishes or best interests of the patient are the standards for defining appropriate care in hospitals and other institutions.[6] But this is a deeply incoherent position: Hands dealt in the hospital often must be played out at home. In fact, harsh as it may sound, it could be right either to refuse to hospitalize an incompetent elderly person or to withdraw care

from her in the hospital on the grounds that her continued existence is too burdensome for her family, especially her caregivers. To think otherwise is to reduce the caregiver to a means to the ends of the elderly person.

5. What is owed to mentally competent elderly persons depends partly on how they act. Competent elderly persons who act badly toward their family and/or caregivers merit less care, and care of lower quality, than those who behave well. In fact, an elderly person who behaves badly enough (in avoidable ways) may even merit her "abuse." Acknowledging this point is part and parcel of treating the elderly as morally capable persons: Any competent member of a family who regularly behaves badly enough toward the others merits less care from them. People, morally competent people, of any age can be nasty, mean, brutal, hateful, selfish, domineering, petty, vengeful, excessively demanding, etc. Members of their families rightfully may and often should take steps to protect themselves and their lives from such a person.

6. What is owed to an elderly person, competent or incompetent, depends partly on how they treated others when they were younger, especially on how they treated those who now care for them. A woman who, as a girl, was physically and sexually abused by her father certainly owes him much less when he becomes old than she would if he had been loving, generous, and supportive. Thus, not only the present situation, but also the history of relationships is relevant to defining the obligations of caregivers.

7. Grossly imprudent earlier activity diminishes an elderly person's claim to assistance. There is a bumper sticker that sometimes appears on the back of motor homes: "I'm spending my children's inheritance." While it may (or may not) be morally permissible to spend your children's inheritance, it is not permissible to spend lavishly and then come to them for financial assistance in your old age.

These, then, are a few of the moral principles that we must use to contextualize our accounts of elder abuse. Of course, such principles are not formulas which will enable us simply to read off the answer to questions about elder abuse. But they are considerations always to bear in mind when formulating judgments about cases of possible elder abuse.

IV. SOCIAL ABUSE AND NEGLECT OF THE ELDERLY

At this point, if not long before, some will want to object strongly: "Any demented woman who is locked in her room or tied in her bed is being abused! Only she is being abused by society, not by her caregiver. Perhaps her husband is being abused by society, as well."

"After all," the objection continues, "if appropriate social services were in place, this old couple would not be in such a desperate situation and there would be no need and no temptation to tie the wife to her bed. Recognizing the responsibility of society for its elderly citizens would allow us to identify cases of elder abuse in the moral sense without examining the situation of the caregiver. It is social abuse of the elderly that Hudson's story illustrates."

Our conference dealt largely with elder abuse on an "up close and personal" level. That seems to make sense, since abuse requires an abuser, presumably some specifiable individual. It also makes sense if our goal is to identify specific activities that constitute elder abuse, or if we are wondering whether or not to intervene in a particular situation.

But the individual level is also the level on which we Americans are most comfortable with moral analysis. Social responsibility or community obligations do not get very far with us. This preference for individual responsibility can easily slide into a kind of moral isolationism: "I'll take care of me and mine; you worry about you and yours."

Such moral isolationism would leave us with insoluble problems about dependent elderly people who have no children, no surviving children, or children who either simply cannot or will not care for their parents. If we do not think it appropriate for elderly people with limited financial resources and no family caregivers simply to be left to die in the streets or in their apartments, such moral isolationism cannot be justified.

If moral isolationism cannot be justified, and if we nonetheless wish to keep our moral discussion on the level of individual responsibility, we need to learn to ask: What do we individually owe to old people who are not part of our families or personal friends? We also need to ask this question whenever our social institutions fail to meet their responsibilities to the elderly.

I cannot even begin here to give an account of the social obligations to the elderly, but a few basic points will suffice to show that the notion of social responsibility to the elderly must also be contextualized.

1. In order to generate a theory of elder abuse by society, we will need a theory of what a society such as ours owes its older people.   "A society such as ours"—social responsibility is thus contextualized from the very beginning, as wealthy societies owe their elderly much more than societies that exist on the margin of subsistence.

Even in a wealthy society such as ours, this theory of social responsibility cannot simply be a litany of what old people need. Just because someone has an unmet need, it does not follow that society has an obligation to meet that need. There may be some needs, e.g., the need for individual affirmation or personal care, that just cannot be met by any society. In addition, it may be impossible to meet everyone's needs, as satisfying one person's needs is incompatible with satisfying the needs of others. For example, a frail, terrified, old man may need his daughter around at all times, but she needs time to herself.

What is more, there are other Americans who have needs every bit as pressing as those of the elderly. Thus, huge questions of intergenerational justice will have to be addressed. For example, old people get better health care than children in this country, and it is arguable that they get better health care than working people, as well. Is that just? We provide nursing home care for elderly people who have nowhere else to go. We do not, however, provide a shelter of even remotely comparable quality for homeless people, including homeless children. Is that just?

2. We will also need a theory of what ought to be done if a society is not going to meet its obligations to all its members.   We face a burgeoning taxpayer revolt in this country. In this context, it may well be that our society simply will not meet its theoretical obligations to all its members in need, either through public or private assistance. We citizens of the United States simply may not feel the obligations which a theory of justice to the elderly states that we have.

Where there are severe budgetary constraints, should we provide decent shelter for all Americans before we provide nursing home care for the demented elderly? Is hunger in children less morally justifiable than hunger in the elderly? Should we provide basic health care for all Americans before we contemplate transferring elderly people to hospitals for expensive, high-tech care? Answers to questions like these are what policy makers most need, not an account of what a wealthy society theoretically owes each of its citizens.

Thus, even the concept of social abuse of the elderly has to be contextualized. In the setting of the United States in the 1990s, we might argue that American voters are abusing the elderly. However theoretically sound such an argument might be, it does not seem likely to get very far. Alternatively, we might argue that politicians who divide up the tax money ought to have been more generous with funding social programs for older people, but it is far from clear that that is true.

Still, even if such arguments were successful, they show only that our social situation should be different. They do not tell us what should be done for old people in our situation. Answers to the question of what social agencies should do in our situation might throw the couple in Hudson's example back on their own resources. Given our limited social will to help others in need, it may well be that we ought not to devote the available resources to nursing home care for this man's demented wife or even to temporary relief for him.

Thus, we again face the very real possibility that the demented wife is not being abused. Given limited funding, social institutions ought not assume care of this demented woman. So, given the context, this couple is not a victim of social abuse in the moral sense ... unless perhaps by American voters. Since her husband is providing the best care he can for this woman, she is not being abused in the moral sense by him, either.

V. ABUSE, INTERVENTION, AND CONTEXT

Increased attention to the situation and interests of caregivers could I think, yield genuine benefits. I turn now to a few practical implications of a more contextualized discussion of elder abuse.

1. We must sharply distinguish abuse in the moral sense from virtually any list of abusive activities. There will be only an **extremely** short list, if any at all, of activities which are always abusive. The fact that an elderly person is physically pushed into her room and locked there, physically restrained, threatened with physical harm, shouted at and frightened, or even hit does not necessarily mean that she is abused. To find out whether she is abused, we must know much more about the situation.

2. We must also recognize that "abusive activities" are not necessarily signs that genuine care or concern is lacking. Since many apparently abusive activities are not abuse in the moral sense, these activities do not necessarily reflect badly on the intentions or character of the caregiver. Blame and accusations will, in such cases, be inappropriate. Moreover, even if something genuinely is abuse (in the moral sense), it may be that the caregiver should be excused for what she did. We all experience lapses from good behavior even within contexts of genuine care—when we are angry, fatigued, harried or rushed, depressed, or simply frustrated due to lack of time to do what we want. Like the rest of us, caregivers will occasionally do things that are wrong, but for which they should be excused.

Where genuine care is present, it may be possible to help the caregiver to reform or to "do better." But we must also recognize that attempts to get caregivers to reform or to do better may be misguided. The husband in Hudson's story got into trouble because he was already trying to do too much for his wife. But even more important for our purposes, "doing better" would often only require even more heroic sacrifices on the part of caregivers; and that might well mean that their legitimate interests would be even more dramatically short-changed. When this is the case, it may be wrong even to suggest that the caregiver try to do better. Such suggestions may be rightfully resented.

3. If we are to respond effectively to the plight of those who seem to be victims of elder abuse, we must, paradoxically, stop focusing exclusively on harm to them. We must also consider the situation of the caregivers. If we can get some relief for the husband in Hudson's story, it will translate into better conditions for his wife, assuming he still genuinely cares for her. If we cannot get relief for him, no amount of investigation and intervention short of removing her from her home will help her much in the long run.

4. An "abusive" situation may be the best situation available for an elderly person, even if it is occasionally genuinely abusive. Removing "abused" old persons from their abusive environments may be contrary to their interests. If a husband still genuinely cares for his wife, then continuing to live with him may be the best alternative for her, even if she is "abused." After all, he is familiar with her particular desires and emotional responses. For this reason, he may be both willing and able to respond more appropriately to those needs. In their home, he is also much more likely to be there when she needs him than if he must visit her in an institution. For that matter, their home is where she feels at home. Finally, there is genuine personal affirmation in being cared for by those who love us, even if they are sometimes abusive, rather than by paid strangers. In fact, an abusive situation may be the best situation for an old person even in cases that involve physical abuse and the risk of serious bodily injury.

This observation was recently corroborated by a social worker who reported that fear of being removed from their homes is one of the primary reasons elderly people do not report abuse.[7] If she is correct, many old people believe they are better off where they are, their abuse notwithstanding. Moreover, if—as seems likely—social funding for alternatives to home care becomes more skimpy and families must shoulder even more of the burdens of long-term care of the elderly, there will be more and more cases in which an abusive situation is the best available situation for an old person. We must face the fact that this is one of the consequences of our declining willingness to provide a social safety net for people, including the elderly.

5. Since an abusive situation may be the best situation for an elderly person, intervention may be unwarranted in cases of abuse.   Attempts to empower an old person so that she will request intervention may also be misguided. We must face the fact that an elderly person may not be requesting intervention because she quite correctly believes her present situation, abusive though it be, is the best available situation for her. Intervention may thus be paternalism gone awry—paternalism that does not even manage to promote the best interests of the victim. When the abusive situation is the best situation for an old person, if no intervention seems likely to improve that situation, none is warranted.

6. On the policy level, we must break the conceptual connection between intervention and abuse (or neglect).   In many situations, applying the concepts of abuse and neglect will actually be counterproductive. Abuse and neglect are accusations. Good people caught in intolerable situations rightly resent such labels. Those caring for the elderly often need assistance, and we must find ways to help them without resorting to the rationale that we are intervening to protect the elderly from abuse.

7. Those working in social agencies must not see themselves as advocates for the elderly victims.   We must not focus only on harm to the victim of abuse even if our ultimate aim is to help the abused. More basically, our ultimate aim ought not to be simply helping the abused. Instead, those dealing with elder abuse must be sensitive to the needs and interests of all involved, fair-minded about what is reasonable to expect of caregivers in their particular situations, and genuinely interested in designing interventions that would improve the lives of all members of the family. If family caregivers recognized that they and their families were being approached in this fair-minded way, there would be much less resistance to intervention. Indeed, intervention would then normally be welcomed by caregivers as long-sought, much needed assistance.

8. All of the above notwithstanding, there remain genuine cases of inexcusable elder abuse (in the moral sense). Often, even criminal prosecution will be part of the appropriate intervention.   Although my purpose in this paper has been to call attention to a badly neglected "other side of the story," I certainly do not deny that there are also many cases of elder abuse in the moral sense. Caregivers are not all good people stuck in intolerable situations. The variation among caregivers is immense—caregivers (and the elderly) are just about as good and as bad as the rest of us. That is part of the reason we need a contextual account of "elder abuse." Intervention, too, must be tailor-made to the specific situation. Consequently, appropriate intervention cannot always be designed and justified by the one, simple rationale that intervention is needed to stop elder abuse or neglect.

In sum, we need richer, subtler, more contextual (and more complicated!) thinking and policies about "elder abuse." Both in our thinking and in our interventions, we need to contextualize—to consider the situation and intentions of the caregiver, the relationship (including the history of the relationship) between the elderly person and her caregiver, the situation they share, the available alternatives, and much, much more.

A contextualized account is a theoretically more sound account both of what caregivers owe the elderly and of what elder abuse is. It also yields important practical benefits. We must not only sensitize ourselves to the situation of caregivers, but also generate ethical analyses that adequately reflect such sensitivity. We must begin to think in terms of what is fair to all, rather than simply what is best, or merely not harmful, for the elderly. Though the stance of an advocate for the "abused" elderly may seem a noble stance, morally adequate analyses or plans for intervention cannot be generated from an advocacy standpoint. Advocacy in such situations implicitly reduces caregivers to mere means to the ends of the elderly and often one-sidedly misdescribes the moral situation. It also tends to obscure appropriate interventions. All are morally unacceptable.

NOTES

1. M. Hudson, "Expert and Public Perspectives in Defining Elder Abuse and Neglect." *Violence, Neglect, and the Elderly.* Ed. R. B. Edwards & E. E. Bittar. Greenwich, CT. JAI Press; 1996. (pp. 1–21).

2. Murray, T. "Ethical Obligations to the Elderly in a Changing Society." Advances in Bioethics, *Violence, Neglect, and the Elderly.* Ed. R. B. Edwards & E. E. Bittar. Greenwich, CT. JAI Press; 1996. (pp. 139–154).

3. B. Rich, "Elements Compromising the Autonomy of the Elderly." *Violence, Neglect, and the Elderly.* Ed. Edwards, R. B. & Bittar, E. E. Greenwich, CT. JAI Press; 1996. (pp. 57–90).

4. J. Hardwig. "What About the Family?—The Role of Family Interests in Medical Decision Making." *Hastings Center Report* 20 (1990): 5–10.

5. J. Hardwig. "The Problem of Proxies with Interests of Their Own—Toward a Better Theory of Proxy Decisions." *Journal of Clinical Ethics* 4 (1993): 20–27.

6. B. Collopy, N. Dubler, and C. Zuckerman. "The Ethics of Home Care: Autonomy and Accommodation." *Hastings Center Report* 20, special supplement (1990): 1–16.

7. National Public Radio. Morning Edition 5/16/95.

ETHICS AND ALZHEIMER'S DISEASE

Life Past Reason

Ronald Dworkin

We turn finally to what might be the saddest of the tragedies we have been reviewing. We must consider the autonomy and best interests of people who suffer from serious and permanent dementia, and what the proper respect for the intrinsic value of *their* lives requires. The most important cause of dementia is Alzheimer's disease, a progressive disease of the brain named after a German psychiatrist and neuropathologist, Alois Alzheimer, who first identified and described it in 1906. Patients in the late stages of this disease have lost substantially all memory of their earlier lives and cannot, except perodically and in only a fragmented way, recognize or respond to other people, even those to whom they were formerly close. They may be incapable of saying more than a word or two. They are often incontinent, fall frequently, or are unable to walk at all. They are incapable of sustaining plans or projects or desires of even a very simple structure. They express wishes and desires, but these change rapidly and often show very little continuity even over periods of days or hours.

Alzheimer's is a disease of physiological deterioration. Nerve terminals of the brain degenerate into a matted plaque of fibrous material. Though researchers have expressed some hope that treatment can be developed to slow that degeneration,[1] no such treatment has yet been established, and there is apparently little prospect of dramatically reversing very advanced brain deterioration. A specialist describes the degeneration as occurring "gradually and inexorably, usually leading to death in a severely debilitated, immobile state between four and twelve years after onset."[2] But according to the US Office of Technology Assessment, death may be delayed for as long as twenty-five years.[3]

Our discussion will focus only on the disease's late stages. I shall not consider, except in passing, the present structure of legal rights and other provisions for demented or mentally incapacitated people, or the present practices of doctors and other custodians or officials who are charged with their care. Nor shall I attempt any report of the recent research into genetic and other features of such diseases, or into their diagnosis, prognosis, or treatment. All these are the subjects of a full literature.[4] I will concentrate on the question of what moral rights people in the late stages of dementia have or retain, and of what is best for them. Is some minimum level of mental competence essential to having any rights at all? Do mentally incapacitated people have the same rights as normally competent people, or are their rights altered or diminished or extended in some way in virtue of their disease? Do they, for example, have the same rights to autonomy, to the care of their custodians, to dignity, and to a minimum level of resources as sick people of normal mental competence?

These are questions of great and growing importance. In 1990, the Alzheimer's Association estimated that four million Americans had the disease, and as Alzheimer's is a disease of the elderly, the number is expected to increase as the population continues to age. In 1989, a Harvard Medical School study estimated that 11.3 percent of the American population sixty-five or over probably had Alzheimer's. The estimated prevalence increased sharply with age: 16.4 percent of people between seventy-five and eighty-four were estimated to have Alzheimer's, and a stunning 47.55 percent of those over eighty-five.[5] (Other studies, using a narrower definition of the disease, suggest a significantly lesser but still alarming prevalence.[6]) The incidence of the disease is comparable in other countries. According to the Alzheimer's Disease Society in Britain, for example, 20 percent of people over eighty are afflicted, more than half a million people have the disease, and that figure will rise to three-quarters of a million in thirty years.[7] Alzheimer's cost is staggering, both for the community and for individuals. Dennis Selkoe, a leading expert on the disease, said in 1991, "The cost to American society for diagnosing and managing Alzheimer's disease, primarily for custodial care, is currently estimated at more than $80 billion annually."[8] In 1992, the annual cost of nursing home care in the United States for one individual with Alzheimer's ranged from $35,000 to $52,000.[9]

Each of the millions of Alzheimer's cases is horrible, for the victims and for those who love and care for them. A recent book dedicated "to everyone who gives a '36-hour day' to the care of a person with a dementing illness" describes the lives of some of these patients in chilling detail, not just in the final, immobile last stages, but along the way.

> Often, Mary was afraid, a nameless shapeless fear. . . . People came, memories came, and then they slipped away. She could not tell what was reality and what was memory of things past. . . . The tub was a mystery. From day to day she could not remember how to manage the water: sometimes it all ran away, sometimes it kept rising and rising so that she could not stop it. . . . Mary was glad when her family came to visit. Sometimes she remembered their names, more often she did not. . . . She liked it best when they just held her and loved her.
>
> Even though Miss Ramirez had told her sister over and over that today was the day to visit the doctor her sister would not get into the car until she was dragged in, screaming, by two neighbors. All the way to the doctor's office she shouted for help and when she got there she tried to run away.
>
> Mr. Lewis suddenly burst into tears as he tried to tie his shoelaces. He threw the shoes in the wastebasket and locked himself, sobbing, in the bathroom.[10]

When Andrew Firlik was a medical student, he met a fifty-four-year-old Alzheimer's victim whom he called Margo, and he began to visit her daily in her apartment, where she was cared for by an attendant. The apartment had many locks to keep Margo from slipping out at night and wandering in the park in a nightgown, which she had done before. Margo said she knew who Firlik was each time he arrived, but she never used his name and he suspected that this was just politeness. She said she was reading mysteries, but Firlik "noticed that her place in the book jumps randomly from day to day; dozens of pages are dog-eared at any given moment. . . . Maybe she feels good just sitting and humming to herself, rocking back and forth slowly, nodding off liberally, occasionally turning to a fresh page." Margo attended an art class for Alzheimer's victims—they all, including her, painted pretty much the same picture every time, except near the end, just before death, when the pictures became more primitive. Firlik was confused, he said, by the fact that "despite her illness, or maybe somehow because of it, Margo's undeniably one of the happiest people I have ever known." He reports, particularly, her pleasure at eating peanut-butter-and-jelly sandwiches. But, he asks, "When a person can no longer accumulate new memories as the old rapidly fade, what remains? Who is Margo?"[11]

I must now repeat an observation that I have made before: we are considering the rights and interests not of someone who has always been demented, but of someone who was competent in the past. We may therefore think of that person, in considering his rights and interests, in two different ways: as a *demented* person, emphasizing his present situation and capacities, or as a person who has *become* demented, having an eye to the course of his whole life. Does a competent person's right to autonomy include, for example, the power to dictate

that life-prolonging treatment be denied him later, or that funds not be spent on maintaining him in great comfort, even if he, when demented, pleads for it? Should what is done for him then be in his contemporary best interests, to make the rest of his life as pleasant and comfortable as possible, or in the best interests of the person he has been? Suppose a demented patient insists on remaining at home, rather than living in an institution, though this would impose very great burdens on his family, and that we all agree that people lead critically better lives when they are not a serious burden to others. Is it really in his best interests, overall, to allow him to become such a burden?

A person's dignity is normally connected to his capacity for self-respect. Should we care about the dignity of a dementia patient if he himself has no sense of it? That seems to depend on whether his past dignity, as a competent person, is in some way still implicated. If it is, then we may take his former capacity for self-respect as requiring that he be treated with dignity now; we may say that dignity now is necessary to show respect for his life as a whole. Many prominent issues about the rights of the demented, then, depend on how their interests now relate to those of their past, competent selves.[12]

AUTONOMY

It is generally agreed that adult citizens of normal competence have a right to autonomy, that is, a right to make important decisions defining their own lives for themselves. Competent adults are free to make poor investments, provided others do not deceive or withhold information from them, and smokers are allowed to smoke in private, though cigarette advertising must warn them of the dangers of doing so. This autonomy is often at stake in medical contexts.[13] A Jehovah's Witness, for example, may refuse blood transfusions necessary to save his life because transfusions offend his religious convictions. A patient whose life can be saved only if his legs are amputated but who prefers to die soon than to live a life without legs is allowed to refuse the operation. American law generally recognizes a patient's right to autonomy in circumstances like those.[14] But when is that right lost? How far, for example, do mentally incapacitated people have a right to make decisions for themselves that others would deem not in their best interests?[15] Should Mary, the woman who couldn't recognize relatives or manage a tub, be allowed to spend or give away her money as she wishes, or to choose her own doctors, or to refuse prescribed medical treatment, or to decide which relative is appointed as her guardian? Should she be allowed to insist that she be cared for at home, in spite of her family's opinion that she would get better care in an institution?

There may, of course, be some other reason, beyond autonomy, for allowing Mary and other demented people to do as they please. For example, if they are prevented from doing as they wish, they may become so agitated that we do them more harm than good by opposing them, even though the decision they make is not itself in their interests. But do we have reason to respect their decision even when this is not so, even when we think it would be in their best interests, all things considered, to take some decision out of their hands?

We cannot answer that question without reflecting on the point of autonomy, that is, on the question of why we should ever respect the decisions people make when we believe that these are not in their interests. One popular answer might be called the *evidentiary* view: it holds that we should respect the decisions people make for themselves, even when we regard these decisions as imprudent, because each person generally knows what is in his own best interests better than anyone else.[16] Though we often think that someone has made a mistake in judging what is in his own interests, experience teaches us that in most cases we are wrong to think this. So we do better, in the long run, to recognize a general right to autonomy, which we always respect, than by reserving the right to interfere with other people's lives whenever we think they have made a mistake.

If we accepted this evidentiary account of autonomy, we would not extend the right of autonomy to decisions made by the seriously demented, who, having altogether lost the power to appreciate and engage in reasoning and argument, cannot possibly know what is in their own best interests as well as trained specialists, like doctors, can. In some cases, any presumption that demented people know their own interests best would be incoherent: when, for example, as is often the case, their wishes and decisions change radically from one bout of lucidity to another.

But in fact the evidentiary view of autonomy is very far from compelling. For autonomy requires us to allow someone to run his own life even when he behaves in a way that he himself would accept as not at all in his interests.[17] This is sometimes a matter of what philosophers call "weakness of the will." Many people who smoke know that smoking, all things considered, is not in their best interests, but they smoke anyway. If we believe, as we do, that respecting their autonomy means allowing them to act in this way, we cannot accept that the point of autonomy is to protect an agent's welfare. And there are more admirable reasons

for acting against what one believes to be in one's own best interests. Some people refuse needed medical treatment because they believe that other people, who would then have to go without it, need it more. Such people act out of convictions we admire, even if we do not act the same way, and autonomy requires us to respect their decisions. Once again, the supposed explanation of the right to autonomy—that it promotes the welfare of people making apparently imprudent decisions—fails to account for our convictions about when people have that right. All this suggests that the point of autonomy must be, at least to some degree, independent of the claim that a person generally knows his own best interests better than anyone else. And then it would not follow, just because a demented person may well be mistaken about his own best interests, that others are entitled to decide for him. Perhaps the demented have a right to autonomy after all.

But we must try to find another, more plausible account of the point of autonomy, and ask whether the demented would have a right to autonomy according to it. The most plausible alternative emphasizes the integrity rather than the welfare of the choosing agent; the value of autonomy, on this view, derives from the capacity it protects: the capacity to express one's own character—values, commitments, convictions, and critical as well as experiential interests—in the life one leads. Recognizing an individual right of autonomy makes self-creation possible. It allows each of us to be responsible for shaping our lives according to our own coherent or incoherent—but, in any case, distinctive—personality. It allows us to lead our own lives rather than be led along them, so that each of us can be, to the extent a scheme of rights can make this possible, what we have made of ourselves. We allow someone to choose death over radical amputation or a blood transfusion, if that is his informed wish, because we acknowledge his right to a life structured by his own values.

The integrity view of autonomy does not assume that competent people have consistent values or always make consistent choices, or that they always lead structured, reflective lives. It recognizes that people often make choices that reflect weakness, indecision, caprice, or plain irrationality—that some people otherwise fanatical about their health continue to smoke, for example. Any plausible integrity-based theory of autonomy must distinguish between the general point or value of autonomy and its consequences for a particular person on a particular occasion. Autonomy encourages and protects people's general capacity to lead their lives out of a distinctive sense of their own character, a sense of what is important to and for them. Perhaps one principal value of that capacity is realized only when a life does in fact display a general, overall integrity and authenticity. But the right to autonomy protects and encourages the capacity in any event, by allowing people who have it to choose how far and in what form they will seek to realize that aim.

If we accept this integrity-based view of the importance of autonomy, our judgement about whether incapacitated patients have a right to autonomy will turn on the degree of their general capacity to lead a life in that sense. When a mildly demented person's choices are reasonably stable, reasonably continuous with the general character of his prior life, and inconsistent and self-defeating only to the rough degree that the choices of fully competent people are, he can be seen as still in charge of his life, and he has a right to autonomy for that reason. But if his choices and demands, no matter how firmly expressed, systematically or randomly contradict one another, reflecting no coherent sense of self and no discernible even short-term aims, then he has presumably lost the capacity that it is the point of autonomy to protect. Recognizing a continuing right to autonomy for him would be pointless. He has no right that his choices about a guardian (or the use of his property, or his medical treatment, or whether he remains at home) be respected for reasons of autonomy. He still has the right to beneficence, the right that decisions on these matters be made in his best interests; and his preferences may, for different reasons, be important in deciding what his best interests are. But he no longer has the right, as competent people do, himself to decide contrary to those interests.

"Competence" is sometimes used in a task-specific sense, to refer to the ability to grasp and manipulate information bearing on a given problem. Competence in that sense varies, sometimes greatly, even among ordinary, nondemented people; I may be more competent than you at making some decisions and less competent at others. The medical literature concerning surrogate decision making for the demented points out, properly, that competence in this task-specific sense is relative to the character and complexity of the decision in question.[18] A patient who is not competent to administer his complex business affairs may nevertheless be able to grasp and appreciate information bearing on whether he should remain at home or enter an institution, for example.

But competence in the sense in which it is presupposed by the right to autonomy is a very different matter.

It means the more diffuse and general ability I described: the ability to act out of genuine preference or character or conviction or a sense of self. There will, of course, be hard cases in which we cannot know with any confidence whether a particular dementia patient is competent in that sense. But we must make that overall judgement, not some combination of judgements about specific task capability, in order to decide whether some mentally incapacitated patient has a right to autonomy.[19] Patients like Mary have no right that *any* decision be respected just out of concern for their autonomy. That may sound harsh, but it is no kindness to allow a person to take decisions against his own interests in order to protect a capacity he does not and cannot have.

So neither the evidentiary view of autonomy nor the more plausible integrity view recommends any right to autonomy for the seriously demented. But what about a patient's *precedent* autonomy? Suppose a patient is incompetent in the general, overall sense but that years ago, when perfectly competent, he executed a living will providing for what he plainly does not want now. Suppose, for example, that years ago, when fully competent, Margo had executed a formal document directing that if she should develop Alzheimer's disease, all her property should be given to a designated charity so that none of it could be spent on her own care. Or that in that event she should not receive treatment for any other serious, life-threatening disease she might contract. Or even that in that event she should be killed as soon and as painlessly as possible? If Margo had expressed any of those wishes when she was competent, would autonomy then require that they be respected now by those in charge of her care, even though she seems perfectly happy with her dog-eared mysteries, the single painting she repaints, and her peanut-butter-and-jelly sandwiches?

If we had accepted the evidentiary view of autonomy, we would find the case for respecting Margo's past directions very weak. People are not the best judges of what their own best interests would be under circumstances they have never encountered and in which their preferences and desires may drastically have changed. But if we accept the integrity view, we will be drawn to the view that Margo's past wishes must be respected. A competent person making a living will providing for his treatment if he becomes demented is making exactly the kind of judgement that autonomy, on the integrity view, most respects: a judgement about the overall shape of the kind of life he wants to have led.

This conclusion is troubling, however, even shocking, and someone might want to resist it by insisting that the right to autonomy is *necessarily* contemporary: that a person's right to autonomy is only a right that his present decisions, not past ones that he has since disowned, be respected. Certainly that is the normal force of recognizing autonomy. Suppose that a Jehovah's Witness has signed a formal document stipulating that he is not to receive blood transfusions even if out of weakness of will he requests one when he would otherwise die. He wants, like Ulysses, to be tied to the mast of his faith. But when the moment comes, and he needs a transfusion, he pleads for it. We would not think ourselves required, out of respect for his autonomy, to disregard his contemporary plea.

We can interpret that example in different ways, though, and the difference is crucial for our present problem. We might say, first, that the Witness's later plea countermanded his original decision because it expressed a more contemporary desire. That presumes that it is only right to defer to past decisions when we have reason to believe that the agent still wishes what he wanted then. On that view, precedent autonomy is an illusion: we treat a person's past decision as important only because it is normally evidence of his present wishes, and we disregard it entirely when we know that it is not. On the other hand, we might say that the Witness's later plea countermanded his original decision because it was a fresh exercise of his autonomy, and that disregarding it would be treating him as no longer in charge of his own life. The difference between these two views about the force of precedent autonomy is crucial when someone changes his mind *after* he has become incompetent—that is, when the conditions of autonomy no longer hold. Suppose that the same accident that made a transfusion medically necessary for the Witness also deranged him, and that while still plainly deranged he demands the transfusion. On the first view, we would not violate his autonomy by administering it, but on the second, we would.

Which of the two views about the force of past decisions is more persuasive? Suppose we were confident that the deranged Witness, were he to receive the transfusion and live, would become competent again and be appalled at having had a treatment he believed worse for him than dying. In those circumstances, I believe, we would violate his autonomy by giving him the transfusion. That argues for the second view about the force of past decisions, the view that endorses precedent autonomy as genuine. We refuse to give the deranged Witness a transfusion not because we think he really continues to want what he wanted before—this is not like a case in which someone who objects to a given

treatment is unconscious when he needs it—but because he lacks the necessary capacity for a fresh exercise of autonomy. His former decision remains in force because no new decision by a person capable of autonomy has annulled it.

Someone might say that we are justified in withholding the transfusion only because we know that the Witness would regret the transfusion if he recovered. But that prediction would make no difference if he was fully competent when he asked for the transfusion and desperate to live at that moment, though very likely to change his mind again and be appalled tomorrow at what he has done. Surely we should accede to his request in those circumstances. What makes the difference, when we are deciding whether to honor someone's plea even though it contradicts his past deep convictions, is whether he is now competent to make a decision of that character, not whether he will regret making it later.

Our argument for the integrity view, then, supports a genuine doctrine of precedent autonomy. A competent person's right to autonomy requires that his past decisions about how he is to be treated if he becomes demented be respected even if they contradict the desires he has at that later point. If we refuse to respect Margo's precedent autonomy—if we refuse to respect her past decisions, though made when she was competent, because they do not match her present, incompetent wishes—then we are violating her autonomy on the integrity view. This conclusion has great practical importance. Competent people who are concerned about the end of their lives will naturally worry about how they might be treated if they become demented. Someone anxious to ensure that his life is not then prolonged by medical treatment is worried precisely because he thinks that the character of his whole life would be compromised if it were. He is in the same position as people who sign living wills asking not to be kept alive in a hopeless medical condition or when permanently vegetative. If we respect *their* past requests, as the Supreme Court has decided American states must do then we have the same reasons for respecting the wishes not to be kept alive of someone who dreads not unconsciousness but dementia.

The argument has very troubling consequences however. The medical student who observed Margo said that her life was the happiest he knew. Should we really deny a person like that the routine medical care needed to keep her alive. Could we ever conceivably *kill* her? We might consider it morally unforgivable not to try to save the life of someone who plainly enjoys her life, no matter how demented she is, and we might think beyond imagining that we should actually kill her. We might hate living in a community whose officials might make or license either of those decisions. We might have other good reasons for treating Margo as she now wishes, rather than as in my imaginary case, she once asked. But still that violates rather than respects her autonomy.

NOTES

1. Doctors are now investigating treatments that include reducing the presence in the brain of toxic substances that may play a role in neurodegeneration, enhancing the supply of trophic factors (which facilitate neuronal repair and growth) and neurotransmitters that are missing or deficient in Alzheimer's patients, and controlling diet-related factors such as blood glucose levels that appear to affect mental functioning in the elderly. See Dennis J. Selkoe, "Aging Brain, Aging Mind," *Scientific American*, 135 (September 1992); Robert J. Joynt, "Neurology," *Journal of the American Medical Association*, 268 (1992), 380; and Andrew A. Skolnick, "Brain Researchers Bullish on Prospects for Preserving Mental Functioning in the Elderly." *Journal of the American Medical Association*, 267 (1992), 2154.

2. Selkoe, "Amyloid Protein and Alzheimer's Disease," *Scientific American* (November 1991), 68.

3. OTA document. "Losing a Million Minds." OTA-BA-323 (1987), 14.

4. Legal provision and practices of custodial care are discussed in several of the papers contained in the OTA document, "Losing a Million Minds." For discussions of clinical diagnosis and histopathology, see, for example, Guy McKhann et al., "Clinical Diagnosis of Alzheimer's Disease: Report of the NINCDS-ADRDA Work Group Under the Auspices of Department of Health and Human Services Task Force on Alzheimer's Disease," *Neurology*, 34 (1984), 939; Christine M. Holette et al., "Evaluation of Cerebral Biopsies for the Diagnosis of Dementia." *Archives of Neurology*, 49 (1992), 28; Selkoe, "Amyloid Protein and Alzheimer's Disease"; and M. Farlow et al., "Low Cerebrospinal-fluid Concentrations of Soluble Amyloid β-protein Precursor in Hereditary Alzheimer's Disease," *The Lancet*, 340 (1992), 453.

5. Evans et al., "Estimated Prevalence of Alzheimer's Disease in the United States," *Milbank Quarterly*, 68 (1990), 267.

6. In 1992, the continuing Framingham Study determined the prevalence of dementia in its study cohort as 23.8 percent from ages eighty-five to ninety-three. See Bachman et al., "Prevalence of Dementia and Probable Senile Dementia of the Alzheimer Type in the Framingham Study," *Neurology*, 42 (January 1992), 42. For a discussion of the differences between the studies cited in this and the preceding note, see Selkoe, "Aging Brain, Aging Mind."

7. See "UK: Dementia Condition Alzheimer's Disease Will Hit 750,000 in 30 Years," *The Guardian*, July 6, 1992.

8. Selkoe, "Amyloid Protein and Alzheimer's Disease," 68.

9. See Abstract, *Journal of the American Medical Association*, 267 (May 27, 1992), 2809 (summarizing Welch et al., "The Cost of Institutional Care in Alzheimer's Disease," *Journal of the American Geriatric Society*, 40 [1992], 221).

10. Nancy L. Mace and Peter V. Rabins, *The 36-Hour Day: A Family Guide to Caring for Persons with Alzheimer's Disease. Related Dementing Illnesses, and Memory Loss in Later Life* (Baltimore: Johns Hopkins University Press, 1981, 1991).

11. See Andrew D. Firlik, "Margo's Logo," *Journal of the American Medical Association*, 265 (1991), 201.

12. I should mention another great practical problem about the relationship between a demented person and the competent person he once was. Should the resources available to a demented patient depend on what he actually put aside when he was competent, by way of insurance for his own care in that event? Insurance schemes, both private schemes and mandated public schemes, play an important part in the way we provide resources for catastrophes of different sorts. But is the insurance approach the proper model to use in thinking about provision for the demented? That must depend on whether we believe that a competent person has the appropriate prudential concern for the incompetent person he might become, and that in turn depends on knotty philosophical problems about the concept of personal identity. I cannot discuss, in this book, either that philosophical problem or any of the other serious problems about the justice of financing the extraordinarily expensive care of demented patients in different ways. I have discussed both at some length, however, in a report. "Philosophical Problems of Senile Dementia," written for the United States Congress Office of Technology Assessment in Washington, DC, and available from that office.

13. See discussion in Allen E. Buchanan et al., "Surrogate Decision-Making for Elderly Individuals Who Are Incompetent or of Questionable Competence," November 1985, a report prepared for the Office of Technology Assessment.

14. See George J. Annas and Leonard H. Glantz, "Withholding and Withdrawing of Life-Sustaining Treatment for Elderly Incompetent Patients. A Review of Appellate Court Decisions," September 16, 1985, a report prepared for the Office of Technology Assessment.

15. I am assuming, in this discussion, that it can be in a person's overall best interests, at least sometimes, to force him to act otherwise than as he wants—that it can be in a person's overall best interests, for example, to be made not to smoke, even if we acknowledge that his autonomy is to some degree compromised, considered in itself, as against his interests.

16. Buchanan et al., "Surrogate Decision-Making."

17. There is an important debate in the economic literature on the question of whether it can be rational to act against one's own best interests. The better view is that it can. See, for example, Amartya Sen, "Rational Fools: A Critique of the Behavioral Foundations of Economic Theory," *Philosophy and Public Affairs*, 6, no. 4 (Summer 1977).

18. See Buchanan et al., "Surrogate Decision-making." Questions of task-sensitive competence are plainly relevant to the issues considered in the Buchanan report. But when the argument against surrogate decision making relies on the autonomy of the demented person affected by these ideas, the overall, non-task-sensitive sense of competence is also relevant.

19. Problems are presented for this judgement of overall integrity capacity when a patient appears only periodically capable of organizing his life around a system of desires and wishes. He seems able to take command of his life sometimes, and then lapses into a more serious stage of dementia, becoming lucid again only after a substantial intervening period, at which time the desires and interests he expresses are very different, or even contradictory. It would be a mistake to say that such a patient has the capacity for autonomy "periodically." The capacity autonomy presupposes is of necessity a temporally extended capacity: it is the capacity to have and act out of a personality.

Dworkin on Dementia: Elegant Theory, Questionable Policy

Rebecca Dresser

In his most recent book, *Life's Dominion: An Argument About Abortion, Euthanasia, and Individual Freedom*,[1] Ronald Dworkin offers a new way of interpreting disagreements over abortion and euthanasia. In doing so, he enriches and refines our understanding of three fundamental bioethical concepts: autonomy, beneficence, and sanctity of life. It is exciting that this eminent legal philosopher has turned his attention to bioethical issues. *Life's Dominion* is beautifully and persuasively written; its clear language and well-constructed arguments are especially welcome in this age of inaccessible, jargon-laden academic writing. *Life's Dominion* also is full of rich and provocative ideas; in this article, I address only Dworkin's remarks on euthanasia, although I will refer to his views on abortion when they are relevant to my analysis.

Professor Dworkin considers decisions to hasten death with respect to three groups: (1) competent and seriously ill people; (2) permanently unconscious people; and (3) conscious, but incompetent people, specifically, those with progressive and incurable dementia. My remarks focus on the third group, which I have addressed in previous work,[2] and which in my view poses the most difficult challenge for policymakers.

I present Dworkin's and my views as a debate over how we should think about Margo. Margo is described by Andrew Firlik, a medical student, in a *Journal of the American Medical Association* column called "A Piece of My Mind."[3] Firlik met Margo, who has Alzheimer disease, when he was enrolled in a gerontology elective. He began visiting her each day, and came to know something about her life with dementia.

Upon arriving at Margo's apartment (she lived at home with the help of an attendant), Firlik often found Margo reading; she told him she especially enjoyed mysteries, but he noticed that "her place in the book jumped randomly from day to day." "For Margo," Firlik wonders, "is reading always a mystery?" Margo never called her new friend by name, though she claimed she knew who he was and always seemed pleased to see him. She liked listening to music and was happy listening to the same song repeatedly, apparently relishing it as if hearing it for the first time. Whenever she heard a certain song, however, she smiled and told Firlik that it reminded her of her deceased husband. She painted, too, but like the other Alzheimer patients in her art therapy class, she created the same image day after day: "a drawing of four circles, in soft rosy colors, one inside the other."

The drawing enabled Firlik to understand something that previously had mystified him:

> Despite her illness, or maybe somehow because of it, Margo is undeniably one of the happiest people I have known. There is something graceful about the degeneration her mind is undergoing, leaving her carefree, always cheerful. Do her problems, whatever she may perceive them to be, simply fail to make it to the worry centers of her brain? How does Margo maintain her sense of self? When a person can no longer accumulate new memories as the old rapidly fade, what remains? Who is Margo?

Firlik surmises that the drawing represented Margo's expression of her mind, her identity, and that by repeating the drawing, she was reminding herself and others of that identity. The painting was Margo, "plain and contained, smiling in her peaceful, demented state."

In *Life's Dominion*, Dworkin considers Margo as a potential subject of his approach. In one variation, he asks us to suppose that

> years ago, when fully competent, Margo had executed a formal document directing that if she should develop Alzheimer's disease . . . she should not receive treatment for any other serious, life-threatening disease she might contract. Or even that in that event she should be killed as soon and as painlessly as possible. (p. 226)

He presents an elegant and philosophically sophisticated argument for giving effect to her prior wishes, despite the value she appears to obtain from her life as an individual with dementia.

Dworkin's position emerges from his inquiry into the values of autonomy, beneficence, and sanctity of life. To understand their relevance to a case such as Margo's, he writes, we must first think about why we care about how we die. And to understand that phenomenon, we must understand why we care about how we live. Dworkin believes our lives are guided by the desire to advance two kinds of interests. Experiential interests are those we share to some degree with all sentient creatures. In Dworkin's words:

> We all do things bemuse we like the experience of doing them: playing softball, perhaps, or cooking and eating well, or watching football, or seeing Casablanca for the twelfth time, or walking in the woods in October, or listening to The Marriage of Figaro, or sailing fast just off the wind, or just working hard at something. Pleasures like these are essential to a good life—a life with nothing that is marvelous only because of how it feels would be not pure but preposterous. (p. 201)

But Dworkin deems these interests less important than the second sort of interests we possess. Dworkin argues that we also seek to satisfy our critical interests, which are the hopes and aims that lend genuine meaning and coherence to our lives. We pursue projects such as establishing close friendships, achieving competence in our work, and raising children, not simply because we want the positive experiences they offer, but also because we believe we should want them, because our lives as a whole will be better if we take up these endeavors.

Dworkin admits that not everyone has a conscious sense of the interests they deem critical to their lives, but he thinks that "even people whose lives feel unplanned are nevertheless often guided by a sense of the general style of life they think appropriate, of what choices strike them as not only good at the moment but in character for them" (p. 202). In this tendency, Dworkin sees us aiming for the ideal of integrity, seeking to create a coherent narrative structure for the lives we lead.

Our critical interests explain why many of us care about how the final chapter of our lives turns out. Although some of this concern originates in the desire to avoid experiential burdens, as well as burdens on our families, much of it reflects the desire to escape dying under circumstances that are out of character with the prior stages of our lives. For most people, Dworkin writes, death has a "special, symbolic importance: they want their deaths, if possible, to express and in that way vividly to confirm the values they believe most important to their lives" (p. 211). And because critical interests are so personal and widely varied among individuals, each person must have the right to control the manner in which life reaches its conclusion. Accordingly, the state should refrain from imposing a "uniform, general view [of appropriate end-of-life-care] by way of sovereign law" (p. 213).

Dworkin builds on this hierarchy of human interests to defend his ideas about how autonomy and beneficence should apply to someone like Margo. First,

he examines the generally accepted principle that we should in most circumstances honor the competent person's autonomous choice. One way to justify this principle is to claim that people generally know better than anyone else what best serves their interests; thus, their own choices are the best evidence we have of the decision that would most protect their welfare. Dworkin labels this the evidentiary view of autonomy. But Dworkin believes the better explanation for the respect we accord to individual choice lies in what he calls the integrity view of autonomy. In many instances, he contends, we grant freedom to people to act in ways that clearly conflict with their own best interests. We do this, he argues, because we want to let people "lead their lives out of a distinctive sense of their own character, a sense of what is important to them" (p. 224). The model once again assigns the greatest moral significance to the individual's critical interests, as opposed to the less important experiential interests that also contribute to a person's having a good life.

The integrity view of autonomy partially accounts for Dworkin's claim that we should honor Margo's prior choice to end her life if she developed Alzheimer disease. In making this choice, she was exercising, in Dworkin's phrase, her "precedent autonomy" (p. 226). The evidentiary view of autonomy fails to supply support for deferring to the earlier decision, Dworkin observes, because "[p]eople are not the best judges of what their own best interests would be under circumstances they have never encountered and in which their preferences and desires may drastically have changed" (p. 226). He readily admits that Andrew Firlik and others evaluating Margo's life with dementia would perceive a conflict between her prior instructions and her current welfare. But the integrity view of autonomy furnishes compelling support for honoring Margo's advance directives. Margo's interest in living her life in character includes an interest in controlling the circumstances in which others should permit her life as an Alzheimer patient to continue. Limiting that control would in Dworkin's view be "an unacceptable form of moral paternalism" (p. 231).

Dworkin finds additional support for assigning priority to Margo's former instructions in the moral principle of beneficence. People who are incompetent to exercise autonomy have a right to beneficence from those entrusted to decide on their behalf. The best interests standard typically has been understood to require the decision that would best protect the incompetent individual's current welfare.[4] On this view, the standard would support some (though not necessarily all) life-extending decisions that depart from Margo's prior directives. But Dworkin invokes his concept of critical interests to construct a different best interests standard. Dworkin argues that Margo's critical interests persist, despite her current inability to appreciate them. Because critical interests have greater moral significance than the experiential interests Margo remains able to appreciate, and because "we must judge Margo's critical interests as she did when competent to do so" (p. 231), beneficence requires us to honor Margo's prior preferences for death. In Dworkin's view, far from providing a reason to override Margo's directives, compassion counsels us to follow them, for it is compassion "toward the whole person" that underlines the duty of beneficence (p. 232).

To honor the narrative that is Margo's life, then, we must honor her earlier choices. A decision to disregard them would constitute unjustified paternalism and would lack mercy as well. Dworkin concedes that such a decision might be made for other reasons—because we "find ourselves unable to deny medical help to anyone who is conscious and does not reject it" (p. 232), or deem it "morally unforgiveable not to try to save the life of someone who plainly enjoys her life" (p. 228), or find it "beyond imagining that we should actually kill her" (p. 228), or "hate living in a community whose officials might make or license either of [Margo's] decisions" (pp. 228–29). Dworkin does not explicitly address whether these or other aspects of the state's interest in protecting life should influence legal policy governing how people like Margo are treated.

Dworkin pays much briefer attention to Margo's fate in the event that she did not explicitly register her preferences about future treatment. Most incompetent patients are currently in this category, for relatively few people complete formal advance treatment directives.[5] In this scenario, the competent Margo failed to declare her explicit wishes, and her family is asked to determine her fate. Dworkin suggests that her relatives may give voice to Margo's autonomy by judging what her choice would have been if she had thought about it, based on her character and personality. Moreover, similar evidence enables them to determine her best interests, for it is her critical interests that matter most in reaching this determination. If Margo's dementia set in before she explicitly indicated her preferences about future care, "the law should so far as possible leave decisions in the hands of [her] relatives or other people close to [her] whose sense of [her] best interests . . . is likely to be much sounder than some universal, theoretical, abstract judgment" produced through the political process (p. 213).

Life's Dominion helps to explain why the "death with dignity" movement has attracted such strong support in the United States. I have no doubt that many people share Dworkin's conviction that they ought to have the power to choose death over life in Margo's state. But I am far from convinced of the wisdom or morality of these proposals for dementia patients.

ADVANCE DIRECTIVES AND PRECEDENT AUTONOMY

First, an observation. Dworkin makes an impressive case that the power to control one's future as an incompetent patient is a precious freedom that our society should go to great lengths to protect. But how strongly do people actually value this freedom? Surveys show that a relatively small percentage of the U.S. population engages in end-of-life planning, and that many in that group simply designate a trusted relative or friend to make future treatment decisions, choosing not to issue specific instructions on future care.[7] Though this widespread failure to take advantage of the freedom to exercise precedent autonomy may be attributed to a lack of publicity or inadequate policy support for advance planning, it could also indicate that issuing explicit instructions to govern the final chapter of one's life is not a major priority for most people. If it is not, then we may question whether precedent autonomy and the critical interests it protects should be the dominant model for our policies on euthanasia for incompetent people.

Dworkin constructs a moral argument for giving effect to Margo's directives, but does not indicate how his position could be translated into policy. Consider how we might approach this task. We would want to devise procedures to ensure that people issuing such directives were competent, their actions voluntary, and their decisions informed. In other medical settings, we believe that a person's adequate understanding of the information relevant to treatment decisionmaking is a prerequisite to the exercise of true self-determination. We should take the same view of Margo's advance planning.

What would we want the competent Margo to understand before she chose death over life in the event of dementia? At a minimum, we would want her to understand that the experience of dementia differs among individuals, that for some it appears to be a persistently frightening and unhappy existence, but that most people with dementia do not exhibit the distress and misery we competent people tend to associate with the condition. I make no claims to expertise in this area, but my reading and discussions with clinicians, caregivers, and patients themselves suggest that the subjective experience of dementia is more positive than most of us would expect. Some caregivers and other commentators also note that patients' quality of life is substantially dependent on their social and physical environments, as opposed to the neurological condition itself.[8] Thus, the "tragedy" and "horror" of dementia is partially attributable to the ways in which others respond to people with this condition.

We also would want Margo to understand that Alzheimer disease is a progressive condition, and that options for forgoing life-sustaining interventions will arise at different points in the process. Dworkin writes that his ideas apply only to the late stages of Alzheimer disease, but he makes implementation of Margo's former wishes contingent on the mere development of the condition (pp. 210, 226). If we were designing policy, we would want to ensure that competent individuals making directives knew something about the general course of the illness and the points at which various capacities are lost. We would want them to be precise about the behavioral indications that should trigger the directive's implementation. We would want them to think about what their lives could be like at different stages of the disease, and about how invasive and effective various possible interventions might be. We would want to give them the opportunity to talk with physicians, caregivers, and individuals diagnosed with Alzheimer disease, and perhaps, to discuss their potential choices with a counselor.

The concern for education is one that applies to advance treatment directives generally, but one that is not widely recognized or addressed at the policy level. People complete advance directives in private, perhaps after discussion with relatives, physicians, or attorneys, but often with little understanding of the meaning or implications of their decisions. In one study of dialysis patients who had issued instructions on treatment in the event of advanced Alzheimer disease, a subsequent inquiry revealed that almost two-thirds of them wanted families and physicians to have some freedom to override the directives to protect their subsequent best interests. The patients' failure to include this statement in their directives indicates that the instructions they recorded did not reflect their actual preferences. A survey of twenty-nine people participating in an advance care planning workshop found ten agreeing with both of the following inconsistent statements: "I would never want to be on a respirator in an intensive care unit"; and "If a short period of extremely intensive medical care could return me to near-normal condition, I would want it"[9] Meanwhile, some promoters of advance care planning

have claimed that subjects can complete directives during interviews lasting fifteen minutes.[10]

We do not advance people's autonomy by giving effect to choices that originate in insufficient or mistaken information. Indeed, interference in such choices is often considered a form of justified paternalism. Moreover, advance planning for future dementia treatment is more complex than planning for other conditions, such as permanent unconsciousness. Before implementing directives to hasten death in the event of dementia, we should require people to exhibit a reasonable understanding of the choices they are making.[11]

Some shortcomings of advance planning are insurmountable, however. People exercising advance planning are denied knowledge of treatments and other relevant information that may emerge during the time between making a directive and giving it effect. Opportunities for clarifying misunderstandings are truncated, and decisionmakers are not asked to explain or defend their choices to the clinicians, relatives, and friends whose care and concern may lead depressed or imprudent individuals to alter their wishes.[12] Moreover, the rigid adherence to advance planning Dworkin endorses leaves no room for the changes of heart that can lead us to deviate from our earlier choices. All of us are familiar with decisions we have later come to recognize as ill-suited to our subsequent situations. As Dworkin acknowledges, people may be mistaken about their future experiential interests as incompetent individuals. A policy of absolute adherence to advance directives means that we deny people like Margo the freedom we enjoy as competent people to change our decisions that conflict with our subsequent experiential interests.[13]

Personal identity theory, which addresses criteria for the persistence of a particular person over time, provides another basis for questioning precedent autonomy's proper moral and legal authority. In *Life's Dominion*, Dworkin assumes that Margo the dementia patient is the same person who issued the earlier requests to die, despite the drastic psychological alteration that has occurred. Indeed, the legitimacy of the precedent autonomy model absolutely depends on this view of personal identity. Another approach to personal identity would challenge this judgment, however. On this view, substantial memory loss and other psychological changes may produce a new person, whose connection to the earlier one could be less strong, indeed, could be no stronger than that between you and me.[14] Subscribers to this view of personal identity can argue that Margo's earlier choices lack moral authority to control what happens to Margo the dementia patient. These shortcomings of the advance decisionmaking process are reasons to assign less moral authority to precedent autonomy than to contemporaneous autonomy. I note that Dworkin himself may believe in at least one limit on precedent autonomy in medical decisionmaking. He writes that people "who are repelled by the idea of living demented, totally dependent lives, speaking gibberish," ought to be permitted to issue advance directives "stipulating that if they become permanently and seriously demented, and then develop a serious illness, they should not be given medical treatment except to avoid pain" (p. 231). Would he oppose honoring a request to avoid all medical treatment, including pain-relieving measures, that was motivated by religious or philosophical concerns? The above remark suggests that he might give priority to Margo's existing experiential interests in avoiding pain over her prior exercise of precedent autonomy. In my view, this would be a justified limit on precedent autonomy, but I would add others as well.

CRITICAL AND EXPERIENTIAL INTERESTS: PROBLEMS WITH THE MODEL

What if Margo, like most other people, failed to exercise her precedent autonomy through making an advance directive? In this situation, her surrogate decisionmakers are to apply Dworkin's version of the best interests standard. Should they consider, first and foremost, the critical interests she had as a competent person? I believe not, for several reasons. First, Dworkin's approach to the best interests standard rests partially on the claim that people want their lives to have narrative coherence. Dworkin omits empirical support for this claim, and my own observations lead me to wonder about its accuracy. The people of the United States are a diverse group, holding many different world views. Do most people actually think as Dworkin says they do? If I were to play psychologist, my guess would be that many people take life one day at a time. The goal of establishing a coherent narrative may be a less common life theme than the simple effort to accept and adjust to the changing natural and social circumstances that characterize a person's life. It also seems possible that people generally fail to draw a sharp line between experiential and critical interests, often choosing the critical projects Dworkin describes substantially because of the rewarding experiences they provide.

Suppose Margo left no indication of her prior wishes, but that people close to her believe it would be in her critical interests to die rather than live on in her current condition. Dworkin notes, but fails to address, the argument that "in the circumstances of dementia, critical interests become less important and experiential interests more so, so that fiduciaries may rightly ignore the former and concentrate on the latter" (p. 232). Happy and contented Margo will experience clear harm from the decision that purports to advance the critical interests she no longer cares about. This seems to me justification for a policy against active killing or withholding effective, nonburdensome treatments, such as antibiotics, from dementia patients whose lives offer them the sorts of pleasures and satisfactions Margo enjoys. Moreover, if clear evidence is lacking on Margo's own view of her critical interests, a decision to hasten her death might actually conflict with the life narrative she envisioned for herself. Many empirical studies have shown that families often do not have a very good sense of their relatives' treatment preferences.[15] How will Margo's life narrative be improved by her family's decision to hasten death, if there is no clear indication that she herself once took that view?

I also wonder about how to apply a best interests standard that assigns priority to the individual's critical interests. Dworkin writes that family members and other intimates applying this standard should decide based on their knowledge of "the shape and character of [the patient's] life and his own sense of integrity and critical interests" (p. 213). What sorts of life narratives would support a decision to end Margo's life? What picture of her critical interests might her family cite as justification for ending her life now? Perhaps Margo had been a famous legal philosopher whose intellectual pursuits were of utmost importance to her. This fact might flit toward a decision to spare her from an existence in which she can only pretend to read. But what if she were also the mother of a mentally retarded child, whom she had cared for at home? What if she had enjoyed and valued this child's simple, experiential life, doing everything she could to protect and enhance it? How would this information affect the interpretation of her critical interests as they bear on her own life with dementia?

I am not sure whether Dworkin means to suggest that Margo's relatives should have complete discretion in evaluating considerations such as these. Would he permit anyone to challenge the legitimacy of a narrative outcome chosen by her family? What if her closest friends believed that a different conclusion would be more consistent with the way she had constructed her life? And is there any room in Dworkin's scheme for surprise endings? Some of our greatest fictional characters evolve into figures having little resemblance to the persons we met in the novels' opening chapters. Are real-life characters such as the fiercely independent intellectual permitted to become people who appreciate simple experiential pleasures and accept their dependence on others?

Finally, is the goal of respecting individual differences actually met by Dworkin's best interests standard? Although Dworkin recognizes that some people believe their critical interests would be served by a decision to extend their lives as long as is medically possible (based on their pro-life values), at times he implies that such individuals are mistaken about their genuine critical interests, that in actuality no one's critical interests could be served by such a decision. For example, he writes that after the onset of dementia, nothing of value can be added to a person's life, because the person is no longer capable of engaging in the activities necessary to advance her critical interests (p. 230). A similar judgment is also evident in his discussion of an actual case of a brain-damaged patient who "did not seem to be in pain or unhappy," and "recognized familiar faces with apparent pleasure" (p. 233). A court-appointed guardian sought to have the patient's life-prolonging medication withheld, but the family was strongly opposed to this outcome, and a judge denied the guardian's request. In a remark that seems to conflict with his earlier support for family decisionmaking, Dworkin questions whether the family's choice was in the patient's best interests (p. 233). These comments lead me to wonder whether Dworkin's real aim is to defend an objective nontreatment standard that should be applied to all individuals with significant mental impairment, not just those whose advance directives or relatives support a decision to hasten death. If so, then he needs to provide additional argument for this more controversial position.

THE STATE'S INTEREST IN MARGO'S LIFE

My final thoughts concern Dworkin's argument that the state has no legitimate reason to interfere with Margo's directives or her family's best interests judgment to end her life. A great deal of Life's Dominion addresses the intrinsic value of human life and the nature of the state's interest in protecting that value. Early in the book, Dworkin defends the familiar view that only conscious individuals can possess interests in not being destroyed or otherwise harmed. On this view, until the advent of sentience and other capacities, human fetuses lack interests of their own that would

support a state policy restricting abortion. A policy that restricted abortion prior to this point would rest on what Dworkin calls a detached state interest in protecting human life. Conversely, a policy that restricts abortion after fetal sentience (which coincides roughly with viability) is supported by the state's derivative interest in valuing life, so called because it derives from the fetus's own interests (pp. 10–24, 168–70). Dworkin believes that detached state interests in ensuring respect for the value of life justify state prohibitions on abortion only after pregnant women are given a reasonable opportunity to terminate an unwanted pregnancy. Prior to this point, the law should permit women to make decisions about pregnancy according to their own views on how best to respect the value of life. After viability, however, when fetal neurological development is sufficiently advanced to make sentience possible, the state may severely limit access to abortion, based on its legitimate role in protecting creatures capable of having interests of their own (pp 168–70).

Dworkin's analysis of abortion provides support, in my view, for a policy in which the state acts to protect the interests of conscious dementia patients like Margo. Although substantially impaired, Margo retains capacities for pleasure, enjoyment, interaction, relationships, and so forth. I believe her continued ability to participate in the life she is living furnishes a defensible basis for state limitations on the scope of her precedent autonomy, as well as on the choices her intimates make on her behalf. Contrary to Dworkin, I believe that such moral paternalism is justified when dementia patients have a quality of life comparable to Margo's. I am not arguing that all directives regarding dementia care should be overridden, nor that family choices should always be disregarded. I think directives and family choices should control in the vast majority of cases, for such decisions rarely are in clear conflict with the patient's contemporaneous interests. But I believe that state restriction is justified when a systematic evaluation by clinicians and others involved in patient care produces agreement that a minimally intrusive life-sustaining intervention is likely to preserve the life of someone as contented and active as Margo.

Many dementia patients do not fit Margo's profile. Some are barely conscious, others appear frightened, miserable, and unresponsive to efforts to mitigate their pain. Sometimes a proposed life-sustaining treatment will be invasive and immobilizing, inflicting extreme terror on patients unable to understand the reasons for their burdens. In such cases, it is entirely appropriate to question the justification for treatment, and often to withhold it, as long as the patient can be kept comfortable in its absence. This approach assumes that observers can accurately assess the experiential benefits and burdens of patients with neurological impairments and decreased ability to communicate. I believe that such assessments are often possible, and that there is room for a great deal of improvement in meeting this challenge.

I also believe that the special problems inherent in making an advance decision about active euthanasia justify a policy of refusing to implement such decisions, at the very least until we achieve legalization for competent patients without unacceptable rates of error and abuse.[16] I note as well the likely scarcity of health care professionals who would be willing to participate in decisions to withhold simple and effective treatments from someone in Margo's condition, much less to give her a lethal injection, even if this were permitted by law. Would Dworkin support a system that required physicians and nurses to compromise their own values and integrity so that Margo's precedent autonomy and critical interests could be advanced? I seriously doubt that many health professionals would agree to implement his proposals regarding dementia patients whose lives are as happy as Margo's.

We need community reflection on how we should think about people with dementia, including our possible future selves. Dworkin's model reflects a common response to the condition: tragic, horrible, degrading, humiliating, to be avoided at all costs. But how much do social factors account for this tragedy? Two British scholars argue that though we regard dementia patients as "the problem," the patients are rather less of a problem than we. They are generally more authentic about what they are feeling and doing; many of the polite veneers of earlier life have been stripped away. They are clearly dependent on others, and usually come to accept that dependence; whereas many "normal" people, living under an ideology of extreme individualism, strenuously deny their dependency needs. They live largely in the present, because certain parts of their memory function have failed. We often find it very difficult to live in the present, suffering constant distraction; the sense of the present is often contaminated by regrets about the past and fears about the future.[17]

If we were to adopt an alternative to the common vision of dementia, we might ask ourselves what we could do, how we could alter our own responses so that people with dementia may find that life among us need not be so terrifying and frustrating. We might ask ourselves what sorts of environments, interactions, and relationships would enhance their lives.

Such a "disability perspective" on dementia offers a more compassionate, less rejecting approach to people with the condition than a model insisting that we should be permitted to order ourselves killed if this "saddest of the tragedies" (p. 218) should befall us. It supports as well a care and treatment policy centered on the conscious incompetent patient's subjective reality; one that permits death when the experiential burdens of continued life are too heavy or the benefits too minimal, but seeks to delay death when the patient's subjective existence is as positive as Margo's appears to be. Their loss of higher-level intellectual capacities ought not to exclude people like Margo from the moral community nor from the law's protective reach, even when the threats to their well-being emanate from their own former preferences. Margo's connections to us remain sufficiently strong that we owe her our concern and respect in the present. Eventually, the decision to allow her to die will be morally defensible. It is too soon, however, to exclude her from our midst.

REFERENCES

1. Ronald Dworkin, *Life's Dominion: An Argument About Abortion, Euthanasia, and Individual Freedom* (New York: Alfred A. Knopf, 1993).

2. See, for example, Rebecca Dresser, "Missing Persons: Legal Perceptions of Incompetent Patients," *Rutgers Law Review* 609 (1994): 636–47; Rebecca Dresser and Peter J. Whitehouse, "The Incompetent Patient on the Slippery Slope," *Hastings Center Report* 24, no. 4 (1994): 6–12; Rebecca Dresser, "Autonomy Revisited: The Limits of Anticipatory Choices," in *Dementia and Aging: Ethics, Values, and Policy Choices,* ed. Robert H. Binstock, Stephen G. Post, and Peter J. Whitehouse (Baltimore, Md.: Johns Hopkins University Press, 1992), pp. 71–85.

3. Andrew D. Firlik, "Margo's Logo," JAMA 265 (1991): 201.

4. See generally Dresser, "Missing Persons."

5. For a recent survey of the state of advance treatment decision-making in the U.S., see "Advance Care Planning: Priorities for Ethical and Empirical Research," Special Supplement, *Hastings Center Report* 24, no. 6 (1994).

6. See generally "Advance Care Planning." The failure of most persons to engage in formal end-of-life planning does not in itself contradict Dworkin's point that most people care about how they die. It does suggest, however, that people do not find the formal exercise of precedent autonomy to be a helpful or practical means of expressing their concerns about future life-sustaining treatment.

7. Ashwini Sehgal et al., "How Strictly Do Dialysis Patients Want Their Advance Directives Followed?" *JAMA* 267 (1992): 59–63.

8. See generally Dresser, "Missing Persons," 681–91; Tom Kitwood and Kathleen Bredin, "Towards a Theory of Dementia. Care: Personhood and Well-Being," *Ageing and Society* 12 (1992): 269–87.

9. Lachlan Forrow, Edward Cogel, and Elizabeth Thomas, "Advance Directives for Medical Care" (letter), *NEJM* 325 (1991): 1255.

10. Linda L. Emanuel et al., "Advance Directives for Medical Care—A Case for Greater Use," *NEJM* 324 (1991): 889–95.

11. See Eric Rakowski, "The Sanctity of Human Life," *Yale Law Journal* 103 (1994): 2049, 2110–11.

12. See Allen Buchanan and Dan Brock, "Deciding for Others," in *The Ethics of Surrogate Decisionmaking* (Cambridge: Cambridge University Press, 1989), at 1017 for discussion of these and other shortcomings of advance treatment decision-making.

13. See generally Rebecca Dresser and John A. Robertson, "Quality-of-Life and Non-Treatment Decisions for Incompetent Patients: A Critique of the Orthodox Approach," *Law, Medicine & Health Care* 17 (1989): 234–44.

14. See Derek Parfit, *Reasons and Persons* (New York: Oxford University Press, 1985), pp. 199–379.

15. See, e.g., Allison B. Seckler et al., "Substituted Judgment: How Accurate Are Proxy Predictions?" *Annals of Internal Medicine* 115 (1992): 92–98.

16. See generally Leslie P. Francis, "Advance Directives for Voluntary Euthanasia: A Volatile Combination?" *Journal of Medicine & Philosophy* 18 (1993): 297–322.

17. Kitwood and Bredin, *"Towards a Theory of Dementia Care,"* 273–74.

ETHICAL PERSPECTIVES ON LIFE EXTENSION

An Unnatural Process: Why it is not Inherently Wrong to Seek a Cure for Aging

Arthur L. Caplan

Not everyone thinks it is a good idea to live longer lives. Some writers, perhaps, most notably Daniel Callahan, the cofounder of the Hastings Center, argue that the quest to extend life is not a self-evident good (Callahan, 1995; Barlow, 2002). A longer life, Callahan contends, is not necessarily a better life. Other writers, such as the philosopher/physician Leon Kass (2002), the political theorist Francis Fukuyama (Fukuyama, 2002), and the theologian Gilbert Meilander (2002) argue that the extension of life should not be pursued because lengthening life is not consistent with human nature. It is "unnatural" to extend human lives beyond the proverbial three score and ten that the demographers assure us is what the average citizen of an economically developed nation can expect.

Still, scientists are eagerly pursuing research in many species that might lead to life extension in human beings (Herndon et al., 2002). French scientists have produced mice that live 26% longer through genetic engineering (Fukuyama, 2002; Kristol and Cohen, 2002). Other scientists have produced longer-lived mice, rats, and primates by placing them early in life on low-calorie diets. Still others believe that by genetically engineering the telomeres of our chromosomes or replacing human growth hormone in our bodies, the changes associated with aging can be slowed or reversed and our lives extended by 30, 40, or even 50 years. We do not know enough about aging to know if any of these interventions can deliver a longer life. But research may provide answers to the question of what does and does not work. Are the scientists, physicians, and others working on techniques that might lead to significantly longer life spans for human beings engaged, as Callahan, Kass, Fukuyama, and others suggest, in unethical activities?

Callahan and those who worry about the personal, social, and economic consequences of life extension must show that our culture or other cultures are not clever enough or flexible enough to figure out how to cope with more life. In part, the resolution of the debate about the consequences of life extension rests on empirical facts.

Have we adjusted to changes in the life span in the past in our species such that longer lives are viewed as better lives? The answer to that question if one compares life for, say, the ancient Hittites, Hebrews, Greeks, and Romans and life for Americans or Italians or Japanese today would seem to be yes.

Few could seriously maintain that an average life span of 35 years would be preferable to the 75 enjoyed today even if many do spend their final years weak, demented, or debilitated. And it would be hard to argue that despite the problems of overpopulation and ageism, the quality of life for the average person has slipped so much during those years added from those lived by the ancients that we live more poorly or less happily today. Few, in other words, would trade their longer life span for the much shorter lives lived by their ancestors thousands of years ago.

Caplan, Arthur. "An Unnatural Process: Why It Is Not Inherently Wrong To Seek A Cure For Aging," *The Fountain of Youth: Cultural, Scientific, and Ethical Perspectives on a Biomedical Goal*, ed. Stephen G. Post and Robert H. Binstock, New York: Oxford University Press, 2004: pp. 271–285. Copyright © 2004. Reprinted by permission of Oxford University Press.

Callahan is right to wonder about the consequences of both a longer life and the costs to society of pursuing a longer life. But the empirical evidence does not seem to bear out his case that trying to live longer must of necessity either bankrupt society or lead to lives of pain and misery. We need policies that ensure that a fair proportion of resources are devoted to the young, that seniority on the job does not become stasis in the workplace, and that we do not use medical technology over-aggressively once life has become a burden or simply too painful to endure.

Those such as Kass, Fukuyama, and Meilander pose a more powerful critique of the war on aging. For theirs is an in-principle objection, not one linked to the possible negative consequences of life extension. They maintain that it is unnatural to live much longer than we now do. Of course, to make this argument hold, they must show why the extension of life is unnatural. Or to put the point another way, they must be able to show that aging and senescence are both natural processes and, as such, intrinsically good things. They need to show that the life span we now have is part of our human nature. Can that case be made? I do not think so.

NORMALITY, NATURALNESS, AND DISEASE

It may seem somewhat odd to question the naturalness of a process as familiar and universal as aging. After all, if aging is not a natural process, what is? While the prospect of aging may be greeted with mixed feelings, there would seem to be little reason to doubt the fact that aging is understood to be a normal and inevitable feature of human existence. The belief that aging is a normal and natural part of human existence is reflected in the practice of medicine. For example, no mention is made in most textbooks of medicine and pathology of aging as abnormal, unnatural, or indicative of disease. It is true that such texts often contain a chapter or two on the related subject of diseases commonly associated with aging or found in the elderly. But it is the diseases of the elderly, such as pneumonia, cancer, or atherosclerosis, rather than the aging process itself, that serve as the focus of description and analysis.

What is so different about the physiological changes and deteriorations concurrent with the aging process that these events are considered to be unremarkable, natural processes, while other, very similar, debilitative changes are deemed diseases constituting health crises of the first order when they occur in younger people?

Surely it cannot simply be the life-threatening aspects of diseases, such as cancer or atherosclerosis, that distinguish these processes from aging. For while it may be true that hardly anyone manages to avoid contracting a terminal disease at some point in life, aging itself produces the same ultimate consequence as these diseases—death. Our bodies break down, and death inevitably is the consequence.

Nor can it be the familiarity and universality of aging that inures medical science to its unnatural aspects. Malignant neoplasms, viral infections, gingivitis, acne, and hypertension are all ubiquitous phenomena. Yet medicine maintains a radically different stance toward these physical processes from that which it holds toward the so-called natural changes that occur during aging.

It might be argued that the processes denoted by the term *aging* do not fit the standard conception of disease operative in clinical medicine. However, in medical dictionaries, disease is almost always defined as any pathological change in the body. Pathological change is inevitably defined as constituting any morbid process in the body. And morbid processes are usually defined in terms of disease states of the body.[1] Regardless of the circularity surrounding this explication of the concept of somatic disease, aging would seem to have a prima facie claim to being counted as a disease. Pathological or morbid changes are often the sole criteria by which age is assessed in the human body. Coroners and medical examiners determine age by morbid changes and pathological alterations in a dead body.

What does seem to differentiate aging from other processes or states traditionally classified as diseases is the fact that aging is perceived as a natural or normal process. Medicine has traditionally viewed its role as that of ameliorating or combatting the abnormal, either through therapeutic interventions or prophylactic regimens. The natural and the normal, while not outside the sphere of medicine, are concepts that play key roles in licensing the intervention of the medical practitioner. For it is in response to or in anticipation of abnormality that physicians' activities are legitimated. And as E.A. Murphy, among many other doctors, has noted, "the clinician has tended to regard disease as that state in which the limits of the normal have been transgressed" (Murphy, 1966; Murphy, 1976, p. 122; Risse, 1978). Naturalness and normality have historically been used as baselines to determine the presence of disease and the necessity of medical activity.

In light of the powerful belief that the abnormal and unnatural are indicative of medicine's range of interest, it is easy to see why many biological processes are not thought to be the proper subject of medical intervention of therapy. Puberty, growth, and maturation *as processes in themselves* all appear to stand outside the sphere of medical concern since they are normal and natural occurrences among human beings. Similarly, it seems odd to think of sexuality or fertilization as possible disease states precisely because these states are commonly thought to be natural and normal components of the human condition.

Nonetheless, it is true that certain biological processes, such as contraception, pregnancy, and fertility, have been the subjects in recent years of heated debates as to their standing as possible disease states. The notions that it is natural and normal for only men and women to have sexual intercourse or for women to undergo menopause have been challenged in many quarters. The question arises as to whether the process of aging in itself can be classified as abnormal and unnatural in a way that will open the door for the reclassification of aging as a disease process and thus as a proper subject of medical attention, concern, and control.

AGING AND MEDICAL INTERVENTION

The past few years have seen the rise of a powerful movement for the *right to die*. Some have even gone so far as to claim that physicians and health professionals have a moral obligation to play an active role in allowing patients to die under certain circumstances. To a great extent, the status of aging and dying as natural processes looms large in discussions about the *right to die* and *death with dignity*. Often those who debate the degree to which the medical profession should intervene in the process of dying disagree about the naturalness of the phenomena of aging and dying. If the alleged right to die is to be built on a conception of the naturalness of aging and dying, then the conceptual status of these terms vis-à-vis *naturalness* must be thoroughly examined.

The perception of biological events or processes as natural or unnatural is frequently decisive in determining whether physicians treat states or processes as diseases (Socarides, 1970; Illich, 1974; Goldberg, 1975). One need only think of the controversies that swirl around allegations concerning the biological naturalness of homosexuality or schizophrenia to see that this is so. This claim is further borne out by an argument that is frequently made by older physicians to new medical students.

Medical students often find it difficult to interact with or examine elderly patients. They may feel powerless when confronted with the seemingly irreversible debilities of old age. To overcome this reluctance, older physicians are likely to point out that aging and senescence are processes that happen to everyone, even young medical students. Aging is simply part of the human condition; it should hold no terror for a young doctor. Students are told that aging is natural and that, while there may be nothing they can do to alter the inevitable course of this process, they must learn to help patients cope with their aging as best they can. It is as if teaching physicians feel obligated to label the obviously debilitative and disease-like states of old age as natural in order to discourage the students' inclination to treat the elderly as sick or diseased.

WHAT IS AGING?

What are the grounds on which this label is applied? Why do we think of aging as a natural process? The reason that comes immediately to mind is that aging is a common and normal process. It occurs with a statistical frequency of 100%. Inevitably and uniformly, bones become brittle, vision dims, joints stiffen, and muscles lose their tone. The obvious question that arises is whether commonality, familiarity, and inevitability are sufficient conditions for referring to certain biological states as natural. To answer this question, it is necessary to first draw a distinction between aging and chronological age.

In a trivial sense, given the existence of a chronological device, all bodies that exist can be said to age relative to the measurements provided by that device. But since physicians have little practical interest in making philosophical statements about the time-bound nature of existence, or empirical claims about the relativity of space and time, it is evident that they do not have this chronological sense in mind in speaking about the familiarity and inevitability of aging. In speaking of aging, physicians are interested in a particular set of biological changes that occur with respect to time. In the aged individual, cells manifest a high frequency of visible chromosomal aberrations. The nuclei of nerve cells become distorted by clumps of chromatin, and the surrounding cytoplasm contains fewer organelles, such as mitochondria. Collagen fibers become increasingly rigid and inflexible, as manifest in the familiar phenomenon of skin wrinkling. The aorta becomes wider and more tortuous. The immunological system weakens, and the elderly person becomes more susceptible to infections. Melanin pigment formation decreases and, consequently, hair begins to whiten (Hayflick, 1994).

NATURALNESS, DESIGN, AND FUNCTION

Changes of this kind, in association with aging, are universal and inevitable. Universality and inevitability do not, however, seem to be sufficient conditions for referring to a process as natural. Coronary atherosclerosis, neoplasms, high blood pressure, sore throats, colds, tooth decay, and depression are all nearly universal in their distribution and seemingly inevitable phenomena, and yet we would hardly agree to call any of these things natural processes or states. The inevitability of infection by microorganisms among all humans does not cause the physician to dismiss these infections as natural occurrences of no particular medical interest. The physician may not intervene, or even attempt to prevent such diseases, but such behavior is a result of a decision concerning an unnatural disease, not a natural process.

So, if universality and inevitability are not adequate conditions for naturalness, are any other criteria available by which naturalness can be assessed and used to drive a wedge between aging and disease? There is a further sense of *natural*[2] that may prove helpful in trying to understand why physicians are reluctant to label aging a disease, preferring to think of it as a natural process.

This sense of naturalness is rooted in the notions of design, purpose, and function. Axes are designed to serve as tools for cutting trees. Scalpels are meant to be used in cutting human tissue. It would seem most unnatural to use axes for surgery and scalpels for lumber-jacking. In some sense, although a skillful surgeon might in fact be able to perform surgery with an axe, it would be unnatural to do so. Similarly, many bodily organs—the liver, spleen, blood vessels, kidneys, and many glands—can perform compensatory functions when certain other organic tissues are damaged or removed. But these are not the purposes or functions they were designed to perform. While the arteries of many organisms are capable of constricting to maintain blood pressure and reduce the flow of blood during hemorrhage-induced shock, the function of arteries is not to constrict in response to such circumstances. The presence of vasoconstriction in arteries is in fact an unnatural state that signals the physician that something has gone seriously awry in the body. It would seem that much of our willingness to accept aging as a natural process is parasitic upon this sense of natural function.

Two answers are commonly given to the question What is the function of aging? The first is a theological explanation. God, as a punishment for the sins of our ancestors in the (proverbial) garden of Eden, caused humans to age and die. On this view, people age because the Creator saw fit to design them that way for retribution or punishment. Aging serves as a reminder of our moral fallibility and weakness.

The second view, which is particularly widespread in scientific circles, is that the purpose or function of aging is to clear away the old to make way for the new for evolutionary reasons. This theory was first advanced by the German cytologist and evolutionary biologist August Weisman (1891). Weisman argued that aging and debilitation must be viewed as adaptational responses on the part of organisms to allow for new mutational and adaptive responses to fluctuating environments. Aging benefits the population by removing the superannuated to make room for the young. The function of aging is to ensure the death of organisms to allow evolutionary change and new adaptation to occur.

On both of these views, aging has an intended purpose or function. And it is from this quasi-Aristotelian attribution of a design that the concept of the naturalness of aging is often thought to arise (Kass, 2002).

THE CONCEPT OF BIOLOGICAL FUNCTION

If the naturalness of aging resides in a functional interpretation, there is a rich and abundant literature on the subjects of function and purpose. However, rooting the source of the naturalness of biological processes in ideas of function or purpose also has its drawbacks, the primary problem being that philosophers have by no means reached anything even vaguely resembling a consensus about the meaning of such terms as *function* or *purpose*.

Fortunately, it is possible to avoid becoming bogged down in an analysis of functional or purposive statements in analyzing the function of aging. The only distinction required for understanding the function of aging is that between the aim of explaining the existence of a particular state, organ, or process and that of explaining how a state, organ, or process works in a particular system or organism. Functional or purposive statements are sometimes used to explain the existence of a trait or process historically. At other times, such statements are used mechanistically to explain how something works or operates. If we ask what is the function, or role, or purpose of the spleen in the human body, the question can be interpreted in two ways: How does the spleen work—what does it do in the body? or Why does the spleen exist in its present state in the human body—what is the historical story that explains why persons have spleens?[3]

It is this latter sense of function, the historical sense, that is relevant to the determination of the naturalness or unnaturalness of aging as a biological process. For while there is no shortage of theories purporting to explain how aging works or functions, these theories are not relevant to the historically motivated question about the function of aging. The determination of the naturalness of aging, if it is to be rooted in biology, will depend not on how the process of aging actually operates, but rather on the explanation one gives for the existence or presence of aging humans.[4] This is the sense of naturalness that Kass, Fukuyama, and others must rely upon to make their case that extending life by conquering aging is wrong because it is unnatural.

DOES AGING HAVE A FUNCTION?

Two purported explanations—one theological, one scientific—of the function or purpose of aging have been given. Both are flawed. While the theological explanation of aging may carry great weight for numerous individuals, it will simply not do as a scientific explanation of why aging occurs in humans. Medical professionals may have to cope with their patients' advocacy of this explanation and their own religious feelings on the subject. But, from a scientific perspective, it will hardly do to claim that aging, as a result of God's vindictiveness, is a natural biological process and hence not a disease worthy of treatment.

More surprisingly, the scientific explanation of aging as serving an evolutionary role or purpose is also inadequate. It is simply not true that aging exists to serve any sort of evolutionary purpose or function. The claim that aging exists or occurs in individuals because it has a wider role or function in the evolutionary scheme of things rests on a faulty evolutionary analysis. There is nothing natural about aging and, contrary to the views of Kass, Fukuyama, and many others, aging is not a natural attribute of being human.

To assign a purpose to aging incorrectly assumes that it is possible for biological processes to exist that directly benefit or advance the evolutionary success of a species or population. In other words, it supposes that processes such as aging exist because they serve a function or purpose in the life history of a species—in this case, that of removing the old to make way for the

new. However, evolutionary selection rarely acts to advance the prospects of an entire species or population. Selection acts on individual organisms and their phenotypic traits and properties. Some traits or properties confer advantages in certain environments on the organisms that possess them, and this fact increases the likelihood that the genes responsible for producing these traits will be passed on to future organisms.

Given that selective forces act on individuals and their genotypes and not on species, it makes no sense to speak of aging as serving an evolutionary function or purpose to benefit the species. How then do evolutionary biologists explain the existence of aging (Williams, 1966; Ghiselin, 1974)? Briefly, the explanation is that features, traits, or properties in individual organisms will be selected for if they confer a relative reproductive advantage on the individual, or his or her close kin. Any variation that increases inclusive reproductive fitness has a very high probability of being selected and maintained in the gene pool of a species. Selection, however, cannot look ahead to foresee the possible consequences of favoring certain traits at a given time; the environment selects for those traits and features that give an immediate return. An increased metabolic rate, for example, may prove advantageous early in life, in that it may provide more energy for seeking mates and avoiding predators; it may also result in early deterioration of the organism due to an increased accumulation of toxic wastes or genetic mutations in the body of an individual thus endowed (Herndon et al., 2002). Natural selection cannot foresee such delayed debilitating consequences.

Aging exists, then, as a consequence of lack of evolutionary foresight; it is simply a by-product of selective forces working to increase the chances of reproductive success in the life of an organism. Senescence has no function; it is simply the inadvertent subversion of organic function, later in life, in favor of maximizing reproductive advantage early in life.

The common belief that aging serves a function or purpose, if this belief is based on evolutionary theory, is mistaken. And, if this is so, it would seem that the common belief that aging is a natural process, as a consequence of the function or purpose it serves in the life of the species, is also mistaken. Consequently, unless it is possible to motivate the description on other grounds, it would seem that aging cannot be understood as a natural process. And if that is true, and if it is actually the case that what goes on during the aging process closely parallels the changes that occur during paradigmatic examples of disease,[5] then it would be unreasonable not to consider aging a disease.

THEORIES OF AGING AND THE CONCEPT OF DISEASE

A consideration of the changes that constitute aging in human beings reinforces the similarities existing between aging and other clear-cut examples of somatic diseases. There is a set of external manifestations or symptoms: graying hair, increased susceptibility to infection, wrinkling skin, loss of muscular tone, and, frequently, loss of mental ability. These manifestations seem to be causally linked to a series of internal cellular and subcellular changes. The presence of symptoms and an underlying etiology closely parallels the standard paradigmatic examples of disease. If the analogy is pushed a bit further, the cause for considering aging a disease appears to become even stronger.

There are many theories as to what causes changes at the cellular and subcellular levels that produce the signs and symptoms associated with aging (Comfort, 1964, 1970; Hayflick, 1973). One view argues that aging is caused by an increase in the number of cross-linkages that exist in protein and nucleic acid molecules. Cross-linkages lower the biochemical efficiency and dependability of certain macromolecules involved in metabolism and other chemical reactions. Free radical by-products of metabolism are thought to accumulate in cells, thus allowing for an increase in available linkage sites for replicating nucleic acid strands and activating histone elements. This sort of cross-linkage is thought to be particularly important in the aging of collagen, the substance responsible for most of the overt symptoms we commonly associate with aging, such as wrinkled skin and loss of muscular flexibility.

Another view holds that aging results from an accumulation of genetic mutations in the chromosomes of cells in the body. The idea underlying this theory is that chromosomes are exposed over time to a steady stream of radiation and other mutagenic agents. The accumulation of mutational hits on the genes lying on the chromosomes results in the progressive inactivation of these genes (Herndon et al., 2002). The evidence of a higher incidence of chromosomal breaks and aberrations in the aged is consistent with this mutational theory of aging.

Along with the cross-linkage and mutational theories, there is one other important hypothesis concerning the cause of aging. The autoimmune theory holds that, as time passes and the chromosomes of cells in the human body accumulate more mutations, certain key tissues begin to synthesize antibodies that can no longer distinguish between self and foreign material. Thus, a number of autoimmune reactions occur in the body as the immunological system begins to turn against the individual it was *designed* to protect. Arthritis and pernicious anemia are symptomatic of the sorts of debilities resulting from the malfunction of the immunological system. While this theory is closely allied to the mutation theory, the autoimmune view of aging holds that accumulated mutations do not simply result in deterioration of cellular activity but, rather, produce lethal cellular end products that consume and destroy healthy tissue.

It would be rash to hold that any of the three hypotheses cited—the cross-linkage, mutational, or autoimmune hypotheses—will, in the end, turn out to be the correct explanation of aging. All three views are, in fact, closely related in that cross-linkages can result from periodic exposure to mutagenic agents and can, in turn, produce genetic aberrations that eventuate in cellular dysfunction or even autoimmunological reactions. What is important, however, is not whether one of these theories or *any* of them is in fact the correct theory of aging, but that all of them postulate mechanisms that are closely analogous to those mechanisms cited by clinicians in describing disease processes in the body.

The concept of disease is, without doubt, a slippery and evasive notion in medicine (Veatch, 1973). Once one moves away from what can be termed *paradigmatic* examples of disease, such as tuberculosis or diphtheria, toward more nebulous examples, such as acne or jittery nerves, it becomes difficult to say exactly what are the criteria requisite for labeling a condition a somatic disease. However, even though it is notoriously difficult to concoct a set of necessary and sufficient conditions for employing the term *organic disease*, it is possible to cite a list of general criteria that seem relevant in attempting to decide whether a bodily state or process is appropriately labeled a disease.

One criterion is that the state or process produces discomfort or suffering. A second is that the process or state can be traced back to a specific cause, event, or circumstance. A third is that there is a set of clear-cut structural changes, both macroscopic and microscopic, that follow in a uniform, sequential manner subsequent to the initial precipitating or causal event. A fourth is that there is a set of clinical symptoms or manifestations (headache, pain in the chest, rapid pulse, shortness of breath) commonly associated with the observed physiological alterations in structure. Finally, there is usually some sort of impairment in the functions, behavior, or activity of a person thought to be diseased (Boorse, 1975). Not all diseases will satisfy all or any of the criteria I have suggested. One need only consider the arguments surrounding the classification of astigmatism, alcoholism, drug addiction, gambling, and hyperactivity to realize the inadequacy of these criteria as necessary and sufficient conditions for the determination of disease. But that the suggested criteria are relevant to such determination is shown by the fact that advocates of all persuasions regarding controversial states and processes commonly resort to considerations of causation, clinical manifestations, etiology, functional impairment, and suffering in arguing the merits of their various views concerning the status of controversial cases.

With respect to the conceptual ambiguity surrounding the notion of disease, it is important to remember that medicine is by no means unique in being saddled with what might be termed *fuzzy-edged* concepts. One need only consider the status of terms such as *species, adaptation,* and *mutation* in biology, or *stimulus, behavior,* and *instinct* in psychology, to realize that medicine is not alone in the ambiguity of its key terms. It is also true that, just as the biologist is able to use biological theory to aid in the determination of relevant criteria for a concept, the physician is able to use his or her knowledge of the structure and function of the body to decide on relevant criteria for the determination of disease. If one accepts the relevance of the five suggested criteria, aging as a biological process is seen to possess all the key properties of a disease. Unlike astigmatism or nervousness, aging possesses a definitive group of clinical manifestations or symptoms; a clearcut etiology of structural changes at both the macroscopic and microscopic levels; a significant measure of impairment, discomfort, and suffering; and, if we are willing to grant the same tolerance to current theories of aging as we grant to theories in other domains of medicine, an explicit set of precipitating factors. Aging has all the relevant markings of a disease process. It has none of the attributes of a functional process. The explanation of why aging occurs has many of the attributes of a stochastic or chance phenomenon. And this makes aging unnatural and in no way an intrinsic part of human nature.

As such, there is no reason why it is intrinsically wrong to try to reverse or cure aging. There may be external reasons—cost, inequity, or even a fear that the overall quality of life will diminish—but those who want to make the case against treating aging as a disease must show why human beings are not capable of solving the challenges that a longer life expectancy would create.

NOTES

1. See, for example, *Dorland's Illustrated Medical Dictionary,* 25th ed. (Philadelphia: W.B. Saunders, 1974).

2. Cf. D.B. Hausman, "What is Natural?," *Perspectives in Biology and Medicine,* 19 (1975), 92–101, for an illuminating discussion of the concept.

3. For a sample of the extant explications of the concept of function see L. Wright, "Functions," *Philosophical Review,* 82 (1973), 139–168; R. Cummins, "Functional Analysis," *Journal of Philosophy,* 72 (1975), 741–765; and M.A. Boden, *Purposive Explanation in Psychology* (Cambridge, MA: Harvard, 1972). See also E. Nagel, *Teleology Revisited* (New York: Columbia University Press, 1979).

4. Further discussion of the distinction between explaining the operation of a trait or feature and explaining the origin and presence of a trait or feature can be found in A.L. Caplan, "Evolution, Ethics and the Milk of Human Kindness," *Hastings Center Report,* 6(2), (1976), 20–26.

5. For an interesting attempt to analyze the concepts of illness and disease, see C. Boorse, "On the Distinction Between Illness and Disease," *Philosophy and Public Affairs,* 5(1), (1975), 49–68.

Why not Immortality?

Leon R. Kass

If life is good and more is better, should we not regard death as a disease and try to cure it? Although this formulation of the question may seem too futuristic or far-fetched, there are several reasons for taking it up and treating it seriously.

First, reputable scientists are today answering the question in the affirmative and are already making large efforts toward bringing about a cure. Three kinds of research, still in their infancy, are attracting new attention and energies. First is the use of hormones, especially human growth hormone (hGH), to restore and enhance youthful bodily vigor. In the United States, over ten thousand people—including many physicians—are already injecting themselves daily with hGH for anti-aging purposes, with apparently remarkable improvements in bodily fitness and performance, though there is as yet no evidence that the hormones yield any increase in life expectancy. When the patent on hGH expires in 2002 and the cost comes down from its current $1,000 per month, many more people are almost certainly going to be injecting themselves from the hormonal fountain of youth.

Second is research on stem cells, those primordial cells that, on different signals, turn into all the different differentiated tissues of the body—liver, heart, kidney, brain, etc. Stem cell technologies—combined with techniques of cloning—hold out the promise of an indefinite supply of replacement tissues and organs for any and all worn-out body parts. This is a booming area in commercial biotechnology, and one of the leading biotech entrepreneurs has been touting his company's research as promising indefinite prolongation of life.

Third, there is research into the genetic switches that control the biological processes of aging. The maximum life span for each species—roughly one hundred years for human beings—is almost certainly under genetic control. In a startling recent discovery, fruit-fly geneticists have shown that mutations in a *single* gene produce a 50 percent increase in the natural lifetime of the flies. Once the genes involved in regulating the human life cycle and setting the midnight hour are identified, scientists predict that they will be able to increase the human maximum age well beyond its natural limit. Quite frankly, I find some of the claims and predictions to be overblown, but it would be foolhardy to bet against scientific and technical progress along these lines.

But even if cures for aging and death are a long way off, there is a second and more fundamental reason for inquiring into the radical question of the desirability of gaining a cure for death. For truth to tell, victory over mortality is the unstated but implicit goal of modern medical science, indeed of the entire modern scientific project, to which mankind was summoned almost four hundred years ago by Francis Bacon and René Descartes. They quite consciously trumpeted the conquest of nature for the relief of man's estate, and they founded a science whose explicit purpose was to reverse the curse laid on Adam and Eve, and especially to restore the tree of life, by means of the tree of (scientific) knowledge. With medicine's increasing successes, realized mainly in the last half century, every death is increasingly regarded as premature, a failure of today's medicine that future research will prevent. In parallel with medical progress, a new moral sensibility has developed that serves precisely medicine's crusade against mortality: anything is permitted if it saves

life, cures disease, prevents death. Regardless, therefore, of the imminence of anti-aging remedies, it is most worthwhile to reexamine the assumption upon which we have been operating: that everything should be done to preserve health and prolong life as much as possible, and that all other values must bow before the biomedical gods of better health, greater vigor, and longer life.

Recent proposals that we should conquer aging and death have not been without their critics. The criticism takes two forms: predictions of bad social consequences and complaints about distributive justice. Regarding the former, there are concerns about the effect on the size and age distribution of the population. How will growing numbers and percentages of people living well past one hundred affect, for example, work opportunities, retirement plans, hiring and promotion, cultural attitudes and beliefs, the structure of family life, relations between the generations, or the locus of rule and authority in government, business, and the professions? Even the most cursory examination of these matters suggests that the cumulative results of aggregated decisions for longer and more vigorous life could be highly disruptive and undesirable, even to the point that many individuals would be *worse off* through most of their lives, and worse off enough to offset the benefits of better health afforded them near the end of life. Indeed, several people have predicted that retardation of aging will present a classic instance of the Tragedy of the Commons, in which genuine and sought-for gains to individuals are nullified or worse, owing to the social consequences of granting them to everyone.

But other critics worry that technology's gift of long or immortal life will not be granted to everyone, especially if, as is likely, the treatments turn out to be expensive. Would it not be the ultimate injustice if only some people could afford a deathless existence, if the world were divided not only into rich and poor but into mortal and immortal?

Against these critics, the proponents of immortality research answer confidently that we will gradually figure out a way to solve these problems. We can handle any adverse social consequences through careful planning; we can overcome the inequities through cheaper technologies. Though I think these optimists woefully naive, let me for the moment grant their view regarding these issues. For both the proponents and their critics have yet to address thoughtfully the heart of the matter, the question of the goodness of the goal. The core question is this: Is it really true that longer life for individuals is an unqualified good?

How *much* longer life is a blessing for an individual? Ignoring now the possible harms flowing back to individuals from adverse social consequences, how much more life is good for us as individuals, other things being equal? How much more life do we want, assuming it to be healthy and vigorous? Assuming that it were up to us to set the human life span, where would or should we set the limit and why?

The simple answer is that no limit should be set. Life is good, and death is bad. Therefore, the more life the better, provided, of course, that we remain fit and our friends do, too.

This answer has the virtues of clarity and honesty. But most public advocates of conquering aging deny any such greediness. They hope not for immortality, but for something reasonable—just a few more years.

How many years are reasonably few? Let us start with ten. Which of us would find unreasonable or unwelcome the addition of ten healthy and vigorous years to his or her life, years like those between ages thirty and forty? We could learn more, earn more, see more, do more. Maybe we should ask for five years on top of that? Or ten? Why not fifteen, or twenty, or more?

If we can't immediately land on the reasonable number of added years, perhaps we can locate the principle. What is the principle of reasonableness? Time needed for our plans and projects yet to be completed? Some multiple of the age of a generation, say, that we might live to see great-grandchildren fully grown? Some notion—traditional, natural, revealed—of the proper life span for a being such as man? We have no answer to this question. We do not even know how to choose among the principles for setting our new life span.

Under such circumstances, lacking a standard of reasonableness, we fall back on our wants and desires. Under liberal democracy, this means the desires of the majority for whom the attachment to life—or the fear of death—knows no limits. It turns out that the simple answer is the best: we want to live and live, and not to wither and not to die. For most of us, especially under modern secular conditions in which more and more people believe that this is the only life they have, the desire to prolong the life span (even modestly) must be seen as expressing a desire *never* to grow old and die. However naive their counsel, those who propose immortality deserve credit: they honestly and shamelessly expose this desire.

Some, of course, eschew any desire for longer life. They seek not adding years to life, but life to years. For them, the ideal life span would be our natural (once thought three-, now known to be) fourscore and ten, or if by reason of strength, fivescore, lived with full powers right up to death, which could come rather suddenly, painlessly, at the maximal age.

This has much to recommend it. Who would not want to avoid senility, crippling arthritis, the need for hearing aids and dentures, and the degrading dependencies of old age? But, in the absence of these degenerations, would we remain content to spurn longer life? Would we not become even more disinclined to exit? Would not death become even more of an affront? Would not the fear and loathing of death increase in the absence of its harbingers? We could no longer comfort the widow by pointing out that her husband was delivered from his suffering. Death would always be untimely, unprepared for, shocking.

Montaigne saw it clearly:

> I notice that in proportion as I sink into sickness, I naturally enter into a certain disdain for life. I find that I have much more trouble digesting this resolution when I am in health than when I have a fever. Inasmuch as I no longer cling so hard to the good things of life when I begin to lose the use and pleasure of them, I come to view death with much less frightened eyes. This makes me hope that the farther I get from life and the nearer to death, the more easily I shall accept the exchange. . . . If we fell into such a change [decrepitude] suddenly, I don't think we could endure it. But when we are led by Nature's hand down a gentle and virtually imperceptible slope, bit by bit, one step at a time, she rolls us into this wretched state and makes us familiar with it; so that we find no shock when youth dies within us, which in essence and in truth is a harder death than the complete death of a languishing life or the death of old age; inasmuch as the leap is not so cruel from a painful life as from a sweet and flourishing life to a grievous and painful one.

Thus it is highly likely that even a modest prolongation of life with vigor or even only a preservation of youthfulness with no increase in longevity would make death less acceptable and would exacerbate the desire to keep pushing it away—unless, for some reason, such life could also prove less satisfying.

Could longer, healthier life be less satisfying? How could it be, if life is good and death is bad? Perhaps the simple view is in error. Perhaps mortality is not simply an evil, perhaps it is even a blessing—not only for the welfare of the community, but even for us as individuals. How could this be?

I wish to make the case for the virtues of mortality. Against my own strong love of life, and against my even stronger wish that no more of my loved ones should die, I aspire to speak truth to my desires by showing that the finitude of human life is a blessing for every human individual, whether he knows it or not.

I know I won't persuade many people to my position. But I do hope I can convince readers of the gravity—I would say, the unique gravity—of this question. We are not talking about some minor new innovation with ethical wrinkles about which we may chatter or regulate as usual. Conquering death is not something that we can try for a while and then decide whether the results are better or worse—according to, God only knows, what standard. On the contrary, this is a question in which our very humanity is at stake, not only in the consequences but also in the very meaning of the choice. For to argue that human life would be better without death is, I submit, to argue that human life would be better being something other than human. To be immortal would not be just to continue life as we mortals now know it, only forever. The new immortals, in the decisive sense, would not be like us at all. If this is true, a human choice for bodily immortality would suffer from the deep confusion of choosing to have some great good only on the condition of turning into someone else. Moreover, such an immortal someone else, in my view, will be less well off than we mortals are now, thanks indeed to our mortality.

It goes without saying that there is no virtue in the death of a child or a young adult, or the untimely or premature death of anyone, before they had attained to the measure of man's days. I do not mean to imply that there is virtue in the particular *event* of death for anyone. Nor am I suggesting that separation through death is not painful for the survivors, those for whom the deceased was an integral part of their lives. Instead, my question concerns the fact of our finitude, the fact of our mortality—the fact *that we must die,* the fact that a full life for a human being has a biological, built-in limit, one that has evolved as part of our nature. Does this fact also have value? Is our finitude good for us— as individuals? (I intend this question entirely in the realm of natural reason and apart from any question about a life after death.)

To praise mortality must seem to be madness. If mortality is a blessing, it surely is not widely regarded as such. Life seeks to live, and rightly suspects all counsels of finitude. "Better to be a slave on earth than the king over all the dead," says Achilles in Hades to the visiting Odysseus, in apparent regret for his prior choice of the short but glorious life. Moreover, though some cultures—such as the Eskimo—can instruct and moderate somewhat the lust for life, liberal Western society gives it free rein, beginning with a political philosophy founded on a fear of violent death, and reaching to our current cults of youth and novelty, the cosmetic replastering of the wrinkles of age, and the widespread anxiety about disease and survival. Finally, the virtues of finitude—if there are

any—may never be widely appreciated in any age or culture, if appreciation depends on a certain wisdom, if wisdom requires a certain detachment from the love of oneself and one's own, and if the possibility of such detachment is given only to the few. Still, if it is wisdom, the rest of us should hearken, for we may learn something of value for ourselves.

How, then, might our finitude be good for us? I offer four benefits, first among which is *interest and engagement.* If the human life span were increased even by only twenty years, would the pleasures of life increase proportionally? Would professional tennis players really enjoy playing 25 percent more games of tennis? Would the Don Juans of our world feel better for having seduced 1,250 women rather than 1,000? Having experienced the joys and tribulations of raising a family until the last had left for college, how many parents would like to extend the experience by another ten years? Likewise, those whose satisfaction comes from climbing the career ladder might well ask what there would be to do for fifteen years after one had been CEO of Microsoft, a member of Congress, or the President of Harvard for a quarter of a century? Even less clear are the additions to personal happiness from more of the same of the less pleasant and less fulfilling activities in which so many of us are engaged so much of the time. It seems to be as the poet says: "We move and ever spend our lives amid the same things, and not by any length of life is any new pleasure hammered out."

Second, *seriousness and aspiration.* Could life be serious or meaningful without the limit of mortality? Is not the limit on our time the ground of our taking life seriously and living it passionately? To know and to feel that one goes around only once, and that the deadline is not out of sight, is for many people the necessary spur to the pursuit of something worthwhile. "Teach us to number our days," says the Psalmist, "that we may get a heart of wisdom." To number our days is the condition for making them count. Homer's immortals— Zeus and Hera, Apollo and Athena—for all their eternal beauty and youthfulness, live shallow and rather frivolous lives, their passions only transiently engaged, in first this and then that. They live as spectators of the mortals, who by comparison have depth, aspiration, genuine feeling, and hence a real center in their lives. Mortality makes life matter.

There may be some activities, especially in some human beings, that do not require finitude as a spur. A powerful desire for understanding can do without external proddings, let alone one related to mortality; and as there is never too much time to learn and to understand, longer, more vigorous life might be simply a boon. The best sorts of friendship, too, seem capable of indefinite growth, especially where growth is somehow tied to learning—though one may wonder whether real friendship doesn't depend in part on the shared perceptions of a common fate. But, in any case, I suspect that these are among the rare exceptions. For most activities, and for most of us, I think it is crucial that we recognize and feel the force of not having world enough and time.

A third matter, *beauty and love*. Death, says Wallace Stevens, is the mother of beauty. What he means is not easy to say. Perhaps he means that only a mortal being, aware of his mortality and the transience and vulnerability of all natural things, is moved to make beautiful artifacts, objects that will last, objects whose order will be immune to decay as their maker is not, beautiful objects that will bespeak and beautify a world that needs beautification, beautiful objects for other mortal beings who can appreciate what they cannot themselves make because of a taste for the beautiful, a taste perhaps connected to awareness of the ugliness of decay.

Perhaps the poet means to speak of natural beauty as well, which beauty—unlike that of objects of art—depends on its *im*permanence. Could the beauty of flowers depend on the fact that they will soon wither? Does the beauty of spring warblers depend upon the fall drabness that precedes and follows? What about the fading, late afternoon winter light or the spreading sunset? Is the beautiful necessarily fleeting, a peak that cannot be sustained? Or does the poet mean not that the beautiful is beautiful because mortal, but that our appreciation of its beauty depends on our appreciation of mortality—in us and in the beautiful? Does not love swell before the beautiful precisely on recognizing that it (and we) will not always be? Is not our mortality the cause of our enhanced appreciation of the beautiful and the worthy and of our treasuring and loving them? How deeply could one deathless "human" being love another?

Fourth, there is the peculiarly human beauty of character, *virtue and moral excellence*. To be mortal means that it is possible to give one's life, not only in one moment, say, on the field of battle, but also in the many other ways in which we are able in action to rise above attachment to survival. Through moral courage, endurance, greatness of soul, generosity, devotion to justice—in acts great and small—we rise above our mere creatureliness, spending the precious coinage of the time of our lives for the sake of the noble and the good and the holy. We free ourselves from fear, from bodily pleasures, or from attachments to wealth—all largely connected with survival—and in doing virtuous

deeds overcome the weight of our neediness; yet for this nobility, vulnerability and mortality are the necessary conditions. The immortals cannot be noble.

Of this, too, the poets teach. Odysseus, long suffering, has already heard the shade of Achilles' testimony in praise of life when he is offered immortal life by the nymph Calypso. She is a beautiful goddess, attractive, kind, yielding; she sings sweetly and weaves on a golden loom; her island is well-ordered and lovely, free of hardships and suffering. Says the poet, "Even a God who came into that place would have admired what he saw, the heart delighted within him." Yet Odysseus turns down the offer to be lord of her household and immortal:

> Goddess and queen, do not be angry with me. I myself know that all you say is true and that circumspect Penelope can never match the impression you make for beauty and stature. She is mortal after all, and you are immortal and ageless. But even so, what I want and all my days I pine for is to go back to my house and see that day of my homecoming. And if some god batters me far out on the wine-blue water, I will endure it, keeping a stubborn spirit inside me, for already I have suffered much and done much hard work on the waves and in the fighting.

To suffer, to endure, to trouble oneself for the sake of home, family, community, and genuine friendship, is truly to live, and is the clear choice of this exemplary mortal. This choice is both the mark of his excellence and the basis for the visible display of his excellence in deeds noble and just. Immortality is a kind of oblivion—like death itself.

But, someone might reasonably object, if mortality is such a blessing, why do so few cultures recognize it as such? Why do so many teach the promise of life after death, of something eternal, of something imperishable? This takes us to the heart of the matter.

What is the meaning of this concern with immortality? *Why* do we human beings seek immortality? Why do we want to live longer or forever? Is it really first and most because we do not want to die, because we do not want to leave this embodied life on earth or give up our earthly pastimes, because we want to see more and do more? I do not think so. This may be what we say, but it is not what we finally mean. Mortality as such is not our defect, nor bodily immortality our goal. Rather, mortality is at most a pointer, a derivative manifestation, or an accompaniment of some deeper deficiency. The promise of immortality and eternity answers rather to a deep truth about the human soul: the human soul yearns for, longs for, aspires to some condition, some state, some goal toward which our earthly activities are directed but which cannot be attained in earthly life. Our soul's reach exceeds our grasp; it seeks more than continuance; it reaches for something beyond us, something that for the most part eludes us. Our distress with mortality is the derivative manifestation of the conflict between the transcendent longings of the soul and the all-too-finite powers and fleshly concerns of the body.

What is it that we lack and long for, but cannot reach? One possibility is completion in another person. For example, Plato's Aristophanes says we seek wholeness through complete and permanent bodily and psychic union with a unique human being whom we love, our "missing other half." Plato's Socrates, in contrast, says it is rather wholeness through wisdom, through comprehensive knowledge of the beautiful truth about the whole, that which philosophy seeks but can never attain. Yet again, biblical religion says we seek wholeness through dwelling in God's presence, love, and redemption—a restoration of innocent wholeheartedness lost in the Garden of Eden. But, please note, these and many other such accounts of human aspiration, despite their differences, all agree on this crucial point: man longs not so much for deathlessness as for wholeness, wisdom, goodness, and godliness—longings that cannot be satisfied fully in our embodied earthly life, the only life, by natural reason, we know we have. Hence the attractiveness of any prospect or promise of a different and thereby fulfilling life hereafter. The decisive inference is clear: none of these longings can be answered by prolonging earthly life. Not even an unlimited amount of "more of the same" will satisfy our deepest aspirations.

If this is correct, there follows a decisive corollary regarding the battle against death. The human taste for immortality, for the imperishable and the eternal, is not a taste that the biomedical conquest of death could satisfy. We would still be incomplete; we would still lack wisdom; we would still lack God's presence and redemption. Mere continuance will not buy fulfillment. Worse, its pursuit threatens—already threatens—human happiness by distracting us from the goals toward which our souls naturally point. By diverting our aim, by misdirecting so much individual and social energy toward the goal of bodily immortality, we may seriously undermine our chances for living as well as we can and for satisfying to some extent, however incompletely, our deepest longings for what is best. The implication for human life is hardly nihilistic: once we acknowledge and accept our finitude, we can concern ourselves with living *well,* and care first and most for the *well-being* of our souls, and not so much for their mere existence.

But perhaps this is all a mistake. Perhaps there is no such longing of the soul. Perhaps there is no soul. Certainly modern science doesn't speak about the soul; neither does medicine or even our psychiatrists, whose name means "healers of the soul." Perhaps we are just animals, complex ones to be sure, but animals nonetheless, content just to be here, frightened in the face of danger, avoiding pain, seeking pleasure.

Curiously, however, biology has its own view of our nature and its inclinations. Biology also teaches about transcendence, though it eschews talk about the soul. Biology has long shown us a feasible way to rise above our finitude and to participate in something permanent and eternal: I refer not to stem cells, but to procreation—the bearing and caring for offspring, for the sake of which many animals risk and even sacrifice their lives. Indeed, in all higher animals, reproduction *as such* implies both the acceptance of the death of self and participation in its transcendence. The salmon, willingly swimming upstream to spawn and die, makes vivid this universal truth.

But man is natured for more than spawning. Human biology teaches how our life points beyond itself—to our offspring, to our community, to our species. Like the other animals, man is built for reproduction. More than the other animals, man is also built for sociality. And, alone among the animals, man is also built for culture—not only though capacities to transmit and receive skills and techniques, but also through capacities for shared beliefs, opinions, rituals, traditions. We are built with leanings toward, and capacities for, perpetuation. Is it not possible that aging and mortality are part of this construction, and that the rate of aging and the human life span have been selected for their usefulness to the task of perpetuation? Could not extending the human life span place a great strain on our nature, jeopardizing our project and depriving us of success? Interestingly, perpetuation is a goal that *is* attainable, a transcendence of self that *is* (largely) realizable. Here is a form of participating in the enduring that is open to us, without qualification—provided, that is, that we remain open to it.

Biological considerations aside, simply to covet a prolonged life span for ourselves is both a sign and a cause of our failure to open ourselves to procreation and to any higher purpose. It is probably no accident that it is a generation whose intelligentsia proclaim the death of God and the meaninglessness of life that embarks on life's indefinite prolongation and that seeks to cure the emptiness of life by extending it forever. For the desire to prolong youthfulness is not only a childish desire to eat one's life and keep it; it is also an expression of a childish and narcissistic wish incompatible with devotion to posterity. It seeks an endless present, isolated from anything truly eternal, and severed from any true continuity with past and future. It is in principle hostile to children, because children, those who come after, are those who will take one's place; *they* are life's answer to mortality, and their presence in one's house is a constant reminder that one no longer belongs to the frontier generation. One cannot pursue agelessness for oneself and remain faithful to the spirit and meaning of perpetuation.

In perpetuation, we send forth not just the seed of our bodies, but also the bearer of our hopes, our truths, and those of our tradition. If our children are to flower, we need to sow them well and nurture them, cultivate them in rich and wholesome soil, clothe them in fine and decent opinions and mores, and direct them toward the highest light, to grow straight and tall—that they may take our place as we took that of those who planted us and made way for us, so that in time they, too, may make way and plant. But if they are truly to flower, we must go to seed; we must wither and give ground.

Against these considerations, the clever ones will propose that if we could do away with death, we would do away with the need for posterity. But that is a self-serving and shallow answer, one that thinks of life and aging solely in terms of the state of the body. It ignores the psychological effects simply of the passage of time—of experiencing and learning about the way things are. After a while, no matter how healthy we are, no matter how respected and well placed we are socially, most of us cease to look upon the world with fresh eyes. Little surprises us, nothing shocks us, righteous indignation at injustice dies out. We have seen it all already, seen it all. We have often been deceived, we have made many mistakes of our own. Many of us become small-souled, having been humbled not by bodily decline or the loss of loved ones but by life itself. So our ambition also begins

to flag, or at least our noblest ambitions. As we grow older, Aristotle already noted, we "aspire to nothing great and exalted and crave the mere necessities and comforts of existence." At some point, most of us turn and say to our intimates, Is this all there is? We settle, we accept our situation—if we are lucky enough to be able to accept it. In many ways, perhaps in the most profound ways, most of us go to sleep long before our deaths—and we might even do so earlier in life if death no longer spurred us to make something of ourselves.

In contrast, it is in the young where aspiration, hope, freshness, boldness, and openness spring anew—even when they take the form of overturning our monuments. Immortality for oneself through children may be a delusion, but participating in the natural and eternal renewal of human possibility through children is not—not even in today's world.

For it still stands as it did when Homer made Glaukos say to Diomedes:

> As is the generation of leaves, so is that of humanity. The wind scatters the leaves to the ground, but the live timber burgeons with leaves again in the season of spring returning. So one generation of man will grow while another dies.

And yet it also still stands, as this very insight of Homer's itself reveals, that human beings are in another respect unlike the leaves; that the eternal renewal of human beings embraces also the eternally human possibility of learning and self-awareness; that we, too, here and now may participate with Homer, with Plato, with the Bible, yes with Descartes and Bacon, in catching at least some glimpse of the enduring truths about nature, God, and human affairs; and that we, too, may hand down and perpetuate this pursuit of wisdom and goodness to our children and our children's children. Children and their education, not growth hormone and perpetual organ replacement, are life's—and wisdom's—answer to mortality.

Longevity, Identity, and Moral Character: A Feminist Approach

Christine Overall

Increases in human life expectancy over the past century and the possibility of growth in the total human life span raise empirical questions about the differences

that greater longevity is making and will make in how we human beings live our lives, how we think of ourselves, and how we relate to each other. They raise

Overall, Christine. "Longevity, Identity, and Moral Character: A Feminist Approach," *The Fountain of Youth: Cultural, Scientific, and Ethical Perspectives on a Biomedical Goal*, ed. Stephen G. Post and Robert H. Binstock, New York: Oxford University Press (2004), 286–303. Copyright © 2004. Reprinted by permission of Oxford University Press.

factual questions about what human beings have and will have time to learn, to do, to experience, and to become habituated to, whether individually or collectively. However, the significant ethical question is normative: in a context of increasing longevity, how *ought* we to live our lives, think of ourselves, and relate to each other?

Life expectancy refers to the average number of years an individual will live; this figure varies by sex, race, and socioeconomic class. *Life span* refers to the maximum amount of time actually lived by any human being, a figure that now stands at around 120 years. There is indisputable evidence that, because of better living conditions and improved medical care, life expectancies have improved markedly over the past century and a half and are likely to continue to do so in the developing nations as well as in the West. There is, however, no scientific consensus as to whether significant increases in maximum life span are attainable. I will nonetheless assume that life span extension is also possible.

In my book (Overall, 2003), I explore a wide range of arguments for and against the value for human beings of an extended life. I will not recapitulate the details of those arguments here. Instead I assume that, other things being equal, a longer life is a better one, provided that one is in a minimally good state of health. The main reason, simply stated, is that a longer life is the prerequisite for almost everything else that one might want. "For anyone who has desires about future states requiring his own existence, it is rational that he regret the anticipation of his nonexistence" (Veatch, 1989, p. 236). The case for valuing longer life is based not on any allegation about the supposed intrinsic value of longevity, of life itself, or of human lives. Instead, it is founded on a genuine appreciation of human potential, of what people want in their lives and are capable of doing and experiencing when given more opportunities. An increased life span gives human beings the chance for activities and experiences that they would not otherwise have enjoyed. Collectively, extending average life expectancy provides for the society in which it occurs the value of increased experience, know-how, labor, loving relationships, and so on—that is, whatever healthy old(er) people can contribute.[1]

I therefore take for granted that increases in life expectancy and life span are worth seeking and, in particular, that society should follow a policy that I call *affirmative prolongevitism* (Overall, 2003), in which efforts are made to increase the life expectancy of members of disadvantaged groups such as poor people, native people, and people of color, whose current life expectancy is lower than that of more privileged white people. In

this chapter, I consider not what the value of longer life is to the individual and to society, but rather what longer life implies for the values that we learn, promulgate, and adhere to, both individually and collectively. My focus here is not on what future moralities will be like. That is, I am not trying to make predictions about the future of moral change. Instead, I am making a case for not just the possibility but also the desirability of moral change, both individually and collectively, given the fact that lives are getting longer. In a context of increasing length of life, what kinds of persons should we be and strive to become, and what ought our responsibilities and values to be? I shall try to delineate, from a feminist philosophical perspective, why this problem arises and is important. I shall also propose a theoretical framework from which these normative questions can best be answered.[2]

THE PROBLEM AND ITS IMPORTANCE

If human lives become significantly longer, we might be tempted to believe that we human beings can just go on in the same way that we have in the past, and that no moral changes are necessary. Daniel Callahan, who for 25 years has argued against increasing either the human life span or human life expectancy, states that there is no good case to show that a longer life would be better, for, he says, "More of the same is not, by itself, a very good argument" (Callahan, 1977, p. 37).[3] Callahan claims that those who seek longer lives want "the clock of the life cycle stopped at a particular point" (1998, pp. 131–132). The realization of this wish, he says, would result in "boredom and ennui, with the possibility of significant change arrested and frozen" (1998, p. 132). Indeed, he suggests that there is no reason to believe that an increased life expectancy would lead to "a better family life, greater economic productivity, a richer cultural and scientific life, or a generally higher standard of collective happiness and sense of well-being" (1998, p. 134).

But Callahan fails to offer arguments to show that longer life would necessarily be "more of the same." The empirical evidence from the distant and near past provides strong evidence both of the capacity of human beings to adapt to and change with the opportunities afforded by increasing age, and of the difficulty, if not the impossibility, of resisting social and technological changes and carrying on in the same way. The accelerating pace of transformation, especially since the Industrial Revolution, indicates that there will be even more to which we must adjust. Even if there can reasonably be said to be a fixed human nature, it nonetheless possesses sufficient plasticity and versatility to allow considerable adaptation to changing conditions, conditions created both through human volition and independent of it. Contrary to Aristotle, human character is not unchangeable, and the plasticity of human nature is not mere passivity to being shaped but the product of active choices in interaction with social and nonsocial environments.

Biomedical ethicists who oppose increasing human life argue that with current life expectancies, individuals already are able to live a full life, so that its ending at the current life expectancy is not an evil (Callahan, 1977, p. 37; 1987, pp. 66–67; 1998, pp. 130–135; see also Hardwig, 2000). But what is a full life? Callahan claims that it is an existence in which "one's life possibilities have on the whole been accomplished" (1987, p. 66). Yet one's life possibilities might well mean one thing under the current life expectancy and something else rather different with a longer life expectancy and a greater maximum life span.

Today, our "life possibilities" are defined and understood within contemporary strictures, not by reference to potentially greater longevity. For example, Callahan says that a "natural death" arrives when, among other conditions, "one's life work has been accomplished" and "one's moral obligations to those for whom one has had responsibility have been discharged" (1977, p. 33; 1987, p. 66). But notice that if our lives become increasingly long, then the concepts of "one's life work" and "one's moral obligations" are likely to change and their dimensions to expand. It is an error, the fallacy of begging the question, to make use of the limited parameters set by current life expectancies in order to argue against increasing human longevity.

For Callahan, one's life's work means "primarily one's vocational or professional work" (1977, p. 33). Even setting aside the possible limitations on or lack of clarity in this definition (does it include familial work, domestic work, volunteer work, hobbies and avocations?), it is also likely that as lives get longer, the scope of individuals' goals will become greater, and people will play a variety of working roles during their lifetimes. Generally, our ideas of what we are capable of taking on will evolve and develop. As they do today, people will undertake new tasks, projects, and interests at different life stages, but if those life stages are longer, then the range of tasks, projects, and interests can become broader.

In addition, our moral obligations may change and grow. As longevity increases, the number of relationships in which one engages and the number of people for whom one has moral responsibility may enlarge. Responsibilities may last longer; the nature of the responsibilities may change; and one may acquire and then discharge responsibilities at various points in a longer life. Once again, to assume that current social and moral exigencies—defined by Callahan in a limited fashion as responsibility for one's immediate biological children (1987, p. 69)—delineate the outward limits of what human beings should expect and do is to beg the question.

The future itself will mean something quite different when there is, reliably, more of it for the average individual. Short lives such as those that prevailed in much of the past and still prevail in poverty-stricken areas of the world must necessarily be more concerned with the basics of physical survival and social reproduction than with education, investigation, creativity, and personal and social development. By contrast, a longer life can be concerned not only with physical maturation but also with individual and cultural maturity and the living of an *optimal life*, a life of fulfillment or meaningfulness (Baier, 1974, pp. 4–5). A society in which lives are longer can aim at the enrichment and enhancement of citizens' lives. I therefore suggest that with increases in longevity, we should not expect more of the same, and we should prepare for and see the necessity of moral change.

It might be objected that, just as individuals ought not to be expected to have different values and responsibilities because of their gender or race, so also is it an error to attribute different values and responsibilities to people because of their age. To ascribe moral responsibilities on the basis of gender or race is to fall prey to sexism and racism, the stereotyping of people, respectively, on the basis of gender and racialization. Therefore, the objection goes, it is an error to suppose that age, even the possibly much greater age that might be achieved through socially steered research and policies to extend life expectancy and life span, should make a difference to one's moral values and responsibilities.

However, my point is not that merely getting older demands new values and responsibilities. My point is that greater longevity, as a widespread social phenomenon, requires the development of new moral systems. The reason is that as the human life span increases, different stages of life are being and will continue to be redefined. I contend that this redefinition of life stages will, unlike gender and racial identities, necessitate moral change. The evidence already shows that increasing longevity creates opportunities for new ways of living (Goddard, 1982, p. 152). For example:

- The enormous growth in research and technology and the concomitant expansion of the knowledge and skills required for many jobs and occupations will have two effects. First, they will continue to increase the time during which offspring are financially dependent or obtaining formal education and are considered to be children and young adults. Thus, what it means to be a child and a young adult will be redefined. Second, the growth in research and technology and the concomitant expansion of knowledge and skills will continue to make it necessary for individuals to move into and out of educational institutions and training environments at a variety of points during their lives. *Lifelong learning* in the form of formal and informal schooling will permit people to continue to acquire skills, information, and understanding as need and interest dictate. Thus, what *schooling* and *education* mean will be redefined.

- Familial, romantic, and amical relationships could last longer. In addition, there would be opportunities for more relationships at various points during the longer life. There may be an increase in the current trend of postponing decisions to enter into permanent and/or legally sanctioned relationships such as marriage. For many, it might be normal and unsurprising to have several legal or common-law marriages or other intimate relationships during one's life, along with divorces and breakups. Moreover, since sexual orientation and gender are becoming more fluid in some people, there may be more variations in sexual and gender identities. Thus, what *marriage, partnership, friendship, sexuality,* and *gender* mean will be redefined.

- Better health and increasing technological control over conception, contraception, gestation, and birth make it possible not only to change the period of time that women devote to reproductive behaviors, but also to have children later in life. Extended or intermittent periods of childbearing and childrearing could be aided by adoption both within and outside national borders, and by the use of new reproductive technologies and practices, whether or not they are legally sanctioned, including sperm donation, in vitro fertilization, contract motherhood, and cloning. One would have much more of a chance not only to raise one's children but to know them well past what we now call middle age. The ideas of, and the length of time committed to, parenthood and childrearing could change as the relationship of parent to child becomes ever longer. We would live to see our great-grandchildren and even our great-great-grandchildren grow to adulthood, and large multigenerational extended families, not necessarily all living in the same place or even the same country, would be possible. Changes in family configurations would include more single parents, blended families, gay couples, and lesbian couples. Thus, *father, mother, parent, grandparent,* and *family* will be redefined.

- With the evolution of technology, changes in resources, and growth in knowledge, there will also be changes to work, work lives, and the number of jobs or careers that an individual may hold (for all of these, see Madigan, 1999, p. 43). Longer lives and the rapid pace of change provide the opportunity and even the necessity of engaging in several careers during one lifetime, and of both self-employment and moving from one employer to another rather than working for a single institution for all one's working days. With changes in access to employment and work, there will be changes

in material security, living environments, and mobility. The life stage called *retirement,* when individuals with adequate financial means can be relieved of all or most paid work, engage in leisure activities, and enjoy relatively good health for a longer period of time is becoming a reality for many in the West. The age of retirement may change, becoming more flexible, and work sabbaticals may be available. *Work, job, career,* and *retirement* will therefore be redefined.

In enumerating these possible changes to life stages, I am not suggesting that they are all unavoidable, or that they are necessarily all desirable and good. My point is just that as human longevity increases, life stages will be re-created and reinterpreted; we will adopt new roles and new identities. Even within current life spans, we can see that some human beings are capable of changing their lives, of making new beginnings, of virtually becoming different selves (Overall, 2003). The religious convert, the reformed alcoholic, the dedicated first-time parent, the newly disabled individual, the immigrant to a different society, the recently released prisoner, and the adult who learns to read at the age of 40 are all persons who are engaged in processes of re-creating themselves. Given the resources and the opportunities, human beings are capable of changing their lives, often even in the face of oppressive or debilitating circumstances.

Many human beings today, perhaps the vast majority, never have the chance fully to explore and express all of their potential as physical/emotional/moral/intellectual beings. What type of person we can reasonably want and intend to be depends in part on what our social and environmental context permits, forbids, or encourages. A more prolonged life would provide at least some of that missed opportunity. With new and redefined life stages, human beings will have the prospect of taking up new values and responsibilities. What type of person we *ought* to be depends on what kind of person we can be. When we get a glimpse of how our identities—who we are—may change as a result of increasing years, we may also see in what ways our character—who we ought to be—should change.

RETHINKING MORALITY

To answer the question of how we should live in the context of extended life expectancies and life spans, I propose a feminist virtue ethics approach. The word *virtue* has acquired, within the past century, a connotation of chastity, especially women's chastity and sexual purity. This association is unfortunate. In its older sense, *virtue* meant "moral excellence," and this is the sense in which it is used within virtue ethics. In general, virtue ethics is less concerned with the modern ethical questions "What are my moral obligations?" and "What is my duty?" than with problems that are both ancient and yet enduring: "How should I live?" and "What kind of person should I be?"

In virtue ethics, the unit of ethical appraisal and judgment is not an action or a class of actions, but the character and life of an individual. Although it is "neither desirable nor feasible" entirely to separate actions from agents (Tong, 1998, p. 136); the focus of virtue ethics is on the individual agent and his or her character, from which actions flow. Thus, morality is rooted more in persons and their characters than in acts or rules. What is foundational is not right and wrong action alone, but rather good and bad character, which predispose one to right or wrong action. Character is a "complex disposition" to act in certain ways (S. Leighton, personal communication); one's character is the composite of the psychological qualities, both mental and moral, that make one a distinct person.

Virtue theorists believe there is an important connection between virtue and human flourishing. Virtues may be variously other-regarding and self-regarding, and possessing moral virtues, being morally virtuous, benefits both other people and oneself. Thus, becoming a good person and cultivating moral virtues is closely tied to the creation of good both for oneself and for others. In the words of Rosalind Hursthouse, "A virtuous agent is one who acts virtuously, that is, one who has and exercises the virtues" (1996, p. 23), and "An action is right if [if and only if] it is what a virtuous agent would characteristically (i.e., acting in character) do in the circumstances" (p. 22). Asking oneself what a virtuous person would do in a given case need not generate hard and fast rules; virtue is not a fixed feature, but something that one repeatedly chooses and expresses in action. The virtuous person has moral knowledge that enables him or her to choose the appropriate actions within ethical contexts; he or she is a moral role model whose behavior is a guide to a moral way of life.

What distinguishes feminist from nonfeminist ethics? What would make virtue ethics feminist? I shall describe three main characteristics of feminist virtue ethics, characteristics that demonstrate, I think, how well suited virtue ethics is to being the morality for increased human longevity.

Personal and social context

Modern Western philosophy advocates impartial reasoning as the method for moral decisionmaking. However, "in requiring the absence of bias toward or against any subjective interests, impartiality thereby demands that the moral agent reason in detachment from her own loyalties, projects, and emotions. These forms of detachment . . . are inimical to what is required for the maintenance of close personal relationships" (Friedman, 1998, p. 394). Moreover, "[I]mpartiality requires that persons and situations be conceptualized in terms of generalizable categories. This approach ignores the rich contextual detail of particular situations" (1998, p. 397). By contrast, feminism advocates what Alisa Carse calls "qualified particularism," which "highlight[s] concrete and nuanced perception and understanding— including an attunement to the reality of other people and to the actual relational contexts we find ourselves in" (Carse, quoted in Tong, 1998, p. 134). We are not just individual moral actors, but also workers, children, parents, friends, colleagues, creators, consumers, and citizens. We are situated, and we live within relationships. Feminist virtue ethics therefore bids moral actors and appraisers to take personal and social contexts into account when making moral decisions and judgments. Virtues (and vices) do not develop in a social vacuum, and the expression of good character involves connections and interactions with other human beings. As Sarah Conly acknowledges, virtue ethics emphasizes "the personal nature of moral life"; it implies that "our personal commitments should inform our moral choices" (Conly, 2001, p. 12).

Feminist virtue ethics allows for the possibility that appropriate and genuine virtues may be defined in relation to the specific communities in which they are needed and valued (Blum, 1996, p. 233). For example, a community whose existence depends on agriculture in an unstable climate may require of many of its members the characteristics of patience, stoicism, versatility, and acceptance. A community that is under constant attack from hostile neighbors may require the characteristics of courage, strength, and endurance. Some virtues, then, are both generated by and also function to sustain the communities within which they exist (Blum, 1996, p. 234). This is not to say that patience, versatility, courage, and so on are not virtues outside of those communities, or that they may not be needed in other communities with different characteristics and in different environments. I am not advocating ethical relativism. It is merely to emphasize that the pragmatic salience of certain virtues can ebb and flow, and that some virtues may be of greater value for the flourishing of some communities, and of individuals in those communities, than for others.

Since feminist ethics emphasizes the importance of personal and social contexts both in shaping moral challenges and in providing the data for responding to them, it requires us to be aware of contexts of aging and of increasing longevity. Philosophical sensitivity to the ways social contexts affect ethics and morality must be extended to take into account the increasing length of human lives. Some virtues, like honesty and truthfulness, may be important for a lifetime, while others, such as receptiveness or assertiveness, may be more useful at some life stages than at others. As communities change and evolve, in part because people live longer and have different and wider opportunities, the nature of the virtues that are relevant to life within those communities may change, requiring, for example, versatility, resilience, tolerance, compassion, courage, and openness to differences and diversity.

The influence of oppression and marginalization on morality

So feminists insist that the individual and cultural contexts of moral characteristics, problems, and judgments must be acknowledged. As Margaret Urban Walker puts it, "moral knowledge like other knowledge is situated (that is, it is made possible and is limited by where it comes from and how it is achieved)" (Walker, 1998, p. 6). Ethicists ought not to make moral evaluations or construct moral theory within a vacuum. Morality and moral systems cannot be analyzed and assessed without attention to the social context in which moral values are transmitted and moral decisions are made. Ethicists and policy makers must take into account the effects and implications of cultural categories such as gender, race, class, sexual orientation, ability, and age, and their attendant belief systems and stereotypes.

Feminism helps us to consider how these assigned and acquired identities influence what kinds of persons we choose to become and are shaped to be. It alerts us to the significance of systematic forms of oppression such as sexism, racism, classism, ableism, and heterosexism, which differentially advantage and disadvantage members of different groups, shape social images of what different groups are like and should be like, and constrain people's lives in order to force them to conform to norms derived not from their best interests but from presumptions about their place in society. Individual communities, even small ones, are not monocultures, and some of the differences within a community come from the inequities they encompass and the relationships of dominance and subordination that prevail between different subgroups.

Feminists also draw attention to the influence of ageism and age categories on personal identities and social interactions (e.g., Copper, 1988; Macdonald, 1991; Walker, 1999). Western society is rife with stereotyping on the basis of age, stereotyping that is empirically and morally unjustified:

> Old people in American society constitute a minority group whose members are victims of ageism. For decades, there has been widespread acceptance of negative stereotypes about the aged involving references to their intellectual decline, conservatism, sexual decline, lack of productivity, and preference for disengagement. Though most such images are based on halftruths or outright falsities, they continue to be used to justify the maltreatment of the aged by American society.
>
> (Levin and Levin, 1980, p. 95)

For, as Phillida Salmon points out, contrary to ageist biases, it is "supremely improbable that a person's age should define her better than anything else about her— that the mere passage of time should tell us all we need to know of her. It might even be said that a standardized, age-governed view is less and less appropriate as people get older.... [I]t may be that the person becomes more themselves and less like anyone else, the further they advance through life" (Salmon, 1985, p. 41). Contrary to ageist stereotypes about aging people, the potential to adapt and change is a fundamental characteristic of all human beings at all ages. Hence, as human lives get longer, it will be essential to be critical of categories such as *the elderly, the aging,* and *senior citizens.* We would have to give up, once and for all, the unthinking assumption that adulthood is the apex of life, for which childhood is the preparation and from which old age is merely the decline and downward deterioration (Salmon, 1985, pp. 3–4).

Feminists point out that many of our present moral categories, concepts, and expectations are tainted by prevailing conditions of inequality, marginalization, and injustice. Feminist ethicists argue that traditional philosophical concepts of personhood, autonomy, obligation, rules, and the nature of morality itself, purported to be objective and neutral, have been skewed by philosophers' failure to be critical of these social categories and their implications. As Walker puts it, "moral theories end up encoding specific social positions and cultural assumptions in highly idealized forms" (Walker, 1998, p. x). "These theories idealize relations of nonintimate, mutually independent peers seeking to preserve autonomy or enhance self-interest in rule- (or role-) bound voluntary interactions. They mirror spheres of activity, social roles, and character ideals associated with socially advantaged men." (Walker, 1998, p. 20).

Feminist virtue ethics is founded upon this critical analysis of subordinated identities and the necessity of a politically grounded evaluation of moral systems. Prevailing concepts of moral goodness and virtue are not immune to cultural influence and must be subjected to evaluation. Persons of different sexes, races, classes, and so on learn different sorts of virtues and come to ascribe moral value to different activities and goals. Many virtues are gendered, racialized, and reflective of other categories such as class. In the past, for example, the virtues expected from the slave were not the same as the virtues expected from the free man. The virtuous child was not supposed to act in the same ways as the virtuous adult. Being good was different for a *lady* than for a more *common* woman. Because slavery is wrong, we must be critical of the virtues assigned to slaves and to their masters. If the social categories of lady and of the common woman demean women and limit their potential, then we must also consider how the virtues associated with these categories uphold marginalization. And if children have traditionally been treated as chattels or commodities, then we must investigate how the virtues assigned to children may uphold their status as object and prevent them from being recognized as developing persons.

Moreover, just as the virtues traditionally attributed to women both arose from and helped to sustain the sexism that kept women down, so also, as Sara Ruddick points out, "[T]he alleged virtues of age often mirror the values responsible for ageism" (Ruddick, 1999, p. 45). Feminist virtue ethics casts a critical eye upon the supposed virtues typically assigned to the aged. In the not so far off past, old people were expected to be quiet, complaisant, cooperative, and helpful. More recently, aging people have been expected to be cheery, active, and independent. Both prescriptions appear designed to counteract the supposed weaknesses and moral failings of elderly people. That is, they both arise from and reinforce invidious stereotypes of elderly people. They also serve an oppressive function: as Ruddick comments, prescriptive "portraits of productive and plucky 'good elderly'" may intimidate people who are already dealing with exhaustion, sadness, and fear (Ruddick, 1999, p. 46).

With increasing longevity, it becomes even more important to be cognizant of how ageism and age categories influence morality and moral theory, and to consider how morality might justifiably change if an anti-ageist stance is taken. Feminist virtue ethics mandates political assessment of existing ideas about the virtues of aging, old people, and great longevity.

Unacknowledged moral virtues

The perspective of feminist virtue ethics also helps us to see that members of oppressed groups cultivate and possess genuinely valuable virtues, sometimes partly as a result of coping with and responding to the subordinated position assigned to them. Yet these virtues under oppression are often unrecognized, actively shunned, or perceived as being not appropriate for more privileged persons. For example, Susan Moller Okin talks about the virtues women have historically needed to sustain and care for other human beings, such characteristics as "the capacity to nurture, patience, the ability to listen carefully and to teach (sometimes mundane things) well, and the readiness to give up or postpone one's own projects in order to pay attention to the needs or projects of others" (Okin, 1996, pp. 227–228). Because the kind of labor that is sustained by these capacities is not always recognized as true work or as truly valuable, the capacities themselves have not always been acknowledged as virtues, yet they deserve to be recognized. The cultivation of traditional "women's" virtues such as caring and sympathy seems to "promise a more humane, benevolent world than does mere action according to duty" (Conly, 2001, p. 12).

Therefore, when we think about the kinds of virtues needed for extended life, we should not simply adhere to traditional notions of middle-class, white, masculine, and youthful (or age-neutral) virtue. We should recognize that many of the characteristics actually acquired by aging people and people gifted with unusual longevity could be genuine virtues and would be genuinely beneficial for other members of the community to cultivate. These might include reflective thought, caring, innovativeness, determination, and a commitment to (some forms of) continued independence, along with the recognition that (some forms of) dependence may be inevitable. Ruddick lists as virtues of old people "curiosity; a capacity for pleasure and delight; concern for near and distant others; capacities to forgive and let go, to accept, adjust, and appreciate; and 'wise independence,' which includes not only the ability to plan and control one's life but also the ability to acknowledge one's limitations and accept help in ways that are gratifying to the helper" (Ruddick, 1999, p. 50). Although it's likely that developing many of these characteristics requires, as a necessary condition, maturity and years of living, the claim is not that all elderly people possess them. The point is that they are significant virtues, recognizable as such through the antiageist political analysis afforded by feminist virtue ethics. If ageism inhibits us from recognizing the virtues of aging long and well, feminist virtue ethics provides a remedy.

FEMINIST VIRTUE ETHICS AND EXTENDED LIVES

As I suggested earlier, the extension of human life is of significant value because it provides human beings with opportunities for engaging in activities and seeking experiences that they would not otherwise have enjoyed if their lives had ended sooner. This is not to say that any experience or any activity is necessarily valuable. Nor is it to assume that every prolonged life is necessarily better, that no one may ever rationally reject a longer life, or that all persons will inevitably make good use of the years they have. But it is to say that what is deeply evil about death, especially a death that is earlier than necessary, is that it terminates all possibilities for anything more.

A longer life provides a greater chance for human flourishing, for learning virtues, and for living a good life. The person who seeks to foster in herself the appropriate virtues and who is successful to at least some degree is the person who will best be able to adapt to a changing environment, who will be more likely to transform herself, and who will be able to flourish within the context of a longer life. I suggest that if, within the context of increasing longevity, we adopt feminist virtue ethics, we will find ourselves reflecting about not just what kind of person we should be, but what kind of person we should *become*. We will need to ask ourselves not just what kind of life we should *lead*, but also what kind of life we should *leave*—that is, what aspects of ourselves we should voluntarily choose to abandon because they no longer contribute to individual or collective well-being. Moreover, in a world in which people are able to enjoy extended lifetimes, our moral lives will not, and probably cannot and should not, be monolithic. Salmon comments, "We all carry within us, encompass within ourselves, something of the people we have been. It is to these people, intimately familiar, though partly 'other,' that we constantly turn" (Salmon, 1985, p. 15). By the same token, by living longer, we acquire many more people to whom we can turn.

Conly, however, objects that virtue ethics, including feminist appropriations of it, has a fundamental flaw: because virtue ethics is concerned with "our whole internal orientation—our emotions, our commitments, our attitudes towards others, our whole psychology"— it is highly intrusive. It makes ethics inescapable; no area of one's life is immune to it: "The cultivation of virtue is a moral task from which there is no respite" (Conly, 2001, p. 13). Moreover, because it is concerned

with one's character, with who one fundamentally is, attempts to adopt virtue ethics will produce personal fragmentation when the demands of different virtues conflict with each other, as they inevitably will. Hence, "[t]he problem [with virtue ethics] is not that living virtuously may make one unhappy . . . but that it promotes a condition in which the very goal we want to achieve, a unified and integrated character, becomes impossible" (Conly, 2001, p. 14).

I think this objection is founded upon an error, and that error becomes even more obvious if we contemplate adopting virtue ethics within the context of lengthening human lives. Conly assumes that a "unified and integrated character" is necessarily a goal for those who hope to live good lives. She fears the development of "an unacceptable fragmentation into incoherent parts, each pulling in a different direction, with no mediating principle" (Conly, 2001, p. 14). But the idea of a unified self is something of an illusion, born precisely of the modernist tendency to see the self as the contained, independent, nonrelational individual that feminism has criticized. Attention to the relational nature of human social life makes it clear that a human person is a composite of many identities, roles, characteristics, skills, relationships, desires, and needs. Moreover, this composite self, far from being pathological, is a highly adaptive means of handling the variegated demands of postindustrial human life. Within an extended life we will more and more be asking ourselves not just what kind of *life* we should lead, but also what kind of *lives* we should lead. Longer life provides the potential for an extended learning process, for more experience and activities, and for opportunities to develop one's character. Within an extended life we will play more roles: son or daughter, parent, student, friend, worker, employer, role model, leader, grandparent, volunteer, caregiver, partner, great-grandparent, colleague, owner, consumer, citizen, voter, artist, athlete, business person, hobbyist, lobbyist. These new roles will generate moral questions about cultivating and changing one's character and one's community that are best handled through feminist virtue ethics. With its emphasis on personal and social contexts, its awareness of the effects of stereotyped identities and forms of oppression such as ageism, and its attention to the virtues of aging and longevity, feminist virtue ethics suggests ways of reforming morality as the human life span and life expectancies become longer.

My goal in this chapter has not been to establish that feminist virtue ethics is the best approach to ethics in general but, somewhat more modestly, to show that feminist virtue ethics is ideally suited to the challenges posed by increasing human longevity. My aim is not moral prescription or the promotion of moral uniformity, but rather to make plausible the theoretical point that feminist virtue ethics provides a general framework for thinking about our future moral lives. While I have named what I think are some important virtues, I offer here no definitive answers to questions about the specific characteristics that should be cultivated within the context of longer lives.[4] Elderly people "are neither more nor less virtuous than people of other age groups" (Ruddick, 1999, p. 47). Yet the virtues needed for longevity may be found in the characters of people who live longer and age well, who acquire them through the experiences and activities of flourishing within an extended lifetime.

NOTES

1. Within a longer life there is more time to acquire moral wisdom and insight, although, of course, there's nothing inevitable about that. I do not want to romanticize old age or what can be learned or experienced by living long. That is why the question of how to live as lives become longer is a normative issue, not an empirical one. In this chapter I am not concerned with what people do achieve, acquire, experience, or learn, but rather with the prospects for what they both can and ought to do.

2. This discussion is based upon two further assumptions. First, I assume a secular context for the discussion. I shall not make use of specifically religious values (although some values advocated by some religions may well be relevant to the discussion), and I shall not assume the existence of an omnipotent, omniscient god. Therefore, second, I assume that ethical issues generated by the prospect of longer human life arise in the context of existence here on earth, not in connection with any purported afterlife, whether in heaven or in the form of a reincarnated state of existence.

3. Callahan fails to provide an argument showing why more of the same cannot be good. One could reasonably say that whether or not more of the same is good depends on what one's life has already been like. If more of same includes additional fulfilling relationships, interesting activities, and personal challenges, then more of the same sounds desirable to me.

4. Some questions about the virtues needed for greater longevity are self-reflexive. For example, what should our moral attitude toward future generations be? Should we cultivate a disposition to increase human lives?

Chapter 10

Issues at End of Life

A Compassionate Ending: An Interview with Dr. Jack Kevorkian

Jack Kevorkian, M.D., is one of the most controversial physicians in the world. He attracted a lot of media attention in the early to mid-nineties due to his outspoken ideas about euthanasia, or "a good death," and was recently released from prison after serving an eight-year sentence for practicing active euthanasia. Between 1990 and 1998, Dr. Kevorkian assisted in the suicide of over one hundred terminally ill people.

In the following excerpted interview, Dr. Kevorkian discusses his ideas about personal freedom, why the practice of euthanasia is so important, and how the availability of euthanasia might actually prolong the lives of terminally-ill patients.

Q:　　　*What do you think are some of the biggest problems with modern medicine and what do you think needs to be done to help correct the situation?*

Dr. Kevorkian:　*The biggest problem with Western medicine is that there is a need for establishing an appropriate system and structure for death with dignity. For those who are facing a terminal illness, who are in irremediable pain and suffering, and wish to exercise their right to die with dignity, a system should be available to them. We also need more structured and reasonable organ donation and transplant systems. 18,000 people die each year waiting for organs. To help correct this situation there has to be an organized public response and outcry—which I believe is now occurring. The current system has not worked well enough to meet the medical needs.*

Q:　　　*Why do you think it's so important for physicians to be able to practice euthanasia without the fear of legal prosecution?*

Dr. Kevorkian:　*Medical art and science are entirely secular and serve a dual purpose: to lengthen life and to preserve or enhance its quality. Theoretically both aims are equally important, but arbitrary (and mainly sectarian) bias fostered an obsession to prolong life, no matter how inimical to its quality. The benefits of medicine permit its practitioners to perform acts that ordinarily are crimes. Thus we condone and even laud surgical mutilation like open heart surgery or organ transplants and tolerate for cancer treatment nearly lethal poisoning with chemotherapy. The resultant quality of life is always subordinate to the chief aim of prolonging it. Why shouldn't the ranking order sometimes be reversed? Why should we not just as readily praise and support the chief aim of relieving pain and suffering for those with terminal illnesses—humanely, expediently and with certainty—an intolerably low quality of individual life through a medical act ordinarily deemed to be homicide? As a secular profession medicine is relevant to the full spectrum of human existence from conception through death. I think that any arbitrary legal constriction of that relevance is irrational, cruel, and barbaric.*

Q:　　　*What are your thoughts about how the availability of euthanasia might prolong the lives of terminally-ill patients?*

Dr. Kevorkian: *The mere availability of the euthanasia option often improves the quality of, and even prolongs, the lives of many terminal and incurably suffering patients. Having such a choice seems to dissipate the panic and helplessness by assuring a modicum of personal control. Consequently the vast majority of patients went on to die "naturally" and with few complaints despite continued excruciating suffering. This was the case with most patients who contacted me.*

Q: *How do you envision euthanasia being put into practice by physicians?*

Dr. Kevorkian: *Not all physicians will want or, by temperament, be able to perform euthanasia. For them, and for patients alike, it's a matter of free choice based on personal belief, faith, or philosophy of life. The service should be a kind of medical specialty staffed by experienced and competent practitioners to whom reticent colleagues may refer inquiries. Because medical guidelines change frequently as a result of research and clinical experience, such procedural details cannot be dictated by law.*

Excerpted from "A Compassionate Ending: An Interview with Dr. Jack Kevorkian" in *Mavericks of Medicine: Exploring the Future of Medicine* with Andrew Weil, Jack Kevorkian, Bernie Siegel, Ray Kurzweil and Others by David Jay Brown, Smart Publications, 2006. The full interview is available at http://www.smart-publications.com/articles/MOM-kevorkian.php

CASE STUDY: DEATH WITH DIGNITY?

Jason Good is a middle-aged college professor from Oregon who has been a cancer survivor for the past 5 years. When Professor Good was initially diagnosed with cancer, it was a stunning and unexpected blow. He had just finished a year of studying abroad in Greece, completing work on his book project. He exercised regularly, drank moderately, and did not smoke; and he always took special care to avoid foods purported to cause cancer. Professor Good returned to the United States feeling quite well, until he started to experience severe headaches that led to episodes of blindness and numbness in his body. He made an appointment to see his physician, who, after detecting a mass, referred Good to an oncologist. The oncologist regretfully informed Professor Good that he did, indeed, have a brain tumor, which was later determined to be malignant and fairly aggressive.

Professor Good in turn elected for the most aggressive approach to his cancer treatment, undergoing months of surgery, chemotherapy, and radiation. Though the side effects were often harsh (including severe nausea and vomiting, loss of appetite, mouth sores, and hair loss), he saw it through and was eventually rewarded by a huge reduction in the brain mass, with stoppage in its growth. The treatment regimen definitely affected him physically and mentally, changing him from his usual assertive and confident self to someone more introverted and uncertain. After his first experience with cancer, he did not relish a recurrence, and was not sure how he would react if it came back.

The cancer did return, however, with a vengeance. When Professor Good returned to his oncologist and was told the mass was growing again, the rate of the tumor's growth was quite alarming. He quickly developed a new mass about the same size as the one that had taken several years to develop, and his oncologist reported that there was not much they could do, though a repeat treatment cycle was recommended.

Professor Good took stock of his situation. He had completed a major book project, had traveled and spent quality time with his family, and felt that he could not bear another series of treatments. He was tired and defeated. But he did not want to wait for the several weeks to months that it would take to die a slow and painful death; he was a strong believer in being in charge of his own life, and wanted control over the time and mode of his death. Having heard that Oregon has a "Death with Dignity" act, Professor Good went to his physician to look into it further.

The physician told Professor Good that, as a resident of Oregon, he could use the Death with Dignity Act to secure his death, if he followed the Act's guidelines. The physician did talk to him about other options, including good pain control and the use of hospice services, but the professor was not interested in these other modes of dealing with his cancer. So Professor Good secured a second opinion, indicating that he was likely to die within the next six months; and he wrote a letter to his physician indicating his wish to die, following up 15 days later with a reiteration of his request. He also contacted his family members to inform them of his decision.

Professor Good was given a prescription for barbiturates, with instructions for how to take them to achieve his death. The night before his death, he held a dinner party that included his friends and loved ones; he expressed his regret that his time with them was coming to an end, but emphasized the fulfilling and happy life he had lived. The next morning he lay on the couch and took the barbiturates as instructed. He died peacefully, with the sun streaming into his living room.

Professor Good's situation, and the circumstances surrounding his death, represents the ideal scenario that advocates have in mind when they petition for physician-assisted suicide. This man was lucid, competent, rational, and, though obviously upset about the return of his cancer, was not suffering clinical depression. He had terminal cancer and was given a prognosis of 6 months to live. Professor Good was committed to living his conception of the good life, which included deciding the time, place, and mode of his death. His death, while sad, was not a tragedy; it was an expression of his intolerance of further pain and suffering, and the kind of death he wanted to have. While some people would have chosen to see the cancer through to its end, Professor Good elected to end things on what he saw as a "high note."

Even given such ideal circumstances, however, Professor Good's actions (and his use of a statute that *entitles* him to those actions) raise profound concerns about physician-assisted suicide and active euthanasia. Should a person's autonomy and freedom of choice extend to determining how and when he or she will die? On one view of it, the right to choose how and when to die is one of the most basic applications of patient autonomy, since control over how one dies is central to having bodily autonomy and respecting individual conceptions of the good life. On a contrary view, extending autonomy to include determining how and when we die reflects and even encourages the idea that we are masters over ourselves and that there is nothing "natural" about the dying process; it suggests that, to the bitter end, we can and should control life.

Some people are still surprised to learn that physician-assisted suicide is, indeed, legal in the United States (Figure 10.1). While Oregon and Washington are the only states that currently allow the practice, there are other states (like New York) where unsuccessful attempts have been made to legalize it. The procedures connected with statutes like the Oregon Death with Dignity Act are meant to protect the individual, the medical profession, and society from the misapplication of physician-assisted suicide; but still, critics argue that such statutues are deeply flawed and that no legislation, no matter how carefully crafted, can protect against the abuse and misapplication of the law

Whatever one's view of Professor Good's choice, and statutes like the Death with Dignity Act, practices of active euthanasia and physician-assisted suicide are not likely to go away. On the contrary, there is a long and complex human history in connection to different forms of suicide and/or euthanasia.

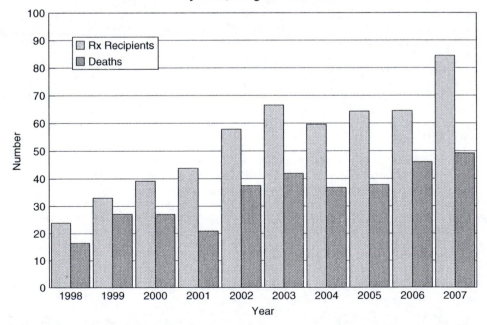

FIGURE 10.1   Death with Dignity Act Prescriptions and Deaths.

Among Romans, for example, suicide and euthanasia were considered to be legitimate practices; in some cultures, ill or "defective" infants have been killed by exposure to the elements, to spare that infant and its community the harm of continued existence; and even in contemporary societies, many people have elected to take their lives (whether legally or illegally) rather than live with certain illnesses or diseases.

The question that plagues us, then, is not whether these acts take place or not, but how a society should *respond* to them. Do statutes like the Death with Dignity Act represent socially endorsed killing, or simply the acknowledgment that people will find ways to achieve death, and that monitoring the conditions under which it happens is better than letting it happen in secret? Does acknowledgment of the practice chip away at respect for life, and possibly erode physicians' commitments to providing the best care possible for all patients? These are the questions that Professor Good's act of physician-assisted suicide raises, and that we must continue to address within bioethics.

DEFINITIONS AND TERMINOLOGY

To begin with, and to keep our categories clear, let's consider the difference between **euthanasia** and **physician-assisted suicide.** In the case of euthanasia—literally meaning "the good death"—doctors take or omit actions that may result in the death of their patients: at patients' requests, they may turn off respirators, or fail to start treatments that would normally be implemented, or they may even give lethal injections. But in the case of physician-assisted suicide, doctors give patients the means to end their *own* lives (e.g., by writing prescriptions for lethal doses of barbiturates), but are not directly involved in the patients' deaths. This means patients can go off on their own with the proper means to effectively end their lives.

As a case in point, in 1991 Dr. Timothy Quill, a medical doctor, published a now-famous article in the *New England Journal of Medicine* (see this chapter) in which he admitted to participating in physician-assisted suicide.[1] Dr. Quill gave one of his cancer patients, Diane, a prescription for pills that he knew she would use to take her life when she felt it was appropriate. Quill says that when he gave her the prescription, "I made sure that she knew how to use the barbiturates for sleep, and also that she knew the amount needed to commit suicide." Quill's admission raised questions about a doctor's role in helping patients to end their lives, and in fact violated laws against aiding and abetting people in suicide attempts; he was investigated following the publication of his article, but was never convicted of any wrongdoing.

In addition to the distinction between euthanasia and physician-assisted suicide, there is also a distinction between different *kinds* of euthanasia. The difference between **active euthanasia** and **passive euthanasia** is most often characterized as the difference between killing versus letting die. Active euthanasia occurs when doctors take direct action to end patients' lives, usually by giving them lethal injections. Bioethicists refer to active euthanasia as entailing acts of **commission,** since physicians are direct agents, *committing* acts that are intended to end the lives of dying patients. Passive euthanasia is conversely referred to as involving acts of **omission,** since in those cases physicians *omit* acts that might extend dying patients' lives (such as doing cardiopulmonary resuscitation, or starting a course of antibiotics to treat an underlying infection). The distinction has been an important one, drawing a line that physicians must not cross between "letting nature take its course" and actively ending patients' lives.

THE CASE OF KAREN ANN QUINLAN

The case of Karen Ann Quinlan set the stage for the active/passive distinction that we now see applied in the clinical context. In 1975, at 21 years of age, Quinlan suffered a collapse at a friend's party, and was taken home and put to bed. She was found not breathing when her friends checked on her shortly thereafter; an ambulance was called, and mouth-to-mouth resuscitation was performed. Quinlan did not regain consciousness, however, and after 9 days in a hospital she was transferred to a larger facility, where she was kept alive by respirator and regular tube feedings (Figure 10.2).

It was determined that Quinlan had suffered severe and irreversible brain damage caused by anoxia, the sustained lack of oxygen to her brain. She was in a **persistent vegetative state,** a deep form of unconsciousness from which patients do not recover. After several months of seeing her in this

FIGURE 10.2   The 1975 case of Karen Ann Quinlan brought out the distinction between active and passive euthanasia that we now see applied in the clinical context.

condition, Quinlan's family decided to remove her from the ventilator, deeming her situation to be beyond hope. But the hospital refused to allow this action, and Quinlan's family turned to the New Jersey Supreme Court, which in 1976 ruled in the family's favor.[2] The ventilator was removed, but much to the surprise of all, Karen Quinlan continued to breathe on her own; she lived on, breathing unaided and being fed through a nasogastric tube, for 9 years. In 1985, Karen died from pneumonia.

As a Catholic, Quinlan's father held to a moral theology that allowed for the removal of the artificial intervention that was keeping her alive. The intention was not to kill his daughter, but to remove the respirator to let nature "take its course." The ventilator was treated as an **extraordinary means** of keeping Quinlan alive; it was viewed as an intervention that could be removed, even if doing so might hasten her natural death. To this day, many bioethicists and moral theologians adhere to this distinction between killing versus letting die.

The distinction between active and passive euthanasia, or killing versus letting die, is problematic, although it has been broadly endorsed by bodies such as the American Medical Association. Some critics (see James Rachels in this chapter) point out that there is no moral or practical difference between killing and letting die. In both cases, the patient is terminally ill, and death is the desired goal. And again, in both cases, whether the physician stands by and "does nothing" or actively takes the life, the patient does, indeed, die. So, according to this criticism, there is no real difference between the two, and actively taking a life is no morally worse than allowing a patient to die.

The difference between active euthanasia and physician-assisted suicide has also been the subject of considerable debate. Some bioethicists would again want to draw a bright line between physician-assisted suicide and active euthanasia, given the difference in the degree to which in these practices physicians are involved in the taking of lives. While some bioethicists are committed to both kinds of practices, many endorse physician-assisted suicide (where physicians merely provide the means for patients to take their own lives) but reject active euthanasia (where physicians themselves become the agents of death). The reason for this split is the concern that physicians should not become too directly involved in taking patients' lives, since the implications of doing so can be grave for both individual practitioners and for the culture of medicine itself.

Ethicists opposed to active euthanasia and physician-assisted suicide make a number of claims concerning the moral wrongness of these practices. These claims are as follows:

• Helping patients to die violates the doctor's duty to save lives.
• Human beings do not have a right to take their own lives—this is playing God.

- The consequences of allowing active euthanasia and physician-assisted suicide would be very bad, indeed, for society; patients would no longer trust doctors, and we might end up killing patients who do not want to die, or who cannot state their wishes in that regard.
- We need to maintain a distinction between killing patients and letting them die; if we cross the line between passive and active euthanasia, we go too far.
- Active euthanasia and physician-assisted suicide are most likely to target and be practiced on society's "undesirables"—older adults, those with disabilities or mental handicaps, and the poor. It could result in a kind of social eugenics.
- Doctors should not be making value judgments about which lives are worth living and which ones aren't.

By contrast, those ethicists who favor practices of active euthanasia and physician-assisted suicide offer the following arguments:

- Doctors have a duty to prevent pain and suffering, and helping terminally ill patients to die is just an extension of that duty.
- Each individual has the right to die, and should have help by willing doctors in exercising that right.
- The consequences of policies against these practices are bad for patients. They end up forced to withstand slow and painful deaths.
- We can no longer distinguish a "natural" death from an "unnatural" one. Medicine has been used to extend lives far beyond what nature intended, so we can't appeal to letting "nature take its course" in any meaningful way.
- Refusing a patient's wish to die is unwarranted medical paternalism, and it is wrong.

While there is a real difference between ethical and legal questions surrounding physician-assisted suicide and active euthanasia, the question quickly arises of how (and whether) a community's moral views of these practices should be addressed by the law. In the United States, physician-assisted suicide is legal in only two states: Oregon and Washington; in all the others, it is either illegal or not specifically mentioned. This means that several stances are available in response to these practices: We could maintain laws against them and punish all those who violate the laws; we could legalize physician-assisted suicide and/or active euthanasia; or we could maintain a kind of "don't ask, don't tell" approach, having laws against the practices, but ignoring cases where physicians violate those laws.

DR. JACK KEVORKIAN'S PRACTICE OF PHYSICIAN-ASSISTED SUICIDE

However, individuals intent on pressing the issue of physician-assisted suicide and active euthanasia may not be content to accept a "don't ask, don't tell" approach to them. One such notable figure is Dr. Jack Kevorkian (see "An Interview with Dr. Jack Kevorkian" at the opening of this chapter), a Michigan physician who publicized the fact that he practiced physician-assisted suicide on people who asked for his help. Kevorkian, known as "Dr. Death," created the "mercitron" machine, which was set up to administer lethal doses of medication; all his clients had to do was pull the paper clip off the tube, and the machine delivered the lethal dose. Kevorkian publicized his participation in physician-assisted suicide cases, even doing the talk show circuit and appearing in newsprint. Over a number of years, he continued to push the envelope, videotaping or tape recording his clients' deaths so that he could present them to the public.

Interestingly, no jury in Michigan would convict him for his acts of physician-assisted suicide, since he always had evidence of the autonomous and free choice made by his clients. It was only when Dr. Kevorkian crossed the line to practice active euthanasia, again presenting it to the public, that he was tried, convicted, and served time in prison for violating Michigan law (Figure 10.3).

Kevorkian's practice was questionable on several grounds. First, he lacked a long-standing relationship in all of the cases in which he assisted people in dying. He had no prior knowledge of his clients, and no context for considering their requests (other than the brief meetings at motels or on park benches). He often made the determination that an individual was a good candidate for his services on the basis of one to two short meetings. Second, he did not consult with colleagues to get a second

FIGURE 10.3   Dr. Jack Kevorkian addresses reporters following his arraignment on the charge of assisting in a suicide.

opinion prior to committing himself to physician-assisted suicide. Third, Kevorkian helped individuals to die who were not terminally ill. In his first application of life-ending services in 1990, he assisted a woman named Janet Atkins who had been diagnosed with Alzheimer's disease, and who wanted to end her life before she was no longer competent to do so. In another case, Judith Curren was suffering chronic fatigue syndrome and fibromyalgia, neither of which are terminal conditions. Curren had a history of depression and had filed abuse complaints against her husband. In neither of these cases were the women suffering terminal illnesses, yet Kevorkian agreed that physician-assisted suicide was an appropriate response to their situations.

More troubling for some bioethicists, however, are the social justice concerns raised by Kevorkian's practice and by the threat of active euthanasia. As some critics have noted, when considering the social and legal acceptance of active euthanasia and physician-assisted suicide, we must consider the implications for individuals who are already socially marginalized and/or devalued. Concerns for persons with disabilities, older adults with dementia, persons with severe cognitive impairments, minorities, and women have been raised by a variety of bioethicists who point to the likelihood that people from these groups may be targeted for killing. For example, as bioethicist Susan Wolf points out, Jack Kevorkian assisted in the suicides of eight women before fulfilling a man's death request, which suggests that there might be a gender bias in how physician-assisted suicide or active euthanasia are carried out.[3] Others have argued that laws favoring these practices will likely have a negative impact on persons with disabilities, who are already marginalized on the basis of their disabilities.[4] The availability of physician-assisted suicide or active euthanasia may put undue pressure on individuals with disabilities to end their lives, especially considering the degree to which society already views disability as undesirable, and the degree to which a life with disabilities is seen as a life not worth living.

THE CASE OF TERRI SCHIAVO

The concern regarding persons with disabilities came to a head in the notable case of Terri Schiavo. In 1990, Schiavo collapsed in her home, and suffered respiratory and cardiac arrest that resulted in extensive brain damage. Like Karen Quinlan, she was diagnosed as being in a persistent vegetative state (PVS) and ultimately spent 15 years being institutionalized (Figure 10.4).

FIGURE 10.4   Terri Schiavo and her mother at Terri's Hospital Bed in Gulfport, Florida, 2003.

In 1998 her husband and guardian Michael Schiavo petitioned the Pinellas County Circuit Court to remove her feeding tube. Terri's parents, Robert and Mary Schindler, strongly opposed the removal of artificial nutrition and hydration, arguing that this is basic care that should be provided and that Terri was conscious. The court determined that Schiavo would not wish to continue life-prolonging measures. This controversy dragged on for 7 years and was taken up by politicians and advocacy groups, particularly pro-life groups and disability rights activists such as Not Dead Yet (see Chapter 5).

The court's decision was finally carried out on March 18, 2005, but before then the governments of Florida and the United States tried to pass laws that would prevent the removal of Schiavo's feeding tube. The legal wrangling resulted in widespread national and international media coverage.

Schiavo was 41 years old when she finally died at a Pinellas Park hospice. Supporters of the Schindlers' cause to save their daughter saw the removal of Terri's feeding tube as a form of murder. Her parents alleged that Michael Schiavo was abusive and that this had led indirectly to her condition, but the Florida Department of Children and Family Services (DCFS) rejected these allegations.

Upon autopsy, examiners found extensive injury to Schiavo's nervous system. Her brain weighed only 615 grams, less than half of a normal adult woman's brain, and microscopic examination indicated severe damage to all regions of her brain. In short, the damage to Schiavo's brain was determined to have been irreversible, indicating that no amount of therapy or treatment would have offered any hope of regenerating her massive loss of neurons.

The case of Terri Schiavo leads to even more questions that arise within the arena of euthanasia and physician-assisted suicide. Is removing artificial nutrition and hydration on par with removing a respirator? Some ethicists claim it is, while others argue that removing a feeding tube goes beyond "letting nature takes its course." Within the parameters of this debate we often find appeals to notions of ordinary versus extraordinary care, and disagreement about whether feeding tubes constitute ordinary care that must be provided, or a medical technology that becomes an extraordinary measure to keep a patient alive. Schiavo's case also raises significant questions about who should have decision-making authority over a loved one when the loved one is no longer capable of making self-regarding decisions. Attempts to override Michael Schiavo's authority to represent his wife's wishes are problematic in light of the current legal recognition of one's spouse as the first-order decision-maker in cases where the individual is not capable of stating his or her wishes. Some ethicists hope that Americans will learn from the Schiavo case and put their wishes in writing about who should make medical decisions for them and what values should inform their medical care. Terri Schiavo had not left any written instructions or clear communications about her wishes or preferences, which in large part fueled the debate and disagreement concerning what she really wanted.

The issues surrounding physician-assisted suicide, active euthanasia, and passive euthanasia have certainly not gone away. Periodically, cases arise that bring this issue to the forefront, and public debates ensue. Next to the abortion debate in the United States, it is perhaps one of the most divisive and complicated bioethical issues; for that reason, it is not likely to be resolved any time in the near future.

Looking Ahead

- Following the case of Terri Schiavo, we may see legislation put into place that limits palliative care medicine, curtailing the use of advance directives and undermining the principle of autonomy in medical care. The legislative campaigns following the Schiavo case have attempted to create laws to prevent the withdrawal or refusal of some forms of life-sustaining medical treatment even when a patient has an advance directive clearly indicating her personal decision in the matter.
- The increasing focus on human longevity, and the use of technology to extend human life (see Chapter 9) will detract from a focus on and conversations about death and dying, and ways to die well. As a result, we may also see the continued struggle for hospice care to take hold, since patients and families will not be prepared to accept the facts of dying and death.
- Laws that limit assisted suicide to those persons with a terminal diagnosis will be questioned in the courts, since this condition creates a duality with regard to the standard of care that doctors owe their patients. In Oregon, a suicidal person can be confined against her will for suicidal ideation; but assisted suicide is permitted for others. This paradox will likely be explored in upcoming legal cases.

Endnotes

1. See Timothy Quill, "Death and Dignity—A Case of Individualized Decisionmaking" included in this chapter.
2. See *In Re* Quinlan, 355 A.2d (N.J. 1976).
3. Susan Wolf, Gender, "Feminism, and Death: Physician-Assisted Suicide and Euthanasia," *Feminism and Bioethics: Beyond Reproduction,* ed. Susan Wolf (New York: Oxford University Press, 1996), 282–317.
4. See Jerome E. Bickenbach, "Disability and Life-Ending Decisions," *Physician Assisted Suicide: Expanding the Debate,* Margaret P. Battin, Rosamond Rhodes, and Anita Silvers, eds. (New York: Routledge, 1998), 123–133.

END–OF–LIFE DECISIONS FOR THE VULNERABLE AND INCOMPETENT

Rejecting the Baby Doe Rules and Defending a "Negative" Analysis of the Best Interests Standard

Loretta M. Kopelman

I. INTRODUCTION

The Best Interests Standard is a widely defended moral and legal standard for guiding decisions when individuals lack decision-making capacity, including infants, children, and adults lacking advance directives. Another newer policy, however, exists for infants under one year of age based on the 1984 Amendments to the Child Abuse Prevention and Treatment Act (CAPTA, 1985) Law. They are called the "Baby Doe Rules," and went into effect in 1985. Many neonatologists and other pediatricians soon charged that the Baby Doe Rules and the Best Interests Standard were incompatible; they reported that the Baby Doe Rules altered standards of care and limited clinicians' and parents' ability to make individualized and compassionate decisions about what was in the best interests of infants. Some defenders of the Baby Doe Rules, such as President Ronald Reagan, his Surgeon General, C. Everett Koop, and other "right-to-life" advocates, however, claimed the Baby Doe Rules were best for infants and were needed to stop unacceptable "quality of life" interpretations about what was best for them. Other defenders, including some members of the American Academy of Pediatrics leadership, held that the Baby Doe Rules were compatible with the Best Interests Standard for radically different reasons; they claim that properly understood, these rules allow doctors and parents to select the same sort of compassionate, individualized medical choices using reasonable medical judgments permitted by the Best Interests Standard. Both defenses are considered and rejected.

I will argue that the Best Interests Standard and Baby Doe Rules offer incompatible guidance about how to treat infants. After discussing why there were two sets of almost identical Baby Doe Regulations, I use a case to display differences between the Baby Doe Rules and the Best Interests Standard. I argue that the Baby Doe Rules should be rejected because they sometimes require actions that violate duties to act compassionately, provide individualized treatment decisions at the end of life, and minimize unnecessary suffering. Moreover, the Baby Doe Rules unfairly single out one group, infants under one, for treatments adults do not want for themselves, violating duties to treat others as we want to be treated. In contrast, the Best Interests Standard offers the same guidance for all incompetent individuals, directing decision-makers to select the sort of individualized and compassionate decision-making that adults want for themselves and that are recommended by professional groups such as the American Academy of Pediatrics and Hospice organizations for end-of-life treatments. Finally, I articulate and briefly defend what I call the "negative" analysis of the Best Interests Standard for many forms of decision-making for incompetent persons, arguing it reflects how this standard is used, avoids common criticisms, and is superior to the Baby Doe Rules.

II. BACKGROUND

The current Baby Doe Rules are formally known as the Child Abuse Amendments to Public Law 98–457 or the Child Abuse and Prevention and Treatment Act. They went into effect on May 15, 1985, about three years after the death of the Baby Doe from Bloomington, Indiana, after whom two sets of rules were named. After summarizing the Baby Doe Rules, I will discuss how there came to be two substantially similar sets of regulations, one promulgated under civil rights law and rejected by the Supreme Court and the other still on the books as federal funding requirements for states to receive money to combat child abuse and neglect.

The current Baby Doe Regulations prohibit anyone from withholding or withdrawing food, water, medications, or other treatments appropriate to maintain survival, allowing only three exceptions for withholding life-supporting treatments:

(i) The infant is chronically and irreversibly comatose;

(ii) The provision of such treatment would merely prolong dying, not be effective in ameliorating or correcting all of the infant's life-threatening conditions, or otherwise be futile in terms of the survival of the infant; or

Abridged from Loretta M. Kopelman, "Rejecting the Baby Doe Rules and Defending a 'Negative' Analysis of the Best Interests Standard," *Journal of Medicine and Philosophy* 2005, 30(4):331–352. Copyright © 2005. Reprinted by permission of Oxford University Press.

(iii) The provision of such treatment would be virtually futile in terms of the survival of the infant and the treatment itself under such circumstances would be inhumane.

Some defenders support these restrictions, applauding their "right-to-life" stance. Other defenders insist these rules are misunderstood and allow the same sort of discretion that doctors may consider for other persons. In what follows, I will criticize both defenses, arguing that these rules should be rejected in favor of the older Best Interests Standard, which applies to all persons lacking competency, not just infants under one year of age.

The first set of rules that came to be called the Baby Doe Regulations was promulgated by the Reagan Administration using civil rights laws. They responded to the events surrounding an infant born with a tracheosophageal fistula and trisomy 21 or Down Syndrome in Bloomington, Indiana, on April 9, 1982. The fistula had to be repaired for the baby to live but physicians disagreed about how the baby ought to be treated. Some wanted to do the repair and others, principally the obstetrician, recommended against it. (Today more is known about trisomy 21 and it seems likely that doctors would not offer such diverse recommendations to parents.) The family elected not to operate.

Some pediatricians and hospital administrators sought an emergency session with a circuit judge, who ruled that the parents had the right to make this decision, especially given disagreements among the physicians about the recommended course of treatment. Upon appeal, both the County Circuit Court and the Indiana Supreme Court also ruled in favor of the parents. An appeal was made to the Supreme Court for an emergency stay, but the baby who became known as Baby Doe died, making the request moot. The legal principle, then and now, is that parents are the primary decision makers for infants and may select the option that they believe is in their child's best interests, and unless there is an emergency, doctors should seek a court order if they disagree with the parents.

These events became widely publicized. President Ronald Reagan ordered the Department of Justice and the Department of Health and Human Services to issue regulations that came to be called the "Baby Doe Rules," under Section 504 of the Rehabilitation Act of 1973. The theory was that the failure to provide infants maximal treatments, unless one or more of the three stated exceptions existed, was discriminatory and violated their civil rights. Because of these Baby Doe Rules, neonatal intensive care units were required by March 22, 1983, to display prominently a large poster stating the rules and a hotline phone number so that anyone could call the Department of Health and Human Services if they believed an infant was not being treated appropriately. If a notice was received, a team was sent to investigate.

The first set of Baby Doe Rules were challenged in the courts after the birth on October 11, 1983, of a baby who came to be known as Baby Jane Doe at St. Charles Hospital in New York. She was soon transferred to the neonatal intensive care unit at State University of New York at Stony Brook because of her spina bifida, hydrocephalus, microcephaly, and kidney damage. Her parents were told she would be severely retarded, paralyzed below the lesion, and suffer from frequent kidney and bladder infections. There was considerable disagreement among doctors about whether it was in her best interest to have corrective surgery. The parents declined surgery and a legal battle ensued that eventually reached the Supreme Court. The Supreme Court in *Bowen vs. American Hospital Association, et al.* (1986) decided in favor of the American Hospital Association and the Stony Brook Hospital, thereby supporting the parents' right to decide. The court held that the first set of Baby Doe Rules could not be issued using Section 504 of the Civil Rights Act and that no need for these rules had been shown.

When it became clear that the courts were rejecting the Reagan Administration's interpretation of the Civil Rights Act (Section 504 Rehabilitation Act of 1973) upon which the first set of Baby Doe Rules were based, the U.S. Congress adopted a similar set of Baby Doe Rules as requirements for states to receive funds to combat child abuse. Unlike civil rights laws, these federal funding requirements are technically optional, although most states adopted them. The second set of Baby Doe Rules went into effect in 1985; but, unlike the first set of Baby Doe Rules, they have not been tested by the U.S. Supreme Court.

As the courts were rejecting the first set of Baby Doe Rules, the second set was being fashioned in a political compromise among members of the leadership of the American Academy of Pediatrics, "right-to life" groups, Congress, and the Reagan Administration. As soon as the second set of Baby Doe Rules were adopted "right-to-life" groups, influential political figures such as Reagan and Koop, and the leadership of the American Academy of Pediatrics all claimed victory, but, as we shall see, the Academy's leadership had very different views from the others about what the rules meant.

In the next section, I discuss a case to illustrate what is at stake, and then I turn to defenses and criticisms of both the Baby Doe Rules and the Best Interests Standard, arguing that the Best Interests Standard is better than the Baby Doe Rules at allowing the sort of compassionate and individualized decision-making recommended by hospice groups for adults and by the American Academy of Pediatrics for children.

III. FINDING A GOOD TREATMENT PLAN FOR ANGEL

The Baby Doe Regulations are linked in my mind to the controversies in which I was involved over finding a good treatment plan for an infant whom I will call "Angel." Disputes over how to care for Angel illustrate why many neonatologists and other pediatricians and the courts were hostile to the Baby Doe Rules. Angel was born shortly after Congress enacted the second set of Baby Doe Regulations.

Angel was at the center of impassioned disagreements among doctors, nurses, social workers, and hospital administrators for over two years. Angel was born at full term, and doctors quickly agreed that there had been prenatal damage to her central nervous system of unknown origin. Her prognosis was that she would continue to be functionally quadriplegic, with severe respiratory distress, and dependent upon a ventilator to breathe. Her lungs were often infected and she had frequent seizures associated with apoxic spells. Interventions necessary to sustain her life were not only painful but caused complications. She did not feed well by mouth and hardly responded to stimuli. Her family was poor and overwhelmed with a variety of other social and economic problems; they stopped visiting after a few weeks, leaving treatment decisions to clinicians.

From the day of her birth, clinicians, social workers, nurses, and others met frequently to consider whether palliative treatment, focusing upon relieving her suffering, was a better goal for Angel than aggressive care to prolong her life. The overwhelming consensus was that palliative care would be in her best interest and what we would choose for ourselves or our family members in such circumstances. Yet, aggressive life-support continued because a few people wanted more data, feared legal entanglements in light of the Baby Doe Regulations, or worried about bad publicity.

After a few months, she was transferred to the Pediatric Intensive Care Unit (PICU) from the NICU. For the sake of continuity, several nurses, a social worker and a pediatric neurologist provided most of her care. The conferences continued and three groups quickly formed. Group 1, composed of her long-term caregivers, favored maximal life saving and aggressive treatments as being in her best interest; they believed that she would eventually do well enough to interact with people and enjoy her life.

Members of Group 2 disagreed with those in Group 1 on factual grounds, arguing that evidence showed her prognosis was grim and that her development was arrested at less than three months; they believed she would develop more life-threatening complications and die slowly and painfully. The pediatricians, other than her neurologist, agreed with members of Group 2, and as the controversy became known throughout the hospital so did most of the other clinicians. They believed that palliative care was the most compassionate approach because there was too much suffering and too little compensatory benefit to justify such burdensome interventions. One consultant grumbled that her long-term caregivers had lost their objectivity and they were like unrealistic parents.

Although these two groups had factual disputes about whether Angel would get past the suffering of a barely conscious, pain-filled existence to a life worth living, they agreed in principle that their actions should be guided by the Best Interests Standard or what was in Angel's best interest, given the available options. They could not agree what was best for her as long as disputes about her prognosis existed.

A third group of clinicians and administrators (Group 3) insisted upon aggressive treatment because of the (then) newly adopted Baby Doe Regulations. Since Angel was not in a coma, not dying, and treatments were not virtually futile in terms of survival, they reasoned that maximal care must be provided. They were unconvinced by arguments that Angel met the second exception that treatment would "merely prolong dying, not be effective in ameliorating or correcting all of the infant's life-threatening conditions, or otherwise be futile in terms of the survival of the infant..." because she was not dying or terminally ill. Moreover, the members of Group 3 did not want their hospital to test the meaning or legal standing of the second set of Baby Doe Rules, including how it relates to the older Best Interests Standard. Institutionally, the safest legal course, they concluded, was to provide Angel maximal life-saving treatments.

Members of Groups 1 and 3 agreed that clinicians should continue maximal life-saving treatment, but for different reasons. Members of Group 1 believed Angel would eventually do well and maximal treatment was in her best interest. Members of Group 3, however, agreed that it was probably in her best interest to have palliative care and would be what they would want for themselves or their family members facing an existence like that of Angel. Yet, since treatment was keeping her alive, she was not in an irreversible coma, and none could say she was dying, they believed the prudent option was to follow what they regarded as their duties under the law, given the Baby Doe Rules.

Month after month, the three groups continued to discuss treatment plans for Angel. Although they agreed that she was in pain and barely conscious, they disagreed about her prognosis and whether to be guided by the Best Interests Standard or the second set of Baby Doe Rules. Because there was no consensus, maximal treatment continued. Angel's room, filled with stuffed animals and bright pictures, showed how much people cared about her. In the center was a tiny infant surrounded by large machines. She scarcely moved, struggled to breathe, and looked uncomfortable from the very technologies keeping her alive. Eventually all three groups agreed, but it took over two years. After a series of medical complications, it was clear that treatments were only prolonging her death.

Unlike the members of Group 3, some defenders of the Baby Doe Rules hold that the regulations serve infants' best interests because they defend a "right-to-life" view. Other defenders hold that these rules are misunderstood and that properly understood, the Baby Doe Regulations do not restrict doctors and families from using reasonable medical judgment in selecting individualized treatment plans, and serving the best interests of infants. I will argue that this benign interpretation cannot be supported by the language or purposes of the Baby Doe Rules. I conclude that neither the "right-to-life" defense nor the "benign" interpretation of the Baby Doe Rules are compatible with individualized and compassionate decision-making favored by adults, and advocated by the courts, the American Academy of Pediatrics, and professional organizations about how to make end of life treatment decisions.

A. The "right-to-life" defense

"Right-to-life" groups claimed that the second set of Baby Doe Rules represented a victory because these regulations severely restricted the quality-of-life considerations that parents and doctors can use in making treatment choices.

The Reagan Administration used the Baby Doe Regulations to set strict parameters about what treatments for imperiled infants like Baby Doe were "appropriate," "useless," "reasonable," or "futile". Reagan wrote, " . . . the real issue is whether to affirm and protect the sanctity of all human life, or to embrace a social ethic where some human lives are valued and others are not. As a nation we must choose between the sanctity of life ethic and the 'quality of life ethic'". Reagan wanted to insure that institutions would never again use quality of life determinations to withhold or withdraw appropriate medications, hydration, or

nutrition. His Surgeon General, C. Everett Koop, strongly supported these regulations, agreeing with Reagan that Baby Doe was mistreated:

> . . . medicine, nutrition and fluids are life itself and regardless of age individuals should be protected; they should receive whatever treatment is indicated. That does not mean prolonging the act of dying. But it does at least mean providing her with the nutrition and fluids needed to sustain life at its most basic level.

The Baby Doe Rules reflect the "right-to-life" position defended by Reagan and Koop. Appropriate medication, hydration, and nutrition may never be withheld, and one and only one quality of life consideration is permissible for withholding or withdrawing maximal life saving treatment, namely, for chronic and irreversible coma (the first exception); "futile" treatments must be understood strictly as those that would only prolong dying (second exception); there is a provision to withhold or withdraw interventions that are "virtually futile in terms of survival" and "under such circumstances" would be inhumane (the third exception).

Even before the Baby Doe Rules were enacted, some theologians criticized the attempt by "right-to-life" advocates, such as Reagan, to link the view that maximal treatment was required for all non-dying minimally conscious life to religious beliefs about the "sanctity of life." Richard McCormick, a well-known Jesuit theologian, argued that when people lack the potential for interpersonal relationships, there is no obligation to require life-saving treatments. Even if there is a duty to protect life, this does not mean it should be treated as an absolute value. In fact, if it were treated as an absolute value, respirators could never be turned off for adults or children. We would not only have to bankrupt our country to provide resources for this, but also limit the liberty of most adults, giving them no choice in the matter about when to withdraw life-saving treatments.

K. D. Clouser also objected to attempts to link "sanctity of life" to a "life at all costs" position. It is more plausible, he argued, to understand sanctity of life as the duty to preserve life unless there is a higher duty. In some cases, preserving a life violates duties to avoid unnecessary suffering, for example, when there is too little compensatory benefit to justify the pain. Life is not always the highest value, and we generally agree there are sometimes higher duties, such as relieving suffering, or risking one's life to save others.

William May, a well-known Protestant theologian, argued that taking death as absolute evil is not a sanctity of life position, but an idolatry of the physical. Sanctity of life should be understood as a duty to prevent untimely death, and not as some have argued, a justification for preserving life at all costs, no matter how minimal.

These theologians argued that selecting medical treatments for imperiled and incompetent individuals should, to the extent possible, be based on their best interests. Yet, we do not always agree about what is best; and/or parents and clinicians often struggle with difficult treatment decisions such as how to balance duties to prolong life and relieve suffering when dealing with severely ill individuals. Some argue that special rules are needed for infants less than one year of age because parental choices may reflect poor bonding rather than what is best for the baby. There is a paucity of data to reach such a sweeping conclusion.

Recommendations for compassionate and individualized decision-making are the norm in many policies for older children and incompetent adults and are widely supported in the pediatric literature and in other American Academy of Pediatrics policies. This "right-to-life" position advocates a policy adults would not want for themselves.

B. The benign and misunderstood defense

In sharp contrast, some members of the leadership of the American Academy of Pediatrics supported the second set of Baby Doe Regulations, because they believed that the rules were reasonable and would not alter standards of care. Properly understood, on this account, the Baby Doe Rules leave doctors free to use reasonable medical judgment in making treatment plans, act in infants' best interests in providing palliative care, and use their discretion to withhold or withdraw hydration, nutrition, or medication. The American Academy of Pediatrics' President when the Baby Doe Regulations were passed was Robert Haggerty, M.D., who is reported as saying, "It would appear that the final rule reaffirms the role of reasonable medical judgment and that decisions should be made in the best interests of infants". These rules leave standards of care unchanged, these defenders contend, allowing doctors to use all reasonable medical judgment in framing treatment plans. This view persists. The 1996 Committee on Bioethics of the American Academy of Pediatrics contend that these rules use the words "reasonable medical judgments," "appropriate," and "inhumane" in ways that allow considerable discretion. I will argue that the text does not support their benign interpretations and the "right-to-life" advocates who applauded these rules and the Academy's rank and file and the Supreme Court who criticized them got their meaning right.

First, the rules permit reasonable medical judgment, but only insofar as it is necessary to apply the Baby Doe Rules. Doctors, for example, must use reasonable medical judgment and practice standards to make the diagnosis that an infant is dying or in an irreversible coma. As noted, Reagan and Koop sought to restrict choices about what was "reasonable."

Second, the regulations state that "appropriate nutrition, hydration, and medication" may never be withheld, and the Committee on Bioethics is mistaken in saying they may be removed when doctors judge that they are not "appropriate." Appropriate can mean what is appropriate for a particular condition (it is appropriate to give antibiotics for bacterial pneumonia) or what is appropriate treatment for a particular patient. Traditional medical judgment is individualized, determining the benefits of a proposed treatment for a particular patient. Parents and physicians may decide it is not appropriate to give antibiotics to a dying infant who has bacterial pneumonia. The 1996 Committee on Bioethics seems to have mistakenly read "appropriate" in its traditional way in thinking that clinicians may omit what they consider inappropriate hydration, nutrition and medication. This interpretation is not only implausible in terms of what the guidelines say, but also in terms of Reagan's and Koop's intention in framing these rules. On the Committee's interpretation, parents and doctors could have turned to the Baby Doe Rules for support in allowing them to stop all medications, nutrition, or hydration from babies like Baby Doe and Baby Jane on the grounds that they thought that they were "inappropriate" given their overall condition. Yet, blocking such discretion is what caused the Baby Doe Rules in the first place.

Thus, defenders' interpretation on this point misrepresents the intention as well as the language of the regulations. Clearly, the Reagan Administration and disability groups did not want to permit this kind of discretion. They framed rules to require doctors to provide all appropriate nutrition, hydration, and medication for the condition and exceptions are impermissible unless the infant is in an irreversible coma, is dying, or if treatment would be virtually futile in terms of survival and therefore inhumane. Physicians may use reasonable medical judgment, but only to apply these rules.

Third, defenders may look to the second clause of the second exception to defend their view: "The provision of such treatment would merely prolong dying, not be effective in ameliorating or correcting all of the infant's life-threatening conditions, or otherwise be futile in terms of the survival of the infant". Defenders may say that this means anytime one cannot correct *all* the infant's life-threatening conditions, life-saving treatments may be withheld or withdrawn. This interpretation, however, is implausible when taken in context since it is clear that "ameliorating or correcting all of the infants' life threatening conditions" must be assessed in terms of whether this would "merely prolong dying" (the first clause) or "otherwise be futile" (the third clause). Moreover, if taken out of this context of "prolonging dying" (in the first clause) and "otherwise futile in terms of survival" (in the third), we get an interpretation that might offer too little protection. If you were at liberty to discontinue life-saving measures *anytime* you could not improve or correct all life-threatening conditions, the door of discretion would be opened so widely that families and doctors could settle on non-treatment for infants likely to die of their conditions when death is years away. Moreover, all finite creatures must die and there is nothing effective in ameliorating or correcting *that* condition. This interpretation, then, is implausible in light of the text of the Baby Doe Rules and the clear intent of the Reagan Administration to prohibit such discretion.

Fourth, defenders argue that the third exception allows adequate consideration of duties to relieve suffering because it states doctors need not provide "inhumane" treatments. Although the word "inhumane" is used, the text does not support this interpretation. It states, "The provision of such treatment would be virtually futile in terms of the survival of the infant and the treatment itself under such circumstances would be inhumane". This passage does not permit consideration of the infant's suffering *unless* survival is "virtually futile" and this is generally understood to mean the infant is dying, especially in the context of an intensive care unit.

Thus, claims by some members of the leadership of the American Academy of Pediatrics that the Baby Doe Rules are misunderstood and allow all reasonable discretion are implausible. The words "reasonable medical care," "appropriate," and "inhumane" taken in context do not permit the discretion these defenders assert. Consequently, these members of the American Academy of Pediatrics' leadership got the meaning wrong. As discussed, those who got it right included Reagan, Koop, and other "right-to-life" defenders, such critics as the Supreme Court, and many neonatologists and other pediatricians.

Critics of the Baby Doe Rules say that the text clearly singles out one group, infants under the age of one, for a set of rules that most adults would not tolerate for themselves. Adults faced with a choice

between prolonging unconscious life or prolonging life and preventing pain and suffering, sometimes believe that there are worse things than dying. This attitude is reflected in the first priority of palliative care as the relief of pain and suffering. If we agree that it is wrong to do to others what we would not want for ourselves and that we would not want a Baby Doe policy for ourselves, then we should not adopt such a policy for infants under one year of age. The Best Interests Standard applies to all persons lacking decision-making capacity or competency, and permits the sort of compassionate and individualized decision-making widely recommended. It is a matter of debate and regional practice how much influence the current Baby Doe Regulations exert on patient care. Some doctors, hospital attorneys, and administrators may find them irrelevant and use the older Best Interests Standard as they would for all other children and incompetent adults. Unless a survey similar to that conducted by my colleagues and me years ago is repeated, it is hard to estimate how many neonatologists and pediatricians are guided by the Best Interests Standard and how many by the Baby Doe Regulations.

IV. THE "NEGATIVE" ANALYSIS OF THE BEST–INTERESTS STANDARD

In this section, I will argue that the Best Interests Standard is a better standard than the Baby Doe Rules for making decisions for imperiled infants. After offering an analysis of the meaning of the Best Interests Standard when used to make many decisions for incompetent persons, I defend it against two criticisms (that it requires what is ideal and that it is too vague).

The Best Interests Standard is a well-established legal principle. For example, the Maryland Court of Appeals recently stated, "we have long stressed that the 'best interests of the child' is the overriding concern of this Court in matters relating to children. . . ." The Supreme Court of Texas, in *Miller v. HCA* (2003), held that parents have the right to consent or refuse treatments for infants, and that other than in emergencies, a court order must be obtained to overrule parental refusals. This Court reaffirmed that parents have the primary responsibility to choose because such a policy will promote children's best interest, welfare, and safety in evaluating the various factors that shape complicated medical decisions. To override parental authority in a non-emergency case, the state must prove, often by clear and convincing evidence, that the child has suffered or is in danger of suffering serious harm.

Parents or others given the authority to make choices for an incompetent individual should justify decisions in terms of established moral and legal duties to them. Parents or guardians are the primary decision-makers because it is assumed they are most knowledgeable about the needs of the individual and because the family bears the consequences. In addition, families need support and privacy to make personal decisions in a way that accommodates different values, religious, ethical, social or philosophical views.

The Best Interests Standard is sometimes used to express an ideal (all children should have excellent education) but in many kinds of decision making for incompetent persons, it is used differently. It is used to find choices that are at least not unacceptable given the different values, needs, and duties of the decision makers. To capture the way it is used in such decisions for incompetent individuals and answer common criticisms, I defend what I will call the *"negative version of the Best Interests Standard," which applies to incompetent individuals of all ages and*

1. instructs decision makers to decide what act(s) are in the incompetent individual's immediate and long-term interests and maximize his or her net benefits and minimize net burdens, setting that act(s) as a prima facie duty;

2. presupposes a consensus among reasonable and informed persons of good will about what choices for the incompetent individual are, all things considered, not unacceptable; and

3. determines the scope of the Best Interests Standard in terms of the scope of established moral or legal duties to incompetent individuals.

One advantage in analyzing the Best Interests Standard in this way is that we make room for differences of opinion about what is best given the available options. Some people may decide to forego painful and highly experimental treatment to save their dying infant for pain-free weeks at home, while others might want to pursue every chance no matter how small. Neither choice is unreasonable as judged by what adults want for themselves and established moral and legal duties.

A second advantage of this moral analyzing of the Best Interests Standard is that it clarifies that the decision about what is best may set a *prima facie* not an actual duty for decision makers. For example, we should acknowledge if it would be best for an individual if he or she received a liver transplant and thus set as a *prima facie* duty seeing if it can be obtained. However, it may not be an actual duty to get it since not every individual who needs this scarce resource can have it. It might be marginally beneficial to prolonging the infants' life

for a day for him or her to get an expensive drug, but it may not be an actual duty if his or her getting it bankrupts the family or community, or denies it to someone who could have many years of life.

This analysis, which I can only sketch here, avoids some criticisms that are often aimed at the Best Interests Standard and corresponds to how it is generally used in making medical decisions for children. Critics of the Best Interests Standard have argued that it is self-defeating, individualistic, unknowable, vague, dangerous and open to abuse.

In every neonatal intensive care unit, certain cases will elicit sustained disagreement. The disagreement may be based upon insufficient data, different understandings of one's duties, miscommunications, misunderstandings, or value conflicts. If disagreements were the rule rather than the exception among informed and competent people of good will, it would be hard to justify the consensus that is presupposed in using the Best Interests Standard. Occasional disagreements do not undermine the Best Interests Standard, however, since disputes about difficult or borderline cases arise in all fields. The analysis I have offered sometimes permits different choices.

The Best Interests Standard in use does not use vague or suspect categories since it should be guided by established moral and legal duties to incompetent individuals and a consensus grounded upon what reasonable and informed competent adults of good will would want for themselves or others in similar situations. These choices should guide what we should want for these infants in similar situations. Most adults want choices and not the sort of inflexible regulations found in the Baby Doe Rules; for example, there is wide legal, moral, and social support to withdraw some medication, nutrition, and hydration or give sufficient pain medication to fulfill palliative goals. Surveys of adults show adequate pain control is a top concern in end-of-life care. Most adults want compassionate and individualized decision-making where families and doctors decide what is best under the circumstances within a framework of established moral and legal duties and a consensus about what acts are not acceptable. We should provide the same consideration to infants.

V. CONCLUDING REMARKS

The Best Interests Standard and the Baby Doe Rules are incompatible and the Baby Doe Regulations should be rejected. Enacted two decades ago as requirements for states to receive federal funding to combat child abuse and neglect, they, if followed, thwart important duties to prevent unnecessary pain, fail to promote individualized and compassionate decision-making by parents and doctors, and do not treat others as we would wish to be treated. Adults do not want Baby-Doe-type rules for themselves because they want individualized decision-making, and the opportunities for families and doctors to give adequate pain medication and to withdraw some medication, hydration, and nutrition to fulfill palliative goals. Moreover, most adults do not want to prolong minimally or permanently unconscious life. Many neonatologists and other pediatricians have been critical of the Baby Doe Rules and their objections resemble the reasons given by the Supreme Court for rejecting an earlier set of rules promulgated under the Civil Rights Law. I have considered and rejected defenses of the Baby Doe Rules coming from two extremes, both of which hold they are consistent with the Best Interests Standard. One view, held by Reagan, Koop, and others is that these rules are in infants' best interests because they honor a "right-to-life" stance. Another view held by members of the American Academy of Pediatrics' leadership is that the Baby Doe Rules allow doctors to use their reasonable medical judgments to make informed decisions that are compatible with the sort of end-of-life care recommended for older children and adults.

I have defended the Best Interests Standard for making medical and other decisions for incompetent individuals that reflects how it is often used. Properly understood, it does not, as critics charge, require people to do what is ideal for the incompetent individual, ignoring all other interests, resources or perspectives. It would not be possible for the Best Interests Standard to provide practical guidance for decision makers if it required what was ideal for the incompetent person. For example, parents can balance interests among their children within their families and have legal protections from critics who complain that the parents are not doing what is ideal from the critics' perspectives. As long as the parents' choices are acceptable to reasonable and informed people of good will and fulfill basic duties, they have considerable freedom to make such important choices as relates to their child's schooling, religion, education. Families of infants, as well as incompetent adults and older children, should also have some freedom, within acceptable limits and with the agreement of clinicians, about how to rank duties for their imperiled relatives, such as whether to provide comfort care, to pursue remote life-saving strategies or to support permanent non-conscious biological life. I have argued that the Best Interests Standard should be understood in terms of established moral and legal duties to the incompetent individual and a consensus about what choices are unacceptable as judged by informed and reasonable people of good will. It is not, as critics have charged, too vague to serve as a guide. I have argued that this analysis which I have called the "negative" analysis of the Best Interests Standard for making many medical and other decisions for incompetent individuals, is superior to the Baby Doe Rules when clinicians and parents make decisions for extremely premature, imperiled, or terminally ill infants. This analysis of the Best Interests Standard offers the same guidance for all incompetent individuals allowing the sort of individualized and compassionate decision-making that adults want for themselves.

Terri Schiavo—A Tragedy Compounded

Timothy E. Quill

The story of Terri Schiavo should be disturbing to all of us. How can it be that medicine, ethics, law, and family could work so poorly together in meeting the needs of this woman who was left in a persistent vegetative state after having a cardiac arrest? Ms. Schiavo had been sustained by artificial hydration and nutrition through a feeding tube for 15 years, and her husband, Michael Schiavo, was locked in a very public legal struggle with her parents and siblings about whether such treatment should be continued or stopped. Distortion by interest groups, media hyperbole, and manipulative use of videotape characterized this case and demonstrate what can happen when a patient becomes more a precedent-setting symbol than a unique human being.

Let us begin with some medical facts. On February 25, 1990, Terri Schiavo had a cardiac arrest, triggered by extreme hypokalemia brought on by an eating disorder. As a result, severe hypoxic-ischemic encephalopathy developed, and during the subsequent months, she exhibited no evidence of higher cortical function. Computed tomographic scans of her brain eventually showed severe atrophy of her cerebral hemispheres, and her electroencephalograms were flat, indicating no functional activity of the cerebral cortex. Her neurologic examinations were indicative of a persistent vegetative state, which includes periods of wakefulness alternating with sleep, some reflexive responses to light and noise, and some basic gag and swallowing responses, but no signs of emotion, willful activity, or cognition.[1] There is no evidence that Ms. Schiavo was suffering, since the usual definition of this term requires conscious awareness that is impossible in the absence of cortical activity. There have been only a few reported cases in which minimal cognitive and motor functions were restored three months or more after the diagnosis of a persistent vegetative state due to hypoxic-ischemic encephalopathy; in none of these cases was there the sort of objective evidence of severe cortical damage that was present in this case, nor was the period of disability so long.[2]

Having viewed some of the highly edited videotaped material of Terri Schiavo and having seen other patients in a persistent vegetative state, I am not surprised that family members and others unfamiliar with this condition would interpret some of her apparent alertness and movement as meaningful. In 2002, the Florida trial court judge conducted six days of evidentiary hearings on Ms. Schiavo's condition, including evaluations by four neurologists, one radiologist, and her attending physician. The two neurologists selected by Michael Schiavo, a court-appointed "neutral" neurologist, and Ms. Schiavo's attending physician all agreed that her condition met the criteria for a persistent vegetative state. The neurologist and the radiologist chosen by the patient's parents and siblings, the Schindler family, disagreed and suggested that Ms. Schiavo's condition might improve with unproven therapies such as hyperbaric oxygen or vasodilators—but had no objective data to support their assertions. The trial court judge ruled that the diagnosis of a persistent vegetative state met the legal standard of "clear and convincing" evidence, and this decision was reviewed and upheld by the Florida Second District Court of Appeal. Subsequent appeals to the Florida Supreme Court and the U.S. Supreme Court were denied a hearing.

So what was known about Terri Schiavo's wishes and values? Since she unfortunately left no written advance directive, the next step would be to meet with her closest family members and try to understand what she would have wanted under these medical circumstances if she could have spoken for herself, drawing on the principle of "substituted judgment." Some families unite around this question, especially when there is a shared vision of the patient's views and values. Other families unravel, their crisis aggravated by genuine differences of opinion about the proper course of action or preexisting fault lines arising from long-standing family dynamics.

Here Ms. Schiavo's story gets more complex. Michael Schiavo was made her legal guardian under Florida law, which designates the spouse as the decision maker above other family members if a patient becomes irreversibly incapacitated and has not designated a health care proxy. After three years of trying traditional and experimental therapies, Mr. Schiavo accepted the neurologists' diagnosis of an irreversible persistent vegetative state. He believed that his wife would not want to be kept alive indefinitely in her condition, recalling prior statements that she had made, such as "I don't want to be kept alive on a machine." The Schindler family, however, did not accept the diagnosis of a persistent vegetative state, believing instead that Ms. Schiavo's condition could improve with additional rehabilitative treatment.

The relationship between Mr. Schiavo and the Schindler family began breaking down in 1993, around the time that a malpractice lawsuit revolving around the events that led to Ms. Schiavo's cardiac arrest was settled. In 1994, Mr. Schiavo attempted to refuse treatment for an infection his wife had, and her parents took legal action to require treatment. Thus began wide-ranging, acrimonious legal and public-opinion battles that eventually involved multiple special-interest groups who saw this case as a *cause célèbre* for their particular issue. Michael Schiavo was criticized for being motivated by financial greed, and his loyalty to his wife was questioned because he now lives with another woman, with whom he has two children. The Schindlers were criticized for not accepting the painful reality of their daughter's condition and for expressing their own wishes and values rather than hers.

The right of competent patients to refuse unwanted medical treatment, including artificial hydration and nutrition, is a settled ethical and legal issue in this country—based on the right to bodily integrity. In the Nancy Cruzan case, the Supreme Court affirmed that surrogate decision makers have this right when a patient is incapacitated, but it said that states could set their own standards of evidence about patients' own wishes.[3] Although both the Schiavo and Cruzan cases involved the potential withdrawal of a feeding tube from a patient in a persistent vegetative state, the family was united in believing that Nancy Cruzan would not want to be kept alive in such a state indefinitely. Their challenge, under Missouri law, was to prove to the court in a clear and convincing manner that this would have been Nancy Cruzan's own wish. The Schiavo case raises much more challenging questions about how to define family and how to proceed if members of the immediate family are not in agreement.

The relevant Florida statute requires "clear and convincing evidence that the decision would have been the one the patient would have chosen had the patient been competent or, if there is no indication of what the patient would have chosen, that the decision is in the patient's best interest." Since there is no societal consensus about whether a feeding tube is in the "best interest" of a patient in a persistent vegetative state, the main legal question to be addressed was that of Terri Schiavo's wishes. In 2001, the trial court judge ruled that clear and convincing evidence showed that Ms. Schiavo would have chosen not to receive life-prolonging treatment under the circumstances that then applied. This ruling was also affirmed by the Florida appeals court and denied a hearing by the Florida Supreme Court. When Terri Schiavo's feeding tube was removed for the second time, in 2003, the Florida legislature created "Terri's Law" to override the court decision, and the tube was again reinserted. This law was subsequently ruled an unconstitutional violation of the separation of powers.

On March 18, 2005, Ms. Schiavo's feeding tube was removed for a third time. The U.S. Congress then passed an "emergency measure" that was signed by the President in an effort both to force federal courts to review Ms. Schiavo's case and to create a legal mandate to have her feeding tube reinserted yet again. The U.S. District Court in Florida denied the emergency request to reinsert the feeding tube, and this decision was upheld on appeal. Multiple subsequent legal appeals were denied, and Ms. Schiavo died on March 31, 2005, 13 days after the feeding tube was removed.

This sad saga reinforces my personal belief that the courts—though their involvement is sometimes necessary—are the last place one wants to be when working through these complex dilemmas. Although I did not examine her, from the data I reviewed, I have no doubt that Terri Schiavo was in a persistent vegetative state and that her congnitive and neurologic functions were unfortunately not going to improve. Her life could have been further prolonged with artificial hydration and nutrition, and there is some solace in knowing that she was not consciously suffering. I also believe that both her husband and her family, while seeing the situation in radically different ways, were trying to do what was right for her. Her family and the public should be reassured and educated that dying in this way can be a natural, humane process (humans died in this way for thousands of years before the advent of feeding tubes).[4]

In considering such profound decisions, the central issue is not what family members would want for themselves or what they want for their incapacitated loved one, but rather what the patient would want for himself or herself. The New Jersey Supreme Court that decided the case of Karen Ann Quinlan got the question of substituted judgment right: If the patient could wake up for 15 minutes and understand his or her condition fully, and then had to return to it, what would he or she tell you to do? If the data about the patient's wishes are not clear, then in the absence of public policy or family consensus, we should err on the side of continued treatment even in cases of a persistent vegetative state in which there is no hope of recovery. But if the evidence is clear, as the courts found in the case of Terri Schiavo, then enforcing life-prolonging treatment against what is agreed to be the patient's will is both unethical and illegal.

Let us hope that future courts and legislative bodies put aside all the special interests and distractions and listen carefully to the patient's voice as expressed through family members and close friends. This voice is what counts the most, and in the Terri Schiavo case, it was largely drowned out by a very loud, self-interested public debate.

NOTES

1. Jennett B. The vegetative state: medical facts, ethical and legal dilemmas. New York: Cambridge University Press, 2002.
2. The Multi-Society Task Force on PVS. Medical aspects of the persistent vegetative state, N Engl J Med 1994;330:1499–508, 1572–9. [Erratum, N Engl J Med 1995;333:130.]
3. Gostin LO. Life and death choices after Cruzan. Law Med Health Care 1991;19:9–12.
4. Ganzini L, Goy ER, Miller LL, Harvath TA, Jackson A, Delorit MA. Nurses' experiences with hospice patients who refuse food and fluids to hasten death. N Engl J Med 2003;349:359–65.

After Terri Schiavo:
Why the Disability Rights Movement Spoke Out, Why Some of Us Worried, and Where Do We Go from Here?

Mary Johnson

The controversy over Clint Eastwood's Oscar-winner *Million Dollar Baby* in February gave both the National Spinal Cord Injury Association and Not Dead Yet at least fifteen seconds of fame, if not the fifteen minutes Andy Warhol prophesied.

Those fifteen minutes came two weeks later.

Terri Schiavo's feeding tube was removed March 18. We knew it was coming. We'd known it since March 1, when Pinellas County Circuit Judge George Greer, saying he was "no longer comfortable" issuing any more stays in the years-long court battle, announced the date.

But few disability groups were prepared for the right-to-life, right-to-die political circus the nation was forced to watch between that date and Terri Schiavo's death from starvation and dehydration on March 31. One could almost think that the Eastwood protest had been just for practice.

After the first few days—in which the story was reported as the latest round in the sniping war between conservative Christian right-to-life activists calling for government intervention and progressives and liberals horrified at the assault on a family's right to privacy and individual choice in dying—the disability rights perspective began to emerge.

The *Boston Globe* noted it first, with its story "Rights Groups for Disabled Join in Fight," but by and large, most reporters finally came to see that there was a third ring at this circus. A glaring exception was the *New York Times,* which steadfastly downplayed the disability rights perspective.

Not Dead Yet seemed to be the group taking the lead. And that was appropriate, given that they exist to "oppose public policy that singles out individuals for legalized killing based on their health status." One didn't hear much from any other disability group, although American Association of People with Disabilities (AAPD) head Andy Imparato, interviewed in news stories and on CNN, spoke cogently about the disability rights point of view.

Now that the sawdust is being swept up, there are a number of objects lying around that we want to take a look at before we move on:

WHAT WAS THE DISABILITY RIGHTS POINT OF VIEW? WAS THERE ONE?

That this question can even be asked with seriousness points to the way people—including disabled people—understand the concept of a "disability rights movement." Not all African Americans (formerly called Blacks, and before that, Negroes) supported the civil rights proposals advanced by groups such as the NAACP or, during its day, the Southern Christian Leadership Conference. However, there was no doubt in anyone's mind—certainly not the media's—that there were groups that spoke for the issues; that collectively were seen to represent the issues of the "civil rights movement." The women's rights movement has its groups as well, as does the gay rights movement.

However, perhaps more than with any other group, people who have disabilities seem unaware of not only any national disability rights groups, but of any central issues that might unite them. Not Dead Yet (NDY) repeatedly noted that over two dozen national disability groups had in one way or another spoken out over the years about Terri Schiavo's situation with alarm; and that over a dozen had joined NDY on friend-of-the-court briefs raising disability rights concerns about the case.

But most people—even most disabled people—don't know these groups well. To add to the problem, the term "disability group" can be equally applied to a group supportive of rights and to one who rights groups have often seen as part of our national disability problem. Rights groups, charity groups (like the MDA Telethon), groups like the March of Dimes (whose solution to the disability problem is to end disabled lives before they're born), and service and "disease groups" like the MS Society, are all mixed together in the public's mind. Many haven't a clue what their own thinking is on any issue like that we faced with Terri Schiavo. Many were secretly horrified that groups protested Eastwood's movie. "The Brain Injury Association of America, the Christopher Reeve Paralysis Foundation, the Parkinson's Action Network, and the ALS Association—were noticeably silent on the Schiavo case," wrote the *Washington Post*'s Ceci Connolly.

Johnson, Mary. "After Terri Schiavo: Why the Disability Rights Movement Spoke Out, Why Some of Us Worried, and Where Do We Go From Here?" *Ragged Edge Magazine,* April 2, 2005, http://www.raggededgemagazine.com/focus/postschiavo0405.html. Reprinted by permission of The Advocate Press.

"Cowardice in the face of controversy is not a virtue," said Arthur Caplan, the celeb bioethicist NDY loves to hate, in an MSNBC commentary. "Not Dead Yet spoke up," he noted. "But where were the many other groups who also speak for those with Alzheimer's, Parkinson's, ALS, cancer, AIDS, spinal cord injuries, cystic fibrosis, Huntington's disease? . . . Ducking commentary on the Schiavo case should not be an option."

The disability groups who refuse to speak out do so mostly because they seem to still think that disability is, as disability rights scholar Paul Longmore put it, "a private matter between patient and doctor." That belief has done us far more harm than good, yet it is at the heart of why such groups do not speak out on issues that affect the lives of people with disabilities in America.

Another group created the slogan "silence = death." But it might be useful for disability rights groups to now adopt it as their motto, and act accordingly.

Still, a number of national disability rights groups have been trying for years to be seen as purveyors of a national disability rights sensibility. They have a long way to go; but that doesn't mean they should be treated any differently than national rights groups of other rights movements.

Will the events of February and March make the head-in-the-sand groups reconsider their ostrich policy? Maybe. But that reconsideration may take the form of simply trying to find a deeper hole in the sand in which to bury their heads. All the more reason to appreciate groups like Not Dead Yet, AAPD, and the Disability Rights Education and Defense Fund, all of whose spokespeople were quoted about the Schiavo case.

WHY DO CRIP SPOKESPEOPLE, AND INDIVIDUAL CRIPS, KEEP COMPARING THEMSELVES TO TERRI SCHIAVO?

Of all the comments we've received at Ragged Edge in recent weeks, this is the most common.

"That's ridiculous. Disabled people aren't like Terri Schiavo."

"Terri Schiavo isn't 'disabled'—she's brain-dead!" a number of e-mailers practically shouted at us. "Can't you people see the difference?"

"I'm disabled but I'm far from being like Terri Schiavo. If I ever ended up like her, I'd want the plug pulled."

A number of you felt that by "getting in bed with Terri Schiavo," as one put it, we were doing the cause of disability rights grave harm. The *Washington Post*'s Ceci Connolly, in an April 2 story ("Schiavo Raised Profile of Disabled"), quoted a number of disabled people who felt that way. Particularly telling was Karen Hwang's comment. Hwang, described as a thirty-seven-year-old quadriplegic from New Jersey, told Connolly, "We're independent; we're working, living in the community. . . . Just to have somebody say we are vulnerable, that's patronizing and insulting."

People like Hwang continually return to the issue that what we need to be pressing for is better access, an end to job discrimination, access to education, better healthcare access.

We understand why people want to assert a distinction between themselves and Terri Schiavo. Hwang's comment captures its essence well. And on surface—if what you are comparing are the individual disabilities—the distinctions are vast. But those who make the comparison aren't basing their comparison on individual disabilities but on societal bigotry.

It's the "better dead than disabled" mindset these crips are focusing on. And to that mindset, it's disability itself that seems horrific. And as long as that's the case, the kinds of things that functioning crips want will always be considered too much trouble, too expensive, too bothersome to mainstream society.

The only way disability bigotry of the "better dead than disabled" school has any chance of being stamped out—or even dislodged a bit—is if the disability rights movement is willing to speak forcefully and publicly about the tie-in between emerging public policies that in the guise of cost containment and choice in dying both promote futile care policies and define feeding tubes as "medical care," and the look-the-other-way stances of progressives and right to lifers alike as Medicaid is cut, healthcare services are cut, and anti-access judges are appointed to the federal bench.

Disabled people who see their lives as mainstreamed and OK may not want to acknowledge this, may not want to think about the connect, perhaps hoping that it will go away. They too may want to join the groups playing ostrich. The stretch of sand is going to fill up pretty soon with lots of us digging holes to stick our heads into.

Here are the reasons, as we understand them, that "functioning crips" aligned with groups like Not Dead Yet compared themselves to Terri Schiavo:

1. She was not terminally ill. She was simply a person who would never "recover." Both points, they said, apply also to their lives.

Those are the two related but distinct points that keep getting made by Not Dead Yet members. And the reason they keep bringing them up, it seems, is because they believe that the public doesn't make the distinction. And not making the distinction, they believe, is dangerous for all disabled people.

It is accurate that Terri Schiavo was not terminally ill. Left as she was, with a feeding tube, and with care, she could have lived decades longer. But people ignore that distinction between permanent disability and terminal illness—Not Dead Yet has been making that point for years. Ignoring it, the group says, has allowed right-to-die groups to press for legal sanction for things like feeding tube removal, and ventilator removal, which allow healthy but seriously disabled people to have their lives ended prematurely—often to save medical costs.

It is also accurate to say that Terri Schiavo would not have "recovered." A number of times that point was made in news stories, often as the final sentence, used as an explanation as to why Michael Schiavo justified the removal of her feeding tube. The "will not recover" phrase also appeared in stories explaining why the Schindlers pressed so hard to gain guardianship—that they believed she could receive therapy and perhaps "improve."

When such stories were reported, they also usually contained comments by medical professionals insisting that therapy would be of no use because Terri Schiavo "would not recover." And the phrase also appeared in "context stories" about the issue of people "like" Terri Schiavo who "will not recover"—how much their care cost taxpayers, how court rulings in recent years had made it easier to turn off ventilators, and so on.

In all these cases, the phrase "will not recover" was used, it seemed to Not Dead Yet protesters, as a kind of shorthand to justify the withdrawal of life-sustaining measures.

And this, perhaps more than any other point, was one we heard made from the Not Dead Yet camp: that people who were seriously disabled with "no hope of recovery" were seen as burdens on society in terms of their costs, their medical care, their needs.

People in the disability rights movement, by and large, are people who have serious disabilities. Virtually none of them will "recover." To them, the phrase—its constant and patently unexamined use—signaled an attitude much in evidence throughout society: that people who could not recover would be better off dead. Or that their families, or society, would be better off—economically, certainly—if they were dead.

That is a hard message to hear. And even if your disability is not on the surface anything like Terri Schiavo's, even if you can think and speak and write and work, if your disability is so serious that you require a feeding tube or a breathing tube or even a catheter—and if

you're not going to recover—you fear being treated like Terri Schiavo. Maybe sooner, if you're admitted to the hospital for something unrelated like pneumonia or a tubal ligation and told that you should sign a "do not resuscitate" order—something a number of our readers have reported happening to them. Maybe later, if your disability progresses to a point where you need more equipment, more assistance. But looming always.

2. A feeding tube is not medical treatment. A story in yesterday's *Washington Post* ("Feeding Tube Benefit Questioned") noted 1977 research (much reported in recent days) that showed that nursing home residents "who had feeding tubes did not live longer on average than those without them"—the study, done using elderly "nursing home patients with dementia," seems to be one of those factoids that get dropped into stories willy-nilly when it serves to ground a hot topic. However, what the research doesn't bother to point out but which crips know is that what this primarily shows is that feeding tubes are not "medical treatment"—they're just an alternative device for delivering nutrition. You can live for years—decades—with a feeding tube if you're otherwise healthy. As many crips upset about the "feeding tube debate" are. As Terri Schiavo was.

Yes, Terri Schiavo was healthy. Brain damaged for sure. Unable to "recover," for sure. But healthy. She could have lived a long long time with that feeding tube.

Now maybe that horrifies you—it horrifies many people who are coming at the issue with the mindset of "I couldn't stand to live like that"—but that is beside the point. The point is that Terri Schiavo was not unhealthy. She was not "ill." She was most assuredly not "terminally ill." As the pope is. Pope John Paul II is dying. That is what "terminally ill" is supposed to mean. He will likely be dead when you read this. But he is dying from old age. Terri was not.

It is this distinction that Not Dead Yet crips feel got almost completely lost in the feeding tube discussion, and it is why they latched so quickly onto their "Tube Pride" concept.

That's what this is all about: The feeding tube represents—stands for—all sorts of equipment without which severely disabled people would not be alive. And, they say, slowly but surely the presence of that equipment is being used as justification for encouraging a person to end their life. "How, exactly, did a feeding tube get reclassified as 'medical treatment'?" asks Boston Not Dead Yet's John Kelly.

"Twelve years ago I made a decision to have a feeding tube placed in my stomach in order to prolong life," wrote David Jayne recently. Jayne, who has had ALS for seventeen years, created RespiteMatch.com and lobbies for a change in Medicare's "Homebound Rule."

"I had lost the ability to swallow due to the progression of the disease," he explained.

"Seven years ago last week," he wrote, when he "had one foot in death's door, because my diaphragm muscle was becoming increasingly disabled," he made the decision "contrary to society"—and contrary to what 95 percent of people with ALS say they want—to begin using a respirator. It was, he noted, also **contrary to what he would have wanted before he contracted the disease.**

> It is extremely easy for a healthy individual to say how they would not live. I am guilty myself. If someone had told me prior to the diagnosis that I would be totally paralyzed, fed by a feeding tube, communicate via computer with a voice synthesizer and tethered to a ventilator, [yet] that I would find more meaning in life and living, I am certain [I would have thought] that person telling me such a tale was insane.

The night before his tracheotomy surgery, he says, "my now ex-wife told me how selfish I was for wanting to live—that my young children had suffered enough and it would cause them only more pain. It was a sickening sense of abandonment. I have absolutely no doubt if I did not have the ability to communicate my desires the surgery would not have taken place."

This is why the feeding tube issue upsets Not Dead Yet crips so much.

They raise these foregoing points again and again. They focus on those points that they say kept getting made over and over in the Terri Schiavo discussion. The attitude with which progressive right-to-die advocates viewed the Terri Schiavo situation is an attitude that they say they feel is often applied to their lives as well.

Another way of putting this: It is not they who see Terri Schiavo as being identical to them; it is the public, which, although it says that Terri Schiavo's situation and condition is very different than that of a severely disabled but conscious person, nonetheless continues to hold beliefs about nonrecovering severely disabled people which to crips seem very similar. Yes, when pressed, now progressives are making distinctions. But very often, the crips say, the same progressives apply the same kind of thinking toward them—and they say they see it all around them.

In other words, Terri Schiavo represents something to the public that they believe they also represent. She is an example of why people think the disabled person is better off dead.

Another lesson learned: then is not now; now is not the future.

Something else we heard, coming through the opinion pieces and letters to the editor from crips, and from e-mails to Ragged Edge, was that people who are not disabled, despite what they think they understand and would want, have no real clue as to what it is like to live as a disabled person. And there is no way . . . that they can know now what they would really want once they became disabled. Once they had time to adjust, that is.

"[W]hen I discovered I was paralysed in almost 90 per cent of my body," wrote Canadian commentator Ed Smith at the height of the *Million Dollar Baby* controversy, "I pleaded with my wife to have me shot or put down in some merciful fashion. At the time, I didn't even care if it was merciful. That was for the first two days. Now, six years later, I'm rather glad she didn't. Actor Christopher Reeve had a similar experience. So did many people I know who have suffered from catastrophic injury."

This point drove many crips' animus against *Million Dollar Baby*. While it might be true that "Maggie" wanted to end her life—many newly paralyzed people do; even Christopher Reeve did—most people get over that suicidal feeling and get on with their lives, said Eastwood's critics. Only paralyzed people are encouraged to act on that suicidal wish—and given society's blessing and help to speed them to the end, they say. That was Frankie's message, they say. And they hated it.

Thus the general solution to this entire sorry saga— get a "durable power of attorney for medical decision making"—which is what every "expert" on TV has preached in the past few days—may be a snare and a delusion.

Wellesley College bioethicist Adrienne Asch, one of the few bioethicists to come out of the disability rights movement, was quoted in Ellen Goodman's syndicated column on Thursday. Asch told Goodman, "The typical advance directive or living will does not ask the right questions. It asks what sort of medical intervention we want or don't want. The question that we ought to be asked is what am I experiencing? What will make me feel that I have something to live for? What is enough?"

> Asch, who is blind and very conscious of societal attitudes toward disabilities, says that if she wrote the living will form, it would ask people to imagine themselves in a range of scenarios. When would we want our lives prolonged by medicine? In her own advance directive she has written that "as long as the people who know me believe that I recognize them and can differentiate them from strangers, I want to be alive."

In the morass of news coverage quoting bioethicists and other "medical experts" on the need for advance directives, Asch's analysis stands out as the only one making the clear point that we hear over and over from disability groups: That people don't really know until they are disabled what it is that they might want. A study reported in the recent issue of the *Journal of Experimental Psychology* found that nondisabled people ("healthy people," the term researchers Jason Riis and colleagues used) consistently "underestimate the self-reported well-being of people with disabilities and serious illnesses." In other words, they consistently believe disabled people are far less happy than they actually are, and imagine life to be far more horrid with a disability than people with disabilities themselves believe it to be. This is not the first study to discover this, but these studies don't seem to have made it into the popular media.

Thus, it is the unusual person who, never having faced disability or lived with others with happily disabled lives, would sign a directive asking to be kept alive if the future meant ventilator or feeding tube dependency. However, what this means is that many many people now rushing to sign directives will say just that—and who knows how they might feel had they had a chance to live with disability?

But why should it matter, you say. If I want my life ended before I wake up on a ventilator for the rest of my life, what does it matter to anyone else? If it's my decision?

It matters very much, it seems, to the community of severely disabled people who make up Not Dead Yet. Although Not Dead Yet's Coleman and Drake are insistent that had Schiavo clearly expressed her wishes, so that there was no debate, they would not be involved in the case, and would not have filed several court briefs in the case over the years, they say they know that many people in "guardianship" who can no longer express their views have lives that are seen as expendable.

Because of those people, the slogan "silence = death" has renewed meaning.

In a recent interview, Coleman told a reporter, "[W]hat we are seeing here is the dismantling of the constitutional rights of people in guardianship. No longer will there be the presumption for life.

"The social presumption that [Schiavo] would be better off dead appears to have influenced the decisions in the case," Coleman said. "We feel threatened by this, almost as if there is a cognitive test for personhood under the law."

Both the evangelical right-to-life movement and the progressive right-to-die movement have broader agendas that go beyond Terri Schiavo. In coming months, as the U.S. Supreme Court prepares to rule on the constitutionality of Oregon's assisted-suicide law, both groups will be pushing their agendas with politicians. And there are plenty of politicians who are already loyal to one or the other side.

But if disability rights movement leadership has learned anything from the past few weeks, one of those lessons should be that it needs to now build on its assertion that it is the one group which can most accurately claim to speak for people like Terri Schiavo. Certainly the disability rights movement can produce a focused agenda—and beyond that, one free of the kind of political overreaching we all grew thoroughly sick of in the last few weeks.

It is, because of this, the agenda most able to lift our nation beyond the left-right hand-wringing we seem mired in.

Not Dead Yet has proposed:

- Meaningful federal civil rights review of contested third-party decisions to withhold treatment in the absence of an advance directive or personally appointed surrogate. Senator Tom Harkin (D-IA) is already working on a bill providing for this. Movement leaders want congressional hearings on how to protect people from death based on decisions of guardians or healthcare providers.
- State-by-state review of guardianship and healthcare decisions laws. They want the review conducted by disability rights monitoring groups like the Disability Rights Education and Defense Fund; they want the review to result in reforms to safeguard against what they call "nonvoluntary euthanasia."
- A moratorium on the removal of food and water from people diagnosed in a "persistent vegetative state" or "minimally conscious state" until they have undergone newer diagnostic MRI procedures, which they say must be a requirement. A recent study done by doctors at Columbia Medical Center noted that patients "who are treated as if they are almost completely unaware may in fact hear and register what is going on around them but be unable to respond."
- Enforcement of the 1999 U.S. Supreme Court Olmstead decision, which ruled that people with disabilities must be allowed to live in the "least restrictive" setting. For well over a decade, the movement has called for changing the Medicaid law to allow people to receive services at home rather than being placed in nursing homes, saving the government millions. It's time for Congress to get serious about passing the Medicaid Community Services and Supports Act.
- Serious and substantive public discussion about "the difference between end-of-life decisions and decisions to end the lives of disabled people who are not otherwise dying." Disability rights movement experts, they say, must be given equal time in media debates with bioethicists; reporters and editors must begin to turn to disability rights spokespeople as experts rather than relying on doctors, ethicists, and spokespersons on the religious right "to pontificate about our lives."

Now if disability rights movement leadership will only press ahead with them.

We can only hope they will.

THE DYING PROCESS

When Race Matters

Annette Dula and September Williams

Many studies show that African Americans want all the care they can get at the end of life, even when it is futile.[1-5] What's the problem here? One might be tempted to think that African Americans' desires are ignorant and uninformed. Yet African Americans are behaving rationally when one considers their historical relation to the health care system.

PART I: FALSE ASSUMPTIONS ON END-OF-LIFE CARE FROM AN AFRICAN AMERICAN PERSPECTIVE

Several widely held assumptions shape end-of-life discussion in the United States. On their face, these assumptions are sensible, and it would seem that all could agree with them. They are embedded in mainstream bioethics and biomedical discourse, debate, and discussion, as well as in the popular media. We have come to regard them as the conventional wisdom. Despite their apparent reasonableness, however, all United States citizens do not hold the assumptions universally, particularly those of color. The assumptions hold contradictions that at least partially explain why fewer African Americans than whites complete advance directives, and why African Americans tend to desire aggressive care at the end of life.

Assumption 1: People want to die with dignity. Quality of life is preferred over quantity of life

A major assumption in end-of-life care is that people want to die with dignity. Associated with quality of life over quantity of life, dying with dignity means avoiding the physical pain, demeaning disability, and spiritual, psychological, and emotional suffering connected with a "bad death." Value is placed on the quality of life and a "good death" as one approaches the end—not on the number of years, months, or days lived.

Death with dignity has a wider and different connotation in African American communities: to an African American, death with dignity is likely to mean that he or she deflected indignity of death caused by the health care system's racism and accumulated neglect, escaped early death caused by poverty, and survived

discriminatory policies that disproportionately affect the health and well-being of African Americans. It is unsurprising, then, that African Americans might place more emphasis on quantity of life (time lived) than on others' conceptions of quality of life (good death) when confronted with decisions about dying. Thus, African Americans associate dying with dignity with aggressive or curative treatment rather than palliative care.

Studies do show that African Americans want all the intervention they can get at the end of life. Contrary to whites, they want aggressive intervention, including dialysis, artificial nutrition, surgery, and antibiotics. They want treatment even if they are in a coma or a permanent vegetative state and have little chance of survival, or even if it means losing all their savings.[1-4,6] Some academics may assume that African Americans want this seemingly futile care because they are unsophisticated, and once properly educated, they will see just how unreasonable their beliefs are. However, black physicians (who certainly are educated) have similar preferences for end-of-life care as black patients. Moreover, any talk about shortening the lives of African Americans must be understood in the context of their already shorter life span as a group compared with whites.[7] In this context, it is understandable that they might opt for longevity over so-called "quality of life."

Assumption 2: People will receive unwanted and unnecessary health care at the end of life

Closely related to the previous assumption is the belief that people will get unwanted health care at the end of life. In fact, most African Americans believe the opposite. Because care has historically been denied, they are afraid they won't get any treatment (let alone unwanted treatment) at the end of life.

The fear of not receiving needed care is based on reality. For example, the procedure to restore coronary blood flow after acute myocardial infarction is underused for blacks, women, and the elderly.[8-10] African Americans are significantly less likely to have access to a neurologist and therefore receive less noninvasive cerebrovascular testing and cerebral angiography.[11] The higher mortality of blacks with early-stage lung cancer is due to the lower rates of surgery.[12] Kidney transplantation is overused in whites and underused in blacks.[13–16]

In March 2002, the Institute of Medicine (IOM) released its astounding report "Unequal Treatment: Confronting Ethnic and Racial Disparities in Health Care." The IOM, drawing on over 100 studies conducted over the past 10 years, found that (1) racial and ethnic disparities exist and are associated with worse health outcomes for black Americans and (2) that sources of disparities include health systems and providers' bias, stereotyping, prejudice, and clinical uncertainty.[17,18]

For people of color, withholding care for ill patients, then, is already a practice. Getting unwanted care at the end of life is not the issue; rather, getting preventive and routine quality care has always been and continues to be the issue.

Assumption 3: Advance directives are planning tools. They help African Americans plan for their death. They are a good thing and everybody ought to fill one out

Bioethicists, health care workers, and government policy encourage people to prepare for their deaths by completing advance directives.[19] Advance directives are a good move for a small number of middle-class well-educated whites who have a sense of empowerment and control over their lives. However, for most people, especially people of color, advance directives have not lived up to their designers' hopes.[1,6] Studies offer various reasons for the low completion rates by African Americans. For example, African Americans, as a group, are less knowledgeable than whites about advance directives, proxies, living wills, and surrogates.[4,5,20] Even when familiar with the terminology, older African Americans may look at formal advanced planning as something that white folks do. Often when they do sign an advance directive, it is to make things easier for the family rather than for providers or hospitals.

The most widespread, deeply held, and troubling reason that African Americans do not complete advance directives is that they are suspicious and afraid that any formal document could be used to justify inferior and inadequate treatment, limit autonomy, and needlessly hasten death.[2,3,21] As some African Americans see it, completing an advance directive is tantamount to signing a death warrant. There is little motivation to put their beliefs down in a formal contract to be executed by white

people whom they neither know nor trust. Doctors and families may "get it wrong," but given a choice, African American patients would rather have their families make the decisions.[5,6]

Assumption 4: When care becomes futile, treatment should be discontinued

The assumption here is that the patient understands through discussions with his or her physician that at some point in the illness further treatment will become futile and expensive. Treatment should then end. This assumption directly conflicts with a widely held African American belief in God as the ultimate decision maker; God's will determines the time, manner, and place of death. Accordingly, you will not die until God is ready for you to die, no matter how ill you may be. Accepting futility means giving up before God is ready for you to give up.

Although African Americans do not live as long as whites, they still expect to have a long life. Expectations of longevity and belief in God create barriers to participating in certain programs deemed beneficial by the dominant culture. For example, most whites see hospice as a good, whereas many blacks disagree with hospice philosophy because it advocates a palliative rather than a curative approach. Hospice care for most African Americans means giving up on living; they aren't interested in going to hospice to wait for death.

African Americans have historically exhibited a keen ability to survive despite overwhelming odds and incredible adversity. This belief in the possibility of overcoming the odds partly explains disagreement with physician-assisted-suicide, indifference to hospice care, and desire for aggressive treatment at the end of life. For many elderly African Americans, futility is a foreign concept that they neither understand nor accept.

Assumption 5: Doctor/patient communication improves end-of-life care and allows health care workers to honor patients' preferences about that care

The assumption here is that communication about end-of-life preferences is a powerful guide to treatment. This is false even for the dominant culture and certainly for communities of color.[22–24] According to SUPPORT[i] findings, 2 years of clinical intervention to

---

[i]The SUPPORT (The Study to Understand Prognoses and Preferences for Outcomes and Risks of Treatment) project enrolled 9105 seriously ill and terminally ill hospital patients in a study to observe their treatment preferences and their end-of-life care and to develop an intervention to improve that care. The intervention was declared as largely ineffective. The study, which began in 1989 and ended in 1994, included 79% whites; 15% African Americans, and 5% other minorities. It generated nearly 100 publications.

improve doctor-patient communication, understanding, pain control, and decision making made no difference in end-of-life care; doctors still did not know what their patients wanted, often did not put preferences in the medical records, and even when they did record preferences, often got them wrong.[23,25]

Blacks, more than whites, want to discuss end-of-life issues, yet physicians are less likely to have this conversation with black patients than with white patients.[1,22] Other studies have substantiated poorer communication with black patients.[26,27] Clearly, the quality of communication between doctors and patients at the end of life is poor for all, but particularly so for people of color.

Assumption 6: Once properly trained in pain management, health professionals will administer adequate pain medication for all patients

This assumption asserts that seriously ill patients need not suffer the excessive pain associated with death from certain conditions but ignores the fact that race and ethnicity are risk factors for inadequate pain medication, especially in public hospitals and emergency departments where a significant proportion of ethnic minorities receive their health care.[28] One quarter of all patients receive insufficient pain medication, but blacks and Latinos are even more likely to receive inappropriate doses of pain medicine. Twenty-eight percent of Latinos and 31% of African Americans in public hospitals do not receive enough medicine to manage cancer pain.[29] Todd and colleagues[30] found that Latinos with long-bone fractures are twice as likely as whites to get no pain medication at all. In a later study they found that 74% of whites in a public hospital's emergency department received pain medicine for long-bone fractures, compared with 57% of blacks.[2,31]

One reason that professionals don't give enough pain relief is their inability to adequately assess pain in patients. Race is an added concern, as health care providers especially fear drug addiction in their black, Latino, and American Indian patients. For example, researchers asked health professionals to assess drug dependency in sickle cell patients. Estimates varied: staff physicians, residents, and nurses respectively thought that 8%, 17%, and 13% were addicted. In reality, less than 1% of sickle cell patients are dependent on opium-based drugs.[32] Additionally, some providers may believe that people of color do not feel pain in the same way or as much as whites feel it. Even if people of color are adequately assessed for pain, there is a good chance they can't get their prescription filled

in their inner city neighborhood pharmacy because inner-city pharmacies do not stock enough medication to treat patients with severe pain.[33]

Assumption 7: Physician-assisted suicide is a means of expressing autonomy

A final assumption is that physician-assisted suicide (PAS) is a means of expressing individual autonomy so that death is not unnecessarily prolonged, expensive, or painful. It is promoted as a way of controlling how and when one dies. However, for African Americans, PAS is not an expression of autonomy. It appears to African American communities as quite the contrary. A history of intentional medical abuse and neglect, medical experimentation, and general disrespect for the health and well being of African Americans has demonstrated that their lives are less valuable to society than white lives.[3] Consider the rule that a slave was worth three-fifths of a white person; consider also that access, use, and delivery of health care services are still unequal between blacks and other ethnic minorities and whites.

As health care costs increase, and if PAS becomes more widespread, black mistrust of the health care system will be heightened. Many fear that vulnerable and historically oppressed people will be among the first to feel the pressure for PAS; that if PAS is legal, more powerful people will find a way to manipulate the law so that "undesirables" are eliminated from society through PAS. With the reemergence of states' rights and public policy that is increasingly hostile to ethnic minority populations, many worry that PAS would disproportionately affect people of color and immigrants.

African Americans have long harbored fears of genocide. Horrible as the actual facts of Tuskegee Syphilis Study are, many wrongly believed (and some still believe) that doctors in the Tuskegee Syphilis Study *deliberately* infected 400 African American men with syphilis.[34] The involuntary sterilization programs of the 1970s and the sickle cell screening programs of the 1960s were widely perceived as genocidal attempts to wipe out the black race.[35] In the early days of the AIDS epidemic, many blacks thought of AIDS as a genocidal plot against African Americans.[36] Given the strong, deep, and justifiable mistrust of societal institutions, many African Americans would see PAS as a continuation of genocidal intentions.[21] Instead of PAS, African Americans would prefer policies that promote health and well-being throughout their lives, leading to a reduction in health disparities.

Summary

Through the analysis of these seven assumptions, the author has revealed the contradictions of mainstream discourse about end-of-life care. These assumptions are certainly false for African Americans, and although they are based on white values and norms, they do not work for most white people either.[37]

The contradictions are symptoms of serious structural and ethical problems of justice in the health care system and in United States society. As long as health care policies, institutions, and individual providers discriminate against the nation's most vulnerable citizens, health care professionals will continue to encounter what appear to be irrational demands for treatment at the end of life.

To address some of the contradictions around end-of-life care, the author suggests the following:

- Bioethicists, providers, and the public need new ways of talking about end-of-life issues that reflect people's real experiences, especially those experiences of people of color. Advance directives should be rethought, acknowledging that as currently conceptualized, they don't meet the needs of most citizens, no matter their ethnicity.
- Provider-patient relationships should change so that providers listen and respond to patients' goals and preferences, and are not penalized for doing so because listening takes time, and time costs insurers. Only then can providers begin to accurately understand and act on patients' needs and desires. They can only "get it right" if they have time to listen. Providers must know not only about pain management generally but must also eliminate biases based on patient race, class, and gender that result in differential pain assessment and medication.
- The role that families have in end-of-life decision making should be acknowledged. To accept a family-centered model would require the adoption of a less-individualized concept of decision sharing, where end-of-life care focuses on the patient and the patient's family. Such an approach may be more beneficial than a discussion of what to write down in a formal document.[38]
- Effective means of eliminating the disparities in health status and access to services and care throughout the life cycle need to be implemented. Such a mission would reduce the demand (based on suspicion) for aggressive and futile health care at the end of life.
- To ensure that these strategies work, institutional racism and provider bias in the allocation of resources needs to be acknowledged and eliminated.

PART II: A SYNTHETIC APPROACH TO PALLIATIVE CARE, CLINICAL ETHICS AND ELDERLY AFRICAN AMERICANS

Geriatric African Americans frequently share a historical and current reality that makes them suspicious of the operational assumptions used in the practice of palliative care medicine. Why these assumptions ring false for African Americans is well outlined in this volume and elsewhere.[39,40] Ironically, it is that same reality which leaves elderly African Americans disproportionately under-using palliative care services.[41,42] The standard presentation of palliative care medicine by clinicians, media, and the nation at large apparently leaves those African Americans most vulnerable to negative aspects of the dying process without needed care near life's end. This circumstance presents clinically as a medical ethical conflict. This can be characterized as a conflict between the competing goods of medically indicated palliative care and patient preferences/perceptions; the latter of which African Americans are loath to abandon as they have ensured cultural/physical survival.

A two-tiered clinical device, extrapolated from standard informed consent procedures, in conjunction with the common paradigm of clinical ethical decision making may assist clinicians in bedside management of clinical ethical conflict. This approach considers palliative care a consentable entity, presented in a clinical medical ethically charged context. The case selected here illustrates how the two-tiered process of disclosure and assessment of barriers to capacity informs more individualized clinical action, subsequently acknowledging concerns and values of dying elderly in African American families.

Disclosure and capacity

Palliative care is a new medical subspecialty in the United States and as such should be considered a new technology. Clinical use of palliative care should be weighted by medical indications and patient preferences, which service the bioethical principles of beneficence and autonomy respectively in the Jonsen, Seigler, and Winslade paradigm.[43] Issues related to justice (ie, quality of life and social contextual features) should inform but cannot be the principal determinants of clinical ethical application of palliative care, or bedside activity may grind to a halt in the milieu of policy and administrative development.

Recommending palliative care, especially across cultures, is an ethically charged high-risk clinical circumstance likened to surgery or transfusion. Accompanying such charged therapies is an obligation of increased stringency in disclosure and concomitant assessment of capacity of the patient to consent or, at the least, assent. Such capacity is demonstrated by ability to reflect back understanding of the policies and procedures that constitute the modern field of palliative care.

If a patient is unable to reflect back such understanding, an assessment of barriers to capacity should be explored. It is in the exploration of these barriers that the clinician and action are most informed. This approach requires that the clinician understand, and the patient be able to reflect that, palliative care is a patient-centered, team-based approach that expects to alleviate pain and noxious symptoms in their physical, psychological, spiritual and fiscal manifestations while neither intentionally hastening nor preventing death.[44]

The following case has been selected to illustrate a circumstance where many of the commonly presented operational assumptions of end-of-life care ring false with one African-American family. Further, the case presents a nononcological indication for palliative care resulting from multiple comorbidities. It also underscores quandaries arising in interpreting patient desires upon invoking the durable power of attorney for health care proxy—a frequent presentation in geriatric populations, and particularly for those of color arising from dementia and late diagnosis of life threatening diseases.

The case

Mr. Moses is an 84-year-old long-term resident of a nursing home where he worked in his younger years. He is postcolostomy for colon cancer, with renal tubular acidosis, chronic obstructive pulmonary disease, morbid obesity, hypercapnea, sleep apnea, normopressure hydrocephalus, and paranoid delusions. On good days, he interacts with family and staff and participates in nursing home recreational activities. He has been transferred to the intensive care unit seven times in 3 months, where he has been intubated for impending respiratory arrest. All clinical options short of frequent intubations have been explored and rejected on clinical grounds.

Palliative care and code status are raised with the patient's son, who is the durable power of attorney for health care proxy, by each acute care admitting medical team as well as his primary provider. The patient's last documented treatment preferences, several years ago, state that he wants full resuscitation as long as he is "able to eat and talk with people." The patient, via his proxy, rejects palliative care so Mr. Moses continues to be "a full code." The nursing home staff is concerned there may be a delay in the recognition of the patient's respiratory compromise, yielding cardiac arrest that would likely end badly. Transfer to a subacute unit has also been rejected by the patient's proxy.

Case analysis

Stating the ethical conflict. In Mr. Moses' case, the conflict is defined as "medical indication for palliative care

versus patient/proxy preference" for continued periodic intubations and full code status.

Clinical ethical considerations. Ethical considerations are best framed as questions and answers regarding the specific case:

Is palliative care medically indicted? Yes. Mr. Moses' case meets nononcological criteria for palliative care referral based on his lung disease.[45]

Is intubation for respiratory support a viable alternative to palliative care? If the patient is intubated, he is unable to "eat or talk" with his family members. He must be sedated to avoid removal of the tube and lines in the intensive care setting, which exacerbates his paranoia and dementia. However, because the respiratory episodes are separated by days to weeks, and the patient reaches baseline function during the interval, this approach of supportive intubation (which cannot be provided in the nursing home) may transiently appear to be an alternative to palliative care. However, it is likely more appropriate to consider intubation or bipap as a part of palliative care and attempt to decrease risk of discomforting impending respiratory arrest associated by anticipating and scheduling the palliative interventions based on clinical need, before emergency need. This approach is not without risk, which should be explained to the patient/proxy.

Is the patient/proxy able to reflect back the first-tier elements of disclosure? No. The patient/proxy believes that the medical staff's expectation is that palliative care will hasten the patient's death and that it is being proposed to decrease the bother of multiple medical admissions for the acute medical team. Also, the proxy mistakenly believes that a risk of palliative care will be that the patient will die sooner because he will be made DNR (do not resuscitate) simultaneously. It is likely that Mr. Moses' demise will result from delayed recognition of respiratory compromised due to placement in a facility, which is inappropriately staffed for the level of care the patient needs. This low staffing ratio will likely result in cardiopulmonary arrest with anticipated poor outcome due to advanced age and multiple comorbidities. Failure to reflect back the expected outcome if palliative care is instituted, and if it is not, should result in exploration of the second tier considerations with the proxy.

Does the second-tier assessment of decisional capacity yield information bearing on the clinical action? Yes. Second-tier evaluation of Mr. Moses proxy yielded a history of family perceptions of discrimination secondary to Mr. Moses' obesity, dementia, delusions, and the family's racial background. The patient's residence in the facility where he had worked for many years and where he had many long-time friends among the current staff serves as an extended family for the patient, augmenting the capacity of his proxy and his siblings to provide support to the patient. This extended family trumped all other considerations in the proxy's mind. It was the proxy's perception, based on his experience with biases directed toward his father in the past that his father's preference would be to live his final days in an environment that accepted him for who he was, as this would be protective to the patient's life *and* spirit.

Recommendations. Knowing that palliative care is medically indicated, and with a better understanding of the patient/proxy wishes, the clinician/team members who know the patient/proxy best should individualize the care of this patient by

1. Actively separating dialog about code status from dialog about the other goals of patient's care in an attempt to establish where the clinical team and the patient/proxy share a common view of the patient's needs and desires

2. Carefully outlining the parameters of goals of care for the patient in general narrative form and in terms of specific life-sustaining and supportive therapies. The proxy is in denial about the eminent demise of his father, fostered by the frequent "resurrection" facilitated by intubation. The goal of palliative care is to help the patient/proxy anticipate and successfully complete final developmental stages of the patient's life. The clinical response to this patient's care should be a palliative approach, short of DNR. The menu of options offered to the patient/proxy should anticipate the patient's future needs and be in accordance with medical indications of each anticipated therapy, individualized for this patient, and guided by evidence-based geriatric medicine.[46] Clinical considerations would include dialysis, antibiotics, artificial nutrition, transfusion, treatment for pain and apnea, attention to spiritual needs and burial planning, organ donation, and financial concerns.

3. Leaving the patient a full code, documenting that the proxy has accepted the risk of delayed response, if the patient is in the long-term facility through a specific contract. Inform the proxy that documentation of the same is being charted and that all measures will be taken to avoid cardiac arrest, but preventing the patient's suffering is the principle intent of all therapies. Clinicians should remember and share that there is no therapy that is automatically precluded from the palliative care armamentarium, nor should DNR status be requisite for admission to a palliative care inpatient service. However, it may impact implementation of hospice care (final stage of palliative care). The presence/absence of assent to DNR orders can be used to gauge the patient/proxy's sense of the extent of disease and underscore work that the palliative care team needs to address.

4. Establish a regular point of contact to review and revise goals of care anticipated by the patient/proxy rather than waiting for a crisis to determine a reactive revision of the treatment plan.

Summary

Recommending palliative care is an ethically charged clinical circumstance, especially when it involves cross-cultural competency. African American culture is a culture of relationships, not data. Operationalizing the process of assent to palliative care establishes stronger patient/proxy—provider relationships. This relationship may discover points of congruency between the goals of the African American patient/proxy and palliative care, dwarfing the significance of incongruence and breaking down impediments to rational clinical care. Framing assent to palliative care and its procedures in a clinical ethical context forces an intimacy between patient perspectives and clinical action.

Medicine is entering an era of earnest commitment to ending health disparities. It is time that more clinicians invest in learning the clinical medical ethics and palliative care principles, hard wrought over the last quarter century. This investment will likely improve implementation of palliative care and the dying process across generations, particularly for people most vulnerable to health care disparities near life's end, as is the case with elderly African Americans.

REFERENCES

1. Caralis PV, Davis B, Wright K, Marcial E. The influence of ethnicity and race on attitudes toward advance directives, life-prolonging treatments, and euthanasia. *J Clin Ethics* 1993;4(2):155–65.

2. Borum ML, Lynn J, Zhong Z. The effects of patient race on outcomes in seriously ill patients in SUPPORT: an overview of economic impact, medical intervention, and end-of-life decisions Study to Understand Prognoses and Preferences for Outcomes and Risks of Treatments. *J Am Geriatr Soc* 2000;48(5 Suppl):S194–8.

3. King PA, Wolf LE. Empowering and protecting patients: lessons for physician-assisted suicide from the African-American experience. *Minn Law Rev* 1998;82:1015–43.

4. Morrison RS, Zayas LH, Mulvihill M, et al. Barriers to completion of health care proxies: an examination of ethnic differences. *Arch Intern Med* 1998;158(22):2493–7.

5. Murphy ST, Palmer JM, Azen S, et al. Ethnicity and advance directives. *J Law Med Ethics* 1996;24(2):5–14.

6. Hornung CA, Eleazer GP, Strothers III HS, et al. Ethnicity and decision-makers in a group of frail older people. *J Am Geriatr Soc* 1998;46(3):280–6.

7. Mebane EW, Oman RF, Kroonen LT, Goldstein MK. The influence of physician race, age, and gender on physician attitudes toward advance care directives and preferences for end-of-life decision-making. *J Am Geriatr Soc* 1999;47(5):579–91.

8. Kressin NR, Peterson LA. Racial differences in the use of invasive cardiovascular procedures: review of the literature and prescription for future research. *Ann Intern Med* 2001;135(5):352–66.

9. Laouri M, Kraavitz RL, French W. Underuse of coronary revascularization procedures: application of a clinical method. *J Am Coll Cardiol* 1997;29:891–7.

10. Peterson ED, Shaw LK, DeLong ER, Pryor DB. Racial variation in the use of coronary-revascularization procedures—are the differences real? Do they matter? *N Engl J Med* 1997;336(7):480–6.

11. Mitchell B, Ballard DJ, Matchar DB, et al. Racial variation in treatment for transient ischemic attacks: impact of participation by neurologists. *Health Serv Res* 2000;34(7):1413–28.

12. Bach PB, Cramer LD, Warren JL. Racial differences in the treatment of early-stage lung cancer. *N Engl J Med* 1999;341:1198–205.

13. Gaston RS, Ayres I, Dooley LG, Diethelm AG. Racial equity in renal transplantation: the disparate impact of HLA-based allocation. *JAMA* 1993;270(11):1352–6.

14. Epstein A. Ayanian J, Keogh J, Noonan S. Racial disparities in access to renal transplantation. *N Engl J Med* 2000;343(21):1537–44.

15. Starzl TE, Aliasziw EM, Gjertson D. HLA and cross-reactive antigen group matching for cadaver kidney allocation. *Transplantation* 1997;64(7):983–91.

16. Schneider EC, Zaslavsky AM, Epstein AM. Racial disparities in the quality of care for enrollees in Medicare managed care. *JAMA* 2002;287(10):1288–94.

17. Institute of Medicine. *Unequal treatment: confronting racial and ethnic disparities in health care.* Washington (DC): National Academy Press: 2002.

18. Stone J, Dula A. Wake-up call: health care and racism. *Hastings Cent Rep* 2002;32(4):48.

19. Emanuel L. Stoeckle BL. Advance directives for medical care—a case for greater use. *N Engl J Med* 1995;324:889–95.

20. Waters CM. End-of-life care directives among African Americans: lessons learned—a need for community-centered discussion and education. *J Community Health Nurs* 2000;17(1):25–37.

21. Dula A. African American suspicion of the healthcare system is justified: What do we do about it? *Camb Q Healthc Ethics* 1994;3(3):47–57.

22. Hofmann JC, Wenger NS, Davis RB, et al. Patient preferences for communication with physicians about end-of-life decisions SUPPORT Investigators Study to Understand Prognoses and Preference for Outcomes and Risks of Treatment [see comments]. *Ann Intern Med* 1997; 127(1):1–12.

23. Covinsky KE, Fuller JD, Yaffe K, et al. Communication and decision-making in seriously ill patients: findings of the SUPPORT project The Study to Understand Prognoses and Preferences for Outcomes and Risks of Treatments. *J Am Geriatr Soc* 2000;48(5 Suppl):S187–93.

24. Cooper-Patrick L, Gallo JJ, Gonzales JJ, et al. Race, gender, and partnership in the patient-physician relationship. *JAMA* 1999;282(6):583–9.

25. Phillips RS, Hamel MB, Covinsky KE, Lynn J. Findings from SUPPORT and HELP: an introduction Study to Understand Prognoses and Preferences for Outcomes and Risks of Treatment Hospitalized Elderly Longitudinal Project. *J Am Geriatr Soc* 2000;48(5 Suppl):S1–5.

26. Curtis JR, Patrick DL, Caldwell E, et al. The quality of patient-doctor communication about end-of-life care: a study of patients with advanced AIDS and their primary care clinicians. *AIDS* 1999;13(9):1123–31.

27. Mouton C, Teno JM, Mor V, Piette J. Communication of preferences for care among human immunodeficiency virus-infected patients Barriers to informed decisions. *Arch Fam Med* 1997; 6(4):342–7.

28. Cone DC, Richardson LD, Todd DH, Betancourt JR. Heath care disparities in emergency medicine. *Acad Emerg Med* 2003;10(11):1176.

29. Anderson KO, Mendoza TR, Valero V, et al. Minority cancer patients and their providers: pain management attitudes and practice. *Cancer* 2000;88(8):1929–38.

30. Todd KH, Samaroo N, Hoffman JR. Ethnicity as a risk factor for inadequate emergency department analgesia [see comments]. *JAMA* 1993;269(12):1537–9.

31. Todd KH, Deaton C, D'Adamo AP, Goe L. Ethnicity and analgesic practice [see comments]. *Ann Emerg Med* 2000;35(1):11–6.

32. Waldrop RD, Mandry C. Health professional perceptions of opioid dependence among patients with pain. *Am J Emerg Med* 1995;13(5):529–31.

33. Freeman HP, Payne R. We don't carry that. *N Engl J Med* 2000;343(6):442–5.

34. Dalton H. AIDS in blackface. *Daedalus* 1989;118:205–27.

35. King P. The past as prologue: race, class, and gene discrimination. In: Annas G, Elias S, editors. *Gene mapping: using law and ethics as guides.* New York: Oxford University Press; 1992. p. 94–114.

36. Thomas SB, Quinn SC. The Tuskegee Syphilis Study, 1932 to 1972: implications for HIV education and the AIDS risk programs in the black community. *Am J Public Health* 1991;81(11):1498–505.

37. Hickey DP. The disutility of advance directives: we know the problems, but are there solutions? *J Health Law* 2003;36(3):455.

38. Tong E, McGraw SA, Dobihal E, Baggish R. What is a good death? Minority and non-minority perspectives. *J Palliat Care* 2003;19(3):168.

39. Dula A, Goering S, editors. *It just ain't fair: The ethics of health care for African Americans.* West Port (CT): Prager; 1994.

40. Williams S. The need for autonomy driven HIV prevention and treatment: strategies for African Americans. In: Secundy MG, Dula A, Williams S, editors. *Bioethics research concerns and directions for African Americans.* Tuskegee (AL): Tuskegee University National Center for Bioethics in Research and Health Care; 2000. p. 100–6.

41. Payne R, Medina E, Hampton JW. Quality of life concerns in patients with breast cancer, evidence of disparity outcomes and experiences in pain management and palliative care among African American women. *Cancer* 2003;97(1):311–7.

42. Virnig BA, Morgan RO, Persily NA, DeVito CA. Racial and income differences in use of hospice benefit between the Medicare and managed care and Medicare fee-for-service. *J Palliat Med* 1999;2(1):23–31.

43. Jonsen A, Siegler M, Winslade W. *Clinical ethics: a practical guide to ethical decisions in clinical medicine.* 5th ed. New York: McGraw Hill Companies Inc.; 2002. p. 5–11.

44. World Health Organization. *Cancer pain relief and palliative care: technical report series.* Geneva: World Health Organization; 1990.

45. National Hospice Organization. Hospice referral guidelines for non-cancer diagnoses. In: Weed-Seaman L, editor. *Symptom management algorithms: a handbook for palliative care.* 2nd ed. Yakima (WA): Intellicard Inc.; 1999. p. 166–7.

46. McNicoll L, Inouye S. Common disorders of the elderly. In: Landefeld CS, Palmer R, Johnson MA, et al, editors. *Current geriatric diagnosis and treatment.* New York: McGraw-Hill; 2004. p. 53–8.

Understanding Cultural Difference in Caring for Dying Patients

Barbara A. Koenig and Jan Gates-Williams

Experiences of illness and death, as well as beliefs about the appropriate role of healers, are profoundly influenced by patients' cultural background. As the United States becomes increasingly diverse, cultural difference is a central feature of many clinical interactions. Knowledge about how patients experience and express pain, maintain hope in the face of a poor prognosis, and respond to grief and loss will aid health care professionals. Many patients' or families' beliefs about appropriate end-of-life care are easily accommodated in routine clinical practice. Desires about the care of the body after death, for example, generally do not threaten deeply held values of medical science. Because expected deaths are increasingly the result of explicit negotiation about limiting or discontinuing therapies, however, the likelihood of serious moral disputes and overt conflict increases. We suggest a way to assess cultural variation in end-of-life care, arguing that culture is only meaningful when interpreted in the context of a patient's unique history, family constellation, and socioeconomic status. Efforts to use racial or ethnic background as simplistic, straightforward predictors of beliefs or behavior will lead to harmful stereotyping of patients and culturally insensitive care for the dying.

In providing care at the end of life, a salient category of difference is cultural variation, which in the United States is usually understood as reflecting differences that divide along lines of race or ethnicity and, to some extent, religion. Death is inevitably understood and experienced within a complex web of cultural meanings.[1-3] How should physicians take culture into account when providing medical care for patients nearing the end of their lives?

We focus on two questions: How does culture shape the experience of illness and death in clinically meaningful ways, such as mediating the response to pain? and How is cultural difference relevant to implementing the new "bioethics practices" that govern end-of-life care in US health care institutions? Practices such as writing do-not-resuscitate orders have become central rituals of death in our society, replacing other markers of transition from life to death.

Central to our discussion is a strong argument about the complexity of cultural interpretation and the need to draw clear distinctions between culture, race, and ethnicity as categories of difference. Dangers exist— for example, creating negative stereotypes—in simply supplying clinicians with an atlas or map of "cultural traits" common among particular ethnic groups.

TWO CASE VIGNETTES

As medical anthropologists, we have done research on how culturally diverse patients with cancer, their family members, and their health care providers have approached decisions about care at the end of life.[4,5] The following case vignettes, collected through in depth interviews in the course of longitudinal anthropologic research, reveal the complexity of cross-cultural medical care.

Patient 1

A diagnosis of pancreatic cancer led this patient's care providers to initiate discussions about her resuscitation status on five separate occasions during the last months of her life. A note written in her medical record during a hospital admission for pain control stated: "Pt urged to consider DNR/DNI [do-not-resuscitate or do-not-intubate orders] given her horrible prognosis." But the patient persistently resisted her care professionals' view of what her course of illness should look like. A 46-year-old African-American woman with strong religious beliefs, she rejected "meals on wheels," refused hospice, and until right before her death, wanted cardiopulmonary resuscitation in the event of cardiopulmonary arrest.

The patient described the following exchange with a physician after her diagnosis, established with great difficulty after several procedures, was finally confirmed:

> But they told me—asked me did I want them to tell me how long I had to live. I told them no, because I said only God has priority over living. That's something man can't tell you—how long you got to live. I said only God can heal you. And they looked at me so funny.

The patient's physicians were compassionate, even visiting her at home during one attempt to verify her resuscitation status. But her medical management was complicated by fragmented care; her only insurance was Medi-Cal (California's Medicaid), and she had not seen a physician for more than five years before being diagnosed with cancer. In the end, frail, immobile, and full of ascites, she was cared for by a large extended family. Her efforts to manage her pain may have been complicated by her fear that medications sometimes "disappeared." Administrative hurdles set up by Medi-Cal made it difficult to get her prescriptions filled. Whereas from her physician's point of view, getting the do-not-resuscitate order was the key decision the patient faced, she was concentrating on getting well.

Patient 2

This patient was diagnosed with locally invasive nasopharyngeal cancer in China before he emigrated to the United States with his family. The oldest son, who attends college, always accompanied his monolingual father to the clinic. Despite treatment with irradiation and chemotherapy—along with traditional Chinese medicine—the cancer progressed to the point of being immediately life-threatening due to hemorrhage. Although aware of the nature and severity of the diagnosis, family members avoided the use of the word cancer, preferring the more neutral Cantonese term for tumor when discussing the patient's illness. The family's ideas about appropriate disclosure varied from the health care team's view. The patient's son complained, "For us Chinese, we are not used to telling the patient everything, and patients are not used to this either. If you tell them, they can't tolerate it and they will get sicker."

During one visit to the clinic, the physician wanted the patient's son to explain that chemotherapy had not been effective in his case and that there were no more treatments available. The son became distressed.

> I did not want to translate this to my father, but the doctor insisted on telling him everything. The doctor found the Chinese-speaking nurse to translate for him and told him everything.

Because of the family's reluctance to discuss the prognosis openly, the team's well-intentioned efforts to manage the patient's death at home were thwarted.

These case presentations reveal a range of ways in which culture is relevant to terminal care. Patient 2's use of Chinese herbal medicines in combination with biomedical therapies represents a successful blending of traditions. The two cases also show the potential for serious disputes and dissatisfaction when patients from a minority group are confronted with practices routinely accepted within US biomedicine. The patient's son did not share the high value his father's physician placed on open disclosure of a cancer diagnosis and

limited prognosis. Patient 1 did not comprehend her physician's view that further treatment of her illness, including resuscitation, was futile.

RACE, CULTURE, CLASS, ETHNICITY—THE NATURE OF DIFFERENCE

Patient 1's race varies from that of most of the physicians who cared for her. Patient 2's ethnicity derives from his country of birth, his language, and his immigrant status. What do these categories mean, and how do they intersect with culture and with social class? One distinction—that the designation "race" reflects biologic difference whereas "ethnicity" refers to cultural variation—is outmoded. Adopting the term ethnicity was a change from 19th-century conceptions of race (or biologic variation) as the bedrock of difference. Although the word "race" remains in popular use, as a scientific classification it is based on "outmoded concepts and dubious assumptions about genetic difference."[6(p 248)] Genetic variation within races is always greater than variation between races.[7] Races do not exist as natural categories; rather, they are social constructions, meaningful only within particular historical contexts, and subject to change.

In the United States, cultural and social class differences are often confused because ethnicity and class are closely correlated. Culture is not reducible to class, however. (A full discussion of the culture concept is beyond the scope of this review.) The medical anthropologist Arthur Kleinman explains how the concept has evolved and changed[8,9(pp113–114)]:

> Culture is now viewed not merely as a fixed, top-down organization of experience by the symbolic apparatuses of language, aesthetic preference, and mythology; it is also "realized" from the bottom up in the everyday negotiation of the social world, including the rhythms and processes of interpersonal interactions.

We focus here on interpretive approaches, on "reading" patients, as opposed to thinking about culture as a demographic variable that predicts specific behavioral traits. Gender differences must be approached in similarly sensitive ways. Culture is constantly redefined and negotiated, meaningful only when interpreted within the context of a patient's unique history, family constellation, and socioeconomic status.

Considering culture as a predictive variable is inherently limited—that is, simply plugging race or ethnicity into a multiple-regression analysis or, in a clinical context, assuming someone's name, appearance, or national origin is a predictive factor. The image that comes to mind is of a young medical resident, recently returned from a lecture on cultural sensitivity in health care, who pulls his or her index card from a pocket when dealing with a patient like patient 2 and, assuming that there is no need to discuss his care directly with him—because Chinese culture is family-oriented—concludes that the resident's only responsibility is to follow the son's wishes.

CHANGING DEMOGRAPHICS

As the United States becomes increasingly diverse, situations often occur in which the cultural background of a physician or other health care professional differs from that of a patient and family.[6] According to the 1990 census, the percentage of foreign-born residents in the United States is 8%. In the state of California, that figure has increased to 22%, with a concentration in urban areas. A third of residents of San Francisco and Los Angeles, for example, are foreign-born. In the United States, 12% of the population identifies itself as African American. Dramatically changing demographics offer only a partial explanation of the urgency of respecting cultural differences in clinical work. Equally salient are the political forces of multi-culturalism.[10] The call for the recognition of minority voices in US society will inevitably surface as a serious concern during discussions of ethical issues in end-of-life care, particularly the appropriate allocation of ever-scarcer medical resources.

CROSS-CULTURAL VARIATIONS IN DEATH AND DYING

The culturally constructed boundaries between life and death are more variable than scientific definitions, based on cellular death or organ system failure, suggest. In Vanatinai, a small island close to Papua New Guinea, those who would be considered unconscious by western-trained physicians are viewed as already dead, leading to cases where a person may "die" many times.[11]

Similarly, cultural practices at the beginning of life shape the definition of death. In some traditional Native American societies, an infant was not considered a full member of the community until a "naming ceremony" or other ritual is performed, often at 1 month of age or older.[12] If an infant dies before this important ceremony, no funeral is required because the infant is not yet a part of the social group and hence not fully alive.

Death is socially constructed in the United States as well. The life of a bedridden, isolated, demented elderly woman could be described as a form of social death that precedes biologic death. Our familiarity with existing social definitions of life and death disguises the strangeness of a concept such as brain death. In the past three decades, the relationship between biologic and social death in the United States has been transformed by the new concept of brain death. Perhaps not surprisingly, this new construction has not been universally embraced. Empirical evidence documents a lower rate of organ donation by minority groups in the United States.[13,14]

The response to the loss of particular persons also varies considerably through time and place. In the contemporary United States, the loss of an infant or child is considered one of the most tragic experiences a family can face. By contrast, in less economically privileged societies, the loss of the family's primary worker may be much more tragic. In the northeast of Brazil where anthropologist Scheper-Hughes studied impoverished mothers, child deaths, which happened frequently, were understood to be inevitable, a function of the child's will to life; mourning lasted only a few days.[15]

Emotional expressions of grief are also highly culturally patterned. Although some form of ritual or ceremony to mark a death is universal, expressions of grief vary widely. Two societies that share the Muslim religion—Egypt and Bali—condone opposite expressions of grief. In Bali, a person in mourning must remain calm and cheerful, keeping a strict separation between inner and outer feelings. By contrast, in Egypt a woman who remains "withdrawn, mute, and inactive" for seven years while mourning the death of a child is considered sane and healthy.[16] In the dominant European-American tradition, both these patterns would be considered disorders.

A problem with blanket statements about cultural patterns is that they disguise the often important intracultural variation that exists in most societies and has always existed, even before the modern era of instant worldwide communication and massive migration. The notion that culture can be simply and easily "mapped" onto geographically isolated human groups has been abandoned by anthropologists.[17] Calls for "culturally competent care" ignore the dynamic nature of culture. It cannot be assumed that patients' origins will lead them to approach decisions about their death in a culturally specified manner.

CULTURAL DIFFERENCE IN THE UNITED STATES

Differences between nations are generally not ethically troubling for clinicians. That physicians in Japan or Italy choose not to reveal a diagnosis of cancer to a patient is not a problem if this is accepted and expected practice in a homogeneous society.[18,19] The situation in the United States is notably different. Maneuvering within cross-cultural encounters requires familiarity with the possible range of variation, both around the world and in the United States. Physicians need to know the possible range of variation in response to illness and death to respond to the needs of their patients.

In the care of dying patients, managing pain is often a central task. Sociologists have observed that the experience of pain and its expression varies among American immigrants.[20,21] Models have been developed that describe how cultural groups have different standards of appropriate behavior when in pain, which in turn lead to variation in how patients perceive, interpret, and respond to pain. More recent models integrate biologic, psychological, and sociocultural aspects of pain.[22] Researchers continue to demonstrate differences in how ethnic groups express and respond to pain, both acute and long-term.[23,24]

To understand the relationship between pain control and cultural difference, it is necessary to consider the historical and political context. Health care workers in urban clinics struggle with the issue of managing pain in an environment of poverty where drug abuse may be present. Social class-based divisions that separate the lives of health care professionals and patients are further accentuated by decades of overt racism and open discrimination. Pain management of Hispanic and white patients with similar trauma was compared in an emergency department.[25] Undertreatment of Hispanic patients in pain by health care professionals—perhaps because of overt discrimination—could not be ruled out, as later research showed that physicians were not simply making inaccurate evaluations of the amount and intensity of pain experienced by these patients.[26]

What constitutes a "good" death? As with the experience of pain, cultural narratives of dying vary. The ideal of hospice care, with its emphasis on a peaceful, accepted death at home in familiar surroundings with family members present, demonstrates unexamined white middle-class assumptions. African Americans have more negative attitudes toward hospice.[27] Admission to a hospice facility generally requires accepting the inevitability of death, expressed through the idea of a prognosis of less than six months to live and an agreement to forgo aggressive care and resuscitation.

Chinese immigrants may choose to avoid death at home because of traditional beliefs about ghosts inhabiting dwellings where someone has died. Indeed, a recent death may affect the market value of real estate in some Chinese neighborhoods (Evelyn Lee, EdD,

oral communication, Richmond Area Multi-Services, San Francisco, California, June 1992).

Beliefs about the integrity of the body and its proper treatment after death are also areas of possible cross-cultural conflict. The idea of an autopsy may be repugnant to some groups, particularly if the request is made while the patient is still alive.[28]

NEW RITUALS OF BIOETHICS

Implications for culturally diverse patients

Understanding that the experience of pain varies across cultural groups may lead to improved clinical management. More problematic is the observation that notable differences exist among cultural groups in the United States in accepting and using the bioethics practices that regulate end-of-life care. Inevitably, each ill person reaches a point when medical interventions can do little to stave off death and may, indeed, prolong the process of dying. Because expected deaths are increasingly the result of explicit negotiation about limiting or discontinuing therapies,[29] the likelihood of serious moral disputes and overt conflict increases. Negotiated deaths lead to bioethics rituals as a new rite of passage to death. In many American hospitals, the decision not to resuscitate a patient or to limit or discontinue therapy is the primary indication that the end of life is approaching. In a sense, because of changing medical technology, death has moved from the realm of nature to that of culture in our society. The cultural values and beliefs that inform the new bioethics practices are white, middle-class, and based on western philosophical and legal traditions that emphasize the individual and individual decision making.[30] Successfully implementing "death by decision" depends on a set of cultural attributes, including the open disclosure of distressing information, the desire for control, and future orientation, described elsewhere as the "autonomy paradigm" in bioethics.[31]

Surveys have documented the lack of fit between bioethics innovations and minority populations in the United States. Substantially fewer minorities make use of advance directives to guide their care at life's close. African Americans differ notably from European Americans both in their unwillingness to complete advance directives and in the desires about life-sustaining treatment expressed.[32] Substantially more African Americans and Hispanics "wanted their doctors to keep them alive regardless of how ill they were, while more... whites agreed to stop life-prolonging treatment under some circumstances."[33(pp157–158)]

A study comparing elderly persons from four cultural groups in Los Angeles found that 80% of Hispanics and Korean Americans endorsed the statement, "Life-sustaining machines should never be stopped because even if the patient appears to be dying, there is always the chance of a miracle." Fewer than a third of the European Americans agreed. The research demonstrated equally striking ethnic differences in beliefs about discussing death openly with patients; most Koreans and Hispanics believed that this was harmful to dying patients.[34]

AN INDIVIDUAL APPROACH VERSUS CULTURAL 'TRAITS'

The challenge of respecting diversity is great. Because culture is fluid and dynamic, how can we respect differences while avoiding stereotyping of patients? The answer is clear. Patients should never be approached as empty vessels, as the bearers of particular cultures. Rather, it is essential to approach patients first as unique persons, assessing them within the context of their family or other key social support system. General knowledge about theoretical differences among groups is helpful. For example, it is useful to bear in mind that in many Asian societies, ideas about "selfhood" vary from the western ideal of an autonomous individual. A sociocentric or relational sense of self often leads to decision-making styles at odds with western bioethics ideals. Likewise, it is helpful to keep in mind that African Americans, with a complex history of limited access to services, may not trust physicians to act in a patient's best interest.[35] Nonetheless, clinical inferences about cultural difference must be evaluated for relevance to a particular patient or family.

We propose an approach with patients and families nearing the end of life. Rather than memorizing the traits associated with different groups, we suggest evaluating each patient and family using the following guidelines:

- Assess the language used to discuss this patient's illness and disease, including the degree of openness in discussing the diagnosis, prognosis, and death itself;
- Determine whether decisions are made by the patient or a larger social unit, such as the family;
- Consider the relevance of religious beliefs, particularly about the meaning of death, the existence of an afterlife, and belief in miracles;
- Determine who controls access to the body and how the body should be approached after death;
- Assess how hope for a recovery is negotiated within the family and with health care professionals;
- Assess the patient's degree of fatalism versus an active desire for the control of events into the future;
- Consider issues of generation or age, gender and power relationships, both within the patient's family and in interactions with the health care team;
- Take into account the political and historical context, particularly poverty, refugee status, past discrimination, and lack of access to care;
- To aid the complex effort of interpreting the relevance of cultural dimensions of a particular case, make use of available resources, including community or religious leaders, family members, and language translators.

POLITICS OF MULTICULTURAL CARE

Assessing patients and families against the dimensions of cultural variation is an important first step. But in the complex setting of managed death, health care professionals have no guarantee that even the most skillful assessment will avoid or resolve conflicts, improve care, or eliminate dilemmas. Some adjustments to clinical management are relatively simple and straightforward. For example, it is relatively easy to respect the wishes of an Islamic patient and family who request that the patient's body be turned to face the east after death. This act does not interfere with clinical management before death, it is not offensive to medically trained staff, and it does not raise costs. Only a small adjustment in the routine of managing the body after death is required; respecting difference is easy because it does not challenge the physician's own values.

In direct contrast are those differences that create serious disputes and the potential for conflict. Like their patients, physicians act in accord with deeply held values; scientific biomedicine has its own set of "cultural" practices surrounding death and dying.

What of a family who requests indefinite life support for a brain-dead patient in an intensive care unit? Situations like this occur, demanding skillful clinical interventions while presenting complex policy dilemmas. The state of New Jersey has enacted revised brain death legislation that allows for an exemption based on religious beliefs.[36]

The ideal of respecting diverse cultural perspectives is based on deeply held American beliefs in the value of tolerance. This does not mean, however, that patients may demand unlimited treatment based on their beliefs or cultural identity. The challenge for clinical practice is to allow ethical pluralism—a true engagement with and respect for diverse perspectives—without falling into the trap of absolute ethical relativism.

REFERENCES

1. Hellman C: *Culture, Health and Illness*, 3rd edition. Newton, Mass, Butterworth & Heinemann, 1995

2. Kleinman AM: *Patients and Healers in the Context of Culture* Berkeley. Calif. University of California Press, 1980

3. Kagawa-Singer M: Diverse cultural beliefs and practices about death and dying in the elderly, In Wieland (Ed): *Cultural Diversity and Geriatric Care*. New York. NY, 1994, pp 101–116

4. Orona CJ, Koenig BA, Davis AJ: Cultural aspects of nondisclosure. *Cambridge Q Health Care Ethics* 1994; 3:338–345

5. Koenig BA, Marshall PA: *Bioethics and the Politics of Race and Ethnicity: Respecting (or Constructing) Difference.* Presented at the annual meeting of the American Anthropological Association. Atlanta, Georgia, December 1994

6. Barker JC Cultural diversity—Changing the context of medical practice, In *Cross-cultural Medicine—A Decade Later* (Special Issue). West J Med 1992; 157:248–254

7. Lock M: The concept of race: An ideological construct. *Transcult Psychiatry Res Rev* 1993; 30:203–227

8. Kleinman A. Kleinman J: Suffering and its professional transformation: Toward an ethnography of interpersonal experience. *Cult Med Psychiatry* 1991; 15:275–301

9. Hinton L. IV. Kleinman A: Cultural issues and international psychiatric diagnoses. In Costa e Silva JA: Nadelson CC (Eds): International Review of Psychiatry. Washington, DC. *American Psychiatric Press*, 1993, pp. 111–129

10. Taylor C: *Multiculturalism and the 'Politics' of Recognition.* Princeton. NJ. Princeton University Press, 1992

11. Lepowsky M: Gender, aging, and dying in an egalitarian society. In Counts DR. Counts DA (Eds): *Aging and Its Transformations—Moving Toward Death in Pacific Societies.* Lanham, Md, University Press of America, 1985, pp 157–178

12. Opler MP. Reactions to death among the Mescalero Apache. *Southwest J Anthropol* 1946; 2:454–467

13. Kjellstand CM: Age, sex, and race inequality in renal transplantation. *Arch Intern Med* 1988; 148:1305–1309

14. Kasiske BL. Neylan JF 3d. Riggio RR. et al: The effect of race on access and outcome in transplantation. *N Engl J Med* 1991; 324:302–307

15. Scheper-Hughes N: *Death Without Weeping: The Violence of Everyday Life in Brazil.* Berkeley, Calif, University of California Press, 1992

16. Rosenblatt PC: Cross-cultural ariation in the experience, expression, and understanding of grief. In Irish DP, Lundquist KF, Nelsen VJ (Eds): *Ethnics Variations in Dying, Death, and Grief.* Washington, DC, Taylor & Francis, 1993, pp 13–19

17. Gupta A, Ferguson J: 1992 Beyond 'culture'—Space, identity, and the politics of difference. *Cult Anthropol* 1992; 7:623

18. Tanida N: Japanese attitudes towards truth disclosure in cancer. *Scand J Soc Med* 1994; 22:50–57

19. Gordon DR: Embodying illness, embodying cancer. *Cult Med Psychiatry* 1990; 14:275–297

20. Zborowski M: Cultural components in response to pain. *J Soc Issues* 1952; 8:16–30

21. Zola JK: Culture and symptoms: An analysis of patients' presenting complaints. *Am Sociol Rev* 1966; 31:615–630

22. Bates MS: Ethnicity and pain: A biocultural model. *Soc Sci Med* 1987; 24:47–50

23. Bates MS, Edwards WT: Ethnic variation in the chronic pain experience. *Ethnicity Dis* 1992; 2:63–83

24. Calvillo ER, Flaskerud JH: Evaluation of the pain response by Mexican-American and Anglo-American women and their nurses. *J Adv Nurs* 1993; 18:451–459

25. Todd KH, Samaroo N. Hoffman JR: Ethnicity as a risk factor for inadequate emergency department analgesia. *JAMA* 1993; 269:1537–1539

26. Todd KH, Lee T. Hoffman JR: The effect of ethnicity on physician estimates of pain severity in patients with isolated extremity trauma. *JAMA* 1994; 271:925–928

27. Neubauer BJ, Hamilton CL: Racial differences in attitudes toward hospice care. *Hospice J* 1990; 6:37–48

28. Perkins HS, Supik JD, Hazuda HP: Autopsy decisions: The possibility of conflicting cultural attitudes. *J Clin Ethics* 1993; 4:145–154

29. Slomka J: The negotiation of death: Clinical decision-making at the end of life. *Soc Sci Med* 1992; 35:251–259

30. Fox RC: The evalution of American bioethics. A sociological perspective, In Weisz G (Ed): *Social Science Perspectives on Medical Ethics.* Boston, Mass, Kluwer, 1990, pp 201–217

31. Koenig PA: *Cultural Diversity in Decision-making About Care at the End of Life.* Presented at the Institute of Medicine Workshop, Dying, Decision-making and Appropriate Care, December 1993

32. Garrett J, Harris RP, Norburn JK, Patrick DL, Danis M: Life-sustaining treatments during terminal illness: Who wants what? *J Gen Intern Med* 1993; 8:361–368

33. Carals PV, Davis B, Wright K, Marcial E: The influence of ethnicity and race on attitudes toward advance directives, life-prolonging treatments, and euthanasia *J Clin Ethics* 1993; 4: 155–165

34. Frank G. Blackhall L, Murphy S. Michel V: *Ethnicity and Attitudes Toward Patient Autonomy: From Cultural Pluralism to Structuration in End of Life Decision-Making.* Presented at the annual meeting of the American Anthropological Association, Atlanta. Georgia December 1994

35. Adler NE, Boyce NF, Chesney MA, Folkman S, Syme SL: Socioeconomic inequalities in health. No easy solution. *JAMA* 1993; 269:3140–3145

36. NJ Stat §26 6A-5 (1992)

Is There a Duty to Die?

John Hardwig

Many people were outraged when Richard Lamm claimed that old people had a duty to die. Modern medicine and an individualistic culture have seduced many to feel that they have a right to health care and a right to live, despite the burdens and costs to our families and society. But in fact there are circumstances when we have a duty

Abridged from Hardwig, John. "Is There a Duty to Die?" *Hastings Center Report* 27:2 (1997), 34–42. Copyright © 1997. Reprinted by permission of The Hastings Center.

to die. As modern medicine continues to save more of us from acute illness, it also delivers more of us over to chronic illnesses, allowing us to survive far longer than we can take care of ourselves. It may be that our technological sophistication coupled with a commitment to our loved ones generates a fairly widespread duty to die.

When Richard Lamm made the statement that old people have a duty to die, it was generally shouted down or ridiculed. The whole idea is just too preposterous to entertain. Or too threatening. In fact, a fairly common argument against legalizing physician-assisted suicide is that if it were legal, some people might somehow get the idea that they have a duty to die. These people could only be the victims of twisted moral reasoning or vicious social pressure. It goes without saying that there is no duty to die.

But for me the question is real and very important. I feel strongly that I may very well some day have a duty to die. I do not believe that I am idiosyncratic, morbid, mentally ill, or morally perverse in thinking this. I think many of us will eventually face precisely this duty. But I am first of all concerned with my own duty. I write partly to clarify my own convictions and to prepare myself. Ending my life might be a very difficult thing for me to do.

This notion of a duty to die raises all sorts of interesting theoretical and metaethical questions. I intend to try to avoid most of them because I hope my argument will be persuasive to those holding a wide variety of ethical views. Also, although the claim that there is a duty to die would ultimately require theoretical underpinning, the discussion needs to begin on the normative level. As is appropriate to my attempt to steer clear of theoretical commitments, I will use "duty," "obligation," and "responsibility" interchangeably, in a pretheoretical or pre-analytic sense.[1]

CIRCUMSTANCES AND A DUTY TO DIE

Do many of us really believe that no one ever has a duty to die? I suspect not. I think most of us probably believe that there is such a duty, but it is very uncommon. Consider Captain Oates, a member of Admiral Scott's expedition to the South Pole. Oates became too ill to continue. If the rest of the team stayed with him, they would all perish. After this had become clear, Oates left his tent one night, walked out into a raging blizzard, and was never seen again.[2] That may have been a heroic thing to do, but we might be able to agree that it was also no more than his duty. It would have been wrong for him to urge—or even to allow—the rest to stay and care for him.

This is a very unusual circumstance—a "lifeboat case"—and lifeboat cases make for bad ethics. But I expect that most of us would also agree that there have been cultures in which what we would call a duty to die has been fairly common. These are relatively poor, technologically simple, and especially nomadic cultures. In such societies, everyone knows that if you manage to live long enough, you will eventually become old and debilitated. Then you will need to take steps to end your life. The old people in these societies regularly did precisely that. Their cultures prepared and supported them in doing so.

Those cultures could be dismissed as irrelevant to contemporary bioethics; their circumstances are so different from ours. But if that is our response, it is instructive. It suggests that we assume a duty to die is irrelevant to us because our wealth and technological sophistication have purchased exemption for us . . . except under very unusual circumstances like Captain Oates's.

But have wealth and technology really exempted us? Or are they, on the contrary, about to make a duty to die common again? We like to think of modern medicine as all triumph with no dark side. Our medicine saves many lives and enables most of us to live longer. That is wonderful, indeed. We are all glad to have access to this medicine. But our medicine also delivers most of us over to chronic illnesses and it enables many of us to survive longer than we can take care of ourselves, longer than we know what to do with ourselves, longer than we even are ourselves.

The costs—and these are not merely monetary—of prolonging our lives when we are no longer able to care for ourselves are often staggering. If further medical advances wipe out many of today's "'killer diseases"— cancers, heart attacks, strokes, ALS, AIDS, and the rest— then one day most of us will survive long enough to become demented or debilitated. These developments could generate a fairly widespread duty to die. A fairly common duty to die might turn out to be only the dark side of our life-prolonging medicine and the uses we choose to make of it.

Let me be clear. I certainly believe that there is a duty to refuse life-prolonging medical treatment and also a duty to complete advance directives refusing life-prolonging treatment. But a duty to die can go well beyond that. There can be a duty to die before one's illnesses would cause death, even if treated only with palliative measures. In fact, there may be a fairly common responsibility to end one's life in the absence of any terminal illness at all. Finally, there can be a duty to die when one would prefer to live. Granted, many of the conditions that can generate a duty to die also seriously undermine the quality of life. Some prefer not to live under such conditions. But even those who want to live can face a duty to die. These will clearly be the most controversial and troubling cases; I will, accordingly, focus my reflections on them.

THE INDIVIDUALISTIC FANTASY

Because a duty to die seems such a real possibility to me, I wonder why contemporary bioethics has dismissed it without serious consideration. I believe that most bioethics still shares in one of our deeply embedded American dreams: the individualistic fantasy. This fantasy leads us to imagine that lives are separate and unconnected, or that they could be so if we chose. If lives were unconnected, things that happened in my life would not or need not affect others. And if others were not (much) affected by my life, I would have no duty to consider the impact of my decisions on others. I would then be free morally to live my life however I please, choosing whatever life and death I prefer for myself. The way I live would be nobody's business but my own. I certainly would have no duty to die if I preferred to live.

Within a health care context, the individualistic fantasy leads us to assume that the patient is the only one affected by decisions about her medical treatment. If only the patient were affected, the relevant questions when making treatment decisions would be precisely those we ask: What will benefit the patient? Who can best decide that? The pivotal issue would always be simply whether the patient wants to live like this and whether she would consider herself better off dead.[3] "Whose life is it, anyway?" we ask rhetorically.

But this is morally obtuse. We are not a race of hermits. Illness and death do not come only to those who are all alone. Nor is it much better to think in terms of the bald dichotomy between "the interests of the patient" and "the interests of society" (or a third-party payer), as if we were isolated individuals connected only to "society" in the abstract or to the other, faceless members of our health maintenance organization.

Most of us are affiliated with particular others and most deeply, with family and loved ones. Families and loved ones are bound together by ties of care and affection, by legal relations and obligations, by inhabiting shared spaces and living units, by interlocking finances and economic prospects, by common projects and also commitments to support the different life projects of other family members, by shared histories, by ties of loyalty. This life together of family and loved ones is what defines and sustains us; it is what gives meaning to most of our lives. We would not have it any other way. We would not want to be all alone, especially when we are seriously ill, as we age, and when we are dying.

But the fact of deeply interwoven lives debars us from making exclusively self-regarding decisions, as the decisions of one member of a family may dramatically affect the lives of all the rest. The impact of my decisions upon my family and loved ones is the source of many of my strongest obligations and also the most plausible and likeliest basis of a duty to die. "Society," after all, is only very marginally affected by how I live, or by whether I live or die.

A BURDEN TO MY LOVED ONES

Many older people report that their one remaining goal in life is not to be a burden to their loved ones. Young people feel this, too: when I ask my undergraduate students to think about whether their death could come too late, one of their very first responses always is, "Yes, when I become a burden to my family or loved ones." Tragically, there are situations in which my loved ones would be much better off—all things considered, the loss of a loved one notwithstanding—if I were dead.

The lives of our loved ones can be seriously compromised by caring for us. The burdens of providing care or even just supervision twenty-four hours a day, seven days a week are often overwhelming.[4] When this kind of caregiving goes on for years, it leaves the caregiver exhausted, with no time for herself or life of her own. Ultimately, even her health is often destroyed. But it can also be emotionally devastating simply to live with a spouse who is increasingly distant, uncommunicative, unresponsive, foreign, and unreachable. Other family members' needs often go unmet as the caring capacity of the family is exceeded. Social life and friendships evaporate, as there is no opportunity to go out to see friends and the home is no longer a place suitable for having friends in.

We must also acknowledge that the lives of our loved ones can be devastated just by having to pay for health care for us. One part of the recent SUPPORT study documented the financial aspects of caring for a dying member of a family. Only those who had illnesses severe enough to give them less than a 50 percent chance to live six more months were included in this study. When these patients survived their initial hospitalization and were discharged about one-third required considerable caregiving from their families; in 20 percent of cases a family member had to quit work or make some other major lifestyle change; almost one-third of these families lost all of their savings; and just under 30 percent lost a major source of income.[5]

If talking about money sounds venal or trivial, remember that much more than money is normally at stake here. When someone has to quit work, she may well lose her career. Savings decimated late in life cannot be recouped in the few remaining years of employability, so the loss compromises the quality of the rest of the caregiver's life. For a young person, the chance to go to college may be lost to the attempt to pay debts due to an illness in the family, and this decisively shapes an entire life.

A serious illness in a family is a misfortune. It is usually nobody's fault; no one is responsible for it. But we face choices about how we will respond to this misfortune. That's where the responsibility comes in and fault can arise. Those of us with families and loved ones always have a duty not to make selfish or self-centered decisions about our lives. We have a responsibility to try to protect the lives of loved ones from serious threats or greatly impoverished quality, certainly an obligation not to make choices that will jeopardize or seriously compromise their futures. Often, it would be wrong to do just what we want or just what is best for ourselves; we should choose in light of what is best for all concerned. That is our duty in sickness as well as in health. It is out of these responsibilities that a duty to die can develop.

I am not advocating a crass, quasi-economic conception of burdens and benefits, nor a shallow, hedonistic view of life. Given a suitably rich understanding of benefits, family members sometimes do benefit from suffering through the long illness of a loved one. Caring for the sick or aged can foster growth, even as it makes daily life immeasurably harder and the prospects for the future much bleaker. Chronic illness or a drawn-out death can also pull a family together, making the care for each other stronger and more evident. If my loved ones are truly benefiting from coping with my illness or debility, I have no duty to die based on burdens to them.

But it would be irresponsible to blithely assume that this always happens, that it will happen in my family, or that it will be the fault of my family if they cannot manage to turn my illness into a positive experience. Perhaps the opposite is more common: a hospital chaplain once told me that he could not think of a single case in which a family was strengthened or brought together by what happened at the hospital.

Our families and loved ones also have obligations, of course—they have the responsibility to stand by us and to support us through debilitating illness and death. They must be prepared to make significant sacrifices to respond to an illness in the family. I am

far from denying that. Most of us are aware of this responsibility and most families meet it rather well. In fact, families deliver more than 80 percent of the long-term care in this country, almost always at great personal cost. Most of us who are a part of a family can expect to be sustained in our time of need by family members and those who love us.

But most discussions of an illness in the family sound as if responsibility were a one-way street. It is not, of course. When we become seriously ill or debilitated, we too may have to make sacrifices. To think that my loved ones must bear whatever burdens my illness, debility, or dying process might impose upon them is to reduce them to means to my well-being. And that would be immoral. Family solidarity, altruism, bearing the burden of a loved one's misfortune, and loyalty are all important virtues of families, as well. But they are all also two-way streets.

OBJECTIONS TO A DUTY TO DIE

To my mind, the most serious objections to the idea of a duty to die lie in the effects on my loved ones of ending my life. But to most others, the important objections have little or nothing to do with family and loved ones. Perhaps the most common objections are: (1) there is a higher duty that always takes precedence over a duty to die; (2) a duty to end one's own life would be incompatible with a recognition of human dignity or the intrinsic value of a person; and (3) seriously ill, debilitated, or dying people are already bearing the harshest burdens and so it would be wrong to ask them to bear the additional burden of ending their own lives.

These are all important objections; all deserve a thorough discussion. Here I will only be able to suggest some moral counterweights—ideas that might provide the basis for an argument that these objections do not always preclude a duty to die.

An example of the first line of argument would be the claim that a duty to God, the giver of life, forbids that anyone take her own life. It could be argued that this duty always supersedes whatever obligations we might have to our families. But what convinces us that we always have such a religious duty in the first place? And what guarantees that it always supersedes our obligations to try to protect our loved ones?

Certainly, the view that death is the ultimate evil cannot be squared with Christian theology. It does not reflect the actions of Jesus or those of his early followers. Nor is it clear that the belief that life is sacred requires that we never take it. There are other theological possibilities.[6]

In any case, most of us—bioethicists, physicians, and patients alike—do not subscribe to the view that we have an obligation to preserve human life as long as possible. But if not, surely we ought to agree that I may legitimately end my life for other-regarding reasons, not just for self-regarding reasons.

Secondly, religious considerations aside, the claim could be made that an obligation to end one's own life would be incompatible with human dignity or would embody a failure to recognize the intrinsic value of a person. But I do not see that in thinking I had a duty to die I would necessarily be failing to respect myself or to appreciate my dignity or worth. Nor would I necessarily be failing to respect you in thinking that you had a similar duty. There is surely also a sense in which we fail to respect ourselves if in the face of illness or death, we stoop to choosing just what is best for ourselves. Indeed, Kant held that the very core of human dignity is the ability to act on a self-imposed moral law, regardless of whether it is in our interest to do so.[7] We shall return to the notion of human dignity.

A third objection appeals to the relative weight of burdens and thus, ultimately, to considerations of fairness or justice. The burdens that an illness creates for the family could not possibly be great enough to justify an obligation to end one's life—the sacrifice of life itself would be a far greater burden than any involved in caring for a chronically ill family member.

But is this true? Consider the following case:

An 87-year-old woman was dying of congestive heart failure. Her APACHE score predicted that she had less than a 50 percent chance to live for another six months. She was lucid, assertive, and terrified of death. She very much wanted to live and kept opting for rehospitalization and the most aggressive life-prolonging treatment possible. That treatment successfully prolonged her life (though with increasing debility) for nearly two years. Her 55-year-old daughter was her only remaining family, her caregiver, and the main source of her financial support. The daughter duly cared for her mother. But before her mother died, her illness had cost the daughter all of her savings, her home, her job, and her career.

This is by no means an uncommon sort of case. Thousands of similar cases occur each year. Now, ask yourself which is the greater burden:

a. To lose a 50 percent chance of six more months of life at age 87?
b. To lose all your savings, your home, and your career at age 55?

Which burden would you prefer to bear? Do we really believe the former is the greater burden? Would even the dying mother say that (a) is the greater burden? Or has she been encouraged to believe that the burdens of (b) are somehow morally irrelevant to her choices?

I think most of us would quickly agree that (b) is a greater burden. That is the evil we would more hope to avoid in our lives. If we are tempted to say that the mother's disease and impending death are the greater evil, I believe it is because we are taking a "slice of time" perspective rather than a "lifetime perspective."[8] But surely the lifetime perspective is the appropriate perspective when weighing burdens. If (b) is the greater burden, then we must admit that we have been promulgating an ethics that advocates imposing greater burdens on some people in order to provide smaller benefits for others just because they are ill and thus gain our professional attention and advocacy.

A whole range of cases like this one could easily be generated. In some, the answer about which burden is greater will not be clear. But in many it is. Death—or ending your own life is simply not the greatest evil or the greatest burden.

This point does not depend on a utilitarian calculus. Even if death were the greatest burden (thus disposing of any simple utilitarian argument), serious questions would remain about the moral justifiability of choosing to impose crushing burdens on loved ones in order to avoid having to bear this burden oneself. The fact that I suffer greater burdens than others in my family does not license me simply to choose what I want for myself, nor does it necessarily release me from a responsibility to try to protect the quality of their lives.

I can readily imagine that, through cowardice, rationalization, or failure of resolve, I will fail in this obligation to protect my loved ones. If so, I think I would need to be excused or forgiven for what I did. But I cannot imagine it would be morally permissible for me to ruin the rest of my partner's life to sustain mine or to cut off my sons' careers, impoverish them, or compromise the quality of their children's lives simply because I wish to live a little longer. This is what leads me to believe in a duty to die.

WHO HAS A DUTY TO DIE?

Suppose, then, that there can be a duty to die. Who has a duty to die? And when? To my mind, these are the right questions, the questions we should be asking. Many of us may one day badly need answers to just these questions.

But I cannot supply answers here, for two reasons. In the first place, answers will have to be very particular and contextual. Our concrete duties are often situated, defined in part by the myriad details of our circumstances, histories, and relationships. Though there may be principles that apply to a wide range of cases and some cases that yield pretty straightforward answers, there will also be many situations in which it is very difficult to discern whether one has a duty to die. If nothing else, it will often be very difficult to predict how one's family will bear up under the weight of the burdens that a protracted illness would impose on them. Momentous decisions will often have to be made under conditions of great certainty.

Second and perhaps even more importantly, I believe that those of us with family and loved ones should not define our duties unilaterally, especially not a decision about a duty to die. It would be isolating and distancing for me to decide without consulting them what is too much of a burden for my loved ones to bear. That way of deciding about my moral duties is not only atomistic, it also treats my family and loved ones paternalistically. They must be allowed to speak for themselves about the burdens my life imposes on them and how they feel about bearing those burdens.

Some may object that it would be wrong to put a loved one in a position of having to say, in effect, "You should end your life because caring for you is too hard on me and the rest of the family." Not only will it be almost impossible to say something like that to someone you love, it will carry with it a heavy load of guilt. On this view, you should decide by yourself whether you have a duty to die and approach your loved ones only after you have made up your mind to say good-bye to them. Your family could then try to change your mind, but the tremendous weight of moral decision would be lifted from their shoulders.

Perhaps so. But I believe in family decisions. Important decisions for those whose lives are interwoven should be made together, in a family discussion. Granted, a conversation about whether I have a duty to die would be a tremendously difficult conversation. The temptations to be dishonest could be enormous. Nevertheless, if I am contemplating a duty to die, my family and I should, if possible, have just such an agonizing discussion. It will act as a check on the information, perceptions, and reasoning of all of us. But even more importantly, it affirms our connectedness at a critical juncture in our lives and our life together. Honest talk about difficult matters almost always strengthens relationships.

However, many families seem unable to talk about death at all, much less a duty to die. Certainly most families could not have this discussion all at once, in one sitting. It might well take a number of discussions to be able to approach this topic. But even if talking about death is impossible, there are always behavioral clues—about your caregiver's tiredness, physical condition, health, prevailing mood, anxiety, financial concerns, outlook, overall well-being, and so on. And families unable to talk about death can often talk about how the caregiver is feeling, about finances, about tensions within the family resulting from the illness, about concerns for the future. Deciding whether you have a duty to die based on these behavioral clues and conversation about them honors your relationships better than deciding on your own about how burdensome you and your care must be.

I cannot say when someone has a duty to die. Still, I can suggest a few features of one's illness, history, and circumstances that make it more likely that one has a duty to die. I present them here without much elaboration or explanation.

1. A duty to die is more likely when continuing to live will impose significant burdens—emotional burdens, extensive caregiving, destruction of life plans, and, yes, financial hardship—on your family and loved ones. This is the fundamental insight underlying a duty to die.

2. A duty to die becomes greater as you grow older. As we age, we will be giving up less by giving up our lives, if only because we will sacrifice fewer remaining years of life and a smaller portion of our life plans. After all, it's not as if we would be immortal and live forever if we could just manage to avoid a duty to die. To have reached the age of, say, seventy-five or eighty years without being ready to die is itself a moral failing, the sign of a life out of touch with life's basic realities.[9]

3. A duty to die is more likely when you have already lived a full and rich life. You have already had a full share of the good things life offers.

4. There is greater duty to die if your loved ones' lives have already been difficult or impoverished, if they have had only a small share of the good things that life has to offer (especially if through no fault of their own).

5. A duty to die is more likely when your loved ones have already made great contributions—perhaps even sacrifices—to make your life a good one. Especially if you have not made similar sacrifices for their well-being or for the well-being of other members of your family.

6. To the extent that you can make a good adjustment to your illness or handicapping condition, there is less likely to be a duty to die. A good adjustment means that smaller sacrifices will be required of loved ones and there is more compensating interaction for them. Still, we must also recognize that some diseases—Alzheimer or Huntington chorea—will eventually take their toll on your loved ones no matter how courageously, resolutely, even cheerfully you manage to face that illness.

7. There is less likely to be a duty to die if you can still make significant contributions to the lives of others, especially your family. The burdens to family members are not only or even primarily financial, neither are the contributions to them. However, the old and those who have

terminal illnesses must also bear in mind that the loss their family members will feel when they die cannot be avoided, only postponed.

8. A duty to die is more likely when the part of you that is loved will soon be gone or seriously compromised. Or when you soon will no longer be capable of giving love. Part of the horror of dementing disease is that it destroys the capacity to nurture and sustain relationships, taking away a person's agency and the emotions that bind her to others.

9. There is a greater duty to die to the extent that you have lived a relatively lavish lifestyle instead of saving for illness or old age. Like most upper middle-class Americans, I could easily have saved more. It is a greater wrong to come to your family for assistance if your need is the result of having chosen leisure or a spendthrift lifestyle. I may eventually have to face the moral consequences of decisions I am now making.

These, then, are some of the considerations that give shape and definition to the duty to die. If we can agree that these considerations are all relevant, we can see that the correct course of action will often be difficult to discern. A decision about when I should end my life will sometimes prove to be every bit as difficult as the decision about whether I want treatment for myself.

CAN THE INCOMPETENT HAVE A DUTY TO DIE?

Severe mental deterioration springs readily to mind as one of the situations in which I believe I could have a duty to die. But can incompetent people have duties at all? We can have moral duties we do not recognize or acknowledge, including duties that we never recognized. But can we have duties we are unable to recognize? Duties when we are unable to understand the concept of morality at all? If so, do others have a moral obligation to help us carry out this duty? These are extremely difficult theoretical questions. The reach of moral agency is severely strained by mental incompetence.

I am tempted to simply bypass the entire question by saying that I am talking only about competent persons. But the idea of a duty to die clearly raises the specter of one person claiming that another—who cannot speak for herself—has such a duty. So I need to say that I can make no sense of the claim that someone has a duty to die if the person has never been able to understand moral obligation at all. To my mind, only those who were formerly capable of making moral decisions could have such a duty.

But the case of formerly competent persons is almost as troubling. Perhaps we should simply stipulate that no incompetent person can have a duty to die, not even if she affirmed belief in such a duty in an advance directive. If we take the view that formerly competent people may have such a duty, we should surely exercise extreme caution when claiming a formerly competent person would have acknowledged a duty to die or that any formerly competent person has an unacknowledged duty to die. Moral dangers loom regardless of which way we decide to resolve such issues.

But for me personally, very urgent practical matters turn on their resolution. If a formerly competent person can no longer have a duty to die (or if other people are not likely to help her carry out this duty), I believe that my obligation may be to die while I am still competent, before I become unable to make and carry out that decision for myself. Surely it would be irresponsible to evade my moral duties by temporizing until I escape into incompetence. And so I must die sooner than I otherwise would have to. On the other hand, if I could count on others to end my life after I become incompetent, I might be able to fulfill my responsibilities while also living out all my competent or semi-competent days. Given our society's reluctance to permit physicians, let alone family members, to perform aid-in-dying, I believe I may well have a duty to end my life when I can see mental incapacity on the horizon.

There is also the very real problem of sudden incompetence—due to a serious stroke or automobile accident, for example. For me, that is the real nightmare. If I suddenly become incompetent, I will fall into the hands of a medical-legal system that will conscientiously disregard my moral beliefs and do what is best for me, regardless of the consequences for my loved ones. And that is not at all what I would have wanted!

SOCIAL POLICIES AND A DUTY TO DIE

The claim that there is a duty to die will seem to some a misplaced response to social negligence. If our society were providing for the debilitated, the chronically ill, and the elderly as it should be, there would be only very rare cases of a duty to die. On this view, I am asking the sick and debilitated to step in and accept responsibility because society is derelict in its responsibility to provide for the incapacitated.

This much is surely true: there are a number of social policies we could pursue that would dramatically reduce the incidence of such a duty. Most obviously, we could decide to pay for facilities that provided excellent long-term care (not just health care!) for all chronically ill, debilitated, mentally ill, or demented people in this country. We probably could still afford to do this. If we did, sick, debilitated, and dying people might still be morally required to make sacrifices for their families. I might, for example, have a duty to forgo personal care by a family member who knows me and really does care for me. But these sacrifices would only rarely include the sacrifice of life itself. The duty to die would then be virtually eliminated.

I cannot claim to know whether in some abstract sense a society like ours should provide care for all who are chronically ill or debilitated. But the fact is that we Americans seem to be unwilling to pay for this kind of long-term care, except for ourselves and our own. In fact, we are moving in precisely the opposite direction—we are trying to shift the burdens of caring for the seriously and chronically ill onto families in order to save costs for our health care system. As we shift the burdens of care onto families, we also dramatically increase the number of Americans who will have a duty to die.

I must not, then, live my life and make my plans on the assumption that social institutions will protect my family from my infirmity and debility. To do so would be irresponsible. More likely, it will be up to me to protect my loved ones.

I don't know about others, but these reflections have helped me. I am now more at peace about facing a duty to die. Ending my life if my duty required might still be difficult. But for me, a far greater horror would be dying all alone or stealing the futures of my loved ones in order to buy a little more time for myself. I hope that if the time comes when I have a duty to die, I will recognize it, encourage my loved ones to recognize it too, and carry it out bravely.

REFERENCES

1. Given the importance of relationships in my thinking, "responsibility"—rooted as it is in "respond"—would perhaps be the most appropriate word. Nevertheless, I often use "duty" despite its legalistic overtones, because Lamm's famous statement has given the expression "duty to die" a certain familiarity. But I intend no implication that there is a law that grounds this duty, nor that someone has a right corresponding to it.

2. For a discussion of the Oates case, see Tom L. Beauchamp, "What Is Suicide?" in *Ethical Issues in Death and Dying*, ed. Tom L. Beauchamp and Seymour Perlin (Englewood Cliffs, N.J.: Prentice-Hall, 1978).

3. Most bioethicists advocate a "patient-centered ethics"—an ethics which claims only the patient's interests should be considered in making medical treatment decisions. Most health care professionals have been trained to accept this ethic and to see themselves as patient advocates. For arguments that a patient-centered ethics should be replaced by a family-centered ethics see John Hardwig, "What About the Family?" *Hastings Center Report* 20, no. 2 (1990): 5–10; Hilde L. Nelson and James L. Nelson, The Patient in the Family (New York: Routledge, 1995).

4. A good account of the burdens of caregiving can be found in Elaine Brody, *Women in the Middle: Their Parent-Care Years* (New York: Springer Publishing Co., 1990). Perhaps the best article-length account of these burdens is Daniel Callahan, "Families as Caregivers; the Limits of Morality" in *Aging and Ethics: Philosophical Problems in Gerontology*, ed. Nancy Jecker (Totowa N.J.: Humana Press, 1991).

5. Kenneth E. Covinsky et al., "The Impact of Serious Illness on Patients' Families," *JAMA* 272 (1994): 1839–44.

6. Larry Churchill, for example, believes that Christian ethics takes us far beyond my present position: "Christian doctrines of stewardship prohibit the extension of one's own life at a great cost to the neighbor...And such a gesture should not appear to us a sacrifice, but as the ordinary virtue entailed by a just, social conscience." Larry Churchill, *Rationing Health Care in America* (South Bend, Ind.: Notre Dame University Press, 1988), p. 112.

7. Kant, as is well known, was opposed to suicide. But he was arguing against taking your life out of self-interested motives. It is not clear that Kant would or we should consider taking your life out of a sense of duty to be wrong. See Hilde L. Nelson, "Death with Kantian Dignity," *Journal of Clinical Ethics* 7 (1996): 215–21.

8. Obviously, I owe this distinction to Norman Daniels. Norman Daniels, *Am I My Parents' Keeper? An Essay on Justice Between the Young and the Old* (New York: Oxford University Press, 1988). Just as obviously, Daniels is not committed to my use of it here.

9. Daniel Callahan, *The Troubled Dream of Life* (New York: Simon & Schuster, 1993).

Access to Hospice Care: Expanding Boundaries, Overcoming Barriers

Bruce Jennings, True Ryndes, Carol D'Onofrio, and Mary Ann Baily

Too many Americans approach death without adequate medical, nursing, social, and spiritual support. In the last stage of a long struggle with incurable, progressive diseases such as cancer, heart or lung disease, AIDS, Alzheimer's, Parkinson's, or amyotrophic lateral sclerosis, their pain is untreated or inadequately controlled. Their depression or other mental health problems are not addressed. Debilitating physical symptoms rob them of energy, dignity, and sometimes the will to carry on. Family members who provide care are

Jennings, Bruce, True Ryndes, Carol D'Onofrio, and Mary Ann Baily. "Access to Hospice Care: Expanding Boundaries, Overcoming Barriers" *Hastings Center Report* Special Supplement 33:2 (2003), S3–S7. Copyright © 2003. Reprinted by permission of The Hastings Center.

stressed, inadequately supported by professionals, and often rendered ill themselves by the ordeal. Patients who wish to remain in familiar surroundings at home are often forced to spend their final days or weeks in a hospital or nursing home. Neither dying patients nor their families are provided with the kind of emotional and spiritual support they desire and need.

In sum, too many Americans die unnecessarily bad deaths—deaths with inadequate palliative support, inadequate compassion, and inadequate human presence and witness. Deaths preceded by a dying marked by fear, anxiety, loneliness, and isolation. Deaths that efface dignity and deny individual self-control and choice. And too many Americans have their access to better care and services, through hospice and other forms of palliative care, blocked by a lack of information, misunderstandings, ambivalence about treatment options, unfairly restrictive governmental policies, financial limitations, and other factors that can and must be changed.

Death is an inevitable aspect of the human condition. Dying badly is not. Yet it usually cannot be avoided by single individuals and families acting alone. Dying badly is a social problem that requires a social solution. It is an artifact of the way our health care system is organized and financed. And it is a product of our societal failure to perceive the ethical and human cost of limited access to, and inadequate provision of, hospice care. Although the acceptance and utilization of palliative and hospice care have grown, there are still over one million Americans who die each year without receiving the hospice or hospice-type services that would have benefited them and their families.

These are difficult, even daunting, problems in the American health care system today. Who opposes improvements in palliative and end of life care in the abstract? The challenge is to find new practical approaches to hospice care, building on the strengths that this movement has developed over the years and correcting those policies and practices that have shown themselves to be unduly restrictive, unworkable, or unwise.

The challenge of end of life care will grow more serious over the next three decades. The population of seniors in the United States is projected to more than double over the next 30 years, rising from 34 million in 1997 to over 69 million by 2030. At that time, one in five Americans will be age 65 or older. One in nine baby boomers is expected to live to age 90, and by 2040, the number of Americans over age 85 will be nearly four times greater than today. The United States already struggles to provide basic primary care to its population;

more than 40 million Americans are without consistent or adequate health insurance coverage. Either they do not have access to health care at all, or they do not get it in a timely or efficient way. Out-of-pocket expenses for prescription drugs are a significant burden to many, and families must shoulder most of the financial and emotional burden for long-term care. We have been remarkably slow to acknowledge the impending health care crisis that looms ahead, much less the serious problems already with us. Health insurance reform has failed several times since the end of World War II, despite the bipartisan efforts of several presidents. Some incremental efforts are under way, but there is no public or governmental vision of a just health care system as a whole. And there is certainly no vision of a health care system adequate to meet our growing needs for chronic and palliative care. Americans are talking and worrying quietly about this, as focus group and opinion survey studies reveal.

A redesign of the end of life care system must be accomplished in this decade if the nation is to have time to prepare for the challenges ahead. It has taken decades to build the present system of hospice care, and efforts to improve palliative care in hospital settings are only just beginning, yet these achievements will soon have to be substantially improved and augmented.

The purpose of this report is to contribute to the broad goal of improving end of life care by addressing specific problems in access to and delivery of hospice care. Several groups are addressing these problems from various points of view. The distinctive contribution of our study is that we pay explicit attention to the human values involved in hospice care policy and practice. The report examines the problem of access from the perspective of social justice and equity, or fairness, and we make an ethical case for equitable access on the basis of the moral importance of the needs met and the values served by comprehensive, high-quality hospice care.

We also offer a new vision of hospice, one that holds firmly to many of the traditions and values of the past, but finds new and more flexible organizational forms through which to express those values. The vision we offer is based on the notions of condition-management, community-responsiveness, and continuity-oriented practices. The new organizational forms appropriate to this vision are the model of the "community hospice" and the "comprehensive hospice center." The past emphasis on eligibility must be replaced by a focus on continuity and appropriateness of services given changes in the patient's and the family's condition over time. And the model of traditional hospice as a specialized service and an independent agency with a limited mission will gradually be transformed into a more comprehensive model in which hospice becomes the coordinating center for a range of services and types of expertise that can be accessed by patients in various ways as the patient's underlying condition evolves from diagnosis to death.

Providing access to hospice care is not simply a question of expanding a given service to more people who could benefit from it. The nature and goals of the service itself need to be redefined. We must envision hospice as a potentially new paradigm of social health care for an aging society. If we can learn how to define, organize, finance, and deliver hospice care properly, then we may have found the key to coping with the major problem of caring for staggering numbers of persons with chronic, degenerative disease—the number one problem of the health care systems of the developed world for the next fifty years. Chronic, degenerative disease requires patients and families to make difficult adjustments and transitions in their lives as they pass through various stages and phases of their disease. The experience of chronic disease blends gradually into the experience of dying. The flow and rhythms of hospice, as well as its goals and care plans, must be allowed to match the rhythms of chronic illness, as chronic illness becomes an increasingly wide-spread social condition. Of all the existing structures and specialties in health care today, hospice has the best chance of successfully transforming itself into this chronic care social medicine of the future.

The promise for a larger mission in the future, perhaps as much as the end of life care that many people lack access to today, is the principal reason for being urgently and deeply concerned about policy reforms in the finance and delivery of hospice.

A course for reform

There are two broad approaches to reforming and restructuring hospice and palliative care financing and delivery systems. First, we might supplement existing hospice services with enhanced, high-quality palliative care integrated into non-hospice care settings to form a continuum of care, of which hospice is a part. Second, we might expand the scope and mission of hospices, which have proved their capacity to provide effective palliative care, beyond their current confines to serve populations of patients who have longer to live and who are in various health care settings. These approaches are not mutually exclusive; in fact, both are needed. In order to further both, we must return to the issue of organizing the financing and delivery of hospice care so as to provide "equitable access." For

the purposes of this report, we define equitable access in the following way: equitable access to health care requires that all citizens can secure an adequate level of care without excessive burdens.

This conception of just or equitable access leads to the following claims:

- Equitable access to hospice services does not exist in the United States, and this constitutes a violation of justice and fairness in our society that should be rectified.
- Many factors limit access to and utilization of hospice services, but governmental policies and professional practices are especially significant. Understanding what steps are appropriate to increase access to and utilization of hospice care services will reveal why we should not define the mission of hospice care narrowly.
- Steps taken to increase access to hospice care and to design the new system should be driven, first and foremost, by an explicit discussion of the ethical values that the end of life caregiving system should embody.

Beyond justice, when individuals who are dying or who are in the later stages of an incurable illness do not attain access to hospice care services, fundamental social values are not fulfilled. The dying persons, their families and loved ones, and society as a whole are diminished by this failure to respect the autonomy and dignity of the person, to respond to the person's suffering, and to offer care, compassion, and vigilance at the end of life. When so many die without the support of good hospice or palliative care, we have not met our obligation to the most vulnerable in our society, and we have not kept faith with our highest moral ideals.

The nation has the technical expertise and financial resources to provide universal access to much higher-quality hospice care today. A just increase in access should take place principally in three ways: first, by making more people eligible for hospice admission and insurance coverage; second, by lengthening the average time spent in hospice, primarily through earlier referral; and third, by maintaining both high-quality care and good stewardship of scarce resources through a professionally rigorous case management system within hospice programs.

Each of these three elements of access is ethically important. Justice pertains not only to getting in and staying in, but also to what types of services a patient and family receive once they are in a hospice program. It would do little good overall to expand hospice admission or length of stay while cutting services so drastically that they are of poor quality or little benefit to dying persons. Thinning the soup—"hospice lite," as it is sometimes referred to—is not the answer to the challenge of just or equitable access.

At the same time, justice does not require the provision of all services that patients and families want—indeed, not even all services that they might marginally benefit from—since there are always other ethically important claims on scarce resources, even in the richest countries. Hence, justice requires that hospices be given sufficient funds to provide adequate care, not a blank check. Historically hospice has operated under a system of fiscal discipline that has worked reasonably well, at least in terms of its case management system and the efficiency of its professional staff. We expect this commitment to case management and quality improvement to continue in the future forms that hospice takes. If the expansion of hospice access we call for here turns out to require a large additional expenditure of Medicare funds, for example, the increase will not be—and should not be permitted by policymakers to be—undisciplined.

In fact, it is not clear how much more money should be spent on hospice, nor what the net increase might be after we take into consideration other health care cost savings produced by broader, better hospice care. We are not in a position to estimate such costs in this study.

In any case, we do not begin this study with a dollar amount. We begin with a description of the system our society needs and should have. We first ask what justice and other ethical values call on us to do in hospice care, and for whom. There will be time enough to devise an efficient way to pay for what ought to be done.

I. WHAT IS HOSPICE CARE?

When the first hospice program in the United States was started in Connecticut in 1973, end of life care was an orphan field of little interest to mainstream medicine, which was busy fighting President Nixon's war on cancer. Death and dying were such socially and culturally taboo subjects that even clergy were uncomfortable discussing them, let alone physicians, family, and friends.

Pioneered in England, hospice took root in the United States during the 1970s and was added as a benefit to the Medicare program in the early 1980s. Its origins lie in a grassroots movement that lay outside the medical mainstream and was informed by an ethic of compassion, dignity, and service. More or less self-consciously, hospice care was initially designed for people who were dying of cancer, and who had a functional family support system and a home where they could be cared for away from the high-tech hospital environment. Over time, the vision and the values of the hospice movement have developed and matured.

The spectrum of hospice services and the hospice philosophy

In the view of most practitioners today, hospice is not limited to any single disease or to any one set of life circumstances for its patients and families. Accordingly, hospice has been expanding in recent years to reach people dying of something other than cancer, who lack family support systems, and who live in institutional settings. Its growth and its capacity to assist dying patients and their families demonstrate the health care and human benefit hospice offers. And although it is still a separate and distinct system in many ways, hospice has become a component of standard of end of life care and a part of accepted medical practice. Hospice cannot rightfully be a matter of optional purchase for the affluent. If nothing else, the landmark public policy decision in 1983 to include hospice care in the Medicare program put an end to such thinking. Whatever unfairly or unreasonably limits access to hospice care should be seen as a moral problem.

In the past, ignorance about hospice and about appropriate palliative measures has also been viewed as an educational problem. Over the past six years, the Robert Wood Johnson Foundation and other foundations have dedicated tremendous resources to advancing professional and community education initiatives in support of improved end of life care. It is hard to imagine a North American health care provider that has not had the opportunity to learn more about hospice.

"Hospice" is both a concept (that is, a philosophy and a paradigm of care) and an organizational form of health care delivery. Hospice services include professional nursing care, personal assistance with activities of daily living, various forms of rehabilitation therapy, dietary counseling, psychological and spiritual counseling for both patient and family, volunteer services, respite care, provision of medical drugs and devices necessary for palliative care, and family bereavement services following the patient's death. Hospice care is provided by an interdisciplinary care team comprised of nurses, social workers, pastoral counselors, nursing assistants, and other health professionals under the management of a physician, who may be the patient's own primary care physician or may be affiliated directly with the hospice program. Caring for the dying is a complex social enterprise that must involve the families of the dying, religious organizations, the health care system, and the community at large, from the very local to the national level.

The specific needs of dying persons to which care must respond can be grouped under the headings of physical, emotional, and social well-being. Within each category, the health care system plays an important role in meeting these needs but is never the only actor and not always even the chief actor. Physical needs include a safe, clean, and comfortable place for dying; control of pain and symptoms; appropriate food and nutrition; personal care (aid with bathing, feeding, dressing, and other activities of daily living); information about how best to manage the physical condition of the dying person; and information about the changes in physical condition to be expected over time. Emotional needs include respect for the dying person's dignity as a human being; respect for the dying person's wishes, to the extent possible; information about the emotional changes to expect; counseling to help the patient come to terms with what is happening; assistance with advance planning for death; and attending to spiritual concerns. Social needs include companionship; maintenance of social functioning, to the extent possible; assistance in "telling one's life story" to others; and help in resolving relationships and taking care of other "unfinished business."

Responding to these needs requires access to a complex continuum of care. As a group, people who are dying make use of virtually the entire array of health care goods and services, including acute care, long-term care, mental health care, and health education. Managing pain and other distressing symptoms may require sophisticated treatment regimens and technologies, ranging from carefully tailored drug regimens to palliative radiation and surgery to mechanical ventilation. Feeding and hydration issues may be addressed by special diets or supportive counseling when patients stop eating. Careful nursing care is required, including bathing, feeding, skin care, and other personal care activities that make a great difference to a sick person's comfort. Health education is necessary to provide information about the physical and emotional changes to expect and to explain what the patient and family can do about them. Mental health services may also be needed, including counseling and the treatment of depression. Patients' symptoms vary tremendously, and with them the appropriate pattern of care.

Some of the care needed must be provided by highly skilled health care workers, but much of it can and should be undertaken by families, friends, and members of the dying person's faith community. Family caregivers may take care of the patient's home, provide meals, help with personal care, offer companionship, and help the patient maintain social functioning. Friends and community organizations may help family members with these caregiving activities. Religious organizations may provide spiritual support to the patient. There is no sharp line separating the care provided by the health care system and the care provided by others; the division of labor depends on the patient's situation and community resources.

Family members themselves also need care and support from the health care system, religious organizations, and the community. Family members are usually the front-line providers of daily care, working in tandem with professional health care providers. To perform their caregiving role well, they need information and training. At the same time, they are themselves patients of the health care system. They need care to prevent and, if necessary, to treat the physical and mental health problems that can be associated with caregiving and bereavement. Again, there is no bright line separating care for family members and care for the dying themselves; their well-being is profoundly interdependent. What hospice care offers family members includes: information about how to provide care to the dying patient; caregiver support, emotional support, and practical assistance; caregiver respite; help with preparation and advance planning for death; resolution of relationships; and grief counseling.

The subjective preferences of patients vary widely. The objective situation of patients also varies with age, diagnosis, income, family circumstances (some have many caring family members while others have none), social class, type of residence (home, nursing home, hospital, board and care facility, prison, or the streets), race/ethnicity/culture, religion, and geographic location. Therefore, someone must manage the patient's access so the patient can receive care that is compassionate, timely, and in accord with individual needs and preferences. The patient and family members can do some of the coordination, but the task is too complicated for them to handle alone. Given the importance of health care in the care mix and the specialized knowledge it requires, the health care system reasonably takes on the role of integrating the care provided by health care providers with the care provided by family and community.

The distinction between hospice and palliative care

What is the relationship between hospice care and palliative care? It is a more complicated question than may at first appear. The two labels are often thought to be virtually synonymous, particularly if one bears in mind that the hospice philosophy (if not the Medicare Hospice benefit) has been expanding its ambit over time to include persons who are dying not only of cancer but of many other fatal diseases as well, and not only those who are thought to have less than six months to live but those whose dying process may follow a longer, more chronic and unpredictable course—who may be referred to as the "chronically dying" or the "chronically terminally ill." This perspective is consistent with the definition of palliative care formulated by the World Health Organization, which makes it virtually identical with hospice: "The active total care of patients whose disease is not responsive to curative treatment. Control of pain, of other symptoms, and of psychological, social, and spiritual problems is paramount. The goal of palliative care is achievement of the best possible quality of life for patients and their families."

From another perspective, however, the two terms are often taken to refer to different caregiving orientations, time frames, institutional settings. WHO's definition of palliative care goes on to add that "Many aspects of palliative care are also applicable earlier in the course of the illness, in conjunction with anti-cancer treatment." From a medical perspective, then, palliative care may be taken as the broader term, covering all forms of the prevention and treatment of suffering, while "hospice," in a narrow medical sense, has been viewed as a subset of palliative care especially targeted to the needs of those near death. This usage seems consistent with the Medicare program, which after all is a hospice benefit and not a palliative care benefit. Palliative care is appropriate whenever symptoms causing pain and suffering are present, and good counsel regarding the consequences of illness and treatment is required, regardless of the underlying medical condition and prognosis of the patient. A child receiving chemotherapy for leukemia, with an excellent chance for recovery and long life, should still receive palliative care as a component of the care plan. Traditional hospice care, on the other hand, has always included addressing the patient's impending death and the reaction to that prospect, whatever additional medical and nursing services it might also involve.

ACTIVE AND PASSIVE EUTHANASIA

The Wrongfulness of Euthanasia

J. Gay-Williams

My impression is that euthanasia—the idea, if not the practice—is slowly gaining acceptance within our society. Cynics might attribute this to an increasing tendency to devalue human life, but I do not believe this is the major factor. The acceptance is much more likely to be the result of unthinking sympathy and benevolence. Well-publicized, tragic stories like that of Karen Quinlan elicit from us deep feelings of compassion. We think to ourselves, "She and her family would be better off if she were dead." It is an easy step from this very human response to the view that if someone (and others) would be better off dead, then it might be all right to kill that person.[1] Although I respect the compassion that leads to this conclusion, I believe the conclusion is wrong. I want to show that euthanasia is wrong. It is inherently wrong, but it is also wrong judged from the standpoints of self-interest and of practical effects.

Before presenting my arguments to support this claim, it would be well to define "euthanasia." An essential aspect of euthanasia is that it involves taking a human life, either one's own or that of another. Also, the person whose life is taken must be someone who is believed to be suffering from some disease or injury from which recovery cannot reasonably be expected. Finally, the action must be deliberate and intentional. Thus, euthanasia is intentionally taking the life of a presumably hopeless person. Whether the life is one's own or that of another, the taking of it is still euthanasia.

It is important to be clear about the deliberate and intentional aspect of the killing. If a hopeless person is given an injection of the wrong drug by mistake and this causes his death, this is wrongful killing but not euthanasia. The killing cannot be the result of accident. Furthermore, if the person is given an injection of a drug that is

Gay-Williams, J. "The Wrongfulness of Euthanasia," as reprinted in *Intervention and Reflection: Basic Issues in Medical Ethics,* 5th ed., Ronald Munson, ed., Wadsworth, (1996) pp. 168–171. Copyright © 1996. Reprinted by permission of Ronald Munson.

believed to be necessary to treat his disease or better his condition and the person dies as a result, then this is neither wrongful killing nor euthanasia. The intention was to make the patient well, not kill him. Similarly, when a patient's condition is such that it is not reasonable to hope that any medical procedures or treatments will save his life, a failure to implement the procedures or treatments is not euthanasia. If the person dies, this will be as a result of his injuries or disease and not because of his failure to receive treatment.

The failure to continue treatment after it has been realized that the patient has little chance of benefiting from it has been characterized by some as "passive euthanasia." This phrase is misleading and mistaken.[2] In such cases, the person involved is not killed (the first essential aspect of euthanasia), nor is the death of the person intended by the withholding of additional treatment (the third essential aspect of euthanasia). The aim may be to spare the person additional and unjustifiable pain, to save him from the indignities of hopeless manipulations, and to avoid increasing the financial and emotional burden on his family. When I buy a pencil it is so that I can use it to write, not to contribute to an increase in the gross national product. This may be the unintended consequence of my action, but it is not the aim of my action. So it is with failing to continue the treatment of a dying person. I intend his death no more than I intend to reduce the GNP by not using medical supplies. His is an unintended dying, and so-called "passive euthanasia" is not euthanasia at all.

1. The Argument from Nature   Every human being has a natural inclination to continue living. Our reflexes and responses fit us to fight attackers, flee wild animals, and dodge out of the way of trucks. In our daily lives we exercise the caution and care necessary to protect ourselves. Our bodies are similarly structured for survival right down to the molecular level. When we are cut, our capillaries seal shut, our blood clots, and fibrogen is produced to start the process of healing the wound. When we are invaded by bacteria, antibodies are produced to fight against the alien organisms, and their remains are swept out of the body by special cells designed for clean-up work.

Euthanasia does violence to this natural goal if the processes of nature are bent towards the end of bodily survival. Euthanasia defeats these subtle mechanisms in a way that, in a particular case, disease and injury might not.

It is possible, but not necessary, to make an appeal to revealed religion in this connection.[3] Man as trustee of his body acts against God, its rightful possessor, when he takes his own life. He also violates the commandment to hold life sacred and never to take it without just and compelling cause. But since this appeal will persuade only those who are prepared to accept that religion has access to revealed truths, I shall not employ this line of argument.

It is enough, I believe, to recognize that the organization of the human body and our patterns of behavioral responses make the continuation of life a natural goal. By reason alone, then, we can recognize that euthanasia sets us against our own nature.[4] Furthermore, in doing so, euthanasia does violence to our dignity. Our dignity comes from seeking our ends. When one of our goals is survival, and actions are taken that eliminate that goal, then our natural dignity suffers. Unlike animals, we are conscious through reason of our nature and our ends. Euthanasia involves acting as if this dual nature—inclination towards survival and awareness of this as an end—did not exist. Thus, euthanasia denies our basic human character and requires that we regard ourselves or others as something less than fully human.

2. The Argument from Self-Interest   The above arguments are, I believe, sufficient to show that euthanasia is inherently wrong. But there are reasons for considering it wrong when judged by standards other than reason. Because death is final and irreversible, euthanasia contains within it the possibility that we will work against our own interest if we practice it or allow it to be practiced on us.

Contemporary medicine has high standards of excellence and a proven record of accomplishment, but it does not possess perfect and complete knowledge. A mistaken diagnosis is possible, and so is a mistaken prognosis. Consequently, we may believe that we are dying of a disease when, as a matter of fact, we may not be. We may think that we have no hope of recovery when, as a matter of fact, our chances are quite good. In such circumstances, if euthanasia were permitted, we would die needlessly. Death is final and the chance of error too great to approve the practice of euthanasia.

Also, there is always the possibility that an experimental procedure or a hitherto untried technique will pull us through. We should at least keep this option open, but euthanasia closes it off. Furthermore, spontaneous remission does occur in many cases. For no apparent reason, a patient simply recovers when those all around him, including his physicians, expected him to die. Euthanasia would just guarantee their expectations and leave no room for the "miraculous" recoveries that frequently occur.

Finally, knowing that we can take our life at any time (or ask another to take it) might well incline us to give up too easily. The will to live is strong in all of us, but it can be weakened by pain and suffering and feelings of hopelessness. If during a bad time we allow ourselves to be killed, we never have a chance to reconsider. Recovery from a serious illness requires that we fight for it, and anything that weakens our determination by suggesting that there is an easy way out is ultimately against our own interest. Also, we may be inclined towards euthanasia because of our concern for others. If we see our sickness and suffering as an emotional and financial burden on our family, we may feel that to leave our life is to make their lives easier.[5] The very presence of the possibility of euthanasia may keep us from surviving when we might.

3. *The Argument from Practical Effects* Doctors and nurses are, for the most part, totally committed to saving lives. A life lost is, for them, almost a personal failure, an insult to their skills and knowledge. Euthanasia as a practice might well alter this. It could have a corrupting influence so that in any case that is severe doctors and nurses might not try hard enough to save the patient. They might decide that the patient would simply be "better off dead" and take the steps necessary to make that come about. This attitude could then carry over to their dealings with patients less seriously ill. The result would be an overall decline in the quality of medical care.

Finally, euthanasia as a policy is a slippery slope. A person apparently hopelessly ill may be allowed to take his own life. Then he may be permitted to deputize others to do it for him should he no longer be able to act. The judgment of others then becomes the ruling factor. Already at this point euthanasia is not personal and voluntary, for others are acting "on behalf of" the patient as they see fit. This may well incline them to act on behalf of other patients who have not authorized them to exercise their judgment. It is only a short step, then, from voluntary euthanasia (self-inflicted or authorized), to directed euthanasia administered to a patient who has given no authorization, to involuntary euthanasia conducted as part of a social policy.[6] Recently many psychiatrists and sociologists have argued that we define as "mental illness" those forms of behavior that we disapprove of.[7] This gives us license then to lock up those who display the behavior. The category of the "hopelessly ill" provides the possibility of even worse abuse. Embedded in a social policy, it would give society or its representatives the authority to eliminate all those who might be considered too "ill" to function normally any longer. The dangers of euthanasia are too great to all to run the risk of approving it in any form. The first slippery step may well lead to a serious and harmful fall.

I hope that I have succeeded in showing why the benevolence that inclines us to give approval of euthanasia is misplaced. Euthanasia is inherently wrong because it violates the nature and dignity of human beings. But even those who are not convinced by this must be persuaded that the potential personal and social dangers inherent in euthanasia are sufficient to forbid our approving it either as a personal practice or as a public policy.

Suffering is surely a terrible thing, and we have a clear duty to comfort those in need and to ease their suffering when we can. But suffering is also a natural part of life with values for the individual and for others that we should not overlook. We may legitimately seek for others and for ourselves an easeful death, as Arthur Dyck has pointed out.[8] Euthanasia, however, is not just an easeful death. It is a wrongful death. Euthanasia is not just dying. It is killing.

NOTES

1. For a sophisticated defense of this position see Philippa Foot, "Euthanasia," *Philosophy and Public Affairs,* vol. 6 (1977), pp. 85–112. Foot does not endorse the radical conclusion that euthanasia, voluntary and involuntary, is always right.

2. James Rachels rejects the distinction between active and passive euthanasia as morally irrelevant in his "Active and Passive Euthanasia," *New England Journal of Medicine,* vol. 292, pp. 78–80. But see the criticism by Foot, pp. 100–103.

3. For a defense of this view see J. V. Sullivan, "The Immorality of Euthanasia," in *Beneficent Euthanasia,* ed. Marvin Kohl (Buffalo, N.Y.: Prometheus Books, 1975), pp. 34–44.

4. This point is made by Ray V. McIntyre in "Voluntary Euthanasia: The Ultimate Perversion," *Medical Counterpoint,* vol. 2, pp. 26–29.

5. See McIntyre, p. 28.

6. See Sullivan, "Immorality of Euthanasia," pp. 34–44, for a fuller argument in support of this view.

7. See, for example, Thomas S. Szasz, *The Myth of Mental Illness,* rev. ed. (New York: Harper & Row, 1974).

8. Arthur Dyck, "Beneficent Euthanasia and Benemortasia," Kohl, op. cit., pp. 117–129.

Active and Passive Euthanasia

James Rachels

The traditional distinction between active and passive euthanasia requires critical analysis. The conventional doctrine is that there is such an important moral difference between the two that, although the latter is sometimes permissible, the former is always forbidden. This doctrine may be challenged for several

Rachels, James. "Active and Passive Euthanasia," *The New England Journal of Medicine* 292:2 (1975), 78–80. Copyright © 1975. Reprinted by permission of Massachusetts Medical Society.

reasons. First of all, active euthanasia is in many cases more humane than passive euthanasia. Secondly, the conventional doctrine leads to decisions concerning life and death on irrelevant grounds. Thirdly, the doctrine rests on a distinction between killing and letting die that itself has no moral importance. Fourthly, the most common arguments in favor of the doctrine are invalid. I therefore suggest that the American Medical Association policy statement that endorses this doctrine is unsound.

The distinction between active and passive euthanasia is thought to be crucial for medical ethics. The idea is that it is permissible, at least in some cases, to withhold treatment and allow a patient to die, but it is never permissible to take any direct action designed to kill the patient. This doctrine seems to be accepted by most doctors, and it is endorsed in a statement adopted by the House of Delegates of the American Medical Association on December 4, 1973.

> The intentional termination of the life of one human being by another—mercy killing—is contrary to that for which the medical profession stands and is contrary to the policy of the American Medical Association.
> The cessation of the employment of extraordinary means to prolong the life of the body when there is irrefutable evidence that biological death is imminent is the decision of the patient and/or his immediate family. The advice and judgment of the physician should be freely available to the patient and/or his immediate family.

However, a strong case can be made against this doctrine. In what follows I will set out some of the relevant arguments, and urge doctors to reconsider their views on this matter.

To begin with a familiar type of situation, a patient who is dying of incurable cancer of the throat is in terrible pain, which can no longer be satisfactorily alleviated. He is certain to die within a few days, even if present treatment is continued, but he does not want to go on living for those days since the pain is unbearable. So he asks the doctor for an end to it, and his family joins in the request.

Suppose the doctor agrees to withold treatment, as the conventional doctrine says he may. The justification for his doing so is that the patient is in terrible agony, and since he is going to die anyway, it would be wrong to prolong his suffering needlessly. But now notice this. If one simply withholds treatment, it may take the patient longer to die, and so he may suffer more than he would if more direct action were taken and a lethal injection given. This fact provides strong reason for thinking that, once the initial decision not to prolong his agony has been made, active euthanasia

is actually preferable to passive euthanasia, rather than the reverse. To say otherwise is to endorse the option that leads to more suffering rather than less, and is contrary to the humanitarian impulse that prompts the decision not to prolong his life in the first place.

Part of my point is that the process of being "allowed to die" can be relatively slow and painful, whereas being given a lethal injection is relatively quick and painless. Let me give a different sort of example. In the United States about one in 600 babies is born with Down's syndrome. Most of these babies are otherwise healthy—that is, with only the usual pediatric care, they will proceed to an otherwise normal infancy. Some, however, are born with congenital defects such as intestinal obstructions that require operations if they are to live. Sometimes, the parents and the doctor will decide not to operate, and let the infant die. Anthony Shaw describes what happens then:

> When surgery is denied [the doctor] must try to keep the infant from suffering while natural forces sap the baby's life away. As a surgeon whose natural inclination is to use the scalpel to fight off death, standing by and watching a salvageable baby die is the most emotionally exhausting experience I know. It is easy at a conference, in a theoretical discussion, to decide that such infants should be allowed to die. It is altogether different to stand by in the nursery and watch as dehydration and infection wither a tiny being over hours and days. This is a terrible ordeal for me and the hospital staff—much more so than for the parents who never set foot in the nursery.[1]

I can understand why some people are opposed to all euthanasia, and insist that such infants must be allowed to live. I think I can also understand why other people favor destroying these babies quickly and painlessly. But why should anyone favor letting "dehydration and infection wither a tiny being over hours and days?" The doctrine that says that a baby may be allowed to dehydrate and wither, but may not be given an injection that would end its life without suffering, seems so patently cruel as to require no further refutation. The strong language is not intended to offend, but only to put the point in the clearest possible way.

My second argument is that the conventional doctrine leads to decisions concerning life and death made on irrelevant grounds.

Consider again the case of the infants with Down's syndrome who need operations for congenital defects unrelated to the syndrome to live. Sometimes, there is no operation, and the baby dies, but when there is no such defect, the baby lives on. Now, an operation such as that to remove an intestinal obstruction is not prohibitively difficult. The reason why such operations are not performed in these cases is, clearly, that the child has Down's syndrome and the parents and doctor judge that because of that fact it is better for the child to die.

But notice that this situation is absurd, no matter what view one takes of the lives and potentials of such babies. If the life of such an infant is worth preserving, what does it matter if it needs a simple operation? Or, if one thinks it better that such a baby should not live on, what difference does it make that it happens to have an unobstructed intestinal tract? In either case, the matter of life and death is being decided on irrelevant grounds. It is the Down's syndrome, and not the intestines, that is the issue. The matter should be decided, if at all, on that basis, and not be allowed to depend on the essentially irrelevant question of whether the intestinal tract is blocked.

What makes this situation possible, of course, is the idea that when there is an intestinal blockage, one can "let the baby die," but when there is no such defect there is nothing that can be done, for one must not "kill" it. The fact that this idea leads to such results as deciding life or death on irrelevant grounds is another good reason why the doctrine should be rejected.

One reason why so many people think that there is an important moral difference between active and passive euthanasia is that they think killing someone is morally worse than letting someone die. But is it? Is killing, in itself, worse than letting die? To investigate this issue, two cases may be considered that are exactly alike except that one involves killing whereas the other involves letting someone die. Then, it can be asked whether this difference makes any difference to the moral assessments. It is important that the cases be exactly alike, except for this one difference, since otherwise one cannot be confident that it is this difference and not some other that accounts for any variation in the assessments of the two cases. So, let us consider this pair of cases:

In the first, Smith stands to gain a large inheritance if anything should happen to his six-year-old cousin. One evening while the child is taking his bath. Smith sneaks into the bathroom and drowns the child, and then arranges things so that it will look like an accident.

In the second, Jones also stands to gain if anything should happen to his six-year-old cousin. Like Smith, Jones sneaks in planning to drown the child in his bath. However, just as he enters the bathroom Jones sees the child slip and hit his head, and fall face down in the water. Jones is delighted: he stands by, ready to push the child's head back under if it is necessary, but it is not necessary. With only a little thrashing about, the child drowns all by himself, "accidentally," as Jones watches and does nothing.

Now Smith killed the child, whereas Jones "merely" let the child die. That is the only difference between them. Did either man behave better, from a moral point of view? If the difference between killing and letting die were in itself a morally important matter, one should say that Jones's behavior was less reprehensible than Smith's. But does one really want to say that? I think not. In the first place, both men acted from the same motive, personal gain, and both had exactly the same end in view when they acted. It may be inferred from Smith's conduct that he is a bad man, although that judgment may be withdrawn or modified if certain further facts are learned about him—for example, that he is mentally deranged. But would not the very same thing be inferred about Jones from his conduct? And would not the same further considerations also be relevant to any modification of this judgement? Moreover, suppose Jones pleaded, in his own defense. "After all, I didn't do anything except just stand there and watch the child drown. I didn't kill him: I only let him die." Again, if letting die were in itself less bad than killing, this defense should have at least some weight. But it does not. Such a "defense" can only be regarded as a grotesque perversion of moral reasoning. Morally speaking, it is no defense at all.

Now, it may be pointed out, quite properly, that the cases of euthanasia with which doctors are concerned are not like this at all. They do not involve personal gain or the destruction of normal healthy children. Doctors are concerned only with cases in which the patient's life is of no further use to him, or in which the patient's life has become or will soon become a terrible burden. However, the point is the same in these cases: the bare difference between killing and letting die does not, in itself, make a moral difference. If a doctor lets a patient die, for humane reasons, he is in the same moral position as if he had given the patient a lethal injection for humane reasons. If his decision was wrong—if, for example, the patient's illness was in fact curable—the decision would be equally regretable no matter which method was used to carry it out. And if the doctor's decision was the right one, the method used is not in itself important.

The AMA policy statement isolates the crucial issue very well: the crucial issue is "the intentional termination of the life of one human being by another." But after identifying this issue, and forbidding "mercy killing," the statement goes on to deny that the cessation of treatment is the intentional termination of a life. This is where the mistake comes in, for what is the cessation of treatment, in these circumstances, if it is not "the intentional termination of the life of one human being by another?" Of course it is exactly that, and if it were not, there would be no point to it.

Many people will find this judgment hard to accept. One reason. I think, is that it is very easy to conflate the question of whether killing is, in itself, worse than letting die, with the very different question of whether most actual cases of killing are more reprehensible than most actual cases of letting die. Most actual cases of killing are clearly terrible (think, for example, of all the murders reported in the newspapers), and one hears of such cases every day. On the other hand, one hardly ever hears of a case of letting die, except for the actions of doctors who are motivated by humanitarian reasons. So one learns to think of killing in a much worse light than of letting die. But this does not mean that there is something about killing that makes it in itself worse than letting die, for it is not the bare difference between killing and letting die that makes the difference in these cases. Rather, the other factors—the murderer's motive of personal gain, for example, contrasted with the doctor's humanitarian motivation—account for different reactions to the different cases.

I have argued that killing is not in itself any worse than letting die: if my contention is right, it follows that active euthanasia is not any worse than passive euthanasia. What arguments can be given on the other side? The most common. I believe, is the following:

"The important difference between active and passive euthanasia is that, in passive euthanasia, the doctor does not do anything to bring about the patient's death. The doctor does nothing, and the patient dies of whatever ills already afflict him. In active euthanasia, however, the doctor does something to bring about the patient's death: he kills him. The doctor who gives the patient with cancer a lethal injection has himself caused his patient's death: whereas if he merely ceases treatment, the cancer is the cause of the death."

A number of points need to be made here. The first is that it is not exactly correct to say that in passive euthanasia the doctor does nothing, for he does do one thing that is very important: he lets the patient die. "Letting someone die" is certainly different, in some respects, from other types of action—mainly in that it is a kind of action that one may perform by way of not performing certain other actions. For example, one may let a patient die by way of not giving medication, just as one may insult someone by way of not shaking his hand. But for any purpose of moral assessment, it is a type of action nonetheless. The decision to let a patient die is subject to moral appraisal in the same way that a decision to kill him would be subject to moral appraisal: it may be assessed as wise or unwise, compassionate or sadistic, right or wrong. If a doctor deliberately let a patient die who was suffering from a routinely curable illness, the doctor would certainly be to blame for what he had done, just as he would be to blame if he had needlessly killed the patient.

Charges against him would then be appropriate. If so, it would be no defense at all for him to insist that he didn't "do anything." He would have done something very serious indeed, for he let his patient die.

Fixing the cause of death may be very important from a legal point of view, for it may determine whether criminal charges are brought against the doctor. But I do not think that this notion can be used to show a moral difference between active and passive euthanasia. The reason why it is considered bad to be the cause of someone's death is that death is regarded as a great evil—and so it is. However, if it has been decided that euthanasia—even passive euthanasia—is desirable in a given case, it has also been decided that in this instance death is no greater an evil than the patient's continued existence. And if this is true, the usual reason for not wanting to be the cause of someone's death simply does not apply.

Finally, doctors may think that all of this is only of academic interest—the sort of thing that philosophers may worry about but that has no practical bearing on their own work. After all, doctors must be concerned about the legal consequences of what they do, and active euthanasia is clearly forbidden by the law. But even so, doctors should also be concerned with the fact that the law is forcing upon them a moral doctrine that may well be indefensible, and has a considerable effect on their practices. Of course, most doctors are not now in the position of being coerced in this matter, for they do not regard themselves as merely going along with what the law requires. Rather, in statements such as the AMA policy statement that I have quoted, they are endorsing this doctrine as a central point of medical ethics. In that statement, active euthanasia is condemned not merely as illegal but as "contrary to that for which the medical profession stands," whereas passive euthanasia is approved. However, the preceding considerations suggest that there is really no moral difference between the two, considered in themselves (there may be important moral differences in some cases in their *consequences*, but, as I pointed out, these differences may make active euthanasia, and not passive euthanasia, the morally preferable option). So, whereas doctors may have to discriminate between active and passive euthanasia to satisfy the law, they should not do any more than that. In particular, they should not give the distinction any added authority and weight by writing it into official statements of medical ethics.

REFERENCE

1. A. Shaw 'Doctor, Do We Have a Choice?' *New York Times Magazine.* January 30, 1972, p. 54.

Rachels on Active and Passive Euthanasia

Tom L. Beauchamp and James F. Childress

James Rachels contends that killing is not, in itself, worse than letting die; the "bare difference" between acts of killing and acts of letting die is not in itself a morally relevant difference.[1] We agree with Rachels that the acts in his two cases are equally reprehensible because of the agents' motives and actions, and we agree that killing as a type of act is in itself no different *morally* than allowing to die as a type of act. However, we do not accept his conclusion that his examples and arguments show that the distinction between killing and letting die and passive and active euthanasia are morally irrelevant in the formulation of public policy. We also do not agree that his cases demonstrate what he claims.

PROBLEMS IN RACHELS'S ANALYSIS

First, Rachels's cases and the cessations of treatment envisioned by the AMA are so markedly disanalogous that Rachels's argument is misdirected. In some cases of unjustified acts, including both of Rachels's examples, we are not interested in moral distinctions between killing and letting die (per se). As Richard Trammell points out, some examples have a "masking" or "sledgehammer" effect; the fact that "one cannot distinguish the taste of two wines when both are mixed with green persimmon juice, does not imply that there is no distinction between the wines."[2] Because Rachels's examples involve two morally unjustified acts by agents whose motives and intentions are despicable, it is not surprising that some other features of their situations, such as killing and letting die, are not morally compelling considerations in the circumstances.

Second, Smith and Jones are morally responsible and morally blameworthy for the deaths of their respective cousins, even if Jones, who allowed his cousin to drown, is not causally responsible. The law might find only Smith, who killed his cousin, guilty of homicide (because of the law's theory of proximate cause), but morality condemns both actions alike because of the agents' commissions and omissions. We find Jones's actions reprehensible because he should have rescued the child. Even if he had no other special duties to the child, there is an affirmative obligation of beneficence in such a case.

Third, the point of the range of cases envisioned by the AMA is consistent with Rachels's arguments, though he thinks them inconsistent. The AMA's central claim is that the physician is always morally prohibited from killing patients but is not morally bound to preserve life in all cases. According to the AMA, the physician has a right and perhaps a duty to stop treatment if and only if three conditions are met: (1) the life of the body is being preserved by extraordinary means, (2) there is irrefutable evidence that biological death is imminent, and (3) the patient or the family consents. Whereas Rachels's cases involve two unjustified actions, one of killing and the other of letting die, the AMA statement distinguishes cases of unjustified killing from cases of justified letting die. The AMA statement does not claim that the moral difference is entirely predicated on the distinction between killing and letting die. It also does not imply that the bare difference between (passive) letting die and (active) killing is the major difference or a morally sufficient difference to distinguish the justified from the unjustified cases. The point is only that the justified actions in medicine are confined to letting die (passive euthanasia).

The AMA statement holds that "mercy killing" in medicine is unjustified in all circumstances, but it holds neither that letting die is right in all circumstances nor that killing outside medicine is always wrong. For an act that results in an earlier death for the patient to be justified, it is necessary that it be an act of letting die, but this condition is not sufficient to justify the act; nor is the bare fact of an act's being a killing sufficient to make the act wrong. This AMA declaration is meant to control conduct exclusively in the context of the physician-patient relationship. The rationale for the prohibition is not stated, but the scope of the prohibition is quite clear.

Even if the distinction between killing and letting die is morally irrelevant in many cases, it does not follow that it is morally irrelevant in all contexts. Although we quite agree that Rachels does effectively undermine all attempts to rest moral judgments about ending life on the "bare difference" between killing and letting die, his target may nonetheless be made of straw. Many philosophers and theologians have argued that there are independent moral, religious, and other reasons both for defending the distinction and for prohibiting killing while authorizing allowing to die in some circumstances or based on some motives.

One theologian has argued, for example, that we can discern the moral significance of the distinction between killing and letting die by "placing it in the religious context out of which it grew."[3] That context is the biblical story of God's actions toward his creatures. In that context it makes sense to talk about "placing patients in God's hands," just as it is important not to usurp God's prerogatives by desperately struggling to prolong life when the patient is irreversibly dying. But even if the distinction between killing and letting die originated within a religious context, and even if it makes more sense in that context than in some others, it can be defended on non-theological grounds without being reduced to a claim about a "bare difference." We turn next to this defense of the distinction.

HOW AND WHERE TO DEFEND THE DISTINCTION BETWEEN KILLING AND LETTING DIE

Even if there are sufficient reasons in some cases to warrant mercy killing, there may also be good reasons to retain the distinction between killing and letting die and to maintain our current practices and policies against killing *in medicine,* albeit with some clarifications and modifications.

Acts and practices

The most important arguments for the distinction between killing and letting die depend on a distinction between acts and practices.[4] It is one thing to justify an act; it is another to justify a general practice. Many beliefs about principles and consequences are applied to rules rather than directly to acts. For example, we might justify a rule of confidentiality because it encourages people to seek therapy and because it promotes respect for persons and their privacy, although such a rule might lead to undesirable results in particular cases where confidentiality should not be maintained.

Similarly, a rule that prohibits "active killing" while permitting some "allowed deaths" may be justifiable, even if it excludes some particular acts of killing that in themselves are justifiable. For example, the rule would not permit us to kill a patient who suffers from terrible pain, who will probably die within three weeks, and who rationally asks for a merciful-assisted death. In order to maintain a viable practice that expresses our principles and avoids seriously undesirable consequences, it may be necessary to prohibit some acts that are not otherwise wrong and in some cases may be morally justified. Thus, although particular *acts* of killing may be humane and compassionate, a *policy* or *practice* that authorizes killing in medicine—in even a few cases—might create a grave risk of harm in many cases and a risk that we find it unjustified to assume.

The prohibition of killing even for "mercy" expresses principles and supports practices that provide a basis of trust between patients and health-care professionals. When we trust these professionals, we expect them to ask for our consent and to do us no harm without a prospect of correlative benefit. The prohibition of killing is an attempt to promote a solid basis for trust in the role of caring for patients and protecting them from harm. This prohibition is both instrumentally and symbolically important, and its removal could weaken a set of practices and restraints that we cannot easily replace.

Wedge or slippery slope arguments

This last argument—an incipient wedge or slippery slope argument—is plausible but needs to be stated carefully. Because of the widespread misuses of such arguments in biomedical ethics, there is a tendency to dismiss them whenever they are offered. However, as expressions of the principle of nonmaleficence, they are defensible in some cases. They also force us to consider whether unacceptable harms may result from attractive and apparently innocent first steps. Legitimation of acts such as active voluntary euthanasia run the risk of leading to other acts or practices that are morally objectionable even if some individual acts of this type are acceptable in themselves. The claim made by those who defend these arguments is that accepting the act in question would cross a line that has already been drawn against killing; and once that line has been crossed, it will not be possible to draw it again to preclude unacceptable acts or practices.

However, wedge arguments of some types may not be as damaging as they may seem at first. As Rachels correctly contends, "there obviously are good reasons for objecting to killing patients in order to get away for the weekend—or for even more respectable purposes, such as securing organs for transplantation—which do not apply to killing in order to put the patient out of extreme agony."[5] In other words, the counterreply is that relevant distinctions can be drawn, and we are not subject to uncontrollable implications from general principles. Some versions of the wedge argument, therefore, do not assist supporters of the distinction between killing and letting die as much as they might suppose.

Indeed, the argument can be used against them: If it is rational and morally defensible to allow patients to die under conditions X, Y, and Z, then it is rational and morally defensible to kill them under those same conditions. If it is in their best interests to die, it is (*prima facie*) irrelevant how death is brought about. Rachels makes a similar point when he argues that reliance on the distinction between killing and letting die may lead to decisions about life and death made on irrelevant grounds—such as whether the patient will or will not die without certain forms of treatment—instead of being made in terms of the patient's best interests.

In the now famous Johns Hopkins Hospital case, an infant with Down syndrome and duodenal atresia was placed in a back room and died eleven days later of dehydration and starvation. This process of dying, which senior physicians had recommended against, was extremely difficult for all the parties involved, particularly the nurses. If decision makers legitimately determine that a patient would be better off dead (we think the parties mistakenly came to this conclusion in this case), how could an act of killing violate the patient's interests if the patient will not die when artificial treatment is discontinued? A morally irrelevant factor would be allowed to dictate the outcome.

The lack of empirical evidence to determine the adequacy of slippery slope arguments is unfortunate, but it is not a sufficient reason to reject them. Some arguments of this form should be taken with the utmost seriousness. They force us to think carefully about whether unacceptable harm is likely to result from attractive and apparently innocent first steps.

NOTES

1. James Rachels. "Active and Passive Euthanasia," *New England Journal of Medicine* 292 (1975):78–80.
2. Richard L. Trammell. "Saving Life and Taking Life," *Journal of Philosophy* 72 (1975):131–137.
3. Gilbert Meilaender. "The Distinction between Killing and Allowing to Die," *Theological Studies* 37 (1976):467–470.
4. This distinction and our arguments are indebted to John Rawls, "Two Concepts of Rules," *Philosophical Review* 64 (1955):3–32.
5. James Rachels. "Medical Ethics and the Rule against Killing: Comments on Professor Hare's Paper." S. F. Spicker and H. T. Engelhardt (eds.). p. 65. In *Philosophical Medical Ethics*, Dordrecht, Holland: D. Reidel, 1977.

When Self-Determination Runs Amok

Daniel Callahan

The euthanasia debate is not just another moral debate, one in a long list of arguments in our pluralistic society. It is profoundly emblematic of three important turning points in Western thought. The first is that of the legitimate conditions under which one person can kill another. The acceptance of voluntary active euthanasia would morally sanction what can only be called "consenting adult killing." By that term I mean the killing of one person by another in the name of their mutual right to be killer and killed if they freely agree to play those roles. This turn flies in the face of a long-standing effort to limit the circumstances under which one person can take the life of another, from efforts to control the free flow of guns and arms, to abolish capital punishment, and to more tightly control warfare. Euthanasia would add a whole new category of killing to a society that already has too many excuses to indulge itself in that way.

The second turning point lies in the meaning and limits of self-determination. The acceptance of euthanasia would sanction a view of autonomy holding that individuals may, in the name of their own private, idiosyncratic view of the good life, call upon others, including such institutions as medicine, to help them pursue

Callahan, Daniel. "When Self-Determination Runs Amok," *Hastings Center Report* 22:2 (1992) 52–55 (excerpt). Copyright © 1992. Reprinted permission of The Hastings Center.

that life, even at the risk of harm to the common good. This works against the idea that the meaning and scope of our own right to lead our own lives must be conditioned by, and be compatible with, the good of the community, which is more than an aggregate of self-directing individuals.

The third turning point is to be found in the claim being made upon medicine: it should be prepared to make its skills available to individuals to help them achieve their private vision of the good life. This puts medicine in the business of promoting the individualistic pursuit of general human happiness and well-being. It would overturn the traditional belief that medicine should limit its domain to promoting and preserving human health, redirecting it instead to the relief of that suffering which stems from life itself, not merely from a sick body.

I believe that, at each of these three turning points, proponents of euthanasia push us in the wrong direction. Arguments in favor of euthanasia fall into four general categories, which I will take up in turn: (1) the moral claim of individual self-determination and well-being; (2) the moral irrelevance of the difference between killing and allowing to die; (3) the supposed paucity of evidence to show likely harmful consequences of legalized euthanasia; and (4) the compatibility of euthanasia and medical practice.

SELF-DETERMINATION

Central to most arguments for euthanasia is the principle of self-determination. People are presumed to have an interest in deciding for themselves, according to their own beliefs about what makes life good, how they will conduct their lives. That is an important value, but the question in the euthanasia context is, What does it mean and how far should it extend? If it were a question of suicide, where a person takes her own life without assistance from another, that principle might be pertinent, at least for debate. But euthanasia is not that limited a matter. The self-determination in that case can only be effected by the moral and physical assistance of another. Euthanasia is thus no longer a matter only of self-determination, but of a mutual, social decision between two people, the one to be killed and the other to do the killing.

How are we to make the moral move from my right of self-determination to some doctor's right to kill me—from *my* right to *his* right? Where does the doctor's moral warrant to kill come from? Ought doctors to be able to kill anyone they want as long as permission is given by competent persons? Is our right to life just like a piece of property, to be given away or alienated if the price

(happiness, relief of suffering) is right? And then to be destroyed with our permission once alienated?

In answer to all those questions, I will say this: I have yet to hear a plausible argument why it should be permissible for us to put this kind of power in the hands of another, whether a doctor or anyone else. The idea that we can waive our right to life, and then give to another the power to take that life, requires a justification yet to be provided by anyone.

Slavery was long ago outlawed on the ground that one person should not have the right to own another, even with the other's permission. Why? Because it is a fundamental moral wrong for one person to give over his life and fate to another, whatever the good consequences, and no less a wrong for another person to have that kind of total, final power. Like slavery, dueling was long ago banned on similar grounds; even free, competent individuals should not have the power to kill each other, whatever their motives, whatever the circumstances. Consenting adult killing, like consenting adult slavery or degradation, is a strange route to human dignity.

There is another problem as well. If doctors, once sanctioned to carry out euthanasia, are to be themselves responsible moral agents—not simply hired hands with lethal injections at the ready—then they must have their own *independent* moral grounds to kill those who request such services. What do I mean? As those who favor euthanasia are quick to point out, some people want it because their life has become so burdensome it no longer seems worth living.

The doctor will have a difficulty at this point. The degree and intensity to which people suffer from their diseases and their dying, and whether they find life more of a burden than a benefit, has very little directly to do with the nature or extent of their actual physical condition. Three people can have the same condition, but only one will find the suffering unbearable. People suffer, but suffering is as much a function of the values of individuals as it is of the physical causes of that suffering. Inevitably in that circumstance, the doctor will in effect be treating the patient's values. To be responsible, the doctor would have to share those values. The doctor would have to decide, on her own, whether the patient's life was "no longer worth living."

But how could a doctor possibly know that or make such a judgment? Just because the patient said so? I raise this question because, while in Holland at the euthanasia conference, the doctors present agreed that there is no objective way of measuring or judging the claims of patients that their suffering is unbearable. And if it is difficult to measure suffering, how much more difficult to determine the value of a patient's statement that her life is not worth living?

However one might want to answer such questions, the very need to ask them, to inquire into the physician's responsibility and grounds for medical and moral judgment, points out the social nature of the decision. Euthanasia is not a private matter of self-determination. It is an act that requires two people to make it possible, and a complicit society to make it acceptable.

KILLING AND ALLOWING TO DIE

Against common opinion, the argument is sometimes made that there is no moral difference between stopping life-sustaining treatment and more active forms of killing, such as lethal injection. Instead I would contend that the notion that there is no morally significant difference between omission and commission is just wrong. Consider in its broad implications what the eradication of the distinction implies: that death from disease has been banished, leaving only the actions of physicians in terminating treatment as the cause of death. Biology, which used to bring about death, has apparently been displaced by human agency. Doctors have finally, I suppose, thus genuinely become gods, now doing what nature and the deities once did.

What is the mistake here? It lies in confusing causality and culpability, and in failing to note the way in which human societies have overlaid natural causes with moral rules and interpretations. Causality (by which I mean the direct physical causes of death) and culpability (by which I mean our attribution of moral responsibility to human actions) are confused under three circumstances.

They are confused, first, when the action of a physician in stopping treatment of a patient with an underlying lethal disease is construed as *causing* death. On the contrary, the physician's omission can only bring about death on the condition that the patient's disease will kill him in the absence of treatment. We may hold the physician morally responsible for the death, if we have morally judged such actions wrongful omissions. But it confuses reality and moral judgment to see an omitted action as having the same causal status as one that directly kills. A lethal injection will kill both a healthy person and a sick person. A physician's omitted treatment will have no effect on a healthy person. Turn off the machine on me, a healthy person, and nothing will happen. It will only, in contrast, bring the life of a sick person to an end because of an underlying fatal disease.

Causality and culpability are confused, second, when fail to note that judgments of moral responsibility and culpability are human constructs. By that I mean that we human beings, after moral reflection, have decided to call some actions right or wrong, and to devise moral rules to deal with them. When physicians could do nothing to stop death, they were not held responsible for it. When, with medical progress, they began to have some power over death—but only its timing and circumstances, not its ultimate inevitability—moral rules were devised to set forth their obligations. Natural causes of death were not thereby banished. They were, instead, overlaid with a medical ethics designed to determine moral culpability in deploying medical power.

To confuse the judgments of this ethics with the physical causes of death—which is the connotation of the word *kill*—is to confuse nature and human action. People will, one way or another, die of some disease; death will have dominion over all of us. To say that a doctor "kills" a patient by allowing this to happen should only be understood as a moral judgment about the licitness of his omission, nothing more. We can, as a fashion of speech only, talk about a doctor *killing* a patient by omitting treatment he should have provided. It is a fashion of speech precisely because it is the underlying disease that brings death when treatment is omitted; that is its cause, not the physician's omission. It is a misuse of the word *killing* to use it when a doctor stops a treatment he believes will no longer benefit the patient—when, that is, he steps aside to allow an eventually inevitable death to occur now rather than later. The only deaths that human beings invented are those that come from direct killing—when, with a lethal injection, we both cause death and are morally responsible for it. In the case of omissions, we do not cause death even if we may be judged morally responsible for it.

This difference between causality and culpability also helps us see why a doctor who has omitted a treatment he should have provided has "killed" that patient while another doctor—performing precisely the same act of omission on another patient in different circumstances—does not kill her, but only allows her to die. The difference is that we have come, by moral convention and conviction, to classify unauthorized or illegitimate omissions as acts of "killing." We call them "killing" in the expanded sense of the term: a culpable action that permits the real cause of death, the underlying disease, to proceed to its lethal conclusion. By contrast, the doctor who, at the patient's request, omits or terminates unwanted treatment does not kill at all. Her underlying disease, not his action, is the physical cause of death; and we have agreed to consider actions of that kind to be morally licit. He thus can truly be said to have "allowed" her to die.

If we fail to maintain the distinction between killing and allowing to die, moreover, there are some disturbing possibilities. The first would be to confirm many physicians in their already too-powerful belief that, when patients die or when physicians stop treatment because of the futility of continuing it, they are somehow both morally and physically responsible for the deaths that follow. That notion needs to be abolished, not strengthened. It needlessly and wrongly burdens the physician, to whom should not be attributed the powers of the gods. The second possibility would be that, in every case where a doctor judges medical treatment no longer effective in prolonging life, a quick and direct killing of the patient would be seen as the next, most reasonable step, on grounds of both humaneness and economics. I do not see how that logic could easily be rejected.

CALCULATING THE CONSEQUENCES

When concerns about the adverse social consequences of permitting euthanasia are raised, its advocates tend to dismiss them as unfounded and overly speculative. On the contrary, recent data about the Dutch experience suggests that such concerns are right on target. From my own discussions in Holland, and from the articles on that subject in this issue and elsewhere, I believe we can now fully see most of the *likely* consequences of legal euthanasia.

Three consequences seem almost certain, in this or any other country: the inevitability of some abuse of the law; the difficulty of precisely writing, and then enforcing, the law; and the inherent slipperiness of the moral reasons for legalizing euthanasia in the first place.

Why is abuse inevitable? One reason is that almost all laws on delicate, controversial matters are to some extent abused. This happens because not everyone will agree with the law as written and will bend it, or ignore it, if they can get away with it. From explicit admissions to me by Dutch proponents of euthanasia, and from the corroborating information provided by the Remmelink Report and the outside studies of Carlos Gomez and John Keown, I am convinced that in the Netherlands there are a substantial number of cases of nonvoluntary euthanasia, that is, euthanasia undertaken without the explicit permission of the person being killed. The other reason abuse is inevitable is that the law is likely to have a low enforcement priority in the criminal justice system. Like other laws of similar status, unless there is an unrelenting and harsh willingness to pursue abuse, violations will ordinarily be tolerated. The worst thing to me about my experience in Holland was the casual, seemingly indifferent attitude toward abuse. I think that would happen everywhere.

Why would it be hard to precisely write, and then enforce, the law? The Dutch speak about the requirement of "unbearable" suffering, but admit that such a term is just about indefinable, a highly subjective matter admitting of no objective standards. A requirement for outside opinion is nice, but it is easy to find complaisant colleagues. A requirement that a medical condition be "terminal" will run aground on the notorious difficulties of knowing when an illness is actually terminal.

Apart from those technical problems there is a more profound worry. I see no way, even in principle, to write or enforce a meaningful law that can guarantee effective procedural safeguards. The reason is obvious yet almost always overlooked. The euthanasia transaction will ordinarily take place within the boundaries of the private and confidential doctor-patient relationship. No one can possibly know what takes place in that context unless the doctor chooses to reveal it. In Holland, less than 10 percent of the physicians report their acts of euthanasia and do so with almost complete legal impunity. There is no reason why the situation should be any better elsewhere. Doctors will have their own reasons for keeping euthanasia secret, and some patients will have no less a motive for wanting it concealed.

I would mention, finally, that the moral logic of the motives for euthanasia contain within them the ingredients of abuse. The two standard motives for euthanasia and assisted suicide are said to be our right of self-determination, and our claim upon the mercy of others, especially doctors, to relieve our suffering. These two motives are typically spliced together and presented as a single justification. Yet if they are considered independently—and there is no inherent reason why they must be linked—they reveal serious problems. It is said that a competent, adult person should have a right to euthanasia for the relief of suffering. But why must the person be suffering? Does not that stipulation already compromise the principle of self-determination? How can self-determination have any limits? Whatever the person's motives may be, why are they not sufficient?

Consider next the person who is suffering but not competent, who is perhaps demented or mentally retarded. The standard argument would deny euthanasia to that person. But why? If a person is suffering but not competent, then it would seem grossly unfair to deny relief solely on the grounds of incompetence. Are the incompetent less entitled to relief from suffering than the competent? Will it only be affluent, middle-class people, mentally fit and savvy about working the medical system, who can qualify? Do the incompetent suffer less because of their incompetence?

Considered from these angles, there are no good moral reasons to limit euthanasia once the principle of taking life for that purpose has been legitimated. If we really believe in self-determination, then any competent person should have a right to be killed by a doctor for any reason that suits him. If we believe in the relief of suffering, then it seems cruel and capricious to deny it to the incompetent. There is, in short, no reasonable or logical stopping point once the turn has been made down the road to euthanasia, which could soon turn into a convenient and commodious expressway.

EUTHANASIA AND MEDICAL PRACTICE

A fourth kind of argument one often hears both in the Netherlands and in this country is that euthanasia and assisted suicide are perfectly compatible with the aims of medicine. I would note at the very outset that a physician who participates in another person's suicide already abuses medicine. Apart from depression (the main statistical cause of suicide), people commit suicide because they find life empty, oppressive, or meaningless. Their judgment is a judgment about the value of continued life, not only about health (even if they are sick). Are doctors now to be given the right to make judgments about the kinds of life worth living and to give their blessing to suicide for those they judge wanting? What conceivable competence, technical or moral, could doctors claim to play such a role? Are we to medicalize suicide, turning judgments about its worth and value into one more clinical issue? Yes, those are rhetorical questions.

Yet they bring us to the core of the problem of euthanasia and medicine. The great temptation of modern medicine, not always resisted, is to move beyond the promotion and preservation of health into the boundless realm of general human happiness and well-being. The root problem of illness and mortality is both medical and philosophical or religious. "Why must I die?" can be asked as a technical, biological question or as a question about the meaning of life. When medicine tries to respond to the latter, which it is always under pressure to do, it moves beyond its proper role.

It is not medicine's place to lift from us the burden of that suffering which turns on the meaning we assign to the decay of the body and its eventual death. It is not medicine's place to determine when lives are not worth living or when the burden of life is too great to be borne. Doctors have no conceivable way of evaluating such claims on the part of patients, and they should have no right to act in response to them. Medicine should try to relieve human suffering, but only that suffering which is brought on by illness and dying as biological phenomena, not that suffering which comes from anguish or despair at the human condition.

Doctors ought to relieve those forms of suffering that medically accompany serious illness and the threat of death. They should relieve pain, do what they can to allay anxiety and uncertainty, and be a comforting presence. As sensitive human beings, doctors should be prepared to respond to patients who ask why they must die, or die in pain. But here the doctor and the patient are at the same level. The doctor may have no better an answer to those old questions than anyone else; and certainly no special insight from his training as a physician. It would be terrible for physicians to forget this, and to think that in a swift, lethal injection, medicine has found its own answer to the riddle of life. It would be a false answer, given by the wrong people. It would be no less a false answer for patients. They should neither ask medicine to put its own vocation at risk to serve their private interests, nor think that the answer to suffering is to be killed by another. The problem is precisely that, too often in human history, killing has seemed the quick, efficient way to put aside that which burdens us. It rarely helps, and too often simply adds to one evil still another. That is what I believe euthanasia would accomplish. It is self-determination run amok.

When Abstract Moralizing Runs Amok

John Lachs

Moral reasoning is more objectionable when it is abstract than when it is merely wrong. For abstractness all but guarantees error by missing the human predicament that needs to be addressed, and worse, it is a sign that thought has failed to keep faith with its mission. The function of moral reflection is to shed light on the difficult problems we face; it cannot perform its job without a clear understanding of how and why certain of our practices come to seem no longer satisfactory.

It is just this grasp of the problem that is conspicuously lacking in Daniel Callahan's assault on euthanasia in "Self-Determination Run Amok"[1] [*sic*]. The rhetoric Callahan unleashes gives not even a hint of the grave contemporary moral problems that euthanasia and assisted suicide, a growing number of people now think, promise to resolve.

Instead, we are offered a set of abstract distinctions calculated to discredit euthanasia rather than to contribute to a sound assessment of it. Thus, Callahan informs us that suffering "brought on by illness and dying as biological phenomena"[2] is to be contrasted with suffering that comes from "anguish or despair at the human condition." The former constitutes the proper concern of medicine (so much for psychiatry!), the latter of religion and philosophy. Medication is the answer to physical pain; euthanasia can, therefore, be only a misconceived response to worries about the meaning of existence. Those who believe in it offer a "swift lethal injection" as the "answer to the riddle of life."

This way of putting the matter will come as a surprise to those who suffer from terrible diseases and who no longer find life worth living. It is grotesque to suppose that such individuals are looking for the meaning of existence and find it, absurdly, in a lethal injection. Their predicament is not intellectual but existential. They are not interested in the meaning of life but in acting on their belief that their own continued existence is, on balance, of no further benefit to them.

Those who advocate the legalization of euthanasia and the practice of assisted suicide propose them as answers to a serious and growing social problem. We now have the power to sustain the biological existence of large numbers of very sick people, and we use this power freely. Accordingly, individuals suffering from painful terminal diseases, Alzheimer's patients, and those in a persistent vegetative state are routinely kept alive long past the point where they can function as human beings. They must bear the pain of existence without the ability to perform the activities that give life meaning. Some of these people feel intensely that they are a burden to others, as well as to themselves, and that their speedy and relatively dignified departure would be a relief to all concerned. Many observers of no more than average sensitivity agree that the plight of these patients is severe enough to justify such desires.

Some of these sufferers are physically not in a position to end their lives. Others could do so if they had the necessary instruments. In our culture, however, few have a taste for blowing out their brains or jumping from high places. That leaves drugs, which almost everyone is accustomed to taking, and which everyone knows can ease one peacefully to the other side.

The medical profession has, however, acquired monopoly power over drugs. And the danger of legal entanglement has made physicians wary of helping patients hasten their deaths in the discreet, humane way that has been customary for centuries. The result is that people who want to die and for whom death has long ceased to be an evil can find no way out of their misery. Current and growing pressures on the medical profession to help such sufferers are, therefore, due at least partly to medicine itself. People want physicians to aid in their suicides because, without such help, they cannot end their lives. This restriction of human autonomy is due to the social power of medicine; it is neither surprising nor morally wrong, therefore, to ask those responsible for this limitation to undo some of its most noxious effects. If the medical profession relinquished its hold on drugs, people could make effective choices about their future without the assistance of physicians. Even limited access to deadly drugs, restricted to single doses for those who desire them and who are certified to be of sound mind and near the end of life, would keep physicians away from dealing in death.

Unfortunately, however, there is little sensible public discussion of such policy alternatives. And these policy alternatives may, in any case, not satisfy Callahan, who appears to believe that there is something radically wrong with anyone terminating a human life. Because he plays coy, his actual beliefs are difficult to make out. He says the notion that self-determination extends to suicide "might be pertinent, at least for debate."[3] But his argument against euthanasia sidesteps this issue: he maintains that even if there is a right to kill oneself, it is not one that can be transferred. The reason for this is that doing so would lead to "a fundamental moral wrong"—that of one person giving over "his life and fate to another."

One might wonder how we know that transferring power over oneself is "a fundamental moral wrong." Callahan appears to entertain the idea with intuitive certainty, which gives him the moral and the logical high ground and entitles him to demand a justification from whoever disagrees. But such intuitions are problematic themselves: is fervent embrace of them enough to guarantee their truth? Morality would be very distant from the concerns of life if it depended on such guideposts placed here and there in the desert of facts, unrelated to each other or to anything else. Their message, moreover, makes the guideposts suspect: it comes closer to being an echo of tradition or an expression of current views than a revelation of eternal moral truths.

Most important, the very idea of a right that intrinsically *cannot* be handed on is difficult to grasp. Under normal circumstances, to have a right is to be free or to be entitled to have or to do something. I have a right, for example, to clean my teeth. No one else has the right to do that without my consent. But I can authorize another, say my sweetheart or my dental hygienist, to do it for me. Similarly, I can assign my right to my house, to my left kidney, to raising my children, to deciding when I rise, when I go to sleep, and what I do in between (by joining the Army), and by a power of attorney even to pursuing my own interest.

To be sure, the transfer of rights is not without limits. My wife and I can, for example, give over our right to our children, though we cannot do so for money. I can contract to slave away for ten hours a day cooking hamburgers, but I cannot sell myself to be, once and for all, a slave. This does not mean, however, that some rights are intrinsically nontransferable. If my right to my left kidney were nontransferable, I could neither sell it nor give it away. But I can give it away, and the only reason I cannot sell it is because sales of this sort were declared, at some point, to be against public policy. We cannot sell ourselves into slavery for the same reason: human societies set limits to this transfer of rights on account of its unacceptable costs.

The case is no different with respect to authorizing another to end my life. If I have a right to one of my kidneys, I have a right to both. And if I can tell a needy person to take one of them, I can tell two needy people to take one each. There is nothing *intrinsically* immoral about this, even though when the second helps himself I die. Yet, by dying too soon, I may leave opportunities unexplored and obligations unmet. Unscrupulous operators may take advantage of my goodwill or naiveté. The very possibility of such acts invites abuse. For these or similar reasons, we may decide that giving the first kidney is morally acceptable, but giving the second is not. The difference between the two acts, however, is not that the first is generous while the second is "a fundamental moral wrong," but that the second occurs in a context and has consequences and costs that the first does not.

Only in terms of context and cost, therefore, can we sensibly consider the issue of the morality of euthanasia. Moving on the level of abstract maxims, Callahan misses this point altogether. He declares: "There are no good moral reasons to limit euthanasia once the principle of taking life... has been legitimated."[4] Serious moral reflection, though it takes principles into account, is little interested in legitimating *them*. Its focus is on determining the moral acceptability of certain sorts of actions performed in complex contexts of life. Consideration of the circumstances is always essential: it is fatuous, therefore, to argue that if euthanasia is ever permissible, then "any competent person should have a right to be killed by a doctor for any reason that suits him."[5]

We can achieve little progress in moral philosophy without the ability and readiness to make relevant distinctions. Why, then, does Callahan refuse to acknowledge that there are important differences between the situation of a terminally ill patient in grave pain who wants to die and that of a young father in the dental chair who wishes, for a moment, that he were dead? Callahan's reason is that he thinks all judgments about the unbearability of suffering and the worthlessness of one's existence are subjective and, as such, parts of a "private, idiosyncratic view of the good life."[6] The amount of our suffering "has very little directly to do" with our physical condition, and so the desire to end life is capricious and unreliable. If medicine honored such desires, it would "put its own vocation at risk" by serving "the private interests" of individuals.

I cannot imagine what the vocation of medicine might be if it is not to serve the private interests of individuals. It is, after all, my vision of the good life that accounts for my wish not to perish in a diabetic coma. And surgeons certainly pursue the private interests of their patients in removing cancerous growths and in providing face-lifts. Medicine does not surrender its vocation in serving the desires of individuals: since health and continued life are among our primary wishes, its career consists in just this service.

Nevertheless, Callahan is right that our judgments about the quality of our lives and about the level of our suffering have a subjective component. But so do the opinions of patients about their health and illness, yet physicians have little difficulty in placing these perceptions in a broader, objective context. Similarly, it is both possible and proper to take into account the objective circumstances that surround desires to terminate life. Physicians have developed considerable skill in relating subjective complaints to objective conditions; only by absurd exaggeration can we say that the doctor must accept either all or none of the patient's claims. The context of the young father in the dental chair makes it clear that only a madman would think of switching from novocaine to cyanide when he moans that he wants to be dead. Even people of ordinary sensitivity understand that the situation of an old person whose friends have all died and who now suffers the excruciating pain of terminal cancer is morally different.

The question of the justifiability of euthanasia, as all difficult moral questions, cannot be asked without specifying the details of context. Dire warnings of slippery slopes and of future large-scale, quietly conducted exterminations trade on overlooking differences of circumstance. They insult our sensitivity by the suggestion that a society of individuals of good will cannot recognize situations in which their fellows want and need help and cannot distinguish such situations from those in which the desire for death is rhetorical, misguided, temporary, or idiotic. It would indeed be tragic if medicine were to leap to the aid of love-lorn teenagers whenever they feel life is too much to bear. But it is just as lamentable to stand idly by and watch unwanted lives fill up with unproductive pain.

Callahan is correct in pointing out that, in euthanasia and in assisted suicide, the physician and the patient must have separate justifications for action. The patient's wish is defensible if it is the outcome of a sound reflective judgment. Such judgments take into account the current condition, pending projects, and long-term prospects of the individual and relate them to his or her permanent interests and established values. As all assessments, these can be in error. For this reason, persons soliciting help in dying must be ready to demonstrate that they are of sound mind and thus capable of making such choices, that their desire is enduring, and that both their subjective and their objective condition makes their wish sensible.

Physicians must first decide whether their personal values permit them to participate in such activities. If they do, they must diligently examine the justifiability of the patient's desire to die. Diagnosis and prognosis are often relatively easy to ascertain. But we are not without resources for a sound determination of the internal condition of individuals either: extensive questioning on multiple occasions, interviews with friends and loved ones, and exploration of the life history and values of people contribute mightily to understanding their state of mind. Physicians who are prepared to aid individuals with this last need of their lives are not, therefore, in a position where they have to believe everything they hear and act on every request. They must make independent judgments instead of subordinating themselves as unthinking tools to the passing desires of those they wish to help. This does not attribute to doctors "the powers of the gods." It only requires that they be flexible in how they aid their patients and that they do so with due caution and on the basis of sound evaluation.

Callahan is once again right to be concerned that, if allowed, euthanasia will "take place within the boundaries of the private and confidential doctor-patient relationship."[7] This does, indeed, invite abuse and permit callous physicians to take a casual attitude to a momentous decision. Callahan is wrong, however, in supposing that this constitutes an argument against euthanasia. It is only a reason not to keep euthanasia secret, but to shed on it the wholesome light of publicity. Though the decision to terminate life is intensely private, no moral consideration demands that it be kept the confidential possession of two individuals. To the contrary, the only way we can minimize wrong decisions and abuse is to require scrutiny of the decision, prior to action on it, by a suitable social body. Such examination, including at least one personal interview with the patient, should go a long distance toward relieving Callahan's concern that any law governing euthanasia would have "a low enforcement priority in the criminal justice system."[8] With formal social controls in place, there should be very little need for the involvement of courts and prosecutors.

To suppose, as Callahan does, that the principle of autonomy calls for us to stand idly by, or even to assist, whenever and for whatever reason people want to end their lives is calculated to discredit both euthanasia and autonomy. No serious moralist has ever argued that self-determination must be absolute. It cannot hold unlimited sway, as Mill and other advocates of the principle readily admit, if humans are to live in a society. And morally, it would cut no ice if murderers and rapists argued for the legitimacy of their actions by claiming that they flow naturally and solely from who they are.

The function of the principle of autonomy is to affirm *a* value and to shift the burden of justifying infringements of individual liberty to established social and governmental powers. The value it affirms is that of individual agency expressed in the belief that, through action and suffering and death, the life of each person enjoys a sort of private integrity. This means that, in the end, our lives belong to no one but ourselves. The limits to such self-determination or self-possession are set by the demands of social life. They can be discovered or decided upon in the process of moral reflection. A sensible approach to euthanasia can disclose how much weight autonomy carries in that context and how it can be balanced against other, equally legitimate but competing values.

In the hands of its friends, the principle of self-determination does not run amok. What runs amok in Callahan's version of autonomy and euthanasia is the sort of abstract moralizing that forgets the problem it sets out to address and shuts its eye to need and suffering.

NOTES

1. D. Callahan, "Self-Determination Run Amok," *Hastings Center Report* 22 (March–April 1992): 52–55.
2. Ibid., 55.
3. Ibid., 52.
4. Ibid., 54.
5. Ibid.
6. Ibid., 52.
7. Ibid., 54.
8. Ibid.

PHYSICIAN–ASSISTED SUICIDE

Death and Dignity:
A Case of Individualized Decision Making

Timothy E. Quill

Diane was feeling tired and had a rash. A common scenario, though there was something subliminally worrisome that prompted me to check her blood count. Her hematocrit was 22, and the white-cell count was 4.3 with some metamyelocytes and unusual white cells. I wanted it to be viral, trying to deny what was staring me in the face. Perhaps in a repeated count it would disappear. I called Diane and told her it might be more serious than I had initially thought—that the test needed to be repeated and that if she felt worse, we might have to move quickly. When she pressed for the possibilities, I reluctantly opened to the door to leukemia. Hearing the word seemed to make it exist. "Oh, shit!" she said. "Don't tell me that." Oh shit! I thought, I wish I didn't have to.

Diane was no ordinary person (although no one I have ever come to know has been really ordinary). She was raised in an alcoholic family and had felt alone for much of her life. She had vaginal cancer as a young woman. Through much of her adult life, she had struggled with depression and her own alcoholism. I had come to know, respect, and admire her over the previous eight years as she confronted these problems and gradually overcame them. She was an incredibly clear, at times brutally honest, thinker and communicator. As she took control of her life, she developed a strong sense of independence and confidence. In the previous 3½ years, her hard work had paid off. She was completely abstinent from alcohol, she had established much deeper connections with her husband, college-age son, and several friends, and her business and her artistic work were blossoming. She felt she was really living fully for the first time.

Not surprisingly, the repeated blood count was abnormal, and detailed examination of the peripheral-blood smear showed myelocytes. I advised her to come into the hospital, explaining that we needed to do a bone marrow biopsy and make some decisions relatively rapidly. She came to the hospital knowing what we would find. She was terrified, angry, and sad. Although we knew the odds, we both clung to the thread of possibility that it might be something else.

The bone marrow confirmed the worst: acute myelomonocytic leukemia. In the face of this tragedy, we looked for signs of hope. This is an area of medicine in which technological intervention has been successful, with cures 25 percent of the time-long-term cures. As I probed the costs of these cures, I heard about induction chemotherapy (three weeks in the hospital, prolonged neutropenia, probable infectious complications, and hair loss; 75 percent of patients respond, 25 percent do not). For the survivors, this is followed by consolidation chemotherapy (with similar side effects; another 25 percent die, for a net survival of 50 percent). Those still alive, to have a reasonable chance of long-term survival, then need bone marrow transplantation (hospitalization for two months and whole-body irradiation, with complete killing of the bone marrow, infectious complications, and the possibility for graft-versus-host disease—with a survival of approximately 50 percent, or 25 percent of

Quill, Timothy E. "Death and Dignity: A Case of Individualized Decision Making," *The New England Journal of Medicine* 324:10 (1991), 691–694.

the original group). Though hematologists may argue over the exact percentages, they don't argue about the outcome of no treatment—certain death in days, weeks, or at most a few months.

Believing that delay was dangerous, our oncologist broke the news to Diane and began making plans to insert a Hickman catheter and begin induction chemotherapy that afternoon. When I saw her shortly thereafter, she was enraged at his presumption that she would want treatment, and devastated by the finality of the diagnosis. All she wanted to do was go home and be with her family. She had no further questions about treatment and in fact had decided that she wanted none. Together we lamented her tragedy and the unfairness of life. Before she left, I felt the need to be sure that she and her husband understood that there was some risk in delay, that the problem was not going to go away, and that we needed to keep considering the options over the next several days. We agreed to meet in two days.

She returned in two days with her husband and son. They had talked extensively about the problem and the options. She remained very clear about her wish not to undergo chemotherapy and to live whatever time she had left outside the hospital. As we explored her thinking further, it became clear that she was convinced she would die during the period of treatment and would suffer unspeakably in the process (from hospitalization, from lack of control over her body, from the side effects of chemotherapy, and from pain and anguish). Although I could offer support and my best effort to minimize her suffering if she chose treatment, there was no way I could say any of this would not occur. In fact, the last four patients with acute leukemia at our hospital had died very painful deaths in the hospital during various stages of treatment (a fact I did not share with her). Her family wished she would choose treatment but sadly accepted her decision. She articulated very clearly that it was she who would be experiencing all the side effects of treatment and that odds of 25 percent were not good enough for her to undergo so toxic a course of therapy, given her expectations of chemotherapy and hospitalization and the absence of a closely matched bone marrow donor. I had her repeat her understanding of the treatment, the odds, and what to expect if there were no treatment. I clarified a few misunderstandings, but she had a remarkable grasp of the options and implications.

I have been a longtime advocate of active, informed patient choice of treatment or nontreatment, and of a patient's right to die with as much control and dignity as possible. Yet there was something about her giving up a 25 percent chance of long-term survival in favor of almost certain death that disturbed me. I had seen Diane fight and use her considerable inner resources to overcome alcoholism and depression, and I half expected her to change her mind over the next week. Since the window of time in which effective treatment can be initiated is rather narrow, we met several times that week. We obtained a second hematology consultation and talked at length about the meaning and implications of treatment and nontreatment. She talked to a psychologist she had seen in the past. I gradually understood the decision from her perspective and became convinced that it was the right decision for her. We arranged for home hospice care (although at that time Diane felt reasonably well, was active, and looked healthy), left the door open for her to change her mind, and tried to anticipate how to keep her comfortable in the time she had left.

Just as I was adjusting to her decision, she opened up another area that would stretch me profoundly. It was extraordinarily important to Diane to maintain control of herself and her own dignity during the time remaining to her. When this was no longer possible, she clearly wanted to die. As a former director of a hospice program, I know how to use pain medicines to keep patients comfortable and lessen suffering. I explained the philosophy of comfort care, which I strongly believe in. Although Diane understood and appreciated this, she had known of people lingering in what was called relative comfort, and she wanted no part of it. When the time came, she wanted to take her life in the least painful way possible. Knowing of her desire for independence and her decision to stay in control, I thought this request made perfect sense. I acknowledged and explored this wish but also thought that it was out of the realm of currently accepted medical practice and that it was more than I could offer or promise. In our discussion, it became clear that preoccupation with her fear of a lingering death would interfere with Diane's getting the most out of the time she had left until she found a safe way to ensure her death. I feared the effects of a violent death on her family, the consequences of an ineffective suicide that would leave her lingering in precisely the state she dreaded so much, and the possibility that a family member would be forced to assist her, with all the legal and personal repercussions that would follow. She discussed this at length with her family. They believed that they should respect her choice. With this in mind, I told Diane that information was available from the Hemlock Society that might be helpful to her.

A week later she phoned me with a request for barbiturates for sleep. Since I knew that this was an essential ingredient in a Hemlock Society suicide, I asked her to come to the office to talk things over. She was more than willing to protect me by participating in a superficial conversation about her insomnia, but it was important to me to know how she planned to use the drugs and to be sure that she was not in despair or overwhelmed in a way that might color her judgment. In our discussion, it was apparent that she was having trouble sleeping, but it was also evident that the security of having enough barbiturates available to commit suicide when and if the time came would leave her secure enough to live fully and concentrate on the present. It was clear that she was not despondent and that in fact she was making deep, personal connections with her family and close friends. I made sure that she knew how to use the barbiturates for sleep, and also that she knew the amount needed to commit suicide. We agreed to meet regularly, and she promised to meet with me before taking her life, to ensure that all other avenues had been exhausted. I wrote the prescription with an uneasy feeling about the boundaries I was exploring—spiritual, legal, professional, and personal. Yet I also felt strongly that I was setting her free to get the most out of the time she had left, and to maintain dignity and control on her own terms until her death.

The next several months were very intense and important for Diane. Her son stayed home from college, and they were able to be with one another and say much that had not been said earlier. Her husband did his work at home so that he and Diane could spend more time together. She spent time with her closest friends. I had her come into the hospital for a conference with our residents, at which she illustrated in a most profound and personal way the importance of informed decision making, the right to refuse treatment, and the extraordinarily personal effects of illness and interaction with the medical system. There were emotional and physical hardships as well. She had periods of intense sadness and anger. Several times she became very weak, but she received transfusions as an outpatient and responded with marked improvement of symptoms. She had two serious infections that responded surprisingly well to empirical sources of oral antibiotics. After three tumultuous months, there were two weeks of relative calm and well-being, and fantasies of a miracle began to surface.

Unfortunately, we had no miracle. Bone pain, weakness, fatigue, and fevers began to dominate her life. Although the hospice workers, family members, and I tried our best to minimize the suffering and promote comfort, it was clear that the end was approaching. Diane's immediate future held what she feared the most—increasing discomfort, dependence, and hard choices between pain and sedation. She called up her closest friends and asked them to come over to say goodbye, telling them that she would be leaving soon. As we had agreed, she let me know as well. When we

met, it was clear that she knew what she was doing, that she was sad and frightened to be leaving, but that she would be even more terrified to stay and suffer. In our tearful goodbye, she promised a reunion in the future at her favorite spot on the edge of Lake Geneva, with dragons swimming in the sunset.

Two days later her husband called to say that Diane had died. She had said her final goodbyes to her husband and son that morning, and asked them to leave her alone for an hour. After an hour, which must have seemed an eternity, they found her on the couch, lying very still and covered by her favorite shawl. There was no sign of struggle. She seemed to be at peace. They called me for advice about how to proceed. When I arrived at their house, Diane indeed seemed peaceful. Her husband and son were quiet. We talked about what a remarkable person she had been. They seemed to have no doubts about the course she had chosen or about their cooperation, although the unfairness of her illness and the finality of her death were overwhelming to us all.

I called the medical examiner to inform him that a hospice patient had died. When asked about the cause of death, I said, "acute leukemia." He said that was fine and that we should call a funeral director. Although acute leukemia was the truth, it was not the whole story. Yet any mention of suicide would have given rise to a police investigation and probably brought the arrival of an ambulance crew for resuscitation. Diane would have become a "coroner's case," and the decision to perform an autopsy would have been made at the discretion of the medical examiner. The family or I could have been subject to criminal prosecution, and I to professional review, for our roles in support of Diane's choices. Although I truly believe that the family and I gave her the best care possible, allowing her to define her limits and directions as much as possible, I am not sure the law, society, or the medical profession would agree. So I said "acute leukemia" to protect all of us, to protect Diane from an invasion into her past and her body, and to continue to shield society from the knowledge of the degree of suffering that people often undergo in the process of dying. Suffering can be lessened to some extent, but in no way eliminated or made benign, by the careful intervention of a competent, caring physician, given current social constraints.

Diane taught me about the range of help I can provide if I know people well and if I allow them to say what they really want. She taught me about life, death, and honesty and about taking charge and facing tragedy squarely when it strikes. She taught me that I can take small risks for people that I really know and care about. Although I did not assist in her suicide directly, I helped indirectly to make it possible, successful, and relatively painless. Although I know we have measures to help control pain and lessen suffering, to think that people do not suffer in the process of dying is an illusion. Prolonged dying can occasionally be peaceful, but more often the role of the physician and family is limited to lessening but not eliminating severe suffering.

I wonder how many families and physicians secretly help patients over the edge into death in the face of such severe suffering. I wonder how many severely ill or dying patients secretly take their lives, dying alone in despair. I wonder whether the image of Diane's final aloneness will persist in the minds of her family, or if they will remember more the intense, meaningful months they had together before she died. I wonder whether Diane struggled in that last hour, and whether the Hemlock Society's way of death by suicide is the most benign. I wonder why Diane, who gave so much to so many of us, had to be alone for the last hour of her life. I wonder whether I will see Diane again, on the shore of Lake Geneva at sunset, with dragons swimming on the horizon.

Assisted Suicide, Terminal Illness, Severe Disability, and the Double Standard

Felicia Ackerman

Here are three positions about assisted suicide.

1. Physician-assisted suicide should be legally available to all competent adults.
2. Physician-assisted suicide should be legally available just to the terminally ill, or possibly just to the terminally ill and to the severely and permanently disabled. (Note that positions 1 and 2 hold that the law should *allow* doctors to provide suicide assistance, not that the law should *require* them to do so.)
3. Physician-assisted suicide should be legally available to no one.

For the most part, the current debate over physician-assisted suicide is between positions 2 and 3.[1] This essay aims to reorient the debate. I think it should be between positions 1 and 3. Positions 1 and 3 both embody reasonable, although opposing, outlooks, and this essay will not try to decide between them. What it will argue is that position 2, although popular with "death with dignity" advocates and many liberals, is morally untenable.

Although assisted-suicide advocates do not characteristically endorse position 1, they often give arguments that can be used to support it. For example, on the very day I am writing this, the *New York Times* has a news story saying that

> In Florida, [AIDS patient Charles E.] Hall's legal arguments for assisted suicide [for the terminally ill] hinge on a state constitutional amendment . . . that asserts a stronger right of privacy than that offered in the United States Constitution. With few exceptions, the amendment says, "every natural person has the right to be let alone and free from government intrusion into his private life."[2]

Appeals to privacy and autonomy are characteristic of assisted-suicide advocates. They have filtered into popular culture in the form of slogans like "Whose life is it, anyway?" These appeals have intuitive force. But why not apply them to all competent adults? If the issues are really autonomy and privacy, then why legalize suicide assistance only for the terminally ill?[3] Why not grant this right of privacy equally to the young and healthy—the very people our society values most—if they come to decide, for whatever reason, that they do not want to go on living? Such people could doubtless use suicide assistance in the form of prescriptions for lethal drugs, advice about administration, etc. What factors could justify granting this right of privacy only to the terminally ill?

EXTREME PAIN

Assisted-suicide advocates frequently paint a picture of the terminally ill in extreme and unrelievable pain, begging to die, and frustrated in this desperate wish by religious fanatics and reactionaries who insist each human life is sacred, regardless of how much the bearer of that life wants to end it. Some terminally ill people do suffer great unrelievable pain. But as a reason for legalizing physician-assisted suicide for only the terminally ill, this rationale is a failure. First, it is obviously false that all and only the terminally ill have severe and unrelievable pain. Many non-life-threatening illnesses, such as rheumatoid arthritis, cause severe unrelievable pain, and many terminal illnesses do not. In fact, a recent study found that "severe, uncontrolled pain or the fear of it" was a less influential factor than (treatable) clinical depression in terminally ill patients who requested suicide assistance.[4] Second, as Yale Kamisar points out, where extreme and unrelievable pain is present, there is a stronger rationale for allowing suicide assistance in cases where the pain will *not* soon be ended by death.[5] For people who find that severe pain makes their life an intolerable burden, surely thirty years of such life is a greater burden than six months. A possible reply is that, the longer the projected lifespan, the more likely that some cure or new form of pain relief may eventually be found. But respect for privacy and autonomy would seem to require that it be each pain-wracked patient, rather than his government, who gets to decide in his own case whether it is worth going for such a long shot. Finally, if severe and intractable pain, rather than terminal illness, is made the condition for legalizing suicide assistance, we have the problem that this revised condition is still out of accord with the rhetoric of privacy and autonomy. True privacy and autonomy would allow each person to determine for himself what conditions would justify suicide.

LOSS OF "DIGNITY" AND OTHER "QUALITY OF LIFE" CONSIDERATIONS

Even aside from the question of pain, assisted-suicide advocate Dr. Timothy Quill has suggested that "suicide could be appropriate for patients if they did not want to linger comatose, demented, or incontinent."[6] Arguments of this sort are common among assisted-suicide advocates, often involving recourse to patients' right to "die with dignity," rather than linger in the "undignified" conditions just mentioned. For example, the Philosophers' Brief in favor of legalizing assisted suicide for the terminally ill holds that "it is intolerable for government to dictate that doctors may never, under any circumstances, help someone to die who believes that further life means only degradation."[7]

This sort of thinking invites a flip reply: Haven't Dr. Quill and his ilk ever heard of Depend?[8] To put the matter less flippantly, I think we need to question our society's bigoted and superficial view of human dignity, which holds that the old, ill, and disabled have less human dignity than the young and strong. Does Dr. Quill really want to endorse the view that human dignity resides in the bladder and the rectum? If being unable to control the discharge of one's urine and feces deprives one of human dignity, then what about being unable to

control the discharge of one's menstrual blood? Should physician-assisted suicide also be legalized for all premenopausal women who believe that the milder "remedy" of a hysterectomy would also undermine their dignity?

Of course, the autonomy reply can be invoked here. The point is not what Dr. Quill or the signatories to the Philosophers' Brief or I believe is inimical to human dignity, but what each individual person believes about his own dignity. And of course, this is the position of mainstream assisted-suicide advocates, who do not endorse the "indignity" of incontinence as a reason for suicide except for patients who themselves want to die for this reason. To be consistent, however, such a position would also have to endorse legalizing assisted suicide for people who believe their menstruation, or their irremediable stuttering, clumsiness, or foolishness deprives them of human dignity. It was not so long ago in American history that most white Americans had difficulty recognizing the human dignity of black Americans. If there are black Americans nowadays who buy into this, would Dr. Quill want suicide assistance to be legalized for them? If not, why legalize assisted suicide for people who believe it is their incontinence, rather than their skin color, that deprives them of human dignity? A similar point applies to people who believe it is their "dependence," rather than their skin color, that deprives them of human dignity.[9] In all these cases, it seems clear that the supposed lack of dignity is a social construct arising from the low value our society places on people of a certain sort, rather than from anything inherent in the person's condition itself. The case of a person's becoming comatose or demented is in some ways different, as being comatose or demented directly and intrinsically undermines one's personality. But whether this would undermine one's human dignity more than incontinence, menstruation, stuttering, or the "wrong" skin color should be each person's own decision if we truly accept each person's "right to make momentous personal decisions which invoke fundamental religious or philosophical convictions about life's value for himself."[10]

The most general of all "quality of life" considerations is unhappiness. Although the National Hospice Organization opposes the legalization of assisted suicide,[11] its "philosophy of hospice" includes a statement that "[p]sychological and spiritual pain are as significant as physical pain."[12] But "psychological and spiritual pain" (the contemporary psychobabble for unhappiness and despair) are hardly limited to the terminally ill. So if "psychological and spiritual pain" are really as "significant" as physical pain, why not allow suicide assistance to every competent adult in these conditions who requests it?[13]

NEGLIGIBLE PROSPECTS
FOR IMPROVEMENT

The standard reply is that many cases of unhappiness and despair are transient and/or can be alleviated. For example, the introduction to the Philosophers' Brief holds that "[s]tates may be allowed to prevent assisted suicide by people who—it is plausible to think—would later be grateful if they were prevented from dying,"[14] such as "a sixteen-year-old suffering from a severe case of unrequited love."[15] Putting the condition this way skews the criterion in favor of limiting suicide assistance to people with little time left to live. The less time people have left to live, the less likely they are to change their minds about *anything* during the time they have left. But not all people with predictably little time left to live are terminally ill. Would the authors of the Philosophers' Brief endorse the legalization of assisted suicide for Death Row inmates who have used up all their appeals, whose executions are due to occur in less than six months, and whose chance of a reprieve is no greater than a terminal patient's chance of a miracle cure?

The reasoning of the Philosophers' Brief can also be applied to actions other than assisted suicide. Selling one's kidney is illegal in the United States. But suppose a Death Row inmate in the above-mentioned situation or a terminally ill person has a strong and stable desire to sell his kidney. Such a person seems unlikely ever to be grateful if he is prevented from doing this—as unlikely as he would ever be to be grateful for having been denied suicide assistance. Why not let him make this "momentous personal [decision] which invoke[s] fundamental religious or philosophical convictions about life's value for himself"?[16]

Another problem, of course, is that it is not just people with predictably little time left to live who are unlikely ever to be grateful for having been denied suicide assistance. Suppose Barnes and Starnes both have the same strong, stable, and longstanding reason for finding life unbearable and wanting suicide assistance (being paralyzed from the neck down, for example, a condition many suicide advocates readily accept as a reasonable ground for wanting to die). Then, as I have suggested, it may be argued that if Barnes is terminally ill but Starnes is not, giving Barnes but not Starnes suicide assistance may well prevent less misery than would the reverse decision.

I do not know how the authors of the Philosophers' Brief would handle the cases about Death Row inmates and selling kidneys. But the introduction to the brief does consider the third sort of case. The introduction suggests that "if the [Supreme] Court adopted [the brief's] argument, the federal courts would no doubt be faced with a succession of cases in years to come testing whether, for example, it is plausible to assume that a desperately crippled patient in constant pain but with years to live, who has formed a settled and repeatedly stated wish to die, would one day be glad he was forced to stay alive."[17] The brief itself grants that "[a] state might assert . . . that people who are not terminally ill, but who have formed a desire to die are, as a group, very likely later to be grateful if they are prevented from taking their own lives. It might then claim that it is legitimate" to deny all such people suicide assistance.[18] But on what grounds would the state make this claim about likelihood? And why does the example involve a "desperately crippled" (does that mean "severely crippled"?) person, rather than a young, healthy, and able-bodied person who is serving a life sentence without possibility of parole or who is desperately poor, unskilled, and stupid, and able to earn a living only by working at drudge work he detests? Such people may be just as unlikely as the "desperately crippled" person to have their lives improve to the point where they are ever glad they were forced to stay alive. How would Ronald Dworkin, author of the introduction to the Philosophers' Brief, feel about such cases?

I do not know, but one possible rationale for treating the "desperately crippled" case differently from the other two would be to say that the misery of the "desperately crippled" person arises directly from the medical facts of his situation, while the misery in the latter two cases arises from correctable social injustices. Prisons need not be unbearable places, and poverty can be alleviated. Such a rationale would face two objections. First, if unbearable misery arises from a social injustice that is not being corrected, it is hard to see how justice is served by forcing the victims to live with it, rather than by correcting the injustice or by allowing the victims suicide assistance if the injustice is not corrected. Second, it is implausible that the poor "quality of life" of even a severely disabled person in constant pain arises solely from his physical condition.[19] In real life, Stephen Hawking is about as "desperately crippled" as a man can be, but by all accounts he is happy. Nor does one have to be a scientific genius to be happy although "desperately" paralyzed. The local paper of the city where I live has an editor who, like Hawking, is almost completely paralyzed by Lou Gehrig's disease. This editor lives happily at home, aided by a family eager to help him stay alive—as eager as many families nowadays are to help their terminally ill loved ones die. He also has an accommodating employer who is "pledged to supply him with whatever he [needs] to write from home"[20] and who has spent thousands of dollars on an eye-activated computer. The fact that he produces, not great works of physics, but hackneyed prose like "[w]e can gaze at a spectacular sunset, listen with rapture to a Beethoven symphony, or smile at the face of a loved one, and the experience leaves us transformed and enlarged" seems not to dim his happiness one bit.[21] Since there are severely disabled and terminally ill people who can live so happily, however, it is worth considering whether those who want to die are, like Tristram, prisoners—not prisoners in actual dungeons, but prisoners of inadequate support and backup services, a result of the low value our society places on the lives of the severely disabled and/or terminally ill.

Arguments of this sort can be found in the disability-rights movement,[22] a source of progressive opinion that seems to have had no effect on the Philosophers' Brief.[23] But an obvious reply here is that even given excellent backup services, some people will find life with Lou Gehrig's disease bearable (and even enjoyable) and some will not. This is plausible, but it is also plausible that some people will prefer death to a life sentence in even a humane prison, and even that some widows and widowers will prefer death to living without their beloved spouses.[24] Some disability-rights activists hold that the only drawbacks of disability result from prejudice and discrimination, and that, inherently, "it is . . . good to be disabled."[25] But one does not have to hold such extreme views in order to recognize that allowing assisted suicide for the terminally ill or for the terminally ill and for the severely and permanently disabled, but not for people facing other severe and irremediable misfortunes, involves a systematic devaluation of the lives of the terminally ill or of the terminally ill and the severely and permanently disabled.

DESIRE NOT TO BE A "BURDEN"

A popular figure in popular culture, as well as in contemporary medical ethics, is the terminally ill person who would rather die quickly than linger to be a burden to his family.[26] Although some writers oppose legalizing assisted suicide on the grounds that legalization may lead to pressure to bow out quickly, others of course disagree. The most prominent grounds for such disagreement fall into two categories.

First, some writers hold that, as Marcia Angell puts it, "Admittedly, overburdened families or cost-conscious doctors might pressure vulnerable patients to request suicide, but similar wrongdoing is at least as likely in the case of withdrawing life-sustaining treatment. . . . Yet there is no evidence of widespread abuse" of the latter sort.[27] But this overlooks the evidence disability-rights groups and other sources offer.[28] Moreover, as David Velleman points out, having the option of ending one's life can harm the patient even if no one is actively pressuring him to use it. The option may create a generally pressured climate where patients feel the need to justify their decisions to go on living.[29] I will not try to settle here whether, given existing healthcare conditions, legalizing physician-assisted suicide would be likely to do patients overall more harm than good. As I have indicated, this essay has the limited scope of arguing that if physician-assisted suicide is to be legalized, it should be legalized for all competent adults, not just for the terminally ill or for the terminally ill and the severely and permanently disabled. And clearly, the danger of pressure toward suicide is apt to be much greater with the terminally ill and the severely and permanently disabled than with the able-bodied and healthy.

But there is another response to the claim that legalizing suicide assistance might lead to pressure on patients to request it in order to avoid being a burden to their families. This is the view that such a motivation would not be a bad thing—or, at least, would not be something that the state should interfere with. Here is how the Philosophers' Brief disposes of the risk "that a patient will be unduly influenced [to request suicide assistance] by considerations that the state might deem it not in his best interests to be swayed by, for example, the feelings and views of close family members."[30]

[W]hat a patient regards as proper grounds for [deciding to request suicide assistance] . . . reflects . . . the judgments of personal ethics—of why his life is important and what affects its value—that patients have a crucial liberty interest in deciding for themselves. Even people who are dying have a right to . . . if they wish, act on what others might wish to tell or suggest or even hint to them, and it would be dangerous to suppose that a state may prevent this on the ground that it knows better than its citizens when they should . . . yield to particular advice or suggestions. . . . It is not a good reply that some people may not decide as they really wish—as they would decide, for example, if free from the "pressure" of others. That possibility could hardly justify the most serious pressure of all—the criminal law which tells them that they may not decide for death if they need the help of a doctor in dying, no matter how firmly they wish it.[31]

This overlooks Velleman's sort of point that, even on the nonpaternalistic assumption that patients will always make the right decision, they may be made worse off simply by having the option of physician-assisted suicide. The presence of this option may cause families to treat patients differently, and in any case, this option deprives patients of the option of staying alive *without* explicitly choosing to do so and being seen as choosing to do so, and thus without having to justify their decisions to stay alive.[32] Whether losing this latter option would be worse on the whole for patients than lacking the option of physician-assisted suicide needs far more discussion, both philosophical and empirical, than the Philosophers' Brief provides. The Philosophers' Brief claims that the number of terminally ill people who correctly believe it would be in their best interest to die but who could not get suicide assistance under a blanket prohibition against it "would undoubtedly be . . . vastly greater" than the number of people who would "mistakenly" get suicide assistance under the system the brief advocates.[33] But the brief gives no good reason to believe this far-from-obvious claim.

The Philosophers' Brief's view about patients' lives and families' burdens is, by current standards, relatively mild. John Hardwig holds a harsher view, that sometimes sick people have a *duty* to die (including a duty to commit suicide) in order to avoid burdening their families. Such a view would not automatically preclude Velleman's sorts of concerns. One might fear that the legalization of assisted suicide would lead to pressure on patients to end their lives even when the burden on their families was not great enough to "justify" this. But Hardwig's conception of what constitutes an intolerable family burden seems amazingly weak. He mentions living "with a spouse who is increasingly distant, uncommunicative, unresponsive, foreign, and unreachable," as well as that "[f]or a young person, the chance to go to college may be lost to the attempt to pay debts due to an illness in the family," and that "there is no opportunity to go out to see friends and the home is no longer a place suitable for having friends in."[34] He also offers a detailed discussion of the question of whether a person with a duty to die should carry out his own suicide or solicit suicide assistance from his loving family or from doctors.[35]

Hardwig's views invite obvious objections. Should being distant, uncommunicative, and unresponsive really be a capital offense anywhere, let alone in a "loving" family? Does a loving family really welcome a beloved member's suicide in order to keep a young person from having to work (and borrow) his way through college? Hardwig's views also illustrate how communitarianism, a movement that bills itself as humane, can have ruthless implications for the old and ill. Rather than recognizing the old and ill as citizens with a right to healthcare, communitarianism can be used to argue that the costs of keeping such people alive are not worth it to the "family" or "community" (i.e., to its younger and/or healthier members). Paradoxically, this would give communitarianism just the sort of brutal consequence for which individualism is often condemned—the consequence that the weak get winnowed out. Hardwig says that "[w]e fear death too much."[36] But to the extent that his views are widespread, I think that what we fear too much is the possibility of being burdened by the dependence of our sick and disabled loved ones—loved ones who are accordingly apt to be endangered if assisted suicide is made legal.

Both the views of Hardwig and of the Philosophers' Brief also raise a problem that elsewhere I have called "the paradox of the selfless invalid."[37] That is, either the patient's loved ones want him to die quickly in order to save money or otherwise make their lives easier, or they do not. If they do not, the patient does them no favor by ending his life for their sake. If they do, why is the patient sacrificing what would otherwise be left of his life for people who love him so little that they value his life less than money or freedom from encumbrance? Wouldn't a truly loving family find such a sacrifice appalling? Of course, families can have mixed feelings, which include both the desire to have the patient stay alive and the self-interested desire to get it all over with and to keep expenses down.[38] But the basic point remains. Decent and loving families, as part of their decency and lovingness, will recognize the latter desire as ignoble and, on balance, will not want patients to pander to it.

A possible exception here, pointed out by Donna Harvey in discussion, might be a case involving an old couple, both of whom have medical problems, but only one of whom is terminally ill, and where the couple's life's savings would be exhausted by medical care for the terminal one, leaving nothing for the ongoing medical needs of the other. But this is a far cry from a case involving a "loving" wife who would welcome her "beloved" husband's suicide in order to spare her the burden of living with a spouse who is distant, uncommunicative, and unresponsive.

Another objection, offered by Joseph Goldfarb in discussion, is as follows. Suppose that the motivation of the selfless invalid is paternalistic; i.e., suppose the invalid is choosing suicide in order to promote what he takes to be his family's long-term welfare, even though he knows that such a sacrifice goes against his family's wishes. Goldfarb offers the case of a terminally ill patriarch whose whole adult life has been dedicated to providing for his family and insuring their financial security and position in the community. Such a patriarch may think he is benefiting his family by forgoing an extra month of life that would use up his family's savings, even if he is aware that his family disagrees. But this case invites the question of when it is appropriate to override other people's wishes because of what you take to be their own good. Clearly, such paternalism can be justified with respect to the irrational or unwise desires of one's own small children. It may also at times be justifiable when dealing with grossly irrational desires of adults with impaired judgment. But there is nothing inherently irrational about loving one's husband or father enough to value his life above money and social standing. There is nothing inherently irrational about being appalled at the prospect of financial security and social position that are bought at the price of an extra month of a beloved husband or father's life. A truly loving (or even minimally decent) family values each member as an end in himself, not as a means to money and social position. A man who paternalistically overrides his loving family's wishes in this regard insults them by showing a lack of respect for their love for him—as a beloved family member, not as a meal ticket—and for the role this love plays in their life.

Of course, this argument cuts both ways. The family that opposes the patriarch's beneficent desire to end his life is also behaving paternalistically toward him. It is tempting to say, once again, that the point is not what any medical ethicist thinks is a good reason to end one's life, but what each patient thinks. But what would the authors of the Philosophers' Brief say about a healthy young man who has a strong, stable, and longstanding desire to kill himself because he thinks his life insurance will be more valuable to his family than he is?[39] People who endorse legalizing assisted suicide in this case because they regard this decision about "why [one's] life is important and what affects its value" as being on a par with the decision of a terminally ill or severely and permanently disabled person who requests suicide assistance in order to avoid burdening his family are genuinely advocating autonomy. Those who favor legalizing suicide assistance only in the latter case, however, are using a double standard that devalues the lives of the severely and permanently disabled and/or terminally ill.

So far, the thrust of this essay has been to argue that position 2 that I sketched at the beginning is morally untenable. But I have not tried to decide between positions 1 and 3. Each has a respectable philosophical outlook behind it. Many ethicists have defended position 3.[40]

Position 1, however, deserves more consideration than it has received. Position 1 is the true expression of the notions of privacy and autonomy. After all, our society allows its adult members to engage in all sorts of risky and potentially lethal activities: race-car driving, jumping across the Snake River canyon on a motorcycle, hanggliding.[41] We allow people to assist others who engage in such activities. We do not require the participants to undergo counseling or psychological assessment to prove their rationality.[42] Why not treat suicide the same way?

Daniel Callahan offers one possible answer, the answer that there is something inherently wrong with an individual's seeking that much control over his own death.[43] But this invites an obvious reply. If you are not supposed to control your own death, who or what is? God? This answer cannot be a basis for law in a secular society. The vicissitudes of nature? Then why take antibiotics or get yourself vaccinated? Other people? Well, whose life is it, anyway? Callahan's lack of respect for individual choice about one's own life and death makes his views unsuitable as a basis for law in a pluralistic society, although the considerations stressed by Velleman, Kamisar and disability-rights groups make me wary of position 1 as well. My aim in this essay, however, has been simply to undermine position 2.[44]

NOTES

1. Although Yale Kamisar and some disability-rights groups seem more sympathetic to position 1 than to position 2, the thrust of their arguments is to oppose any legalization of assisted suicide, rather than to offer position 1 as a serious contender. See the amicus brief of Not Dead Yet and ADAPT (*Vacco V. Quill*, and *State of Washington* v. *Glucksberg*, October 1995). See also Yale Kamisar, "Against Assisted Suicide—Even a Very Limited Form," *University of Detroit Mercy Law Review* 72 (4) (1995): 735–69; "Physician-Assisted Suicide: The Last Bridge to Active Voluntary Euthanasia," in John Keown, ed., *Euthanasia Examined* (Cambridge: Cambridge University Press, 1995), pp. 225–60; "The Reasons So Many People Support Physician-Assisted Suicide—And Why These Reasons Are Not Convincing," *Issues in Law and Medicine* 12 (2) (1996): 113–31, and "The 'Right to Die': On Drawing (and Erasing) Lines," *Duquesne Law Review* 35 (1) (1996): 481–521.

2. Mireya Navarro, "Assisted Suicide Decision Looms in Florida," *New York Times*, July 3, 1997, A14.

3. All the references cited in note 1 raise this question. See also Leon Kass and Nelson Lund, "Courting Death: Assisted Suicide, Doctors, and the Law," *Commentary* 100 (December 1996): 23.

4. Jane Brody, "Personal Health" column, *New York Times*, June 18, 1997. See also H. M. Chochinov, et al., "Desire for Death in the Terminally Ill," *American Journal of Psychiatry* 152 (8) (1995): 1185–91.

5. Kamisar, "Against Assisted Suicide—Even a Very Limited Form," 740–41.

6. Jane Gross, "Quiet Doctor Finds a Mission in Assisted Suicide Case," *New York Times*, January 2, 1997, p. B1.

7. R. Dworkin, et al., "Assisted Suicide: The Philosophers' Brief," *New York Review of Books,* March 27, 1997, p. 44.

8. Incontinence underpants, available in any drug store.

9. For criticisms of the view that human dignity requires youth, health, able-bodiedness, and independence, see my "No, Thanks, I Don't Want to Die With Dignity," op-ed, *Providence Journal-Bulletin,* April 19, 1990; and "Goldilocks and Mrs. Ilych: A Critical Look at the 'Philosophy of Hospice,'" *Cambridge Quarterly of Healthcare Ethics* 6 (1997): 318; as well as J. David Velleman, "Against the Right to Die," *The Journal of Medicine and Philosophy* 17 (1992): 666–67.

10. Dworkin, introduction to "Assisted Suicide: The Philosophers' Brief," p. 41.

11. See Linda Greenhouse, "Before the Court, the Sanctity of Life and Death," *New York Times,* January 5, 1997, p. 5. As I have argued elsewhere, since hospices also eschew life-prolonging treatment for the terminally ill, the National Hospice Organization seems committed to an arbitrary "Goldilocks Principle" for the terminally ill, holding that "death by assisted suicide is too soon, death after high-tech life-prolonging treatment is too late, [but] 'natural' death is just right, [even though] hospices do not eschew intervention through technology or other forms of human ingenuity in other areas" ("Goldilocks and Mrs. Ilych: A Critical Look at the 'Philosophy of Hospice,'" 317). For further critical treatment of the hospice approach to death and dying, see my short story, "Flourish Your Heart in This World," in M. Nussbaum and C. Sunstein, eds., *Clones and Clones: Facts and Fantasies About Human Cloning* (New York: Norton, 1998), pp. 312–33.

12. B. Menard and C. Perrone, *Hospice Care: An Introduction and Review of the Evidence* (Arlington, VA: National Hospice Organization, 1994), p. 4. The term "philosophy of hospice" is theirs.

13. Yale Kamisar stresses this sort of point in "Against Assisted Suicide—Even a Very Limited Form," 744–45.

14. R. Dworkin, introduction to "Assisted Suicide: The Philosophers' Brief," *New York Review of Books,* March 27, 1997, p. 41.

15. Ibid.

16. Ibid.

17. Ibid.

18. Dworkin, et al., "Assisted Suicide: The Philosopher's Brief," pp. 46–47. Note that the formulations in these two quoted passages need improvement. The crucial issue can hardly be simply whether "one day" or "later" (for how long?) the patient would be glad he was forced to stay alive. What if he is glad for only one day out of thousands—or for only five minutes?

19. While we are on the subject of quality of life, let me suggest that the reader's own quality of life will be immeasurably increased if he reads *Le Morte D'Arthur.*

20. Gerald S. Goldstein, "How to Live," *Brown Alumni Monthly,* March 1996, p. 32.

21. Ibid.

22. For example, psychologist and disability-rights activist Carol Gill claims that, "In the vast majority of cases, when a severely disabled person persists in wanting to die, there is an identifiable problem in the support system" (Mary Johnson, "Unanswered Questions," *The Disability Rag,* September/October 1990, p. 17). See also the ADAPT/Not Dead Yet brief. Surprisingly, however, some (although definitely not all) disability-rights activists do not apply such considerations to the terminally ill, but instead write as though suicide can be reasonable for the terminally ill, but not for the severely and permanently disabled. For examples, see Anne Peters, "A Misunderstood Case," *The Disability Rag,* February/March 1984, pp. 9–10 and Kathi Wolfe, "Death—Take a Holiday," *The Disability Rag,* January/February 1994. For criticisms of this double standard for the severely and permanently disabled and the terminally ill, see my letter to the editor, ibid. (July/August 1994), as well as the letter from Wesley J. Smith, ibid. (March/April 1995).

23. This oversight is also found in *Life's Dominion,* by Ronald Dworkin, one of the signatories to the Philosophers' Brief and the author of its introduction. Although he respects people like Stephen Hawking, who live happily with severe disability, Dworkin approvingly cites the case of quadriplegic Nancy B., who successfully sued to have her respirator turned off because, as she put it, "The only thing I have is television and looking at the walls. It's enough. It's been two and a half years…." (Ronald Dworkin, *Life's Dominion,* (New York: Knopf, 1993), p. 184. It is remarkable that this prominent liberal does not even mention that Nancy B.'s having nothing to do but look at the walls or watch television is a result not of her disability but of her lacking the sort of backup services readily available to Stephen Hawking. Nor does Dworkin's book suggest the life-ending option for people whose poverty makes life unbearable by their standards. His book's use of the word "vegetable" for comatose people further betrays his readiness to devalue the lives of the ill and disabled. Even more surprisingly, Yale Kamisar, who generally shows great respect for the lives of the terminally ill and/or severely disabled, approvingly quotes Jed Rubenfield's claim that denying patients the right to terminate life supports would force them into "a particular, all-consuming, totally dependent, and indeed rigidly standardized life: the life of one confined to a hospital bed" (Kamisar, "The Reasons So Many People Support Physician-Assisted Suicide—And Why These Reasons Are Not Convincing," p. 126). This grim description does not fit the life of Stephen Hawking, the Providence editor described above, or many other severely disabled respirator-users who have adequate backup services. But I am not claiming that a ban on physician assistance in removing life supports would be as defensible as a ban on physician-assisted suicide. For some relevant differences, see Ibid., 120–28.

24. The example about widows and widowers echoes a question from the ADAPT/Not Dead Yet Brief.

25. Disability-rights activist Cyndi Jones, as quoted in Joseph Shapiro, *No Pity* (New York: Times Books, 1993), p. 12.

26. For example, see Steven Erlanger, "A Scholar's Suicide: Trying to Spare a Family Anguish," *New York Times,* October 26, 1987, p. B1, which admiringly recounts the suicide of seventy-five-year-old Richard Schlatter, who committed suicide because he wanted to spare his family the burden of coping with his terminal illness. See also my letter to the editor, November 4, 1987.

27. Marcia Angell, "The Supreme Court and Physician-Assisted Suicide—The Ultimate Right," *New England Journal of Medicine,* 336 (January 2, 1997): 52. See also The Philosophers' Brief, pp. 45–46 [Appendix B], as well as Bioethicists' Brief Supporting Respondents, *Vacco* v. *Quill* and State of *Washington* v. *Glucksberg.*

28. See the ADAPT/Not Dead Yet Brief, as well as the references in my "Goldilocks and Mrs. Ilych: A Critical Look at the 'Philosophy of Hospice,'" notes 21, 61, and 62. See also Ann Hood, "Rage Against the Dying of the Light," op-ed, *New York Times,* August 2, 1997.

29. See Velleman, "Against the Right to Die." (His view have some complexities that I am not addressing.)

30. Dworkin, et al., "The Philosophers' Brief," p. 46.

31. Ibid. Note that the first occurrence of the word "pressure" in this passage is in double quotes, suggesting remarkably, that such pressure is always merely alleged rather than real. (But see ibid., pp. 44 and 45, where the brief does mention the possibility of pressure from relatives.)

32. See Velleman, "Against the Right to Die."

33. Dworkin, et al., "The Philosophers' Brief," p. 46.

34. John Hardwig, "Is There a Duty to Die?" *Hastings Center Report* 27 (2) (March/April 1997): 36.

35. John Hardwig, "Dying at the Right Time: Reflections on (Un)assisted Suicide," in H. LaFollette (ed.), *Ethics in Practice* (Cambridge, MA: Blackwell, 1997), pp. 53–65.

36. Hardwig, "Is There a Duty to Die?" p. 40.

37. Ackerman, "Goldilocks and Mrs. Ilych: A Critical Look at the 'Philosophy of Hospice,'" p. 318. See also my "The Forecasting Game," in W. Abrahams, ed., *Prize Stories 1990: The O. Henry Awards* (New York: Doubleday, 1990), pp. 318–19, and my letter to the editor *New York Times*, November 4, 1987.

38. I owe this point to Sara Ann Ketchum.

39. Yale Kamisar offers another possibility, the case of "a healthy septuagenarian, who has struggled to overcome the hardships of poverty all his life [and] wants to assure that his two grandchildren have a better life than he did. So he decides he will sell his heart for $500,000 and arrange to have a trust fund established for his grandchildren" ("The Reasons So Many People Support Physician-Assisted Suicide—And Why These Reasons Are Not Convincing," 114). "But would 'society' allow this transaction to take place?" Kamisar asks, answering, "I think not." (Ibid.) While I think he is correct, I consider the case less clear-cut than the one I offer. There is so much ageism in our society that I suspect there are people who would object to sacrificial suicide in my case of a healthy young person but who would admire it in

Kamisar's case of the septuagenarian grandfather. See also Kamisar, "The 'Right to Die'—On Drawing and Erasing Lines," note 116, p. 507–508.

40. For example, see the Kamisar references in note 1 here, as well as Daniel Callahan, *What Kind of Life?* (New York: Simon and Shuster, 1990), and Kass and Lund, "Courting Death: Assisted Suicide, Doctors, and the Law."

41. See Dworkin, *Life's Dominion*, p. 222–24.

42. Positions 1 and 2 have variants, depending on whether such safeguards as counseling waiting periods, proof of rationality, etc. would be required of those seeking suicide assistance from physicians. Space limitations prevent me from discussing these issues in detail here. But it is worth noting two objections to requiring counseling or even certification of rationality by a therapist, beyond such basic competence tests as giving consistent answers to questions like "Do you want suicide assistance?" and "Do you want to stay alive?" First, such a requirement would give therapists enormous power over people's lives. Second, judgments of rationality in this context seem particularly subject to therapists' own ideologies about suicide. Is it really likely that disability-rights psychologist Carol Gill (quoted in note 22, above) and a therapist who favors assisted suicide will agree about a severely and permanently disabled person's underlying rationality in requesting suicide assistance?

43. Callahan, *What Kind of Life?*, chapter 8.

44. I thank James Dreier, Joseph Goldfarb, Donna Harvey, Sara Ann Ketchum, Thomasine Kushner, Lynn Pasquerella, and James Van Cleve for helpful discussions of this material.

Why Gender Matters to the Euthanasia Debate: On Decisional Capacity and the Rejection of Women's Death Requests

Jennifer A. Parks

The euthanasia debate has typically addressed the tension between patient autonomy and physician obligations. Where physician-assisted suicide and active euthanasia are concerned, ethicists balance a patient's request to die against both the physician's role as healer and her duty of nonmaleficence. The physician is seen to be in a moral dilemma in which her commitments to healing and saving lives conflict with her commitment to serving her patients' needs, respecting their autonomy, and maintaining their trust. The focal question for ethical debate has thus been: how much should patient autonomy govern the practices of physician-assisted suicide and active euthanasia?

Such questions are too narrowly formulated because they fail to address the background conditions that may affect a patient's death request. Besides individual agency, we must take into account the ways gender roles and social circumstances affect patients' requests to die, and the way those requests are received by our culture. Feminist approaches raise such contextual and cultural

questions, yet there is little available feminist literature on physician-assisted suicide and euthanasia. Although feminists are concerned about the cultural context within which women make medical decisions, they have primarily focused on women's reproductive decisions; only recently have feminist bioethicists turned to issues beyond reproduction.

Susan Wolf offers one of the few feminist treatments to date of euthanasia. She argues that women are more likely to request euthanasia and physician-assisted suicide in an attempt to avoid burdening their families—a perversion of the feminine ethic of care that takes women's caring for and about others to the extreme—and that physicians are simultaneously more likely to fulfill women's death requests, based on "the same historical valorization of women's self-sacrifice and the same background sexism."[1] In a culture that valorizes their altruism and caring for others, women who suffer from severe pain or terminal illness may perceive themselves as failing in their appointed duties; unable to care for others,

Parks, Jennifer A. "Why Gender Matters to the Euthanasia Debate: On Decisional Capacity and the Rejection of Women's Death Requests," *Hastings Center Report* 30:1 (2000), 30–36. Copyright © 2000. Reprinted by permission of The Hastings Center.

they may see themselves as actually burdening them. For Wolf, the authenticity and rationality of a woman's request to die seems suspect at the very least, given the extent to which cultural expectations about not burdening others have likely affected her. Indeed, Wolf chastens physicians "not to accede to the request for assisted suicide and euthanasia" for this very reason (p. 308).

Wolf also discusses the unequal social conditions that may encourage women to seek death, such as poverty, higher incidences of depression, poor pain relief, lack of good medical care, and poor social support networks—essential topics in any ethical analysis of physician-assisted suicide and active euthanasia. While other feminists have shared these concerns for women's social conditions, Wolf is the first to relate them to the issue of euthanasia. Her analysis thus ushers in important theoretical and practical concerns regarding women's death requests and their implementation.

I have isolated Wolf as an influential feminist voice because she brings depth to a debate that has, until recently, focused almost exclusively on the issue of patient autonomy. I suggest, however, that Wolf's reasoning may actually lead to very different conclusions. While some women in particular can exhibit a preoccupation with and overemphasis on relationships, terminally ill women's death requests can also, like men's, stem from basic personal concerns for pain, psychic suffering, and the determination that their lives have become meaningless or burdensome to them. In taking Wolf's feminist account seriously, I suggest that women's requests to die may be discounted, trivialized, and ignored for the same reasons that Wolf claims they are too likely to be heeded. By virtue of the expectation that women will be altruistic, self-abnegating caregivers, women's own voices, and their claims to autonomy in requesting death, are easily dismissed. I conclude that women's choices, their capacity to reason, and their ability to accurately represent their own interests are undermined in our culture and as a consequence that women's claims to pain and suffering are often disregarded. Yet in cases of intolerable pain and suffering, a woman's request to die should not be questioned on the grounds that she is incapable of determining her own good; women, like men, should be extended the right to decide when their life is burdensome, meaningless, and no longer worth living.

SOME BACKGROUND

Both in Canada and the United States there has been growing support for social policies that would legalize active euthanasia and physician-assisted suicide. This increasing support is not surprising given North Americans' commitment to an individualistic ethic: the primary focus, socially, politically, and medically, is on the individual, and the protection of his or her autonomy. Ethicists are also primarily concerned with the individual and his rights: their debates largely concern the conflict between patient and physician and how to navigate the tensions between these two parties and their conflicting goals. For example, Dan Brock argues that the patient has a right to choose active euthanasia or physician-assisted suicide because, "If self-determination is a fundamental value, then the great variability among people on this question makes it especially important that individuals control the manner, circumstances, and timing of their dying and death."[2]

Conversely, arguments against euthanasia have also taken the individual's self-governance to be the main issue. Gay-Williams argues against euthanasia on the ground that, "Because death is final and irreversible, euthanasia contains within it the possibility that we will work against our own interest if we practice it or allow it to be practiced on us."[3] Plainly, traditional liberal concerns for protecting individual autonomy remain the primary focus of debates over euthanasia.

Autonomy is valued in a liberal society because it secures the interest that each citizen has in directing her life; it dominates liberal theories because self-government is an essential feature of a nonoppressive society. Autonomy is a cornerstone of the euthanasia debate because our interest in directing our own lives has special force when it comes to determining our mode and time of death. The choice of how and when to die is indeed a deeply personal decision. As Wolf critically states,

> Advocacy of physician-assisted suicide and euthanasia has hinged to a great extent on rights claims. The argument is that the patient has a right of self-determination or autonomy that entitles her to assistance in suicide or euthanasia. The strategy is to extend the argument that self-determination entitles the patient to refuse unwanted life-sustaining treatment by maintaining that the same rationale supports patient entitlement to more active physician assistance in death. Indeed, it is sometimes argued that there is no principled difference between termination of life-sustaining treatment and more active practices.[4]

On the autonomy model, if the rights-bearer asserts her right to die, then the appropriate response is to secure her death. And while this model intends the positive goal of individuals pursuing their own good as they see fit, the liberal conception of the individual as a rational, independent, rights-bearing agent choosing her own time and mode of death is impoverished. By contrast, a feminist approach to the euthanasia debate regards women's experiences in a gendered culture as relevant to determinations regarding the legitimacy of their death requests.

THE IMPORTANCE OF CONTEXT

The demand for euthanasia, and the interaction between the patient requesting death and the physician considering the request, is largely understood as a private matter. Timothy Quill, for example, relates a case involving Diane, a patient who is dying of cancer and who is requesting his assistance in securing a painless death. He entitles this case "Death and Dignity: A Case of Individualized Decision-Making."[5] But feminist ethicists argue that practices like active euthanasia and physician-assisted suicide are not merely cases of individualized decisionmaking: such individual decisions are made within a social context that informs and affects individuals' choices. Thus, unlike liberal accounts of the self, feminist approaches view the individual as a socially embedded, interdependent, relational subject whose choices are made within a complex web of social relationships. Where the euthanasia debate is concerned, the situated subject is not an isolatable, independent, atomistic subject: her choice to die has implications for both self and society, and her choices can be either upheld or undermined by the prevailing social ethos.[6]

That gender matters where physician-assisted suicide and active euthanasia are concerned is contentious. The individual expression of autonomy is held to be a right in which we all share an objective, equal interest. Thus the particular features of a patient's life are considered irrelevant once we have determined that her choices are unconstrained by coercion, irrationality, ignorance, or the limited options available to her. But here a feminist account of euthanasia departs from traditional liberal accounts; feminists assert that deep social inequalities affect individual agents in ways not recognized on traditional liberal approaches to autonomy. For example, liberal accounts of euthanasia fail to address the wide-spread sexism that serves to undermine respect for women's choices.

It is imperative that a feminist account of euthanasia consider the feminine ethic of care to which women have been held, an ethic that requires women's unselfish commitment to the nurturance and care of others, especially their husbands, children, and elderly parents. The imperative to care for others—to the point of giving up their sense of self completely—encourages people to dismiss women's self-concerns, and it makes society less willing to consider euthanasia for women. A liberal, rights-based account of euthanasia fails to account for such difficulties because it does not countenance contextual features of this sort. A feminist account, however, can show how sexism may lead to the medical and social rejection of a woman's request for death.

As Wolf indicates, the valorization of women's self-sacrifice and self-abnegation has been criticized by feminist ethicists. Bonnelle Lewis Strickling, for example, argues that women's self-abnegation is such that there is often no "self" beyond their identification with others. Strickling recognizes two forms of self-abnegation: in its virtuous form, it accomplishes a "sympathetic understanding between and among persons" in which both parties' interests and feelings are taken into consideration.[7] In its negative form, the self-abnegator abandons any sense of being a particular self outside of her relationships with others. Self-abnegation in this form demands no less than that women renounce, discount, and deny the self: only if one has no self (or no conception of self) can one commit entirely to the service of others. And service to others is exactly what is expected of women in our culture. As Strickling claims,

> traditionally women have been asked to be helpful, loving without expectation of return, emotionally dependable, supportive, and generally nurturing to both children and husband both physically and in the sense of nurturing their respective senses of self, all without complaining . . . taken together, these expectations comprise the expectation of self-renunciation on an extremely large scale. (p. 197)

Furthermore, women have been held to a feminine ethic of care, a conception of "womanly" virtues according to which it is part of women's moral obligation to care for and nurture others. This feminine ethic is rooted in women's traditional roles of homemaking, child-bearing and rearing, and the care and nurturing activities that accompany these roles.

That "womanly" virtues require caring for and nurturing others to the detriment of women's self-concern relates to my worries about gender and euthanasia. For if women are expected to be deferential to others, self-effacing, and caring to the point of sacrificing their own happiness, then any self-interested and self-directed claims they make (in this case, the request to die) may be more easily discounted or dismissed as irrational. A woman's capacity for reason and self-determination is not validated in our culture (since women have been historically viewed as emotional, not rational, beings); the presence of severe pain or terminal illness may be used as further support for the view that women are particularly incompetent when it comes to making even deeply personal life and death decisions.

For Daniel Callahan, the acceptance of voluntary active euthanasia and physician-assisted suicide minimally requires that the physician fulfilling or denying the patient's request have her own moral grounds for helping (or refusing to help) a patient to die. As Callahan states,

> If doctors, once sanctioned to carry out euthanasia, are to be themselves responsible moral agents—not simply hired hands with lethal injections at the ready—then they must have their own independent moral grounds to kill those who request such services.... The doctor would have to decide, on her own, whether the patient's life was "no longer worth living."[8]

If doctors have their own independent moral grounds for implementing euthanasia then we must question what those moral grounds are and whence they stem. On a feminist account, physicians' values are informed by a social context within which the undermining of women's self-regarding choices has a long history. One might expect physicians' judgments about patient competence to be more objective because of their medical training, but this is not so. Valerie Hartouni has recently offered an account of the subtle ways in which our vision is "trained," "impaired," and "partial." What we see, and the way we see it, is not merely a physiological event or a mechanical process, but is learned. As she claims, "Seeing is an act of immense construction.... Seeing is a set of learned practices and processes that allow us to organize the visual field and that engage us in producing the world we seem to greet and take in only passively."[9] On this account, our view of euthanasia, and those who have a legitimate claim to it, is not objectively determined, but is strongly influenced by the pre-organized world through which our social and ethical vision is trained. The apparent illegitimacy of a woman's claim to euthanasia is effected by a social world in which her voice is silenced and her capacity for self- or other-regarding choices is questioned.

So a physician's moral grounds for rejecting euthanasia or physician-assisted suicide will—at least partially—reflect a social refusal to acknowledge the legitimacy of such feelings of burdensomeness and meaninglessness in a culture that denies women's competency. Not only does our culture view women as self-abnegating caregivers who lack reason and autonomy: physicians discount or dismiss women's reasoning capacity and ability to govern themselves, making it easier for them to reject women's death requests. For determining that a patient's life has become "meaningless" or "burdensome" involves making a value judgment that, like most value judgments, reflects dominant cultural prejudices, among them (in our society) the assumption that women are primarily nurturers and caregivers who lack the competency to self-govern. That a man may experience his life as "meaningless" or "burdensome" is considered a rational self-evaluation so long as his life is marked by intolerable pain, personal suffering, or terminal illness. But women's similar experiences are much more likely to be rejected, discounted, or unheeded because their capacity for such determinations of personal suffering are questioned. Perhaps, as Kathryn Morgan claims, the denial of women's full moral agency stems from the view that, "simply by virtue of their embodiment as women, women just are closer to nature and, hence, not capable of the kind of thought that is necessary for human moral life."[10]

FURTHER CONSIDERATIONS

I have offered some theoretical worries about the background inequalities that lead doctors to discount or dismiss women's death requests. These worries lead in the opposite direction of Wolf's concerns that women are more likely to be euthanized in our gendered society.

Wolf's feminist account is also not supported by strong empirical evidence, although, as she points out, research on gender and euthanasia remains in its infancy.[11] Until we have strong empirical data relating to gender and euthanasia, and given that the theory alone can lead in different directions, we have equally good reason to suppose that women's legitimate death requests (that is, requests stemming from experiences of intolerable pain, human suffering, and negative experiences of terminal illness) are likely to go unheeded.

In support of her women-at-risk thesis Wolf cites the case of Dr. Jack Kevorkian, an American pathologist who has helped a preponderance of women to die, and the recent data from the Netherlands that has been collected from the Dutch experience with euthanasia. Kevorkian helped eight women to die before fulfilling a man's death request. That a large number of Kevorkian's "patients" have been women is telling on Wolf's account: Kevorkian may be acting out a cultural stereotype that demands women's commitment to caregiving and that rejects women's claims to be cared for in times of sickness or terminal illness. Kevorkian's actions are particularly heinous, then, when placed in the context of women's traditional role expectations as caregivers, nurturers, and self-abnegators.

Like Wolf, I have concerns about Kevorkian's actions and the context within which he is helping people to die. The demand for Kevorkian arises because individuals are not receiving help from a trusted physician in securing their deaths. Kevorkian-esque deaths do not derive from a longstanding relationship with one's physician. On the contrary, what the Kevorkian deaths indicate is not that women in particular are at a high risk of being put to death, but that social conditions for a socially accepted, dignified death through physician-assisted suicide or active euthanasia do not obtain, either at home or in care facilities. Kevorkian's practice does not provide evidence of a widespread social bias in favor of killing women; rather, his actions are witness to the sad position into which both women and men who are seeking death are placed.

Furthermore, the Dutch data that support her women-at-risk thesis are problematic; Wolf indicates that available data from the Netherlands are not decisive and may not be generalizable to the United States. Nevertheless, Wolf argues that the Dutch data indicate a slightly greater percentage of women than men being euthanized, and that we ought to be concerned about the difference since "the differences in Dutch demographics and health care would be reasons to expect no gender differential in the Netherlands in the practices we are examining" (p. 296). Given the differences in health care systems and demographics between the two counties, however, we can draw no conclusions from the Dutch data that would be relevant to the context of the United States. Furthermore, the Dutch data in fact neither support nor undermine Wolf's claim.

Wolf is justified in her concern that gender role socialization and ubiquitous cultural stereotypes may lead women to define themselves—and be defined by others—according to their caregiving role. Yet she errs in concluding that women are therefore more likely than men to have their death requests fulfilled when they are terminally ill or suffering and no longer capable of fulfilling their care-giving duties. On the contrary, a woman's death request—based as it is on her own knowledge claims and experiences of her own pain and suffering—is more easily dismissed. Evidence both inside and outside the medical arena indicates that women's knowledge claims and their claims to self-concern tend to be denied, not (as Wolf argues) too easily upheld. This evidence stems from a variety of sources; and while the data is not entirely conclusive, it suggests that for social reasons, physicians are less likely to heed women's death requests than those made by men.

Our social rejection of women's knowledge has a long history, a history too long to account for in this paper. But consider an early indicator that a female's attempts at independence and independent thinking is socially rejected: the American classroom. A report by Myra and David Sadker indicates that as early as preschool, sexism prevails in the classroom. As they note in their survey of studies done on classroom dynamics,

> teachers gave boys more attention, praised them more often and were at least twice as likely to have extended conversations with them.... [T]eachers were twice as likely to give male students detailed instructions on how to do things for themselves. With female students, teachers were more likely to do it for them instead. The result was that boys learned to become independent, girls learned to become dependent.[12]

The import of such a study is difficult to overestimate. It addresses a concern that feminists have been voicing for a very long time: that women's knowledge, independence, and self-promotion are systemically undermined in our culture. From an early age females are denied the opportunity to think and act independently. It would be unsurprising, then, if later in their lives women's death requests, which would be based on their own perspectives and experiences, were rejected because they were denied the capacity to make such determinations.

Consider also the case of abortion, where women's decisional capacity, their right to self-regarding choices, and their personal experiences have been questioned. Arguments against a woman's right to abortion turn on her alleged moral responsibility for others and her incapacity for rational decisionmaking at a time of great distress. Both nonfeminists and pro-life feminists alike have argued that pregnant women are not entitled to consider only themselves as the subjects of concern: they are chided to place their families, their communities, and in particular their fetuses at the center of their moral deliberations. In the case of abortion, we again see a cultural predilection for imposing an other-oriented ethic on women that is not extended to men: a woman's right to make a self-regarding decision based on her own experiences (for example, her claim that she cannot financially or emotionally support a child at this particular time) comes under heavy attack. As Sidney Callahan claims, "A woman, involuntarily pregnant, has a moral obligation to the now-existing fetus whether she explicitly consented to its existence or not."[13]

In addition, critics of abortion argue that a pregnant woman has questionable decisionmaking capacities and should not be the final arbiter of her own good. Again, to quote Callahan, "It also seems a travesty of just procedures that a pregnant woman now, in effect, acts as the sole judge of her own case under the most stressful conditions". (p. 13).

Commentators on the abortion debate have perverted the ethic of care in order to deny women the right to place their interests ahead of others and to have their decisions respected. A woman's knowledge about her body, her financial situation, her social context, and her own emotional state—knowledge claims that find counterparts in the claims made by terminally ill women requesting death—are dismissed or discounted.

Even women's reports of coronary pain have, until fairly recently, been dismissed as being "all in their heads," resulting in many unnecessary deaths because of late detection of heart disease. Indeed, coronary research (like most other medical research) has targeted white men to the serious detriment of women. Heart disease has historically been understood as a man's affliction, and with physicians guiding their thinking on the subject, women have misunderstood their own symptoms. Since there has been little study of women's own particular experiences with heart disease, their reported symptoms have gone largely unrecognized. Instead, women's knowledge about their condition, their experiences of symptoms, and their request for medical attention tend to be rejected, and their complaints set aside as hyperbole or attributed to emotional causes.[14] If this conception of women is operating in the area of heart disease, one can only imagine how it affects consideration of women's requests to die.

That women have been treated differently from men is borne out by some directly relevant statistics. In a review of "right to die" cases, researchers found that courts honored the death requests of men in 75 percent of reported cases but respected similar requests by women in only 14 percent of reported cases.[15] More recently, the *New England Journal of Medicine* cites a national study of physician-assisted suicide and euthanasia in the United States, according to which men largely outnumber women in receiving undercover prescriptions for lethal doses of medication.[16] The survey reveals that 97 percent of those receiving undercover prescriptions were men, while of those who received an undercover lethal injection—active euthanasia—57 percent were men and 43 percent women. Significantly, in 95 percent of cases in which patients received the means for physician-assisted suicide it was the patient himself who made the request for the prescription (in the remaining 5 percent the request came from a family member or partner); by contrast 54 percent of all active euthanasia requests were made by family members. Such data suggest that in cases of physician-assisted suicide, where the patient characteristically makes the request and terminates his life at a time and place he deems appropriate, men are deemed capable of making such significant choices while women are not. Conversely, in cases of active euthanasia, which usually take place within institutions and are requested by family members, women are far more likely to have death requests fulfilled.[17]

Interestingly, the national survey supports both the thesis that women's death requests are less likely to be heeded than those of men and Wolf's claim that women are typically viewed as "expendable." It is largely when the death request is made *for* women by their family members that the request is fulfilled by physicians. Arguably, when family members request active euthanasia for a kinswoman, the broader society might understand that she is no longer capable of providing the care, nurturing, and self-sacrifice that is expected of women.

DISMISSING SUFFERING

While Wolf's feminist account provides a foundation for a rich ethical analysis of euthanasia, it is not clear that women are more likely than men to be euthanized or extended the means for physician-assisted suicide. Indeed, there is reason to think, and statistical evidence to support the thought, that women are far less likely to be taken seriously, listened to, and supported in their end of life choices than are their male counterparts. While I share Wolf's concern for the way in which the debate over euthanasia and physician-assisted suicide has been decontextualized and governed by an individualistic model, I believe that contextual considerations should lead us to question why women's death requests are taken less seriously and acted on less often than those of men.

Wolf acknowledges that some feminists "will see this problem differently. That may be especially true of women who feel in control of their lives, are less subject to subordination by age or race or wealth, and seek yet another option to add to their many."[18] She makes an important point: contingencies such as poverty, poor education, age, and race are important to a feminist account of euthanasia. But rather than making a woman's death request more likely to be respected, these contingencies make it less so: the less social weight a woman carries, the less likely she is to have her death requests taken seriously. A woman who is white, well educated, articulate, wealthy, or politically powerful is far less likely to be denied decisionmaking capacity than is her uneducated, poor, powerless counterpart. The more a woman is like the autonomous, rational, independent agent that is the traditional focus of the euthanasia debate, the more likely her death request will be taken seriously.

A person's access to euthanasia and physician-assisted suicide should not be affected by conditions over which she has no control: it is alarming to think that in a sexist society, only some members' claims to pain and psychic suffering will be taken seriously.

REFERENCES

1. S. Wolf, "Gender, Feminism, and Death: Physician-Assisted Suicide and Euthanasia," in *Feminism & Bioethics: Beyond Reproduction,* ed. S. Wolf (New York: Oxford University Press, 1996), pp. 282–317, at 284.

2. D. Brock, "Voluntary Active Euthanasia," *Hastings Center Report* 22, no.2 (1992):11–21, at 11.

3. J. Gay-Williams, "The Wrongfulness of Euthanasia," reprinted in *Intervention and Reflection: Basic Issues in Medical Ethics,* ed. Ronald Munson, 5th ed. (Belmont, Calif.: Wadsworth Publishing Co., 1996), pp. 168–71, at 170.

4. See ref. 2, Wolf, "Gender, Feminism, and Death," p. 298.

5. T. Quill, "Death and Dignity: A Case of Individualized Decision-Making," reprinted in *Ethical Issues in Modern Medicine,* ed. J. D. Arras and B. Steinbock, (London: Mayfield Publishing Co., 1991), pp. 292–95.

6. Note, however, that feminists are concerned with both under-contextualizing and over-contextualizing women's lives. While ethicists should not ignore the situational aspects of women's lives, they also should not subordinate women's self-regarding choices to the requirements of maintaining social relationships.

7. B. L. Strickling, "Self-Abnegation," in *Feminist Perspectives: Philosophical Essays on Method and Morals,* ed. C. Overall, L. Code, and S. Mullet (Toronto: University of Toronto Press, 1988), pp. 190–201, at 194.

8. D. Callahan, "When Self-Determination Runs Amok," in *Ethical Issues in Modern Medicine,* ed. J. Arras and B. Steinbock, 4th ed. (London: Mayfield Publishing Co, 1996): 295–309, at 311.

9. V. Hartouni, *Cultural Conceptions: On Reproductive Technologies and the Remaking of Life* (Minneapolis: University of Minnesota Press, 1997), pp. 12–13.

10. K. Morgan, "Women and Moral Madness," in *Feminist Perspectives: Philosophical Essays on Method and Morals,* ed. C. Overall, L. Code, and S. Mullet (Toronto: University of Toronto Press, 1988), pp. 146–67, at 150.

11. See ref. 2, Wolf, "Gender, Feminism, and Death," p. 294.

12. M. Sadker and D. Sadker, "Sexism in the Schoolroom of the '80s," *Psychology Today* 19, no. 3 (1985): 54–57, at 55.

13. S. Callahan, "Abortion and the Sexual Agenda: A Case for Pro-life Feminism," *Commonweal,* 25 April 1986: 9–17, at 15.

14. E. Nechas and D. Foley, *Unequal Treatment: What You Don't Know About How Women are Mistreated by the Medical Community* (New York: Simon & Schuster, 1994), p. 66.

15. S. H. Miles and A. August, "Courts, Gender and the 'Right to Die'," *Journal of Law, Medicine and Health Care* 18 (1990): 85–95.

16. D.E. Meier et al., "A National Survey of Physician-Assisted Suicide and Euthanasia in the United States," *NEJM* 338 (1998): 1193–200.

17. This study also indicates that when patients received a prescription for a lethal dose of medication (that is, the means to implement physician-assisted suicide), 90 percent of lethal prescriptions were given to patients who were at home, and only 5 percent were given to patients in nursing homes. However, in cases of active euthanasia, 99 percent of patients were hospitalized at the time of lethal injection (p. 1197).

18. See ref. 2. Wolf, "Gender, Feminism, and Death," p. 308.

Lessons for Physician-Assisted Suicide from the African-American Experience

Patricia A. King and Leslie E. Wolf

THE INCREASING MEDICALIZATION of death has led to widespread fear that death is unnecessarily prolonged, painful, expensive, and without dignity. This fear has given momentum to the desire of patients to have more control over their dying and to the movement to legalize physician-assisted suicide (PAS) and active voluntary euthanasia (AVE). Others may have a different fear. They may be concerned that their lives are not highly valued in this society and thus fear that they will not have access to life-prolonging treatment or palliative care that for them represents death with dignity. Moreover, many others may not share either of these fears, considering death a "welcome friend" to

be greeted with family or, in any event, a process that is beyond their control. Making sure that all of these voices are heard in the PAS debate is a challenge.

An examination of the African-American patient will expand the array of portraits of patients who face death and worry about dying with dignity. In expanding the images of patients faced with end-of-life decision-making, we enhance our understanding of patients' cultural, religious, and family values and the complexity of decision-making with respect to PAS. Some of these patients will prefer life-prolonging treatment or palliative care. Other patients will not seek access to PAS and AVE because they mistrust healthcare professionals and medical institutions.

Abridged from King, Patricia A., and Wolf, Leslie E. "Lessons for Physician-Assisted Suicide from the African-American Experience," *Physician Assisted Suicide: Expanding the Debate,* Margaret P. Battin, Rosamond Rhodes, and Anita Silvers, eds., New York: Routledge (1998). Copyright © 1998. Reprinted by permission of Copyright Clearance Center on behalf of Taylor & Francis Group LLC.

Yale Kamisar points out that, "[m]any people, understandably, are greatly affected by the heart-wrenching facts of individual cases." There is no doubt that the suffering and anguish of some patients is compelling. Many people identify with these patients and worry that they will find themselves in the same position. We are understandably reluctant to deny interventions that would relieve suffering and bring about desired relief through death. There are also moving stories that point out the dangers of too quickly acceding to requests for physician-assisted suicide and euthanasia. Yet, the portraits of potential victims of PAS and euthanasia have attracted less public attention. John Arras, a philosopher and bioethicist, writes:

> The victims of the current policy are easy to identify: they are on the news, the talk shows, the documentaries, and often on Dr. Kevorkian's roster of so-called "patients." The victims of legalization, by contrast, will be largely hidden from view: they will include the clinically depressed 80-year-old man who could have lived for another year of good quality if only he had been treated; the 50-year-old woman who asks for death because doctors in her financially stretched HMO cannot/will not effectively treat her unrelenting but mysterious pelvic pain; and perhaps eventually, if we slide far enough down the slope, the uncommunicative stroke victim whose distant children deem an earlier death a better death. Unlike Dr. Kevorkian's "patients," these victims will not get their pictures in the paper, but they will have faces and they will all be cheated of good months or perhaps even years.

Most descriptions of potential victims of legalizing PAS, however, fail to include images of members of stigmatized minority groups.

There is evidence that members of groups considered vulnerable have different attitudes about end-of-life treatment than the majority of Americans who support assisting the terminally ill to die. Disparities are greatest, however, in attitudes, values, and beliefs about end-of-life decision-making with racial and ethnic minorities. Studies show that blacks are substantially less likely than whites to support legalization of physician-assisted suicide. Although the support for legalization has increased over time in both groups, the gap in support between blacks and whites persists. There is also evidence that these differences arise in attitudes towards other end-of-life issues such as use of life-prolonging treatment, advance directives and living wills.

Why these substantial gaps in attitudes about end-of-life decision-making exist is not clear. The available evidence indicates that these differences persist even when researchers control for education, age, and socioeconomic status. Possible reasons for this difference in attitude include religious preferences, blacks'

distrust of physicians, medical institutions and the healthcare system generally, and cultural characteristics such as trusting families more than physicians.

Specifically, these differences in attitude towards PAS may reflect differences in black expression of health and illness as well as concerns about death. Not only have African-Americans experienced disrespect for their autonomy, they have suffered injustice in medicine as well as in the broader society. As a group, blacks have been abused, neglected and exploited. They have reason to believe that their lives are not valued in the same way as whites' and rationally perceive that, in their encounters with the healthcare system, they are frequently treated differently solely because of their race. African-Americans have reason to be suspicious of physicians and rightly worry about giving them too much authority. In the medical context, physician paternalism builds on and reinforces ubiquitous race differentials in power and authority. In short, historical and current experiences with American medicine have made African-Americans acutely aware of the difficulty of looking after their own interests because they lack power in the society and in the healthcare system, and in their relationships with physicians.

Ordinary practices, norms, and habits of well-intentioned institutions and professions can result in unjust practices for some groups. Those with power in the society are able to impose their norms, values, and beliefs on those who lack power. The dominant group's ideas, beliefs, and judgments serve to stigmatize and mark other groups as different and deficient. Behaviors and practices of the stigmatized group are often considered unworthy of study or respect.

The myth of white superiority persists and has profoundly affected both whites and blacks. As Professor Charles Lawrence notes, "[w]e do not recognize the ways in which our [shared] cultural experience has influenced our beliefs about race or the occasions on which those beliefs affect our actions." Stereotypes that capture and reflect negative attitudes towards African-Americans flourish and become embedded in the culture to the point where they may not be consciously noticed. Thus, injury frequently is inflicted on blacks without the actors being consciously aware of racial motivation.

It is not only the dominant group, however, that is affected. Negative messages are also absorbed by blacks themselves. Feelings of inferiority and unworthiness are among the psychic injuries inflicted on blacks. As a result, they carry the additional burden of not always appreciating their own worth as human beings. As Herbert Nickens points out, "such stigma is never far from consciousness for minorities and is one of the lenses through which life is perceived."

Although other racial and ethnic groups have separate and distinct experiences with American medicine, an additional reason for examining the African-American experience is that African-Americans are the paradigmatic minority group in this country. They constitute approximately 12 percent of the population. Although they were not willing immigrants and endured slavery and its aftermath of rigid segregation, as people of color they have not been easily assimilated and do not share the Western European heritage and culture of some immigrants. Features of black health experience such as persistent poverty, limited access to healthcare, poorer health status, and low numbers of healthcare professionals are common to other minorities as well.

It is important to reflect on the African-American experience because it offers insights into the nature of society's responsibilities for those who are competent but whose autonomy and well-being may be compromised by historical, social, and cultural forces at work in society itself. Sadly, some individuals are in need of protection because they have been rendered vulnerable by their own society.

AN INHERENT DISTRUST OF MEDICINE

The relationship between blacks and medicine has in the main not been beneficial for blacks. Medicine played a critical role in the development of racial differences that stamped blacks as an inherently inferior people. It provided much of the theory and data that supported beliefs about biological differences observed in differences in skin color, hair appearance, and behavior between blacks and whites and confirmed the superiority of whites.

The assumption that blacks were biologically inferior to whites paved the way for abuse and exploitation of blacks in medical research, education, and experimentation. Racial ideology posed obstacles to the development of adequate healthcare for blacks. Biological explanations were sometimes invoked to explain black-white differences in health. Indeed, race is still used, without appropriate explanation, along with age and gender, as a key variable in medical and epidemiological research because of the assumption that race conveys important health information. Medicine's interest in black health status historically was motivated by the self-interest of whites rather than the needs of African-Americans. This legacy of suspicion of medical professionals and institutions explains why African-Americans are likely to approach PAS with caution.

A MEANS TO ACHIEVE THE ENDS OF OTHERS

The rise of medical institutions in the nineteenth century affected blacks in at least two ways: 1) blacks were used as specimens for clinical instruction and public display and 2) blacks were disproportionately involved in research and experimentation. And, although there was widespread public sentiment opposed to dissection and autopsy, black bodies were used because blacks were in no position to protect their dead. Professor Todd Savitt notes that "[s]outhern medical schools could and did boast that their cities' large black populations provided ample supplies of clinical and anatomical material. And white physicians trained at these institutions carried with them into their own careers this idea of the medical usefulness of blacks."

Use of black bodies for dissection and autopsy is just one example in a long history of blacks being exploited or used as a means to achieve the ends of others in medical research and experimentation. During slavery blacks were subject to experimental procedures that were exploitive. After slavery, the extent to which blacks were experimental subjects without their consent has not been documented. Professor Vanessa Northington Gamble's examination of folklore in the late nineteenth and early twentieth centuries, however, makes clear that blacks believed that these practices persisted. Concerns about such abuse and exploitation of blacks in medical experimentation were used to press for the creation of black-controlled hospitals in the early twentieth century.

The best known twentieth-century example of the use of blacks as unconsenting experimental subjects is the Tuskegee Syphilis Study. It illustrates the nature of the relationship between medicine and blacks that evolved during slavery, continued during the post-emancipation period, and in some aspects is still prevalent today.

The United States Public Health Service (PHS) sponsored the Tuskegee Syphilis Study, which began in 1932 and lasted forty years. It involved 399 black men who lived in Macon County, Alabama. The study was intended to observe the effects of untreated syphilis on blacks and thus held out no promise of benefit to the subjects. The subjects never consented. They were misled and never given important information about the study. When effective treatment for syphilis became available, the subjects were not provided with penicillin. Indeed, measures were taken to prevent their being treated.

Assumptions about biologically based differences in disease between blacks and whites and negative stereotypes about blacks played an important role in the creation and implementation of the Tuskegee Study. For example, the investigators accepted the medical view prevailing in the United States that syphilis affected blacks differently than whites. The PHS doctors believed that blacks had different sexual natures than whites and that blacks were more promiscuous. They also wrongly believed that blacks would not seek medical care.

The PHS investigators took advantage of the subjects' bleak social and economic situation. These men were poor and lived in a rural and segregated county in the deep South. They were accustomed to responding to the authority of whites. Offers of free healthcare and payment of burial expenses were powerful incentives for participation in the Tuskegee Study. In sum, although these men were capable of making rational decisions for themselves in terms of their own interests and preferences, they were vulnerable to exploitation because of conditions in their environment. They were powerless and in no position to protect themselves from those who would take advantage of them. They understood the limitations of their lives and environment and were powerless to change it.

The lesson of Tuskegee is not only that vulnerable people can be easily exploited, but also that healthcare professionals do not always act in the best interests of their patients. It shows how scientific objectivity can be infected with bias. It suggests that abstract concepts like autonomy, self-determination, and informed consent have little meaning in circumstances where an individual's ability to protect himself or herself is blunted by persons and forces that are authoritative and powerful.

Black experience with being used as objects in medical research and experimentation has left a legacy of distrust that continues to affect the behavior and beliefs of blacks. There is concern that, despite reforms in the conduct of human experimentation, blacks are still devalued in the modern research context. Distrust is also evident in organ donation. Historically, blacks have been less likely than whites to agree to organ donation. Blacks have consistently linked their reluctance to the concern that if they were potential organ donors they might not be given adequate care. Nation of Islam minister Louis Farrakhan's statement in a 1994 speech that whites do not stop black-on-black violence because it provides a source of organs for whites, while controversial, echoes the fear expressed by many blacks that their lives are valued less than the lives of white recipients.

This distrust of the medical profession and the feeling that black lives are devalued in our society is also reflected in the allegations of genocide that are frequently voiced within the African-American community. The Tuskegee Syphilis Study left its mark in the widespread and often repeated (mis)understanding that the men of Tuskegee were deliberately infected with syphilis. The allegation of genocide also arose in connection with efforts to establish sickle cell anemia screening programs and birth control programs. More recently, the allegation has arisen in connection with the AIDS epidemic. Professor Gamble cites surveys indicating that up to one-third of African-Americans believe either that the AIDS virus was created to infect African-Americans or that it could have been created for that purpose.

In short, African-Americans with reason believe that they are not always viewed as persons of unconditioned worth who are deserving of respect. These beliefs are reinforced because so little progress has been made in improving the health status of African-Americans.

THE ABSENCE OF EQUAL OPPORTUNITY IN HEALTHCARE ACCESS AND DISTRIBUTION

From the time blacks were first brought to America, one fact has been overwhelming. Blacks by any measure have been sicker and died younger than whites. Initially medical theories affirmed race-based explanations, as opposed to social and economic ones, for the difference in health status between blacks and whites. For example, during the post-emancipation period, census reports, insurance statistics, and military data all indicated high mortality and morbidity rates among blacks. It was believed that the peculiar susceptibility of blacks to disease, vice, and crime were responsible for these differences.

At times, belief in the inherent differences between blacks and whites even posed obstacles to sorting through the complexities of disease such as tuberculosis and syphilis. It was reassuring for whites to believe that diseases affected whites and blacks differently (and blacks more harshly) or that close observation confirmed the presence of two diseases rather than one. Negative stereotypes about blacks were frequently employed to justify perceived disease or health status disparities between blacks and whites. Often these stereotypes involved sexual promiscuity, intellectual performance, or susceptibility of blacks to disease and vice.

Explicit discrimination against African-Americans in all areas of medicine was the norm until the mid-1960s. As P. Preston Reynolds notes, "African-American students were denied admission to most medical and nursing schools, African-American physicians were rejected from membership to state and national medical societies, and African-Americans were refused care at most hospitals in this country." Moreover, the Hospital Survey and Construction Act (Hill-Burton Act) passed in 1946 contained a provision that required hospital facilities of equal quality to be built for minorities, thus introducing "separate but equal" into healthcare. As Justice Harlan points out in his dissent in *Plessey* v. *Ferguson,* the "real meaning" of segregation is "that colored citizens are so inferior and degraded that they cannot be allowed to sit in public coaches [or to share hospital wards and doctors' waiting rooms] occupied by white citizens."

This explicit segregation in healthcare did not begin to change until the passage of the Civil Rights Act of 1964, which prohibited provision of federal funds to programs and institutions that discriminated on the basis of race. The creation of the Medicare program in 1965 virtually assured that every hospital in the nation would be subject to the act.

Although hospitals, unlike public schools, were required by the federal government to comply immediately with federal guidelines promulgated to achieve integration, resistance was strong. Eventually progress towards integration of facilities providing healthcare services was achieved. Yet, there is little reason to believe, in the health domain any more than in public education, that desegregation brought about equal access or equal quality of healthcare for blacks. There is evidence to suggest that contemporary changes in the United States healthcare system is causing a further decline in an admittedly small pool of African-American physicians. In 1890 there were fourteen black medical schools. Today there are only four predominantly black schools training African-American physicians. Moreover, the persistent disparities in healthcare status between blacks and whites suggests that equal opportunity in health access and distribution remains an illusive goal.

African-Americans perceive that they are treated differently within the healthcare system and are more likely than whites to report difficulties in obtaining access to the healthcare system and, once they obtain care, dissatisfaction with the care they receive, including their communications with healthcare providers. This perception of racial disparities in the healthcare system is supported by a host of studies demonstrating racial differences in health status, access to healthcare and quality of health across a variety of conditions and healthcare settings. While the majority of African-Americans may not be familiar with these studies, reports about them in the media reinforce the perception that African-American lives are devalued in our society. The results of a recent study of Medicare beneficiaries, combined with other studies of racial disparities in health which persist after controlling for other factors thought to influence health, such as age, sex, insurance status, income, disease severity, other health conditions, and underlying incidence and prevalence rates, led one commentator to conclude that: "although both race and income have effects, race was the overriding determinant of disparities in care" and that "[h]igher incomes for blacks had a modifying—but never an equalizing—effect on black-white ratios for" certain types of care.

Evidence of the racial disparities in health and healthcare comes in a number of different forms. For example, the United States mortality statistics have provided dramatic evidence of the racial difference in health status year after year. These statistics reveal that African-Americans have an overall mortality rate that is approximately 70 percent higher than that of whites. The mortality differences exist across disease categories, so that the 1995 age-adjusted death rates for blacks were higher for most of the leading causes of death. Indeed, a recent study reported that declines in breast cancer mortality were found only among white, not black, women.

African-Americans also experience higher morbidity with respect to various disease categories, including diabetes, high blood pressure, and AIDS. Similarly, numerous studies have demonstrated that African-Americans, when they are given care, receive different care than whites for the same conditions. For example, a number of studies have shown that blacks are less likely to receive angiography or to undergo coronary artery bypass surgery or angioplasty than whites. Some of these differences in health status, but not all, may be explained by the fact that blacks are less likely than whites to have access to healthcare. For example, blacks are less likely than whites to have insurance and they make fewer visits to office-based physicians than whites.

Recent studies suggest that these disparities in access to treatment remain, even when blacks gain access to the healthcare system. For example, a number of studies have shown that blacks still have fewer physician visits and receive different treatments than whites, even within the Medicare or Veteran's Affairs populations where disparities in access have been minimized or eliminated. Not only have studies shown that blacks are less likely than whites to receive certain, more common treatments, but that blacks were more likely than whites to receive certain, less common treatments. For example, blacks were more than 3.5 times more likely than whites to undergo amputation of all or part of the lower limb, even though diabetes mellitus (the most common reason for the amputation) is only 1.7 times as prevalent in elderly blacks as in whites. In addition, there is evidence that, among patients seen in similar hospitals, blacks receive poorer quality of treatment than whites.

While the racial disparities in treatment decisions cannot be denied, the reasons for the disparities are harder to identify. Because race is often used as a proxy for socioeconomic status, the racial disparities seen in health and healthcare could reflect socioeconomic or class differences, rather than racial differences. However, racial differences in health and healthcare persist in studies that control or adjust for indicators of socioeconomic status, such as income, educational level, and insurance status. For example, a recent study which compared mortality rates among blacks and among whites living in comparable areas demonstrated that, although both poor blacks and poor whites experienced mortality rates higher than nationwide rates, poor blacks had lower survival rates than poor whites in all but one location. This and other studies indicate that socioeconomic status alone cannot account for all of the documented racial differences in health and healthcare.

If racial disparities in health and healthcare access persist as they do among populations in which access issues have been equalized or minimized and among populations which face similar economic difficulties and barriers, we must look beyond access to explain the continuing disparities. Are there differences in the clinical encounter itself that might explain the disparities in health status between blacks and whites?

In addressing this question, some commentators have suggested that blacks and whites may differ in their treatment preferences. Some evidence supports this hypothesis. For example, the Coronary Artery Surgery Study (CASS) found that whites were more likely than blacks to elect bypass surgery, even when some other, less invasive therapy was recommended and that blacks were 10 percent more likely than whites to decline an invasive treatment. Differences by race have also been documented with respect to preferences for using life-sustaining treatments. However, blacks still are treated differently, even when their preferences are the same.

Cultural differences in the clinical encounter may account for some of these disparities. Clinical decision-making takes place within the context of a clinical relationship. Accordingly, clinical decisions are necessarily influenced by the social structure and context in which they are made. The "sociologic influences" on the clinical decision include the social characteristics of patients and physicians, the patterns of social interaction and authority in clinical settings, and the structure of healthcare organizations. For example, cultural differences can result in medical advice that does not "fit" the patient's values and conceptions. They can also result in a physician's ignoring the patient's values and conceptions. In neither case will optimum health be achieved. To the extent that medicine's approach to a problem does not coincide with a patient's beliefs, patient noncompliance and dissatisfaction with healthcare become more likely.

Cultural differences also give rise to communication problems between patient and healthcare provider. Studies have documented that white and black patients express themselves differently within the medical encounter. To the extent that black patients downplay or fail to discuss their symptoms, their healthcare is likely to suffer. More importantly, to the extent that African-American patients use different language or frame their decisions differently from that of their physicians, they are at greater risk of having their decisions ignored or overridden. One study of physician-patient encounters found that

> the person who hears a vernacular [e.g., Black English] dialect spoken tends to devalue the speaker of that dialect. Consciously or unconsciously, dialect speakers tend to get worse treatment, wait longer for service, are considered ignorant, and are told what to do rather than asked what they would like to do. Therefore, the effect of the patient's vernacular dialect in the medical interview is a potential source of interference to the effective exchange of information.

Cultural differences may create difficulties not only in communication, but also because they may make health providers less comfortable in their dealings with their patients. This discomfort may hinder effective communication or preclude some communication altogether. For example, at least two studies have suggested that blacks are less likely to be approached for organ donation by predominately white medical teams.

Finally, physicians' unconscious stereotypes and biases, generally influenced by cultural differences, although sometimes influenced by views of biological differences, may affect healthcare decision-making. Some have suggested that the medical criteria used in clinical decision-making may reflect or incorporate unconscious biases. Others have suggested that perceptions of the patient's support system, which may reflect the physician's racial and cultural biases, may influence the decision-making process. Anecdotes of

African-American patients support this view. In a recent article, Vanessa Northington Gamble relates two powerful examples of racial stereotyping experienced in the emergency room. In one, an African-American professor of nursing describes how her symptoms of severe abdominal pain were met immediately with questions regarding the number of sexual partners she had, recalling persistent stereotypes of black women as sexually promiscuous. The other (reported in the *Los Angeles Times*) describes the experience of an African-American medical school administrator with a broken arm who was assumed to be a welfare mother and told to hold her arm as if she were holding a can of beer. In a similar vein, Herbert Nickens refers to his own experience in comparing the ways in which white healthcare workers treat those with cystic fibrosis (affects primarily whites) and sickle cell anemia (affects primarily blacks). He opines that healthcare workers often question whether those with sickle cell disease are having real pain or are exhibiting analgesic drug-seeking behavior. Finally, physicians' racial and cultural biases can be inferred from their behavior. For example, the Coronary Artery Surgery Study demonstrated that providers are more likely to recommend whites for bypass surgery than blacks, "despite similar clinical and angiographic characteristics." In a similar vein, researchers found that physicians in one Florida county were almost ten times as likely to report a black woman for substance abuse during pregnancy than a white woman, even though rates of drug use were similar. In addition, a 1987 review of cases of court-ordered cesarean section demonstrated that 81 percent of the women were women of color (specifically, African-American, Asian, or Latina), 25 percent of the women did not speak English as their primary language, and all of the women were being treated at a teaching hospital clinic or were receiving public assistance.

The enduring disparities in health status between blacks and whites perpetuate the legacy of mistrust of medicine. African-Americans rightly wonder what sort of society would allow such disparities to continue unchecked. They are understandably suspicious, therefore, of those who express concern that blacks will not be given a fair opportunity to assistance in ending their lives.

CONCLUSION

What lessons does the African-American experience with medicine and the healthcare system have for efforts to ensure that the interests and preferences of all patients will be respected should PAS be legalized?

What does it mean to be rendered vulnerable because of poverty, prejudice, negative stereotypes, societal indifferences, or membership in a stigmatized group?

Given the general distrust of medical institutions and the medical profession and the belief that their lives are undervalued, African-Americans are likely to view the legalization of physician-assisted suicide with suspicion. Rather than see it as an opportunity to exercise their autonomy at the end of life, African-Americans may sense that this is yet another way through which less valued African-American lives can be eliminated. This distrust makes it less likely that African-Americans will be easily manipulated in making their end-of-life decisions. African-Americans may question more vigorously the judgments of their healthcare providers and be noncompliant with the medical regimes recommended to them. While mistrust serves to protect blacks in their contacts with the healthcare system, it also presents obstacles for them. The distrusting patient may have limited his or her access to desirable services. It is important that patients trust their healthcare providers, especially in end-of-life decision-making. If patients are to participate in managing and controlling their illnesses, patients and their families need to have confidence in the information they have received about diagnosis, prognosis, and options for care. If the patient's mistrust motivates him or her to ignore these recommendations, the patient may have lost an important opportunity to manage his or her dying. Conflicts between patients and families on the one hand and healthcare providers on the other can severely compromise patients' desires to die with dignity.

Difficulties that exist in the clinical encounter also have significant implications for PAS. Assuming the very best intentions, cultural differences between African-American patients and their healthcare providers may give rise to communication difficulties, either because of differences in values or because of differences in communication styles. However, those cultural differences may create a barrier that prevents even the attempt at communication regarding such important and personal issues as end-of-life care. In a worst-case scenario, cultural differences may cause a physician to discount his African-American patient's values and wishes to such an extent that those wishes are not honored.

The African-American experience with medicine also cautions against placing too much confidence in the ability of physicians and other healthcare providers to insure that patient preferences are honored and respected. In the context of the patient-physician relationship, physicians have power. This power derives from several sources. The physician has superior knowledge and skill. The physician has broad discretion and is not easily held accountable for actions by patients or society. Dying patients and their families are disadvantaged in terms of questioning physicians by virtue of the crisis that they find themselves in. They may also be disadvantaged by a sense of helplessness that results from low socioeconomic status or low self-esteem. In the face of the power inequities in this relationship and the historical instances of misuse of power, African-Americans appreciate that making PAS available as an option for terminally ill patients does not necessarily empower those who have been disadvantaged. Thus, an important implication of the power inequities in physician-patient relationships is that greater equality for the seriously disadvantaged may be a precondition for the meaningful exercise of autonomy.

Moreover, physicians do not exist in isolation from the social milieu in which they find themselves any more than patients do. Both physicians and patients absorb the prevailing norms, values, and beliefs of the society. Physicians may have assimilated the negative messages about some groups. For example, physicians may be too quick to interpret ambivalent statements made by patients as being pleas to die, because at an unconscious level they perceive the patient as not deserving of money, resources, or other efforts that might be needed for care. Alternatively, patients may have absorbed the negative messages that society has heaped upon them and perceive themselves to be unworthy of the efforts that might be needed to prolong their treatment or provide them with palliative treatment. These patients might be easily coerced into believing that it would be easier for them and for others if their lives ended sooner. As a consequence these patients will not be able to effectively manage end-of-life care decisions. They may not be willing to discuss their medical problems with healthcare professionals. Still others may be unwilling to risk the contempt and lack of respect that they have encountered with health professionals in the past. In neither scenario will the patient receive optimum care. Thus, requirements for concurring physician diagnoses or that patients make repeated requests for PAS may not provide meaningful protection. The essential point is that physicians have broad discretion and power. Unless there is confidence in physician objectivity and lack of unconscious bias, such cynicism is valid.

A commentator perceptively notes, "[h]ow in the world . . . is a white, middle class, twenty-five year old male doctor, who wants to perform his role in the most intelligent and beneficent way, to approach a poor, aging, folk-educated, black, female patient?" At a minimum, before healthcare providers can maximize the participation of African-American patients in end-of-life decisions, they must know and appreciate the realities of their patients' lives. Essentially, however, the appeal to develop thick descriptions of patients as persons situated in broader social, historical, and cultural contexts is really an invitation to conversation before PAS becomes an option in our healthcare system. This conversation should be about the changes and modifications that are required in the training of healthcare providers and the delivery of healthcare services before we can be confident that all patients will have the opportunity to die with dignity.

Chapter 11

Future Directions in Bioethics

"... plague first began to occur in Athens... In the first place doctors, who treated it in ignorance, had no effect (being themselves the ones who died in proportion to having the most contact with it), nor did any other human agency, and their supplications at sanctuaries and recourse to prophecies and the like were all of no avail. In the end they abandoned these, vanquished by the disaster... Some died in neglect; others, when they had been given a great deal of attention. And no single cure was established, practically speaking, whose application could bring relief; for what had helped one person actually harmed someone else. No constitution, as to strength or weakness, showed sufficiency against it, but it devastated every sort, cared for by every sort of regimen. What was most terrible in the whole affliction was the despair when someone realized he was sick (for immediately forming the judgment that there was no hope, they tended much more to give themselves up instead of holding out), and the fact that from tending one another they died like a flock of sheep; this brought on the most destruction."[1]

Thucydides, The Peloponnesian War, Book 2, 47-51

"A very great pestilence broke out particularly in the province of Liguria. For suddenly there appeared certain marks among the dwellings, doors, utensils and clothes, which, if anyone wished to wash away, became more and more apparent. After the lapse of a year indeed there began to appear in the groins of men and in other rather delicate places a swelling of the glands, after the manner of a nut or date, presently followed by an unbearable fever, so that upon the third day the man died. But if anyone should pass over the third day he had a hope of living. Everywhere there was grief and everywhere tears. For as common report had it that those who fled would avoid the plague, the dwellings were left deserted by their inhabitants, and the dogs alone kept house. The flocks remained alone in the pastures with no shepherd at hand. You might see villages (villas) or fortified places lately filled with crowds of men, and on the next day all had departed and everything was in utter silence. Some fled, leaving the corpses of their parents unburied; parents forgetful of their duty abandoned their children in raging fever. If by chance long-standing affection constrained anyone to bury his near relative, he remained himself unburied, and while he was performing funeral rites he perished; while he offered obsequies to the dead, his own corpse remained without obsequies. You might see the world brought back to its ancient silence; no voice in the field; no whistling of shepherds; no lying in wait of wild beasts among the cattle; no harm to domestic fowls. The crops, outliving the time of the harvest, awaited the reaper untouched; the vineyard with its fallen leaves and its shining grapes remained undisturbed while winter came on; a trumpet as of warriors resounded through the day and night; something like the murmur of an army was heard by many; there were no footsteps of passers by, no murderer was seen, yet the corpses of the dead were more than the eye could discern; pastoral places had been turned into a desert, and human habitations had become places of refuge for wild beasts."[2]

Paul the Deacon, *History of the Lombards*

As we consider in this final chapter the future of bioethics, it may seem strange to begin with these descriptions of plagues reported by authors from so long ago. Indeed, the first passage is a part of Thucydides' description of the plague that hit Athens in 430 B.C. and the second is Paul the Deacon's account of a plague in northern Italy in the 560's. But keeping in mind the topics and issues of the earlier chapters, we trust that certain ethical themes are evident in these passages. In other places, Thucydides includes more graphic descriptions of the physical symptoms of the plague; however, in these passages he is focused on the loss of lives, the lack of a cure, and the resulting despair. What is especially striking about these accounts is that they address the human side of a massive disease **epidemic**—the effects of the disease on human relationships, such as parent–child and doctor–patient, and the disruption to human lives and social order caused by contagious disease. These issues, of course, are still with us today and will be with us in the future.

Yet there are other ways of relating these accounts of plagues to the topics in this chapter. Several issues seem to be on the horizon for bioethics. One such issue is the question of what to study and research, that is, how to best spend the time and resources of scientists, bioethicists, and societies. Thucydides says that there was no effective treatment for the plague and that doctors, sanctuaries, and prophecies were equally useless. For us, then, what should be our priorities in the new millennium as we plan the best ways to preserve and improve human lives? Are our goals of health and well-being furthered best by technological discoveries, public health measures, human rights efforts, preventative education, or something else? We have to make decisions today that will impact the health and well-being of ourselves and others in the future.

A second issue is the possibility of future occasions where health care needs may be acute and the question of how to respond may be difficult. Just like the plagues of long ago, there may be future epidemics, **pandemics,** or acts of **bioterrorism.** Where there is a catastrophic disaster or infectious illness, there will be ethical questions about how to protect people, how to appropriately treat people, and how to allocate scarce resources. There will also be questions about human relationships and social roles. As the reports about the plagues indicate, some people who died were given a lot of attention while others were neglected. Some parents abandoned dying children while some grown children left untended the bodies of their parents. As Paul the Deacon hauntingly reports, "the dogs alone kept house." The doctors who tended to the sick were themselves likely to contract the disease. What can we say about the values of compassion, care, nonmaleficence, beneficence, justice, and professional responsibility at the time of an epidemic? What rules can be drawn up for times in which the need for medical care far surpasses the resources available to provide such care? Are physicians or other health care professionals required to treat the sick when doing so puts them at significant risk of contracting a disease (Figure 11.1)? According to Thucydides, "from tending one another they died like a flock of sheep."

A third issue follows from the second and concerns the relationship between the health care professional and the society within which the professional practices. Suppose, for example, that the government of a country recognizes a certain medical need and asks that health care professionals respond to the need (Figure 11.2). Let's say that there are not enough surgeons in the U.S. Army to adequately care for the soldiers. Would it be morally acceptable for the U.S. government to solicit volunteers, to offer incentives to civilian surgeons willing to serve, to "draft" surgeons, or to mandate military service of surgeons? What obligations do physicians and other health care providers have when the government or military or citizens of their countries have need of their medical services?

FIGURE 11.1   Plague doctor's clothing including a beak filled with herbs and spices.

FIGURE 11.2   WWII nurse recruiting poster.

Or, in the case of an epidemic or plague, do you think there would be morally acceptable reasons to conscript health care providers into caring for the sick? Judging from the reports given by Thucydides and Paul the Deacon, in times of tremendous social need and human peril, some people flee while others stay to help and some are cared for while others are abandoned. Under these types of conditions, what is the physician's duty and responsibility and what is the relationship between health care and a society's needs?

CASE STUDY: MEG'S NIGHTMARE

On the Friday after Thanksgiving, multiple bombs are simultaneously detonated at two shopping malls near a big city. It is unclear what or who is responsible for the bombings. The explosions have caused the buildings to crumble and collapse. Many people are hurt or killed, some from the bombs themselves and others from the collapsing buildings. Emergency personnel respond quickly and ambulances begin to ferry patients to the nearest hospital, Westside Community.

As the first ambulances arrive, the hospital staff works to stabilize patients and to control bleeding. More patients arrive. The medical staff is treating patients with wounds, burns, and broken bones. The emergency room soon fills with patients waiting to be seen.

The head physician, Dr. Fuller, takes a look around the emergency room and directs staff to call all medical personnel in to work and to "implement the capacity triage plan." Meg, an orthopedic resident who has just completed her shift at the hospital, receives the call in her car as she is driving home. Meg knows that the plan directs staff to treat only those who are likely to be saved through medical intervention. Those who are not likely to be salvageable must be passed over in order to save the greatest number of lives. Meg hoped that the triage plan would never be implemented because she hates the idea of having to make these judgments concerning who receives treatment and who does not. She turns her car around and heads back to the hospital.[3]

It sounds as though Meg and the rest of the hospital's staff have received training for situations like this one where a disaster overwhelms the capacity of the hospital to provide care. Meg is uncomfortable with what the **triage** plan requires her to do. Although she is officially off-duty, she decides to do what she can to help save lives. We, on the other hand, can ask the following questions:

Must Meg return to the hospital?
Do medical personnel have a duty to report to work in cases of disasters or epidemics?
Can hospitals or the government force medical personnel to work in emergencies?
Is the triage plan appropriate?

How should triage plans be developed and who should have input in formulating them?
Are medical personnel required to carry out emergency plans if they are opposed to what the
plans require them to do?

Many of these questions concern issues we have considered in previous chapters, such as professional
roles and responsibilities, and the values of beneficence and justice. But they also raise the following
themes treated in this chapter: the priorities of bioethics, pandemics and disasters, and the conscription
of health care workers. Let's consider each of these in more detail.

BIOETHICS PRIORITIES

Here we are looking at proposals for what sorts of issues *will* occupy or *should* occupy the bioethicists of
the future. Put another way, we are reflecting on what direction the discipline of bioethics may be or
should be moving. Of course, bioethicists are free to study and comment on whatever issues they like
in order to advance knowledge or truth. But realistically, bioethics is connected with politics, public policy, law, and social values and priorities. Some countries such as the Netherlands (and the states of Oregon and Washington) have decided that physician-assisted suicide is morally acceptable, although other
countries and U.S. states disagree. The laws of a particular country often dictate what health-related
practices are allowed, for example, whether abortion is legal or whether research on embryos is permitted. These laws tend to reflect the moral and social climates of the countries that enact them. Hence,
different social communities may have different senses of what the significant bioethical issues are.
There may also be bioethical issues that transcend national boundaries and are especially significant
either because of their potential impact on the world community or because of some fundamental question of value, principle, or human rights. The readings in this chapter offer different pictures of these
future bioethical issues, but, taken as a whole, they propose four areas: (1) globalization; (2) social conditions that impact health and disease, such as wealth or poverty; (3) the status and condition of women
and children, and (4) scientific progress in medicine, genetics, and diagnostics. Obviously, these are not
exclusive categories; many bioethical topics can be discussed in the context of several of them.

By **globalization,** we mean in one sense that the issues of bioethics are worldwide. It is commonplace
now to say that the world has grown smaller. Given the availability of worldwide travel and excellent communication systems, many people are able to travel far from their homes and receive almost instant notification of world events. We hear about scientific discoveries in South Korea and Ebola outbreaks in
Uganda. We are aware of organizations—such as, Médecins sans Frontières (Doctors without Borders),
Partners in Health, and Unite for Sight—that provide health care resources in remote and generally
underserved areas. Many health care professionals have traveled on mission or outreach trips to bring medicine and health care to countries around the world. We compare our health care system in the United
States to the systems in other countries, such as Canada, the United Kingdom, and the Netherlands. We
can see the way that a need in one part of the world (say, persons who need organ transplants and can
afford to pay for them) has an effect on other parts of the world (where people in poverty may willingly
or unwillingly give up their organs). In short, given that illness and disease occur everywhere in the world
(Figure 11.3) and that moral questions can arise in the diagnosis, treatment, and research of disease, it
is clear that bioethics cannot now be, if it ever was, a narrow, nationalistic discipline; its scope is the world.

The second direction for bioethics pays attention to the social conditions that impact health and
disease. A good example of this is the field of public health. As we have come to understand the relationship between living conditions (clean water, dry houses, sewage systems, etc.) and health, we have
learned how to prevent disease by improving living conditions. Those who live under the worst conditions are the most impoverished and often the most powerless. There is a correlation between wealth
and health and between poverty and disease. According to the World Health Organization (WHO),
in 2005, almost 500,000 women died from maternal causes and 99% of these women lived in developing countries.[4] WHO also reports that over 80% of the deaths attributed to diabetes occur in low- and
middle-income countries.[5] Within the United States, a 1995 study showed that poverty is correlated with
higher rates of preventable hospitalization and that uninsured people have more trouble accessing

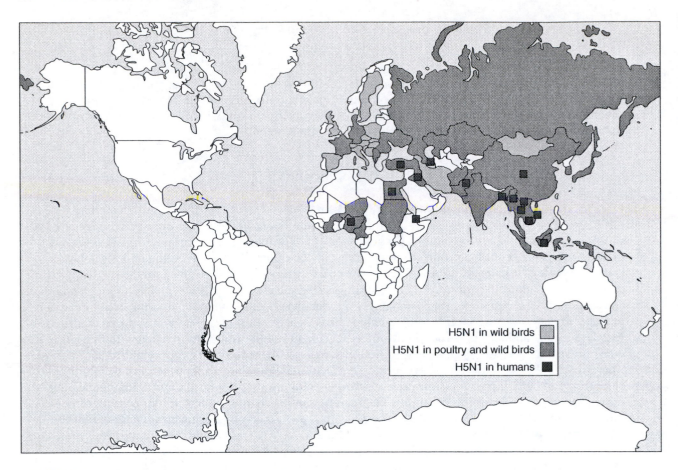

FIGURE 11.3   Map of Avian Flu sites in the world.

care than do privately insured people.[6] In March 2008, a government study showed that the life expectancy for affluent Americans is 4.5 years longer than that for poorer Americans and that the gap is widening.[7] Perhaps we need an economic solution in order to rectify these inequalities, say, a cap on the salaries of the most highly paid CEOs and athletes or a significant raise in the minimum wage paid to employees. Or perhaps we need a health care system not tied to one's ability to pay, where one could receive necessary care or prescriptions regardless of whether one has insurance or not.

Another way that the economic gap has an effect on health care can be seen in the distinction between health care needs and health care desires. Joe may need surgery to repair a torn ligament in his knee so that he can walk again without pain. Jim may want or desire surgery that will rebuild his nose to fit his idea of a pleasing appearance. Joan may need human growth hormone supplements because she lacks a normal amount of the hormone. Judy may desire human growth hormone supplements in order to enhance her career as a softball player. Of course, it is not always easy to determine whether a treatment satisfies a need or a desire. We have different senses of what our medical needs are. But it is still possible to explain the difference between a **health care need** and a **health care desire.** According to one definition, health care needs "assume some existing or potential condition of illness or disease and seek to restore some level of normalcy, whether the need be life-rescuing, life-sustaining, or life-improving" while health care desires "assume a normal condition and seek to enhance this already normal condition."[8] The main point is that medical research and health care resources, including a health care provider's time, can be spent either tending to medical needs or serving medical desires. Bioethicists in the future may consider whether the nature of medicine or the physician's role is threatened by patient requests to satisfy medical desires and whether there should be any attempt to control or regulate the way resources are spent.

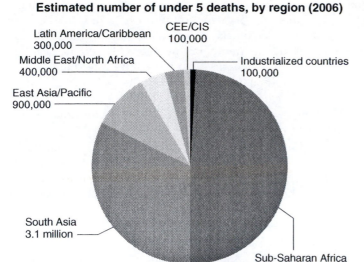

Estimated number of under 5 deaths, by region (2006)

Latin America/Caribbean
300,000

Middle East/North Africa
400,000

East Asia/Pacific
900,000

CEE/CIS
100,000

Industrialized countries
100,000

South Asia
3.1 million

Sub-Saharan Africa
4.8 million

FIGURE 11.4   Children who die before their fifth birthday.

A third topic that bioethics may focus on in the future is the status and condition of women and children. When women are uneducated and powerless in society, their health and their families' health is likely to suffer. The World Health Organization issues reports on how gender inequalities are related to diseases, such as blindness, mental health, HIV/AIDS, and more. To take one example, among those who are blind, 64% are female. In Asia and Africa, the major source of blindness is cataracts. Cataracts can be cured by surgery but women are less likely to get cataract surgery than men. The report lists these reasons, as well as others, for why women are less likely to get eye care: women have less access to family resources to pay for eye care, they have fewer options to travel to get eye care, women are less likely to have family support to obtain care, and female literacy is low and women are less likely to know about available eye care.[9] WHO also recognizes that "gender equality is a major determinant of health."[10] Improving the status and condition of women helps women achieve their potential, improves the community, and benefits the health of their children and families.

According to UNICEF, the United Nations Childrens Fund, every day an average of 26,000 children under the age of 5 die of largely preventable conditions. Most of them live in developing countries (Figure 11.4).[11] UNICEF reports: "Most deaths result from five causes, or a combination of them: acute respiratory infections (ARI), diarrhea, measles, malaria and malnutrition. Poverty and the failure to ensure universal access to basic social services are to blame."[12] Without a doubt, a person's social condition has a bearing on her level of health and on whether health care resources are liable to be spent on her. Poverty and inequality take a great toll on women's and children's health.

Finally, a fourth likely focus for bioethicists in the future is scientific progress in medicine, genetics, and diagnostics. Bioethicists will consider the ethical implications of the newest discoveries and will monitor the ways in which research is conducted. As medical science experiments with new ways to diagnose and fight disease, bioethicists will continue to reflect on the human impact of medicine, the provision of health care, and science.

RESPONSES TO PANDEMICS AND DISASTERS

The second topic considered in this chapter's readings is catastrophic illness or disaster. As the beginning passages on the plagues describe, there have been occasions of epidemic disease, war, natural disaster, and terrorist acts that challenge our ability to provide care, save lives, and minimize harm. How ought we to prepare for such events and how ought we to think about our obligations, responsibilities, rights, and values in such cases?

Think of the health care needs after Hurricane Katrina or of the annual worries about influenza outbreaks. In 2005, there were 758 terrorist events that took place in 45 countries.[13] These are the kinds of disasters in which health care would need to be provided quickly and on a large scale. One significant feature of these large scale disasters or epidemics is that the number of people who need medical care far exceeds the number of people who on a regular, daily basis are seen by health professionals and at hospitals. If medical centers are staffed only for the normal daily patient load, they will be unprepared to treat people in a large scale disaster. On March 11, 2004, after the Madrid train bombings, the closest hospital received 272 patients in 2½ hours.[14] Hospitals and medical centers must plan for how they will accommodate these patients, how they will add staff, beds, equipment, and medicine.

One part of this planning is discussed under the name of **surge capacity.** This refers to "a health care system's ability to expand quickly to meet an increased demand for medical care in the event of bioterrorism or other large-scale public health emergencies."[15] Surge capacity planning involves developing procedures for what to do when capacity has been reached, how to coordinate needed resources and staff, and so on. One study showed that many health care workers, over 40%, would hesitate to show up for work during a disaster out of concern for their own well-being or the well-being of their families.[16] Some direction is provided by the U.S. Health Resources and Services Administration (HRSA), which sets certain benchmarks for hospitals on disaster preparedness. States are required to develop a response system that provides for:

1. The triage, treatment, and disposition of 500 adult and pediatric patients per one million population who suffer from acute illness or trauma requiring hospitalization from a biological, chemical, radiological, or explosive terrorist incident;
2. Immediate deployment of 250 or more additional patient care personnel per million in urban areas; and
3. Immediate deployment of 125 or more additional patient care personnel per million in rural areas.[17]

In addition to those who are hurt or infected at the time of a disaster, there will also be the "worried well" who present themselves to health care workers and hospitals because they are anxious and worried that they might become ill.

CONSCRIPTION OF HEALTH CARE PROVIDERS

Finally, one more issue for the future may be the conscription of health care workers. The question debated in the United States and Canada is whether there are or should be conditions under which physicians and other health care providers could be "drafted" into service. Perhaps a national emergency or pandemic or perhaps the need of the military for medical workers are sufficient reasons to conscript medical providers. In 1987, the U.S. Congress authorized the Health Care Personnel Delivery System (HCPDS), a "draft" for medical workers in times of emergency need.[18] If the President and Congress activated the plan, then health care workers between the ages of 18 and 44 would be required to register with the Selective Service. Within a few weeks, the U.S. could begin drafting civilian medical personnel into service. In Canada, there are also several pieces of legislation, such as the federal Emergencies Act and Ontario's proposed Emergency Management and Civil Protection Act, designed to give the government more authority during emergencies. Many physicians in Canada are said to fear that the laws could force physicians and other health professionals into service during an emergency. These laws call us to reconsider the relationship of the health professional and the larger society.

THE FUTURE OF BIOETHICS

You might still be asking yourself: Why should we hypothesize on the future directions of bioethics? Aren't we only spinning our wheels here and dealing with idle speculations? In fact, there are two reasons for thinking that this undertaking is important. First, by considering what may be ahead of us, we can better prepare for the future. We can make choices now that will enable us to respond better to future events. This is certainly the idea behind fire drills and mock emergency training. If we practice now, if we make the hard planning and prioritizing choices now, then if and when the time comes to handle triage for a massive epidemic, we will be ready.

Second, and at least as important, the future is in part made out of what we decide and choose today, therefore we must plan now for the future we will create. We can make choices today that will affect the future we will have. Choices that we make now will affect us as citizens, taxpayers, patients, parents, children, and world citizens. For example, if the U.S. decides to commit funds to rapidly stockpile vaccines against avian flu, then fewer U.S. citizens may be exposed to harm, supposing a worldwide pandemic occurs. Of course, this stockpiling may divert funds from other sources so that Medicaid or Medicare benefits are reduced to low-income families or older adults. As we choose to address one health care goal, others may be sacrificed. Or, suppose that a country were to decide, in keeping with one of the **Millennium Development Goals of the United Nations,** that it would commit resources to: "Reduce by two-thirds the mortality rate among children under 5." Then more money, research time, and direct health care would be spent on mothers-to-be and children and this would likely require taking money and resources from other groups of people and disease categories. On the other hand, perhaps we will not take steps to stockpile vaccines or reduce the child mortality rate. In either case, whether we do or do not, there will be consequences for the health and well-being of people. In the new millennium, there will continue to be a need for bioethical awareness, sensitivity, reflection, analysis, and decision making.

Keep in mind that we already have many of the tools that will help us address the bioethical questions of the future. Granted, there will be new techniques, new medical drugs, new health care challenges, and new institutional structures and social contexts for providing health care, doing research, and practicing medicine. But we won't face this future completely unarmed.

First, we have the accumulated wisdom of the past. By this, we mean that we have the history of bioethics as a resource. Philosophers, theologians, lawyers, physicians, nurses, and many more have contributed to our understanding of bioethical concepts and arguments. While many issues have not been decided once and for all, we have collected a vocabulary of important concepts and distinctions (passive vs. active euthanasia, the child's right to an open future, etc.) that assist careful and precise bioethical thinking. We can use the ground-breaking cases in bioethics, such as the Karen Ann Quinlan case and the Molly Nash case, to preserve a kind of collective memory that will enable us to recognize similarities and differences in cases. This shared vocabulary and historical memory gives us a base from which to comment on future cases and issues.

Second, we can make use of the published codes and statements of professional societies and organizations. Health care professionals of various sorts, doctors, nurses, physical therapists, and so on, are members of professional associations and as such are governed by their own codes of ethics. National and international organizations such as the U.S. Department of Health and Human Services and the World Health Organization focus money and resources on issues of health and medicine. There are also many grassroots and community organizations that raise money for medical research or offer opportunities for people to contribute both directly and indirectly to improving health care. Thus, we can expect that guidance on future bioethical issues will continue to come both from the associations of health care professionals and from the larger social, national, and international communities within which they practice.

A third tool is the collected wisdom of moral philosophy, namely, the values, theories, and forms of reasoning that moral philosophy uses to describe and guide moral experience. As we have seen, there are many ways of thinking ethically about a situation. Utilitarian values and commitments are different from deontological values and commitments and both differ in significant ways from a care approach or a four principles approach to bioethics. Because we are familiar with various ways of thinking ethically, we may be more aware of the myriad components of any ethically complex situation. We may be better able to anticipate the consequences or more inclined to employ dialogue in order to facilitate a decision by consensus. We have used case analysis procedures in order to identify and balance values and to improve the clarity and comprehensiveness of our moral thinking. All of these tools of moral philosophy give us ways of talking about, understanding, and analyzing bioethical issues of the past, the present, and even the future.

And finally, as Meg recognized in our earlier case study and as Thucydides and Paul the Deacon knew, medicine and the care of the ill and disabled happen in the context of communities and affect communities. Families and communities can come together or fall apart in the face of disease and disability. It is communities that have the resources to train and educate, to engage in research, and to provide direct care. The choice of how best to do these things must be made by communities, be they families, towns, countries, or international organizations. The same is true of bioethicists. As a group of ethical thinkers, we aim to make our own contribution to the larger community. We promote ethical awareness of and sensitivity to bioethical issues, highlight human values and rights, and promote moral and just decision making in bioethics. Thus, for all of us, it is in the context of this connectedness that we must plan for our future, decide how to respond to the medical and health care needs of people, and promote scientific research.

The future of bioethics is thus in our hands. While we have attempted in this textbook to look ahead toward some of the bioethical topics on the horizon, there is no sure way for us to know what events will happen and what issues will be most pressing. In this spirit, this chapter includes only a few articles pointing to some of the possible future goals of bioethics and to problems facing bioethics. No doubt there are many other topics and concerns that we have not anticipated, but one measure of the effectiveness of this text will be whether its readers feel equipped to move on, to identify, analyze, and resolve, future issues in bioethics.

Endnotes

1. Thucydides, *The Peloponnesian War*, Book 2, 47–51 (trans. S. Lattimore) (Indianapolis, IN: Hackett, 1998), 98–100; also cited in Lester K. Little, "Life and Afterlife of the First Plague Pandemic," in *Plague and the End of Antiquity* (New York: Cambridge University Press, 2007), 4.

2. Paul the Deacon, *History of the Lombards* (ed. E. Peters, trans. W.D. Foulke) (Philadelphia: University of Pennsylvania Press, 1974), 56–58. See John Maddicott, "Plague in Seventh-Century England," in *Plague and the End of Antiquity* (New York: Cambridge University Press, 2007), 197–198.

3. See James F. Childress, "Disaster Triage," *Virtual Mentor (American Medical Association Journal of Ethics)* 6:5 (May 2004) at http://virtualmentor.ama-assn.org/2004/05/ccas2-0405.html for discussion of a similar case. [Accessed on February 11, 2008]

4. See the World Health Organization website at http://www.who.int/research/en/ [Accessed on March 21, 2008].

5. See http://www.who.int/infobase/report.aspx [Accessed on March 21, 2008].

6. A.B. Bindman, K. Grumbach, D. Osmond, M. Komaromy, K. Vranizan, N. Lurie, et al. "Preventable Hospitalizations and Access to Health Care," *Journal of the American Medical Association*, 274:4 (1995), 305–311.

7. Robert Pear, "Gap in Life Expectancy Widens for the Nation," *New York Times*, March 23, 2008, http://www.nytimes.com/2008/03/23/us/23health.html?_r=1&oref=slogin. [Accessed on March 23, 2008]

8. Michael C. Brannigan and Judith A. Boss, *Healthcare Ethics in a Diverse Society* (Mountain View, CA: Mayfield, 2000), 626. Others distinguish inherent needs from subjective or socially induced needs. See Thomas M. Garrett, Harold W. Baillie, Rosellen M. Garrett, *Health Care Ethics: Principles and Problems*, 3rd ed. (Upper Saddle River, NJ: Prentice Hall, 1998), 91–92.

9. See http://www.who.int/gender/other_health/en/genderblind.pdf. [Accessed on March 23, 2008]

10. See http://www.who.int/gender/mainstreaming/investing/en/index.html. [Accessed on March 23, 2008]

11. See http://www.unicef.org/sowc08/profiles/child_survival.php. [Accessed March 23, 2008]

12. See http://www.unicef.org/health/index_bigpicture.html. [Accessed March 23, 2008]

13. Terrorism Research Center, Inc. (see www.Terrorism.com) [Accessed on April 27, 2008]; cited in the National Center for Injury Prevention and Control, "In a Moment's Notice: Surge Capacity for Terrorist Bombings" (Atlanta, GA: Centers for Disease Control and Prevention, 2007).

14. National Center for Injury Prevention and Control, "In a Moment's Notice: Surge Capacity for Terrorist Bombings" (Atlanta, GA: Centers for Disease Control and Prevention, 2007), 1.

15. National Association of Public Hospitals and Health Systems, "Hospital Staffing and Surge Capacity during a Disaster Event," *Research Brief*, May 2007, 1.

16. See Steven Reinberg, "Many Health Care Workers Won't Show Up in Flu Pandemic: Poll results a 'wake-up call' for better preparedness training, experts say," *HealthDay News*, April 18, 2006, cited at http://www.covenanthealth.org/HealthDay/4_2006/532153?Mode=Print [Accessed on April 27, 2008]

17. See the Agency for Healthcare Research and Quality (AHRQ), "Bioterrorism and Health System Preparedness—Optimizing Surge Capacity: Hospital Assessment and Planning," Issue Brief No.3 (January 2004) at http://www.ahrq.gov/news/ulp/btbriefs/btbrief3.pdf. [Accessed on April 27, 2008]

18. J. Wesley Boyd, David U. Himmelstein, Karen Lasser, Danny McCormick, David H. Bor, Sarah L. Cutrona, Steffie Woolhandler, "U.S. Medical Students' Knowledge about the Military Draft, the Geneva Conventions, and Military Medical Ethics," *International Journal of Health Services* 37:4 (2007), 644.

BIOETHICS PRIORITIES

Bioethics and Public Policy in the Next Millennium: Presidential Address

Ruth Macklin

Alastair Campbell, President of the Fifth World Congress of Bioethics, has described our mission as that of confronting major opportunities and challenges to be faced in a global context in the next millennium. We are bioethicists—philosophers, physicians, lawyers, nurses, theologians, social scientists, policy analysts, and other practitioners in our multidisciplinary field. To my knowledge, none of us is a fortuneteller, so we are unable to predict what fortunes or misfortunes the new millennium will bring. But we can look around us today and see what challenges face us here and now— challenges that are urgent and will not disappear unless public policy on a global scale rises to meet them.

I want to focus on two phenomena that are well described in the public health literature. The first is the gross inequalities in health and health care that exist between rich and poor classes within nations, as well as among industrialized countries and many developing countries. The second phenomenon that requires public policy remedies, most notably in developing countries, is the health status of women. Both of these are situations of grave injustice on a broad social scale.

Global inequalities go beyond health status and health care. They exist, as well, in access to such prerequisites for good health as clean water and adequate nutrition. Add to that the demographic picture of the burden of diseases such as HIV in sub-Saharan Africa, and we see that the problem cannot be solved by policies developed solely within nation states. In South Africa and Zimbabwe, 20 to 25% of the adult population is infected with HIV. In Botswana, about one in three adults is infected. Peter Piot, the executive director of the Joint United Nations Programme on AIDS, recently noted that 'Because of AIDS, poverty is getting worse just as the need for more resources to curb the spread of HIV and alleviate the epidemic's impact on development is growing.'[1] But there is a need not only for drugs to treat people with HIV infection. Other diseases, such as malaria, wreak havoc in tropical countries. Malaria annually affects some 500 million people, and 90% of the cases are in Africa.[2] Countries with an annual healthcare budget of less than US $10 per person can no more afford drugs to treat malaria in their populations than they can to treat HIV/AIDS. Without concerted efforts to forge public policies that address these international inequities, there is little hope for much improvement.

In early August of this year, the United States government made an offer of $1 billion in annual loans to finance the purchase of anti-AIDS drugs in sub-Saharan Africa. By late August, South Africa and Namibia rejected the offer of the loan, and officials at the Southern Africa Development Community, which represents 12 other African countries, also expressed doubts about the proposal. They would prefer the United States to pressure American drug companies to reduce prices and to support countries that seek to produce generic drugs more cheaply.[3] But that is a step the United States has so far been unwilling to take. Interest-bearing loans cannot be the answer to the problem. That is a market solution, not one that stems from considerations of justice.

Issues related to justice have attracted interest among some bioethicists in the past quarter century, but they have not taken center stage, and they have mostly focused on allocation of health care resources within nations. Only recently have bioethicists begun to explore inequalities in health and health care in the international sphere.[4]

Philosophers have argued that health care is a special form of social good, one not strictly commensurate with or replaceable by commodities in the marketplace.

Macklin, Ruth. "Bioethics and Public Policy in the Next Millennium: Presidential Address," *Bioethics* 15:5/6 (2001), 373–381. Copyright © 2001. Reprinted by permission of Blackwell Publishing Ltd.

[1] AIDS cases devastating hardest-hit countries, *The Nation's Health,* August 2000, p. 12.

[2] D. C. Jayasuriya. Health and Human Rights in the Third World. Paper delivered at the World Association of Medical Law Congress, Helsinki, Finland, August 8, 2000, published in Congress Proceedings, p. 516.

[3] R. L. Swarns. Loans to Buy AIDS Drugs Are Rejected By Africans. *New York Times,* August 22, 2000.

[4] N. Daniels, B. P. Kennedy, and I. Kawachi. Why Justice is Good for Our Health: The Social Determinants of Health Inequalities. *Daedalus* 1999; 128: 215–251; S. Marchand, D. Wikler, and B. Landesman. Class, Health, and Justice. *Milbank Quarterly* 1998; 76: 449–467; D. W. Brock. Broadening the Bioethics Agenda. *Kennedy Institute of Ethics Journal* 2000; 10: 21–38; S. R. Benatar. Global Disparities in Health and Human Rights: A Critical Commentary. *American Journal of Public Health* 1998; 88:295–300.

Following the concept introduced by Rawls[5] and elaborated by Norman Daniels in his writings related to justice in health care,[6] this line of reasoning adopts the premise that health is a 'primary good.' 'Primary goods' are things that every rational person would want because they are needed to carry out a personal life plan. Although health care and medications are not sufficient to guarantee good health, they are surely among the necessary conditions for attaining or restoring health in the case of treatable diseases. Daniels has made the compelling argument that access to basic health care is a requirement of justice. A goal of public health and medicine is to keep people as close as possible to the ideal of normal functioning, under reasonable resource constraints.[7] The question is how can this goal be accomplished on a global scale, and what sorts of public policies are needed to make progress toward that goal?

The second injustice that requires public policy remedies—the health status of women—has several dimensions. Maternal mortality remains unacceptably high in many developing countries, a consequence of limited health infrastructure, poorly trained birth attendants, and women's inevitable recourse to illegal and unsafe abortions. In the past decade, the rate of maternal mortality remained highest in Africa, with 9.4 deaths per 1000 live births. The death rate for Southeast Asian women was 6.1. In contrast, the rate was 1.4 for North and South America taken together, 0.6 for Europe, and 0.1 for the United States.[8] The platforms of the U.N.-sponsored international conferences in Cairo in 1994 and Beijing in 1995 called for increased access for women to appropriate, affordable and quality health, information, and related services throughout the life cycle; the strengthening of preventive programs that promote women's health; the undertaking of gender-sensitive initiatives that address sexually transmitted diseases, including HIV/AIDS, and sexual and reproductive health issues, among other goals. Yet a variety of factors continue to thwart progress toward these goals.

For at least the last ten years, scholars have documented a significant imbalance in the ratio of females to males in several Asian countries. The most recent census in one Asian country reported about 900 women for every 1000 men, and in another, only 929 females for every 1000 males. The single most important cause of the excess mortality rate among females in these Asian countries is thought to be systematic neglect of the health and nutrition needs of girls and women, especially among girls from birth to 4 years of age.[9] Other causes are high rates of maternal mortality, female infanticide, and abortion of female fetuses. This imbalance in the sex ratio has its roots in the low status of women in these cultures, which place a high priority on the health and education of male children to the exclusion of girl children in poor families.

A 1998 report of the World Health Organization revealed the role that attitudes toward sexuality and family planning play in contributing to unwanted pregnancy and sexually transmitted diseases, including HIV/AIDS, in women. In several African countries, condoms are associated with sex workers and premarital and extramarital sex, so many men are unwilling to use them within their marriage. The idea of using condoms with a marriage partner was rejected especially by men since 'condom use in marriage portends unfaithfulness which leads to mistrust.'[10] Groups interviewed in one study agreed that a woman who feared infection by her partner should try to convince him to use a condom, but all also believed that this would not be easy, as women have to submit to male demands or face rejection or violence. Similar groups in another study also said that refusing sex or asking a man to use a condom was likely to lead to violence, rejection and separation.

Lest those of us from industrialized countries and long-established democracies be too complacent, I want to emphasize that inequalities in women's health status and access to health care are not confined to developing countries. An article entitled 'Human Rights Is a US Problem, Too'[11] documents the limited access to medical care of HIV-infected women in the United States, most of whom are poor. 81% of women recently diagnosed with AIDS in the US are black or Hispanic. The article

---

[5]J. Rawls. 1971. *A Theory of Justice*. Cambridge, MA. The Belknap Press.

[6]N. Daniels. 1985. *Just Health Care*. Cambridge. Cambridge University Press.

[7]Daniels, Kennedy, and Kawachi, 1998, p. 228.

[8]W. H. Helfand, J. Lazarus, and P. Theerman. Safe Motherhood Means: Social Equity for Women. *American Journal of Public Health* 2000; 90: 1382.

[9]A. Cohen. Excess Female Mortality in India: The Case of Himachal Pradesh. *American Journal of Public Health* 2000; 90: 1369–1371, p. 1369.

[10]E.K. Baaui, C.O. Garimoi, P. Maharaj, A.C.S. Mushingeh, S. Neema, E. Ngirwamungu, and P. Riwa. Attitudes to sexuality and family planning. *Progress in Human Reproduction Research* No. 48. 1998. UNDF/UNFPA/WHO/World Bank Special Programme of Research, Development and Research Training in Human Reproduction. Geneva, Switzerland: 7.

[11]E. L. Gollub. Human Rights Is a US Problem, Too: The Case of Women and HIV. *American Journal of Public Health* 1999; 89: 1479–1482.

faults the public health prevention messages from the government as 'punitive and rigid' and the government's response generally as paternalistic and condescending. As an example, the article cites the US public health message insisting that women convince men to wear condoms 100% of the time or refuse sex. Yet, the author notes, most women at greatest risk of HIV infection fail to accomplish these preventive steps.

The continued subordinate status of women in so many parts of the world is a gross injustice, one that stems from a conception of justice different from that of the maldistribution of health and health care in the world. The form of injustice that results in the poor health status of women is gender discrimination, plain and simple. Women and girls are disvalued, treated as inferior to men and boys, and in some countries, both married and unmarried women are limited by law and custom in the exercise of their autonomy. Given these phenomena with deep cultural roots, what role can public policy play in seeking to change the fundamental cultural values?

As we reflect on past institutions and episodes from history, some quite recent or even still current, we cannot help but wonder how intelligent and otherwise morally upstanding human beings could have tolerated and endorsed them. To name only a few: the hideous human experiments conducted by otherwise reputable German doctors during the Nazi era; the infamous Tuskegee syphilis study sponsored by the United States Public Health Service; the forced sterilization of women in government-sponsored programs to control population. It is an interesting thought experiment to imagine what ethical judgments will be made 100 or 1,000 years from now regarding the current global inequities in health status and health care. Might future generations judge wealthy nations to have been unconscionably remiss in failing to make genuine efforts to close the gap? Might bioethicists 200 years from now ask why public policy at the turn of the 21st century was not directed more forcefully at eliminating violence against women and addressing the problem of excess female mortality in countries where that demographic situation exists?

Perhaps most striking of all, will bioethicists in future generations be flabbergasted by the situation in the super-rich and powerful United States of America, where 44 million people are without health insurance—that is 18.4 percent of the population—and necessary medications are beyond the reach even of many people who have a minimal form of health insurance? Will they

be even more amazed to learn that in 1999, when the US economy was booming, 31 million people in the country grappled with hunger or often could not afford to eat balanced meals? And that number is tiny in comparison with those who are starving or near starvation in the developing world. When bioethicists of the future read the mainstream literature of our field from the last three decades of the 20th century, they may very well wonder about us: Why was only a very small percentage of the literature in our field devoted to the injustice in health status, access to health care and adequate nutrition, and morbidity and mortality of women over these decades as bioethics has come to maturity?

If the hope for rectifying at least some of these injustices lies in developing responsive public policies, several key questions need to be addressed. One of the most vexing is: Whose responsibility is it to develop and implement such public policies? If politicians in the wealthy United States cannot see fit to ensure universal health care and adequate food to all citizens of their own nation, what hope is there for resource-poor countries that cannot begin to afford comprehensive health care for their citizens? Is it reasonable to expect wealthy countries to devote a substantial portion of their own resources to helping the poorest countries to improve the health status of their citizens? Is it plausible to hold that considerations of justice give rise to such obligations?

One place to begin is in the vast and growing international research enterprise. Professor Coovadia from South Africa has written:

> A major consideration in research among third world populations is the application of the basic ethical principle of distributive justice. No intervention is supportable unless it is made widely available to the affected population. This principle requires that studies should benefit, not only participants in a trial, but also the class of persons they represent.[12]

This sentiment is echoed in international ethical guidelines for research, such as those issued by the Council of International Organizations of Medical Sciences (CIOMS):

> As a general rule, the sponsoring agency should agree in advance of the research that any product developed through such research will be made reasonably available to the inhabitants of the host community or country at the completion of successful testing. Exceptions to this general requirement should be justified and agreed to by all concerned parties before the research begins.'[13]

---

[12]H. M. Coovadia. The Expectations of Resource-poor Countries in Clinical Research. *Good Clinical Practice Journal* 1999; 6: 16–17, p. 16.

[13]Council of International Organizations of Medical Sciences. 1993. *International Ethical Guidelines for Biomedical Research Involving Human Subjects*. Geneva: 45, Guideline 15.

Yet concurrence with this viewpoint is by no means universal. Speaking from my own experience, I witnessed disagreement among participants at a meeting sponsored by the Nuffield Council in London in 1999. One researcher from a developing country argued that the clause in the CIOMS guidelines that seeks to ensure that products are made 'reasonably available' is too weak, since it does not promise enough. Yet another participant, a researcher from the UK, contended that a requirement to make a product reasonably available to inhabitants of a poor country is too strong, since the country or industry sponsoring the research would never want to undertake such an obligation and the result would be that research simply could not be done in those countries.

In another personal experience, I spent the last year serving as a consultant to the National Bioethics Advisory Commission in the United States, working on its forthcoming report on international collaborative research. When the Commission tackled the question, 'What obligations do industry and industrialized country sponsors of research have to the population in resource-poor countries *after* the research is completed?' they found it most difficult to reach agreement. Individual commissioners reversed their positions from one meeting to the next, and often disagreed with one another. The Commission readily agreed that sponsors of research should provide successful products of the research to the individuals who participated in a study if they still need those products after the study has ended, and also that sponsors should assist in capacity building in those countries. A final version of the Commission's report is just now being prepared, so we will soon learn what was the consensus on making products available to the host country or community after research is concluded.

Several prominent bioethicists from the United States have stated a clear and persuasive position on what is owed to developing countries in international collaborative research, as follows:

> If the research only has the potential to benefit the limited number of individuals who participate in the study, it cannot offer the benefit to the underdeveloped country that legitimizes the use of its citizens as research subjects. It should be emphasized that research whose goal is to prevent or treat large populations is fundamentally public health research, and public health research makes no sense (and thus should not be done) if its benefits are limited to the small population of research subjects.[14]

In recent years, some promising activities have been taking place on the international scene. We can see the beginnings of efforts to address the overwhelming health needs of resource-poor countries in several initiatives to make the successful products of research available to developing countries where experimental products are tested. The use of prior agreements—outlining a realistic plan for making the proposed research product available after a study is completed—is a relatively new phenomenon, and appears to be growing.

The World Health Organization (WHO), the International Aids Vaccine Initiative (IAVI), a non-profit organization founded in 1996, and UNAIDS, the Joint United Nations Programme on HIV/AIDS, have all entered into some types of agreement in advance of beginning research. WHO collaborates with industry to promote the development of health-related products and technologies stemming from agreements aimed at ensuring that successful products will be made widely available at low cost to both the public sector and developing countries. IAVI has managed to broker novel pricing and intellectual property agreements with industrial partners, designed to increase global access to AIDS vaccines developed with IAVI support. And UNAIDS has succeeded in getting certain manufacturers to agree to preferential pricing agreements for developing countries prior to the initiation of research.[15] These efforts demonstrate that arriving at prior agreements is indeed possible. Yet these efforts are just bare beginnings. Granted, a shift from marketplace values to those of distributive justice cannot and will not take place all at once. The challenge for the next decades is to expand such agreements, and to create and implement broader public policies that have a good likelihood of diminishing the inequities in health and health care that exist within nations and throughout the world. Expressed in the language of the international human rights framework, we need to work toward a 'progressive realization' of this goal.

As for the injustices related to discrimination against women and the resulting morbidity and excess mortality of women in many countries, there is a role for human rights activists and watchdog organizations to play. The campaign launched by the late Jonathan Mann to join public health and human rights had already begun in attention to women's health in the United Nations conferences in Cairo and Beijing in the mid-1990s. A summit meeting of world leaders at the United Nations in New York that concluded on

---

[14]L. Glantz, G. J. Annas, M. Grodin, and W. Mariner. Research in Developing Countries: Taking 'Benefit' Seriously. *Hastings Center Report* 1998: 41.

[15]For additional details, see the draft report of the National Bioethics Advisory Commission, Chapter 4, at www.bioethics.gov

September 8, 2000 resulted in a Millennium Declaration from the General Assembly. The Declaration included the following fundamental values as essential in international relations in the 21st century:

Under the heading of *equality:* 'The equal rights of women and men must be assured'.

Under the heading of *solidarity:* 'Those who suffer, or who benefit least, deserve help from those who benefit most.'

The United Nations Millennium Declaration also included the following resolutions: 'By the year 2015, to have reduced maternal mortality by three-quarters, and under-5 child mortality by two-thirds, of their current rates'; and further, 'To encourage the pharmaceutical industry to make essential drugs more widely available and affordable by all who need them in developing countries.'[16]

In conclusion: if these United Nations resolutions are to be more than aspirational ideals, governments, nongovernmental organizations, and the private sector need to work together on an international scale to establish public policies that take meaningful steps to implement these goals. It is my sincere hope that we, as bioethicists, will do our part.

Examining American Bioethics: Its Problems and Prospects

Renée C. Fox and Judith P. Swazey

In 1986, philosopher-bioethicist Samuel Gorovitz published an essay entitled "Baiting Bioethics," in which he reported on various criticisms of bioethics that were "in print, or voiced in and around . . . the field" at that time, and set forth his assessment of their legitimacy.[1] He gave detailed attention to what he judged to be the particularly fierce and "irresponsible attacks" on "the moral integrity" and soundness of bioethics contained in two papers: "Getting Ethics" by philosopher William Bennett[2] and "Medical Morality Is Not Bioethics," coauthored by us.[3] Gorovitz attributed some of the criticisms that bioethics was eliciting to the fact that this new, rapidly rising, and increasingly visible field had brought "scholars and practitioners together who otherwise would have little exposure to one another's disciplines. Their interactions are mutually enriching at times," he declared, "but mutually baffling and even infuriating at other times." In this latter regard, he suggested that "perhaps" Fox and Swazey's characterization of bioethics in the article he dissected "reflects a general revulsion at endeavors they see as inadequately like the social sciences or insufficiently respectful of them."[4] He went on to say that despite his objections to our "complaints" about bioethics—especially to our claim that "autonomy [had] been an unduly emphasized value" in the field—he had "a lingering sense" that there might be "a grain of truth" in them.[5] Gorovitz ended his essay with an affirmation about the "benefit" that bioethics can derive from "responsible" and even from "irresponsible" criticism.

"The unexamined discipline invites the philosopher's critical scrutiny no less than the unexamined life," he aphoristically concluded.[6]

It may seem incongruous to introduce our reflections on the future of bioethics with a commentary by Gorovitz published almost two decades ago. We have done so because we consider it pertinent to some of the characteristics of the outlook, agenda, and atmosphere of present-day bioethics that, in our view, need to be addressed and altered in order to advance the state of the field in ways that would enlarge and enrich its perspective, concerns, and content. To begin with, Gorovitz's spirited observations and opinions indicate that bioethics evoked a considerable amount of criticism and controversy then, as it does now, both from within and from outside the field. His riposte reflects a highly ambivalent attitude toward this criticism—an espousal of its potential intellectual value for improving the field and of its moral virtuousness on the one hand and, on the other, a strong disapproval and sharp rejection of what he considered to be erroneous, "misguided," or "baiting" about it. This kind of ambivalence continues to rend the field.

In addition, Gorovitz identified the multidisciplinary composition of bioethics as a source of the "[d]iverse expectations, disappointments, and criticisms [that] surround [the field],"[7] and he associated our own critique of bioethics with the chagrin that he thought we might be feeling about the subordinate status accorded to the social sciences in this field of

---

[16]B. Crossette. U.N. Meeting Ends with Declaration of Common Values. *New York Times,* September 9, 2000, A4.

"applied ethics" that, however pluridisciplinary it might be, had a closer relationship to moral philosophy. The assumption on the part of certain bioethicists that the criticisms of the field expressed by social scientists like ourselves are rooted in our "desire to supplant philosophy with sociology"[8] or with some other social science discipline has persisted to this day.

AMERICAN BIOETHICS: AREAS OF CONCERN AND CONTENTION

It is both notable and intriguing that despite the relatively short life span of bioethics, a number of differing accounts exist about when and why it began[9] and rapidly evolved into a new arena of public as well as academic and clinical–medical significance. Nevertheless, it is generally agreed that the field began to develop institutionally and underwent its first stage of professionalization in the United States during the late 1960s and 1970s, and that, since that time, it has not only grown exponentially in this country, but has emerged in a wide and diverse array of other societies. There is no bioethics "map" that comprehensively identifies the countries in which bioethics now exists or that provides cartographic information about its salient features in different societal contexts. For this reason, and because virtually since its inception, we have been both participant-observers and observing participants in U.S. bioethics, our commentary on the present state and the potential future of bioethics will be confined to the American setting. Throughout its short historical span, U.S. bioethics has been marked by debate-surrounded criticism regarding its conceptual framework, methodology, multidisciplinary composition and dynamics, agenda of moral issues, relationships with the social institutions and culture of American society, and its international scope and relevance. This ongoing, often tension-ridden, criticism, which has emanated largely from persons working in the field, has clustered around certain nodal areas of concern and contention:[10]

- The privileged place occupied by philosophy and philosophers in a field that is purportedly interdisciplinary and the tenuous, noninterpenetrative relations between the disciplines that compose the field. The predominant influence of Anglo-American analytic philosophy in bioethical thought, and the associated "principlism" view that the four principles of autonomy, beneficence, nonmaleficence, and justice are adequate to treat most moral issues relevant to health, illness, and medicine.[11] The "triumph" of a rational, highly individualistic conception of autonomy over all other moral principles, and an emphasis on individual rights, choice, and welfare that outbalances the invocation of responsibilities, obligations, and duties.

- The insufficient weight accorded to the connections between self and others, interpersonal relationships, human dependency and interdependency, community values, public health, social solidarity, trust, and the common good—and, more generally and basically, to the role and influence of social, cultural, historical, and "contextual" factors in how ethical questions are defined, approached, and debated, and in what James Gustafson calls the "density of experience" that the "lived" moral life involves (Gufstason J, interview, June 17–18, 1999).

- The secondary moral status accorded to virtues and qualities of the heart, like compassion, sympathy, kindness, and caring, and to the principle of beneficence, that entail an active regard for the welfare of others, an emotional response of empathy for their suffering or misfortune, and the humane motivation to help alleviate their distress.

- The appropriateness of incorporating religious scholarship and viewpoints and religiously resonant human condition questions about human origins, identity, nature, and destiny, the meaning of suffering, and the mysteries of life and death into the secularly grounded normative thought of bioethics.

- The narrow biomedical focus of bioethics, its continuous preoccupation with a limited roster of advances in biology, medicine, and medical technology, such as assisted means of reproduction; genetic screening, engineering, and therapy; organ replacement; the use of life support and life-sustaining technologies; and euthanasia, including physician-assisted suicide. The tendency of bioethicists, at particular junctures, to become preoccupied with certain of these biomedical developments—for example, organ transplantation or, at the present time, the human genome, stem cell research, and cloning.

- The field's relative inattention to ethical questions of social justice in American society, framed by the fact that a record 45 million persons currently do not have health insurance and millions more are under-insured, and by the adverse effects on their access to medical care and their health experienced by the increasing number (an estimated 35% of the population) who live below the poverty line in this, the wealthiest country in the world.

- The insular and insulated perspective of U.S. bioethics on global health and health care, particularly the degree to which many bioethicists distance themselves from ethical issues related to health, illness, and poverty in developing countries—most notably, the catastrophic consequences of the epidemic of HIV/AIDS, the emergence and the reemergence of numerous other infectious diseases (such as tuberculosis and malaria), and the dearth of affordable drugs to treat them in such poor, often besieged societies. The concomitant tendency of American bioethics to define these problems as macroeconomic and macropolitical, rather than moral in nature.

- The maintenance of a distinction between bioethical and human rights issues and of a line of demarcation between bioethics and international human rights law—with the unintended consequence of pushing occurrences such as the alleged complicity of U.S. military medical personnel in the abuses of detainees in Iraq, Afghanistan, and Guantanamo Bay to the outer edge of bioethicists' engrossments.

- Concerns about the propensity of individual and institutional participants in bioethics to become "coopted" or "captured" by the medical profession (physicians, medical schools, hospitals), the pharmaceutical and biotechnological industry, the competitive, self-interested aspects of free markets, the media, government agencies, and/or the regnant political atmosphere in the larger society.
- The propensity toward dichotomization and polarization in bioethical thought, with the result (in the words of one participant in bioethics) that it gets "trapped in binaries" that are difficult to reconcile (Gustafson J, interview, June 17–18, 1999). Primary among the dichotomies that have bifurcated bioethical discussion and its literature are (1) conceptions of a universal "common morality," on the one hand, and of ethical and cultural particularism, pluralism, contextualism, and "relativism," on the other (accompanied by disagreement about how Western and American U.S. bioethics is and ought to be); (2) what are considered to be the domains of intrinsically moral considerations versus the spheres of social, cultural, and/or legal issues; (3) the sharp distinction made between descriptive ethics and normative ethics; (4) the split that exists between an espousal of science- and technology-propelled biomedical progress with few constraints, and concern about the bodily damage and the debasing and "technologizing" of human life that may result from unlimitedly pursuing and applying new medical knowledge.

Some of these dichotomously expressed differences and controversies, such as the fissure between what philosopher/bioethicist Tom Beauchamp terms "cultural relativity and moral universality,"[12] the split between what philosopher/bioethics pioneer Daniel Callahan calls "individual and common good,"[13] and the divide between descriptive and normative ethics,[14] "largely arose in philosophy and have been perpetuated [in bioethics] using philosophical discourse,"[15] Some have been supported and augmented by basic American values. This is notably the case, for example, with regard to the role that American individualism—one of the predominant ideas around which the society and culture have been organized since the beginning of the nation's history—has played in the weight that has been accorded to the principle of autonomy and in heightening the tension between individual and common good. In addition, the affect and rhetoric with which these binary issues have been discussed at different stages in the unfolding of bioethics have been influenced by the surrounding political and ideological atmosphere in the country at the time. For example, during the inaugural years of U.S. bioethics, the nascent field attracted a sizable number of persons who had been intensively engaged during their student years in the civil rights, antiwar, and women's movements of the 1960s and 1970s. They carried their militant individualism, antipaternalism, and antiauthority convictions with them into bioethics and helped to shape its individualism-grounded values and rights language. More recently (from the mid-1990s to the present), as Daniel Callahan has noted with concern, a tendency for controversy between bioethicists to become more polarized and acrimoniously polemical has developed in what he characterizes as a previously "irenic field," in which the discussions that took place between bioethicists around areas of debated criticism were once "remarkably friendly."[16] He attributes this change in tone to the incorporation of the American "culture wars" between conservatives and liberals taking place on the current political scene into the matrix of bioethics.[17]

SHAPING THE FUTURE OF BIOETHICS

What bearing does our compressed account of the persistent foci of criticism, controversy, and structural strain inside bioethics have on our ideas about what could and should be the future of bioethics? To begin with, in our view, fundamental to any endeavor by bioethicists to shape bioethics' future is learned and insightful knowledge and understanding of the patterns of thought and the underlying value commitments that presently characterize the field, its prevailing intellectual and cultural ethos and ambience, and the historical, social, and cultural influences that have contributed to these attributes. Sociologist-bioethicist Adam M. Hedgecoe considers this sort of "reflexivity" to be integral to a "critical bioethics" that is sufficiently "self-aware"—individually and collectively—to take into account where the field and its participants "come from," and to be able to "think about how bioethics came to occupy the position that it does," and the "issues of power and authority" that this raises.[18] We regard such "reflexivity" to be especially important in thinking penetratingly about the present and future state of bioethics, both because of its multidisciplinary composition and because it is not, and never has been, just an academic, medically relevant field. From its inception, the value and belief questions that U.S. bioethics has pursued have paralleled "collective conscience" issues with which American society has been grappling more broadly—"albeit phrased in its own . . . medicalized, ethicized, and secularized vocabulary."[19] Further, debate and deliberation about bioethical questions have not been confined to classrooms and clinics, but have continually taken place in public arenas and within political or quasi-political institutions including print and electronic media, commissions appointed by the U.S. Congress or the President of the United States, and state and federal legislatures and courts.

The need for greater interdisciplinarity

As British philosopher Onora O'Neill has aptly commented, despite the fact that bioethics is "a meeting ground for a number of disciplines, discourses, and organizations concerned with ethical, legal, and social questions raised by advances in medicine, science, and biotechnology,"[20] its "interdisciplinarity" is "tenuous."[21] By and large, the field is made up of enclaves of persons from different disciplines who tolerate each other (up to a point), but seldom allow themselves to be touched or altered by the perspectives of disciplines other than their own. The interchange between bioethicists from different disciplines tends to be substantively thin, characterized by superficial understanding of the ethos, concepts, knowledge base, methods of inquiry, and modes of justification and proof of other disciplines, and fraught with repetitive misunderstandings. Remedying this state of affairs by working concertedly to make bioethics more interpenetratingly interdisciplinary is high on the list of our aspirations and recommendations. We believe that achieving this would go a long way toward breaking through the cleavages that rend the field.

As we have indicated, we do not mean by this that the disciplines that contribute to bioethics should be reshuffled so that moral philosophy and its ethical theory exert a less strong influence than they have until now. Here, we diverge from Beauchamp's opinion, given in a recent, remarkably candid and lucid article, that the bioethics literature has "shifted in the past 15 years or so toward great levels of comfort with law, policy studies, empirical studies, standards of practice, government guidelines, and international guidelines," to a degree that raises the "question, whether ethical theory [any longer] has a significant role in bioethics"—a question, he comments, that is "worth considering."[22] In our view, among the constellation of disciplines that have converged around bioethics, philosophy is the most appropriate one to play a central role in the examination and analysis of the fundamental moral issues that the field addresses. But the philosophical base that we envisage would not be as rigid as it has been until now. Rather, the philosophical underpinnings of bioethics would become more supple and porous so that some of the boundaries in which bioethical–philosophical thought is presently enclosed could be traversed in ways that facilitated the integration of social (including economic and political), cultural (including religious), legal, and historical variables, and other disciplines' ways of thinking about them, into the foundational intellectual structure of the field. The sort of complementarity that we believe is needed is illustrated by Pakistani and American surgeon and bioethicist Fahrat Moazam's call to balance secular philosophical principles and religious virtue ethics in a bioethics that draws upon Abrahamic faiths—Islam, Judaism, and Christianity—and that integrates concerns about "Is this an ethical act?" with "Is the active agent an ethical agent?"[23] The kind of renovated framework that we propose would also increase the theoretical pluralism of American bioethics' philosophical outlook by bringing the standards and principles of analytic philosophy, which dominate the field, into an intersecting relationship with an expanded range of philosophical views (including Continental European schools of thought), in a manner that is less extrinsic and "shotgun" reactive than the current tendency to simply "add on" alternative approaches, such as feminist, virtue, and narrative ethics and casuistry.

There has been some tendency to seize upon "quick-fix" solutions in efforts that have been made to more influentially and effectively incorporate social science and a wider range of philosophical approaches into bioethics' conceptual framework. An example of this is the "bandwagon-like" way in which both philosopher and social scientist participants in bioethics have embraced ethnography as "salvational."[24] A more promising development toward the kind of integration of social science and social thought into bioethics that Hedgecoe envisions seems to have occurred when a small interdisciplinary group (including three philosophers, three sociologists, two religionists, two anthropologists, a jurist, and a political scientist) was invited to spend the 2003–2004 academic year together in residence at the School of Social Sciences of Princeton's Institute of Advanced Studies. Their year-long interchanges appear to have resulted in a socially oriented convergence of their disciplinary perspective that continues to be reflected in their ongoing publications,[25] activities such as organizing conferences,[26] and their plans for collaborative research.[27]

Balancing universalism and particularism

We also feel that it is imperative for the conceptual framework and the outlook of U.S. bioethics to be less tipped in the direction of the kind and degree of intellectual and moral preference for universalism over particularism that it currently displays—a preference that minimizes, and in certain ways denigrates, the particularities of historical circumstances and traditions and of social and cultural contexts and locales, and that (to borrow a phrase from French sociologist Pierre Bordieu), "imperializes universality" by "universalizing its own ... particular [cultural] characteristics."[28] Closely related to this, in our view, is the moral responsibility that U.S. bioethics has to move in the transnational direction of expanding its agenda of ethical concerns beyond its own borders to pay greater attention to issues of global health and to approach these issues in a cross-culturally sensitive, respectful, and knowledgeable manner.

The education and training of bioethicists

The changes that we would like to see take place in the orientation of American bioethics cannot occur simply through the resolution of bioethicists to effect them. They call for a thoughtful, deliberative reconsideration of the education and training involved in equipping people to work in this field—training in their baseline discipline(s), and in Ph.D.[29] and Master's programs. With respect to graduate degrees, we recognize the time and course-work constraints of Master's programs, but nonetheless believe that they could be restructured to include, in a compressed form, the types of educational content discussed below to at least make students more aware of and knowledgeable about the competencies that can be developed.[30]

To begin with, the fundamental competence that every bioethicist ought to have should be grounded in his/her discipline of origin. In a rock-bottom sense, the quality of bioethical thought, research, and analysis depends on disciplinary excellence—no matter which is the primary discipline from whose foundations a participant in bioethics works.

In addition, if our premise that philosophy should have a pivotal place in bioethical theory and reflection is accepted, it follows from this that anyone intending to be seriously involved in the field should have more than a perfunctory introduction to philosophy. That introduction should not be confined to analytic philosophy or to a reductionistic, rotelike understanding of its emanation in principlism. Nor should it consist of a smorgasbord mix of approaches. Rather, the diversity of philosophical outlooks should be brought together and related to one another in a way that maximizes the potentiality of incorporating social, cultural, and historical factors into moral analysis and comprehension.

Because bioethics is a multidisciplinary field with interdisciplinary aspirations, it also requires some degree of training and experience in at least one discipline other than one's "home" field. Achieving and maintaining interdisciplinary competence is intellectually demanding and cannot be accomplished through a packaged set of presentations given by a series of lecturers from an array of fields. In the case of philosopher–bioethicist

Norman Daniels, for example, as he has attested, doing "serious work on issues of social justice in health care" required his "willingness to look at political science and economics." It entailed "an enormous . . . intellectual investment" to attain "a really good mastery of literature and work on distributive justice." He also had to "learn something about the whole design of health care—who gets health care, who doesn't, what were the determinants of health care":

> This really was a full-time intellectual task to master a whole body of literature . . . of vaster scope than most background literature on particular problems that you work on in isolation in bioethics. . . . I . . . read health economics textbooks . . . and bunches of books on the sociology of health care, comparative health care systems, [and] literature on the access to heath care. . . . In effect, I would say I did the equivalent of a Ph.D. in health policy just to get to the point where I felt comfortable talking about health systems. (Daniels N, interview, May 14, 1999)

Whether in the context of M.A. or Ph.D. programs in bioethics, one of the goals of the curriculum should be imparting to students the importance and value of interdisciplinary knowledge and understanding, a solid sense of what it involves, and the kind of long-term motivation to develop it that Daniels describes. A pedagogically effective way of initiating this process might be to organize the interdisciplinary training in at least two fields in a fashion that is equivalent to a major and a minor.[31]

We consider it as critical—perhaps even more so—for American bioethics to strengthen its commitment to dealing with the international and cross-cultural as well as the local and national aspects of the value-laden issues with which it is concerned and to identify and institute ways to forge stronger links between them. In this connection, it seems to us, knowledge in detail and depth of at least one society other than one's own—its history, social institutions and organization, culture, and worldview—is essential. "You rarely know enough about one society, let alone more than one, to generalize usefully—or safely," modern European historian Eugen Weber has cautioned. Nevertheless, he affirms, although it may be "hard to do it well, . . . that's no reason not to try," because developing such comparative knowledge "opens perspectives, suggests questions and possibilities, indicates untried directions and correspondences, and helps us to avoid provincialism and facile assumptions."[32] We would add that it also sharpens recognition of the defining characteristics of one's own society and culture—what is distinctive and idiosyncratic about them, and what they have in common with those of other societies and cultural traditions. Philosopher Martha Nussbaum terms this "cosmopolitan education," through which students "learn to recognize humanity wherever they encounter it, undeterred by traits that are strange to them, and . . . eager to understand humanity in all its strange guises." "They must learn enough about the different to learn about common aims, aspirations, and values," she declares, "and enough about the common ends to see how variously they are instantiated in the many cultures and their histories."[33]

Consonant with Weber and Nussbaum, we urge that, at the very least, Ph.D. programs and, in a more limited way, M.A. programs in bioethics launch their enrollees on the systematic study of a society or societies other than their own, in a manner that provides them with insight about why this knowledge is important. In our view, the comparative perspective that it provides is vital, if U.S. bioethics is to break through the dichotomy between universalism and particularism to which it cleaves, acknowledge some of the specifically American and Western attributes of its premises and concepts, and enlarge the geographical orbit of its medico-moral concerns to pay greater attention to the causes and consequences of the most serious global health problem that besets the present-day world: the rise and ravages of newly emerging and of reemerging infectious diseases.

Bioethics and the culture wars

We feel morally as well as intellectually compelled to end our consideration of American bioethics with an admonitory statement about the escalating ideological and political animosity currently taking place between so-called liberal and conservative bioethicists within the field. This rancorousness has been conspicuous in statements made by bioethicists on both sides of the divide in professional publications, blog sites, and the media about matters such as embryonic stem cell research, therapeutic and reproductive cloning, genetic enhancement, other uses of fetal tissues and embryos, end-of-life issues, the place of religious thought and belief in ethical analysis, and about the potential dangers and harms as well as benefits that advances in medical science and technology can bring in their wake.[34] In many respects, the divisiveness that has developed inside of bioethics mirrors the passion-accompanied divisions between liberals and conservatives about "moral values" in American society, concerning matters such as gay marriage and gay rights more generally, abortion, and stem cells, which have escalated, often flamboyantly, during and since the U.S. Presidential election of 2004. In the realm of bioethics, it runs counter to the composed, fair-minded, rationally thoughtful outlook ideally associated with a philosophically oriented field. And it is indicative of a general lack of awareness by bioethicists of the ways in which the ambience and ethos of their field are being tainted by the harshness and lack of tolerance surrounding the politico-ideological splits on the larger American scene.

We consider the strife that has been mounting among bioethicists to be amoral, destructive, and self-destructive. We agree with Daniel Callahan that "if bioethics is to retain its vitality and be taken seriously, it will have to find a way to extricate itself from the culture wars":

> It will have to remember that it is possible for bioethicists to be wrong without being immoral, that bioethics harms itself if it turns into a moral crusade, either for the values of the left or the right, and that a healthy bioethics will be one where conservatives and liberals understand they have a common cause, one best pursued in lively dialogue rather than as opposing armies.[35]

A particularly revealing manifestation of the way in which the so-called culture wars that have erupted around bioethical issues in the United States has recently played out in a florid, unsettling, and tragic fashion concerns the case of Terri Schiavo, who was in a persistent vegetative state for 15 years and had no written advanced directive indicating how she would want to be treated in this type of circumstance. Michael Schiavo, her husband and legal guardian, believed she would not have chosen to be kept alive with the artificial feeding and hydration that she was receiving at a hospice in Florida. Her parents, Mr. and Mrs. Robert Schindler, fiercely contended that the feeding tube should not be removed, holding that this would go against Terri's wishes if she could make them known and also because they did not accept the medical determination that she was in a persistent vegetative state without hope of recovery.

Beginning in 1998, Terri Schiavo's husband and parents engaged in a moral and legal battle over the removal of her feeding tube that was enacted in state and federal courts and legislatures. Court rulings in April 2001, including the U.S. Supreme Court's refusal to intervene in the case, led to the tube's removal and, then, after another court order, its reinsertion. In October 2003, the tube again was removed after another court order and again reinserted after Florida's lower house passed "Terri's Law," giving Governor Jeb Bush the authority to order her physicians to provide artificial nutrition and hydration. Then, in September 2004, the Florida Supreme Court struck down Terri's Law, upholding a lower court ruling that it was unconstitutional and a violation of the right to privacy. When the U.S. Supreme Court, in January 2005, refused to hear Governor Bush's appeal to change the Florida ruling, the case went back to the Florida courts.

To a virtually unprecedented degree, the case was catapulted into the public square by Terri's desperate parents and their supporters when, on March 16, a Florida Appellate Court refused to block removal of the feeding tube and set March 18 as the date for the discontinuation of artificial feeding. In rapid order, the Schindlers filed another emergency appeal with the U.S. Supreme Court on March 17, arguing that lower courts again needed to review their daughter's case, this time with respect to whether her religious freedom and due process rights had been violated; on March 18 the U.S. Congress moved to block removal of the feeding tube, a strategy rejected by the Florida judge who had previously ordered its removal that day. Next, on March 20 and 21, the U.S. House and Senate passed special emergency legislation for a federal court review of the case, and the bill was promptly signed into law by President George W. Bush. Between March 22 and 27, a series of state judges and courts rejected the Schindlers' emergency appeals and a petition by Governor Bush to be appointed as Terri's legal guardian, and refused to order reinsertion of the feeding tube. The Florida rulings were upheld by a federal judge and appellate court, and the U.S. Supreme Court twice more refused to intervene in the case.

Extensive media coverage of these legal and political events, along with innumerable interviews with Terri Schiavo's husband and parents, their attorneys, other family members, and advocates for both sides of the bitter dispute, all but eclipsed reporting of other news events.[36] Evangelically oriented religious conservatives, including key political figures in Congress, were key actors in the unfolding drama. President Bush and Vatican spokesmen affirmed their unwavering adherence to what they termed "the culture of life." Leaders and members of Catholic and Protestant "right to life" groups voiced their vehement opposition to the cessation of artificial feeding and hydration, with many engaging in public protests and vigils, including those held in front of Terri Schiavo's hospice under the glare of television cameras.

Terri Schiavo, age 41, died on March 31, 2005, at the Pinellas Park, Florida, hospice, 13 days after her feeding tube was removed. In our view, her case ominously epitomizes how societally serious, ideologized, and politicized the entwining of bioethical issues and the cultural split in the country has become. It also sharply frames the question of how, in a secular but nonetheless religiously resonant society under law rather than under men like the United States, such ultimate questions of life and death that are intrinsically religious can be resolved in the name of all its citizens—or even whether this is possible.

In his weekly "Beliefs" column for *The New York Times*, Peter Steinfels has called for "an honest discussion of the moral stances dividing Americans, [with] each side (and there may be more than two) addressing the contending arguments at their best and not their worst."[37] It is our strong conviction that unless this kind of colloquy pervades American bioethics, the future of the field will be so seriously jeopardized that any recommendations proposed for its betterment will be superfluous.[38]

NOTES

1. Gorovitz S. Baiting bioethics. *Ethics* 1986;96(Jan):356–74.

2. Bennett W. Getting ethics. *Commentary* 1980;Dec:62–5.

3. Fox RC, Swazey JP. Medical morality is not bioethics—Medical ethics in China and the United States. *Perspectives in Biology and Medicine* 1984;27(Spring):336–60.

4. See note 1, Gorovitz 1986:365.

5. See note 1, Gorovitz 1986:366, 367.

6. See note 1, Gorovitz 1986:372.

7. See note 1, Gorovitz 1986:356.

8. Chambers T. Centering bioethics. *Hastings Center Report* 2000;30(1):22–9, at 27.

9. The various historiographies of the beginning of bioethics are examined in an essay on "the coming of bioethics" in our forthcoming book on the development and role of bioethics in the United States. Some writers have assigned a "moment of creation" date, such as the Nuremberg Trials in 1947, the issuance of the Harvard Ad Hoc Committee's report on the definition of brain death in 1968, or the founding of the Hastings Center in 1969 and the Kennedy Institute in 1971. Other "origin stories" define a time period rather than a specific date of conception or birth, usually during the mid-1960s to early 1970s, or the late 1960s to mid-1970s. See, for example, Callahan D. The Hastings Center and the early years of bioethics. *Kennedy Institute of Ethics Journal* 1999;9(1):53–71; Chambers T. Retrodiction and the histories of bioethics. *Medical Humanities Review* 1998;12(1):9–22; Jonsen AR, ed. The birth of bioethics. Special supplement. *Hastings Center Report* 1993;23(6):S1–16; Jonsen AR. *The Birth of Bioethics.* New York: Oxford University Press, 1998; Reich WT. Revisiting the launching of the Kennedy Institute: Revisioning the origins of bioethics. *Kennedy Institute of Ethics Journal* 1996;6(4):323–7; Rothman D. *Strangers at the Bedside.* New York: Basic Books: 1991; Stevens T. *Bioethics in America: Origins and Cultural Politics.* Baltimore: Johns Hopkins University Press; 2000; Veatch R. The birth of bioethics: Autobiographical reflections of a patient person. *Cambridge Quarterly of Healthcare Ethics* 2002;11:344–52.

10. The areas identified come both from our reading of the bioethics literature and from the interviews we conducted with bioethicists as part of the Acadia Institute study.

11. The best known exposition of principlism is Tom Beauchamp and James Childress' *Principles of Biomedical Ethics* (New York: Oxford University Press). First published in 1979, the book is now in its fifth edition; a sixth edition is in preparation, and the book has been translated into many languages.

12. Beauchamp TL. Does ethical theory have a future in bioethics? *Journal of Law, Medicine & Ethics* 2004;32:209–17, at 216.

13. Callahan D. Individual good and common good. *Perspectives in Biology and Medicine* 2003;46(4):496–507.

14. Sugarman J. Sulmasy DP. *Methods in Medical Ethics.* Washington, DC: Georgetown University Press; 2001, at 4,10.

15. See note 12, Beauchamp 2004:216.

16. See note 13, Callahan 2003:498.

17. Callahan D. Bioethics and the American culture wars. Unpublished paper, 2003; Callahan D. Bioethics and the culture wars. *The Nation* 1997;264(14):23–4.

18. Hedgecoe AM. Critical bioethics: Beyond the social science critique of applied ethics. *Bioethics* 2004;18(2):120–43, at 138–40.

19. Fox RC. Is medical ethics asking too much of bioethics? Teaching the "nonbiomedical" aspects of medicine: The perennial patterns. *Daedalus* 1999;128:1–25, at 8.

20. O'Neill O. *Autonomy and Trust in Bioethics*. Cambridge, UK: Cambridge University Press; 2002, at 1.

21. O'Neill O. Reason and passion in bioethics [review of L. Kass. *Life, Liberty, and the Defense of Dignity. The Challenge for Bioethics*. San Francisco: Encounter Books; 2002]. *Science* 2002;298(20):2335.

22. See note 12, Beauchamp 2004:216.

23. Moazam F. Foundational ethical concepts in Islam: The Qur'an, Imam al-Ghazali, and Muslim physicians. Plenary speech, Aga Kahn University Symposium on Clinical Ethics, October 7, 2004.

24. See especially Hoffmaster B. Can ethnography save the life of medical ethics? *Social Science & Medicine* 1992;35:1421–36.

25. The fall 2004 issue of the *Hastings Center Report* (35,4), for example, had a cluster of articles discussing ethical concerns associated with the influence of the pharmaceutical industry. Three of the four papers were written by members of the Princeton group: Lemmens T. Piercing the veil of corporate secrecy about clinical trials (pp. 14–18); Elliot C. Pharma goes to the laundry: Public relations and the business of medical education (pp. 18–23); and DeVries R, Bosk C. The bioethics of business: Rethinking the relationship between bioethics consultants and corporate clients (pp. 28–32).

26. The sociologists in the Princeton group (Charles Bosk, Joseph Davis, and Raymond De Vries), for example, were members of the program committee headed by sociologist John Evan that organized a two-day "Sociology of Bioethics" conference, held in March 2005 at Georgetown and the Eastern Sociological Society meeting. In his communication to prospective participants, Evans exuberantly described the conference as "a watershed event in the nascent history of the sociology of bioethics," designed to expand and transform the informal contacts between sociologists working on bioethical topics into a more formally organized group of scholars (Evans J. e-mail communication to possible conference participants, October 11, 2004).

27. Members of the Princeton group have drafted a research proposal to study firsthand how international guidelines for the protection of human subjects in the global marketplace are (and are not) implemented in the regulatory systems of a cross section of different societies, with special attention to the needs of multinational corporations and the rights of national citizens in the area of industrialized drug testing. Sociologist R. G. De Vries, anthropologist A. Petryana, jurist T. Lemmens, and sociologist C. Bosk from the Princeton group, joined by philosopher-bioethicist J. Kahn, will constitute the research team.

28. Bordieu P. Uniting to better dominate. *Items and Issues* (Social Science Research Council) 2001;2(3–4):1–6, at 3.

29. A number of doctoral programs, particularly in philosophy, offer a concentration in bioethics within the degree program field: for example, a Ph.D. in philosophy with a concentration in bioethics. At present, Case Western Reserve University's Department of Bioethics offers the only Ph.D. in bioethics per se. Its program contains some of the types of interdisciplinary training that we recommend, although it has a heavy emphasis on methodology and does not mention social science in its program statement. Its research-oriented program objective is "[t]o train scholars who will have specific expertise in the conceptualization, design, and conduct of empirical research concerning bioethics questions. Training and competency in the methodology of traditional bioethics (philosophy, religious studies, law, and medical humanities) will also be provided" (www.cwru.edu/med/bioethics/phd.htm).

30. The limitations inherent in a Master's program are even more acute in short, intensive bioethics courses, but here too we advocate including a block of materials that would at least begin to make attendees more aware of the knowledge bases that would enhance their work in bioethics.

31. Another model for furthering and deepening fruitful interdisciplinary relations, learning, and collaboration between members of different fields working in the area of bioethics is to bring them together for a period of time in a manner comparable to the experience that was provided for the group working in bioethics at Princeton.

32. Weber E. Time travelers' tales [review of Schivelbusch W. *The Culture of Defeat: On National Trauma, Mourning, and Recovery*. New York: Henry Holt]. *The American Scholar* 2003;72(3):142–4, at 142, 144.

33. Nussbaum MC. Patriotism and cosmopolitanism. In: Cohen J ed. *For Love of Country. Debating the Limits of Patriotism*. Boston: Beacon Press; 1996:2–16, at 9.

34. Much of the criticism of "conservative" bioethics and bioethicists by self-professed "liberal" or "mainstream" bioethicists has focused on Leon R. Kass, Chairman of the President's Council on Bioethics established by George W. Bush, and on the composition of the Council and the contents of its reports. A fresh round of controversy was unleashed in March 2005, when Kass, acting, he maintains, as a private citizen rather than as Chairman of the Council, distributed a document entitled "Bioethics for the second [Bush] term: Legislative recommendations," to members of the U.S. Congress. The position paper was developed during discussions of an informal group led by Kass and Eric Cohen, editor of the conservative bioethics journal, *The New Atlantis*. The "second term" agenda calls for the passage of laws banning the use of various types of novel biotechnological reproductive methods. "We have today," the document concludes, "an administration and a Congress as friendly to human life and human dignity as we are likely to have for many years to come. It would be tragic if we failed to take advantage of this rare opportunity to enact significant bans on some of the most egregious biotechnical practices." The Kass agenda: "Bioethics for the second term." http://www.blog.bioethics.net. March 9, 2005 [*The American Journal of Bioethics* editor's blog]; see also Kintisch E. Anticloning forces launch second-term offensive. *Science* 2005;307 (Mar 18) at 1702–3.

35. See note 17, Callahan 2003.

36. A Google search on April 19, 2005, listed 5,620,000 entries for Terri Schiavo. For a small sample of the coverage of her case, see Brain-damaged Terri Schiavo dies. http://www.new.bbc.co.uk/1/hi/world/americas, March 31, 2005: Cohen E. How liberalism failed Terri Schiavo. http://theweeklystandard.com, Vol. 10(27), March 25, 2005; Feldman L, Richey F. The Terri Schiavo legacy. http://www.csmonitor.com/2005/0401/p01s01-ussc.htm; Glantz LH. The Schiavo tragedy. http://www.boston.com/news/globe/editorialopinion/op-ed/articles/2005/03/22; Quindlen A. The culture of each life. *Newsweek* April 4, 2005 at 62; Timeline: Terri Schiavo case. http://www.new.bbc.co.uk/1/hi/world/americas. March 31, 2005.

37. Steinfels P. Beliefs: Voters say values matter, but it's important to find out what reality is behind this convenient catchall. *New York Times* 2004 Nov 6:A15.

38. It is significant that Tom Beauchamp expressed his concern about the gravity of the partisan divisions in bioethics, and the importance of bridging them, in his acceptance speech, when he, along with James Childress, received a Lifetime Achievement Award at the October 2004 annual meeting of the American Society for Bioethics and Humanities.

RESPONSES TO PANDEMICS AND BIOTERRORISM

Flu Pandemic and the Fair Allocation of Scarce Life-Saving Resources: How Can We Make the Hardest of Choices?

The Hastings Centre

If—many experts say when—the next influenza pandemic strikes the United States, what values should guide our decisions on allocating tragically scarce resources such as vaccines, antiviral drugs, and ventilators? What ethical resources do we have to guide us in making these immensely difficult choices?

THE RISK: UNPREDICTABLE BUT UNAVOIDABLE

In 1918, nearly one in every two deaths in the United States was due to "Spanish influenza." Few Americans living today can remember that pandemic, which killed 675,000 Americans in a single year and tens of millions globally. Recent scientific studies suggest that the devastating influenza of 1918 was a bird flu virus that mutated to permit rapid human-to-human transmission.

Could it happen again? Avian influenza A (H5N1), which has killed 141 people worldwide as of August 2006, has not yet mutated into a virus capable of triggering a pandemic. This particular virus may never make that final, catastrophic change. But, experts agree, a new flu pandemic is inevitable. The US Department of Health and Human Services estimates that a pandemic, spreading rapidly among a much larger US population, could sicken 90 million of us, and kill 1.9 million. Ten million of us will need to be hospitalized; 1.5 million will require intensive care, as wave upon wave of new patients arrives in ERs.

Patients who are admitted to hospitals with acute respiratory infections may need up to 18 days in the ICU, as health care workers in Toronto and Singapore learned from treating SARS patients.

THE RESPONSE: A SHORTFALL IN RESOURCES

According to HHS estimates, during the first *year* of a pandemic, fewer than 10% of us will receive an effective vaccine. While there are federal stockpiles of experimental vaccines that may or may not prove effective, the mutated virus will be transmitted much faster than an effective vaccine, matched to the particular strain of the virus that triggers widespread human-to-human transmission, can be developed, manufactured, and distributed.

We will also probably lack an adequate supply of antiviral medication such as Tamiflu (oseltavimir) for the tens of millions of us who will need it. In addition, we may not have enough ventilators for the hundreds of thousands sick enough to require mechanical ventilation to help us breathe and allow our damaged lungs to heal. And what about the patients who are already in the ICU, or already on ventilators, when the pandemic strikes? Some of the resources we will need in a pandemic will inevitably already be in use by the very sickest patients in our hospitals.

HARD CHOICES: THE NECESSITY OF TRADE-OFFS

The prospect of a pandemic, and the reality of tragically scarce resources, compels all of us—policy makers, bioethicists, public health officials, and health care providers—to answer the hard question posed by Hastings Center Fellow John Arras: "Who shall live when not all can live?" This is not a question most Americans are accustomed to asking about our health care system. As a nation, we tend to be uncomfortable talking about "rationing" in health care. But in a pandemic, rationing is inevitable because there will not be sufficient resources to go around. And rationing, provided it is done in an ethical manner, will serve justice and save lives by conscientiously distributing scarce life-saving resources in harmony with our nation's deepest values, including fairness.

If we accept, as we must, that tragically scarce resources must be rationed, and that rationing decisions should not be left up to first responders, or to administrators and state and local policy makers working in isolation, what do federal policy makers need to know about the ethics of resource allocation to ensure that the nation's pandemic plans are ethically sound?

OPTIONS: DIRECTING SCARCE RESOURCES WHERE THEY WILL DO THE MOST GOOD

In a recent article in *JAMA*, Hastings Center Fellow Lawrence O. Gostin describes seven [sic] ethical options for rationing scarce health resources in a pandemic. These options can be summarized as follows:

- *Prioritize preventing new infection:* As Gostin points out, this is the "historic mission of public health." An ethically sound resource allocation plan should consider the extent to which limited supplies of vaccine or antiviral drugs should be reserved for "feasible, rapid deployment" to "contain localized outbreaks."
- *Prioritize essential medical and scientific personnel:* Protecting professionals who have specialized training and a duty to care for the sick is universally recognized as an ethically sound approach to resource allocation in a public health emergency. In a flu pandemic, essential personnel will also include the scientists working to identify effective vaccines and the public health workers responsible for tracking and responding to outbreaks. Determining who counts as "essential" is a key question: Should all physicians be vaccinated, or only those with training in certain specialties? Should all individuals involved in the vaccine-manufacturing process be vaccinated? What are the obligations of essential personnel once they have been prioritized for vaccination?
- *Prioritize health and safety infrastructure:* This is an extension of the "essential personnel" criterion—ambulance drivers, police, pharmacists, sanitation workers, and many other workers are crucial to the care of the sick, the functioning of health care organizations, and the safety of the general public. As with medical and scientific personnel, determining who counts as "essential," preventing abuses of this category, and describing the obligations of those who have been prioritized to receive scarce resources are essential parts of this ethical analysis.
- *Prioritize those with the greatest medical needs:* Health professionals prioritize patients according to medical need in emergency rooms every day. However, a pandemic will result in surges of acutely ill persons arriving at ERs for weeks or even months. How can pandemic plans help medical personnel make rapid and ethically sound decisions about who gets antiviral drugs or ventilators when all are desperate for care? Past flu pandemics, in 1918, 1957, and 1968, plus data from seasonal flu outbreaks, do not tell us who will be most susceptible to a new avian flu pandemic, or whose medical needs will be greatest. The very old and very young are most vulnerable to seasonal flu, but young adults were most vulnerable to the 1918 virus. What will happen to a hospital's current patients, including those on ventilators and others too sick to be discharged, when a pandemic looms or strikes? How will resource allocation plans address the plight of flu patients whose underlying health care problems make them less likely to respond to available therapies?

- *Prioritize based on life cycle:* Is it ever appropriate to consider age when determining whether one individual should be given priority over another? Some physicians argue that triage, for example, should never be done on the basis of age alone, although it is ethically acceptable to take a patient's overall health into account when determining who is most likely to benefit from care when all cannot be served. But Hastings Center Fellow Ezekiel J. Emanuel argues in favor of a "life-cycle allocation principle" for vaccination in particular. Under this principle, scarce vaccines would go to younger persons, preserving their opportunity to live a long, full life. Families contain persons of all ages, and pandemic planning must also consider how resource allocation decisions will affect different members of the same family and whether families will understand why a pandemic plan may provide different levels of protection to different persons.
- *Prioritize the chronically underserved:* One of the conditions for ethical action is that it must be applied fairly. An ethical plan for resource allocation can never be concerned solely with one's own institution or community, but must take into account existing imbalances in access to health care and to the resources needed in a pandemic. Pandemic planners have an obligation to make sure that low-income, rural, and isolated communities, and the health care institutions that serve them, are prepared for the pandemic and that existing imbalances are not exacerbated when the plan is put into action.
- *Prioritize early detection and response globally:* Gostin points out that avian flu vaccine manufacturing and distribution will take place "almost exclusively in Europe, North America, and Asia." The world's poorest regions will have unequal access to vaccines at a time when a new pandemic is added to HIV/AIDS, malaria, tuberculosis, and other pandemics that already disproportionately affect the world's poorest citizens. Ethics and epidemiological strategy alike argue in favor of thinking globally in pandemic planning, including using surveillance, vaccination, and treatment outside the United States to prevent or contain dangerous outbreaks.
- *Prioritize transparency and public cooperation:* If the public is to trust and comply with a resource allocation plan, the plan must both be fair and be seen to be fair. No one says this will be easy. However, people who are given advance notice of a process and who view that process as fair are more accepting of it than are those who are simply ordered to follow it. This "fair-process effect," as it is known, applies to medical professionals as well as to those in need of health care: hospitals cannot expect physicians to comply with a vaccination priority list unless they understand the ethical reasoning underlying it.

COORDINATING THE RESPONSE: WHAT POLICY MAKERS CAN DO

The inevitability that some people will never trust or comply with a resource allocation plan and will try to obtain scarce resources by any means necessary should not distract us from the central task of devising and implementing resource allocation plans that are consistent with our values, including fairness, and that squarely address the hardest questions: when a pandemic hits, how will we fairly distribute our limited supplies of vaccine, Tamiflu, ventilators, and ICU beds? Pandemic planners at every level will need to consider how each of these rationing criteria, singly or in combination, may apply to different resource allocation scenarios, include vaccination of essential workers, vaccination of members of the public, allocation of Tamiflu, access to hospitals, and access to levels of care within hospitals. They will need to work with regional, state, and local authorities and with health care professionals to put workable resource allocation systems and guidelines into place. They will need to work with the media and with trusted public figures and civic institutions to teach the public about the need for resource allocation during a pandemic. They must be prepared to defend the ethical reasoning underlying resource allocation, acknowledging the inherent tragedy of these hardest of choices while nurturing the conditions for hope, trust, and cooperation to flourish in difficult times.

Physician Obligation in Disaster Preparedness and Response

Karine Morin, Daniel Higginson, and Michael Goldrich for the Council on Ethical and Judicial Affairs of the American Medical Association

The terrorist attacks of 2001 were a reminder that individual and collective safety cannot be taken for granted. Since then, physicians, alongside public health professionals and other healthcare professionals as well as nonhealthcare personnel, have been developing plans to enhance the protection of public health and the provision of medical care in response to various threats, including acts of terrorism or bioterrorism. Included in those plans are strategies to attend to large numbers of victims and help prevent greater harm to even larger populations.[1]

It is important to recognize that unique responsibilities beyond planning rest on the shoulders of the medical profession. Indeed, irrespective of the cause of harm—whether it arises from natural disasters or otherwise—physicians are needed to care for victims. In some instances, this will require individual physicians to place their health or their lives at risk. Many physicians demonstrated their sense of duty and courage by participating in the rescue efforts that followed the events of September 11, 2001, and more recently the aftermath of Hurricane Katrina. These and other circumstances, such as the debate regarding smallpox vaccination of front-line responders and the SARS epidemic, require the medical profession and each of its members to reflect anew on ethical responsibilities that arise in the face of adversity.

A BRIEF HISTORY OF ETHICAL OBLIGATIONS IN THE FACE OF RISKS

Prior to the events of 2001, the most recent profession-wide debate regarding a duty to treat despite personal risks arose when there was limited understanding of HIV transmission. Those who believed there was a duty to treat appeared to rely in part on historical evidence of the role physicians had played during epidemics. However, some historians remained cautious in making any claim that such a duty existed.[2] In fact, they pointed to many instances when physicians had fled in times of the plague,[3] and also showed that physicians who had provided care during epidemics had done so not out of a sense of professional obligation, but either because of religious doctrines, because it was lucrative, or because it could result in fame.

By the time standards of medical ethics became codified, starting with the 1803 code developed by Thomas Percival, a growing sense of the duties owed by professionals had developed. In this vein, the AMA's 1847 code stated that: "When pestilence prevails, it is [physicians'] duty to face the danger, and to continue their labors for the alleviation of the suffering, even at the jeopardy of their own lives." This clear mandate may have been moderated by the introduction of a separate notion that physicians should be free to choose whom to serve in later editions of the code. However, the AIDS epidemic led to a strong reiteration of the obligation to treat.

Much of the historical analysis regarding physicians' obligation to treat despite personal risk has focused on the treatment of infectious diseases. However, threats to personal safety, health, or life come in many different forms, for example, when a natural disaster strikes or during armed conflicts. Along the spectrum of threats, all physicians are confronted with the same question: whether the care needed by a patient or a group of patients calls for the assumption of personal risk.

ETHICS OF THE MEDICAL PROFESSION

The AMA's *Principles of Medical Ethics* recognizes that many situations in medical care call for a delicate balancing. In the context of a physician's general obligations, the preamble notes that: "As a member of this profession, a physician must recognize responsibility to patients, first and foremost, as well as to society, to other health care professionals, and to self." Principle VIII emphasizes physicians' obligations to patients in the following way: "A physician shall, when caring for a patient, regard responsibility to the patient as paramount."

Arguably, the obligation to treat may be counterbalanced by Principle VI, which states: "A physician shall, in the provision of appropriate care, except in emergencies, be free to choose whom to serve . . . and the environment in which to provide medical care." However, several Opinions limit physicians' choice in light of medical need. (See, for example, Opinions 9.06, "Free Choice," 9.065, "Caring for the Poor," 8.11 "Neglect of Patient," and 10.015 "The Patient—Physician Relationship," AMA Code of Medical Ethics.)

In the context of infectious diseases, two opinions clarify the ethical obligation of physicians to provide medical care to patients infected with HIV or AIDS. Specifically, Opinion 2.23, "HIV Testing," states that: "It is unethical to deny treatment to HIV-infected individuals because they are HIV seropositive." Opinion 9.131, "HIV-Infected Patients and Physicians," also states that: "A physician may not ethically refuse to treat a patient whose condition is within the physician's current realm of competence solely because the patient is seropositive for HIV."

The *Principles* not only consider the role of the individual physician vis-à-vis an individual patient, but also recognize the role of physicians regarding the patient population. Specifically, Principle VII calls for participation in activities contributing to the improvement of the community and the betterment of public health, and Principle IX calls upon physicians to support access to medical care for all people.

Emergencies: Individual heroism or professional obligation

It often appears that responsibilities to provide emergency care arise in the context of an individual patient. However, an epidemic, a large-scale disaster, or a bioterrorist attack could result in a significant portion of the population within a community requiring urgent medical care. Under such extraordinary circumstances, it is possible that a number of physicians would exhibit personal courage and provide medical care in the face of risk. However, would the personal courage of individual physicians be sufficient to assure that availability of medical care would not be compromised?

Instead of relying on individual heroism, physicians have a professional commitment to assure adequate availability of care. Indeed, professional ethics, as embodied by a code of conduct such as the AMA's, is intended to put forth a uniform standard of conduct for individuals who belong to a profession. When large-scale disaster strikes, physicians individually and collectively should use their knowledge and skills to address medical needs.

In the context of a threat to the health and safety of a population, the unavailability of healthcare professionals to provide needed medical care, due not to casualties among them but rather to individuals' refusal to assume personal risk, could be viewed as a serious failure of medical professionalism. Is this view of professional obligation morally justified?

Professional obligations in the face of personal risk

One leading philosopher in healthcare argues that relevant expert knowledge gives rise to professional acceptance of "known" risks and that it would be disingenuous to accept the privileges of professional status but not to fulfill the obligations.[4] For example, firefighters and police officers know of the threats they face and are obligated to provide services in spite of those risks; similarly, risks that are foreseeable from a medical perspective cannot be avoided by physicians.

Such a perspective may explain in part that the risks of HIV infection needed to be understood before they could be assumed. This could lead to the conclusion that, although physicians faced unknown risks at the time of the 2001 terrorist attacks and acted beyond their professional obligations, similar conduct is now becoming part of the professional commitment. In this regard, Alexander and Wynia have shown that physicians who felt that they were well "prepared to play a role in responding to a bioterror attack [were more] willing to work under conditions of personal risk."[5]

Another compelling justification for a professional commitment in providing medical care in the face of personal risk can be derived from four general factors that give rise to a widely acknowledged moral obligation to render aid.[6] First is the degree of need: the greater the need, the greater the obligation to assist. This is well recognized in medicine, as expressed in Principle VI of the AMA's *Principles of Medical Ethics,* which allows physicians to choose whom to serve, except in emergencies. Next comes the notion of proximity. This can refer to spatial proximity, such that physicians closest to a disaster site have a greater obligation of offering their services than those far from it. Proximity also can be understood as a function of knowledge, such that those with knowledge of a threat have greater obligations to act than those who are ignorant of it. Closely related is the notion of capability. A lifeguard, even if not on duty, has a greater obligation than the occasional swimmer to assist in the rescue of a drowning person. Similarly, there may be other healthcare professionals available to assist victims, but few would possess the full medical knowledge and skills held by physicians. Finally, it becomes clear that the obligation to provide assistance becomes greater as the possible sources of aid diminish. In this regard, physicians need not be victims' first providers of care, but oftentimes they will be needed when other providers cannot adequately treat victims. Altogether, these four factors justify a strong professional commitment to providing services to victims in need of medical care despite risk to the provider.

Limitations to the duty to treat

An obligation to treat need not be absolute. To the extent that reasonable steps can be taken to protect oneself, it is important that physicians avail themselves of such measures. In the context of infectious diseases, vaccination has played a significant role to minimize risk, along with universal precautions. However, instances where individuals fail or refuse to avail themselves, outside appropriate guidelines, of protective measures may be problematic. For example, if a large number of physicians refused certain vaccinations and if they subsequently claimed that they were unwilling to care for infected patients, a considerable burden would likely be placed upon vaccinated physicians.

Another limitation may exist to the obligation to treat, but needs to be carefully circumscribed. Physicians should not be expected to place themselves at greater risk than the benefit they can provide. Indeed, if the nature of the risk is so lethal that there is little likelihood that a physician can provide care to more than a single patient, then limiting the number of exposed physicians at the onset of an event may be necessary to ensure that a sufficient number remain available to treat patients who can reasonably be expected to survive beyond the acute event.

To address these various possibilities, sound preparedness strategies need to be established through broad physician consultation. This could lead to the preidentification of teams of volunteers willing to accept greater risk. These teams could receive specialized training to respond to specific threats instead of each and every physician being expected to possess the necessary knowledge and willingness to respond to any and every threat. Additionally, as the focal points of preparedness, volunteer teams could be offered due compensation for their training, as well as their assumption of risks. Other physicians' responsibilities would become more clearly defined—namely, to refer patients knowledgeably according to the nature of the threat.

Although such strategies would not eliminate all risk to individual physicians under all circumstances, they could help limit undue risk and assure coordinated, effective, and prompt responses. These strategies also could facilitate the education of patient populations regarding the appropriate actions to take according to various threats. In turn, this could help establish realistic societal expectations toward physicians and other healthcare professionals, alleviate unnecessary confusion or fear, and ultimately help minimize morbidity and mortality.

Another important dimension to consider as planning efforts move forward is the legal environment in which medical care is provided. Specifically, the medical profession should advocate for the establishment of legal protections that facilitate the provision of medical care by all available and specifically trained physicians, expanding upon laws that protect physicians against liability in special circumstances.

CONCLUSION

Preparedness for the threat of epidemics, disasters, or terrorism requires physicians to express a renewed commitment to the ethical foundation of the practice of medicine. Indeed, when the health of large populations is threatened, society should expect that the medical profession will be prepared to provide medical care in a cohesive and comprehensive manner. To accomplish this goal, the obligation to provide care must reside not only with individual physicians, but with the profession as a whole.

RECOMMENDATIONS

National, regional, and local responses to epidemics, terrorist attacks, and other disasters require extensive involvement of physicians. Because of their commitment to care for the sick and injured, individual physicians have an obligation to provide urgent medical care during disasters. This ethical obligation holds even in the face of greater than usual risks to their own safety, health, or life. The physician workforce, however, is not an unlimited resource; therefore, when participating in disaster responses, physicians should balance immediate benefits to individual patients with ability to care for patients in the future.

In preparing for epidemics, terrorist attacks, and other disasters, physicians as a profession must provide medical expertise and work with others to develop public health policies that are designed to improve the effectiveness and availability of medical care during such events. These policies must be based on sound science and respect for patients. Physicians also must advocate for and, when appropriate, participate in the conduct of ethically sound biomedical research to inform these policy decisions.

Moreover, individual physicians should take appropriate advance measures to ensure their ability to provide medical services at the time of disasters, including the acquisition and maintenance of relevant knowledge.

NOTES

1. Wynia MK, Gostin L. The bioterrorist threat and access to health care. *Science* 2002;296:1613.

2. Fox DM. The history of responses to epidemic disease in the United States since the 18th century. *Mount Sinai Journal of Medicine* 1989;56:223–9; Fox DM. The politics of physicians' responsibility in epidemics: A note on history. *Hastings Center Report* 1988;18:S5–10.

3. Zuger A, Miles S. Physicians, AIDS, and occupational risk: Historic traditions and ethical obligations. *JAMA* 1987;258:1924–8, see reference 15.

4. Daniels N. Duty to treat or right to refuse? *Hastings Center Report.* 1991;21:36–46.

5. Alexander GC, Wynia MK. Ready and willing? Physicians' sense of preparedness for bioterrorism. *Health Affairs* 2003;22:189–97.

6. This analysis is adapted from a presentation by Chalmers Clark, while he was a visiting scholar at the Institute for Ethics, which refers to the work of various commentators on the case of Kitty Genovese, who died in 1964, as more than 30 people heard her being stabbed.

Glossary

Active Euthanasia This occurs when doctors take direct action to end patients' lives, usually by giving them lethal injections.

Acute Care Treatment of a severe medical condition that is of short duration and at a crisis level.

Advance Directive A document that outlines a person's health care decisions that is used if a person is unable to speak (or communicate) for him- or herself.

Allocation Distribution (as in the allocation of scarce medical resources).

Alzheimer's Disease A progressive, irreversible disease, most prevalent in late life, characterized by deterioration of the brain cells and leading to impaired mental functioning.

Americans with Disabilities Act (ADA) A U.S. law passed in 1990 that outlaws discrimination against any person with a disability. The areas in which persons with disabilities are protected include housing, public accommodations, employment, government services, transportation, and telecommunications.

Assisted Reproductive Technologies (ART) All fertility treatments in which both egg and sperm are handled. These are clinical procedures that are designed to help achieve pregnancy.

Belmont Report The 1979 report of the U.S. National Commission for the Protection of Human Subjects of Biomedical and Behavioral Research. It presents the principles of autonomy, beneficence, and justice as necessary to ethical research.

Best Interest Standard A decision making standard used by surrogates when there is no way of knowing what the incompetent patient's beliefs or wishes are. Decisions are made in accordance with what is in the best interest of the patient.

Bioterrorism The use of biological agents (bacteria, viruses, pests) as weapons of terror.

Bodily Identity Integrity Disorder (BIID) The overwhelming desire to amputate one or more healthy limbs.

Chronic Care Long-term care of individuals with long-standing, persistent diseases or conditions.

Clinical Trials Trials designed to test the safety and efficacy of drugs or procedures, prior to their being approved for use.

Cloning Inserting the nucleus of an adult somatic cell into an egg cell whose nucleus has been removed.

Commercial Surrogacy A woman contracts with a couple to become pregnant and deliver a child for them. She may be the child's genetic mother (the traditional form of surrogacy), or she may simply be the gestational surrogate, carrying the pregnancy to term after having been implanted with an embryo.

Commission (acts of) In euthanasia, acting as a direct agent to commit an act that is intended to end the life of a dying patient. Acts of commission are usually aligned with active euthanasia.

Commodification The view of or treatment of persons (or embryos, etc.) as commodities, things.

Competency One necessary part of an informed consent. It requires that patients have the rational capacity to make their own decisions.

Confidentiality A value or principle related to privacy that is especially binding in certain types of professional relationships (e.g., physician and patient). It requires that the intimate and private information that a patient discloses must not be shared with third parties.

Consequentialism A type of moral theory in which rightness and wrongness is determined solely by whether the consequences are good or bad (utilitarianism is the best known example).

Cryopreservation The practice of freezing and storing the excess embryos resulting from *in vitro* fertilization so that they can be saved for future treatment cycles.

Cultural Relativism The view that moral standards are not absolute or universal but are different from one culture to another.

Damage-Based Theory of Aging Argues that aging is the result of cumulative damage to living organisms that is caused by the environment.

Dead Donor The gift of an organ, tissue, and so on from a dead person (a cadaver or a brain-dead person).

Deaf Culture A social group of people who consider deafness to be a difference in human experience, rather than a disability.

Declaration of Helsinki A code of ethics for medical research that adds to the principles of the Nuremberg Code (1964).

Deinsurance When health care services that were previously insured are cut in an attempt to control health care costs.

Dementia Significant loss of intellectual abilities such as memory capacity, severe enough to interfere with social or occupational functioning.

Deontology An approach to moral situations and moral decision making that focuses on carrying out duties and obligations.

Direct-to-Consumer Advertising The marketing of pharmaceutical products directly toward patients, rather than to health care professionals. Forms of DTC advertising include television, magazine ads, and other mass media.

Directed Donation A donor's gift of an organ, tissue, and so on to a particular person chosen by the donor.

Disclosure One necessary part of an informed consent. It requires that health care providers disclose important information to patients before the patients make decisions (information such as risks and benefits, alternatives, etc.).

Distributive Justice The passing-out of benefits and burdens (often scarce resources) in terms of what people deserve or are owed or what is fair.

Double-Blind An experimental study in which neither the researcher nor the subject knows to which control or treatment group the subject is assigned.

Ectogenesis Development of an embryo or of embryonic tissue outside the body in an artificial womb.

Embryonic Stem Cell Research Research on stem cells (cells that have the capacity to develop into a variety of specialized cells) from early embryos.

Employment-Based Health Insurance Health insurance offered through one's own employment or through a relative's. It may be offered by an employer or by a union.

Epidemic A rapidly spreading breakout of a contagious disease.

Ethic of Care An approach to moral situations and moral decision making that focuses on the values of care, compassion, and the maintaining and promoting of relationships.

Eugenics The use of science to improve the human species.

Euthanasia Literally meaning "the good death," in cases of euthanasia, doctors take or omit actions that may result in the death of their patients.

Extraordinary Means An aggressive medical procedure performed on a dangerously ill patient that in itself may endanger the patient but which has a possibility of being successful.

Four Principles Approach An approach to moral situations and moral decision making that utilizes four principles: autonomy, nonmaleficence, beneficence, and justice.

Gender Reassignment Surgery (GRS) Sometimes called a "sex change" operation, this is a surgery on the genitals that changes a person's sex from male to female or female to male.

Genetic Determinism The idea that genes determine the lives of organisms.

Germ-Line Cells Reproductive cells, namely, eggs or sperm.

Globalization The adoption of a worldwide scale or perspective.

Health Care Desire A condition in which one wishes to enhance one's normal state.

Health Care Need A condition in which one has an illness or disease that must be addressed to restore a level of normalcy.

Health Insurance Portability and Accountability Act (HIPAA) A 1996 federal law designed in part to improve the privacy and security of information related to health and health care.

Health Maintenance Organization (HMO) A type of medical insurance coverage that specifically states which doctors and medical institutions patients may use and which medical tests and procedures will be paid for by the HMO.

Hippocratic Oath A code of physician ethics, attributed to the Greek physician Hippocrates, from the fourth century B.C.E.

Home Health Care Part-time care that is provided by medical professionals or aides in the home setting rather than in a hospital or skilled nursing facility.

Informed Consent The process by which patients (or research subjects) accept or refuse treatment (or research participation), requiring disclosure, competency, understanding, and voluntariness.

Institutional Review Board (IRB) The committee at universities and medical institutions that is responsible for protecting human subjects of research (reviewing and approving research protocols and upholding federal guidelines).

Intersexed Formerly known as "hermaphrodite." The term for persons born with "ambiguous" genitalia and/or chromosomal anomalies. Babies born intersexed may not clearly have male or female genitalia, and in such cases parents are often convinced by medical professionals to allow them to do "normalizing" surgery on their infants' genitals.

***In Vitro* Fertilization (IVF)** This means "reproduction in a glass." It involves hyperstimulating a woman's ovaries to remove a large number of eggs, then combining them with sperm in a petri dish to create embryos. Some of the embryos are then returned to the woman's uterus for implantation.

Justice Theory An approach to moral situations and moral decision making that focuses on what is fair, what is owed or deserved, or on moral rights.

Kantian Deontology An approach to moral situations and moral decision making that emphasizes carrying out duties and uses the categorical imperative to determine what are our duties.

Living Donor The gift of an organ, tissue, and so on from a living person (e.g., a kidney or a liver lobe).

Managed Care Organizations (MCOs) Managed care plans are health care delivery systems that integrate the financing and delivery of health care. MCOs generally negotiate agreements with providers to offer packaged health care benefits to covered individuals.

Medicaid A program in the United States, jointly funded by the states and the federal government, that reimburses hospitals and physicians for providing care to qualifying people who cannot finance their own medical expenses.

Medical Model of Disability A model by which illness or disability is the result of a physical condition, is intrinsic to the individual (being part of that individual's own body), reduces quality of life, and causes him or her clear disadvantages.

Medicare A federal program in the U.S that pays for certain health care expenses for people age 65 and older. Enrolled individuals must pay deductibles and co-payments, but many of their medical costs are covered by the program.

Millennium Development Goals (of the United Nations) Eight goals adopted in 2000 (with a target completion date of 2015) agreed to by all United Nations member states.

Multiculturalism A belief or policy valuing racial, cultural, and ethnic diversity.

Natural Law A theory developed by Saint Thomas Aquinas and important to Catholic bioethicists that what is natural and rational for human beings (what God has intended) is what is morally right.

Nuremberg Code A code of ethics for medical research drawn up after the Nazi medical experiments during World War II (1946).

Omission (acts of) The absence of an action, or the failure to act.

Paired Exchange A system of matching persons who need organs and who have willing but nonmatching donors with others in similar situations (so donors trade organs—each gives an organ to an unrelated recipient in exchange for an organ for their loved one).

Pandemic An epidemic that spreads over a wide geographical area.

Passive Euthanasia Failing to provide a medical intervention that might extend dying patients' lives (such as doing cardiopulmonary resuscitation, or starting a course of antibiotics to treat an underlying infection).

Paternalism The practice of acting as a father (or parent) toward a child (this includes making decisions for the child in the child's best interest).

Patient Bill of Rights Patient rights were developed with the expectation that hospitals and health care institutions would support them in the interest of delivering high-quality and responsive health care.

Persistent Vegetative State (PVS) A deep state of unconsciousness from which patients do not recover.

Personhood This term is commonly used to refer to an individual human being. In specialized fields of law, philosophy, and medicine, it means the presence of particular characteristics that grant a certain legal, ethical, or moral standing.

Physician-Assisted Suicide (PAS) Doctors give patients the means to end their own lives. This is usually done by writing prescriptions for lethal doses of medications that patients fill and then take at a point where the suffering from their terminal illnesses becomes unbearable.

Pittsburgh Protocol A procedure by which organs are removed from non-heart-beating donors a few minutes after life support systems are removed with their or their surrogate's consent.

Placebo A biologically inert pill or substance.

Preimplantation Genetic Diagnosis (PGD) Techniques by which embryos fertilized *in vitro* are tested for specific genetic disorders (e.g., cystic fibrosis) or other characteristics such as sex before transfer to the uterus.

Programmed Theory of Aging Argues that aging is regulated over the life span by one's biological clock; regulation depends on changes in gene expression that affect the systems responsible for repair, maintenance, and defense responses.

Randomization The process of assigning subjects in a research experiment to a treatment or control group by chance.

Rationing The controlled distribution of resources and scarce goods or services.

Reproductive Cloning Using cloning techniques to create offspring (who are thus genetically identical to the donated adult nucleus cell).

Right A morally justified claim to something.

Sex Selection Methods used to predetermine or diagnose the sex of an embryo for the purpose of selecting only those embryos of a particular sex for transplanting to the uterus of a woman.

Single-Blind An experimental study in which only the researcher (but not the subject) knows to which treatment or control group the subject is assigned.

Single-Payer System   Single-payer health care is an American term describing the payment for doctors, hospitals, and other providers of health care from a single fund. The Canadian health care system, the British National Health Service, Australia's Medicare, and Medicare in the United States for older adults and those with disabilities are single-payer systems.

Social Model of Disability   Prejudice and exclusion by society (either on purpose or by mistake) are the ultimate factors defining who is disabled and who is not in a particular society. The social model recognizes that while some people have physical, intellectual, or psychological differences from a statistical mean, which may sometimes be impairments, these do not have to lead to disability unless society fails to accommodate and include them in the way it would those who are "normal."

Socialized Medicine   A system of health care in which all health personnel and health facilities, including doctors and hospitals, work for the government and draw salaries from the government.

Somatic Cells   Cells not involved in reproduction.

Species-Typical Functioning   The normal level and degree of bodily function that a human being is supposed to achieve; a level of function that is standardly met by any individual within a species group.

Sperm Sorting   A means of choosing what type of sperm cell is to fertilize the egg cell. It can be used to sort out sperm that are most healthy, as well as determination of more specific traits, such as sex selection.

Substituted Judgment Standard   A decision making standard used by a surrogate when the wishes of the formerly competent patient are known. Decisions are made in accordance with the previously competent person's expressed beliefs and wishes.

Surge Capacity   The ability of a health care system or institution to quickly expand its medical services in the event of a large-scale emergency.

Surrogate   A person who is acting as decision maker for another person.

Therapeutic Cloning   Using cloning techniques to create cells, tissues, or even organs to treat diseases.

Therapeutic Privilege   The privilege claimed by a physician to withhold information from a patient when the physician believes the information will be harmful to the patient.

Transsexualism   A condition in which an individual's gender identity does not match the sex that was assigned to him or her at birth. Many transsexual people will seek hormonal and/or surgical treatment in order to bring their body into alignment with their gender identity.

Triage   A system for sorting people into groups based on their need or ability to benefit from treatment.

Tuskegee Syphilis Study   A medical experiment conducted by the U.S. Public Health Service from the 1930s to the 1970s. It studied the course of syphilis in about 400 poor black men in Alabama. In 1997 President Bill Clinton apologized to the survivors and their families for the U.S. Government having acted in a "morally wrong" way.

United Network for Organ Sharing (UNOS)   Operates the Organ Procurement and Transplantation Network in the United States.

United States Public Health Service Syphilis Study   *See* Tuskegee Syphilis Study.

Universal Health Care   A government-sponsored system that ensures health care coverage for all citizens of a nation, regardless of income level or employment status.

Utilitarianism   An approach to moral situations and moral decision making that focuses on utility, that is, maximizing the greatest amount of good for all.

Virtue Ethics   An approach to moral situations and moral decision making that emphasizes character, being a good person through the practice of virtues, such as courage, justice, and so on.

Willowbrook State Hospital Study   A medical experiment conducted from the 1950s to the 1970s at a New York State facility for children with mental disabilities to research hepatitis.

Cases

CASE 1. *Commercial Surrogacy in the Global Context*

Relevant Chapters: 3, 6, 11

Commercial surrogacy has been legal in India since 2002. The cheap medical care, the supply of cheap surrogate mothers, and the absence of legal controls have made India the new world leader in commercial surrogacy. Couples from the United States, Great Britain, and other countries are increasingly using services in India because they are so much more affordable.

In 2008 one such couple, Ikufumi Yamada and his now ex-wife Yuki Yamada, arranged through a surrogacy clinic for an Indian woman to act as their surrogate, using Mr. Yamada's sperm and a donated egg. Mr. Yamada bought the surrogate mother a house worth 325,000 rupees ($7,200) and gave her 50,000 rupees to bear the child. By the time the baby was born, however, the couple divorced, and Mrs. Yamada decided that she did not want to adopt the baby after all.

According to Indian law, a child may not leave the country without a passport and the child's mother must be present in order to get a passport. Although Mr. Yamada wants to keep the baby, he is not allowed to take her out of the country because Indian laws also prohibit single men from adopting girls.

Baby Manji is being cared for in a hospital in the city of Jaipur by Mr. Yamada's 70-year-old mother, who speaks no Hindi or English and who is very distressed that she cannot bring her grandchild home to Japan. She plans to stay in Jaipur to be with her granddaughter for as long as she can, although her travel visa may not allow her to stay in India until the case is settled.

As the industry flourishes, concerns are mounting for the welfare of the poor women who typically become surrogates and for the children they bear. Yet supporters of the practice in India claim that the money a woman can earn as a surrogate is equivalent to the well-paid salary of a blue-collar worker, and that it is a viable choice.

CASE 2. *Assessing the Demands of an Alzheimer's Patient*

Relevant Chapters: 2, 9

Mrs. Goldstein is an 82-year-old woman with Alzheimer's disease. She lives at a Jewish nursing home where she has been a resident for the past 5 years. For all of her rational and competent adult life, Mrs. Goldstein has kept kosher. She is a devout Jewish woman who has always expressed a deep faith and pride in her Jewish heritage.

Lately, however, Mrs. Goldstein has started demanding that the staff give her ham for her meals—something that she would never have requested in her rational state. The staff are uncertain of how to respond. Some believe she should be given the ham in order to quiet her and keep her calm, while other staff members believe it would be a violation of her lifelong commitment to keeping kosher.

The staff wonders which Mrs. Goldstein they are responsible to: the current one with Alzheimer's disease who is demanding the ham, or the past Mrs. Goldstein, who would never break kosher and would probably be horrified at the thought of eating ham. They decide to seek the advice of the nursing home's social worker in the hopes that they will achieve a satisfactory decision.

787

CASE 3.   *Parental Choice for Alternative Therapies*

Relevant Chapters: 2, 10

A 2½-year-old boy named Chad Green developed acute lymphoblastic leukemia (ALL) that, according to physicians, needed chemotherapy if the boy was to have a chance at survival. Chemotherapy involves fighting cancer with chemical drugs and it often has unpleasant side effects such as nausea, vomiting, fatigue, and hair loss. The cure rate using chemotherapy to treat children with ALL is 65–85%. The family, however, believed in an alternative diet. They felt that the chemotherapy would be too toxic and harmful for their son and that it would fail. They preferred treating his leukemia with a special diet of macrobiotic rice and Laetrile, an extract from apricot pits that was believed to be a therapy for cancer by many committed to alternative therapies.

When the family refused the recommended orthodox chemotherapy, the physician, Dr. John Truman of Harvard Medical School, pondered what to do.

CASE 4.   *A Patient's Responsibility for His Own Health*

Relevant Chapters: 2, 3

Jacob Fletcher is a man in his early 60s who has been diagnosed with high cholesterol and high blood pressure, and who is approximately 50 pounds overweight. Jacob is from a poor family, and did not complete his high school education. He smokes almost a pack of cigarettes a day and leads a very unhealthy lifestyle.

Jacob has been seeing his regular physician, Dr. Philips, to work on reducing his blood pressure through medications; and his doctor has recommended a series of life changes in order to reduce his cholesterol level and get his weight down. Dr. Philips has told Jacob that he needs to make good food choices in order to reduce his high cholesterol, to quit smoking, and to get his weight down within a normal range: if he fails to do so, he will remain at very high risk for a heart attack.

While Jacob dutifully keeps his appointments with Dr. Philips, the doctor begins to notice that he is not following her advice. When she asks about an exercise routine, Jacob admits that he hasn't gotten around to it yet, and that he hates to exercise. When he submits his food diaries for her review, Dr. Philips sees that Jacob continues to eat at fast-food restaurants; and his food choices at home continue to be poor. Over several weeks of seeing her patient, Dr. Philips sees no improvement in his cholesterol level or his weight; nor does Jacob show any signs of quitting his smoking habit.

Dr. Philips is becoming increasingly annoyed with Jacob. She is willing to give her time and energy in order to help her patients, but feels that they must do their share to take care of their own health. Jacob is clearly not doing so, and Dr. Philips even ponders the possibility of refusing to see Jacob any longer unless he makes a real effort to make changes.

CASE 5.   *Postmortem Sperm Procurement*

Relevant Chapters: 2, 3, 6, 10

Mr. Z suffered a severe head injury in an accident and died without regaining consciousness soon after being brought to the emergency room. His wife was contacted and she arrived in the emergency room along with his parents. Mrs. Z confided to the doctors that the couple had been trying desperately to conceive a child and she asked whether they could perform postmortem sperm procurement. Mr. Z had no advance directive stating, or implying, his wish to father a child, or specifying his agreement to this procedure in case of his death. Mr. Z's parents argued that their son would never have wished to father a child after his death or one who would be raised with only one parent.

The hospital has the equipment to do the procedure and offers services for sperm collection and storage for various reasons, including posthumous fatherhood. However, it has no policy for this situation, where the father is not a competent participant in the consent process.

Mr. Z's physicians discuss what to do.

CASE 6.   *A Cancer Patient's Interest in a Clinical Trial*

Relevant Chapters: 2, 3, 4, 10

Marvin Williams looked hopeful as his physician of 20 years, Dr. Tasaka, entered the examining room. Marvin was suffering from advanced lung cancer and had been through several rounds of chemotherapy. Recent tests had revealed the presence of tumors in his liver as well. Marvin and his physician both know that his disease is progressing.

Marvin came to see Dr. Tasaka today to see if there were any new medications he could try for relief of his symptoms and pain. He was losing weight and breathing was difficult. As Dr. Tasaka pondered what to recommend, Marvin began talking about his last visit with his oncologist, Dr. Fryberg. "Dr. Fryberg wants me to try one more drug treatment. He's head of a study that is testing a drug that was used very successfully on animals and is now being tested on people. He says there's a chance this drug could help me and I'm thinking that I should give it a try. Here's a description of the study he gave me. What do you think?"

Dr. Tasaka took the paper Marvin handed him. He noted that the top of the paper described the study as a Phase I Clinical Trial. What should he say to Marvin?

CASE 7.   *Organ Donation When the Family Disagrees*

Relevant Chapters: 2, 8, 10

Henri Gilbert is a third-year medical student working a rotation in trauma surgery. He is working the evening shift as the EMTs bring a shooting victim into the emergency room. The patient is a young man who was shot in the head. It appears to be an act of gang violence, although it is unclear whether the patient was an intended or unintended victim. Henri, the attending physician, Dr. Markle, and the rest of the ER staff work diligently, but the patient, although still breathing by means of a respirator, is declared brain dead.

In the patient's wallet, the staff finds identification, a home telephone number, and an organ donor card. The patient's name is Than Lee. The patient's family is called and Henri calls the local organ procurement agency.

Within an hour, Than's parents and siblings are at the hospital, sobbing and wailing. The representative from the organ procurement agency also arrives and introduces himself to the family. Than's mother acknowledges that yes, her son wanted to be an organ donor and help others live, if he were to die. But Than's father does not want his son to be an organ donor; he insists that his boy should be left alone, that he has suffered enough.

As the organ procurement representative considers what to say or do, Dr. Markle orders Henri to continue to provide respirator support to Than until a resolution is reached regarding organ donation.

CASE 8.   *Disclosure, Decision making, and the Uncomprehending Patient*

Relevant Chapters: 2, 9, 11

At a small, rural community hospital, an older Asian woman is brought to the emergency room by her family. She is not a local resident but a Chinese citizen, and she has spent the last 2 months in town visiting with her son's family. She is 82 years old, widowed, frail, and does not speak English.

After an initial evaluation in the emergency room, she is admitted to the hospital. She is suffering from weakness, coughing, weight loss, and a pulmonary mass. Tests confirm that she has pulmonary tuberculosis. This disease can be treated with antibiotics, although the treatment regime is complicated and may involve multiple drugs. In addition, tuberculosis is an infectious disease spread by air so others close to the patient may be at risk.

There are no Chinese translators available at the hospital so the admitting physician, Dr. Albane, decides to speak to her son. First, she asks the son if he will please translate while she explains his mother's condition and recommended course of treatment to her. The son indicates that his mother will not be willing or capable of making decisions about her treatment, not because she is incompetent, but because of cultural traditions. She will expect a male relative to make decisions for her. Dr. Albane does not know anything about Chinese cultural traditions, but since she feels that she has few options, she agrees to let the son be the decision maker if that is his mother's wish. Dr. Albane begins to describe what tests were performed and the diagnosis at which she arrived, when the son interrupts and asks that she not divulge the tuberculosis diagnosis to his mother. According to the son, in China, tuberculosis is considered to be a fatal disease and if this diagnosis is reported to his mother she will give up her will to live. Dr. Albane wonders what to tell her patient.

CASE 9. *Responsibility for a Death in a Clinical Trial*

Relevant Chapters: 2, 3, 4, 7

Jolee Mohr was a 36-year-old married woman with a 5-year-old daughter. Jolee suffered from rheumatoid arthritis, an immune system illness that caused pain and inflammation in her joints. For 8 years, she took Humira, an anti-inflammatory drug that kept her symptoms under control.

Then in 2007, Jolee signed up for a research trial that involved using gene therapy. Her doctor for the past 7 years recruited her into the study. The trial was testing the targeting of genetically altered viruses to specific parts of the body in hopes that this treatment approach would prove safer than existing drug treatments. In Jolee's case, the viruses were injected into her right knee. She died soon after the injection.

Jolee's husband, Robb, says that his wife did not understand that she had signed up for a study testing the safety of gene therapy. She thought the trial stood a chance of benefiting her directly. Her physician notes that Jolee signed a 15-page informed-consent document and that he answered all of the questions she asked him about the study. Both the study and the informed consent document were approved by an institutional review board, as U.S. law requires.

The biotech company that sponsored the for-profit research study halted the trial and is monitoring the other participants. They have suggested that Jolee's death may be due not to the gene therapy but to problems associated with Humira, the arthritis drug she was taking before the trial.

Who is responsible for Jolee's death?

CASE 10. *Drug-Resistant TB and the Homeless, Untrusting Patient*

Relevant Chapters: 2, 3

Maurice Grant is a 40-year-old man who has been diagnosed with multidrug-resistant tuberculosis. He has no close family and has not worked since he was a teenager. The clinic staff suspect that he has alcohol and/or drug dependencies but he has never admitted this to them. Maurice spends his days out of doors, carrying his belongings with him, and his nights either outdoors or in various community or church shelters.

The clinic staff started Maurice on the complicated multidrug regimen for his TB. They emphasized the need for regular visits, and consistent and disciplined administration of medicines. At first, Maurice showed up regularly and seemed to develop a rapport with some of the staff. He especially enjoyed talking about sports with the male staff members. But there was some staff turnover and Maurice complained that the nurses were all "girls" and "foreigners" now. He missed some of his scheduled visits. The clinic physician contacted the social work case manager and asked her to arrange for supervised drug administration. This worked for a few weeks but Maurice seems to not like or trust the female nurses and it is difficult to find him and get him to come to the clinic. What should be done?

CASE 11.   *Creating a Baby to be a Bone Marrow Donor*

Relevant Chapters: 2, 6, 7, 8

Mr. and Mrs. Ortiz are a middle-aged couple (he is 48, she is 42). Their medical histories are uneventful except for the fact that Mr. Ortiz had a vasectomy about 5 years ago. They have two children: their son Eduardo is 19 and their daughter Lucinda is 15.

Almost 2 years ago, Eduardo was diagnosed with leukemia. He has been fairly sick, unable to work or go to school regularly, and his treatment with standard chemotherapy regimens has not led to a remission of his cancer. His physician spoke candidly to Eduardo's parents. The next treatment option he recommended was a bone marrow transplant. This treatment is arduous, requires long hospital stays, and is designed to knock out a patient's own bone marrow and replace it with the transplanted healthy bone marrow. To have the best chance at success, it would be necessary to find a donor match for Eduardo.

Mr. and Mrs. Ortiz immediately volunteer to be tested as possible donors and Lucinda volunteers as well. But none of the three turn out to be good matches for Eduardo. Eduardo's physician is not optimistic about his odds of receiving a donation from someone outside of his family. Mr. and Mrs. Ortiz begin to make a list of cousins, aunts, and uncles who could be asked to submit to matching tests. Suddenly, Mrs. Ortiz's eyes widen and she begins to speak. "What if we have another baby," she says. "What if our next child is a perfect match for Eduardo?" The physician starts to interrupt but Mrs. Ortiz is not finished. "Couldn't we," she continues, "have the vasectomy reversed and then either get pregnant and pray the baby is a match or have the baby conceived by *in vitro* fertilization and then pick a baby who is a perfect match?" The physician pauses and then says, "Well, those are possibilities."

Should Mr. and Mrs. Ortiz pursue these options? Should the physician encourage them or discourage them from pursuing these options?

CASE 12.   *Financial Incentives for Organ Donors?*

Relevant Chapters: 2, 3, 8

Federal and state laws prohibit the buying and selling of human organs and tissues. Recently, a campaign has begun to convince the public to rethink the issue in new ways. With thousands of people on waiting lists for organ transplants, there are not enough donations to go around. Some advocates of financial reimbursement believe that more Americans would donate their organs if there were some incentive to do so. Lloyd Cohen, of George Mason University, has pointed out that a great deal of money is made on transplant operations. Hospitals, doctors, and drug companies all benefit—why not the donor? Also, since people can advertise and sell their sperm and eggs, why shouldn't they be allowed to do the same with their organs?

How might this be done? A financial incentive could be awarded to organ donors after death. For example, Pennsylvania lawmakers considered a proposal that would provide $300 toward the cost of the funeral for any person who donated an organ. Or, the $300 could go into an account to be awarded to the donor's family after the death of the donor. Or, in another type of case, patients with very high medical bills might agree to donate an organ (either as a living donor or upon death) and have a portion of their medical bill waived upon their death.

A bioethics consultant has been called in to advise the President's Commission on Bioethics on the idea of financial incentives for organ donors. What should the consultant say?

CASE 13. *SARS and the Emergency Room Nurse*

Relevant Chapters: 2, 3, 11

In February 2003, Toronto was hit by an outbreak of the highly contagious and poorly understood severe acute respiratory syndrome, or SARS, a new type of corona virus. Over a 4-month period, 247 probable cases of SARS were diagnosed and there were 43 deaths. Local hospitals were forced to quickly develop special examining rooms for SARS evaluations and procedures for isolating suspected cases and protecting the health care workers serving patients.

Suppose that Everett is an emergency room nurse with over 10 years of experience working with trauma patients and doing triage nursing. He is married and has a 6-month-old son. His father, who is recovering from a stroke, also lives with the family.

Everett was on duty for the first 2 days of the SARS outbreak. At the time no one knew what illness was befalling people—where it came from, how it would progress, or how to treat it. By the end of the second day when the severity of the virus became evident, the hospital staff began to talk amongst themselves about the risks of working. Some staff members were considering calling in sick or taking vacation days so as not to have to report to work. Everett is concerned not only about his own risks but about the possibility of taking the virus home and exposing his family members to it. There is talk circulating that the staff might be paid a supplemental salary for continuing to work through the outbreak. What should Everett do? What should the hospital administration do?

CASE 14. *The Doctor as Kidney Donor*

Relevant Chapters: 2, 3, 8

In 2002, Dr. Susan Hou, medical director of the renal transplant center at Loyola University Medical Center in Maywood, Illinois, donated a kidney to her patient, Hermelinda Gutierrez. This is believed to be the first time that a U.S. physician donated a kidney to a patient.

Dr. Hou, 56 years old, had thought about donating a kidney for 30 years, ever since a fellow medical student battled kidney disease. Dr. Hou hadn't found a good antigen match until Mrs. Gutierrez turned up. Mrs. Gutierrez, 34 years old and a mother of two, was also a good size match with Dr. Hou. Both are small; Dr. Hou is 4 feet 10 inches tall and Mrs. Gutierrez is 4 feet 7 inches. Dr. Hou also reported that she wanted to find someone who was going to take care of the kidney.

On Mrs. Gutierrez's first visit with Dr. Hou, Dr. Hou did not mention her intention to donate her own

kidney. Dr. Hou spoke to her husband, her endocrinologist, and her three children. She checked to make sure that her childrens' kidneys were healthy. When Mrs. Gutierrez returned for her second visit, Dr. Hou revealed that she wanted to donate a kidney to her.

The transplant took place in October 2002 and neither donor nor recipient had any major complications. The surgery took place at the Loyola transplant center and Dr. Hou continues to see Mrs. Gutierrez as a patient.

Should a physician give a kidney to his or her patient? If a physician does donate a kidney to a patient, should the physician continue to act as the patient's doctor? Are directed donations morally acceptable? On what basis should a person be chosen to receive a directed donation?

CASE 15. *Indecision Regarding Genetic Abortion*

Relevant Chapters: 5, 6, 7

Susan and her husband Rick have four children. Before they married, Rick indicated his desire to have a large family, something that Susan believed

she would really enjoy. They have been married 10 years and their children are between the ages of 8 and 3.

Now that their youngest is old enough to go to preschool, Susan is hoping she might be able to return to her legal practice, even part time. She feels somewhat embittered by the fact that she had to give up her legal career because of their large family. The thought of spending some time outside the home, doing work of a more intellectual nature, is even more appealing to Susan after spending so many years with young children.

But now Susan discovers she is pregnant, and after undergoing prenatal genetic testing, she is told her fetus has Down syndrome. The testing cannot specify whether the Down syndrome will be mild or severe. As Susan receives this news, tears stream down her face. She was having serious doubts about having any more children at all, let alone a special needs child. The chance is slim that she will ever be able to return to work so long as they have a disabled child, since she has always been the primary caregiver for the children. As her dreams of returning to work and professional life are fading away, Susan seriously considers aborting this fetus, and whether she should even tell Rick about it.

CASE 16. *Genetic Testing, Confidentiality, and Third-Party Interests*

Relevant Chapters: 2, 5, 7

Gina and her husband David visit the obstetrician when Gina is 8 weeks pregnant. Because they tell the doctor that their son Sammy had died from cystic fibrosis at age 3, tissue samples are taken from both Gina and David so that a prenatal diagnosis of cystic fibrosis can be made as accurately as possible. Results of the test indicate that Gina is a carrier for the most common mutation associated with the disease, but her husband David is not, meaning that their son Sammy could not have been his genetic offspring.

Gina returns on her own for the follow-up appointment. When she receives the news about the genetic testing, she immediately begins to cry and begs the genetic counselor not to tell her husband. "We had a rough patch a few years ago," she states, "and for a while I had a relationship with a man that David never knew about. I don't want David to be told anything about this, because he has a bad temper and I'm really afraid what he might do. Please don't tell him!"

The genetic counselor feels very conflicted. On the one hand, she believes that Gina has a right to privacy, and she wants to protect her client from potential harm. On the other hand, since she tested both partners, and since David has an unmarried sister and a brother who just recently married, the genetic counselor is concerned about the third-party interest in knowing the results of the testing. The information about David is relevant to his brother and sister, since down the road they may seek testing to learn of their carrier status before deciding to have children. If David is not a carrier for cystic fibrosis, such testing on his brother and sister is not medically indicated.

The genetic counselor feels conflicted and uncertain. She promises to keep Gina's secret, but wonders what harm will result if she fails to disclose the situation to David.

CASE 17. *Health Care for a Noncitizen*

Relevant Chapters: 2, 3, 11

Maria is a 7-year-old girl diagnosed with relapsed acute lymphoblastic leukemia (ALL). She comes from a very poor country in South America. A few months after her diagnosis, Maria, with her parents and younger brother, presented to the emergency room of a large Catholic teaching hospital in the United States that Maria's family knew had provided treatment to a young girl from their country, without cost, 5 years earlier.

Upon presentation, Maria had fatigue, lethargy, purple spots on the skin, and required a transfusion of platelets and packed red cells. Bone marrow biopsy confirmed ALL of the pre-B type.

Maria began reinduction chemotherapy, although her parents were unable to pay for her medical care. The hospital considered having the leukemia treated with chemotherapy in Maria's home country and was willing to provide the drugs free of charge, but Maria's parents rejected the plan. The hospital then consulted four cancer treatment centers, three of which recommended bone marrow transplant (BMT). Maria has a histocompatible sibling and was in remission for 18 months prior to relapse, but also developed fungal sinusitis (aspergillosis) less than 3 weeks into her hospital course.

Currently the hospital has incurred costs of $800,000 for Maria's care, an additional $100,000 in professional fees, and $20,000 in preparing her brother as a possible transplant donor. Maria's parents have sought the assistance of various Hispanic groups to assist them with fundraising and protect their rights. Several organizations came to their aid.

The hospital administration has requested an "ethics consult" to decide what to do. It believes that Maria's parents intend to seek media attention if it decides not to continue treatment, and it worries that the publicity will lead to further financial damage. Yet it also wonders whether the hospital must continue to provide uncompensated care for Maria. If it performs the BMT, then given its current financial situation, layoffs of up to 15 employees will probably be necessary to offset the additional financial losses. The Emergency Medical Treatment and Active Labor Act (EMTALA) obligates hospitals to provide emergency treatment and stabilization to anyone presenting to an emergency room before asking about insurance or ability to pay. However, having accepted Maria as a patient and initiated treatment, does the hospital incur an ethical obligation to continue to provide ongoing care? If so, does the obligation extend to the point that the hospital must compromise its ability to sustain its mission, provide care to others, and meet its obligations to staff?

CASE 18. *The Demands of a Racist Patient*

Relevant Chapters: 2, 3

Mr. Williams is a 75-year-old white male who was admitted to a Detroit hospital after a fall that fractured his hip. He has proven to be a rather irritable and difficult patient, and particularly strikes out against African American staff members that enter his room. Whether the minority staff member is a care provider, orderly, or cleaning personnel, Mr. Williams hurls racist epithets and demands that the individual get out of his room. He has even struck out at one of the workers who was sent in to help him with his bath. He complains that he "doesn't want black people touching him" or coming into his room, and demands that no African Americans be permitted to enter.

This abusive treatment is extremely upsetting to the hospital staff, but especially painful for the African American employees. The hospital administrator becomes involved and, after speaking to Mr. Williams, decides she must do something to protect her staff from his verbal and physical assaults. In an attempt to prevent potential attacks by this patient, she posts a note outside his hospital room door indicating that nonwhite staff members should not enter the room. Following this action, the hospital administrator is fired from her position.

CASE 19. *Treatment of an Extremely Premature Neonate*

Relevant Chapters: 3, 6

Amillia Taylor was born in Miami 21 weeks and 6 days after conception. She weighed less than 10 ounces at birth and she was just 9½ inches long. Amillia is officially the most premature baby ever to have survived.

Amillia's parents, understandably, are immensely pleased, because, as her mother stated, "She's like a real baby now. Now I can feel her when I hold her." The doctors involved, having initially been prepared to break the news of the baby's death to parents who had already been through a grueling IVF program and scare after scare during the pregnancy, are expressing incredulity. "This is not the norm," says neonatologist Dr. William Smalling. "Really, most of these babies don't survive.... This is a miracle." Even more surprisingly, apart from some expected respiratory issues, Amillia appears to be doing well.

Babies born prematurely face a daunting array of problems, both immediately and in the long term. At less than 23 weeks, fetuses have very little in the way of lung or brain development. In fact, all the organs are extremely immature. The critical issue, however, is the lungs. Even with machines, it's impossible to get oxygen in because the lungs are almost solid. Trying to keep the baby alive may involve inflicting a very high degree of irreparable damage. The skin is often very thin, and the kidneys underdeveloped. The brain is extremely immature, and very prone to injury, especially bleeding. Furthermore, follow-up studies suggest that babies who survive at less than 23 weeks have a very high chance of developmental or neurological problems.

A 1995 study indicates that of 138 babies who showed signs of life after being born at less than 22 weeks, only two survived to be discharged, and a follow-up at 6 years of age found that one of those two had severe disabilities, classed as "likely to make a child highly dependent on caregivers, and involving one or more of the following symptoms: cerebral palsy that prevented the child from walking, an IQ score considerably lower than average, profound sensorineural hearing loss, or blindness." (The other child was classed as mildly disabled.) Quite apart from the state of the child, such levels of disability cause great stress to the parents and to their relationship.

"Should one really be trying at all to keep that baby alive?" asks Professor Richard Nicholson, editor of the *Bulletin of Medical Ethics*. "Chances are it will require an enormous amount to be spent on it for the rest of its life. We have much less experience of death, so we have become much less willing to accept it. In countries where infant mortality is higher it would be seen as absurd. We live in a society where we have become addicted to physical existence. It's totally unsustainable. Our attempts at the moment to keep every human physically alive as long as possible will make it less likely that the human race will survive climate change."

CASE 20. *Plastic Surgery and the Goals of Medicine*

Relevant Chapters: 2, 5

Rebecca Forst is a 30-year-old woman who is considered to be quite beautiful by everyone who meets her. Yet Rebecca doesn't feel beautiful; in fact, every time she looks in the mirror, all she can notice is her nose. By her own estimation, her nose is large, dominates her face, and presents too much of an "ethnic" Jewish appearance. Rebecca goes to her physician to ask for a referral to a good plastic surgeon, since she doesn't quite know where to begin looking for one.

Rebecca's doctor tries to dissuade her from cosmetically altering her appearance. "You're a beautiful woman," he claims, "and I really don't see why you think this is necessary." "I'm miserable," claims Rebecca. "I hate how I look, and it's really affecting my life. If I could get my nose fixed, I know I would feel better about myself."

Her doctor retorts, "Maybe you should try talking to a therapist before you take this step. It's going to be painful, and I don't see the need to alter your perfectly lovely face!" But Rebecca is adamant; she looks at her doctor and states, "But isn't it the goal of medicine to help patients feel better? Does it matter whether my pain is physical or psychological?"

CASE 21. *An Elderly Male Refuses to Eat*

Relevant Chapters: 2, 9, 10

Vivian West, a nurse at a local hospital, has been asked to help feed an 89-year-old Asian man who, despite all attempts otherwise, has been dropping weight steadily. When Vivian first met Mr. Sun in the hospital, he proved to be a thin, frail, weak, but very strong-willed man.

Mr. Sun was not the least interested in eating, and seemed so tired most of the time that he could barely keep his eyes open. Vivian attempted to be cheerful about what was essentially force-feeding this elderly gentleman, but her interactions with him were anything but cheery.

Mr. Sun's command of the English language was not very good, but he did know a few words and was able to express his wishes very clearly to Vivian. Every time she came to the door now, he would look at her and moan "Oh, no!" He knew why she was there, and dreaded what would happen next as much as Vivian did.

Vivian added as many calories as she could to Mr. Sun's food by putting butter pats in his soups and entrees. She would bring the spoon toward his mouth, and the negotiations would begin: "No more!" he would state firmly; Vivian would respond "five more!" The two would continue to negotiate while, in between his sputtering and protestations, she would pop the spoon into his mouth. She usually managed to get a fair bit of pureed food into Mr. Sun before the meal was over.

Mr. Sun made it very clear that he did not want to eat, and that he had little interest left in the world around him. His adult children, however, were paying Vivian extra money to sit with him during mealtimes to ensure that he ate. She started to feel terrible about force-feeding him, and wondered whether it was serving any purpose at all. What he wanted for himself didn't seem to matter to his family, and it seemed disrespectful to force the feedings upon him. Yet this was the purpose for Vivian's being there, and so she continued to feed Mr. Sun against his will, all the time feeling extremely guilty.

CASE 22. *Selective Reporting of Clinical Trials*

Relevant Chapters: 3, 4, 5

Over his coffee and newspaper one morning, Howard Bell sees a headline about a revolutionary new drug called "Mybest." The media buzz is based on a clinical trial that included thousands of participants, the overwhelmingly positive results having just been published in one of the world's leading medical journals. Shortly following this front-page headline, Howard sees television ads that promise significantly improved health and well-being through the use of this drug. The voiceover in the television ad recommends: "Ask your doctor if Mybest is right for you!" Howard starts to think about this new drug, wondering "why not?" After all, the study has been reviewed by experts and the data and conclusions have been judged sound; Mybest may be just the thing that Howard needs.

Is Mybest too good to be true? Howard must seriously consider this question, especially given current clinical reporting guidelines. The manufacturers of Mybest have no obligation to disclose "proprietary information," which may include data from other trials, even if those data suggest that Mybest was less effective than any other medications, completely ineffective, or even potentially harmful to individuals taking it.

Worldwide pharmaceutical sales amount to approximately $350 billion annually, so the makers of Mybest have strong economic incentives to withhold all but the most positive of findings; after all, a drug with questionable efficacy or benefits that are outweighed by associated risks will certainly not succeed on the market. The pharmaceutical industry is a business and is, therefore, entitled to earn a profit; these profits, in turn, help fund further biomedical research and innovation. But is there a point at which that entitlement is superseded by the interests of the patient as consumer, since these "consumers" are inherently vulnerable in their inability to research these new drugs?

CASE 23. *IVF Services for a Lesbian Couple?*

Relevant Chapters: 2, 3, 5

Guadalupe Benitez and her partner, Joanne Clark, had been buying frozen sperm at a bank in Los Angeles and trying to get pregnant at home for 2 years when Benitez finally sought out the services of a fertility specialist. At that point, in 1999, Benitez was 27 years old, Clark was 40 years old, and the couple had been together for 8 years, since Benitez emigrated from Mexico. Benitez, a medical assistant, had some infertility benefits at a nearby obstetrics/gynecological clinic, the North Coast Women's Care Medical Group. There,

Dr. Christine Brody put Benitez on a hormonal drug called Clomid, to treat her polycystic ovarian syndrome, and also told her that she was willing to oversee her treatment but not to perform inseminations because, as a Christian, she disapproved of lesbians having children. Dr. Brody indicated, however, that other physicians at the clinic would be willing to offer them insemination services.

Benitez and Clark tried home inseminations for a few more months, and Dr. Brody even did some exploratory surgery. But when the time came to schedule a more effective in utero insemination—a procedure that involves injecting sperm directly into the uterus—an assistant from North Coast Women's Care called to tell Benitez that no one in the practice would do the procedure, nor would they refill her prescriptions.

Should everybody have the right to have a baby? Who should pay when nature alone doesn't seem to work?